Thailand

The travel guide

Footprint Handbook

Joshua Eliot & Jane Bickersteth

with Natapon Buranakul, Sophia Buranakul,
Heidi El Hosaini and Jasmine Saville

"*Arriving in Thailand…is always a relief.
The taxis smell of flowers. The people are
gracious. Hedonism comes without guilt.
So what if people want your money. And if
the city is a little crass. … Here the king
plays jazz.*"

Ian Buruma, *God's Dust: a Modern Asian
Journey (1989)*

Thailand Handbook
Third edition
© Footprint Handbooks Ltd 2001

Published by Footprint Handbooks
6 Riverside Court
Lower Bristol Road
Bath BA2 3DZ. England
T +44 (0)1225 469141
F +44 (0)1225 469461
Email discover@footprintbooks.com
Web www.footprintbooks.com

ISBN 1 900949 86 5
CIP DATA: A catalogue record for this
book is available from the British Library

Distributed in the USA by
Publishers Group West

Credits

Series editors
Patrick Dawson and Rachel Fielding

Editorial
Editor: Jo Williams
Maps: Sarah Sorensen

Production
Typesetting: Emma Bryers, Richard
Ponsford, Leona Bailey
Maps: Robert Lunn, Claire Benison
Colour maps: Kevin Feeney

Cover: Camilla Ford

Design
Mytton Williams

Photography
Front cover: Damneon Saduak market,
near Bangkok,
Steve Davey/La Belle Aurore
Back cover: Lamphun, Northern
Thailand, Eye Ubiquitous
Inside colour section: Eye Ubiquitous,
Robert Harding Picture Library, La Belle
Aurore, Trip Photographic Library

Print
Manufactured in Italy by LEGOPRINT

Every effort has been made to ensure
that the facts in this Handbook are
accurate. However, travellers should still
obtain advice from consulates, airlines
etc about current travel and visa
requirements before travelling. The
authors and publishers cannot accept
responsibility for any loss, injury or
inconvenience however caused.

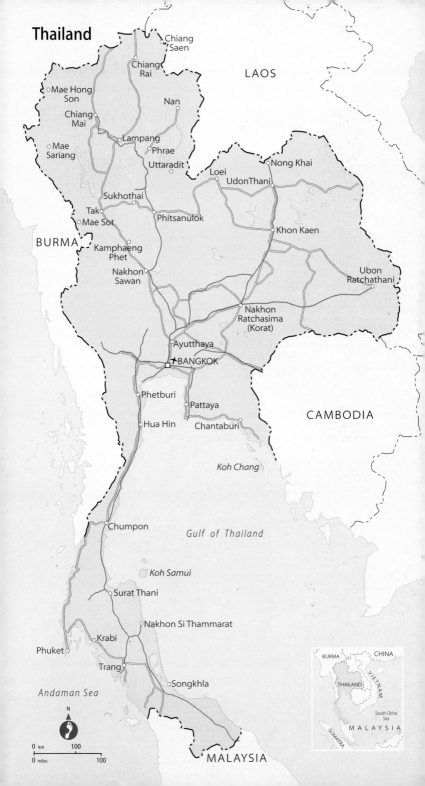

Thailand

LAOS

Chiang Saen

Chiang Rai

Mae Hong Son

Nan

Chiang Mai

Lampang

Phrae

Mae Sariang

Uttaradit

Loei

Nong Khai

UdonThani

BURMA

Sukhothai

Tak

Phitsanulok

Khon Kaen

Mae Sot

Kamphaeng Phet

Nakhon Sawan

Ubon Ratchathani

Nakhon Ratchasima (Korat)

Ayutthaya

BANGKOK

Phetburi

Pattaya

CAMBODIA

Hua Hin

Chantaburi

Koh Chang

Chumpon

Gulf of Thailand

Koh Samui

Surat Thani

Nakhon Si Thammarat

Phuket

Krabi

Trang

Songkhla

Andaman Sea

N

0 km   100

0 miles   100

MALAYSIA

BURMA   CHINA

VIETNAM

THAILAND

South China Sea

SUMATRA   MALAYSIA

Contents

Left: the impressive Phra Pathom Chedi, the world's tallest Buddhist monument, in Nakhon Pathom, western Thailand.

Right: changing faces...masks for sale in the shopper's paradise of Chiang Mai, northern Thailand.

A foot in the door

6

Right: toad kebabs to titillate your tastebuds. *Below*: flower markets and wet markets, festival markets and night markets, buffalo markets and amulet markets...and Damnoen Saduak Floating Market, near Bangkok. *Next page*: Khaosan Road, Bangkok, the spot where many backpackers spend their first night in Thailand. More transcultural than Thailand, it's a haven of backpacker culture offering everything from tattoos to tie-dyed sarongs.

Above: with their distinctive clothing, houses and agricultural systems, settled in the forested hills near the borders of Burma and Laos, the hill people like the Lisu provide a vivid counterpoint to the Tais who dominate the lowlands and the cities. *Right*: elephant in a Karen village, northern Thailand. In 1989 a new logging ban threw hundreds of elephants out of work. Now they and their mahouts carry tourists and beg for food in cities.

Highlights

Thailand is an Asian cliché. Exotic, inscrutable, hot, Oriental, delicate, sumptuous... Take the first few hours of an average visitor's arrival in Bangkok. Off the plane and into a gleaming new airport terminal. Lilting Thai voices, and a strange alphabet. Into the city along an elevated highway in the company of an apparently deranged taxi driver, with a magic diagram inscribed on the roof of his car, a picture of a long-dead king lodged reverently in the tachometer, a cheap gold Buddha glued to the top of the dashboard, and a garland of plastic frangipani hanging from the rear-view mirror. Out of the taxi and into a quiet, cool hotel with copies of the *Asian Wall Street Journal* artfully arranged on reception and CNN in the bedrooms. Or into a small guesthouse run by a Thai bobbing to Bob Marley and offering sweltering rooms the size of chicken coops for the price of a dozen eggs. But aside from the delights of Thailand that can never be planned, what has the country to offer?

The first step

As Thailand's premier city, Bangkok lies at the epicentre of political, economic, social and cultural life. The swankiest restaurants, the richest monasteries, the grooviest music, the finest art, the hippest bars, and the best shopping are all to be found in Bangkok. Enjoy the city for what it is, not for what it isn't. It is not a peaceful, elegant, refined and sedate place. It is a vibrant cornucopia of life where over 10 million people live and love – and battle with perhaps the worst traffic in the world.

Bangkok swank

While some people come to Thailand looking to be pampered and entertained, just as many arrive in search of a simple hut on a quiet beach. The challenge is to find one before the next person – or the next 10,000. Bear in mind that in the early 1970s Phuket was a forgotten backwater. The pace of change is sometimes bewildering. Koh Phangan, Koh Tao, Koh Phi Phi, Koh Samet, Koh Lanta, Koh Chang, Khao Lak and the beaches close to Krabi are now on the tourist trail – in the 1980s and 1990s they were quiet and 'undiscovered' (except, of course, by the people who have always lived there). But while you might not be pushing back the frontiers of knowledge, you will find simple bungalow accommodation for a couple of dollars a night, and probably a quiet beach, clear waters, an empty hammock, and time on your hands.

Tropical idylls

Many who escape from the beaches of the South head for the hills of the North. Here, some might say, is to be found the 'other' Thailand – of hill peoples. Nine 'tribes' make up the great bulk of the country's half a million-plus hill people. Most are comparatively recent immigrants and many are Christian or animist. Taking the time to trek through the hills and forests of the north, rafting down its fast-flowing rivers and staying with the hill peoples is the highlight of many a visitor's stay. These can be relatively demanding one or two week explorations, staying in hill villages and penetrating deep into the hills, or harmless one or two day affairs suitable even for young children and the seriously unfit.

Hill tribes of the north

A few years ago, Thai food was tricky to track down outside Thailand. Now it's everywhere. But even if you regard yourself as something of an expert (and haven't been to Thailand before), expect to be surprised by the range, quality and sheer exuberance of the home-grown real thing. From sophisticated royal cuisine to simple single-dish noodle and rice-based dishes sold from roadside stalls for the cost of a Mars Bar, the Thais take their food very, very seriously. Even the simplest meals are prepared with love and commitment. The major regions of Thailand have their own distinct cuisines, and individual towns their special dishes.

Reality bites

Top: More than nine out of every ten Thais are Buddhist. Here, Buddhist monks go on their morning alms round, Chiang Saen, northern Thailand. *Centre*: Wat Rajaburana, one of the many religious monuments within Ayutthaya Old City, central Thailand.
Right: the festival of songkran, held in April, has become an excuse for uninhibited water-throwing. *Next page*: lazing on a sunny afternoon: a smiling, reclining Buddha awaiting death and enlightenment.

A Buddhist Kingdom

Thailand is a Buddhist kingdom. While there may be significant populations of Muslims in the south and Christians in the north, adherence to Buddhism is viewed by many Thais as a defining characteristic of Thai-ness. A country with a population of 60 million supports some 30,000 monasteries and a quarter of a million monks. That's one wat to every 2,000 people and one monk for every 240. Buddhist ceremonies mark the stages of life, Buddhist monasteries mark the landscape, and Buddhist values mark interpersonal relations. Buddhism has been used as a reason to fight Communism - and a reason to be Communist.

Religion of the people

The most visible sign of Buddhism's hold on Thailand are the country's wats or monasteries. A wat is a place of worship, refuge, meeting, healing and teaching. It is, for many villages, the soul of the community. Men aspire to be ordained for at least one period in their lives and, in the past, women would be wary of marrying a man who had not been ordained, viewing him as *dip* or 'raw'. While some modern wats, to the Western eye at least, may seem garish and gaudy, older monasteries are often beautiful with their sweeping tiled roofs, carved teak pillars, somnolent Buddha images and peaceful cloisters.

The heart of the matter

Near the top of any list of Bangkok's attractions must be the Grand Palace, built in 1782 by the founder of the current Chakri dynasty. The Palace's most important building is Wat Phra Kaeo, the Temple of the Emerald Buddha, housing the Kingdom's most revered image of the Buddha. Bangkok lies at the centre of the country, the Grand Palace lies at the core of Bangkok, and the Emerald Buddha is at the heart of the Grand Palace. But while the Grand Palace may be Bangkok's premier historical sight, there are hundreds of other monasteries in the capital which, in their own ways, are more interesting and beautiful. These range from the gauche Wat Traimitr – with its five-and-a-half tonne solid gold image of the Buddha – through to the elegant Wat Rakhang.

Palatial splendour

Some of the most beautiful monasteries are away from Bangkok, in the provinces. Among the finest is the 13th to 15th-century Wat Phrathat Lampang Luang outside Lamphun, with its surrounding mellow brick walls, expert wood carvings and faded murals. The 16th-century Wat Phumin, adorned with some of the finest late 19th-century murals in Thailand, is another premier division monastery, aesthetically at least. In addition to these big-draw monasteries are many, many village wats which, for their grace, peace and simple beauty, are often even more memorable.

Ancient temples

Most of the country's festivals are ostensibly Buddhist, although many are also spiced with animism and Brahmanism. Perhaps the loveliest is *loi krathong*, held during November's full moon. Model rafts fashioned from banana leaves in the shape of a lotus and carrying a candle, incense, flowers and a coin are pushed out on to rivers, canals and lakes across the kingdom. Dating from the 14th-century Sukhothai period, the boats are said to symbolize the washing away of the past year's sins and heartaches.

Festival goers & water throwers

The most exuberant festival is undoubtedly *songkran*, held in April and marking the end of the dry season. This festival began as a celebration of natural bounty; Buddha images would be bathed in lustral water and, as a mark of respect, monks and the elderly would be sprinkled with water. Nowadays, it has changed somewhat and hoses, buckets – every conceivable container – are used to soak passers-by whether they are dressed in a suit and carrying a briefcase or are wearing shorts and a T-shirt.

Paradise found

On the beach While most people do touch base in effervescent Bangkok, and some grow to love the city, for many it is just a means to an end, a halfway station en route to the islands, beaches and towns of the south. With 2,614 km of coastline, there's a lot of potential.

People have been coming to the beaches of Thailand since the 1920s. Early guidebooks to Thailand called Hua Hin, 150 miles south of Bangkok, Hua Hin-on-Sea, treating it like a sort of Oriental Margate. But mass beach tourism in Thailand had to await the invention of the bikini, the development of cheap air transport, the onset of the Vietnam War, and humanity's love affair with the sun-bronzed body.

Thailand's most developed beach resorts are Phuket and Pattaya. Both have thousands of hotel rooms, restaurants and bars, with entertainment on tap. But these are not for the thin of wallet and shallow of pocket, nor for those after a serene and peaceful time; they are, in the main, high octane places for visitors wanting to rave, not laze. Backpackers head elsewhere. Pattaya's beaches and sea are second rate; Phuket's are rather better.

Koh Samui, Hua Hin and Cha-am are also well developed but are geared to people of most budgets. Hua Hin is suffering some of the problems afflicting Pattaya: unsustainable, unplanned and rather thoughtless development. Koh Samui, with several beaches and a more dispersed pattern of development, has managed to avoid most of these problems. It still has some peaceful places as well as a zingy nightlife and a great choice of restaurants and bars. Cha-am is something else again: more a get-away for Bangkok's middle classes than a place frequented by overseas visitors. Many backpackers have moved on from Koh Samui to Koh Phangan and Koh Tao, smaller and less-developed islands in the same island group.

Forest wealth In 1928 Major Erik Seidenfaden wrote that 'forests and jungle teem with game, large and small', and that 'only a few hours from Bangkok … you may meet tiger, leopard, various tiger cats, wild boar and stags'. Over seventy years later and you are more likely to get disoriented in a shopping mall than lost in a jungle, or run over by a ten-wheel truck than eaten by one of Thailand's 200-odd tigers struggling to survive in a few remnant hideaways. But, with over 80 national parks covering more than 40,000 sq km, Thailand is not quite paradise lost.

Lying at a biological crossroads between mainland and island Southeast Asia, Thailand has an extraordinarily rich variety of flora and fauna. There are 20-25,000 species of plant, 282 species of mammal, 928 bird species, and 405 species of reptile and amphibian and the Kingdom's forest habitats range from true rainforest in the west, to montane forest in the north and savanna forest in the northeast.

Undersea riches More foreign visitors to Thailand, though, come to see Thailand's undersea riches than its forest wealth. Some of the best waters are now protected and increasingly professional dive companies operate from all the main island and beach resorts. While there might not be good diving close to Phuket, it is possible to access the excellent dive sites of the Surin and Similan Islands. The same goes for Koh Samui, which is within easy reach of the Ang Thong Marine National Park (although Koh Tao is even closer). Pattaya, on the eastern seaboard, probably has more dive companies than any other resort and is an excellent place to start, but few experienced divers would compare the dive sites here with those of the Andaman Sea. Whatever, if you have ever had a yen to learn to scuba dive - or even to snorkel - there are few better places than Thailand to start.

Right: impressive limestone pinnacles tower out of the sea near Krabi, southern Thailand.
Next page: Buddha under Naga awaits deliverance.

Thai embassies worldwide

Australia 111 Empire Circuit, Yarralumla, ACT, 2600 Canberra, T06-62731149.
Austria Cottaggasse 48, 1180 Vienna, T431-4783335.
Belgium 2 Square du Val de la Cambre, Brussels, T322-6406810.
Burma 45 Pyay Rd, 65 1/2 Mlie, Hlaing Township, Yangon, T951-525670.
Canada 180 Island Park Drive, Ottawa, Ontario, K1Y 0A2, T613-7224444.
Denmark Norgesmindevej 18, 2900 Hellerup, Copenhagen, T45-39625010.
France 8 Rue Greuze, 75116 Paris, T331-56265050.
Germany Uberstrasse 65, 53173 Bonn, T0228-956860.
Greece 23 Taigetou St, PO Box 65215, Paleo Psychico 15452 Athens, T301-6717969.
Italy Via Nomantana, 132, 00162 Rome, T396-86204381.
Japan 3-14-6, Kami-Osaki, Shinagawa-Ku, Tokyo 141, T813-34472247.
Laos Route Phonekheng, Vientiane, PO Box 128, T85621-214581.
Malaysia 206 Jalan Ampang, 50450 Kuala Lumpur, T093-2488222.
Nepal Ward 3, Bansbari, PO Box 3333, Kathmandu, T9771-371410.
Netherlands Laan Copes Van Cattenburch 123, 2585 E3, The Hague, T3170-3450632.
New Zealand 2 Cook St, Karori, PO Box 17226, Wellington, T644-4678618.
Norway Eilert Sundts Gate 4, 0244 Oslo, T47-22128660.
Portugal Rua de Alcolena 12, Restelo 1400 Lisbon, T3511-3015051.
Spain Calle del Segre 29-2 A, 28002 Madrid, T3491-5632903.
Sweden Floragatan 3, 114 31, Stockholm 100 40, T4608-7917340.
Switzerland Kirchstrasse 56, 3097 Bern, T4131-3722281.
UK 29-30 Queen's Gate, London SW7 5JB, T020-7589 2944.
USA 1024 Wisconsin Avenue, NW, Suite 401, Washington, DC 20007, T202-9443600.

Essentials

Finding out more

The Tourist Authority of Thailand (TAT) publishes a good range of glossy brochures which provide an idea of what there is, where to go, and what it looks like. The main TAT offices are listed in the box on page 24.

Useful websites
See also Useful websites, page 76

www.tourismthailand.org/tat and **www.tat.or.th** The Tourist Authority of Thailand's websites (there are two); a useful first stop and generally well regarded.
www.pata.org/ The Pacific Asia Travel Association, better known simply as PATA, with a useful news section arranged by country, links to airlines and cruise lines, and some information on educational, environmental and other initiatives.
www.TourThai.com A private website with a fair amount of material on transport, national parks, hotels, restaurants and the like (much sourced from the TAT). There is also a photo library of 2,000 images.
www.sabuy.com Named after two Thai cartoon characters. The Thai version is better than the English (http://travel.mweb.co.th/indexeng.html), but the latter is being improved.
www.Siamguide.com Travel information in both Thai and English for destinations across the Kingdom.
http://tmd.motc.go.th/eng/index.html The Thai meteorological office's website so you can find out if you are about to arrive in sun or storm.
www.hotels.siam.net/ The number of hotels listed on the Siam Hotel Network site is limited – online reservations possible. There's also a good range of other information here on clubs, climate, culture, cuisine and more.
www.thaiindex.com A gateway site for a good range of Thai-oriented websites.

Essentials

 TAT offices worldwide

Australia
2nd floor, 75 Pitt St, Sydney, NSW 2000,
T9247-7549, F9251-2465,
info@Thailand.net.au

France
90 Ave des Champs Elysées, 75008 Paris,
T5353-4700, F4563-7888,
tatpar@wanadoo.fr

Germany
Bethmannstr 58 D-60311 Frankfurt/
Main 1, T069-295-704, F281-468,
tatfra@t-online.de

Hong Kong
Room 401 Fairmont House, 8 Cotton Tree
Drive, Central, T2868-0732, F2868-4585,
tathkg@hk.super.net

Italy
Via Barberini 68, 00187 Roma,
T06-487-3479, F487-3500,
tat.Rome@iol.it

Japan
Technoble Yotsubashi Bldg, 3F1, 1-6-8
Kitahorie Bldg, Nishi-ku, Osaka 550-0014,
T6543-6654, F6543-6660,
tatosa@ca.mbn.or.jp; Yurakucho Denki

Building, South Tower 2F, Room 259,
1-7-1, Yurakucho, Chiyoda-ku, Tokyo 100,
T03-218-0337, F03-218-0655,
tattky@crisscross.com; and El Gala Bldg,
6F1, 1-4-2 Tenjin, Chuo-ku, Fukuoka
810-0001, T725-8808, F735-4434,
tatfuk@asahi-net.or.jp

Malaysia
Suite 22.01, level 22, Menara Lion, 165 Jl
Ampang, Kuala Lumpur, T2623480,
F2623486, sawatdi@po.jaring.my

Singapore
c/o Royal Thai Embassy, 370 Orchard Rd,
Singapore, T2357694, F7335653,
tatsin@mbox5.singnet.com.sg

UK
49 Albemarle St, London W1X 3FE,
T020-7499 7679, F7629 5519,
info@tat-uk.demon.co.uk

USA
611 North Larchment Blvd, 1st floor, Los
Angeles, Ca 90004, T461-9814, F461-9834,
tatla@ix.netcom.com; 1 World Trade
Center, Suite No 3729, New York, NY 10048,
T432-0433, F432-0435, tatny@aol.com

---

www.nationgroup.com Homepage for The Nation one of Thailand's main English language daily newspapers.

www.bangkokpost.net/ Homepage for the Bangkok Post including back issues and main stories of the day.

http://asiatravelmart.com includes deals on flights, hotels and more; especially good on cheap hotel deals in the Asian region.

www.yahoo.com/Regional Countries/[name of country] Insert name of country to access practical information including material from other travel guides.

Travel advisories websites **www.travel.state.gov/travel_warnings.html** The US State Department's continually updated travel advisories on its Travel Warnings & Consular Information Sheets page.

www.fco.gov.uk/travel/ The UK Foreign and Commonwealth Office's travel warning section.

Language

See also words & phrases, page 837
The Thai language is tonal and, strictly speaking, monosyllabic. There are five tones: high, low, rising, falling and mid-tone. These are used to distinguish between words which would otherwise be identical. For example: *mai* (low tone, new), *mai* (rising, silk), *mai* (midtone, burn), *mai* (high tone, question indicator) and *mai* (falling tone, negative indicator). Not surprisingly, many visitors find it hard to hear the different tones and it is difficult to make much progress during a short visit (unlike, say, with Malaysian or Indonesian). The tonal nature of the language also explains why so much of Thai humour is based around homonyms and especially when farangs say what

they do not mean. Although tones make Thai a challenge for foreign visitors, other aspects of the language are easier to grasp: there are no marked plurals in nouns, no marked tenses in verbs, no definite or indefinite articles and no affixes or suffixes.

Visitors may well experience two oddities of the Thai language being reflected in the way that Thais speak English. An *l* or *r* at the end of a word in Thai becomes an *n*, while an *s* becomes a *t*. So some Thais refer to the 'Shell' Oil Company as 'Shen', a name like 'Les' becomes 'Let', while 'cheque bill' becomes 'cheque bin'. It is also impossible to have two consonants after one another in Thai. If it occurs, a Thai will automatically insert a vowel (even though it is not written). So the soft drink 'Sprite' becomes 'Sa-prite', and the English word 'start', 'sa-tart'.

In general, English is reasonably widely spoken on the tourist trail and visitors should be able to find someone to help. English is taught to all schoolchildren, and competence in English is regarded as a very useful qualification. Off the tourist trail, making yourself understood becomes more difficult.

Despite Thai being a difficult language to pick up, it is worth trying to learn a few words, even if your visit to Thailand is short. Thais generally feel honoured that a farang is bothering to learn their language and will be patient and helpful. If they laugh at some of your pronunciations do not be put off; it is not meant to be critical.

Essentials

consonant 'y' consonant 'b'

คือ ปูแสมนี้ ส่วนแสมดำลำต้นใหญ่โตมากผิวต้น
เกลี้ยงดำ มีขึ้นทางแถบชายทะเลบางปู่ก็มี

Tone marks

ประโยชน์ทางยา ในแพทย์ตำบลกล่าวว่า
แก่นแสมทะเล· รสเค็มเฝื่อน แก้ลมในกระดูก,
และกษัยขับโลหิต, โดยมากใช้คู่กันกับแก่นแสมสาร
เรียกว่าแก่นแสมทั้งสอง

consonant 's' vowels

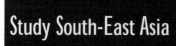

Disabled travellers

Disabled travellers will find Thailand a challenge. The difficulties that even non-disabled travellers encounter in crossing roads, when pedestrian crossings are either nonexistent or ignored by most motorists, are amplified many-fold for disabled people. And the difficulties don't end, having successfully negotiated the road. The high kerbs and lack of ramps will pose a challenge for even the most wheelchair savvy. Furthermore, the cracked concrete and the tendency for pavements to be littered with motorbikes, stall holders, even parked cars, will further exasperate. Buses and taxis are not designed for disabled access and it sometimes takes alacrity for non-disabled people to hop aboard a moving bus. Finally, there are relatively few hotels and restaurants that are disabled-friendly. This is particularly true of cheaper and older establishments.

This is not to suggest that travel in Thailand is impossible for disabled travellers, but merely to point out some of the challenges. On the plus side, you will find Thais to be extremely helpful, and because taxis and tuk-tuks are cheap it is usually not necessary to rely on buses. Best of all, though, is to come to Thailand with a non-disabled companion who can help in sticky situations.

But of course only a minority of disabled people are wheelchair users, and it is now widely acknowledged that your impairments do not stop you from enjoying a great holiday. The website www.geocities.com/Paris/1502 is dedicated to providing travel information for 'disabled adventurers', and includes book reviews and travel tips.

Gay and lesbian travellers

Thailand and Thai society are accommodating towards gays and lesbians. Homosexuality is not regarded as reprehensible as it is in some other cultures, and gays and lesbians are not persecuted. This extends to gay and lesbian travellers who will find Thailand a welcoming place. However, advice given in the conduct section (see page 40) still applies. Outward and overt shows of affection are frowned upon, whether heterosexual or homosexual.

Several of the free tourist magazines in Bangkok, available from lobbies in many hotels, provide information on the gay and lesbian scene, including bars and meeting points. Two websites to browse before you get there are www.utopia-asia.com (see http://www.utopia-asia.com/tipsthai.htm for the Thai section of the site) and www.ithailand.com/living/entertainment/bangkok/gay/index.htm Both provide good material on where to go, current events, and background information on the Thai gay scene in Bangkok and beyond. *Utopia Tours* at *Tarntawan Palace Hotel*, 119/5-10 Surawong Rd, T2383227, www.utopia-tours.com, provides tours for gay and lesbian visitors. There's also a map of gay Bangkok. Gay clubs are listed in *Bangkok Metro* magazine (www.bkkmetro.com), and include *Icon: the Club*, Silom Rd Soi 4, www. iconasia.com, and *Freeman Dance Arena*, 60/18-21 Silom Rd, www.dj-station.com. The main centres of activity in Bangkok are Silom Rd sois 2 and 4 and Sukhumvit soi 23.

Student travellers

ISIC Students are eligible for discounts at some museums but the use of student cards is not widespread so don't expect to save a fortune.

Anyone in full-time education is entitled to an International Student Identity Card (ISIC). These are issued by student travel offices and travel agencies across the world, and offer special rates on all forms of transport and other concessions and services. For more details, see www.isic.org/ The head office is at Herengracht 479, 1017 BS Amsterdam, The Netherlands, T31-20-4212800, F31-20-4212810.

Women travellers

Compared with neighbouring East and South Asia, women in Southeast Asia enjoy relative equality of opportunity. While this is a contentious issue, scholars have pointed to the lack of pronouns in Southeast Asian languages, the role of women in trade and commerce, the important part that women play in reproductive decisions, the characteristically egalitarian patterns of inheritance, and so on. This is not to suggest that there is complete equality between the sexes. Buddhism, for example – at least as it is practised in Thailand – accords women a lower position, and it is notable how few women there are in positions of political power.

The implications of this for women travellers, and especially solo women travellers, is that while they will face some difficulties not encountered by men – for example, the possibility of some low-key sexual harassment – these are not as pronounced as they are in other countries. Nonetheless, women should make sure that rooms are secure at night (there have been reports of unwelcome intrusions) and if travelling in remote regions, should try to team up with other travellers.

Work opportunities

Most visitors to Thailand who also work take on English teaching. Some guesthouses will provide free accommodation for guests who are willing to allot a portion of the day to English conversation classes. There are also opportunities in Bangkok and Chiang Mai. Those with a qualification, for example a TEFL certificate, can usually command a higher salary. There are also various NGOs/voluntary organizations that will employ people. For more information on working in Thailand see www.ethailand.com/LIFESTYLE/work_permit.html, or www.goabroad.com/ The former provides background information on getting a visa while the latter has information on language schools, volunteer work and more.

Travelling with children

Many people are daunted by the prospect of taking a child to Southeast Asia. Naturally, it is not something which is taken on lightly; travelling is slower and more expensive and there are additional health risks for the child or baby. But it can be a most rewarding experience and, with sufficient care and planning, it can also be safe. Children are excellent passports into a local culture. You will also receive the best service and help from officials and members of the public when in difficulty.

Children in Thailand are given 24-hour attention by parents, grandparents and siblings. They are rarely left to cry and are carried for most of the first eight months of their lives; crawling is considered animal-like. A non-Asian child is still something of a novelty and parents may find their child frequently taken off their hands, even mobbed in more remote areas. This can be a great relief (at mealtimes, for instance) or most alarming. Some children love the attention, others react against it; it is best simply to gauge your own child's reactions.

At the hottest time of year, air conditioning may be essential for a baby or young *Sleeping* child's comfort. This rules out many of the cheaper hotels, but air-conditioned accommodation is available in all but the most out-of-the-way spots. When the child is bathing, be aware that the water could carry parasites, so avoid letting him or her drink it.

The advice given in the health section on food and drink (see page 65) should be *Eating* applied even more stringently where young children are concerned. Be aware that expensive hotels may have squalid cooking conditions; the cheapest street stall is

Essentials

Essentials

often more hygienic. Where possible, try to watch food being prepared. Stir-fried vegetables and rice or noodles are the best bet; meat and fish may be pre-cooked and then left out before being re-heated. Fruit can be bought cheaply – papaya, banana and avocado are all excellent sources of nutrition – and can be self-peeled, ensuring cleanliness. Powdered milk is also available throughout the region, although most brands have added sugar. If taking a baby, breast-feeding is strongly recommended. Powdered food can be bought in most towns; the quality may not be the same as equivalent foods bought in the West, but it is perfectly adequate for short periods. Bottled water and fizzy drinks are also sold widely. If your child is at the `grab everything and put it in mouth' stage, a damp cloth and some *dettol* (or equivalent) are useful. Frequent wiping of hands and tabletops can help to minimize the chance of infection.

Transport Public transport may be a problem; trains are fine, but long bus journeys are restrictive and uncomfortable. Hiring a car is undoubtedly the most convenient way to see a country with a small child. Rear seatbelts are rarely fitted, but it is possible to buy child-seats in Bangkok, Chiang Mai and some other larger cities and tourist centres (though they are not necessarily made to international standards).

Health More preparation is probably necessary for babies and children than for an adult, and perhaps a little more care should be taken when travelling to remote areas where health services are primitive. This is because children can be become more rapidly ill than adults (on the other hand, they often recover more quickly). A travel insurance policy which has an air ambulance provision is strongly recommended. When planning a route, try to stay within 24 hours' travel of a hospital with good care and facilities. Many expatriats fly to Singapore for medical care, which has the best doctors and facilities in the region.

Diarrhoea and vomiting are the most common problems, so take the usual precautions, but more intensively. Breastfeeding is best and most convenient for babies, but powdered milk is available in the cities, as are a few baby foods. Bananas and other fruits are all nutritious and can be cleanly prepared. The treatment of diarrhoea is the same for adults, except that it should start earlier and be continued with more persistence. Children get dehydrated very quickly in hot countries and can become drowsy and uncooperative unless cajoled to drink water or juice, plus salts. Upper respiratory infections such as colds, catarrh and middle ear infections are also common, and if your child suffers from these normally take some antibiotics against the possibility. Outer ear infections after swimming are also common and antibiotic eardrops will help. **NB** Never allow your child to be exposed to the harsh tropical sun without protection. A child can burn in a matter of minutes. Loose cotton-clothing with long sleeves and legs and a sunhat are best. High-factor sun-protection cream is essential.

Vaccinations Children should already be properly protected against diphtheria, poliomyelitis and pertussis (whooping cough), measles and HIB, all of which can be more serious infections in Southeast Asia than at home. Measles, mumps and rubella vaccine is also given to children throughout the world, but those teenage girls who have not had rubella (German measles) should be tested and vaccinated. Hepatitis B vaccination for babies is now routine in some countries.

Essentials **Disposable nappies** These can be bought in Thailand but remember that you're adding to the rubbish-disposal problem. If you are staying any length of time in one place, it may be worth taking Terry's (cloth) nappies. All you need is a bucket and some double-strength nappy cleanse (simply soak and rinse). Cotton nappies dry quickly in the heat and are generally more comfortable for the baby or child. Of course, the best way for a child to be is nappy-free – like the local children.

Baby products Many Western baby products are available in Thailand: shampoo, talcum powder, soap and lotion. Baby wipes are expensive and not always easy to find.

Checklist Baby wipes; Child paracetamol; Disinfectant; First aid kit; Flannel; Immersion element for boiling water; Decongestant for colds; Instant food for under-one-year-olds; Mug/bottle/bowl/spoons; Nappy cleanse, double-strength; ORS (Oral Rehydration Salts) such as *Dioralyte*, widely available in Thailand, and the most effective way to alleviate diarrhoea (it is not a cure); Portable baby chair, to hook onto tables – this is not essential but can be very useful; Sarong or backpack for carrying child (and/or lightweight collapsible buggy); Sterilizing tablets (and container for sterilizing bottles, teats, utensils); Cream for nappy rash and other skin complaints, such as *Sudocrem*; Sunblock, factor 15 or higher; Sunhat; Terry's (cloth) nappies, liners, pins and plastic pants; Thermometer; Zip-lock bags for carrying snacks etc.

Pentes, Tina and Truelove, Adrienne (1984) *Travelling with children to Indonesia and South-East Asia*, Hale & Iremonger: Sydney. Wheeler, Maureen, *Travel with children*, Lonely Planet: Hawthorne, Australia.

Further information
See also websites, page 76

Before you travel

Getting in

All tourists must possess passports valid for at least six months longer than their intended stay in Thailand.

Visas
See also box on Thai embassies worldwide, page 23

30-day visa exemptions No visa is required for travellers from some 56 countries, listed below, when entering Thailand for tourist purposes for 30 days or less. If you intend to stay longer, obtain a 60-day tourist visa (see below). Visitors are fined ฿100 per day each day they exceed the 30-day limit, to a maximum of ฿20,000 or 200 days. Payment can be made at the airport before departure or at the Immigration Department (see below). While, in theory, visitors can be denied entry if they do not have an onward ticket and sufficient funds for their stay, in practice customs officials almost never check. The same is true of tourists who arrive via the Thai-Malaysian border by sea, rail or road. The 30-day exemption applies to nationals of the following countries: Algeria, Argentina, Australia, Austria, Bahrain, Belgium, Brazil, Brunei, Burma, Canada, Denmark, Djibouti, Egypt, Fiji, Finland, France, Germany, Greece, Iceland, Indonesia, Ireland, Israel, Italy, Japan, Kenya, Korea, Kuwait, Luxembourg, Malaysia, Mauritania, Mexico, Morocco, The Netherlands, New Zealand, Norway, Oman, Papua New Guinea, Philippines, Portugal, Qatar, Saudi Arabia, Senegal, Singapore, Slovenia, South Africa, Spain, Sweden, Switzerland, Tunisia, Turkey, UAE, UK, USA, Vanuatu, Western Samoa, Yemen. Malaysian nationals arriving by road from Malaysia do not need evidence of an onward journey. Visitors from Hong Kong (China) do not require a visa for visits of up to 15 days.

Visas on arrival For visitors from 99 countries not in the list above, it is possible to have a visa issued on arrival. There is a visa booth at Don Muang (Bangkok) Airport, at customs control, and even a photo booth to provide passport snaps (one photograph required). Note that these visas are valid for 15 days only (฿300). Applicants must also have an outbound (return) ticket. There are similar desks at Chiang Mai, Phuket and Hat Yai airports.

Essentials

Tourist visas These are valid for 60 days from date of entry (single entry) and must be obtained from a Thai embassy before arrival in Thailand. They can be extended for a further 30 days. Multiple entry visas are also available.

90-day non-immigrant visas These are also issued and can be obtained in the applicant's home country (about US$30). A letter from the applicant's company or organization, guaranteeing their repatriation, should be submitted at the same time.

Re-entry permit For those who wish to leave and then re-enter Thailand before their visa expires, it is possible to apply for a re-entry permit from the Immigration Department (see below) (฿500).

Visa extensions These are obtainable from the Immigration Department in Bangkok (see below) for ฿500. The process used to be interminable, but the system is now much improved and relatively painless. Extensions can also be issued in other towns, such as Koh Samui (see page 665) and Chiang Mai (page 299). Applicants must bring two photocopies of their passport ID page and the page on which their tourist visa is stamped, together with three passport photographs. It is also advisable to dress neatly. It may be easier to leave the country and then re-enter having obtained a new tourist visa. Visas are issued by all Thai embassies and consulates. The length of time a visa is extended varies according to the office and the official. However, those on a 30-day no-visa entry can usually have their stay extended by a week, sometimes 10 days; those with a 60-day tourist visa can usually expect a 30-day extension.

For the latest information on visas and tourist visa exemptions, see the Consular Information section of the Thai Ministry of Foreign Affairs website: www.mfa.go.th/ConsInfo/

In the UK there is now a **visa information line**, operating 24 hours a day, T0891-600150. Calls are charged at 60p a minute.

Immigration Department Soi Suan Plu, Thanon Sathorn Tai, Bangkok 10120, T02-2873101. Open 0930-1630 Monday-Friday, 0830-1200 Saturday (tourists only).

Lost or stolen passports 1. File a report with the local police. 2. Take the report to your local embassy or consulate and apply for a new travel document or passport. (If there is no representation, visit the Passport Division of the Ministry of Foreign Affairs). 3. Take the new passport plus the police report to Section 4, Subdivision 4, Immigration Bureau, room 311 (third floor), Old Building, Soi Suan Plu, Sathorn Tai Rd, Bangkok, T02-2873911, for a new visa stamp.

Vaccinations

See also Vaccination & immunization, page 63 No vaccinations required, unless coming from an infected area. If visitors have been in a yellow fever infected area in the 10 days before arrival, and do not have a vaccination certificate, they will be vaccinated and kept in quarantine for six days, or deported.

Money

Plastic is increasingly used in Thailand and just about every town of any size will have a bank with an ATM. Because Thailand has embraced the ATM with such exuberance, many foreign visitors no longer bother with travellers' cheques and rely entirely on plastic. However, travellers' cheques denominated in most major currencies can be exchanged in provincial centres, whether they are recognized tourist destinations or not. A small stash of US dollars cash can come in handy in a sticky situation; keep it separate from your travellers' cheques.

The unit of Thai currency is the **baht** (฿), which is divided into 100 **satang**. Notes in circulation include ฿20 (green), ฿50 (blue), ฿100 (red), ฿500 (purple) and ฿1,000 (orange and grey). Coins include 25 satang and 50 satang, and ฿1, ฿5 and ฿10. The two smaller coins are gradually disappearing from circulation and the 25 satang coin, equivalent to the princely sum of US$0.003 (3 c), is rarely encountered. The colloquial term for 25 satang is *saleng*.

Currency

The exchange rate can be found in the daily newspapers or on the web. One website is the Bangkok Bank's: www.bbl.co.th/bankrates/ Another useful site is www.oanda.com/converter/classic, which will provide exchange rates for any specified currencies. It is best to change money at banks or money changers, which give better rates than hotels. There is no black market. First-class hotels have 24-hour money changers. There is a charge of ฿13 per cheque when changing travellers' cheques (passport required), so it works out cheaper to travel with large denomination travellers' cheques (or avoid them altogether). Indonesian Rupiah, Nepalese Rupees, Burmese kyat, Vietnamese dong, Lao kip and Cambodian riels cannot be exchanged for baht at Thai banks. Money changers will sometimes exchange kyat, dong, kip and riel, and it can be a good idea to buy the currencies in Bangkok before departure for these countries as the black market rate often applies.

Exchange rates
See inside front cover for a quick reference guide to exchange rates

For 13 years until 2 July 1997, the Thai baht was pegged to the US dollar, and you could be sure, on arrival, that US$1 would buy you ฿25, give or take a saleng. Since the baht was forced from its peg and allowed to float, it has fluctuated a great deal more. At the time of going to press there were around ฿44 to US$1.

Visa and MasterCard are the most widely taken credit cards, and cash cards with the Cirrus logo can also be used to withdraw cash at many banks. Generally, Amex can be used at branches of the Bangkok Bank; JCB at Siam Commercial Bank; MasterCard at Siam Commercial and Bangkok Bank; and Visa at Thai Farmers' Bank and Bangkok Bank. Most larger hotels and more expensive restaurants take credit cards as well. In theory, Thai businesses should not pass on the credit card commission; there is a law against this. In practice many do (although generally not hotels), adding 3% or 4% to the bill.

Credit cards

Notification of credit card loss American Express, IBM Bldg, Phahonyothin Rd, T2730040; Diners Club, Dusit Thani Bldg, Rama IV Rd, T2332645/2335775/ 2335644/2383660; JCB, T2561361/2561351; Visa and MasterCard, Thai Farmers Bank Bldg, Phahonyothin Rd, T2522212, T2701801-10.

Visitors staying in first class hotels and eating in hotel restaurants will probably spend a minimum of ฿1,000 per day and conceivably much more. Tourists staying in cheaper air-conditioned accommodation and eating in local restaurants will probably spend about ฿500-750 per day. A backpacker, staying in fan-cooled guesthouses and eating cheaply, might expect to be able to live on ฿200 per day. In Bangkok, expect to pay 20-30% more.

Cost of living

Customs

250 g of cigars or cigarettes (or 200 cigarettes) and one litre of wine or spirits. One still camera with five rolls of film or one movie camera with three rolls of 8 mm or 16 mm film.

Duty free allowance

Non-residents can bring in up to ฿2,000 per person and unlimited foreign currency, although amounts exceeding US$10,000 must be declared. Maximum amount permitted to take out of the country is ฿50,000 per person.

Currency regulations

Essentials

Essentials

Prohibited items	All narcotics; obscene literature, pornography; firearms (except with a permit from the Police Department or local registration office).

Some species of plants and animals are prohibited; for more information contact the Royal Forestry Department, Phahonyothin Rd, Bangkok, T02-5792776. Permission of entry for animals by air is obtainable at the airport. An application must be made to the Department of Livestock Development, Bangkok, T02-2515136 for entry by sea. Vaccination certificates are required; dogs and cats need rabies certificates.

Export restrictions No Buddha or Bodhisattva images or fragments should be taken out of Thailand, except for worshipping by Buddhists, for cultural exchanges or for research. However, obviously many people do and you only have to look in the antique shops to see the abundance for sale. A licence should be obtained from the Department of Fine Arts, Na Prathat Rd, Bangkok, T02-2241370, from Chiang Mai National Museum, T053-221308, or from the Songkhla National Museum, Songkhla, T074-311728. Five days' notice is needed; take two passport photographs of the object and photocopies of your passport.

What to take

Travellers usually tend to take too much. Almost everything is available in Thailand's main towns and cities and often at a lower price than in the West. Even apparently remote areas will have shops that stock most things that a traveller might require, from toiletries and batteries to pharmaceuticals and film.

Suitcases are not appropriate if you are intending to travel overland by bus. A backpack, or even better a travelpack (where the straps can be zipped out of sight), is recommended. Travelpacks have the advantage of being hybrid backpacks-suitcases; they can be carried on the back for easy porterage, but they can also be taken into hotels without the owner being labelled a 'hippy'. **NB** For serious hikers, a backpack with an internal frame is still by far the better option for longer treks.

In terms of clothing, dress in Thailand is relatively casual, even at formal functions. Jackets and ties are not necessary except in a few of the most expensive hotel restaurants. However, though formal attire may be the exception, dressing tidily is the norm. This does not apply on beaches and islands where (almost) anything goes, and sarongs, thongs and such like are *de rigeur*. However, while dress may be casual, this does not extend to undress, ie topless sunbathing. This does increasingly occur, but it is frowned upon by Thais who are usually too polite to say anything. This is particularly true in the Muslim areas of the South.

There is a tendency, rather than to take inappropriate articles of clothing, to take too many of the same article. Laundry services are cheap and the turnaround rapid.

Checklist Bumbag; earplugs; first aid kit; hiking boots (if intending to visit any of the national parks); insect repellent and/or electric mosquito mats, coils; international driving licence; money belt; passports (valid for at least six months); photocopies of essential documents; short wave radio; slip-on shoes (handy when you have to take your shoes off before entering houses and monastery buildings); spare passport photographs; sun hat; sun protection; sunglasses; Swiss Army knife; torch; umbrella; wet wipes; zip-lock bags.

Those intending to stay in budget accommodation might also include: cotton sheet sleeping bag; padlock (for hotel room and pack); soap; student card; toilet paper; towel; travel wash. All items listed above are available in Thailand, so don't think that you have to pack six weeks' supply of toilet paper!

Discount flight agents in the UK and Ireland

Council Travel, 28a Poland St, London, W1V 3DB, T020-7437 7767, www.destinations-group.com
STA Travel, T0870-1606070, www.statravel.co.uk Branches in London, as well as in Brighton, Bristol, Cambridge, Leeds, Manchester, Newcastle-Upon-Tyne and Oxford, and on many university campuses. Specialists in low-cost student/youth flights and tours, also good for student IDs and insurance.

Trailfinders, 194 Kensington High Street, London, W8 7RG, T020-7938 3939.
Usit Campus, 52 Grosvenor Gardens, London, SW1 0AG, T0870-2401010, www.usitcampus.co.uk Student/youth travel specialists, with branches also in Belfast, Brighton, Bristol, Cambridge, Manchester and Oxford. The main Ireland branch is at 19 Aston Quay, Dublin 2, T01-6021777.

Essentials

Getting there

Air

The majority of visitors arrive in Thailand through Bangkok's Don Muang airport. Chiang Mai in the north and Phuket, Hat Yai and Koh Samui in the south are also international airports. More than 35 airlines and charter companies fly to Bangkok. Thai International, or Thai, is the national carrier.

The approximate flight time from London to Bangkok (non-stop) is 12 hours. There are direct flights from most major cities in Europe. From **London** Heathrow, airlines offering non-stop flights include Qantas, British Airways, Thai Airways and Eva Air. Philippine Airlines flies a two-stop service from **Gatwick**. There are non-stop flights from **Athens** on Thai and Olympic, **Amsterdam** on KLM and China Airlines, **Copenhagen** on Thai and SAS, **Frankfurt** on Thai, Lufthansa and Garuda, **Paris** on Thai and Air France, and **Zurich** on Thai and Swiss Air.
From Europe

The approximate flight time from Los Angeles to Bangkok is 21 hours. There are one-stop flights from **Los Angeles** on Thai and two stops on Delta; one-stop flights from **San Francisco** on Northwest and United and two stops on Delta; and one-stop flights from **Vancouver** on Canadian.
From the USA & Canada

There are flights from **Sydney** and **Melbourne** (approximately nine hours) daily, with Qantas and Thai Airways. There is also a choice of other flights with British Airways, Alitalia, Lufthansa and Lauda Air, which are less frequent. There are flights from **Perth** with Thai Airways and Qantas. From **Auckland**, Air New Zealand, Thai Airways and British Airways fly to Bangkok.
From Australasia

Thai Airways, Air India, Indian Airlines and Aeroflot fly from **Delhi**. Air Lanka, Thai Airways and Cathay Pacific fly from **Colombo**. From **Dhaka** there are flights with Biman Bangladesh Airlines or Thai Airways. PIA and Thai Airways fly from **Karachi**. Balkan flies from **Male**. Royal Nepal Airlines and Thai Airways fly from **Kathmandu**.
From South Asia

Gulf Air fly from **Bahrain**, and Egyptair from **Cairo**. Numerous airlines fly from **Hong Kong**, **Tokyo** and **Manila**, as well as regional destinations like **Kuala Lumpur**, **Singapore** and **Jakarta**.
From the Middle & Far East

Essentials

 Discount flight agents in North America

Air Brokers International, 323 Geary St, Suite 411, San Francisco, CA94102, T01-800-883 3273, www.airbrokers.com Consolidator and specialist on RTW and Circle Pacific tickets.

Council Travel, 205 E 42nd St, New York, NY 10017, T1-888-COUNCIL, www.counciltravel.com Student/budget agency, with branches in many other US cities.

Discount Airfares Worldwide On-Line, www.etn.nl/discount.htm A hub of consolidator and discount agent links.

International Travel Network/Airlines of the Web, www.itn.net/airlines Online air travel information and reservations.

STA Travel, 5900 Wilshire Blvd, Suite 2110, Los Angeles, CA 90036, T1-800-777 0112, www.sta-travel.com Also branches in New York, San Francisco, Boston, Miami, Chicago, Seattle and Washington DC.

Travel CUTS, 187 College St, Toronto, ON, M5T 1P7, T1-800-667 2887, www.travelcuts.com Specialist in student discount fares, Ids and other travel services. Branches in other Canadian cities.

Travelocity, www.travelocity.com Online consolidator.

Links to South East Asia Bangkok is a transport hub for air connections with Rangoon (Burma), Vientiane (Laos), Hanoi and Ho Chi Minh City/Saigon (Vietnam), and Phnom Penh (Cambodia). Partly as a result, it also has a concentration of tour companies specializing in Indochina and Burma and is a good place to arrange a visa.

International links with other Thai airports It is possible to fly direct to **Chiang Mai** from Dusseldorf and Munich in Germany and from Kunming (China), Singapore and Kuala Lumpur. From **Phuket** there are links with Dusseldorf and Munich, as well as Hong King, Kuala Lumpur, Penang, Singapore, Taipei and Tokyo. **Hat Yai** has daily connections with Singapore and Kuala Lumpur, and **Koh Samui** with Singapore.

Train

Regular rail services link Singapore and Bangkok, via Kuala Lumpur, Butterworth and the major southern Thai towns. Express a/c trains take two days from Singapore, 34 hours from Kuala Lumpur, 24 hours from Butterworth (road connections to Penang). The *Magic Arrow Express* leaves Singapore on Sunday, Tuesday and Thursday, Bangkok-Singapore (฿899-1,965), Bangkok-Kuala Lumpur (฿659-1,432) and to Ipoh (฿530-1,145). An additional train from Butterworth departs at 1340, arriving Bangkok 1130 the next day. The train from Bangkok to Butterworth departs 1400, arriving Butterworth 1240 (฿457-1,147). All tickets should be booked in advance.

Orient-Express Hotels, which operate the Venice Simplon Orient-Express, also run the luxury *Eastern & Oriental Express* between Bangkok, Kuala Lumpur and Singapore. (The train now continues north to Chiang Mai, see page 295.) The air-conditioned train of 22 carriages, including a saloon car, dining car, bar and observation deck and carrying just 132 passengers, runs once a week from Singapore to Bangkok and back. Luxurious carriages, fine wines and food designed for European rather than Asian sensibilities make this not just a mode of transport, but an experience. This locomotive extravaganza departs from Bangkok on Wednesday and returns from Singapore every Sunday. The journey takes 41 hours (two nights, one day) to cover the 2,000 km one-way trip. Passengers can disembark at Hua Hin, Butterworth (Penang) and Kuala Lumpur. Reservations can be made at *Orient-Express Hotels*, Sea Containers House, 20 Upper Ground, London SE1 9PF, UK T020-78055100; *Orient-Express Hotels* also has agents in Bangkok, Singapore and Kuala Lumpur to

Discount flight agents in Australia and New Zealand

Flight Centres, *82 Elizabeth St, Sydney,* *Ultimo, Sydney, and 256 Flinders St,*
T13-1600; 205 Queen St, Auckland, *Melbourne. In NZ: 10 High St, Auckland,*
T09-309 6171. Also branches in other *T09-366 6673. Also in major towns and*
towns and cities. *university campuses.*
STA Travel, *T1300-360960,* **Travel.com.au**, *80 Clarence St, Sydney,*
www.statravelaus.com.au; 702 Harris St, *T02-929 01500, www.travel.com.au*

handle reservations – in Bangkok T02-2168661; in Singapore contact: 32-01 Shaw Towers, Beach Rd, T3923500, F3923600. Booking and information available in Australia (T02-99059295), France (T01-55621800), Italy (T55180003), Japan (T03-32651200), USA (T630-9542944).

Road

The main road access is to and from Malaysia. The principal land border crossings into Malaysia are near Betong in Yala Province, from Sungei Golok in Narathiwat Province (see page 738) and at Padang Besar, where the railway line crosses the border. In April 1994 the Friendship Bridge linking Nong Khai with Laos opened and became the first bridge across the Mekong River. To cross into Laos here, foreigners no longer need to obtain a visa beforehand; they are issued on arrival and in December 1998 cost US$30. In addition to the Nong Khai/Friendship Bridge crossing, it is also possible to enter Laos from Thailand at the following places: Chongmek, near Ubon Ratchathani, to Pakse; Mukdahan to Savannakhet; Nakhon Phanom to Thakhek; and Chiang Khong to Ban Houei Xai. The latter three crossings involve crossing the Mekong by ferry or boat.

In 1992 an overland crossing at Mae Sai in the north, but only for forays into the immediate vicinity. The border at Saam Ong in the west can also be crossed by foreigners, but again only for day trips into Burma. There has also been talk of opening the border at Mae Sot, but at the time of writing this only applied to Thai passport holders.

Boat

No regular, scheduled cruise liners sail to Thailand any longer, but it is sometimes possible to enter Thailand on a freighter, arriving at Khlong Toey Port in Bangkok. The *Bangkok Post* publishes a weekly shipping post, with details on ships leaving the Kingdom.

There are frequent passenger ferries from Pak Bara, near Satun, in southern Thailand to Perlis and Langkawi Island, both in Malaysia (see page 647). The passenger and car ferries at Ta Ba, near the town of Tak Bai, south of Narathiwat, make for a fast border crossing to Pengkalan Kubor in Malaysia (see page 732). An alternative is to hitch a lift on a yacht from Phuket (Thailand) or from Penang (Malaysia). Check at the respective yacht clubs for information.

Touching down

Airport information

Don Muang Airport lies 25 km north of Bangkok. There are two international terminals (adjoining one another) and one domestic terminal. Terminal 1 serves Asia, and Terminal 2 the rest of the world. A 500 m-long covered and air-conditioned walkway links the domestic and international terminals. Facilities include banks and currency exchange, post office, left luggage (฿70 per item per day – maximum four months, located between terminals 1 and 2), hotel booking agency, airport information, airport clinic, lost and found baggage service, duty-free shops and restaurants and bars, including many newly-opened fast food outlets: *Burger King*, *Svensson's*, *Pizza Hut* and *Upper Crust*. **NB** Food is expensive here; cheap food is available across the footbridge at the railway station. The *Amari Airport Hotel*, T02-5661020/1, is linked to the international terminal by a walkway. It provides a 'ministay' service for passengers who wish to 'freshen-up' and take a room for up to three hours between 0800 and 1800.

Passport control at Don Muang Airport during peak arrival periods (usually 1200-1400) can be choked with visitors – be prepared for a wait of an hour or more before reaching the arrivals hall.

A new airport for Bangkok in 2004 In 2000 a government panel finally decided that **Nong Ngu Hao** – or Cobra Swamp – will become Bangkok and Thailand's new international gateway in 2004, taking over from Don Muang. Nong Ngu Hao is in Bang Phli district, Samut Prakan province, south of Bangkok (Don Muang is north). But Don Muang will remain open for two years while Nong Ngu Hao is expanded and a second runway added. Given the Thai authorities' tendency to change their minds, don't imagine that this is signed and sealed until the first aircraft touches down at Nong Ngu Hao.

Flight information International: T5351386 for departures, T5351301 for arrivals. Domestic: T5351253. The domestic terminal has a hotel booking counter, post office, currency exchange counters, restaurant and bookshop. An elevated air-conditioned walkway connects the international and domestic terminals; a shuttle bus is sometimes available, but beware – taxis grossly overcharge for a drive of under 1 km.

Sleeping **A** *Amari Airport*, 333 Chert Wudthakas Rd, T5661020, F5661941, airport@amari.com, www.amari.com A/c, restaurants, pool, fitness centre, connected to airport by a/c footbridge; 400-plus rooms look onto attractive gardens. Useful hotel for transit passengers, with short-term stays for wash and rest available. Ladies and executive floors, several restaurants including Japanese and *Le Bel-Air* for steaks and seafood. **A** *Rama Gardens*, 9/9 Vibhavadi Rangsit Rd, Bangkaen (7 km from the airport), T561002, F5611025. A/c, restaurants, two attractive large pools, out of town on road to airport, inconvenient for most except those merely stopping over for a few hours, but spacious grounds with fitness centre, tennis, squash, golf, putting. **A-B** *Quality Suites*, 99/401-486 Chaeng Wattana Rd, Soi Benjamitr, T9822022, F9822036. A/c, restaurant, indoor pool, 'mini' stays available (maximum eight hours), slightly cheaper than the *Amari* but 15 minutes from airport, OK for a night's stopover. **A** *Asia Airport*, 99/2 Moo 8 Phahon-yothin Rd, T9926999, F5323193, sale@asiahotel.co.th Huge and impersonal, but all the amenities if you can't face driving into town.

Transport to town **Taxi** Official taxi booking service in the arrivals hall. There are two desks. One for the more expensive official airport taxis (newer, more luxurious vehicles); one for public

Essentials

Essentials

Touching down

Emergency services *Police: T191, T123. Tourist Police: T195.* **Fire:** *T199.* **Ambulance:** *T2522171-5.* **Tourist Assistance Centre:** *Rachdamnern Nok Avenue, Bangkok, T2828129.*

Hours of business *Banks: 0830-1530 Mon-Fri.* **Currency exchange services:** *0830-2200 Mon-Sun in Bangkok, and other tourist centres like Pattaya, Phuket and Chiang Mai. In other towns, opening hours are usually rather shorter.* **Government offices:** *0830-1200, 1300-1630 Mon-Fri.* **Tourist offices:** *0830-1630 Mon-Sun.* **Shops:** *0830-1700, larger shops: 1000-1900 or 2100.*

Official time *7 hrs ahead of GMT.*

Voltage *220 volts (50 cycles) throughout Thailand. Most first and tourist class hotels have outlets for shavers and hair dryers. Adaptors are recommended, as almost all sockets are two-pronged.*

Weights and measures *Thailand uses the metric system, although there are some traditional measures still in use, in particular the rai, which equals 0.16 ha. There are four ngaan in a rai. Other local measures include the krasorp (sack), which equals 25 kg, and the tang, which is 10-11 kg. However, for most purchases (eg fruit) the kilogram is now the norm.*

taxis. The former cost ฿400 downtown; ฿300 to the northern and northeastern bus terminals; ฿450 to the southern bus terminal; ฿1,500 to Pattaya. Note that airport flunkies sometimes try to direct passengers to this more expensive 'limousine' service: walk through the barriers to the public taxi desk. A public taxi downtown should cost about half these prices, roughly ฿200. Note that tolls on the expressways are paid on top of the fare on the meter. If taking a metered taxi, the coupon from the booking desk will quote no fare; ensure that the meter is used or you may find that the trip costs ฿300 instead of ฿200. Keep hold of your coupon – some taxi drivers try to pocket it – as it details the obligations of taxi drivers. Some regular Don Muang visitors recommend going up to the departures floor and flagging down a taxi that has just dropped passengers off. Again, expect to pay ฿200. **Warning** There have been cases of visitors being robbed in unofficial taxis. To tell whether your vehicle is a registered taxi, check the colour of the number plate. Official airport limousines have green plates, public taxis have yellow plates and a white plate means the vehicle is not registered as a taxi. The sedan service into town costs ฿500-650. Cars are newer, more comfortable and better maintained than the average city taxi. It takes 30 minutes to one hour to central Bangkok, depending on the time of day and the state of the traffic. The elevated expressway can reduce journey time to 20 minutes; ask the taxi driver to take this route if you wish to save time, but note, again, that there is a toll fee. Also note that there have been some complaints about taxi drivers at the domestic terminal forming a cartel, refusing to use their meters and charging a fixed rate considerably above the meter rate.

Courtesy car Many upmarket hotels will meet passengers and provide transport to town gratis. Check before arrival or contact the *Thai Hotels Association* desk in the terminal building.

Bus An a/c airport bus service operates every 15 minutes, 0500-2400, ฿70 to Silom Rd (service A1), Sanaam Luang (service A2) (most convenient for Khaosan Road guesthouses) and Phra Khanong (service A3). Stops are as follows: **Silom service (A1):** Don Muang Tollway, Din Daeng, Pratunam, Lumpini Park, Silom. **Sanaam Luang service (A2):** Don Muang Tollway, Din Daeng, Victory Monument, Phayathai, Phetburi, Lan Luang, Democracy Monument, Sanaam Luang. **Phra Khanong service (A3):** Don Muang Tollway, Din Daeng, Sukhumvit, Ekamai, Phra Khanong. While hotel stops are: **Silom service (A1):** *Century, Indra, Anoma, Grand Hyatt, Erawan, Regent,*

Dusit Thani and *Narai* hotels. **Sanaam Luang service (A2)**: Victory Monument, *Siam City Hotel*, Soi King Phet, Saphan Khao, *Majestic* and *Rattanakosin* hotels. **Phra Khanong service (A3)**: Amari Building, *Ambassador* and *Delta Grand Pacific* hotels, Bang Chan Glass House, *Novotel*, Soi Ekkamai (Sukhumvit). **NB** Return buses have slightly different stops.

Although many visitors will see ฿70 as money well spent (but note that for three or four passengers a taxi is as cheap or cheaper), there will still be the hardened few who will opt for the regular bus service. This is just as cheap and slow as it ever was, 1½ to three hours (depending on time of day) (฿7-15). The bus stop is 50 m north of the arrivals hall. Buses are crowded during rush hour and there is little room for luggage. Bus 59 goes to Khaosan Rd, bus 29 goes to Bangkok's Hualamphong railway station, via the Northern bus terminal and Siam Square. A/c bus 10 goes to Samsen Rd and Silom Rd via the Northern bus terminal, a/c bus 4 goes to Silom Rd, a/c bus 13 goes to Sukhumvit Rd and the Eastern bus terminal, a/c bus 29 goes to the Northern bus terminal, Siam Square and Hualamphong railway station. **By minibus**: ฿100 to major hotels, ฿60 shuttle bus to the *Asia Hotel* on Phayathai Rd, ฿50-80 to Khaosan Rd, depending on the time of day. Direct buses to Pattaya at 0900, 1200 and 1700, ฿180.

Train The station is on the other side of the north-south highway from the airport. Regular trains into Bangkok's Hualamphong station, ฿5 for ordinary train, third class (the cheapest option). But only six ordinary trains per day. For 'rapid' and 'express', a supplementary charge of ฿40-60 is levied. The State Railways of Thailand run an 'Airport Express' five times a day (but not on Saturday and Sunday), with a/c shuttle bus from Don Muang station to airport terminal, 35 minutes (฿100).

Ferry A civilized way to avoid the traffic. If booked in the *Oriental*, *Shangri-la* or *Sheraton* hotels, it is possible to get a minibus from the airport to the ferry terminal on the river. Then take the hour-long river crossing by long-tailed boat to the appropriate hotel.

Payable on departure, ฿500 for international flights. Tax on domestic departures is included in the price of the ticket. This does not apply, however, when leaving from one of the airports owned by Bangkok Airways; namely Koh Samui and Sukhothai. **Visitors in transit** for less than 12 hours are permitted to enter the country and not pay departure tax on leaving again. **Airport tax**

Tax clearance Any foreign visitor who has derived income while staying in Thailand must pay income tax. In addition, all travellers who have stayed in Thailand for 90 days or more in any one calendar year must obtain a tax clearance certificate. To avoid delay at the airport, contact the Revenue Department, Chakrapong Rd, Bangkok, T02-2829899.

Tourist information

The **Tourist Authority of Thailand** (TAT) is Thailand's very efficient tourism organization. The head office is on the 10th floor, Le Concorde Building, 202 Rachadaphisek Rd, T6941222, F6941220, towards the northeastern edge of the city centre. Open 0830-1630, Monday-Friday. There is a more convenient office at 4 Rachdamnern Nok Ave, T2829773, F2829775. Open 0830-1630, Monday-Sunday. There is also a third minor office at the Chatuchak Weekend Market, Kamphaeng Phet 2 Road, T2724440-1. Open Saturday and Sunday only, 0900-1700. The TAT's useful website is http://www.tourismthailand.org/tat *See also box, page 24, for TAT offices overseas*

Most major tourist destinations have local offices, see appropriate sections for addresses. TAT offices are a useful source of local information, often providing maps of the town, listings of hotels and guesthouses, as well as information on local tourist attractions. Opening hours are 0830-1630 Monday-Sunday. The tourist information office at Hualamphong Railway Station is not an official one and reportedly provides inaccurate or misleading advice.

Rules, customs and etiquette

Bargaining This is common, except in the large department stores (although they may give a discount on expensive items of jewellery or furniture) and on items like soap, books and most necessities. Expect to pay anything from 25-75% less than the asking price, depending on the bargainer's skill and the shopkeeper's mood. Bargaining is viewed as a game, so enter into it with good humour.

Clothing In towns and at religious sights, it is courteous to avoid wearing shorts and sleeveless tops.. Visitors who are inappropriately dressed may not be allowed into temples (wats). Most Thais always look neat and clean. *Mai rieb-roi* means 'not neat' and is considered a great insult. Beach resorts are a law unto themselves – casual clothes are the norm, although nudity is still very much frowned upon by Thais. In the most expensive restaurants in Bangkok, diners may be expected to wear a jacket and tie.

Conduct Thais are generally very understanding of the foibles and habits of foreigners (*farangs*) and will forgive and forget most indiscretions. However, there are a number of 'dos and don'ts' which are worth observing:

Cool & hot Among Thais, the personal characteristic of *jai yen* is very highly regarded; literally, this
hearts means to have a 'cool heart'. It embodies calmness, having an even temper and not displaying emotion. Although foreigners generally receive special dispensation, and are not expected to conform to Thai customs (all farangs are thought to have *jai rawn* or 'hot hearts'), it is important to try and keep calm in any disagreement – losing one's temper leads to loss of face and subsequent loss of respect. An associated personal characteristic which Thais try to develop is *kreng jai*; this embodies being understanding of other people's needs, desires and feelings – in short, not imposing oneself.

Greeting people Traditionally, Thais greet one another with a *wai* – the equivalent of a handshake. In a wai, hands are held together as if in prayer, and the higher the wai, the more respectful the greeting. By watching Thai's wai it is possible to ascertain their relative seniority, where a combination of class, age, wealth, power and gender all play a part. Juniors or inferiors should initiate a wai, and hold it higher and for longer than the senior or superior. Foreigners are not expected to conform to this custom; a simple wai at chest to chin height is all that is required. You should not wai to children or to waiters, waitresses and other people offering a service. When farangs and Thais do business it is common to shake hands. The respectful term of address is *khun*, which applies to both men and women. This is usually paired with a Thai's first name so that, for example, Somchai Bamruang would be greeted as Khun Somchai. The closest equivalent to the English Mr and Mrs/Miss are *Nai* and *Nang*, which are also used as formal terms of address. Thais also invariably have nicknames like *Kai* (Chicken), *Ooy* (Sugar) or *Kung* (Shrimp), while people from certain professions will also have respectful titles – like *ajaan* for a teacher or lecturer.

Heads & feet Try to not openly point your feet at anyone – feet are viewed as spiritually the lowest part of the body. At the same time, never touch anyone's, even a child's, head, which is the holiest, as well as the highest, part. Resting your feet on a table would be regarded as highly disrespectful, while stepping over someone sitting on the floor is also frowned upon. If sitting on the floor, try to tuck your feet under your body; although Westerners unused to this posture may find it uncomfortable after even a short time.

Never criticize any member of the royal family or the institution itself (see page 765). The **The monarchy** monarchy is held in very high esteem and *lèse majesté* remains an offence, carrying a sentence of up to 15 years in prison (see page 753). You should treat even coins and bank notes with respect as they bear the image of the King, and the same goes for postage stamps which Thais will methodically moisten using a sponge rather than their tongues. In cinemas, the National Anthem is played before the show and the audience is expected to stand. At other events, take your lead from the crowd as to how to behave. A dying custom, but one which is still adhered to in smaller towns as well as certain parts of Bangkok such as at Hualamphong railway station, is that everybody stops in their tracks at 0800 and 1800, when the National Anthem is relayed over loudspeaker.

Remove shoes on entering any monastery building, do not climb over Buddha **Monastery (wat)** images or have your picture taken in front of one, and when sitting in a *bot* or *viharn* **& monk** ensure that your feet are not pointing towards a Buddha image. Wear modest **etiquette** clothing; women should not expose their shoulders or wear dresses that are too short (see above, clothing). Ideally, they should be calf length, although knee length dresses or skirts are usually acceptable. Women should never touch a monk, hand anything directly to a monk, or venture into the monks' quarters. They should also avoid climbing chedis (stupas). As in any other place of worship, visitors should not disturb the peace of a wat.

Observant visitors will quickly notice that men and women rarely show open, public **Open shows of** signs of affection. It is not uncommon, however, to see men holding hands; this is **affection** usually a sign of simple friendship, nothing more. That said, in Bangkok, traditional customs have broken down, and in areas such as Siam Square it is common to see young lovers hand-in-hand.

A quality of *sanuk*, which can be roughly translated as 'fun' or *joie de vivre*, is important **Sanuk** to Thais. Activities are undertaken because they are *sanuk*, others avoided because they are *mai sanuk* ('not fun'). Perhaps it is because of this apparent love of life that so many visitors returning from Thailand remark on how Thais always appear happy and smiling. However, it is worth bearing in mind that the interplay of *jai yen* and *kreng jai* means that everything may not be quite as it appears.

This is prohibited on domestic flights, public buses in Bangkok, department stores and **Smoking** in cinemas. Many fast food restaurants also ban smoking – except at outside tables.

A useful book delving deeper into the do's and don'ts of living in Thailand is Robert **Further reading** and Nanthapa Cooper's *Culture shock: Thailand*, Time Books International: Singapore (1990). It is available from most bookshops.

Safety

In general, Thailand is a safe country to visit. Physical violence against tourists, while it does occur, is rare. Confidence tricksters, touts, pickpockets and other thieves all operate, particularly in more popular tourist centres, but care and common sense usually avoids them. Police usually react efficiently to tourist complaints and the country's health infrastructure, especially in provincial capitals and popular tourist destinations, is good. For background information on staying healthy, see page 62.

Calling one of the emergency numbers will not usually be very productive as few **Dealing with** operators speak English. It is better to call the Tourist Police or have a hotel employee **emergencies** or other English-speaking Thai telephone for you. For more intractable problems, contact your embassy or consulate.

Tourist Police In 1982 the government set up a special arm of the police to deal with the demands of the tourist industry – the Tourist Police – and in 1995 there were around 500 officers stationed in the main tourist destinations. The Thai police have come in for a great deal of scrutiny over recent years. Although most policemen are honest and only too happy to help the lost or luckless overseas visitor, it is worth being aware of some of the complaints that have reached the press or been expressed in letters to us. **Tourist Police:** T2815051 or T2216206. Open 0800-2400.

Personal There have been some worrying attacks on tourists and a handful of murders. It must
security be emphasized that these are very few and far between. Most have occurred when visitors have become involved in local conflicts, or when they have tried to outwit thieves. Robbery is much more common; it ranges from simple pickpocketing to the drugging (and subsequent robbing) of bus and train passengers. As in all countries, watchfulness and simple common sense should be employed. Women travelling alone should be especially careful. Always lock hotel rooms and place valuables in a safe deposit if available (or if not, take them with you).

Insurgency & The Communist Party of Thailand (CPT), which was influential in parts of the South,
security in North and Northeast during the late 1970s and early 1980s, is virtually moribund and
border areas does not pose a threat to visitors. Rather more problematic at the moment is PULO (the Pattani United Liberation Organization), which is agitating for an independent Muslim state in the far south. While it is not thought that armed PULO rebels number more than a few dozen, there have been a handful of bombings during the 1990s. Travel throughout almost all of the country is safe.

Traffic Perhaps the greatest danger is from the traffic, especially if you are attempting to drive yourself. More foreign visitors are killed or injured in traffic accidents than in any other way. Thai drivers have a 'devil may care' attitude towards the highway code, and there are many quite horrific accidents. Be very careful crossing the road; just because there is a pedestrian crossing, do not expect drivers to stop. Be particularly wary when driving or riding a motorcycle (see page 50).

Drugs & Many prostitutes and drug dealers are in league with the police and may find it more
prostitution profitable to report you than to take your custom (or they may try to do both). They receive a reward from the police, and the police in their turn receive a bonus for the detective work. Note that foreigners on buses may be searched for drugs. Sentences for possession of illegal drugs vary from a fine or one year's imprisonment for marijuana, up to life imprisonment or execution for possession or smuggling of heroin. (The death penalty is usually commuted.)

Touts & Inevitably, Thailand's tourist industry has created a side-industry populated by touts
confidence and confidence tricksters. More visitors get 'stung' buying what they hope are
tricksters valuable gems than in any other way (see the box on page 160 and the Tricksters section, page 59). There is also a rich tradition in card scams. Along with the scammers and confidence tricksters, there are scores of touts who make their living guiding tourists towards certain shops and hotels where they are paid a commission for their pains. Ignore touts who claim that hotels have closed, are full, or are dirty or substandard. Likewise, it is best to avoid taxi or tuk-tuk drivers who are offering to drive you to a hotel or guesthouse for free.

Bribery The way to make your way in life, for some people in Thailand, is through the strategic offering of gifts. A Chulalongkorn University report recently estimated that it 'costs'

฿10 million to become Bangkok Police Chief. Apparently this can be recouped in just two years of hard graft. Although bribing officials is by no means recommended, resident farangs report that they often resort to such gifts to avoid the time and hassle involved in filling in the forms and making the requisite visit to a police station for a minor traffic offence. As a visitor, the best first step is to play it straight.

Thai prisons are very grim. Most foreigners are held in two Bangkok prisons: Khlong Prem and Bangkwang. One resident who visits overseas prisoners in jail wrote to us saying: 'You cannot overestimate the horrors! Khlong Prem has 7,000 prisoners, five to a cell, with not enough room to stretch out, no recreation, one meal a day (an egg on Sundays)...' A hundred prisoners in a dormitory is not uncommon, and prisoners on Death Row have waist chains and ankle fetters permanently welded on.

Prisons

Where to stay

As a premier tourist destination and one of the world's fastest-growing economies, Thailand has a large selection of hotels, including some of the very best in the world. However, outside the tourist centres, there is still an absence of adequate 'Western style' accommodation. Most 'Thai' hotels are distinctly lacking in character and are poorly maintained. Due to the popularity of the country with backpackers, there are also a large number of small guesthouses geared to Westerners, serving Western food and catering to the foibles of foreigners.

Hotels

These are listed under eight categories (see below) according to the average price of a double/twin room for one night. It should be noted that many hotels will have a range of rooms, some with air-conditioning (a/c) and attached bathroom facilities, others with just a fan and shared facilities. Prices can therefore vary a great deal. If a hotel entry lists 'some a/c', then these rooms are likely to be in the upper part of the range, perhaps even in the next range. Unlike, say, Indonesia, few hotels in Thailand provide breakfast in the price of the room. A service charge of 10% and government tax of 7% will usually be added to the bill in the more expensive hotels (categories **L**-**B**). Ask whether the quoted price includes tax when checking in. Prices in Bangkok are inflated. **NB** During the off-season, hotels in tourist destinations may halve their room rates, so it is always worthwhile bargaining or asking whether there is a special price. Given the fierce competition among hotels, it is even worth trying during the peak season. Over-building has meant that there is a glut of rooms in some towns and hotels are desperate for business.

For a quick reference guide to our hotel price codes, see inside front cover

L: ฿5,000+ luxury and **AL:** ฿2,500-5,000 **International:** the entire range of business services (fax, translation, seminar rooms etc), sports facilities (gym, swimming pool etc), Asian and Western restaurants, bars and discotheques.
A: ฿1,250-2,500 **First class:** usually offer comprehensive business, sports and recreational facilities, with a range of restaurants and bars.
B: ฿750-1,250 **Tourist class:** these will probably have a swimming pool and all rooms will have air-conditioning and an attached bathroom. Other services include one or more restaurants and 24-hour coffee shop/room service. Some may have televisions in the rooms showing cable films.
C: ฿400-750 **Economy:** rooms should be air-conditioned and have attached bathrooms with hot water. A restaurant and room service will probably be available. Sports facilities are unlikely.
D: ฿200-400 **Budget:** rooms are unlikely to be air-conditioned, although they

Hotel classifications

should have an attached bathroom. Toilets may be either Western-style or of the 'squat' Asian variety, depending on whether the town is on the tourist route. Toilet paper should be provided. Many in this price range, out of tourist areas, are 'Thai' hotels. Bed linen and towels are usually provided, and there may be a restaurant.

E: ฿100-200 **Guesthouse:** fan-cooled rooms, in some cases with shared bathroom facilities. Toilets are likely to be of the 'squat' Asian variety, with no toilet paper provided. Bed linen should be provided, although towels may not. Rooms are small, facilities few. Guesthouses popular with foreigners may be excellent sources of information, and also sometimes offer cheap tours and services such as bicycle and motorcycle hire. Places in this category vary a great deal, and can change very rapidly. One year's best bargain becomes the following year's health hazard. Other travellers are the best source of up-to-the-minute reviews on whether standards have plummeted.

F: under ฿100 **Guesthouse:** fan-cooled rooms, usually with shared bathroom facilities. Toilets are likely to be of the 'squat' Asian variety, with no toilet paper provided. Some of these guesthouses can be filthy, vermin-infested, places. At the same time, others are superb value. As in the category above, standards change very fast and other travellers are the best source of information.

Getting around

Air

Thai Airways is the national flag carrier and is also by far the largest domestic airline. Although it has had a turbulent few years and standards have declined since the halcyon days of the late 1980s – in 1995-96 the airline underwent a major internal review by outside consultants – it is still a good outfit. Planes are maintained to a high standard and crews are professional.

Thai flies to 22 destinations in Thailand, as well as Bangkok. These include: eight destinations in the north – Chiang Mai, Chiang Rai, Lampang, Mae Hong Son, Mae Sot, Nan, Phitsanulok and Phrae; seven in the northeast – Khon Kaen, Nakhon Ratchasima, Sakhon Nakhon, Nakhon Phanom, Ubon Ratchathani, Buri Ram and Udon Thani; and seven in the south – Hat Yai, Krabi, Nakhon Si Thammarat, Narathiwat, Phuket, Surat Thani and Trang. Thai have introduced a multi-destination promotional fare of US$199 for internal routes. The ticket must be bought prior to arrival in Thailand. Head office for Thai is 89 Vibhavadi Rangsit Rd, T02-5130121, but it is better to book flights through one of the local offices or a travel agent displaying the Thai logo, or check out their website: www.thaiair.com In April 2000 domestic fares went up for the first time for many years; a selection of fares is listed on page 846.

Bangkok Airways (see page 846) fly from Bangkok to Koh Samui (nearly 20 flights daily) and Ranong, and from Koh Samui to Krabi, Phuket and Pattaya (U-Tapao). In addition, the airline has opened a second private airport at Sukhothai (in fact, nearer Sawankhalok), and is now operating flights between Bangkok and Chiang Mai via Sukhothai. There are also plans to add Chiang Rai, Udon Thani and Hat Yai to their domestic routes. Bangkok Airways' international connections currently only extend to flights between Bangkok and Phnom Penh and Siem Reap in Cambodia, between Koh Samui and Singapore, and between Sukhothai and Siem Reap. However, there are plans to open routes to Medan (Indonesia), Kuala Lumpur (Malaysia) and Bali (Indonesia) to their international connections. Head office is at 60 Queen Sirikit National Convention Centre, Ratchadapisek Rd, Bangkok, T02-2293456, F2293450, www.bkkair.co.th The airline also has domestic offices at Don Muang Airport, and in Krabi, Pattaya, Phuket, Samui, Ranong, Sukhothai and Chiang Mai.

In September 1998, **Angel Airlines** began operations. They have leased a Boeing 737-500, a 30 seat Dornier 328 and a luxury Beech jet. Head office: 3rd Floor,

Benchachinda Building, Tower B, Vibhavadi Rangsit Road, Bangkok, T02-9532260, www.angelairlines.com Currently their only scheduled service is between Bangkok and Chiang Rai. However, they also have plans to add Udon Thani, Chiang Mai, Hat Yai and Phuket to their list of domestic destinations. The airline also operates international connections with Kunming and Chengdu in China and are negotiating for landing rights in Laos, Myanmar, Cambodia and Singapore. The company says it intends to fly on routes not currently covered by Thai's network. However, while the

Domestic air routes

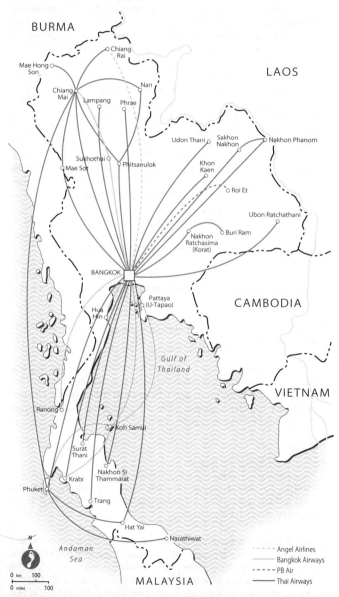

Essentials

company may have grand plans, it is also in debt and its future uncertain; towards the end of 2000 it was trying to find a partner to ease some of its problems. Thailand's newest commercial outfit is **PB Air**. Head office: 17th Floor, UBC II Building, 591 Sukhumvit Soi 33, Bangkok 10110, T02-2610220. The airline currently only runs services between Bangkok and Roi Et (in the Northeast), and Krabi and Wattananakorn. The airline operates 30-seat Dornier 328s.

Train

For rail information, T02-2237010/T2237020

The State Railway of Thailand is efficient, clean and comfortable, with five main routes to the north, northeast, west, east and south. It is safer than bus travel but can take longer. The choice is first class air-conditioned compartments, second class sleepers, second class air-conditioned sit-ups with reclining chairs and third class sit-ups. Travelling third class is often the cheapest way to travel long distance. First and second class are more expensive than the bus, but infinitely more comfortable. Express trains are known as *rot duan*, special express trains as *rot duan phiset* and rapid trains as *rot raew*. Express and rapid trains are faster as they make fewer stops; there is a surcharge for the service. Reservations for sleepers should be made in advance (up to 60 days ahead) at Bangkok's Hualamphong station (T02-2233762/2247788). The Advance Booking Office is open 0700-0400 Monday-Sunday. It is advisable to book the bottom sleeper, as lights are bright on top (in second class compartments). It still may be difficult to get a seat at certain times of year, such as during festivals (like Songkran in April). Personal luggage allowance is 50 kg in first class, 40 kg in second and 30 kg in third class. Children aged 3-12 and under 150 cm in height pay half fare; those under three years old and less than 100 cm in height travel free, but do not get a seat. It is possible to pick up timetables at Hualamphong station (from the information booth in the main concourse): there are two types – the 'condensed' timetable (by region) showing all rapid routes and complete, separate timetables for all classes. Some travel agencies book tickets. A queue-by-ticket arrangement works efficiently, and travellers do not have to wait long. If you change a reservation the charge is ฿10. If travelling north or south during the day, try to get a seat on the side of the carriage out of the sun.

A 'bullet train' may soon transport visitors along the eastern seaboard to Pattaya. See page 847 for fares listing or access .

Tourist passes A 20-day rail pass costs ฿1,100 for adults, ฿550 for children (blue pass), valid on all trains, second and third class; supplementary charges NOT included. A red pass includes supplementary charges, ฿2,000 for adults, ฿1,000 for children. For further details visit the Advance Booking Office at Hualamphong station in Bangkok, T02-2233762/2247788 or F2256068/2263656.

Boat

The waterways of Thailand are extensive. However, most people limit their water travel to trips around Bangkok (see page 107) or to Ayutthaya (page 183). *Hang-yaaws* (long-tailed boats) are the most common form of water travel; they are motorized, noisy, fast and entertaining.

Cruise holidays The following tour operators can organize cruise holidays; all are based in Bangkok (phone code: 02): *Seatran Travel*, 1091/157 Metro Shopping Arcade, Phetburi Rd, T2535307; *Songserm Travel Centre*, 121/7 Soi Chalermla, Phayathai Rd, T2500768; *Phuket Travel and Tour*, 1091/159 Metro Shopping Arcade, Phetburi Rd, T2535510; *Thai Yachting*, 7th Floor, Rachdamri Arcade, Rachdamri Rd, T2531733; *Asia Voyage*,

Ground Floor, Charn Issara Tower, 942/38 Rama IV Rd, T2354100; *Yacht Charter*, 61/3 Mahadlek Luang 3, Rachdamri Rd, T2519668.

An alternative to the usual overland tour of Thailand is to book a berth on the *Andaman Princess*. This large cruise ship sails to Koh Tao and back (three days/two nights). Passengers can snorkel at Koh Tao and the level of service and safety is very high. Large numbers of young, middle-class Thais make the journey and there is lots of entertainment. Around ฿5,000 for a single berth. Contact: *Siam Cruise*, 33/10-11 Sukhumvit Soi Chaiyod (Soi 11), Bangkok, T02-2554563, F2558961.

Bus

Essentials

Private and state-run buses leave Bangkok for every town in Thailand; it is an extensive network and an inexpensive way to travel. The government bus company is called *Bor Kor Sor* (an abbreviation of *Borisat Khon Song*), and every town in Thailand will have a BKS terminal. There are small stop-in-every-town local buses, plus the faster long-distance buses (*rot duan* – express; or *rot air* – air-conditioned). Standard air-conditioned buses come in two grades: *chan nung* (first class) and *chan song* (second class). *Chan song* have more seats and less elbow and leg room. The local buses are slower and cramped, but are a great experience for those wishing to sample local life. The seats at the very back are reserved for monks (why is a mystery), so be ready to move if necessary. For longer/overnight journeys, air-conditioned deluxe (sometimes known as *rot tour*) or VIP buses, stewardess service is provided with food and drink supplied en route, and more leg room (plus constant Thai music or videos). Many fares include meals at roadside restaurants, so keep hold of your ticket. **NB** The overnight air-conditoned buses are very cold and it is a good idea to take a few extra layers of clothing.

Many tour companies operate bus services in Thailand; travel agents in Bangkok will supply information. These buses are normally more comfortable than the state buses but are more expensive. Overnight trips usually involve a meal stop (included in price of ticket) and stewardess service for drinks and snacks. They often leave from outside the company office, which may not be located at the central bus station. (See page 849 for fares listing.)

Private tour buses

Car hire

There are two schools of thought on car hire in Thailand: one, that under no circumstances should farangs drive themselves; and second, that hiring a car is one of the best ways of seeing the country and reaching the more inaccessible sights. Increasing numbers of people *are* hiring their own cars and internationally respected car hire firms are expanding their operations (such as Hertz and Avis). Roads and service stations are generally excellent. Driving is on the left-hand side of the road.

See the box, page 48, for some hot tips on driving in Thailand!

However, there are a few points that should be kept in mind: accidents in Thailand are often horrific. Towards the end of 1990 a gas tanker collided with a tuk-tuk on the Bangkok expressway, exploded, and killed more than 60 people, with many others horrendously burned. If involved in an accident, and they occur with great frequency, you – as a foreigner – are likely to be found the guilty party and expected to meet the costs. Ensure that the cost of hire includes insurance cover. Many local residents recommend that should a foreigner be involved in an accident, they should not stop but drive on to the nearest police station – if possible, of course.

The average cost of hiring a car from a reputable firm is ฿1,000-1,500 per day, ฿6,000-10,000 per week, or ฿20,000-30,000 per month. Some rentals come with insurance automatically included; for others it must be specifically requested and a surcharge is added. An international driver's licence, or a UK, US, French, German,

👉 *A non-comprehensive primer to driving in Thailand*

So you were thinking about hiring a self-drive car for your travels around Thailand, but now your friends all think you must be completely crazy, and after that first trip from the airport in the taxi you are beginning to think they may be right. Well, don't despair. It is possible to enjoy driving in Thailand, and you don't have to be crazy to do so. Not only that, but it does provide opportunities to see places that most tourists never get near. The key to enjoying driving in Thailand is to allow plenty of time to get from A to B. The rigidly law-abiding and the very nervous probably shouldn't attempt a self-drive holiday. But if you do take the plunge, remember:

■ *Bangkok isn't Thailand. While places such as Hat Yai and Chiang Mai do suffer from heavy traffic, it never reaches the levels of Bangkok's infamous traffic jams. For much of the rest of the country traffic is pretty quiet, driving is enjoyable and most people are courteous.*

■ *A combination of corrupt building contractors and overloaded trucks have left roads in parts of Thailand in a terrible state of disrepair. This is often worse the closer one gets to large cities.*

■ *Signposting is often poor – make sure you leave ample time, have a decent map and a good sense of direction.*

■ *Stick to driving during the day. Night-time brings out the police road blocks, the heavy trucks and the speeding pick-up trucks. It also reveals that some Thais don't believe that it is necessary to have lights – or to turn them on – when travelling at night. Other oddities to watch out for: motorcyclists travelling together in a cozy row (three lights all heading in the same direction) or two motorcyclists holding hands as they drive!*

■ *Country driving brings its own hazards: drivers who rarely bother to look when turning onto a road; and buffaloes, dogs, goats and other assorted wildlife that have limited road sense. Slow down, honk the horn and be ultra suspicious of anyone's intentions, human or animal.*

■ *Motorcyclists in the countryside are frequently over-burdened with passengers and other loads. Give them room when passing.*

Australian, New Zealand, Singapore or Hong Kong licence is required. The lower age limit is 20 years (more for some firms). Addresses of car hire firms are included in the sections on the main tourist destinations. If the mere thought of competing with Thai drivers is terrifying, an option is to hire a chauffeur along with the car. For this service an extra ฿300-500 per day is usually charged, more at weekends and if an overnight stay is included. Note that local car hire firms are cheaper, although the cars are likely to be less well maintained and will have tens of thousands of kilometres on the clock.

Other land transport

Towns in Thailand will often have their own distinctive forms of transport for hire. In Chonburi and Si Racha, chariot-like seats have been attached to large motorbikes; in Prachuap Kiri Khan there are motorbikes with side-cars.

Cycling We have had a number of letters from people who have cycled through various parts of Southeast Asia. The advice below is collated from their comments, and is meant to provide a general guideline for those intending to tour the country by bicycle, which is becoming increasingly common. There may be areas, however, where the advice does not hold true. Some of the letters we have received even disagree on some key points.

Bike type Touring, hybrid or mountain bikes are fine for most roads and tracks in Thailand; take an ordinary machine, nothing fancy. Spares are readily available for

Essentials

■ Be aware that motorcyclists are expected to use the shoulder (in some places they are required to by law), and are not generally considered to 'equal' a car.

■ You cannot depend on maps being up-to-date or completely accurate.

■ Road construction projects provide little warning on approach and you should not expect logical traffic management systems to be in place. Heavy machinery is a give-away that something may be just around the corner.

■ Some trucks will use their indicators to let you know if it is safe to pass: flashing the right indicator means oncoming traffic; flashing the left indicator means it is clear to pass. There are variations in different parts of the country, but it is usually fairly clear what is going on.

■ Oncoming traffic flashing the headlights on and off is a warning. It can mean 'I'm not stopping to let you through', 'don't try passing' and in some cases 'get out of the way, I'm coming through'. It is not uncommon to move on to the shoulder to avoid oncoming traffic, particularly if that oncoming traffic is a tour bus or a truck.

■ Recently, many motorists have taken to switching their hazard lights on to indicate they are going straight on when they come to an intersection. This can be very confusing if you can only see one side of the car.

■ Remember that while you may be confident you know the highway code, the same does not apply to everyone else. Junctions, whether with lights or not, are frequently sites of accidents and of long pauses, as each person tries to work out who can go first and who must wait.

■ If you are going on a long drive through a relatively unpopulated area, fill up with petrol whenever you get the opportunity.

■ Road markings make little difference to most drivers. Passing on solid yellow lines, on blind corners and over hills is common. Passing on the left on a dual carriageway or on the shoulder is also very common and adds to the fun.

■ It is worth putting your hazards on if you have to brake very suddenly as most cars are not fitted with two sets of brake lights, and it is not always possible to distinguish between slowing and stopping!

most machines, and even small towns have bicycle repair shops where it is often possible to borrow larger tools such as vices. Mountain bikes have made an impact, so accessories for these are also widely available. What is less common are components made of unusual materials, such as titanium and rarer composites. It is best to use common accessories. Buses are used to taking bicycles (although the more expensive air-conditioned tour buses may prove reluctant) and most carry them free, although some drivers may ask for a surcharge. Many international airlines take bicycles free of charge, provided they are not boxed. Take the peddles off and deflate the tyres. Check your carrier's policy before checking-in. **NB** The maps in this guide are not sufficiently detailed for cycling and a good colour map is useful in determining contours and altitude, as well as showing minor roads.

Attitudes to cyclists It is still comparatively rare to see foreigners cycling in Thailand, so expect to be an object of interest. Cars and buses often travel along the hard shoulder, and few expect to give way to a bicycle. Be very wary, especially on main roads.

Useful equipment Basic tool kit – although there always seems to be help near at hand, and local workshops seem to be able to improvise a solution to just about any problem – including a puncture repair kit, spare tubes, spare tyre, pump, good map of the area, bungee cords, first-aid kit and water filter.

Unnecessary equipment A tent is generally not needed. Every small town will have a guesthouse of some description. Nor is it worth taking a stove, cooking utensils, sleeping bag, food; it is almost always possible to get food and a place to sleep – and cheaply, too. The equipment is simply a burden. The exception to this rule of thumb are National Parks, where camping is common and camping grounds exist.

Essentials

 ### Death highways

It doesn't take very long after arriving in Bangkok to realize that the city has a transport problem. But the emphasis on the capital's congestion and pollution sometimes obscures another, equally serious, issue: the country's stupendous accident rate. The Kingdom has the highest fatality rate from road accidents of any country in the Southeast Asian region. On current trends, it was estimated in November 1998 that by the year 2000 road accidents would claim a staggering 68,000 lives, or eight each hour. In 1995 the number killed was 16,727, but this has been increasing at a rate of over 30% each year. In 1997 the estimated figure was around 28,000, or three deaths every hour. (The number injured in 1995 was 50,546.) Preecha Chosap, the secretary of the Transport and Communications Ministry, announced at the end of 1998 that a new Master Plan on road safety was in the process of being finalized. As he explained to the press, part of the problem is that no one takes responsibility for road safety. "If a full passenger coach overturns", he said, "killing a large number of people and you ask the police, they'll say it's nothing to do with them. If you ask the Land Transport Department or the Highways Department,

they'll say the same thing." The government doesn't even know the true number of people who die in road-related accidents – the figures are collected from hospital admissions where, it is said, some 30% of beds are occupied by patients injured in road accidents.

Songkran carnage 2000   During the Songkran holiday of 2000, between 12-17 April, there was, at first, hope that things had improved on the nation's roads. On 18 April local papers were reporting 'only' 142 deaths and 1,272 injuries in 813 road accidents. But a day later, as information filtered through, it became clear that things were a trifle bloodier. By 19 April it was being reported that 204 people had been killed and 1,599 injured. That's a pretty high attrition rate.

Another piece in the explanatory puzzle is that drivers who infringe the law are dealt with extremely leniently – if they are ever caught. The fine for speeding or drink driving is just ฿1,000. But in some areas of the country there are just 24 highway police patrolling 1,000 km of road, so the chances of being stopped are pretty slim in any case. Getting proof that someone is drunk is also hard when, in 1998, there were only 35 breathalyzers for use throughout the country.

In general   Avoid major roads. Avoid major towns.

Hitchhiking   Thai people rarely hitchhike and tourists who try could find themselves waiting a long time at the roadside. It is sometimes possible to wave down vehicles at the more popular beach resorts.

Motorbike taxi   These are becoming increasingly popular, and are the cheapest, quickest and most dangerous way to get from A to B. Riders wear coloured vests (sometimes numbered) and tend to congregate at key intersections or outside shopping centres, for example. Agree a price before boarding – expect to pay ฿10-20.

Motorbike hire   Mostly confined to holiday resorts and prices vary from place to place. ฿200-300 per day is usual for a 100-150cc machine. Often licences do not have to be shown and insurance will not be available. Off the main roads and in quieter areas, it can be an enjoyable and cheap way to see the country. Borrow a helmet if at all possible and expect anything larger than you to ignore your presence on the road. Be extremely wary. Thousands of Thais are killed in motorcycle accidents each year and large numbers of tourists also suffer injuries. Riding with shorts and flip-flops is dangerous. Koh Samui has been said to have the highest death rate anywhere in the world! Some travellers are now not just hiring motorbikes to explore a local area, but are touring the entire country by motorcycle. It is the cheapest way to be independent of public transport, but the risks rise accordingly.

In December 1992 the Thai government introduced a new – and long overdue – law requiring that motorcyclists wear helmets on Bangkok's 240 main roads. In April 1995 this was extended to all roads and sois (lanes) in the capital. At the end of June 1995, Chiang Mai also made the wearing of helmets mandatory. However, outside Bangkok the wearing of helmets in most areas is not compulsory.

These come in the form of pedal or motorized machines. Drivers of saamlors, or 'three wheels', abound and will descend on travellers in any town. Fares should be bargained and agreed before setting off. Drivers are a useful source of local information and will know most places of interest, plus hotels and restaurants (and sometimes their prices). In Bangkok, and now in some other large towns, the saamlor is a motorized, gas-powered scooter, known affectionately as the tuk-tuk (because of the noise it makes). Pedal-powered saamlors were outlawed in Bangkok a few years ago and they are now gradually being replaced by the noisier motorized version throughout the country. Always bargain and agree a price before setting out on a journey. It will not take long to discover what is a reasonable price, but don't expect to pay the same as a Thai.

Saamlor & tuk-tuks

Songthaews, 'two rows', are pick-up trucks fitted with two benches, and can be found in many up-country towns. They normally run fixed routes, with set fares, but can often be hired and used as a taxi service (agree a price before setting out). To stop a songthaew use the electric buzzers often provided, or tap the side of the vehicle with a coin.

Songthaew

Standard taxis can be found in some Thai towns. This is the most expensive form of public motorized transport, and many now have the added luxury of air conditioning. In Bangkok, almost all taxis have meters. If unmetered, agree a price before setting off, and always bargain. In the south of Thailand, long-distance share taxis are common.

Taxi

Keeping in touch

Local postal charges: ฿1.50 (postcard) and ฿2 (letter, 20 g). **International postal charges**: Europe and Australasia – ฿9 or 12 (postcard, depending on the size), ฿17 (letter, 10 g); US – ฿9 or 12 (postcard, depending on the size), ฿19 (letter, 10 g). Airmail letters cost ฿15. Poste Restante: correspondents should write the family name in capital letters and underline it, to avoid confusion.

Outside Bangkok, most post offices are open from 0800 to 1630 Monday-Friday and only the larger ones will be open on Saturday.

Postal services

From Bangkok there is direct dialling to most countries. Outside Bangkok, it is best to go to a local telephone exchange for phoning outside the country.

Telephone services

For a quick reference guide to phone codes within Thailand, see inside front cover

Codes Local area codes vary according to province. Individual area phone codes are listed throughout this book in the margin, underneath town headings; the code can also be found at the front of the telephone directory.

Directory inquiries Domestic long distance including Malaysia and Vientiane (Laos) – 101, Greater Bangkok BMA – 183, international calls T2350030-5, although hotel operators will invariably help make the call if asked.

Callboxes cost ฿1.

Essentials

Essentials

Fax Now widely available in most towns. Postal and telex/fax services are available in most large hotels.

Mobiles These are common and increasingly popular – reflecting the difficulties of getting a landline as well as a desire to be contactable at all times and places. Coverage is good except in some border areas. Mobile numbers begin '01' and mobile phone users are charged both for receiving and making a call.

Internet & email
For a global internet café listing, see www.netcafeguide.com

Thailand has embraced the internet with alacrity and enthusiasm. There are internet cafés in most towns, especially in areas where there is a tourist presence. Rates clearly vary, but expect to pay ฿2 per minute (often with a minimum of five minutes) in tourist centres and a figure of half this or less in internet cafés frequented by locals. If you are thinking of spending some time at the screen it may be worth searching beyond the tourist hotels and guesthouses; internet cafés are often concentrated around universities.

Media

Newspapers Until recently there were two major English language daily papers: the *Bangkok Post* and the *The Nation*. They provide good international news coverage and are Thailand's best known English language broadsheets. At times of social conflict they have also represented dissenting liberal voices. Both *The Nation* and the *Bangkok Post* have websites: www.nationgroup.com/ and www.bangkokpost.net/ respectively.

In the mid-1990s these two august institutions – which until then had the English language newspaper market to themselves – were joined by three other dailies: the *Business Day*, *Asia Times* and *Thailand Times*. The latter two closed down during the economic slump of 1997, leaving just *Business Day* battling it out with the *Bangkok Post* and *The Nation*. *Business Day* is, as the name suggests, aimed at the business market. It is jointly owned by a group of Thai investors, along with Singapore Press Holdings and Malaysia's New Straits Times group (http://bday.net).

There are a number of Thai language dailies and weeklies, as well as Chinese language newspapers. The Thai press is one of the least controlled in Southeast Asia (although controls were imposed following the coup at the beginning of 1991 and during the demonstrations of May 1992), and the local newspapers are sometimes scandalously colourful, with gruesome annotated pictures of traffic accidents and murder victims. International newspapers and magazines are readily available in Bangkok, Chiang Mai, Pattaya and Phuket, although they are more difficult to come by up-country.

Television Five TV channels, with English language sound track, are available on FM. Channel 3 – 105.5 MHz, Channel 7 – 103.5 MHz, Channel 9 – 107 MHz and Channel 11 – 88 MHz. The *Bangkok Post* stars programmes where English soundtrack is available on FM.

In addition to Thai television many hotels also receive satellite TV channels. These include BBC World, CNN, Star, MTV Asia and ABC. Even guesthouses will often have a communal TV, as will many bars and restaurants in tourist centres. Don't feel that you will necessarily get away from world events (whether you view that as desirable or not).

Radio Shortwave radio can receive the BBC World Service, Voice of America, Radio Moscow and other foreign broadcasts (see below). There are several hundred radio stations in Thailand. In Bangkok there are a number with bilingual presenters and DJs and with good music. FM 107 broadcasts CNN news every hour (also shown in Channel 9) from early evening. The best stations playing Western music in Bangkok are probably FM 102.5 and FM 95.5.

The BBC World Service's *Dateline East Asia* provides probably the best news and views on Asia. Also with a strong Asia focus are the broadcasts of the ABC (Australian Broadcasting Corporation). For information on Asian radio and television broadcasts access http://www.isop.ucla.edu/eas/web/radio-tv/htm, which includes free downloadable software.

Short wave radio British Broadcasting Corporation (**BBC, London**), *Southeast Asian service* 3915, 6195, 9570, 9740, 11750, 11955, 15360; *Singapore service* 88.9 MHz; *East Asian service* 5995, 6195, 7180, 9740, 11715, 11750, 11945, 11955, 15140, 15280, 15360, 17830, 21715. **Voice of America** (**VoA, Washington**), *Southeast Asian service* 1143, 1575, 7120, 9760, 9770, 15185, 15425; *Indonesian service* 6110, 11760, 15425. **Radio Beijing**, *Southeast Asian service (English)* 11600, 11660. **Radio Japan** (**Tokyo**), *Southeast Asian service (English)* 11815, 17810, 21610.

Food and drink

Food

Thai cuisine is an intermingling of Tai (see page 757), Chinese, and to a lesser extent, Indian cuisines. This helps to explain why restaurants produce dishes which must be some of the (spicy) hottest in the world, as well as some which are rather bland. *Laap* (raw – now more frequently cooked – chopped beef, mixed with rice, herbs and spices) is a traditional 'Tai' dish; *pla priaw waan* (whole fish with soy and ginger) is Chinese in origin; while *gaeng mussaman* (beef 'Muslim' curry) was brought to Thailand by Muslim immigrants. Even *satay*, paraded by most restaurants as a Thai dish, was introduced from Malaysia and Indonesia (who themselves adopted it from Arab traders during the Middle Ages).

Despite these various influences, Thai cooking is distinctive. Thais have managed to combine the best of each tradition, adapting elements to fit their own preferences. Remarkably, considering how ubiquitous it is in Thai cooking, the chilli pepper is a New World fruit and was not introduced into Thailand until the late-16th century (along with the pineapple and papaya).

When a Thais asks other Thais whether they have eaten they will ask, literally, whether they have 'eaten rice' (*kin khaaw*). Similarly, the accompanying dishes are referred to as food 'with the rice'. A Thai meal is based around rice, and many wealthy Bangkokians own farms up-country where they cultivate their favourite variety. There are two main types of rice – 'sticky' or glutinous (*khao niaw*) and non-glutinous (*khao jao*). Sticky rice is usually used to make sweets (desserts), although it is the staple in the Northeastern region and parts of the North. *Khao jao* is standard white rice.

A meal usually consists (along with the rice) of a soup like *tom yam kung* (prawn soup), *kaeng* (a curry) and *krueng kieng* (a number of side dishes). Generally, Thai food is chilli-hot, and aromatic herbs and grasses (like lemon grass, coriander, tamarind and ginger) are used to give a distinctive flavour. *Nam pla* (fish sauce) and *nam prik* (nam pla, chillies, garlic, sugar, shrimps and lime juice) are two condiments that are taken with almost all meals. *Nam pla* is made from steeping fish, usually anchovies, in brine for long periods and then bottling the peatish-coloured liquor produced. Chillies deserve a special mention because most Thais like their food HOT! Some chillies are comparatively mild; others – like the tiny, bright red *prik khii nuu* (mouse shit pepper) – are fiendishly hot.

Due to Thailand's large Chinese population (or at least Thais with Chinese roots), there are also many Chinese-style restaurants whose cuisine is variously 'Thai-ified'. Many of the snacks available on the streets show this mixture of Thai and Chinese, not to mention Arab and Malay. *Bah jang*, for example, are small pyramids of leaves stuffed with sticky rice, Chinese sausage, salted eggs, pork and dried shrimp. They were reputedly first created for the Chinese dragon boat festival, but are now available 12 months a year – for around ฿20.

Thai cuisine
See also box, page 54, & food glossary, page 844

Essentials

Essentials

Thai dishes

It is impossible to provide a comprehensive list of Thai dishes. However (and at the risk of offending connoisseurs by omitting their favourites), popular dishes include:

Soups (gaeng chud)

Tom yam kung – *hot and sour prawn soup spiced with lemon grass, coriander and chillies*

Tom ka kai – *chicken in coconut milk with loas (loas, or ka, is an exotic spice)*

Khaaw tom – *rice soup with egg and pork (a common breakfast dish) or chicken, fish or prawn. It is said that the soup can cure fevers and other illnesses. Probably best for a hangover.*

Kwaytio – *Chinese noodle soup served with a variety of additional ingredients, often available from roadside stalls and from smaller restaurants – mostly served up until lunchtime.*

Kaeng juut – *bean curd and vegetable soup, non-spicy*

Rice-based dishes

Single-dish meals served at roadside stalls and in many restaurants (especially cheaper ones).

Khaaw phat kai/mu/kung – *fried rice with chicken/pork/prawn*

Khaaw naa pet – *rice with duck*

Khaaw gaeng – *curry and rice*

Khaaw man kai – *rice with chicken*

Khaaw mu daeng – *rice with red pork*

Noodle-based dishes

Khaaw soi – *a form of Kwaytio with egg noodles in a curry broth*

Phak sii-u – *noodles fried with egg, vegetables and meat/prawns*

Kwaytio haeng – *wide noodles served with pork and vegetables*

Ba-mii haeng – *wheat noodles served with pork and vegetables*

Phat thai – *Thai fried noodles*

Mee krop – *Thai crisp-fried noodles*

Curries (gaeng)

Gaeng phet kai/nua – *hot chicken/beef curry*

Gaeng khiaw waan kai/nua/phet/pla – *green chicken/beef/duck/fish curry (the colour is due to the large number of whole green chillies pounded to make the paste that forms the base of this very hot curry)*

Gaeng phanaeng – *chicken or beef curry*

Gaeng plaa duk – *catfish curry*

Gaeng mussaman – *Muslim beef curry served with potatoes*

Meat dishes

Laap – *chopped (once raw, now more frequently cooked) meat with herbs and spices*

Kai/nua phat prik – *fried chicken/beef with chillies*

Nua priaw waan – *sweet and sour beef*

Mu waan – *sweet pork*

Kai/mu/nua phat kapow – *fried meat with basil and chillies*

Kai tort – *Thai fried chicken*

To sample Thai food it is best to go in a group to a restaurant and order a range of dishes. To eat alone is regarded as slightly strange. However, there are a number of 'one dish' meals like fried rice and *phat thai* (fried noodles), and restaurants will also usually provide *raat khao* ('over rice'), which is a dish like a curry served on a bed of rice for a single person.

The etiquette of eating The Thai philosophy on eating is 'often' and most Thais will snack their way through the day. Eating is a relaxed, communal affair, and it is not necessary to get too worked up about etiquette. Dishes are placed in the middle of the table where diners can help themselves. In a restaurant rice is usually spooned out by a waiter or waitress, and it is considered good manners to start a meal with a spoon of rice. While food is eaten with a spoon and fork, the fork is only used to manoeuvre food onto the spoon. Because most food is prepared in bite-sized pieces, it is usually not necessary to use a knife. At noodle stalls chopsticks and china soup spoons are used, while in the Northeast most people – at least at home – use their fingers. Sticky rice is compressed into a ball using the ends of the fingers and then dipped in the other dishes. Thais will not pile their plates with food,

Kai tua – *chicken in peanut sauce*
Kai yang – *garlic chicken*
Priao wan – *sweet and sour pork with vegetables*
Seafood
Plaa priaw waan – *whole fried fish with ginger sauce*
Plaa too tort – *Thai fried fish*
Haw mok – *steamed fish curry*
Plaa nerng – *steamed fish*
Plaa pao – *grilled fish*
Thotman plaa – *fried curried fish cakes*
Luuk ciin – *fishballs*
Salads (yam)
Yam nua – *Thai beef salad*
Som tam – *green papaya salad with tomatoes, chillies, garlic, chopped dried shrimps and lemon (can be extremely hot)*
Vegetables
Phak phat ruam mit – *mixed fried vegetables*
Sweets (kanom)
Khaaw niaw sankhayaa – *sticky rice and custard*
Khaaw niaw mamuang – *sticky rice and mango (a seasonal favourite)*
Kluay buat chee – *bananas in coconut milk*
Kanom mo kaeng – *baked custard squares*
Kluay tort – *Thai fried bananas*
Leenchee loi mek – *chilled lychees in custard*

Fruits (see page 56)
Chomphu – *rose apple*
Khanun – *jackfruit*
Kluay – *banana*
Lamyai – *longan*
Linchi – *lychee*
Lamut – *sapodilla*
Makham wan – *tamarind*
Malakho – *papaya*
Manaaw – *lime*
Mang khud – *mangosteen*
Maprao – *coconut*
Majeung – *star apple*
Mamuang – *mango*
Ngo – *rambutan*
Noi na – *custard (or sugar) apple*
Sapparot – *pineapple*
Som – *orange*
Som o – *pomelo*
Taeng mo – *watermelon*
Thurian – *durian*
Cookery courses
For those interested in taking a course in Thai cookery, contact: UFM Baking and Cooking, 593/29-39 Sukhumvit Soi 33/1, T2590620; the Thai Cooking School at the Oriental Hotel, 48 Oriental Ave, T4376211; Modern Housewife Centre, 45/6-7 Setsiri Rd, T2792831; all in Bangkok (phone code: 02). For more details on courses in Bangkok, see page 153. Courses are also available in Phuket, page 583, Chiang Mai, page , and guesthouses in many other parts of the country also run informal courses.

but take many small portions from the dishes arranged on a table. It is also considered good manners when invited out to leave some food on your plate, as well as on the serving dishes on the table. This demonstrates the generosity of the host.

It is possible to get a good, tasty and nutritious meal almost anywhere – and at any time – in Thailand. Thais eat out a great deal, so most towns have a range of places. Starting at the top, in pecuniary terms at any rate, are the more **sophisticated restaurants**. These are usually air conditioned, and sometimes attached to a hotel. In places like Bangkok and Chiang Mai they may be Western in style and atmosphere. In towns less frequented by foreigners they are likely to be rather more functional – although the food will be just as good. In addition to these more upmarket restaurants are a whole range of places, from **noodle shops** to **curry houses** and **seafood restaurants**. Many small restaurants have no menus. But often the speciality of the house will be clear – roasted, honeyed ducks hanging in the window, crab and fish laid out on crushed ice outside. Away from the main tourist spots, 'Western' breakfasts are commonly unavailable, so be prepared to eat Thai-style (noodle or rice soup or fried rice).

Where to eat
See inside front cover for a guide to our restaurant price categories

Distinctive fruits

Custard apple (or sugar apple) Scaly green skin; squeeze the skin to open the fruit and scoop out the flesh with a spoon. Season: June-September.

Durian (Durio zibethinus) A large prickly fruit, with yellow flesh, about the size of a football. Infamous for its pungent smell. While it is today regarded by many visitors as simply revolting, early Europeans (16th-18th centuries) raved about it, possibly because it was similar in taste to Western delicacies of the period. Borri (1744) thought it was 'God himself, who had produc'd that fruit'. But by 1880 Burbridge was writing: 'Its odour – one scarcely feels justified in using the word 'perfume' – is so potent, so vague, but withal so insinuating, that it can scarcely be tolerated inside the house'. Banned from hotel rooms throughout the region, and beloved by most Southeast Asians , it has an alluring taste – some maintain it is an addiction. Durian-flavoured chewing gum, ice-cream and jams are all available. Season: May-August.

Jackfruit Similar in appearance to durian but not so spiky. Yellow flesh, tasting slightly like custard. Season: January-June.

Mango (Mangifera indica) A rainforest fruit which is now cultivated; widely available in the West. In Southeast Asia there are hundreds of different varieties with subtle variations in flavour. Delicious eaten with sticky rice and a sweet sauce. The best mangoes in the region are considered to be those from South Thailand. Season: March-June.

Mangosteen (Garcinia mangostana) An aubergine-coloured hard shell covers this small fruit, which is about the size of a tennis ball. Cut or squeeze the purple shell to reach its sweet white flesh, which is prized by many visitors above all others. In 1898, an American resident of Java wrote, erotically and in obvious ecstasy: 'The five white segments separate easily, and they melt on the tongue with a touch of tart and a touch of sweet; one moment a memory of the juiciest, most fragrant apple, at another a remembrance of the smoothest cream ice, the most exquisite and delicately flavoured fruit-acid known – all of the delights of nature's laboratory condensed in that ball of neige parfumée'. Southeast Asians believe it should be eaten as a chaser to durian. Season: April-September.

Papaya (Carica papaya) A New-World fruit that was not introduced into Southeast Asia until the 16th century. Large, round or oval in shape, yellow or green-skinned, with bright orange flesh and a mass of round, black seeds in the middle. The flesh, in texture and taste, is somewhere between a mango and a melon. Some maintain that it tastes 'soapy'. Season: Year round.

Pomelo A large round fruit the size of anything from an ostrich egg to a football, with thick, green skin and pith, and flesh similar to a grapefruit's, but less acidic. Season: August-November.

Rambutan (Nephelium lappaceum) The bright red and hairy rambutan – rambut is the Malay word for 'hair' – with its slightly rubbery but sweet flesh, is a close relative of the lychee of southern China. The Thai word for rambutan is ngoh, which is the nickname given by Thais to the fuzzy-haired Negrito aboriginals in the southern jungles. Season: May-September.

Salak (Salacca edulis) A small pear-shaped fruit about the size of a large plum, with a rough, brown, scaly skin (somewhat like a miniature pangolin) and yellow-white, crisp flesh. It is related to the sago and rattan trees.

Tamarind (Tamarindus indicus) Brown seedpods with dry brittle skins and a brown tart-sweet fruit, which grow on a tree introduced into Southeast Asia from India. The name is Arabic for 'Indian date'. The flesh has a high tartaric acid content and is used to flavour curries, jams, jellies and chutneys, as well as for cleaning brass and copper. Elephants have a predilection for tamarind balls. Season: December-February.

Why all the spice?

People have occasionally considered the vexed question of why tropical countries tend to produce spicy food. Some people have suggested that it is because the spices disguise the taste of bad food. Others have hazarded that spices have some useful nutritional value. Still more ingenious is the argument that spices stimulate sweating and thus increase evaporational cooling in hot climates. However, Jennifer Billing and Paul Sherman have, apparently, resolved the dilemma. In the March 1998 issue of the Quarterly Review of Biology, they revealed that many spices have anti-bacterial properties, particularly useful in hot climates where food spoils rapidly.

Essentials

Towards the bottom of the scale are **stalls and food carts**. These tend to congregate at particular places in town – often in the evening, from dusk – although they can be found just about anywhere: outside the local provincial offices, along a cul-de-sac, or under a conveniently placed shady tree. Stallholders will tend to specialize: noodles, rice dishes, fruit drinks, sweets and so on. Hot meals are usually prepared to order. While stall food may be cheap – a meal costs only around ฿15-20 – they are frequented by people from all walks of life. A well-heeled businessman in a suit is just as likely to be seen bent over a bowl of noodles at a rickety table on a busy street corner as a construction worker.

A popular innovation over the last 10 years or so has been the *suan a-haan* or **garden restaurant**. These are often on the edge of towns, with tables set in gardens, sometimes with bamboo furniture and ponds. Another type of restaurant worth a mention is the **Thai-style coffee shop**. These are sometimes attached to hotels in provincial towns and feature hostesses dressed in Imelda-esque or sparingly spangly costumes. The hostesses, when they are not crooning to the house band, sit with customers, laugh at their jokes and assiduously make sure that their glasses are always full. They may provide other services too, but usually not at the table. In the North, **khantoke dining** is de rigeur – or so one might imagine from the number of restaurants offering it. This is traditional to the North and involves sitting on the floor, usually with cushions provided for Westerners unused to being at ground level for extended periods, and eating regional delicacies accompanied by traditional music and dance.

Tourist centres also provide good European, American and Japanese food at reasonable prices. Bangkok boasts some superb restaurants. Less expensive Western **fast food** restaurants can also be found – McDonald's, Pizza Hut (although these may well be renamed due to a spat between the Thai operator of the franchise), Kentucky Fried Chicken and others.

Drink

Water in smaller restaurants can be risky, so many people recommend that visitors drink bottled water (widely available) or **hot tea**.

Drinking water

Coffee is also now consumed throughout Thailand (usually served with Coffee-mate or creamer). In stalls and restaurants, coffee comes with a glass of Chinese tea. Soft drinks are widely available. Many roadside stalls prepare fresh fruit juices in liquidizers (*bun*), while hotels produce all the usual cocktails.

Soft drinks

Spirits Major brands of spirits are served in most hotels and bars, although not always off the tourist path. The most popular spirit among Thais is *Mekhong* – local cane whisky – which can be drunk straight or with mixers such as Coca-Cola. It can seem rather sweet to the Western palate, but it is the cheapest form of alcohol.

Alcohol

Beer drinking is spreading fast. In 1987, beer consumption was 98,000,000 litres; in 1992, 330,000,000 litres. The most popular local beer is *Singha* beer, brewed by Boon Rowd. The company commands 89% of the beer market. It is said that the beer's distinctive taste is due to the formaldehyde that it contains. When the company removed the chemical (it was no longer needed as bottling technology had been improved), there was such an outcry from Thais that they quickly reincorporated it. Whether or not the story is true, an evening drinking *Singha* can result in quite a hangover. Its alcohol content of 6% must be partly to blame.

Among expatriates, the most popular Thai beer is the more expensive *Kloster* brand (similar to a light German beer), with an alcohol content of 5.7%. *Singha* introduced a light beer called *Singha Gold* a few years back, which is quite similar to *Kloster*. *Amarit* is a third, rather less widely available, brand, but popular with foreigners and brewed by the same company who produce *Kloster*. Between them, *Kloster* and *Amarit* control about 10% of the market. Two 'local' beers to enter the fray in the last 10 years are *Heineken* and *Carlsberg*. At the beginning of the 1990s, Carlsberg built a brewery north of Bangkok and had clearly done their homework. The beer is sweeter and lighter than *Singha* and *Kloster* but still strong, with an alcohol content of 6%. The Carlsberg brew has made considerable inroads into the markets of the established brands – although in so doing they are said to have lost many millions of baht. A little later Carlsberg introduced a new beer specifically for the Thai market, *Bier Chang* or *Elephant Beer*, which is yet more alcoholic at 7%. More recently still, Heineken have opened a local brewery near Sena in the Central Plains, again producing beer with a much higher alcohol content than the equivalent in the West.

These beers have now been joined by a wave of new locally produced beers, often brewed in collaboration with overseas breweries. The cheapest is *Leo* brand beer, which is brewed in Khon Kaen in the Northeast. Their advertising campaign emphasizes that this is a Thai beer, but Bangkok's sophisticates snigger under their breath at anyone stooping to drink the stuff. In fact, though, *Leo Super* is quite palatable; the same can't be said of Lao thammada. Then there's *Amstel* (a Dutch beer) and *Mittweida*. The latter's advertising campaign, in contrast to Leo's, plays on the fact that, apparently, virtually the entire population of Germany drink the stuff for breakfast, lunch and tea. That few Germans seem to have heard of the brew doesn't seem to have tempered the ad company's enthusiasm.

Beer is relatively expensive in Thai terms as it is heavily taxed by the government. But it is a high status drink, so as Thais become wealthier, more are turning to beer in preference to traditional, local whiskies. It is the burgeoning middle class, especially the young, which explains why brewers are so keen to set up shop in this traditionally non-beer drinking country. In a café, expect to pay ฿30-50 for a small beer, in a coffee shop or bar ฿50-70, and in a hotel bar or restaurant rather more than that. Some pubs and bars also sell beer on tap – which is known as *bier sot*, 'fresh' beer.

Wine Thais are fast developing a penchant for wines. Imported wines are expensive by international standards and Thai wines are pretty ghastly – overall. An exception is *Chateau de Loei* which is produced in the northeastern province of Loei by Chaijudh Karnasuta, with the expert assistance of a French wine maker. They produce a *chenin blanc* and a *chenin rouge* and they are eminently drinkable. At the 1996 Asia-Europe meeting (ASEM), Khun Chaijudh managed to get bottles placed in all the heads of state's rooms – what President Chirac thought, and whether he even tried the wine, is not known.

Shopping

Bangkok and Chiang Mai are the shopping 'centres' of Thailand. Many people now prefer Chiang Mai, as the shops are concentrated in a smaller area and there is a good range of quality products, especially handicrafts. Bangkok still offers the greatest variety and choice. But it is difficult to find bargains in Bangkok any longer. The department stores and shopping malls contain high-price, high-quality merchandise (all at a fixed price), much of which is imported.

Thailand has had a reputation as being a Mecca for pirated goods: cassette and video tapes, Lacoste shirts, Gucci leather goods, Rolex watches, computer software and so on. These items are still available, but pressure from the US to protect intellectual copyright is leading to more enthusiastic crackdowns by the police. In Bangkok, 'genuine' cassette tapes can be bought (at what are still bargain prices compared with the West), and buying pirated videos requires, in many cases, a retreat to some back room. This clampdown on buying pirated goods is likely to continue; in 1994-95 Thailand brought a new copyright law onto the statute books, and fearing trade retaliation from the US, the law is being respected to a much greater degree than formerly.

The widest selection of **Thai silk** is available in Bangkok, although cheaper silk as well as good quality cotton can be obtained in the northeast (the traditional centre of silk weaving). **Tailor-made clothing** is available (suits, shirts and dresses), although designs are sometimes rather outdated; it might be better for the tailor to copy an article of your own clothing (see page 162). However, things change and there are now some top designers in Bangkok. **Leather goods** include custom-made crocodile skin shoes and boots (for those who aren't squeamish, after seeing the brutes in one of the crocodile farms).

Bangkok is also a good place to buy **jewellery** – gold, sapphires and rubies – and the same applies to **antiques**, bronzeware and celadon (see page 156). **NB** See section on safety – regarding tricksters. Handicrafts are best purchased up-country. In general, Bangkok has by far the best selection of goods, and by shopping around, visitors will probably be able to get just as good a price as they would up-country.

Competition

Between shopkeepers competition is fierce. Do not be persuaded into buying something before having a chance to price it elsewhere – Thais can be enormously persuasive. **NB** Also watch out for guarantees of authenticity – fake antiques abound, and even professionals find it difficult to know a 1990 Khmer sculpture from a 10th-century one.

Tips

This is generally unnecessary. A 10% service charge is now expected on room, food and drinks bills in the smarter hotels, as well as a tip for any personal service. Increasingly, the more expensive restaurants add a 10% service charge; others expect a small tip.

Tricksters

Tricksters, rip-off artists, fraudsters, less than honest salespeople – call them what you will – are likely to be far more of a problem than simple theft. People may well approach you in the street offering incredible one-off bargains, and giving what might seem to be very plausible reasons for your sudden good fortune. Be wary in all such cases and do not be pressed into making a hasty decision. Unfortunately, more often than not, the salesperson is trying to pull a fast one. Favourite 'bargains' are precious stones, whose authenticity is 'demonstrated' before your very eyes (see the box on page 160). Although many Thais do like to talk to farangs and practise their English, in tourist areas there are also those who offer their friendship for pecuniary rather than linguistic reasons. Sad as it is to say so, it is probably a good idea to be suspicious.

Essentials

Essentials

Entertainment and nightlife

Thais are great clubbers and party-goers, although provincial nightclubs and coffee shops might not be to everyone's tastes. Karaoke is also very popular, across the country. Unsurprisingly, the most sophisticated nightlife is to be found in the largest towns and in tourist centres. Jazz and blues, nightclubs, rock, discos, wine bars, gay and lesbian bars, cabaret, straight bars, karaoke, beer gardens and more are all available. Nightclubs tend to close between 0200 and 0300 while opening hours are more variable, anywhere from 1800 to 2200. Bars tend to open earlier than nightclubs and also close slightly earlier; happy hours are usually between 1700 and 1900. For latest offerings, including music, dance and theatre see (for Bangkok) *Bangkok Metro* and *Bangkok Timeout* and for tourist centres one of the many free newspapers and magazines.

Coffee shops   If you want a taste of tradition, then visit one of the upcountry coffee shops. Some of these are innocuous places where men gather to drink strong coffee, accompanied by Chinese tea, and chat about the price of rice and the latest political scandal. Others are really nightclubs where men drink prodigious quantities of whisky while accompanied by girls dressed in a weird assortment of dresses from figure-hugging little black numbers to Marie Antoinette extravagances. They also take it in turns to croon popular Thai ballads and rock songs to bad backing bands. Upstairs is, commonly, a brothel. An education, if nothing else.

Cinemas   In Bangkok there are a range of cinemas that show films either with an English soundtrack or English subtitles (listed in the *Bangkok Post* and the *Nation*). Upcountry cinemas will often have a separate glass enclosed section where it is possible to listen to the English soundtrack of dubbed films. Generally films are screened at 1200, 1400, 1700, 1900, 2100, and at 1000 on Saturday and Sunday. In Bangkok and Chiang Mai cultural centres such as the Alliance Française and the Goethe Institute show European films. It is also possible to rent videos and have them played in rented rooms in some towns.

Holidays and festivals

See also individual towns for details of local festivals   Festivals with month only are movable; a booklet of holidays and festivals is available from most TAT offices. For movable festivals, check the TAT's website, www.tourismthailand.org/tat This website also provides dates and background information for regional festivals, by month. The dates given here for movable festivals and public holidays are for 2001, except where noted otherwise.

January   *New Year's Day* (1st: public holiday).

February/March   *Chinese New Year* (movable, end of January/beginning of February, 12-14 February 2002), celebrated by Thailand's large Chinese population. The festival extends over 15 days; spirits are appeased, and offerings are made to the ancestors and to the spirits. Good wishes and lucky money are exchanged, and Chinese-run shops and businesses shut down. *Magha Puja* (movable, full-moon: public holiday). Buddhist holy day, celebrates the occasion when the Buddha's disciples miraculously gathered together to hear him preach. Culminates in a candle-lit procession around the temple *bot* (or ordination hall). The faithful make offerings and gain merit.

Chakri Day (6th: public holiday) commemorates the founding of the present Chakri   April
Dynasty. *Songkran* (movable: public holiday) marks the beginning of the Buddhist New
Year. The festival is particularly big in the north, much less so in the south and
(understandably) the Muslim far south. It is a three to five day celebration, with parades,
dancing and folk entertainment. Traditionally, the first day represents the last chance for
a 'spring clean'. Rubbish is burnt, in the belief that old and dirty things will cause
misfortune in the coming year. The wat is the focal point of celebrations. Revered
Buddha images are carried through the streets, accompanied by singers and dancers.
The second day is the main water-throwing day. The water-throwing practice was
originally an act of homage to ancestors and family elders. Young people pay respect by
pouring scented water over the elders' heads. The older generation sprinkle water over
Buddha images. Gifts are given. This uninhibited water-throwing continues for all three
days (although it is now banned in Bangkok). On the third day, birds, fish and turtles are
all released, to gain merit and in remembrance of departed souls.

Labour Day (1st: public holiday). *Coronation Day* (5th May: public holiday)   May/June
commemorates the present King Bhumibol's crowning in 1950. *Ploughing Ceremony*
(movable: public holiday, 16 May 2001), performed by the King at Sanaam Luang near
the Grand Palace in Bangkok. Brahmanic in origin, it traditionally marks the auspicious
date when farmers could begin preparing their riceland. Impressive bulls decorated
with flowers pull a sacred gold plough. *Visakha Puja* (full-moon: public holiday),
holiest of all Buddhist days, it marks the Buddha's birth, enlightenment and death.
Candle-lit processions are held at most temples.

Asalha Puja and Khao Phansa (movable, full-moon: public holiday, 5 July 2001)   July
commemorates the Buddha's first sermon to his disciples and marks the beginning of
the Buddhist Lent. Monks reside in their monasteries for the three-month Buddhist
Rains Retreat to study and meditate, and young men temporarily become monks.
Ordination ceremonies all over the country, and villagers give white cotton robes to
the monks to wear during the Lent ritual bathing.

The Queen's Birthday (12th: public holiday).   August

Chulalongkorn Day (23rd: public holiday) honours King Chulalongkorn (1868-1910),   October/
perhaps Thailand's most beloved and revered king. *Ok Phansa* (three lunar months   November
after Asalha Puja) marks the end of the Buddhist Lent and the beginning of Krathin,
when gifts – usually a new set of cotton robes – are offered to the monks. Particularly
venerated monks are sometimes given silk robes as a sign of respect and esteem.
Krathin itself is celebrated over two days. It marks the end of the monks' retreat and
the re-entry of novices into secular society. Processions and fairs are held all over the
country; villagers wear their best clothes, and food, money, pillows and bed linen are
offered to the monks of the local wat.

Loi Krathong (full-moon of the 12th Thai lunar month, which falls between October
and November, 31 October, 1 November 2001) – a *krathong* is a small model boat
made to contain a candle, incense and flowers. The festival comes at the end of the
rainy season and honours the goddess of water. The small boats are pushed out onto
canals, lakes and rivers. Sadly, few krathongs are now made of leaves: polystyrene has
taken over and the morning after Loi Krathong, lakes and river banks are littered with
the wrecks of the night's festivities. **NB** The 'quaint' candles in flower pots sold in
many shops at this time are, in fact, large firecrackers.

The King's Birthday (5th: public holiday). Flags and portraits of the King are erected all   December
over Bangkok, especially down Rachdamnern Ave and around the Grand Palace.
Constitution Day (10th: public holiday). *New Year's Eve* (31st: public holiday).

Essentials

Non-holiday observances These are holidays when schoolchildren may have the day off and some offices may be closed, but in general the country operates normally:

2nd Saturday in January – Children's Day
16th January – Teachers' Day (schools closed)
24th September – Mahidol Day (commemorates the 'Father' of modern Thai medicine)
25th November – Primary Education Day (marks the death of King Rama VI)

Health

Staying healthy in Thailand is straightforward. With the following advice and precautions you should keep as healthy as you do at home. Most visitors return home having experienced no problems at all beyond an upset stomach. However, in Thailand the health risks, especially in the tropical areas, are different from those encountered in Europe or the USA. It also depends on how you travel and where. The country has a mainly tropical climate; nevertheless, the acquisition of true tropical disease by the visitor is probably conditioned as much by the rural nature and standard of hygiene of the surroundings than by the climate. There is an obvious difference in health risks between the business traveller who tends to stay in international class hotels in the large cities and the backpacker trekking through the rural areas. There are no hard and fast rules to follow; you will often have to make your own judgement on the healthiness or otherwise of your surroundings.

Medical facilities There are English-speaking doctors in Bangkok and other major cities, who have particular experience in dealing with locally occurring diseases. Your embassy representative will often be able to give you the name of local reputable doctors and most of the better hotels have a doctor on standby. If you do fall ill and cannot find a recommended doctor, try the outpatient department of a hospital – there are excellent private hospitals in Bangkok, although they are not cheap but offer a very acceptable standard to foreigners. The likelihood of finding good medical care diminishes very rapidly as you move away from the big cities. Especially in the rural areas there are systems and traditions of medicine wholly different from the Western model, and you will be confronted with less orthodox forms of treatment such as herbal medicines and acupuncture; not that these are unfamiliar to most Western travellers.

Before travelling

See page 27 for advice on travelling with children Take out medical insurance. Make sure it covers all eventualities, especially evacuation to your home country by a medically-equipped plane, if necessary. You should have a dental check-up, obtain a spare glasses prescription, a spare oral contraceptive prescription (or enough pills to last) and, if you suffer from a chronic illness (such as diabetes, high blood pressure, ear or sinus troubles, cardio-pulmonary disease or nervous disorder), arrange for a check up with your doctor, who can at the same time provide you with a letter explaining the details of your condition in English. Check the current practice in countries you are visiting for malaria prophylaxis (prevention). If you are on regular medication, be sure to take enough to cover the period of your travel.

Medicines There is very little control on the sale of drugs and medicines in Thailand. You may be able to buy any and every drug in pharmacies without a prescription. Be wary of this, because pharmacists can be poorly trained and might sell you drugs that are unsuitable, dangerous or old. Many drugs and medicines are manufactured under licence from American or European companies, so the trade names may be familiar to you. This means you do not have to carry a whole chest of medicines with you, but remember that the shelf life of some items, especially vaccines and antibiotics, is markedly reduced in hot conditions. Buy your supplies at the better outlets where there are more refrigerators, even though they are more expensive, and check the expiry date of all preparations you buy. Immigration officials occasionally confiscate scheduled drugs (Lomotil is an example) if they are not accompanied by a doctor's prescription.

Medical supplies

You may like to take some of the following items with you from home: sunglasses – ones designed for intense sunlight; earplugs – for sleeping on aeroplanes and in noisy hotels; suntan cream – with a high protection factor; insect repellent – containing DET for preference; mosquito net – lightweight, permethrin-impregnated for choice; tablets – for travel sickness; tampons – can be expensive in some countries in Southeast Asia; condoms; contraceptives; water sterilizing tablets; anti-malarial tablets; anti-infective ointment – for example, Cetrimide; dusting powder for feet etc – containing fungicide; antacid tablets – for indigestion; sachets of rehydration salts plus anti-diarrhoea preparations; painkillers such as paracetamol or aspirin; antibiotics – for diarrhoea etc; First Aid Kit – small pack containing a few sterile syringes and needles and disposable gloves. The risk of catching hepatitis etc from a dirty needle used for injection is very low in Thailand, but some may be reassured by carrying their own supplies – available from camping shops and airport shops.

Vaccination & immunization

Smallpox vaccination is no longer required anywhere in the world and cholera vaccination is no longer recognized as necessary for international travel by the World Health Organization; it is not very effective either. Yellow fever vaccination is not required either, although you may be asked for a certificate if you have been in a country affected by yellow fever immediately before travelling to Southeast Asia. Vaccination against the following diseases are recommended.

Typhoid A disease spread by the insanitary preparation of food. A number of new vaccines against this condition are now available; the older TAB and monovalent typhoid vaccines are being phased out. The newer, for example Typhim Vi, cause less side effects, but are more expensive. For those who do not like injections, there are now oral vaccines.

Poliomyelitis Despite its decline in the world, this remains a serious disease if caught and is easy to protect against. There are live oral vaccines and in some countries injected vaccines. Whichever one you choose, it is a good idea to have a booster every three to five years if visiting developing countries regularly.

Tetanus One dose should be given with a booster at six weeks and another at six months, and 10-yearly boosters thereafter are recommended.

Infectious hepatitis This is less of a problem for travellers than it used to be because of the development of two extremely effective vaccines against the A and B form of the disease. It remains common, however, in Southeast Asia. A combined hepatitis A and B vaccine is now licensed and has been available since 1997 – one jab covers both diseases.

Other vaccinations These might be considered in the case of epidemics; for example, meningitis. Meningococcal meningitis and Japanese B encephalitis (JVE): there is an extremely small risk of these rather serious diseases. Both are seasonal and vary according to region. Meningitis can occur in epidemic form. JVE is a viral disease transmitted from pigs to humans by mosquitoes. For details of the vaccinations, consult a travel clinic. Consult your doctor for advice on tuberculosis inoculation: the disease is still widespread in Southeast Asia.

Further information

Further information on health risks abroad, vaccinations etc may be available from a local travel clinic. If you wish to take specific drugs with you such as antibiotics, these are best prescribed by your own doctor. Beware, however, that not all doctors can be experts on the health problems of remote countries. More detailed or more up-to-date information than local doctors can provide is available from various sources, including the following.

In the UK there are hospital departments specializing in tropical diseases in London, Liverpool, Birmingham and Glasgow, and the Malaria Reference Laboratory at the London School of Hygiene and Tropical Medicine provides advice about malaria, T0891-600350 (calls cost 60p a minute). In the USA the local Public Health Services can give such information, and information is available centrally from the Centres for Disease Control (CDC) in Atlanta, T404-3324559, www.cdc.gov In Canada information is available from the McGill University Centre for Tropical Diseases, T514-9348049, www.medcor.mcgill.ca/~tropmed/td/txt

There are computerized databases which can be accessed for up-to-the-minute information specific to destinations. In the UK there is MASTA (Medical Advisory Service to Travellers Abroad), T0906-8224100, calls cost 60p a minute. The Scottish Centre for Infection and Environmental Health has an excellent website providing information for travellers at www.fitfortravel.scot.nhs.uk Other information on medical problems overseas can be obtained from the book by Richard Dawood (Editor) – *Travellers' Health, How to Stay Healthy Abroad*, Oxford University Press l992, £7.99. Handbooks on First Aid are produced by the British and American Red Cross and by St. John's Ambulance (UK). The Ross Institute, London School of Hygiene and Tropical Medicine, Keppel Street, London WC1E 7HT, publishes *The Preservation of Personal Health in Warm Climates*. A helpful travel health website is Shoreland's Travel Health Online, www.tripprep.com A more general publication is John Hatt's *The Tropical Traveller* (Penguin, 1993).

On the road

For most travellers a trip to Southeast Asia means a long flight. If this crosses time zones then jetlag can be a problem, where your body's biological clock gets out of synchrony with the real time at your destination. The main symptoms are tiredness and sleepiness at inconvenient times and, conversely, a tendency to wake up in the middle of the night feeling like you want your breakfast. Most find that the problem is worse when flying in an easterly direction. The best way to get over jetlag is probably to try to force yourself into the new time zone as strictly as possible, which may involve, on a westward flight, trying to stay awake until your normal bedtime, and on an eastward flight forgetting that you have lost some sleep on the way out and going to bed relatively early, but near your normal time, the evening after you arrive. The symptoms of jetlag may be helped by keeping up your fluid intake on the journey, but not with alcohol. The hormone melatonin seems to reduce the symptoms of jetlag but is not presently licensed in most of Europe, although it can be obtained from health food stores in the USA.

On long-haul flights it is also important to stretch your legs at least every hour to prevent slowing of the circulation and the possible development of blood clots. Drinking plenty of non-alcoholic fluids will also help.

If travelling by boat then sea sickness can be a problem – dealt with in the usual way by taking anti-motion sickness pills.

Intestinal upsets The thought of catching a stomach bug worries visitors to Southeast Asia, but there have been great improvements in food hygiene and most such infections are preventable. Travellers' diarrhoea and vomiting is due, most of the time, to food poisoning, usually passed on by the insanitary habits of food handlers. As a general rule the cleaner your surroundings and the smarter the restaurant, the less likely you are to suffer.

Foods to avoid Uncooked, undercooked, partially cooked or reheated meat, fish, eggs, raw vegetables and salads, especially when they have been left out exposed to flies. Stick to fresh food that has been cooked from raw just before eating, and make sure you peel fruit yourself. Wash and dry your hands before eating – disposable wet-wipe tissues are useful for this.

Shellfish Eating raw shellfish is risky, and at certain times of the year some fish and shellfish concentrate toxins from their environment and cause various kinds of food poisoning. Liver fluke can also be transmitted. The local authorities notify the public not to eat these foods. Do not ignore the warning.

Heat treated milk (UHT, pasteurized or sterilized) is becoming more available in Southeast Asia, as is pasteurized cheese. On the whole, matured or processed cheeses are safer than the fresh varieties. Fresh unpasteurized milk from whatever animal can be a source of food poisoning germs, tuberculosis and brucellosis. This applies equally to ice-cream, yoghurt and cheese made from unpasteurized milk, so avoid these home-made products – the factory-made ones are probably safer.

Tap water This is rarely safe outside the major cities, especially in the rainy season. Stream water, if you are in the countryside, is often contaminated by local communities. Filtered or bottled water is usually available and safe, although you must make sure that somebody is not filling bottles from the tap and hammering on a new crown cap. If your hotel has a central hot water supply, this water is safe to drink after cooling. Ice for drinks should be made from boiled water but rarely is, so stand your glass on the ice cubes, rather than putting them in the drink. The better hotels have water-purifying systems. There are a number of ways of purifying water in order to make it safe to drink. Dirty water should first be strained through a filter bag (camping shops) and then boiled or treated. Bringing water to a rolling boil at sea level is sufficient to make the water safe for drinking, but at higher altitudes you have to boil the water for longer to ensure that all the microbes are killed. There are sterilizing methods that can be used and there are proprietary preparations containing chlorine (eg Puritabs) or iodine (eg Pota Aqua) compounds. Chlorine compounds generally do not kill protozoa (eg Giardia). There are a number of water filters now on the market available in personal and expedition size. They work either on mechanical or chemical principles, or may do both. Make sure you take the spare parts or spare chemicals with you and do not believe everything the manufacturers say.

Travellers' diarrhoea This is usually caused by eating food that has been contaminated by food poisoning germs. Drinking water is rarely the culprit. Sea water or river water is more likely to be contaminated by sewage and so swimming in such dilute effluent can also be a cause.

Infection with various organisms can give rise to travellers' diarrhoea. They may be viruses, bacteria – for example, Escherichia coli (probably the most common cause worldwide), protozoa (such as amoebas and giardia), salmonella and cholera. The diarrhoea may come on suddenly or rather slowly. It may or may not be accompanied by vomiting, or by severe abdominal pain and the passage of blood or mucus when it is called dysentery.

How do you know which type you have caught and how to treat it? If you can time the onset of the diarrhoea to the minute ('acute'), then it is probably due to a virus or a

Essentials

bacterium and/or the onset of dysentery. The treatment in addition to rehydration is Ciprofloxacin 500 mg every 12 hours; the drug is now widely available and there are many similar ones.

If the diarrhoea comes on slowly or intermittently ('sub-acute') then it is more likely to be protozoal, which is caused by an amoeba or giardia. Antibiotics such as Ciprofloxacin will have little effect. These cases are best treated by a doctor, as is any outbreak of diarrhoea continuing for more than three days. Sometimes blood is passed in amoebic dysentery and for this you should certainly seek medical help. If this is not available then the best treatment is probably Tinidazole (Fasigyn), one tablet four times a day for three days. If there are severe stomach cramps, the following drugs may help but are not very useful in the management of acute diarrhoea: Loperamide (Imodium) and Diphenoxylate with Atropine (Lomotil). They should not be given to children.

Any kind of diarrhoea, whether or not accompanied by vomiting, responds well to the replacement of water and salts, taken as frequent small sips of some kind of rehydration solution. There are proprietary preparations consisting of sachets of powder which you dissolve in boiled water, or you can make your own by adding half a teaspoonful of salt (3.5 g) and four tablespoonfuls of sugar (40 g) to a litre of boiled water.

Thus the linchpins of treatment for diarrhoea are rest, fluid and salt replacement, antibiotics such as Ciprofloxacin for the bacterial types and special diagnostic tests and medical treatment for the Amoeba and Giardia infections. Salmonella infections and cholera, although rare, can be devastating diseases and it would be wise to get to a hospital as soon as possible if these were suspected.

Fasting, peculiar diets and the consumption of large quantities of yoghurt have not been found useful in calming travellers' diarrhoea or in rehabilitating inflamed bowels. Oral rehydration has on the other hand, especially in children, been a life-saving technique and should always be practised, whatever other treatment you use. As there is some evidence that alcohol and milk might prolong diarrhoea, they should be avoided during and immediately after an attack. So should chillies!

Diarrhoea occurring day after day for long periods of time (chronic diarrhoea) is notoriously resistant to amateur attempts at treatment, and again warrants proper diagnostic tests (cities with reasonable sized hospitals have laboratories for stool samples). There are ways of preventing travellers' diarrhoea for short periods of time by taking antibiotics, but this is not a foolproof technique and should not be used other than in exceptional circumstances. Doxycycline is possibly the best drug. Some preventatives such as Enterovioform can have serious side effects if taken for long periods.

Paradoxically, **constipation** is also common, probably induced by dietary change, inadequate fluid intake in hot places and long bus journeys. Simple laxatives are useful in the short term, and bulky foods such as rice, beans and plenty of fruit are also useful.

Heat & cold Full acclimatization to high temperatures takes about two weeks. During this period it is normal to feel a bit apathetic, especially if the relative humidity is high. Drink plenty of water (up to 15 litres a day are required when working physically hard in the tropics), use salt on your food and avoid extreme exertion. Tepid showers are more cooling than hot or cold ones. Large hats do not cool you down, but do prevent sunburn. Remember that, especially in the highlands, there can be a large and sudden drop in temperature between sun and shade and between night and day, so dress accordingly. Warm jackets or woollens are essential after dark at high altitude. Loose cotton is still the best material when the weather is hot.

Sunburn The burning power of the tropical sun, especially at high altitude, is phenomenal. Always wear a wide-brimmed hat and use some form of suncream or lotion on untanned skin. Normal temperate zone suntan lotions (protection factor up to seven) are not much good; you need to use the types designed specifically for the tropics or for mountaineers or skiers, with protection factors up to 15 or above. These are often not available in Thailand. Glare from the sun can cause conjunctivitis, so wear sunglasses especially on tropical beaches, where high protection factor sunscreen should also be used.

Prickly heat This very common, intensely itchy rash is avoided by frequent washing and by wearing loose clothing. It is cured by allowing skin to dry off through use of powder or by spending two nights in an air-conditioned hotel!

Athlete's foot This and other fungal skin infections are best treated with Tolnaftate or Clotrimazole.

There is serious traffic congestion and air pollution in the major cities, especially in Bangkok. Expect sore throats and itchy eyes. Sufferers from asthma or bronchitis may have to increase their regular maintenance treatment.

Air pollution

These are mostly more of a nuisance than a serious hazard and if you try, you can prevent yourself entirely from being bitten. Some, such as mosquitoes, are, of course, carriers of potentially serious diseases, so it is sensible to avoid being bitten as much as possible. Sleep off the ground and use a mosquito net or some kind of insecticide. Preparations containing pyrethrum or synthetic pyrethroids are safe. They are available as aerosols or pumps, and the best way to use these is to spray the room thoroughly in all areas (follow the instructions rather than the insects) and then shut the door for a while, re-entering when the smell has dispersed. Mosquito coils release insecticide as they burn slowly. They are widely available and useful out of doors. Tablets of insecticide which are placed on a heated mat plugged into a wall socket are probably the most effective. They fill the room with insecticidal fumes in the same way as aerosols or coils.

Insects

You can also use insect repellents, most of which are effective against a wide range of pests. The most common and effective is diethyl metatoluamide (DET). DET liquid is best for arms and face (care around eyes and with spectacles – DET dissolves plastic). Aerosol spray is good for clothes and ankles, and liquid DET can be dissolved in water and used to impregnate cotton clothes and mosquito nets. Some repellents now contain DET and permethrin, an insecticide. Impregnated wrist and ankle bands can also be useful.

If you are bitten or stung, itching may be relieved by cool baths, antihistamine tablets (care with alcohol or driving) or mild corticosteriod creams – for example, hydrocortisone (great care: never use if any hint of infection). Careful scratching of all your bites once a day can be surprisingly effective. Calamine lotion and cream have limited effectiveness and antihistamine creams are not recommended – they can cause allergies themselves.

Bites which become infected should be treated with a local antiseptic or antibiotic cream such as Cetrimide, as should any infected sores or scratches.

When living rough, skin infestations with body lice (crabs) and scabies are easy to pick up. Treat with whatever local commercial preparation is recommended.

Crotamiton cream (Eurax) alleviates itching and also kills a number of skin parasites. Malathion lotion – 5% (Prioderm) – kills lice effectively, but avoid the use of the toxic agricultural preparation of Malathion, more often used to commit suicide.

Usually attach themselves to the lower parts of the body, often after walking in areas where cattle have grazed. They take a while to attach themselves strongly, but swell up as they start to suck blood. The important thing is to remove them gently, so that they do not leave their head parts in your skin, because this can cause a nasty allergic reaction some days later. Do not use petrol, Vaseline, lighted cigarettes etc to remove the tick, but with a pair of tweezers remove the beast gently by gripping it at the attached (head) end, and rock it out in very much the same way that a tooth is

Ticks

Essentials

Essentials

extracted. Certain tropical flies which lay their eggs under the skin of sheep and cattle also occasionally do the same thing to humans, with the unpleasant result that a maggot grows under the skin and pops up as a boil or pimple. The best way to remove these is to cover the boil with oil, Vaseline or nail varnish so as to stop the maggot breathing, then to squeeze it out gently the next day.

Other risks and more serious diseases

Remember that rabies is endemic throughout Southeast Asia, so avoid dogs and cover your toes at night from vampire bats, which also carry the disease. If you are bitten by a domestic or wild animal, do not leave things to chance: scrub the wound with soap and water and/or disinfectant, try to have the animal captured (within limits) or at least determine its ownership, where possible, and seek medical assistance at once. The course of treatment depends on whether you have already been satisfactorily vaccinated against rabies. If you have (this is worthwhile if you are spending lengths of time in developing countries), then some further doses of vaccine are all that is required. Human diploid vaccine is the best, but expensive: other, older kinds of vaccine, such as that derived from duck embryos, may be the only types available. These are effective, much cheaper and interchangeable, generally with the human-derived types. If not already vaccinated then anti-rabies serum (immunoglobulin) may be required in addition. It is important to finish the course of treatment whether the animal survives or not.

AIDS
See also box opposite, & page 788, for more information on the spread of AIDS in Thailand & the fight against aids

AIDS is increasing its prevalence in Southeast Asia. It is not wholly confined to the well known high-risk sections of the population – that is, homosexual men, intravenous drug abusers, prostitutes and the children of infected mothers. Heterosexual transmission is now the dominant mode of infection and so the main risk to travellers is from casual sex. The same precautions should be taken as when encountering any sexually transmitted disease. The disease has had a huge impact on Thailand due to the high rates of prostitution and, in some areas, drug abuse. The AIDS virus (HIV) can be passed via unsterile needles that have been previously used to inject an HIV positive patient, but the risk of this is very small indeed. It would, however, be sensible to check that needles have been properly sterilized or disposable needles are used. The chance of picking up hepatitis B in this way is more of a danger. Be wary of carrying disposable needles. Customs officials may find them suspicious. The risk of receiving a blood transfusion with blood infected with the HIV virus is greater than from dirty needles because of the amount of fluid exchanged. Supplies of blood for transfusion are supposed to be screened for HIV in all reputable hospitals, so the risk should be small. Catching the virus that causes AIDS does not necessarily produce an illness in itself; the only way to be sure if you feel you have been put at risk is to have a blood test for HIV antibodies on your return to a place where there are reliable laboratory facilities. However, the test does not become positive for many weeks.

Malaria

Malaria is prevalent in Southeast Asia and remains a serious disease, and you are advised to protect yourself against mosquito bites as above and to take prophylactic (preventative) drugs. Start taking the tablets a few days before exposure and continue to take them six weeks after leaving the malarial zone. Remember to give the drugs to babies and children, pregnant women also.

The subject of malaria prevention is becoming more complex as the malaria parasite becomes immune to some of the older drugs. Nowhere is this more apparent than in Southeast Asia, especially parts of Laos and Cambodia. In particular, there has been an increase in the proportion of cases of falciparum malaria, which is resistant to the normally used drugs. It would not be an exaggeration to say that we are near to the situation where some cases of malaria will be untreatable with presently available drugs.

Modelling AIDS in Southeast Asia

There has been a tendency to assume that there is a single AIDS 'pandemic'. However, in reality it seems that there are possibly three different patterns to the spread of AIDS – one is characteristic of Europe and North America, the second of Sub-Saharan Africa, and the third of Asia. This third pattern, described by Tim Brown and Peter Xenos of the East-West Population Institute in Hawaii, is different in a number of important respects. Furthermore, they argue that these differences are likely to make the disease both more serious and more intractable. The pattern is based on the experience of Thailand, and it is assumed that the Thai experience will soon be seen reflected in other countries in Asia.

It seems that the possibility of transmission per exposure, whether that be through sexual relations or needle sharing, is higher in Asia than in Europe and North America because of the high incidence of sexually transmitted diseases, especially among sex workers. Furthermore, a significant proportion of the male population of the countries of the region visit prostitutes for sex, meaning that the population 'at risk' is also very high. Therefore, in Thailand – and by implication also soon in many other countries of Asia – AIDS quickly made the crossover from the homosexual and drug-using populations to the heterosexual population. Thailand's first AIDS case was reported in 1984. By the end of 1988, 30% of addicts visiting methodone treatment centres were HIV positive. Five years later, by the end of 1993, levels of infection among sex workers had similarly reached 30%. Now, nearly 2% of women visiting pre-natal clinics are testing HIV positive. Thus, in the space of less than 10 years – far faster than in Europe and North America, and even faster than in Africa – AIDS has spread from homosexuals and drug addicts to the wives and babies of heterosexual men.

In August 1994, at a major international conference on AIDS in Asia, James Allen, of the American Medical Association, likened (provoking considerable anger, it should be added) AIDS to the Black Death in Europe. The costs to Asia of the disease are likely to be truly staggering: McGraw-Hill have put a figure of US$38-52bn on the social and economic costs of AIDS in the region.

Southeast Asia: potential for the spread of AIDS/HIV

Rapidly increasing: Burma; Cambodia; Thailand

Potential for rapid increase: Indonesia; Laos; Malaysia; Vietnam

Increasing: Singapore

Not classified: Brunei

Essentials

Before you travel you must check with a reputable agency the likelihood and type of malaria in the countries that you intend to visit. Take note of advice on prophylaxis, but be prepared to receive conflicting advice. Because of the rapidly changing situation in the Southeast Asian region the names and the dosage of the drugs have not been included, but chloroquine and proganil may still be recommended for the areas where malaria is still fully sensitive, while Doxycycline, Mefloquine and Artemether are presently being used in resistant areas. Quinine, Halofantrine and Tetracycline drugs remain the mainstay of treatment. It is still possible to catch malaria even when taking prophylactic drugs, although it is unlikely. If you do develop symptoms (high fever, shivering, severe headache and sometimes diarrhoea), seek medical advice immediately. The risk of the disease is obviously greater the further you move from the cities into rural areas with primitive facilities and standing water.

Information regarding country-by-country malaria risk can be obtained from the World Health Organization (WHO) or in the UK from the Malaria Reference Laboratory, at the London School of Hygiene and Tropical Medicine, T0891-600350 (calls cost 60p a minute).

Infectious hepatitis (jaundice) The main symptoms of this illness are pains in the stomach, lack of appetite, lassitude and yellowness of the eyes and skin. Medically speaking there are two main types. The less serious but more common is hepatitis A, for which the best protection is the careful preparation of food, the avoidance of contaminated drinking water and scrupulous attention to toilet hygiene. The other, more serious, version is hepatitis B, which is acquired usually as a sexually transmitted disease or by blood transfusion. It can less commonly be transmitted by injections with unclean needles and possibly by insect bites. The symptoms are the same as for hepatitis A. The incubation period is much longer (up to six months compared with six weeks) and there are more likely to be complications.

Hepatitis A can be protected against with gamma globulin. It should be obtained from a reputable source and is certainly useful for travellers who intend to live rough. You should have a shot before leaving and have it repeated every six months. The dose of gamma globulin depends on the concentration of the particular preparation used, so the manufacturer's advice should be taken. The injection should be given as close as possible to your departure and as the dose depends on the likely time you are to spend in potentially affected areas, the manufacturer's instructions should be followed. Gamma globulin has really been superseded now by a proper vaccination against hepatitis A (Havrix), which gives immunity lasting up to 10 years. After that, boosters are required. Havrix monodose is now widely available, as is junior Havrix. The vaccination has negligible side effects and is extremely effective. Gamma globulin injection can be a bit painful, but it is cheaper than Havrix and may be more available in some places.

Hepatitis B can be effectively prevented by a specific vaccine (Engerix) – three shots over six months before travelling. If you have had jaundice in the past it would be worthwhile having a blood test to see if you are immune to either of these two types, because this might avoid the necessity and costs of vaccination or gamma globulin. There are other kinds of viral hepatitis (C, E etc) which are fairly similar to A and B, but vaccines are not available as yet.

Typhus Can still occur, carried by ticks. There is usually a reaction at the site of the bite and a fever. Seek medical advice.

Intestinal worms These are common and the more serious ones such as hookworm can be contracted from walking barefoot on infested earth or beaches. Some cause an itchy rash on the feet – 'cutaneous larva migrans'.

Various other tropical diseases can be caught in jungle areas, usually transmitted by biting insects. Examples are leishmaniasis and filariasis.

Leptospirosis Various forms of leptospirosis occur throughout Latin America, transmitted by a bacterium which is excreted in rodent urine. Fresh water and moist soil harbour the organisms, which enter the body through cuts and scratches. If you suffer from any form of prolonged fever, consult a doctor.

Snake bite This is a very rare event indeed for travellers, but if you are unlucky (or careless) enough to be bitten by a venomous snake, spider, scorpion or sea creature, try to identify the creature, without putting yourself in further danger. Snake bites in particular are very frightening, but in fact rarely poisonous – even venomous snakes bite without injecting venom. What you might expect if bitten are: fright, swelling, pain and bruising around the bite, and soreness of the regional lymph glands, perhaps nausea, vomiting and a fever. Signs of serious poisoning would be the following symptoms: numbness and tingling of the face, muscular spasms, convulsions, shortness of breath or a failure of the blood to clot, causing generalized bleeding. Victims should be taken to a hospital or a doctor without delay. Commercial snake bite and scorpion kits are available, but are usually only useful for the specific types of snake or scorpion. Most serum has to be given intravenously, so it is not much good equipping yourself with it unless you are used to making injections into veins. It is best to rely on local practice in these cases, because the particular creatures will be known about locally and appropriate treatment can be given.

Treatment of snake bite Reassure and comfort the victim frequently. Immobilize the limb by a bandage or a splint, or by getting the person to lie still. Do not slash the bite area and try to suck out the poison, because this sort of heroism does more harm than good. If you know how to use a tourniquet in these circumstances, you will not need this advice. If you are not experienced, do not apply a tourniquet.

Precautions Avoid walking in snake territory in bare feet or sandals – wear proper shoes or boots. If you encounter a snake, stay put until it slithers away and do not investigate a wounded snake. Spiders and scorpions may be found in the more basic hotels. If stung, rest and take plenty of fluids and call a doctor. The best precaution is to keep beds away from the walls and look inside your shoes and under the toilet seat every morning.

Marine bites and stings Certain tropical sea fish when trodden upon inject venom into bathers' feet. This can be exceptionally painful. Wear plastic shoes when you go bathing if such creatures are reported. The pain can be relieved by immersing the foot in extremely hot water for as long as the pain persists.

Dengue fever

This is increasing worldwide, including in Southeast Asia. It can be completely prevented by avoiding mosquito bites in the same way as malaria. No vaccine is available. Dengue is an unpleasant and painful disease, presenting with a high temperature and body pains, but at least visitors are spared the more serious forms (haemorrhagic types), which are more of a problem for local people who have been exposed to the disease more than once. There is no specific treatment for dengue – just painkillers and rest.

When you return home

Remember to take your anti-malarial tablets for six weeks after leaving the malarial area. If you have had attacks of diarrhoea it is worth having a stool specimen tested in case you have picked up amoebas. If you have been living rough, blood tests may be worthwhile to detect worms and other parasites. If you have been exposed to schistosomiasis by swimming in lakes etc, check by means of a blood test when you get home, but leave it for six weeks because the test is slow to become positive. Report any untoward symptoms to your doctor and tell the doctor exactly where you have been, and, if you know, what the likelihood of disease is to which you were exposed.

Further reading

Magazines

Asiaweek (weekly). A lightweight *Far Eastern Economic Review*; rather like a regional *Time* magazine in style.

The Far Eastern Economic Review (weekly). Authoritative Hong Kong-based regional magazine; their correspondents based in each country provide knowledgeable, in-depth analysis, particularly on economics and politics.

Metro (monthly). Bangkok's own *Time Out*. The best source for information on new restaurants, bands, clubs and much else. *Metro* has now been joined by a competitor in the listings stakes, *Bangkok Timeout*. This is also monthly and provides much the same information. It also has a website: www.bkktimeout.com

Books

Southeast Asia **Buruma, Ian** (1989) *God's Dust*, Jonathan Cape: London. Enjoyable journey through Thailand, Myanmar, Malaysia and Singapore, along with the Philippines, Taiwan, South Korea and Japan; journalist Buruma questions how far culture in this region has survived the intrusion of the West.

Clad, James (1989) *Behind the Myth: Business, Money and Power in Southeast Asia*, Unwin Hyman: London. Clad, formerly a journalist with the *Far Eastern Economic Review*, distilled his experiences in this book; as it turned out, rather disappointingly – it is a hotch-potch of journalistic snippets.

Dingwall, Alastair (1994) *Traveller's Literary Companion to South-east Asia*, In Print: Brighton. Experts on Southeast Asian language and literature select extracts from novels and other books by Western and regional writers. The extracts are annoyingly brief, but it gives a good overview of what is available.

Dumarçay, Jacques (1991) *The Palaces of South-East Asia: architecture and customs*, OUP: Singapore. A broad summary of palace art and architecture in both mainland and island Southeast Asia.

Fraser-Lu, Sylvia (1988) *Handwoven Textiles of South-East Asia*, OUP: Singapore. Well-illustrated, large-format book with informative text.

Higham, Charles (1989) *The Archaeology of Mainland Southeast Asia from 10,000 BC to the fall of Angkor*, Cambridge University Press: Cambridge. Best summary of changing views of the archaeology of the mainland.

Hope, Sebastian (2001) *Outcasts of the Islands: the Sea Gypsies of South East Asia*, London: Harper Collins. An account of the author's encounters with the marginalized Sea Gypsies of Indonesia, Thailand and Burma.

Keyes, Charles F (1977) *The Golden Peninsula: Culture and Adaptation in Mainland Southeast Asia*, Macmillan: New York. Academic, yet readable, summary of the threads of continuity and change in Southeast Asia's culture. The volume has been recently republished by Hawaii University Press, but not updated or revised.

King, Ben F and Dickinson, EC (1975) *A Field Guide to the Birds of South-East Asia*, Collins: London. Best regional guide to the birds of the region.

Miettinen, Jukko O (1992) *Classical Dance and Theatre in South-East Asia*, OUP: Singapore. Expensive but accessible survey of dance and theatre, mostly focusing on Thailand, Burma and Indonesia.

Osborne, Milton (1979) *Southeast Asia: An Introductory History*, Allen & Unwin: Sydney. Good introductory history, clearly written, published in a portable paperback edition. A new revised edition is not on the shelves.

Rawson, Philip (1967) *The Art of Southeast Asia*, Thames & Hudson: London. Portable general art history of Burma, Cambodia, Vietnam, Thailand, Laos, Java and Bali; by necessity, rather superficial, but a good place to start.

Reid, Anthony (1988) *Southeast Asia in the Age of Commerce 1450-1680: The Lands Below the Winds*, Yale University Press: New Haven. Perhaps the best history of everyday life in Southeast Asia, looking at such themes as physical well-being, material culture and social organization.

Reid, Anthony (1993) *Southeast Asia in the Age of Commerce 1450-1680: Expansion and Crisis*, Yale University Press: New Haven. Volume 2 in this excellent history of the region.

Rigg, Jonathan (1991) *Southeast Asia: A Region in Transition*, Unwin Hyman: London. A thematic geography of the ASEAN region, providing an insight into some of the major issues affecting the region today.

Rigg, Jonathan (1997) *Southeast Asia: The Human Landscape of Modernization and Development*, London: Routledge. A book which covers both the market and former command economies (ie Burma, Vietnam, Laos and Cambodia) of the region. It focuses on how people in the region have responded to the challenges and tensions of modernization.

SarDesai, DR (1989) *Southeast Asia: Past and Present*, Macmillan: London. Skilful but at times frustratingly thin history of the region from the first century to the withdrawal of US forces from Vietnam.

Savage, Victor R (1984) *Western Impressions of Nature and Landscape in Southeast Asia*, Singapore University Press: Singapore. Based on a geography PhD thesis, the book is a mine of quotations and observations from Western travellers.

Steinberg, DJ *et al* (1987) *In Search of Southeast Asia: A Modern History*, University of Hawaii Press: Honolulu. The best standard history of the region; it skilfully examines and assesses general processes of change and their impacts from the arrival of the Europeans in the region.

Tarling, Nicholars (1992) (ed) *Cambridge History of Southeast Asia*, Cambridge University Press: Cambridge. Two-volume edited study, long and expensive, with contributions from most of the leading historians of the region. A thematic and regional approach is taken, not a country one, although the history is fairly conventional.

Waterson, Roxana (1990) *The Living House: An Anthropology of Architecture in South-East Asia*, OUP: Singapore. An academic but extensively illustrated book on Southeast Asian architecture and how it links with lives and livelihoods. Fascinating material for those interested in such things.

Essentials

Collis, Maurice (1982) *Siamese White*, DD Books: Bangkok. A historical novel based in the court of Narai during the 17th century; packed full of slightly unconvincing scheming Orientals.

Novels

For a summary of Thai literary works available in English, see page 801

Diehl, William (1989) *Thai Horse*, Ballantine Books: New York. A novel about the Thai drug trade and the underworld in Thailand and the US.

Garland, Alex *The Beach*. Available just about everywhere in Thailand, but while it is an easy and enjoyable read, it hardly deserves all the media hype and attention that it has received. It is most interesting to read while travelling through the beach resorts of the country, where the observations on Thailand, hedonism and the power of the guidebook (but not this one!) are instructive.

Grey, Anthony (1990) *The Bangkok Secret*, Pan: London. Novel of intrigue based around the murder/assassination of King Ananda; banned in Thailand.

Moore, Christopher G (1991) *Spirit House*, White Lotus: Bangkok. Novel based on life in the red light districts of Bangkok.

Boulle, Pierre (1990) *The Bridge Over the River Kwai*, Bantam Books: New York. The story of the infamous bridge in western Thailand.

History

Manich Jumsai (1972) *Popular History of Thailand*, Chalermit: Bangkok. A rather second-rate history of Thailand; all fact and dates and names and no story line or analysis. Widely available in Thailand though and relatively cheap.

Terwiel, BJ (1983) *A History of Modern Thailand, 1767-1942*, University of Queensland Press: St Lucia, Queensland. Reasonably solid history but not very easily found.

Wright, Joseph (1991) *The Balancing Act: A History of Modern Thailand*, Pacific Rim Press: Oakland. Most detailed modern history (to 1991), but not as scholarly as Wyatt's volume.

Wyatt, David K (1982) *Thailand: A Short History*, Yale University Press: New Haven. Simply the best history of Thailand, from the beginning of recorded Thai history to the 1980s.

Kruger, Rayne (1964) *The Devil's Discus*, Cassell: London. Best investigation into the death of King Ananda; banned in Thailand and rather difficult to get hold of. Worth tracking down in your local library as it is a good read.

Biography & autobiography

Leonowens, Anna [1870] (1988) *The English Governess at the Siamese Court*, Oxford University Press: Singapore. The book on which the play and film *The King and I* was based, starring Yul Brynner. A travesty of history and offensive to many Thais in the manner in which it depicts one of Thailand's greatest monarchs, but entertaining nonetheless and now reprinted.

Warren, William (1970) *The Legendary American: The Remarkable Career and Strange Disappearance of Jim Thompson*, Houghton Mifflin: Boston. The story of the strange life and even stranger disappearance of the so-styled 'saviour' of Thailand's silk industry.

Travel & geography

Bock, Carl (1884) *Temples and Elephants*, White Lotus: Bangkok. An entertaining and informative account of an early European visitor's time in Siam. Reprinted by White Lotus in Bangkok in 1985 and easily available.

Bowring, Sir John (1857) *The Kingdom and People of Siam*, OUP: Kuala Lumpur. An account of Bowring's visit which led to the signing of the important Bowring Treaty in 1855. A remarkable book when one considers how short a time he was in Siam. Reprinted by OUP in 1969.

Maugham, Somerset (1930) *The Gentlemen in the Parlour: A Record of a Journey from Rangoon to Haiphong*, Heinemann: London. An account of Maugham's journey through Southeast Asia, including Thailand, in classic limpid prose.

McCarthy, James (1994) *Surveying and Exploring in Siam with Descriptions of Las Dependencies and of Battles Against the Chinese Haws*, White Lotus: Bangkok. Reprint of an account first published in 1900 telling of the travels of Englishman James McCarthy, who was employed by the government of Siam as a surveyor and adviser; an interesting book to read when travelling, particularly, in the north and northeast.

Shearer, Alistair (1989) *Thailand: the Lotus Kingdom*, John Murray: London. Good background to culture and history of Thailand, rather derivative but entertaining.

West, Richard (1991) *Thailand: the Last Domino*, Michael Joseph: London. An 'alternative' travel book which provides considerable historical and cultural background; entertaining and interesting, occasionally inaccurate.

Economics, politics & development

Ekachai, Sanitsuda (1990) *Behind the Smile: Voices of Thailand*, Thai Development Support Committee: Bangkok. Vignettes of Thai life and the strains of development by a *Bangkok Post* journalist; interesting and informative.

Keyes, Charles, F (1987) *Thailand: Buddhist Kingdom as Modern Nation-State*, Westview Press: Boulder, Colorado. Good, clearly written background to Thailand, especially good on politics and society, widely available in cheaper DK (Duang Kamol) edition in Thailand.

Pasuk Phongpaichit and Baker, Chris (1998) *Thailand's Boom ... and Bust!*, Silkworm Books: Chiangmai. A collaborative book by a well-known Thai economist and her partner, a British historian turned advertising executive. They have written a book that tries to bridge the gap between popular and academic and have been generally pretty successful, although it is rather breathless in tone. This new edition analyzes Thailand's economic collapse (the first edition, published in 1996, had the title *Thailand's boom!*)

Pasuk Phongpaichit and Baker, Chris (2000) *Thailand's Crisis*, Silkworm Books: Chiang Mai. The fullest account of Thailand's fall from economic grace. They do have an axe to grind (namely the need for more community-oriented development), but it is clear and comprehensive.

Rigg, Jonathan (1995) (ed) *Counting the Costs: Economic Growth and Environmental Change in Thailand*, ISEAS: Singapore. The title says it all: an edited collection of papers examining the conflicts between economic growth and the conservation of the environment.

Tapp, Nicholas (1989) *Sovereignty and Rebellion: the White Hmong of Northern Thailand*, Oxford University Press: Singapore. Scholarly study of the tensions under which the Hmong are forced to live their lives.

Art & archaeology

Fickle, Dorothy (1989) *Images of the Buddha in Thailand*, OUP: Singapore. Small, portable book, with background to the main periods in Thailand's plastic arts and outline of the major styles and images.

Labbe, AJ (1985) *Ban Chiang, Art and Prehistory of Northeast Thailand*, Bowers Museum: Santa Ana, California. Only for the truly interested – an illustrated account of the discovery and significance of this important archaeological site in Northeast Thailand.

Moore, Elizabeth, Stott, Phili and Suriyavudh Sukhasvasti, with photographs by Michael Freeman (1996) *Ancient Capitals of Thailand*, Thames & Hudson: London (also published by River Books in Thailand). A heavy-weight coffee table book with marvellous photographs of Sukhothai, Si Satchanalai, Kamphaeng Phet, Phitsanulok and Ayutthaya, and an informative text written by two art historians and a historical geographer. Expensive.

Ringis, Rita (1990) *Thai Temples and Temple Murals*, OUP: Singapore. Good background to Thailand's *wats* and their murals; illustrated and quite widely available in Thailand.

Smitthi Siribhadra and Moore, Elizabeth (1991) *Palaces of the Gods: Khmer Art and Architecture in Thailand*, River Books: Bangkok. Expensive but nicely illustrated coffee table book covering the Khmer monuments of Thailand, text by an art historian at London's School of Oriental and African Studies.

Stratton, Carol and Scott, Miriam M (1981) *The Art of Sukhothai: Thailand's Golden Age*, Oxford University Press: Kuala Lumpur.

Van Beek, S and Tettoni, LI (1991) *The Arts of Thailand*, Thames & Hudson: London (revised). Glossy coffee table book with good photographs and informative text.

A decent map is an indispensable aid to travelling. Although maps are usually available locally, it is sometimes useful to buy a map prior to departure to plan routes and itineraries. Below is a select list of maps. Scale is provided in brackets.

Maps of Thailand & Southeast Asia
See also Useful websites, page 76

Regional maps Bartholomew – Southeast Asia (1:5,800,000); ITM (International Travel Maps) – Southeast Asia (1:6,000,000); Nelles – Southeast Asia (1:4,000,000); Hildebrand – Thailand, Burma, Malaysia and Singapore (1:2,800,000).

Country maps Bartholomew – Thailand (1:1,500,000); ITM (International Travel Maps) – Thailand (1:1,000,000); Nelles – Thailand (1:1,500,000).

City maps Nelles – Bangkok.

Other maps Tactical Pilotage Charts (TPC, US Airforce) (1:500,000); Operational Navigational Charts (ONC, US Airforce) (1:500,000). Both of these are particularly good at showing relief features (useful for planning treks); less good on roads, towns and facilities.

Locally available maps are widely available in Thailand and many are given out free, although the quality of information is sometimes poor. In addition to these gratis maps, there is an increasing number of maps produced by local companies. These range from highway maps (produced by oil companies, for example), to regional (sub-national) maps, to city maps, through to special interest maps (Bangkok's night life, trekking maps etc). All tend to be cheap and usually more up-to-date, if not necessarily more accurate, than those produced by international outfits.

Map shops in London, the best selection is available from Stanfords, 12-14 Long Acre WC2E 9LP, T020-7836 1321; also recommended is McCarta, 15 Highbury Place, London N15 1QP, T020-7354 1616.

Films on and about Thailand

The Beach Filmed in Thailand and released in 2000, this celluloid version of Alex Garland's book of the same title created a mini-environmental crisis (see the box on page 634). Leonardo Di Caprio does a reasonable job, but this is not a film that will be particularly remembered.

Anna and the King Yes, another version of the *King and I* (with Yul Brunner), released in 2000. This time a Hong Kong Chinese actor Chow Yun-Fat plays King Mongkut, while Anna is portrayed as a feisty proto-feminist by Jodie Foster. Of course the historians have lambasted the film as a travesty – Anna would never

Essentials

have been allowed to do these things or get so close to the King – and the Thai authorities banned it (as they do with anything of this sort). The result? Pirated videos and endless letters to the Thai newspapers.

Brokedown Palace The least publicized of the three films about Thailand that have recently been released – this one opened in 1999 – and the least good of a mediocre offering. This recounts the tale of two high-school graduates who go to Thailand, get seduced into carrying drugs, are arrested and thrown in prison, only to be pardoned when they get to see the King. Sure! Also banned in Thailand.

The Bridge Over the River Kwai The best of the bunch, which only goes to show that good old (1957) acting always beats slick technology. Alec Guinness stars in this Academy Award-winning account of the horror of the prison camp in Kanchanaburi province, where prisoners of war (and many Chinese – who don't really feature) were used by the Japanese to build the Burma-Siam Railway and the bridge that gives the film its name.

In addition to these films there are many, many with a Vietnam War focus which were filmed in Thailand, and may have scenes in Thailand, but aren't really about Thailand. These include: **The Killing Fields** (about Cambodia under Pol Pot); **The Deer Hunter** (the dark side of the conflict); and **Good Morning Vietnam** (Robin Williams in good form as a disk jockey). And lastly there's the Bond movie **The Man With the Golden Gun**, which uses Bangkok and Phangnga Bay as a backdrop.

Useful websites

Maps www.lib.utexas.edu/Libs/PLC/Map_collection/asia/htm Up-to-date maps of Asia showing relief, political boundaries and major towns.
www.nationalgeographic.com/resources/ngo/maps/atlas/asia/asia.html National Geographic's cartographic division, which takes maps from their current atlas of the world.
www.expediamaps.com/ US-biased but still pretty comprehensive. Key in a town and wait for it to magically appear.
Weather & geographical information http://metnet.tmd.go.th
Thailand's meteorological department, with weather forecasts for numerous towns.
www.rainorshine.com A simple but effective weather site, with five-day forecasts for 800 cities worldwide.

Travel & health www.cdc.gov/travel/index.htm Managed by the Center for Disease Control and Prevention (CDC) in Atlanta, this is one of the best health sites, providing detailed and authoritative information, including special sections on such diseases, ailments and concerns as malaria, dengue fever, HIV/AIDS, rabies and Japanese encephalitis.
www.tripprep.com/index.html Shoreland's Travel Health Online provides health advice by country.
www.masta.org UK-based centre for travel-related health; good for family advice.
www.medicineplanet.com A useful travel clinic for those travelling with children.
www.uclh.org/htd Site for the UCH-based Hospital for Tropical Diseases.
www.tropicalscreening.com More topical tropical disease advice.

Hotel sites www.siam-travel.com The number of hotels listed on the Siam Hotel Network site is limited – on-line reservations possible.
www.citynet.com/asia/asia Hotel booking information for Asia.
www3.sympatico.ca/donna.mcsherry/asia.htm Stuck overnight at Don Muang airport? Then check out the Budget Traveller's Guide to Sleeping in Airports.
http://asiatravelmart.com Includes deals on flights and hotels; especially good on cheap hotel deals in Asia.

www.bkktimeout.com Bangkok's *Timeout* magazine, with listings and more.　Entertainment

www.netcafeguide.com/ Around 2,000 cybercafés in 113 countries are listed here,　Cyber cafés
and it also provides discussion forums for travellers and a language section.

www.thaiindex.com Mainly business and cultural, but also includes bus, train and air　Transport sites
timetables, along with some other useful travel information (sometimes out of date).
www.thaiair.com Thai Airways site.
http://bkkair.com Bangkok Airways' website.

www.nationgroup.com/ Homepage for *The Nation,* one of Thailand's main English　Newspapers,
language daily newspapers.　news & the
　media

www.bangkokpost.net/ Homepage for the *Bangkok Post* including back issues and
main stories of the day.
www.isop.ucla.edu/eas/web/radio-tv/htm For information on Asian radio and
television. Includes free downloadable software.

www.oanda.com/converter/classic Select your two currencies by clicking on a list,　Currencies
and wham – the exchange rate is provided.

www.stern.nyu.edu/~nroubini/asia/AsiaHomepage.html Homepage of a　Business-
professor of economics – Roubini – who has collated all the information on the Asian　related sites
financial and economic crisis, and there's a lot.

www.nectec.or.th/ Homepage for Thailand in Bangkok, good links to other　General sites
websites in the country.
http://pears.lib.ohio-state.edu/asianstudies/asian studies.html Huge range of
links, with information on topics from sports and travel to economics and
engineering.
**http://coombs.anu.edu.au/WWWVLPages/WhatsNewWWW/asian-www-news.
html** Assortment of material from across the Asian region.
http://coombs.anu.edu.au/asia-www-monitor.html Produced by ANU's Research School of Pacific and Asian Studies, this site provides evaluations and summa-
ries of Asian sites.
www.nbr.org Centre for papers on Asia, covering strategic, economic and political issues.
http://libweb.library.wisc.edu/guides/SEAsia/library.htm 'Gateway to Southeast
Asia' from University of Wisconsin, numerous links.

www.chula.ac.th/INTERNATIONAL/POT/ Managed by Thailand's premier　History &
university, Chulalongkorn, and intended to introduce people to Thailand's history,　culture
culture, society, politics and economics.
www.thaifolk.com Good site for Thai culture from folk songs and handicrafts,
through to festivals like Loi Kratong and Thai myths and legends. Information posted
in both English and Thai – although the Thai version of the site is better.
www.cs.ait.ac.th/~wutt/wutt.html More historical and cultural information at this
site operated from the Asian Institute of Technology, based just north of Bangkok.
www2.hawaii.edu/~tsomo Resources on women and Buddhism.
www.asiasociety.org Homepage of the Asia Society, with papers, reports and
speeches, as well as nearly 1,000 links to what they consider to be the best educational, political and cultural sites on the internet.
www.hmongnet.org.usa Information on Hmong culture, history and language.

Essentials

Environment   **http://nautilus.org** Homepage of the Nautilus Institute, which focuses on issues connected with the environment and sustainability in the Asia-Pacific region.
www.geocities.com/~nesst/ The homepage of the Network for Environmentally So Sustainable Tourism Thailand, with information on tourism in Thailand, book reviews and a discussion page.

Picture libraries   **www.leidenuniv.nl/pun/ubhtm/mjkintro.htm** Library of 100 slides of Thailand
& books   (Phimai, Chiang Mai, Lamphun) and other mainland Southeast Asian countries.
http://thailine.com/lotus Homepage of White Lotus, a Bangkok-based publishing house specializing in English language books (many reprints of old books) on the region.

Bangkok

3

Bangkok

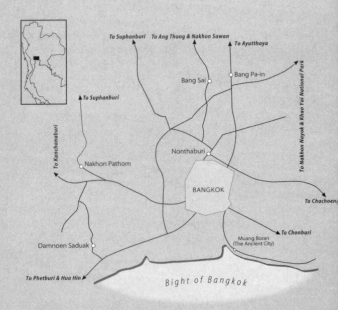

Bangkok is not a city to be trifled with: a population approaching 11,000,000 struggle to make their living in a conurbation with perhaps the worst traffic in the world; a level of pollution which causes some children, so it is (rather improbably) said, to lose four intelligence points by the time they are seven; and a climate which can take one's breath away. (The Guinness Book of Records *credits Bangkok as the world's hottest city because of the limited seasonal and day-night temperature variations.) As journalist Hugo Gurdon wrote at the end of 1992: 'One would have to describe Bangkok as unliveable were it not for the fact that more and more people live here'. But, Bangkok is not just a perfect case study for academics looking into the strains of rapid urban growth. There is charm and fun beneath the grime, and Bangkokians live life with a* joie de vivre *which belies the congestion. There are also numerous sights, including the spectacular Grand Palace, glittering wats (monasteries) and the breezy river, along with excellent food and shopping.*

Ins and outs

Getting there
*See also Transport,
page 166*
Don Muang Airport, around 25 km north of the city, is a regional hub and has connections with Europe, East and South Asia, Australasia and North America. It also has the best connections in the region with Burma, Laos, Cambodia and Vietnam – as well as other Southeast Asian destinations. There are buses, trains and taxis from the airport into town. On a bad day it can take an hour or more to get to the city centre; taking the expressway cuts the travel time down significantly. Bangkok is Thailand's domestic transport hub with flights to more than 20 towns and cities; trains south to the Malaysian border (and onward to Kuala Lumpur and Singapore), north to Chiang Mai and northeast to Nong Khai and Ubon Ratchathani; and buses of every description to all corners of the country. It is often necessary to transit through Bangkok if working your way north to south by whatever means of transport. Some cruise liners dock at Bangkok's port, but this is not a common way to arrive.

Bangkok & vicinity

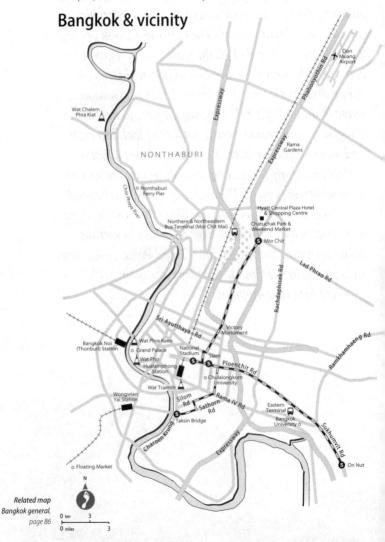

*Related map
Bangkok general,
page 86*

Arriving by air

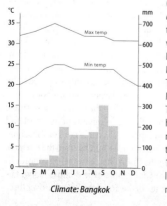

Most flights to Bangkok's Don Muang airport arrive at a reasonable time so weary passengers rarely have to handle a hot, new city in the early hours. However, because Bangkok is a transport hub, transit passenger do sometimes find themselves staying the night before catching an onward early morning flight. There is a good airport hotel – the Amari Airport – just across the highway from the international terminals (along an elevated covered walkway). It has a pool, fitness centre, several restaurants and bars and also offers short-term stays for those who just want to freshen-up. In addition to the Amari, there are several other hotels within a short (5-10 minute) taxi ride of the airport. These are listed on page 37. Along with the hotel, the airport area has quite a number of cheap restaurants and stalls.

If you have a little longer to stay, and don't want to brave Bangkok, then it is easy to leave your bags in the Don Muang left luggage office and travel up to Ayutthaya, Thailand's capital before Bangkok, around 50 km north. There is a good range of budget place to stay here, some great restaurants, and it is possible to get their direct from the airport by bus, train or taxi. See page 175 for more details.

Bangkok (vertical side text)

Bangkok has the unenviable reputation of having some of the worst traffic in the world. It is certainly bad. But the new Skytrain – an elevated railway – has made things a lot easier for those areas of the city it covers (although it is too expensive for most Thais). Metered taxis are everywhere, buses (a/c and non-a/c) cheap, tuk-tuks – motorized 3-wheeled taxis – still fighting off extinction, and motorcycle taxis are a novel way to see your life flashing before your eyes. Walking is not a lot of fun in the heat and fumes, although there are some parts of the city where this can be the best way to get around. One of the best ways to travel is by express river taxi, which ply the Chao Phraya River and some of the *khlongs* (canals).

Buses, both a/c and non-a/c, travel to all city sights. A taxi or tuk-tuk for a centre of town trip should cost ฿50-100. Now that taxis are almost all metered visitors may find it easier, and more comfortable (they have a/c) – not to mention safer – than the venerable tuk-tuk. If travelling by bus, a bus map of the city – and there are several, available from most bookshops and hotel gift shops – is an invaluable aid. This is a far more pleasant way to get around and is also often quicker than going by road (see map, page 108, for piers, and box, page 111).

Getting around
Phone code: 02
Colour map 3, grid B4

The **Tourist Authority of Thailand** (TAT) has its main offices at 4 Rachdamnern Nok Avenue (at intersection with Chakrapatdipong Road), T2829775. ■ *0830-1630 Mon-Sun.* A second office is at Le Concorde Building, 10th Floor, 202 Rachdaphisek Road (in the office block attached to the *Merchant Court Le Concorde Hotel* – north of town and rather inconvenient for most visitors), T6941222. ■ *0830-1630 Mon-Fri.* In addition there is a counter at Don Muang airport (in the Arrivals Hall, T5238972) and the Chatuchak Weekend Market (Kamphaeng Phet 2 Road), T2724440. The two main offices are very helpful and provide a great deal of information for independent travellers – certainly worth a visit. For information, phone 1155 between 0800 and 2400 for English-speaking Tourist Service Centre. A number of good, informative,

Tourist offices

°C / mm

Max temp

Min temp

Climate: Bangkok

Bangkok

A Foot in the Door

★ The Grand Palace is the sight which usually tops the bill in tourist brochures and guidebooks. It is certainly memorable – in a gaudy, rather over-the-top way. It contains Wat Phra Kaeo which houses the Emerald Buddha or the Phra Kaeo, Thailand's holiest image of the Buddha.

★ For something a little different, charter a long-tail boat for a trip on the khlongs. You can negotiate your own route (and price) with the driver and stop off, for example, to see the snake farm, old monasteries like Wat Rakhang or Wat Suwannaram, the prang of Wat Arun, or the Royal Barge Museum. But most fun is just zipping along the khlongs taking a peek into people's lives.

★ Shopping in Bangkok is generally excellent but the Weekend Market at Chatuchak is truly stupendous. This is a weekly gathering of approaching 10,000 stalls just north of the city centre (easily accessible on the new Skytrain).

★ Bangkok is not a terribly venerable city – it only celebrated its bicentenary in 1982

– but there are some – not many, it must be said – beautiful buildings. Jim Thompson's House was the private residence of an American who is said to have breathed life back into Thailand's silk industry (and who mysteriously disappeared in the Malaysian jungle). Not only is the house very attractive, but it also has a wonderful collection of Thai and Asian art. The Suan Pakkard Palace also has a fine art collection.

★ Thai food is wonderful, and Bangkok has a number of superb restaurants. Nor does culinary excellence stop at tom yang kung; there are some fine international restaurants too.

★ If you want to escape from Bangkok for the day there are a number of nifty excursions. Probably the most memorable is Ayutthaya, the capital of Siam until 1767 and a UNESCO World Heritage Site. After it was sacked by the Burmese the city was abandoned and, as a result, the ruins were not built over. It is easily reached by river, road or train.

English-language magazines provide listings of what to do and where to go in Bangkok. *Bangkok Metro*, published monthly (฿100, www.bkkmetro.com) is well designed and produced and covers topics from music and nightlife, to sports and fitness, to business and children. A competitor to *Metro* is *Bangkok Timeout* which is much like its London namesake, but a tad less hip (฿80, published monthly, www.bkktimeout.com). Less independent, and with less quality information, is the oddly named *Guide of Bangkok* or *GoB*. Its advantage is that it is free.

History

The official name for Thailand's capital city begins Krungthep – phramaha – nakhonbawon – rathanakosin – mahinthara – yutthayaa – mahadilok – phiphobnobpharaat – raatchathaanii – buriiromudomsantisuk. It is not hard to see why Thais prefer the shortened version – Krungthep, or the 'City of Angels'. The name used by the rest of the world – Bangkok – is derived from 17th-century western maps, which referred to the city (or town as it then was) as Bancok, the 'village of the wild plum'. This name was only superseded by Krungthep in 1782, and so the western name has deeper historical roots.

In 1767, Ayutthaya, then the capital of Siam, fell to the marauding Burmese for the second time and it was imperative that the remnants of the court and army find a more defensible site for a new capital. Taksin, the Lord of Tak, chose Thonburi, on the western banks of the Chao Phraya River, far from the Burmese and from Phitsanulok, where a rival to the throne had become ensconced. In three years, Taksin had established a kingdom and crowned himself king. His reign was short lived, however; the pressure of thwarting the Burmese over three

Bangkok: primate city of Thailand

	% of national total
Land area	0.3%
Population (end 1998)	9.2%
Gross regional product (1996)	39.1%
Commercial bank deposits (end 1998)	65.3%
Commercial bank loans (end 1998)	76.5%
Passenger car registrations (end 1997)	63.8%
Telephones (end 1998)	50.1%
Physicians (end 1995)	39.4%
Hospital beds (end 1995)	21.1%

Bangkok

arduous years caused him to go mad and in 1782 he was forced to abdicate. General Phraya Chakri was recalled from Cambodia and invited to accept the throne. This marked the beginning of the present Chakri Dynasty.

In 1782, Chakri (now known as Rama I) moved his capital across the river to Bangkok (an even more defensible site) anticipating trouble from King Bodawpaya who had seized the throne of Burma. The river that flows between Thonburi and Bangkok and on which many of the luxury hotels – such as *The Oriental* – are now located, began life not as a river at all, but as a canal (or *khlong*). The canal was dug in the 16th century to reduce the distance between Ayutthaya and the sea by shortcutting a number of bends in the river. Since then, the canal has become the main channel of the Chao Phraya River. Its original course has shrunk in size, and is now represented by two khlongs, Bangkok Yai and Bangkok Noi.

Bangkok: the new capital

This new capital of Siam grew in size and influence. Symbolically, many of the new buildings were constructed using bricks from the palaces and temples of the ruined former capital of Ayutthaya. But population growth was hardly spectacular – it appears that outbreaks of cholera sometimes reduced the population by a fifth or more in a matter of a few weeks. An almanac from 1820 records that "on the seventh month of the waxing moon, a little past 2100 in the evening, a shining light was seen in the northwest and multitudes of people purged, vomited and died".

Bangkok began life as a city of floating houses; in 1864 the French explorer Henri Mouhot wrote that "Bangkok is the Venice of the East (in the process making Bangkok one of several Asian cities to be landed with this sobriquet) and whether bent on business or pleasure you must go by water". In 1861, foreign consuls in Bangkok petitioned Rama IV and complained of ill-health due to their inability to go out riding in carriages or on horseback. The king complied with their request for roads and the first road was constructed running south in the 1860s – Charoen Krung ('New Road'). This did not initially alter Bangkok's watery character, for bridges to span the many canals were in limited supply. In addition, Charoen Krung was frequently under water during the monsoons. It was not until the late 19th century that King Chulalongkorn (Rama V) began to invest large sums of money in bridge and road building; notably, Rachdamnern Avenue ('the royal way for walking') and the Makawan Rungsun Bridge, which both link the Grand Palace with the new palace area of Dusit. This avenue was used at the end of the century for cycling (a royal craze at the time) and later for automobile processions which were announced in the newspapers.

Venice of the East

Bangkok general

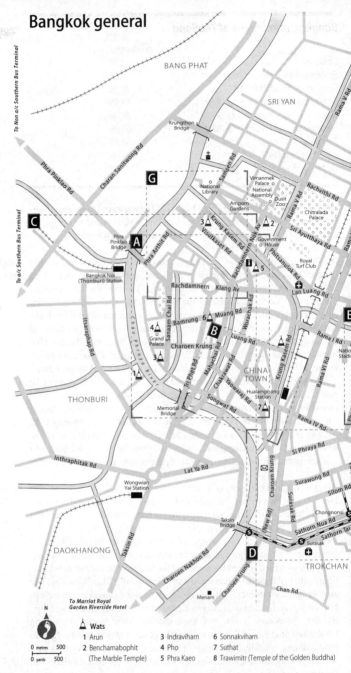

N

0 metres 500
0 yards 500

Wats

1 Arun
2 Benchamabophit
 (The Marble Temple)
3 Indraviharn
4 Pho
5 Phra Kaeo
6 Sonnakviharn
7 Suthat
8 Trawimitr (Temple of the Golden Buddha)

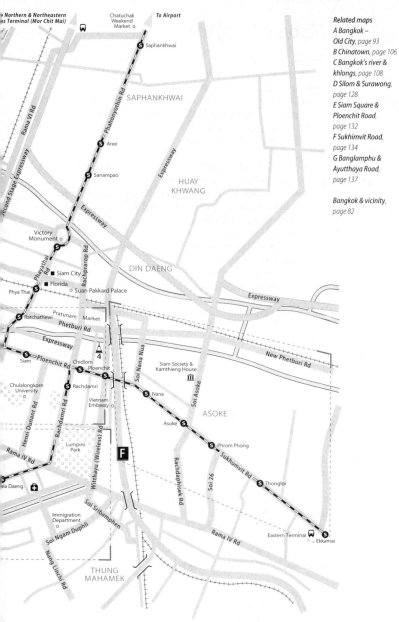

Related maps
A Bangkok –
Old City, page 93
B Chinatown, page 106
C Bangkok's river &
khlongs, page 108
D Silom & Surawong,
page 128
E Siam Square &
Ploenchit Road,
page 132
F Sukhimvit Road,
page 134
G Banglamphu &
Ayutthaya Road,
page 137

Bangkok & vicinity,
page 82

Bangkok

Modern Bangkok

In the rush to modernize, Bangkok may have buried its roots and in so doing, lost its charm. But beneath the patina of modern city life, Bangkok remains very much a Thai city, and has preserved a surprising amount of its past. Most obviously, a profusion of monasteries (wats) and palaces remain. In addition, not all the khlongs have been filled in, and by taking a long-tailed boat through Thonburi (see page 109) it is possible to gain an idea of what life must have been like in the 'Venice of the East'.

First impressions The immediate impression of the city to a first-time visitor is bedlam. The heat, noise, traffic, pollution – the general chaos – can be overwhelming. This was obviously the impression of Somerset Maugham, following his visit in 1930:

'I do not know why the insipid Eastern food sickened me. The heat of Bangkok was overwhelming. The wats oppressed me by their garish magnificence, making my head ache, and their fantastic ornaments filled me with malaise. All I saw looked too bright, the crowds in the street tired me, and the incessant din jangled my nerves. I felt very unwell.'

Population In 1900 Bangkok had a population of approximately 200,000. By 1950 it had surpassed one million, and by the end of 1998 it was, officially, 5,647,799 (don't you just love the spurious accuracy?). But the official figure considerably under-states the true population of the city – 10-11 million would be more realistic. Many people who live in the capital continue to be registered as living up-coun-try, and the physical extent of the capital has long overrun its administrative boundaries. By 2010, analysts believe Bangkok will have a population of 20 mil-lion. As the population of the city has expanded, so has the area that it encom-passes: in 1900 it covered a mere 13.3 sq km; in 1958, 96.4 sq km; while today the Bangkok Metropolitan region extends over 1,600 sq km and the outskirts of the city sprawl into neighbouring provinces. Such is the physical size of the capital that analysts talk of Bangkok as an EMR or Extended Metropolitan Region.

Bangkok & Thailand In terms of size, Bangkok is at least 23 times larger than the country's second city, Chiang Mai (40 times bigger, using the unofficial population estimates). It also dominates Thailand in cultural, political and economic terms. All Thai civil servants have the ambition of serving in Bangkok, while many regard a posting to the poor Northeast as (almost) the kiss of death. Most of the country's industry is located in and around the city, and Bangkok sup-ports a far wider array of services than other towns in the country (see box, page 85). It is because of Bangkok's dominance that people often, and inaccurately, say 'Bangkok is Thailand'.

Flooding Bangkok is built on unstable land, much of it below sea-level, and floods used regularly to afflict the capital. The most serious were in 1983 when 450 sq km of the city was submerged. Each year the Bangkok Metropolitan Authority announced a new flood prevention plan, and each year the city flooded. The former populist Bangkok Governor, Chamlong Srimuang, was perhaps the first politician to address the problem of flooding seriously. His blindingly obvious approach was to clear the many culverts of refuse, and some people believe that at last serious flooding is a thing of the past. This may be over-opti-mistic: like Venice, Bangkok is sinking by over 10 cm a year in some areas and it may be that the authorities are only delaying the inevitable.

Bangkok's architectural nightmare

It doesn't, as they say, take a rocket scientist to realize that Bangkok is short of modern buildings with architectural merit. Indeed, there is a rather cruel joke doing the rounds: what is the difference between Bangkok and a toilet? At least you can flush a toilet. The reasons are manifold for this dearth of decent modern buildings. Of prime importance is the sheer speed of change in the capital. In the early 1970s there were less than 25 buildings over 6 storeys high; today there are well over 1,000. Most of the country's architects are young and inexperienced – and yet they are expected to be able to design high-rise buildings as they step out of college grasping their certificates. There are none of the critical apprenticeship years when architects hone their skills and eye on mundane garage blocks and single-storey old people's homes.

But it is not just that there is a dearth of experienced architects. Sumet Jumsai is possibly Thailand's most respected architect and he has little but derision for Bangkok's modern architecture. "Here – he suggested in a magazine article by John Hoskin – is money in its ugliest aspect, dictating building styles ... [producing] distorted Western neo-classical buildings and bad taste to satisfy the nouveau-riche's

make-believe world".

Bangkok-based architect Robert Boughey also puts the blame on clients who want the largest building at the lowest cost – and young architects without the status or the desire to refuse, comply. As he put it, "Clients deserve the buildings they get." Sometimes, it can all go tragically wrong – as when the Royal Plaza Hotel in Korat collapsed killing 137. Some more cynical observers say that Bangkok's architectural poverty has a long-standing history. In his book Bali and Angkor published in 1936, Geoffrey Gorer wrote that Bangkok was "the most hokum place" he had ever seen, "a triumph of the imitation school". The tendency for buildings to combine Greek Classical with US Ranch style, Spanish Villa with Tudor Beamed seems to indicate that things really haven't progressed very far since the 1930s.

This is not to say that all Bangkok's contemporary architecture is so crass. There are the clean lines and elegance of the Regent Hotel on Rachdamri Road; and the appropriately stratospheric feel of the blue-glass walled HQ of Thai Airways on Phahonyothin Road on the way to the airport. There are also the older buildings which may have fulfilled Gorer's 'hokum' characterization in the 1930s, but which today seem positively refined.

Traffic

Bangkok has become synonymous with traffic congestion. For many years it has been regarded as having some of the worst – perhaps *the* worst – traffic conditions of any capital city in the world. During peak periods the traffic congestion is such that 'gridlock' seems inevitable. The figures are sometimes hard to believe: US$500 mn of petrol is consumed each year while cars wait at traffic lights; average traffic speeds can be less than 10 km per hour; one day in July 1992 it took 11 hours for some motorists to get home after a monsoon storm; in 1996, the Thai Farmers Bank's research centre estimated that Bangkok's congestion costs the economy US$2.3 bn in lost productivity, wasted energy, and health care costs; and the number of cars on the capital's streets was increasing by 800 each day prior to the economic crisis (the figure for the country is 1,300). In 1995 the singer Janet Jackson purposely avoided scheduling her concerts on Friday explaining, "with the traffic, who could make it on Friday?" It seemed that nothing could stop Bangkok simply grinding to a halt (see the box, The mother of all traffic jams). As one analyst observed: "Bangkok is only just beginning to happen". Even editorial writers

Traffic & congestion – the perennial problem

☞ *Racing in the streets*

In Bangkok, bored young men gain short-lived fame and money by racing through the darkened streets of the capital on motorcycles late at night on weekends. Gang members put their reputations (and their lives) on the line, as they power down the wide and almost empty roads at over 160 km per hour. Large sums of money are gambled on the riders while 'rescue squads' wait to pick up the corpses that each night's racing produces. In Thai this dance with death is known as sing – from the English 'racing'. As journalist Gordon Fairclough explains: "Riders see themselves as members of an exclusive brotherhood, bound together by their willingness to risk death and dismemberment in the pursuit of thrills, notoriety and money". Although money is important, few of the riders are poor. Some even come from wealthy families. Critics of Thailand's climb into NIC-dom claim that the racing is a side-effect of the breakdown of traditional family life in the face of modernization. The racers themselves tend not to engage in amateur sociology. They explain "It's fun. It's a high. We like the speed, and its better than taking drugs".

at the *Bangkok Post* who, one might have imagined, would have become inured to the traffic found it a constant topic for comment throughout the 1980s and 1990s. At the end of 1993 the newspaper stated: "Bangkok's traffic congestion and pollution are just about the worst in the world – ever. Never in history have people had to live in the conditions we endure each day".

Ironically perhaps, the economic crisis that hit Thailand at the beginning of July 1997 gave the authorities a breathing space to try and sort out Bangkok's road nightmare. The bottom fell out of the new car market and many people took to alternative forms of transport to save money. This gave the capital's governor time to push through the necessary infrastructural projects designed, on the one hand, to improve the road system while also enticing people out of their cars and into a new and improved public transport network. At the beginning of 2000 Bangkok's first mass transit system opened – the BTS or Bangkok Transit System, popularly known as the Skytrain. This has made a real difference to travel in the areas that the network covers. The only trouble is that it is limited in coverage. In short, Bangkok has not become, overnight, another Singapore.

Solutions Solutions to Bangkok's traffic problem have been suggested, devised, contracts drawn up, shelved, cancelled and then revived since the early 1980s. The process of finding a solution became almost as slow as the traffic itself. In addition to the failure to approach transport planning in a co-ordinated way, Bangkok has a number of characteristics which make its problems particularly intractable. To begin with, Thailand was a city of canals; these have now been built over, but it means that the capital has a lower area of roads relative to its land area than any other capital – some 9% (some commentators put it as low as 5%) to New York's 24% and London's 22%. In addition, Bangkok is really Thailand's only city, making economic activity highly over-centralized. But there is more to it than just a series of historical accidents. Administration of roads is divided between numerous different agencies making co-ordination impossible. "It's like driving a bus with 16 hands on the wheel" one official was quoted as saying. The corruption that has accompanied many of the more grandiose projects, and the competition between various schemes – aerial railways, undergrounds, toll ways, computerized traffic control systems, freeways – has meant that none got off the ground until recently. Even when one project was finished – the 20 km-long,

The mother of all traffic jams

Bangkok's reputation for traffic congestion was already well-founded when, as the Bangkok Post put it, the Songkran exodus of 11-12 April 1995 created the 'mother of all traffic jams'. On Tuesday night, the capital saw the traditional mass movement of people to the provinces to celebrate Songkran. By late Wednesday afternoon, traffic on major routes was still heavily congested. One man telephoned a radio station to say that he had left his home in Bangkok at 2100 on Tuesday night and at 1100 on Wednesday had only made it to the Rangsit junction – barely out of the capital. One highway policeman remarked, perhaps with a touch of pride: "This is the first time in the 20-year history of the Vibhavadi Rangsit Highway that we have had traffic congestion for as long as 20 hours."

Bangkok

US$800 mn Bangkok Expressway which was completed in March 1993 – it didn't open to traffic until September that year. The government, under pressure from the public, tried to get the consortium to lower the agreed toll of ฿30. They refused, saying it would make the venture commercially unviable, so the city authorities gained a court order and opened the road themselves whereupon it promptly became snarled with traffic. Such actions on the part of the government threaten to scare away potential investors who require cast-iron agreements if they are to undertake such BOT (Build, Operate, Transfer) projects.

For wealthier commuters, the solution to the traffic problem is to transform their cars into mobile offices, to leave home at ungodly hours and, in some cases, to move elsewhere – like Chiang Mai (which, partly as a result, is experiencing its own traffic problems). Taxi drivers have taken to 'chicken footing' – skipping through hotel car parks to short-cut intersections. Government attempts to get people to leave their cars in the suburbs and bus in have failed because Bangkokians have an attachment to their cars which seems almost as devout as a Californian's. There was even talk of outfitting special buses with flashing lights declaring 'These passengers are car owners', so they could feel good about themselves!

A few years back, the motorcycle taxi hit the streets of Bangkok – a much faster alternative to sitting in a taxi in stationary traffic. Not that everyone is willing to endure weaving in and out of the traffic and sucking in great lung-fulls of the capital's noxious fumes just to get to their destination a little bit quicker. In June 2000 David Wilson, an executive with British-American Tobacco who was in Bangkok for the launch of the World Health Organisation's World No Smoking Day, likened smoking to taking a ride on one of these machines. "Every day people do things they choose to do that aren't terribly wise on reflection" he said, "like driving a motorbike taxi in Bangkok".

With the traffic comes pollution. Traffic police stationed at busy intersections **Pollution** have 'respite booths' with oxygen tanks, wear face masks to protect them from the fumes, and are entitled to regular health checks. Even so, directing traffic can, apparently, drive you mad. At the end of 1993, Lance Corporal Suradej Chumnet blew a fuse and switched all the traffic lights to green at one of Bangkok's busiest intersections. He then danced a jig amidst the chaos. Afterwards he claimed that he had seen King Rama V coming down the road towards him. A recent study found that 34% of police officers suffered from loss of hearing, and 23% had lung disease. Sitting in an open-sided tuk-tuk at traffic lights can seriously damage your health – or it seems as much with the fumes swirling around. It is for this reason that the tuk-tuk as a mode of transport in the capital is rapidly losing out to the air-conditioned taxi. Even so, one million of the

Bangkok

capital's population are said to be suffering from respiratory ailments of one kind or another. It seems that even Silom Road's barn swallows, that have traditionally wintered on the road's telephone and electricity wires, have decided enough is enough. In 1984 there were an estimated 250,000 birds. In 1996-97 just 10-20,000 were prepared to carry on coughing their way through the winter months.

Bangkok has no sewerage system and most water gets pumped straight into the *khlongs* (canals) and waterways where it poses a health hazard before emptying into the Chao Phraya River which, in its lower stretches, is said to be biologically dead. The reputation of Bangkok's traffic keeps potential investors away, not to mention many tourists. And there are also around 1½ million people in the city living in squatter or slum conditions – a number which is growing due to the effects of the economic crisis. NGOs have identified a worrying increase in drug dealing and prostitution as people struggle to make a living – or struggle to forget their predicament – and there also seems to be a breakdown in some of the community social structures that formerly helped to maintain a semblance of stability.

But, despite the traffic conditions and pollution, Bangkok has a wealth of sights (even the traffic might be classified as a 'sight'): wats and palaces, markets and shopping, traditional dancing and Thai boxing, glorious food, tuk-tuks and water taxis. Ultimately, Bangkok and Bangkokians should win the affections of even the most demanding foreigner – although you may not be there long enough to get past the frustration phase. In Major Erik Seidenfaden's *Guide to Bangkok* published in 1928, the opening few sentences could be describing the city today:

'No other city in Southeastern Asia compares with Bangkok in the gripping and growing interest which leaves a permanent and fragrant impression on the mind of the visitor. It is difficult to set down in words, precisely whence comes the elusive fascination of Bangkok. With a wealth of imposing temples, beautiful palaces, other characteristic buildings and monuments, Bangkok offers a vista of fascinating views. In no other city is it possible to so often turn from the throng of the city street and find oneself, miraculously it would seem, in a little residential quarter. Even the most bitter misanthrope cannot but feel that in the very atmosphere of Bangkok, woven into all the stir and briskness of its daily life, is an impelling and pleasurable sense of more than mere contentment – of rare serenity and happiness everywhere.'

Sights

This section is divided into five main areas: the **Old City**, around the Grand Palace; the **Golden Mount**, to the east of the Old City; **Chinatown**, which lies to the south of the Golden Mount; the **Dusit** area, which is to the north and contains the present-day parliament buildings and the King's residence; and **Wat Arun and the khlongs**, which are to the west, on the other bank of the Chao Phraya River in Thonburi. Other miscellaneous sights, not in these areas, are at the end of the section, under **Other sights**.

The Old City

The Old City contains the largest concentration of sights in Bangkok, and for visitors with only one day in the capital, this is the area to concentrate on. It is possible to walk around all the sights mentioned below quite easily in a single day. For the energetic, it would also be possible to visit the sights in and around the Golden Mount. If intending to walk around all the sights in the old city start from Wat Pho; if you have less time or less energy, begin with the Grand Palace.

The Temple of the Reclining Buddha, or **Wat Pho** as it is known to western-
ers (a contraction of its original name Wat Potaram), has its entrance on Chetuphon Road on the south side of the monastery complex. It is 200 years old and the largest wat in Bangkok. The wat is most famous for its 46-m long, 15-m high gold-plated reclining Buddha contained in a large viharn built during the reign of Rama III in 1832. The soles of the feet of the Buddha are inlaid with intricate mother-of-pearl decoration displaying the 108 auspicious signs of the Buddha.

The grounds of the wat contain more than 1,000 bronze images, rescued from the ruins of Ayutthaya and Sukhothai by Rama I's brother. The bot, or *ubosoth*, houses a bronze Ayutthayan Buddha in an attitude of meditation and the pedestal of this image contains the ashes of Rama I. Also notable is the

Wat Phra Chetuphon

Bangkok

Old City

Related map Bangkok general, page 86

Bangkok highlights

Temples Bangkok's best known sight is the temple of Wat Phra Kaeo, situated within the grounds of the Grand Palace (page 95). Other notable temples include Wat Pho (page 93), Wat Arun (page 109), Wat Suthat (page 103) and Wat Traimitr (page 107).

Museums Bangkok's extensive National Museum houses the best collection in the country (page 100); other significant collections include those in Jim Thompson's House (page 115), the Suan Pakkard Palace (page 114) and Vimanmek Palace (page 113).

Markets The sprawling Chatuchak Weekend Market is the largest (page 117), but other markets include Nakhon Kasem or Thieves' Market (page 105), Pahurat Indian Market (page 105) and Chinatown's Sampeng Lane (page 106).

Boat trips On Bangkok's canals (page 107).

Excursions Day trips to the former capital and ruins of Ayutthaya (page 122), the Bridge over the River Kwai outside Kanchanaburi (page 123), the massive chedi at Nakhon Pathom (page 123), and the floating market at Damnoen Saduak

---

11-piece altar table set in front of the Buddha, and the magnificent mother-of-pearl inlaid doors which are possibly the best examples of this art from the Bangkok Period. They depict episodes from the Ramakien. The bot is enclosed by two galleries which house 394 seated bronze Buddha images. They were brought from the north during Rama I's reign and are of assorted periods and styles. Around the exterior base of the bot are marble reliefs telling the story of the Ramakien as adapted in the Thai poem the *Maxims of King Ruang* (formerly these reliefs were much copied by making rubbings onto rice paper). The 152 panels are the finest of their type in Bangkok. They recount only the second section of the Ramakien: the abduction and recovery of Ram's wife Seeda. The rather – to western eyes – unsatisfactory conclusion to the story as told here has led some art historians to argue they were originally taken from Ayutthaya. Thai scholars argue otherwise.

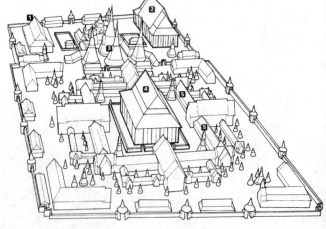

Wat Phra Chetuphon (Wat Pho)
Source: adapted from a drawing by Kittisak Nualvilai based on aerial photographs and reproduced in Beek, Steve van and Tettoni, L (1991) The arts of Thailand, Thames & Hudson: London

1 Sala kan parian or study hall
2 Viharn of the reclining Buddha
3 Enclosure of the royal chedis
4 Ubosoth (bot) or ordination hall
5 Cloister or phra rabieng

A particular feature of the wat are the 95 chedis of various sizes which are scattered across the 20-acre complex. To the left of the bot are four large chedis, memorials to the first four Bangkok kings. The library nearby is richly decorated with broken pieces of porcelain. The large top-hatted stone figures, the stone animals and the Chinese pagodas scattered throughout the compound came to Bangkok as ballast on the royal rice boats returning from China. Rama III, whose rice barges dominated the trade, is said to have had a particular penchant for these figures, as well as for other works of Chinese art. The Chinese merchants who served the King – and who are said to have called him *Chao Sua* or millionaire – loaded the empty barges with the carvings to please their lord. Rama III wanted Wat Pho to become known as a place of learning, a kind of exhibition of all the knowledge of the time and it is regarded as Thailand's first university.

Wat Pho is also probably Bangkok's most respected centre of traditional Thai massage (see page 154), and politicians, businessmen and military officers come here to seek relief from the tensions of modern life. Most medical texts were destroyed when the Burmese sacked the former capital, Ayutthaya, in 1776 and in 1832 Rama III had what was known about Thai massage inscribed on stone and then had these stones set into the walls of Wat Pho to guide and inform students of the art. ■ *Mon-Sun 0900-1700, ฿20.* **NB** *From Tha Tien pier at the end of Thai wang Rd, close to Wat Pho, it is possible to get boats to Wat Arun (see page 109). For westerners wishing to learn the art of traditional Thai massage, special 30-hr courses can be taken for ฿4,500, stretching over either 15 days (2 hrs per day) or 10 days (3 hrs per day). The centre is located at the back of the wat, on the opposite side from the entrance. A massage costs ฿100 for 30 mins, ฿180 for 1 hr with herbal treatment, the fee is ฿260 for 1½ hrs.*

For other centres of traditional Thai massage see page 154

About 10-15 minutes walk from Wat Pho northwards along Sanaam Chai Road is the entrance to the Grand Palace and Wat Phra Kaeo. (**NB** The main entrance is the Viseschaisri Gate on Na Phralan Road.) The Grand Palace is situated on the banks of the Chao Phraya River and is the most spectacular – some might say 'gaudy' – collection of buildings in Bangkok. The complex covers an area of over 1½ sq km and the architectural plan is almost identical to that of the Royal Palace in the former capital of Ayutthaya. It was started in 1782 and was subsequently added to. Initially the palace was the city, the seat of power, surrounded by high walls and built to be self-sufficient.

Grand Palace & Wat Phra Kaeo

The buildings of greatest interest are clustered around **Wat Phra Kaeo**, or the 'Temple of the Emerald Buddha'. On entering the compound, the impression is one of glittering brilliance, as the outside is covered by a mosaic of coloured glass. The buildings were last restored for Bangkok's bicentenary in 1982 (the Wat Phra Kaeo Museum shows the methods used in the restoration process). Wat Phra Kaeo was built by Rama I in imitation of the royal chapel in Ayutthaya and was the first of the buildings within the Grand Palace complex to be constructed. While it was being erected the king lived in a small wooden building in one corner of the palace compound.

● ● ● ● ● ● ● ● ● ● ● ● ● ● ● ● ● ● ● ●
Old City place names

Grand Palace

พระบรมมหาราชวัง

National Museum

พิพิธภัณฑสถานแห่งชาติ

Wat Mahathat

วัดมหาธาตุ

Wat Phra Chetuphon/ Wat Pho

วัดพระเชตุพน/วัดโพธิ์

Wat Phra Kaeo

วัดพระศรีรัตนศาสดาราม

Bangkok

The **Temple of the Emerald Buddha, ubosoth (1)** is raised on a marble platform with a frieze of gilded garudas holding nagas running round the base. Bronze *singhas* (lions) act as door guardians. The inlaid mother-of-pearl door panels date from Rama I's reign (late 18th century). Flanking the door posts are Chinese door guardians riding on lions. Inside the temple, the Emerald Buddha (see box, page 97) sits high up, illuminated above a large golden altar. In addition, there are many other gilded Buddha images, mostly in the attitude of dispelling fear, and a series of mural paintings depicting the *jataka* stories. Those facing the Emerald Buddha show the enlightenment of the Buddha when he subdues the evil demon Mara. Mara is underneath, wringing out his hair, while on either side, the Buddha is surrounded by evil spirits. Those on one side have been subjugated; those on the other have not. The water from the wringing out of Mara's hair drowns the evil army, and the Buddha is shown 'touching ground' – calling the earth goddess Thoranee up to witness his enlightenment. (No photography is allowed inside the ubosoth.)

Around the walls of the shaded cloister that encompasses Wat Phra Kaeo, is a continuous mural depicting the Ramakien – the Thai version of the Indian Ramayana (see box, page 98). There are 178 sections in all, which were first painted during the reign of King Rama I but have since been restored on a number of occasions.

To the north of the ubosoth on a raised platform, are the **Royal Pantheon (2)**, the **Phra Mondop (3)** – the library – two gilt stupas, **a model of Angkor Wat (4)** and the **Golden Stupa (5)**. At the entrance to the Royal Pantheon are gilded *kinarees*. The Royal Pantheon is only open to the public once a year on Chakri Day, 6 April (the anniversary of the founding of the present Royal Dynasty). On the same terrace there are two gilt stupas built by King Rama I in commemoration of his parents. The Mondop was also built by Rama I to house the first revised Buddhist scriptural canon. To the west of the mondop is the large

Wat Phra Kaeo & Grand Palace

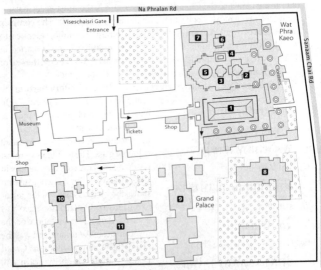

1 Temple of the Emerald Buddha (ubosoth)
2 Royal Pantheon
3 Phra Mondop (library)
4 Model of Angkor Wat
5 Golden Stupa
6 Viharn Yod
7 Viharn Phra Nak
8 Boromabiman Hall
9 Amarinda Hall
10 Chakri Mahaprasart
11 Dusit Hall

The Emerald Buddha

Wat Phra Kaeo was specifically built to house the Emerald Buddha, the most venerated Buddha image in Thailand, carved from green jade (the emerald in the name referring only to its colour), a mere 75 cm high, and seated in an attitude of meditation. It is believed to have been found in 1434 in Chiang Rai, and stylistically belongs to the Late Chiang Saen or Chiang Mai schools. Since then, it has been moved on a number of occasions – to Lampang, Chiang Mai and Laos (both Luang Prabang and Vientiane). It stayed in Vientiane for 214 years before being recaptured by the Thai army in 1778 and placed in Wat Phra Kaeo on 22 March 1784. The image wears seasonal costumes of gold and jewellery; one each for the hot, cool and the rainy seasons. The changing ceremony occurs three times a year in the presence of the King.

Buddha images are often thought to have personalities. The Phra Kaeo is no exception. It is said, for example, that such is the antipathy between the Phra Bang image in Luang Prabang (Laos) and the Phra Kaeo that they can never reside in the same town.

Golden Stupa or chedi, with its circular base, in Ceylonese style. To the north of the mondop is a model of Angkor Wat constructed during the reign of King Mongkut (1851-1868) when Cambodia was under Thai suzerainty.

To the north again from the Royal Pantheon is the Supplementary Library and two viharns – **Viharn Yod (6)** and **Phra Nak (7)**. The former is encrusted with pieces of Chinese porcelain.

To the south of Wat Phra Kaeo are the buildings of the Grand Palace. These are interesting for the contrast that they make with those of Wat Phra Kaeo. Walk out through the cloisters. On your left can be seen **Boromabiman Hall (8)**, which is French in style and was completed during the reign of Rama VI. His three successors lived here at one time or another. The **Amarinda Hall (9)** has an impressive, airy interior, with chunky pillars and gilded thrones. The **Chakri Mahaprasart (10)** – the Palace Reception Hall – stands in front of a carefully manicured garden with topiary. It was built and lived in by Rama V shortly after he had returned from a trip to Java and Singapore in 1876, and it shows: the building is a rather unhappy amalgam of colonial and traditional Thai styles of architecture. Initially the intention was to top the structure with a western dome, but the architects settled for a Thai-style roof. The building was completed in time for Bangkok's first centenary in 1882. King Chulalongkorn (Rama V) found the overcrowded Grand Palace oppressive and after a visit to Europe in 1897, built himself a new home at Vimanmek (see page 113) in the area to the north, known as Dusit. The present King Bhumibol lives in the Chitralada Palace, built by Rama VI, also in the Dusit area. The Grand Palace is now only used for state occasions. Next to the Chakri Mahaprasart is the raised **Dusit Hall (11)**, a cool, airy building containing mother-of-pearl thrones. Near the Dusit Hall is a museum, which has information on the restoration of the Grand Palace, models of the Palace and many more Buddha images. There is a collection of old cannon, mainly supplied by London gun foundries. Close by is a small café selling refreshing coconut drinks. All labels in Thai, but there are free guided tours in English throughout the day. ■ *Mon-Sun 0900-1600. ฿50. Admission to the Grand Palace complex ฿200, ticket office open Mon-Sun 0830-1130, 1300-1530 except Buddhist holidays when Wat Phra Kaeo is free but the rest of the palace is closed. For further information, T2220094 or www.palaces.thai.net The cost of the admission includes a free guidebook to the palace (with plan) as well as a ticket to the Coin Pavilion, with its collection of medals and 'honours' presented to members of the Royal Family and to the Vimanmek Palace in the Dusit area (see page 113). NB Decorum of dress is required (trousers can be hired for ฿10 near the*

The Thai Ramayana: the Ramakien

The Ramakien – literally 'The Story of Rama' – is an adaptation of the Indian Hindu classic, the Ramayana, which was written by the poet Valmiki about 2,000 years ago. This 48,000-line epic odyssey – often likened to the works of Homer – was introduced into mainland Southeast Asia in the early centuries of the first millennium. The heroes were simply transposed into a mythical, ancient, Southeast Asian landscape.

In Thailand, the Ramakien quickly became highly influential, and the name of the former capital of Siam, Ayutthaya, is taken from the legendary hero's city of Ayodhia in the epic. Unfortunately, these early Thai translations of the Ramayana were destroyed following the sacking of Ayutthaya by the Burmese in 1767. The earliest extant version was written by King Taksin in about 1775, although Rama I's rather later rendering is usually regarded as the classic interpretation.

In many respects, King Chakri's version closely follows that of the original Indian story. It tells of the life of Ram (Rama), the King of Ayodhia. In the first part of the story, Ram renounces his throne following a long and convoluted court intrigue, and flees into exile. With his wife Seeda (Sita) and trusted companion Hanuman (the monkey god), they undertake a long and arduous journey. In the second part, his wife Seeda is abducted by the evil king Ravana, forcing Ram to wage battle against the demons of Langka Island (Sri Lanka). He defeats the demons with the help of Hanuman and his monkey army, and recovers his wife. In the third and final part of the story – and here it diverges sharply from the Indian original – Seeda and Ram are reunited and reconciled with the help of the gods (in the Indian version there is no such reconciliation). Another difference with the Indian version is the significant role played by the Thai Hanuman – here an amorous adventurer who dominates much of the third part of the epic.

There are also numerous sub-plots which are original to the Ramakien, many building upon events in Thai history and local myth and folklore. In tone and issues of morality, the Thai version is less puritanical than the Indian original. There are also, of course, differences in dress, ecology, location and custom.

entrance to the Grand Palace) which means no shorts and no sleeveless tops. It also means, slightly weirdly, no thongs. There are some rather nuanced drawings of acceptable footwear at the entrance. If you are considered to have contravened this edict then there are tasteful plastic shoes for hire. For those who fear that they may leave Thailand with some incurable foot disease, socks are also helpfully made available for purchase. There are lots of touts offering to guide tourists around the Palace. It is also possible to hire a personal audio guide for ฿100 (2 hrs), available in English, French, German and some other languages.

Kite fighting

Kite fighting is a sport which is taken very seriously – perhaps because they were used as weapons of war during the Sukhothai Period, as well as being used to ward off evil spirits during Brahmanic rites. King Rama V was an avid kite-flyer and allowed Sanaam Luang to be used for the sport from 1899. There are usually two teams, each with a different kind of kite: the 'chula' or male kite is the bigger of the two and sometimes requires a number of people to fly it. The 'pukpao' or female kite is smaller and more nimble and opposes the chula. The field is divided into two and the aim of the contest is to land the opposition in your half of the field. Attached to the chula kite are a number of hooks (champa) with which the kite-flyer grapples the pukpao and forces it to land in the opposite side of the field. The pukpao meanwhile has a loop with which the flyer lassoes the chula – which then crashes to the ground.

Immediately opposite the entrance to the Grand Palace is **Silpakorn Fine Arts University**. It contains an exhibition hall. ■ *Mon-Sun 0900-1900 (see boards outside entrance for shows).* Turn left outside the Grand Palace and a five-minute walk leads to **Tha Chang pier and market**. The market sells fruit and food, cold drinks and the like. There is also a small amulet (lucky charm) and second-hand section. From Tha Chang pier it is possible to get a boat to Wat Arun for about ฿150 return, or a water taxi (see page 109). To the north of the Grand Palace, across Na Phralan Road, lies the large open space of the Pramane Ground (the Royal Cremation Ground), better known as **Sanaam Luang**. This area was originally used for the cremation of kings, queens and important princes. Later, foreigners began to use it as a race track and as a golf course. Today, Sanaam Luang is used for the annual **Royal Ploughing Ceremony**, held in May. This ancient Brahmanistic ritual, resurrected by Rama IV, signals the auspicious day on which farmers can begin to prepare their riceland, the time and date of the ceremony being set by Royal Astrologers. Bulls decorated with flowers pull a red and gold plough, while the selection of different lengths of cloth by the Ploughing Lord predicts whether the rains will be good or bad. Sanaam Luang is also used by the Thai public simply to stroll around – a popular pastime, particularly at weekends.

In the southeast corner of Sanaam Luang opposite the Grand Palace is Bangkok's **Lak Muang**, housing the City Pillar and horoscope, originally placed there by Rama I in 1782 even before the Grand Palace was built. This original pillar is the taller of the two. However, the original shrine deteriorated due to lack of maintenance and Rama VI erected a second, squatter pillar, with the horoscope of the city inscribed in gold. The original pillar was removed and left to lie against the shrine walls until 1986, when it was reinstated. Rama IV needed to erect a new pillar, with a new horoscope, to legitimate his kingship and to protect the city from new threats – namely, the European colonial powers rather than the traditional Burmese. It is protected by an elaborate pavilion with intricate gold-inlay doors, and is set below ground level. According to Pornpun Kerdphol there is no evidence of this tradition of erecting city pillars prior to 1782. The shrine is believed to grant people's wishes, so it is a hive of activity all day. In a small pavilion to the left of the main entrance, Thai dancers are hired by suppliants to dance for the pleasure of the resident spirits – while providing a free spectacle for everyone else. ■ *Open 24 hrs Mon-Sun.* **NB** *There is no entrance charge to the Lak Muang compound; touts sometimes insist there is. Donations can be placed in the boxes within the shrine precincts.* At the northeast corner of Sanaam Luang, opposite the *Royal Hotel*, is a small statue of the **Goddess of the Earth** erected by King Chulalongkorn to provide drinking water for the public.

Other sights near the Grand Palace

Kite fighting can be seen at Sanaam Luang in the late afternoons between late-Feb & mid-Apr (the Kite Festival season). On Sun, kites are sold for 15-20 baht

Wat Mahathat North along Na Phrathat Road, on the river side of Sanaam Luang is **Wat Mahathat** (the Temple of the Great Relic), a temple famous as a meditation centre, which is tucked behind a façade of buildings and hard to find; walk under the archway marked 'Naradhip Centre for Research in Social Sciences' to reach the wat. For those interested in learning more about Buddhist meditation, contact monks in section five within the compound. The wat is a royal temple of the first grade and a number of Supreme Patriarchs of Bangkok have based themselves here.

The revision of the Tripitaka (the Buddhist Canon) took place at the temple in 1788, and an examination system was established for monks and novices after a meeting at the wat in 1803. In 1801 the viharn was burnt down during an over-enthusiastic fireworks display. In 1824 the future Rama IV began his 24 years as a monk here, and it was again reconstructed between 1844 and 1851. Both viharn and bot, crammed in side-by-side, are undistinguished. Note that there are only four *bai sema* (boundary stones), and they are affixed to the walls of the building – presumably because there is so little room. The main Buddha images in the viharn and ordination hall are of brick and mortar. In the mondop are 28 bronze Buddha images, with another 108 in the gallery around the ordination hall. Most date from the Sukhothai Period. ■ *Mon-Sun 0900-1700*. At No 24 Maharaj Road a narrow soi (lane) leads towards the river and a large amulet market.

See also box, page 101 Attached to the wat is a fascinating daily market selling exotic herbal cures, amulets, clothes and food. It is worth a wander as few tourists venture into either the market or the wat. At weekends, the market spills out onto the surrounding streets (particularly Phra Chan Road) and amulet sellers line the pavement, their magical and holy talismen carefully displayed.

Thammasat & Further north along Na Phrathat Road, is **Thammasat University**, the site of
the National viciously suppressed student demonstrations in 1973. Sanaam Luang and
Museum Thammasat University remain a popular focus of discontent. Most recently, at
This museum is the beginning of May 1992, mass demonstrations occurred here to demand
reputedly the largest the resignation of Prime Minister General Suchinda. The rally was led by for-
in Southeast Asia mer Bangkok Governor Chamlong Srimuang.

Next to Thammasat lies the **National Museum**, an excellent place to view the full range of Thai art before visiting the ancient Thai capitals, Ayutthaya and Sukhothai. Gallery No 1, the gallery of Thai history, is interesting and informative, as well as being air-conditioned, so it is a good place to cool off. The gallery clearly shows kings Mongkut and Chulalongkorn's fascination with western technology. The other 22 galleries and 19 rooms contain a vast assortment of arts and artefacts divided according to period and style. If you are interested in Thai art, the museum alone might take a day to browse around. A shortcoming for those with no background knowledge is the lack of information in some of the galleries and it is recommended that interested visitors buy the *Guide to the National Museum, Bangkok* or join one of the tours. ■ *Wed-Sun 0900-1600. ฿40, together with a skimpy leaflet outlining the galleries, tickets on sale until 1530. For English, French, German, Spanish and Portuguese-speaking tour information call T2241333. The tours are free and start at 0930, lasting 2 hrs (usually on Wed and Thu).*

The Buddhaisawan Chapel, to the right of the ticket office for the National Museum, contains some of the finest Bangkok period murals in Thailand. The chapel was built in 1795 to house the famous Phra Sihing Buddha. Folklore has it that this image originated in Ceylon and when the boat carrying it to Thailand sank, it floated off on a plank to be washed ashore in Southern Thailand, near the town of Nakhon Si Thammarat. This, believe it or not, is probably

Magic designs and tokens: tattoos and amulets

Many, if not most, Thai men wear amulets or khruang. Some Thai women do so too. In the past tattooing was equally common, although today it is usually only in the countryside that males are extensively tattooed – sometimes from the ankle to the neck. In the case of both tattoos and amulets the purpose is to bestow power, good luck or protection on the wearer. (Members of secret societies and criminal gangs also use tattoos to indicate their allegiances.)

Amulets have histories: those believed to have great powers sell for tens of thousands, even millions, of baht and there are several magazines devoted to amulet buying and collecting (available from most magazine stalls). Vendors keep amulets with their takings to protect against robbery, and insert them into food at the beginning of the day to ensure good sales. An amulet is only to be handled by the wearer – otherwise its power is dissipated, and might even be used against the owner.

Amulets can be obtained from spirit doctors and monks and come in a variety of forms. Most common are amulets of a religious nature, known as Phra khruang. These are normally images of the Buddha or of a particularly revered monk. (The most valuable are those fashioned by the 19th-century monk Phra Somdet – which are worth far more than their weight in gold). Khruang rang are usually made from tiger's teeth, buffalo horn or elephant tusk and protect the wearer in very specific ways – for example from drowning. Khruang rang plu sek, meanwhile, are magic formulas which are written down on an amulet, usually in old Khmer script (khom), and then recited during an accident, attack or confrontation.

Tattooing is primarily talismanic: magic designs, images of powerful wild beasts, texts reproduced in ancient Khmer and religious motifs are believed to offer protection from harm and give strength.

(The word tattoo is derived from the Tahitian word tattau, meaning 'to mark'. It was introduced into the English language by Captain James Cook in 1769.) Tattoos are even believed to deflect bullets, should they be sufficiently potent. One popular design is the takraw ball, a woven rattan ball used in the sport of the same name. The ball is renowned for its strength and durability, and the tattoo is believed to have the same effect on the tattooed. The purpose of some tattoos is reflected in the use of 'invisible' ink made from sesame oil – the talismatic effects are independent of whether the tattoo can be seen. Most inks are commercial today (usually dark blue) although traditionally they were made from secret recipes incorporating such ingredients as the fat from the chin of a corpse (preferably seven corpses, taken during a full moon).

The tattooist is not just an artist and technician. He, like the tattoos he creates, is a man of power. A master tattooist is highly respected and often given the title ajarn (teacher) or mor phi (spirit doctor). Monks can also become well-known for their tattoos. These are usually religious in tone, often incorporating sentences from religious texts. The tattoos are always beneficial or protective and always on the upper part of the body (the lower parts of the body are too lowly for a monk to tattoo).

Tattoos and amulets are not only used for protection, but also for attraction: men can have tattoos or amulets instilled with the power to attract women; women, alternatively, can buy amulets which protect them from the advances of men. Khruang phlad khik (or 'deputy penis') are phallic amulets carved from ivory, coral or rare woods, and worn around the wrist or the waist – not around the neck. Not surprisingly, they are believed to ensure sexual prowess, as well as protection from such things as snake bites.

Bangkok

Bangkok

untrue: the image is early Sukhothai in style (1250), admittedly showing Cey-lonese influences, and almost certainly Northern Thai in origin. There are two other images that claim to be the magical Phra Buddha Sihing, one in Nakhon Si Thammarat (see page 698) and another in Chiang Mai (Northern Thai-land). The chapel's magnificent murals were painted between 1795 and 1797 and depict stories from the Buddha's life. They are classical in style, without any sense of perspective (as was usual), and the narrative of the Buddha's life begins to the right of the rear door behind the principal image, and progresses clockwise through 28 panels. ■ *German-speaking tours of the chapel are held at 0930 on the third Tue of the month.*

Next to the National Museum is Thailand's **National Theatre**, a newish, large, Thai-style building on the corner of Na Phrathat and Phra Pinklao Bridge roads. Thai classical drama and music are staged here on the last Friday of each month at 1730 as well as periodically on other days. ■ *0830-1630 Mon-Fri. Current programmes can be checked by calling T2241342.* Opposite the National Theatre is the **National Art Gallery** on Chao Fa Road. It exhibits traditional and contemporary work by Thai artists. ■ *Tue-Thu, Sat and Sun 0900-1600. ฿30.*

The Golden Mount, Giant Swing and surrounding wats

Democracy Monument | The Democracy Monument is a 10-15 minute walk from the north side of Sanaam Luang, in the middle of Rachdamnern Klang Avenue. This rather stolid structure was completed in 1940 to commemorate the establishment of Siam as a constitutional monarchy. Its dimensions signify, in various ways, the date of the 'revolution' – 24 June 1932. For example, the 75 buried cannon which sur-round the structure denote the Buddhist year (BE – or Buddhist Era) 2475 (1932 AD). In May 1992, the monument was the focus of the anti-Suchinda demonstrations, so brutally suppressed by the army. Scores of Thais died here, many others fleeing into the nearby *Royal Hotel.*

Golden Mount | From the Democracy Monument, across Mahachai Road, at the point where Rachdamnern Klang Avenue crosses Khlong Banglamphu can be seen the Golden Mount (also known as the Royal Mount), an impressive artificial hill nearly 80 m high. The climb to the top is exhausting but worth it for the fabulous views of Bangkok. On the way up, the path passes holy trees, memorial plaques and Chinese shrines. The construction of the mount was begun during the reign of Rama III who intended to build the greatest chedi in his kingdom. The struc-ture collapsed before completion, and Rama IV decided merely to pile up the rubble in a heap and place a far smaller golden *chedi* on its summit. The *chedi* contains a relic of the Buddha placed there by the present king after the structure had been most recently repaired in 1966. ■ *Mon-Sun 0800-1800. ฿5.*

● ●

Golden Mount place names

Amulet market	Wat Rachanada
ตลาดพระเครื่อง	วัดราชนัดดา
Golden Mount	Wat Saket
ภูเขาทอง	วัดสระเกศ
Wat Rachabophit	Wat Suthat
วัดราชบพิธ	วัดสุทัศน์เทพวราราม

Wat Saket lies at the bottom of the mount, between it and Damrong Rak Road – **Wat Saket** the mount actually lies within the wat's compound. Saket means 'washing of hair' and Rama I is reputed to have stopped here and ceremoniously washed himself before being crowned King in Thonburi (see Festivals, November, page 156). The only building of real note is the library (*hor trai*) which is Ayutthayan in style. The door panels and lower windows are decorated with wood-carvings depicting everyday Ayutthayan life, while the window panels show Persian and French soldiers from Louis XIV's reign. ■ *Mon-Sun, 0800-1800* .

Also in the shadow of the Golden Mount but to the west and on the corner of **Loha Prasat** Rachdamnern Klang Avenue and Mahachai Road lies Wat Rachanada and the Loha Prasat. Until 1989 these buildings were obscured by the Chalerm Thai movie theatre, a landmark which Bangkok's taxi and tuk-tuk drivers still refer to. In the place of the theatre there is now a neat garden, with an elaborate gilded sala, which is used to receive visiting dignitaries. Behind the garden the strange-looking Loha Prasat or Metal Palace, with its 37 spires, is easily recognizable. This palace was built by Rama III in 1846 as a memorial to his beloved niece Princess Soammanas Vadhanavadi, and is said to be modelled on the first Loha Prasat built in India 2,500 years ago. A second was constructed in Ceylon in 160 BC, although Bangkok's Loha Prasat is the only one still standing. The 37 spires represent the 37 Dharma of the Bodhipakya. In 1996 a major renovation and expansion project was initiated on this wedding cake of a building. Rama III's original plans were never fully realised and so the Loha Prasat Restoration Committee has taken on the task. The pink cement is being peeled off and the chedis coated with bronze. The upper *chedi* was completed by 2000 but work on the smaller *chedis* will continue for another few years yet. The monks who look after the building have had problems with homeless men and woman who use the Prasat's many nooks and crannies as handy places to sleep: they are turfed out (in a suitable meritorious manner) by the monks before the place opens each morning. ■ *Daily 0830-1600.*

Next to the Loha Prasat is the much more traditional Wat Rachanada. Wat **Wat Rachanada** Rachanada was built by Rama III for his niece who later became Rama IV's queen. The principal Buddha image is made of copper mined in Nakhon Ratchasima province to the northeast of Bangkok, and the ordination hall also has some fine doors. ■ *Mon-Sun 0600-1800*. What makes the wat particularly worth visiting is the **Amulet Market** (see page 101) to be found close by, between the Golden Mount and the wat. The sign, in English, below the covered part of the market reads 'Buddha and Antiques Centre'. The market also contains Buddha images and other religious artefacts and is open every day.

A five minute walk south of Wat Rachanada, on Bamrung Muang Road, is the **The Giant Swing** **Sao Ching Cha** or Giant Swing, consisting of two tall red pillars linked by an **& Wat Suthat** elaborate cross piece, set in the centre of a square. The Giant Swing was the original centre for a Brahmanic festival in honour of Siva. Young men, on a giant 'raft', would be swung high into the air to grab pouches of coins, hung from bamboo poles, between their teeth. Because the swinging was from east to west, it has been said that it symbolized the rising and setting of the sun. The festival was banned in the 1930s because of the injuries that occurred; prior to its banning, thousands would congregate around the Giant Swing for two days of dancing and music. The magnificent Wat Suthat faces the Giant Swing. The wat was begun by Rama I in 1807, and his intention was to build a temple that would equal the most glorious in Ayutthaya. The wat was not finished until the end of the reign of Rama III in 1851.

Bangkok

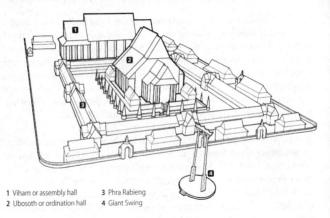

Wat Suthat
Source: adapted
from a drawing by
Kittisak Nualvilai
based on aerial
photographs and
reproduced in Beek,
Steve van and
Tettoni, L (1991) The
arts of Thailand,
Thames & Hudson:
London

1 Viharn or assembly hall 3 Phra Rabieng
2 Ubosoth or ordination hall 4 Giant Swing

The viharn is in early-Bangkok style and is surrounded by Chinese pagodas. Its six pairs of doors, each made from a single piece of teak, are deeply carved with animals and celestial beings from the Himavanta forest. The central doors are said to have been carved by Rama II himself, and are considered some of the most important works of art of the period. Inside the viharn is the bronze Phra Sri Sakyamuni Buddha in an attitude of subduing Mara. This image was previously contained in Wat Mahathat in Sukhothai, established in 1362. Behind the Buddha is a very fine gilded stone carving from the Dvaravati Period (2nd-11th centuries AD), 2½ m in height and showing the miracle at Sravasti and the Buddha preaching in the Tavatimsa heaven.

The bot is the tallest in Bangkok and one of the largest in Thailand. The murals in the bot, painted during the reign of Rama III are traditional Thai in style, and largely unaffected by western artistic influences. They use flat colours and lack perspective. The *bot* also contains a particularly large cast Buddha image. ■ *0900-1700; viharn only opens on weekends and Buddhist holidays.*

Wat Rachabophit The little visited Wat Rachabophit is close to the Ministry of the Interior on Rachabophit Road, a few minutes' walk south of Wat Suthat down Ti Thong Road. It is recognizable by its distinctive doors carved in high relief with jaunty-looking soldiers wearing European-style uniforms. The temple was started in 1869, took 20 years to complete, and is a rich blend of western and Thai art forms (carried further in Wat Benchamabophit 40 years later, see page 114). Wat Rachabophit is peculiar in that it follows the ancient temple plan of placing the Phra Chedi in the centre of the complex, surrounded by the other buildings. It later became the fashion to place the ordination hall at the centre.

Engraving of the Sao Ching Cha, or Golden Swing, from Henri Mouhot's Travels in the central parts of Indo-China (1864)

The 43 m-high gilded chedi's most striking feature are the five-coloured Chinese glass tiles which richly encrust the lower section. The ordination hall has 10 door panels and 28 window panels each decorated with gilded black lacquer on the inside and mother-of-pearl inlay on the outside showing the various royal insignia. They are felt to be among the masterpieces of the Rattanakosin Period (1782-present). The principal Buddha image in the ordination hall, in an attitude of meditation, sits on a base of Italian marble and is covered by the umbrella that protected the urn and ashes of Rama V. It also has a surprising interior – an Oriental version of Italian Gothic, more like Versailles than Bangkok. ■ *Mon-Sun 0800-1700. ฿10.*

North of Wat Rachabophit, on Tanao Road is Wat Mahannapharam, in a large, tree-filled compound. A peaceful place to retreat to, it contains some good examples of high-walled, Bangkok-Period architecture decorated with woodcarvings and mother-of-pearl inlay. Just south of here is the bustling **Chao Phaa Sua**, a Chinese temple with a fine tiled roof surmounted with mythological figures.

Wat Mahannapharam

Bangkok

From Wat Rachabophit, it is only a short distance to the **Pahurat Indian Market** on Pahurat Road, where Indian, Malaysian and Thai textiles are sold. To get there, walk south on Ti Thong Road which quickly becomes Tri Phet Road. After a few blocks, Pahurat Road crosses Tri Phet Road. **Pak Khlong Market** is to be found a little further south on Tri Phet Road at the foot of the Memorial Bridge. It is a huge wholesale market for fresh produce, and a photographer's paradise. It begins very early in the morning and has ended by 1000. The closest pier to the Pak Khlong Market is Tha Rachini, which is remembered for a particularly nasty episode in Thai history. It is said that in the 1840s a troublemaking up-country *chao* or lord was brought to Bangkok and sentenced to death. His eyes were burnt out with heated irons and then the unfortunate man was suspended above the river at Tha Rachini in a cage. The cage was so positioned that the *chao* could touch the water with his finger tips but could not cup water to drink. He died of thirst and sunstroke after three days and for years afterwards people would not live near the spot where he died.

Markets near Wat Rachabophit

Chinatown and the Golden Buddha

Chinatown covers the area from Charoen Krung (or New Road) down to the river and leads on from Pahurat Road Market; cross over Chakraphet Road and immediately opposite is the entrance to Sampeng Lane. This part of Bangkok has a different atmosphere from elsewhere. Roads become narrower, buildings smaller, and there is a continuous bustle of activity. There remain some attractive, weathered examples of early 20th-century shophouses. The industrious Sino-Thais of the area make everything from offertory candles and gold jewellery to metalwork, gravestones and light machinery.

A trip through Chinatown can either begin with the Thieves' Market to the NW, or at Wat Traimitr, the Golden Buddha, to the SE. An easy stroll between the two should not take more than 2 hrs

Nakhon Kasem (strictly speaking Woeng Nakhon Kasem), or the Thieves' Market, lies between Charoen Krung and Yaowarat Road, to the east of the *khlong* that runs parallel to Mahachai Road. Its boundaries are marked by archways. As its name suggests, this market used to be the centre for the fencing of stolen goods. It is not quite so colourful today, but there remain a number of second-hand and antique shops which are worth a browse –

• •
Chinatown place names

Wat Traimitir
วัดไตรมิตรวิทยาราม

Woeng Nakhon Kasem
เวิ้งนครเกษม

such as the *Good Luck Antique Shop*. Amongst other things, musical instruments, brass ornaments, antique (and not so antique) coffee grinders are all on sale here.

Yaowarat Road Just to the southeast of the Thieves' Market are two interesting roads that run next to and parallel with one another: Yaowarat Road and Sampeng Lane. Yaowarat Road, a busy thoroughfare, is the centre of the country's gold trade. The trade is run by a cartel of seven shops, the Gold Traders Association, and the price is fixed by the government. Sino-Thais often convert their cash into gold jewellery, usually bracelets and necklaces. The jewellery is bought by its 'baht weight' which fluctuates daily with the price of gold (most shops post the price daily). Should the owner need to convert their necklace or bracelet back into cash it is again weighed to determine its value. During the economic crisis of 1997-98 the Gold Traders Association encouraged people to hand over gold in exchange for bonds to help support the slumping baht. They set a target of collecting 1 kg of gold per shop, or some 10,000 kg in total.

Sampeng Lane The narrower, almost pedestrian Sampeng Lane, also called **Soi Wanit**, is just to the south of Yaowaraj Road. This road's history is shrouded in murder and intrigue. It used to be populated by prostitutes and opium addicts and was fought over by Chinese gangs. Today, it remains a commercial centre, but rather less illicit. It is still interesting, and shaded with awnings, but there is not much to buy here – it is primarily a wholesale centre specializing in cloth and textiles although it is a good place to go for odd lengths of material, buttons of any shape and size, costume jewellery, and such like. It appears to have changed scarcely at all since James McCarthy wrote of it in his book *Surveying and exploring in Siam* published in 1900 (and since republished by the

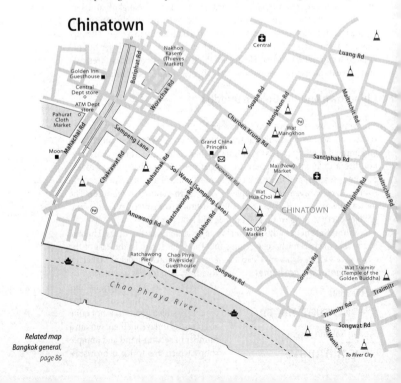

Chinatown

*Related map
Bangkok general,
page 86*

Bangkok-based publisher White Lotus): 'The Chinaman is a born trader, and the country people prefer dealing with him. The consequence is the narrow streets of Sampeng, seen by few Europeans, are thronged with busy crowds, and the little shop-front awnings, meeting in the middle of the street, make the heat more stifling to the half-naked, happy-go-lucky passers-by'.

The most celebrated example of the goldsmiths' art in Thailand sits within Wat Traimitr, or the **Temple of the Golden Buddha**, which is located at the eastern edge of Chinatown, squashed between Charoen Krung, Yaowaraj Road and Traimitr Road (just to the south of Bangkok's Hualamphong railway station). The Golden Buddha is housed in a small, rather gaudy and unimpressive room. Although the leaflet offered to visitors says the 3 m-high, 700 year-old image is 'unrivalled in beauty', be prepared to be disappointed. It is in fact rather featureless, showing the Buddha in an attitude of subduing Mara. What makes it special, drawing large numbers of visitors each day, is that it is made of 5½ tonnes of solid gold. Apparently, when the East Asiatic Company was extending the port of Bangkok, they came across a huge stucco Buddha image which they obtained permission to move. However, whilst being moved by crane in 1957, it fell and the stucco cracked to reveal a solid gold image. During the Ayutthayan Period it was the custom to cover valuable Buddha images in plaster to protect them from the Burmese, and this particular example stayed that way for several centuries. In the grounds of the wat there is a school, crematorium, foodstalls and, inappropriately, a money changer. Gold beaters can still be seen at work behind Suksaphan store. ■ *Mon-Sun, 0900-1700. ฿20.*

> **Wat Traimitr**

Between the river and Soi Wanit 2 there is a warren of lanes, too small for traffic – this is the Chinatown of old. From here it is possible to thread your way through to the River City shopping complex which is air-conditioned and a good place to cool off.

Visitors wishing to explore the wonders of Chinatown more thoroughly, should buy Nancy Chandler's *Map of Bangkok*, a lively, detailed (but not altogether accurate) map of all the shops, restaurants and out of the way wats and shrines. ฿70 from most bookstores.

> **Recommended reading**

Thonburi, Wat Arun and the Khlongs

Thonburi is Bangkok's little-known alter ego. Few people cross the Chao Phraya to see this side of the city, and if they do it is usually only to catch a glimpse from the seat of a speeding *hang yaaw* (long-tailed boat) and then climb the steps of Wat Arun. But Thonburi was, for a few brief years, the capital of Thailand (or Siam, as it was then) under King Taksin. It was only King Rama I's belief that Bangkok would be more easily defended from the Burmese that led him to

> **Thonburi**

switch sides in 1782. Perhaps because history gave Thonburi the cold shoulder, it retains a traditional character which, some people would say, has been lost to Bangkok.

Long-tailed boats & the Floating Market

One of the most enjoyable ways to see Bangkok is by boat – and particularly by the fast and noisy *hang yaaws*. You will know them when you see them; these powerful, lean machines roar around the river and the *khlongs* (canals) at break-neck speed. There are innumerable tours around the *khlongs* of Thonburi taking in a number of sights which include the floating market, snake farm and Wat Arun. Boats go from the various piers located along the east bank of the

Bangkok's river & khlongs

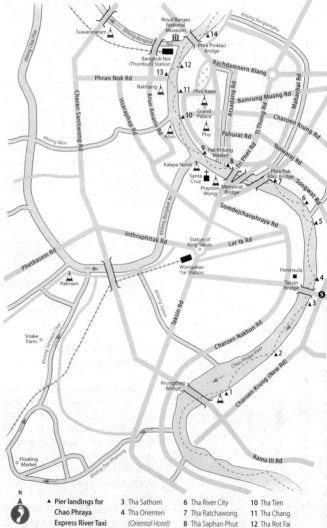

N

Related map
Bangkok general,
page 86

0 metres 400
0 yards 400

▲ Pier landings for Chao Phraya Express River Taxi

1 Tha Wat Rajsingkorn
2 Tha Vorachanyawat

3 Tha Sathorn
4 Tha Orienten *(Oriental Hotel)*
5 Tha Siphya *(Royal Orchid Hotel)*

6 Tha River City
7 Tha Ratchawong
8 Tha Saphan Phut *(Memorial Bridge)*
9 Tha Rachini

10 Tha Tien
11 Tha Chang
12 Tha Rot Fai
13 Tha Maharaj
14 Tha Saphan Phra Pinklao

Chao Phraya River. The journey begins by travelling downstream along the Chao Phraya, before turning 'inland' after passing beneath Krungthep Bridge. The route skirts past laden rice-barges, squatter communities on public land and houses overhanging the canals. This is a very popular route with tourists, and boats are intercepted by salesmen and women marketing everything from cold beer to straw hats. You may also get caught in a boat jam; traffic snarl-ups are not confined to the capital's roads. Nevertheless, the trip is a fascinating insight into what Bangkok must have been like when it was still the 'Venice of the East', and around every bend there seems to be yet another wat – some of them very beautiful. On private tours the first stop is usually the **Floating Market** (*Talaat Nam*). This is now an artificial, ersatz gathering which exists purely for the tourist industry. It is worth only a brief visit – unless the so-called 'post-tourist' is looking for just this sort of sight. The nearest functioning floating market is at Damnoen Saduak (see excursions from Bangkok, page 121).

The **Snake Farm** is the next stop where man fights snake in an epic battle of wills. Visitors can even pose with a python. The poisonous snakes are incited to burst balloons with their fangs, 'proving' how dangerous they are. There is also a rather motley zoo with a collection of crocodiles and sad-looking animals in small cages. ■ *฿70, shows every 20 mins. Refreshments available.* (The other snake farm in Central Bangkok (see page 116) is, appropriately, attached to the Thai Red Cross and is more professional and cheaper.) On leaving the snake farm, boats enter Khlong Bangkok Yai at the site of the large **Wat Paknam**. Just before re-entering the Chao Phraya itself, the route passes by the impressive **Wat Kalaya Nimit**.

To the south of Wat Kalaya Nimit, on the Thonburi side of the river, is **Wat Prayoon Wong**, virtually in the shadow of Saphan Phut (a bridge). The wat is famous for its *Khao Tao* or turtle mountain. This is a concrete fantasyland of grottoes and peaks, with miniature chedis and viharns, all set around a pond teeming with turtles. These are released to gain merit and the animals clearly thrive in the murky water. To coin a phrase, rather grotty, but unusual. Also unusual is the large white chedi with its circular cloister surmounted with smaller chedis, and the viharn with a mondop at each corner, each containing an image of the Buddha. The bot adjacent to the viharn is attractively decayed with gold inlay doors and window shutters, and *bai sema* protected by large mondops. This wat is rarely visited by tourists. ■ *Khao Tao open 0830-1730. Getting there: can be reached by taking a cross-river shuttle boat from Tha Saphan Phut (฿1).* The large white chedi of Wat Prayoon Wong is clearly visible from the Bangkok side of the river. A short walk (five minutes) upstream from here is **Santa Cruz Church**, facing the river. The church, washed in pastel yellow with a domed tower, was built to serve the Portuguese community who lived in this part of Thonburi. ■ *Getting there: cross-river shuttles also stop at Tha Santa Cruz, running between here and Tha Rachini, close to the massive Pak Khlong fresh produce market.*

Facing Wat Pho across the Chao Phraya River is the famous Wat Arun, or the Temple of the Dawn. Wat Arun stands 81 m high, making it the highest prang (tower) in Thailand. It was built in the early 19th century on the site of Wat Chaeng, the Royal Palace complex when Thonburi was briefly the capital of Thailand. The wat housed the Emerald Buddha before the image was transferred to Bangkok and it is said that King Taksin vowed to restore the wat after passing it one dawn. The prang is completely covered with fragments of Chinese porcelain and includes some delicate gold and black lacquered doors. The temple is really meant to be viewed from across the river; its scale and beauty can only be

Snake Farm

Wat Arun
The best view of Wat Arun is in the evening from the Bangkok side of the river when the sun sets behind the prang

Bangkok

Bangkok

Wat Arun
In Myr Pallegoix's Description du Royaume Thai ou Suam (1854)

appreciated from a distance. Young, a European visitor to the capital, wrote in 1898: 'Thousands upon thousands of pieces of cheap china must have been smashed to bits in order to furnish sufficient material to decorate this curious structure. Though the material is tawdry, the effect is indescribably wonderful'.

Until recently, energetic visitors could climb up to the halfway point and view the city, however this is no longer permitted. ■ *Mon-Sun, 0830-1730 ฿20. The men at the pier may demand ฿20 to help 'in the maintenance of the pier'. NB It is possible to get to Wat Arun by water-taxi from Tha Tien Pier (at the end of Thai Wang Road near Wat Pho), or from Tha Chang (at the end of Na Phralan near Wat Phra Kaeo) (฿1).*

Royal Barges   After visiting Wat Arun, some tours then go further upstream to the mouth of Khlong Bangkok Noi where the Royal Barges are housed in a hangar-like boat-house – the Royal Barges National Museum. These ornately carved boats, winched out of the water in cradles, were used by the king at *krathin* (see Ok Phansa festival, page 61) to present robes to the monks in Wat Arun at the end of the rainy season. The ceremony ceased in 1967 but the Royal Thai Navy restored the barges for the revival of the spectacle, as part of the Chakri Dynasty's bicentennial celebrations in 1982. The oldest and most beautiful barge is the Sri Supannahong, built during the reign of Rama I (1782-1809) and repaired during that of Rama VI (1910-1925). It measures 45 m long and 3 m wide, weighs 15 tonnes and was created from a single piece of teak. It required a crew of 50 oarsmen, and two coxwains, along with such assorted crew members as a flagman, a rhythm-keeper and singer. Its gilded prow was carved in the form of a

Wat Arun place names

Royal Barges National Museum
**พิพิธภัณฑสถานแห่งชาติ
เรือพระราชพิธี**

Wat Arun
วัดอรุณราชวราราม

Wat Prayoon Wong
วัดประยูรวงศ์

Wat Rakhang
วัดระฆัง

Wat Suwannaram
วัดสุวรรณาราม

The Chao Phraya River Express

One of the most relaxing – and one of the cheapest – ways to see Bangkok is by taking the Chao Phraya River Express. These boats (or rua duan) link almost 40 piers (or tha) along the Chao Phraya River from Tha Wat Rajsingkorn in the south to Tha Nonthaburi in the north. The entire route entails a journey of about 1¼-1½ hours, and fares are ฿4, ฿6 or ฿8. Adjacent to many of the piers are excellent riverside restaurants. At peak periods, boats leave every 10 minutes, off-peak about every 15-25 minutes. Note that boats flying red or green pennants do not stop at every pier; they also exact a ฿1 surcharge. Also, boats will only stop if passengers wish to board or alight, so make your destination known.

***NB** The boats don't always stop at all the piers; it depends upon the water level.*

Selected piers and places of interest, travelling upstream

Tha Orienten *by the* Oriental Hotel; *access to* Silom Road.

Tha River City *in the shadow of the* Royal Orchid Hotel, *on the south side and close to* River City shopping centre.

Tha Ratchawong Rabieng Ratchawong Restaurant; *access to* Chinatown *and* Sampeng Lane.

Tha Saphan Phut *Under the* Memorial Bridge *and close to* Pahurat Indian Market.

Tha Rachini Pak Khlong Market; *just upstream, the* Catholic seminary *surrounded by high walls.*

Tha Tien *Close to* Wat Pho; Wat Arun *on the opposite bank; and just downstream from Wat Arun the* Vichaiprasit Fort *(headquarters of the Thai navy), lurking behind crenellated ramparts.*

Tha Chang *Just downstream is the* Grand Palace *peeking out above white-washed walls;* Wat Rakhang *with its white corn-cob prang lies opposite.*

Tha Maharat Lan The Restaurant; *access to* Wat Mahathat *and* Sanaam Luang.

Tha Phra Arthit Yen Jai Restaurant; *access to* Khaosan Road.

Tha Visutkasat Yok Yor Restaurant; *just upstream the elegant central* Bank of Thailand.

Tha Thewes Son Ngen Restaurant; *just upstream are boatsheds with royal barges; close to the* National Library.

Tha Wat Chan *Just upstream is the* Singha Beer *Samoson brewery.*

Tha Wat Khema Wat Khema *in large, tree-filled compound.*

Tha Wat Khian Wat Kien, *semi-submerged.*

Tha Nonthaburi *Last stop on the express boat route (see map, page 108).*

hamsa (or goose) and its stern, in the shape of a *naga*. ■ *Mon-Sun 0830-1630 ฿30 (children free), extra for cameras and video cameras (see Festivals, September, page 156).*

Two rarely visited wats are Wat Suwannaram and Wat Rakhang. The royal Wat Rakhang is located just upstream from Wat Arun, almost opposite Tha Chang landing, and is identifiable from the river by the two plaster sailors standing to attention on either side of the jetty. The original wat on this site dates from the Ayutthaya Period: it has since been renovated on a number of occasions including during the reign of King Taksin and Rama I. The **Phra Prang** in the grounds of the wat is considered a fine, and particularly well proportioned example of early Bangkok architecture (late 18th century). The **ordination hall** (not always open – the abbot may oblige if he is available) was built during the reign of Rama III and contains a fine gilded Buddha image in an attitude of meditation, over which is the nine-tiered umbrella used to shelter the urn of Rama I during the Royal Cremation. Also here is a fine mural recording the 10 previous lives of the Buddha (note the trip to hell) painted by Phra Wannavadvichitre, an eminent monk-artist of the time. The bot was extensively renovated in 1995. The

Wat Rakhang

Bangkok

beautiful red-walled wooden **Tripitaka Hall** (originally a library built in the late 18th century) to the left of the viharn and bot when facing away from the river, was the residence of Rama I while he was a monk (before he became king) and Thonburi was still the capital of Siam. Consisting of two rooms, it is decorated with faded but nonetheless highly regarded murals of the Ramakien (painted by a monk-artist), black and gold chests, a portrait of the king, and some odd bits of old carved door. It is one of the most charming buildings in Bangkok. The hall is towards the back of the complex, behind the large white *prang* and it is in excellent condition, having been recently restored. ■ *Mon-Sun 0500-2100 ฿2 (the river ferry stops at the wat).*

Wat
Suwannaram
For plan, see page 444

Wat Suwannaram is a short distance further on from the Royal Barges on Khlong Bangkok Noi, on the other side of the canal. The main buildings – which are particularly well proportioned – date from Rama I's reign (late 18th century), although the complex was later extensively renovated by Rama III. There was a wat on this site even prior to Rama I's reign, and the original name, Wat Thong (Golden Wat) remains in popular use. The *ubosoth* displays some fine wood-carving on the gable ends of the square pillared porches (Vishnu on his vehicle, Garuda), while the interior contains a series of murals, painted by two artists in professional competition with one another and commissioned by Rama III, and regarded by many as among the finest in Bangkok. The murals are in two 'registers'; the murals on the long walls between the windows show the Ten Lives of the Buddha. Entering the building through the right-hand door (with the river behind), on the right-hand wall, is a representation of a boat foundering with the crew being eaten by sharks and sea monsters as they thrash about in the waves. Closer inspection shows that these unfortunates are wearing white skull-caps – presumably they are Muslims returning from the haj to Mecca. The principal image in the bot is made of bronze and shows the Buddha calling the Earth Goddess to witness. Sukhothai in style, it was presumably brought down from the old capital, probably in the first reign, although no records exist of its prior history. Next to the bot is the viharn abutted, unusually, by two cross halls at the front and rear. It was built during the reign of Rama IV. Wat Suwannaram is elegant and rarely visited and is a peaceful place to escape after the bustle of Wat Arun and the Floating Market.

Almost opposite Wat Suwannaram on the opposite bank of the river is the home of an unusual occupational group – Chao Phraya's divers. The men use traditional diving gear – heavy bronze helmets, leaden shoes, air pumps and pipes – and search the bed of the murky river for lost precious objects, sunken boats, and the bodies of those who have drowned or been murdered. How they find anything is one of life's deeper mysteries.

Arranging a
boat tour

Either book a tour at your hotel (see tours, page 124), or go to one of the piers and organize your own customized trip. The most frequented piers are located between the *Oriental Hotel* and the *Grand Palace* (see map, or ask at your hotel), or under Taksin Bridge (which marks the end of the Skytrain line – at Sapan Taksin). The pier just to the south of the Royal Orchid Sheraton Hotel is recommended. Organizing your own trip gives greater freedom to stop and start when the mood takes you. It is best to go in the morning (0700). For the trip given above (excluding Wat Rakhang and Wat Suwannaram), the cost for a *hang yaaw* which can sit 10 people should be about ฿600 for the boat for a half-day. If visiting Rakhang and Suwannaram as well as the other sights, expect to pay about another ฿200-300 for the hire of a boat. Be sure to settle the route and cost before setting out.

The Dusit Area

The Dusit area of Bangkok lies north of the Old City. The area is intersected by wide tree-lined avenues, and has an almost European flavour. The Vimanmek Palace lies off Rachvithi Road, just to the north of the National Assembly. It was built by Rama V in 1901 and designed by one of his brothers. The palace makes an interesting contrast to Jim Thompson's House (see page 115) or Suan Pakkard (page 114). While Jim Thompson was enchanted by Thai arts, King Rama V was clearly taken with western arts. It seems like a large Victorian hunting lodge – but raised off the ground – and is filled with china, silver and paintings from all over the world (as well as some gruesome hunting trophies). The photographs are fascinating – one shows the last time elephants were used in warfare in Thailand. Behind the palace is the Audience Hall which houses a fine exhibition of crafts made by the Support Foundation, an organization set up and funded by Queen Sirikit. Support, rather clumsily perhaps, is the acronym for the Foundation for the Promotion of Supplementary Occupations and Related Techniques. Also worth seeing is the exhibition of the king's own photographs, and the clock museum. Dance shows are held twice a day at 1030 and 1400. Visitors are not free to wander, but must be shown around by one of the charming guides who demonstrate the continued deep reverence for King Rama V (tour approximately 1hr). ■ *Mon-Sun 0900-1600 (last tickets sold at 1500) ฿50, ฿20 for children. Note that tickets to the Grand Palace include entrance to Vimanmek Palace. For further information T2811569, www.palaces.thai.net Refreshments available.* **NB** *Visitors to the palace are required to wear long trousers or a skirt; sarongs available for hire (฿100, refundable). Buses do go past the palace, but from the centre of town it is easier to get a tuk-tuk or taxi (฿50-60).*

Vimanmek Palace
The largest golden teakwood mansion in the world

Bangkok

From Vimanmek, it is a 10-15 minute walk to the Dusit Zoo, skirting around the **National Assembly** (which, before the 1932 coup was the Marble Throne Hall and is not open to visitors). The route is tree-lined, so it is possible to keep out of the sun or the rain. In the centre of the square in front of the National Assembly stands an equestrian statue of the venerated King Chulalongkorn. To the left lie the **Amporn Gardens**, the venue for royal social functions and fairs. Southwards from the square runs the impressive **Rachdamnern Nok Avenue**, a Siamese Champs Elysée. Enter the **Dusit Zoo** through Uthong Gate, just before the square. A pleasant walk through the zoo leads to the Chitralada Palace and Wat Benchamabophit. The zoo has a reasonable collection of animals from the region, some of which look rather the worse for wear. There is a children's playground, restaurants and pedal-boats can be hired on the lake. ■ *Mon-Sun 0800-1800. ฿30, ฿10 children.*

Amporn Gardens & Dusit Zoo

From the Dusit Zoo's Suanchit Gate, a right turn down the tree-lined Rama V Road leads to the present King Bhumibol's residence – **Chitralada Palace**. It was built by Rama VI and is not open to the public. Evidence of the King's forays into agricultural research may be visible. He has a great interest and concern for the development of the poorer, agricultural parts of his country, and invests large sums of his own money in royal projects. To the right of the intersection of Rama V and Sri Ayutthaya

• • • • • • • • • • • • • • • • • • • •
Dusit area place names

Dusit Zoo
สวนสัตว์ดุสิต

Vimanmek Palace
พระที่นั่งวิมานเมฆ

Wat Benchamabophit
วัดเบญจมบพิตร

roads are the gold and ochre roofs of Wat Benchamabophit – about a 10 minute walk from the zoo.

Wat Benchamabophit
The best time to visit this temple complex is early morning, when monks can be heard chanting inside the chapel

The **Marble Temple**, or Wat Benchamabophit, is the most modern of the royal temples and was only finished in 1911. It is of unusual architectural design (the architect was the king's half brother, Prince Naris), with carrara marble pillars, a marble courtyard and two large *singhas* guarding the entrance to the bot. Rama V was so pleased with the marble-faced ordination hall that he wrote to his brother: 'I never flatter anyone but I cannot help saying that you have captured my heart in accomplishing such beauty as this'. The interior is magnificently decorated with crossbeams of lacquer and gold, and in shallow niches in the walls are paintings of important stupas from all over the kingdom. The door panels are faced with bronze sculptures and the windows are of stained-glass, painted with angels. The cloisters around the assembly hall house 52 figures (both original and imitation) – a display of the evolution of the Buddha image in India, China and Japan. The walking Buddha from the Sukhothai Period is particularly worth a look. The rear courtyard houses a large 80-year-old bodhi tree and a pond filled with turtles, released by people hoping to gain merit. ■ *Mon-Sun 0800-1700. ฿10.*

Government House

Government House is south of here on Nakhon Pathom Road. The building is a weird mixture of cathedral gothic and colonial Thai. It is only open on Wan Dek – a once yearly holiday for children held on the second Saturday in January. The little visited **Wat Sonnakviharn** is on Krung Kasem Road, located behind a car park and schoolyard. Enter by the doorway in the far right-hand corner of the schoolyard, or down Soi Sommanat. It is peaceful, unkempt, and rather beautiful, with fine gold lacquer doors, and a large gold tile-encrusted chedi. ■ *Mon-Sun.*

Other sights

Suan Pakkard Palace
The palace grounds are very peaceful

In addition to the Vimanmek Palace, Bangkok has a number of other beautiful Thai-style houses that are open to the public. Suan Pakkard Palace or Lettuce Garden Palace is at 352-354 Sri Ayutthaya Road, south of the Victory Monument (see map page 86). The five raised traditional Thai houses (domestic rather than royal) were built by Princess Chumbhot, a great granddaughter of King Rama IV. They contain her fine collection of antiquities, both historic and prehistoric (the latter

Wat Benchamabophit
Adapted from Döhring, Kar (1920) Buddhistische Tempelanlagen in Siam, Asia Publishing House: Bangkok

are particularly rare). Like the artefacts in the National Museum, those in Suan Pakkard are also poorly labelled. The rear pavilion is particularly lovely, decorated in black and gold lacquerwork panels. Prince Chumbhot discovered this temple near Ayutthaya and reassembled and restored it here for his wife's 50th birthday. ■ *Mon-Sun 0900-1600. ฿100 – including a fan to ward off the heat. All receipts go to a fund for artists.*

Jim Thompson's House is on the quiet Soi Kasemsan Song (2), opposite the National Stadium on Rama I Road. It is an assemblage of traditional teak Northern Thai houses, some more than 200 years old, transported here and re-assembled (these houses were designed to be transportable, consisting of five parts – the floor, posts, roof, walls and decorative elements constructed without the use of nails). Jim Thompson arrived in Bangkok as an intelligence officer attached to the United States' OSS (Office of Strategic Services) and then made his name by reinvigorating the Thai silk industry after the Second World War. He disappeared mysteriously in the Malaysian jungle on 27 March 1967, but his silk industry continues to thrive. (The *Jim Thompson Silk Emporium*, selling fine Thai silk, is at the northeast end of Surawong Road (see map page 128). This shop is a tourist attraction in itself. Shoppers can buy high-quality bolts of silk and silk clothing here – anything from a pocket handkerchief to a silk suit. Prices are top of the scale.) Jim Thompson chose this site for his house partly because a collection of silk weavers lived nearby on Khlong Saensaep. The house contains an eclectic collection of antiques from Thailand and China, with work displayed as though it was still his home. Shoes must be removed before entering; walking barefoot around the house adds to the appreciation of the cool teak floorboards. Bustling Bangkok only intrudes in the form of the stench from the khlong that runs behind the house. Compulsory guided tours around the house and no photography allowed. ■ *฿100, children ฿25 (profits to charity). Mon-Sat 0900-1630. There is a sophisticated little café attached to the museum as well as a shop selling Jim Thompson products. Getting there: bus along Rama I Rd, taxi or tuk-tuk.*

Jim Thompson's House

A 10 minute walk east along Rama I Road is the shopping area known as Siam Square (or *Siam Sa-quare*, see map page 132). This has the greatest concentration of fast-food restaurants, boutiques and cinemas in the city. Needless to say, it is patronized by young Thais sporting the latest fashions and doing the sorts of things their parents would never have dreamed of doing – girls smoking and couples holding hands, for instance. For Thais worried about the direction their country is taking, Siam Square encapsulates all their fears in just a few *rai*. This is crude materialism; this is Thais aping the west; this is the erosion of Thai values and culture with scarcely a thought to the future. Because of the tourists and wealthy Thais who congregate around Siam Square it is also a popular patch for beggars. During the 'miracle' years of rapid economic growth the number of beggars actually increased. It may have been that this economic expansion didn't reached the poor in rural areas (Thailand has become a more unequal society over the last decade or so); or it may be that with greater wealth, begging had become a more attractive – in terms of economic

Siam Square

Bangkok

• •

Other area place names

Chatuchak Weekend Market

ตลาดนัดสวนจัตุจักร

Jim Thompson's House

บ้านจิม ทอมป์สัน

Siam Square

สยามสแควร์

Suan Pakkard Palace

วังสวนผักกาด

Bangkok

return – occupation. A study by the Thai Farmers Bank in the mid-1990s found that beggars could earn more than the minimum wage. They also found that many of the beggars were not even Thai: many were Cambodians.

Chulalongkorn University

The land on which this chequerboard of shops at Siam Square are built is owned by Chulalongkorn University – Bangkok's, and Thailand's, most prestigious. While Thammasat University on Sanaam Luang is known for its radical politics, Chulalongkorn is conservative. Just south of Siam Square, on the campus itself (off Soi Chulalongkorn 12, behind the massive Mahboonkrong or MBK shopping centre; ask for *sa-sin*, the houses are nearby) is a collection of beautiful **traditional Thai houses**, erected to help preserve Thai culture. Also on campus is the **Museum of Imaging Technology** with a few hands-on photographic displays. Occasional photographic exhibitions are also held here. ■ *Mon-Fri 1000-1530 ฿100. To get to the museum, enter the campus by the main entrance on the east side of Phaya Thai Rd and walk along the south side of the playing field. Turn right after the Chemistry 2 building and then right again at the entrance to the Mathematics Faculty. It is at the end of this walkway in the Dept of Photographic Science and Printing Technology.*

Erawan Shrine

East of Siam Square is the Erawan Shrine on the corner of Ploenchit and Rachdamri roads, at the Rachprasong intersection. This is Bangkok's most popular shrine, attracting not just Thais but also large numbers of other Asian visitors. The spirit of the shrine, the Hindu god Thao Maha Brahma, is reputed to grant people's wishes – it certainly has little artistic worth. In thanks, visitors offer garlands, wooden elephants and pay to have dances performed for them accompanied by the resident Thai orchestra. The popular *Thai Rath* newspaper reported in 1991 that some female devotees show their thanks by covorting naked at the shrine in the middle of the night. Others, rather more coy about exposing themselves in this way, have taken to giving the god pornographic videos instead. Although it is unlikely that visitors will be rewarded with the sight of naked bodies, the shrine is a hive of activity at most hours, incongruously set on a noisy, polluted intersection tucked into a corner, and in the shadow of the Sogo Department Store.

Siam Society

One other traditional house worth visiting is the home of the Siam Society, off Sukhumvit Road, at 131 Soi Asoke (see map page 134). The Siam Society is a learned society established in 1904 and has benefited from almost continual royal patronage. The **Kamthieng House** is a 120-year-old Northern Thai house from Chiang Mai. It was donated to the society in 1963, transported to Bangkok and then reassembled a few years later. It now serves as an ethnological museum, devoted to preserving the traditional technologies and folk arts of Northern Thailand. It makes an interesting contrast to the fine arts displayed in Suan Pakkard Palace and Jim Thompson's House. The Siam Society houses a library, organizes lectures and tours and publishes books, magazines and pamphlets. ■ *Mon-Sat 0900-1700 ฿100, T6616470 for information on lectures or info@siam-society.org*

Wat Indraviharn

Wat Indraviharn is rather isolated from the other sights, lying just off Visutkaset Road. It contains a 32 m-high standing Buddha encrusted in gold tiles that can be seen from the entrance to the wat. The image is impressive only for its size. The topknot contains a relic of the Buddha brought from Ceylon. Few tourists. ■ *Mon-Sun.*

For those with a penchant for snakes, the **Snake Farm** of the Thai Red Cross is very central and easy to reach from Silom or Surawong roads (see map page 128).

The Patpong Story

On 30 September 1996, Udom Patpongsiri died at the age of 79. In 1946 his family bought a small plot of land between Silom and Surawong roads for the princely sum of US$3,000 – presumably with some advice from the young Udom who had returned from an overseas education well informed about all the latest business and management trends. (He attended the London School of Economics and the University of Minnesota). At the time of his death half a century later the land was worth around US$100 mn and his name – or a part of it at least – had acquired an international profile: Patpong.

When they bought the land Patpong had no name; indeed there was not even a road on the plot of land to give it a name. Udom's family built a track from Surawong to the canal which is now Silom Road. Later when the canal was covered over, Udom began using his language skills and knowledge of American and British culture to entice foreigners to base their operations on his family's land. The fact that Udom joined the Free Thai Movement during the war and received training from the Offices of Strategic Services (OSS – the forerunner to the CIA) no doubt also introduced Udom to the predilections of US servicemen. When the war in Indochina saw a massive influx of American servicemen into Thailand, Udom saw a market niche crying out to be filled and with his encouragement and guidance Patpong Road and the parallel Patpong 2 Road quickly made the metamorphosis from quiet business streets to a booming red-light emporium.

It was established in 1923, and raises snakes for serum production, which is distributed worldwide. The farm also has a collection of non-venomous snakes. During showtime (which lasts half an hour) various snakes are exhibited, and venom extracted. Visitors can fondle a python. The farm is well maintained and professional. ■ *Mon-Fri 0830-1630 (shows at 1100 and 1430), Sat/Sun and holidays 0830-1200 (show at 1100) ฿70 . The farm is within the Science Division of the Thai Red Cross Society at the corner of Rama IV and Henri Dunant roads.*

Chatuchak Weekend Market
Definitely worth a visit – allocate half a day at least

Slightly further out of the centre of Bangkok is the Chatuchak Weekend Market which is off Phahonyothin Road, opposite the Northern bus terminal (see map page 86). Until 1982 this market was held at Sanaam Luang, but was moved because it had outgrown its original home and also because the authorities wanted to clean up the area for the Bangkok bicentenary celebrations. It is a huge conglomeration of 8,672 stallholders spread over an area of 12 ha (28 acres), selling virtually everything under the sun, and an estimated 200,000 people visit the market over a weekend. It is probably the best place to buy handicrafts and all things Thai in the whole Kingdom. There are antique stalls, basket stalls, textile sellers, shirt vendors, carvers and painters along with the usual array of fish sellers, vegetable hawkers, butchers and candle-stick makers. In the last couple of years a number of bars and food stalls geared to tourists and Thai yuppies have also opened so it is possible to rest and recharge before foraging once more. In addition to the map here, Nancy Chandler's Map of Bangkok has an inset map of the market to help you get around. ■ *Believe it or not, the market is open on weekends, officially from 0900-1800 (although in fact it begins earlier around 0700). It's best to go early in the day. Getting there: a/c buses 2 (from Silom Rd), 3, 10, 13 and 29 go past the market, and non-a/c buses 8, 24, 26, 27, 29, 34, 39, 44, 59, and 96. Or take a taxi or tuk-tuk.* In 1994 plans were announced to transform the market by building a three-storey purpose-built structure with car parking and various other amenities. Such has been the outcry that the planners have retired to think again. But the fear is that this gem of shopping chaos will be reorganized, sanitized, bureaucratized and, in the process, ruined. **Beware pickpockets**. There is a tourist information centre at the entrance gate off Kamphaeng Phet 2 Road, and the clock tower serves as a good reference point should visitors become disoriented. Also here, in the north section of Chatuchak Park adjacent to Kamphaeng Phet Road is the **Railway Museum** with a small collection of steam locomotives as well as miniature and model trains. ■ *0500*.

The **Science Museum and Planetarium** is just past Sukhumvit Soi 40, next to the Eastern bus terminal (see map page 134). It contains a planetarium, aeroplanes and other exhibits but don't expect many of them to work. As one recent report put it, there are lots of interactive buttons, but nothing much happens when you press them. ■ *Tue-Sun 0900-1600. Closed public holidays. ฿40 adults, ฿20 children. Getting there: bus (a/c 1, 8, 11, 13, non-a/c 2, 25, 38, 40, 48, 71, 119), taxi or tuk-tuk.* (There is a newer and much better science museum, the National Science Museum, see page 122).

Chatuchak Weekend Market

1 Decorative rocks & Bonsai	8 Plants & clothing
2 Agricultural products & clothing	9 Plants
3 Miscellaneous	10 Fresh & dried fruits & ceramic wares
4 Pets & handicrafts	11 Antiques
5 Pets	12 Buddha images, plants & books
6 Clothing	13 Paintings & plants
7 Fresh & dried fruits	

Art galleries *The Artist's Gallery*, 60 Pan Rd, off Silom, houses a selection of international works of art. *The Neilson Hays Library*, 195 Surawong Rd, has a changing programme of exhibitions. *The Sunday Gallery*, at Chatuchak Weekend Market, exhibits up and coming Thai artists. The gallery is in Section 3, Soi 2, open 0930-1830 Sunday, T5851556. The *British Council*, on Siam Square, also holds exhibitions, T6116830.

Excursions

Ancient City

Allocate a full day for a trip out to the Ancient City

The Ancient City or *Muang Boran* (T2241057) lies 25 km southeast of Bangkok in the province of Samut Prakarn and is billed as the world's largest outdoor museum. It houses scaled-down constructions of Thailand's most famous wats and palaces (some of which can no longer be visited in their original locations) along with a handful of originals relocated here. Artisans maintain the buildings while helping to keep alive traditional crafts. The 50-ha site corresponds in shape to the map of Thailand, with the wats and palaces appropriately sited. ■ *Mon-Sun 0800-1700. ฿50, ฿25 children. Getting there: there are 3 ways of getting to the Ancient City – either on the a/c city bus 8 or 11, or non-a/c 25 to Samut Prakarn and then a short songthaew ride; or by bus from the Eastern bus terminal to Samut Prakarn; or on one of the innumerable organized tours (see Tours, below).*

Bangkok: animal supermarket of the world

Thailand has few laws restricting the import of endangered species of wildlife – either alive or dead – and the country acts as a collection point for animals from Burma, Cambodia and Laos, as well as further afield. Tiger skins and penises (the latter much prized by the Chinese), ivory, rhino horns and nails, cayman skins (from Latin America), live gibbons and tiger cubs, clouded leopard skins, hawksbill turtle shells, and rare palm cockatoos are all available in Bangkok, a city which has been called the 'wildlife supermarket of the world'. This is nothing particularly new: in 1833, government records show that 50-60 rhinoceros horns were exported, along with 26,000 pairs of deer's antlers and 100,000 deer hides.

But pressure on Thailand's natural environment means that the scale of the threat is different. In 1991 the World Wide Fund for Nature labelled Thailand as 'probably the worst country in the world for the illegal trade in endangered species'. Before the Olympic Games in Seoul, South Korea, in 1988 it is said that 200 Malayan sun bears were smuggled from Thailand to Korea so that local athletes could consume their energy-enhancing gall bladders and meat. Even Korean tourists are able to dine on bear meat in
restaurants in Bangkok – the animals are lowered alive in cages into vats of boiling water. The rear left paw is considered very lucky and cooked and cut off first. A plate of bear paw soup costs US$1,000. A whole bear, US$14,000.

Critics claim that the Thai government flagrantly violates the rules of the Convention on International Trade in Endangered Species (CITES) – which it has officially acceded to – and ignores blatant trading in both live and dead endangered species. At the end of 1994 a house was raided and discovered to contain piles of animal carcasses, frozen bears' paws, and live bears, monkeys and snakes – all destined for the cooking pot. In recent years there has been increasing pressure from conservationists and from other governments to try and force the Thai authorities to clean up their act. Perhaps as evidence of some success, in 1997 the Chatuchak Weekend Market – where hitherto it was possible openly to see and buy endangered species – fenced off the animal-selling sections in an effort to control the trade in protected fauna. They also erected signs and banners telling people to avoid buying protected animals, and set up a permanent information booth to inform the public.

Bangkok

The Samut Prakarn Crocodile Farm and Zoo claims to be the world's oldest **Crocodile** crocodile farm. Founded in 1950 by a certain Mr Utai Youngprapakorn, it **Farm & Zoo** contains over 50,000 crocs of 28 species. Thailand has become, in recent years, one of the world's largest exporters of farmed crocodile skins and meat. Newly rich Asians have a penchant for crocodile skin handbags, briefcases and shoes, and the Chinese are said to have developed a liking for crocodile steaks. Never slow in seeing a new market niche, Thai entrepreneurs have invested in the farming of the beasts – in some cases in association with chicken farms. (The old battery chickens are simply fed to the crocs – no waste, no trouble.) The irony is that the wild crocodile is now, to all intents and purposes, extinct in the country – there are said to be two left alive, and unfortunately living in different areas. The show includes the 'world famous' crocodile wrestling. The farm also has a small zoo, train and playground. ■ *Mon-Sun 0700-1800 (approximately), ฿300, ฿200 children, T7034891. Croc combat and elephant show-time is every hour between 0900 and 1600 Mon-Fri (no show at 1200), and every hour between 0900 and 1700 Sat/Sun and holidays. Getting there: a/c bus 8 or 11, or regular bus 25, 45, 102 or 119 along Sukhumvit Rd; or a bus from the Eastern bus terminal to Samut Prakarn and then take a minibus to the Crocodile Farm; or a tour (see Tours, below).*

Watery excursions

Apart from the *khlong* trips outlined on page 107, there are other places to go on the river. The cheapest way to travel the river is by regular **water taxi**. There are three types (not including the *hang yaaws*):

First, the **Chao Phraya Express River Taxi** (*rua duan*) which runs on a regular route from Wat Rajsingkorn (near Krungthep Bridge, at the south end of Charoen Krung) northwards to Nonthaburi (see box, page 111). Fares range from ฿4-16 and the service operates every 8 to 25 minutes depending on the time of day, 0600-1800 Monday-Sunday (see map page 108 for stops). The boats are long and fast. There are also **ferries** which ply back and forth across the river, between Bangkok and Thonburi. The fare for these slower, chunkier boats is ฿1. Lastly, there are a number of **other boat services** linking Bangkok with stops along the *khlongs* which run off the main Chao Phraya River and into Thonburi. These are a good, cheap way of getting a glimpse of waterside life. Services from Tha Tien pier (by Wat Pho) to Khlong Mon, 0630-1800 Monday-Sunday (every half an hour) ฿4; from Memorial Bridge pier to Khlong Bang Waek, 0600-2130 Monday-Sunday (every 15 minutes) ฿10; from Tha Chang pier (by the Grand Palace) to Khoo Wiang floating market (market operates 0400-0700) and Khlong Bang Yai, 0615-2000 Monday-Sunday (every 20 minutes) ฿10; and from Nonthaburi's Phibun Pier (north of the city) to Khlong Om, 0400-2100 Monday-Sunday (every 15 minutes).

An interesting day trip by long-tailed boat takes visitors to a **traditional Thai house** 30 km from Bangkok, in Nonthaburi (see next entry). A day trip, including lunch costs ฿500. It is possible to stay here as guests of the owner Mr Phaiboon (**A**, the rate includes breakfast, fan rooms, outside bathrooms and no hot water). Call *Asian Overland Adventure*, T2800740, F2800741.

Nonthaburi

Nonthaburi is both a province and a provincial capital immediately to the north of Bangkok (see map page 82). Accessible by express river taxi from the city, the town has a provincial air that contrasts sharply with the overpowering capital: there are saamlors in the streets (now banished from Bangkok) and the pace of life is tangibly less frenetic. About half an hour's walk away are rice fields and rural Thailand. A **street market** runs from the pier inland past the *sala klang* (provincial offices), selling clothes, sarong lengths, dried fish and unnecessary plastic objects. The buildings of the *sala klang* are early 19th century, wooden and decayed. Note the lamp posts with their durian accessories – Nonthaburi's durians are renowned across the Kingdom. Walk through the *sala klang* compound (downriver) to reach an excellent riverside restaurant.

Excursions place names

Ancient City
เมืองโบราณ

Ayutthaya
พระนครศรีอยุธยา

Bang Pa-In
บางปะอิน

Floating market at Damnoen Saduak
ตลาดน้ำดำเนินสะดวก

Hua Hin
หัวหิน

Khao Yai National Park
อุทยานแห่งชาติเขาใหญ่

Nakhon Pathom
นครปฐม

Nonthaburi
นนทบุรี

Phetburi
เพชรบุรี

My kingdom for a durian

To many Thais, durians are not just any old fruit. They are Beaujolais, grouse and dolcellata all rolled into one stinking, prickly ball. The best durian in Thailand – the cognoscenti would say the whole world – come from Nonthaburi, north of Bangkok. And the best varieties are those like the kan yao durian. The problem is that Nonthaburi has been taken over by factories and housing estates. Durian orchards are disappearing as development proceeds and many of the most famous orchards are now under concrete. In early 2000 it was said that there were just 3,000 rai of orchards left in the province (less than 500 ha). Such is the scarcity of these fruit that wealthy Thais reserve their fruit on the tree – each of which sells for ฿1,200-1,500. Nor is it just a case of land being redeveloped. Durian trees are said not to like thundering traffic and the fumes that go with Nonthaburi's gradual industrialization. The sensible things just refuse to fruit or produce second-class offerings.

Bangkok

Across the river and upstream (five minutes by long-tailed boat) is **Wat Chalem Phra Kiat**, a refined wat built by Rama III as a tribute to his mother who is said to have lived in the vicinity. The gables of the bot are encrusted in ceramic tiles; the chedi behind the bot was built during the reign of King Mongkut or Rama IV (1851-1868). ■ *Getting there: by express river taxi (45 mins) to Tha Nonthaburi or by Bangkok city bus (Nos 32, 64, 97 and 203).*

Floating market at Damnoen Saduak
It is possible to combine this trip with a visit to the Rose Garden (see page 123)

Damnoen Saduak floating market, in Ratchaburi Province, 109 km west of Bangkok, is (almost) the real thing. Sadly, it is becoming increasingly like the Floating Market in Thonburi (see page 108), although it does still function as a legitimate market. ■ *Getting there: catch an early morning bus (No 78) from the Southern bus terminal in Thonburi – aim to get to Damnoen Saduak between 0800-1000, as the market winds down after 1000, leaving only trinket stalls. The trip takes about 1½ hrs. A/c and non-a/c buses leave every 40 mins from 0600 (฿30-49) (T4355031 for booking). The bus travels via Nakhon Pathom (where it is possible to stop on the way back and see the Great Chedi – see Nakhon Pathom page 123).* Ask the conduc-

Damnoen Saduak Floating Market

To Bangkok

o Market
Ton — Khem — Market
Hia Kui Market
Sukhaphiban I Rd
78 Bus Stop
Thanarat Bridge
Rte 325
Khun Phithak Market

N
Not to scale

▲ Piers
1 Soem Suk
2 Seri Khemi Kaset
3 Potchawan
4 Lek Silom
5 Mongkhon
6 Soem Suk

To Samut Songkhram

tor to drop you at Thanarat Bridge in Damnoen Saduak. Then either walk down the lane (1½ km) that leads to the market and follows the canal, or take a river taxi for ฿10, or a mini-bus (฿2). There are a number of floating markets in the maze of *khlongs* – Ton Khem, Hia Kui and Khun Phithak – and it is best to hire a *hang yaaw* to explore the back-waters and roam around the markets, about ฿300 per hour (agree the price before setting out). Tour companies also visit the floating market.

Thai Human Imagery Museum

Situated 31 km west of Bangkok on Pinklao-Nakhon Chaisri highway, the Thai Human Imagery Museum is the Madame Tussauds of Bangkok. 'Breath-taking' sculptures include famous monks, Thai kings, and scenes from Thai life; the museum is probably more interesting to Thais than foreigners. ■ *Mon-Fri, 0900-1730, Sat, Sun and holidays 0830-1800. ₿200. T034-332109. Getting there: by bus from the Southern bus terminals (either a/c or non-a/c) towards Nakhon Pathom; ask to be let off at the museum.*

National Science Museum
The National Science Museum or NSM opened in Pathum Thani province in 2000, north of town, past the airport. The money for the project – a cool one billion baht – was allocated before the economic crisis. New buildings, air-conditioned, internet centre, and lots of hands-on exhibits to thrill children and the childlike is the result. The exhibits are labelled in English and Thai and the recorded information is also in both languages. It really is surprisingly good, well designed and with charming student helpers for that human touch. The cafeteria needs some more thought though. ■ *Tue-Sun, 0900-1700. ₿50, ₿20 children. T5774172, Pasopsuk@lox1.loxinfo.com Getting there: not that easy because it is some way north of the city centre. In Thai the Museum is known as Ongkaan Phiphitiphan Withayasaat Haeng Chaat (or Or Por Wor Chor). But even if you can manage that the chances are that the taxi driver will not know where you mean, so get someone from your hotel or guesthouse to make sure. Take the Chaeng Wattana-Bang Pa-in expressway north and exit at Chiang Rak (for Thammasat University's new out-of-town campus). Continue west on Khlong Luang Rd, over Phahonyothin Rd, and follow your nose over khlong 1 to khlong 5 (canals) until the road ends at a 'T' junction. Turn right and the NSM is 4 km or so down here on the left.*

Ayutthaya
See page 175
Ayutthaya, 85 km north of Bangkok, was the capital of Thailand until 1767 when the Burmese razed the city. Despite the efforts of the Burmese – or perhaps because of them – it remains a splendid place with 84 palaces, shrines, monasteries and *chedis*. In December 1991 UNESCO added it to its list of World Heritage sites. Accessible as a day's excursion from Bangkok there are also ample places to stay. ■ *Getting there: it is an easy 1-hr journey from Bangkok's Northern bus terminal to Ayutthaya so it is easily accessible as a day tour. There are also regular train connections with Hualamphong station – and the station in Ayutthaya is centrally located. Another option is to arrive by boat, which takes a leisurely 3 hrs from Tha Tien pier in Bangkok (see page 125).*

Bang Pa-in
Just over 60 km north of Bangkok, Bang Pa-In became the summer residence of the Ayutthayan kings of the 17th century. After the capital of Thailand was moved to Bangkok, Bang Pa-In was abandoned and left to degenerate. It was not until Rama IV stopped here on a journey to Ayutthaya that a restoration programme was begun and both he and his son, King Chulalongkorn (Rama V), visited Bang Pa-In regularly. The palace is now a museum and is easily accessible from Bangkok, by bus or train or on a tour. For more information see page . ■ *Bang Pa-In complex ₿50 (guidebook included). Mon-Sun 0830-1630. Getting there: regular bus connections from Bangkok's Northern terminal (1 hr) and 3 train connections each day from the capital's Hualamphong station.*

Bang Sai
The **Royal Folk Arts and Crafts Centre** is based north of Bangkok at Amphoe (district) Bang Sai, around 24 km from Bang Pa-In, and covers an area of nearly 50 ha. Local farmers are trained in traditional arts and crafts such as basketry, weaving and wood carving. The project is funded by the Royal Family in an attempt to keep alive Thailand's traditions. Visitors are offered a glimpse of traditional life and technologies. All products – artificial flowers, dolls, silk and cotton cloth, wood carvings, baskets and so on – are on sale. Other attractions at Bang Sai include a freshwater aquarium and a bird park. ■ *Tue-Sun, 0830-1600. ₿50, ₿30 children. T366666, bangsai@wnet.net.th Getting there: by bus from the Northern bus terminal, or by boat up the Chao Phraya.*

Khao Yai is Thailand's oldest national park and one of the most accessible, lying only 165 km northeast of Bangkok. ■ *Getting there: 3 hrs by car. Regular connections by bus from the Northern bus terminal to Pak Chong. From here there are regular buses into the park.*

Khao Yai National Park

A Thai 'cultural village' spread over 15 ha of landscaped tropical grounds, 32 km west of Bangkok. Most people go for the cultural show – elephants at work, Thai classical dancing, Thai boxing, hilltribe dancing and a Buddhist ordination ceremony. The resort also has a hotel, restaurants, a swimming pool and tennis courts, as well as a golf course close by. ■ *Mon-Sun, 0800-1800. The cultural show is at 1445 Mon-Sun ฿300. (Bangkok office: 195/15 Soi Chokchai Chongchamron Rama III Rd, T2953261). Daily tour from Bangkok, half day (afternoons only).*

Rose Garden

The ancient city of Nakhon Pathom, less than 70 km from Bangkok, can be reached on a day trip from the capital, whether by train or road, and makes a nifty getaway from the madness of the city. While the Bangkok effect is noticeable even in Nakhon Pathom, the town does still have a provincial charm which makes it a refreshing counterpoint to the capital. For more information see page 518. ■ *Getting there: the train station is to the north of the fruit market, an easy walk to/from the chedi. Regular connections with Bangkok's Hualamphong station, 1 hr. A/c buses also stop to the north of the fruit market, and there are regular connections (every 15 mins) with Bangkok's Southern bus terminal, 1-2 hrs.*

Nakhon Pathom

Situated 122 km northwest of Bangkok, Kanchanaburi is famous for its proximity to the Bridge over the River Kwai – built at such human cost during the Second World War. This is also an area of great natural beauty and is a good jumping-off point for visits to national parks, trips on the River Kwai or excursions to one of a number of waterfalls and caves. ■ *Getting there: the State Railways of Thailand offer a worthwhile all-day tour from Bangkok to Kanchanaburi on weekends and holidays. There are also regular buses from Bangkok's Southern bus terminal, 2-3 hrs.*

Kanchanaburi
See also page 521

Chachoengsao is not on very many visitors' itineraries. However, as it lies just 1½ hours from Bangkok by train or bus, it makes a nifty day excursion from the capital - and offers an insight into 'traditional' Thailand. Chachoengsao lies on the Bang Pakong River, to the east of the capital, and has almost been engulfed by fast-expanding Bangkok. Nonetheless, old-style shophouses and restaurants, as well as some evidence of a much more rustic past, remain. The old heart of the town is near the confluence of the Bang Pakong River and Khlong Ban Mai, on Supakit Road. **Ban Mai market** is worth exploring not for its wares - the main market has moved into the centre of the new town - but for its traditional architecture. A concrete footbridge over Khlong Ban Mai links the two halves of the old market. A Chinese clan house reveals the largely Chinese origin of the population of the market area; most arrived before the outbreak of the Second World War. **Wat Sothorn Woramahavihan** is the town's best known monastery and it contains one of the country's most revered images of the Buddha, Luang Por Sothorn. The image is linked with a revered monk, Luang Por Sothorn, and is said to have magical powers. The monastery is a little over 2 km south of Sala Changwat (the Provincial Hall), on the banks of the Bang Prakong. Most people come here for the day; however, there is a range of hotels for those who might want to remain overnight. The most luxurious are on the edge of town - the *Grand Royal Plaza* (T038-513515) and the *Wang Tara Princess* (T038-512565). There is also a handful of quite serviceable places, some with air conditioning, more centrally positioned in town;

Chachoengsao

recommended are *River Inn* (largely for its position, on the river - T038-511921) and the slightly cheaper *Chachoengsao Hotel*. The best restaurants in town are strung out along Marupong Road which runs along the bank of the river. Specialities are prawn (this is a centre of production) and fish dishes. The *Koong Nang Restaurant* is one of the best known. Trains leaves from Hualamphong station between 0510 and 1805 and the journey takes one hour 40 minutes. Buses depart from both the Mor Chit and Ekkamai terminals but it is quickest from Ekkamai – about two hours, depending on the traffic.

Phetburi   The ancient city of Phetburi lies 160 km southwest of Bangkok. It can just be visited in a day from the capital (see page 542). ■ *Getting there: by bus from the Southern bus terminal (2 hrs) or by train from Hualamphong station, 2½ hrs.*

Hua Hin   Hua Hin, a beach resort, lies 230 km south of Bangkok. It is accessible as a day tour by either bus from the Southern terminal, 3½ hours, or by train from Hualamphong station, 3½-4 hours (see page 550).

Safari World   This is a 300-acre complex in Minburi, 9 km from the city centre, with animals and an amusement park. Most of the animals are African – zebras, lions, giraffes – and visitors can either drive through in their own (closed) vehicles or take one of the park's air-conditioned coaches. There is also a marine park and a bird park. ■ *Mon-Sun 0900-1700. ฿600, ฿360 (children). T5181000, www.safariworld.com Getting there: bus no 26 from the Victory Monument to Minburi where a minibus service runs to the park.*

Siam Water Park   Water World (with artificial surf, fountains, waterfalls and shutes), theme park, zoo, botanical gardens and fair all rolled into one. Thirty minutes east of town, or one hour by bus 26 or 27 from Victory Monument. ■ *Mon-Fri 1000-1800, Sat-Sun 0900-1900 ฿200. 101 Sukhapibarn 2 Rd, Bangkapi, T5170075. Getting there: bus nos 26 and 27 from the Victory Monument.*

Tours

See also Tour operators, page 164   Bangkok has innumerable tour companies that can take visitors virtually anywhere (see page 164 for a listing). If there is not a tour to fit your bill – most run the same range of tours – many companies will produce a customized one for you, for a price. Most top hotels have their own tour desk and it is probably easiest to book there (arrange to be picked up from your hotel as part of the deal). The tours given below are the most popular; prices per person are about ฿400-800 for a half day, ฿1,000-2,000 for a full day (including lunch).

Half-day tours   *Grand Palace Tour*; *Temple Tour* to Wat Traimitr, Wat Pho and Wat Benjamabophit; *Khlong Tour* around the *khlongs* (canals) of Bangkok and Thonburi, to Floating Market, Snake Farm and Wat Arun (mornings only); *Old City Tour*; *Crocodile Farm Tour*; *Rice Barge and Khlong Tour* (afternoons only); *Damnoen Saduak Floating Market Tour*.

Full-day tours   *Damnoen Saduak and Rose Garden*; *Thai Dinner and Classical Dance*, eat in traditional Thai surrounding and consume toned-down Thai food, ฿250-300, 1900-2200. *Pattaya*, the infamous beach resort; *River Kwai*, a chance to see the famous Bridge over the River Kwai and war cemeteries, as well as the great chedi at Nakhon Pathom; *Ayutthaya and Bang Pa-In*. There are also boat tours to Ayutthaya and Bang Pa-In (see below).

A number of so-styled 'alternative' tour companies are springing up in Bangkok. One of the best is run by the Thai Volunteer Services' (TVS) *Responsible Ecological and Social Tour (REST)* project. TVS is a non-governmental organization with links to other up-country NGOs. People visit and stay in rural villages, go trekking and camping, are shown round local development projects and are encouraged to participate in community activities. Costs are around ฿3,000-4,000 for a three- to four-day tour. Contact T6910437/ 6910438. Another similar, and also recommended firm is *Alternative Tour*, 14/1 Soi Rajatapan, Rajaprarop Road, T2452963, F2467020, which offers excellent 'alternative' tours, enabling visitors to see the 'real' Thailand, and not just tourist sights.

Alternative tours

There are more than 30 boats (in addition to the *hang yaaws* and regular ferries) offering cruises on the Chao Phraya. The *Oriental Queen* sails up the Chao Phraya River daily from the *Oriental Hotel* to the old capital, Ayutthaya, returning to Bangkok by air-conditioned bus, ฿1,550 (children 3-10 years old, ฿900), 0800-1700 with mediocre lunch (T2360400). The tour includes rather hurried visits to Bang Pa-In, Wat Phra Sri Sanphet and Wat Khun Inthapramun. The *Ayutthaya Princess* operates from the *Shangri-La Hotel* pier or the *Royal Sheraton* pier. The *Ayutthaya Princess* is a two-level vessel resembling a Royal Barge. Leaving at 0800 daily, there are cruises to Bang Pa-In, an air-conditioned bus tour around Ayutthaya, returning to Bangkok by coach at 1730. You can also do the reverse: coach to Ayutthaya and then a boat back to Bangkok, arriving at 1730, ฿1,100, including buffet lunch on board. (Kian Gwan Building, 140 Wireless Road, T2559200.)

Boat tours

Mekhala is operated by the *Siam Exclusive Tours* on the same route. The difference is that *Mekhala* leaves Bangkok in the late evening and puts ashore for one night in Ayutthaya, supplying a romantic dinner on deck. The *Mekhala* fleet consists of three converted rice barges accommodating 12-16 passengers in six air-conditioned cabins with attached bathrooms. The barge arrives in Ayutthaya at Wat Kai Tia in the evening and departs the following morning for Bang Pa-In. To visit other sights, passengers are transferred to a long-tailed boat. An air-conditioned minibus transports passengers back to Bangkok. The reverse, proceeding by road up to Ayutthaya/Bang Pa-In and returning on the rice barge, is also available ฿5,290 (single), ฿4,200 (twin). Book through travel agents or *Siam Exclusive Tours*, Building One, seventh floor, 99 Witthayu Road, T2566153, F2566665. Cheaper are the day boat tours to Bang Pa-In via Queen Sirikit's handicraft centre at Bang Sai and the stork sanctuary at Wat Phai Lom operated by the *Chao Phraya Express Boat Company*. Tours leave on Saturday and Sunday only from the Maharaj and Phra Athit piers at 0800 and 0805 respectively, returning 1530, ฿180 or ฿240, T2225330.

Another company offering a professional cruise service is *Pearl of Siam* which operates three 'yachts'. Like other companies, they offer passengers either a bus trip up to Ayutthaya and a cruise down, or vice versa (฿1,600). In the evenings the company also offer dinner cruises for ฿1,100.

Chao Phraya, T4335453; *Loy Nava*, T4374932, ฿700. *Wanfah Cruise*, T4335453, ฿650. *Ayutthaya Princess*, T2559200 organizes Sunday dinner cruise for ฿850.

Dinner cruises

Cycling tours around Thailand, tailored to different fitness levels. T9900274, tanin@cyclingthailand.com, www.cyclingthailand.com
Bird tours Monthly field trips to the best birding spots in the country with the Bird Conservation Society of Thailand, T9435965, bcst@box1.a-net.th
Nature trails, T3746610, ntrails@samart.co.th, www.ntrails.co.th

Specialist tours

Train tours The State Railway of Thailand organize day trips to Nakhon Pathom (see page 123) and the Bridge over the River Kwai and to Ayutthaya (see page 122). Both trips run on weekends and holidays. The latter tour leaves Bangkok at 0630 and returns from Ayutthaya by boat along the Chao Phraya River.

International For organizing visas to Vietnam, Laos, Cambodia and Burma, see page 164.

Essentials

Sleeping

See inside front cover for price codes

Bangkok offers a wide range of accommodation at all levels of luxury. There are a number of hotel areas in the city, each with its own character and locational advantages (and disadvantages). Accommodation has been divided into five such areas with a sixth – 'other' – for the handful situated elsewhere. A new type of hotel which has emerged in Bangkok in recent years is the 'boutique' hotel. These are small, with immaculate service, and represent an attempt to emulate the philosophy of 'small is beautiful'.

For the last few years Bangkok has had a glut of hotel rooms – especially 5-star – as hotels planned during the heady days of the late 1980s and early 1990s have opened. Many hotels will offer considerable discounts off the rack rate. Advertisements in the *Bangkok Post* may provide some heavily discounted rates in some more upmarket hotels.

NB For business women travelling alone, the *Oriental*, *Dusit Thani* and *Amari Airport* hotels allocate floors to women travellers, with all-female staff.

Many of the more expensive places to stay are on the **Chao Phraya River** with its views, good shopping and access to the old city. Running eastwards from the river are **Silom** and **Surawong** roads, in the heart of Bangkok's business district and close to many embassies. The bars of Patpong link the two roads. This is a good area to stay for shopping and bars, but transport to the tourist sights can be problematic. Not far to the north of Silom and Surawong roads, close to Hualamphong (the central railway station), is **Chinatown**. This, as one might expect, is a place of feverish commercial activity. There are a handful of hotels and guesthouses here – but it remains very much an alternative location to the better established accommodation centres. A more recently developed, but now well-established area is along **Sukhumvit Road** running east from Soi Nana Nua (Soi 3). The bulk of the accommodation here is in the **A-B** range, and within easy reach is a wide range of restaurants, bars, and reasonable shopping. The hotels are a long taxi or tuk-tuk ride from the sights of the old city, but the long-tailed boats which race along the *khlongs* (canals) provide access in under 20 mins to the historic centre. The journey is cheap and thrilling. There is a pier near the far end of Soi Nana Nua (Soi 3) (see map, page 134). In the vicinity of **Siam Square** are a handful of deluxe hotels and several 'budget' class establishments (especially along Rama 1 Soi Kasemsan Nung). Siam Square is central, a good shopping area, with easy bus and taxi access to Silom and Sukhumvit roads and the sights of the Old City. The main concentration of guesthouses is along and around **Khaosan Road** (an area known as Banglamphu, within walking distance of the Grand Palace). There is a second, smaller and quieter cluster of guesthouses just north of Khaosan Road, at the northwest end of **Sri Ayutthaya Road**. A third concentration of budget accommodation is on **Soi Ngam Duphli**, off Rama IV Road. These hotel areas encompass about 90% of Bangkok's accommodation, although there are other places to stay scattered across the city; these are listed under **Other**, page 141.

Development has not abated, with still more skyscrapers under construction. It is also home to one of the world's best-known red-light districts – Patpong. The opening of the Skytrain has made Silom more accessible to other parts of the city too: the line runs north through Siam Square to Mor Chit and the Weekend Market while another line runs east along Sukhumvit Road.

Silom, Surawong & the river

■ on map, page 128. This area most resembles a western city, with its international banks, skyscrapers, first-class hotels, shopping malls, pizza parlours & pubs

Bangkok

L *Dusit Thani*, 946 Rama IV Rd, T2360450, F2366400, dusitbkk@dusit.com A/c, restaurants, disappointing pool. When it was built, the *Dusit Thani* was the tallest building in Bangkok. Still excellent, it has been continually refurbished and upgraded. Recently played host to several celebrities, including boy band wonders *Ultra*. Excellent service and attention to detail. Recommended. **L** *Evergreen Laurel Hotel*, 88 Sathorn Nua, T2669988, F2667222, elhbkk@loxinfo.co.th A/c, restaurants, pool, looks somewhat undersized compared to some of the newer high-rise blocks. Taiwanese-owned, all facilities and excellent service. **L** *Montien*, 54 Surawong Rd, T2337060, F2365219, montien@kscl5.th.com A/c, restaurants, pool, one of the first high-rise hotels (opened 1967) with good location for business, shopping and bars, slick service, and continuing good reputation with loyal patrons. **L** *Oriental*, 48 Soi Oriental, Charoen Krung, T2360400, F2361937, www.mandarin-oriental.com A/c, restaurants, pool, one of the best hotels in the world, beautiful position overlooking the river, superb personal service despite its size (400 rooms). The hotel claims that Joseph Conrad, Somerset Maugham and Noel Coward all stayed here at one time or another, although the first of these probably did not – he lived aboard his ship or, perhaps, stayed in the now defunct *Universal Hotel*. Good shopping arcade, programme of 'cultural' events, 6 excellent restaurants, and a spa on the other side of the river opposite the hotel. Some of the equipment and bathrooms could be said to be a little old, however the hotel still comes highly recommended. **L** *Peninsula Hotel*, 333 Charoen Nakhon Rd, T8612888, Although not strictly in this Silom/Surawong area, it can be easily reached by river taxi or via Taksin Bridge. The latest newcomer to the 5-star scene; 370 stylish, sumptuous rooms with river views, mood lighting, CD players and 'hand-crafted' furniture. **L** *Royal Orchid Sheraton*, 2 Captain Bush Lane, Si Phraya Rd, T2660123, F2368320, rosht@mozart.inet.co.th A/c, restaurants, pool. At times strong and rather unpleasant smell from nearby *khlong*, lovely views over the river, and close to River City Shopping Plaza (good for antiques). Rooms are average at this price but service is very slick. **L** *Shangri-La*, 89 Soi Wat Suan Plu, Charoen Krung, T2367777, F2368579. A/c, restaurants, lovely pool, and great location overlooking the river. This hotel is preferred by some to the *Oriental* although others consider it dull and impersonal. Claims to be in the Top 10 World Hotels and is certainly an excellent hostelry. Recommended. **L** *The Westin Banyan Tree*, 21/100 Sathorn Tai Rd, T6791200, F6791199, www.westin-bangkok.com A/c, restaurant, pool and health spa. New hotel and the tallest in Bangkok – the spa on the 51st-54th floors has stunning views. It is targetting the business traveller, all rooms are suites with working area, in-room fax and copier, computer port and voice mail. Good location for central business district and set back from busy Sathorn Rd. The atmosphere is quiet sophistication. Recommended. **L-AL** *Holiday Inn Crowne Plaza*, 981 Silom Rd, T2384300, F2385289, admin@hicp-bkk.com A/c, restaurants, pool, vast, pristine marble-filled hotel, all amenities, immensely comfortable, minimum atmosphere and character. **L-AL** *Sukhothai*, 13/3 Sathorn Tai Rd, T2870222, F2874980, beaufort@kscll.th.com A/c, restaurants (especially good poolside Italian restaurant), pool, beautiful rooms and excellent service. The design is clean and elegant, what might be termed Thai postmodern, and there are those who say it is even better than such established hotels as *The Regent* or even *The Oriental*. Since it opened a few years back it has become the favourite place to stay for regular visitors to Bangkok with deep pockets – the fact that their ads don't even bother with an address says it all. Recommended.

Bangkok

AL *Marriott Royal Garden Riverside Hotel*, 257/1-3 Charoen Nakorn Rd, T4760021, F4761120, www.marriott.com A/c, restaurant, excellent swimming pool, almost resort-like, very spacious surroundings with over 10 acres of grounds. On the other side of the river from the *Oriental Hotel*, near the Krung Thep Bridge, with free shuttle-boat service every half an hour between hotel and the *Oriental* and River City piers. Attractive low-rise design with some attempt to create Thai-style ambience. *Trader Vic's* is situated here. **AL** *Menam*, 2074 Charoen Krung, T2891148, F2911048. A/c, restaurant, pool, good value for river-view rooms but inconvenient location; shuttle-boat makes sightseeing easier. **AL** *Monarch Lee Gardens*, 188 Silom Rd, T2381991, F2381999, monarch@ksc9.th.com A/c, restaurants, pool, stark and gleaming high-tech high-rise, all facilities, still trying hard to attract custom, discounts available. **AL** *Pan Pacific Hotel*, 952 Rama IV Rd, T6329000, F6329001, panpacificbkk@loxinfo.co.th A/c, restaurant, pool, 235 room hotel, good central position for business and shopping. **AL** *Sheraton Grande Sukhumvit*, Sukhumvit Rd, T6530333, F6530400, sheraton-sukhumvit@ittsheraton.com A bronzed, gilded affair offering the usual range of international hotel services, opposite the *Delta Grande*. **AL** *Tantawan Place*, 119/5-10 Surawong Rd, T2382620, F2383228, tantawan@mozart.inet.co.th A/c, restaurant, pool, good service and rooms. Recommended. **AL** *Tawana Ramada*, 80 Surawong Rd, T2360361, F2363738, twnaa@loxinfo.co.th A/c, restaurant, pool, average hotel given the stiff competition at this grade. **A** *Mandarin*, 662 Rama IV Rd, T2380230, F2343363. A/c, restaurant, small pool, friendly atmosphere, comfortable rooms, popular nightclub. **A** *Silom*

Silom & Surawong

Related maps
A Soi Ngam Duphli, page 130
Bangkok general, page 86

N

0 metres 200
0 yards 200

To Menam Hotel

■ Sleeping

1 Dusit Thani *B4*
2 Evergreen Laurel *C4*
3 Holiday Inn *C2*
4 Mandarin *A3*
5 Manohra *B2*

6 Monarch Lee Gardens *B3*
7 Montien *A3*
8 Narai *B3*
9 New Peninsula *B2*
10 Oriental *B1*
11 Pan Pacific *B4*

12 Peninsula *B1*
13 River City Guesthouse *B2*
14 River View Guesthouse *A1*
15 Rose *A3*
16 Royal Orchid Sheraton *B1*
17 Shangri-La *C1*

Plaza, 320 Silom Rd, T2368441, F2367566. A/c, restaurant, small pool, caters mainly for East Asian tour groups, central but characterless, gently decaying. **A** *Silom Street Inn*, 284/11-13 Silom Rd, opposite the junction with Pan Rd (between Sois 22 and 24), T2384680, F2384689. A/c, restaurant, pool, small hotel, 30 well equipped but small rooms with CNN News, grubby and rather seedy lobby, set back from the road. **A** *Silom Village Inn*, 286 Silom Rd, T6356816, F6356817. Part of the Silom Village Shopping Complex, nothing to separate it from the masses, and not especially good value. **A** *Tower Inn*, 533 Silom Rd, T2378300, F2378286, towerinn@box1.a.net.th A/c, restaurant, pool, simple but comfortable hotel, with large rooms and an excellent roof terrace, good value. **A** *Trinity Place*, 150 Silom Soi 5, T2380052, F2383984. A/c, restaurant, pool, attractive, small hotel. **A-B** *Narai*, 222 Silom Rd, T2370100, F2367161, narai@marai.com A/c, restaurant, pool, rather non-descript, with cold, marble-clad lobby and small rooms.

B *Collins House (YMCA)*, 27 Sathorn Tai Rd, T2871900, F2871996. A/c, restaurant, large pool. Set back from Sathorn Tai Rd, clean, excellent value and friendly management. Not particularly central for sights and shopping but it is only a 10-15 min walk to the Sala Daeng Skytrain station. **B** *Manohra*, 412 Surawong Rd, T2345070, F2665411. A/c, coffee shop, small pool, unattractive rooms, mediocre service. **B** *New Peninsula*, 295/3 Surawong Rd, T2343910, F2365526. A/c, restaurant, small pool, small rooms. **B** *River City Guesthouse*, 11/4 Charoen Krung Soi Rong Nam Khang 1, T2351429, F2373127. A/c, not very welcoming but rooms are spacious and

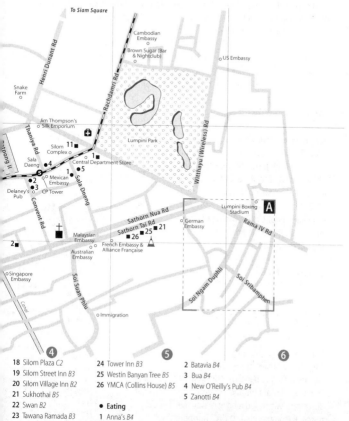

clean, good bathrooms, short walk to River City and the river. **B** *Rose*, 118 Surawong Rd, T2668268, F2668096. A/c, restaurant, pool, opposite Patpong, favourite among single male visitors, but getting seedier by the month. **B** *Swan*, 31 Charoen Krung Soi 36, T2348594. Some a/c, great position, clean but scruffy rooms.

Chinatown
■ *on Chinatown map, page 106, unless otherwise stated*

A *Grand China Princess*, 215 Yaowarat Rd, T2249977, F2247999, gcphotel@loxinfo.co.th High-rise block mainly catering to the Asian market, with choice of Asian cuisine, business facilities, fitness centre (but no pool).

C *Chao Phya Riverside Guesthouse*, 1128 Songwat Rd (opposite the Chinese school), T2226344, F2231696. Some a/c, old-style house overlooking river, clean rooms, atmospheric, unusual location in commercial Chinatown with *sip lors* (10-wheelers) loading rice, and metal workers fashioning steel. Seems to be a little more run-down than a few years back and characteristically brusque management but worth considering for its position and ambience. **C** *River View Guesthouse*, 768 Songwad Soi Panurangsri, T2345429, F2375771 (see map page 128). Some a/c, the restaurant/bar is on the top floor and overlooks the river, food is mediocre. Noisy and rather dirty, some rooms with balconies, some with hot water, overlooking (as the name suggests) the river. This hotel is worth considering for its location away from the bulk of hotels, close to the river. Reasonably good value too.

D *Moon Hotel*, Mahachai Rd, T2357195. A rabbit warren of cellular a/c rooms joined by damp corridors, excellent value however. **D-E** *Golden Inn Guesthouse*, Mahachai Rd, no telephone, excellent situation in the heart of Chinatown. Dark rooms and very noisy, but then this is Chinatown.

Soi Ngam Duphli
■ *on map. Good for the shopping & bars of Silom Rd but inconvenient for many main sights in the old city*

Soi Ngam Duphli is much the smaller of Bangkok's 2 main centres of guesthouse accommodation. Generally, the area is rather rundown these days and nowhere near as happening as Banglamphu. The only exception is *Charlie's*, which is good value. After *Charlie's*, the other places worth considering (at our last visit) are *Lee 3*, *Lee 4*, *Madam* and *Sala Thai*.

AL *Pinnacle Hotel*, 17 Soi Ngam Duphli, T2870111, F2873420. Clean and pleasant rooms with all mod cons, helpful staff, restaurant, nightclub. **B-C** *Malaysia*, 54 Rama IV, Soi Ngam Duphli, T6797127, F2871457, malaysia@ksc15.th.com A/c, restaurant, pool. Once a Bangkok favourite for travellers but now rather seedy and not great value.

C *Charlie's House*, Soi Saphan Khu, T6798330, F6797308. According to its own PR, this place is not a hotel, nor a guesthouse, but a home. It lives up to this description. The owners are helpful, the atmosphere is friendly, the rooms are carpeted and very clean. This is the probably the best place in Soi Ngam Duphli if you are willing to pay that little bit extra. There is a restaurant and coffee corner downstairs with good food at reasonable prices. Recommended. **D** *ETC*, northern

Soi Ngam Duphli

■ **Sleeping**
1	Anna	8	Lee 3
2	Charlie's House	9	Lee 4
3	ETC	10	Madam
4	Freddy 2	11	Malaysia
5	Honey House	12	Pinnacle
6	Lee 1	13	Sala Thai
7	Lee 2	14	TTO

0 metres 100
0 yards 100

end of Soi Ngam Duphli, T2869424, F2871478, etc@mozart.inet.co.th Big, clean rooms with nice sitting area on the fourth floor, but the management are a little *laissez faire*. Price includes breakfast. **D** *Honey House*, 35/2-4 Soi Ngam Duphli, T2863460. An interesting building architecturally. Big and clean rooms with attached bathrooms, some with small balconies, but sloppy management. **D** *Sala Thai Guesthouse*, Soi Saphan Khu, T2871436. At end of peaceful – almost leafy – soi, clean rooms, family run, good food, shared bathrooms. Recommended. **D** *TTO*, 2/48 Soi Sribamphen, T2866783, F2871571. Some a/c, well-run and popular. Homely atmosphere, with only 8 reasonably sized rooms all with attached bathrooms. Not particularly good value, however. **D-E** *Lee 3*, 13 Soi Saphan Khu, T2863042. Some a/c. Wooden house with character, down quiet soi, rooms are clean, shared bathrooms. Recommended. **D-E** *Madam*, 11 Soi Saphan Khu, T2869289. Wooden house, friendly atmosphere, attached bathrooms, no hot water, quiet. Recommended.

E *Lee 2*, 21/38-39 Soi Ngam Duphli, T2862069. Dirty and with sometimes hostile staff. **E** *Lee 4*, 9 Soi Saphan Khu, T2867874. Spotless rooms and bathrooms, some with balconies and views over the city. Recommended. **E-F** *Anna*, 21/30 Soi Ngam Duphli, clean rooms, some with bathrooms, travel desk downstairs. **E-F** *Lee 1*, Soi Sribamphen. OK for what you pay, quite clean, but nothing special. Asian toilets. **F** *Freddy 2*, Soi Sribamphen (next door to *Lee 1*), full on our last visit, so it must be popular. Similar to *Lee 1*.

L *Grand Hyatt Erawan*, 494 Rachdamri Rd, T2541234, F2546308, erawan@ksc.g.th.com The replacement hotel for the much-loved *Erawan Hotel*. A towering structure with grandiose entrance and a plastic tree-filled atrium plus sumptuous rooms and every facility. The hotel is hard to fault in its range of services but old hands maintain it has none of the atmosphere of the old *Erawan*. The *Spasso Restaurant/Club* here is very popular and very pricey. **L** *Novotel*, Siam Square Soi 6, T2556888, F2551824, novotel@ksc.th.com A/c, restaurant, pool, undistinguished but comfortable with a good location in the heart of Siam Square. **L** *Siam Intercontinental*, 967 Rama I Rd, T2530355, F2544388, bangkok@interconti.com A/c, restaurants, small pool, relatively low-rise hotel with a central position yet set in an amazing 11 ha (26 acres) of grounds. Good sports facilities and excellent service. A real haven in over-bearing Bangkok. **L-AL** *Hilton*, 2 Witthayu Rd, T2530123, F2536509, www.hilton.com, bkkhitw@lox2.loxinfo.co.th A/c, restaurants, attractive pool. An excellent hotel set in lovely grounds with a remarkable garden feel for a hotel that is so central. Comparatively small for such a large plot first-class service, good restaurants, attractive rooms, a great hotel. In addition, US$1 is deducted for the WWF to salve environmental consciences and make you feel good about using all those towels. Recommended. **L-AL** *Imperial*, 6-10 Witthayu Rd (on the edge of Siam Square area), T2540023, F2533190. A/c, restaurants, pool, lovely grounds but hotel seems rather jaded next to Bangkok's newer upstarts. 370 rooms and numerous bars and restaurants where, apparently, it is possible to rub shoulders with the city's 'beautiful people'. Partition walls are thin for a hotel of this calibre and recent visitors have been disappointed at how it has declined in quality. **L-AL** *Regent Bangkok*, 155 Rachdamri Rd, T2516127, F2515390, www.regenthotels.com, regent@bkkl.asiaccess.net.th A/c, restaurants (see Thai Restaurants, page 152), pool (although rather noisy, set above a busy road), excellent reputation among frequent visitors who insist on staying here. Stylish and postmodern in atmosphere with arguably the best range of cuisine in Bangkok. It is also perhaps the most impressive piece of modern hotel architecture in Bangkok – which admittedly isn't saying much. Recommended.

Siam Square, Rama I, Ploenchit & Phetburi roads
■ *on map, page 132, unless stated otherwise*

AL *Amari Atrium Hotel* (see map page 134) 1880 New Phetburi Rd, T7182000, F7182002, reservations@atrium.amari.com www.amari.com A/c, restaurants, pool,

Clark Hatch fitness centre, opened early 1996, 600 rooms, all facilities, including babysitting. Reasonably accessible for the airport but not particularly well placed for the sights of the old city or for the central business district. **AL** *Arnoma*, 99 Rachdamri Rd, T2553411, F2553456. A/c, several restaurants, pool, health club, business centre. 403 well-equipped rooms, though much like any others in this price bracket, good location for shopping and restaurants. **AL** *Hotel Mercure*, 1091/336 Phetburi Rd, T2530510, F2530556, mercureb@ksc15.th.com 650 rooms in this rather dated-looking hotel with pool, business centre and health centre. **AL** *Le Meridien President*, 135/26 Gaysorn Rd, T2530444, F2537555, meridien@loxinfo.co.th Pool, health club, 400 rooms in this, one of the older but still excellent luxury hotels in Bangkok (it opened in 1966). Tranquil atmosphere, good service, excellent French food; a new sister hotel, *The President Tower*, was completed in 1996. It towers 36 storeys skywards. The original hotel is still recommended. **AL** *Radisson*, 92 Soi Saengcham, Rama 9 Rd, T6414777, F6414884, radisson@samart.co.th Overblown marble-clad lobby, sells itself as a business hotel, 431 ordinary rooms in this high-rise block, choice of cuisine, bakery, pub and cocktail lounge with good views of the city, fitness centre and pool. **AL** *Siam City*, 477 Sri Ayutthaya Rd, T2470123, F2470165, siamcity@siamhotels.com A/c, restaurants, pool, stylish hotel with attentive staff, large rooms, all facilities (gym, etc) and well managed. Good Mediterranean restaurant and bakery. Recommended.

A *Amari Watergate*, 847 Phetburi Rd, T6539000, F6539045, reservations@watergate.amari.com, www.amari.com A/c, restaurants (including the excellent Thai on 4 – see restaurant section), pool, Clark Hatch fitness centre, squash court, situated close to the Pratunam Market, great freeform pool (which makes swimming lengths a little tricky), but close to 600 rooms makes this a hotel on a grand scale. Lots of marble and plastic trees, uninspired block, good facilities and good value, great views from the

Siam Square & Ploenchit Road

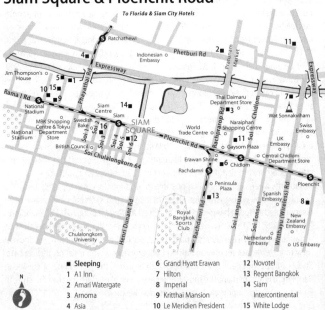

■ Sleeping	6 Grand Hyatt Erawan	12 Novotel
1 A1 Inn	7 Hilton	13 Regent Bangkok
2 Amari Watergate	8 Imperial	14 Siam
3 Arnoma	9 Kritthai Mansion	Intercontinental
4 Asia	10 Le Meridien President	15 White Lodge
5 Bed & Breakfast	& President Tower	16 White Orchid Guesthouse
& Wendy House	11 Mercure	

Related map
Bangkok general,
page 86

0 metres 100
0 yards 100

upper floors on the south side of the building. **A** *Asia*, 296 Phayathai Rd, T2150808, F2154360, techarn@mozart.inet.co.th A/c, several restaurants from different continents (the *Rio Grill* – Brazilian food – has been recommended, with a good and reasonably priced buffet), pool. The jewellers within the hotel is one of the best in Bangkok. Entrance implies a certain degree of sophistication, but rooms are basic and the hotel is situated on a noisy thoroughfare. Overall, this old hotel is showing its age. Good deals available when booking in advance. **A** *Cape House Langsuan*, 43 Soi Langsuan, Ploenchit Rd, T6587444. For anyone not wishing to stay in a hotel, these stylish new serviced apartments make a good alternative. Restaurant, pool, fitness centre and playroom, room service 0600-2400. A good choice for families, as extra beds for under 12's are free. Bookable in the UK 0207 581 8281.

B *Kritthai Mansion*, 931/1 Rama I Rd, T2153042. A/c, restaurant, situated on a noisy thoroughfare. **B** *Florida*, 43 Phayathai Rd, T2470990. A/c, restaurant, pool, one of Thailand's first international hotels – and it shows – average even at this price. **B-C** *Chom's Boutique and Thai Kitchen*, 888/37-39 Ploenchit Rd, T2542070. A/c, central location, good rooms, small boutique hotel. The owner is a well-known chef. **C-D** *A1 Inn*, 25/13 Soi Kasemsan Nung (1), Rama I Rd, T2153029, aoneinn@thaimail.com A/c, well-run, intimate hotel. Recommended. **C-D** *Bed and Breakfast*, 36/42 Soi Kasemsan Nung (1), Rama 1 Rd, T2153004, F2152493. A/c, friendly and efficient staff, clean but small rooms, good security, bright 'lobby', price includes basic breakfast. Recommended. **C-D** *Wendy House*, 36/2 Soi Kasemsan Nung (1), Rama I Rd, T2162436, F2168053. A/c, spotless but small rooms, eating area downstairs, hot water. **C** *White Lodge*, 36/8 Soi Kasemsan Nung (1), Rama I Rd, T2168867, F2168228, pnktour@hotmail.com A/c, hot water, airy, light reasonably sized rooms. Recommended. **C** *White Orchid Guesthouse*, Soi 2 Siam Square, T2552186. 8 small rooms with pleasant atmosphere. **C-E** *Alternative Tour Guesthouse*, 14/1 Rachaprarop Soi Rachatapan, T2452963, F2467020. Friendly, excellent source of information, attached to *Alternative Tour Company*, promoting culturally and environmentally sensitive tourism, clean.

Sukhumvit is not one of Bangkok's traditional centres of tourist accommodation and really only emerged as such in the 1970s. Since then there has been almost continual expansion so that today almost all the facilities that a tourist might need – shops, tour and travel agencies, stalls, bars and restaurants – are to be found here. The main disadvantage of staying in this area is its distance from the main places of interest in the Old City like the Grand Palace, Wat Pho and the National Museum. However it is possible to take a long-tailed boat in under 20 mins from the pier near the far end of Soi Nana Nua (Soi 3) (see map). In addition, the opening of the Skytrain (which runs down Sukhumvit all the way to On Nut) has made the area much more convenient for travel to Siam Square and Silom.

Sukhumvit Rd
■ *on map, page 134*

L *Amari Boulevard*, 2 Sukhumvit Rd Soi 5, T2552930, F2552950, boulevard@amari.com, www.amari.com Great location in the heart of Sukhumvit, good rooms, adequate fitness centre, small pool with terraced Thai restaurant. Popular place with European visitors. **L** *Imperial Queen's Park*, Sukhumvit Soi 22, T2619000, F2619546, reservations@imperialhotels.com A massive hotel with a mind boggling 1,400 rooms. How service can, in any sense, be personal is hard to imagine, but it provides all possible facilities and an excellent French restaurant, *Les Nymphéas*, is also based here. Its remoteness from most sights and the main business district means battling with traffic to do most things. **L** *Landmark*, 138 Sukhumvit Rd, T2540404, F2534259, landmark@mozart.inet.co.th One of the most glamorous hotels in the area. Excellent facilities, 12 restaurants, pool, health centre, smart shopping plaza and business facilities. Terrific views from the 31st floor. Recommended. **L** *Marriott*, 4

Sukhumvit Soi 2, T6567700, F6567711. Extremely elegant, with hints of art-deco design. 4 restaurants, pool, health club and spa, shops, bakery, the works. Recommended. **L** *Windsor Suites*, 8 Sukhumvit Soi 20, T2580160, F2581491, varaport@mozart.inet.co.th A/c, restaurants, pool, next door to the entrance hall has a Paddington-Station ambience, now under new ownership. **AL** *Delta Grand Pacific*, 259 Sukhumvit Rd, T6511000, F2544431, deltabkk@kscll.th.com, www. grandpacifichotel.com A/c, restaurants, pool, a very elegant hotel with a good pool and 4 restaurants. Even the standard rooms are expensive – but better value than the others, as ridiculous price increases are not reflected by a corresponding growth in amenities. **AL** *Rembrandt*, 15-15/1 Sukhumvit Soi 18, T2617100, F2617017, sales @rembrandtbkk.com, www.rembrandtbkk.com A/c, restaurants, pool, lots of marble but limited ambience. Pool, restaurant and usual facilities.

A *Ambassador*, 171 Sukhumvit Rd, T2540444, F2534123, amtelkksc7.th.com A/c, restaurants, pool. Large, impersonal and rather characterless hotel but with great food hall (see Eating, page 142). No email as yet **A** *Comfort, The Promenade*, 18 Sukhumvit Soi 8, T2534116, F2547707. A/c, restaurant, small pool, fitness centre, rather kitsch. **A** *Manhattan*, 13 Sukhumvit Soi 15, T2550166, F2553481. Smart hotel with 3 good, but expensive, restaurants, pool. Lacks character but rooms are comfortable enough. Tours available and tri-weekly cabaret. **A** *The Park*, 6 Sukhumvit Soi 7, T2554300, F2554309.

Sukhumvit Road

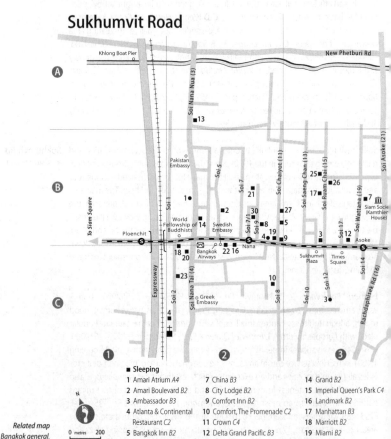

■ **Sleeping**

1 Amari Atrium *A4*	7 China *B3*	14 Grand *B2*
2 Amari Boulevard *B2*	8 City Lodge *B2*	15 Imperial Queen's Park *C4*
3 Ambassador *B3*	9 Comfort Inn *B2*	16 Landmark *B2*
4 Atlanta & Continental	10 Comfort, The Promenade *C2*	17 Manhattan *B3*
Restaurant *C2*	11 Crown *C4*	18 Marriott *B2*
5 Bangkok Inn *B2*	12 Delta Grand Pacific *B3*	19 Miami *B2*
6 Bourbon Street *C4*	13 Grace *A2*	20 Nana *C2*

Related map
Bangkok general,
page 86

0 metres 200
0 yards 200

A/c, restaurant. A peaceful oasis but showing signs of shabbiness and is overpriced given the competition in the area. **A** *Ruamchit*, 199 Sukhumvit Soi 15, T2540205, F2532406. A fairly well-furnished hotel with good views and excellent pool. The staff speak little English and it mainly serves Asian clientele. **A** *Swiss Park*, 23-24 Sukhumvit Soi 11, T2540228, F2540378. A/c, restaurant, excellent roof-top pool, business centre, another overbearing neo-classical hotel, but friendly service. **A** *Tai-pan*, 25 Sukhumvit Soi 23, T2609888, F2597908, taipanbkk@loxinfo.co.th A/c, tastefully decorated with restaurant and pool. **A-B** *Somerset*, 10 Sukhumvit Soi 15, T2548500, F2548538. A/c, restaurant, small but rather ostentatious hotel with shallow indoor pool. Rooms are non-descript but comfortable, bath-tubs are designed for people of small stature. Reception on the second floor.

B *Bourbon Street*, 29/4-6 Sukhumvit Soi 22 (behind Washington Theatre), T2590328, F2594318. A/c, a handful of rooms attached to a good Cajun restaurant. Recommended. **B** *Comfort Inn*, 153/11 Sukhumvit Soi 11, T2519250, F2543562. Small a/c hotel with rather dark, slightly musty rooms, coffee shop and friendly service. **B** *Grace*, 12 Sukhumvit Soi Nana Nua (Soi 3), T2530651, F2530680. A/c, restaurant, pool, bowling alley, disco. Once *the* sex hotel of Bangkok now trying to redeem itself but still overshadowed by its seedy reputation and rather gauche feel. **B** *Grand*, 2/7-8 Sukhumvit Soi Nana Nua (Soi 3), T2549021, F2549020. A/c, small hotel with rather

Bangkok

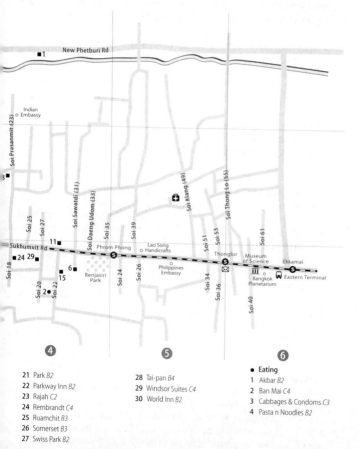

dark rooms, café. **B** *Rajah*, 18 Sukhumvit Soi 2, T2550040. A rather dated hotel but with an attractive pool area, good-value restaurant, travel agents and craft shop. The atrium is reminiscent of the former eastern bloc. **B-C** *Atlanta*, 78 Sukhumvit Soi 2, T2521650. Basic a/c or fan-cooled rooms. A good large pool and a children's pool are a big plus. 'Oiks, lager louts and sex tourists' are requested to go elsewhere! 'Those who cannot behave themselves abroad are advised to stay at home'. Good restaurant, *Señor Pico* (see Eating, page 151). Prides itself on its literary, peaceful atmosphere. Appears to be the cheapest and is certainly the most appealing hotel in the area at this price, particularly suited for families, writers and dreamers, 24-hr email available. Highly recommended. **B-C** *China*, 19/27-28 Sukhumvit Soi 19, T2557571, F2541333. A/c, restaurant, a small hotel masquerading as a large one, but rooms are up to the standard of more expensive places, so good value. Beware the karaoke lounge. **B-C** *City Lodge*, Soi 9 Sukhumvit, T2537705, F2554667, citylodge@amari.com, www.amari.com A fairly smart, small hotel with bright rooms and a personal feel. Good room discounts at time of writing. The absence of a pool is counteracted by free access to the pool at the *Amari Boulevard*. Trendy *Pasta n Noodles* restaurant (see Eating, page 150). **B-C** *Parkway Inn*, 132 Sukhumvit Rd, T2553711, F2542180. Small establishment centred around the bar, which is a cross between an English pub lounge and Thai decor, basic rooms, book exchange. **B-C** *Nana*, 4 Sukhumvit Soi Nana Tai (Soi 4), T2520121, F2551769. A/c, coffee bar, cocktail bar, disco, shops, pool and travel agency. Frequented by dozens of unregistered female guests; like the *Grace*, this hotel has a long-standing reputation for its links with the sex industry.

C *Bangkok Inn*, 12-13 Sukhumvit Soi 11/1, T2544834, F2543545. German management, clean, basic rooms, with a/c, TV and attached shower. **C** *Miami*, 2 Sukhumvit Soi 13, T2530369, F2531266, miamihtl@asiaaccess.net.th A/c, a distinctly run-down hotel, but quite good value considering its central Sukhumvit location. Reasonable pool. **C** *World Inn*, 131 Sukhumvit Soi 7/1, T2535391, F2637728. Basic rooms with the standard TV, minibar and en suite bathroom. Coffee shop with Thai and Western food. **C-D** *Crown Hotel*, Sukhumvit Soi Lahet 29, T2580318, F2584438. Friendly with transport-style café, a/c rooms, nothing special even by backpacker standards. **C-D** *Reno Hotel*, Rama 1 Soi Kasemsan 40, T2150026, F2153430, a/c, laundry, etc, grocery store on site.

Banglamphu (Khaosan Road) & surrounds
■ *on maps, pages 138 & 137 & 140*

Khaosan Road lies northeast of Sanaam Luang, just off Rachdamnern Klang Ave, close to the Democracy Monument. It is continually expanding into new roads and sois, in particular the area west of Chakrapong Rd. The *sois* off the main road are often quieter, such as Soi Chana Songkhran or Soi Rambutri. Note that rooms facing on to Khaosan Rd tend to be very noisy. Khaosan Rd is not just a place to spend the night. Also here are multitudes of restaurants, travel and tour agents, shops, stalls, tattoo artists, bars, bus companies – almost any and every service a traveller might need. (Note that toiletries and bottled water, etc are considerably cheaper in the Thai supermarkets, just outside the main tourist drag.) In general, the guesthouses of Khaosan Rd itself have been eclipsed in terms of quality and cleanliness by those to the north, closer to the river. The useful little post office that used to be at the top of Khaosan Rd and operated a Poste Restante service and a fax facility has recently closed; whether it will reopen is not certain.

AL *Royal Princess*, 269 Lan Luang Rd, T2813088, F2801314, larnluang@dusit.com A/c, restaurants, pool, part of the Dusit chain of hotels, good facilities and good deals if booked through *Vieng Travel*. **A** *Royal*, 2 Rachdamnern Klang Ave, T2229111, F2242083, www.rattanakosin-hotel.com (*Rattanakosin* is the name of the hotel in Thai). A/c, restaurant, pool. Another old (by Bangkok standards) hotel which acted as a refuge for demonstrators during the 1991 riots. Rooms are dated and featureless. This hotel is popular amongst Thais. **A** *Viengtai*, 42 Tanee Rd, Banglamphu, T2805434, F2818153. A/c, restaurant, pool. Rooms here are good, if a little worn, clean and relatively spacious, with all the advantages of this area in terms of proximity to the Old City. Helpful management.

B *Pra Arthit Mansion*, 22 Phra Arthit Rd, T2800744, F2800742. Leafy though slightly dated hotel, popular with German tour operators. Rooms are good value with all the trimmings. Well-run with helpful management. **B** *Trang Hotel*, 99/1 Visutkaset Rd, T28221414, F2803610, www.trang-hotel.co.th A/c, restaurant, pool. Clean and friendly mid-range hotel which comes recommended by regular visitors to Bangkok. It opened way back in 1962 but is still a good establishment at this price. Discount vouchers available from *Vieng Travel* in the same building, with breakfast included.

C *New Siam*, Phra Arthit 21 Soi Chana Songkram, T2824554, F2817461. Some a/c, good restaurant, modern and clean, friendly and helpful staff, airy rooms, but featureless block with scarcely an ounce of atmosphere. Extensive services include tickets and tour information, fax facilities, email, lockers available. Quiet and a popular place – but it remains overpriced. **C-E** *Baan Sabai*, 12 Soi Rongmai, T6291599, F6291595, baansabai@hotmail.com A large, colonial style building with a green pillared

Bangkok

Banglamphu & Ayutthaya Road

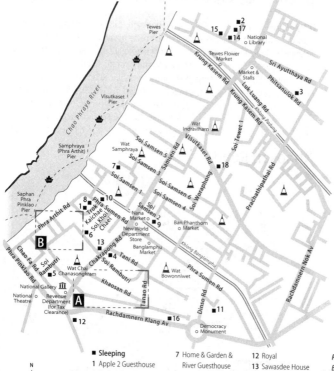

■ Sleeping

1 Apple 2 Guesthouse
2 Backpacker's Lodge
3 Bangkok Youth Hostel
4 BK Guesthouse
5 Chai's House
6 Chusri Guesthouse

7 Home & Garden & River Guesthouse
8 KC Guesthouse
9 New World Guesthouse
10 PS Guesthouse
11 Pra Suri Guesthouse

12 Royal
13 Sawasdee House
14 Sawatdee
15 Shanti Lodge
16 Sweety
17 Tavee
18 Trang

Related maps
Bangkok general,
page 86
A Khaosan Road,
page 138
B Phra Arthit
Road, page 140

0 metres 200
0 yards 200

entrance in front. Construction work being done on a new building at the back at the time of writing. Although it is not very expensive, it is not the typical backpacker's scene. Rooms are simple but large and airy. Storage is available at ฿10 per bag/suitcase. Occasionally local Thai bands are invited to play here. **C-E** *Chart Guesthouse*, 58 Khaosan Rd, T2820171. Restaurant, some a/c, majority of rooms are directly over a busy restaurant, so it can be noisy till early in the morning. Some rooms are small and a bit tatty, others are relatively spacious by Khaosan standards, while still others have no windows – so ask to see a range. **C-E** *New World Lodge Hotel and Guesthouse*, 2 Samsen Rd, T2815596 (hotel), T2812128 (guesthouse), F2825614, www. new-lodge.com Some hotel rooms have a/c whereas the guesthouse only offers fans, good location for the Old City yet away from the hurly-burly of Khaosan Rd. Not particularly inviting or characterful, rooms are large but barren and beginning to look worn. The Lodge has satellite TV for a higher price. Safety boxes are free for guests, as is the use of a small but worn-out gym. **C-E** *Sawasdee House*, 147 Chakrapong Soi Rambutri, T2818138, F6290994, sawasdee_house@hotmail.com Feels like a cross between a guesthouse and a hotel. Shared loos and showers are kept clean, and rooms, though box-like, are fine. Outside at the front is an atmospheric, wooden lounging area and beer 'garden'. Cocktails are slightly overpriced, but jazz and reggae music at night may make it worth the extra. This place has all the travellers' trimmings – email, travel service, TV, etc. **C-E** *Sawasdee Krungthep Inn*, 30 Praathi Rd, T6290072, F6290079. Recently opened, with a lively communal atmosphere. Clean and simple rooms, all with cable TV. Family rooms available with 2 double beds for ฿560.

D *My House*, 37 Phra Arthit Soi Chana Songkram, T2829263. Helpful and friendly management, rooms are very clean and the place maintains excellent standards of cleanliness. Popular, good travel service (minibus to airport every hour). **D** *7 Holder*, 216/2-3 Khaosan Rd, T2813682. Some a/c, some rooms a little grubby, but clean shared toilets. Friendly, located on the narrow soi behind Khaosan Rd, so quieter than those places situated right on the street. **D-E** *Arunthai (AT)*, 90/1, 5, 12 Khaosan Soi Rambutri, T2826979. Situated in a quiet little courtyard with 4 or 5 other guesthouses. Rooms are adequate but staff are unfriendly. **D-E** *Buddy*, 137/1 Khaosan Rd, T2824351. Off main street, some a/c, rooms are small and dingy but it remains

Khaosan Road

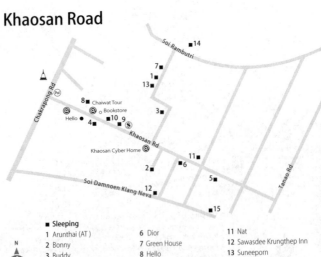

Related map
Bangkok General,
page 86
Banglamphu,
page 137

N

Not to scale

■ **Sleeping**		
1 Arunthai (AT)	6 Dior	11 Nat
2 Bonny	7 Green House	12 Sawasdee Krungthep Inn
3 Buddy	8 Hello	13 Suneeporn
4 Chart Guesthouse	9 Lek	14 Viengtai
5 CH Guesthouse	10 Mam's	15 7 Holder Guesthouse

Khaosan Road: a world of its own

Banglamphu, as the place for backpackers to stay, dates from the mid-1970s. The Viengtai Hotel opened in 1962, and as it gained a reputation for budget accommodation, so some local families began to rent out rooms to tourists. Most of these places were concentrated along Khaosan Road, which as Marc Askew has written in his study The Banglamphu District: a portrait of change in inner Bangkok *(TDRI, 1993), soon became known as Thanon Farang Khaosan. As he explains, and which is evident from first sight: "There is nothing Thai about the character of Khao San Road: everything is for the Farang, from the clothing, the jewellery, to the food. Most local residents in surrounding neighbourhoods tend to keep the road at*

an arms length and do not claim a close familiarity with it ...". Prior to this transformation Khaosan Road was an ordinary street of middle-class Thai educated families, with a commercial specialization of dress-making and tailoring. Today, the tourist focus has spilt over into surrounding streets, particularly to the north and east. The Tourist Authority of Thailand estimated at the beginning of the 1990s that there were 83 guesthouses in the area and that 238,000 tourists stayed in the district each year. The irony perhaps is that the group of tourists which is usually perceived to live closest to the Thai way of living – backpackers – have helped to create a world which is wholly their own.

popular for some reason. Large open restaurant area bustles with people exchanging information. **D-E** *Chai's House*, 49/4-8 Chao Fa Soi Rongmai, last house down Soi Rambutri, so away from the competition, T2814901, F2818686. Some a/c, friendly atmosphere. Rooms are in traditional Thai style, with wood panelling. They vary in size but are clean and the a/c rooms are good value. Colourful with bougainvillea growing from the balconies and bamboos and orchids in the restaurant, making it a cool, quiet and relaxing place to eat. Recommended. **D-E** *CH Guesthouse*, 216/1 Khaosan Rd, T2822023. Some a/c, good reputation, and very popular – fully booked on our last visit, so unable to check the rooms. Probably the cheapest dorm rooms on Khaosan Rd. Left luggage (฿7 per day, ฿40 per week). **D-E** *Green House*, 88/1 Khaosan Soi Rambutri, T2820323. Some a/c. Rooms are spacious but variable, and some can be quite noisy. Helpful staff and a large and airy restaurant with a pleasant sitting area (a/c with TV and books). **D-E** *Hello*, 63-65 Khaosan Rd, T2818719. Some a/c, popular place, which means that we were unable to check rooms on our last visit. Internet café and popular restaurant with big screen downstairs (7 films shown daily). **D-E** *New Merry V*, 18-20 Phra Athit Rd, T2829267, merryv@loxinfo.co.th Adequately sized rooms but many are dark with windows facing onto an unlit shaft within the building (make sure the slats and curtains into the shaft are shut if you don't want to share everything with your neighbours). Excellent baguettes at cheap prices in the restaurant downstairs. **D-E** *Peachy Guesthouse*, 10 Phra Arthit Rd, T2816659. Some a/c, the courtyard – which was its selling point – is starting to look neglected. Rooms are large but dark if you don't have a window, but clean. **D-E** *Pra Suri Guesthouse*, 85/1 Soi Pra Suri (off Dinso Rd), T2801428, F2801428. 5 mins east of Khaosan Rd not far from the Democracy Monument, fan, restaurant, own bathrooms (no hot water), clean, spacious and quiet, very friendly and helpful family-run travellers' guesthouse with all the services to match – videos, travel details, western food. Recommended. **D-E** *Privacy Tourist House*, 69 Tanow Rd, T2814708. Popular, quiet. Recommended. **D-E** *Sawasdee Smile Inn*, 35 Soi Rongmai, T6292340, F6292341. Large, spacious, sitting area in front under a gaudy looking green, Thai-style roof. Restaurant and 24 hr bar, so ask for a room at the back if you want an early night. Rooms are clean and simple, all with cable TV. Free safety boxes available.

E *Dior*, 146-158 Khaosan Rd, T/F2829142. Tiny, dirty rooms, unhelpful staff, avoid.
E *KC Guesthouse*, 60-64 Phra Sumen Rd Soi Khai Chae, T2820618, kc_guesthouse
@hotmail.com Small friendly place with a cosy and personal ambiance. Rooms and
toilets are clean and well kept. Not far enough off the main road to be quiet. **E** *Lek*,
90/9 Khaosan Soi Rambutri, T2812775. Up a long flight of steps off the main road.
Rooms are clean but boxy. Rooms at the front can suffer from the noise of Khaosan Rd.
Helpful staff and friendly atmosphere, popular. **E** *Mam's*, 119 Khaosan Rd. Double
rooms only. Adequately clean, and friendly staff. Some rooms are a little dark and
noisy. **E** *Merry V*, 33-35 Phra Arthit Soi Chana Songkram, T2829267. Clean, tidy and
cheap. Some rooms with good views out over the city from the upper floor balconies,
although not from the rooms (some of which have no windows), which are small and
dirty around the edges. Toilets kept clean. A well run place with good information.
E *Nat*, 217 Khaosan Rd. Small, stuffy rooms which face onto a balcony overhanging
the restaurant (thus noise disturbance into the early hours). **E** *PS Guesthouse*, 9 Phra
Sumen Rd, T2823932. Kept clean and well-run, with good security. Rooms at the back
have windows over the river (but it's not scenic). Some rooms have no windows.
Aligns with main road, so noisy at the front. There is an airy, open restaurant in the
front downstairs that does some of the best filtered coffee in the area (almost everywhere else serves instant sachets of Nescafé). It offers an international and reasonably
priced menu, and guests may help out in the kitchen if they want to learn a bit of Thai
cookery on the side. **E** *Suneeporn*, 90/10 Khaosan Soi Rambutri, T2826887. The
entrance looks like a junk shop, with a ramshackle, characterful appearance. Run by a
friendly old lady who keeps the rooms and toilets clean. Quiet location and recommended by guests. **E** *Sweety*, 49 Thani Rd, T2802191, F2802190, sandwiched
between 2 roads, so noisy. Rooms are large and clean, with adequately clean shared
toilets. **E** *Vimol Guesthouse*, 358 Samsen Soi 4, T2814615. Good value, friendly guesthouse in quiet location, shared bathrooms, good breakfast. **E-F** *Apple 2 Guesthouse*,
11 Phra Sumen Rd, T2811219. Quite hard to find: if you turn off Phra Arthit Rd, take the
soi opposite Baan Chaophraya (with Compost 9 in front of it). If turning off the Phra
Sumen Rd, take Trok Kaichee (soi). Not to be confused with *Apple*, which is grimy and
unfriendly. Very friendly management (run by the same lady for 20 years, who exer-
cises a tough love policy), this place, with
its homely feel and quiet, clean rooms in
an old wooden house, remains a firm
favourite. Dorm beds available.
E-F *Bonny*, 132 Khaosan Rd, T2819877.
Situated down a narrow alley off
Khaosan itself, a quiet location and family-run, but rooms are dirty. Cheap dorm
beds available. **E-F** *Chusri Guesthouse*,
1-2 Soi Rambutri, T2829941,
chusri_gh@hotmail.com Rooms are
very simple, but not particularly clean.
Cheap and open restaurant area in front.
E-F *Green Guesthouse*, 27 Phra Arthit Soi
Chana Songkram, T2828994. Not to be
confused with the *Green House*, rooms
are very small but are clean and cheap.
E-F *Home and Garden*, 16 Samphraya
Rd (Samsen 3), T2801475. Away from the
main concentration of guesthouses,
down a quiet soi, a small house in a
delightful leafy compound and with a
homely atmosphere. The rooms are a fair
size with large windows, some face onto

Phra Arthit Road

■ **Sleeping**
1 Baan Sabai
2 Bella Bella
3 Chusri Guesthouse
4 Green Guesthouse
5 Krungthop Inn
6 Merry V
7 My House

8 New Merry V
9 New Siam
10 Peachy Guesthouse
11 Popiang House
12 Pra Arthit Mansion
13 Rose Garden
14 Sawasdee House
15 Sawasdee Smile Inn

a balcony. Friendly owner and excellent value. Recommended. **E-F** *The River Guesthouse*, 18 Samphraya Rd (Samsen 3), T2800876. A small, family house with a homely and friendly atmosphere. Small but clean rooms. **F** *Clean and Calm Guesthouse*, 17 Samphraya Rd (Samsen 3), T2822093. It may be clean and calm, but this is probably due to the lack of visitors as there is no communal area.

It is a central location with restaurants and foodstalls nearby, but does not suffer the overcrowding and sheer pandemonium of Khaosan Road and so is considerably quieter and more peaceful. It is also close to the Tewes Pier for the express river boats (see the Banglamphu map). The guesthouses are, overall, a little more expensive than those in Khaosan Road but the rooms are better and the places seem to be generally better managed. One family runs 4 of the guesthouses, and with a fifth one opened in late 2000, this means that if one is full you will probably be moved on to another.

Sri Ayutthaya Road
■ *on map, page 137*
Sri Ayutthaya is emerging as an 'alternative' area for budget travellers

Bangkok

D-E *Shanti Lodge*, 37 Sri Ayutthaya Rd, T2812497, F6287626. Reservation necessary during high season. Range of rooms from large a/c rooms to dorm beds for ฿80. Most rooms are housed in an old wooden house full of character. Rooms are clean and cosy and there is an attractive garden. Friendly management. Expensive but good restaurant with extensive menu (and a turtle). Very popular (particularly with long-term guests), good location for bus connections. Recommended. **D-F** *Bangkok Youth Hostel*, 25/2 Phitsanulok Rd (off Samsen Rd), T2820950, F6287416. North of Khaosan Rd, away from the bustle, the dorm beds are great value (฿90) being newly furnished and with a/c. Other rooms are clean, small and basic and remain good value. If you don't have a valid YHA membership card, it will cost an extra ฿50 per night. **D-F** *Tavee*, 83 Sri Ayutthaya Rd, Soi 14, T2825983. Restaurant, a quiet, relaxed, and respectable place with a small garden and a number of fish tanks. Friendly management – a world away from the chaos of Khaosan Rd. The Tavee family keep the rooms and shared bathrooms immaculately clean and are a good source of information for travellers. Dorms are also available for ฿80 per night. This place has been operating since 1985 and has managed to maintain a very high standard. Highly recommended.

E *Backpackers Lodge*, 85 Sri Ayutthaya Rd, Soi 14, T2823231. Very similar to its neighbour, *Tavee* (whose owner is brother of the *Backpackers'* manager). The rooms are a little small but it has friendly service and there is an intimate feel to the place. Quiet and recommended. **E** *Sawatdee*, 71 Sri Ayutthaya Rd, T2825349. Western menu, pokey rooms, popular with German travellers, management brusque and off-hand.

L *Central Plaza Hotel*, 1695 Phahonyothin Rd, T5411234, F5411087, centel @ksc5.th.com Out of town, close to Chatuchak Market, huge 600-room block, pool, fitness centre, tennis, jogging track, 18-hole golf course, extensive business/conference facilities, good location for shopping either in Central Plaza or at the market. **L** *Merchant Court Hotel*, 202 Ratchadapisek Rd, Huay Kwang, T6942222, F6942223, info@merchantcourt-bkk.com, www.raffles-intl.com Recently renovated hotel (which used to be *Le Concorde*), struggling with low occupancy rates, but banking on the opening of the underground by 2002 which will mean a station right outside the hotel and an easy link to the skytrain and other areas of the city. Impeccably high standard, with friendly staff, faultless rooms and good facilities including pool and gym. A spa on the fourth floor will be completed by the time this book goes to press. Meeting rooms and conference amenities also extensive. *Doc Cheng's* restaurant (original one to be found in *Raffles Hotel*, Singapore) provides sumptuous fusion food (see page 152). 24-hr coffee shop and Japanese restaurant. 50% off rack rate through 2001. **A-B** *Ramada Renaissance Bridge View*, 3999 Rama III Rd, T2923160, F2923164. A/c, numerous restaurants, pools, tennis, squash, new 476 room high-rise overlooking Chao Phraya River, all facilities, poor location for sights, shopping and business.

Other
For hotels at, or close to, the airport, see page 37

C-E *The Artists Club*, 61 Soi Tiem Boon Yang, T8620056. Some a/c, run by an artist, this is a guesthouse-cum-studio cum gallery in Thonburi (ie the other side of the river), clean rooms and a really alternative place to stay with concerts and drawing lessons, away from the centre of guesthouse activity.

Eating

See inside front cover for our restaurant price categories. For bars with live music also see Music, page 154

Bangkok has the largest and widest selection of restaurants in Thailand; everyone eats out, so the number of places is vast. Food is generally very good and cheap; this applies not just to Thai restaurants but also to places serving other Asian cuisines and western dishes. Roadside food is good value and many Thais eat on the street, businessmen and civil servants rubbing shoulders with factory workers and truck drivers.

Until a few years ago, with one or two notable exceptions, it was best to recommend that visitors stick to Thai restaurants if they are gastronomes who know their foie gras from their fettucini. This has changed. There is now a good range of excellent restaurants in the city and an increasing number of first-rate foreign chefs.

NB Many restaurants – especially Thai ones – close early (between 2200 and 2230). Many of the more expensive restaurants listed here take credit cards. Not that most bars also serve food. For those with either a large or an empty stomach who want a blow out, a number of restaurants, especially in hotels, offer (usually lunchtime) good-value buffet meals where you can eat till you drop or explode. See the box on page 143 for a listing. For a fuller listing of places to eat see *Bangkok Metro Magazine* or *Bangkok Timeout*, both published monthly. The former is better. Both magazines are also good for bars, music venues, shopping, etc.

Silom, Surawong & the River
See map, page 128

Thai Expensive: *Anna's*, 118 Silom Soi Sala Daeng, T6320619. Great Thai-cum-fusion restaurant in a vegetation-surrounded villa off Silom Rd named after Anna of *King & I* fame. Some classic Thai dishes like *laap*, *nua yaang* and *somtam* along with **fusion** dishes such as Alaska clams and **Western** food including apple crumble and banoffee pie. Refined atmosphere and a good place to linger for coffee and conversation. Open daily 1100-2200. *Benjarong*, *Dusit Thani Hotel*, 946 Rama IV Rd, T2360450. Elegant surroundings, exquisite Thai food, very expensive wines. *Bua Restaurant*, Convent Rd (off Silom Rd). Classy post-modern Thai restaurant with starched white table linen and cool, minimalist lines, the food also reflects the décor (or the other way around?): refined and immaculately prepared. *Bussaracum*, Sethiwan Building, 139 Pan Rd (off Silom Rd), T2666312. Changing menu, popular, classy Thai restaurant with prices to match. Recommended. *Jesters*, *Peninsula Hotel*, 333 Charoen Nakorn Rd, T8611112. Open 1800-0200. Exotic **fusion** cuising (recommended are the crispy duck pancakes arranged like a mini-pagoda). Disappointing desserts. Live music every night except Mon and a dance floor from 2230. Private shuttle boat service between *Peninsula* and *Shangri-la Hotel* Pier until midnight. *Once Upon a Time*, 32 Phetburi Soi 17 (opposite Pantip Plaza), T2528629. Upmarket and inventive Thai cuisine including seafood soufflé in coconut and more traditional dishes like a delectable duck curry. Open for lunch and dinner, Tues-Sun. *Thaniya Garden Restaurant*, Thaniya Plaza, 3rd Floor, Room 333-335, 52 Silom Rd, T2312201. Open Mon-Sat 1100-2200, excellent Thai food and enormous portions.

Mid-range: *Banana Leaf*, Silom complex (basement floor), Silom Rd, T3213124. Excellent and very popular Thai restaurant with some unusual dishes, including *kai manaaw* (chicken in lime sauce), *nam tok muu* (spicy pork salad, Isan style) and fresh spring rolls 'Banana Leaf', along with excellent and classic *laap kai* (minced chicken Isan style), booking recommended for lunch. There are several excellent Thai restaurants in *Silom Village*, a shopping mall, on Silom Rd (north side, opposite Pan Rd), excellent range of food from hundreds of stalls, all cooked in front of you, enjoyable village atmosphere. Recommended. *Ban Krua*, 29/1 Saladaeng Soi 1, Silom Rd.

Buffet meals in Bangkok

The following restaurants offer buffet 'eat all you like' meals. They are often very good value. Phone to check. The prices quoted are 2000 prices; children are usually charged half price or less and under 12s are sometimes allowed to gorge gratis. Daily newspapers also often provide information on new promotions as do listings magazines like Bangkok Timeout.

Sukhumvit Road

Ambassador Café, Ambassador Hotel, T2540444. Buffet Amercian breakfast (฿210), international lunch (฿260) and seafood dinner (฿300).
Grand Pacific Hotel, T6511000. Buffet Sunday brunch (฿480).
Tara Coffee Shop, Imperial Tara Hotel, T2592900. Porridge buffet Monday-Saturday, 1800-2400 (฿200).
Atrium, Landmark Hotel, T2540404. International lunch buffet (฿515).

Silom, Suriwong and Charoen Krung roads

The Pavilion, Dusit Thani Hotel, T2360450. Changing buffet themes, lunch and dinner (around ฿450-500)
Coffee Garden and Mae Nam Terrace,

Shangri-La Hotel, T2367777. Sunday brunch featuring Asian dishes as well as international cuisine (฿625).

Sathorn and Wittayu roads

Café Laurel, Evergreen Laurel Hotel, T2669988. International buffet, Monday-Friday (฿380)
Colonnade Restaurant, The Sukhothai, T2870222. Sunday brunch – one of the classiest (฿950).

Phetburi, Rama 1, Ploenchit and Rachdamri roads

The Garden Bar, Indra Regent Hotel, T2080022. International buffet, daily lunch and dinner.
Sivalai Restaurant, Siam Intercontinental Hotel, T2530355. Special children oriented Sunday brunch (฿450).
The Dining Room, Grand Hyatt Erawan Hotel, T2541234. Sunday brunch, live music (฿650).
The Expresso, Le Royal Meridien Hotel, T6560444. Sunday brunch with live music (฿690).

Sri Ayutthaya Road

Patummat Restaurant, Siam City Hotel, T2470123. Sunday brunch (฿580).

Simple decor, friendly atmosphere, a/c room, traditional Thai food, unfortunately the old garden sitting area has gone. *MK*, Silom Complex, basement, Silom Rd. Thai. Very popular DIY restaurant. *Side Walk*, 855/2 Silom Rd (opposite *Central Dept Store*). Grilled specialities, also serves **French**. Recommended.

Cheap: *Banana House*, Silom Rd/Thaniya Rd (2nd floor). Very good and reasonably priced Thai food; few tourists here but lots of locals. *Isn't Classic*, 154 Silom Rd. Excellent barbecue, king prawns and **Isan** specialities like spicy papaya salad (*somtam*). *Rung Pueng*, 37 Saladaeng, Soi 2, Silom Rd. Traditional Thai food at reasonable prices.

Chinese Mid-range: *Shangarila*, 154/4-7 Silom Rd, T2340861. Bustling **Shanghai** restaurant with *dim sum* lunch.

French Expensive: *La Normandie, Oriental Hotel*, 48 Oriental Avenue, T2360400. **French** food. Despite many competitors, *La Normandie* maintains extremely high standards of cuisine and service (with guest chefs from around the world), jacket and tie required in the evening but the service is still not overbearing. Very refined and while it is expensive for Thailand it is not pricey considering the quality of the food and service – set lunch and dinner menus are the best value. Open Mon-Sat for lunch and dinner and Sun for dinner. Recommended. *Le Bouchon*, 37/17 Patpong 2, T2349109, open daily 1100-0200, **French** country cuisine (Provence), family run, reasonable prices. **Mid-range**: *Le Café de Paris*, Patpong 2 Rd, T2372776. Traditional French food from steaks to pâté. Open for lunch and dinner, daily. Recommended.

Bangkok

 Food courts

If you want a cheap meal with lots of choice, then a food court is a good place to start. They are often found along with supermarkets and in shopping malls. Buy coupons and then use these to purchase your food from one of the many stalls – any unused coupons can be redeemed. A single-dish Thai meal like fried rice or noodles should cost around ฿25-30. The more sophisticated shopping malls will have stalls servings a wider geographical range of cuisines including, for example, Japanese and Korean.

There are food courts in the following (and many more) places:

***Central Plaza Pinkalao's Colosseum Food Centre**, large area with 28 stalls and not much choice.*

***Mah Boon Krong** (MBK), Phayathai Rd (just west of Siam Square, BTS Siam station).*

***Panthip Plaza**, Phetburi Road. 15 years in operation, with 90 stalls and seating for 2,500.*

***Ploenchit Centre**, 2 Ploenchit Road (BTS Nana station).*

***Robinson**, 139 Ratchadapisek Road.*

***Siam Discovery Centre**, Rama 1 Road (BTS Siam station).*

***The Garden Terrace**, The Emporium, 622 Sukhumvit Road (corner of Soi 24), 20 stalls and seating in wooden window booths.*

***United Centre Building**, 323 Silom Road (near intersection with Convent Road, BTS Sala Daeng station).*

***World Trade Centre**, Ratchdamri Road (BTS Chitlom station).*

Indian Mid-range: *Himali Cha Cha*, 1229/11 Charoen Krung, T2351569. Good choice of Indian cuisine, mountainous meals for the very hungry, originally set up by Cha Cha and now run by his son – 'from generation to generation' as it is quaintly put. **Cheap**: *Nawab*, 64/39 Soi Wat Suan Plu, Charoen Krung. **North and South Indian** dishes. *Tamil Nadu*, 5/1 Silom Soi (Tambisa) 11, T2356336. Good, but limited **South Indian** menu, cheap and filling, *dosas* are recommended, there are 4 or 5 **Indian** restaurants in a row on Sukhumvit Soi 11.

Indonesian Mid-range: *Batavia*, 1/2 Convent Rd, T2667164. 'Imported' Indonesian chefs, good classic dishes like *saté*, *gado-gado* (vegetable with peanut sauce and rice) and *ayam goreng* (deep-fried chicken).

Italian Expensive: *Angelini*, Shangri-La Hotel, 89 Soi Wat Suan Plu, T2367777, open 1130 'till late', one of the most popular Italian restaurants in town – a lively place with open kitchens, pizza oven and the usual range of dishes. Menu could be more imaginative. *Zanotti*, 21/2 Sala Daeng Colonnade, Silom Soi Sala Daeng, T6360002. Sophisticated Italian restaurant just off Silom Rd with wide-ranging menu including pizzas and pasta, risotto dishes, meat and poultry, all served in a clean modern atmosphere (no raffia chianti bottles here) with starched table clothes in a renovated early 20th-century building. Open daily for lunch and dinner. **Mid-range**: *Ristorante Sorrento*, 66 North Sathorn Rd (next to the Evergreen Laural Hotel), T2349841. Excellent Italian food along with imported steaks. *Terrazzo*, Sukhothai Hotel, 13/3 South Sathorn Rd, T2870222. Stylish al fresco Italian restaurant overlooking the pool, wonderful Italian breads and good pasta dishes. Recommended.

Mediterranean Expensive: *Tiara*, Dusit Thani Hotel, 946 Rama IV Rd. At the top of the hotel, so excellent views. A long-established Mediterranean restaurant with a limited but sophisticated menu; grilled octopus, stuffed vine leaves, hummus and goats' cheese. Rabbit stew and Mediterranean sausage for the main course. **Mid-range**: *Café Bongo*, 44 Convent Rd, T6320920/2663545(pm). Mediterranean food, trendy place for a younger crowd. Modern décor, the tapas are popular. *Willy 2*, Charn Issara II Building,

New Phetburi Rd, T3082071. Mediterranean food in a lively 'music' café. Long happy hour and live music on Mon nights.

Mexican Cheap: *Tia Maria*, 14/18 Patpong Soi 1, T2588977. For the price, this is the best Mexican restaurant in Bangkok. Nachos, *enchiladas*, *fajitas* and more of the usual. Open daily for lunch and dinner 1100-2300.

Polynesian Expensive: *Trader Vic's*, *Marriott Riverside Hotel*, 257/1-3 Charoen Nakhon Rd, T4760021. Bangkok's only restaurant serving Polynesian food which is sea-food based and takes inspiration from Chinese culinary traditions. Open for lunch and dinner (1200-1400, 1800-0100).

Vietnamese Mid-range: *Sweet Basil* (branch at Sukhumvit also, see above) 1 Silom Soi Srivieng (opposite Bangkok Christian College), T2383088. Vietnamese food in an attractive 1930s house with live music. Open daily for lunch and dinner.

Western Expensive: *The Barbican*, 9/4-5 Soi Thaniya, Thaniya Plaza, Silom Rd, T2343590. Chic café bistro with duck, steaks, sophisticated sandwiches, fish, open 1100-0200, DJ on Thu, Fri and Sat evenings. *T.G.I. Friday's*, Kamol Sukosol Building, 317 Silom Rd, T2667488. Large and popular **American** joint with burgers, **Cajun** food, pasta, steaks and salads. Frozen drinks too. Open 1100-0200. **Mid-range**: *Bobby's Arms*, 2nd Floor, Car Park Building, Patpong 2 Rd, T2336828. **English pub** and grill, with jazz on Sun from 2000, open 1100-0100. Roast beef, fish and chips, pies and mixed grill – in other words English food which is increasingly difficult to get in the more chic restaurants in London. **Cheap**: *Harmonique*, 22 Charoen Krung. Good food and a great atmosphere.

Children Expensive: Rom Sai, Westin Banyan Tree Hotel, Sathorn Rd. Hosts a kids' club every weekend, with brunch menu and entertainment.

Afternoon tea and morning coffee *The Authors' Lounge*, *Oriental Hotel*. Also for after-noon tea go to the *Dusit Thani Hotel* library, Rama IV Rd. *Starbucks*, six branches by 2000 and more opening as the drug spreads: Central Plaza, Phahonyothin Rd (Lad Phrao); Sivadol Building, Convent Rd (off Silom); 54 Surawong Rd (5 mins from Sala Daeng BTS station); Central Chitlom, Ploenchit Rd; Bumrungrad Hospital, Sukhumvit Soi 3 (Nana BTS station) Amarin Plaza, Ploenchit Rd – Californian coffee culture comes to Bangkok. **Bak-eries Jimmy**, 1270-2, near Oriental Lane, Charoen Krung. A/c, **cakes** and **ice creams**, very little else around here, so it's a good stopping place.

Bars The greatest concentration of bars are in the 2 'red light' districts of Bangkok – Patpong (between Silom and Surawong roads) and Soi Cowboy (Sukhumvit). Patpong was transformed from a street of 'tea houses' (brothels serving local clients) into a high-tech lane of go-go bars in 1969 when an American made a major invest-ment. In fact there are 2 streets, side-by-side, Patpong 1 and Patpong 2. Patpong 1 is the larger and more active, with a host of stalls down the middle at night (see page 157); Patpong 2 supports cocktail bars and, appropriately, pharmacies and clinics for STDs, as well as a few go-go bars. The *Derby King* is one of the most popular with expats and serves what are reputed to be the best club sandwiches in Asia, if not the world. Opposite Patpong, along Convent Rd is *Delaney's*, an Irish pub with draft Guinness from Malaysia (where it is brewed) and a limited menu, good atmosphere and well-patronized by Bangkok's expats – sofas for lounging and reading (upstairs). Limited and predictable menu – beef and guinness pie, etc. Daily 1100-0200. *O'Reilly's* , corner of Silom and Thaniya is another themed Irish pub, run by a Thai (Chak) but with all the usual cultural accoutrements – Guinness and Kilkenney, rugby on the satellite, etc. 2300-0100.

Bangkok

Soi Cowboy is named after the first bar here, the **Cowboy Bar**, established by a retired US Air Force officer. Although some of the bars also offer other forms of entertainment (something that quickly becomes blindingly obvious), there are, believe it or not, some excellent and very reasonably priced bars in these two areas. A small beer will cost ฿45-65, with good (if loud) music and perhaps videos thrown in for free. However, if opting for a bar with a 'show', be prepared to pay considerably more.

Warning Front men will assure customers that there is no entrance charge and a beer is only ฿60 (or whatever), but you can be certain that they will try to fleece you on the way out and can become aggressive if you refuse to pay. Even experienced Bangkok travellers find themselves in this predicament. Massages and more can also be obtained at many places in the Patpong and Soi Cowboy areas. **NB** AIDS is a significant and growing problem in Thailand so it is strongly recommended that customers practice safe sex (see page 68).

A particularly civilized place to have a beer and watch the sun go down is on the veranda of the *Oriental Hotel*, by the banks of the Chao Phraya River, expensive, but romantic (and strict dress code of no backpacks, no flip flops and no T-shirts). **Boh**, Tha Tien, Chao Phraya Express Boat Pier, Maharat Rd, open 1900-2400. A popular student hangout, with good sunset views over Wat Arun. **Hyper**, 114/14 Silom Soi 4. A very trendy joint, popular with celebrities. **King's Castle**, Patpong 1 Rd. Another long-standing **bar** with core of regulars. **Royal Salute**, Patpong 2 Rd. **Cocktail bar** where local farangs end their working days. **Soho**, Convent Rd. Terraced area and 2-level a/c where jazz bands play Mon-Wed. Open 1700-0200.

Soi Ngam
Duphli
See map, page 130

Expensive *Chandraphen*, Rama 1V Rd. Popular, classy, catering for a superior clientele. Expensive but worth it. *Ratstube*, Goetegasse. German food, good quality but rather pricey. *Basement Pub* (and restaurant), 946 Rama IV Rd. A **bar** with live music, also serves international food, open 1800-2400.

Bakeries *Folies*, 309/3 Soi Nang Linchee (Yannawa) off southern end of Soi Ngam Duphli, T2869786. French expats and bake-o-philes maintain that this bakery makes the most authentic **pastries** and **breads** in town, coffee available, a great place to sit, eat and read.

Siam Square,
Rama I,
Ploenchit &
Phetburi
See map, page 132.
Price categories:
see inside front cover

Thai Expensive: *Spice Market*, *Regent Hotel*, 155 Rachdamri Rd, T2516127. **Westernized Thai**, typical hotel decoration, arguably the city's best Thai food – simply delectable. If the lists of dishes bamboozle, then choose the excellent set menu. Open daily for lunch and dinner. *Thai on 4*, *Amari Watergate Hotel*, 847 Phetburi Rd, T6539000. Classy, modernist restaurant on the fourth floor of this hotel. The food is excellent: some very traditional, some more like nouvelle cuisine, bordering on fusion. Pricey for Thai but good value for a hotel restaurant with high standards. The laid-back jazz music gives lie to the image the restaurant is trying to project.

Mid-range: *Ban Khun Phor*, 458/7-9 Siam Square Soi 8, T2501732. Good Thai food in stylish surroundings. *Moon Shadow*, 145 Gaysorn Rd. Thai food, good seafood, choice of dining-rooms – a/c or open air. *Sarah Jane's*, 36/2 Soi Lang Suan, Ploenchit Rd, T2526572. Run by American woman, married to a Thai, best Thai salad in town and good duck, **Isan** food especially noteworthy, excellent value. Recommended. *Wannalee Earth Kitchen*, 63/12 Soi Langsuan 2, Ploenchit Rd, T6522939. 'Mother Earth' theme to this Thai restaurant, with background whale music and simple decor, there's a good choice of food from each region of the country. Open daily for lunch and dinner.

Cheap: *Princess Terrace*, Rama I Soi Kasemsan Nung (1). Thai and **French** food with barbecue specialities served in small restaurant with friendly service and open terrace down quiet lane. Recommended. *Seafood Market*, Sukhumvit Soi 24. A deservedly famous restaurant which serves a huge range of seafood; 'if it swims we have it', choose your seafood from the 'supermarket' and then have it cooked to your own specifications before consuming the creatures at the table, very popular.

Burmese   Mid-range: *Mandalay*, 23/17 Ploenchit Soi Ruamrudee. Authentic Burmese food, most gastronomes of the country reckon their food is the best in the capital. Recommended.

Chinese   Most Thai restaurants sell Chinese food, but there are also many dedicated Chinese establishments. **Siam Square** has a large number, particularly those specializing in shark's fin soup. Those who are horrified by the manner by which fins are removed and the way in which fishing boats are decimating the shark populations of the world should stay clear. But Siam Square also has two of the best noodle shops around, side-by-side on Siam Square Soi 10. *Hong Kong Noodles* is usually packed with university students and serves stupendously good *bamii muu deang kio kung sai naam* (noodle soup with red pork and stuffed pasta with shrimp) while *Kuaytiaw Rua Khuan Boke* is equally popular. More expensive than most noodle shops, but definitely worth the extra few baht. **Mid-range**: *China*, 231/3 Rachdamri Soi Sarasin. Bangkok's oldest Chinese restaurant, serving full range of Chinese cuisine. *Noble house*, 2nd floor of Promenade Decor next to *Hilton International Hotel*, 2 Witthaya Rd, T2530123. Upmarket Chinese restaurant in the style of an old China trading house. Cantonese and *dim sum* lunch.

French   Expensive: *Auberge Dab*, Ground flr, Mercury Tower, 540 Ploenchit Rd, T6586222. Exclusive French cuisine and excellent service. *Ma Maison*, 2 Witthayu Rd, T2530123. Classic French cuisine from duck escoffier to wild mushroom soup and great soufflés. Restaurant is in a traditional Thai teak house which adds something to the ambience. Pricey. Open for lunch Mon-Fri and dinner every day.

Indonesian   Mid-range: *Bali*, 20/11 Ruamrudee Village, Soi Ruamrudee, Ploenchit Rd, T2500711. Those who know say that this is the only authentic Indonesian food in Bangkok. Friendly proprietress and a charming old-style house with garden. Open for Mon-Sat for lunch and dinner and Sun for dinner only.

Italian   Expensive: *Biscotti*, *Regent Hotel*, 155 Rachdamri Rd, T2555443. Italian 'fusion', a second superb restaurant at this top-class hotel. Cuisine here is difficult to categorise. The chef is Italian and while there are pizzas and porcini mushrooms, there is also salmon and smoked duck. Excellent. *Paesano*, 96/7 Soi Tonson (off Soi Langsuan), Ploenchit Rd, T2522834. Italian food in friendly atmosphere. This long-established restaurant has a loyal following and is very popular with farangs and westernized Thais. Our last visit was a mediocre culinary experience, but many disagree and come here time and again. **Mid-range**: *Peppers*, 99/14 Soi Langsuan, T2547355. Open during the day from 1030 to 1700, closed on Sun, small restaurant with just 20 seats run by Aussie-trained Sunissa Hancock, home-cooked Italian food and international dishes, friendly atmosphere, wholesome, tasty food. Great for a lunch stop. *Vito's Spaghetteria*, Basement, Gaysorn Plaza, Ploenchit Rd (next to *Le Meridien Hotel*). Bright and breezy pasta bar, make up your own dish by combining 10 types of pasta with 12 sauces and 29 fresh condiments, smallish servings but good for a hurried lunch.

Japanese   Mid-range: *Kobune*, 3rd Floor, Mahboonkhrong (MBK) Centre, Rama 1 Rd. Sushi Bar and tables, very good value. Recommended. *Otafuku*, 484 Siam Square Soi 6, Henri Dunant Rd. Sushi Bar or low tables.

Vegetarian Mid-range: *Vegetarian House*, 4/1-4/2 6th Floor, Isetan World Trade Centre, Rachdamri Rd, T2559898. Wide-ranging menu from Asian to western. This bright and airy vegetarian restaurant is a place where vegetables are made to look like meat: beef stroganoff, shark's fin soup and the like, all cunningly crafted from soybean. *Whole Earth*, 93/3 Soi Langsuan, Ploenchit Rd, T2525574. Thailand's best-known and arguably first vegetarian restaurant. This is the second and slightly less plush of the two branches (the other is on Sukhumvit Rd), but both have the same eclectic menu from Thai to Indian dishes, lassis and herbal teas and coffees. They have recently introduced some meat dishes. A trifle expensive, but good ambience. Open daily for lunch and dinner.

Vietnamese Expensive: *Pho*, 2F Alma Link Building, 25 Soi Chidlom, T2518900. Supporters claim this place (there are 3 other branches) serves the best Vietnamese in town even though the owner is not Vietnamese herself, but Thai. Modern trendy setting, non-smoking area. Open daily for lunch and dinner. *Tan Dinh*, 20/6-7 Soi Ruamrudee, Ploenchit Rd, T6508986. Gourmet Vietnamese food. Small but exclusive menu.

Western Expensive: *The Bay*, 2032 New Phetburi Rd, T7160802, **American** restaurant but serving more than just the usual burgers and fries – pork, duck, seafood, attached micro-brewery and live music in the evening from 2130. Good atmosphere, enjoyable décor. *Wit's Oyster Bar*, 20/10 Ruamrudee Village, T2519455. Bangkok's first and only **Oyster Bar**, run by an eccentric Thai, one of the few places where you can eat late, good salmon fishcakes, international cuisine.

  Mid-range: *Fisherman's*, Basement, Gaysorn Plaza, 999 Ploenchit Rd, T6561013. Best **seafood** in town. *Hard Rock Café*, 424/3-6 Siam Square Soi 11, T2510792. Home-from-home for all burger-starved farangs, overpriced, videos, live music sometimes, and all the expected paraphernalia, a couple of **Thai** dishes have been included, large portions but it is appalling that a place serving burgers at ฿250 a shot (twice the daily salary of a farm worker) can't even offer water gratis. Moreover, the food is poor (over-cooked chicken, second-rate fries...); it's living off its name. *Planet Hollywood*, Gaysorn Plaza, 1st Floor, Ploenchit Rd, T6561358. Open 1100-0200 7 days a week. Live music nightly, typical American chow, salads, nachos, burgers, ribs and the decor you would expect from this showbiz-linked place.

  Cheap: *Caravan Coffee House*, Siam Square Soi 5. Large range of coffee or tea, food includes pizza, curry and some Thai dishes.

Afternoon tea and morning coffee The *Bakery Shop*, Siam Intercontinental Hotel. *The Cup*, 2nd floor of Peninsula Plaza, Rachdamri Rd. *The Regent Hotel* lobby (music accompaniment), Rachdamri Rd. *Starbucks*, Central Chitlom, Ploenchit Rd and Amarin Plaza, Ploenchit Rd – the usual Starbucks' fare.

Bakeries *Basket of Plenty*, Peninsula Plaza, Rachdamri Rd (another branch at 66-67 Sukhumvit Soi 33). Bakery, deli and trendy restaurant, very good things baked and a classy (though expensive) place for lunch. *La Brioche*, ground floor of *Novotel Hotel*, Siam Square Soi 6. Good range of French patisseries. *Au Bon Pain*, Ground Floor Siam Discovery Centre, Rama 1 Rd. Excellent bakery and coffee shop with French pastries, croissants, muffins, cookies and great sandwiches as well as salads and some other dishes. *Sweet Corner*, *Siam Intercontinental Hotel*, Rama I Rd. One of the best bakeries in Bangkok. *Swedish Bake*, Siam Square Soi 2. Good Danish pastries.

Bars *Mingles*, *Amari Atrium Hotel*, New Phetburi Rd. Open 1700-0100. Calls itself a 'Rustic Thai Fun Pub', but the vodka bar suggests otherwise, theme nights throughout the week, some food available. *Round Midnight*, 106/12 Soi Langsuan. A bar with live blues and jazz, some excellent bands play here, packed at weekends, good atmosphere and worth the trip, also serves Thai and Italian food, open 1700-0400.

Thai Mid-range: *Lemon Grass*, 5/1 Sukhumvit Soi 24, T2588637. Thai food and Thai-style house, rather dark interior but very stylish, one step up from *Cabbages and Condoms*. Open daily for lunch and dinner. Recommended. *Seven Seas*, Sukhumvit Soi 33, T2597662. Quirky 'nouvelle' Thai food, popular with young sophisticated and avant garde Thais. *Tum Nak Thai*, 131 Rachdapisek Rd, T2746420. Thai food, 'largest' restaurant in the world, 3,000 seats, rather out of the way (฿100 by taxi from city centre), classical dancing from 2000-2130. **Cheap**: *Ambassador Food Centre*, Ambassador Hotel, Sukhumvit Rd. A vast self-service, up-market hawkers' centre with a large selection of *Asian* foods at reasonable prices: Thai, Chinese, Japanese, Vietnamese, etc. Recommended. *Ban Mai*, 121 Sukhumvit Soi 22, Sub-Soi 2. Thai food, in old Thai-style decorations in an attractive house with friendly atmosphere, good value. *Cabbages and Condoms*, Sukhumvit Soi 12 (around 400 m down the soi). Population and Community Development Association (PDA) restaurant so all proceeds go to this charity, eat rice in the Condom Room, drink in the Vasectomy Room, good *tom yam kung* and honey-roast chicken, curries all rather similar, good value. Recommended. *Continental*, Atlanta Hotel, 78 Sukhumvit Soi 2. Not clearly signed but worth seeking out at the end of Soi 2. The proprietor is a self-confessed foodie and his enthusiasm is reflected in the quality of the fare. A 1930s feel is created by the classical and jazz music played and art-deco fittings. Terrific menu, delicious food, excellent value. Highly recommended. *September*, 120/1-2 Sukhumvit Soi 23. **Thai**. Art nouveau setting, also serves Chinese and European, good value for money. *Trumpet Pub* (and restaurant), 7 Sukhumvit Soi 24. A **bar** with live blues and jazz, also serves Thai food, open 1900-0200. *Wannakarm*, 98 Sukhumvit Soi 23, T2596499. Well established, very Thai restaurant, grim decor, no English spoken, but rated food. **Seriously cheap**: *Suda*, 6-6/1 Sukhumvit Rd, Soi 14. Rather basic looking but popular with westerners. Wide menu. Recommended.

Chinese Mid-range: *Art House*, 87 Sukhumvit Soi 55 (Soi Thonglor). Country house with traditional Chinese furnishings, surrounded by gardens, particularly good seafood.

Egyptian Mid-range: *Nasir al-Masri*, 4-6 Sukhumvit Soi Nana Nua, T2535582. Reputedly the best **Eastern** (Egyptian) food in Bangkok, *felafale, taboulie, humus*, frequented by large numbers of Arabs who come to Sayed Saad Qutub Nasir for a taste of home.

French Expensive: *Le Banyan*, 59 Sukhumvit Soi 8, T2535556. Classic French food from foie gras to crêpes suzette, expensive with tougher dress code than most places. Open only for dinner, Mon-Sat. Highly regarded food, a shade stuffy. *Beccassine*, Sukhumvit, Soi Sawatdee. **English** and French home cooking. Recommended. *La Grenouille*, 220/4 Sukhumvit Soi 1, T2539080. Traditional French cuisine, French chef and manager, small restaurant makes booking essential, French wines and French atmosphere. Recommended. *L'Hexagone*, 4 Sukhumvit Soi 55 (Soi Thonglor), T3812187. French cuisine, in 'posh' surroundings. *Les Nymphéas*, Imperial Queen's Park Hotel, Sukhumvit Soi 22, T2619000. An excellent restaurant (the interior theme is *Monet's Waterlillies* – hence the name) in an over-large and inconveniently located (unless you are staying here!) hotel – but don't be put off. The English chef creates probably the best 'modern' French cuisine in Bangkok.

German Mid-range: *Bei Otto*, 1 Sukhumvit Soi 20, T2600869. Thailand's best-known German restaurant; sausages, bread, pastries all made on the premises, good provincial food, large helpings. *Haus Munchen*, 4 Sukhumvit Soi 15, T2525776. German food in quasi-Bavarian lodge, connoisseurs maintain cuisine is authentic enough.

Sukhumvit

See map, page 134.

Price categories:
see inside front cover

Bangkok

Indian Expensive: *Rang Mahal*, *Rembrandt Hotel*, Sukhumvit Soi 18, T2617100. Best Indian food in town, very popular with the Indian community and spectacular views from the roof-top position, sophisticated, elegant and expensive. **Mid-range**: *Akbar*, 1/4 Sukhumvit Soi 3, T2533479. A long established Indian restaurant serving **Indian, Pakistani** and **Arabic** food on 3 floors. *Mrs Balbir's*, 155/18 Sukhumvit Soi 11, T2532281. **North Indian** food orchestrated by Mrs Balbir, an Indian originally from Malaysia, regular customers just keep going back, chicken dishes are succulent, Mrs Balbir also runs cookery classes.

Italian Expensive: *Hibiscus*, 31st Floor, *Landmark Hotel*, 138 Sukhumvit Rd, T2540404. Italian food which extends to more than pasta and pizza. Worth it for the views. Open for lunch and dinner. *L'Opera*, 55 Sukhumvit Soi 39, T2585606. Italian restaurant with Italian manager, conservatory, good food (excellent salted baked fish), professional service, lively atmosphere, popular, booking essential. Recommended. *Rossini*, *Sheraton Grande Sukhumvit*, Sukhumvit Rd, T6530333. This hotel-based Italian restaurant is open for lunch and dinner. A limited, but tantalizing array of dishes. Particularly good is the seafood. Italian chef. Vies for the 'best Italian in town' award. **Mid-range**: *Gino's*, 13 Sukhumvit Soi 15. Italian food in bright and airy surroundings, set lunch is good value. **Cheap**: *Pasta n Noodles*, attached to *City Lodge* hotel, Sukhumvit Soi 9. A trendy Italian and **Thai** restaurant, a/c, spotless open-plan kitchen.

Korean Cheap: *New Korea*, 41/1 Soi Chuam Rewang, Sukhumvit Sois 15-19. Excellent Korean food in small restaurant. Recommended.

Laotian Mid-range: *Bane Lao*, Naphasup Ya-ak I, off Sukhumvit Soi 36. Laotian open-air restaurant (doubles as a travel agent for Laos), Laotian band, haphazard but friendly service.

Mediterranean Expensive: *Manja*, Sukhumvit Soi 24, Easy to find near skytrain steps. Recently opened, run by a Greek lady, who is also the chef so the food is distinctly **Greek**, eg Corfu lamb shank stew. *Talisman Restaurant Club*, Sukhumvit Soi 20, T2588008. Recently opened Mediterranean restaurant, set in a large garden, with interior decked out like a Moroccan tent. Live music Fri and Sat nights. French chef, good food; try the tajine of lamb. **Mid-range**: *Aioli*, 18/5 Sukhumvit Soi 23, T2584237, French Mediterranean food. This bistro serves country-style food with some good seafood. *Crêpes & Co*, 18/1 Sukhumvit Soi 12, T2512895. Mediterranean food. Specializes in crêpes but the '& Co' is the addition of some Mediterranean food to the menu. The owner Philippe is a Swiss Bulgarian, raised in Spain, Morocco and Greece. Particularly good Moroccan fare and Greek specialities such as moussaka. Some local culinary touches – like the *crêpe musssaman* (a Thai curry). Open 0900-2400.

Scandanavian Mid-range: *Den Hvide Svane*, Sukhumvit Soi 8. Scandinavian and **Thai** dishes, former are good, efficient and friendly service.

Vegetarian Mid-range: *Whole Earth*, 71 Sukhumvit Soi 26, T2584900. This is the slightly swisher of the two Whole Earth **vegetarian** restaurants (the other branch is on Soi Langsuan). Both offer the same eclectic menu from Thai to Indian dishes, live music, *lassis* and good range of coffee. Ask to sit at the back downstairs, or Thai-style upstairs on cushions. They have recently introduced some meat dishes. A trifle expensive, but good ambience. Open daily for lunch and dinner. **Cheap**: *Veg House*, 2nd Floor, 1/6 Sukhumvit Soi 3 (Nana Nua). Friendly place with a menu of Thai and Indian vegetarian dishes. Good value and tasty.

Vietnamese Mid-range: *Le Dalat Indochine*, 47/1 Sukhumvit Soi 23, T6617967. Reputed to serve the best Vietnamese food in Bangkok, arrive early or management may hassle. Open daily for lunch and dinner.

Western Expensive: *Cucina Bangkok Steak and Seafood*, 29/1 Sukhumvit Soi 49, T6626015. Run by a Thai who learnt about steaks in New York and returned to Thailand to spread the word. The name says it all, pricey but the quality of the ingredients is first rate and the service slick. **Mid-range**: *Bourbon Street*, 29/4-6 Sukhumvit Soi 22 (behind Washington Theatre), T2590328. **Cajun** specialities including gumbo, jambalaya and red fish, along with steaks and **Mexican** dishes (Mexican buffet for ฿170 every Tue), served in a/c restaurant with central bar – good for breakfast, excellent pancakes. Open 0700-0100. *Gourmet Gallery*, 6/1 Soi Promsri 1 (between Sukhumvit Soi 39 and 40), T2600603. Interesting interior, with art work for sale, unusual menu of **European** and **American** food. *Larry's Dive*, 8/3 Sukhumvit Soi 22, T6634563. **American** bar which bills itself as the 'only private beach restaurant in Bangkok'. Burgers, nachos, ribs, chicken wings – what you would expect. Happy hours 1600-2000. Good value. *Longhorn*, 120/9 Sukhumvit Soi 23. **Cajun** and **Creole** food. *Señor Pico*, *Rembrandt Hotel*, 18 Sukhumvit Rd, T2617100. **Mexican**, pseudo-Mexican decor, staff dressed Mexican style, large, rather uncosy restaurant, average cuisine, live music, open only for dinner 1700-0100 daily.

Other Mid-range: *Grand Pacific Kid's Club*, *Delta Grand Pacific Hotel*, Sukhumvit Rd. **Children** aged 8-15 yrs get a 20% discount on food and drink. Talent show on first Sun of the month.

Bakeries Bangkok has a large selection of fine bakeries, many attached to hotels like the *Landmark*, *Dusit Thani* and *Oriental*. There are also the generic 'donut' fast-food places although few lovers of bread and pastries would want to lump the two together. *The Bakery Landmark Hotel*, 138 Sukhumvit Rd. Many cakes and pastry connoisseurs argue that this is the best of the hotel places, popular with expats, wide range of breads and cakes. *Bei Otto*, Sukhumvit Soi 20. A **German bakery** and **deli**, makes really very good pastries, breads and cakes. *Cheesecake House*, 69/2 Ekamai Soi 22. Rather out of town for most tourists but patronized enthusiastically by the city's large Sukhumvit-based expat population, as the name suggests **cheesecakes** of all descriptions are a speciality – and are excellent.

Bars There are plenty of bars in the Sukhumvit area, a couple of trendy nightspots are *Café 50*, Thonglor Rd (Sukhumvit Soi 50), *Gitanes*, 52 Soi Pasana 1, Sukhumvit Soi 63. A bar with live music, open 1800-0100, *Half Moon Street*, Ground Floor, Times Square, Sukhumvit. British pub with jukebox and band at the weekend. Jam session, Sun from 1600. Darts and pool also available. *Black Scene*, 120/29-30 Sukhumvit Soi 23. A bar with live jazz, also serves Thai and French food, open 1700-0300. *Hemingway Bar and Grill*, 159/5-8 Sukhumvit Soi 55. A bar with live jazz and country music at the weekend, plus **Thai** and **American** food, open 1800-0100. *The Londoner Brew House*, UBC II Building, Sukhumvit Soi 33, Micro-brewery with London Best Bitter. Bistro-style restaurant with english food, caters for children. Live bands from 2200. Open 1100-0100. *Riley's*, corner of Sukhumvit and Soi 3 (Soi Nana). Sportsman bar upstairs and British food served downstairs. Open 0900-0200. *The Rock and Roll Bar*, 2nd Floor, Nana Plaza, Sukhumvit Soi 4. Good place to view rock concerts, movies and famous sports events on large screens. Open from 1200 till late. *See, Too*, Ekamai Rd, T7116089, open until 0200, also serves reasonably priced Thai food. Undoubtedly the bar of the moment is the *Q Bar*, Sukhumvit Soi 11, T2523274. Opened in Dec 1999. Housed in a modern building, it is the reincarnation of photographer David Jacobson's bar of the same name in Ho Chi Minh City. Highly sophisticated, designed for conversation, not for posing. Come here to drink, not to eat – the food is said to be poor and pricey. Live acid jazz on Sun.

Banglamphu
See maps, pages 138 & 137.
Price categories: see inside front cover

Japanese Expensive: *Teketei*, 202 Khaosan Rd, same entrance as *Nana Plaza Inn*, T6290173. A new Sushi restaurant, open 1130-0100. Excellent but pricey.

Vegetarian Seriously cheap: *May Kaidee*, 117/1 Tanao Rd, Banglamphu. This is a tiny, simple vegetarian restaurant tucked away down a soi at the eastern end of Khaosan Rd. Delicious, cheap **Thai vegetarian** dishes served at tables on the street.

There are a number of trendy café and bars along Phra Arthit Rd offering good cheap food and beer, popular with young Thais. **Cheap**: *Dog Days* and *Commé* are particularly good. **Seriously cheap**: *Riverside Restaurant*, between the canal and *New World Guesthouse*, off Samsen Rd, nr Soi 2. Very good value restaurant.

Travellers' food available in the guesthouse/travellers' hotel areas (see above). Nearly all the restaurants in Khaosan Rd show videos all afternoon and evening. If on a tight budget it is much more sensible to eat in Thai restaurants and stalls where it should be possible to have a good meal for ฿15-30.

Bars *Buddy Beer*, 153 Khaosan Rd. A popular spot with beer garden, pool table and even a swimmng pool! *Dali*, 227 Soi Rambutri. Open 1600-0200, huge choice of alcohol and vintage music too. *Blues Bar and Marjan Reech*, 4th and 5th Floor, Sukhumvit Plaza, 212/34 Sukhumvit Soi 12, open 1900-0200. A tiny Japanese bar selling whisky and sake. *Cheap Charlie's*, 1 Sukhumvit Soi 11, open 1500 until very late. As the title suggests; alcohol at very reasonable prices. *Gullivers*, Khaosan Rd. Popular with young travellers, happy hours 1700-2000 and 2300-0200. *Jools Bar*, 21/3 Nana Tai, Sukhumvit Soi 4. A favourite watering hole for Brits. Open 0900-0100, also serves classic English food. *The Londoner Brew Pub*, Basement, UBC II Building, Sukhumvit 33, open 1100-0200. A large pub, now brewing its English-style ales and also sells usual lagers. *Tasman Pub*, 159/9 Sukhumvit Soi, 55, opposite Bangkok Bank. The only place in Thailand to serve Boag's Beer from Tasmania. Open 1700-2400.

Sri Ayutthaya

Thai Expensive: *Kaloang*, 2 Sri Ayutthaya Rd, T2819228. 2 dining areas, one on a pier, the other on a boat on the Chao Phraya River, attractive atmosphere, delicious Thai food. Recommended.

Other areas

Thai Expensive: *Ban Chiang*, 14 Srivdieng Rd, T2367045. Thai food, quite hard to find – ask for directions, old style Thai house, large menu of traditionally prepared food. *D'jit Pochana Oriental*, 1082 Phahonyothin Rd, T2795000. Extensive range of Thai dishes, large and rather industrial but the food is good. *Kanasa*, 34 Soi Phahonyothin 9, T6183414. This is not an easy place to get to for many casual visitors to Bangkok – it is in a residential area, north of town. Large garden as well as rooms in an European-style house. Serves what can best be described as nouvelle Thai – good, sometimes excellent but variable. Popular with Bangkok's intelligentsia. **Fusion Expensive**: *Doc Cheng's*, 202 Ratchadapisek Rd (in the *Merchant Court Hotel*), Huay Kwang, T694222. A newly opened branch of the well-known Doc Cheng's in Singapore. Although the restaurant is none too happy with being described as concocting fusion cuisine (because the terms is viewed as hackneyed) that's exactly what it does. However the food and the restaurant are excellent. Imaginative creations, stylish presentation. Recommended.

Fast food

Bangkok now has a large number of western fast-food outlets, such as *Pizza Hut*, *McDonalds*, *Kentucky Fried Chicken*, *Mister Donut*, *Dunkin' Donuts*, *Shakey's*, *Baskin Robbins* and *Burger King*. These are located in the main shopping and tourist areas – Siam Square, Silom/Patpong roads, and Ploenchit Rd, for example.

Scattered across the city for a rice or noodle dish, where a meal will cost ฿15-30 instead **Foodstalls** of a minimum of ฿50 in the restaurants. For example, on the roads between Silom and Surawong Rd, or down Soi Somkid, next to Ploenchit Rd, or opposite on Soi Tonson.

Entertainment

The headquarters of the World Fellowship of Buddhists is at 33 Sukhumvit Rd (between **Buddhism** Soi 1 and Soi 3). Meditation classes are held in English on Wed at 1700-2000; lectures on Buddhism are held on the first Wed of each month at 1800-2000.

At the *Goethe Institute*, 18/1 Sathorn Tai Soi Atthakan Prasit; check newspapers **Classical music** for programme.

All programmes and show times may change without notice. To double-check, ask **Cinemas** your concierge to help you as most cinemas do not have English-speaking operators. It is obligatory to stand when The Royal Anthem is being played in the cinemas.

Bangkae 10, 4th Floor, Future Park, Phetkasem Rd, T4550148. *Central 5, 6, 7*, 4th Floor, Central Plaza Ladprao, T5411065. *Fashion Island 7*, 3rd Floor, Fashion Island, Ram Indra Rd. T9476475. *Fortune 1, 2, 3, 4*, Basement & 4th Floor, Fortune Town, Ratchadapisek Rd, T2485855. *Grand Pata*, Pata Square, Pinklao, T5230568. *Indra*, Indra Plaza, Pratunam, T2516230. *Ladprao 7*, 6th Floor, Imperial World, Ladprao, T9349399. *Lido*, Siam Square, Rama I Rd, T2526498. *Mackenna*, Phayathai Rd, T2526215. *Major Cineplex Pinklao*, Pinklao Rd, T88179709. *Major Cineplex Sukhumvit*, Sukhumvit Soi 61, Sukhumvit Rd, T714282843. *Major Cineplex Ratchayothin*, Paholyothin, T511555. *The Mall Bangkapi*, 4th Floor, The Mall, Bangkapi, T7341953. *Pantip*, Pantip Plaza, Petchburi Rd, T2512390. *Pinklao 10*, 5th Floor, Central Plaza Pinklao, T88485704. *Rangsit 14*, 3rd Floor, Future Park Rangsit, T9580607. *Scala*, Soi Siam Square 1, Rama I Rd, T2526498. *Seacon 14*, Seacon Square, Srinakarin Rd, T7219418, 7219426. *Seri Center Multiplex 6*, Seri Center, Srinakarin Rd, T7460609. *Siam Square Multiplex 5*, Siam Square, Rama I Rd, T2526498. *UMG 5*, Royal City Avenue, Petchburi Rd, T64159114. *United Artists*, 6th Floor, Emporium, Sukhumvit Soi 24, Sukhumvit Rd, T664871130. *United Artists*, 7th & 8th Floor, Central Plaza Rama III, Rama III Rd, T673606088. *Warner*, Mahesak Rd, Silom, T23437009. *World Trade Major*, Basement & 6th Floor, World Trade Center, Ratchaprasong, T2559500.

The *Oriental Hotel* organizes an intensive 4-day course, with different areas of Thai cui- **Cookery courses** sine covered each day, 0900-1200. ฿2,500 per class or ฿11,500 for 5 classes. T4376211 or 4373080. The classes take place in an old teak house on the other bank of the Chao Phraya – student gastronomes are ferried across from the hotel. For US$2,500 it is possible to combine the course with staying at the hotel, breakfast and a jet lag mas- sage. *Wandee's Kitchen School*, 134/5-6 Silom Rd (on the 5th Floor, above the *Dokya Book Shop*), T2372051. Also offer a 5-day, 40-hr course from Mon-Fri but at the slightly cheaper rate of ฿5,200. Successful students emerge with a certificate and reeking faintly of chillies and *nam plaa*. Yet cheaper courses still are run by Mrs Balbir every Fri 0930-1130, in which she instructs small classes of 10 or so, ฿100, 155/18 Sukhumvit Soi 11, T2352281. At *UFM Baking and Cooking School*, 593/29-39 Sukhumvit Soi 33, T2590620, classes are held Mon-Fri 0900-1000, again in groups of about 10; and at the prosaically and politically incorrectly named *Modern Housewife Centre*, 45/6-7 Sethsiri Rd, T2792831, 2792834.

Dianas, 3rd Floor, Oriental Plaza, Charoen Krung Soi 38. *Grand Palace*, 19th Floor, **Discos** Rajapark Building, Sukhumvit Soi Asoke, 2100-0200. *Spasso's*, *Grand Hyatt Erawan Hotel*, 494 Rachdamri Rd, T2541234. This Italian restaurant turns into a dance floor as the evening progresses, 1800-0100.

Bangkok

Traditional Thai massage

While a little less arousing than the Patpong-style massage, the traditional Thai massage or nuat boraan is probably more invigorating, using methods similar to those of Shiatsu, reflexology and osteopathic manipulation. It probably has its origins in India, and is a form of yoga. It aims to release blocked channels of energy and soothe tired muscles. For Thais, this form of massage is as much a spiritual experience as a physical one – hence its association with monasteries and the Buddha (see page 93). A full massage should last one to two hours and cost around ฿150 per hour, although rates vary considerably. NB Make sure you are getting raksaa tang nuat (traditional Thai massage), otherwise you'll be in for the more pornographic variety.

The thumbs are used to apply pressure on the 10 main 'lines' of muscles, so both relaxing and invigorating the muscles. Headaches, ankle and knee pains, neck and back problems can all be alleviated through this ancient art (a European visitor

to the Siamese court at Ayutthaya 400 years ago noted the practice of Thai massage). Centres of massage can be found in most Thai towns – wats and tourist offices are the best sources of information on where to go.

Many hotels in Bangkok offer this service; guesthouses also, although most masseuses are not trained. Also in Bangkok is Wat Pho, the most famous centre (see page 95) and a Mecca for the training of masseuses. Murals on the temple buildings' walls help to guide the student. Wat Pho specializes in the more muscular Southern style. The Northern-style is less exhausting, more soothing. Other centres offering quality massages by properly trained practitioners include: Marble House, 37/18-19 Soi Surawong Plaza (opposite Montien Hotel), T2353519. Open Mon-Sun 0100-2400, ฿300 for 2 hrs, ฿450 for 3 hrs and Vejakorn, 37/25 Surawong Plaza, Surawong Rd, T2375576. Open Mon-Sun 1000-2400, ฿260 for 2 hrs, ฿390 for 3 hrs.

Dream World Mixed fairground-cum-fantasy land-cum-historical recreation located 10 mins drive from Don Muang Airport at Km 7 on the Rangsit-Ong Kharak Rd (T5331152). ■ *Mon-Fri 1000-1700, Sat and Sun 1000-1900. ฿450. Getting there: bus nos 39, 59 and 29 to Rangsit and then local bus.*

Fortune tellers There are up to ten soothsayers in the *Montien Hotel* lobby, Surawong Rd, on a regular basis.

Magic Land 72 Phahonyothin Rd, T5131731. Amusement park with ferris wheel, roller coaster, etc. ■ *Mon-Fri 1000-1700, Sat and Sun 1000-1900. ฿100, plus additional charges for rides. Getting there: near Central Plaza Hotel – ask for 'Daen Neramit'.*

Music
See also Bars, listed under respective areas in Eating, above

Blues-Jazz, 25 Sukhumvit Soi 53. Open Mon-Sun 1900-0200, 3 house bands play really good blues and jazz, food available, drinks a little on the steep side. *Blue Moon*, 73 Sukhumvit 55 (Thonglor). Open Mon-Sun 1800-0300, for country, rhythm, jazz and blues – particularly Fri and Sun for jazz – some food available. *Brown Sugar*, 231/20 Sarasin Rd (opposite Lumpini Park). Open Mon-Fri 1100-0100, Sat and Sun 1700-0200, 5 regular bands play excellent jazz, a place for Bangkok's trendies to hang out and be cool (there are a couple of other popular bars close by too). *Cool Tango*, 23/51 Block F, Royal City Av (between Phetburi and Rama IX roads). Open Tue-Sat 1100-0200, Sun 1800-0200, excellent resident rock band, great atmosphere, happy hour 1800-2100. *El Niño Latin Heat*, Le Royal Meridien Hotel, Ploenchit Rd. High-energy South American dance music with resident band 'Tropicaribe'. Open 2100-0200. *Front Page*, 14/10 Soi Saladaeng 1. Open Mon-Fri 1000-0100, Sat and Sun 1800-0100, populated, as the name might suggest, by journos who like to hunt in packs more than most, music is country, folk and blues, food

Meditation and yoga

Wat Mahathat, facing Sanaam Luang, is Bangkok's most renowned meditation centre (see page 100). Anyone interested is welcome to attend the daily classes – the centre is located in Khana 5 of the monastery. Apart from Wat Mahathat, classes are held at **Wat Bowonniwet** *in Banglamphu on Phra Sumen Rd (see the Bangkok – Old City map 93), and at the* **Thai Meditation Centre** *in the World Fellowship of Buddhists building on 33 Sukhumvit Rd, (between sois 1 and 3), T2511188 (Mon-Fri 0900-1630).* **International Buddhist Meditation Centre**, *Mahachulalongkorn Buddhist University, Wat Mahadhatu, Ta-Prachan, T2222835 Ext 130. For weekend retreats, talks, meditation sessions.* **House of Dhamma**, *26/9 Soi Chompol Laadprao Lane 15 Chatuchak, T5113549. The* **Dharma Study Foundation**, *128 Soi Thonglor 4, Sukhumvit Soi 55, T3916006 (Mon-Fri 0900-1800) Offers classes in meditation and some religious discussions. Yoga classes available at* **Baan Yoga**, *310/1 Ekamai Soi 16, Sukhumvit Soi 63, T3929869 Mon-Fri 0730-1000, 1400-1500. Sat 0730-1000, 1330-1500.*

available. *Hard Rock Café*, 424/3-6 Siam Square Soi 11. Open Mon-Sun 1100-0200, speaks for itself, burgers, beer and rock covers played by reasonable house band, food is expensive for Bangkok though. *Magic Castle*, 212/33 Sukhumvit Plaza Soi 12. Open Mon-Thu 1800-0100, Fri and Sat 1800-0200, mostly blues, some rock, good place for a relaxed beer with skilfully performed covers. *The Metal Zone*, Langsuan Rd, Ploenchit. Probably the only real heavy metal music venue in Thailand. Open 2000-0100. *Picasso Pub*, 1950-5 Ramkamhaeng Rd (close to Soi 8). Open Mon-Sun 1900-0300, house rock band, adept at playing covers. *Q Bar*, Sukhumvit Soi 11, T2523274, acid jazz on Sun (but phone to check) in one of Bangkok's hippest bars. *Radio City*, Patpong I, Silom Rd. A place to hear the 'Golden Oldies', with Elvis and Tom Jones lookalikes making regular appearances. Open 1700-0200. *Round Midnight*, 106/12 Soi Langsuan. Open Mon-Thu 1900-0230, Fri and Sat 1900-0400, jazz, blues and rock bands. *Taurus Brew House*, Sukhumvit Soi 26. American-style beer brewed on the premises, bands start at 2200.

Sanaam Luang, near the Grand Palace, is a good place to sample traditional Thai sports. From late Feb to mid-Apr there is a traditional Thai Sports Fair held here. It is possible to watch **kite-fighting**, and **takraw** (the only Thai ball game – a *takraw* ball is made of rattan, 5 inches to 6 inches in diameter. Players hit the ball over a net to an opposing team, using their feet, head, knees and elbows – but not hands – and the ball should not be touched by the same team member twice in succession. Regions of Thailand tend to have their own variants of the sport; *sepak takraw* is the competition sport with a nationwide code of rules), **Thai chess**, **krabi** and **krabong** (a swordfighting contest). For Thai boxing, see below.

Spectator sports

Classical dancing and music is often performed at restaurants after a 'traditional' Thai meal has been served. Many tour companies or travel agents organize these 'cultural evenings'. *National Theatre*, Na Phrathat Rd (T2214885 for programme). Thai classical dramas, dancing and music on the last Fri of each month at 1730 and periodically on other days. *Thailand Cultural Centre*, Rachdaphisek Rd, Huai Khwang, T2470028 for programme of events. *College of Dramatic Arts*, near National Theatre, T2241391. *Baan Thai Restaurant*, 7 Sukhumvit Soi 32, T2585403, 2100-2145. *Chao Phraya Restaurant*, Pinklao Bridge, Arun Amarin Rd, T4742389. *Maneeya's Lotus Room*, Ploenchit Rd, T2526312. 2015-2100. *Piman Restaurant*, 46 Sukhumvit Soi 49, T2587866, 2045-2130. *Ruen Thep*, Silom Village Trade Centre, T2339447, 2020-2120. *Suwannahong Restaurant*, Sri Ayutthaya Rd, T2454448, 2015-2115. *Tum-Nak-Thai Restaurant*, 131 Rachdaphisek Rd, T2773828 2030-2130.

Thai Performing Arts

Bangkok

Bangkok

Theme parks See individual entries – *Magic Land*, *Siam Water Park*, *Dream World*, *Safari World*.

Festivals and major events

January *Red Cross Fair* (movable), held in Amporn Gardens next to the Parliament. Stalls, classical dancing, folk performances, etc.

January/ *Chinese New Year* (movable), Chinatown closes down, but Chinese temples are
February packed. *Handicraft Fair* (mid-month), all the handicrafts are made by Thai prisoners.

March-April *Kite Flying* (movable, for 1 month), every afternoon/evening at Sanaam Luang there is kite fighting (see page 99). An **International Kite Festival** is held in late Mar at Sanaam Luang when kite fighting and demonstrations by kite-flyers from across the globe take place.

May *Royal Ploughing Ceremony* (movable), this celebrates the official start of the rice-planting season and is held at Sanaam Luang. It is an ancient Brahman ritual and is attended by the king (see page 99).

September *Swan-boat races* (movable), on the Chao Phraya River.

November *Golden Mount Fair* (movable), stalls and theatres set-up all around the Golden Mount and Wat Saket. Candles are carried in procession to the top of the mount. *Marathon* road race, fortunately at one of the coolest times of year.

December *Trooping of the Colour* (movable), the elite Royal Guards swear allegiance to the king and march past members of the Royal Family. It is held in the Royal Plaza near the equestrian statue of King Chulalongkorn.

Shopping

See also page 59. Most shops do not open until 1000-1100. Nancy Chandler's Map of Bangkok is the best shopping guide

Bangkok still stocks a wonderful range of goods, but do not expect to pick up a bargain – prices are high. Having said that, there are many items which find their way to smart London shops at double the price. Stallholders, entirely understandably, are out for all they can get – so bargain hard here. The traditional street market, although not dying out, is now supplemented by other types of shopping. Given the heat, the evolution of the a/c shopping arcade and a/c department store in Bangkok was just a matter of time. Some arcades target the wealthier shopper, and are dominated by brand-name goods and designer wear. Others are not much more than street side stalls transplanted to an arcade environment. Most department stores are now fixed price. For shoppers with limited time and little knowledge of Bangkok there is a new service available in the city. *ShopS I am Co Ltd* runs full-day or half-day shopping tours for private individuals or couples. Run by an Englishman, the company will provide a car, driver and personal shopping expert to take customers to the best places with the minimum of stress. The company charges a fee and takes no commission from shops. For more information and prices contact *ShopsS I am Co Ltd*, Bangkok, Thailand, T662-3821849, F662-3902750, www.shoppingsiam.com

Bangkok's main shopping areas are:

Sukhumvit Sukhumvit Rd, and the sois to the north are lined with shops and stalls, especially around the *Ambassador* and *Landmark* hotels. Many tailors and made-to-measure shoe shops are to be found in this area. Higher up on Sukhumvit Rd particularly around Soi 49 are various antique and furnishing shops. The big Emporium

Department Store and Shopping Mall is to be found near Soi 24 (get off at the BTS Phrom Phong station which has a direct escalator link), where the top brand names are to be found, along with some bargain designer items.

Central

Two areas close to each other centred on Rama I and Ploenchit roads. At the intersection of Phayathai and Rama I roads there is Siam Square (for teenage trendy western clothing, bags, belts, jewellery, bookshops, some antique shops and American fast-food chains) and the massive – and highly popular – *Mah Boonkhrong Centre* (MBK), with countless small shops and stalls and the *Tokyu Department Store*. Siam Square used to be great for cheap clothes, leather goods, etc, but each year it inches further up-market. The arrival of the six-floored *Siam Tower* has made it even more chi-chi (all the top designers have a presence here). Peninsular Plaza, between the *Hyatt Erawan* and *Regent* hotels is considered one of the smarter shopping plazas in Bangkok. A short distance to the east, centred on Ploenchit/Rachprarop roads, are more shopping arcades and large department stores, including the *World Trade Centre*, *Thai Daimaru*, *Robinsons*, *Gaysorn Plaza*, *Naraiphan* shopping centre (more of a market-stall affair, geared to tourists, in the basement) and *Central Chidlom* (which burnt down in a catastrophic fire in 1995 but is now completely renovated. North along Rachprasong Rd, crossing over Khlong Saensap, at the intersection with Phetburi Rd is the *Pratunam Market*, good for fabrics and clothing.

Patpong/Silom

Patpong is more of a night market (opening at 2100), the streets are packed with stalls selling the usual array of stall goods which seem to stay the same from year to year (fake designer clothing, watches, bags, etc), although some welcome additions include such items as binoculars, all-in-one pliers, etc (and other boys' toys). **NB** Bargain hard. The east end of Silom has a scattering of similar stalls open during the day time, and Robinsons Department Store. Surawong Rd (at the other end of Patpong) has Thai silk, antiques and a few handicraft shops.

West Silom/ Charoen Krung (New Road)

Antiques, jewellery, silk, stamps, coins and bronzeware. Stalls set up here at 2100. A 15 min walk north along Charoen Krung (close to the *Orchid Sheraton Hotel*) is the *River City Shopping Plaza*, specializing in art and antiques.

Banglamphu/ Khaosan Road

Vast variety of low-priced goods, such as ready-made clothes, shoes, bags, jewellery and cassette tapes.

Lardphrao- Phahonyothin

Some distance north of town, not far from the Weekend Market (see page 117) is the huge *Central Plaza* shopping complex. It houses a branch of the *Central Department Store* and has many boutiques and gift shops.

Antiques

Chinese porcelain, old Thai paintings, Burmese tapestries, wooden figures, hilltribe art, Thai ceramics and Buddhist art. Be careful of fakes – go to the well-known shops only. Even they, however, have been known to sell fake Khmer sculpture which even the experts find difficult to tell apart from the real thing. Permission to take antiques out of the country must be obtained from the *Fine Arts Department* on Na Phrathat Rd, T2214817. Shops will often arrange export licences for their customers. Buddha images may not be taken out of the country – although many are. A large number of the more expensive antique shops are concentrated in *River City*, a shopping complex next to the *Royal Orchid Sheraton Hotel* and an excellent place to start. Reputable shops here include *Verandah* on the top floor, *The Tomlinson Collection Room* 427-428 and *Acala Room* 312 for Tibetan and Nepalese art. More antique shops can be found in *Gaysorn Plaza* on Ploenchit Rd and at the *Jewellery Trade Centre* 919/1 Silom Rd in the shopping mall on the ground floor called *The Galleria Plaza* or *Silom Galleria*. At the time of writing the management of this building has been taken over by the Central Group and it has been successful in attracting some of the more up-market antique shops of River City ilk. *NeOld*, 149 Surawong Rd has a good selection of new and old objects, but it's pricey. *Peng Seng*, 942/1-3 Rama IV Rd, on the corner of Surawong Rd, has an excellent selection of antiques. *Thai House Antiques*, 720/6 Sukhumvit (near Soi 28). *L'Arcadia*, 12/2 Sukhumvit Soi 23, Burmese antiques, beds, ceramics, carvings, doors, good quality and prices are fair. The affable owner Khun Tum is helpful and informative. Another quality shop off Sukhumvit is *Paul's Antiques*, 41 Sukhumvit Soi 19 (behind the *Grand Pacific Hotel*), mostly furniture from Thailand and Burma. *Jim Thompson's*, Surawong Rd, for a range of antiques, wooden artefacts, furnishings and carpets. For the serious, see Brown, Robin (1989) *Guide to buying antiques and arts and crafts in Thailand*, Times Books: Singapore.

Books　*Asia Books*, has branches at 221 Sukhumvit Rd, between Sois 15 and 17; 2nd Floor Peninsula Plaza, Rachdamri Rd; Thaniya Plaza (3rd Floor), Silom Rd; 2nd Floor, Times Square, Sukhumvit Rd between Sois 12 and 14; and World Trade Centre (3rd Floor), Rachdamri Rd. Siam Discovery Centre, Siam Square, Emporium, Sukhumvit Rd between Sois 22 and 24. *Bookazine* has several outlets: in Patpong (CP Tower) Silom Complex, Ploenchit (Sogo Dept store) and Siam Square, opposite Siam centre. Good for foreign newspapers, magazines and bestsellers. *The Bookseller*, 81, Patpong I. Strong on coffee table books, some German, French and Spanish books available. *Chulalongkorn University Book Centre*, in University compound (ask for 'suun nang suu Chula') for academic, business and travel books. *DK (Duang Kamol) Books* in Siam Square, on the 3rd floor of the Mahboonkhrong Centre, at 180/1 Sukhumvit (between Sois 8 and 10), and 90/21-25 Rachprarop Rd is the best source of locally published books in English. They also have branches on the 3rd floor of the Mahboonkrong Centre (MBK) at the corner of Phayathai and Rama I roads, and at 180/1 Sukhumvit (between Sois 8 and 10). *Elite Used Books*, 593/5 Sukhumvit Rd, near Villa Supermarket (and with a branch at 1/2 Sukhumvit Soi Nana Nua [Soi 3]), offers a good range of second-hand books in several languages. *White Lotus Press*, 11/2, Soi 58, Sukhumvit Rd, T3324915, ande@loxinfo.co.th, www.thailine.com/lotus for collectors' books on Southeast Asia and reprints of historical volumes under their own imprint (also available from many other bookshops). *Dokya*, 258/8-10 Soi Siam Square 3. Books are also sold in the various branches of *Central Department Stores*, 1027 Ploenchit Rd, 1691 Pahonyothin Rd, and 306 Silom Rd. Second-hand books are also available at the *Chatuchak Weekend Market* (see page 117) in sections 22 and 25. For **Maps**, see below.

Bronzeware　Thai or the less elaborate western designs are available in Bangkok. There are a number of shops along Charoen Krung, north from Silom Rd, eg *Siam Bronze Factory* at No 1250 also at 714/6-7 Sukhumvit Road between Sois 26 and 28. The cutlery has become particularly popular and is now even available at the big department stores.

Camping　*Sanam Dernpa*, 8-10 Soi Praeng Phuthorn, off Tanao Rd. Well stocked with every-
equipment　thing from sleeping bags to torches, to jungle boots.

Celadon　Distinctive ceramic ware, originally produced during the Sukhothai Period (from the late 13th century), and recently revived. *Thai Celadon House*, 8/8 Rachdapisek Rd, Sukhumvit Rd (Soi 16), also sells seconds, or from *Narayana Phand*, 127 Rachdamri Rd.

Clothes　Cheap designer wear with meaningless slogans and a surfeit of labels (on the outside) available just about everywhere and anywhere, and especially in tourist areas like Patpong and Sukhumvit. Imitation *Lacoste* and other garments are less obviously on display now that the US is pressurizing Thailand to respect intellectual copyright laws but they are available. Note that the less you pay, generally, the more likely that the dyes will run, shirts will spontaneously down-size, and buttons will eject themselves at will. For unique funky designer clothes of Indian inspiration visit *Vipavee* on the first floor of *The Emporium* at Sukhumvit Soi 24 (there are lots of other places here as well). *Kai Boutique* on the 4th floor of Times Square Building is worth visiting for those interested in what the best designers in Thailand are doing. Many of Bangkok's smartest ladies patronise this establishment.

Central is the largest chain of department stores in Bangkok, with a range of Thai and imported goods at fixed prices; credit cards are accepted. Main shops on Silom Rd, Ploenchit Rd, and in the Central Plaza, just north of the Northern bus terminal. Other department stores include *Thai Daimaru* on Rachdamri and Sukhumvit (opposite Soi 71). *Robinson's* on corner of Silom and Rama IV roads, Sukhumvit (near Soi 19) and Rachdamri roads. *Tokyu* in MBK Tower on Rama I Rd. *Sogo* in the Amarin Plaza on Ploenchit Rd, and *Zen*, World Trade Centre, corner of Rama I and Rajdamri roads, soon to have an ice rink.

Department stores

Clothing, watches, leather goods, etc, all convincing imitations, can be bought for very reasonable prices from the many roadside stalls along Sukhumvit and Silom roads, Siam Square and in other tourist areas. Times Square, on Sukhumvit 14, has several 'designer clothing' shops.

Designer ware

There is a Thai doll factory on Soi Ratchataphan (Soi Mo Leng) off Rachprarop Rd in Pratunam. The factory sells dolls to visitors and also has a display. ■ *Mon-Sat 0800-1700, T2453008.*

Dolls

Between Soi 43 and Soi 45, Sukhumvit Rd, is an area where rattan furniture is sold. *Rattan House*, 795-797 Sukhumvit Rd (between Soi 43 and 45). *Corner 43*, 487/1-2 Sukhumvit Rd (between Soi 25-27). For stylish modern furniture visit the shopping mall attached to the Hilton Hotel on Witthayu Rd or *Home Place*, a shopping mall on Sukhumvit Soi 55 (Thonglor) at sub-soi No.13

Furniture

This is considerably cheaper than in USA or Europe; there is a concentration of shops along Yaowaraj Rd (Chinatown), mostly selling the yellow 'Asian' gold. Price is determined by weight (its so-called 'baht weight').

Gold

The *State Handicraft Centre* (*Narayana Phand*), 127 Rachdamri Rd, just north of Gaysorn, is a good place to view the range of goods made around the country. *House of Handicrafts*. *Regent Hotel*, 155 Rajdamri Rd. *House of Handicrafts*, 3rd Floor, Amarin Plaza, 496-502 Ploenchit Rd. On the opposite side of the road on the corner is *Gaysorn Plaza*. On the top two floors of the building is a collection of stalls called *The Thai Craft Museum* shop. This has a bit more style than Narayana Phand and feels less like a tour bus shopping stop. Also here on the 3rd floor is a relatively new and very "in" shop called *Cocoon*. Here traditional Thai objects have been transformed by altering the design slightly and using bright colours. Great for unusual and fun gifts.

Handicrafts

Aesthetic Studio, 22 Phahonyothin Rd, Soi 8. Trendy designer interior bits and pieces from glasses to candlesticks and boxes. *Back to the Origin*, 5th flr, Zen Building, Ratchadamir Rd. Attractive range of small pieces made from natural products; from bamboo handbags to rattan wine-racks. *Orientations*, President Park, corner of Sukhumvit Soi 22 and 24. Attractive furniture and accessories from Thailand, India, China and Indonesia. *Siam Discovery Centre*, otherwise known as Siam Tower, has some great interior design shops, including *Habitat*, and *Anyroom*, on the fourth floor.

Interior design/home furnishings

Thailand has become the world's largest gem cutting centre and it is an excellent place to buy both gems and jewellery. The best buy of the native precious stones is the

Jewellery
see box, overleaf

Bangkok

Buying gems and jewellery

More people lose their money through gem and jewellery scams in Thailand than in any other way (60% of complaints to the TAT involve gem scams). **DO NOT** *fall for any story about gem sales, special holidays, tax breaks – no matter how convincing.* **NEVER** *buy gems from people on the street (or beach) and try not to be taken to a shop by an intermediary. Any unsolicited approach is likely to be a scam. The problem is perceived to be so serious that in some countries Thai embassies are handing out warning leaflets with visas. For more background to Thailand and Burma's gems see page 501.*

Rules of thumb to avoid being cheated:

Choose a specialist store in a relatively prestigious part of town (the TAT will informally recommend stores).

Note that no stores are authorized by the TAT or by the Thai government; if they claim as much they are lying.

It is advisable to buy from shops which are members of the Thai Gem and Jewellery Traders Association.

Avoid touts.

Never be rushed into a purchase.

Do not believe stories about vast profits from re-selling gems at home.

Do not agree to have items mailed ("for safety").

If buying a valuable gem, a certificate of identification is a good insurance policy. The Department of Mineral Resources (Rama VI Rd, T2461694) and the Asian Institute of Gemological Sciences (484 Rachadapisek Rd, T5132112) will both examine stones and give such certificates.

Compare prices; competition is stiff among the reputable shops; be suspicious of 'bargain' prices.

Ask for a receipt detailing the stone and recording the price.

For more information (and background reading on Thailand) the Buyer's Guide to Thai Gems and Jewellery, *by John Hoskin can be bought at Asia Books.*

---

sapphire. Modern jewellery is well designed and of a high quality. Always insist on a certificate of authenticity and a receipt. *Ban Mo*, on Pahurat Rd, north of Memorial Bridge is the centre of the gem business although there are shops in all the tourist areas particularly on Silom Rd near the intersection with Surasak Rd, eg *Rama Gems*, 987 Silom Rd. *Uthai Gems*, 28/7 Soi Ruam Rudi, off Ploenchit Rd, just east of Witthayu Rd are recommended, as is *P. Jewellery* (Chantaburi), 9/292 Ramindra Rd, Anusawaree Bangkhan, T5221857. For western designs, *Living Extra* and *Yves Joaillier* are to be found on the 3rd floor of the Charn Issara Tower, 942 Rama IV Rd. *Jewellery Trade Centre* (aka Galleria Plaza), next door to the *Holiday Inn Crowne Plaza* on the corner of Silom Rd and Surasak Rd contains a number of gem dealers and jewellery shops on the ground floor. *Tabtim Dreams* at Unit 109 is a good place to buy loose gems.

Maps   *Asia Books* sell a very accurate map of Bangkok called *Bangkok, Central Thailand Travel Map*, published by Periplus Editions, ฿85. *Nelles* also publish a good Bangkok map with an excellent detailed map of the city centre.

Markets
Nancy Chandler's map of Bangkok, available from most bookshops, is the most useful guide to the markets of the capital

The markets in Bangkok are an excellent place to browse, take photographs and pick up bargains. They are part of the life blood of the city, and the encroachment of more organized shops and the effects of the re-developer's demolition ball are inimical to one of Bangkok's finest traditions. The largest is the *Weekend Market* at Chatuchak Park (see page 117). The *Tewes Market*, near the National Library, is a photographer's dream; a daily market, selling flowers and plants. *Pratunam Market* is spread over a large area around Rachprarop and Phetburi roads, and is famous for clothing and fabric. Half of it was recently bulldozed for redevelopment, but there is still a multitude of stalls here. The *Bai Yoke Market* is next door and sells mostly fashion garments for teenagers – lots of lycra. A short distance south of here on Rachprarop Rd is the *Naraiphan Shopping*

Centre and *Narayana Bazaar* an indoor stall/shopping centre affair (concentrated in the basement) geared to tourists and *farang* residents. *Nakhon Kasem* known as the *Thieves' Market*, in the heart of Chinatown, houses a number of 'antique' shops selling brassware, old electric fans and woodcarvings (tough bargaining recommended, and don't expect everything to be genuine – see page 105). Close by are the stalls of *Sampeng Lane* (see page 106), specializing in toys, stationery, clothes and household goods, and the *Pahurat Cloth Market* (see page 105) – a small slice of India in Thailand, with mounds of sarongs, batiks, buttons and bows. *Bangrak Market*, south of the General Post Office, near the river and the *Shangri-La Hotel*, sells exotic fruit, clothing, seafood and flowers. *Pak Khlong Market* is a wholesale market selling fresh produce, orchids and cut flowers and is situated near the Memorial Bridge. An exciting place to visit at night when the place is a hive of activity, (see page 105). *Phahonyothin Market* is Bangkok's newest, opposite the Northern bus terminal, and sells potted plants and orchids. *Banglamphu Market* is close to Khaosan Rd, the backpackers' haven, on Chakrapong and Phra Sumen roads. Stalls here sell clothing, shoes, food and household goods. The nearby *Khaosan Rd Market* (if it can be called such) is much more geared to the needs and desires of the foreign tourist: CDs and cassettes, batik shirts, leather goods and so on. *Patpong Market*, arranged down the middle of Patpong Rd, linking Silom and Surawong roads, opens up about 1700 and is geared to tourists, selling handicrafts, T-shirts, leather goods, fake watches, cassettes and videos. *Penang Market*, Khlong Toey, situated under the expressway close to the railway line specializes in electronic equipment from hi-fis to computers, with a spattering of other goods as well. Watch out for pick-pockets in this market! A specialist market is the *Stamp Market* next to the GPO (see map page 128) on Charoen Krung which operates on Sun only. Collectors come here to buy or exchange stamps.

Music

Tapes and CDs can be bought from many stalls in tourist areas, although the choice is limited to better-known artists. Cheap copies are harder to come by these days although as the genuine article is just ฿100 for a cassette or ฿500 for a CD it makes sense to buy the real McCoy. For a wider range of choice visit *Tower Records* on the top floor of *Siam Centre*, Rama 1 Rd or on the 3rd floor of *The Emporium* at Sukhumvit Soi 24.

Pottery

There are several pottery 'factories' on the left-hand side of the road on the way to the Rose Garden, near Samut Sakhon (see page 123).

Shoes

The *Siam Bootery* is a chain of shops for handmade footwear.

Shopping malls

No longer do visitors to Bangkok need to suffer the heat of the market stall, Bangkok is fast becoming another Singapore or Hong Kong, with shopping malls springing up all over the place. Some, like the long established *MBK* on the corner of Phayathai and Rama 1, are down-market and packed full of bargains, whilst others, like the *Siam Discovery Centre* (or Siam Tower), across the road from Siam Square, are more sophisticated and you are unlikely to pick up many cut-price goods. *The Emporium*, on Sukhumvit Soi 24 (directly accessible from BTS Phrom Phong Station) is an enormous place, dominated by the *Emporium Department Store* but with many other clothes outlets as well as record and book shops, designer shops and more. The ground and first floors are monopolised by the big names in fashion – *Kenzo, Chanel, Versace* are all there along with some expensive looking watch and jewellery shops. For the less extravagant there are a number of trendy clothes shops on the 2nd floor namely, *Phalene* and *Soda* (the names of two different shops as opposed to a new drink). The 3rd floor has the more prosaic offerings in the way of shops – *Boots the Chemists* have recently opened a store here. *Exotique Thai* occupies the space between the escalators on the 4th Floor. Here you can find a nice selection of decorative items for the home while the 5th Floor is dedicated to household goods along with a large food hall.

Bangkok

Silk Beware of 'bargains', as the silk may have been interwoven with rayon. It is best to stick to the well-known shops unless you know what you are doing. Silk varies greatly in quality. Generally, the heavier the weight the more expensive the fabric. One-ply is the lightest and cheapest (about ฿200 per metre), four-ply the heaviest and most expensive (about ฿300-400 per metre). Silk also comes in 3 grades: Grade 1 is the finest and smoothest and comes from the inner part of the cocoon. Finally, there is also 'hard' and 'soft' silk, soft being rather more expensive. Handmade patterned silk, especially *matmii* from the northeast region, can be much more expensive than simple, single-coloured industrial silk – well over ฿10,000 per piece. There are a number of specialist silk shops at the top of Surawong Rd (near Rama IV), including the famous *Jim Thompson's* (which is expensive, but has the best selection). ■ *Mon-Sun 0900-2100*. There are also a number of shops along the bottom half of Silom Rd (towards Charoen Krung) and in the Siam Centre on Rama I Rd. *Anita Thai Silk*, 294/4-5 Silom Rd, slightly more expensive than some, but the extensive range makes it worth a visit. *Home Made (HM) Thai Silk*, 45 Sukhumvit Soi 35 (silk made on premises), good quality *matmii* silk. *Jagtar* at 37 Sukhumvit Soi 11 has some lovely silk curtain fabrics as well as cushion covers in unusual shades and other accessories made from silk. Originality means prices are high. Village-made silks also available from *Cabbages and Condoms* (also a restaurant) on Sukhumvit Soi 12 and Raja Siam, Sukhumvit Soi 23. *Khompastr*, 52/10 Surawong Rd, near *Montien Hotel*, distinctive screen-printed fabric from Hua Hin. Factory (industrial) silk available from *Shinawatra* on Sukhumvit Soi 31. Numerous stalls at the *Chatuchak Weekend Market* also sell lengths from Laos and northeast Thailand (see page 117).

Spectacles Glasses and contact lenses are a good buy in Bangkok and can be made up in 24 hrs. Opticians are to be found throughout the city.

Supermarkets *Central Department Store* (see Department stores listing). *Isetan* (World Trade Centre), Rachdamri Rd. *Robinsons* – open until midnight (see Department stores listing). *Villa Supermarket*, between Sois 33 and 35, Sukhumvit Rd (and branches elsewhere in town) – for everything you are unable to find anywhere else. The *Villa* supermarkets are the best place to go for the more exotic imported foods and the branch on Sukhumvit road is open 24 hrs a day.

Tailoring services Bangkok's tailors are skilled at copying anything; either from fashion magazines or from a piece of your own clothing. Always request a fitting, ask to see a finished garment, ask for a price in writing and pay as small a deposit as possible. Tailors are concentrated along Silom, Sukhumvit and Ploenchit roads and Gaysorn Square. Indian tailors appear to offer the quickest service. *N and Y Boutique*, 11 Chartered Bank Lane (Oriental Avenue), near the *Oriental Hotel* (for ladies' tailored clothes), *New Devis Custom Tailors*, 179/2 Sukhumvit Rd, Soi 13 and *Rajawongse*, 130 Sukhumvit Rd (near Sukhumvit Soi 4) have both been recommended. There are many other places, though.

Textiles *Prayer Textile Gallery*, 197 Phayathai Rd, good range and excellent quality traditional and Laotian textiles.

Woodworking Lots of woodworking shops along Worachak Rd at the point where it crosses Khlong (canal) Banglamphu. *Bua Thong* is recommended, although the sign is only in Thai. Good places to buy bracelets, curtain rings and other knobs and trinkets fashioned from tropical hardwoods.

Sport

Facilities for sports such as badminton, squash or tennis are either available at the 4 to 5-star hotels or are listed in Bangkok's Yellow Pages and the monthly publications *Bangkok Metro Magazine* and *Bangkok Timeout*.

PS Bowl, 1191 Ramkamhaeng Rd, Huamark. ■ *Mon-Thu 1000-0100, Fri-Sun 1000-0200*. *Sukhumvit Bowl*, 2 Sukhumvit Soi 63 (Ekamoi). ■ *Mon-Sun 1000-0100*. **Bowling**

Dive Master, 110/63 Ladprao Soi 18, T5121664, F5124889. Organize dive trips, NAVI and PADI courses and sell (or rent) diving equipment. **Diving**

Most courses open at 0600 and play continues till dusk. Green fees vary from ฿400-2,000. Most also have clubs for hire. Telephone beforehand to check on availability. *Rose Garden*, Mu 4, Tambon Tha Talaat, Nakhon Pathom, T03-4322771. Green fees weekdays ฿450, weekends and holidays ฿1,100, club hire ฿260, caddy fee ฿180, 18 holes. *Royal Dusit*, Phitsanulok Rd, T2811330. Green fees ฿320 weekdays, ฿530 weekends, club hire ฿200. *Navatanee*, Ratana Samakee Rd, T3761031, Green fee ฿1,605 Mon-Fri, ฿2,140 weekends. Mature challenging course. *Muang-Ake*, 34 Mu 7, Phahonyothin Rd, Amphoe Muang, Pathum Thani, T5359335. 40 mins from city centre. Green fees ฿300 weekdays, ฿600 weekends, club hire ฿300. Phone to check regulations for temporary membership. There are also a number of golf **practice/driving ranges** off New Phetburi and Sukhumvit roads. Check the Yellow Pages, *Bangkok Metro Magazine* or *Bangkok Timeout*, for details. **Golf**

Low-key runs with heavy bouts of drinking. There are mixed hashes on Mon 1715. Call: Tod Wilkie, T8657137, www.bangkokhhh.com; men only hashes on Sat at 1630, call Randell Burke on T6475590. **Hash House Harriers (H3)**

Phillip Wain International, 8th Floor, Pacific Place, 140 Sukhumvit Rd, T2542544. ■ *Mon-Sat 0700-2200*. **Health club**

At the *Royal Turf Club* and *Royal Sports Club* on alternate Sun from 1230 to 1800, each card usually consists of 10 races. Check newspapers for details. **Horse racing**

Floor 8, World Trade Centre (Isetan end), 4 Ratchadamri Rd. Mon-Fri 1000-2030, Sat-Sun 1000-1445, 1530-2030. **Ice skating**

Kites are sold at Sanaam Luang for ฿15-20 on Sun and public holidays during the 'season' (see page 99). **Kite flying**

NTT Sports Club, 612/26 Soi Lao Lada, Phra Pinklao Bridge Rd. Large pool open to public with sports centre, just north of Sanaam Luang, on the river (฿100). Another reasonably priced and central pool is at the *Department of Physical Education*, Rama I Rd (next to Mahboonkrong Shopping Centre). Open Tue-Sun 1500-1800. There are a number of other public pools as well as private pools which allow non-members/non-residents to swim for a small fee. For a full listing with addresses and rates, see the capital's two listing magazines, *Bangkok Metro Magazine* or *Bangkok Timeout*. **Swimming**

This is both a sport and a means of self-defence and was first developed during the Ayutthaya Period, 1350-1767. It differs from western boxing in that contestants are allowed to use almost any part of their body. Traditional music is played during bouts. There are 2 main boxing stadiums in Bangkok – Lumpini (T2514303) on Rama IV Rd, near Lumpini Park, and Rachdamnern Stadium (T2814205) on Rachdamnern Nok **Thai boxing**

Ave. At Lumpini, boxing nights are Tue and Fri (1800-2200) and Sat (1700), up to and over ฿1,000 for a ringside seat (depending on the card); cheaper seats cost from about ฿150. At Rachdamnern Stadium, 1 Rachdamnern Rd (near the TAT office), boxing nights are Mon and Wed (1800-2200), Thu (1700 and 2100), Sun (1600 and 2000), seats from ฿160-500. Bouts can also be seen occasionally at the National Stadium on Rama I Rd (Pathumwan) and at Hua Mark Stadium near Ramkhamhaeng University on Khlong Ton Rd. Or you can just turn on the television – bouts are often televised live. If you want to learn more about the sport contact the Muai Thai Institute, 336/932 Prachathiphat, Pathum Thani, www.muaythai.th.net

Tennis Courts in many hotels. Public courts available at: *Central Tennis Club*, Sathorn Tai Soi Attakarnprasit, T2867202. ■ *Mon-Fri 0700-2200, Sat and Sun 1100-2100, ฿80-150 per hour, 5 courts, showers, racket hire and food available*. *Volvo Sports Club*, Ramkhamhaeng Soi 13 (near mall 3), T3180322. ■ *Mon-Sun 0700-2200, ฿120 per hour, good facilities, 6 courts, racket hire, hot showers.*

Tour operators

See also Tours, page 124

Travel agents abound in the tourist and hotel areas of the city – Khaosan Rd/Banglamphu, Sukhumvit, Soi Ngam Duphli, and Silom (several down Pan Rd, a soi opposite Silom Village). All major hotels will have their own in-house agent. Most will book airline, bus and train tickets, arrange tours, and book hotel rooms. Because there are so many to choose from, it is worth shopping around for the best deal. For those wishing to travel to Vietnam, Laos, Cambodia and Burma, specialist agents are recommended as they are usually able to arrange visas – for a fee. *Asian Holiday Tour*, 294/8 Phayathai Rd, T2155749. *Asian Lines Travel*, 755 Silom Rd, T2331510, F2334885. *Asian Trails*, 15th floor, Mercury Tower, 540 Ploenchit Rd, T6586080, F6586099, res@asiantrails.org, www.asiantrails.net *Banglamphu Tour Service*, 17 Khaosan Rd, T2813122, F2803642. *Dee Jai Tours*, 2nd Flr, 491/29 Silom Plaza Building, Silom Rd, T2341685, F2374231. *Diethelm Travel*, Kian Gwan Building II, 140/1, Witthayu Rd, T2559150, F2560248. *Dior Tours*, 146-158 Khaosan Rd, T2829142. *East-West*, Building One, 11th floor, 99 Witthaya Rd, T2567164, F2566665, celia@east-west-siom.com, www.east-west.com *Educational Travel Center (ETC)*, Room 318 Hotel, Rajdamnoen Avenue, T2240043, F6221420, etc@etc.co.th, www.etc.co.th *Exotissimo*, 21/17 Sukhumvit Soi 4, T2535240, F2547683 and 755 Silom Rd, T2359196, F2834885. *Fortune Tours*, 9 Captain Bush Lane, Charoen Krung 30, T2371050. *GM Tour & Travel*, 273 Khaosan Rd, T2823979, T2810642. One of the more efficient operations, with impartial flight information. *Guest House and Tour*, 46/1 Khaosan Rd, T2823849, F2812348. *MK Ways*, 57/11 Witthayu Rd, T2555590, F2545583. *Patco Chiang Mai*, Hualamphong Railway Station tourist office, organizes treks in the north, it comes recommended. *Pawana Tour and Travel*, 72/2 Khaosan Rd, T2678018, F2800370. *Roong Ruang Tour Travel Centre Co*, 183-185 Samsen Rd, T2534757, F2366808. *Siam Wings*, 173/1-3 Surawong Rd, T2331864, F2366585. *Skyline Travel Service*, 491/39-40 Silom Plaza (2nd Flr), Silom Rd, T2121583, F2121583. *Thai Travel Service*, 119/4 Surawong Rd, T2349360. *Top Thailand Tour*, 61 Khaosan Rd, T2802251, F2823337. *Tour East*, Rajapark Building (10th Flr), 163 Asoke Rd, T2593160, F2583236. *Transindo*, Thasos Building (9th Flr), 1675 Chan Rd, T2873241, F2873246. *Vieng Travel*, branch on the ground floor of the Trang Hotel, 99/8 Wisutkaset Rd, T2803537. *Vista Travel*, 244/4 Khaosan Rd, T2800348. *Western Union*, branch in the foyer of *Atlanta Hotel*, 78 Sukhumvit Soi 2, T2552151. Good all-round service.

Transport

See also Ins & outs, page 83.

More people have their belongings stolen on Bangkok's city buses than almost anywhere else

Bangkok

Local

Bus This is the cheapest way to get around town. A bus map marking the routes is indispensable. The *Bangkok Thailand* map and *Latest tours guide to Bangkok and Thailand* are available from most bookshops as well as many hotel and travel agents/ tour companies. Major bus stops also have maps of routes and instructions in English displayed. There is quite a range of buses, including a/c and non-a/c, micro, express and new improved, generally colour coded. Standard non-a/c buses (with blue stripe) cost ฿3.50. Beware of pickpockets on these often-crowded buses. Red-striped express buses are slightly more expensive, slightly less crowded, and do not stop at all bus stops. A/c buses cost ฿6-18 depending on distance and are coloured solid blue. Travelling all the way from Silom Rd to the airport by a/c bus, for example, costs ฿14; most inner city journeys cost ฿6. There are also smaller a/c 'micro buses' (a bit of a misnomer as they are not micro at all, not even 'mini'), which follow the same routes but are generally faster and less crowded because officially they are only meant to let passengers aboard if a seat is vacant. They charge a flat fare of ฿20. New arrivals on Bangkok's complicated bus system are white a/c buses which charge a flat fare of ฿10 and orange a/c buses which cost ฿12.

Car hire Approximate cost, ฿1,000-1,200 per day, ฿6,000-8,000 per week; Hertz and Avis charge more than the local firms, but have better insurance cover. See page 47 for general advice on driving in Thailand. *Avis*, 2/12 Witthayu Rd, T2555300. *Central Car Rent*, 115/5 Soi Ton-Son, Ploenchit Rd, T2512778. *Dollar Car Rent*, 272 Si Phraya Rd, T2330848. *Grand Car Rent*, 233-5 Asoke-Din Daeng Rd, T2482991. *Hertz*, 420 Sukhumvit Soi 71, T3900341. *Highway Car Rent*, 1018/5 Rama IV Rd, T2357746. *Inter Car Rent*, 45 Sukhumvit Rd, T2529223. *Silver International*, 102 Esso Gas Station, 22 Sukhumvit Rd, T2596867. *SMT Rent-a-Car*, 931/11 Rama I Rd, T2168020, F2168039.

Skytrain (BTS) At last Bangkok has a mass transit system! It may have taken years to make an appearance, and it may not cover even most of the city, but at least it's here. It runs on an elevated track several storeys up in the sky – hence its popular name, Skytrain. But it is officially know as BTS or the Bangkok Transit System, which are the letters emblazoned at the stations. There are two lines which cross at Siam Station (Siam Square): one runs from Mor Chit on Phahonyothin Road (close to the Chatuchak Weekend Market, to the north of the city centre) to Phrakanong on Sukhumvit Rd. The second lines runs from the National Stadium on Rama I Rd to Taksin Bridge (Saphan Taksin) at the end of Silom Rd in the heart of the business district. While the Skytrain doesn't cover anywhere close to all of the city, it does include a large chunk of the tourist, business and shopping areas so is very useful. It is also quick and cool – although the tramp up to the stations can be a fag (10 stations were having escalators installed in mid-2000) and the stations themselves are not air-conditioned. Trains run from 0600-2400, every 3-5 mins during peak periods and every 10-15 mins out of the rush hour. Fares are steep by Thai standards but worth it for most overseas visitors: ฿10 for one stop, ฿40 for the whole route. See the map on page 86 for its planned route. Although the Skytrain is a boon to visitors, it has not yet attracted the numbers the authorities were hoping for; despite the distribution of 1,000,000 leaflets, only 170,000 passengers take the train each day (instead of the hoped for 600,000). The reason perhaps – it is overpriced for locals. The skytrain may be the first mass transit system in the capital, but there are others being mooted and one already under construction: an underground which is scheduled for completion in 2002. For up-to-date information T6177300 or www.bts.co.th

Express boats Travel between Nonthaburi in the north and Wat Rajsingkorn (near Krungthep bridge) in the south. Fares are calculated by zone and range from ฿10 upwards. At peak hours boats leave every 10 mins, off-peak about 15-25 mins (see map, page 108 for piers, and page 107). The journey from one end of the route to the other takes 75 mins. Note that boats flying red or green pennants do not stop at all piers (they also exact a ฿2 express surcharge). Also, boats will only stop if passengers wish to board or alight, so make your destination known. Be warned that Thais trying to sell boat tours will tell you that the express boats are not running and will try to extort grossly inflated prices from you. Walk away and find the correct pier!

Bangkok's public transport numbers

taxis	*145,000*
tuk tuks	*127,405*
motorcycle taxis	*120,000*
illegal taxis	*126,000*

Ferries Small ferries take passengers across the Chao Phraya River, ฿1 (see map on page 108 for piers).

Khlong or long-tailed boats can be rented for ฿200 per hour, or more (see page 112).

Motorcycle taxi A relative newcomer to Bangkok (and now present in other towns in Thailand) they are the fastest, and most terrifying, way to get from A to B. Riders wear numbered vests and tend to congregate in particular areas; agree a fare, hop on the back, and hope for the best. Their 'devil may care' attitude has made them bitter enemies of many other road users. Expect to pay ฿10-20.

Taxi Taxis are usually metered (they must have a/c to register) – look for the 'Taxi Meter' illuminated sign on the roof. There are a number of unmarked, unofficial taxis which are to be found around the tourist sites. Flag fall is ฿35 for the first 3 km, and ฿5 per kilometre thereafter. Most trips in the city should cost ฿40-100. If the travel speed is less than 6 km per hour – always a distinct possibility in the traffice choked capital – a surcharge of ฿1 per minute is automatically added. Passengers also pay the tolls for using the expressway. Taxi drivers sometimes refuse to use the meter despite the fact that they are required to do so by law. We have had numerous complaints about Bangkok's taxi drivers who view foreign visitors to the city as ripe for ripping-off. If they refuse to use the meter simply get out and hail another – there are usually scores around. Another popular ruse is for drivers to deny they have any change. It's best to make sure you have sufficient 20s and 100s to pay but if not just get out and get change from a nearby shop. They'll wait! Taxis should not be tipped, although it is usual to round fares up to the nearest ฿5. For most tourists the arrival of the metered taxi has lowered prices as it has eliminated the need to bargain (assuming, of course, that the meter is being used). To call a taxi T1545 or T1661, they charge ฿20 plus the fare on the meter. Note that taxi drivers are not renowned for their knowledge of Bangkok. Many are up-country boys and with *farang* visitors massacring their language it is handy to have a rough idea of where you want to go, and a map (preferably with Thai lettering too).

Check that the meter is 'zeroed' before setting off

Tuk-tuk The formerly ubiquitous motorized saamlor is rapidly becoming a piece of history in Bangkok, although they can still always be found near tourist sites. Best for short journeys: they are uncomfortable and, being open to the elements, you are likely to be asphyxiated by car fumes. Bargaining is essential and the fare must be negotiated before boarding, most journeys cost at least ฿40. Both tuk-tuk and taxi drivers may try to take you to restaurants or shops – do not be persuaded; they are often mediocre places charging high prices.

Bangkok lies at the heart of Thailand's transport network. Virtually all trains and buses end up here and it is possible to reach anywhere in the country from the capital. Bangkok is also a regional transport hub, and there are flights to most international destinations. For international transportation, see page 33.

Long distance

See also Ins & outs, page 83

Bangkok

Air Don Muang Airport is 25 km north of the city. Regular connections on Thai to many of the provincial capitals. For airport details see page 37. There are a number of Thai offices in Bangkok, Head Office for domestic flights is 89 Vibhavadi Rangsit Rd, T5130121, but this is inconveniently located north of town. 2 more central offices are at 6 Lan Luang Rd (T2800070) and 485 Silom Rd. Tickets can also be bought at most travel agents. Bangkok Airways flies to Koh Samui, Hua Hin, Phuket, Sukhothai, Chiang Mai, Ranong, Hat Yai, U-Tapao (Pattaya) and Mae Hong Son. They have an office in the domestic terminal at Don Muang, and 2 offices in town. Note that Bangkok Airways have their own check-in area and departure lounge on the ground floor of the domestic terminal (not on the first floor).

Train Bangkok has 2 main railway stations. The primary station, catering for most destinations, is Hualamphong, Rama IV Rd, T2237010/2237020; condensed railway timetables in English can be picked up from the information counter in the main concourse. Trains to Nakhon Pathom and Kanchanaburi leave from the Bangkok Noi or Thonburi station on the other side of the Chao Phraya River. See page 34 for more information on Thailand's railways.

Bus There are 3 main bus stations in Bangkok serving the north and northeast, the east, and the south and west. Destinations in the Central Plains are also served from these terminals – places north of Bangkok from the northern and northeastern bus terminal, southwest of Bangkok from the southern terminal, and southeast from the eastern bus terminal. The new **Northern bus terminal** or *Mor Chit Mai* (new Mor Chit), aka Mor Chit 2, is at the western side of Chatuchak Park on Kamphaeng Phet 2 Rd. It serves all destinations in the north and northeast as well as towns in the Central Plains that lie north of Bangkok like Ayutthaya and Lopburi. Non-a/c buses 77, 134, 136 and 145 and a/c buses 3, 8, 12, 134, 136 and 145 all pass the terminal. Note that the original Mor Chit bus terminal, on Phahonyothin Rd, closed in 1998. The non-a/c **Southern bus terminal** is on Phra Pinklao Road (T4110061) near the intersection with Route 338. Buses for the west (places like Nakhon Pathom and Kanchanaburi) and the south leave from here. A/c town bus no 7 travels to the terminal. A/c buses to the south and west leave from the terminal on Charan Santiwong Rd, near Bangkok Noi Train Station in Thonburi, T4351199. The **Eastern bus terminal**, Sukhumvit Rd (Soi Ekamai), between Soi 40 and Soi 42, T3912504, serves Pattaya and other destinations in the eastern region.
  Buses leave for most major destinations throughout the day, and often well into the night. There are overnight buses on the longer routes – Chiang Mai, Hat Yai, Chiang Rai, Phuket, Ubon Ratchathani. Even the smallest provincial towns such as Mahasarakham have deluxe a/c buses connecting them with Bangkok. Note that in addition to the government-operated buses there are many private companies which run 'tour' buses to most of the major tourist destinations. Tickets bought through travel agents will normally be for these private tour buses which leave from offices all over the city as well as from the public bus terminals listed above. Shop around as prices may vary. Note that although passengers may be picked up from their hotel/guesthouse therefore saving on the ride (and inconvenience) of getting out to the bus terminal, the private buses are generally less reliable and less safe. Many pick up passengers at Khaosan Rd, for example.

Directory

Airline offices
For airport enquiries
call T2860190

Aeroflot, Regent House, 183 Rachdamri Rd, T2510617. *Air China*, 2nd Flr, CP Building, 313 Silom Rd, T6310731. *Air France*, Vorawat Building, 20th Flr, 849 Silom Rd, T6351199. *Air India*, SS Building, 10/12-13 Convent Rd, Silom, T2350557. *Air Lanka*, Ground Flr, Charn Issara Tower, 942 Rama IV Rd, T2369292. *Alitalia*, SSP Tower 3, 15th Flr, Unit 15A, 88 Silom Rd, T6341800. *American Airlines*, 518/5 Ploenchit Rd, T2511393. *Asiana Airlines*, 18th Flr, Ploenchit Center, 2 Sukhumvit 2 Rd, T6568610.

Bangkok Airways, Queen Sirikit National Convention Centre, New Rajdapisek Rd, Klongtoey, T2293456/2293454, and 140 Pacific Place Building, Sukhumvit Rd, T2293434. *Bangladesh Biman*, Ground Flr, Chongkolnee Building, 56 Surawong Rd, T2357643. *British Airways*, 14th Flr, Abdulrahim Place, 990 Rama 1V Rd, T6361747. *Canadian Airlines*, 6th Flr, Maneeya Building, 518/5 Ploenchit Rd, T2514521. *Cathay Pacific*, 11th Flr, Ploenchit Tower, 898 Ploenchit Rd, T2630606. *China Airlines*, 4th Flr, Peninsula Plaza, 153 Rachdamri Rd, T2534242. *Continental Airlines*, CP Tower, 313 Silom Rd, T2310113. *Delta Airlines*, 7th Flr, Patpong Building, Surawong Rd, T2376838. *Eva Airways*, Green Tower, 2nd Flr, 425 Rama IV Rd, opposite Esso Head Office. *Egyptair*, 3rd Flr, CP Tower, 313 Silom Rd, T2310504. *Finnair* 6th Flr, Vorawat Bldg, 849 Silom Rd, T6351234. *Garuda*, 27th Flr, Lumpini Tower, 1168 Rama IV Rd, T2856470. *Gulf Air*, 12th Flr, Maneeya Building, 518 Ploenchit Rd, T2547931. *Japan Airlines*, 254/1 Ratchadapisek Rd, T6925151. *KLM* 19th Flr, Thai Wah Tower 11, 21/133-134 South Sathorn, T6791100. *Korean Air*, Ground Flr, Kong Bunma Building (opposite *Narai Hotel*), 699 Silom Rd, T6350465. *Kuwait Airways*, 12th Flr, RS Tower, 121/50-51 Ratchadapisek Rd, T6412864. *Lao Aviation*, 491 17 Ground Flr, Silom Plaza, Silom Rd, T2369822. *Lufthansa*, 18th Flr, Q-House (Asoke), Sukhumvit Rd Soi 21, T2642400. *MAS (Malaysian Airlines)*, 20th Flr, Ploenchit Tower, 898 Ploenchit Rd, T2630565. *Myanmar Airways*, 23rd Flr, Jewellery Trade Centre, Silom Rd, T6300334. *Orient Express*, 17th Flr, 138/70 Jewellery Centre, Naret Rd, T2673210. *Pakistan International*, Chongkolnee Building, 56 Surawong Rd, T2342961. *Qantas*, 14th Flr, Abdulrahim Place, 990 Rama IV Rd, T6361747. *Royal Brunei*, 4th Flr, Charn Issara Tower, 942 Rama IV Rd, T2330056. *Royal Air Cambodge*, 17th Flr, 2 Pacific Place, 142 Sukhumvit Rd, T6532261. *Royal Nepal Airlines*,9th Flr, Phyathai Plaza Building, 128/108 Rajthevee Rd, T2165691. *Sabena*, 12th Flr, Charn Issara Tower, Rama 1V Rd, T2672100. *SAS*, 8th Flr, Glas Haus I, Sukhumvit Rd Soi 25, T2600444. *Saudi*, 19th Flr, United Centre Building, Silom Rd, T2667393. *Singapore Airlines*, 12th Flr, Silom Centre, 2 Silom Rd, T2365295/6. *Swissair*, 21st Flr Abdulrahim Place, 990 Rama 1V Rd, T6362160. *THAI*, 485 Silom Rd, T2343100. 89 Vibhavadi-Rangsit Rd, T5130121. *Vietnam Airlines*, 7th Flr, Ploenchit Centre, 2 Sukhumvit 2 Rd, T6569056.

Banks There are countless exchange booths in all the tourist areas open 7 days a week, mostly 0800-1530, some from 0800-2100. Rates vary only marginally between banks, although if changing a large sum, it is worth shopping around.

Church services *Evangelical Church*, Sukhumvit Soi 10 (0930 Sun service). The *International Church* (interdenominational), 67 Sukhumvit Soi 19 (0800 Sun service). *Baptist Church*, 2172/146 Phahonyothin Soi 36 (1800 Sun service). *Holy Redeemer*, 123/19 Wittayu Soi Ruam Rudee (Catholic, 5 services on Sun). *Christ Church*, 11 Convent Rd (Anglican – Episcopalian – Ecumenical, 3 Sun services at 0730, 1000 and 1800).

Communications Internet cafés abound, especially in the backpackers' centres. Eg *Khaosan Cyber Home*, Khaosan Rd. Open 0900-2200. *Bangkok Internet Café*, Khaosan Rd. *Chaiwat Tour*, Khaosan Rd. *Byte in @ cup*, Rm 401, 4th Flr, Siam Discovery Centre, 989 Rama I Rd, open 1000-1900, www.byte-in-a-cup.com 4 laptops available for ฿150 per 2 hrs (free if you bring your own laptop). Coffee, cakes and sandwiches as well as maps and books available. *The Café*, Surawong Rd, Corner of Soi Thaniya (ryoidii@rms.ksc.co.th). Open 1100-2200. 4 terminals and modern plugs for bringing your own laptops. *Cyberia*, 654/8 Sukhumvit Rd, corner of Soi 24. Open Sun-Wed 1030-2300. Thu-Sat 1030-2400. 18 terminals, ฿250 per hour, classy joint, food and live music towards the end of the week. *Explorer Internet Café*, Patpong Soi 1, a new place with plans to expand; they hope to be open 24 hrs a day, at present they are open 1700-0100. **Central GPO** (*Praysani Klang* for taxi drivers): 1160 Charoen Krung, opposite the *Ramada Hotel*. Open 0800-2000 Mon-Fri and 0800-1300 weekend and holidays. The money and postal order service is open 0800-1700, Mon-Fri, 0800-1200 Sat. Closed on Sun and holidays. 24-hr telegram and telephone service (phone rates are reduced 2100-0700) and a packing service.

Cultural centres *British Council*, 254 Chulalongkorn Soi 64 (Siam Square), T6116830, F2535311. For films, books and other Anglocentric entertainment; check in 'What's On' section of *Sunday Bangkok Post's* magazine for programme of events. *Alliance Française*, 29 Sathorn Tai Rd. *Goethe Institute*, 18/1 Sathorn Tai Soi Atthakan Prasit. *Siam Society*, 131 Soi 21 (Asoke) Sukhumvit, T2583494. Promotes Thai culture and organizes trips within (and beyond) Thailand. Open Tue-Sat.

Bangkok

Embassies & consulates Australia 37 Sathorn Tai Rd, T2872680. **Austria** 14 Soi Nandha, off Soi Attakarnprasit (Soi 1), Sathorn Tai Rd, T2873970. **Belgium** 44 Soi Phya Pipat, off Silom Rd, T2360150. **Burma** 132 Sathorn Nua Rd, T2332237. **Canada** 11th and 12th Floors, Boonmitr Building, 138 Silom Rd, PO Box 2090, T2374125. **Denmark** 10 Soi Attakarn Prasit, Sathorn Tai Rd, T2132021. **France** 35 Soi Rong Phasi Kao (Soi 36), Charoen Krung Rd, T2668250. **Germany** 9 Sathorn Tai Road, T2132331. **Greece** 79 Sukhumvit Soi 4 (Nana Tai), Sukhumvit Rd, Prakanong, T2542939. **Italy** 399 Nang Linchee Rd, Thungmahamek, T2854090. **Japan** 1674 New Petchburi Rd, T2526151. **Laos** 520, 520/1-3 Soi Ramkamhaeng 39, Bangkapi, T5383696. **Malaysia** 15th Floor, Regent House, 183 Rajdamri Rd, Pathumwan, T2541700. **Nepal** 189 Soi 71 Sukhumvit Rd, Prakanong, T3902280. **Netherlands** 106 Wireless Rd, T2547701. **New Zealand** 93 Wireless Rd, T2542530. **Norway** 1st Floor, The Bangkok of America Building, 2/2 Wireless Rd, T2530390. **Portugal** 26 Bush Lane, T2342123. **Spain** 7th Floor (701-702), Deithelm Towers (Tower A), 93/1 Wireless Rd, T2526112. **Sweden** 20th Floor, Pacific Place, 140 Sukhumvit Rd, T2544955. **Switzerland** 35 North Wireless Rd, PO Box 821, T2530156. **UK** 1031 Wireless Rd, T2530191. **USA** 120-122 Wireless Rd, T2054000.

Language schools Bangkok has scores of language schools. The best known is the *AUA school, 179 Rachdamri, T2528170.*

Libraries *British Council Library*, 254 Chulalongkorn Soi 64 (Siam Square). Open Tue-Sat 1000-1930, membership library with good selection of English-language books. *National Library*, Samsen Rd, close to Sri Ayutthaya Rd. Open Mon-Sun 0930-1930. *Neilson Hays Library*, 195 Surawong Rd, T2331731. Next door to British Club. Open 0930-1600 Mon-Sat, 0930-1230 Sun. A small library of English-language books housed in an elegant building dating from 1922. It is a private membership library, but welcomes visitors who might want to see the building and browse; occasional exhibitions are held here. Open Mon-Sat 0930-1600, Sun 0930-1230. *Siam Society Library*, 131 Sukhumvit Soi 21 (Asoke). Membership library with excellent collection of Thai and foreign language books and periodicals (especially English) on Thailand and mainland south east Asia. Open Tue-Sat 0900-1700.

Medical services *Bangkok Adventist Hospital*, 430 Phitsanulok Rd, Dusit, T2811422/2821100. Efficient vaccination service and 24-hr emergency unit. *Bangkok General Hospital*, New Phetburi Soi 47, T3180066. *Bangkok Nursing Home*, 9 Convent Rd, T2332610. *St Louis Hospital*, 215 Sathorn Tai Rd, T2120033. **Health clinics:** *Dental Polyclinic*, New Phetburi Rd, T3145070. *Dental Hospital*, 88/88 Sukhumvit 49, T2605000, F2605026. Good, but expensive. *Clinic Banglamphu*, 187 Chakrapong Rd, T2827479.

Useful addresses *Tourist Police*, Unico House, Ploenchit Soi Lang Suan, T1699 or 6521721. There are also dedicated tourist police offices in the main tourist areas. **Immigration:** Sathorn Tai Soi Suanphlu, T2873101.

The Central Plains

4

The Central Plains

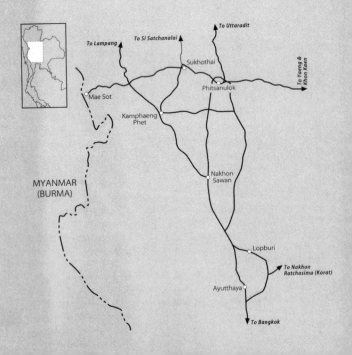

The history of Thailand, for over 700 years, has been focused on the Central Region. The two former capitals of Thailand – Sukhothai and Ayutthaya – were founded here and Thai cultural traditions are, to a significant extent, defined by those of Central Thailand. Any visitors wishing to immerse themselves in Thailand's past should spend some time travelling up through the Central region rather than rushing through straight to the north. For many the highlight of their trip to Thailand is a day spent exploring these 'lost' cities.

This region encompasses the fertile and productive valley of the Chao Phraya River where much of Thailand's rice is grown. Scenically, the area is rather monotonous. The valley is too wide (200 km in the south, 60 km in the north) and the gradient too shallow to be noticeable. Historically and economically though, the Central Plains has been of critical significance. The key to Thailand's wealth before the Second World War was the flood plain of the Chao Phraya and the rich rice farming areas that it encompasses. The Chao Phraya River proper begins at the town of Nakhon Sawan, 240 km north of Bangkok and situated at the confluence of the Ping, Wang, Nan and Yom rivers.

Although it is not always obvious, the Chao Phraya River and its tributaries are enclosed by the Phetchabun range of hills to the east and the Tenasserim range to the west. The former separates the Central Plains from the Northeast and divides two of Thailand's major natural and cultural regions. The latter was heavily forested until relatively recently and marks the divide between Thailand and Burma. There is trekking to be found in the western hills of Thailand, from towns like Mae Sot and Umphang.

Bang Pa-In   บางปะอิน

Colour map 2, grid C1 Bang Pa-In became the summer residence of the Ayutthayan kings of the 17th century. King Prasat Thong (1630-56) started the trend of retiring here during the hot season, and he built both a palace and a temple, Wat Chumphon Nikayaram, on an island in the middle of the Chao Phraya River. The palace is in turn located in the middle of a lake that the king had created on the island. It is said that his fondness for Bang Pa-In was because he was born on the island.

After the capital of Thailand was moved to Bangkok, Bang Pa-In was abandoned and left to degenerate. It was not until Rama IV stopped here on a journey to Ayutthaya that a restoration programme was begun, and both he and his son, King Chulalongkorn (Rama V), visited Bang Pa-In regularly. King Chulalongkorn also had a number of new halls built in the period 1872-89, and today the only original (although much restored) buildings that remain are those of **Wat Chumphon Nikayaram**, outside the palace walls, near the bridge and close to the railway station. The wat is an example of the third period of Ayutthayan architecture, while all the other buildings at Bang Pa-In date from the late 19th and early 20th centuries and are a strange mixture of Oriental, Italian and Victorian styles.

The description below follows the suggested 'official' route, passing through immaculately kept gardens. The **Varophat Phiman Hall** is essentially Corinthian in style and was built by Chulalongkorn in 1876 as his private residence. From here, a covered bridge leads to the inner palace. Immediately on the right, the **Thewarat Khanlai Gate** (not really a gate at all but a pavilion) overlooks the much-photographed **Isawan Thipaya-at Hall** in the middle of the lake. It is modelled on the Aphorn Phimok Hall in the Grand Palace, Bangkok. Facing the gate and bridge is the **Phra Thinang Uthayan Phumisathian**, painted a two-tone green. Designed to resemble a Swiss chalet, it looks more like a New England country house. Behind the 'chalet', the **Vehat Chamroon Hall**, built in 1889, is Chinese in style and was a gift from Chinese traders to King Chulalongkorn. It is the only building open to the public and contains some interesting Chinese artefacts and uncomfortable furniture. In front of the Vehat Chamroon Hall stands the **Hor Vithun Thasna**, a tall observation tower. Another bridge leads to a pair of memorials; the second commemorates Queen Sunanda, Rama V's half-sister and favourite wife who drowned here; it is said her servants watched her drown because of the law that forbade a commoner from touching royalty. South of the palace, over the Chao Phraya River, is the gothic-style **Wat Nivet Thamaprawat**, built in 1878 and resembling a Christian church. Currency exchange are facilities available. ■ *0830-1630 Mon-Sun. ฿50 (guidebook included).*

Excursions The **Royal Folk Arts and Crafts Centre** at Bang Sai is 24 km from Bang Pa-In (see page 122).

Transport **Boat** Boats can be hired from the pier opposite the Chandra Kasem Palace in
61 km to Bangkok Ayutthaya – ฿250-300, one-way; ฿400, return (3 hrs). For transport by boat from Bangkok, see Tours, page 124. **Bus** There is a regular minibus service from Ayutthaya's Chao Prom Market, 50 mins (฿30). Also regular bus connections from Bangkok's Northern terminal (1 hr). **Train** Three connections each day with Bangkok's Hualamphong station (1½ hrs) and connections north to Chiang Mai.

A Foot in the Door

★ The Central region's great draw is its historical sights: the ruined monuments, monasteries and palaces of the former capitals of Sukhothai and Ayutthaya as well as lesser cities such as Kamphaeng Phet, Si Satchanalai and Lopburi.

★ In the hills to the west are two important trekking bases, Mae Sot and Umphang. From here is it possible to explore the natural wealth – parks, caves and waterfalls – of the area and come into contact with assorted hill peoples.

★ The eastern edge of the central region divides the Central and Northeastern regions. The otherwise rather ugly town of Phitsanulok – much of it destroyed by a devastating fire in the 1960s – is home to one of Thailand's most important monasteries, Wat Phra Sri Ratana Mahathat.

Ayutthaya พระนครศรีอยุธยา

The Central Plains

Walking around the old city of Ayutthaya in the evening, with the setting sun illuminating the deep red brick ruins, it is not hard to imagine the grandeur of this place which so amazed early European visitors. Here is a stunning complex of palaces, shrines, monasteries and chedis, despite the disappearance of 84 of the original 384 monuments first listed in 1935 by the Fine Arts Department. The so-called historical park, which was made a UNESCO World Heritage site in 1991, covers some 3 sq km. Rama V (1868-1910) was the first person to appreciate the value of the site, both in terms of Thailand's national identity and in terms of its artistic merit.

Population: 65,000
Phone code: 035
Colour map 2, grid C1

Ins and outs

Most people get here by bus from Bangkok's Northern bus terminal. It is an easy 1½ hr journey, making a day trip from Bangkok possible. The station is centrally located in Ayutthaya. Another option is to arrive by boat, which takes a leisurely 3 hrs from Tha Tien pier in Bangkok.

Getting there
See also Transport, page 189

The wats are spread over a considerable area, too large to walk around comfortably, and the best way to cover quite a bit of ground is to hire a saamlor by the hour. That way, you can decide your route and instruct accordingly. There are long-tailed boats which transport people around the perimeter of the town, in order to visit the outlying sites, or many of the guesthouses hire out bicycles.

Getting around

TAT (temporary office), Si Sanphet Rd (next to the Chao Sam Phraya Museum), T246076, F246078. Areas of responsibility are Ayutthaya, Ang Thong, Suphanburi and Nonthaburi.

Tourist offices

History

Ayutthaya is reputed to have been founded in 1350 by Prince Uthong (later King Ramathibodi I) on the site of an ancient Indianized settlement. It is said that the Prince and his court were forced to leave Uthong following an outbreak of cholera and, after a brief interlude at the nearby Wat Panancherng, founded the city of Ayutthaya. The Royal Chronicles of Ayutthaya record: "In 712, a Year of the Tiger, second of the decade, on Friday, the sixth day of the waxing moon of the fifth month, at three *nalika* and nine *bat* after the break of dawn, the capital city of Ayutthaya was first established [that is, Friday 4 March 1351, at about 0900]". Another account reports that it was not until the

King Naresuan the Great of Ayutthaya

One of Thailand's great kings, King Naresuan of Ayutthaya (1590-1605), was one of only five who have posthumously been awarded the sobriquet 'the Great'. In 1569 the Burmese had taken Ayutthaya and placed a puppet monarch on the throne. The great kingdom appeared to be on the wane. But Naresuan, who in David Wyatt's words was "one of those rare figures in Siamese history who, by virtue of dynamic leadership, personal courage, and decisive character, succeed in herculean tasks that have daunted others before them", proceeded to challenge the Burmese. He confronted their forces in 1585, 1585-86 and in 1586-87, defeating armies that grew larger by turn. Finally, at the beginning of 1593, the decisive battle occurred at Nong Sarai, to the northwest of Suphanburi. The Burmese had assembled an army of monumental proportions. During the initial skirmish, Naresuan saw the Burmese crown prince mounted on his war elephant and, according to the chronicles, shouted across the battle field: "Come forth and let us fight an elephant duel for the honour of our kingdoms". When the Burmese prince lunged with his lance, Naresuan ducked beneath the blow to rake, and kill, his opponent with his sword. The battle was won and Ayutthaya was once again in a position to flourish.

surrounding marsh was drained that the town was freed from epidemics and could prosper.

Ayutthaya's name derives from 'Ayodhya', the sacred town in the Indian epic, the Ramayana. It became one of the most prosperous kingdoms in the Southeast Asian region, and by 1378 the King of Sukhothai had been forced to swear his allegiance and submit to the suzerainty of Ayutthaya. Ultimately, the kingdom stretched from Angkor (Cambodia) in the east to Pegu (Burma) in the west. In 1500 it was reported that the kingdom was exporting 30 junk loads (10,000 tonnes) of rice to Malacca (Melaka) each year. Ayutthaya was also an important source of animal skins, ivory, resins and other forest products.

The city is situated on an island at the confluence of three rivers – the Chao Phraya, Pasak and Lopburi. Its strong defensive position proved a distinct advantage as Ayutthaya was attacked by the Burmese alone on no less than 24 occasions. Recent research on sea level changes in the Gulf of Thailand also indicate that in 1350, when the city was founded, the coastline was much further north and the city therefore was considerably closer to the sea. Thus Ayutthaya, unlike the previous Thai capitals of Sukhothai and Si Satchanalai, was a trading port and not purely a land-based kingdom.

Given that the Ayutthayan Period lasted for over 400 years from 1350 to 1767, the town exudes history. One of Ayutthaya's most famous kings was Trailokant (1448-88), a model of the benevolent monarch. He is best known for his love of justice and his administrative and legislative reforms. This may seem surprising in view of some of the less than enlightened legal practices employed later in the Ayutthayan Period. A plaintiff and defendant might, for example, have to plunge their hands into molten tin, or their heads into water, to see which party was the guilty one.

A succession struggle in the mid-16th century heralded the beginning of 20 years of intermittent warfare with the Burmese, who managed to seize and occupy Ayutthaya. This led to the emergence of another Thai hero, King Naresuan (1590-1605), who recaptured the city and led his country back to independence. Under King Narai (1656-88), Ayutthaya became a rich, cosmopolitan trading post. Merchants came to the city from Portugal, Spain, Holland, China, Arabia, Persia, Malaya, India and Japan. In its heyday, Ayutthaya was said to have 40 different nationalities living in and around the city walls, and in the 16th century it supported a population larger than London at that time.

The city was strongly fortified, with ramparts 20 m high and 5 m thick, and was protected on all sides by waterways: rivers on three sides and a linking canal on the fourth. Accounts by foreign visitors clearly record their awe at the size and magnificence of the city which, with its temples (over 400 – many gilded or decorated in mosaic) and canals, was an Oriental Venice. The cosmopolitan atmosphere was evident on the waterways where royal barges rubbed shoulders with Chinese junks, Arab dhows and ocean-going schooners. Jean de Lacombe, a French visitor of the 17th century, wrote of the house of Juric that 'the richness of its materials, transcending every other building of the world, renders it a Dwelling worthy of an Emperor of the whole world', while Glanius, in 1682, described the city as being so gilded that in the sunshine the light reflected from the spires "disturbed the eyes". Visitors found endless sources of amusement in the city. There were elephant jousts, elephant and tiger fights, Thai boxing (*muay Thai*), masked plays and puppet theatre. It was said that the King of Ayutthaya was so wealthy that even the elephants were fed from vessels of gold.

Indeed, early western visitors to Ayutthaya often commented on the king's elephants and the treatment they received. One of the earliest accounts is by Jacques de Countres, a merchant from Bruges who resided in the city for eight months in 1596 (during Naresuan's reign). His son later recorded his father's experiences:

> *The palace is surrounded by stables where live the favourite elephants ridden by the king ... The sumptuosity of their treatment deserves to be mentioned. Each one had its silk cushion, and they slept on it as if they were small dogs. Each one of them had six very large bowls of gold. Some contained oil to grease their skins; others were filled with water for sprinkling; others served for eating; others for drinking; others for urinating and defecating. The elephants were indeed so well trained that they got up from their beds when they felt the urge to urinate or defecate. Their attendants understood at once and handed them the bowls. And they kept their lodges always very sweet-smelling and fumigated with benzoin and other fragrant substances. I would not have believed it if I had not actually seen it (quoted in Smithies, Michael (1995) Descriptions of Old Siam, Kuala Lumpur: OUP).*

One European became particularly influential: King Narai's Greek foreign affairs officer (and later Prime Minister), Constantine Phaulcon. It was at this time the word 'farang' – to describe any white foreigner – entered the Thai vocabulary, derived from 'ferenghi', the Indian for 'French'. In 1688, Narai was taken ill and at the same time the French, who Phaulcon had been encouraging, became a serious threat, gaining control of a fortress in Bangkok. An anti-French lobby arrested the by now very unpopular Phaulcon and had him executed for suspected designs on the throne. The French troops were expelled and for the next century Europeans were kept at arm's length. It was not until the 19th century that they regained influence in the Thai court.

In the mid-18th century, the kingdom was again invaded, by the Burmese, reputedly for the 24th time. In 1767 they were finally successful in vanquishing the defenders. The city was sacked and its defences destroyed, but, unable to consolidate their position, the Burmese left for home, taking with them large numbers of prisoners and leaving the city in ruins. The population was reduced from one million to 10,000. Ayutthaya never recovered from this final attack, and the magnificent temples were left to deteriorate.

Sights

Sites with an entrance
fee generally open
from 0800-1700.
For more background
on Ayutthayan style,
see page 807

The modern town of Ayutthaya is concentrated in the eastern quarter of the old walled city, and beyond the walls to the east. Much of the rest of the old city is green and open, interspersed with abandoned wats and new government buildings. Unfortunately, Bangkok's sprawl has even made itself felt up here. The new town is eating its way eastwards into the countryside, roads and flyovers are spreading like cancerous growths, and concepts such as urban planning, zoning and green belts are clearly not on the city fathers' agenda. Fortunately though, the core old city is protected (3 sq km of the 8 sq km of the 'island' are part of the park) and survives relatively unscathed from the onslaught.

The route below takes in the most important wats. Ayutthaya's other fine ruins are described in the second half of this section. The sheer size of the site means that the considerable numbers of tourists are easily dispersed among the ruins, leaving the visitor to wander in complete tranquillity along shaded brick-paved walkways, among chedis built of a mellow red brick, which stand among trees reminiscent of the olive and cork trees of Southern France. Away from the vendors' stalls, the quietness comes as a stark contrast to the high-pressure bustle of Bangkok.

NB Ayutthaya is one of the most popular day tours from Bangkok (see page 124), but for those with an interest in ruins or Thai history, there is more than enough to occupy a whole day. The day tour allows about two hours; a frustratingly short time for a superficial glance at this ancient capital. Ignore tour operators who maintain there is no accommodation here; it is perfectly adequate.

Tours A number of companies run boat tours up the Chao Phraya to Ayutthaya. For further information, see page 125. River tours around Ayutthaya can also be arranged through a number of guesthouses.

Wat Ratchaburana This wat was built by King Boromraja II in 1424 on the cremation site of his two brothers (princes Ai and Yo), who were killed while contesting the throne. The Khmer-style prang (which has been partially restored) still stands amidst the ruins of the wat. Remains of figures supporting the structure surround the prang, along with some stucco work, garuda figures and poorly restored standing Buddha images in the niches. Half-way up the prang, steep stairs lead downwards into the bowels of the structure where disappointing murals can just be discerned in the dim light. Some of the most important treasures yet found in Ayutthaya were discovered here when the site was excavated in 1958: bronze Buddha images, precious stones and golden royal regalia, belonging, it is assumed, to the two brothers. Much of the viharn to the east of the prang remains intact, giving an idea of how the compound must have looked. Scattered remains of countless Buddha images litter the grounds. ∎ ฿30.

Wat Phra Mahathat Across the road from Wat Ratchaburana, on the opposite corner of Chee Kun and Naresuan roads, is this wat, the Monastery of the Great Relic. It was founded in 1384, making it one of the earliest prangs in Ayutthaya, and was the largest of all Ayutthaya's monasteries, built to house holy relics of the Buddha (hence its name). It was also the place where Ayutthaya's Supreme Patriarch based himself. It is said that King Boromraja I (1370-88) was meditating one dawn when he saw a glow emanating from the earth; he took this to mean that a relic of the Buddha lay under the soil and ordered a wat to be founded. Following his successful assault on Angkor, King Boromraja II (1424-48) is said to have brought a hoard of bronze statues of wild animals back with him as booty, and these were arranged around the base of the main chedi. The Burmese, in their turn, plundered the statues after their first successful assault on Ayutthaya in 1569. This interest in artefacts that have little instrinsic value – they were bronze – is linked to the traditional belief that only emperors could own them. They were viewed, then, as a sort of guarantee of greatness. Only the large base remains of the original Khmer-style prang, which collapsed during the reign of King Song Tham (1610-28). BC – before collapse – it was an impressive 50 m high and built of laterite and brick. Just before the Burmese army's second, and final, assault on the city in 1767, two crows were seen fighting over Wat Mahathat. One spiked itself on the chedi's finial - a bad omen! When the Fine Arts Department excavated the site in 1956, they found a number of gold Buddha images as well as relics of the Buddha inside a gold casket, now exhibited in the National Museum, Bangkok. The prang is surrounded by walls, which are in turn surrounded by smaller prangs and chedis, some of which are rather precariously supported. Like Wat Ratchaburana, remnants of Buddha torsos and heads are scattered in the grounds. ■ ฿30.

Wat Phra Ram Travelling west on Naresuan Road (Chao Phrom Road), to the south is another of the older wats, begun in 1369 by King Ramesuan (1369-70), the son of Ayutthaya's founder. The entrance to the compound is through tall archways, designed to be high enough for elephants to pass under. The slender prang has been partially restored, but there are still some original stucco nagas and garudas, as well as standing Buddha images in the niches. ■ ฿30. There is a pleasant little noodle stall to the right of the entrance to this wat.

Ayutthaya Historical Study Centre
An excellent place to begin a tour of Ayutthaya

To the south of Wat Phra Ram, on Rojana Road, is this new museum and research centre. It is housed in a surprisingly sensitively-designed modern building, proving there are some creative architects in the country, funded by a large donation from Japan and opened in 1990. The museum tries to recreate Ayutthaya life and does so with some excellent models. The entrance fee might be regarded as slightly steep for Thailand. ■ *0900-1630 Wed-Fri, 0900-1700 Sat and Sun, ฿100.*

Wat Boromaphutharam

Colloquially known as Wat Krabueng Klueb (the Ceramic Monastery), this wat is not far away on Si Sanphet Road. It was built in 1683, according to the annals, during the reign of King Petracha (1682-97) and is said to be based on a monastery in the Central Plains town of Lopburi which the king particularly admired. One 'block' west, close to the moat, is **Wat Som**. This is notable for its well-preserved Khmer-style early-Ayutthaya prang, perhaps the best example surviving in the city. **Wat Sala Poon** just to the west has been extensively renovated; the bot has worthwhile murals, some incorporating western subject matter and techniques, such as a modest stab at perspective.

• •

Ayutthaya main places

Wang Luang
วังหลวง

Wat Phra Ram
วัดพระราม

Viharn Phra Mongkol Bopitr
วิหารพระมงคลบพิตร

Wat Phra Sri Sanphet
วัดพระศรีสรรเพชญ์

Wat Phra Mahathat
วัดพระมหาธาตุ

Wat Ratchaburana
วัดราชบูรณะ

Wat Phra Sri Sanphet

Within the extensive grounds of Wang Luang (the Royal Palace) was the largest and most beautiful wat in Ayutthaya, the equivalent of Wat Phra Kaeo in Bangkok. It was built in 1491, and subsequently extended during the reigns of several kings. The wat was only used on royal religious occasions, and unlike most wats it had no quarters for monks. Three highly-regarded restored Ceylonese-style chedis dominate the compound. They contain the ashes of King Trailokant (1448-88) and his two sons (who were also kings of Ayutthaya). There are no prangs here; the three central chedis are surrounded by alternate smaller chedis and viharns. Remains of walls and leaning pillars give an impression of the vastness of the wat. In 1500 it is alleged that a 16 m standing Buddha was cast by King Ramathipodi II (1491-1529), using a staggering 5,500,000 kg of bronze and covered in 340 kg of gold leaf. The image's name, Phra Sri Sanphet, later became the name of the wat. When the Burmese invaded the city in 1767 the image was set on fire in order to release the gold, in the process destroying both it and the temple. A model of this Buddha can be seen in Wat Pho in Bangkok (see page 93). ■ ฿30.

Close to Wat Phra Ram and Wat Phra Sri Sanphet is a newly restored 100-year-old Thai house, **Khum Khun Paen**. The house was built in 1894 as the residence of the governor of Monthon Ayutthaya. ■ *Mon-Sun.*

Ayutthaya

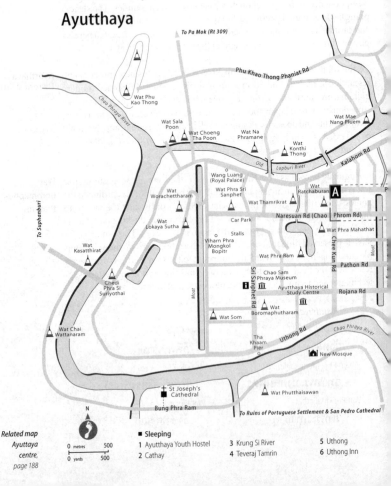

N

0 metres 500
0 yards 500

■ **Sleeping**
1 Ayutthaya Youth Hostel
2 Cathay

3 Krung Si River
4 Teveraj Tamrin

5 Uthong
6 Uthong Inn

Looking north from Wat Phra Sri Sanphet, it is possible to see the extensive foundations of **Wang Luang**. The palace was constructed by King Trailokant and was only one of three palaces used by the Ayutthayan kings. It originally consisted of five main buildings, although the Burmese did such an effective demolition job that today only the foundations remain. This was aided by the fact that the palace was built of wood; only religious buildings and monuments were allowed to be built of brick or stone. Within the palace's double walls were stables to house 100 elephants, and the extent of the foundations gives some idea of how impressive the palace must have been. ■ β30.

Viharn Phra Mongkol Bopitr

South of Wat Phra Sri Sanphet stands this 'new' viharn, built in 1956 and modelled on the 15th-century original which was razed by the Burmese. It houses one of the largest bronze Buddhas in the world, the Phra Mongkol Bopitr, after which the monastery is named. It is nearly 12.5 m high, seated in an attitude of subduing Mara, on a raised platform. It stares imperiously down on the many pilgrims who pay homage by sticking copious amounts of gold leaf to its base. This black image is made of sheets of copper-bronze, fastened onto a core of brick and plaster. It probably dates from the 16th century as it is early Ayutthayan in style – by which it is meant showing Sukhothai's influence. It was certainly mentioned in a royal order of 1603 when it was moved on the order of King Song Tham. Until 1956, when it was restored, the image had been left exposed to the elements and was badly damaged.

The Central Plains

Other sights

Wat Lokaya Sutha

Taking the road west beside the Viharn Phra Mongkol Bopitr, cross over the moat and a winding road leads to the small Wat Lokaya Sutha, of which little remains except a large white reclining Buddha (which faces a row of foodstalls) and a small prang. Close by is **Wat Worachettharam**, the Monastery of the Beloved Brother, built in 1587 on King Naresuan's death. His younger brother, King Ekathosaroth, built this monastery as a monumental epitaph in stone to his great predecessor. The chronicles record that 10,000 monks from across the Kingdom attended the cremation. Today not much remains to hint at the scale of the place: a large but badly damaged chedi and a few crumbling walls. The Fine Arts Department, though, is carrying out renovation work.

Travel back past Wang Luang to the main road, turn east and after 250 m the road crosses the Old Lopburi River. From the bridge one can see

(Map)

Elephant Kraal o

Pasak River

Lopburi River

Hua Ro Market amanakot o

Chandra Kasem ace & Museum

Pier

Canal ✉

■5
■2

aphrao Rd

Wat Pradu Songtham

Wat Kuti Tao

Wat Samanakot

To Wat Maheyong →

Pasak River

Chao Phrom Market Samanakot

■4

Uthong Rd

To Wat Ayutthaya

1
■3

Pridi Damrong Bridge

Rojana Rd

6■

To Ayutthaya Grand Hotel, Wat Suwan Dararam, Uthong & Bangkok (Rt 309)

Wat Suwan Dararam

1

Phom Phet Fortress

RT 3059

Wat Phanan Choeng

Wat Yai Chai Mongkol

To Bang Pa-In

● **Eating**
1 Phae Krung Kao

Wat Na Phramane, a restored wat which dates from 1503 and is one of the most complete examples of Ayutthayan architecture. It is reputed to have been built by one of King Ramathibodi's concubines, Pra Ong, at which time it was known as Wat Pramerurachikaram. A treaty to end one of the many wars with Burma was signed here in 1549. Over two centuries later in 1767, the Burmese used the position to attack the city once again, and it is said that the King of Burma suffered a mortal blow from a cannon which backfired during the initial bombardment. Perhaps because of this, the Burmese – unusually – left the wat intact. Even without the helping hands of the Burmese, the wat still fell into disrepair and was not restored until 1838. The lovely early Ayutthayan bot is the largest in the city and contains an impressive crowned bronze Buddha image in an attitude of subduing Mara. Unusually, the Buddha is dressed – in king's dress of the Ayutthayan Period. The ceiling is painted with red and gold stars. Next to the bot is the beautiful **Viharn Noi** ('little' or 'lesser' viharn), which houses a small green stone Buddha image, seated in the 'European manner' and dating from the Dvaravati Period. It was found in the ruins of Wat Mahathat, but is believed to have come from Nakhon Pathom. Some people even maintain that it originally came from Ceylon some 1,300 years ago, although this is unlikely. This bot antedates the rest of the complex, having been built by Rama III (1824-51) specifically to house the Dvaravati Buddha. **NB** The image cannot always be viewed. ■ ฿10.

Wat Thamrikrat A short distance to the east of Wat Na Phramane, across a small tributary of the Old Lopburi River, are the ruins of **Wat Konthi Thong**. South over the bridge again and a short distance east along Kalahom Road is Wat Thamrikrat, the Monastery of the Pious Monarch, with stucco lions (singha) surrounding an overgrown chedi. Scholars are not sure exactly when it was built, but they are largely agreed that it predates the reign of King Boromtrailokant (1448-88). The lions show some stylistic links with similar lions of the Khmer Bayon period (13th century), and it has been suggested that when King Boromraja II (1424-48) overcame the Khmer he brought back craftsmen, ideas and artefacts from Angkor.

● ●

Ayutthaya other places

Chao Sam Phraya Museum
พิพิธภัณฑสถาน–
แห่งชาติเจ้าสามพระยา

Chandra Kasem Palace
พระราชวังจันทรเกษม

Elephant kraals
เพนียดคล้องช้าง

Viharn Noi
วิหารน้อย

Wat Chai Wattanaram
วัดไชยวัฒนาราม

Wat Lokaya Sutha
วัดโลกยสุธา

Wat Na Phramane
วัดหน้าพระเมรุ

Wat Phanan Choeng
วัดพนัญเชิง

Wat Phu Kao Thong
วัดภูเขาทอง

Wat Phuttaisawan
วัดพุทธไทสวรรค์

Wat Suan Dararam
วัดสวนดาราราม

Wat Yai Chai Mongkol
วัดใหญ่ชัยมงคล

The Central Plains

Also on the north bank of the river, not far from the confluence of the Chao Phraya and Old Lopburi rivers, is this wat. It is not known when it was originally built – it has been restored on a number of occasions – but it is said to have been constructed by a man whose daughter ran away with her lover and never returned; it was known as Wat Koy Tha, the Monastery of Waiting. The Ayutthaya-style prang is in reasonable condition, as is the *sala kan parian*, although the bot and viharn are both in poor condition.

Wat Choeng Tha

Set apart from the other wats is this little-visited wat, the Monastery of the Golden Star. To get there, take Uthong Road, south of Pridi Damrong Bridge, and just before the remnants of Phom Phet turn down a narrow lane. The wat was razed by the Burmese during their sacking of the city in 1767, and Rama I, the founder of the present Chakri dynasty, took charge of its rebuilding when he was still an officer in the Ayutthaya army. When he acceded to the throne and became Rama I, he ordered the restoration to be continued and then renamed it Suwan Dararam in honour of his parents. (It had previously been called Wat Thong.) It is still in use today. The bot dips towards the centre, a feature of the architecture of the period, and contains a series of vivid murals depicting the Jataka stories, images of heaven and hell and, facing the main Buddha image, the Buddha subduing Mara with the earth goddess as his witness. The principal image is an enlarged stone copy of the Emerald Buddha in Bangkok. The viharn is also notable for its fine murals. Completed in 1931, they show episodes from the life of King Naresuan (1590-1605). This choice of subject matter seems to be linked to Rama I's wish to gain legitimacy in the eyes of lords and commoners alike. It was an attempt to link the new dynasty with the most glorious of Ayutthaya's kings. As at Wat Na Pramane, however, the buildings are not always open. If arriving by tuk-tuk, the driver will probably know who to ask for the key; otherwise, ask one of the monks. It is worth persevering as the murals are unique in Ayutthaya. **Phom Phet** or Diamond Fort was built as a stronghold after the first successful assault on Ayutthaya by the Burmese in 1549.

Wat Suwan Dararam

Located on Rojana Road, this museum was opened in 1961. Votive tablets excavated from Wat Ratchaburana were auctioned off to raise funds for its construction. It houses many of Ayutthaya's relics, in particular the Mongkol Buddha. ■ *0900-1200, 1300-1600 Wed-Sun (except public holidays), ฿30.*

Chao Sam Phraya Museum

The extensive waterways of Ayutthaya (over 50 km of them) are a pleasant way to see some of the less accessible sights. Long-tailed boats can be taken from the landing pier opposite Chandra Kasem Palace, in the northeast corner of the town. During the dry season, it is not possible to circle the entire island; the Old Lopburi River becomes unnavigable. The usual route runs south down the Pasak River and round as far as Wat Chai Wattanaram on the Chao Phraya River.

Waterways

This palace, the Palace of the Happy Moon (also known as Wang Na, or Front Palace), was built during the reign of the 17th King of Ayutthaya, Maha Thammaraj (1569-90), for his son Prince Naresuan. Afterwards it became the traditional residence of the Crown Prince. Like most other buildings, the palace was destroyed by the Burmese. It was later restored by King Mongkut in the 19th century for use as one of his provincial residences. Within the palace is Ayutthaya's second, and smaller, **museum** housed in the wooden Chaturamuk Pavilion built by Rama IV (1851-68). It offers more interesting surroundings than the Chao Sam Phraya Museum, but has an inferior collection. Buddha

Chandra Kasem Palace

heads, torsos and other works of art line the walls of the palace grounds, sadly enclosed by thick wire mesh. ■ *0900-1200, 1300-1600 Wed-Sun, ₿30.*

Wat Phanan Choeng
All the wats described from hereon can also be reached by road

Situated close to the junction of the Pasak and Chao Phraya rivers, this is the first wat to be reached by boat, travelling clockwise from the Chandra Kasem pier. It is a restored wat, which cannot be accurately dated. However, the 19 m high seated Buddha image in the viharn (immediately behind the bot) is mentioned in a chronicle as having been made in 1324, some 26 years before Ayutthaya became the capital. It is likely that the wat was founded at the same time, making it the oldest in Ayutthaya. The Buddha, sitting in an attitude of subduing Mara, is made of brick and plaster and is gilded. It sits crammed into the viharn, dark, somnolent and atmospheric. Unusually in Thailand, behind the image, the wall is pockmarked with tiny niches, each containing a small Buddha. The principal image was popular with Chinese traders, who would worship before it prior to embarking on long journeys. It is still worshipped by people from all over the country and is popularly known as 'Luangpor To'. Judging from the Chinese characters that adorn the entrance, it is still popular with the Chinese community. This image is said to have wept tears when Ayutthaya was sacked by the Burmese in 1767.

Wat Phutthaisawan

This active wat contains within its compound a large recently restored 'corn cob' prang. The monastery has a fine array of buildings and images and is worth exploring. A ferry carries passengers over to the monastery from the Tha Khaam pier immediately opposite. It can also be reached by road. Travelling further west along the Chao Phraya, the handsomely restored **Catholic Cathedral of St Joseph** comes into view. It was built in 1666 to serve the large European community living in Ayutthaya during its heyday as a trading centre. The Burmese used it as a base in 1767; it was destroyed, to be renovated under Father Pallegoix's supervision from 1831.

Wat Chai Wattanaram

Turning north, this wat occupies a magnificent position on the west bank of the Chao Phraya River, to the west of the city. Constructed in 1630, it is a large complex, and the latest to be 'restored'. A decapitated Buddha sits overlooking the river in front of the ruins, while the large central prang is surrounded by two rows of smaller chedis and prang-like chedis, arranged on the cardinal and sub-cardinal points of the cloister that surrounds the central structure. The wat was built by King Prasat Thong (1630-56) in honour of his mother and he initially planned to build a monument of Angkor-esque proportions. He later adopted a less ambitious plan, but even so the complex has a Khmer quality about it, particularly in the early evening when the fading light gives this place a wonderful glow. Sadly, the fine stucco work depicting scenes from the lives of the Buddha has all but disappeared. This wat was particularly badly damaged during the Burmese assault on the city in 1767. A row of headless Buddhas and Buddha remnants sit on raised plinths around the walls. Relatively few tours of Ayutthaya include Wat Chai Wattanaram on their itineraries, which is a great shame as this is a marvellous site. It is also possibly the best restored of all the monasteries, avoiding the rather cack-handed over-restoration that mars some of the other sites. ■ *₿30.* North of here is **Wat Kasatthirat**. This wat represents the end of a river tour unless the Old Lopburi River is navigable in which case Wat Na Phramane (see page 182) and Wat Konthi Thong can also be reached, returning, full circle, to the Chandra Kasem pier.

Wat Yai Chai Mongkol

Two active wats are to be found southeast of the town, along Route 3059 (which goes on to the Summer Palace at Bang Pa-In, see page 174). The first is

Wat Yai Chai Mongkol, also known as Wat Chao Phraya Thai, or simply Wat Yai ('Big' Wat). It was built by King Uthong, also known as King Ramathibodi I, in 1357 for a group of monks who had studied, and been ordained, in Ceylon. The imposing 72 m high chedi was built in the Ceylonese style (now with a rather alarming tilt) to celebrate the victory of King Naresuan over the Prince of Burma in 1592, in single-handed elephant combat. It was at this time that the wat received its current name – previously it had been known as Wat Pa Keo. The viharn contains a massive reclining Buddha image. What is unusual about it is that its eyes are open. Reclining images traditionally symbolize death or sleep, so the eyes are closed. It has been suggested that in this instance the image relates to an episode in the Buddha's life when he confounded a truculent demon by making himself several times larger. The wat remained unused from the fall of Ayutthaya until 1957, when a group of monks took up residence and began to restore it. ■ *♭30*. The second active wat is the above-mentioned Wat Phanam Choeng.

About 4 km north of Ayutthaya off the road to Pa Mok is Wat Phu Kao Thong, or the Golden Mount Chedi. The principal chedi was built by the Burmese King Burengnong after he had conquered Ayutthaya in 1549, and at 80 m high it towers above the surrounding countryside. The wat is rather older, having been founded by King Uthong's son in 1387. After King Naresuan regained Ayutthaya's independence in 1584, the chedi was remodelled in Ayutthayan style. As a result, the bottom portion of the chedi up to the balustrade is Mon in style and the upper storeys are Thai. In 1956 a 2,500-gramme gold ball was mounted on top of the chedi by PM Phibun Songkram to mark 2,500 years of Buddhism; it was stolen by an agile thief just five years later. Only a few people will bother to make the journey by tuk-tuk to this wat which is artistically inferior to those within the city walls. **Wat Phu Kao Thong**

Northeast of the city, on the banks of the Old Lopburi River, are the only remaining elephant kraals in Thailand. *En route* to the kraals the road passes **Wat Mae Nang Pluem**. This wat may well pre-date the Ayutthaya period and it seems to have been the place where the Burmese set up camp in 1767 before their final assault on the city. The kraals were built in the reign of King Maha Chakrapat in 1580 to capture wild elephants. The kraals are square-shaped enclosures with double walls. The inner walls are made of massive teak posts fixed firmly to the ground at close intervals. The outer walls are made of earth, faced with brick and are 3 m high. The kraals have two entrances: one to allow the decoy elephant to lure the herd into the enclosure, and the other to lead them out again, to be trained for war or work. The outer wall on the west side is slightly wider to provide a platform from which the king, seated in a pavilion, could watch the elephant round-up. The last round-up of wild elephants occurred in May 1903, to entertain royal guests during King Chulalongkorn's reign. The kraal has been extensively restored and is rather clinical as a result. ■ *Getting there: take a saamlor from Chee Kun Rd northwards over the Old Lopburi River to reach the kraal. If coming from Wat Phu Kao Thong, cross the Pa Mok highway and drive for 3½ km.* **Elephant kraals**

There are also a handful of monasteries to the east of the old city and the Pasak River. **Wat Samanakot** is in poor condition; more interesting is **Wat Kuti Tao**, which dates from the early Ayutthaya period but has been much changed since its foundation. There is even evidence of western, perhaps Persian, influence in the arches of the window frames. **Wat Maheyong**, just east of Wat Kuti Tao, was built during the reign of King Boromraja II (1424-48). The bot is a **Wats east of the old city** fine building (well, ruin) with its elegant *bai sema* (boundary stones), as is the principal chedi which clearly takes its inspiration from Sukhothai, with its Sri Lankan bell shape and surrounding elephants. Worth a detour.

Wat Pradu Songtham is also amongst this group of monasteries to the east of the Pasak River, and is the most interesting. The wat is first mentioned in 1620 and was abandoned for a while after the fall of Ayutthaya to the Burmese. The bot is a renovated, but still classic late Ayutthaya building. Inside it is even better: three Buddha images raised up on plinths gaze serenely over a cool, bare interior, where moulding murals provide hints of subdued colour. The murals in the viharn are in better condition and depict episodes in the former lives of the Buddha – the jataka tales. They date from the early Bangkok (Ratanakosin) period.

Excursions

Wat Khun Inthapramun
Contains the largest reclining Buddha in Thailand, 50 m in length, 11 m high

This monastery lies 7 km north of Ang Thong (a town 40 km north of Ayutthaya), just short of the district town of Pho Thong. Turn left at a red sign in Thai, identifiable by the reclining Buddha above the lettering. About 2 km along the road is the wat, which dates from the Sukhothai period. The image is contained within a ruined viharn for which funds are currently being sought for renovation. The wat is named after a tax collector, Khun Inthapramun, who spent the king's revenue lengthening the original image and was promptly flogged to death by his king. So much for religious devotion. It is said that during the reign of Rama V, the image spoke; muffled sounds were heard coming from the Buddha, so the abbot enquired "Are you not well, Sir?", to which the image responded "Thank you, I am quite well ... but trouble is on its way; within two months, there will be a bad outbreak of cholera". The abbot asked what measures should be taken and the Buddha is said to have provided a herbal remedy which proved effective. ■ *Getting there: buses to Ang Thong from Chao Phrom Rd and then a local bus to Pho Thong; ask to be let off at the Wat.*

Wat Phra Phuttha Saiyat Pa Mok

This wat, simply Wat Pa Mok, is located 12 km north of town in the Amphoe district Pa Mok. Of note in the wat is a 22.5 m long reclining Buddha which, it is said, King Narai visited while he was leading his troops to fight King Maha Uparacha of Burma. If so, it must be several hundreds of years old. The image is contained within a fine viharn and approached, unusually, along a long covered walkway. ■ *Getting there: songthaews from Chao Phrom Rd to Pa Mok and ask for directions.*

San Pedro Cathedral

Lying 11 km south outside the city, this was the site of the original Portuguese settlement in Ayutthaya, dating from 1511. At one point as many as 3,000 Portuguese and their mixed-blood offspring were living here, although with the sacking of Ayutthaya by the Burmese in 1767 the community was abandoned. Since the mid-1980s the Fine Arts Department, with financial support from Portugal, has been excavating the site and the cathedral itself is now fully renovated. It was opened to the public in 1995. ■ *Getting there: charter a tuk-tuk or songthaew, or take a motorcycle taxi. Buses may be available.*

Bang Pa-In

This summer residence of former kings lies 20 km down river. It makes a pleasant contrast to the ruins of Ayutthaya. (See page 174.)

Ayutthaya excursions

Wat Khun Inthapramun

วัดขุนอินทาประมูล

Wat Phra Phuttha Saiyat Pa Mok

วัดพระพุทธไสยาศน์ป่าโมก

Essentials

It is not entirely clear why, but one of the features of guesthouses in Ayutthaya is that they all seem to be rather confusingly named by their initials. So be prepared to battle with the *TMT Guesthouse*, the *PS Guesthouse*, the *Old BJ Guesthouse*, the *PU Guesthouse*, the *TR Guesthouse* and the *New BJ Guesthouse*.

Sleeping

■ *on maps, page 180 & page 188*
Price codes: see inside front cover

L-B *Uthong Inn*, 210 Rojana Rd, Amphoe Phra Nakhon Si, T242236, F242235, BT5124843, BF9383929, uthong@ksc.th.com, www.uthonginn.com Inconvenient location 2 km or so east of town, some a/c. A strikingly attractive 100 room hotel, primarily aimed at the business and conference market. Japanese restaurant, snooker club and pool. **A** *Ayutthaya Grand*, 55/5 Rojana Rd, T335483, F335492. A/c, a large, rather run-down luxury hotel remote from the main sights. Restaurants, karaoke and a huge pool. **A** *Krung Si River Hotel*, 7/2 Rojana Rd, to the east of town, T244333, F243777. A 200 room-plus hotel with all facilities including restaurant, pool sauna and fitness centre; a/c, situated on the banks of the Pasak River. On paper at least this is the best hotel in town, but it is rather impersonal. A major road spoils the views and it is too far out of town for residents to explore the old city on foot. **A-B** *Ayutthaya Hotel*, Naresuan Rd (Chao Phrom Rd), T232855, F251018. This is probably the best hotel on the riverine island on which the historic city of Ayutthaya was centred. Good pool, attractive décor, although now feeling a little run-down, restaurant. (There is a cheaper guesthouse wing – also called *Ayutthaya Hotel*, see below.) **B** *Teveraj Tamrin Hotel*, 91 Mu 10, Tambon Ka Mung, T243139, F244139. Close to the train station, with views over the river Pasak. Pleasant rooms with good western bathrooms. Floating restaurant (see Eating below).

C-D *Uthong Hotel*, 86 Uthong Rd, T251063. Some a/c, large cleanish rooms, some with Thai TV and attached western bathrooms. **C-E** *Cathay*, 36/5-6 Uthong Rd, T251663. Rather grubby hotel with some a/c rooms. Basic squat loos and showers in every room (check the bathrooms, they can be filthy), Thai TV. **D** *Ayutthaya Hotel*, Naresuan Rd (Chao Phrom Rd), T252249, F251018, Naresuan Rd, T252249, F251018. Attached to the more expensive *Ayutthaya Hotel* (see above), this is the cheaper guesthouse wing. Rather tatty fan-cooled rooms but with TV and shower rooms attached. A ฿70 supplement gives access to the main hotel pool. Check in at the main hotel. **D** *Thai Thai*, 13/1 Naresuan Rd (Chao Phrom Rd), T244702. Some a/c, a

The Central Plains

Reclining Buddha at Wat Phra Phutta Saiyat Pa Mok

well-positioned guesthouse, but a bit rundown and the management speak no English. **D** *Thongchai Guesthouse*, 9/1 Maharaj Rd, T245210. Some a/c (good value), clean rooms. **D-F** *Tony's Place*, 12/18 Soi Thor Kor Sor, T252578. Not yet opened at the time of writing, but plans are to have some a/c and some fan as well as dorm rooms, as well as a pub and restaurant. **D-F** *Old BJ Guesthouse*, Soi Thor Kor Sor, Naresuan Rd, T251526. Owned by the same people as the *Ayutthaya Guesthouse*. Some a/c rooms and cheaper dorms, but squat toilets only which are less well maintained, shared bathrooms. Rundown and rather dirty, but friendly staff and good restaurant. Bicycles for hire (฿50 per day or ฿40 if you stay here).

E *Ayutthaya Youth Hostel*, 48/2 Uthong Rd, T241978. Interesting house, clean rooms, friendly people. **E** *TR Guesthouse*, Pa Maphrao Rd. This very small and quiet guesthouse is run by a teacher and his family. There are 4 basic, but fairly clean, fan-cooled rooms in a house on stilts set back from the road, behind a garden. **E-F** *Ayutthaya Guesthouse*, 12/34 Soi Thor Kor Sor, Naresuan Rd (Chao Phrom Rd), T232658. The fan-cooled rooms and communal facilities in this attractive teak house are kept spotless. Dorm beds also available. Restaurant, international payphone, helpful staff and very popular. Recommended. **E-F** *New BJ Guesthouse*, 19/29 Naresuan Rd, T246046. Positioned close to the old part of the city but also on a busy road so noisy, attached restaurant. Bicycle rental (฿50 per day) and motorbike rental (฿300 per day), trekking tours arranged from here. Friendly management. **E-F** *PS Guesthouse*, 23/1 Maharaj Rd (moved from Soi Thor Kor Sor), no phone. Run by teacher Phatsaphorn, with an English manager and a Japanese receptionist. Very friendly and quiet place, with a large garden in front. Bicycles and motorbikes can be rented from here. **E-F** *PU Guesthouse*, 20/1 Soi Thor Kor Sor, Naresuan Rd, T251213. Recently renovated, some a/c and some fan rooms, Thai owner with very good English and very helpful. Good food in a new a/c restaurant, dorms for ฿60, satellite TV, internet services, bicycle (฿50) and motorbike hire (฿250). Recommended. **E-F** *TMT Guesthouse*, 14/9 Soi Thor Kor Sor, Naresuan Rd, T251474. Good clean, fan-cooled rooms, with good service, basic showers and squat toilets, cheap dorm rooms. Restaurant and minibar in front.

Eating

• *on maps, page 180 & below*
Price categories: see inside front cover

Restaurants in Ayutthaya are good places to sample Chao Phraya river fish like *plaa chon, plaa nam ngen* and *snake head*. **Expensive** *Ku-Choeng Chinese Restaurant*, at the *Krung Si River Hotel*. The flashiest restaurant in town, serving a wide choice of good but expensive Chinese food. **Mid-range** *Ruan Thai Mai Suay (Thai House)*, Route 3059 (south of the city). This restaurant is 2 km or so to the south, on Route 3059, but getting here is worth the effort: good Thai food in an open, wooden traditional Central Plains house, very popular with wealthier locals. *Uthong Café*, part of the *Uthong Inn*. As with the hotel, the décor is striking. It serves sushi and Thai food.

Ayutthaya centre

■ Sleeping
1 Ayutthaya
2 Ayutthaya Guesthouse
3 New BJ Guesthouse
4 Old BJ Guesthouse
5 PS Guesthouse
6 PU Guesthouse
7 Thai Thai
8 Thong Chai Guesthouse
9 TMT Guesthouse
10 Tony's Place

● Eating
1 Bohemian Bar
2 Good Luck Bar & Restaurant
3 Moon Café

Related map
Ayutthaya, page 180

0 metres   200
0 yards   200

Floating Restaurant at the *Teveraj Tanrin*, on the Pasak River. This pleasing restaurant is divided into a/c and open air sections. It serves sushi and a very large choice of Thai and Western food. *Phae Krung Kao*, 4 Uthong Rd. Floating restaurant to the south of Pridi Damrong bridge, excellent Chao Phraya river fish – try the *plaa chon* and the tasty deep-fried snake head (a fish!) with chillies. **Cheap** *Siam Restaurant*, Chee Kun Rd, T211070. A smart a/c restaurant. Tables upstairs in the open air have a terrific view of Wat Phra Mahathat. Good value Thai and Vietnamese food offered. Recommended.

Foodstalls There is a night market with cheap foodstalls in the parking area in front of Chandra Kasem Palace; stalls are also concentrated at the west end of Chao Phrom Rd and in the market at the northeast corner of the city on Uthong Rd. The covered Chao Phrom Market is also an excellent place for cheap food.

Bars *Moon Café*, Soi Thor Kor Sor, Naresuan Rd (Chao Phrom Rd). More of a bar than a café. This immensely stylish, but small, venue offers a limited Thai and Western menu. An exciting mix of rock reggae and rhythm and blues is played nightly. They have a piano that anyone is encouraged to play, even if it's just a quick afternoon practice. Recommended. *Bohemian Bar*, just opposite the Moon Café on Soi Thor Kor Sor. Cheap food and drinks. Chilled out seating area on logs and straw mats with chairs and tables extending out onto the road, and a range of music from techno to jazz. Opening times vary depending on how lively it is, but generally from around 1600 to 0300. Recommended. *Home Pub*, 51/1 Naresuan Rd, opposite *BJ Guesthouse*. Open daily 1900-0200, live music every night, country pub style, warm atmosphere. *Good Luck Bar and Restaurant*, Soi Thor Sor Khor. Also does cheap food and drinks, recommendations of good tuna spaghetti.

Festivals Nov *Loi Krathong*, festival of lights (see page 61).

Transport **Local Bicycles**: can be hired from many guesthouses (eg *Ayutthaya Guesthouse*); expect to pay about ฿50 per day. **Long-tailed boats**: can be hired at the jetty opposite the Chandra Kasem Palace in the northeast corner of town. Expect to pay ฿250 for 1 hr (boats can take 10 people). The *Ayutthaya Guesthouse* and several other guesthouses also arrange boats. **Saamlors**: around town should not cost more than ฿20-30; they can also be hired by the hour. **Songthaews**: from the train station into town cost ฿5. They run about the old town for a flat fare of ฿3. They can also be chartered for about ฿300 per day. **Tuk-tuks**: around town for ฿30-50.

See also Ins & outs, page 175
85 km N of Bangkok

Long distance Train: the station is just off Rojana Rd, across the Pasak River. Nine connections daily with Bangkok's Hualamphong station (1½ hrs), and with all stops north to Chiang Mai (12 hrs). It is possible to catch a train from Don Muang Airport, making it unnecessary to enter Bangkok. The easiest way to get from the station in Ayutthaya to the old city is to take the small track facing the station down to the river; from the jetty here ferries cross over to the other side every 5 mins or so (฿2).

Bus: the station is on Chao Phrom Rd. Regular a/c and non-a/c connections with Bangkok's Northern bus terminal (1½ hrs) and stops north including Lopburi (2 hrs), Phitsanulok, Chiang Mai and Sukhothai (5 hrs).

Boat (See Bangkok Tours, page 124.) From Tha Tien pier in Bangkok daily at 1000. Private boats can also be hired from the pier opposite Chandra Kasem Palace in Ayutthaya, the most popular destination being the Summer Palace at Bang Pa-In (see page 174). ฿250-300 one-way, ฿400 return (3 hrs). Boat trips around the river from the pier cost ฿600 per trip for up to 12 people. The Benjarang boat does a tour south along the Chao Phraya River, stopping at Wat Chai Wattanaram, Wat Phutthaisawan and Wat Phanam Choeng for ฿180 per person.

Directory **Banks** Most of the banks are either on Uthong Rd or Naresuan Rd (Chao Phrom Rd) and change TCs and have ATMs. *Thai Military*, Chao Phrom Rd. *Thai Farmers*, Chao Phrom Rd. *Siam City*, Uthong Rd (close to *Uthong Hotel*). *Bangkok*, Uthong Rd (next to *Cathay Hotel*). **Communications** Post Office: Uthong Rd (south from the Chandra Kasem Palace). International calls available here. **Internet & email facilities:** a number of internet cafés have opened up on Naresuan Rd and Soi Thor Kor Sor. **Useful addresses** Tourist Police: across the street from TAT office, Si Sanphet Rd, T242352.

Around Ayutthaya

Lopburi ลพบุรี

Population: 45,000
Phone code: 036
Colour map 2, grid C1

To the west is the old city with its historical sights. To the east is the new town with its major military base. Inevitably, most visitors will be attracted to the palace, museum, monasteries and prangs of the old city. This part of Lopburi is also teeming with monkeys that clamber from one telegraph pole to another, laze around the temples – particularly Sam Phra Karn – feast on the offerings left by worshippers and grasp playfully at the hair of unwitting tourists.

History Lopburi has been seemingly caught between competing powers for over 1,000 years. The discovery of neolithic and bronze age remains indicate that the site on the left bank of the Lopburi River was in use in prehistoric times. The town became a major centre during the Dvaravati period (sixth-11th century), when it was known as Lavo (the original settlers were the 'Lavah', related to the Mon). In 950 Lopburi fell to the expanding Khmers who made it a provincial capital: in Thailand, the Khmer period of art and architecture is known as 'Lopburi' because of their artistic impact evident in the town and surrounding area (see page 804). By the 14th century, Khmer influence had waned and the Thais reclaimed Lopburi. In 1350 King Uthong of Ayutthaya gave his son – Prince Ramesuan – governorship of the town, indicating its continued importance. It fell into obscurity during the 16th century, but was resuscitated when King Narai (1656-88) restored the city with the assistance of European architects. With Narai's death in Lopburi, the town entered another period of obscurity but was again restored to glory during Rama IV's reign. Today, Lopburi is a major military base, with the new town located to the east of the railway line. Most of the historic sights are to the west.

Tourist offices *TAT* (temporary office), HM The Queen's Celebration Building, Narai Maharat Road (in the new town and 4 km from the Old City, 1 km after the bus station), T422768, F422769. Helpful staff. Areas of responsibility are Lopburi, Nakhon Sawan, Uthai Thani, Ayutthaya, Suphanburi and Singburi. Do not be put off by the apparent lack of an obvious entrance; climb over the small wall. There are plans, which seem to be extremely drawn out, to move the office to the old city, probably to a location near Wat Phra Sri Ratana Mahathat.

Sights
It is more convenient for sightseeing to be based in the old city; all the sights here are within walking distance of one another

The **Narai Ratchaniwet Palace** represents the historical heart of Lopburi, encased by massive walls and bordered to the north by the Lopburi River. When King Narai declared Lopburi his second capital in the 17th century, he set about restoring the town with the help of Italian and French architects. He built his palace (also known as the Lopburi Palace, or King Narai's Palace) between 1665 and 1677, which became his 'summer' retreat (he lived here for more than six months each year). The main gate is on Sorasak Road, opposite the *Asia Lopburi Hotel*. The well-kept palace grounds are divided into three sections: an outer, a middle and an inner courtyard.

The outer courtyard, now in ruins, contained the 'functional' buildings: a **tank** to supply water to the palace (transported down terracotta pipes from a lake some distance away), **storage warehouses** for hides and spices, and **elephant and horse stables**. There was also a **Banquet Hall** for royal visitors, and on the south wall, an **Audience Hall** (Tuk Phrachao Hao). It was here that those plotting against King Narai, while he was seriously ill, are reputed to have met to discuss their plans. The niches that line the inner side of the walls by the main gates would have contained oil lamps, lit during festivals and important functions.

An archway leads to the middle courtyard. On the left are the tall ruins of the **Dusitsawan Thanya Mahaprasat Hall**, built in 1685 for audiences with visiting dignitaries. When the French ambassador Chevalier de Chaumont was received here, his account records that the hall was lined with French mirrors. The front portion of the hall is French in style, the rear Thai. The king would have received visitors from the window throne in the centre of the hall. Next to this is the **Phiman Mongkut Pavilion**, now the **King Narai Museum**. It was built in 1863 by King Rama IV for his own use and is in colonial style. It is made up of several buildings all connected with each other and acts as the museum, housing a fine collection spanning all periods of Thai art, but concentrating, not surprisingly, on Lopburi period sculpture. Some of the Buddha images are exquisite. To the north, the **Chantra Paisan Pavilion**, looking like a wat, was

The Central Plains

Narai Ratchaniwet Palace

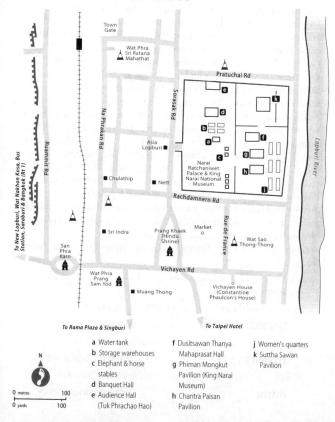

a Water tank	**f** Dusitsawan Thanya	**j** Women's quarters
b Storage warehouses	Mahaprasat Hall	**k** Suttha Sawan
c Elephant & horse	**g** Phiman Mongkut	Pavilion
stables	Pavilion (King Narai	
d Banquet Hall	Museum)	
e Audience Hall	**h** Chantra Paisan	
(Tuk Phrachao Hao)	Pavilion	

0 metres 100
0 yards 100

N

one of the first structures built by King Narai and served as his audience hall until the Suttha Sawan Pavilion was completed. Restored by King Mongkut in 1863, the pavilion houses more artefacts; notably, a collection of Thai cabinets. Behind these buildings were the **women's quarters**, again built by Rama IV. One of them has been turned into a Farmer's Museum displaying traditional Central Plains farming technology and other implements used in rural life, for pottery and iron production, weaving and fishing. The other buildings in the women's quarters are in the process of being restored.

The inner courtyard contains the ruins of King Narai's own residence, the **Suttha Sawan Pavilion**. It is isolated from the rest of the complex and was surrounded by gardens, ponds (where the king took his bath under huge canopies) and fountains. King Narai died in this pavilion on 11 July 1688 while his opponents plotted against him. It is said that to protect those who had remained loyal, he dedicated the building and its grounds as a monastery, and ordained those who had remained with him as monks. As a result, when King Mongkut began to renovate the palace in the 19th century he had to deconsecrate the 'temple' before starting work. After King Narai's death, the palace was used for his successor's (one of his regimental commanders) coronation ceremony and was then abandoned until the mid-19th century, when Rama IV ordered a restoration programme. ■ *0830-1200, 1300-1630 Wed-Sun, ฿30.*

Wat Phra Prang Sam Yod (Wat of Three Prangs) is a very good example of Khmer provincial art. It is a laterite and sandstone shrine whose three spires originally represented the three Hindu deities: Brahma, Vishnu and Siva. Another interpretation has it that because the Khmer king of the time, Jayavarman VII (1181-1217), was a strict Mahayana Buddhist, the three prangs symbolize the Buddha (the central tower), Bodhisattva Avalokitasvara or the future Buddha (the south tower) and Prajnaparamita, the Mahayana Goddess of Wisdom (the north tower). Depending on one's viewpoint, either King Narai converted it to a Buddhist temple in the 17th century, or it was always Buddhist. Whatever the case, it still reflects the syncretic religions of the time. The south prang has remnants of some fine stucco friezes and naga heads; also note how the stone door frames are carved to resemble their wooden antecedents. In mid-1994 the Fine Arts Department completed a major restoration programme of the monument, to considerable local criticism. The wat lies north of Vichayen Road, next to the railway line. Nearby, on the other side of the railway track, is the Brahmanic shrine **San Phra Karn**, constructed in 1951. The shrine contains a stone statue of Vishnu with a Buddha's head. Up some steps behind the shrine is a guardian house, probably built by King Narai, containing a strange assortment of Buddhist and Hindu images. It lies on top of the remains of a Khmer laterite structure. Monkeys are obviously a problem here, as the entire shrine has been enclosed in a cage, in order to keep them at bay. The shrine is interesting for its activity rather than for any artistic merit.

● ●

Lopburi place names

Narai Ratchaniwet Palace	Wat Phra Buddhabat
นารายณ์ราชนิเวศน์	วัดพระพุทธบาท
Prang Khaek	Wat Phra Prang Sam Yod
ปรางค์แขก	วัดพระปรางค์สามยอด
Si Thep	Wat Phra Sri Ratana Mahathat
ศรีเทพ	วัดพระศรีรัตนมหาธาตุ

Constantine Phaulcon: Greek adventurer, Siamese Minister, Catholic Zealot

Constantine Phaulcon (1647-88) was a Greek adventurer who became, for a short time, the most influential man in Siam barring the king. He arrived in Ayutthaya in 1678 with the English East India Company, learnt Thai and became an interpreter in the court. By 1682 he had worked his way up through the bureaucracy to become the Mahatthai, the most senior position. But it was also at this time that, in retrospect, he sealed his fate. Phaulcon acted as interpreter for a French mission led by Mgr Pallu. An avid Catholic, having recently been converted by Jesuit priests, Phaulcon was enthralled by the idea of converting King Narai and his subjects to Christianity. He discussed with Narai – who was the King's most trusted adviser – the superiority of Catholicism versus Buddhism, and seemed to be representing the interests of the French in negotiations, rather than those of Siam. Phaulcon made many enemies among powerful Siamese, who doubted his integrity and his intentions. By 1688, Phaulcon's activities were becoming increasingly unacceptable, and he was also linked by association with the excesses of French and British troops, with the proselytizing of priests, and with the effect that foreign traders were having upon the interests of local businessmen. A plot was hatched to kill the foreigner on the king's death. In March 1688, when Narai fell seriously ill, Phra Phetracha – a claimant for the throne – had Phaulcon arrested, tried and convicted for treason, and then executed on 5 June.

West along Vichayen Road is the Khmer **Prang Khaek**. Built in the late eighth century, this, like Prang Sam Yod, was also originally a Hindu shrine. The three brick spires represent the oldest Khmer prangs found in the Central region of Thailand. It was restored by King Narai in the 17th century, but today lies in ruins.

Further west along Vichayen Road are the remains of **Vichayen House**, better known as **Constantine Phaulcon's House**, the highly influential adviser to King Narai (see box above). The house, European in style, was initially constructed for Chevalier de Chaumont, the first French ambassador to Thailand who lived here in 1685. Later, it was used by the Greek Prime Minister, Phaulcon, as his residence. On entering the gates, his residence lay on the left-hand side, a Roman Catholic Chapel was straight ahead and a reception hall to the right. ■ ฿30.

Opposite the railway station is the entrance to **Wat Phra Sri Ratana Mahathat**. This monastery has two claims to fame: it is the oldest wat in Lopburi and also houses the tallest prang. The prang, slender and elegant (rather than squat like those of the Northeast), is of laterite, faced in places, with the last fragments of what must have been fine stucco-work. Dating it has presented something of a problem. Originally it was thought to be contemporary with Angkor Wat in Cambodia (that is 12th century). Now, it is considered to date from the 14th century and to belong to the Uthong School, when the Thais had captured the town from the Khmers. Indeed, it may represent the first example of a 'Tai' as opposed to a Khmer prang, symbolizing the eclipse of the Khmers in the region. The problem is that numerous (and on-going) restorations have tended to obscure the origins of the buildings. In front of the prang is a viharn dating from King Narai's reign, with traditional Thai style doors and gothic windows. ■ ฿30.

Northwest of the palace is **Wat Sao Thong-Thong**, on France Road (Rue de France in Roman characters). There is nothing much here except a viharn built by Narai in western style, as a church for the Christian envoys. Within the viharn (now Buddhist) is a large seated Buddha, while along the walls are niches containing more assorted Buddha images.

The Central Plains

Excursions **Wat Phra Buddhabat** lies 24 km south of the old city in the town of Phra Buddhabat. The wat is founded on the site of a large and revered footprint of the Buddha. The habit of modelling footprints of the Buddha with the 108 auspicious signs and the Wheel of Law seems to have begun in the 14th century. As Steve van Beek and Luca Tettoni write in *The Arts of Thailand*: 'Little did [the Sukhothai artists] know what they had begun because today, nearly every hill of any size is topped by a small shrine whose object of veneration is a Buddha Footprint, usually of gargantuan dimensions'. The most renowned is that at Wat Phra Buddhabat. A short stairway, flanked by two well-wrought many-headed nagas, leads up to a cluster of shrines, salas, chedis and pavilions set at different levels. The ornate tile-encrusted mondop, built to cover the footprint, was constructed during Rama I's reign. It has four pairs of exquisite mother-of-pearl doors. The footprint itself, which is a natural impression made in the limestone rock (depending on one's beliefs), was first discovered in the reign of King Song Tham (1610-28). It is 150 cm long, edged in gold and set down below floor level. The print must be special: pilgrims not only rub gold leaf onto it, but also rain down coins and banknotes; hence the protective grill. It is said that King Song Tham ordered officials to search for the footprint, having been told by Ceylonese monks that one might be found in Thailand. A hunter stumbled across it while trailing a wounded deer – which was miraculously healed of its injury – and the site was declared a shrine. Behind the mondop, there is a viharn with two large Buddha images, unusually back-to-back: a large seated Ayutthayan Buddha in front and a reclining Buddha behind. A large annual festival is held here (see below, Festivals). About 40 km southeast of Phra Buddhabat is another related Buddhist pilgrimage site – **Phra Buddhachai**, the Buddha's shadow. This is a faint image of the Buddha painted on a cliff face and many pilgrims combine a trip to the footprint with an excursion to the shadow. ■ *Getting there: take Route 1 south and after 23 km turn onto Route 310. By public transport, catch a Saraburi bus from the bus station; passengers are let off on the main road, so either walk the 1 km to the shrine or take a saamlor.*

The **Si Thep Historical Park** is a little-visited historical park 80 km northeast of Lopburi, 8 km off Route 21. It is a former city which predates Lopburi and which has, in turn, been Hindu and then Buddhist. During the sixth to eighth centuries it was part of the Mon Dvaravati Kingdom, before being incorporated into the Khmer Empire in the 10th century. The city forms two distinct sections: an inner, earlier city designed by Dvaravati architects, and a later,

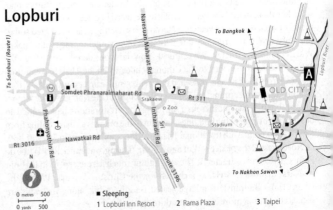

Lopburi

To Sarabu (Route 1)

To Bangkok ▲

Naresuan Maharat Rd

Lopburi River

A

OLD CITY

■ 1
Somdet Phranaraimaharat Rd

Srakaew

Rt 311

o Zoo

Phahonyothin Rd

Sri Intharadit Rd

Stadium

■ 3
■ 2

Rt 3016

Nawatkai Rd

Route 3196

To Nakhon Sawan ▼

Related map
A Narai Ratchaniwet
Palace & Museum,
page 191

N

0 metres   500
0 yards   500

■ **Sleeping**
1 Lopburi Inn Resort   2 Rama Plaza   3 Taipei

outer city which envelopes the inner and which was designed by Khmer planners. In all, it measures 4 km 1,500 m, making it one of the largest archaeological sites in Thailand. Work on excavating and renovating the temples is at an early stage, and many are still choked with vegetation. The earlier Mon period produced some superb sculpture: the eighth-century sandstone Vishnus are particularly sensitively carved and are regarded by some art historians as being among the finest pieces produced in Southeast Asia. The later Khmer pieces are derivative, and though fine, are not regarded as highly as similar works from other sites in the Northeast of Thailand. Few Buddha images have been unearthed. There are four sections to the park: the archaeological excavation site (digging began in 1988) where five skeletons were found (one a woman wearing a carnelian necklace and a bronze bangle, her head turned to the north – as, oddly, was the skeleton of an elephant found nearby – Khao Klang Nan with stucco reliefs; Prang Song Phi Nong which consists of two brick prangs dating from the 11th-12th centuries; and Prang Si Thep which is square with a laterite base and a lotus top, again dating from the 11th to 12th centuries. There is simple food available at the park. ■ *0830-1630, Mon-Sun, ฿20. Getting there: take a bus north towards Phetchabun on Route 21 and get off 5 km or so after the town of Si Thep. The ruins lie 8 km off the main road, not far from the village of Ban Nok Charoen. It should be possible either to take a motorcycle taxi or a local songthaew (ask for muang boraan Si Thep or muang kao Si Thep).*

Sleeping
■ *on map*
Price codes:
see inside front cover

A *Lopburi Inn Resort*, Phahonyothin Rd, T411625, F412010. Slightly overpowering monkey theme employed in this hotel's décor and it is also a long way out of town. Nevertheless, the smartest in the area, with good facilities including a gym and a large pool. C *Lopburi Inn*, 28/9 Narai Maharat Rd, T412300, F411917. Large and clean with reasonable a/c rooms, but now beginning to show its age. Out of town location, but regular buses travel the 4 km into the old town. Pricey restaurant. D *Asia Lopburi*, 1/7-8 Sorasak Rd, T411892, F411892. Fairly clean rooms, some of which have a/c, western bathrooms and views over the Narai Palace. Rather dingy pair of Chinese restaurants. Avoid the rooms close to busy Sorasak Rd. D *Rama Plaza*, 4 Banphom Rd, north of Old City, T411663, F411484. Smart hotel for the price, quiet but dark a/c rooms. Restaurant. D-E *Muang Thong*, almost opposite Wat Phra Prang Sam Yod, T411036. Some a/c, some bathrooms, not clean, and noisy on this road. D-E *Taipei*, 24/6-7 Surasongkhram Rd, T411524. Some a/c. A simple, reasonably priced hotel, clean rooms with attached bathrooms, very ordinary. E *Nett*, 17/1-2 Rachdamnern Soi 2, T411738. Clean, central and quiet, with attached shower rooms, the best of the cheaper hotels. E *Sri Indra*, 3-5 Na Phrakan Rd, T411261. Good position but grubby and distinctly rundown. Some a/c. F *Chulathip*, 17-18 Na Phrakan Rd, T411672. Cheap and central, but dingy and dirty and doubles as a brothel.

Eating
● *on map*
Price categories:
see inside front cover

The orchards around Lopburi are reputed to produce the finest *noi naa*, or custard apples, in Thailand. A local speciality is coconut jelly, served with ice. The jelly is a mixture of coconut and glycerine. Another local delicacy are marl salted eggs. Lopburi has a good selection of Chinese-Thai restaurants, especially along Na Phrakan Rd and Sorasak Rd. The *market* between Rachdamnern Rd and Rue de France provides the usual range of stall foods, as do the stalls along Sorasak Rd. The best places to eat in the evening in Lopburi are at the *foodstalls* along Na Phrakan Rd in the Old City. They serve a good range of Thai dishes at very good prices. Also in this category is *Chulathip*, corner of Na Phrakan and Rachdamnern roads. Nothing to do with the hotel, this 24-hr open-air restaurant is good value and serves a wide range of Thai food. Recommended. **Cheap** *White House Garden*, Phryakamjad Rd. Appealing open-air seating area with white wrought iron chairs and plenty of greenery. Imaginative Thai menu and good food. *Mr Sontose*, Phryakamjad Rd. A somewhat

The Central Plains

expensive Thai restaurant with outdated, scrappy décor. *Ice-cream parlour*, northern end of Sorasak Rd. Also serves Thai food.

Festivals Feb *King Narai Reign Festival* (15-17), processions, stalls and traditional dancing, centred around King Narai's Palace. Mar *Phra Bhuddhabat fair and festival* (movable) at Wat Phra Bhuddhabat draws large crowds; folk music and handicraft market.

Transport **Local** Frequent buses and songthaews ferry passengers between the old and new towns. **Long distance** Train: regular connections with Bangkok's Hualamphong station (2¾ hrs), Ayutthaya (1 hr) and destinations to the north. **Bus**: the bus station for both a/c and non-a/c buses is in the new town, 2 km from the old town, close to the roundabout where Routes 311 and 3016 cross (Wongwian Sra Kaeo). Regular connections with Bangkok's Northern bus terminal (2-3 hrs) and with Ayutthaya (1 hr). Buses from Kanchanaburi via Suphanburi and Singburi (6 hrs), and destinations north.

155 km to Bangkok,
75 km to Ayutthaya

Directory **Banks** *Krung Thai*, 74 Vichayen Rd; *Thai Military*, corner of Sorasak and Rachdamnern roads. **Communications** Post Office: on road to Singburi, not far from Prang Sam Yod. A second Post Office is to be found near the bus station. **Medical services** Hospital, Phahonyothin Rd.

Suphanburi   สุพรรณบุรี

Population: 30,000
Phone code: 035
Colour map 3, grid B3

Suphanburi languished in obscurity until it achieved national fame as the home province of former Prime Minister Banharn Silapa-Archa (1995-96). It is sometimes referred to as Banharnburi (Banharntown), and it is hard not to notice his influence: streets, parks, bus shelters, shops and squares are named after him. The term 'pork barrel' was clearly invented for Suphanburi: it has excellent roads, a telephone system which is the envy of other up-country provinces, and Mr Banharn, the local MP since 1976, won more votes than any other candidate in the elections in 1995. Suphanburi is a veritable boom province.

Even with Banharn's influence, it has to be said that not many visitors make it to Suhanburi. But there are a couple of interesting monasteries, some reasonable hotels, and it also has the added attraction of being the closest town to Don Chedi where a major fair is held each January to celebrate a famous victory over the Burmese (see Festivals below).

Suphanburi was founded in the latter part of the ninth century, and became an important centre during the Dvaravati period, when it was known as Phanchumburi. However, different kings seem to have been unsure as to exactly where the town should be positioned; it has switched from one bank of the Tha Chin River to the other on a number of occasions. It was not until Rama VI came to the throne in 1910 that its final location on the east bank of the river was, so to speak, cemented.

Sights **Wat Phra Rup** is an active wat which lies across the Tha Chin River on Malimaen Road and left down Khunchang Road. The viharn to the right as you enter the compound houses a striking, large reclining Buddha: Phra Phut Sai Yaat or, more popularly, 'Nen Kaew'. On the upper floor of one of the buildings to the left of the central bot is a beautiful, carved wooden footprint of the Buddha. Both date from the late Uthong period (14th century). The carving is kept in a locked room which will be willingly opened, upon request.

Take a saamlor or
tuk-tuk to visit the sights

Returning to Malimaen Road, the prang of **Wat Phra Sri Ratana Mahathat** (locally known as Wat Phrathat) can be clearly seen on the other side of the road. The road leading to the wat is marked with a fish sign. The wat was built between the late 14th and early 15th centuries during the reign of either King Uthong (1350-69) or King Ramatibodhi II (1424-48), and features a large

Khmer prang containing relics of the Buddha. Some of the original stucco remains. Close to the prang is a ruined bot with a seated Buddha. Some renovations took place during the second half of the Ayutthaya period.

Continuing down Malimaen Road, towards Kanchanaburi, about 3 km from town, is **Wat Palelai**, also known as Wat Pa ('Forest' Wat). It dates from the Uthong period. The **Viharn Luang Phor Tor** (meaning 'Viharn of the Immense Buddha Image') contains a large seated Buddha (in the unusual attitude of a wandering forest monk) believed to possess great powers. The image has not always been in this attitude, though. For some unspecified reason, when it was being restored a decision was taken to change the mudra from that of preaching the first sermon. It is an important pilgrimage place for Thais, as the Buddha image (and two other seated Buddha images in the side aisles) is plastered in gold leaf. There are good foodstalls in the compound. East of Wat Palelai is an ornate Chinese temple, **Sao Chao Pho**.

The **Uthong National Museum**, a regional branch of the National Museum, is situated 7 km west of town on Route 321, the continuation of Malimaen Road. The museum houses a modest collection of bronze and stone pieces, largely from the Uthong and Dvaravati periods, unearthed in the vicinity. ■ *0900-1600 Wed-Sun, ₿10.*

Suphanburi is most famous for its **Don Chedi Fair**, held in January at the site of the Battle of Nong Sarai, now known as Don Chedi; see Festivals, below.

Excursions

A *Khum Suphan*, 28/2 Meunhan Rd, T523553/522273, F523553. A/c. The décor indicates that this hotel is past its best. It does, however, still have fairly attractive rooms, a pool and a restaurant (see Eating below). **B-C** *Kalapruek*, 135/1 Prachatipatai Rd, T522555. A/c, restaurant. Modern hotel with comfortable rooms and reasonable service, good value. **C** *Songphanburi Thani*. A/c, restaurant, pool. Good value for a hotel of this standard. Smartly decorated rooms and attractive pool area. Prices may rise when all the facilities in this new hotel are completed. Dine elsewhere, the food is expensive, poor quality and, in the evenings, diners are forced to put up with intrusive Thai crooners. **D-E** *KAT*, 433 Phra Phanvasa, T521619. Some a/c. A little grubby but reasonable value considering its central position. It has a garden. **D-E** *King Pho Sai*, 678 Nen Kaew Rd, T522412. Some a/c, a good budget place to stay with reasonable rooms and also quite peaceful. **D-E** *Pachara*. Some a/c, simple, clean rooms at reasonable prices, restaurant.

Sleeping

Cheap *Song*. Reasonably smart a/c restaurant with a wide menu offering Thai and a little western food. *Khum Suphan* 28/2 Meunhan Rd. A tastefully decorated a/c restaurant in the hotel of the same name with an extensive Thai and European menu. *Pachara*. Surprisingly smart a/c restaurant connected to the hotel, offering reasonably priced Thai food.

Foodstalls Suphanburi is blessed with a large number of street restaurants and these are, by far, the best places to eat in town. A dish costs just ₿20 and guests are able to choose their own vegetables from an elaborate display of fresh produce.

Eating
The greatest concentration of restaurants is along Muunhan Rd

· ·
Suphanburi place names

Wat Palelai

วัดป่าเลไลยก์

Wat Phra Rup

วัดพระรูป

Wat Phra Sri Ratana Mahathat

วัดพระศรีรัตนมหาธาตุ

Jan *Don Chedi Fair* (week of 25th – Thai Armed Forces Day), held at Don Chedi, 23 km northwest of town on Route 322. On 18 Jan 1593, King Naresuan of Ayutthaya won an elephant duel against the Burmese Crown Prince and liberated the Thai Kingdom. A memorial (Don Chedi)

Festivals

was constructed to commemorate the event, but was then allowed to fall into disrepair. In 1913 the original memorial was rediscovered by Prince Damrong and 40 years or so later in 1951 (these decisions take time) it was decided to construct a new monument to this great moment in Thai history. As a result, a Ceylonese-style pagoda was built over the original structure and a statue of King Naresuan placed in front of the structure, depicted astride an elephant, swords held high in a victory salute (presumably). The fair is the Memorial Day of King Naresuan. There are the usual festivities: beauty contests, folk music, processions, craft fair etc. As there are precious few recent victories to celebrate (and, admittedly, few defeats), the week-long celebrations have also been embraced by the Thai armed forces as their 'day'. While the fair is on there are ample buses from Suphanburi, but out of festival time take a taxi.

Transport   **Road**   170 km north of Bangkok, 95 km from Singburi. **Bus**: regular connections with Bangkok's northern bus terminal (1½ hrs), Kanchanaburi, Singburi and Lopburi.

Uthai Thani   This charming little town situated about 35 km south of Nakhon Sawan consists of
Phone code: 056   a small number of shops, one hotel and a handful of restaurants. One major road
Colour map 3, grid A3   runs through the town and most of the attractions are concentrated along this road.

At one end, there is a fitness park surrounded with trees and topiary, and just beyond the fitness area is a large **monastery**. This dates from the 19th century and the complex is a good example of Bangkok-style architecture. In the centre is a large pond which is said to have provided the holy water used in the coronation of King Rama VI. Next to the pond is a cemetery. The wat is well endowed and prosperous. The town's **main market**, which sells mainly clothes and kitchen utensils, takes up much of the central square, where there are also food stalls. There are regular connections with Bangkok's Northern and Northeastern bus terminal, and with other destinations in the Central Plains and North.

There is not a great deal of interest to see in the local area, but for those searching for something to do, there is a **Bat Cave** nearby and cave paintings at **Kao Plara**, 30 km from town.

Sleeping and eating   **C** *Huay Kha Khaeng Jesthasilpa Hotel*. The only hotel in town and perhaps somewhat surprisingly it is a very elegant establishment, with friendly and efficient service and a good restaurant (see below). Excellent a/c rooms with views over Uthai Thani, room rate includes American breakfast.

Cheap   *Huay Kha Khaeng Jesthasilpa Hotel*. A wide range of very good Thai food, and a few Western dishes, at very reasonable prices. *Easy Corner*, at one corner of the market. Disney-themed restaurant serving tasty Thai food. Thai menu only. **Foodstalls**   Street restaurants can be found near the bus station.

Nakhon Sawan   นครสวรรค์

Phone code: 056   This major commercial centre, also known as Paknam Pho ('river mouth'), is
Colour map 3, grid A3   regarded as the gateway to the north, but is rarely visited by tourists for the simple reason that there is not much to see here. The town is situated at the confluence of four rivers: the Ping, Wang, Yom and Nan. It became an important centre for the teak trade as rafts travelling down from the north were broken up into smaller rafts for the journey south. As Thailand's teak forests were decimated, so this activity declined until finally, in early 1989, the Thai government announced a ban on all logging in the kingdom. Now the town's ties with water are bound up with irrigation: close by is one of the major diversion dams which help to control flooding and the supply of water for rice cultivation in the Central Plains.

Wat Chomkiri Nagaproth stands on a hill just before Dejativong Bridge, with a good view over the city. The wat dates from the Sukhothai period (although extensive renovation has succeeded in obliterating this fact). It contains a fine seated Buddha image from the Ayutthaya period and a footprint of the Buddha. Two giant seated Buddhas overlook the town. They can be seen from Matuli and Autthakavi roads.

Bung Boraphet is an area of swampland covering over 22,000 ha, about 10 km from the city. It is famous for the *sua* fish that abound in the swamp and which are regarded as a delicacy. There is also an aquarium here. ■ *Getting there: by chartered car or by boat from the landing behind the city market (40 mins).*

AL-A *Nakhon Sawan Lagoon Hotel* (formerly known as the *NSC Sports Hotel*), Jakkawan Rd, T228845, F228649. This is without doubt the most luxurious place to stay in town. Spacious and well decorated rooms. Reasonably priced restaurant, fitness centre and impressive olympic-sized pool. Rather eccentric mix of native American and Oriental décor, but with a fabulous fountain at the front. The disadvantage is that it is far out of town and difficult to reach without private transport. **C** *Piman*, 605/244 Asia Rd (a little out of town, but accessible by songthaew), T222097/312222, F221253. A/c, restaurant, comfortable but dull hotel with good facilities including nightclub and ballroom dancing. Some rooms have views over the hillsides. **D** *Penung Hotel*, 249/7-8 Sawanvithi Rd, T222462. Clean, pleasant a/c rooms, restaurant. **D** *Thaivisanu Hotel*, 26-28 Autthakavi Rd, T212932. The sign for this place is in Thai script only. Perhaps a little overpriced but clean, a/c rooms available. **D** *Visanuin Hotel*, 217-225 Matuli Rd, T222938. Clean and reasonably decorated hotel. Rooms have a/c and TV, but are a little dark. **D-E** *Anodard Hotel*, 473-479 Kosi Rd, T221844. Simple, clean and spacious rooms with TV, some a/c, but a restaurant which is best avoided. **D-E** *Irawan*, 1-5 Matuli Rd, T221889. A/c, friendly staff, though this hardly compensates for the rather high prices for dirty rooms. Filled with mangy cats and numerous cockroaches.

Sleeping

Hotels are usually booked up in the week of the Dragon & Lion Parade, late Jan-Feb

Mid-range *Suki Yaki* (part of the *Thaivisanu Hotel*), 26-28 Autthakavi Rd. Fast food-style Japanese restaurant selling good, interesting dishes at reasonable prices. **Cheap** *Hong Faa*, Autthakavi Rd. Thai and Chinese food. *Corner Café*, on the corner of Sawanvithi Rd. A convivial atmosphere, tasty Thai food available, though the menu for this place is only in Thai. Cheap cocktails. Recommended. **Foodstalls** Almost exclusively concentrated along the riverside; good place for a quick bite.

Eating

Late Jan-Feb *Dragon and Lion Parade* (movable), associated with Chinese New Year which (due to Nakhon Sawan's large ethnic Chinese population) is celebrated more enthusiastically and colourfully here than in almost any other town in Thailand. There are lion dances, music and parades of virgins. **Nov/Dec** (12th lunar month) Celebrations are held at *Wat Chomkiri Nagaproth*.

Festivals

Local Yellow songthaews link the town with the bus station, while green songthaews ferry passengers between town and the train station. Songthaews travel throughout the town for a flat fare of ฿5. Saamlors and motorbike taxis are also available.

Transport

35 km S of Uthai Thani, 241 km N of Bangkok

Long distance Train: the station is quite a distance out of the town. Songthaews can be found immediately outside the station; they all carry you into the centre of town (฿5). Regular connections with Bangkok's Hualamphong station (4 hrs).

Bus: the government bus terminal (*bor kor sor*) is on the main road through town (Route 117), about 1 km from the intersection with Route 1. The bus company *Tavorn Farm* have their terminal on Daowadung Rd. Songthaews following routes through town stop at the *bor kor sor* (฿5) and motorcycle taxis are also available. Regular connections with Bangkok's Northern bus terminal. Also buses from Ayutthaya and other towns on the route running north towards Chiang Mai and from towns in the Northeast, including Khon Kaen and Nakhon Ratchasima.

The Central Plains

Routes north to Si Satchanalai

From Nakhon Sawan, Route 117 runs north to Phitsanulok (where buses link up with the northeast). From here it is 50 km west to Sukhothai town and its histori- cal sights. Continuing north from Sukhothai, Route 101 passes through the ancient city of Si Satchanalai before reaching the Northern region, and the beau- tiful towns of Lampang, Lamphun and Chiang Mai. Alternatively, Route 11 to the east of Phitsanulok and the Yom River passes close by the provincial capital of Uttaradit, and from there into the Northern region.

Phichit
Phone code: 056
Colour map 2, grid B1

This small provincial capital in the so-called Lower North lies off the main routes linking the north with the Central and Northeastern regions and with Bangkok. Its roots are said to date back to 1058 when the town was founded by Phraya Khot Thabong, a local lord. It was known as Sa Luang during the Sukhothai period (1238-1350) and was recognized as a province during the administrative reforms of King Chulalongkorn at the end of the 19th century.

Wat Tha Luang, not far from the Sala Klang on Busaba Road and overlook- ing the Nan River, is notable for its fine bronze image of the Buddha cast in the Chiang Saen style. The image is known as Luang Pho Phet and is portrayed in the mudra of subduing Mara. In style it is reminiscent of the image at Wat Phra Sri Ratana Mahathat in Phitsanulok, although the latter is much finer. Wat Tha Luang is also the site of **Phichit's annual boat racing festival** (appropriately, as *tha* means port or jetty, so *tha luang* can be roughly translated as Royal Jetty), which is held over the first Saturday and Sunday in September (see Fes- tivals, below).

Muang Kao (simply 'Old Town'), or the original site of Phichit, lies about 10 km from the modern urban centre. The site has been turned into a public garden and nearby are two important monasteries. **Wat Nakhon Chum** has a fine Viharn dating from the Sukhothai period (1238-1350), containing an 800-year-old image of the Buddha. About 300 m from Wat Nakhon Chum is **Wat Mahathat**, which also dates, so it is thought, from the Sukhothai period and contains a ruined chedi and the remains of various monastery buildings. As this site is on almost anyone's itinerary, it remains unrenovated; a substantial plus for those looking for the Lost City in the Jungle. ■ *Getting there: by songthaew.*

Hotels are basic & not geared to overseas visitors; most visitors are travelling salesmen, truck drivers & officials

Sleeping Most hotels are concentrated in the centre of town near the main market area, by the river. **B** *Rose Inn Taphanhin Hotel*, 57-59 Chomteravej Rd, T621044, F621808. A/c, restaurant. The best place to stay in Phichit. **C** *Okhaa Nakhon*, 2/91 Srimala Rd, T611206. Eighty a/c rooms, situated in the western quarter of town, the best place to stay here before the *Rose Inn* was opened, but it is still very plain. **E** *Muang Thong*, 28 Thitacaree Rd, T611128. Forty-five rooms, some with a/c. **E** *Srimala I*, 9/29 Srimala Rd, T611238. Twelve fan rooms.

Festivals Sep *Phichit Boat Races* (first Sat and Sun in the month) held at Wat Tha Luang in town, when local teams paddle boats up and down the Nan River which flows through the provincial capital. As with just about every festival in the Kingdom, the organizers have also seen fit to run a beauty competition to find the most beauti- ful Phichit maiden.

340 km N of Bangkok **Transport Train**: Phichit lies on the northern rail line between Bangkok and Chiang Mai, although not all trains stop here. The station is to the north of the Nan River (the town lies largely to the south). Regular connections with Bangkok's Hualamphong

The Central Plains

station and towns on the north-south rail route. **Bus**: the *bor kor sor* (BKS – main bus terminal) lies to the west of town; saamlors wait to take passengers into the throbbing metropolis. The Thavorn bus company, which runs a/c tour buses to Bangkok, operates from its office on Chanot Sawang Rd, in the centre of town. Regular a/c and non a/c bus connections with Bangkok and provincial centres in the north, northeast and Central Plains regions.

Directory Communications Post Office: corner of Busaba and Busaba 6 roads, not far from Wat Tha Luang. **Telephone office:** to the south of the centre of town on Bung Si Fai Rd, next to Phichit Hospital. **Medical services** *Phichit Hospital*, Bung Si Fai Rd, to the south of the centre of town.

Phitsanulok   พิษณุโลก

At first glance, Phitsanulok appears an ugly modern town; most of the old wooden buildings which graced the city were destroyed in a disastrous fire in the 1960s, and their replacements are uninspired to say the very least. However, this large, bustling town is attractively positioned on the banks of the river Nan, with houseboats lining the steep banks, and is home to one of the most important shrines in Thailand – Wat Phra Sri Ratana Mahathat. It is also a transport hub, linking the Central Plains with the north and northeast. With its collection of comfortable Western-style hotels, it is a convenient base from which to visit the historic cities of Sukhothai and Si Satchanalai.

Population: 85,000
Phone code: 055
Colour map 2, grid B1

The Central Plains

Getting there Phitsanulok is a very easy place to get to by bus, as it connects the north, northeast and Central Plains. The bus terminal is not central, but Bus No 10 travels between the local bus station and the terminal every 10 mins (and takes 30 mins). The journey from Bangkok takes 5-6 hrs. It is possible to fly here, with plenty of daily connections with Bangkok and also with other northern towns.

Ins & outs
See also Transport, page 207

Getting around Phitsanulok is easy enough to get around on foot, with the main site of interest being in the northern part of town. A walk along the river road is worthwhile at night, when the night market gets into full swing.

Tourist offices *TAT*, 209/7-8 Surasi Shopping Centre, Boromtrailokant Rd, T252742, tatphs@loxinfo.co.th, welcome.to/tatphs Areas of responsibility are Phitsanulok and Sukhothai. Helpful and informative, with good maps of the town and surrounding area. Open 0830-1630 Mon-Sun.

Phitsanulok was the birthplace of one of the heroes of Thai history: King Naresuan the Great of Ayutthaya (reigned 1590-1605) (there is a shrine to the king on the west side of the river facing Wat Mahathat). However, shortly after his birth the young Naresuan was bundled off to Burma as a guarantee of his father's – King Thammaracha – good behaviour. He did not return to Phitsanulok until he was 16, when he was awarded the principality to govern by his father. Here he developed his military and political skills which were to stand him in good stead when he assumed the throne of Ayutthaya 19 years later in 1590 (see box). For the short period of 25 years, during the reign of King Boromtrailokant (1448-88) of Ayutthaya, Phitsanulok was actually the capital of Siam, and over the four centuries prior to the fall of Ayutthaya to the Burmese in 1767 it was effectively the Kingdom's second city.

History

The 'lost wax' process of bronze casting

A core of clay is moulded into the desired form and then covered in beeswax and shellac. Details are engraved into the beeswax. The waxed core is then coated with a watery mixture of clay and cow's dung, and built up into a thick layer of clay. This is then fired in a kiln, the wax running out through vents cut into the clay. Molten bronze is poured into the mould where it fills the void left by the wax, and after cooling the mould is broken open to reveal the image.

Sights

Wat Phra Sri Ratana Mahathat
This is a very sacred site & visitors wearing shorts or revealing clothing will not be admitted

The Monastery of the Great Relic, known locally as Wat Yai – 'Big Wat' – is to be found on the east bank of the river Nan, close to the Naresuan Bridge. It was built in the reign of King Phya Li Thai of Sukhothai, in 1357. Originally the chedi probably took the form of the classic Sukhothai-style lotus bud, and art historians believe that it was only on the instructions of King Boromtrailokant (1448-88) that the chedi was remodelled into the classic Ayutthaya prang that exists today.

The viharn contains one of the most highly regarded and venerated Buddha images in Thailand – the *Phra Buddha Chinaraj*. Through the centuries, successive Thai kings have come to Phitsanulok to pay homage to the image and to make offerings of gifts from royal raiments to precious utensils. The image is cast in bronze in an attitude of subduing Mara and is said to have been made on the orders of King Lithai in 1357, although the date cannot be confirmed. In the early 17th century, King Eka Thossarot is said to have given some gold to the wat so that it could be beaten into sheets and used to plate the Buddha. The image is a superlative example of late Sukhothai style – corpulent body, rounded face, serene, almost grave expression, and fingers all the same length (see section on Sukhothai style, page 805). The head is covered in tight spiralled curls and is surrounded by a flame-like ketumala. The whole effect is accentuated by lighting from below and a dark backdrop. This Buddha is said to have wept tears of blood when the city was captured by the Ayutthayan army in the early 14th century. The three-tiered viharn in which the image is contained is also impressive. It was built during the Ayutthaya period and shows a fusion of Ayutthayan and Lanna (Northern) Thai architectural styles. The low sweeping roofs, supported by black and gold pillars, accentuate the massive gilded bronze Buddha image seated at the end of the nave. The entrance is through inlaid **mother-of-pearl doors**, made in 1756 in the reign of King Boromkot to replace the original ones of carved wood. The small viharn in front of the main building houses another significant Buddha image, also in the mudra of subduing Mara. This image is known as the 'Remnant Buddha' because it was cast from the bronze remaining after the main image had been produced. Behind the main viharn is the bot, with a stucco image of the Buddha, thought to have been made during the residence of King Naresuan in the city while he was Crown Prince. The 36 m high prang in the centre of the complex was rebuilt in the popular Ayutthayan style when King Boromtrailokant visited Phitsanulok. Stairs lead up to a niche containing relics of the Buddha. Also in the wat compound is the **Buddha Chinnarat National Museum**, with a small collection of Sukhothai Buddhas and assorted ceramics. ■ *0800-1700 Mon-Sun, a donation of ฿50 is recommended.*

Other sights The excellent TAT Office (see Ins and outs above), in some might say a futile attempt to lure more people to the city, are promoting walking tours of the capital. One of the sights being promoted is the **Folk Museum** on Wisutkaset

Road which exhibits items from everyday rural life, in particular agricultural implements and tools, children's games, festival and ceremonial items, and other bits and pieces. By all accounts it has improved markedly as a museum and is now full of interest and, for what it is, is well laid out and informative. The museum is run by Dr Thawi who has a national reputation. ■ *0830-1200, 1300-1630 Tue-Sun*. Across the street, and run by the same man, is a **factory casting Buddha images**. These are produced using the lost wax method (see box opposite) and range in size from diminutive to monstrous. It is usually possible to see at least some of the production processes. ■ *The door is always shut; open it and go in, 0800-1700, Mon-Sat*. The **riverside night market**, south of the new bridge, is open from 1800 to midnight and is a great bustle of activity, colour and smell. Stalls include food of every variety and a range of goods including handicrafts, amulets, clothes and other trinkets.

Excursions

Wat Chulamani, 6 km to the south of Phitsanulok on Route 1063, was probably the original town centre. During the Khmer period it was known as Muang Song Kwae ('Two River Town'), as it lies between the Nan and the Kwae Noi. It was built by King Boromtrailokant (1448-88) in 1464. The wat compound houses the remains of an ornate Khmer prang which pre-dates the Sukhothai period (but was probably remodelled in the Ayutthaya period), a bot, some monastery walls, and Buddha images housed under a makeshift shelter. The finest element of the rather ramshackle complex is the fine stucco work of the prang – note the well-modelled *hamsas* (geese) that ring the 'corn cob'. Nonetheless, the site will probably be rather disappointing for those who have just experienced the wonders of the ancient city of Sukhothai. ■ *₿5-7. Getting there: catch Bus No 5 which leaves from the City bus centre, near the railway station on Ekathosarot Rd, every 10 mins, 20-min journey*.

Wat Chulamani

Phu Hin Rongkla National Park is situated 120 km east of Phitsanulok, off Route 2113, which links Phitsanulok with Loei. It covers 5,000 sq km over three provinces: Phitsanulok, Phetchabun and Loei. The park, which has been partly deforested, was a stronghold of the Communist Party of Thailand (CPT) until the early 1980s, and hundreds of disaffected students fled here following the Thammasat University massacre of 1976. (As the tourist blurb rather opaquely puts it: 'the place used to be a bloody battlefield due to the conflict in political idealism.') The government encouraged farmers to settle in the park to deny the guerrillas refuge; now that the CPT has been vanquished, the same farmers have been told they are illegal squatters and must move. So much for helping in the fight against Communism. The buildings used by the CPT for training and indoctrination (3 km southwest of the park headquarters) have been preserved and in some cases rebuilt, and have now become sights of historical interest to the Thais, particularly those former students and their families who joined the movement after the student demonstrations of 1973-76. The base supported a political and military school – with printing press and communications centre, a small hospital, cafeteria and air raid shelter.

Phu Hin Rongkla National Park

The Central Plains

● ●
Phitsanulok place names

Phu Hin Rongkla National Park
อุทยานแห่งชาติภูหินร่องกล้า

Wat Chulamani
วัดจุฬามณี

Wat Phra Sri Ratana Mahathat
วัดพระศรีรัตนมหาธาตุ

Rising to 1,780 m, the park has a diverse flora ranging from dry dipterocarp forest at low altitudes to pine forest on the upper slopes, and including numerous orchids and lichens. Wildlife, though it has suffered from hunting, includes small populations of tiger, bear, sambar deer and hornbills. Bungalows are available at park headquarters (book in advance, T5795734) and there is a camping ground (tents for hire, ฿40), two restaurants (take own food if self-catering) and money changer. ■ *Getting there: catch a bus towards Loei and get off at Nakhon Thai, 3 hrs (฿35), and then a songthaew to the park (฿15-25). If travelling by car or motorcycle, drive to Ban Yaeng at the Km 68 marker and turn left towards Nakhon Thai; turn right after another 24 km at Ban Nong Krathao. The headquarters are 28 km along this road.*

Thung Salaeng National Park

The **road between Phitsanulok and Lomsak**, Highway 12, is increasingly popular with visitors. The Thung Salaeng National Park is here (see below), and so too are a number of waterfalls and resort hotels. The **Sakunothayon Botanical Gardens** is located off the Phitsanulok-Lomsak road (Highway 12) at the Km 33 marker. A 500 m-long access road leads to the gardens, which are best known for the picturesque, 10 m-high **Waeng Nok Aen Waterfall**. ■ *Getting there: take one of the regular buses running between Phitsanulok and Lomsak and get off at the Km 33 marker.*

The Thung Salaeng Luang National Park, consisting of forest (much of it degraded) and grasslands, covers more than 1,250 sq km of Phitsanulok and Phetchabun provinces, rising from 300 m to over 1,000 m. The word *thung* in Thai means open meadow and these are the most notable features of the park. The meadows allow good viewing of a rich variety of birdlife (190 recorded species), including hornbills, pheasants (including the Siamese fireback pheasant), eagles and owls. Of the park's 17 mammal species the most notable is the park's small population of elephants; tigers are also said to inhabit the park, but these are rarely seen. The best time for trekking is during the cool season between November and March. During the 1970s this area was a stronghold of the Communist Party of Thailand and it was closed to visitors until the mid-1980s. There are guesthouses and a dormitory block at the headquarters and four campsites. Tents are available for hire. A more comfortable alternative is to stay in one of the resort hotels scattered along Highway 12, between Phitsanulok and Lomsak. Recommended is *Rainforest Resort* at Km 44 (T55-241185), which overlooks the Khek River and offers attractive wooden bungalows with air conditioning. ■ *Getting there: the park office is located at Km 80 on the Phitsanulok-Lomsak Highway (Highway 12). Regular buses run between Phitsanulok and Lomsak.*

Essentials

Sleeping
■ *on map*
Price codes:
see inside front cover

AL-B *Amarin Lagoon Hotel*, 52/299 Phra Ong Khao Rd, T220999, F220994, BT6684277, BF6685222, amarin@psnulok.loxinfo.co.th A/c, restaurant, pool, opened in 1995, 305-room hotel on 10-ha site some way from the town centre. However, the management provide a shuttle service, and a long time resident of Thailand reports that the hotel is well-run, with courteous and efficient staff, superb views from the back over the lagoon and open countryside to the far hills, and a sumptuous buffet lunch for ฿150. Good value. Recommended. **A** *Phailyn*, 38 Boromtrailokant Rd, T252411, F258185, BT2157110, BF2155640. A/c, restaurant, professionally managed. Don't be put off by the rather dreary exterior which makes the hotel look like a grubby block of flats; inside it is clean, modern and well kept. **A** *Topland Plaza Hotel*, 68/33 Akathodsarod St, T247800, F247815, BT2156108, BF2150511. A/c, restaurant, multi-storey hotel associated with the *Topland Plaza*, good views over the city from the upper floors. **A-B** *Golden Grand Hotel*, 66 Thambucha Rd, T210234, F210887. Proclaims itself as a first class hotel, though maybe not by Western standards (first-class hotels don't have to make a point of saying 'individual controlled air-conditioning' in their brochures). Still comfortable, but a bit overpriced. Restaurant with international and Thai food. There's also a 'Fizzy' karaoke bar. **A-B** *Phitsanulok Thani Hotel*, 39 Sanambin Rd, T211065, F211071, BT3189101, BF3189104, sale_phl@ksc.th.com, www.phitsanulokthani.th.com A/c, restaurant, pub, pool, new luxury hotel, one of the *Dusit* chain, so standards are high. The room rate includes breakfast and there are a few pleasant garden restaurants just across the road. A little out of town, but within walking distance. **A-C** *Rajapruk*, 99/9 Phra Ong Dam Rd, T258788, F251395. A/c, restaurant, pool. Ugly, scruffy looking hotel with an almost Soviet or Eastern European flavour, cluttered and impersonal. **A-C** *Thep Nakhon*, 43/1 Sri Thamtripodok Rd, T244070, F251897, BT398208, BF3982227. A/c, large hotel, cocktail lounge, all usual first class facilities, Asian in atmosphere. Beginning to look rather tatty, but the staff are helpful and friendly. (Thep Nakhon means the 'City of Angels'.)

Phitsanulok

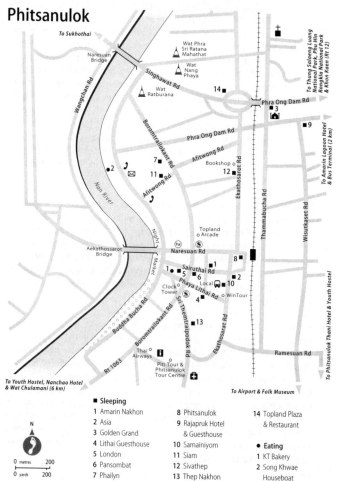

The Central Plains

C *Amarin Nakhon*, 3/1 Chaophraya Rd, T219069, F219500. A/c, restaurant, 'Thai businessman's hotel' which is doing a good job maintaining standards despite its age. **C** *Nanchao*, 242 Boromtrailokant Rd, T252510. A/c, comfortable modern hotel with views from the upper floors, good value. Recommended. **D** *Asia Hotel*, 176/1 Ekathosarot Rd, T258378, F230419. Some a/c (reasonably priced), some fan, no character. Noisy street. **D** *Rajapruk Guesthouse*, Phra Ong Dam Rd (behind the *Rajapruk Hotel* above a row of garages), T258477. Some a/c, characterless and tatty, poor value, guests have access to the facilities of the *Rajapruk Hotel*, for what it's worth. **D** *Samainiyom Hotel*, 175 Ekathosarot Rd, T247527. Open marble entrance, but warm and quiet. All rooms a/c or cool air ventilation, though it still feels quite warm. Satellite TV and clean en suite bathrooms for those willing to pay a little bit more. Very reasonable prices. **D** *Sivathep Hotel*, 110/21 Ekathosarot Rd, T244933, F219148. Some fan, some a/c, all rooms ensuite with satellite TV. **D-E** *Lithai Guesthouse*, 73/1 Phaya Lithai Rd., T219626, F219627, maka@loxinfo.co.th Some fan, some a/c, satellite TV, en suite rooms, telephones in rooms to make international calls. Breakfast included with a/c rooms, and free morning coffee for fan rooms. Coffee shop downstairs open 0700-1400, 1700-2100. Not an attractive building, with room views of either dirty rooftops or busy streets below. Still, good value for money. **D-E** *Phitsanulok*, 82 Naresuan Rd, T258425. Near the railway station, making it a very noisy choice. Rooms are dark, dirty and gloomy. If the noise doesn't keep you awake, the concrete beds certainly will. **D-E** *Siam Hotel*, 4/8 Atitwong Rd, T258844. Some a/c, some fan, unenthusiastic management. Kamikaze restaurant and pub across the road. **D-E** *Youth Hostel*, 38 Sanambin Rd, T242060. Southeast of the railway, slightly out of town. This has become the travellers' hang out, so it is very popular and often full. Relaxing atmosphere in an attractive wooden building, large clean rooms with some a/c and some style, helpful owner, dorm beds available, breakfast included, bicycles for rent. Outdoor sitting area for relaxing with bamboo hammocks. Possibly the only place in Thailand where you'll wake up to classical music. The best option in town for those on a budget. Highly recommended.

E *Hollywood Guesthouse*, out of town, T258108 for free transport, there is also an office at 112 Boromtrailokant Rd. Some rooms with own toilet, some dorm beds, recently opened. **E** *Pansombat*, 4/1 Sairuthai Rd, T258179. Rather dirty and tatty Chinese-style hotel with interesting graffiti on the wall to keep you entertained when sleep seems a million miles off; no hot water. A last resort. **E** *London Hotel*, 21-22 Puttabucha Soi, T225145. Cheap fan rooms, simple, but the management have made an effort to give the place a wooden 'country house' effect by nailing small planks into the walls. Very little English spoken.

Eating
● *on map, page 205*
Price categories:
see inside front cover

As the largest town in this area of the country there is a wide choice of restaurants, catering for all tastes and pockets. They are concentrated in the centre of town around Naresuan, Sairuthai and Phaya Lithai roads, and many are truly excellent. Phitsanulok has 2 specialities for which it is known across Thailand. The first is its excellent *kluay thaak* or sweet bananas. Dry bananas are also processed in this area – the best place to buy them is in the compound of Wat Phra Si Rattana Mahathat. The second is its *thao mai luai* or morning glory. This vegetable is flash-fried in a wok with a great burst of flame and then tossed onto the plate (the dish is usually known as *phak bung loi fan*). 'Flying Vegetable' artistes can be seen at work in the night market and at a few restaurants. Not to be missed! Several houseboat restaurants are to be found along Buddha Bucha Rd, near Naresuan Bridge.

Thai Mid-range: *Song Khwae Houseboat*, Buddha Bucha Rd. Also serves Chinese food. *Bi Bi's Pub*, Sithamtripidok Rd. European steaks, grills and a few Thai dishes. **Cheap**: *Sor Lert Rod*, 4/5 Boromtrailokant Rd, near *Phailyn Hotel*. Recommended.

Tiparot, 9 Soi Lue Thai Rd. Also serves Chinese food. *Viroys*, 99/18-19 Phra Ong Dam Rd. Excellent Chinese food, with morning glory frying for the uninitiated. **Seriously cheap**: *Poon Sri*, Phaya Lithai Rd. Recommended.

Muslim There are 2 Muslim restaurants on Phra Ong Dam Rd. Of these: **Cheap**: *Fab Ke Rab* (80 m east of the level crossing) is recommended – friendly staff, good food and very well priced. The other (adjacent to the level crossing) hasn't had a very good press!

Foodstalls The riverside night market is open from 1800 to midnight, excellent stalls selling Thai and Chinese food. Thai sweets (desserts) like *khao niaw sangkayaa* (sticky rice and custard) can be bought from the foodstalls on Phaya Lithai Rd in the evening. Basement of Topland Arcade, Boromtrailokant Rd, has a good selection of clean, well presented foodstalls.

Bakery *KT*, Phaya Lithai Rd. Excellent range of cakes and pastries.

Bi Bi's Pub, Sithamtripidok Rd (down soi near *Thep Nakhon Hotel*). Cocktails and a wide range of drinks in an a/c 'chalet'. **Thip Beer House** (opposite *Phailyn Hotel*), Boromtrailokant Rd. Ice-cold beer in open bar.

Bars
Most bars & pubs are near expensive hotels

Jan/Feb *Phra Buddha Chinarat* (movable), a 6-day fair which honours the Phra Buddha Chinarat, held at Wat Phra Sri Ratana Mahathat, with entertainment and stalls selling local products. **Oct** *Boat Races* (first weekend) on the stretch of the Nan overlooked by Wat Mahathat.

Festivals

Antiques and handicrafts *Mondok Thai*, 10 Sithamtripidok Rd. *Hat Tim*, 1/1 Sithamtripidok Rd. **Sri Satchanalai Traditional Gold** Gold shops line the streets throughout town. Some jewellery and ornaments are handmade locally, with their designs taken from ruins and remains in the Sri Satchanalai area.

The *night market* on Buddha Bucha Rd, on the river, sells everything from handicrafts, clothes and toys to amulets (see page 101); something Phitsanulok has a reputation for. The *Topland Arcade* is a large a/c shopping centre on Boromtrailokant Rd, while the *Topland Plaza* is a similar affair on Singhawat Rd, near the *Topland Plaza Hotel*.

Shopping

Piti Tour and Phitsanulok Tour Centre, 55/45 Surasri Trade Center, 43/11 Boromtrailokant Rd, T242206. Organizes city tours and tours to Sukhothai and Si Satchanalai by private car. *Able Group Company Ltd*, 55/45 Sri Thammatripidok Rd, T243851, F242206. Runs sightseeing and trekking tours and rents out cars.

Tour operators

Local Songthaews, tuk-tuks, saamlors and buses – both a/c and non-a/c (₿10-20). **Car hire**: *Able Group Company Ltd*, see Tour operators above.

Transport
See also Ins & outs, page 175
498 km N of Bangkok

Long distance **Air**: airport is just out of town on Sanambin Rd, T258029. **Thai Airways**, T2800060, BT6282000, have multiple daily connections with Bangkok. There are also connections with Loei, Tak, Lampang, Chiang Mai (daily), Mae Hong Son, Mae Sot and Nan. From the airport, take a songthaew into town or buses run to/from the city bus centre near the railway station every 10 mins (₿4-6).

Train: Swiss 'chalet' style station, with steam locomotive parked outside, Ekathosarot Rd, T258005. A copy of the train timetable in English is available from the TAT office (see under Ins and outs, page 201). Regular connections with Bangkok's Hualamphong station (6 hrs), Lopburi (5 hrs), Ayutthaya (7 hrs). Also with Uttaradit, Nakhon Sawan, Lampang (4-5 hrs) and Chiang Mai (6-7 hrs). For those travelling straight on to Sukhothai, take a tuk-tuk the 4 km to the bus station on the road east (Route 12) to Lom Sak.

The Central Plains

Bus: terminal on the road east to Lom Sak (Route 12) 2 km out of town, T242430. There's a good, cheap Thai restaurant at the western end of the station, on the ground floor of a shophouse. If the bus travels through town en route to the bus terminal, ask the driver to let you off at the train station and save an additional journey. Bus No 7 leaves the local bus station for the bus terminal every 10 mins (30 min journey). Regular connections with Bangkok from the Northern bus terminal (5-6 hrs), Kamphaeng Phet (2 hrs), Uttaradit (2 hrs), Nan (5 hrs, via Uttaradit), Phrae (3 hrs), Udon Thani, Sukhothai, Pattaya, Tak (3 hrs), Mae Sot (5 hrs), Nakhon Sawan (2 hrs), Chiang Mai (5-6 hrs), Lampang (4 hrs), Khon Kaen (5 hrs), Korat (6 hrs) and Chiang Rai (6-7 hrs). There are hourly departures for Tak, Kamphaeng Phet, Uttaradit and Phetchabun and half-hourly departures for Sukhothai. Private a/c and VIP tour buses leave from offices in the centre of town, eg *Win Tour*, T243222 (see map) or *Tavorn Farm Tour* (slightly cheaper).

Directory **Airline offices** *Thai Airways*, 209/26-28 Boromtrailokant Rd, T2800060, BT6282000. **Banks** *Bangkok*, 35 Naresuan Rd. *Krung Thai*, 31/1 Naresuan Rd. *Thai Farmers*, 144/1 Boromtrailokant Rd, TCs & ATM. **Communications** Post Office and telephone centre: Buddha Bucha Rd. **Internet & email services**: internet café on Sanambin Rd, just before the Phitsanulok Thani Hotel. More internet cafés are opening around town. **Medical services** Hospital: Sithamtripidok Rd, T258812. **Tourist Police**: Boromtrailokant Rd, next to TAT office, T251179.

Sukhothai สุโขทัย

Population: 28,000
Phone code: 055
Colour map 1, grid C3

Travelling along Route 12 towards Muang Kao, ruined chedis and the brick foundations of ancient religious structures appear in the rice fields, interspersed between wooden shophouses until, magically, the road pierces the eastern moat and ramparts of the city. The old city and its surroundings are a national histori-cal park covering 640 ha which was officially opened in 1988, after a decade of restoration work, when a total of 192 wats were restored. Old Sukhothai is very well cared for, with lotus ponds, flowering trees and manicured lawns which have become a haven for birdlife. Twelve kilometres east of the old city is the modern, and unattractive, New Sukhothai, which was rebuilt after being destroyed by a fire in the late 1950s. It doesn't have much to offer, although it makes a pleasant enough spot to stay while exploring the glories of Old Sukhothai.

Ins and outs

Getting there
See also Transport, page 221

In 1994 a new airport opened at Sukhothai – in fact it is nearer Sawankhalok – run by Bangkok Airways which flies between here and Bangkok and Chiang Mai. The alterna-tive is to fly to Phitsanulok, about 50-odd km away and served by Thai. But most people arrive by bus and there are regular connections with Bangkok, Chiang Mai, Phitsanulok and Khon Kaen as well as other major towns in the North and Central Plains.

Getting around

Most people come to Sukhothai to see the ruins of the former capital. But most accommodation is situated in the new town which is 12 km to the east. Regular buses and songthaews ply the route between the two and it is also easy to hire a motorcy-cle. The ruins themselves are spread over a considerable area. See page 217 for details on getting around the historical park.

History

If you ask a Thai about the history of Sukhothai, he or she will say that King Intradit ('Glorious Sun-King') founded the Sukhothai Kingdom in 1240, hav-ing successfully driven off the Khmers following a single-handed elephant duel with the Khmer commander. King Intradit then founded Wat Mahathat, the geographical and symbolic heart of the new kingdom. Revisionist historians and archaeologists reject this view, regarding it as myth-making on a grand scale (see page 211). They maintain that Sukhothai evolved into a great kingdom over a long period and find the Big Bang theory ultimately unconvincing.

Like Angkor to the east in Cambodia, until comparatively recently Sukhothai was a 'lost city in the jungle'. It was only in 1833 that the future King Mongkut discovered the famous inscription No 1 and not until 1895 that the French scholar Lucien Fournereau published an incomplete description of the site. The key date though is 1907 when crown Prince Maha Vajiravudh – later King Vajiravudh – made an eight-day visit to Sukhothai, during a two-month excursion to Northern Thailand between January and March. It was his account that laid the foundations for the Sukhothai 'myth'. It seems that he was concerned at Siam's rush into westernization and his trip gave him the chance to construct a proud, glorious and civilized past for a country which, he felt, was on the verge of being submerged by an alien culture. What, as Elizabeth Moore, Philip Stott and Suryavudh Sukhasvasti argue in their book *Ancient Capitals of Thailand* (Thames and Hudson, 1996), is remarkable is that Prince Vajiravudh's account, based on a cursory visit, was accepted for so long and by so many. Western scholars like Georges Coedès, Jean Boisselier, Alexander Griswold and Reginald S Le May may have put more flesh on the bones, but they never challenged the basic thesis. It has only been since the mid-1980s that people have begun to question the conventional history.

Sukhothai, meaning 'dawn of happiness', became the **first capital of Siam**, and the following 200 years (until the early 15th century) is considered the pinnacle of Thai civilization. There were nine kings of the Sukhothai Dynasty, the most famous being King Intradit's third son, Ramkhamhaeng, whose reign is disputed but believed to have been 1275-1317. He was the first ruler to leave accounts of the state inscribed in stone stelae (now displayed in the National Museum in Bangkok). These provide a wealth of information on conquests, taxation and political philosophy. Realizing the importance of a national language as a unifying force, the King created the Thai script, derived from Mon and Khmer, and the inscription No 1 of 1292 is regarded by many as the first work of Thai literature (see page 746, but also see the box on page 211).

King Ramkhamhaeng vastly expanded his kingdom, which at its peak encompassed much of present-day Thailand, except the northern kingdom of Lanna Thai, Lopburi and the Khorat Plateau (which were still controlled by the waning Khmer Empire). The Sukhothai Kingdom also extended south down the Malay Peninsula and west into Lower Burma.

Ramkhamhaeng is commonly portrayed as an absolute monarch, but one who governed his people with justice and magnanimity. It is written, for example (or rather, inscribed), that if anyone wanted to lodge a complaint, he or she would ring a bell at the gate and the king would grant them an audience. Naturally, the inscriptions on which much of our knowledge of Sukhothai and King Ramkhamhaeng is based are rather fanciful. Even so, his reign was a brilliant one. King Ramkhamhaeng was responsible for the introduction of Theravada Buddhism, when he brought Ceylonese monks to his kingdom – partly intended to displace the influence of the Khmers. He displayed considerable diplomatic powers and cultivated good relations with his northern neighbours in order to form an alliance against the Khmers. In addition, he opened relations with China, establishing both economic and cultural links. The fine pottery produced at Sukhothai and Si Satchanalai is thought by some scholars to have developed only after the arrival of expert Chinese potters, with their knowledge of advanced glazing techniques (see box page 223).

The Central Plains

If historical records are to be believed (and the story sounds ominously apocryphal), his closest brush with death came when he was foolish enough to fall in love with the wife of the King of Phayao whom he was visiting. Princess Ua Chiengsaen returned his affection, but when her husband discovered the affair, he arrested Ramkhamhaeng. The love-stricken King was about to be put to death when Phya Mengrai, the great King of Chiang Mai, called on them to resolve their differences. Ramkhamhaeng apologized and was ordered to pay 999,000 cowrie shells in penance. Then the three kings went to the River Ping and swore perpetual friendship by drinking a cup of water, mixed with blood from their fingers.

The Sukhothai period saw a flowering not just of ceramic arts, but of art in general (see page 805). The Buddha images are regarded as the most beautiful and original to have ever been produced in Thailand. And the walking Buddha image carved in the round is perhaps the greatest innovation of the artists of the period. There had previously been walking Buddhas in bas-relief, but never free-standing. The style is graceful and languid, with an expression of bliss and an enigmatic smile. It was not to last: by the second half of the 14th century, the smile had become a smirk and the general expression degenerated into one of haughtiness.

King Ramkhamhaeng's son, Lo Thai (1327-46), was an ineffectual leader, overshadowed even in death by his father, and much of the territories gained by the previous reign were lost. By the sixth reign of the Sukhothai Dynasty, the kingdom was in decline, and by the seventh, Sukhothai paid homage to Ayutthaya. In 1438 Ayutthaya officially incorporated Sukhothai into its realm, and the first Thai kingdom had succumbed to its younger and more vigorous neighbour.

Sights

New Sukhothai Guesthouses here are generally of a high standard (although the 'better' hotels are poor), there is good stall food at the night market on Ramkhamhaeng Road, a fresh day market off Charodwithithong Road (see map) and a useful range of tourist amenities.

The old city The old city is 1.8 km long and 1.4 km wide, and originally it was encompassed by triple earthen ramparts and two moats, pierced by four gates. Within the city there are 21 historical sites; outside the walls are another 70 or so places of historical interest. At one time the city may have been home to as many as 300,000 people, with an efficient tunnel system to bring water from the mountains into the city and a network of roads. It was an urban centre to rival any in Europe at the time. Within the city are monuments of many different styles – as if the architects were attempting to imbue the centre with the magical power of other Buddhist sites: there are Mon chedis, Khmer prangs and Sri Lankan chedis, as well as monuments of clearly Sukhothai inspiration.

Sukhothai walking Buddha, late 14th century

Sukhothai: a 'Golden Age' or mother of invention?

At the beginning of March 1989, several hundred people – mostly scholars – assembled at the Bangkok Bank's headquarters on Silom Road, to debate an issue that threatened to undermine the very identity of the Thai people. Some archaeologists had begun to argue that the famous inscription number 1 on which the interpretation of King Ramkhamhaeng's reign is based (see page 746) is a forgery. They maintained that the then Prince Mongkut's remarkably timely 'discovery' of the inscription in 1833 served Siam's political purposes – it showed to the expansionist British and French that the country was a 'civilized' kingdom that could govern itself without outside interference. Along with certain literary and artistic anomalies, this led some commentators to maintain that King Mongkut created King Ramkhamhaeng – or at least his popular image – to protect his kingdom from the colonial powers.

Before Mongkut stumbled upon inscription number 1, knowledge of Sukhothai's history was based upon myth and legend. The great king Phra Ruang – who was believed to have hatched from the egg of a naga (serpent) and to be so powerful that he could make trees flower – was clearly the stuff of imagination. And some scholars also argued the same was true of King Ramkhamhaeng. Since the meeting of 1989, academic opinion has swung back to viewing Mongkut's discovery as genuine. For most Thais, of course, who have been raised to believe that Sukhothai was Thailand's Golden Age and Ramkhamhaeng its chief architect, this is beyond reproach.

However, this does not detract from the fact that inscription number 1 – and the other inscriptions – are fanciful portrayals of history carved to serve the interests of an élite, not to reflect 'reality'. As Betty Gosling writes in Sukhothai: its history, culture and art (1991) "... the controversy emphasizes the need to consider Sukhothai inscriptions ... not in the golden afterglow of Thai mythology, but in the harsh daylight of objective research".

Situated just inside the **Kamphanghek** (Broken wall) **Gate (a)** – the entrance gate – is **The Ramkhamhaeng National Museum (b)**, which is a good place to begin a tour of the site (bicycles and motorbikes can be hired close by). The museum contains a copy of Ramkhamhaeng's stela and some wonderful Buddha images, along with explanatory information. It also houses a range of household goods which give some indication of the sophistication of Sukhothai society. ■ *0900-1600 Mon-Sun, ฿30, T612167.*

The letters after the place names in bold relate to the map, page 213

The centre of the Sukhothai Kingdom was **Wat Mahathat (c)** and the royal palace (the earliest example of a royal palace in Thailand), to be found west of the museum. This was both the religious and the political centre of the Kingdom and is usually regarded as the first truly 'Sukhothai' monument. The complex was begun by King Intradit, expanded by King Ramkhamhaeng and finally completed by King Lo Thai in 1345, or thereabouts. In total, the shrine contains nearly 200 chedis (containing the ashes of the Sukhothai royal family), 10 viharns and a plethora of other structures.

The principal building is the central sanctuary, which has a large lotus-bud chedi at its core. King Lo Thai is said to have rebuilt the sanctuary in the 1340s to house the hair and neckbone relics of the Buddha which had been brought back from Ceylon. The central tower is surrounded by four smaller chedis in Srivijaya-Ceylonese style, alternating with four Khmer prangs. The entire ensemble is raised up on a two-tiered base with a stucco frieze of walking monks in relief (rather poorly restored and probably later in date). They are shown walking clockwise around the monument; pilgrims to the wat would have circumambulated in the same fashion (known as pradaksina).

The Khmer prangs would originally have had stucco decorations on their superstructure, depicting mythical animals and spirits. Most have long since eroded away. However, on the pediments of the east prang can be seen two scenes from the life of the Buddha: his birth and his death (there were 12 such scenes). Such decoration was not designed just to beautify the monument; most pilgrims would have been illiterate and the panels would also have helped to guide and educate the worshipper. In its original form, the wat was encrusted in stucco decoration and then covered in gold leaf. The central summit of the wat represented the mythical Mount Meru, and the whole sanctuary was in effect a magic diagram.

Mount Meru was located in the centre of the universe and ... Kalisa was on its summit. Gods dwelt at the highest levels, the many mythical creatures and earth spirits inhabited the terraced slopes. Around Mount Meru rose the lesser pinnacles arranged in six and seven concentric rings. At their feet lay the continents and islands which in turn were surrounded by vast oceans whose far boundaries were demarcated by a wall of rock (Stratton & Scott, 1981: 54-5).

Some original Buddha images still sit among the ruins. Particularly unusual are the two monumental standing Buddhas, in an attitude of forgiveness, either side of the central sanctuary, enclosed by brick walls, with their heads protruding over the top.

The **Royal Palace (d)** or **Phra Ruang Palace** – sometimes known as the **Noen Prasat** or 'Palace Mound' – is found just to the east of Wat Mahathat. Little remains of the original structure. It was here that King Mongkut, while he was still the Crown Prince, found the famous inscription No 1 of King Ramkhamhaeng, the Manangsilabat stone throne, and the stone inscription of King Lithai in 1833. All three objects – which became talismans for the Thai people – were carted off to Bangkok. Whether the Royal Palace really was a palace is a subject for conjecture. The site appears rather too small and, although it has revealed a mass of objects, some scholars believe it was the site of a royal pavilion rather than a royal palace. To the north of Wat Mahathat is **San Da Pa Deng (e)**, the oldest existing structure from the Sukhothai era. It is a small Khmer laterite prang built during the first half of the 12th century.

Wat Trapang Ngoen and Wat Trapang Thong flank Wat Mahathat and the Royal Palace. **Wat Trapang Ngoen (f)** (Wat Silver Pond) lies to the west and contains a large lotus-bud chedi, similar in style to that at Wat Mahathat. The difference here is that the Buddha images found in the niches towards the summit of the chedi are all in the walking attitude. It seems that one passage from

● ●

Sukhothai: inside city walls

Ramakhamhaeng National Museum	Wat Mahathat
พิพิธภัณฑสถานแห่ง–	วัดมหาธาตุ
ชาติรามคำแหง	
	Wat Sra Sri
Phra Ruang Palace	วัดสระศรี
วังพระร่วง	
	Wat Sri Sawai
Wat Chedi Si Hong	วัดศรีสวาย
วัดเจดีย์สี่ห้อง	
	Wat Trapang Ngoen
Wat Chetuphon	วัดตระพังเงิน
วัดเชตุพน	

inscription No 1 of 1292 refers to this wat: "In the middle of this city of Sukhothai the water of the Pho Si Pond is as clear and as good to drink as the river of the Khong [Mekong] in the dry season". **Wat Trapang Thong (g)** lies to the east of Wat Mahathat and the Royal Palace on an island in the middle of a lake, after which the monastery is named. It is approached along a rickety bridge. Particularly fine are the stucco reliefs, of which perhaps the most beautiful is that on the south side of the mondop. It shows the Buddha descending from the Tavatimsa Heaven with the attendant Brahma on his left and Indra on his right. Although Hindu gods, Brahma and Indra are said to have converted to Buddhism. Being deities themselves, they too have divinities in attendance. The Buddha is protected by two parasols, above which are more deities. Particularly striking is the simplicity of the Buddha's flowing, monastic robes, and the elaborate garments of the other deities and divinities. The sculpture is considered the finest piece of stucco work from the Sukhothai period. Wat Trapang Thong is an active monastery.

Wat Sra Sri (h), to the north of Wat Trapang Ngoen, is a popular photo-spot, as the bot is reflected in a pond. A Ceylonese-style chedi dominates the complex, which also contains a fine, large seated Buddha image enclosed by columns. To the east of here is **King Ramkhamhaeng's statue (j)**, seated on a copy of the stone throne (the Phra Thaen Manang Silabat) that was found on the site of the Royal Palace and which is now in the Wat Phra Kaeo Museum in Bangkok. The statue was erected in 1969 and the high relief carvings depict famous episodes from the life of the illustrious king.

To the southwest of Wat Mahathat is **Wat Sri Sawai (k)**, enclosed within laterite walls. It was built during the time that Sukhothai was under Khmer

Sukhothai Old City

domination. The prang is in the three-tower style, with the largest central prang (rather badly restored) being 20 m tall. The stucco decoration was added to the towers in the 15th century, as were their upper brick portions. The lower laterite levels are the original sections, built under Khmer influence. It must originally have been a Hindu shrine, as carvings of Vishnu and other Hindu divinities have been found on the site. Only later was it converted into a Buddhist shrine.

A 2 km ride to the south of the city is **Wat Chetupon**, built in the late 13th or perhaps early 14th century. It is not a very exciting wat, but the journey there gives one an idea of the scale of the whole site and the road passes through an attractive village. Slate slabs run round the viharn while the bridges across the moat are also of slate. On the four walls of the mondop are two stucco images of the Buddha in high relief, walking and standing. East of Wat Chetupon is **Wat Chedi Si Hong**, with small but interesting stucco figures of elephant heads and human figures in bas relief.

Wats outside the city walls

You could cycle around these, but they're far apart & in the hot season it can be exhausting. Take plenty of water & start early! Or hire a tuk-tuk for half a day (around ฿200)

The main reason to take the trouble to see the monasteries outside the city walls is that they give a better idea of what Sukhothai was like before it became a historical park and was cleared of undergrowth. Some of the lesser known monasteries still sit in the forest.

Take the northwest gate out of the city to visit the impressive **Wat Sri Chum**. A large mondop, with a narrow vaulted entrance, encloses an enormous brick and stucco seated Buddha image; possibly the *Phra Atchana* mentioned in the stele of Ramkhamhaeng. Georges Coedès interpreted *atchana* as *acala* – meaning 'immovable' – and certainly the sheer size of the image and its snug encasing within the walls of Wat Sri Chum make this the Immovable Buddha. The temple was probably built during the seventh reign of the Sukhothai Kingdom (mid-14th century) and is said to have caused a Burmese army to flee in terror, such is the power of its withering gaze. The large Buddha seems almost suffocated by the surrounding walls which must have been added at a later stage. There is a stairway in the mondop which leads up to a space behind the head of the image (closed since 1988). Here there are line carvings recounting the jataka tales, covering the slate slab ceiling. Each slab depicts one story, skilfully carved with free-flowing lines – which originally would have been enlivened with paint. These are the finest and earliest (c.1350) to be found in Thailand (there are examples from Wat Sri Chum in the National Museum, Bangkok). What is surprising is that they should be positioned in such a dark and inaccessible place. It is thought that they were designed to instruct pilgrims, but they could hardly do so in this location. Some scholars maintain that they were originally produced for Wat Mahathat and were only later moved to Wat Sri Chum for safe-keeping. The image here is said to have talked on a number of occasions – although the back stairs provide a useful hiding place for someone to play a practical joke.

East of Wat Sri Chum is **Wat Phra Pai Luang**, the Monastery of the Great Wind, primarily interesting for the remains of three laterite prangs. It was

Sukhothai: outside city walls

kilns
เตาสังคโลก

Ramkhamhaeng National Park
อุทยานแห่งชาติรามคำแหง

Wat Phra Pai Luang
วัดพระพายหลวง

Wat Saphan Hin
วัดสะพานหิน

Wat Sri Chum
วัดศรีชุม

built during the reign of King Jayavarman VII (a Khmer king who ruled 1181-1217) and therefore dates from the Khmer period that preceded the rise of Sukhothai. Its Khmer inspiration is clearly evident in the square base and indented tiers. Only the north prang retains some of the original fine stucco-work with naga-makara arches bordering the pediment. To the east of the prang is a later stupa, with niches on all four sides containing damaged Buddha images. Further east still is a ruined mondop with the remains of large stucco Buddha images, standing, walking and reclining. In total Wat Phra Pai Luang contains over 30 stupas of assorted styles. It is thought that not only was it originally a Hindu shrine, but that it was also the site of an earlier Khmer town.

To visit **Wat Saphan Hin**, take the northwest road 3 km beyond the city walls (rather than the longer, rougher route from Oa Gate). A large standing Buddha image (in an attitude of forgiveness) stands on a hill here (possibly the *Phra Attharot* image referred to in the inscriptions). The name of the wat means 'stone bridge', a reference to the steep slate path leading to the wat, which is still in place.

Not far away from Wat Saphan Hin are the remains of two other monasteries. **Wat Khao Phrabat Noi**, the Monastery on the Hill of the Lesser Buddha Footprint, lies about 2½ km northwest of the city walls and it is approached along a stone lined footpath. The chedi here is unusual in that it is not really Sukhothai in style and it is presumed that it was remodelled during the Ayutthaya period. The graceful bell is very different from the almost corpulent Sukhothai stupas. There are four niches in each of the faces of the square base which would have contained images of the Buddha. Four Buddha footprints were found here, hence the name, but these have been removed to the National Museum in Bangkok. To the south is **Wat Aranyik**, the Monastery of Forest Dwellers, sited on a hillside. There is not much here, but the position is attractive: a few *kuti* (monks' quarters), the laterite columns of a viharn, a handful of phra chedi and a bot. At the southeast corner of the site there is a pool lined with laterite blocks.

South from this group of three monasteries is the better-known **Wat Chang Rob**, the Monastery Encircled by Elephants. The most notable structure here is the large bell-shaped Sri Lankan-style chedi with its elephant caryatid base. In Buddhist mythology, elephants – the holiest of beasts – support Mount Meru, the centre of the universe. North of Wat Chang Rob are ruins of 14th-15th century **kilns**, where Chinese-inspired ceramics were made. Although the raw material was of poor quality, and the firing techniques comparatively primitive, the pottery produced is very appealing to the western eye. Free-flowing and uninhibited in style, the decorations are based upon T'zu Chou and Annamese (north Vietnamese) prototypes. The more famous Sawangkhalok wares were produced at Sukhothai's sister city of Si Satchanalai, to the north.

Continuing south to Route 12 is the impressive, at least in size, **Wat Chedi Ngam**, the Monastery of the Beautiful Chedi. The large chedi, pure and simple in its form, has been well preserved. Also here are the remains of a large viharn with some standing columns, and what is thought to have been a *kuti* (monk's quarters) or place for bathing. As the monastery seems not to be mentioned in any of the inscriptions, scholars know little about the wat.

On the north side of Route 12 is **Wat Mangkon**, the imposingly named Dragon Monastery. This is a relatively large complex. The bot, surrounded by large *bai sema* – leaf-shaped boundary stones – has an unusual slate-tiled brick base. To the west of the bot is the base of a pavilion or *sala*, and to the north the remains of a Sri Lankan-style bell-shaped phra chedi. This chedi was originally supported at its four corners by stucco elephants. They have since crumbled but it explains the wat's original name – Wat Chang Lom, or the Monastery

Surrounded by Elephants. **Wat Phra Yuen**, the Monastery of the Standing Buddha, is around 200 m from Wat Mangkon and 1,500 m from the city walls, just to the south of Route 12. The remains of a bot can be identified by the *bai sema* that surround it and a mondop houses a large standing Buddha image, but in a poor state of preservation.

The truly enthused, or those for whom the sun has addled their brains, can continue south to visit two other minor sites, which are notable for their hill top positions rather than their artistry. **Wat Tham Hip**, the Monastery of the Casket Cave, is set on a small hill about 2½ km from the city walls. A path leads up to the ruins of two viharn and a phra chedi. **Wat Khao Phrabat Yai**, the Monastery on the Hill of the Greater Buddha Footprint, is almost 3 km from the city. The name of the monastery comes from an inscription which says that King Lithai asked for a footprint of the Buddha in Sri Lanka to be copied and the replica to be placed here, in 1360. All very exciting, except that there is not much left of the place – just a ruined viharn.

But for the majority who just want to get back to a cold drink, turn east back along Route 12. The first monastery on the way back is **Wat Si Thon**, the Monastery of the Glorious Tooth Relic, although not much remains. Today it comprises a brick base, a small mondop surrounded by minor acolyte phra chedi, and a viharn. From inscriptions found near the site, scholars have surmised that a senior monk resided here. Nearby is **Wat Tuk**, or the Masonry Monastery, which lies about 500 m west of the city walls, just to the north of Route 12. This complex consists of a viharn and mondop raised on a square brick base. The mondop contains a badly damaged image of the Buddha and the building was originally covered in high relief stucco work, of which only a small portion remains. On one face of the mondop the Buddha is shown descending from the Tavatimsa Heaven. Just south of Route 12, **Wat Pa Mamuang**, the Mango Grove Monastery, was one of Sukhothai's more important monasteries, although few visitors come to see it. Inscriptions unearthed at the site indicate that it was built for a Sri Lankan monk who was enticed to take up residence in Sukhothai in 1361. The name of the monastery is linked to a mango grove which the great Sukhothai king Ramkhamhaeng is said to have planted here, and it consisted of a bot, a large stupa and 12 smaller phra chedi.

There are also a series of monasteries to the south and east of the city. Leaving the city by the south gate, the first is **Wat Ton Chan**, the **Sandalwood Tree Monastery**, about 1½ km away. Although large, the monastery is nothing very special, although it is moated and has a bathing pool along with the usual array of viharn and chedi. Far more impressive is **Wat Chetuphon**, one of Sukhothai's more important monasteries. The building materials are more varied than the usual brick and stucco; stone, slate and brick have also been used in its construction. However, archaeologists and art historians suspect that the monastery was renovated and expanded on a number of occasions, so how much of the structure is Sukhothai in date, and how much post-Sukhothai, is a source of conjecture. The mondop, with its four stucco Buddha images – walking, seated, standing and reclining – is surrounded by a beautiful balustraded wall made of slate. In Khmer architecture, walls like this were carved from laterite with rounded uprights; here they are angular and solid.

On the other side of the road, about 500 m from Wat Chetuphon, is **Wat Chedi Si Hong**, the Monastery of the Four Bays. The most notable feature of this wat is the fine stucco work on the base of the viharn and chedi. The stucco figures are of devas – heavenly beings – humans and – on the base of the phra chedi – repeated images of garuda riding on an elephant. Visible from here across the rice fields is the rather ponderously named **Wat Si Pichit Kirati Kalayaram** which, in English, means even more ponderously, the Monastery of the

Glorious, Honourable and Beautiful Building. There is not much point in tramping through the ricefields as it looks best from a distance – the Sri Lankan-style phra chedi rising above the bright green ricefields (at the right time of year).

Leaving the city by the eastern gate and the road that leads back to Sukhothai new town are a handful of other buildings. Most important is **Wat Chang Lom**, the Monastery Surrounded by Elephants (rather than Wat Chang Rob, which is merely encircled!), just under 2 km from the city walls and on the northern side of the river. Like Wat Chang Rob, the most notable building here is the large phra chedi, supported by 36 elephant brick and stucco caryatids which protrude from the base. On the opposite side of the river, to the south of the road, is **Wat Trapang Thong Lang**, the Monastery of the Coral Tree Pond. The stucco images of the Buddha in the mondop's niches were relatively well preserved when King Rama VI visited the site in 1907; today they are much deteriorated. Further south still, off the road and into the agricultural countryside, are two minor sites, **Wat Chedi Soong** and **Khao Luang**. Wat Chedi Soong has a massive, rather ungainly chedi. The name means the Monastery of the High Chedi, and it is raised high above the ground on an ugly, elongated square base. This is characteristic of chedi of the late Sukhothai period.

Best time to visit Sukhothai is spread over a large area and this part of Thailand is one of the hottest. If visiting the site during the hot or rainy seasons (roughly Mar-Oct), it is best to explore either early in the morning or at the end of the day.

Park essentials
Open 0600-1800
Mon-Sun

Admission The park is divided into 5 zones, each with an admission charge: ฿40 for the central section, and ฿30 for each of the north, south, east and west sections. If you intend to visit all the zones, then it makes sense to purchase the so-called 'Total' ticket which costs ฿150, thus saving ฿10. However, as this 'all in' ticket also includes entrance to the Si Satchanalai Historical Park, the Ramkhamhaeng National Museum, the Sangkaloke Kiln Education & Preservation Center (45 km outside Sukhotai) and the Sawankha Woranayok National Museum (at Sawankhalok), you could end up saving more than ฿100. The Total ticket is valid for 30 days (each site can only be visited once within this time). There are also some additional charges: ฿50 per car, ฿10 per bike, ฿20 per motorcycle. Food and souvenir stalls are to be found just north of Wat Trapang Ngoen.

Getting around If arriving by public bus, either hire a bicycle (฿20 per day) or moped (฿250 per day) from the entrance gate close to the museum, or take the little yellow trolley bus which tours the major sights (฿20, but it waits for a minimum of 10 people before leaving). If bicycling around the site it is worth taking a bottle of water. There are a number of ways of travelling the 12 km from Sukhothai new town to the old city. Cheapest is to catch one of the quaint buses that run from the station on Charodwithithong Rd, 200 m or so from the bridge towards the old city, leaving every 10 mins, 0600-1730 (฿10). Songthaews also make the trip for the same fare – catch one on Charodwithithong Rd. Tuk-tuks should take visitors to the park for about ฿80 (they congregate on Nikhon Kasem Rd). Alternatively, either go on a tour (see below), hire a motorbike (฿250), or charter a tuk-tuk for the trip there and back, along with trips around the site (฿150-200 for 3 hrs).

Excursions and tours

Si Satchanalai, see page 222. **Ramkhamhaeng National Park** is 30 km southwest of New Sukhothai in Amphoe Khiri Mat. The highest peak here, Khao

Luang, rises to nearly 1,200 m. This park is not really yet on any tourist route, so transport there can be difficult. However, some guesthouses (for example, *Somprasong* and *Ban Thai*) are beginning to organize trips. Alternatively, take a local bus along Route 101 towards Kamphaeng Phet and ask to be let off at the road to the national park (*Uthayaan Haeng Chart Ramkhamhaeng*); it is a 16-km drive from here and we have had reports that motorcycle taxis are sometimes available at the turn-off. Another protected area which is even more worthwhile, but even more difficult to reach, is **Paa Khaa** to the west. *Ban Thai Bungalows* organize trips here for swimming and exploring.

Many hotels and guesthouses arrange tours to Sukhothai, Kampaeng Phet and Si Satchanalai, for example *Rachthani Hotel, Somprasong Guest House, Yupa Guest House, Ban Thai, Northern Palace Hotel, Chinawat Hotel, Sawatipong Hotel, Lotus Village* and *No 4*. Prices vary a great deal depending on whether the tour is organized by a guesthouse or a more expensive hotel – and on the quality of the transport provided. But expect to pay roughly ฿300 for a tour to Sukhothai and ฿500 for Si Satchanalai.

Essentials

Sleeping
■ *on maps,*
page 213 & 219
Price codes:
see inside front cover

The Old City AL-B *Paylin*, Charodwithithong Rd, about 4 km from the old city on the road leading to Sukhothai New Town, T613310, F613317, BT2157110, BF2155640. A/c, restaurants, pool, sauna, disco, monster of a hotel rather out of place on the road to the old city. Guests rattle around in empty corridors and lobbies, but this is without doubt the most luxurious place to stay, if not the most characterful. The position is hardly handy for a stroll around town. **C** *The Old Sukhothai Cultural Centre* (aka *Thai Village House*), 214 Charodwithithong Rd, Muang Kao, advance booking is needed between Oct and Apr, T612275, F612583. A/c, good restaurant, attractive teak bungalows set on a semi-island, almost surrounded by water. Large, clean and simply decorated rooms. During the day the restaurant and stall area becomes rather overrun with tour groups, detracting from the peaceful image, buffet breakfast included. The *Nam Kang Garden Restaurant* is a good outdoor restaurant here.

C-D *Vitoon Guesthouse*, 49/3 Jarodvithithong Rd, T697045, near the entrance to the park, at the bend in the road. Not as peaceful as the *Suwan Guesthouse*, but rooms are spotless with some a/c, some fan, and immaculate western toilets attached. Bicycle hire. Good value, despite noise pollution. **D-E** *Suwan Guesthouse*, 28/4 Jarodvithithong Rd, T613015, near the entrance to the park, at the bend in the main road, but set 50 m back. Quieter than its rival just down the road, this tipsy, old teak house offers small but clean rooms, with clean shared toilets. A characterful old place with friendly management, although service can sometimes be hard to come by. There are 3 a/c rooms in a new block; good value at ฿300.

New Sukhothai C *Northern Palace*, 43 Singhawat Rd, T611193, F612038. A/c, TV (Thai), restaurant, unattractive pool due to lack of maintenance. This markets itself as the best hotel in town, but it is very disappointing, the service is unenthusiastic and the rooms can be tatty, though the bathrooms are usually clean. Popular with tour groups, members of which can't, of course, make a decision before checking in. **B** *Rachthani*, 229 Charodwithithong Rd, T611031, F612878. West of the bridge, a/c, restaurant. Noisy location, popular with tour groups, but despite (or because of?) this, it is rundown with poorly maintained rooms. Managed with a distinct lack of friendliness, with most of the staff, apparently, half asleep. **B-E** *Lotus Village* (formerly the *No 4 Guesthouse*), 170 Rachthani Rd, T621484, F621463, lotusvil@yahoo.com This large leafy compound is scattered with several ponds (mosquitoes a problem), and has a number of attractive teak houses on stilts as well as several spotless bungalows, some with a/c. Tastefully decorated, clean and peaceful, tropical gardens. A selection of informative books and magazines in the lobby. Internet facilities (though quite pricey) available. Managed by a Thai/French couple, English-speaking and a good source of information. Very popular, with western breakfasts of toast, yoghurt, fresh juice and fresh coffee. Excursions organized and bikes (β30 per day) and motorbikes (300β per day) for rent. Highly recommended. **B-E** *River View Hotel*, 92 Nikon Kasem Rd, T611516, F613373. Coffee shop (24 hrs), minibar, snooker room, a/c, hot showers, TV (Thai). Large, echoey corridors, with comparatively small rooms cluttered with excessive furnishing.

D-E *Friend House*, T620910, F610172, atanawan@hotmail.com The Friendship Foreign Language Centre rents out several rooms in its quiet compound. Rooms are basic and a bit dirty, but with their own toilet and shower. Restaurant and table tennis table, bikes (β40 per day) and motorbikes for rent (β300 per day). Discounts for longer stay visitors. It is also possible to offer services at the local school teaching English to Thai children; the owners will pay β100 per hour and provide a room for free, if you can committ yourself to a minimum of 2-3 months. **D-E** *J&J Guesthouse*, just before you come to *No 4 Guesthouse*, T620095, jjguest@hotmail.com This place is run by one of the women who used to work at the *No 4 Guesthouse*, see below, and is managed in much the same way (ie emphasis on cleanliness). Attractive bungalows with a number of rooms, small pleasant restaurant, friendly management with very good English. Possibly the cheapest motorbike rental in Sukhotai (β200 per day). Comfortable and quiet. **D-E** *No 4*, 234/6 Charodwithithong Rd, T611315, Soi Panitsan, about 1 km from the town centre, west of the bridge, the lane runs off the main road opposite the Caltex garage. Very friendly lady owner rents out spotless bamboo bungalows, tucked into a small compound in a wonderfully secluded location. Clean rooms with western toilets and shower; very well kept. Excellent Thai food in the restaurant. The owner speaks good English, so is a useful source of information. She also runs cookery classes. Tours organized from here. Good value. Highly recommended. **D-E** *Sawatdipong*, 56/2-5 Singhawat Rd, T611567, F612268. Large, clean rooms if a little dark. A/c rooms seem overpriced, but fan rooms are fair value. Helpful management, but a characterless hotel on a busy road. **D-E** *Sky*, 58/1-7 By Pass Rd, T612237, F611212 (office at 28-30 Prasert Pong Rd – close to the government bus stop on the

The Central Plains

Sukhothai New Town

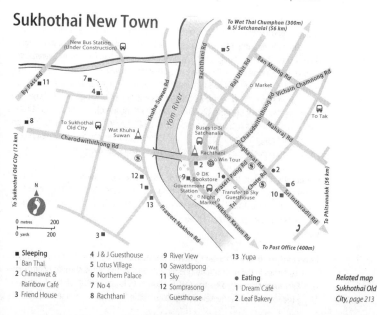

same street, free transfer to the hotel from this office). Some a/c, restaurant (rather unreliable standard), this hotel is about 2 km from the centre of town towards Sukhothai Historical Park (turn onto the By Pass Rd at the first main intersection) – an inconvenient location, despite free transportation to town. Range of rooms available from simple fan rooms to a/c rooms with hot water (deluxe rooms are no better than standard) – all kept very clean, popular with German tour groups, friendly and well run, good information. Recommended. **D-E** *Somprasong Guesthouse*, 32 Prawert Nakhon Rd, T611709. Overlooking the Yom River (not a very romantic river at this point), this 40-year-old teak house has been expanded to accommodate tourists. The newer bungalows are very clean and spacious. Friendly management, restaurant, bicycles for rent, ฿30. **D-F** *Chinnawat Hotel*, 1-3 Nikhon Kasem Rd, T611385. Some fan, some a/c, dark and gloomy but clean, Western toilets, hot water, friendly management. Rainbow cafeteria downstairs with international news. Internet service, money exchange and overseas calls.

E *Ban Thai*, 38 Prawert Nakhon Rd, T610163. Overlooking the Yom River, an assortment of clean, well kept rustic bungalows and rooms in a large natural-style house. Rooms are rather small, but shared toilets are kept clean (you can pay more for an ensuite room). A good source of information, with friendly English-speaking management. Maps of area provided free and bike rental for ฿40 per day. Restaurant with vegetarian food, and they recycle all their plastic water bottles. **E-F** *Yupa*, 44 Prawet Nakhon Rd, T612578, yupa-house@excite.com On the west bank of the river. Old house run by disinterested management. Rooms are large and airy, but a little worn and dirty. Many rooms have shared balconies with great views.

Eating
● *on map, page 219*
Price categories:
see inside front cover.
Fresh coffee seems to
have made an impact
on Sukhothai

Art's Fresh Coffee and Beer, by the bus station for the old city on Charodwithithong Rd, is a good place for a steaming mug of early morning coffee while waiting in the chill for the bus. Most other restaurants also serve variants on 'fresh coffee'. *Chinnawat*, 1-3 Nikhon Kasem Rd. A/c restaurant with satellite TV and reasonable food, they offer the rather novel option of small and large portions – the latter are for the very hungry.

Mid-range *Kho Joeng Hong*, Nikhon Kasem Rd. Closes at 2000, Chinese food. **Cheap** *Dream Café 1*, Ramkhamhaeng Rd (next to *Win Tour*). Thai and international dishes in cool, relaxing interior, good for breakfasts, similar dishes to sister restaurant *Dream Café 2*, near *Sawatdipong Hotel*, Singhawat Rd. Similar fare to *Dream Café*; *Dear House*, Nikhon Kasem Rd (next to the *Chinnawat Hotel*). American breakfasts, Thai and Chinese dishes and what is rather disturbingly referred to as 'sandwich parade', all served in western – that is cowboys and Indians – style surroundings; *Leaf Bakery*, 23/6 Singhawat Rd. *Rainbow Café*, off Nikhon Kasem Rd (near night market). Good breakfasts and sometimes patrons can watch CNN or BBC World News (when it isn't set on Thai TV), although the road is a bit noisy. Also serves international food. *Sukhothai Coca*, 56/2-5 Singhawat Rd (*Sawatdipong Hotel*), Thai food and sandwiches.

Foodstalls Cheap: the night market or *talaat to rung*, on Ramkhamhaeng Rd off Nikhon Kasem Rd, opposite the cinema, for good stalls. Open 1800-0600. Excellent *Kai yaang* (barbecue chicken) is also sold from a small stall by the bridge, near the park, in the evenings from about 1730. Other stalls open up at about the same time along the walls of Wat Rachthani.

Food in the old city There are a number of stalls and small restaurants selling simple Thai dishes in the old city, and one more sophisticated outfit, the *Nam Kong Garden Restaurant*, attached to the Old Sukhothai Cultural Centre, about 1 km back along the road towards the New Town. Reasonable food in a garden setting.

Several pubs are scattered along the bypass approaching *Sky House*, such as **Bars**
Focus Bar and *Top Country Pub*; rather out of the way for an evening drink unless you
have your own transport. There is also the ***Chopper Beer Bar*** on Charodwithithong Rd,
about 20m after the bridge, on the left.

Oct/Nov *Loi Krathong and Candle festival* (movable), candles are lit, there are fire- **Festivals**
work displays, folk dancing and a sound and light show at the Old City. Sukhothai is
reputed to be the 'home' of this most beautiful of Thai festivals. It is said that one of
the king's mistresses carved the first *krathong* from a piece of fruit and floated it down
the river to her king. Today the festival symbolizes the floating away of the previous
year's sins, although traditionally it was linked to the gift of water. The Thai word for
irrigation, *chonprathaan*, literally means the 'gift of water', and the festival comes at
the end of the rainy season when the rice is maturing in the paddy fields. Krathongs
used to be made from leaves; now, polystyrene is used, and the boats are laden with
candles, sticks of incense and other gifts for Mae Khong Kha, the Goddess of water.

Cultural Centre, near the Historical Park, offers antiques, weaving and handicrafts **Shopping**
such as Sangkhalok pottery. ***Phra Mae Ya Shrine*** shop, in front of the Municipal Hall
for antiques and local cloth. ***Hat Sieo village***, near Si Satchanalai, is noted for its weaving. ***DK Bookstore***, Nikon Kasem Rd (opposite the Riverview Hotel). Very small English
section, though it's worth a browse. Mostly books on Thai historical sites and culture,
Buddhism, guidebooks and cookery. Also a few translated pieces by Thai authors.

Local For transport to the old city, see page 217. **Bicycle hire**: ฿50 per day at the res- **Transport**
taurants on the road opposite the museum (old city) or from *Sawatdipong Hotel* and *See also Ins & outs,*
many guesthouses (see Sleeping, above). **Motorbike hire**: ฿250-300 per day from *page 208*
many guesthouses (*Sky Guesthouse, Sawatipong Hotel, Chinawat Hotel, No 4* guest- *466 km to Bangkok,*
houses, *J&J Guesthouse* and *Lotus Village*). **Tuk-tuks**: for town trips and for excursions *56 km to Phitsanulok*
further afield; they congregate on Nikhon Kasem Rd, opposite the *Chinnawat Hotel*.

Long distance Air: Bangkok Airways, T633266/T612167, BT02-2293456, began flying to Sukhothai – in fact, the airport is nearer Sawankhalok – at the end of 1994 and
the route is Bangkok-Sukhothai-Chiang Mai. Because Bangkok Airways have been
having some difficulty getting people to use the route, there are some good discounts available. But note that transport from town to the airport is expensive (by Thai
standards) because this is a private airport (owned by Bangkok Airways). They also
charge a 'departure tax' of ฿100. Sukhothai Airport, T647224. Even with the opening
of Sukhothai airport, most people arriving by air fly to Phitsanulok, 56 km east of
Sukhothai, which is served by Thai Airways 4 times a day.

Bus: for Bangkok, Phitsanulok, Chiang Mai and Khon Kaen, the station is at 9 Prasert
Pong Rd – this is the government 'station' or *bor kor sor*. However, buses for other
parts of the Kingdom leave from offices at assorted points around town. For Tak and
Mae Sot, buses leave from Ban Muang Rd; for Si Satchanalai (or, simply, Si Sat) from
the corner of Raj Uthit and Charodwithithong roads, near Wat Rachthani. Regular connections with Bangkok's Northern bus terminal (7-8 hrs), Chiang Mai via Lampang
(4-6 hrs), Khon Kaen, Phitsanulok, Nakhon Sawan, Chiang Rai, Uttaradit, Nan, Phrae
and Tak. A new bus station is under construction along the bypass, which will probably mean that the bus stops around town will become redundant once it is completed. **Private bus companies**: *Win Tour* are on Ramkhamhaeng Rd, T611039, and
operate buses to some of the destinations noted above.

Airline offices *Bangkok Airways*, 10 Moo 1, Jarodvithithong Rd, T613310, F613317. **Directory**
Banks *Bangkok*, 49 Singhawat Rd. ***Bangkok Bank of Commerce***, 15 Singhawat Rd. ***Thai Farmers***,

The Central Plains

134 Charoen Withi Rd. There is also a currency exchange booth by the Ramkhamhaeng Museum in the old city. **Communications** Post Office: Nikhon Kasem Rd. There is also a **sub post office and overseas telephone service** in the old city (see map). **Internet & email:** a number of cafés have opened up in both the old and new cities; some guesthouses provide internet services, such as *Chinnawat* and *Lotus Village*. **Medical services** *Sukhothai Hospital*, Charodwithithong Rd, T611782 (about 4 km out of town on the road towards the Old City). **Useful addresses** Police: Nikhon Kasem Rd, T611010.

Si Satchanalai ศรีสัชนาลัย

Phone code: 055
Colour map 3, grid B3

Referred to by Thais as Si Sat, this is the twin city to Sukhothai and lies to the north, on the west bank of the Yom River. It remained relatively undiscovered by tourists until 1987, when a grant was provided to prepare the town for 'Visit Thailand Year'. The sight has been 'cleaned up', rather as Sukhothai has been, and in the process has lost some of its charm, at least to romantic westerners brought up on images of vegetation-choked lost cities. Even so, Si Satchanalai makes a fascinating side trip from Sukhothai. In architectural terms, it is also more varied than Sukhothai, with examples of Sri Lankan-style bell-shaped chedis, Khmer prangs and Sukhothai-influenced buildings. There is no modern town here; the whole area has become a 'Historical Park'. The most regal way to visit the sights is by elephant; an elephant 'rank' is to be found by Wat Chang Lom. The Si Satchanalai Historical Park Information Centre is to be found just outside Ram Narong Gate, to the southeast. There's not much information here, just a scale model and map of the park and a few books for sale. ■ *Admission fee to Si Satchanalai of ฿40, ฿50 for a car, ฿30 for a motorbike and ฿10 for a bicycle. (See the admission information under the entry for Sukhothai for details on the 'Total' ticket which provides entry to both Si Sat and Sukhothai.)*

History   During the fourth reign of Sukhothai it became the seat of the king's son – the Uparaja, and the two cities were linked by a 50 km-long road, the Phra Ruang Highway. Si Satchanalai was probably built on the site of a Khmer town called Chaliang. It was bounded by a moat 10 m wide and by town walls that stood three rows deep on three sides and a single row deep on the east side (which was protected by the river). Six gates pierced these walls. During its heyday it was the equal of Sukhothai in splendour, and probably superior in terms of its defences. Protected by rapids, swamp and mountains, not to mention a triple moat filled with barbed spikes and impressive walls, Si Sat must have seemed immensely daunting to any prospective attacker.

Critical to Si Sat's vitality was the ceramic industry based at Ban Pha Yang and Ban Ko-noi, to the north of the city. With the technical assistance of Chinese potters these villages produced probably the finest of all Thai ceramics

• •

Si Satchanalai place names

ceramic kilns	Wat Chedi Jet Thaew
เตาเครื่องปั้นดินเผา	วัดเจดีย์เจ็ดแถว
Wat Chang Lom	Wat Khao Phanom Phloeng
วัดช้างล้อม	วัดเขาพนมเพลิง
Wat Chao Chan	Wat Suan Kaeo Utthayanyai
วัดเจ้าจันทร์	วัดสวนแก้วอุทยานใหญ่

Ceramics of Si Satchanalai and Sukhothai

Popular history has it that the technology of ceramics production was introduced into Thailand after King Ramkhamhaeng visited the Yuan court of China in 1292 and requested that a group of Chinese potters accompany him back to his kingdom. This is almost certainly false. It seems far more likely that Chinese potters arrived in Thailand on their own initiative, trying to escape from the wars and instability of late 13th-century Southern Sung China. Their skills recognized, they would have been welcomed by the Thais. There was probably already a primitive ceramics industry in Thailand; the Chinese were able to build upon this and immeasurably improve the quality and range of output, incorporating their own designs and techniques.

Important centres of production included Pha Yang and Ko-noi, just outside the walls of Si Satchanalai (where Sangkhalok ware was produced) and Sukhothai. The best work was produced at Pa Yang, with the best known being the wonderful Sangkhalok celadons, and probably the finest the incised brown and

pearl wares. Celadon refers to the colour of the glaze, which ranges from blue-green to grey. Some connoisseurs regard the celadon produced at Si Satchanalai during the 14th and 15th centuries as being almost as fine in quality as that of the famous Longquan kilns in China's Zhejiang province. Production of Sangkhalok ware is usually said to have come to an end in the early to mid-15th century, although recent work indicates that production probably continued as late as the mid-16th century.

The terminology for the different wares is somewhat confusing. Sukhothai ware should refer to all products of the kingdom; foreigners often use it to mean only those wares from Old Sukhothai town. Sangkhalok is ware from the kilns in the vicinity of Si Satchanalai. The word Sangkhalok is taken from Sawangkhalok, a town a short distance south of Si Satchanalai. The origins of the word Sawangkhalok are disputed. Some scholars argue that it means the 'Celestial World'; others that it is derived from the Chinese words Song Golok, meaning Sung period ceramic kilns.

The Central Plains

(see box). These were not just for local consumption; Sangkhalok ware has been found as far afield as Java, Borneo and the Philippines. The city was redis-covered by a retired British Consular official called Reginald le May, whose particular love became Si Satchanalai.

Wat Chang Lom, the Monastery surrounded by Elephants, probably the fin-est wat in the park, lies in the heart of the old city and is the most sacred wat in Si Satchanalai. It lies in front of the gates to the park and is specifically men-tioned in Ramkhamhaeng's inscriptions. The principal chedi was built by the King between 1285 and 1291 to contain sacred relics of the Buddha which, according to Inscription No 1, he dug up, worshipped for a month and six days, buried and then had a chedi built over them which took three years to complete. The Ceylonese-style chedi is the earliest example of its kind in Thai-land and became the prototype for many others (like the wat of the same name in Sukhothai). It is made of laterite and stucco and sits on a two-storey square base. On the low tier are the remains of 39 standing elephant caryatids (proba-bly post-dating the chedi) separated by columns, which would have been sup-ports for lanterns. Stairs take the pilgrim from the lower, earthly levels, upwards towards the more spiritual realm of the Buddha. Here, on the second tier, 20 niches contain stucco seated Buddha images, portrayed in quiet medi-tation (all now mutilated). Above the second tier is an octagonal plinth, four circular mouldings, the smooth bell-shaped stupa, and finally an honorific

Sights
Si Satchanalai is littered with monuments; only major ones are included here. Most hotels in Sukhothai run day tours here, see page 218

umbrella spire towering into the heavens both physically and symbolically. The chedi is enclosed by 50 m long laterite walls, and in front of it are the ruins of a large viharn, together with another smaller stupa and viharn.

Wat Chedi Jet Thaew (30 m south of Wat Chang Lom), or the Monastery of the Seven Rows of Chedi, stands within a ditch and two rows of laterite walls pierced by four gates. The wat contains the remnants of seven rows of lotus-bud chedis, some 34 in total, which house the ashes of members of the Si Satchanalai ruling family. The largest stands on a square base, and was probably built by King Li Thai (1347-68). The 14th-century mondop tower displays a fusion of stylistic elements: the corbelled archway of overlapping blocks was a technique used by both Khmer and Sukhothai architects; above this are niches holding Buddha images which are then crowned by a Ceylonese bell and umbrella spire. Other noteworthy elements are the Burmese-style stucco decorations on a chedi in the northeast corner and a Srivijaya-style Buddha – sadly, it has been unsympathetically restored – sitting under a naga on the north side. A number of the chedis display remnants of fine naga-makara arches: five-headed nagas issue forth from the makaras which form the double curve of the arch.

South of here is **Wat Suan Kaeo Utthayanyai** and the southernmost wat within the walls, **Wat Nang Phaya** (Monastery of the Queen). The latter is enclosed by single walls of laterite, with four gateways. A Ceylonese-style chedi dominates the compound. The fine stucco floral motifs (now protected by a shed) on the west wall of the large laterite viharn are early Ayutthayan in style (15th century), and are the best preserved of any such decoration in either Sukhothai or Si Sat.

Wat Khao Phanom Phloeng lies on a 20 m high hillock on the north side of the town and is reached by a laterite staircase of 144 steps. It comprises a Ceylonese-style chedi, a large seated Buddha and some stone columns. Recent excavations at this site have revealed an early animist shrine, the **Sala Chao Mae Laong**

The Central Plains

Si Satchanalai & Chaliang

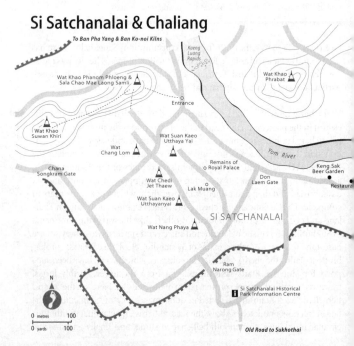

To Ban Pha Yang & Ban Ko-noi Kilns

Kaeng Luang Rapids

Wat Khao Phrabat

Wat Khao Phanom Phloeng & Sala Chao Mae Laong Samli

Entrance

Wat Khao Suwan Khiri

Wat Suan Kaeo Utthaya Yai

Wat Chang Lom

Yom River

Chana Songkram Gate

Remains of Royal Palace

Keng Sak Beer Garden

Wat Chedi Jet Thaew

Don Laem Gate

Restaura

Lak Muang

Wat Suan Kaeo Utthayanyai

SI SATCHANALAI

Wat Nang Phaya

Ram Narong Gate

Si Satchanalai Historical Park Information Centre

N

0 metres 100
0 yards 100

Old Road to Sukhothai

Samli, which predates both the Khmer and Tai periods here, showing that Si Sat was occupied – and important – long before the rise of the Sukhothai Kingdom. To the west of Wat Khao Phanom Phloeng and linked by a path and staircase, on a higher hillock, are the remains of **Wat Khao Suwan Khiri**.

To the southeast, 2 km outside the Si Satchanalai city walls, is the area known as Chaliang. The name 'Chaliang' is thought to be derived from the Khmer and Northern Thai words for 'askew' or 'leaning'. Scholars have surmised that this refers to the original city's location within a meander of the Yom.

Chaliang

The first wat you come to along the road to Chaliang is **Wat Kok Singh Karam**, on the right-hand side, which includes three chedis on the same base. In front of these stupas a viharn and bot are to be found. While this wat is not notable in terms of scale, refinement or its condition, the bot is the only known ordination hall in Si Sat where a chedi is placed inside the bot building. It is thought that this is derived from a Polonnarua Dynasty prototype (Sri Lanka).

Positioned on the banks of the Yom River is **Wat Phra Sri Ratana Mahathat Chaliang** (or **Wat Phra Prang**), an impressive laterite prang originally built in the mid 15th century, probably during the reign of King Boromtrailokant (1448-88), and then rather badly restored later in the Ayutthaya period during the reign of King Boromkot (1733-58). However, its origins are older still as the prang is thought to have been built on top of an earlier Khmer prasat. In front of the prang are the ruins of a viharn which houses a large seated Sukhothai Buddha image, with long, graceful fingers 'touching ground'. Even more beautiful is the smaller walking Buddha of brick and stucco to the left. It is thought to be one of the finest from the Sukhothai Period displaying that enigmatic 'Sukhothai smile' (see illustration, page 210). The wat also contains a number of other interesting Buddha images.

Wat Chom Chuen – the Monastery of Prince Chan, 500 m west of Wat Phra Prang – contains a prang built in the time of the Khmer King Jayavarman VII

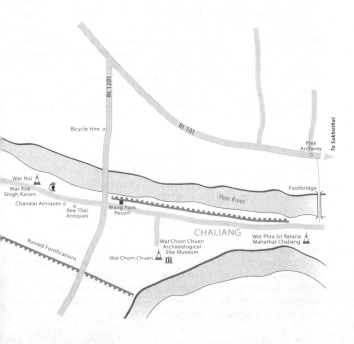

(1181-1217). It seems that Chaliang, presumably because of its incomparable defensive position, was chosen by the Khmer as the site for one of its outposts, right at the far northwestern extremity of the Khmer Empire. Next to this wat is an **Archaeological Site Museum**; a great building set into the riverbank with a grass roof. Admission is free and there are some excavations to view. These were undertaken between 1993 and 96. They have revealed 15 inhumation burials. The bodies were buried during the Dvaravati period (sixth-11th centuries). They comprise four adult females, one adult male, four children and six adults of unknown sex. Most of the dead bodies found here were laid out on their sides and not on their backs. This ritual is completely different to other archaeological sites in Thailand. Grave goods devoted to the dead comprise glass beads, iron tools and clay paddles. Head orientation is to the west.

Wat Noi (Small Wat) is to be found within the boundary walls of Chaliang. The main stupa has a lotus bud shape and there is the base of a small viharn evident to the front. King Vajiravudh (Rama Vl) spent a night near here when he visited Si Satchanalai as a prince in 1907.

North of the city, at Ban Pha Yang and Ban Ko-noi, remains of **ceramic kilns** have been discovered, dating from the 1350s. The pottery produced from here is known as 'Sangkhalok', after the early Ayutthaya name for the district (there is a town of the same name to the south). The kilns of **Ban Pha Yang** lie 500 m north of the old city walls, and so far 21 kilns have been found, all of the closed kiln variety. It is thought that they produced architectural and high quality ceramics (see above).

Excursions The village of **Had Siaw** lies to the southeast of Si Sat. It is unusual to the extent that it is inhabited by Tai Phuan, an immigrant group from Laos who are thought to have settled here in the late 19th century. The Tai Phuan probably originated in the Xieng Khouang area of Laos from where they migrated south and west to the Vientiane area, and from there into Thailand. The Tai Phuan are renowned for their weaving skills and these have been maintained in Had Siaw. In particular, they weave beautiful ceremonial blankets in orange, yellow, green and purple, from both silk and cotton. Their textiles are characterized by bold blocks of colour and regimented motifs. Examples of Tai Phuan textiles can be obtained either from Ban Had Siaw itself or from shops in Sawankhalok. In April there is a special reason to go to the village: to witness the Sangha (monkhood) Induction Ceremony. This ceremony begins with a parade along the main street to the local village wat, with the monks to be ordained perched on an elephant's back, dressed in colourful costume, with sunglasses and top-headed decoration and sacred offerings held in both hands. The small monastery of Wat Hat Siaw has an inscription indicating it was built in 1844.

Sleeping Other than the *Wang Yom*, Si Sat has no other places to stay which is one reason why people tend to visit the park on a day trip. The nearest town with a range of accommodation is Sawankhalok, 10 km south (see below). **A-B** *Wang Yom Resort*, off Route 101 to Sawankhalok, T611179. Overpriced bungalows set in beautiful gardens, those with riverside location being more expensive. Frugal interiors and some cheaper fan-cooled bungalows. Caters for the tour group market and can afford to keep its prices high, but bargain on a slow day. Attached restaurant serves Thai food (**mid-range**).

Eating **Mid-range** *No Name*, east of Don Laem Gate (see map). Basic place selling noodles and rice dishes. A good place for lunch if you are keen to avoid the overpriced restaurants aimed at the tour group market. **Cheap** *Kong Sok Beer Garden*, restaurant with a large veranda overstretching the river (good views). Built to accommodate the tour buses which swarm here for a lunch/dinner stop. Overenthusiastically decorated, but run by under-enthusiastic staff. Limited choice of Thai food.

Antiques *Ree Thai Antiques*, a small quaint Walt Disney-style house. *Chanalai* **Shopping** *Antique*, grotesque bright red brick house with a rum collection of antiques (see map for locations).

Local Si Satchanalai is more compact than Sukhothai Old City and the main monu- **Transport** ments can be seen on foot. However, to reach Chaliang and the sights outside the city *54 km N of Sukhothai* walls it is best to hire a **bicycle** (฿20 per day) from the shop, 1 km down Route 1201 towards the site, or at the pink archway that leads to Chaliang, or at the Admission Gate. **Bus**: regular connections from 0600 to 1800 with Sukhothai from Raj Uthit Rd, 1 hr. Ask to be dropped off at the *muang kao* (old city). For Chaliang, get off at the pink archway on Route 101, 2 km before Route 1201, which leads to a suspension footbridge crossing the Yom River to Chaliang. **Motorbike**: for hire in Sukhothai – see page 221.

Today, Sawankhalok, meaning the Celestial World, is a small, unassuming **Sawankhalok** sort of place, a town that one might breeze through without a second thought. *The best place to stay* But historically this was an important centre, lying within the merit of the kings *when exploring the* of Sukhothai and its sister city, Si Satchanalai. There are regular bus connec- *ruins of Si Satchanalai,* tions with Si Satchanalai and Sukhothai. Places to stay include **C-E** *Sangsin* *10 km to the north* *Hotel*, Thetsabarn Damri Road, T641859, with some air conditioning, clean rooms; quite serviceable. **D-E** *Muang In*, 21 Kasemrat Road, T642622, some air conditioning, slightly cheaper than the *Sangsin*, and slightly grottier.

Most people's only contact with this dusty provincial capital is during a brief **Uttaradit** stop at the bus terminal. The area in the vicinity of Uttaradit seems to have *Phone code: 055* been at the very edge of the Khmer sphere of influence during the 13th century. *Colour map 1, grid B3* Later, it lay at the heart of King Ramkhamhaeng's emerging Kingdom of Sukhothai. When Sukhothai began to collapse with Ramkhamhaeng's death in 1317, so Uttaradit again came to mark the northern frontier of Sukhothai.

In the centre of the town is **Wat Tha Thanon**, which contains a revered seated image of the Buddha – cast in bronze – from the Chiang Saen period. **Wat Phra Boromthat**, also known as Wat That Thung Yang, is a wat with ancient origins, although many of the structures have had to be rebuilt. It lies 5 km west of town near Thung Yang market. ■ *Getting there: by local bus*. **Wat Phra Yun Buddhabat Yukhon** is a hilltop wat 6 km from the city. Its unusual architecture dates from the Chiang Saen period. **Sirikit Dam** lies 58 km from town. Like the other dams that control the waters of the tributaries of the Chao Phraya River north of its confluence at Nakhon Sawan, the Sirikit was built to improve flood control and generate power. It is named after the Queen of Thailand. ■ *Getting there: by bus*.

Sleeping A-B *Seeharaj*, 163 Borom Art Rd, T411106, F412172. A/c, pool, large hotel with 124 rooms and surprisingly plush for a place like Uttaradit. **C-D** *Wiwat*, 159 Borom Art Rd, T411779. Eighty rooms, some a/c. **D-E** *Numchai*, 213/3-4 Borom Art Rd, T411253. Fifty basic rooms. **E-F** *Heaven*, 185/1 Chonpratan-Sirikit Rd, T412866. Fifteen very basic rooms.

Festivals Sep The *Langsat Fair*, a fruit for which Uttaradit is well known in Thailand, is held early in the month in the grounds of Wat Mae Plu School.

Transport Train: connections with Bangkok's Hualamphong station (9 hrs) and sta- *481 km to Bangkok* tions north to Chiang Mai (5 hrs). **Bus**: connections with Bangkok's Northern bus ter- minal (7 hrs) and with other towns in the Central Plains and the north. Some buses also leave here and travel up to the Khorat Plateau and the northeast.

The Central Plains

Routes north to Mae Sot

A second, less frequently used, route from Nakhon Sawan northwards runs up Route 1 to the historical city of Kamphaeng Phet and on to Tak. From Tak it is possible to travel west to the border town of Mae Sot, with trekking and views over to Burma. The trip itself is interesting. Tak is clearly a Central Plains city. The architecture of the monasteries is Central Thai and the town is situated on the edge of the rice growing lands of the Ping River. Travelling west, the road climbs into the forested (surprisingly) Tenasserim hills and after 80 km arrives at Mae Sot. Here the monasteries are Burmese in inspiration, and Karen and Burmese people are in evidence. Travelling north from Tak, the route passes from the Central to the Northern region, and thence to Lampang, Lamphun and Chiang Mai.

Kamphaeng Phet   กำแพงเพชร

Population: 27,500
Phone code: 055
Colour map 1, grid C3

Like the better-known ruins of Sukhothai and Ayutthaya, Kamphaeng Phet's old city is a historical park and has been selected by UNESCO as a World Heritage Site. However, few tourists bother to come here, which gives the place a certain attractiveness. It is possible to wander through the ruined monasteries, many overgrown with trees (it has not been 'cleaned up' like Sukhothai), without meeting another person. In total the Old City encompasses an area of over 400 ha. Modern Kamphaeng Phet is sleepy and easygoing; traffic still seems to move in an entirely random fashion. With a proportion of its older, wooden, shuttered and tiled buildings still surviving, the town retains a modicum of character, something which cannot be said for many Thai towns.

Kamphaeng Phet (or 'Diamond Wall') acted, as its name suggests, as a garrison town for the capital, Sukhothai, 80 km to the north. It was built by King Li Thai (1347-68) on the banks of the River Ping, in his attempts to consolidate the Sukhothai Kingdom at a time when surrounding states were growing in influence. The Ayutthayan chronicles refer to the town as Chakangrao, while earlier Sukhothai inscriptions refer to Muang Nakhon Chum. Although King Li Thai does not have the reputation of his illustrious predecessor King Ramkhamhaeng, he was by all accounts a skilful and scholarly man. He entered the monkhood in 1362, legitimizing Theravada Buddhism as the 'state' religion. He wrote the Traiphum (The Three Worlds), a Buddhist treatise, and it was also during his reign that Sukhothai sculpture arguably attained its purest form. Evidence of this flowering of art is to be seen in and around Kamphaeng Phet.

Ins & outs
See also Transport, page 232

Getting there Buses connect with Bangkok's Northern terminal at regular intervals. It's a 5 hr journey. The bus station is out of town, but songthaews transport visitors to the market. **Getting around** It is worth hiring a saamlor or tuk-tuk to visit the ruins to the north of town.

Sights

Within the walls

The 6-m high defensive walls still stand – earthen ramparts topped with laterite – beyond which is a moat to further deter attackers. Within the walls, encompassing an area of 2½ km by 500 m, lie two old wats, Wat Phra Kaeo and Wat Phrathat, as well as the **Provincial Museum**. The museum contains, in the

The Central Plains

entrance hall, what is commonly regarded as one of the finest bronzes of Siva in Thailand. Cast in 1510, in the Khmer 'Bayon' style, its head and hands were removed by an overzealous German visitor in 1886. Fortunately, he was intercepted, and his limbs and head (the statue's, not the German's) were reunited with the torso. The museum contains some good examples of Buddha images found in the locality. ■ *0800-1200, 1300-1600 Wed-Sun, ฿30.* The **Tourist Information Office** in the Kamphaeng Phet Local Handicraft Centre, Thesa Road (near Soi 13), hardly deserves such a title. It provides no maps, no help, in short, no information (bar a colour brochure which details useful sights such as the Sirikit Oil Field in Larn Krabu District). Open 0800-2000 (though these hours seem to be open subject to personal convenience). There is a second Tourist Information Centre next to Wat Phra Kaeo. This is, again, not much help. It simply sells publications of the Fine Arts Department and postcards.

From the museum, walk west to **Wat Phrathat**, the Monastery of the Great Relic. Not much remains except a chedi and a well-weathered seated Buddha (of laterite) sitting in the viharn. Immediately north, **Wat Phra Kaeo** was probably the largest and most important wat in Kamphaeng Phet. It was initially built during the Sukhothai period and then extensively remodelled in the Ayutthaya period. The wat is surrounded by laterite walls, with a central Ceylonese-style chedi, resting on a square base. The bottom tier of niches once contained 32 singha, whilst the niches above held 16 Buddha images, none of which is intact. Two weathered Buddha images sit facing the chedi, as well as much later images of a reclining Buddha and two seated Buddhas. Like the other buildings, Wat Phra Kaeo would have been faced in stucco, and probably painted. There would also, of course, have been many wooden buildings which have long since weathered away. Just beyond the ticket office is Kamphaeng Phet's *lak muang* or **City Pillar Shrine**. Many saamlor drivers mainly ring their bells when passing the shrine in recognition of the power of the spirits that reside here. ■ *For information on admission prices see the end of the next section.*

The Central Plains

Ruins outside the old city's ramparts
The ruins are best seen early morning, when it is cooler & the deep red laterite is bathed in golden light

Most of the more interesting ruins lie outside the ramparts, to the north of town. Start with the outer ruins, returning to view Wat Phra Kaeo, Wat Phrathat and the museum (which opens at 0900). Although it is possible to walk to, and around, the site, by far the easiest way to get about is by chartering a saamlor or tuk-tuk. Expect to pay about ฿100-150 for one hour. It costs ฿40 to visit both the area within the ancient city walls and the forested area to the north, known as Aranyik. It is possible to walk within the city walls, but vehicles are useful for the Aranyik area, for which the following charges are levied: ฿10 for a bike, ฿20 for a motorbike, ฿30 for a tuk-tuk, and ฿50 for a car. ■ *Open 0800-1630 Mon-Sun.*

The first wat of significance to be reached travelling north from the New Town to the Old City is **Wat Phra Non** which, like many of the structures here, dates from the 15th to 16th centuries. The monastery is surrounded by laterite walls and walking through the complex from the road the buildings are, in turn, the bot, viharn, the main chedi, and then a secondary viharn. There are also the remains of monks quarters, wells and washing areas. The viharn, with its

· ·
Kamphaeng Phet place names

Wat Chang Rob
วัดช้างรอบ

Wat Phra Non
วัดพระนอน

Wat Phra Si Iriyaboth
วัดพระสี่อิริยาบถ

Wat Phrathat
วัดพระธาตุ

Wat Singh
วัดสิงห์

massive square columns, would have contained a reclining Buddha. Note the stone 'windows' which, though less finely wrought, resonate with those at Angkor in Cambodia and some Khmer temples in northeast Thailand. Behind the viharn is a large square-based and eight-sided laterite stupa. Most of the images and other ornamentation have been pillaged through the years.

North from here, there is the slightly better preserved **Wat Phra Si Iriyaboth**, locally known as **Wat Yuen** or the Monastery of the Standing Buddha. This wat derives its name from the large Buddha images that were to be found in the mondop at the end of the viharn. The name of the wat literally means 'four postures' – standing, reclining, sitting and walking. They were all in high stucco relief, one on each side of the mondop. The impressive standing image is the only one in reasonable repair and is a good example of Sukhothai sculpture, dating from the 14th to 15th centuries. The remains of the walking image give the impression of grace, so typical of the Sukhothai period. The viharn was built on a raised platform so that it is higher than the bot. It is thought that this was done to show the greater religious significance of the images in the viharn.

Adjacent to Wat Phra Si Iriyaboth is **Wat Singh**, again built in the 15th – possibly the 16th – century. The most important structure here is the stupa at the back of the compound, with porches for Buddha images on each side. In front is the bot, with its *bai sema* or boundary stone still evident.

This is probably the most impressive structure outside the city walls

Walking through the forest behind Wat Singh is **Wat Chang Rob** (the Shrine of the Elephants). The forested position of this monastery is appropriate for it was built for the use of forest-dwelling monks of a meditational sect. This consists of a huge Ceylonese-style laterite chedi (or what is left of it), with its base surrounded by 68 elephant caryatids (also of Ceylonese influence). Only one row of elephants, on the south side, are preserved. Numerous other ruins of wats are scattered around the area, some in thick undergrowth, others amidst paddy fields – particularly to the northeast and southwest. Only the most interesting have been described above.

On the right-hand side of the approach road to Kamphaeng Phet (Route 1) are the remains of a laterite fort, **Phom Seti**, which pre-dates the existing town. The fort was built to replace an earlier settlement called Muang Nakhon Chum or sometimes Chakangrao. This walled and moated settlement had similar dimensions to Khamphaeng Phet. It seems that the location of the city was switched to the other bank of the Ping after successive attacks by Ayutthaya from 1373. Inscriptions indicate that the walls of the 'new' city were built in 1403 and would seem to tie in with the assaults from the increasingly powerful kingdom to the south.

Past the bus terminal and before the bridge over the Ping, set back on the left-hand side, is **Wat Phra Boromthat**, also known as Wat Phra Mahathat Nakhon Chum. Just before the bridge, on the right-hand side, is the unusually shaped, square, restored chedi of **Wat Chedi Klang**, also built before Kamphaeng Phet was established by King Li Thai.

A ruined **bot** (ordination hall) in the heart of the city, which few even notice, let alone see, is on Thesa Road between Sois 6 and 8. The abandoned brick structure is simply falling into ruin; within the 'building' a Buddha calling the Earth Goddess to witness serenely remains, revered clearly by some local residents.

As with any Thai town, Kamphaeng Phet has its share of **markets**. On Thesa Road, opposite the tourist information centre, is a small fresh market; a little further south, also on Thesa Road, is a **night bazaar**, a good place to eat stall food in the evening (near Soi 13). But the main day market occupies a large area, sandwiched between Wichit and Charoensuk roads.

Essentials

All hotels are situated in the new town. There is nowhere to stay here that is geared to the budget traveller, although the hotels are well-priced with good a/c rooms available in our **D** category. The *Chakungrao Hotel*, at 123/1 Thesa Rd, used to be the place where tour groups housed their guests, but it was closed in mid-2000.

Sleeping
■ *on map*
Price codes:
see inside front cover

Kamphaeng Phet

The Central Plains

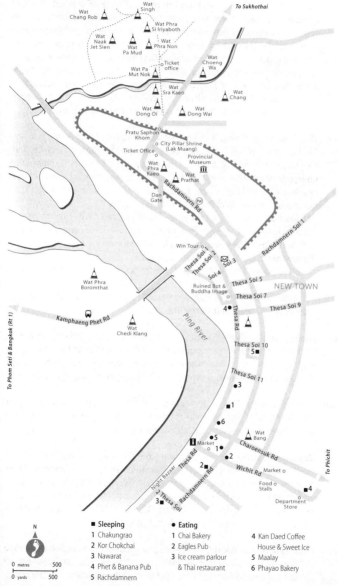

■ **Sleeping**
1 Chakungrao
2 Kor Chokchai
3 Nawarat
4 Phet & Banana Pub
5 Rachdamnern

● **Eating**
1 Chai Bakery
2 Eagles Pub
3 Ice cream parlour
& Thai restaurant

4 Kan Daed Coffee
House & Sweet Ice
5 Maalay
6 Phayao Bakery

N

0 metres 500
0 yards 500

A-C *Phet Hotel*, 189 Bumrungraj Rd, T712810, F712816, BT2701520, BF2714374, phettl@cscoms.com Definitely the most comfortable hotel in town with what passes in provincial Thailand for first class facilities. A/c, small pool (open to non-residents), restaurant serving Thai and international food, snooker club. Usual coffee shop artistes belt out Thai pop songs, beer garden with good barbecue king prawns. The *Banana Pub* is found here. **B-C** *Nawarat*, 2 Thesa Soi Prapan, T711106, F711961, BT5891686. A/c, TV (Thai), restaurant. Big price differences between rooms are hard to fathom. You seem to pay an extra ฿200 if you want an American breakfast included, and another ฿150 for a minibar (ie fridge). Rooms are decent and clean but some are only separated by a wooden door, making it very noisy if someone is watching TV in the next room. Very overpriced for the extras. The hotel might market itself as a 'gem of a hotel', 'founded on the best location beyond the most romantic river', but don't raise your expectations too high. The upper floors have good views. **D** *Kor Chokchai*, 7-31 Rachdamnern Soi 6, T711247. Some a/c, some fan. Large, clean rooms and bathrooms, Western toilets, very reasonable for this price category. **D-E** *Rachdamnern*, 114 Rachdamnern Rd, T711029. Some a/c, largish hotel with dark airy corridors and basic wooden interiored rooms. Adequately clean, although Thai squat toilets attached leave a bit to be desired.

Eating
● *on map*
Price categories: see inside front cover

Thai Two excellent cheap Thai restaurants are the *Kitti* and *Khrua Wibun*, at 101 and 102 Thesa Rd (near Thesa Soi 2). They serve *khao muu daeng* (red pork and rice), *khao man kai* (chicken and rice) and most simple rice and noodle dishes. Recommended. **Cheap**: *Maalay*, 77 Thesa Rd, look out for the rice baskets hanging outside – serves excellent Isan (Lao) food, very traditional, no attempt to conform with western tastes here. Recommended. *Yaat Phet*, Thesa Rd (corner of Soi 10).

Foodstalls In the evening the best selection of foodstalls can be found at the night bazaar on Thesa Rd. A 2nd group of stalls can be found on Wichit Rd (see map, page 231).

Bakery *Chai Bakery*, Rachdamnern Rd (near intersection with Charoensuk Rd). *Phayao Bakery*, Thesa Rd (near Charoensuk Rd).

Coffee house *Kan Daed*, Thesa Rd. Coffee house inside an attractive wooden shophouse.

Ice-cream Two a/c ice-cream parlours on Thesa Rd are *Tasty* (sign in Thai only) near Thesa Soi 2, and *Sweet Ice* near Thesa Soi 7.

Bars
Banana Pub, *Phet Hotel*, 99 Wichit Soi 3. A popular nightspot, with live bands playing regularly. Probably the most reputable nightclub in town. *Eagles Pub*, at the crossroads of Wichit and Rachdamnern roads, a US western-style pub serving Thai and Western food (**Mid-range**), which often has live folk music playing till the early hours.

Festivals
Sep/Oct *Kluai Khai (Banana) Festival* (movable); Kamphaeng province produces over 200,000,000 bahts' worth of bananas annually. This annual event honours the fruit and features an entirely innocent Miss Banana Pageant.

Shopping
Department stores *Great Department Store*, Charoensuk Rd (opposite the *Phet Hotel*). **Fruit** One of Kamphaeng Phet's claims to fame is its bananas and especially its *kluai khai*, sweet banana, of which some 160 m worth is said to be sold annually. **Hammocks** Between Nakhon Sawan and Khampaeng Phet, on Route 1, is one of the best places to buy hammocks in Thailand. Made out of kenaf (*bor kaew*), an inferior jute substitute, they are sold at roadside stalls, ฿50-150.

Transport
See also Ins & outs, page 228
358 km to Bangkok, 114 km NW of Nakhon Sawan

Local Saamlor or tuk-tuk: can be hired for a tour of the ruins. **Songthaews** to local destinations depart from the main market (the municipal or *Thetsabarn*) for the bus station; and from Kamphaeng Phet Rd, at the roundabout by the bridge. **Long distance Bus**: terminal is 2 km from the bridge, some way out of town. Songthaews run from the bus terminal to the market in town (฿5). Regular connections with Bangkok's Northern bus terminal (5 hrs) and with Phitsanulok, Chiang Mai, Tak (2 hrs), Nan, Phrae and Chiang Rai. *Win Tour*, on Kamphaeng Phet Rd, operates a/c tour buses to Bangkok.

Banks *Thai Farmers*, 233 Charoensuk Rd, and *Bangkok Bank* both have ATMs. **Directory**
Communications Post Office: corner of Thesa Rd and Thesa Soi 3. Also available at this office, fax and overseas telephone facilities.

Tak ตาก

Sprawling along the east bank of the Ping River, Tak was once a junction in the river trade but is now better known as a smuggling centre; drugs, teak and gems from Burma are exchanged for guns and consumer goods from Thailand. The Phahonyothin Highway is often lined with logging lorries carrying timber from Burma; a trade which has the political and commercial support of the Thai Army. Still small and distinctly provincial, Tak has managed (so far) to retain some of its traditional architecture: attractive wooden houses with tiled roofs are scattered amongst the ubiquitous concrete shophouses. Like a number of other areas in the more peripheral areas of Thailand, Christian missionaries have been active in Tak Province and there is a large Catholic Church on the Phahonyothin Highway. The **tourist office**, TAT, is situated on Thaksin Rd, T514341. It covers Tak, Pichit and Kamphaeng Phet.

Population: 24,000
Phone code: 055
Colour map 1, grid C1

The Central Plains

Wat Bot Mani Sibunruang (or **Wat Mani Banphot**) is a Lanna Thai monastery on the Phahonyothin Highway. Inside the bot is a fine and highly revered Chiang Saen period Buddha image dating from the late 1200s, Luang Pho Phutthamon. Nearby is a scenic garden known as **Nang Mani Banphot**. **Khao Tham** (Hill Cave) is located in Tambon Mai Ngam; it is a rocky hillock near Phahonyothin Highway, containing an impression of the Lord Buddha's footprint on the summit. Tak residents pay homage throughout the year, most particularly during Songkran.

Sights
Official sights in Tak are pretty few & far between

To the north of town, on the other side of Route 12 to Sukhothai at the intersection of Charotwithithong and Mahatthai Bamrung roads, is a **statue of King Taksin** (1734-82), one of the heroes and father figures of the Thai nation. He is depicted seated with a sword across his lap. In addition to the road bridge across the Ping to the south of town, there is also a long, slender and rather unusual **suspension bridge** for motorcycles and pedestrians north of the *Viang Tak 2 Hotel*. As in any other town, Tak has its share of markets and wats. There is a large **general market** between Chompon and Rimping roads, and a smaller **food market** opposite the *Viang Tak Hotel* on Mahatthai Bamrung Road. The wats in Tak are undistinguished, although Wat Phra Boromthat 36 km to the northwest is worth a detour (see Excursions below).

● ●

Tak place names

Bhumibol Dam
เขื่อนภูมิพล

Lan Sang National Park
อุทยานแห่งชาติลานสาง

Wat Phra Boromthat
วัดพระบรมธาตุ

Lan Sang National Park is 13 km **Excursions** southwest of Tak, 1 km off Route 105 to Mae Sot (the turn-off is just west of the village of Lang Sang). It covers just over 100 sq km and supports small populations of leopard, various deer and bear; much of the wildlife has been denuded through years of hunting (usually illegal). There are a number of trails leading to waterfalls, together with the Doi Musur Hilltribe

Shophouses: combining domestic and working worlds

The shophouse is one of Asia's great architectural innovations, at least functionally, if not always artistically. It combines domestic life and work in a single building. Mothers with children can work and meet their 'reproductive' demands at the same time, whereas in the West the spatial separation of the domestic world and the world of work means that either women cannot work or they must send (and pay for) their children to attend a crèche.

The family live upstairs; work is carried

out on the ground floor. Today, shophouses are still being built, although architecturally they may be inferior, illustrating their functional beauty and flexibility even in rapidly developing, and westernizing, Thailand. Today, it is common to see the family pick-up parked next to the refrigerator, while children play among sacks of produce. The Romanesque shophouse may have arrived, replacing the far more aesthetically pleasing wooden shophouse, but their functional logic remains the same.

Development and Welfare Centre. Limited accommodation is available (T02-5790529 to book) in the park and camping is permitted. ■ ฿3, ฿20 (car). Hilltribe products are for sale at Km 29 on the Tak-Mae Sot highway.

Wat Phra Boromthat and **Chedi Yuttha Hatti (Wat Prathat)** are 36 km from Tak, some way off Route 1, northwest towards Thoen and Lampang. Although they are rather difficult to get to, the journey is worth the effort, not least because it is via **Ban Tak**, an attractive village of wooden houses situated on the banks of the Ping River (see page 235). ■ *Getting there: take a bus north on Route 1 to the district town of Ban Tak, then another (infrequent) bus going towards Sam Ngao (on Route 1107). The bus crosses the Ping River then turns north on Route 1107. Get off at the junction with Route 1175 (after about 5 km) and walk the final kilometre up the hill to the wat.*

Bhumibol Dam (*Khuan Bhumipon*), named after the present King of Thailand, represents the first of Thailand's multi-purpose dams and was officially opened in May 1964. The operations area below the dam is immaculately maintained, with gardens, an information centre (where visitors must collect a pass to visit the dam), shops, some guesthouse accommodation (T02-4240101/4363179) and homes for the engineers. This impressive dam is over 150 m high and holds back a reservoir 100 km long with, apparently, a capacity of 12,200,000,000 cu m of water. Long-tailed boats take daytrippers across the reservoir and stalls at the top of the dam sell dried fish and other delicacies. ■ *0700-1730. Getting there: take a bus north up Route 1 to the turn off for the dam (43 km from Tak), then another bus to the dam (a further 17 km away). Ask for 'Khuan Bhumipon'. Alternatively, there are direct minibuses to the dam.*

Mae Sot can also be visited as a day trip from Tak (see page 236). There are regular buses, journey time about two hours.

Sleeping
Hotels are limited here, with no guesthouses that can be recommended for budget travellers. The ones listed make up virtually all there is in Tak

AL-B *Viang Tak 2*, 236 Chumphon Rd, T512507, F512169, T02-2332690, F02-6338086, www.viangtak.com A/c, overlooking the Ping River, the best hotel in Tak – well-run, well-maintained, clean and contemporary-looking reception with great views over the river. Pool, coffee shop, snooker, nightclub, shopping plaza with 24-hr supermarket. Significant discounts available during low season (as little as ฿550-800, which is excellent value). Recommended. **C** *Viang Tak*, 25/3 Mahatthai Bamrung Rd, T512507, F512687, BT2332690, BF2355137. Comfortable a/c hotel with 'Western' bar and restaurant out the front. Breakfast included in room price. Spacious rooms with optional TV. Good value. **C-D** *Racha Villa*, 307/1 Pahonyothin Rd, T512361. On the outskirts of town, this hotel accommodates mainly Thais. Situated on the main road, it is more like a motel than a

The Central Plains

hotel. Facilities include a/c, TV and western toilet, and the rooms are large and clean if a little tatty. **D** *Sa Nguan Thai*, 619 Taksin Rd, T51153. Chinese hotel with rooms set around a courtyard. Clean and well kept but overpriced, being bland and characterless. Some fan, some a/c. **E** *Mae Ping*, 231/4-6 Mahatthai Bamrung Rd, T511918. Smelly courtyard off a busy road, reception is in an old wooden house in the centre of the courtyard. Rooms are dark and dirty with grubby Thai squat toilets. Noisy and characterless. A truly last resort.

There are a number of large 'garden' restaurants along Phahonyothin Rd, eg **Eating** *Jintanaa*. Stall food from the market on Mahatthai Bamrung Rd.

Nov *Loi Krathong Sai*, Thailand's annual Festival of Light, is worth seeing here, as peo- **Festivals** ple thread their *krathongs* together and launch these illuminated necklaces simultaneously onto the Ping River. **28 Dec-3 Jan:** *Taksin Maharachanusorn Fair*, celebrated annually at the Taksin Shrine and provincial sports field, features religious ceremonial processions, displays and nightly folk entertainment.

Local Tuk-tuks, saamlors and motorcycle taxis are available to whisk passengers to their **Transport** hotels and guesthouses. Local songthaews also leave from this station. **Air**: airport is 14 *65 km N of* km out of town off Route 12, east towards Sukhothai. Four connections a week with Bang- *Kamphaeng Phet* kok (via Phitsanulok), Chiang Mai and Mae Sot. Transfer to the airport is available twice *423 km to Bangkok* daily; contact *Thai Airways*, T512164. **Bus**: non-a/c and a/c buses leave from the station on Route 12 near crossroads of Phahonyothin Rd. There are connections with Bangkok's Northern bus terminal (7 hrs), Chiang Mai (4 hrs), Mae Sot (1½ hrs), Kamphaeng Phet (1 hr, departures hourly), Sukhothai (1-1½ hrs, departures hourly), Chiang Rai, Mae Sai, Lampang and elsewhere in the Northern and Central Plains regions.

Tak

Airline offices *Thai*, 485 Taksin Rd, **Directory** T512164. **Banks** *Krung Thai*, Taksin Rd (corner of Soi 9). *Siam City*, 125 Mahatthai Bamrung Rd. *Thai Military*, 77/2 Mahatthai Bamrung Rd. **Communications** Post Office: off Mahatthai Bamrung Rd in the north of town.

Twenty kilometres north of Tak on **Ban Tak** the Ping River is this lovely little *Phone code: 055* town, as yet only marginally *Colour map 1, grid C2* afflicted by the curse of the concrete mixer. This was the original site of Tak City. It has one place to stay and is the most convenient base for visiting Wat Phra Boromthat and Chedi Yuttha Hatti (see below). The countryside around here is well worth exploring, but few people bother to spend much time in the area. The town has a night market with food vendors opposite the bus terminal, several restaurants, a bank and a post office. There are regular bus connections with Tak and with Bangkok. At the time of writing

■ **Sleeping**
1 Mae Ping
2 Racha Villa
3 Sa Nguan Thai
4 Viang Tak
5 Viang Tak 2

The Central Plains

there is only one place to stay. **D-E** *Bantak Youth Hostel*, 9/1 Muu 10, T591286, F591286. Run by a Thai-English couple, Alvin and Petchlat Goodwin, rooms are housed in a modern villa with a large garden and good views of the surrounding mountains. Dorm beds available, restaurant, good Thai food can be ordered in advance, bicycles for hire, customized tours arranged. Recommended.

Wat Phra Boromthat is set on a hill, about 5 km from Ban Tak, with views over paddy fields. The chedi is Burmese in style and there is an attractive old viharn in the compound, with rustic carvings on the window shutters and doors. On the other side of the road from the wat is **Chedi Yuttha Hatti (Wat Prathat)**, a lotus-shaped chedi said to have been built as a memorial to King Ramkhamhaeng's victory in elephant combat over King Khun Sam Chon, ruler of Mae Sot. ■ *Getting there: take a (rather infrequent) bus going towards Sam Ngao (on Route 1107). The bus crosses the Ping River then turns north on Route 1107. Get off at the junction with Route 1175 (after about 5 km) and walk the final kilometre up the hill to the wat.*

Mae Sot แม่สอด

Phone code: 055
Colour map 1, grid C2

Mae Sot lies 5 km from the Burmese border, near the end of Route 105 which, from Tak, swoops its way through hills and forest to Mae Sot and the Moei River valley. The town has developed into a locally important trading centre and just about every ethnic group can be seen wandering the streets: Tais, Chinese, Burmese, Karen, Hmong and other hilltribes. Although Mae Sot has quietened down over the last few years, it still has a reputation as being one of the more lawless towns in Thailand. With a flourishing, and sometimes illicit, trade in drugs, teak and gems, this is perhaps unsurprising.

The importance of teak has grown since the Thai government imposed a ban on all logging in Thailand, and companies have turned instead to concessions in eastern Burma, close to Mae Sot, to secure their wood. Whether the army and police force are protecting the forests or are making a tidy profit out of the industry is never quite clear. At the beginning of 1992, Burmese army incursions into Thailand near Mae Sot pursuing Karen rebels led to a diplomatic incident, and once again underscored Mae Sot's reputation as a slightly 'dangerous' frontier town. The Thai-Burmese border in this area is strewn with anti-personnel mines and many local people refuse to graze their cattle because of the danger.

The authorities in Mae Sot are now attempting to diversify the town's economy and build a reputation as a tourist destination and trekking centre. They have been fairly successful in this regard and there is now a modern, western-style hotel on the outskirts of the town – the *Mae Sot Hills*. Even so, there still appear to be more darkened-windowed Mercedes and BMWs plying the road from Mae Sot to Tak than along most other stretches of highway in Thailand.

Sights **Wat Moni Phraison**, on Intharakit Road, has an unusual chedi in which a golden central spire is surrounded by numerous smaller chedis rising in tiers, behind each of which is a small image of the Buddha. **Wat Chumphon**, also on Intharakit Road but on the western side of town, is worth visiting. Many of Mae Sot's older **wooden shophouses** are still standing, especially on Intharakit Road. There is an unusually busy **morning market** running off and between Prasat Withi and Intharakit roads in the centre of town. Many Burmese make their way here to sell produce and even shops acknowledge

Mae Sot place names

Burmese border
ชายแดนพม่า

Umphang
อุ้มผาง

The Central Plains

their presence, seemingly, by providing signs in Burmese and Thai. Much of the cheap labour is provided by day commuters from Burma; average wages for Thais are already so high (relatively) that they have priced themselves out of the market. Burmese day migrants can be identified by their dress (many wear *lungyis* or sarongs), language and their finely featured and powdered faces.

Excursions

The **Burmese border** lies 5 km west of Mae Sot, and runs down the middle of the Moei River. The construction of a 420 m bridge across the river, directly linking Mae Sot with the Burmese town of Myawady, was completed and formally opened in August 1997. Predictably, it is known as the Friendship Bridge; just make sure you don't get a lift to the other Friendship Bridge outside Nong Khai over 500 km to the east. With the opening of the bridge, local businesses were hoping for a tourist boom on the scale of that at Mae Sai, in the north. From here it is a 400 km drive to Yangon (Rangoon), although such is the state of the road that it takes a pick-up five days to make the journey. Thai and Burmese nationals can currently cross the border here (they can be seen in Mae Sot town, see above), but not (yet) overseas visitors.

There is a busy market at the border selling Burmese goods (hats, blankets, gems, silver, baskets and agricultural produce like dried mushrooms), with gun-toting Thai rangers, powder-covered Burmese girls and a few restaurants. A fire in 1993 destroyed a large section of the market and for a period in 1995 and 1996 the border was closed. However, a new custom-built shopping market/arcade is now complete – the **Mae Moei City** (but many of the shops are standing empty) – and the border was reopened on 14 August 1996. This new market does not have the ramshackle attractiveness of the old market and it is possible that the latter may be encouraged to close. Nonetheless, the tantalizing view over to Burma is worth the short journey out here. Check in town at your hotel/guesthouse or at the **Mae Sot Travel Centre** to see whether foreign (that is, non-Thai) visitors can make day trips to Burma; there is talk of restrictions being eased.

Around 1 km from the bridge, back along the road to Mae Sot, is **Wat Thai Wattanaram**. This monastery is notable mainly for the massive, recently built, Burmese-style reclining Buddha in the rear courtyard. Also here is a gallery of over 25 smaller sitting Buddhas. A hotel was under construction with a riverside location as part of the Mae Moei City development, but the economic crisis intervened to slow things down. It should now be completed and will probably be in our **B-C** categories. ■ *Getting there: regular blue songthaews to the Moei River and the Burmese border leave from the west end of Prasat Withi Rd, not far from the Thai Airways office (฿10).*

Umphang lies 164 km south of Mae Sot (see page 237). Several songthaews a day leave from the stop near the telephone office (see map, page 238), starting at about 0600 with the last departure around 1400, four to five hours (฿100). It is also possible to go by motorbike, but a scooter will not be powerful enough to make it up the hills; or rent a car with driver for the day, costs around ฿1,500.

Trekking & tours
See also page 360

Mae Sot offers some of the best trekking in northern and western Thailand because the trekking routes here are relatively untouched by mass tourism. But its potential as another Mae Hong Son or Pai has not gone unnoticed. Its popularity is increasing and in the immediate future there are likely to be new or improved bus services, as well as more guesthouses, trekking companies and associated services. It is now possible to cross the border into Burma, for an immigration fee of approximately US$10 to Burma's military government. This fee tends to fluctuate regularly between US$5 and US$18. Treks tend to either go south to Umphang or north towards Mae Sariang, and incorporate visits to caves, waterfalls, hilltribe villages and Karen refugee camps. The usual array of raft trips and elephant rides are

The Central Plains

available, in addition to straightforward trekking. **NB** the Thai-Burmese border in this area is heavily mined and visitors should not hike without a guide. This applies particularly to Pang Ma Pha and Pai districts. Approximate rate ฿3,500 for a three day/two night trek, ฿4,500 for four days/three nights, dependent upon whether raft trips and elephant rides are part of the deal. The *Mae Sot Conservation Tour*, 415/7 Tang Khim Chiang Road, T532818, premat@ ksc15.th.com, runs educational and soft adventure tours for families and the elderly (contact *Pim Hut Restaurant*); *Eco-trekking* is run from *No 4 Guesthouse*. They do seven-day tours at special request for an extortionate US$400, though it's a truly unique experience. *SP Tours* (run from *SP Guesthouse*) organizes day sightseeing trips to surrounding places of interest and trekking. *Queen Bee Tours and Trekking* is run out of *Mae Sot Guesthouse*; it is quite expensive. *Max One Tours* (opposite *DK Hotel*) operates in a similar way, but also organizes birdwatching tours and tours to refugee camps.

Sleeping
■ *on map*
Price codes:
see inside front cover

A *Mae Sot Hill*, 100 Asia Rd, T532601, F532600. Restaurant, 2 pools, tennis courts and 120 rooms on the outskirts of town, the only luxury place to stay. Clean and well-maintained, although the grounds are looking neglected. Shuttle to town ฿50.

C-D *Duang Kamol (DK) Hotel*, 298 Intharakit Rd, T542648, F531378. Built by the DK publishing group (not Dorling Kindersley, but Duang Kamol), the lower floor is a large Thai language bookshop. A/c and fan rooms available in this hotel which sparkles with cleanliness (tiled walls give the impression of one enormous bathroom), but it's a desolate place. Very spacious rooms, quieter ones are at the back. Good value. **C-D** *Pornthep*, 25/4 Prasart Withi Rd, T532590, F532596. Some a/c and some fan, restaurant, hideous great barn of a place with 50-odd rooms. Lifeless and noisy but staff are helpful enough. Avoid rooms with TV (Thai & CNN); they're overpriced, though there's a 20% discount for some of the more expensive rooms during the low season. There's also a small but dark café area behind the reception. **C-E** *Siam*, 185 Prasat Withi Rd, T531176, F531974. Some a/c, a 3-storey Chinese-style hotel in the centre of town near the market, noisy and rather unrestful. Rooms are variable but mostly old and tatty with grubby squat toilets, though there are some a/c rooms with Western toilets.

D *First*, 444 Sawat Withi Rd, T531770. Some a/c, large, clean rooms, some character, recently changed hands and there are some renovations under way. **D-F** *Mae Sot*

Mae Sot

■ **Sleeping**
1 Bai Fern Guesthouse & Restaurant
2 Duang Kamon (DK) & Bookstore
3 First
4 Mae Sot Guesthouse
5 No 4 Guesthouse
6 Pornthep
7 Siam
8 Suwanavit

● **Eating**
1 Fah Fah Bakery
2 Neung Nuk
3 Pim Hut
4 River
5 Seafood

To Umphang

N
Not to scale

Guesthouse, 208/4 Intharakit Rd, T532745, F532745. Teak house in largish garden compound, set back from the road, 50 m from a wat. Quiet, small simple rooms in main house, bigger rooms with attached cold water bathrooms and a/c in motel-esque bungalow (dorm beds available). The a/c rooms are very good value. Attractive dining and seating area in a large airy teak barn on the side of the house, with satellite TV and lots of information. The guesthouse organizes trekking tours and collect unwanted clothing and medicines to distribute to Burmese refugees in the area.

E-F *Bai Fern*, 660/2 Intharakit Rd, T533343, rungrapee@hotmail.com A few rooms are available in the back of what is really a restaurant. Generally this comprises a mattress on the floor or on a raised wooden platform. Communal toilets with hot showers, dorm rooms also available. The *Bai Fern Restaurant* in front is a popular spot with travellers (see Eating below). **E-F** *No 4 Guesthouse*, 736 Intharakit Rd, T544976, F544976, no4guesthouse@yahoo.com Another of the *No 4 Guesthouse* empire which seem to have a stranglehold on the region. The owner is the nephew of the lady owner of *No 4 Guesthouse* in Sukhothai. Wooden floors in this large teak building set back on a big plot to the west of town on the road to the Moei River (about 10-15 mins' walk from the bus station). Rooms are large, airy and basic with mattresses on the floor and rather dirty shared toilets, but hot showers. Seating area with Thai TV, and a few books and magazines. *Eco-trekking* is run from here (see Trekking above). **E-F** *SP Guesthouse*, 14/21 Asia Rd, T531409, F532279, BT5737942. Clean and well-run (dorm beds available), free cold drinking water.

Resort **A-C** *Thaweechailand*, 9 km outside Mae Sot on the road to Tak, T531287. Restaurant.

Several small restaurants have recently opened along the western part of Intharakit Rd; notable are the Burmese restaurants at the southern end of Tang Khim Chiang Rd. **Mid-range** *Sea Food Restaurant*, Intharakit Rd. Attractive teak sitting area with a good range of lobster, crab, squid, seabass and prawns served in a variety of ways.

Eating
● *on map*
Price categories:
see inside front cover

Cheap *Bai Fern Restaurant*, 660/2 Intharakit Rd, serves Thai and Western food, with a range of pizzas and vegetarian options. Pleasant indoor sitting area. Popular with travellers. *Canton* (*Kwangtung*), 2/1 Soi Sriphanich. Locals say that this place serves the best Chinese food in town. *Café Myawaddy*, Prasat Withi Rd (opposite the songthaew stop for the Moei River). Open 0700-2100, run by a Burmese and spotlessly maintained a/c restaurant; also an attached shop selling Burmese lacquerware and providing some information. *Kaan Buun Restaurant*, Intharakit Rd. Only open in the evening when it becomes the place for Mae Sot's hippest people to hang out, average to good food, great ambience, occasional live music. Recommended. *Pim Hut*, Thang Kim Chiang Rd. This place serves almost everything from pizzas to ice-creams to frog, food is generally good, nice atmosphere in open-air surroundings, serves breakfast from 0700. *Neung Nuk*, Intharakit Rd. Garden restaurant, geared to Thais (the name is only in Thai), but the food is good, especially the fish.

To Mae Sot Hill Hotel, Tak, Moei River & Border (5 km)

Wat Moni Phraison

Tak, Lampang, Chiang, Chiang Rai & Mae Sai

Mae Sot Reservation Tours

Soi Sapphakan

Suwanwit Rd

Soi Phoen Chitr

Prasat Withi Rd

Night Market

-ket

To Um Phang

To Hospital

Seriously cheap   *Fah Fah*, Thang Kim Chiang Rd. Bakery/Thai. *The River*, Intharakit Rd. Thai and Western food with a distinct American flavour (peanut butter and banana shakes!), and a range of fresh ground coffees. Run by a man called Prasong and his wife, who speak good English and are an excellent source of information. They also run a range of special package tours, for reservations T534593. Pleasant atmosphere, open 0600-2100. Recommended.

Foodstalls There are 2 excellent stall restaurants by the Chiang Mai bus stop on Intharakit Rd. One specializes in superb *phat thai* (fried noodles), the other in seafood dishes. The night market just off Prasat Withi Rd is a good place to eat cheaply in the evening.

Shopping **Books** *DK Bookstore*, under the *DK Hotel* (see Sleeping above), has a large range of English-language Penguin classics, the only literature in English stocked. **Burmese goods** On sale in the market on the Moei River and in the market behind the *Siam Hotel*. For better quality objects, try the Burmese lacquerware shop on Prasat Withi Rd, almost opposite the songthaew stop for the Moei River. For better deals it is also worth catching a songathew to Moei (see map for location, 10-15 mins, ฿10) in the morning. **Department store** 100/3-7 Prasat Withi Rd. **Gems** A good buy; most of the jewellery shops are concentrated on Prasat Withi Rd around the *Siam Hotel*.

Tour operators
See also Trekking above
Mae Sot Travel Centre (aka *SP Tour*), 14/21 Asia Rd, T531409, F532279, BT5737942. The main office is out of town, but Mr Sunny can also be contacted through the *Mae Sot Hills Guesthouse* or the *Siam Hotel*, see Sleeping above, and has a desk at a small office not far from the songthaew stop for the Moei River.

Transport
87 km W of Tak,
230 km to Mae Sariang,
510 km to Bangkok
Local Saamlors, tuk-tuks, songthaews. **Motorbike hire**: Prasat Withi Rd (close to the Bangkok Bank), ฿160 per day. **Long distance Air**: airport 1½ km out of town on Route 105 to Burmese border. Thai operate services to 2 destinations: Bangkok and Chiang Mai on Mon, Tue, Thu and Sat. **Bus**: Mae Sot does not have a single bus terminal; buses and songthaews depart from various places around town (see map, page 238). A/c and non-a/c bus connections with Bangkok's Northern bus terminal (10 hrs), from the stop out of town near Asia Rd at 0800, 0830, 1900, 2000, 2030, 2100 (and VIP buses at 2115, 2130 and 2145). A/c and non-a/c buses for Chiang Mai (6½ hrs) leave at 0600 and 0800, Chiang Rai, Tak (1½ hrs), Lampang and Mae Sai (12 hrs) leave from the bus stop on Intharakit Rd, either in the morning or at night. Songthaews for Mae Sariang leave in the morning from the road running past the police station, off Intharakit Rd (5 hrs) (see description of this route, below). For transport to the Burmese border see Excursions, above.

Directory **Airline offices** *Thai*, 76/1 Prasat Withi Rd, T531730. **Banks** *Siam Commercial*, 544/1-5 Intharakit Rd. *Thai Farmers*, 84/9 Prasat Withi Rd. *Thai Military*, 179/7 Prasat Withi Rd. **Communications** Overseas telephone service: at Post Office on Intharakit Rd. **Post Office**: Intharakit Rd (opposite the *DK Hotel*). The main post office is also on Intharakit Rd, but past the *No 4 Guesthouse* about 1 km out of town on the road to the Moei River. **Email & internet facilities:** a few internet cafés have opened up at the western end of Prasat Withi Rd. **Useful addresses** Tourist Police: office on Intharakit Rd (next to *No 4 Guesthouse*), T533523.

Route between Mae Sot and Mae Sariang

On most maps this road – Route 105 – appears indistinct, as if it is no more than a track. In fact, it is made up over its entire length of 230 km and is in better shape than many other, busier, roads. The reason why the Thai government has invested so much in Route 105 is clear: it follows the Moei River and the Burmese border for a considerable distance and is therefore of strategic and military importance. Police checkpoints are interspersed along its length. Travelling south to north, the road is fast to the district town of **Tha Song Yang**. It then follows the Moei River – which surprisingly flows south to north too (and then loops south as it joins the Salween River) – and the Burmese border. The landscape becomes wilder, less populated, more mountainous and the road slower with each kilometre. Karen refugee camps are scattered along the road. A beautiful, if sometimes uncomfortable, five hour journey. There are a few **places to stay** en route. Almost where the road stops following the river and climbs into the hills is the **E** *Mae Sali Guesthouse* (121 km from Mae Sariang, 109 km from Mae Sot), a clean and relaxing place to stay with a welcoming Burmese host. Further on still, about two-thirds of the way to Mae Sariang, is the **C** *Pa Pa Valley Resort*.

Umphang อุ้มผาง

Umphang lies 164 km south of Mae Sot along a rollercoaster road. This district is one of the least developed in Western Thailand, and rugged terrain and large expanses of forest, including the **Khlong Lan National Park**, make it ideal for trekking. Until the early 1980s it was under the control of the Communist Party of Thailand, explaining why it remains comparatively pristine. Although an organized trek is the best way to see and experience the area's natural beauty (see Trekking, page 237, or take a trek arranged by one of the guesthouses in Umphang), it is possible to explore the area to a limited extent on one's own. Malaria is a problem, not so much in Umphang itself but in the surrounding countryside. Precautions should be taken if trekking outside the town. Umphang is not much more than an oversized village and the majority of its population are Karen.

Phone code: 055
Colour map 3, grid A2

The Central Plains

If travelling to Umphang by your own transport, leave early in the morning as there are quite a number of worthwhile stops en route, including waterfalls and Karen villages. The **Thara Rak waterfall** is just over 25 km from Mae Sot. At the base of the falls is a pool for swimming and it is being gradually developed into a small park. It's a popular spot for locals at the weekend when vendors set up and sell various Thai snacks and cold drinks. Turn-off the road after the Km 24 marker. Note that if you are travelling here by motorbike or car the road is treacherous: sharp bends, mist and, during the wet season, a good deal of rain.

Umphang

To Morning Market,
Songthaews to
Mae Sot & Hospital

To Mae Sot (164 km)

Wat Nilaman

Nong Koong

BL Tour

Um Phang House

PM Tour

Veera Tour

Palata Rd

Garden Huts

Rafting Point

Huai Umphang

Umphang.com

Aing Doi Resort

Um Phang Hill Resort

To Palatha (27 km)

To Karen Village (6 km)

N

Not to scale

Ta Ka Su

There is some excellent trekking in the vicinity of Umphang. Many of the trekking companies in Mae Sot come out this way and the guesthouses and resorts in Umphang itself also offer similar packages, as do a few tour companies. Most of the tour companies (aside from those arranged by guesthouses) are on Palata Rd. *Veera Tours*, T561239, *PM Tours*, T561059, F561293, and *BL Tours*, T561021, do the usual treks similar to those found elsewhere in Thailand –

Trekking
See page 360

rafts, hill villages, elephant rides – but the relatively pristine forest hereabouts, not to mention the villages, makes the experience a more exciting and authentic one (whatever that might mean). *The Ecotourist Center*, T561063, F561065, T02-5737941, F02-5735924, umpanghill@hotmail.com, www.umpanghill.com, now offers the environmentally correct tourist a six-night, seven-day trek from Umphang down to Sangkhlaburi, a route that has only been trekked once before at the time of writing (August 2000), and costs around β12,000 (see page 533).

Sleeping Umphang has only come onto the *farang* tourist itinerary in the last couple of years, but it has been popular with Thais for a while (hence the concentration of karaoke bars blaring out over an otherwise tranquil village). For the budget traveller the accomodation here is good value for money, but if you are looking for the minibar and executive lounge experience, expect to be disappointed. In fact there is not even a hotel or guesthouse with a/c, although the cool weather usually makes this unnecessary in any case. **D-E** *Um Phang House*, T561073. Range of rooms with attached facilities, some separate bungalows. Basic, with mattresses on raised wooden platforms, a bit dark and gloomy. Cheaper rooms have squat toilets, bungalows (2-3 people) have Western toilets though there's little other difference. **A-F** *Um Phang Hill Resort*, Palata Rd, T561063, F561065, umpanghill@ hotmail.com, www.umpanghill.com Mostly patronized by Thais getting away from it all; rooms have an ersatz frontier feel with wagon wheels and the like. Wooden bungalows on a small hill with attractive gardens, ranging from dorm rooms to large, comfortable rooms with hot showers, TV (Thai plus MTV) and fridges. *Umphang Hill Restaurant* at the bottom of the hill is pleasant enough, until the karaoke starts. Very friendly management with excellent English. This guesthouse also runs the *Ecotourist Center* which offers treks to Sangkhlaburi (see Trekking above). Recommended. **D-E** *Garden Huts*, 106 Palata Rd, T561093, boonyaporn.com Sometimes cramped bamboo and wooden bungalows (they vary in size), some with beds on raised platforms. Some also offer Western toilets, others are of the squat variety. More expensive rooms have a river view and a small sitting area out the back of the bungalow (though these are noisy at night with the karaoke from the *Umphang Hill Restaurant* across the river). Five more wooden bungalows were under construction in mid-2000. Filter coffee available, restaurant, very friendly management with a little English. Tours available. **D-E** *Ta Ka Su*, Palata Rd, T561295, F561295, Cell01-8258238. Attractive setting in well-maintained gardens with pebble paths. Wooden and bamboo bungalows, some with loft beds. All have attached bathrooms, some open air, but very clean and attractively decorated with plants and pebbles. Very clean and pleasant atmosphere, good English spoken. Bicycles for rent, and the usual treks organized. Restaurant area. Recommended. **E** *Aing Doi Resort*, Palata Rd. Large, open, well-kept garden with simple bungalows. Some of the outside bathrooms are housed in rather grotty corrugated metal huts, with concrete floors and squat toilets. Bamboo bungalows may be 'naturally' ventilated, but that's not necessarily what you want with so many vicious mosquitoes.

Eating Almost all guesthouses and resorts have their own restaurants attached, with Thai food at prices in our cheap to seriously cheap range. There is also **cheap** *Nong Koong*, on the corner of Palata Rd, opposite *BL Tours*. A few tables spread out in a simple wooden bungalow, a local place serving simple Thai dishes (you'll need your phrasebook to order).

Transport **Road** Several songthaews a day connect Umphang with Mae Sot. The first leaves Mae *164 km S of Mae Sot* Sot around 0600 and the last at about 1400, 4-5 hrs (β100). For the return journey they leave Umphang for Mae Sot at 0700, 0800, 0900, 1300, 1400 and 1500. It is also possible to go by motorbike – but a scooter will not be powerful enough due to the steep inclines.

Directory **Police** T055-561112 (see map for location). **Banks** No banks in Umphang – make sure you bring plenty of money with you! **Communications** Internet & overseas calls from *Umphang.com* on Palata Rd (though there's only 1 computer and usually a handful of children glued to it).

The Northern Region

5

The Northern Region

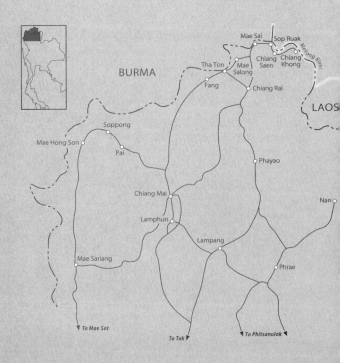

This region is best known for the hilltribes who inhabit the mountains that fringe its borders. Those looking for an energetic outdoor holiday, with trekking, perhaps a raft trip and visits to hilltribe communities, should head here. The North also contains many historically important sights, perhaps the most notable being in and around Lampang, Lamphun and Chiang Mai.

The North was only firmly incorporated into the Thai state in the early 20th century. Before then the lowland valleys were controlled by local princes. The hills were sparsely settled, largely by hill peoples. The Khon Muang, the people of the lowlands, and the Phu Khao, the hill people, inhabited different worlds. But only since the end of the Second World War have the Khon Muang and the Phu Khao found themselves competing over the same resources.

Although geographical constraints prevented northern rulers gaining power further south, they have left their imprint in fine city walls (Chiang Mai, Phrae, Chiang Saen, Lamphun) and some of the most beautiful monasteries in Thailand. Because the north developed autonomously it also has its distinctive cultural traditions reflected in cuisine, fine arts, music and language. The hill people, in turn, have their own unique cultures.

In the 1970s the northern mountains became a haven for rebels of the Communist Party of Thailand (CPT). The area also became a centre for heroin poppy production with land controlled by opium warlords beyond the reach of the Thai state. That has all changed. There is very little opium grown in Thailand, the CPT has been vanquished, and the hill peoples have been increasingly incorporated into the Thai state.

Lampang to Chiang Mai

From the ancient town of Lampang, Route 11 runs northwestwards to Lamphun (77 km) and from there to Chiang Mai (another 26 km), the unofficial capital of the north. Close to Lampang is arguably the most beautiful wat in Thailand: Wat Lampang Luang. Lamphun, the former capital of the Mon kingdom of Haripunjaya, features highly unusual stepped chedis, to be seen nowhere else in the country. The walled city of Chiang Mai is the tourist centre of the North, with multitudes of hotels, restaurants and trekking companies, beautiful wats and the centre of handicraft production and Northern culture.

Lampang ลำปาง

Phone code: 054
Colour map 1, grid B3
Population: 50,000

Lampang – now the second largest city in the north, after Chiang Mai – was one of Thailand's most attractive provincial capitals. It still retains a number of its old wooden buildings and horse-drawn carriages – the town's symbol – are still used as taxis rather than the frenetic tuk-tuk. But, unfortunately, the municipal authorities failed to appreciate the treasure in their grasp: they have allowed the town to sprawl out of control with, seemingly, no building restrictions whatsoever. In places – especially towards the Wang River – the Lampang of just 10 years ago is there still to be found, but it appears to be an endangered species.

Ins and outs

Getting there
See also Transport, page 252

As the trip from Chiang Mai, whether by bus or train, takes just 2 hrs, it is possible to visit Lampang on a day trip. Both the bus and train stations are around 1 km southwest of the town centre.

Getting around

Lampang's one way road system does seem to complicate matters and getting your bearings here is not always straightforward. Don't miss the opportunity to take a horse-drawn carriage around town, see page 252 for details.

Tourist offices

A tourist office is at Boonyawat Rd, in the front of the police station, first floor, T218823. Good map and brochure.

History

Established in the seventh century Dvaravati Period, Lampang became a prosperous trading centre, with a wealth of ornate and well-endowed wats. Built as a fortified *wiang* (a walled city) during the 19th century, it became an important centre for the teak industry. British loggers made this one of their key centres, exploiting the town's location on the Wang River. The influence of the Burmese is reflected in the architecture of some of the more important wats – a number still have Burmese abbots.

Sights

Wat Phra Kaeo Don Tao & Wat Chadaram
It's easiest to visit wats here by saamlor or horse-drawn carriage

Wat Phra Kaeo Don Tao and its 'sister' Wat Chadaram are to be found on Phra Kaeo Road, north across the Rachada Phisek Bridge. Wat Phra Kaeo housed the renowned Emerald Buddha (the Phra Kaeo – now in Wat Phra Kaeo, Bangkok) for 32 years during the 15th century, and is reputed to have been founded by Queen Chama Devi of Lamphun's son in the seventh century.

A Foot in the Door

★ The North is best known for its colourful hilltribes who inhabit the highland borderlands of the area. Tour companies in all the major centres will organise treks through the hills and often include rafting trips and elephant rides into the bargain.

★ Chiang Mai is the cultural capital of the North – and of Thailand – with an excellent range of hotels, restaurants and bars as well as good shopping and some fine monasteries.

★ The attractive historic towns of Nan, Chiang Saen and Lamphun are worth a visit.

★ The highland town of Mae Hong Son has Burmese-style monasteries, a large tribal population, cool climate, and an attractive position encircled by hills.

★ Chiang Rai is an alternative base to border towns like Mae Sai (for Burma) and Chiang Khong (for Laos), with their distinctive markets.

★ Wat Phrathat Lampang Luang, near Lampang, which is arguably the most beautiful monastery in Thailand, and Wat Phumin in Nan has some of the finest murals.

This, a royal temple, is said to be imbued with particular spiritual power and significance, largely because of its association with the Phra Kaeo. The ceilings and columns of the 18th-century viharn are carved in wood and are intricately inlaid with porcelain and enamel. In the compound, there is also a Burmese-style chapel (probably late-18th century) and a golden chedi. ■ ฿10.

Next door, Wat Chadaram is less highly regarded, although it contains possibly the most attractive building in the whole complex: a small, intimate, well proportioned, wooden viharn.

Wat Chedi Sao

This wat, the 'temple of the 20 chedis', is 3 km northeast of the town, 1 km off the Lampang-Jae Hom road at Ban Wang Moh. A principal white chedi surrounded by smaller acolytes stand amongst the rice fields, together with a strange assortment of concrete animals and monks. The most important Buddha image here is a gold, seated image cast in the 15th century. Its importance stems both from its miraculous discovery – by a local farmer in his rice field in 1983 – and from the fact that it is said to contain a piece of the Lord Buddha's skull in its head. The image is contained in a pavilion. ■ Daily, 0800-1700. Getting there: saamlors from town quote extortionate prices; it is much cheaper to walk over the bridge to the junction of Jhamatawee and Wangkhon roads and hail one there for ฿5.

Wat Sri Chum

This beautiful wat, on Tippowan Road (also known as Sri Chum Road), was constructed 200 years ago and is registered with the Fine Arts Department as a 'national treasure'. The monastery is regarded as one of the finest Burmese-style wats in Thailand. Tragically, the richly carved and painted viharn, one of the finest structures in the compound, was destroyed by fire in 1993. The compound exudes an ambience of peaceful meditation, although the wat is in urgent need of funds to complete the restoration of its delicate buildings and, possibly, to rebuild the razed viharn. ■ 0700-1830, ฿10.

Wat Rong Muang is also south of the river and can be found close to the intersection of Wangkhwa and Thakrawnoi roads. Yellow and faded red, built of wood and corrugated iron, it rises up in tiers almost like a fantasy building.

Other architecture

In addition to its wats, Lampang also has a number of interesting secular buildings. The old wooden **railway station** is a charming point of arrival and departure, while the streets off Boonyawat Road contain a number of traditional

Northern-style wooden houses. The river road – Tipchang Road – also retains a number of wooden shophouses, until recently the characteristic house style of most Thai towns. In the 19th century, the British made Lampang the centre of the teak trade with neighbouring Burma, and many of the Chinese, Burmese and 'Western' shophouses are reputed to have been built at this time. Near the *Riverside Restaurant* is a Chinese pagoda, the **Sala Chao Mae Thap Tim**. A short distance west, also on Tipchang Road, is **Wat Singh Chai**, notable for its rather fine plaster guardian lions, or *singh* (reproduced on bottles of the local beer of the same name).

Excursions

Wat Phra That Lampang Luang
One of the finest & most beautiful wats in Thailand. The letters in bold correspond to the map

To the wat cognoscente, this magnificent wat, some 20 km southwest of Lampang off Route 1, is the reason to come not just to Lampang, but to the North. Nothing in Chiang Mai compares.

The monastery stands on a slight hill, surrounded by a mellow brick wall – all that remains of the original fortressed city which was sited here more than 1,000 years ago. Sand and tiles, rather than concrete, surround the monuments. While the buildings have been restored on a number of occasions over the years, it remains beautifully complete and authentic.

Originally this wat was an ancient *wiang* – a fortified site, protected by walls, moats and ramparts – and was one of a series of such fortresses linked with Lampang and following the course of the Wang River. The wat is approached by a staircase flanked by guardian lions and nagas, and is entered through an archway of intricate stone carving, built around the late-15th century. The large central viharn, **Viharn Luang (a)**, also dates from the late-15th century and is open on all four sides. It houses a ku – a brick, stucco and gilded pyramid peculiar to Northern wats – containing a Buddha image (dating from 1563), a collection of thrones, and some lively wall paintings dating from the early 19th century or possibly even the 18th century. These are now faded and deteriorated but among the scenes that can be discerned are farmers ploughing, women weaving, houses and temples, fruit pickers, and tattooed men. (Because they have been painted onto wood, and not onto stuccoed walls as is usually the case in Thailand's monasteries, they have survived rather better. There are few murals older than 100 years in Thailand.) The building, with its intricate woodcarving and some fine pattern work on the pillars and ceiling, is dazzling.

Behind the viharn is the principal **chedi (b)**, 45 m high and containing not one but three relics of the Buddha: a hair, the ashes of the Buddha's right forehead and his neck bone ashes. Made of beaten copper and brass plates over a brick core, it is typically Lanna Thai in style and was erected in the late-15th century. The **Buddha Viharn (c)** to the left of the chedi is thought to date from the 13th century and was restored in 1802. Beautifully carved and painted, it contains a seated Buddha image. Immediately behind this viharn is a small,

Lampang place names

Thai Elephant Conservation Centre

ศูนย์อนุรักษ์ช้างไทย

Wat Chadaram

วัดชฎาราม

Wat Chedi Sao

วัดเจดีย์ซาว

Wat Phra Kaeo Don Tao

วัดพระแก้วดอนเต้า

Wat Phra That Lampang Luang

วัดพระธาตุลำปางหลวง

Wat Sri Chum

วัดศรีชุม

raised building housing a **footprint of the Buddha (d)**. This building and the Buddha Viharn have two other claims to fame: at certain times of day the sun's rays pass through a small hole in each building's walls and project an inverted image of the chedi and the surrounding buildings. If you happen to be here at the right time (from late morning through to early afternoon), it really is a rather magical experience. Unfortunately, though, only men are permitted into the Buddha footprint building.

To the right of the main viharn are two more small, but equally beautiful, viharns: the **Viharn Nam Taem (e)** and the **Viharn Ton Kaew (f)**. The former is thought to date from the early 16th century, and may be the oldest wooden building in Thailand. It also contains some old wall paintings, although these are difficult to see in the gloom. Finally within the walls are the **Viharn Phra Chao Sila (g)**, built to enshrine a stone image of the Buddha (hence its name), and the bot, towards the back of the compound and built in 1476, restored in 1924.

Outside the walls, through the southern doorway, is an enormous and ancient **bodhi tree (h)**, supported by a veritable army of crutches. Close by is a small, musty and rather unexciting **museum (j)**. Next to this is a fine raised scripture library and a **viharn**, within which is another revered **Emerald Buddha (k)**, rumoured to have been made from the same block of jasper as the famous Emerald Buddha in Bangkok. It dates from the Chiang Saen Period (1057-1757) and shows the Buddha meditating. Obscured by two rows of steel bars, the image does not begin to compare with the wat buildings in terms of beauty. It can only be viewed 0900-1200, 1300-1700. ■ *Donation. There are drinks and foodstalls in the car park area across the road from the wat. Getting there: by songthaew to Ko Kha and then by motorbike taxi the last 2½ km to the wat. Songthaews for Ko Kha run regularly along Phahonyothin Rd. Alternatively, charter a songthaew from Lampang (฿150-200). If travelling by private transport from Lampang, drive along Route 1 towards Ko Kha. In Ko Kha pass through the town, over the bridge, and then turn right at the T-junction onto Route 1034. The wat is 2½ km away – just off Route 1034 (the chedi can be seen rising up behind some sugar palms). From Chiang Mai, turn right off Route 11 just past the Km 80 marker, signposted to Ko Kha.*

Wat Phra That Lampang Luang

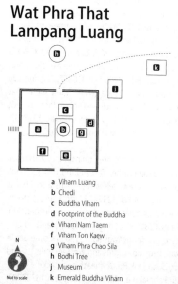

a Viharn Luang
b Chedi
c Buddha Viharn
d Footprint of the Buddha
e Viharn Nam Taem
f Viharn Ton Kaew
g Viharn Phra Chao Sila
h Bodhi Tree
j Museum
k Emerald Buddha Viharn

N
Not to scale

Thai Elephant Conservation Centre

The Thai Elephant Conservation Centre lies 38 km northwest of town near Thung Kwian, on the road to Chiang Mai (Highway 11). Approximately a dozen elephants are trained each year for forest work and there are about 100 animals here in total. Calves are three to five years old when they arrive and they undergo five years' training. Rather less crowded than the training centres nearer Chiang Mai, the shows are more authentic and put the elephants through their paces, stacking, carrying and pulling logs. The most highly prized elephants of all are 'white' elephants – in fact, they are a pale pink. These animals are considered so holy that they used to be fed off gold platters. Rama IV wrote a treatise on their characteristics, of which one was the possession of a 'beautiful snore'. This centre is also the location of an Elephant Hospital. There is also a small restaurant, souvenir shop and toilets. ■ *'Taught' between 0900 and 1100 daily, except public and Buddhist holidays and the dry season from Mar to May, ฿50. Elephant rides ฿100 for 10 mins, ฿300 for 30 mins, ฿600 for 1 hr (overpriced), T227051. Getting there: by early morning bus towards Chiang Mai; get off at the Km 37 marker (ask the bus driver to let you off at the Conservation Centre). NB From the road it is a 1.8 km walk by road or take a short cut through the forest.*

Pha Thai caves The Pha Thai caves are some of the most spectacular caves in Thailand, found on the road to Ngao. These are associated with a wat and are located about 20 km before Ngao. ■ *Getting there: take a bus on from Ban Pang La towards Ngao.*

Jai Sorn National Park for hot volcanic springs in the waterfall pools, ask at *TT and T Guesthouse* for directions.

Essentials

Sleeping
■ *on map*
Price codes:
see inside front cover

Because Lampang is only 2 hrs from Chiang Mai, few tourists seem to stay here. There is one good hotel and a great mass of indistinguishable and undistinguished Chinese-style places: often clean and comfortable enough, but with no ambience whatsoever. There are also a number of good guesthouses, especially down by the river.

A *Lampang Wiengthong Hotel*, 138/109 Phahonyothin Rd, T225801, F225803. A/c, restaurant, pool, 250 rooms in this, the smartest and largest of Lampang's hotels, and easily the most luxurious place to stay in town. Nonetheless, the feel is distinctly provincial when compared with the sophisticated places 2 hrs up the road in Chiang Mai. **A-B** *Lampang River Lodge*, 330 Moo 11 Tambon Chompoo, T2241173; 6 km south of Lampang on the banks of the Wang River, a/c, restaurant, 60 individual Thai-style bungalows on stilts, in an attractive position. **B-C** *Tipchang Lampang*, 54/22 Thakrawnoi Rd, T226501, F225362. A/c, restaurant, dirty pool, rather tacky, unfriendly staff, overpriced – and has been all of these things for a number of years now. It also has a disco (supper club) and guests can use the tennis courts nearby. **C** *Asia Lampang*, 229 Boonyawat Rd, T227844, T224436. A/c, restaurant, large, non-descript rooms, but good value. Friendly staff and with the added bonus of the 'Sweety Room' for 'the romantic of your ambience moods'. Recommended. **C** *Pin*, 8 Suan Dok Rd, T221509, F322286. Some a/c, fridge, satellite TV, squeaky clean and quiet. **C-D** *Wieng Fah Hotel*, 13 Wiang Lakorn Rd, T310674, F310677. A/c, friendly staff trying to make the most of an almost entirely characterless hotel, with what would be best described as minimalist rooms. A good mid-range place for those not seeking local atmosphere. **C-D** *Khelangnakorn*, 719-720 Suan Dok Rd, T217137. Some a/c, restaurant, comfortable rooms. Smells, feels and looks like a hospital.

D *Kim*, 168 Boonyawat Rd, T217721, F226929. Some a/c, grey, uninspired 1970s block with rooms in keeping. Not particularly good value either. **D** *Lampang*, 696 Suan Dok Rd, T217311, F227313. Some a/c, another Chinese hotel with perhaps a touch less frosty staff than most. **D** *Siam*, 260/29 Chatchai Rd, T217472. Some a/c, 4-storey block, bare rooms. Friendly management, restaurant has live music and dancing. **D** *9 Mituna*, 285 Boonyawat Rd, T217438, F2815596. Some a/c, fairly standard Chinese place and rather noisy. **D-E** *Romsri*, 142 Boonyawat Rd, T217054. Some a/c. A bland looking place but clean inside, with large tidy rooms and Western toilets. Good value in this price range. **E** *Sri Sangar*, Suan Dok Rd. A cheap, backpackers place. **E** *TT&T Backpackers Guesthouse*, 55 Pahmai Rd, T225361, mobile 014729827,

TTT@hotmail.com A 10 min walk from town. The traveller's hang out. A friendly English-speaking family run this compound by the riverside, with several old teak houses set in a peaceful garden. The rooms are clean and well kept with fans, shared Western toilets and hot showers. Relaxed atmosphere, good source of information. Motorbike and cycle hire. Recommended.

Thai Mid-range: *Krua Thai*, Phahonyothin Rd (near the *Lampang Wiangthong Hotel*). Good Thai food in an immaculate a/c restaurant or in the adjoining garden. *MacKenna Restaurant*, Tipchang Rd. Reasonable food in open-air wooden house overlooking the river, great place for a drink and a meal. **Cheap**: *Riverside* (*Baan Rim Nam*), 328 Tipchang Rd. Wooden house overlooking the river, attractive ambience, reasonable Thai and international food including Thai salads, rice and noodle dishes, curries, steaks, sandwiches, burgers and spaghetti. Pizzas only served in the evenings and not on every day. Recommended. *Oey Thong Café*, Tipchang Rd (near the bridge), good Thai food in cosy surroundings.

International Lampang seems to have embraced Western culture (that is the Wild Western) with some enthusiasm and Western steakhouse-style restaurants with live bands are popular. Two on Thakrawnoi Rd are the **Mid-range**: *Old Town* and *Larn Ngern* (Million Money).

Fast food *KFC* and *Pizza Hut* in the town centre along Boonyawat Rd.

Foodstalls Near the railway station and around the market (see map, page 251).

Eating
● *on map*
Price categories:
see inside front cover

The Northern Region

Lampang

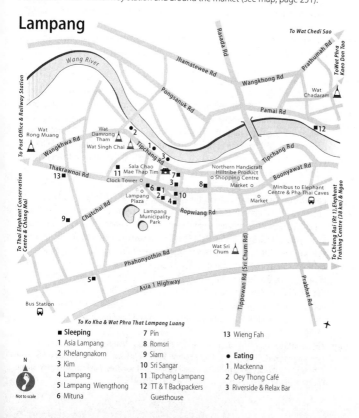

■ **Sleeping**
1 Asia Lampang
2 Khelangnakorn
3 Kim
4 Lampang
5 Lampang Wiengthong
6 Mituna
7 Pin
8 Romsri
9 Siam
10 Sri Sangar
11 Tipchang Lampang
12 TT & T Backpackers Guesthouse
13 Wieng Fah

● **Eating**
1 Mackenna
2 Oey Thong Café
3 Riverside & Relax Bar

Bars *Relax*, Tipchang Rd (next to Riverside Restaurant), modern style bar in wooden building overlooking the river. Cold beer and more, open-air verandah. Riverside (see above) live music most nights, eclectic selection ranging from rock and roll to romantic Thai ballad groups.

Festivals Feb *Luang Wiang Lakon* (movable), 5 important Buddha images are carried through the streets in procession. Traditional dancing and a sound and light show at Wat Lampang Luang.

Massage *Northern Herbal Medicine Society*. Traditional Thai massage in the capable hands of Mrs Lamduan. Good value at ฿150 per hour, 108 herbs available for the full treatment. Opposite Wat Prakaew Don Tao.

Shopping **Ceramics** Lampang is famous for its ceramics. There are more than 50 factories in and around the town; a number are to be found to the west along Phahonyothin Rd (eg, *Chao Lampang* and *Ceramic Art* at 246/1) and Route 1 towards Ko Kha (eg, *Art Lampang*). International outlets selling seconds very cheaply can also be found near Lampang – ask at the TAT office in Chiang Mai for details.

Handicrafts The *Lampang Plaza*, on Ropwiang Rd near the clock tower, sells an assortment of knick-knacks like wind chimes, shells and ceramics from a series of stalls. Another similar outlet is the *Northern Handicraft Hilltribe Shopping Centre*, a small teak house and, unfortunately, not as grand as it sounds.

Department stores *Texas Department Store* in the centre of town, Boonyawat Rd.

Sport **Swimming** The rather small, and at weekends rather crowded, pool at the *Lampang Wiengthong Hotel* is open to non-residents. Open 0800-1800, Mon-Sun.

Transport
See also Ins & outs, page 246
604 km N of Bangkok, 93 km S of Chiang Mai

Local Horse-drawn carriages: ฿80/120 for a tour around town. They generally take 2 routes, the cheaper one takes about 20 mins, the more expensive 45 mins or ฿120 per hour. The drivers, rather incongruously, insist on wearing stetsons, giving the impression that they have been translated from some cowboy epic to small town Lampang. Haggling is required with these John Wayne wannabes. **Saamlors**: ฿10 around town, ฿50 per hour to hire. **Songthaews** run routes around town (although these are flexibly interpreted); the *rop muang* or *rop wiang* ('around town') are the most useful (฿10 anywhere in town).

Long distance **Air**: airport is on the south edge of town, off Prabhat Rd. Daily flights to Bangkok via Phitsanulok. **Train**: station is on the west side of town, at the end of Surain Rd. Regular connections with Bangkok's Hualamphong station (12 hrs) and Chiang Mai (2 hrs). **Bus**: station is on Route 1, just east of the railway line (15 min walk to town centre). It is possible to leave luggage at the information counter in the terminal. Regular connections with Bangkok's Northern bus terminal (9 hrs), Chiang Mai (2 hrs), Chiang Rai, Sukhothai, Tak and Phitsanulok. Buses from Chiang Mai leave from the Old Chiang Mai-Lamphun Rd, near the tourist office. Buses also go east to Phrae and on to Nan; these leave throughout the day, about 1 every hour. **Taxi**: taxis from Chiang Mai leave from the corner of Chang Klan and Tha Phae roads.

Directory **Airline offices** *Thai*, 314 Sanambin Rd, T217078. **Banks** *Thai Farmers*, 284/8 Chatchai Rd. *Siam Commercial*, Chatchai Rd. *Thai Military*, 173-75 Chatchai Rd. **Communications** Post Office: Surain Rd (opposite the railway station). **Medical services** *Khelang Nakom Hospital*, Phahonyothin Rd (near *Lampang Wiengthong Hotel*), T217045.

Lamphun   ลำพูน

Lamphun is perhaps Thailand's oldest preserved town and is easily reached on a day trip from Chiang Mai. It is also one of the region's success stories in terms of inward investment; thousands of local people are employed in export-oriented factories, built on industrial estate around (but out of sight of) the city. If travelling to Lamphun from Chiang Mai it is worthwhile taking the old road, which is lined over a 10 km stretch with an avenue of magnificent yang trees. Only the action of activist monks who ordained the trees saved them from felling a few years back (see page 272 for details).

Phone code: 053
Colour map 1, grid B2
Population: 18,000

The city is situated on the banks of the Ping River and was formerly the capital of the Haripunjaya Kingdom, founded in 660 AD by Queen Chama Devi. The moat and parts of the old defensive walls are still present. Lamphun became a powerful centre of the Mon culture that resisted the advances of the kingdom of Lanna, until King Mengrai succeeded in taking the city in 1281. In so doing, he brought to an end the Chama Devi Dynasty and the last vestige of the once powerful Mons. The Haripunjaya Kingdom was perhaps the most fervently Buddhist of all – unlike other areas, no images of Hindu gods have been found here. Today the town is quietly provincial, clean and neat. The town is also famous for its longans, so much so that in August there is a **Longan Fair**, with a contest to judge the best fruit and another to select the year's Miss Lamyai (longan). Lamphun is a small town and easy enough to walk around – although it is very hot in the hot season. Saamlors are available for the incurably exhausted.

Wat Phra That Haripunjaya is a famous and venerated place of Buddhist teaching. It is best entered from the riverside where *singhas* (guardian lions) flank the entrance. To the right of the singhas the TAT has erected a map detailing the location of the monastery's main structures. Within the wat compound are an assortment of buildings from different eras. The 50 m tall central chedi behind the main central viharn, with its gold nine-tiered honorific umbrella (weighing, apparently, 6,498.75 g), was started in 1043 AD. Also notable is the rare five-stepped pyramid chedi (similar to that at Wat Chama Devi, see below), pierced by niches which originally housed standing Buddha images of decreasing size. Most have long since disappeared. A gigantic bronze gong is housed to the right of the main central viharn and an ancient raised library is on the left. The main central viharn has a phalanx of Buddha images, all in the altitude of subduing Mara, and some lively murals on the inner and outer walls. Outside the main walls of the monastery to the right is a large associated monastery school with two more viharns, an old stupa and several school buildings, and a good selection of sleeping manky dogs. The ubosoth is in a small enclosure just before the main entrance to the wat, on the right, which has fine gilded doors. The wat

Sights

has a small museum. ■ *0900-1200, 1300-1600 Wed-Sun.* Around the monastery, stallholders sell amulets and other Buddhist paraphernalia. During the sixth lunar month a festival and fair are held at the wat on full moon day.

Leaving the wat by the back entrance and almost opposite on Inthayongyot Road is the **Haripunjaya**, or **Lamphun National Museum**. Housed in a

• • • • • • • • • • • • • • • • •
Lamphun place names

Wat Chama Devi
วัดจามเทวี

Wat Kukut
วัดกู่กุด

Wat Phra That Haripunjaya
วัดพระธาตุหริภุญชัย

The Northern Region

modern building, it contains a small but fine collection of Buddhas and other artefacts from the area. ■ *0900-1200, 1300-1600 Wed-Sun, ฿10.*

Better known as Wat Kukut, **Wat Chama Devi** lies 1 km west of the moat on Chama Devi Road. It is said that Princess Chama Devi selected the spot by having an archer shoot an arrow to the north from town: he must have been a very strong man. The wat was originally founded in 755 AD by the Mon. Although many of the wat buildings are unspectacular, this wat is of great architectural significance as it contains the prototype for the rare stepped-pyramid chedi. There is another at Wat Phra That Haripunchaya, also in Lamphun, and another example at Wat Chedi Luang, a few kilometres south of Chiang Mai (see page 267). Built in 1218, this square-based chedi of brick and stucco has five tiers of niches. Each contains a standing Buddha of great beauty in an attitude of dispelling fear, diminishing in size upwards, and thereby giving an illusion of height. The style of the Buddha images is noticeably Dvaravati, with their rather attractive wider faces and elongated ears. Originally the top of the chedi was encased in gold, but this was subsequently removed and the wat became known as Wat Kukut or Wat 'without top'. The chedi contains the ashes of Queen Chama Devi. It is similar in style to Satmahal at Polannaruwa in Sri Lanka. Next to it, in the shadow of the viharn, is the smaller – and also unusual – 12th-century Ratana Chedi, with an octagonal base and standing Buddhas in each layer of niches.

Excursions The **cotton weaving centre** of **Pasang** lies 12 km southwest of Lamphun on Route 106. The market here sells batiks, silk, woodcarvings and other local crafts, as well as cotton cloth. ■ *Getting there: regular songthaews from Lamphun.*

Sleeping Few people stay in Lamphun; most use
Price codes: Chiang Mai as a base and visit here only
see inside front cover as a day trip. **D** *Suphamit Hotel*, Chama Devi Rd (opposite Wat Chama Devi, 1 km west of town), T534865, F534355. New hotel with 70 a/c rooms; hot water showers, large restaurant – rather a barn of a place but comfortable – little English spoken here. **D** *Suan Kaew Bungalow*, 209 Lamphun-Lampang Highway. On the edge of town and offering reasonable rooms with Western bathrooms at good prices. **D-E** *Sri Lamphun*, 51/2 Inthayongyot Rd, T2244176. Just south of Wat Phra That Haripunjaya, rooms are grubby but it is OK for a night or two.

Eating **Cheap** Within and around Wat Phra
● on map That Haripunjaya are several stalls selling
Price categories: simple dishes and drinks. On the road
see inside front cover running down the south wall of the monastery is *Lamphun Ice*, an a/c place good for ice-cream, coffee and cooling off, and with a menu which runs to 16 pages with such delicacies as pig's knuckle and chicken tendon. The name is in Thai only, but it's hard to miss. On the east side of

Lamphun

Rt 106 to Chiang Mai (26 km) & Train Station (2 km)

Rop Muang Nai Rd
Wat Chang Si
Intha Yongyot Rd
To Wat Chama Devi (1 km) & Suphamit Hotel
Rop Muang Rd
Rachawong Rd
Waem Kham (Vankam) Rd
Provincial Office
Wat Mahawan
Rot Kaew Rd
Wat Phra That Haripunjaya
Moat
White Buses to Chiang Mai
Lamphun National Museum
Main Entrance
3 ●
Wat Suphanrangsi
Chaimongkon Rd
2 ●
● 1
Wang Khwa (Wangkaui) Rd
Kuang River
To Lampang
(Pol)

N

To Bus Station

0 metres (approx) 300
0 yards (approx) 300

● Eating
1 Duck Noodle Soup Shop
2 Lamphun Ice
3 Wai Pub & Restaurant

the Wat, just to the left of the main entrance, is the **_Wai Pub and Restaurant_**, another a/c place with OK but scarcely spectacular food. For _Kuaytiaw_ fans, there is a tremendous **_Duck Noodle Soup Shop_** on Inthayongyot Rd, just south of Wat Phra That Haripunjaya (see map).

Aug _Lamyai festival_ (movable), parades, elephant shows, beauty pageant and a competition to judge the sweetest and juiciest lamyai (or longan) fruit.

Festivals

Train The station is just under 2 km north of the city centre off Charoenrat Rd, 5 connections each day with Bangkok and with Chiang Mai. **Bus** The main bus terminal is 500 m south of Wat Haripunjaya on Inthayongyot Rd. There are 2 a/c and 3 non-a/c departures per day from Bangkok's Northern bus terminal (10 hrs). Most people visit Lamphun from Chiang Mai and regular (blue) songthaews run along the Old Lamphun-Chiang Mai Rd, leaving Chiang Mai just over the Nawarat Bridge, near the TAT office (30-40 mins), ∅7. They pass through the middle of Lamphun town, down Inthayong Yot Rd, and can be picked up by the National Museum too.

Transport
26 km to Chiang Mai,
77 km to Lampang,
668 km to Bangkok

Banks Exchange booth within the grounds of Wat Phra That Haripunjaya. **Communications** Post Office: Inthayongyot Rd. **Medical services** _Lamphun Hospital_, Rimping Rd, T511233.

Directory

Chiang Mai   เชียงใหม่

When Reginald Le May wrote about Chiang Mai back in 1938, this was, in his view, one of the loveliest cities imaginable. Life, as they say, has moved on since then. But while old Thailand hands may bemoan lost innocence, Chiang Mai is still a city worth visiting. The monasteries are the most beautiful in the North, there is a rich tradition of arts and crafts, and the moated old city still gives a flavour of the past. And as it is the unofficial 'capital of the North', there are also some good practical reasons to base yourself here. It is an important transport hub, there is an excellent range of hotels and restaurants, the shopping is the best in the North (some say, in all of Thailand), and there are also scores of trekking and other companies offering everything from whitewater rafting to elephant treks. The average length of stay of visitors to Chiang Mai is 2.3 days – perhaps implying that there is not much to do here. This figure, though, reflects itchy feet rather more than it does a lack of distractions or attractions.

Phone code: 053
Colour map 1, grid B2
Population: 200,000

Ins and outs

The quickest way of getting to Chiang Mai is by air. There are multiple flights from Bangkok and also links to some other provincial centres. If travelling from the beaches of the south, travelling by air cuts out a bum-numbing overland journey of 20 hrs or more. Booked locally, flights are also relatively cheap. An attractive alternative is to take the sleeper train – a great experience. Finally, there are scores of buses that make the journey from Bangkok in around 10 hrs – from super-luxury VIP buses through to bone-shaking and nerve-tingling ordinary buses. The network of regional bus connections is also the best outside Bangkok.

Getting there
See also Transport,
page 295

Chiang Mai used to be the quiet sort of place you could wander around on foot or rattle through on a saamlor (bicycle rickshaw). No longer. The traffic may be less frenetic than Bangkok, but this isn't saying much. Sii-lors – converted pick-ups – operate as the main mode of public transport, ferrying people around for a fixed fare. There are also tuk-tuks, some taxis, and a good number of car, motorbike and bicycle hire companies.

Getting around

The Northern Region

Tourist offices *TAT*, 105/1 Chiang Mai-Lamphun Rd, T248604, F248605 (open 0830-1630 Mon-Sun). Helpful and informative, with a good range of maps and leaflets, including information on guesthouses and guidelines for trekking. Areas of responsibility are Chiang Mai, Lamphun, Lampang and Mae Hong Son. *Chiang Mai Municipal Tourist Information Centre*, corner of Tha Phae and Charoen Prathet roads. The only one of its type in Thailand, good maps and some other handouts, but not yet up to TAT standard. Open Mon-Fri 0830-1200, 1300-1630. In addition to these tourist offices, there are also a number of free tourist-oriented magazines, namely: *Trip Info*, *Chiang Mai This Week*, *Le Journal* (in French), *Guidelines Chiang Mai*, *Chiang Mai Newsletter*, *What's On Chiang Mai*, *Good Morning Chiang Mai* and Welcome to Chiang Mai and Chiang Rai These are regularly updated and, although not very selective or critical, have good maps. The *Chiang Mai Newsletter* has the most informed articles. *Nancy Chandler* and *DK Maps* are both good sources of information on Chiang Mai. *Welcome to Chiang Mai & Chiang Rai*, is the best magazine on the market, with information on what's on, where to go, Thai customs, Thai culture and the environment.

History

Around 1290 King Mengrai succeeded in annexing Haripunjaya (Lamphun), the last of the Mon kingdoms. Up until that point, the capital of his kingdom had been Chiang Rai, but with the defeat of Lamphun he decided to move his capital south to a more central location. In 1296 he chose a site on the banks of the Ping River and called his new capital Nopburi Sri Nakawan Ping Chiang Mai, later shortened to Chiang Mai or 'New City'. It is said that he chose the site after seeing a big mouse accompanied by four smaller mice scurry down a hole beneath a holy Bodhi tree (*Ficus religiosa* – the tree under which the Buddha attained enlightenment). This he took to be a good omen, and with his friends King Ramkhamhaeng of Sukhothai and King Ngarm Muang of Phayao, who agreed with the portents, he made this the heart of his kingdom of Lanna *(laan naa)* or a 'million rice fields'. Through his reign, Mengrai succeeded in expanding his kingdom enormously: in 1259 he became King of Chiang Saen; from there he extended the areas under his control to Fang and Chiang Rai; and then, finally, to Haripunjaya. The land in itself was unimportant; King Mengrai was concerned with the control of people, and he spent much of his reign founding new towns which he would settle with people who would then owe him allegiance.

Like his friend King Ramkhamhaeng, Mengrai was a great patron of Theravada Buddhism. He brought monks from Ceylon to unify the country through promoting this religion of both King and commoner. From Mengrai's reign up until the 15th century, Chiang Mai flourished. Towards the end of the 15th century, during the reign of King Tiloka (1442-88), relations with up-and-coming Ayutthaya became strained. The two kingdoms engaged in a series of wars with few gains on either side, although many stories recount the bravery and cunning of each side's warriors. Muen Loknakorn, one of Tiloka's most skilful commanders, is said to have defeated the Ayutthayan army on one occasion by creeping into their camp at night, and cutting the tails off their elephants. With the elephants rampaging around the camp in pain, the Ayutthayans thought they were being attacked and fled in confusion.

Although relations between Chiang Mai and Ayutthaya were fractious, it was actually the Burmese who eventually captured the city of Chiang Mai in 1556. King Bayinnaung, who had unified all of Burma, took Chiang Mai after a battle of three days and the city remained a Burmese regency for the next 220 years. There was constant conflict during these years and by the time the Burmese succeeded in overthrowing Ayutthaya in 1767, the city of Chiang Mai was decimated and depopulated. In 1775, General Taksin united the kingdom of Thailand and a semi-autonomous prince of the Lampang Dynasty was appointed to rule the North. It was not until 1938 that Chiang Mai lost its semi-independence and came under direct rule from Bangkok.

Modern Chiang Mai

Today, Chiang Mai is possibly the second largest city in Thailand, with a population of between 200,000 (the official figure) and perhaps 400,000 (the unofficial, and more likely, figure), a thriving commercial centre as well as a favourite tourist destination. The TAT estimates that 12% of Thailand's tourists travel to Chiang Mai. Its attractions to the visitor are obvious: the city has a rich and colourful history, still evident in the architecture of the city which includes over 300 wats; it is manageable and still relatively 'user friendly' (unlike Bangkok); it has perhaps the greatest concentration of handicraft industries in the country; and it is also an excellent base from which to go trekking and visit the famous hilltribe villages in the surrounding highlands. Chiang Mai has developed into a major tourist centre with a good infrastructure, including excellent hotels and restaurants in all price categories.

In pursuing the tourist dollar, some longtime visitors argue that the city has lost some of its charm in the process. Bangkok's problems of traffic congestion, pollution and frantic property development are now much in evidence in Chiang Mai, albeit on a smaller scale. This is rather ironic in that part of the cause is people escaping congestion, pollution and development in Bangkok – and in so doing bringing the problems with them. Various tax breaks have attracted around 100 companies to Chiang Mai and the surrounding area, which is dotted with industrial estates, factories and warehouses.

In December 1995 Chiang Mai hosted the Southeast Asian Games and in 1996 the city celebrated its 700th anniversary. Although all this attention was intended to mark Chiang Mai's 'coming of age', some locals and long time visitors regret the attention that it has received. In 1998, 1.8 million tourists visited the city – several times more than its total population – and some tourists are returning disappointed that 'what was clearly once a beautiful place is now a concrete wilderness of bleak treeless highways, snarling exhausts and very few Thai smiles' (letter from a foreign tourist to the *Bangkok Post*). Nonetheless, Reginald Le May's observations of 1938 are not entirely redundant:

> Chiangmai possesses a singular beauty. I was stationed there in 1913, and again in 1915, and completely succumbed to its charms; and when I visited it afresh in 1927, after 12 years' absence, I found it more enchanting than ever, with its brick-red palace-fort surrounded by a lotus-filled moat dating from about 1350, its shady avenues, its broad flowing river, and its innumerable temples each within its leafy garden, where the tiled roofs and stately stupas, the swept courtyards, the green mango trees and the heavenly blue sky above all combined to induce a feeling of such peace and happiness as it would be hard to match elsewhere.

On a clear day at the beginning of the cold season, or perhaps after the rains have begun towards the end of the hot season, Chiang Mai's strategic location becomes all too evident. Mountains surround the city to the north, west and east, enclosing a large and rich bowl of rice fields drained by the Ping River. With Doi Suthep to the west still clothed in trees, and the famous golden chedi of Wat Phrathat Doi Suthep glittering on its slopes, it is still a magical place.

The Northern Region

Sights

Chiang Mai is centred on a square moat and defensive wall built during the 19th century, although their origins lie in the late 13th century. The four corner bastions are reasonably preserved (although parts of the wall have been rather insensitively rebuilt) and are a useful reference point when roaming the city. Much of the rest of the town's walls were demolished during the Second World War and the bricks used for road construction. Not surprisingly, given Chiang Mai's turbulent history, many of the more important and interesting wats are located within the city walls which is – surprisingly – the least built-up part. Modern commercial development has been concentrated to the east of the city, and now well beyond the Ping River.

Wat Chiang Man
Within the Old City map, page 275

Situated in the northeast of the walled town, Wat Chiang Man is on Rachpakinai Road within a peaceful compound. The wat is the oldest in the city and was built by King Mengrai soon after he had chosen the site for his new capital in 1296. It is said that he resided here while waiting for his new city to be constructed and also spent the last years of his life at the monastery. The wat is Northern Thai in style, most clearly evident in the gilded woodcarving and fretwork which decorate the various pavilions. The gold-topped chedi *Chang Lom* is supported by rows of elephants, similar to those of the two chedis of the same name at Si Satchanalai and Sukhothai. Two ancient Buddha images are contained behind bars within the viharn, on the right-hand side as you enter the compound. One is the tiny crystal Buddha, *Phra Sae Tang Tamani* (standing 10 cm high). This image, possibly originally from Lopburi, is thought to have been brought to Chiang Mai from Lamphun by King Mengrai in 1281, where it had already resided for 600 years. The second is the stone Buddha, *Phra Sila* (literally, 'Stone Buddha'), in bas-relief, believed to have originated in India or Ceylon about 2,500 years ago. It is supposed to have been made by Ajatacatru at Rajagriha in India, after the death of the Buddha and contains his relics. From India it was taken to Ceylon, and from there was brought by monks to Chiang Mai after first residing at both Sukhothai and Lampang. The image is carved in a dark stone, later gilded over, and shows the Buddha taming the wild elephant Nalagiri, sent to kill him by Ajatacatru. Both the Phra Sae Tang Tamani and the Phra Sila are believed to have the power to bring rain, and are paraded through the streets of Chiang Mai and drenched in water during the Songkran Festival in April at the end of the dry season. Wat Chiang

Chiang Mai place names

Folk Art Museum	Wat Ku Tao
พิพิธภัณฑ์ศิลปพื้นบ้าน	วัดกู่เต่า
Wat Chedi Luang	Wat Phra Singh
วัดเจดีย์หลวง	วัดพระสิงห์
Wat Chiang Man	Wat Suan Dok
วัดเชียงมั่น	วัดสวนดอก
Wat Duang Dii	Wat Umong
วัดดวงดี	วัดอุโมงค์
Wat Jed Yod	
วัดเจ็ดยอด	

Man is an excellent place to see the full range of wat buildings, and how architectural designs have evolved. The largest structure is an extensively renovated viharn; gaudy to most Western tastes. Behind it is the Chedi Chang Lom; to the left of the chedi, a raised *hor trai* or scripture library (raised to protect the scriptures from pests and flooding); to the left of this a fine, old *bot* or ordination hall, identifiable from the *bai sema* that surround it. On the right-hand side of the compound are monks' dormitories or *kutis*, the abbot's own abode, a second, smaller viharn and a bell tower. Taken together, these structures make up the main elements of a large monastery.

To the northeast of Chiang Man, just outside the city walls, is the lesser known Wat Pa Pao. It is worth rooting out because it is so different in style from other monasteries in the city; it is Shan. The wat is just outside the northeastern corner of the moat. A narrow soi leads off the busy road through an archway and into the wat's peaceful and rather ramshackle compound. The wat's name means 'Grove [Pa] of Pao Trees'. The wat was founded more than 400 years ago by a Shan monk. King Inthawichayanon (r 1871-97) – whose consort was Shan – built the chedi and the distinctive viharn which stands close by, in 1891. The chedi is a melange of stuccoed animals from singhas to nagas, while the flat-roofed viharn, with its dark and atmospheric interior, contains three Buddha images. The bot, which is usually locked, is at the back of the compound – identifiable by its tiered, Shan-style roof. The interior is rather plain though, with three more Buddha images and little else. The monks at the wat are, as one would expect, Shan – most having come here from Burma over the last few years – and it continues to serve Chiang Mai's Shan community. What is particularly charming about Wat Pa Pao is its rather abandoned and forgotten air, a result of the fact that it does not receive the funds and patronage of the city's better known monasteries.

Wat Phra Singh, or 'Temple of the Lion Buddha', is arguably Chiang Mai's most important and certainly its largest wat. There is a useful plan of the temple compound in Thai and English, just inside the main entrance on the right. It is situated in the west quarter of the old city and is impressively positioned at the end of Phra Singh Road. The wat was founded in 1345 and contains a number of beautiful buildings decorated with fine woodcarving. Towards the back of the compound is the intimate *Lai Kham Viharn*, which houses the venerated Phra Buddha Singh image. It was built between 1385 and 1400 and the walls are decorated with early 18th-century murals. Two walls are painted in the more rustic Lanna Thai style, and depict women weaving and the traditional costumes of the north. Another two walls are printed in central Thai style: here there are Burmese noblemen, central Thai princes, court scenes and battles. The two sets of murals make a fascinating contrast. The former concentrate on the lives of ordinary people; the latter on the élites. The *Phra Buddha Sihing* is yet another image, with a colourful and rather doubtful provenance. It is said to have come from Ceylon by a rather roundabout route (see page 698), but as art historians point out, is Sukhothai in style. The head, which was stolen in 1922, is a copy. Among the other buildings in the wat is an attractive raised library (*hor trai*), with intricate carved wood decorations, inset with mother-of-pearl.

On Phra Pokklao Road, to the east of Wat Phra Singh, is the 500-year-old ruined chedi or Wat Chedi Luang, which once stood some 90 m high. Built initially in 1401 and then substantially enlarged between 1475 and 1478 by King Tiloka, the chedi was partially destroyed during an earthquake in 1545 and

The Northern Region

Wat Phra Singh
*Chiang Mai map,
page 260.
The best time to come
here is shortly after 1700
when the sun is setting;
the buildings are aglow
& the monks are up &
about in the cool of the
early evening*

**Wat Chedi
Luang**
*Within the Old City map,
page 275*

never rebuilt. After an interlude of a mere 450 years, the Fine Arts Department recently restored the chedi. It is now a charming place to wander around, set in a sizeable compound with huge trees at the boundaries, protected due to their presence within the wat compound. Judging by the remains, it must have been an impressive monument, especially as the entire chedi was encased in metal plates, covered with gold leaf. The wat has two particular claims to fame: during the 15th century, the east niche of the chedi housed the famous Emerald Buddha, now in Bangkok; and second, King Mengrai is believed to have been

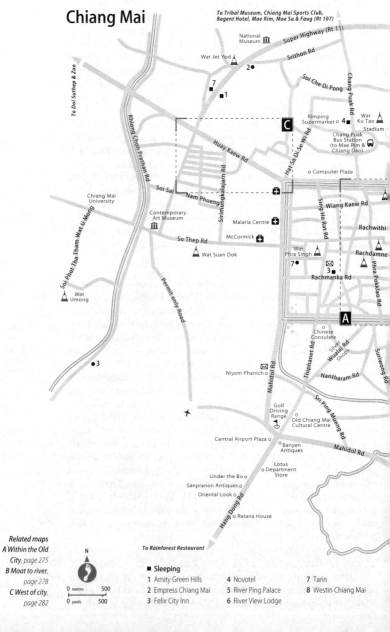

Chiang Mai

To Tribal Museum, Chiang Mai Sports Club,
Regent Hotel, Mae Rim, Mae Sa & Faug (Rt 107)

National Museum
Super Highway (Rt 11)
Wat Jet Yod
Srithon Rd
2
Soi Che Di Pong
7
1
Chiang Puak Rd
Wat Ku Tao
Rimping Supermarket
4
Stadium
Chang Puak Bus Station (to Mae Rim & Chiang Dao)
Computer Plaza
Huay Kaew Rd
Sirimungkalajarn Rd
Hat Sa Di-Sae Wi Rd
C
Soi Sai
Nam Phueng Rd
Khlong Chon Prathan Rd
Wiang Kaew Rd
To Doi Suthep & Zoo
Chiang Mai University
Contemporary Art Museum
Malaria Centre
Sing Ha Rat Rd
Rachwithi
Su Thep Rd
McCormick
Rachdamne
Wat Suan Dok
Wat Phra Singh
7
Phra Pokklao Rd
Rachmanka Rd
3
Soi Phut Tha Tham Wat U Mong
Wat Umong
A
Permit only Road
Chinese Consulate
Silver Wualai Rd Shops
Suriwong Rd
3
Niyom Phanich
Mahidol Rd
Thiphanet Rd
Nantharam Rd
Golf Driving Range
Old Chiang Mai Cultural Centre
Sri Ping Mung Rd
Central Airport Plaza
Banyen Antiques
Mahidol Rd
Lotus Department Store
Under the Bo
Sanpranon Antiques
Oriental Look
Hang Dong Rd
Ratana House

To Rainforest Restaurant

Related maps
A Within the Old City, page 275
B Moat to river, page 278
C West of city, page 282

N
0 metres 500
0 yards 500

■ **Sleeping**
1 Amity Green Hills
2 Empress Chiang Mai
3 Felix City Inn
4 Novotel
5 River Ping Palace
6 River View Lodge
7 Tarin
8 Westin Chiang Mai

killed by a bolt of lightning in the temple compound. Only the Buddha in the northern niche is old; the others are reproductions. To the west of the chedi is a reclining Buddha in an open pavilion. The airy viharn still contains a mid-15th century standing Buddha, along with a series of framed paintings depicting some of the jataka stories. **NB** Women are not permitted to climb the steps of the chedi. Chiang Mai's rather uninteresting **Lak Muang**, or city pillar, is found in a small shrine close to the large viharn, at the western side of the monastery compound. This phallic-looking pillar – some scholars maintain that it

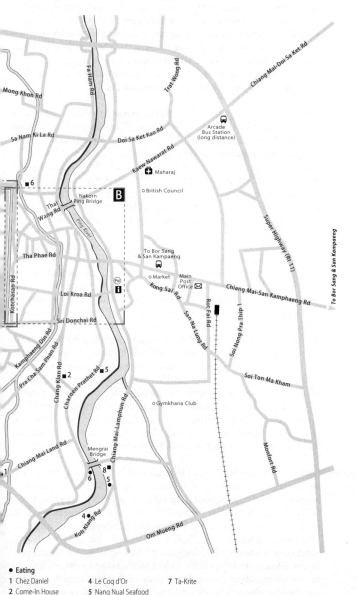

The Northern Region

● **Eating**

1 Chez Daniel	4 Le Coq d'Or	7 Ta-Krite
2 Come-In House	5 Nang Nual Seafood	
3 Gallery	6 Our Place	

is meant to symbolize an emerging rice seedling – is the foundation stone of the city and home to Chiang Mai's guardian spirits. These must be periodically appeased if the city is to prosper. So while it might not be very beautiful or exciting, it is significant.

Wat Duang Dii
Within the Old City map, page 275

Also within the city walls, just north of the intersection of Rachdamnern and Phra Pokklao roads, is a haven of peace at Wat Duang Dii. The compound contains three Northern Thai wooden temple buildings, with fine woodcarving and attractively weathered doors. Note the small, almost Chinese-pagoda roofed, structure to the left of the gate with its meticulous stucco work. Behind the viharn and bot is a square-based chedi with elephants at each corner, and topped with copper plate. Close by is the less attractive **Wat Umong** – not to be confused with the other of the same name, see below – with a pair of formerly stucco-clad chedis, now weathered down to brick. **Wat Mengrai** is situated in the southern quarter of the city.

Wat Suan Dok
Chiang Mai map, page 260

Outside the walls, Wat Suan Dok (or Wat Bupharam [not to be confused with the monastery of the same name on Tha Phae Road]) lies to the west of town on Suthep Road. Originally built in 1371 but subsequently much restored and enlarged, the wat contains the ashes of Chiang Mai's royal family, housed in many white, variously-shaped, mini-chedis. Much of the monastery was erected during the reign of King Kawila (1782-1813). Not content with just one relic, the large central chedi is said to house eight relics of the Lord Buddha. On the sides of its base are four finely moulded brick and stucco naga slipways and gates. The large, open-walled viharn which confronts the visitor on entering the complex displays some good woodcarving on its exterior walls, but in other respects is rather disappointing: impressive only for its sheer size. The two large Buddha images, placed back-to-back at one end of the building, are regarded by art historians as artistically inferior. However, while their style may be crude, the standing Buddha which faces out of the back of the viharn is unusual for its mudra. Initially it seems that this large monastery has no bot or ordination hall. To find it, walk around the 'university' buildings (the wat is an important teaching monastery) behind the viharn. The bot is usually open to the public and has a large, brightly-lit, gilded bronze Buddha image in the Chiang Saen style, seated in an attitude of subduing Mara. The walls are decorated with lively, rather gaudy, scenes from the jataka stories. Above the entrance is a mural showing the Buddha's mother being impregnated by a white elephant (highly auspicious), while on the left-hand wall is depicted (along with several other episodes from the Buddha's life) the moment when, as a prince (note the fine clothes and jewellery), he renounces his wealth and position and symbolically cuts his hair. The wat is also a centre of Thai traditional massage – ask one of the monks for information.

Wat Umong
Chiang Mai map, page 260

Continuing west on Suthep Road is the turn-off for Wat Umong, about 1 km off the road down a narrow lane (turn left almost opposite the gates to CMU, just past a market travelling west). The wat was founded in 1371 by King Ku Na (1355-85) who promoted the establishment of a new, ascetic school of forest dwelling monks. In 1369 he brought a leading Sukhothai monk to Chiang Mai – the Venerable Sumana – and built Wat Umong for him and his followers. Sumana studied here until his death in 1389. Although the wat is at the edge of the city, it feels much more distant, with areas of woodland, a ruined chedi and the artificial tunnels after which the wat is named. Inside the tunnels are niches with Buddha images. The wat was abandoned in the 19th century and the chedi pillaged for its treasures some years later. It became a functioning wat again in 1948. From the trees hang Thai proverbs and sayings from the Buddhist texts, extolling pilgrims to lead good and productive lives. Above the tunnels is a modern statue of the fasting Buddha, reduced to skin and bones. Vivid, almost lurid, murals decorate one building and the wat is a centre for meditation and teaching, with a small library. ■ *Getting there: take a songthaew or bus (Nos 1 and 4) along Suthep Rd and ask to be let off at the turning for Wat Umong. It is about a 1 km walk from here.*

The Chiang Mai Contemporary Art Museum opened in 1998 on the corner of Nimmahaemin and Suthep roads. Housed in a large modern structure, this Chiang Mai University-run museum displays modern fine art, including paintings, sculpture, installation works and prints by mostly Thai artists. There are occasional temporary exhibitions of work by non-Thais. Other activities include concerts and puppet shows (T933833 for information). It is interesting for displaying the progress of Thai fine art, but hardly world class. The small but chic attached Art Café and shop (selling books and ceramics) is classier than the works displayed. ■ *0930-1700 Tue-Sun, ฿50.*

The Chiang Mai Contemporary Art Museum
Chiang Mai map, page 260

The beautiful Wat Jet Yod (literally, 'seven spires'), is just off the 'superhighway' at the intersection with Ladda Land Road, northwest of the city and close to the National Museum. It was begun in 1453 and contains a highly unusual square chedi with seven spires. These represent the seven weeks the Buddha resided in the gardens at Bodhgaya, after his enlightenment under the Bodhi tree. According to the chronicles the structure is a copy of the 13th-century Mahabodhi temple in Pagan, Burma, which itself was a copy of the famous temple at Bodhgaya in Bihar (although it is hard to see the resemblance). On the faces of the chedi are an assortment of superbly modelled stucco figures in bas relief, while at one end is a niche containing a large Buddha image – dating from 1455 – in an attitude of subduing Mara (now protected behind steel bars). The stucco work represents the 70 celestial deities and are among the finest works from the Lanna School of art. They are wonderfully modelled, flying, their expressions serene. At the back of the compound is the small **Phra Chedi** and associated bot, both raised off the ground on a small brick platform. Next to this is a much larger chedi, with four niches containing images of the Buddha subduing Mara. Unfortunately, the wat was ransacked by the Burmese in 1566 and its buildings were badly damaged. The stucco facing of the original structures has in large part disappeared, leaving only attractively weathered brick. A new, gaudy, gold and red viharn rather detracts from the 'lost city' atmosphere of the compound.

Wat Jed Yod
Chiang Mai map, page 260

The National Museum lies just to the east of Wat Jet Yod on Highway 11. It is a cool relief from 'wat spotting' and has a fine collection of Buddha images and Sawankhalok china downstairs, as well as some impressive ethnological exhibits upstairs. ■ *0900-1600 Wed-Sun, ฿30. Getting there: on bus No 6.*

The National Museum
Chiang Mai map, page 260

Wat Ku Tao (on Chiang Mai map, page 260), to the north of the city off Chotana Road, dates from 1613. It is situated in a leafy compound and has an unusual chedi, shaped like a pile of inverted alms bowls.

Other wats

Given that Chiang Mai has over 300 wats, there are a great many to choose from. Others worth a fleeting visit for those not yet 'watted out' include: **Wat Chetawan**, **Wat Mahawan**, **Wat Saen Fang** and **Wat Bupharam**– all on Tha Phae Road (all Moat to River map, page 278) – between the east walls of the city and the Ping River. **Wat Mahawan** displays some accomplished woodcarving on its viharn, washed in a delicate yellow, while the white stupa is guarded by a fearsome array of singhas – mythical lions – some with bodies hanging from their gaping jaws. **Wat Bupharam** has two, fine old viharns (*viharn yai*, 'big'; *lek*, 'small'), a new and rather gaudy raised viharn, a small bot and a white stupa. Of the viharns, the finest is the viharn lek, built about 300 years ago in Lanna Thai style. The small 'nave' is crowded with Buddha images and features Chinese plates, adhered to the wooden ceiling. The façade of the viharn – which is in need of funds for renovation – has some fine woodcarving. Also impressive are the carved doors of the viharn yai; note the carving of the Buddha subduing the wild elephant Nalagiri, sent to attack him.

Night Market
Moat to River map, page 278

The Night Market or Night Bazaar dominates the west side of Chang Klan Road; it consists of a number of purpose-built buildings with hundreds of stalls, selling a huge array of tribal goods as well as clothing, jewellery, tapes etc (see page 289). The market has been expanding year-by-year so that it now extends virtually down the whole length of Chang Klan Road, from the intersection with Tha Phae south to Loi Kroa. For a completely different atmosphere, walk through Chiang Mai's 'Chinatown' which lies to the north of Tha Phae Road, between the moat and the river. True to form, this area buzzes with business activity. Small workshops run by entrepreneurial Sino-Thais jostle between excellent small restaurants serving reasonably priced Thai and Chinese food. Near the river, and running two or three streets in from the river, is the Warorot Market (on Moat to River map, page 278), Chiang Mai's largest. Close to the river, along Praisani Road, it is a flower market. But walking away from the river, it becomes a mixed market with fruit and vegetables, dried fish, pigs' heads and trotters, great dollops of buffalo flesh, crabs, dried beans, and deep fried pork skin. Further on still, there are several large covered market areas with clothes, textiles, toys, shoes, leather goods, Chinese funeral accessories, stationery and baskets. Showing that this is truly the heart of Chiang Mai's Chinese community, there is a small Chinese temple one street in from the river on Vichayanon Road – Wat Poong Tao Kong, with fine dragons, lots of incense and two imaginative fish ponds. You can buy paper money – which is burnt during funeral celebrations so that the dead person has sufficient funds to live in the manner to which they were accustomed (or would have liked to have been) – from the market. Very practical; very Chinese. Another much smaller, but charming, market is Thon Payom Market (on West of the City map, page 282), on the corner of Suthep Road and the 'Canal Road' (Thanon Chonprathaan). There's not much for the tourist to buy here, but it is colourful and the food is good: snacks of barbecue chicken, sticky rice and mango (in season), great fruit and cold drinks. It is a mixed fresh and dried goods market, with assorted other stalls selling clothes, knives, baskets and the like. In the evening, stalls open up all along this side of Suthep Road from the market running east back towards town.

Museum of World Insects & Natural Wonders
West of the City map, page 282. This quirky little bug museum makes for some light entertainment on a hot afternoon

Established in 1999 by Manop and Rampa Rattanarithikul, this eccentric couple take pleasure in showing you around their house which has become a mausoleum for thousands of creatures you would rather not find in your shoes, let alone your pants. Rampa's specialism is mosquitoes: there are 420 species of mosquito in Thailand (all on show here, not that they make for particularly scintillating viewing), 18 of which she personally identified and categorized, travelling to London to check the type specimens in the National History Museum. Interesting collection of shells, fossils, petrified wood and, of course, case after case of bugs including beetles, moths, roaches and butterflies. ■ *0900-1630 daily, ฿100, ฿50 for children. Situated west of town at 72 Nimanhaemin Soi 13 (near Sirimungkalajarn 3), T211891, F410916, insects_museum@hotmail.com*

At the end of Huay Kaew Road, west of town at the foot of Doi Suthep, is Chiang Mai Zoo, which occupies a huge area – 85 ha in all – on a steep wooded hillside overlooking Chiang Mai. If you have time on your hands, it is well worth a visit – but be prepared for a considerable amount of steep walking, which can be exhausting, especially in the hot season. But there are plenty of drinks stops and some good foodstalls to keep you going. The highlights are the hippos: about six of them stand at the bottom of a water filled pit with their mouths open, waiting to be fed by the public. The game is to toss the food into their gaping jaws. Other notable animals incarcerated here – along with the usual rhinos, elephants, crocs, deer et al – are the giant catfish (pla buk, from the Mekong) and the open piranha tank (watch toddlers here). While it is not up to top zoo standards, Chiang Mai Zoo is a much better example than most in the region. There is an Arboretum (0900-1730, ฿10 adults, ฿5 children) and Fitness Park next to the zoo. ■ 0800-1700 Mon-Sun, ฿10, adults, ฿5 children. Getting there: No 3 bus from Chang Puak Gate, or songthaew.

Chiang Mai Zoo
Around Chiang Mai map, page 267

Excursions

Overlooking Chiang Mai, 16 km to the northwest, is Doi Suthep, Suthep mountain. A steep winding road climbs 1,000 m to the base of a 300-step naga staircase, which in turn leads up to **Wat Phrathat**, usually known by visitors simply as Doi Suthep (*doi* is the Northern word for mountain; in Thai, *Khao*). Come here on Sundays to see Thais at worship; or come here during the week for a slightly quieter experience. Avoid the climb by taking the cable car, which was due for completion in 2000. A white elephant is alleged to have collapsed here, after King Kuena (1367-85) gave it the task of finding a propitious site for a shrine to house a holy relic of the Lord Buddha. A chedi was built to house the relic, which was embellished and extended two centuries later.

Doi Suthep
A very popular pilgrimage spot for Thais, perched on the hillside & offering spectacular views of the city & plain below

The 24 m high chedi, recently replated, is topped with a five-tiered honorific parasol. There are a number of Buddha images in both Sukhothai and Chiang Saen styles, arrayed in the gallery surrounding the chedi. The whole compound is surrounded by bells (which visitors can ring) and meditation instruction is available at the wat. When James McCarthy visited Chiang Mai and Doi Suthep at the end of the 19th century (he was employed by the government of Siam as a surveyor and adviser), the city had just suffered a prolonged dry spell. As water was channelled the 12 km from the hill, it was assumed that the chief of Chiang Mai had somehow offended the spirits of the chedi. An angel, allegedly, appeared to the man and insisted he surmount it with a new, precious stone-encrusted finial. He was then enjoined to parade around the city with his finest elephants to propitiate the offended spirits. ■ Getting there: songthaew from Mani Noparat Rd, by Chang Puak Gate (฿30 up, ฿20 down), or take bus No 3 to the zoo and then change onto a minibus. A taxi should cost about ฿200 return. The temple is closed after 1630.

Five kilometres past Wat Phrathat, Phu Ping Palace is the winter residence of the King. The immaculate gardens are open 0830-1630 Friday-Sunday and public holidays, when the Royal Family is not in residence. ■ Getting there: the Doi Suthep minibus continues on to the Phu Ping Palace.

Phu Ping Palace

Four kilometres past Phu Ping Palace, down a deteriorating track, is this rather commercialized Meo village. Nonetheless, it is worth a visit for those unable to get to other, more traditional, villages. There are two second-rate museum huts, one focusing on opium production, the other on the different hilltribes. On the hillside above the village is a rather unexpected English flower garden, which is in full bloom in January. ■ Getting there: charter a songthaew or take a

Doi Pui

The Northern Region

minibus from Mani Noparat Rd, by Chang Puak Gate, and then charter a songthaew from Doi Suthep.

Tribal Museum A new Tribal Museum, attached to the Tribal Research Institute, has opened overlooking a lake in Rachamangkhla Park, 5 km north of town off Chotana Road. The building itself looks like a cross between a rocket and a chedi and it houses the fine collection of tribal pieces that were formerly held at Chiang Mai University's Tribal Research Centre. Carefully and professionally presented, the pieces on show include, for example, textiles, agricultural implements, musical instruments, jewellery and weapons. The museum has plans to set up a website. A slide and video show is screened at 1000 and 1400. The museum is particularly worth visiting for those intending to go trekking (see page 273). ■ *0900-1600 Mon-Fri, T221933.*

Wiang Kum Kam

The gardens & ruins here are very beautiful & peaceful, dotted with bodhi trees

Wiang Kum Kam is a ruined former city, 5 km south of Chiang Mai. A *wiang* is a fortified site, and Wiang Kum Kam was an outlier of the Mon Haripunjaya Kingdom which had its capital at Lamphun. The city was established by the Mon in the 12th or 13th centuries (according to tradition it was built in 1286) and was not abandoned until the 18th century. Today, archaeologists are gradually beginning to uncover the site which covers an area of about 9 sq km and contains the remains of at least 20 wats. The site was discovered in 1984 when rumours surfaced that a hoard of valuable amulets were to be found in the grounds of Wat Chang Kham. Treasure seekers began to dig up the grounds of the monastery until the Fine Arts Department intervened and began a systematic survey of the site to reveal Wiang Kum Kam. The most complete monument is **Wat Kan Thom** (in Thai, Wat Chang Kham), which has a marvellous bronze naga outside. In front of the wat is the spirit chamber of the great King Mengrai (?-1317), who founded the city of Chiang Mai and who through military prowess and diplomatic verve substantially enlarged the kingdom of Lanna Thai. It is believed his spirit still resides here and consequently is a highly revered place. Nearby are the ruins of **Wat Noi** and two dilapidated chedis. Perhaps the most impressive single structure is the renovated chedi at **Wat Chedi Liam**. This takes the form of a stepped pyramid – a unique Mon architectural style of which there are only a handful of examples in Thailand (the best example hereabouts is at Wat Phra That Haripunjaya in Lamphun, see page 253). Each of the niches, which diminish in size up the pyramidal tower, contains an image of the Buddha in a different mudra. The chedi is surmounted by a gold harmika. The original chedi was probably built around 1286, although it has been extensively renovated over the years. While Wat Chedi Liam may be the most impressive building, the most important

* *

Chiang Mai excursions

Bor Sang	Mae Sa Valley
บ่อสร้าง	แม่สาวาเลย์
Chiang Dao Caves	Pasang
ถ้ำเขียงดาว	ป่าซาง
Doi Pui	Phu Ping Palace
ดอยปุย	พระราชตำหนักภูพิงค์ราชนิเวศน์
Doi Suthep	Wiang Kum Kam
ดอยสุเทพ	เวียงกุมกาม

archaeological discovery has been a series of inscriptions which seem to indicate that King Ramkhamhaeng was not the 'inventor' of the Thai script, but rather made adaptations to a script that was already in use (see box, page 211).

Transport Accessible by bicycle or motorbike, or by tuk-tuk. There are 2 ways to get here. Either take Route 106 south towards Lamphun; the ruins are signposted off to the right about 5 km from Chiang Mai – but only in Thai – from where it is another 2 km. Look out for a ruined chedi on the right and ask along the way for confirmation. To get to Wat Kan Thom, take the yellow sign to the left about 800 m from the main road. It's about a 10-15 min walk from the main road. For Wat Chedi Liam, follow the land all the the way to the river road (Koh Klang Rd), about 2 km or so, and turn left. The Wat is about 200 m down here, on the left – impossible to miss. An alternative route is to drive south down Koh Klang Rd, which runs off Om Muang Rd and follows the east bank of the river south. Wat Chedi Liam is on the left a couple of kilometres down here.

A pleasant day round trip takes you out east of the city, visiting craft centres, a couple of interesting wats, some incredible caves, and a hot spring – in total, a 75 km trip. This can only be undertaken by private transport.

Bor Sang & San Kamphaeng Circuit

Almost immediately after leaving the built-up area of the city driving along Route 1006 (Charoen Muang Road) running east, workshops and showrooms start to appear, and continue for a full 15 km all the way to **Bor Sang**. This ribbon development has become a very popular jaunt for tour groups, who visit kilns, paper factories, lacquerware establishments and (hopefully) spend plenty of money along the way. If you can't face the crowds in the Night Market, this kind of shopping might suit you better. Bor Sang is best known for its paper umbrellas, handmade and then painted. The shaft is crafted from local

The Northern Region

Around Chiang Mai

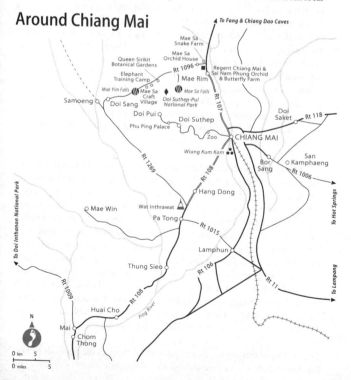

softwood, the ribs from bamboo, and the covering from oiled rice paper. The Umbrella Festival in January is a colourful affair. While Bor Sang is best known for its umbrellas, there's a lot more here. There is also one interesting monastery: Wat Buak Khrok Luang. To get here, turn right off Route 1006 down a soi before entering Bor Sang proper (it is signposted). The wat is 100 m or so down the soi. It is worth coming here for two reasons: one, because few people do so, and two, because the 19th-century Lanna-style viharn has some great murals. As usual the most arresting are those depicting visions of hell, on the right-hand wall, near the main door. All manner of gruesome fates await miscreants: boiling, impaling, disembowelling and various other things. Beyond Bor Sang is **San Kamphaeng**, another craft village which has expanded and diversified so that it has effectively merged with Bor Sang – at least in terms of shopping. If you make it as far as San Kampaeng, there is a good Muslim restaurant at the intersection with the main road (left hand, near side) serving chicken biryani, other Indian dishes, ice-creams and cappuccino.

For **Wat Pa Tung**, which is 10 km on from San Kamphaeng, take a right-hand fork onto route 1147. At the junction with route 1317, cross over the road (signposted towards the Chiang Mai-Lamphun Golf Club). Where the road takes a sharp right (with another signpost for the Golf Club), continue straight ahead on the minor road. About 3 km on is Wat Pa Tung. This wat is a lively and popular modern wat, set amongst sugar palms and ricefields. Its popularity rests on the fact that the revered Luang Phu La Chaiya Janto lived here to the ripe old age of 96. When he died in 1993 his rather diminutive body was placed in a sealed glass coffin, and a stilted modern kuti built to house it and him.

From Wat Pa Tung, return to Route 1317 and turn right. After about 10 km, on the left, you will see a rocky outcrop with flags fluttering from the top; this is the only marker for the **Muang On Caves**. Take a left turning (no sign in English) and wind up a lane, past a forest of ordained (*buat*) trees, to the car park. From here there are around 170 steps up a naga staircase to the entrance to the caves, with great views over the valley. Once inside, you probably take about the same number of steps down again. Watch out; the entrance is tricky and the steps are very steep, with low overhangs of rock. But it is worth the sweating and bending: the cave opens up into a series of impressive caverns. The lower one has a large stalagmite wrapped with sacred cloth and a number of images of the Buddha. Drink stalls at the car park. ■ ฿10.

At the foot of the hill (before returning to the main road), take a left turn for the back route to the **Roong Arun Hot Springs** (2½ km). Here, sulphur springs bubble up into an artificial pond, where visitors can buy chicken or quail eggs to boil in wicker baskets hung from bamboo rods. The springs reach around 107°C, so no chance of a quick dip here. However, the 'resort' provides public baths, where the water is cooled (฿60), or a whole range of massages, mud baths, saunas, herbal or otherwise. There is also a swimming pool (฿80) and attractive and colourful gardens. The resort sells Visunee Cosmetics, made from the Roong Arun spring water (Lancôme are no doubt quaking in their elegant shoes). There is **A-B** *Roong Arun Hot Springs Resort*, T248475, with air-conditioned bungalows with pleasant sitting rooms (which have open fires for the cool season) and access to the resort's swimming pool, jacuzzi, sauna etc. ■ *Entrance to the Springs is ฿20 adult, ฿10 children.*

The final leg of this day trip is a 10 km wander through the ricefields to **Wat Doi Saket**. Follow your nose meandering along with country lane until you reach a T-junction – here, turn right towards Wat Doi Saket. Set impressively on top of a hill (but views obscured by trees), this large modern wat is not particularly interesting. But the viharn has some unusual modern murals, painted in the 1990s in 'magic realist' style. Gruesome painted images line the route to the wat. More fun is the market at the foot of the hill. Return to Chiang Mai by way of Route 118 – around a 20 minutes' drive.

There is an attractive loop drive that can easily be accomplished in a day from Chiang Mai, along the Mae Sa Valley to Samoeng and then back along Route 1269 – a little over 100 km in total. For those who want to pootle, there is accommodation available along the route. Travel north on Route 107 out of town and then turn west onto Route 1096, in the district town of Mae Rim. At the corner, during the season (January-April), it is usually possible to buy strawberries at about ฿40 a kilo (make sure they are well washed before you eat them though – pesticides are used with abandon by many farmers). From here the road follows the course of the Mae Sa River. There are a number of attractions that have developed along this route, largely because it is within reach of Chiang Mai and is on the tour group itinerary. At the 20 km mark, about 4 km from the main road, is a turning to the *Regent Chiang Mai*, the most exclusive hotel in the Chiang Mai region (see page 283). Near the entrance to the hotel are a couple of exclusive shops selling 'antiques' (rather pretentious and overpriced), one being Lanna House (no children under 12 allowed inside). Better is the TiTa art gallery, about 500 m further on past the Regent Chiang Mai's main entrance (see Shopping below, under art, page 290). The **Sai Nam Phung Orchid and Butterfly Farm** is to be found here too. It has the best selection of orchids in the area as well as a small butterfly enclosure (unusual jewellery for sale).

The **Mae Sa Snake Farm** is just a short distance on from there, on the main road. There are three shows daily at 1130, 1415 and 1530, ฿100. At the Km 5 marker is the sign for the Tad Mok Waterfalls, which lie 9 km off the main road to the right. These are less popular than the Mae Sa Falls a couple of kilometres on from here (see below), but worthwhile. The road to the falls is sealed; continue on along a dirt track (four-wheel drive only) to some Hmong villages. Continuing west on the main road, there are two more **orchid gardens**: the first (Suan Bua Mae Sa Orchid) between the Km 5 and Km 6 markers and the second (Mae Rim Orchid and Butterfly Farm) at the Km 6 marker. The orchids are beautiful, the butterflies even more so (watch them emerge from their chrysalises), and the food average and overpriced. With a ฿20 entrance change they are worthwhile (but eat elsewhere).

The **Mae Sa Waterfall** is located in the **Doi Suthep-Pui National Park**, 1 km off Route 1096 (to the left) and about 1 km beyond the orchid farm. The waterfall is in fact a succession of mini-falls – relatively peaceful, with a visitors' centre and a number of stalls. Special parking for 'Royal' cars. ■ *0800-1800 Mon-Sun, ฿3 per person, ฿20 per car.*

But the most popular destination of all in the valley is the **Elephant Training Camp**, 3 km further on from the waterfall. Around 100 elephants are well cared for here (with a number of babies, which must be a good indicator of their happiness). Visitors can see the elephants bathing, feed them bananas and sugar-cane and then watch an elephant show, when the pachyderms play harmonicas, kick footballs, stand on one leg and finally, as a brief nod to their former work, drag a few logs about. Elephant rides available between 0700 and 1400. ■ *฿80, 2 shows a day at 0800 and 0940 and an additional show at 1330 during peak periods, T297060.*

The recently opened **Queen Sirikit Botanical Gardens** was established in 1993, on a little under 1,000 acres of steeply sloping land on the edge of the Doi

Mae Sa Valley-Samoeng circuit

The Northern Region

Suthep-Pui National Park, 27 km from Chiang Mai and 12 km from the Mae Rim turnoff. The great bulk of the gardens was designated a protected watershed and conservation area even before 1993, and hence there are a number of large trees. It is Thailand's first botanical gardens and a truly impressive enterprise. The fact that it was initiated before Thailand's economic crisis probably explains the 'no expense spared' feel to the place. There are three marked trails (rock garden and nursery plus waterfall, arboreta and climber trail), a museum (largely empty in mid-2000, but plans are afoot) and an information centre. But the highlight of the gardens – or it will be – is the glasshouse complex, which should be fantastic. The largest will feature a waterfall and elevated broadwalk, and there are also glasshouses for desert flora, savannah flora and wetland plants. The glasshouses were well advanced in mid-2000 and should be completed by the time this book goes to press. To check, T298171 or email qbg@chmai.loxinfo.co.th What is surprising is how few people make it here. ■ *0800-1700, Mon-Sun. ฿20 adult, ฿10 child, ฿ 50 car.*

The **Mae Sa Craft Village** is a leafy resort spread over a hillside, with immaculately kept gardens of brightly coloured annual flowers. Non air-conditioned accommodation is available (**B**), with an average restaurant (avoid non-Thai food) and a smallish swimming pool. The primary reason to visit this place is to take part in the activities provided, from ceramic painting to batik dyeing and sa paper-making. There is also a working farm where visitors can help with the rice cultivation, a Thai cookery school or, for people who find all this activity just too exhausting, there's a health centre for massage and relaxation. ■ *Small entrance fee for those who just want to wander. For their activity programme, T290052 or maesa1@ksc.th.com, www.maesa.th.com.*

Continuing further on along Route 1096 there are, in turn, the **Mae Yim Falls** (17 km), **Doi Sang** – a Meo tribal village (25 km) – and the **Nang Koi Falls** (34 km). At the furthest point in this loop is Samoeng, the district capital. Don't have your hopes raised by the tourist information shack – this shows enterprise more than it indicates a plethora of things to do and see. It is Samoeng's annual strawberry festival held in January or February that really puts the place on the map. Otherwise it is just a town to stop and have a cold drink or a bowl of soup. There is **B** *Samoeng Resort*, northwest of town, T487074, F487075, with restaurant, pool, hot water showers. There is a conference room and cottages set in spacious gardens; an isolated spot. More popular with Thai holidaymakers than farangs; a little down-at-heel.

Continuing on from Samoeng, the road skirts around the Doi Suthep-Pui National Park. This is an attractive upland area, still forested though degraded. A number of resorts (**B**) have been established along the road. Most cater for Thais. The largest and most luxurious are *Suan Bua* in the village of Ban Don, 22 km from Samoeng, set in attractively landscaped gardens in a valley basin, and *Belle Villa*, 19 km from Samoeng, where there are cottages for longer term rental (and purchasing too) as well as some hotel accommodation, T365318, belle_villa@hotmail.com About 2 km on from here are the *Ban Klang Doi* and *Golden Orchid Hill* resorts. This winding road finally descends from the hills and comes out by the north-south irrigation canal at the village of Ban Ton Khwen. Just before you reach the canal, and before a government office, is a turning to the right. Follow your nose, over a minor road, for about 100 m to the bare brick walls of **Wat Inthrawat (Wat Ton Kwen)**. The entrance at the back is by a cluster of sugar palms. This spectacular viharn was built in 1858 in Lanna style. Its graceful roofs and detailed woodcarving are a fine sight. Unfortunately, the new teak doors are usually well and truly padlocked, but it is still worth the two minute detour. Return to Chiang Mai by way of the canal road (turn left at the junction) or on Route 108 (the Hang Dong road), which is a little further to the east of the canal road. ■ *Getting there: there are buses and songthaews along this route, but it would be much more convenient to do the round trip by hire car or motorbike.*

The **Chiang Dao Elephant Training Centre** at Chiang Dao is 56 km from Chiang Mai on the route north to Fang, about 15 km south of Chiang Dao. Shows daily at 0900 and 100. Elephant riding and rafting available too. ■ ฿60 *adults,* ฿30 *children. Getting there: numerous companies offer tours to the Centre from Chiang Mai, although it is easy enough to get here by public transport as it is on the main road. Catch a bus or songthaew from the Chang Puak bus station.* (**NB** *There is a second elephant camp 17 km south of Chiang Dao, the Mae Ping Elephant Camp. This is not as good.*)

Probably the most authentic of the several elephant training camps around Chiang Mai

Chiang Dao, a district town 70 km north of Chiang Mai, is a useful stopping off point for visitors to the Chiang Dao caves (see below). The surfaced road running east from the town leads to a series of hilltribe villages: Palong, Mussur, Lahu and Karen. Most of these are situated on public Forest Reserve land and many of the inhabitants do not have Thai citizenship. They have built simple huts where tourists can stay (฿20 a night) and a number of trekking companies in Chiang Mai begin or end their treks in the villages here. The town has a number of good restaurants; of particular note is the locally renowned *Bun Thong Phanit* (on the left-hand side travelling north in a wooden shophouse), which serves excellent *khao kha muu* (baked pork with rice). ■ *Getting there: as Chiang Dao is on the main Chiang Mai-Fang road, there are numerous buses and songthaews from the Chang Puak bus station.*

Chiang Dao

These caves, located 78 km north of Chiang Mai on Route 107, penetrate deep into the limestone hills that represent the eastwards extension of the Himalayas and are associated with a wat, **Wat Chiang Dao**. They are amongst the most extensive in Thailand and are a popular pilgrimage spot for monks and ordinary Thais. There is a profusion of stalls here, many selling herbal remedies said to cure most ailments known to woman and man. The caverns contain an assortment of Buddha and hermit images, as well as some impressive natural rock formations. Electric lights have been installed, but only as far as the Tham Phra Non (Cave of the Reclining Buddha), where a royal coat of arms on the cave wall records Queen Sirikit's visit to the caves early in King Bhumibol's reign. To explore further it is necessary to hire one of the guides with kerosene lamps and (rather disconcertingly) candles in their top pockets. The tour of the cave takes about 40 minutes, but even this covers just a small portion of the system. At times oversized farang bodies may have to squeeze through narrow openings, but on the whole the exploration is easy. As with caves the world over, guides relish pointing out rock formations. **F** (dorm), **D** (bungalow) *Malee's Nature Lovers Bungalows*, 144/2 Mu 5, Chiang Dao, T01 (mobile) 9618387. These bungalows are about 1 km from the caves, it can be cold at night and in the early morning, especially between November and February, restaurant, good for trekking and walking. ■ ฿5 *to go as far as the electric light system extends.* ฿60 *to hire a guide with lamp for a 40 min tour deeper into the caves (the guides congregate 100 m or so into the caves where a rota system ensures an equal share of business). Getting there: catch a bus to Fang from the Chang Puak bus station on Chotana Rd and get off at Chiang Dao. Songthaews take visitors the final 6 km from the main road to the caves. A taxi to the caves and back should cost about* ฿1,000 *(1½ hrs each way) which, shared four ways, is an easier and reasonable alternative. It is also possible to hire motorbikes and bicycles in Chiang Dao itself – from the 'Tourist Corner' on the left-hand side of the*

Chiang Dao Caves

The Northern Region

main road, shortly before reaching the turn-off for the caves (turn left in the town of Chiang Dao, just after the Km 72 marker, it is clearly signposted).

Lamphun This historic city lies 26 km south of Chiang Mai (see page 253). The route is along a beautiful 15 km avenue of massive yang khao trees (*Dipterocarpus alatus*). The latex from these trees is used for waterproofing and as a fuel for torches (it is flammable). A few years ago there were suggestions that the road would be widened and the *yang* trees felled. Environmentalists, appalled at the prospect, solicited the help of local activist monks to ordain (*buat*) the trees by wrapping lengths of saffron cloth around them. Every tree on a 10 km stretch from just outside Chiang Mai is ordained and carefully numbered, and the development plans have been shelved. ■ *Getting there: buses leave regularly from the Old Lamphun-Chiang Mai Rd, just over the Nawarat Bridge and near the TAT office, 30-40 mins (฿12).*

Lampang lies 93 km south of Chiang Mai and is easily visited on a day trip (see page 246). Outside Lampang is the incomparable **Wat Phra That Lampang Luang** (see page 248). **The Young Elephant Training Centre,** en route to Lampang, is also worth a visit (see page 249). ■ *Getting there: by bus from Nawarat Bridge or from the Arcade terminal.*

The **Cotton weaving centre** of Pasang is 12 km southwest of Lamphun. ■ *Getting there: regular songthaews from Lamphun and from Chiang Mai (same stop as for Lamphun).*

The district town of **Chom Thong,** with its fine monastery, is the entry point to the **Doi Inthanon National Park** (see page 300). ■ *Getting there: buses, mini-buses and songthaews for Hang Dong and Chom Thong leave from around the Chiang Mai Gate. From Hang Dong there are songthaews to Doi Inthanon.*

Trekking

See also Tour operators, page 294, & Hilltribes & trekking, page 360

There are scores of trekking companies in Chiang Mai and hundreds of places selling trekking tours (this includes restaurants, photo shops, launderettes). Not many places actually organize the trek themselves and it is rare to meet the guide – or other people in the group – before leaving for the trek. Competition is stiff and most companies provide roughly the same assortment of treks, ranging from one night to over a week.

Like many other areas of tourism, trekking is suffering from its own success. Companies organizing treks are finding it increasingly difficult to present their products as authentic get-away-from-it-all adventures when there is such a high probability of bumping into another group of tourists, also under the false impression that they are enjoying a unique experience walking through an area untouched by Timberland-shod feet. This is especially true in the more overtrekked areas like the Doi Inthanon National Park. Yet, just at the time when pressure of numbers is making it increasingly difficult to keep tourists at arm's length from one another, travellers are demanding more authenticity in their trekking experiences. The answer is to avoid the environs of Chiang Mai and trek in less pressured areas like Mae Hong Son, Nan and Pai. Many trek operators – like those along Moon Muang Road – are advertising special non-tourist routes, although this is disingenuous to say the least as they are only pandering to the wishes of tourists. Almost all of these so-called special routes are virtually indistinguishable from established routes, so avoid paying more for them. With many travellers demanding the real thing and bypassing

Chiang Mai for other lesser-known towns, business has slowed and competition has intensified. This has put downward pressure on prices, so it is worth shopping around.

Treks can also incorporate raft trips and elephant rides. Motorcycle trekking is also becoming popular, although it is environmentally destructive – bringing noise to otherwise quiet areas and promoting soil erosion. Some companies, in order to convince potential customers that they will be pioneers, offer a money-back guarantee should they come into contact with other trekkers. The TAT office distributes a list of recommended trekking operators and a leaflet on what to look out for when choosing your trip. **The Tribal Research Institute** (see page 266), situated at the back of the Chiang Mai University campus on Huay Kaew Road, provides information on the various hilltribes, maps of the trekking areas, and a library of books on these fascinating people. ■ *0900-1600 Mon-Fri.* There is also a small ethnographic museum attached to the centre. An informative book on the hilltribes can be bought here for ฿35. ■ *0830-1200, 1300-1630 Mon-Fri.*

When choosing a guide for the trip, ensure that he or she can speak the hilltribe dialect as well as good English (or French, German etc). **NB** Guides must hold a 'Professional Guide Licence'. Treks must be registered with the Tourist Police; to do this the guide must supply the Tourist Police with a photocopy of the Identity page of your passport and your date of entry stamp. You can check on a company's reputation by contacting the police department. **Beware of leaving valuables** in guesthouses in Chiang Mai; however reliable the owner may appear, it is always safer to deposit valuables such as passport, jewellery and money in a bank (banks on Tha Phae Road have safety deposits and charge about ฿200 per month). **Insects**: remember to take protection against mosquitoes; long trousers and long-sleeved shirts are essential for the night-time.

Choosing a trekking company & guide

Prices for treks are highly variable, with low season prices of ฿1,300-1,400 for a three day/four night trek with elephant rides and rafting. During the rest of the year, ฿1,500 is a good benchmark. There are scores of trekking companies in Chiang Mai (a list can be obtained from the TAT office) and guesthouses also often provide a trekking service. Many of the companies are concentrated along Tha Phae, Chaiyaphum, Moon Muang and Kotchasan roads. We have decided to stop recommending companies because standards change so very rapidly. Note that it is the guide, rather than the company, who is important in determining a 'successful' trek, and guides swap allegiances constantly; as noted above, many are freelance in any case. A recommendation from another visitor is hard to beat.

Tours

A range of day tours run from Chiang Mai. Prices seem to vary between companies; examples of day tours include: Wat Phrathat Doi Suthep, the Phu Ping Palace and a Meo village (฿350-500); the Mae Sa Valley to visit a waterfall, orchid farm and elephants at work (฿400-500); Doi Inthanon National Park (฿900-1,300); Bor Sang (the Umbrella village) and San Kampaeng (฿100); Chiang Rai and the Golden Triangle (฿750-1,200); even the Sukhothai Historical Park over 200 km south (฿1,500). A ride on an elephant, some bamboo rafting and a visit to an orchid farm cost about ฿600. **NB** Make sure you know exactly what is included in the price, some travellers have complained of hidden costs such as road tolls, tips for guides, entrance fees etc. It is advisable to shop around to secure the best deal.

See also Tour operators, page 294

The Northern Region

Most tour operators are concentrated around Tha Phae Gate, so this process is not as time consuming as it may seem. There are numerous companies, making it impossible to provide any kind of listing, but one company which comes recommended is *North Pearl Travel*, 332/334 Tha Phae Road, T232976, F232976. Another notable operator is *Chiang Mai Green Tour and Trekking*, which tries to provide eco-friendly and culturally sensitive tours. However, they also run motorbike treks which can hardly be said to be the former. *Click and Travel Ltd*, www.clickandtravelonline.com, etienne@loxinfo.co.th, a young 'Soft Adventure Company' specializing in bicycle tours.

Many of the larger tour companies and travel agents will also arrange visas and tours to **Burma**, **Cambodia**, **Laos** and **Vietnam**. For Laos, at the beginning of 1999, it was possible to obtain visas on arrival when crossing via the Friendship Bridge near Nong Khai in the Northeast.

Essentials

Sleeping
■ *on maps*
Price codes:
see inside front cover

Chiang Mai has a huge range of accommodation to choose from, mostly concentrated to the east of the old walled city, although there is a significant group of guesthouses to be found west of Moon Muang Rd, south of Tha Phae Gate. There are well over 100 guesthouses and also more than 100 hotels in Chiang Mai, so below is only a selection. Stiff competition, a proliferation of new hotels and a stagnant industry mean room rates are slashed in many instances. It is rare for visitors to have to pay the set room rate. Some guesthouse owners complain that tourists have moved on to other pastures – notably Burma and the countries of Indochina. Perhaps because times are difficult for the guesthouse owners; we've had reports that the backpacker places are now putting pressure on their guests to book tours through them, or not stay there – something you need to be aware of.

All hotels are on the
Within the Old City
map, unless
otherwise stated

Within the old city walls and the moat is the greatest concentration of guesthouses, plus one or two small(ish) mid-range places. Most are to be found in the eastern half of the old city. The old city is relatively quiet and tree-filled and away from the main centre of commercial activity. It is about a 15-min walk to the night market, although there are bars, restaurants, tour operators, laundries and motorbike and jeep rental outfits. This listing is not comprehensive.

B *Felix City Inn* (on Chiang Mai map, page 260), 154 Rachmanka Rd, T270710, F270709. A/c, restaurant, small second floor pool, price includes breakfast, internet service provided, 132 rooms, mediocre, mid-range place situated within the city walls in a quiet location, but away from most of the action east of the moat. **B-C** *Vista*, 252/19-23 Phra Pokklao Rd, T210663, F214563. Quite attractive small-scale hotel, but in a strange location for exploring town. Popular with Asian visitors. **C** *Gap House*, 3 Soi 4 Rachdamnern Rd, T278140. Restaurant, includes breakfast, positioned down a quiet soi in the heart of the walled city (turn off Rachdamnern Rd after the offices of the American Universities Alumni Language Centre [AUA]), attractive rooms, good value. Recommended. **C** *Montri's*, 2-6 Rachdamnern Rd, T211070, F217416, am-intl@cm.ksc.co.th Some a/c, restaurant, clean, good central position near Tha Phae Gate, large rooms sparsely furnished, the restaurant here (*JJ's*) is one of Chiang Mai's more popular places – but rooms tend to be very noisy due to hotel's position on an intersection. **C-D** *Anodard*, 57 Rachmanka Rd, T270755, F270759. Restaurant, pool, one of Chiang Mai's older large hotels and there is no attempt in terms of design to make the place in any sense 'Thai'. Rooms in this classic 1960s-style concrete block are functional, but it is the only large place within the old city walls – erected before restrictions pushed developers to build elsewhere. **C-D** *Top North*, 15 Soi 2 Moon Muang Rd, T278900, F278485. Some a/c, small pool, modern concrete block, well-run but rather sterile, check rooms as many are

Within the Old City

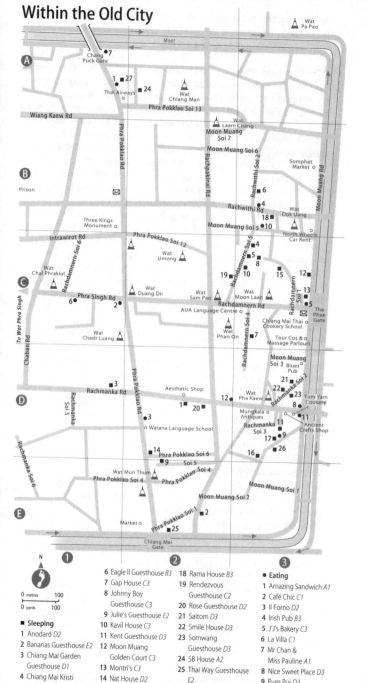

■ **Sleeping**
1 Anodard *D2*
2 Bananas Guesthouse *E2*
3 Chiang Mai Garden
  Guesthouse *D1*
4 Chiang Mai Kristi
  House *C3*
5 Chiang Mai
  White House *C3*

6 Eagle II Guesthouse *B3*
7 Gap House *C3*
8 Johnny Boy
  Guesthouse *C3*
9 Julie's Guesthouse *E2*
10 Kavil House *C3*
11 Kent Guesthouse *D3*
12 Moon Muang
  Golden Court *C3*
13 Montri's *C3*
14 Nat House *D2*
15 Nice Apartments *C3*
16 North Star House *D3*
17 Pathara House *D3*

18 Rama House *B3*
19 Rendezvous
  Guesthouse *C2*
20 Rose Guesthouse *D2*
21 Saitom *D3*
22 Smile House *D3*
23 Somwang
  Guesthouse *D3*
24 SB House *A2*
25 Thai Way Guesthouse
  E2
26 Top North *D3*
27 Vista *A1*

● **Eating**
1 Amazing Sandwich *A1*
2 Café Chic *C1*
3 Il Forno *D2*
4 Irish Pub *B3*
5 J'J's Bakery *C3*
6 La Villa *C1*
7 Mr Chan &
  Miss Pauline *A1*
8 Nice Sweet Place *D3*
9 Pum Pui *D3*
10 Siam Kitchen *B3*
11 Tiger *D3*
12 Wok *D2*

*Related map
Chiang Mai,
page 260*

0 metres 100
0 yards 100

rather grubby. Popular but needs to maintain standards, slightly overpriced – largely because people are willing to pay extra for access to a pool. Good reports on its tour operations; the hotel runs its own fleet of minibuses.

D *The Chiang Mai White House*, 12 Rachdamnern Soi 5, T357130. A new 3-storey block with 18 rooms (some a/c), an immaculate garden and very high standard of cleanliness but not oozing character. **D** *Pathara House*, 24 Moon Muang Soi 2, T206542, F206543. Some a/c, new small hotel-cum-guesthouse, rooms are clinically clean, and also clinically bare, attached bathrooms with hot water, raised rather exposed patio and beer 'garden'. The a/c rooms are well priced and considerably cheaper than the *Top North* just up the soi – but then there's no pool. **D** *Smile House*, 5 Rachmanka Soi 2, T208661, F208663, smile208@ mail.cscoms.com A new place in a quiet compound with 32 spotless spacious rooms, some with a/c and hot water showers. Breakfast available, bikes for rent, tours and trekking organized. Recommended. **D-E** *Chiang Mai Garden Guesthouse*, 82/86 Rachmanka Rd, T278881. Good food (homemade yoghurt), very clean large rooms with bathroom, second floor rooms are better than first floor. Remains popular. **D-E** *Eagle II Guesthouse* , 26 Rachwithi Rd, Soi 2, T210620, trekeagl@ cm.ksc.co.th Dorms for ฿70. Run by an Irish woman and her Thai husband. Friendly staff, spotless rooms with a/c and some attached bathrooms and excellent food. Also organizes treks and will collect from railway or bus station. Attractive area to sit, efficient and friendly set up. Appropriately, there's a good Irish pub next door. Recommended. **D-E** *Moon Muang Golden Court*, 95 Moon Muang Rd, T212779. Some a/c, set back from the road, large hotel at this price bracket with dark, gloomy corridors. The rooms are OK but bare and very plain, bathrooms with hot water, discounts for long stays. **D-E** *North Star House*, 38 Moon Muang Soi 2, T278190. Some a/c, much like the *Thailand Guesthouse* over the road, though perhaps with a touch more character. On our last visit the dining area was being used as a car park, with construction going on around the entrance. **D-E** *Rendezvous Guesthouse*, 3/1 Rachdamnern Soi 5, T213763, F217229. Some a/c, situated down a quiet soi close to Wat Sam Pao, good rooms – though a little gloomy because it is arranged around a covered lobby – with clean bathrooms, hot showers, cable TV and some rooms with fridge. Attractive atmosphere with relaxing plant-filled lobby, satellite TV, books and comfy chairs, good value.

E *Bananas Guesthouse*, 4 Rachpakinai Rd (near intersection with Phra Pokklao Soi 1), T278458. Set on a rather noisy road and almost irritatingly cool and trendy, with lots of signs stating how hip the management are. That aside, the rooms are OK and the food here is good. **E** *Chiangmai Kristi House*, 14/2 Rachdamnern Soi 5, T418165. A largish place with over 30 rooms, down quiet soi. Rooms are well kept, very clean and a good size, with very clean attached bathrooms, hot water and a well in the lobby for some reason. Great views from the rooms at the back. **E** *Johnny Boy Guesthouse (JB House)*, 7/3 Rachdamnern Soi 1, T213329. Small restaurant, no hot water, clean, quiet and friendly, good trekking from here (although you need to check that it's not compulsory if you book a room here). Ramshackle courtyard but quite a nice feel to the place. **E** *Kavil House*, 10/1 Rachdamnern Soi 5, T224740. Some a/c, quiet, clean and tidy place down a long narrow soi, attached bathrooms with hot water, good food. **E** *Kent Guesthouse*, 5 Rachmanka Soi 1, T217578. One of the more peaceful guesthouses in this area, house in large, leafy compound down a quiet dead-end soi, the rooms are well maintained with attached bathrooms. **E** *Nice Apartments*, 15 Rachdamnern Soi 1, T210552. Clean but bare and rather sterile in feel, fine for a short stay but lack of character could be rather disturbing long-term. **E** *Rama House*, 8 Moon Muang Soi 5 (or main entrance on Rachwithi Rd), T216354. Some a/c, a well run friendly and popular place. Large, clean but a little shabby, rooms with attached bathrooms in a fairly ugly block. Garden to relax in, good food, laundry and left luggage facilities. Good reports on its trekking services from residents. Various rental services. **E** *SB House*, 1/1 Phra Pokklao Soi 13 (not far from Wat Chiang Man), T210644. Some a/c, this is one of the few places to stay well within the city walls. A little hard to locate with a small reception in an apartment block. Quiet and good value but lacks atmosphere or character. Service is intermittent. **E** *Thong Koon House*, 27/5 Moon Muang Rd Soi 9, T418174, F418161. A/c, hot showers and private bathrooms, small, very clean guesthouse, friendly set up and good information about trekking.

E-F *Julie's Guesthouse*, 7/1 Phra Pokklao Soi 5, T274355. Run by a Swiss guy, Steff, who recently bought this place and is gradually making improvements. Small basic fan rooms, some with own bathroom and hot water. Friendly atmosphere and plenty of communal space for chilling out, including a rooftop that is being developed. Thai and Western food offered and treks organized from here. Recommended. **E-F** *Nat House*, 7 Phra Pokklao Soi 6, T277878. Rooms are clean, with some attempt to create a local feel, small balconies, clean attached bathrooms with hot water, views over the old city to Doi Suthep from upper floor, but nowhere very comfortable to chill out – rather a gloomy sitting area. Seems popular, but unclear why. **E-F** *Saitom*, 21 Moon Muang Soi 2, T278575. Rooms in a group of traditional wooden houses in large compound, peaceful and a refreshing absence of concrete – although the bathrooms could be cleaner. **E-F** *Somwang Guesthouse*, Rachmanka Soi 2, T278505. The cheaper, older rooms have shared bathrooms. Ugly, rather uninspired concrete block and stable-like wooden fronted huts, which are dark and gloomy with no character. **F** *Rose Guesthouse*, 87 Rachmanka, T273869. Large guesthouse at an intersection of 2 quite busy roads, rooms are very plain, slightly scruffy, although the shared bathrooms (hot water showers) are kept clean. Not much provincial charm here. **F** *Thai Way Guesthouse*, 63A Bamrungburi Rd (by Chiang Mai Gate), T276737, F279043. A new place which used to be the *Chiang Mai Youth Hostel*. Friendly woman owner provides good value accommodation. Garden and restaurant are a little scruffy, but the place is busy and is frequently fully booked.

This area of town includes 2 sections of hotels and guesthouses. On Chang Klan Rd and close by are a number of large, upmarket hotels. This is the shopping heart of Chiang Mai, with the night market and many other stalls and shops. It is busy and noisy (although the hotels need not be), with a good range of restaurants. West of here, down the sois or lanes between Loi Kroa and Tha Phae roads, are a number of guesthouses and small mid-range hotels. This area, though quiet and peaceful (usually), is still close to many restaurants and the shops and stalls of Chang Klan Rd.

Between the eastern city wall & Chang Klan Rd
Moat to River map, page 278

AL *Royal Princess* (formerly the *Dusit Inn*), 112 Chang Klan Rd, T281033, F281044. A/c, restaurant, small pool and gym. One of the Dusit chain of hotels, so the service is to a high standard. Central location, squashed up against the *Suriwong Hotel* by the night market and quite noisy (on the main road). With 200 rooms, the hotel makes an effort to be more Thai than Western in image and style. Of the top-range hotels in town, this is recommended. **AL-A** *Chiang Inn*, 100 Chang Klan Rd, T270070, F274299. A/c, restaurant, pool, one of Chiang Mai's older first-class hotel blocks, very central in the heart of the night market area. Still a good match in terms of price and quality, though reception staff could be friendlier. **AL-A** *Mae Ping*, 153 Sri Donchai Rd, T270160, F270181. A/c, restaurant, large ugly tower block on a big plot, Chinese in character, popular with Asian tourists. At this price there are other places with more style and finesse. **AL-A** *Zenith Suriwong*, 110 Chang Klan Rd, T270051, F270063. A/c, good restaurants, pool, all facilities, the slightly frayed exterior betrays a renovated interior, central. Recommended, although some rooms look out directly onto neighbouring blocks and noise pollution is particularly bad here. **A** *Chiang Mai Plaza*, 92 Sri Donchai Rd, T270040, F272230. A/c, restaurant,

Moat to river

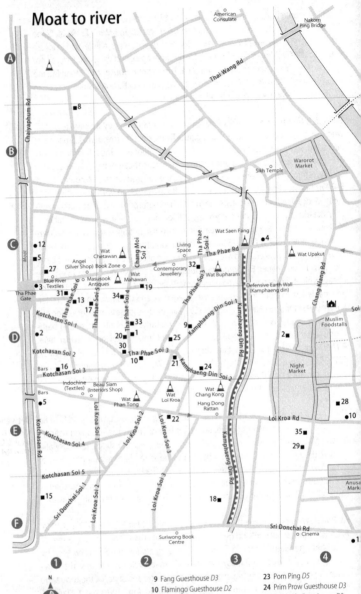

Not to scale

■ **Sleeping**
1 Bang Jong Come Guesthouse *D2*
2 Chiang Inn *D4*
3 Chiang Mai Plaza *F5*
4 Chiang Mai Souvenir *F5*
5 Daret's *C1*
6 Diamond Riverside *E5*
7 Downtown Inn *E5*
8 Eagle House I *B1*

9 Fang Guesthouse *D3*
10 Flamingo Guesthouse *D2*
11 Galare *D5*
12 Green Lodge *E5*
13 Home Place *D1*
14 Kim House *E5*
15 Lai Thai *F1*
16 Little Home Guesthouse *D1*
17 Living House *D1*
18 Mae Ping *F3*
19 Midtown House *C2*
20 Mr John Guesthouse *D2*
21 Nice Place Inn *D2*
22 Phucome Inn *E2*

23 Porn Ping *D5*
24 Prim Prow Guesthouse *D3*
25 Ratchada Guesthouse *D2*
26 River View Lodge *D5*
27 Roon Ruang *C1*
28 Royal Lanna *E4*
29 Royal Princess *E4*
30 Sarah's Guesthouse *D2*
31 Syntax Guesthouse *D1*
32 Tapae Place *C3*
33 Thana Guesthouse *D2*
34 Tha Phae Guesthouse *D2*
35 Zenith Suriwong *E4*

Related map
Chiang Mai,
page 260

The Northern Region

pool, large (444 rooms), impersonal but central to night market and restaurants.

C *Lai Thai*, 111/4-5 Khotchasan Rd, T271725, F272724. Some a/c, restaurant, good clean pool, free baby cots, spotless rooms, cross between a North Thai house and Swiss chalet. Popular and well-run, good facilities, attractive surroundings, tours, trekking and motorbike rental. Note that the cheaper rooms at the back are noisy, so expect an early wake-up. Nonetheless recommended. **C** *Phucome Inn*, Loi Kroa Rd, T206390. A/c, restaurant, small modern hotel in central location, rooms are on the small side but come with hot water bathrooms and cable TV, reasonable at the price. Loi Kroa, though, is a comparatively busy through-street. **C** *Tapae Place Hotel*, 2 Tha Phae Soi 3, T270159, F271982. A/c, restaurant next to Wat Bupharam, small hotel in the mid-range bracket, refined for a place in this price category and surprisingly stylish. Good central location but set off the busy Tha Phae Rd – no pool, though. Room rate includes breakfast. **C-D** *Bang Jong Come Guesthouse*, 47 Tha Phae Soi 4, T274823. This is larger than most guesthouses, almost like a small hotel. Rooms are good: light and airy with attached hot water showers and some with a/c. Attached restaurant and trekking available. **C-D** *Home Place*, 9 Tha Phae Soi 6, T276468, F273494. Some a/c, clean, quiet, good service, helpful advice, clean rooms of a good size, with some attempt to infuse the place with Thai-ness, central location. Recommended.

D *Fang Guesthouse*, 46-48 Kamphaeng Din Soi 1, T282940. Some a/c, quiet place in good central location, attached restaurant, rooms are very clean although a little dark, good attached bathrooms (some with hot water), a/c rooms are an especially good deal. **D** *Little Home Guesthouse*, 1/1 Kotchasarn Soi 3, T206754, F206754. Not a little guesthouse at all, but a large place more like a small hotel. Don't be put off: it is peaceful, down a quiet soi within a leafy compound. The rooms are clean and well maintained and Roger, the Dutch manager, has insisted on no TV, no videos and no music – professionally run and popular, with cheaper package tours. Recommended. **D** *Roon Ruang Hotel*, 398 Tha Phae Rd, T234746, F252409. Twenty-two rooms set in a quiet courtyard, just off the busy Tha Phae Rd. Some rooms with a/c, more expensive rooms upstairs. Basic and rather scruffy, but friendly people and a great location. **D-E** *Living House*, 4 Tha Phae Soi 5, T275370. Some a/c, hot water, rooms with bathrooms, clean and quiet, but at our last visit rather unenthusiastic reception – probably just a bad day, as it has been recommended by visitors. Lots of travellers' information here. **D-E** *Nice Place Inn*, 77/1 Kampaeng Din Soi 1, T272919, F26068. Some a/c, a guesthouse with pretensions of hotel grandeur, for an extra ฿150 they will turn the a/c on. Rooms are plain but clean, quiet but central location, trekking company attached, hot water and lots of services from car hire to visas. Popular and well-organized. **D-E** *Thana Guesthouse*, 27/8 Tha Phae Soi 4, T279794, F272285. A/c rooms available, all with attached hot water showers. Sometimes rather unfriendly but very popular, especially with Israeli visitors. Serves kosher food. Jeeps for hire and lots of trekking organized. Thai massage on site.

E *Eagle House I*, 16 Chiangmai Gao Soi 3, T874126, F216368, trekeagl@cm.ksc.co.th Basic rooms, but well run and *Eagle Treks* here. **E** *Flamingo Guesthouse*, 71 Tha Phae Soi 3. Small guesthouse in a converted private residence. Basic rooms, quiet, simple, restaurant attached. **E** *Lek House*, 22 Chaiyaphum Rd, T252686. Quiet compound down narrow soi, rooms are good on the upper floor, slightly murky below, small bathrooms in need of upkeep, but good information and peaceful atmosphere. French restaurant sells buffalo steak. **E** *Midtown*, 7 Tha Phae Soi 4, T209062, F273191. Clean, plain rooms with hot water. Centrally located down quiet soi near Wat Mahawan. However, while it may be away from the traffic, there is a choir of frogs on the roof which more than makes up for it. Trekking, motorbike and car rental. **E** *Mr John Guesthouse*, Tha Phae Soi 4. Small guesthouse virtually opposite the much more popular Thana Guesthouse. Rooms are rather small and murky, but it is reasonably run. **E** *Prim Prow Guesthouse*, Kamphaeng Din Soi 2. Unattractive place: a single storey barrack-like place, with simple rooms and little atmosphere. **E** *Ratchada Guesthouse*, 55 Tha Phae Soi 3, T272559, F275556. Friendly guesthouse. Rooms are a little small and can be hot, but they are clean with reasonable attached bathrooms. Treks arranged, restaurant attached, well run. **E** *Sarah's*, 20 Tha Phae Soi 4, T208271, F279423, jack21@loxinfo.co.th Run by an English woman married to a Thai. Twelve basic but clean rooms, with attached bathrooms and shared hot water showers. Trekking and tour services available. This well-established guesthouse in the heart of the guesthouse area remains very popular and continues to turn people away, even in the low season when most other places are empty. Recommended. **E** *Syntax Guesthouse*, 2/2 Tha Phae Rd Soi 6, T206272. Five rooms down a quiet soi in a very central location. One a/c room, but no bathrooms in any room. Modern block with no charm. **E** *Tha Phae Guesthouse*, Tha Phae Soi 4, T271591. Large guesthouse down a quiet soi backing onto Wat Mahawan. Rooms are reasonable: attached hot water showers and Western loos. Not a buzzing place. **E-F** *Daret's*, 4/5 Chaiyaphum Rd, T235440. Popular restaurant, good source of information. Standards have declined, with rather grubby rooms, but it's good value, with rooms having own toilet and shower; check out time 1000, rather detached service, good trekking centre, motorbikes and bicycles for hire.

On the west bank of the river & off Charoen Prathet Rd
Moat to River map, page 278, unless otherwise stated

This area includes a number of mid- and upper-range hotels on the river. Some of the smaller places are particularly recommended. They are peaceful, often on large plots of land, and have the added bonus of the Ping River. They are within easy walking distance of many restaurants and not too far from the markets and shops of Chang Klan Rd.

AL *The Empress Chiang Mai* (Chiang Mai map, page 260), 199/42 Chang Klan Rd, T270240, F272977. Several restaurants, pool and fitness centre. Part of the Empress

Hotels Group, this hotel has made every effort to emphasize the Lanna Thai heritage of the area, with a reception which is decorated with traditional Thai artefacts. Its 375 rooms are spacious and attractive, with silk wall panelling, carved teakwood furniture and decorated with local products. Recommended. **A** *Diamond Riverside*, 33/10 Charoen Prathet Rd, T270081, F271482. A/c, restaurant, pool, large, ugly and charmless 4-storey hotel, river views from rather spartan rooms, riverside pool and verandah. **A** *Porn Ping*, 46-48 Charoen Prathet Rd, T270099, F270119. A/c, restaurant, pool. This towering block of 300 plus rooms is built on to one of Chiang Mai's older hotels erected in the 1970s. There's not much to set it apart from other similar places across the world. Very small rooms and cramped bathrooms. The only thing to recommend it is its position close to the night market and the top floor restaurant, from which there are splendid views of the city – when haze allows. **A** *Royal Lanna*, 119 Loi Kroa Rd, T818773, F818776, price includes breakfast. This high-rise block has little to recommend it except its location. The rooms are spartan and charmless, but spotlessly clean. There's a small fourth-floor pool and views from the upper floors are great. **A-C** *River Ping Palace* (Chiang Mai map, page 260), 385/2 Charoen Prathet Rd, T274932, F2338493. Some a/c, restaurant, traditional northern Thai teak buildings on the banks of the river. Once the most romantic place to stay in Chiang Mai, but now taken over by lacklustre management and an overabundance of mosquitoes, dirty verandah and broken furniture. Just shows how quickly a place can go downhill. **B** *Downtown Inn*, 172/1-11 Loi Kroa Rd, T270662, F272406. A/c, 72 rooms in this ugly hotel block close to the night market, rooms are a good size. **B** *River View Lodge* (Chiang Mai map, page 260), 25 Soi 2 Charoen Prathet Rd, T271109, F279019, tucked away down a narrow soi. A/c, restaurant, pool, small, quiet, riverside hotel, with large, rather plain rooms, some with wonderful views, attractive verandah and pool overlooking the Mae Ping, breakfast included. The hotel is well run by a very friendly Thai family, who have good English, and the place is small enough to feel personal and have such amenities as a book lending service. Recommended.

C *Galare*, 7 Soi 2 Charoen Prathet Rd, T273885, F279088. A/c, restaurant, small hotel in leafy compound, lovely position on the river. Large, clean rooms and efficient service, the open-air restaurant overlooks the Ping and serves simple but tasty food. A great little place. Recommended. **C** *Green Lodge*, 60 Charoen Prathet Rd, T279188, F279188. Some a/c, clean rooms with attached bathrooms in small, but featureless, hotel block on busy road. **D** *Kim House*, 62 Charoen Prathet Rd, T282441, F274331. Some a/c, small hotel in leafy compound down a secluded soi, with clean rooms and hot showers. Friendly, welcoming atmosphere. **E** *Chiang Mai Souvenir*, 118 Charoen Prathet Soi Anusarn, T818786. Good sized rooms, but shared hot water bathrooms. A popular place – even though it has become rather tatty – in a converted private house, with large leafy garden and peaceful atmosphere (apart from the dogs barking and the traffic!). Early checkout at 0900, popular. Recommended.

AL *Novotel*, 183 Chang Puak Rd, north of the city centre, T225500, F225505, novotel@chiangmai.a-net.net.th A/c, restaurants, pool, an unattractive block in a hopeless position for exploring the city. **AL** *Westin Chiang Mai*, 318/1 Chiang Mai-Lamphun Rd, T275300, F275299. A/c, restaurant, over 500 rooms in this grandiose, over-blown high-rise hotel, on the east bank of the Ping River. Hoards of smiling staff open doors, carry bags, park cars and do virtually everything except attend to your most personal needs. Despite rather inconvenient location, remains popular with upmarket and business travellers as there really isn't any other choice.

Elsewhere in the city
Chiang Mai map, page 260

The Northern Region

Huay Kaew Rd (W of city towards Doi Suthep)

West of the City, map, below unless otherwise stated

There are a number of large hotels on Huay Kaew Rd, which runs northwest towards Doi Suthep from the northwestern corner of the city walls. Until a few years ago this area of the city was comparatively quiet; Huay Kaew now has a string of shopping plazas and other developments along its length. It is some distance from the shops and markets of the town centre – too far to walk with any ease – but some people prefer to be away from the bustle of the commercial heart of the city in any case.

AL *Amity Green Hills* (Chiang Mai map, page 260), 24 Chiang Mai-Lampang Super Highway, T220100, F221602, once the *Holiday Inn*, this big tower block stands on its own, away from the action, and doesn't have much to recommend it. Popular for tour groups and conferences, but nothing special otherwise. **AL** *Chiang Mai Orchid*, 23 Huay Kaew Rd, T222099, F221625. Situated right next to the large Pang Suan Kaew shopping complex. A/c, restaurants, pool, large but attractive hotel recently expanded, health club, efficient service, relatively peaceful, very good Chinese restaurant. Recommended. **AL-A** *Amari Rincome* Nimanhaemin Rd, T221130, F221915, rincome@amari.com, www.amari.com West of town, a/c, restaurant (Italian), pool, tennis court and 158 rooms. Located out of the town centre, this hotel remains popular with tour groups. It also has 14 apartments that can be rented on a monthly basis. Friendly and professional service puts it ahead of some of the glitzier newer places. **A** *Lotus Pang Suan Kaew Hotel*, 99/4 Huay Kaew Rd, T224333, F224493. A/c, restaurants, pool, gym, massive ugly hotel, set behind Central shopping centre (Pang Suan Kaew) and rather hard to navigate around. Although they've invested in lots of teak cladding, it still lacks ambience. Competitive rates are a plus and the rooms are large, and so is the pool, very popular conference centre because of its sheer size. **A-B** *Holiday Garden Hotel*, 16/16 Huay Kaew Rd, T211333, F210905. Two grades of room, cheaper rooms being in older 2-storey building set around the pool, whilst more expensive are in an ugly high-rise block. Quiet situation down a lane, but small and gloomy rooms do not justify the cost. Smallish pool. **B** *Tarin* (Chiang Mai map, page 260), 10/7 Moo 2, Chiang Mai-Lampang Super Highway . An uninspired block with no garden and a pool, which should be described as a bath-tub. Rooms might be slightly bigger than average, but perhaps they just seem bigger as there's no furniture in them. **D** *Green Palace Hotel*, 70 Sirimungkalacharn Rd, T894718, F894721, tucked away

West of city

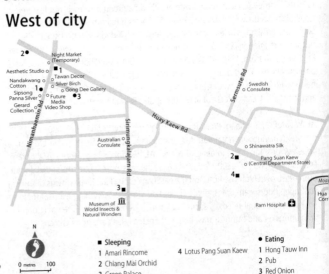

Night Market (Temporary)

Aesthetic Studio

Tawan Decor

Silver Birch

Nandakwang Cotton

Gong Dee Gallery

Sipsong Panna Silver

Future Media Video Shop

Gerard Collection

Nimanhaemin Rd

Sermsuke Rd

Swedish Consulate

Huay Kaew Rd

Australian Consulate

Sirimungkalajarn Rd

Shinawatra Silk

Pang Suan Kaew (Central Department Store)

Museum of World Insects & Natural Wonders

Ram Hospital

Mod

Hua Corr

N

Related map
Chiang Mai, page 260

0 metres 100
0 yards 100

■ **Sleeping**
1 Amari Rincome
2 Chiang Mai Orchid
3 Green Palace

4 Lotus Pang Suan Kaew

● **Eating**
1 Hong Tauw Inn
2 Pub
3 Red Onion

next to the Insect Museum on a road parallel to Nimanhaemin Rd. This small block is quite pleasant really, with comfortable and good value rooms and friendly staff. It's not a great location though.

L *Chiang Mai Regent Four Seasons Resort* (on Around Chiang Mai map, page 267), situated on the Mae Rim, Samoeng Old Rd, about 10 km north of town, T298181, F298190, www.regenthotels.com This has 64 Pavilion Suites and 11 luxury 2- and 3-bedroom Residences, set in exquisitely landscaped grounds. The hotel overlooks a small amphitheatre of ersatz rice fields, owned and managed by the hotel, providing guests with an opportunity to witness the rice cycle first-hand, from the comfort of their hotel room. Lovely pool and heavenly spa provides all pampering required; a couple of excellent restaurants complete the picture. All in all, an immaculately managed hotel with first rate service, in a beautiful setting. **AL** *Chiangmai Sports Club*, 284 Moo 3, Don Kaew, Mae Rim (7 km north of the city on the Chiang Mai-Mae Rim road), T298330, F297897. A/c, restaurant, large lengths pool. This sports club on a 10 ha site also has 45 rooms and excellent facilities, including squash and tennis and horse riding, free shuttle service to town – an alternative hotel for people keen on sports and not wishing or needing to be in the city.

Eating

For listing of where to have a Northern Khantoke meal plus cultural show, see Entertainment. Some of the best Thai food, particularly seafood, is served from numerous small and large restaurants, and countless stalls, in the *Anusarn market* area (on map Moat to River, page 278). The best place to see what is on offer in a small area; food available all day, but best at night when there is a cacophony of talking, frying and chopping. Note that some bars and pubs also serve food. They are listed under **Bars**.

Thai Mid-range: *Antique House 1* (page 278), 71 Charoen Prathet Rd (next to the *Diamond Riverside Hotel*). Well prepared Thai food in wonderful garden with antiques and an old teak house, built in 1870s (and listed as a National Heritage Site), very nice candlelit ambience, tasty but small servings and rather slow service, live music – though a busy road can be intrusive. Open 1100-2400. *Antique House 2*, 154/1 Chiang Mai/Lamphun Rd, T240270. A terraced restaurant overlooking the River Ping, live music. Open 1600-0500. *Aroon Rai* (page 278), 43-45 Kotchasan Rd. Very big restaurant, good value Thai food, North Thai specialities, very popular – try and get a table on the quieter upper floor. *Come-In House* (page 278), 79/3 Srithon Rd, Chang Puak, down a soi opposite Wat Jet Yod, set in traditional Thai house and pleasant garden, not easy to locate. *The Gallery* (page 278), 25-29 Charoenrat Rd, T248601. Quiet and refined Thai restaurant on the Ping River, in a century-old traditional Thai house, superb food, highly recommended for a special night out, art gallery attached, either sit in a leafy verandah (under an ancient makiang tree) overlooking the river, or inside. Particularly recommended are the fish dishes, including steamed sea bass with lime and deep fried *plaa chon*. *The Gallery* (page 278), 122/1 M.6 Chon Prathan Rd (otherwise known as the Canal road). Southwest of town, this has no connection with the other *Gallery*. Recently constructed teak house in attractive position overlooking fish ponds (also new), this big restaurant was empty on our last visit. Very pleasant spot to watch the sun go down. Good food, if you can decipher the menu which is only in Thai. Classical Thai music and dance performed daily. *The Good View Bar and Restaurant* (page 278), 13 Charoenrat Rd, T249029. Situated on the Ping River, outdoor or a/c dining available. Good live music and bar and very reasonably priced. The atmosphere is more modern than its long-established neighbour, the *Riverside Restaurant*, and it is frequented by Chiang Mai's yuppies. Not open for lunch. *Hong Tauw Inn* (page 282), Nimanhaemin Rd (about 20 m south of the *Amari Rincome Hotel*). A great little Thai restaurant with an abundance of clocks. Elegant surroundings, relaxed, friendly service, northern Thai specialities from regional sausage to crispy catfish, plus ice-cold beer. Slightly more expensive than the average Thai restaurant. Recommended. *Our Place Brewery and Restaurant*, 411 Charoen Prathet Rd (page 260), large and popular open-air bar and restaurant, with a menu about as long as the Oxford English Dictionary covering European, Thai, Chinese and more dishes. The attached brewery produces a rather watery brew known as Eagle Beer. Live music in the evenings from a revolving stage, range of cocktails. *Rainforest*, rather out-of-the-way Thai restaurant, only really worth considering for those with own transport. Set around a lake about 8 km out of town running south, east off the Hang Dong road. Good Thai food; seafood and northern specialities. *Riverside* (page 278), 9-11 Charoenrat Rd, T243239. A rambling, very popular place that stretches along the Ping River. Thai specialities include jungle curry and unusual fried rice dishes. Also serves international food. Live music, good, fast service, good food and value for money, booking advised in the evenings. Open for late breakfast (1000) and lunch. Recommended. *Ta-Krite Thai Restaurant* (page 260), Samlarn Rd Soi 1 (down the road which runs along the southern wall of Wat Phra Singh towards the moat), excellent Thai restaurant in an attractive, plant-filled house, with table cloths and amenable atmosphere. *Whole Earth* (page 278), 88 Sri Donchai Rd. Also serves Indian, traditional house, set in a Thai house, situated in lovely garden, very civilized, with unobtrusive live Thai classical music. Open 1100-2300. Recommended.

Cheap: *The Corner*, Rachmanka/Moon Muang Rd. Range of Thai classics and some vegetarian dishes. Also a popular place for breakfast. Sa paper products sold here. *Galae*, 65 Suthep Rd, T278655. In the foothills of Doi Suthep on the edge of a reservoir, Thai and North Thai dishes in garden setting. *Nang Nual Seafood* (page 260), 27/2-5 Koh Klang Rd. On the east bank of the Ping River, just south of *Westin Hotel*, also serves Chinese and international food, popular with tour groups.

Seriously cheap: *Rot Nung* (page 278), Charoen Prathet Rd (opposite the *Diamond Riverside Hotel*). Excellent Thai noodle soup (*kway tiaw*) in a restaurant almost entirely frequented by Thais – few sacrifices to farang tastes here. *Thanom Pochana* (page 278), 8 Chaiyaphum Rd. Clean, 'dress appropriate', full of locals.

Other Asian cuisines Cheap: *Shere Shiraz*, 23-25 Charoen Prathet Soi 7, T276132. Popular Indian restaurant with good tandoori. **Seriously cheap** *Sophia*, Charoen Prathet Soi 1 (down narrow soi between the night market and the river road). Cheap and very popular Muslim restaurant, this soi also usually supports a number of stalls, serving Malay/Muslim dishes from *roti* to mutton curry.

● *on maps (page numbers in brackets after restaurant names) Price categories: see inside front cover*

International Expensive: *Casa* (page 282), Canal Rd, just north of Huay Kaew Rd, set in an attractive wooden house, good range of authentic Italian cuisine (heavy on the garlic), apparently a popular restaurant with the Queen of Thailand. Fairly pricey. *Chez Daniel Le Normand* (page 260), corner of Mahidol and Chiang Mai Land roads, T204600. Next door to *Kazoo Discotheque*, good Normandy-style food – home-made charcuterie, wide choice of French wine, French music in the background. Daniel has cooked for the Queen of Thailand and members of the Royal Family, who frequent this restaurant. *Le Coq d'Or* (page 260), 68/1 Koh Klang Rd, T282024. A long-established international restaurant, set in a pleasant house south of the *Westin Chiang Mai Hotel*. Over-zealous waiters anticipate your every need. High standard of cuisine (including mouth-watering steaks), choice of wines, not heavily patronized, pricey.

Mid-range: *Art Café* (page 278), 291 Tha Phae Rd (on the corner facing Tha Phae Gate). In a great position for trade, this place serves Italian specialities including pizzas and pasta, as well as Thai favourites. They source their ingredients locally and their meats and cheese come from Dacheeso, a local dairy. Takeaway cheeses, meats and some great cakes (including brownies) available. *Babylon*, Huay Kaew Rd (about 100 m past the entrance to the university, on the right travelling out of town). Open lunch and dinner. Long-established Italian restaurant with an Italian owner. Favourite with Chiang Mai's expat population, scarcely seems to have changed over the last 10 years, pasta, pizza, salads, steaks, veal – unpretentious and reasonable food. *Bacco* (page 278), 158 Tha Phae Rd, eastern end. Italian restaurant in restored teak house, the chef and manager is an Italian and though the food is just mediocre it has style, with rattan chairs, white table linen and soothing lighting and music. *Café Chic* (page 275), 105/5 Phra Pokklao Rd, T814651. A groovy little place serving a limited menu of Thai and western food, its strength lies in its great range of cakes, coffees and teas. Small shop here selling a range of products, artfully displayed and therefore probably overpriced. Recommended. Open 1000-2000, closed Wed. *Daret's*, 4/5 Chaiyaphum Rd. Good travellers' food and fruit shakes, very popular but rather smug, slow service. *Four Regions* (page 278), Kotchasan Rd (by *DK Books* – easy parking). A/c place which could do with an ambience transplant. Food is OK and the staff are enthusiastic – must be one of the few restaurants in the northern hemisphere which still serves crêpes Suzette (which are flamed on a trolley at your table). *German Beer Garden* (page 278), 48 Charoen Prathet Rd (opposite *Diamond Riverside Hotel*). German specials served in roadside 'garden', good barbecue. *Irish Pub* (page 275), Rachwithi Rd, lamb chops, Irish stew, steaks, pasta, lasagne etc. Pretty good fare in a pub atmosphere. See Bars below. *Piccola Roma* (page 278), 3/2-3 Charoen Prethet Rd, T271256. Good Italian food prepared by the Italian chef and owner Angelo Faro, excellent wine cellar. *La Villa* (page 275), 145 Rachdamnern Rd, T277403. Italian, mostly pizza, but good pasta dishes too, traditional wooden house in large garden compound; slow, rather surly service on our last visit, and seems to be less popular these days.

Cheap: *The Amazing Sandwich* (page 275), 252/3 Phra Pokklao Rd, T218846. Only 4 tables in this sandwich bar (and a couple more outside), which makes it feel a little cramped. However, the sandwiches are to a very high quality (good bread too). Some of the meat pies are to be avoided, but the sweet pies are good. Also serves a typical English breakfast. Takeaway and limited delivery service available. Open 0900-2030, closed Sun. *Il Forno* (page 275), Phra Pokklao Rd, range of pastas and pizzas, ice-cream and cappuccino. *JJ's Bakery* (*Montri Hotel*) (page 275), Tha Phae Gate and in the *Chiang Inn Plaza*, Chang Klan Rd. Excellent breakfasts and delicious sandwiches (including ones with focaccia bread). Consistently good service and very popular, this is one of the best places to come to cool off and enjoy some good Western fare. Note that unlike *Daret's* opposite, this is not just a travellers' place – locals also meet here. *Mr Chan and Miss Pauline* (page 275), 5/2-3 Sriphum Rd, T223989, close to Chang Puak Gate, just inside the city walls (with awnings marked 'pizza' and 'steak'). This unusual restaurant serves a great selection of pizzas (including calzone), Thai food and Swedish food (excellent meatballs and good fish, baked on a board). The owner-cum-chef is Sopit Vatanasombut, who learnt to cook pizzas and Swedish food whilst studying in Sweden for 10 years. Fab atmosphere and great food at very reasonable prices. *Milk Garden*. This milk bar is very popular with local students – a groovy little hang out that serves frozen yoghurt drinks out of handcrafted ceramic mugs, while Carole King warbles in the background. Some food served too. *Nice Sweet Place* (page 275), 27/1 Moon Muang Rd. A/c restaurant with attached bakery, good pastries, serves breakfast – could do with a name change. *Pum Pui Restaurant and Bar* (page 275), 24/1 Moon Muang Soi 2. Traditional Thai house with large garden converted into an Italian restaurant – reasonable Italian, good value and pleasant location. *Red Lion* (page 278),123 Loi Kroa Rd, T818847. Not a bad imitation of an English pub, with pub grub to match – sausages and mash, beans on toast, fish and chips, as well as a range of salads and sandwiches. *Sizzler*, Pang Suan Kaew, Huay Kaew Rd. For slap-up steaks, this place is pretty good. Their 'all you can eat' salad bar is extremely good value (as it includes fruit and chocolate mousse!). *The Tea Shop*, Huay Kaew Rd, on south side, near Chiang Mai University. A tiny little place, easy to miss, just beyond the *Black Canyon Coffee Shop*. Delightful place for a cappuccino or herbal tea. Also serves a good range of desserts and has a limited menu of such things as spaghetti and lasagne. Recommended. *Tiger Restaurant* (page 275), 1 Rachmanka Rd. Good breakfast stop – yoghurts and lassis. *El Tori*, Kotchasan Soi 1. Mexican, good and cheap with great *tostadas*.

Fast food *Burger King, Pizza Hut, Svenson's Icecream* and *Mister Donut* have outlets in *Chiang Inn Plaza*, near the night market on Chang Klan Rd (page 278). *McDonald's*, in the *Chiang Mai Pavilion* on corner of Chang Klan and Loi Kroh roads (page 275). Other fast food outlets in the *Lotus Pang Suan Kaew* (page 282), shopping centre on Huay Kaew Rd.

Foodstalls *Anusarn Market* (page 278), southeast of the Night Market. Stalls mostly at night, but also smaller number throughout the day, cheap (฿10-15 single dish meals), lively and fun. Recommended. Stalls along Chang Klan Rd sell delicious pancakes, ฿3-7. *Somphet market* (page 275), on Moon Muang Rd, for takeaway curries, fresh fish, meat and fruit. North of *Chang Phuak Gate*, outside the moat, is another congregation of good foodstalls. *Warorot Market* (page 278), north of Chang Klan and Tha Phae roads, is a great place for foodstalls at night. If you need a/c comfort, then there are some excellent food courts in the basement of both the *Airport Plaza* (page 260) and *Pang Suan Kaew* (aka Central) (page 282), on Huay Kaew Rd. The former is better – quieter and slightly less frenetic than Pang Suan Kaew, which is a bit like eating in a crowd of pedestrians. Buy coupons (they can be redeemed if you don't spend them all) and then browse the stalls: wide range of noodle and rice dishes, drinks, kanom, Korean, Japanese and some other Asian cuisines, along with cold drinks including bottled and draft beer.

Bars

Many of the bars are concentrated around the southeast wall of the city. See under Music, page 287, for more bars with live music

There are quite a few pubs at the western end of Loi Kroa Rd. There is a group of bars within leafy gardens at the entrance to Moon Muang Soi 2: *Golden Triangle Beer Garden*, *John's Place*, *The Blue's Pub* and *Cheers Pub*. The *Golden Triangle Bar* serves reasonable food (**cheap**) and is set within and without a teak house, while the *Cheers Pub* is down a narrow soi and serves pub food like pork pies and pea and ham soup (**cheap**). *Swiss Wine-Pub*, 95/10 Nimanhaemin Rd, opposite Amari Rincome Hotel, also acts as a wine shop, open 1700-0200. *The Red Lion*, 123 Loi Kroa Rd, near *McDonald's*, an English pub (and restaurant, see under Eating, Cheap, above) with satellite sports TV. *The Pub*, 88 Huay Kaew Rd, bar and restaurant in a traditional wooden Thai house in a large leafy compound. Food is overpriced (**mid-range**) but includes steaks, some British dishes as well as Thai favourites. The pub is still relaxing in the afterglow of a review over 20 years ago in *Newsweek*, which judged it one of the world's best pubs. It has recently been voted 'Top Pub' in Asia by website Asia Travel Tips (though it's hard to see why). It's pleasant enough but hardly world-class. Open 1730 until midnight. *Overlander Bar*, Moon Muang Rd (facing the moat), good atmosphere, extremely cold beer. *Irish Pub*, Rachwithi Rd, good atmosphere and food available (**cheap**, see International food above). The name speaks for itself – management (which is Australian, but who cares) help to organize the (small) annual St Patrick's Day (17 Mar) parade. Draught Carlsberg and some Irish beer in cans. Garden, along with a large upstairs room where it is possible to lounge and watch Rachwithi's limited world go by.

Entertainment

Boat trips Evening departures from the *Riverside Restaurant* on Charoenrat Rd for trips along the Ping River. ฿50 a head, minimum 2 people.

Cinema *Lotus Pang Suan Kaew*, Huay Kaew Rd, top floor of this shopping centre, 3 screens, latest blockbusters, changes every Fri. Call 'Movie line' for information, T262661. Across the road at 12 Huay Kaew, also shows English language movies. ฿80.

Future Media, Nimanhaemin Rd, south of *Amari Rincome* hotel on same side of road. Possible to rent a room to watch movies on big TV screens. ฿200. Good choice of movies here.

Cookery   There are numerous cooking schools and only a few are listed here. One of the best is at the *Chiang Mai Thai Cookery School*, booking at 1-3 Moon Muang Rd (by Tha Phae Gate), T206388, nabnian@loxinfo.co.th The courses run over 1-5 days between 1000 and 1600. Contact Samphon and Elizabeth Nabnian. The location of the course is at The Wok, 44 Rachmanka Rd, although some sessions take place in a charming rural location outside town. *Thai Kitchen Cookery School*, 25 Moon Muang Rd, Soi 9, T219896. Run by Prathuang (Tim) Impraphai, who speaks good English (having worked as a chef in Canada for 3 years), a full day's course with a recipe book costs ฿700 – a good deal. *Tom Yam Cookery School*, Lake View Park II, Maejo Rd, T844877, 15 mins from Chiang Mai (free pick-up, swimming pool available at lunchtime), but bookable (and more information) at 2 Rachmanka Rd. *Siam Kitchen*, Moon Muang Soi 5, beside *Rama Guesthouse*, T213415, siam-kitchen@bangkok.com Attractively laid out, with pleasant seating areas to relax in after slaving over a hot stove.

Cultural centres   *Alliance Française*, 138 Charoen Prathet Rd, T275277. Presents French cultural (and some Northern Thai) activities. French films with English subtitles are screened on Tue (1630) and Fri (2000). Entrance to non-members, students ฿10, public ฿20. *AUA (American University Alumni)*, 24 Rachdamnern Rd, T278407, F211973. Library open 1200-1800 Mon-Fri, 0900-1200 Sat. English and Thai classes; films and other shows. *British Council*, 198 Bumrungrat Rd, T242103, F244781.

Cultural shows and Khantoke dinners   These traditional Northern Thai meals get a lot of coverage – just about every tour company seems to offer some variation on the theme. Food is served at low tables by traditionally dressed women while diners sit uncomfortably on the floor – shifting around to ease cracking joints and numbed muscles. Average food (usually) is then consumed to the sound of plink-plunk music and the languid movements of dancers. *Khun Kaew Palace*, 252 Phra Pokklao Rd (north end), next to Vista Hotel, T210663. Admission ฿180 (book in advance), open 1900-2200 Mon-Sun. *Old Chiang Mai Cultural Centre*, 185/3 Wualai Rd, T275097. Admission ฿180 (book in advance), Khantoke dinner, followed by hilltribe show, 1900-2200, Mon-Sun. The *Diamond Riverside Hotel* on Charoen Prathet Rd and the *Galare Food Centre* in the Night Bazaar, Chang Klan Rd, also organize Khantoke dinners, 1900, ฿180.

Discos   *Bubble*, Pornping Tower Hotel, 46048 Charoen Prathet Rd, T270099, very popular. *Kazoo*, 68/2 Lamphun Rd, T240880, 300 m from TAT office, open daily, very popular. *Porn Ping Hotel*, Charoen Prathet Rd. *Chiang Mai Orchid Hotel*, Huay Kaew Rd.

Music   *Early Times*, Kotchasan Rd, open air and live heavy metal music. *Baritone*, 96 Praisani Rd, live jazz from 2100. *Riverside Bar and Restaurant*, 9-11 Charoenrat Rd, assorted music from blues to Thai rock, owner is a big Beatles fan. *The Hill*, 122 Bumrungburi Rd, Thai rock and heavy metal – more of a venue than a bar.

Jan   *Chiang Mai Winter Fair* (movable), a 10-day festival held late Dec/early Jan, based in the Municipal Stadium. Exhibitions, Miss Beauty Contest, musical performances. *Bor Sang Umbrella Fair* (outside Chiang Mai, mid-month) celebrates traditional skills of umbrella making, and features contests, exhibitions and stalls selling umbrellas and other handicrafts. Miss Bor Sang, a beauty contest, is also held. **Festivals**

Feb   *Flower Festival* (1st Fri, Sat and Sun of month). This is a great festival and is centred on the inner moat road, at the south-west corner of the old city. It is a sort of Chelsea flower show-comes-to-Chiang Mai affair, with small displays of flowers and plants arranged by schools, colleges and professional gardeners and garden shops from across the North. There are also, as you would expect in Thailand, lots of foodstalls as well as handicrafts. If you have ever felt the urge to grow a papaya tree then this is the place to get your seeds. The highlight is a parade of floral floats along with the requisite beauty contest. If you want to avoid the crowds, come on the Fri evening.

Apr *Songkran* (13th-16th public holiday), traditional Thai New Year celebrated with more enthusiasm in Chiang Mai than elsewhere. Boisterous water-throwing, particularly directed at farangs; expect to be soaked to the skin for the entire 4 days. Given that it is the hottest time of year, no bad thing – unless you are going out for a business lunch or dinner (leave your camera in your hotel). See also box opposite.

Nov *Yi Peng Loi Krathong* (mid-month), a popular Buddhist holiday when boats (krathong) filled with flowers and lit candles are floated down the river. Fireworks at night – small hot-air balloons are launched into the sky.

Massage

For a truly traditional Thai massage, it is best to avoid the places geared to tourists around Tha Phae Gate. See also page 154

Traditional Thai massage There are umpteen places in town offering palm, head, foot and full body massage (not all of these are traditional Thai massage – but reflexology). They tend to charge around the same amount (฿200 per hr). Note that many masseuses seem to have had rudimentary training and the massage rooms consist of mattresses laid on the floors of upper rooms. The experience may be pleasant enough, but don't expect your sinuses to clear or your lower colon to sort itself out. The greatest concentration of massage outfits is to be found around Tha Phae Gate – just to the south on Moon Muang Rd, or to the east, on the corner of Tha Phae Rd. For a more upmarket experience, *Let's Relax*, Chiang Mai Plaza (basement), Chang Klan Rd, T818498, and Chiang Mai Pavilion Plaza (2nd floor, above McDonald's), both branches in the Night Market, offer foot, hand and back massage in clean, comfortable, a/c surroundings, and the masseuses seem to know a little bit more about what they are doing. More expensive at around ฿250 for 45 mins. For those who want to find out more about Thai massage, a number of courses are available: *ITM (Institute of Thai Massage)*, 17/7 Morokot Rd, T218632, F224197, 5-10 day courses in basic, intermediate and advanced Thai massage, 0900-1600; courses begin on Mon and cost ฿1,500 – the 'Master Teacher' Chongkol Setthakorn is well qualified. Courses are also available at the *Moh Shivagakomarpaj Foundation*, Old Chiang Mai Traditional Hospital, 78/1 Soi Moh Shivagakomarpaj (opposite Old Chiang Mai Cultural Centre, Chiang Mai-Hod Rd), T275085. Courses last 11 days (fee ฿2,770) and run from the beginning and middle of each month.

Shopping

Chiang Mai is a shopper's paradise. It provides many of the treasures of Bangkok, in a compact area, and is fast becoming very sophisticated too. The craft 'villages' on the San Kampaeng and Hang Dong (Ban Tawai) roads are a popular jaunt of the coach tour, whilst the Night Market, with its array of handicrafts, antique shops and fake designer shirts, continues to pack the tourists in night after night. A quieter, less frequented spot, is the group of sophisticated shops that have opened up near the *Amari Rincome Hotel* (see West of the City map, page 282). Prices are higher, but there is no tack here. Tha Phae Rd is an old favourite and this too is smartening up its act, with the likes of *Living Space* and *Contemporary Jewellery* recently opening up. Two department stores at Pang Suan Kaew on Huay Kaew Rd and the Airport Plaza, south of town near the airport, provide focal points for a vast array of shops, including plenty of cheap clothes outlets. For anyone interested in exporting products, visit Sarah Leelaphat, an Englishwoman who will act as your agent, 20 Tha Phae Rd, Soi 4, sarahlee123@hotmail.com, jack21@loxinfo.co.th, T208271.

Rough guide to Songkran in Chiang Mai

11 April Bathing ceremony at Wat Phra Singh (0900-2400). Traditional games and dancing at Wat Phra Singh.

12 April Homage to three founding kings of Chiang Mai (0900-1000, Three Kings Monument). Bathing Ceremony at Wat Phra Singh and more games and cultural shows (0900-2400). Drum competitions at Tha Phae Gate (1800-2400). Cultural performances and a mass of foodstalls along Rachdamnoen (1800-2400).

13 April Opening ceremony at Tha Thae Gate, with contests and games (0500-1200). Wat Phra Singh parade, cultural performances, merit making, alms offerings and more (0900-2400). Candle-lit procession and other events including body-building competition (around Wat Upakut, at the northern end of the Night Market, 1800-2400). Miss Songkran beauty contest and music (Tha Phae Gate, 2000-2400). Foodstalls (Rachdamnoen Rd, 1800-2400).

14 April Buddha image bathing ceremony (0900-2300, Wat Phra Singh). Drum competitions (0800-1800, Wat Phra Singh). Traditional games and beauty contest (1000-2400, Tha Phae Gate). Music competition and cultural performances (around Wat Upakut, 1300-2400). Foodstalls (Rachdamnoen Road, 1800-2400).

15 April Merit making and Buddha bathing ceremony (0800-2100, Wat Chedi Luang). Buddha image bathing ceremony (0900-2400, Wat Phra Singh). Ceremonial bathing of Chiang Mai governor and city elders (1230-1500, Governor's residence). Music contest (around Wat Upakut, 1800-2400). Foodstalls (Rachdamnoen Road, 1800-2400).

Night markets Situated on the west and east sides of Chang Klan Rd, Chiang Mai's multiple night markets are now a major tourist attraction and consist of 2 or 3-storey purpose-built structures containing countless stalls. The set-up is no longer a ramshackle affair and many would say the whole area has been rather sanitized. However, it is an excellent place to browse and, along with a wide range of tribal handicrafts, it is possible to buy T-shirts, watches, cheap tapes, leather goods, children's clothes and Burmese 'antiques'. Beware of wood carved products which may well be made of polymer resin. In addition, there are some better quality shops selling jewellery, antiques and silks (both ready-made and lengths) on the first floor of the Viang Ping Building. Most stalls and shops open at about 1800 and close around 2300. *Warorot Market*, north of Tha Phae Rd for clothing, fabric, sportswear, hilltribe handicrafts. Open 0700-1600. *Fruit stalls and market* on both sides of moat north of Tha Phae Gate. Some tuk-tuk drivers are subsidized by factories, so will take you to see silver, silk, enamel factories for about ฿20 each, with no obligation to buy. A new market has opened at *Mae Jo* (287 Chiang Mai-Mae Jo Rd), selling fresh food, plants and household items.

Antiques Beware of fakes. There are a number of shops on Tha Phae Rd. Another good road to wander along is Loi Kroa, which supports a large number of antique and hilltribe handicraft shops. Route 108, otherwise known as the Hang Dong road, has several places worth a browse, as does the San Kampaeng Rd, towards Bor Sang (to get there, take a tuk-tuk or a bus from the north side of Charoen Muang Rd. *Ancient Crafts*, 11/3 Rachmanka Rd.Small antique shop selling mostly Burmese lacquerware and northern Thai artefacts with some Chinese pieces. *Lanna House*, at the entrance of *Regent Chiang Mai Hotel*, north of town and west of Mae Rim, T861257. Set in a very attractive wooden building and exquisitely displayed, this place is obviously cashing in on being so close to the *Regent*. It does have some interesting pieces, but prices are high and it is probably only worth visiting as a detour up the Mae Sa Valley. *Antique House*, 71 Charoen Prathet Rd. *Masusook Antiques*, 263/2-3 Tha Phae Rd, T275135. This place has been around for years, which must be a good sign. Good range of antique ceramics, some textiles and some metalwork (opium weights

The Northern Region

and figurines from Burma). *Sanpranon Antiques*, west side of Hang Dong Rd, about 4 km from Airport Plaza. Set off the road in a traditional Thai house, this is well worth a visit, just to rummage about in this huge place. There's an overwhelming amount of stock (from lacquerware to ceramics to woodcarvings), much of which is clearly not antique, but it's fun to nose.

Art *TiTa Gallery*, opposite *Regent Chiang Mai Hotel* (see Sleeping above), on Samoeng Rd, Mae Rim, T298373, tita@cm.ksc.co.th Chiang Mai is short on really good local art and this is one of the few places where you will be able to find anything of quality. TiTa displays changing exhibitions, so it's best to call to find out about the latest show. In addition, TiTa sells some very attractive ceramics, cutlery, textiles and jewellery in a sophisticated environment.

Bookshops *DK Bookstore*, Kotchasarn Rd, just south of Loi Kroa Rd. This big new store has a good range of English language books and magazines, plus stationery, maps and cards. *Suriwong Book Centre*, 54/1-5 Sri Donchai Rd. Most extensive collection of books in English on Thailand in Chiang Mai. *Book Zone*, 318 Tha Phae Rd, part of *Asia Books*. This small store sells a range of Thai coffee table books, a good range of guidebooks, some English language novels, children's books, magazines and maps. Open 0900-2130. *Bookazine*, basement of Chiang Inn Plaza, Chang Klan Rd. Good range of coffee table books, children's books and magazines. *Book Exchange*, 21/1 Soi 2 Rachmanka. Books bought and sold, probably has the largest range of English second-hand novels, but no intellectual challenges here. *The Lost Bookshop*, Rachmanka Rd (close to Soi 4). Second-hand books.

Ceramics Beautiful celadon-glazed ceramics can be found in proliferation in Chiang Mai. The San Kampaeng road is as good a place as any to see a number of set ups. Several of the establishments on this road are selling outlets for small scale factories on the same site, which are open to visitors. One such place is *Baan Celadon*, 7 Moo 3, Chiangmai-Sankampaeng Rd, T338288, F338940. A good range of ceramics for sale, from simple every day bowls to elaborate vases. *Mengrai Kilns*, 79/2 Arak Rd, T272063. A showroom only, with a good range of celadonware, although the glazes are not as vibrant as some of the other kilns in Chiang Mai. Range of seconds at reasonable prices. *Suan Buak Haad,* in the southwest corner of the city on Aruk Rd. A selection of rustic pottery and large tongs. *Naiyana*, 283-286 Chang Moi Rd, for large ceramic tongs.

Clothing Huge assortment of T-shirts, cotton clothing and tribal clothing in the 3 night markets on Chang Klan Rd. Other shops along Tha Phae Rd or for more contemporary styles, the 2 shopping centres (Pang Suan Kaew on Huay Kaew Rd and Airport Plaza) have a good range. The former has some excellent bargains on both the top and basement floors. Also see textiles and silk entries below. *Pang Suan Kaew*, Huay Kaew Rd. This is the place to come for cheap and groovy clothes – lots of small shops and stalls mostly concentrated on the top floor, with a few more in the basement and scattered through the complex.

Computer equipment and software The best place for computers and software is the *Computer Plaza*, Mani Noparat Rd (north side of the moat, west of Chang Puak Rd). Along with well-priced hardware, this is a good place for software and games – bona fide and copies.

Cotton products *Fai Ngam*, Nimanhaemin Soi 1, opposite *Amari Rincome Hotel*. An attractive range of cotton products – some clothing, scarves, tableware and strange soft toys.

Electrical goods Thailand can provide some bargains here at the moment. As good a place as any to shop is *Niyom Panich*, Mahidol Rd, where there is a good range and tourists can claim VAT back.

Furniture If you are prepared to ship furniture home, Chiang Mai is an excellent place to rummage around for it. For locally made products, Hang Dong Rd is your best bet, with plenty of choice (and they can make furniture to order too). As well as there being several shops on the main north-south road, the best area to look is immediately to the east of Hang Dong – turn left at the junction. There is a strip of shops along here selling an excellent range of furniture, both old and new. The road to Bor Sang (the San Kampaeng Rd, to northeast of town) is also worth a visit. There are also quite a few shops selling furniture imported from the region. *Under the Bo*, 22-23 Night Bazaar, also has a shop on the west side of Hang Dong Rd, about 4 km south of the Airport Plaza. Fascinating mixture of Indonesian, Bhutanese, Afghan and Pakistani pieces. Worth a visit. Also custom-made pieces, from *Chiangmai Sudaluck*, 99/9 Chiang Mai-San Kamphaeng Rd. *Lanna House*, Km 4.5, Mae Rim-Samoeng Rd, close to The Regent Hotel. *Beau Siam*, 41 Loi Kroa Rd, great collection of contemporary furniture, some decorative items and unusual ceramics.

Handicrafts Chiang Mai is the centre for hilltribe handicrafts. There is a bewildering array of goods, much of which is of poor quality (Tha Phae Rd seems to specialize in a less good range of products). Bargain for everything. *Co-op Handicraft*, next to *Thai Farmer's Bank* on Tha Phae Rd. *Hilltribe Products Foundation*, next to *Wat Suan Dok* on Suthep Rd. *Thai Tribal Crafts*, 208 Bumrungrat Rd, near McCormick Hospital – run by Karen and Lahu church organizations on a non-profit basis, good selection, quality and prices. The *night market* on Chang Klan Rd also has a lot on offer, although generally of poor quality; better pieces can be found at the more exclusive shops on Loi Kroa Rd.

See Hilltribe section, on page 372, for more detailed information on the various styles of clothing

Honey Good range of local honeys from *Bees Knees*, 17 Chang Klan Rd.

Interior design Chiang Mai is undoubtedly the best place outside Bangkok to find good quality 'decorative items' and contemporary furniture for your home. Probably the best concentration of shops of this kind are on Nimanhaemin Rd, west of town, opposite the Amari Rincome Hotel, but Charoenrat Rd is also well worth a visit. *Beau Siam*, 41 Loi Kroa Rd, T209111. Very sophisticated range of contemporary furniture, decorative items and modern ceramics. *Gong Dee Gallery*, soi just south of Amari Rincome Hotel and factory on San Kampaeng Rd, T225032. Great range of mango-wood boxes, vases, bowls and frames and other beautiful decorative items. Also sells great range of coffee table books and serves drinks in sophisticated little café area. Sells to John Lewis Partnership in the UK, so he's well established. *Aesthetic Accessories*, 50-60 Rachmanka Rd, opposite *Anodard Hotel*, T278659. Not to be confused with the other *Aesthetic* opposite *Amari Rincome Hotel*, this is a groovy little place selling beautiful small-scale 'accessories'. It's quite expensive by Thai standards. It also serves a range of teas and cold drinks and some snacks. *Aesthetic Studio*, 95/12 Nimanhaemin Rd, opposite *Amari Rincome Hotel*, T222026, shop@aesthetic-studio.com Fabulous little place with some really interesting pieces, from clocks to lamps to glass and ceramics. *Living Space*, 276-78 Tha Phae Rd, T874299, livingsp@loxinfo.co.th It is incredible how much better artefacts look if they are displayed properly. This place is a pleasure to visit and is full of beautiful things from celadon to Vietnamese-lacquered mango wood bowls to silverware. Worth a visit, but it's pricey. *Oriental Look*, Chiang Mai-Hang Dong Rd, on west side of the road about 5 km from Airport Plaza, T280106, F280107. Range of painted and decorated mango wood bowls, vases, dishes etc, as well as some locally made furniture. Attractive stuff, but not to the highest quality. *Villa Cini*, 30, 32 and 34 Charoenrat Rd, T244025, F244867. Beautiful range of textiles and antiques, high-quality products displayed in sophisticated surroundings makes for inflated prices, but it's fun to browse here. Also has a small restaurant in the courtyard. *Oriental Style*, 36 Charoenrat Rd, T243156, F245725, oriental@loxinfo.co.th Set in this renovated shophouse, amongst other antique and interior design shops, their content holds no surprises. Much of this stuff can be bought for half the price in the Night Market, but then it's a more peaceful experience shopping here. *The Good View*, 13 Charoenrat Rd, T241866, F249726, goodview@chmai.loxinfo.co.th A tiny shop attached to the restaurant of the same name with an eclectic mix, ranging from dining equipment (attractive ceramics) to photo frames to T-shirts to food products. High quality products at reasonable prices.

Jewellery and silverwork Chiang Mai now offers not only a proliferation of hilltribe jewellery, but also some better quality, contemporary designed jewellery. A good starting point is Tha Phae Rd, where there is a strip of about 5 shops near the *Thai Farmers Bank*. *Shiraz Co*, 170 Tha Phae Rd, T252382. A long-established gem shop. Several of the more sophisticated 'interior design' shops around town sell the odd silver pieces, for instance *Silver Birch* behind *Amari Rincome Hotel* on Nimanhaemin Rd or *Living Space* on Tha Phae Rd. *Contemporary Jewellery*, Tha Phae Rd, T/F206134, nova@thaiway.com, www.thaiway.com/nova Attractive contemporary silver jewellery at reasonable (by Western standards) prices. Commissions undertaken. Owned and work designed by long-term Canadian resident. *Old Silver*, 59/3 Loi Kroa Rd, and *Sipsong Panna Silver*, 95/19 Nimanhaemin Rd. Both sell traditional and modern silver jewellery. *CM Silver Jewellery Co*, Tha Phae Rd, just to west of *Book Zone*. Good cheap range of jewellery. For more traditional, Thai-style silverwork, make your way to Wualai Rd which runs off the southern moat road. There are quite a number of shops and workshops down here on both sides of the road.

Lacework *Sarapee Handmade Lace*, 2 Rachwithi Rd. Claims to be the only workshop in Southeast Asia using silk thread.

Lacquerware *Vichaikul*, near *Wat Nantharam*. *Masusook Antiques*, 263/2-3 Tha Phae Rd. Also cheaper stuff available from the Night Bazaar.

Paper products There is now a proliferation of shops selling handmade paper products. The paper is made from the bark of the Sa tree, is unsized and is rough in texture, but quite beautiful when leaves or flowers are interspersed among it. The best place to find paper is along San Kampaeng Rd, where there are numerous small scale operations making paper out the back. Take the lane to the west just before Chiang Mai Sudaluck, and before the Bor Sang junction, signposted to Preservation House. There are several places down here, where all manner of paper products can be seen being made or for sale. If you are stuck in town, then try *HQ Paper Maker*, 3/31 Samlarn Rd, behind Wat Phra Singh.

Rattanware *Hang Dong Rattan*, Loi Kroa Rd (near intersection with Kampaeng Din Rd). High quality rattan products. There is also a good range of cheaper stalls strung out along Route 108 towards Hang Dong, about 10 km south of town.

Silk *Shinawatra Silk*, Huay Kaew Rd (opposite the *Chiang Mai Orchid Hotel*). For the usual array of silk products: specs cases, silk frames, ties, scarves, and endless bolts of fabric. Hardly funky, but a good stop for stocking fillers for the grandparents/parents. *City Silk*, 360 Tha Phae Rd. Extensive range of colours and some ready-made garments. *Capital Silk*, 35/4 Moon Muang Rd. Similar to City Silk and Shinawatra Silk, lots of choice for silk on the roll, as well as ready mades and some small silk items like frames. *Blue River*, Tha Phae Rd, west end. Good range of silk and loose weave cotton. Some interesting ready-made clothing too. *Classic Lanna Thai*, Night Bazaar, upper floor, far right-hand corner. Fabulous range of well designed jackets, dresses and blouses. Also sells antique silk. Will make to measure.

Supermarkets and department stores *Rimping Supermarket*, 171 Chotana Rd, by *Novotel Hotel*. One of the better small central supermarkets for Western foods (including good cheeses, salads, cold meats and pâtés). The largest department store is the ugly *Central Department Store*, in the *Pang Suan Kaew* shopping complex on Huay Kaew Rd, next door to the *Chiang Mai Orchid Hotel*; there is a *Tops* supermarket in the basement where a good range of food is available. *Airport Plaza*, at the intersection of Hang Dong Rd and the ring road, *Robinsons* department store and *Tops* supermarket provide good selection of clothing, household goods and Western food. *Lotus/Tesco*, Hang Dong Rd, about 3 km south of Airport Plaza. Enormous place selling household goods, clothing, electrical goods and a big supermarket, with a good range of fresh fruit and vegetables and some western foods.

Tailors *Far Mee*, 66 Square U Pakut, Tha Phae Rd. Many of the stalls in and around Warorot Market will make up clothes. Walk north along Vichayanon Rd from Tha Phae Rd.

Terracotta Plaques, murals, statues, pots at *Ban Phor Liang Meun*, 36 Phra Pokklao Rd. A factory showroom.

Textiles *Pothong House*, 4 Moon Muang Soi 5. For Khmer, Lao and hilltribe fabrics. *The Loom*, 27 Rachmanka Rd, attractive little wooden Thai house with a good range of textiles, old and new. *Chatraporn*, 194 Tha Phae Rd. For silks, cotton and made-up garments. *Nandakwang*, 6/1-3 Nimanhaemin Rd, opposite *Amari Rincome Hotel*, T222261 or 3rd floor, Chiang Inn Plaza, Chiang Klan Rd, T281356. Loose weave cotton 'homespun creations', ranging from napkins to cushion covers to bedspreads to made up clothing. Attractive range of colours. Also sells some ceramics (brightly coloured coffee cups). *Studio Naenna*, 138/8 Soi Changkhian, Huay Kaew Rd, T226042. Handwoven cloth, made up. *Le Bombyx*, 3 km out of town on the San Kampaeng Rd. Ready-to-wear and made-to-measure silk and cotton clothing. *Folk Art*, 326 Tha Phae Rd. For textiles, *matmii*, handwoven cotton.

For a good range of textiles, it is worth walking down Loi Kroa Rd, east of the city wall

Woodcarving Western tastes accommodated for along Tha Phae Rd, with many outlets selling woodcarved trinkets. *Banyen*, 201/1 Wualai Rd, on the junction of the Superhighway and the Hang Dong Rd, opposite Airport Plaza. This long-established shop still sells a range of wooden products, but has been rather overshadowed by newcomers to the market. *Ratana House*, 284 Chiang Mai-Hang Dong Rd, east side, T271734. Huge range of goods from Burmese lacquerware to wood products of all descriptions – both large (chests and cupboards) and small (candlesticks and wooden frogs). Also sells china. *Silver Birch*, 40 Soi 1, Nimanhaemin Rd, behind *Amari Rincome Hotel*. Quirky collection of wooden products, from mobiles to toilet-roll holders to giant frogs. Particularly good are the pigs in a poke. Also sells some silverwork items. Ban Tawai is a woodcarving centre about 3 km east of Hang Dong (itself 15 km south of town). This place began life as a woodcarving village, and has been colonized and now overgrown by shops and stalls selling many of the products available in the city's better known Night Bazaar. However the specialist products here are still woodcarvings, from cheap and cheerful frogs to grandiose sculptures which will cost more than your holiday to ship home. Packing services available for those who have lost leave of their senses. It is quite a good place to come if you have transport and there are places to eat and drink too (try the *Coffee Corner*, serving coffee, cakes and simple Thai dishes, with attached art gallery displaying contemporary works).

Sport

Latest information on sports listed in most free newspapers & newsletters, available from many shops, hotels & guesthouses

Fitness and sports centres *Club House Inn Chiang Mai Sports Club*, Km 10 Mae Rim Rd (Rt 107), large pool, tennis, squash, badminton, gym, aerobics, horse riding. *Huay Kaew Fitness Park* is on Huay Kaew Rd at the bottom of Doi Suthep, near the zoo. *Hillside Fitness Centre*, 4th floor, Hillside Plaza 4, Huay Kaew Rd, T225984, fitness centre, sauna and herbal steam rooms, beauty treatment.

Go-kart racing *Chiang Mai Speedway*, 8 km out of town on Route 108, T430059, racing every Sat and Sun afternoon, open 0930-1900, Mon-Sun. *Chiang Mai Gokart*, San Kampaeng Rd, near Bor Sang intersection.

Golf *Lanna Public Golf Course*, Chotana Rd (at Nong Bua, 4 km north of the city), a woodland course, part of the Chiang Mai Sports Club. Green fee ฿500, ฿700 at weekends, club hire ฿300. Open 0600-1930. There is also a driving range here. *Gymkhana Club*, Chiangmai-Lamphun Rd, 9-hole course, green fees ฿100 weekdays, ฿400 weekends. *Chiang Mai Golf Driving Range*, opposite *Airport Plaza*, where Route 108 meets the superhighway. *Green Valley Golf Club*, 183/2 Chotana Rd, Mae Rim, north of town, green fees ฿430-750, getting more expensive through the week, ฿1,500 weekends, club hire ฿500. *Chiang Mai Lamphun Golf Club*, San Kamphaeng-Ban Thi, north-east of town, the newest of the golf courses in the region, a championship course situated in the heart of a forested area. Green fee ฿1,168, club hire ฿351. Open 0600-1930.

Hash House Harriers Hashes are fortnightly, Sat evening for men and women, Mon evening for men. Contact either David or Martin on T278503, or John on T271950, or the *Domino Bar*, T278503.

Horse racing Next to the *Lanna Public Golf Course*, Chotana Rd (4 km north of the city), races every Sun from 1200 to 1730.

Horse riding *Lanna Sports Centre*, Chotana Rd (north of town), ฿250 per hour, call Janet on T217956 for details. *The Chiang Mai Sports Club,* on the Chiang Mai-Mae Rim Rd (T298327), also offers riding (see Sleeping, above, under Outside the city). *The Army Horseriding Club*, Km 10 Mae Rim Rd, the hourly rate is a very competitive ฿100, but not much English spoken.

Squash *Gymkana Club*, Chiang Mai-Lamphun Rd, T247352, every Thu 1730.

Microlight flying Chiang Mai Sky Adventure, 143 Moo 6, Chiang Doi, T868460, flying@cmnet.co.th Sessions of 15 and 30 mins.

Swimming *Amari Rincome Hotel*, Huay Kaew Rd. *Top North Guesthouse*, 15 Moon Muang Rd Soi 2, ฿50. *Anodard Hotel*, 57 Rachmanka Rd. *Padungsilpa Sports Club*, Rasada Rd, large pool, clean with snack bar, open 0830-2030. *Pang Suan Kaew Hotel* on Huay Kaew Rd – large pool.

Tennis Fees are about ฿100 per hour; rackets for hire. *Amari Rincome Hotel*, Huay Kaew Rd. *Anantasiri Courts*, Superhighway (near the National Museum). *Padungsilpa Sports Club*, Rasada Rd (฿40 per hour, ฿80 per hour under floodlights).

Thai boxing *Dechanukrau boxing ring*, south of San Pakoi market, on Bumrungrat Rd. Matches every weekend at 2000 (฿20/70).

Yoga *Khun Wai*, Huay Kaew Rd, 0800-1800, Mon-Sat ฿100 per hour. *Raja Yoga Meditation Centre*, 218/6 Chotana Rd, T214904.

Tour operators

See also Trekking, page 272, & Tours, page 273

There are numerous travel agents along Tha Phae, Chang Klan and Moon Muang (in the vicinity of Tha Phae Gate) roads, most of whom will offer tours and treks over the north. They will also book air, train and bus tickets out of Chiang Mai. **NB** The TAT recommend that services should only be bought from companies that register with the tourist Business and Guide Registration Office; they provide a list of all such companies. As noted in the trekking section (see page 272), we have decided not to list or recommend companies because standards vary between treks (and guides) within individual outfits, and because these standards can change rapidly. Word of mouth is the best guarantee. **Visas** can be arranged in Chiang Mai for Laos, Burma, Vietnam and Cambodia. Going rates in Jan 2001 were: Laos, ฿US$30 on arrival or US$20 pre-arranged (30 days); Burma,

฿1,500 (30 days); Vietnam, ฿2,600 (30 days). Visas take between 3 and 7 days to arrange. There are direct flights to Vientiane and Luang Prabang in Laos.

Local   Bicycle hire: from Chang Phuak Gate and at the southern end of Moon Muang Rd, ฿50 per day, or on Nakhon Ping Bridge, plus some guesthouses. Two establishments are *The Wild Planet Adventure*, Charoen Prathet Rd, next to *SK Money Changer*, T277178, or *Bike & Bite*, 23/1 Sri Phum Rd, T418534. A deposit or your passport will probably be required. Mountain bikes should be locked up and always tie your bag to the basket.

Transport
See also Ins & outs, page 255; 697 km to Bangkok

Bus: ฿3-5 (the latter is for a/c) anywhere in town (the bus routes are given in Nancy Chandler's Map of Chiang Mai; see Tourist information, under Ins and outs, page 255). Buses operate 0600-1800.

Car or jeep hire: there are numerous places to hire vehicles and motorbikes, and rates start at ฿800-1800 per day, ฿6,000 per week. Many guesthouses will arrange rental or there are outfits along Chaiyaphum and Moon Muang roads. *National* and *Avis* are slightly more expensive, but are more reliable. *Avis*, *Royal Princess Hotel*, T281033, or the airport, T201574. *SMT Rent-a-car* (aka *National*), *Amari Rincome Hotel*, 301 Huay Kaew Rd, T210118, smtcar@samart.co.th *North Wheels*, 127/2 Moon Muang Rd, T216189, www.northwheels.com Some of the cars have seen better days, but rates are competitive here and they are a local operator who have been established for at least a decade. There are plenty of others, but check insurance cover and the car before setting off.

Motorbike hire: along Chaiyuphum and Moon Muang roads and at many guesthouses. Rates start at around ฿150-200 for a Honda Dream and rise up to ฿1,200 or so for a mean machine. Insurance is not available for small motorbikes and most policies only protect you from 50% of the repair costs. Companies include: *Ladda Motorcycle Rental*, Moon Muang Soi 2 (at the *Panda Guest House*). *POP*, 51 Kotchasan Rd, T276014, ฿250 for 24 hrs. **NB** the wearing of helmets in Chiang Mai city is compulsory (but you wouldn't know it).

Saamlor: ฿8-10 within city, ฿20 for longer distances. **Sii-lor** ('4 wheels'): these converted red pick-ups are known as songthaews ('2 rows') in most other towns, but in Chiang Mai they are usually referred to as sii-lors. They are the most common means of transport around town. Travelling on regular routes costs ฿8, ฿10 if you want them to take you somewhere off their route. Before boarding, tell the driver where you want to go and they will either say 'yes' or, if it's not on the route, they will quote you a price for the trip. Use landmarks (such as hotels, bridges, gates etc) rather than street names as a guide for where you want to go. **Tuk-tuk**: minimum ฿20 per trip, ฿30-40 for longer journeys.

Long distance   Air: the airport is 3 km southwest of town. It contains a bank (currency exchange vans also park outside the terminal building), hotel booking counter, post office, *Avis* rent-a-car counter, tourist information counter, *Pizza Hut* and snack bar. Regular connections on Thai with Bangkok (1 hr). Also flights to Chiang Rai (40 mins), Mae Hong Son (30 mins), Nan (45 mins), Mae Sot (50 mins), Phuket (2 hrs), Phitsanulok (35 mins) and Khon Kaen (1 hr 25 mins). Bangkok Airways also operate a daily service to Bangkok and Sukhothai, with connections on to Koh Samui.

   International air connections with Singapore, Kunming in South China, Vientiane in Laos (twice a week), Kuala Lumpur in Malaysia, and Dusseldorf and Munich in Germany. Lao Aviation, LTU International, Silk Air and Malaysian Airlines all serve Chiang Mai. International Passenger Service Charge of ฿500. **Transport to town**: taxis to town cost ฿90 (fixed price from the taxi booking counter). Thai Airways operate a shuttle bus service between the airport and their office in town (but you can get off anywhere in town), ฿40. **Airport information**: T270222.

The Northern Region

From Chiang Mai Arcade Bus Station

Bus No & Company	Destination	Length (hours)	Distance (km)	Non a/c	A/c Std	A/c Lux	VIP
99/Orange	Bangkok	10	726	190	287	369	570
166/Green	Chiang Rai (new route)	3	194	66	92	119	
148/Green	Chiang Rai (old route)	6	337	79			
166/Green	Chiang Saen & Golden Triangle	5	265	83			
619/Green	Mae Sai	4	256	83	116	149	
198/Green	Phayao	3	160	59	83	106	
170/Orange	Mae Hong Son (via Mae Sariang)	8	359	115	206	239	
612/Orange	Pai	4	137	45	93		
617/Green	Chiang Khong	6	337	108	151	194	
169/Green	Phrae	4	216	65	91	117	
169/Green	Nan	6	338	114	160	205	
152/Green	Lampang	2	97	29			
672/Green	Mae Sot (via Tak)	6	393	115		207	
155/Orange	Pitsanulok (old route)	6	428	126	176	227	
623/Orange	Pitsanulok (new route)	6	352	104			
155/Orange	Sukhothai	5	373	109	153	196	
118/Orange	Nakhon Sawan	6	468	115	193		
636/Orange	Udon Thani (via Loei)	12	712	205		369	
635/Blue	Nakhon Ratchasima	12	756	218		392	
175/Orange 177/Blue	Khon Kaen (Route 1)	12	774	230	332	414	
633/Orange 633/Blue	Khon Kaen (Route 2)	12	686	205	287	369	
587/Blue	Ubon Ratchathani	15	1055	300		540	
659/Blue	Rayong (via Pattaya)	15	990	282		575	

NB Prices quoted are 2000

Train: station is in the east of the town, on Charoen Muang Rd, across the Ping River, ticket office open 0500-2100. Left luggage 0600-1800, ฿5 per bag for first 5 days, ฿10 per bag from then on. Transport into town: frequent songthaews and tuk-tuks, or take city bus numbers 1, 3 or 6 which stop outside the station. Regular connections with Bangkok's Hualamphong station and towns along the route, 11-15 hrs. The overnight Special Express train (first and second class sleepers only, fan or a/c, T02-4911193) leaves Bangkok at 1800 and arrives in Chiang Mai at 0710, whilst the Sprinter (second class a/c carriage only) leaves at 1925 and arrives at 0720, the Nakornping Special Express (first and second class sleeper only, T02-6111193) leaves at 1940, arriving at 0905, and the Rapid Train (second and third class only, T02-161471) leaves at 2200 and arrives in Chiang Mai at 1305. The *Eastern and Oriental Express* now runs a luxury service from Bangkok to Chiang Mai, with 1 night on board and a stop at Sukhothai en route. Waiter service in the beautiful dining car and a cabin with en suite bathroom

Train information: T244795. Reservations: T242094. For a full listing of trains from Bangkok, see page 847

The Northern Region

Buses from Chotana Road

	Fare	Journey time (approx)
Chiang Dao	฿35	1½ hrs
Fang	฿48	3½ hrs
Tha Ton	฿55	4 hrs
Lamphun	฿12	1 hr
Pasang via Lamphun	฿27	1 hr 40 mins
Mae Rim	฿7	20 mins
Phrao	฿90	3 hrs

NB Prices quoted are mid-2000.

are all part of the service, departures at 2030, arrival 1830 the following afternoon. Booking and information available in Australia (T02-99059295), France (T01-55621800), Italy (T055-180003), Japan (T03-32651200), Singapore (32-01 Shaw Towers, Beach Rd, T3923500, F3923600), USA (T630-9542944).

Bus: the long distance bus station or Bor Kor Sor (BKS) is at the Chiang Mai Arcade, on the corner of the super highway and Kaew Nawarat roads, northeast of town, T242664. Most companies will provide a transfer service to the station: pick-up points are Anusarn Market, Narawat Bridge, *Sang Tawan Cinema* and Chiang Inn Hotel Lane. Tuk-tuks and sii-lors wait at the station to take passengers into town. There is an information desk within the main terminal building, with information on all departure times and prices. The tourist police also have a desk here. Regular connections with Bangkok's Northern bus terminal (9-12 hrs), Phitsanulok (6 hrs), Sukhothai (5 hrs), Chiang Rai (3-4 hrs), Mae Sariang (4-5 hrs), Mae Hong Son (8-9 hrs), Pai (4 hrs), Nan (6 hrs) and other northern towns. A number of tour companies organize coaches to the capital; these are concentrated in the Anusarn Market area and usually provide transport to the Arcade terminal, from where the buses depart. Buses to closer destinations (such as Mae Rim, Phrao, Chiang Dao, Fang, Tha Ton and Lamphun) go from Chotana Rd, north of Chang Puak Gate. For Pasang, there are direct buses from the Arcade Bus Station, or catch a bus to Lamphun (฿12, 1 hr) and then a connecting bus to Pasang (฿15, 45 mins). For Bor Sang and San Kampaeng take a red bus running along the north side of Charoen Muang Rd, opposite the San Pa Khoi Market east of the Narawat Bridge, or take a bus from Chang Puak Gate.

See also tables, above & page 297

Directory **Airline offices** *Air Mandalay* (*Skybird Tour*), 92/3 Sri Donchai Rd, T818049. *Bangkok Airways*, Chiang Mai International Airport, T922258, F281520. *Lao Aviation*, 840 Phra Pokklao Rd, T418258. *Malaysian Airlines (MAS)*, *Mae Ping Hotel*, 153 Sri Donchai Rd, T276523. *Silk Air*, *Mae Ping Hotel*, 153 Sri Donchai Rd, T276459, F216549. *Angel Airlines*, Chiang Mai International Airport, T270222. *PB Air*, Chiang Mai International Airport, T279172. *Thai*, 840 Phra Pokklao Rd, T210210, open 0830-1630, Mon-Sun.

Banks Several banks on Tha Phae Rd and plenty of exchange services along Chang Klan and Tha Phae roads. Many exchange booths open 0800-2000, Mon-Sun. Most banks offer a safety deposit service (useful for leaving valuables when embarking on a trek), expect to pay about ฿200 per month. Good rates at *SK*, 73/8 Charoen Prathet Rd.

Communications General Post Office: Charoen Muang Rd (west of the railway station), telegram counter open daily 24 hrs, T241056. Chiang Mai's other main post office is the new *Mae Ping Post Office* on Praisani Rd, near the Nawarat Bridge. This post office has a packing service and is more conveniently situated than the GPO out near the train station. It also offers an international telephone facility. Other post offices include the *Phra Singh Post Office*, near Wat Phra Singh,

Sriphum Post Office on Phra Pokklao Rd, *Night Bazaar Post Office*, in the basement of the bazaar, Chang Klan Rd, open until 2300. *Rachdamnern Post Office* (opposite *JJ's*, by Tha Phae Gate), convenient for many guesthouses on Moon Muang Rd, packing service available, open 0830-2200 Mon-Sun, run by Mi Tui, who speaks perfect English and some French, very reliable. Post Office at the airport offers telegram and international telephone services. Many travel agents in town offer overseas call and fax services. **Telephone:** International calls can be made from many tour companies; the post offices on Charoen Muang and Praisani roads also have international telephone services. **Email:** there are dozens of email/internet places all around town, especially in the tourist and university areas of town. It's a lot cheaper around the university; about ฿15 per hour as against ฿1-2 per minute in tourist areas. **Shipping & packing companies:** packers available around the Post Offices; shippers along Wualai Rd, many south from the Superhighway.

Embassies & consulates *British*, Unit 201, Airport Business Park, 90 Mahidol Rd, T203405, F203408. *French Honorary Consulate*, 138 Charoen Prathet Rd, T281466, F215719. *India*, 113 Bamrungrat Rd, T243066. *Japanese*, Suite 104-107, Airport Business Park, 90 Mahidol Rd, T203367. *People's Republic of China*, 111 Changlor Rd, T276125, F274614. *Sweden*, The International Hotel, 11 Sermsute Rd, T220844, F210877. *USA*, 387 Vichayanon Rd, T252629, F252633.

Language schools *Watana Language Centre*, Phra Pokklao Rd, T278464. Open 0900-2000, ฿20 per hour and learn about Thai culture. *AUA*, 73 Rachdamnern Rd, T278407, F211973. For a more serious look at the Thai language, AUA teaches in 60 hr modules, it also offers some conversation classes. *CEC*, Nimanhaemin Rd, west side, T895202. Open 0800-2100, private tuition possible here for around ฿200 per hour.

Libraries 21/1 Rachmanka Rd, Soi 2. Open 0800-1700 Mon-Sat. Advice on routes, books on Thailand and novels available. Chiang Mai University's Tribal Research Institute is a useful information source for people going trekking – see page 273. *Raintree Resource Centre*, Charoenrat Rd (by Nawarat Bridge). Small English-language lending library, open 1000-1200, Mon-Sun.

Medical services Chiang Mai's medical services have a good reputation. The most popular expat hospital is Ram, where there is 24 hr service available and good English speaking doctors. *Chiang Mai Ram Hospital*, Boonruangrit Rd, T224851/224861. *McCormick Hospital*, Kaew Nawarat Rd, T241107; 1700-2000 Mon-Fri. *Chiang Mai Central Hospital*, Chang Klan Rd, near *Lanna Palace Hotel*. *Malaria Centre*, Boonruangrit Rd, north of Suan Dok Gate. Outpatient fees around ฿100-140, emergency fees are not exorbitant either. **Dentists** also have excellent reputations here and people travel from around the world to have dental work done, as it is relatively inexpensive. Two recommended clinics are *Seventh Day Adventist Clinic*, Doi Saket Rd, T491813, and *Dr Promote's Clinic*, 206 Vichayanon Rd, T234453. Ram Hospital also has a good clinic.

Places of worship Churches: *Chiang Mai Community Church*, Charoen Rasada Rd, services on Sun at 1600 and 1800 (children of all ages cared for) in English. *Christian Church of Thailand*, Kaew Nawarat Rd, English service on Sun 1700. *Seven Fountains Catholic Chapel*, 97 Huay Kaew Rd, English service on Sun 0930.

Useful addresses Fire Emergency: T199. **Immigration:** Fang Rd, 300 m before the entrance to the airport, T277510. Open 0830-1200, 1300-1630, Mon-Fri (visa extensions possible, see page 30). **Main Police station:** corner of Phra Singh and Jhaban roads. **Police Emergency:** T191. **Tourist Police:** in the same building as the TAT office on the Chiang Mai-Lamphon Rd, T248974, at the Arcade Bus Station, the Night Market and at the airport. **Samaritans:** T274150, hotline counselling centre.

NB Chiang Mai's several local English newsletters have useful community services pages, listing such things as yoga classes, women's groups, Alcoholics Anonymous meetings and meditation sessions.

The Northern Region

The western loop: Mae Sariang, Mae Hong Son and Pai

Some of the most spectacular scenery in Thailand lies to the west of Chiang Mai, where the Tenasserim range divides Burma from Thailand. Travelling southwest from Chiang Mai on Route 108, the road passes close to Doi Inthanon, one of the country's most famous peaks and national parks, and passes through Chom Thong (50 km). From here the road follows narrow river valleys before reaching Mae Sariang, not far from the Burmese border – a good trekking point – and 188 km from Chiang Mai. The hill town of Mae Hong Son, with its Burmese-style wats, is 160 km due north of Mae Sariang and is another popular trekking centre. Until recently the northern section of this loop was almost impassable during the rainy season. Today it is much improved and Pai is accessible from both east and west. From Pai the road returns to Chiang Mai, through the Mae Sa Valley and south along Route 107, a total of 140 km.

Chom Thong
Colour map 1, grid B2

This featureless roadside town is a necessary stopping-off point for trips on public transport to Doi Inthanon, and is situated 58 km from Chiang Mai on the Chiang Mai-Hod highway (Route 108). There are regular connections with Chiang Mai by yellow songthaew from the Chiang Mai Gate. It is notable only for the historic **Wat Phrathat Si Chom Thong**, situated on the left-hand side of the main road from Chiang Mai. This impressive wat has a gilded Burmese chedi, dated 1451, and a Burmese-style bot and viharn built in 1516. Both are of great beauty, and the raised bot (on the left as you enter the complex) exhibits some fine woodcarving. The ancient viharn is cluttered with Buddha images. A smaller white chedi is faced with four standing Buddhas, and there is also an impressive assorted collection of miniature Buddha images.

Doi Inthanon and the National Park ดอยอินทนนท์

Colour map 1, grid B2

Located off Route 108, on Route 1009, Doi Inthanon is Thailand's highest peak at 2,595 m (see map, page 153). The mountain is a national park and the winding route to the top is stunning, with terraced rice fields, cultivated valleys and a few hilltribe villages. The park covers 482 sq km and is one of the most visited in Thailand. Although the drive to the top is dramatic, the park's flora and fauna can only really be appreciated by taking one of the hiking trails off the main road. The flora ranges from dry deciduous forest on the lower slopes, to moist evergreen between 1,000 and 1,800 m, to 'cloud' forest and a sphagnum (moss) bog towards the summit. There are even some relict pines. Once the habitat of bears and tigers, the wildlife has been severely depleted through overhunting. However, it is still occasionally possible to see flying squirrel, red-toothed shrew, Chinese pangolin and Pere David's vole, as well as an abundance of butterflies and moths. Although the mountain, in its entirety, is a national park, there are several thousand Hmong and Karen living here and cultivating the slopes.

Just beneath the summit, in a spectacular position, are a pair of bronze and gold-tiled chedis, one dedicated to the King in 1989 and the other dedicated to Queen Sirikit at the end of 1992, and opened at the beginning of 1993. Both chedis contain intricate symbolism and have been built to reaffirm the unity of the Thai nation. The ashes of Chiang Mai's last king, Inthawichayanon, are contained in a small white chedi on the summit itself – the ultimate reflection of the idea that no one should be higher than the king, in life or in death.

Disappointingly, the views from this point are obscured by trees. The radar station on the peak must not be photographed. Close by is a small wat, and next to that a shrine dedicated to two pilots whose plane crashed into the peak. There are a number of **waterfalls** on the slopes: the **Mae Klang Falls** (near the 8 Km marker and not far from the visitors' centre) **Wachiratan Falls** (26 km down from summit and near the Km 21 marker, restaurant here) and **Siriphum Falls** (3-4 km off the road near the Km 31 marker and not far from the park headquarters), as well as the large **Borichinda Cave** (a 2 km hike off the main road near the visitors' centre at the Km 9 marker). Note that it is a tiring climb up steep steps to the Mae Klang and Wachiratan falls. The **Mae Ya Falls** in the south of the park are the most spectacular, plunging more than 250 m (they lie 15 km from park headquarters and are accessible from Chom Thong town). Ask for details at the visitors' centre a few kilometres on from the park's entrance checkpoint. ■ *0600-1800, ฿30 for car, ฿10 for motorbike, ฿50 for songthaew and minibus. Best time to visit: just after the end of the rainy season, in late Oct or Nov. By Jan and Feb the air becomes hazy, not least because of forest fires.*

Sleeping There are bungalows (**A-C**, sleeping 4-30 people) at the 31 km outstation on the route up the mountain. To book, phone T02-5790529 or write to the Superintendent, Doi Inthanon National Park, Chom Thong District, Chiang Mai 50160. Advance reservation recommended as this is a very popular park. A relatively new Karen eco-resort has been set up by 4 villages with support from the National Parks Authorities. The bungalows have been built in the traditional style and the location is fantastic. The resort organizes treks, teaches about medicinal plants, introduces visitors to Karen dance etc. To find the resort, it is on the road to the summit, before the second check point. There is a camping ground at the Km 31 mark (฿5 per person). Small tents (฿50 per night) and blankets are available for hire.

Eating A small park shop at the Km 31 mark will serve meals. There are no stalls on the summit, although there is a restaurant near the chedis, close to the summit.

Transport Take a yellow songthaew for the 58 km from Chiang Mai Gate to Chom Thong (฿10). *105 km to Chiang Mai* From Chom Thong market, take another yellow songthaew to the Mae Klang Falls (฿5) or the Wachiratan Falls (฿10). To reach Mae Ya Falls and Doi Inthanon summit, a songthaew must be chartered (this will seat 10 people); ฿350 and ฿500 respectively; 1¼ hrs to the summit from Chom Thong.

Mae Sariang แม่สะเรียง

The capital of Amphoe (District) Mae Sariang, this small market town on the *Phone code: 053* banks of the Yuam River is a good departure point for trekking. The road from *Colour map 1, grid B1* Chom Thong runs up the Ping valley, before turning west to follow the Chaem River, climbing steadily through beautiful dipterocarp forest, the Op Luang National Park (17 km from Hod), and into the mountains of western Thailand. There is little to draw people here, except as a stopping-off point for Mae Hong Son or as a starting point for trekking. The town is small, leafy, indeed overgrown by the river, with many of the houses still built of wood, making it seem a comparative oasis after the dusty urban centres. It is easily negotiated by foot and the roads are virtually empty.

There are a handful of unremarkable wats; **Wat Utthayarom**, known locally as Wat Chom Soong, is Burmese in style but also displays two Mon-inspired white chedis. Other monasteries include **Wat Sri Bunruang** (in town) and **Wat Joom Thong** (on a hill overlooking town). The latter has a large and recently constructed white seated Buddha image surveying the valley below. The town also has a better stock of wooden shophouses than most Thai towns – that is on Laeng Phanit Road (the river road). The **morning market** operates from a plot on Sathit Phon Road; there is also an **evening market** – good for stall food – at the end of Wiang Mai Road.

Trekking
See Hilltribes & trekking, page 360

The owners of the *Riverside Guesthouse* organize treks through *Salawin Tours*. Treks include rafting, elephant rides, or visits to caves, waterfalls, Karen villages within the area or to the Burmese border. *Chan* trekking company operates through the *Roj Thip Restaurant* at 661 Wiang Mai Rd. The *Sea View Resort* also organizes treks.

Sleeping
■ on map
Price codes:
see inside front cover

There are 3 reasonable guesthouses in Mae Sariang, a couple of passable mid-range places, but nowhere more sophisticated. Guesthouses are a 5-15 min walk from the bus station.

B-D *Mitaree Hotel/New Mitaree Guesthouse/Somsri Resort*, 34 Wiang Mai Rd, T681109. About 1 km from town, near the night market. This is a compound consisting of a resort, a hotel and a guesthouse, all run by the same management. The resort (**B**) consists of Thai-styled bungalows, clustered together rather too closely, limiting views of the beautiful scenery. All have a/c, fridge and TV – it's overpriced. The hotel (**C-D**) offers featureless rooms, with a/c and hot water and fairly clean bathrooms. Only breakfast is served. The guesthouse (**E**) has 15 fair-sized rooms. Lovely views from the hotel balcony over ricefields. **C-E** *Mitaree Hotel and Guesthouse*, 158 Mae Sariang Rd, T681110, F681280. Some a/c and hot shower, more expensive rooms are in a grotesque block with bare scruffy rooms, cheaper rooms across the courtyard in an old wooden Thai house which is equally grubby and uninviting.

E *Riverside*, 85/1 Laeng Phanit Rd, T681188. A 5-min stroll from the bus station, on the riverfront, this attractive wooden building has large, clean rooms overhanging the river. Wonderful views from a nice dining/seating area, serving the usual Western breakfast and a small range of rice, chicken, pork and vegetable Thai dishes. (only breakfast is served). This remains a popular choice for travellers and as a result is a good source of information; visas can be arranged from here. **E** *See View*, 70 Wiang Mai Rd (across the river – and overlooking it – on the edge of town), T681556. Good sized rooms in stone bungalows, smaller wooden rooms also available, with shared facilities. New bungalows opposite the restaurant should now be completed, but are less appealing. The place is quiet and peaceful, a touch shabby but still recommended. It is a good source of information, partly because the owner speaks English and is very helpful. **E-F** *Mae Sariang Guesthouse*, 1 Laeng Phanit. Filthy – to be avoided. **E** *Lotus Guesthouse*, 73/5 Wiang Mai Rd, T681048. Clean rooms, but pretty featureless little place, with restaurant and karaoke. **E** *North West Guest House*, 87/1 Laeng Phanit Rd, T332464, info@faz.co.th A new spick-and-

Mae Sariang

To Mae Hong Se

Wat Utthayarom
(Wat Chom Soong)

Mae Sariang Rd

Bakery

6 ■ ■ 5

Black &
White Bar

2 ■
3 ■

Laeng Phanit Rd

Yuam River

Wiang Mai Rd

Inthira

4

Night Market

Sathit Phon Rd

Amphoe
Office

Morning
Market

Vaisuksa Rd

Wat Chong Kham

7 ■

N

Not to scale

To Mae Sot & Tak

Wat Joon
Thong

■ **Sleeping**
1 Lotus Guesthouse
2 Mae Sariang Guesthouse
3 Mitaree

4 New Mitaree Guesthou
5 Northwest Guesthou
6 Riverside
7 See View

span guesthouse (for the moment at least), with the only internet in town. A curious mixture of fairy lights and the Wild West, this is a friendly and personal place to stay with high standards of presentation. Restaurant (**seriously cheap**) serves a large range of Thai dishes, with good vegetarian soups.

Cheap *Ruan Phrae*, down soi to Wat Sri Bunruang, off Wiang Mai Rd. Thai and Chinese. Recommended. **Seriously cheap** *Inthira Restaurant*, Wiang Mai Rd. Tasty dishes and good prices, probably the best Chinese/Thai restaurant in town. Open for breakfast, frog specialities. **Foodstalls** At the night market on Wiang Mai Rd (about 1 km from the centre of town).

Eating
Price categories:
see inside front cover

VIP Karaoke, Wiang Mai Rd (opposite the bus station). Dark and cheesy. *Black and White Bar*, see map for location, al fresco ambience and some live music.

Entertainment

Treks, specialist birdwatching and star gazing trips available through *Baan Nam Ngao*, www.faz.co.th, T3110314, info@faz.co.th

Tours

Local Songthaews: to local destinations, congregate at the morning market on Sathit Phon Rd. **Bus**: station is on Mae Sariang Rd in the centre of town, 5 mins' walk from the *Riverside Guesthouse*, next to Wat Jong Sung. Seven buses daily each way to Chiang Mai and Mae Hong Son (both 4 hrs) and several a/c and non-a/c connections a day with Bangkok. The road south to Mae Sot, following the Burmese border, though slow (5 hrs), is excellent – it is kept in good repair for security reasons and is little used. (See page 240 for a description.) Songthaews depart 4 times a day from the bus station for Mae Sot, 5 hrs (฿150).

Transport
188 km to Chiang Mai,
230 km to Mae Sot

Banks *Thai Farmers*, 150/1 Wiang Mai Rd. *Krung Thai Bank*, Laeng Phanit Rd. *Thai Military Bank*, Wiang Mai Rd (ATM). **Communications** Post Office (and overseas telephone): 31/1 Wiang Mai Rd.

Directory

Mae Hong Son   แม่ฮ่องสอน

Mae Hong Son lies in a forested valley, surrounded by mountains, and lives up to its claim to being the 'Switzerland of Thailand'. Arriving by air, the plane spirals down, banking continuously, to deposit passengers almost in the middle of the town. During the winter months, the temperatures can get as low as 2°C at night, so you will need to take a sweater. During the day, though, it is warm enough. It is also often misty. An excellent centre for trekking, the town is changing rapidly (some would say has changed) from a backpackers' hideaway to a 'tour' centre, with the construction of two major hotels and a proliferation of 'resort'-style hotels. It is expanding at a rate of knots, and the arrival of the likes of KFC and Swensen's seem just around the corner.

Phone code: 053
Colour map 1, grid A1
Population: 10,000

Ins and outs

The airport is almost in the town. Regular connections with Chiang Mai and Bangkok. The bus station is at the northern end of town; there are plenty of buses travelling to and from Chiang Mai and connections with other destinations in this area of western Thailand, as well as Bangkok's Northern bus terminal.

Getting there
See also Transport,
page 311

Mae Hong Son is small enough to walk around with ease – no need to take a tuk-tuk except, perhaps, at midday during the hot season. It is a friendly, accessible and amenable place, a pleasant change after the rigours of frenetic Chiang Mai or Chiang Rai.

Getting around

There is a poor tourist information booth at the Night Market.

Tourist offices

The Northern Region

Background

Mae Hong Son Province is about as far removed from 'Tailand' as you are likely to get, with only an estimated 2% of the population here being ethnic Tais. (This figure is suspiciously low, and the town itself has a far larger population of ethnic Tais than the figure would suggest.) The great majority belong to one or other of the various hilltribes; mostly Karen, but also Lisu, Hmong and Lahu.

Mae Hong Son has always been caught between the competing powers of Burma and Siam/Thailand. For much of recent history the area has been under the (loose) control of various Burmese kingdoms. The influence of Burmese culture is also clearly reflected in the architecture of the town's many monasteries. The clash between Burma and Thailand continues today. Towards the end of 1992 Burmese forces occupied the Thai village of Huay Pleung, to the northwest of Mae Hong Son. The Burmese have been fighting Karenni rebels who killed 50 Burmese troops in a skirmish at the beginning of September that year. The Burmese authorities perceived that the rebels had received support from the Thai authorities and this led to an angry exchange between officials of the two countries. At the time, journalist Bertil Lintner reported that the Burmese referred to the Thai troops as *yeme* or 'female soldiers', and quoted a source in Mae Hong Son as saying that the 'Thais, for their part, mention the Burmese army in a whisper, as if they were talking about a ghost or an evil spirit'. In 1995 Burmese forces again intruded onto Thai territory – albeit to the south of Mae Hong Son, nearer Mae Sot.

Mae Hong Son also has a murky reputation for illegal logging – this area has some of the richest forests in the country. At the beginning of 1998, revelations about an alleged ฿5,000,000,000 bribe to officials of the Royal Forestry Department, to overlook logging in the Salween conservation area, surfaced.

Sights

Wats Most postcards of the town picture the lake, with **Wat Jong Klang**, a Burmese wat, in the background. It is particularly beautiful in the early morning, when mist rises off the lake. Wat Jong Klang started life as a rest pavilion for monks on pilgrimage, with a wat being built by the Shans living in the area between 1867 and 1871. The monastery contains some 50 carved Burmese wooden dolls (or *tukata*) depicting characters from the *Jataka* stories (ask to see them), as well as a series of mediocre painted glass panels on the same theme. Next door, in the same compound, is **Wat Jong Kham**. The most important building here is the pink-washed, reminiscently colonial structure at the far (northern) side of the compound. This contains a large seated Buddha in an attitude of subduing Mara – the Luang Por Tor. **Wat Hua Wiang**, next to the market (see below), contains an important Burmese-style brass Buddha image – the *Phra Chao Phla La Khaeng* – in an attitude of subduing Mara. It is said that the image was cast in nine pieces in Burma and transported to Mae Hong Son along the Pai River. For want of nothing better to do, you can feed the fish in Jong Kham Lake (stalls on the lakeside provide puffed wheat for sale); the fish practically jump out of the water! The dragonflies on the lake are also worth watching.

• •
Mae Hong Son place names

Mae Aw
แม่ออ

Wat Jong Klang
วัดจองกลาง

Doi Kong Mu, the hill overlooking the town, provides superb views of the valley (on a good day) and is home to a Burmese-style wat, **Wat Phrathat Doi Kong Mu**, known locally as Wat Plai Doi. The wat was constructed by the first King of Mae Hong Son in the mid-19th century. A path from the town winds its way up the hill, or alternatively go by tuk-tuk. At the foot of Doi Kung Mu Hill is **Wat Phra Non,** which contains a 12 m-long Burmese-style reclining Buddha. The main **fresh market** in town is on Phanit Watana Road, next to Wat Hua Wiang. The usual commodities from slippery catfish to synthetic clothing are sold here, together with some produce from Burma.

Mae Aw, officially known in Thailand as Ban Rak Thai, is a Hmong and KMT (Kuomintang – the remnants of Chiang Kai Shek's army) village in the mountains, 22 km to the north of Mae Hong Son, on the border with Burma. There are stunning views over Burma and the trip here is almost as worthwhile as the arriving. This area of the border has been a flashpoint in recent years as Burmese government forces have battled for control against various rebel groups. During periods of tension, public songthaew services are usually suspended. ■ *Getting there: by songthaew (2 hrs) (from Singhanat Bamrung Rd at about 0800), or arrange a trek. The alternative to taking a public songthaew, which tend to be intermittent, is to charter a vehicle for the day – which makes sense if there are 8-10 people.*

Excursions

Tham Plaa or **Fish Cave**, 16 km northeast of town off Route 1095, is another worthwhile excursion, which can be combined with a trip to Mae Aw (see above). The cave and the surrounding area have recently been gazetted as a national park. The name of the cave refers to the large numbers of carp that live in the cave pools – several hundred, some exceeeding 1 m in length – which can be viewed through a natural opening in the cave wall. The carp are believed to be sacred and local people have traditionally fed them; now visitors have taken over the task and fishy titbits can be purchased at the park gate. From the gate, a path leads across a river to the cave. ■ *Getting there: Tham Plaa is close to Mae Aw (see above), around 18 km from Mae Hong Son, just off Route 1095.*

Most guesthouses will organize treks, ranging from trips down the Salween River to the Burmese border, to Mae Sot, elephant treks, and rafting on the Pai River. Treks can be organized from one day to one week; the average price is ฿800 per day for a group of at least four people (this does not include rafting and elephant rides). There are both dedicated trekking companies, and trekking outfits attached to guesthouses. The former include: *TN Tours*, Pradit Jong Kham Rd; *Rose Garden Tour*, 86/4 Kunlum Praphat, T/F611577; *Well Tour*, Khunlum Praphat Rd (near the Post Office); *Sawasdee Tour*, Khunlum Praphat Rd (by bus station). Guesthouses which run treks include: *Friend House*; *Jean's House*; *Johnnie House*; *Piya Guesthouse, Golden Huts* and *Yok Guesthouse (Sawasdee Tours)*.

Trekking

See Hilltribes & trekking, page 360

There are assorted day tours to such sights as Pha Sua Waterfall, Pang Tong Summer Palace, the KMT village of Mae Aw, Tham Plaa (Fish Cave) and Tham Nam Lot (Water Cave). A number of companies also advertise trips to the 'long-necked' Padaung, which involves a bumpy one hour trip to their two villages. Many people deplore this type of tourism: see the box on page 306. Most trekking companies also run tours.

Tours

The Northern Region

The selling of the Padaung or 'Long-Necked Karen'

The Padaung, a Burmese people from the state of Kayah, are better known as the 'Long-Necked Karen' or, derogatorily, as the 'giraffe people'. Forced out of Burma during their long struggle for autonomy, they have become refugees in Thailand and objects of tourist fascination. Their name says it all: female Padaung 'lengthen' their necks using brass rings, which they add from the age of five. An adult Padaung can have a neck 30 cm long, and be weighed down with 5 kg or more of brass. Their heads supported by the brass coils, the women's neck muscles waste away, and if they were ever removed they would suffocate. The collarbones are forced down by the weight of brass, while the neck is pushed up. The women claim that although the rings might mean they take a little longer to get dressed in the morning, and they have to sleep with a bamboo pillow supporting their necks, they are otherwise able to lead full and productive lives.

Why the Padaung should do this, in one sense, is clear: it is regarded as beautiful. But their explanations of how the custom arose in the first place take several forms. Some Padaung maintain that women began to add rings to their necks to protect themselves from tiger attack. Another explanation is that they were designed to disfigure the body so that Padaung women would not be taken to the Burmese court as concubines or prostitutes. A third reason relates to the myth of the origins of the Padaung people. It is said that they arose after a dragon had been impregnated by the wind, and that the lengthening of the neck is designed to mimic the dragon's long and beautiful neck.

Sadly, Thai entrepreneurs, in allegiance with the army and Karen rebels, have exploited the Padaung's refugee status (they have few rights in Thailand), their relative naivety regarding matters commercial, and their only asset from a tourist perspective – their long necks. Most tourists who take tours to the two refugee camps (paying ฿250 to enter the villages) in Mae Hong Son Province leave disgusted at the 'selling' of these people. Thais sell bottled drinks to visitors, while the 'Karenni Culture Department' collects the entrance fee before tourists gawp at what

Essentials

Sleeping
■ on map, page 308
Price codes:
see inside front cover

Most of the more expensive hotels are located at the south end of town, off the map. There are a number of good guesthouses set around Lake Jong Kham, perhaps the most romantic spot to stay, and also a number to the northeast, some situated outside the town.

AL *Golden Pai and Suite Resort*, 285/1 Ban Pang Moo, T612265, 33 modern yet traditional Thai-Yai style chalets, well furnished, a/c, private terrace and 30 deluxe rooms. Set in landscaped gardens with 2 swimming pools, open-air restaurant overlooking Pai River. Tours organized. **AL** *Imperial (Tara Mae Hong Son)*, 149 Moo 8, Tambon Pang Moo, T611021, F611252. A/c, restaurant, pool, situated 3 km south of town in extensive attractive gardens, raised balcony restaurant, smallish pool for so many rooms (104), but all have satellite TV, well run. Gym, sauna, conference rooms and good restaurant. **AL-A** *Rooks Holiday Resort and Hotel*, 114/5-7 Khunlum Praphat Rd, T612324, F611524, rooksgroup@hotmail.com A/c, several restaurants, pool, large hotel outside town, good facilities including tennis courts, conference rooms, Thai massage and cookery courses and romantic location with good hill views. Ask for low season rates. **B** *Baiyoke Chalet*, 90 Khunlum Praphat Rd, T611486, F611533. Looks rather like a cross between a Swiss chalet and a Burmese monastery. Central location by the Post Office, rooms at the front are a little noisy. The best mid-range place to stay, with 40 a/c comfortable rooms with fridge and TV, good restaurant.

is less a village and more of a human display. John Davies, a Chiang Mai resident who runs culturally-sensitive tours to the hill peoples, observes: "It's a freak show brought into Thailand for commercial gain – tourism at its worst". And yet even he caved into the demands of Asia Voyages, who insisted that the Padaung be included in his tour if they were to feed their clients into his operation. The tourist dollar speaks.

Even more tragic and contemptible is the case of a village near Tha Ton, where a small group of Padaung were held against their wishes on land controlled by the Thai army. At the end of 1997, journalist Andrew Drummond quoted from a tape smuggled out by these kidnapped people: "Please come now. Things cannot be any worse. ... I feel so sorry when foreigners come and ask about our children's schooling. They won't let us take our children to school. We cannot eat the food they give us. They shout and scream if we do not make the foreigners [tourists] happy." (Bangkok Post, 8.11.98).

Notwithstanding this particularly tragic and repugnant case, the hard fact is that the Padaung have little else to sell. One woman, Ba Nang, is paid 1,000 baht a month simply to pose for photographs. Does she like it in Thailand? "I love Thailand. Here it's easy to find food; easy living and no problems." Stephen Sparkes found much the same. He writes: 'They [the Padaung women] were unanimous in praise of the new system of receiving tourists ... Now they looked upon it as 'work' ... preferring it to the hard, back-breaking labour of slash and burn cultivation' (1996). With the money, the villagers were improving their community, planning to build a school and health clinic. Like so many other indigenous peoples in Southeast Asia, the Padaung find themselves caught in a web of poverty, oppression, exploitation and powerlessness. It is hard not to accept that these people have little choice but to sell themselves in the name of development. Ironically, a custom which had almost died out has been revived. Every young girl is now bedecked with coils, parents hoping to cash in on their attractiveness to tourists searching for the exotic.

B *Fern House*, 2 km from Highway 108 at the turn off for Ban Nua Hum Mae Sakut Village (5 km from town), T611374, F612363, ferngroup@softhome.net Wooden bungalows built on rice paddies, Shan style. Simple yet comfortable and tasteful. Set in lovely grounds, friendly and helpful staff; a good eco-friendly place, with good walks from here. **B** *Mae Hong Son Group*, 3 km further from Rim Nam Klang Doi on same road, T234069, F252260. 40 a/c rooms, set by the river in pleasant gardents. Good restaurant, pool, right next to elephant rides and boat to long-neck tribes. Friendly, helpful owner speaks English, German and Thai. **B** *Mountain Inn*, 112 Khunlum Praphat Rd, T612284, F611309. A/c, restaurant, about 1 km from town centre, so not very conveniently positioned. Rather motel-esque, once clean, but apparently gone downhill, overpriced. **B-C** *Saammok Villas*, 28/1 Tambon Tapon Daeng, T611478 (3 km from town off route to Mae Sariang – turn right after the police station). A/c, restaurant. This place has become a little shabby, with a neglected garden and pool, but the rooms remain clean. **B-D** *Sang Tong Huts*, T620680, sangtonghuts@hotmail.com Secluded setting northwest of town (near *Yok Guesthouse*), with great views. Range of huts, the more expensive have balcony, fridge and tasteful (Habitat style) furniture and décor (but unpretentious). Dining area with open cooking fire, great food to order (set dinner), hilltribe coffee, red wine, menu in German and English. Friendly and helpful owners. Highly recommended.

C *Mae Hong Son Hill Hotel*, near the stadium, behind *99 Restaurant*. 22 chalet-style clean and comfortable rooms, with own hot water showers. Set back from the road, but a little cramped and holiday camp feel. **C** *Panorama*, 51 Khunlum Praphat Rd, T611757. A/c, 40 rooms with a/c and hot water, TV, fridge, all the amenities although short on character and rather listless management. **C** *Rim Nam Klang Doi Resort*, signposted 4 km from traffic lights on Highway 108, T611086. Overlooking the river, peaceful garden setting. Thirty chalets with verandahs, some a/c. Rooms run down and musty but clean – you pay for the setting more than for the room. Restaurant. **C-D** *Piya Guesthouse*, 1 Soi 3 Khunlum Praphat Rd, T611260. In a garden setting, 14 clean rooms next to the lake, all with a/c and TV. Some with doubles, others 2 singles. Restaurant at front. Nice but a bit soulless. **C-D** *TN Family House*, Khunlum Praphat Rd, on southern outskirts of town opposite Weekend Market. Ten rooms (8 single, 2

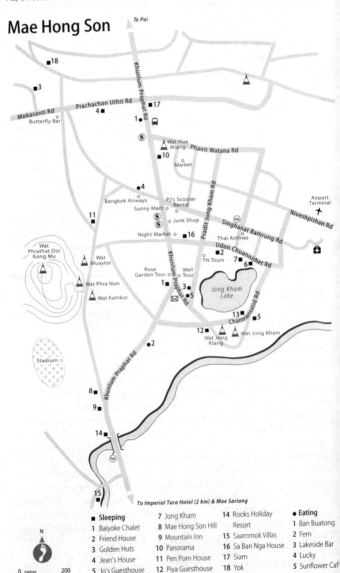

Mae Hong Son

■ **Sleeping**	7 Jong Kham	14 Rooks Holiday	● **Eating**
1 Baiyoke Chalet	8 Mae Hong Son Hill	Resort	1 Ban Buatong
2 Friend House	9 Mountain Inn	15 Saammok Villas	2 Fern
3 Golden Huts	10 Panorama	16 Sa Ban Nga House	3 Lakeside Bar
4 Jean's House	11 Pen Porn House	17 Siam	4 Lucky
5 Jo's Guesthouse	12 Piya Guesthouse	18 Yok	5 Sunflower Caf
6 Johnnie House	13 Rim Nong		

double), all with own hot water showers and fans or a/c. Very lean big rooms, pleasant field behind. Nice breakfast area. The same friendly family runs *TN Tours*, which provides off road 4x4 adventures, trekking and rafting. **D** *Golden Huts*, 253 Mokasanti Rd, T611554. Set around a garden, some distance from the centre of town, 15 overpriced rooms with double bed and shower. Nice quiet location, but a bit rundown and damp. Motorbikes for rent and will organize tours. **D** *Pen Porn House*, 16/1 Padungmuai Tor Rd, T611577. Situated on an increasingly noisy junction, this consists of a row of 10 motel-style rooms in a barrack-like building overlooking the town. All rooms are a decent size and have hot shower and fan, friendly and helpful owner. There are other more attractive and central places to stay. **D** *Wichitporn House*, on main road parallel to and north of airstrip, T612163. Ten clean rooms in 2 longhouses set around nice garden. Each room has 2 single beds and hot shower and fan. **D-E** *Friend House*, 20 Pradit Jong Kham Rd, T620119, F620060. Set back from the road, 10 rooms in this teak house are very clean with solid wooden floors, the shared showers are even cleaner, upstairs rooms have a view of the lake, well managed and carefully maintained, small café downstairs for breakfast, laundry service. Recommended. **D-E** *Siam Hotel*, 23 Khunlun Praphat Rd, T612148. Centrally located, clean but characterless hotel. **D-F** *Jean's House*, 6 PrachaUthit Rd, T/F611662. Almost in the countryside, this place looks inviting, but the rooms are dark and smelly and the shared squat toilets are filthy. **D-F** *Jo's Guesthouse*, 3 Chamnansatid Rd, T612417. Small personal place, 6 small clean rooms with mattresses on the floor and fans in an old teak house. More expensive rooms have own hot shower.

E *Chan Guesthouse*, first left after a bridge on Khunlum Prapaht Rd, heading north towards Pai. Clean but small fan rooms, 3 upstairs and 3 down in a traditional wooden family house. Communal showers, nice atmosphere. **E** *Jong Kham*, on Udon Chuannithet Rd, T611420, lakeside, run down bamboo bungalows with 'leaf' roofs (good for softening the sound of the rain) and some cheaper rooms in the main house, largish garden, very popular, only breakfast available. **E** *Mae Hong Son Hotel*, up a quiet street just north and parallel to the airstrip, T612023. Eight clean, good sized rooms, all with 2 single beds, with fan and shower, balcony upstairs. Small restaurant, friendly owner. **E** *Rim Nong*, 4/1 Chamnansatid Rd, T611052. Restaurant. Lakeside position, a mismatched ramshackle place with a few rooms crammed into this claustrophobic guesthouse, dormitory accommodation available, cheap and friendly backpacker place. **E** *Sa Ban Nga House*, 14 Udon Chuannithet Rd, a raised barrack-like structure divided into 8 rooms (as in a longhouse), verandah area pleasant for socializing. Shared bathrooms, hot water, reasonable place but not as clean as some others in town, popular with backpackers. Breakfast available. **E** *Yok Guesthouse*, 14 Sri Mongkol Rd, T611532. Tucked away behind a wat, this is a great place with 9 rooms with fan, and hot shower with soap and towels. Very clean and comfortable. Set around a little garden, it's a peaceful, friendly and safe place with caring owners. Small restaurant with good food. Free transport to and from the bus station and airport. Manager Susie is very helpful and organizes tours.

F *Johnnie House*, 5/2 Udon Chuannithet Rd. Peaceful position on the lakeside, 7 clean and simple rooms, shared hot water showers. Breakfast menu, laundry facilities. Friendly and quiet. **F** *Neelan Guesthouse*, Pracha Uthit Rd, next door to *Jean's Guesthouse*. Six fan rooms, but shared cold water shower. Nothing to write home about. **F** *Nui's Backpacker Lodge*, on corner before *Mae Hong Son Guest House*. Five concrete and bamboo huts with shower and double bed. Laundry service and some food. Nui speaks English. **F** *Paradise Huts*, 189/1 Mokasanti Rd. Five very basic bamboo huts. Mattresses on floor and no mosquito nets. Basic Thai bathroom, cold shower, far from 'paradise'.

Eating
● on map
Price categories:
see inside front cover

The largest concentration of restaurants is on Khunlum Praphat Rd. The cheapest place to eat is in the night market, also on Khunlum Praphat Rd. Internet cafés are proliferating on the main street amongst the coffee shops, see Directory below.

Thai/Chinese Cheap: *99 Restaurant*, on the road out of town near the stadium. Thai dishes at reasonable prices, set breakfast, barbecue, curries and salads. Open-air roadside place. *Fern Restaurant*, 87 Khunlum Praphat Rd. Large restaurant (making it popular with tour groups) in rambling, raised wooden house on road towards Mae Sariang, on edge of town. Smart yet unpretentious and affordable, mostly Thai dishes including good frog, spicy salads and crispy fish, also ice-creams. *Kin's House*, 89 Khunlum Praphat Rd (past *Fern Restaurant*). Selection of traditional and local Thai cuisine and Western food. Nice décor, café/bar atmosphere. Open front with a few tables on the street. Average prices and portions and good music. *Lakeside Bar*, 2/3 Khunlum Praphat Rd. Bar and restaurant with tables overlooking the lake, excellent place to eat and drink in the evening, the owner and manager, Khun Sirot, runs the place professionally and produces pancakes, milkshakes and cookies, along with more usual Thai dishes, live music in the evening. *Lucky Restaurant*, 5 Singhanat Bamrung Rd. Excellent restaurant in wooden house, run by Lucky, a man with a smile. Good atmosphere and décor and choice of Thai and Western dishes, specialities include deep fried catfish and steaks, also serves breakfast. Friendly and affordable. *Paa Dim*, Khunlum Praphat Rd (near the 7-11), popular with locals, varied but small selection of Thai dishes, good portions and cheap. *Ton Restaurant*, Pradit Jong Klang Rd (near the lake). Great little local roadside restaurant run by Ton. Good Thai dishes (especially red and green curries), sticky rice, salads and soups. Menu is in French and English. Extensive, cheap and tasty. *Thip Restaurant*, Pradit Jong Klang Rd (next to the lake). A newer touristy restaurant with upstairs balcony overlooking lake. Reasonable prices and reasonable food. **Seriously cheap**: *Baby Corn Restaurant*, Khunlum Praphat Rd (at the traffic lights), Thai rice and noodles, small menu but very cheap. Good shakes. *No name restaurant*, next to Tourist Police on Singhanat Bamrung Rd. A good local restaurant that does some vegetarian dishes. Tasty and cheap, but menu in Thai only.

Western Cheap: *Ban Buatong (aka JiJi's)*, 34 Khunlum Praphat Rd. This lady can cook. Breakfasts (American, Continental, Mexican and muesli), soups, spaghetti, sandwiches, Indian curries, salad, vegetarian dishes (moussaka, falafel, burrito, bruchetta, shepherd's pie, lasagna), also serves Thai food. Friendly, family atmosphere in a typical wooden Thai Yai house. *KK Bakery*, near *Pen Porn House*, fresh-baked cakes and bread, small selection of Thai dishes, set breakfasts, snacks and drinks. A bit like a diner, inexpensive. *Reaun Pap Restaurant*, Singhanat Bamrung Rd. Good atmosphere, décor and music. Real coffee and good orange juice. A few café items and good breakfasts; a cool place to hang out, also has internet access. *Sunflower Café and Tours*, 2/1 Khunlum Phraphat Soi 3, T620549, suncafetourmhs@cmnet.co.th Cosy café run by an Australian/Thai couple, popular with farangs. Good spot for breakfast and the best bread in town (it has its own bakery), also sells home-made cakes, pizzas and cheesecake. Good coffee, internet access and organizes tours. A great place with friendly service, a good source of information

Foodstalls Night market, also on Khunlum Praphat Rd.

Bars The best bar in town is *Butterfly*, at the crossroads on the way to *Mae Kong Son Guesthouse*. A swanky Thai Lounging bar with karaoke, big 1970s style kitsch chairs, live music and open as long as you care to drink. *Lakeside Bar*, 2/3 Khunlum Praphat Rd. See Eating above for details.

Traditional massage and herbal steam bath is a Mae Hong Son speciality; particularly **Massage**
welcome for those just back from strenuous treks. Available at several places around
town, for example *Piya Guesthouse* or on Pracha Uthit Rd. *Tubtim Thai Massage*, next
door to the *Lakeside Bar*, T620553, and above *Sunny Supermarket* (Khunlum Praphat
Rd), has been recommended (฿100-150 per hour).

Apr *Poi Sang Long* (movable, beginning of month), 10-16 year old boys are ordained **Festivals**
into the monkhood. Beforehand, they are dressed up as princes (the historic Buddha
was a prince), and on the following day there is a colourful procession through town
starting from Wat Kham Ko. **Oct** *Tak Bak Devo* (movable). Celebrates the Buddha's
descent from the Tavatimsa heaven. Festivities centre on the hill-top Wat Phrathat
Doi Kong Mu.

Books *Asia Books*, Khunlum Praphat Rd (next to *Panorama Hotel*), for English lan- **Shopping**
guage novels and magazines. **Handicrafts** *Thai Handicraft Centre*, Khunlum
Praphat Rd. *Chokeadradet*, 645 Khunlum Praphat Rd for antiques, tribal handicrafts
and junk. Recommended. Also a number of places on Singhanat Bamrung Rd. **Supermarkets** A 24 hr 7-11 and 2 good supermarkets, both near the crossroads in the centre of town. **Photo developing** Kodak and Fuji shops on Singhanat Bamrung Rd
(though developing quality varies).

Fitness Park (not as grand as it sounds) around the lake. **Sport**

The following have been recommended by a long-term resident of Mae Hong Son: **Tour operators**
TN Tour, 10 Udom Chuannithet Rd, T620059. Trekking, jeep adventure, rafting, *See also Trekking &*
licenced guides. *Sunflower Tours*, *Sunflower Café*, eco-conscious birdwatching and *Tours above*
nature treks. *Friend Tour* at *Friend Guesthouse*, T620119. Trekking, bamboo rafting,
elephant rides, boat trips, *Rose Garden Tours*, 86/4 Khunlum Prapaht Rd, T611577.
Cultural and ecological tours. French also spoken.

Local Mountain bike hire: from *22 Singhanat Bamrun Rd*, ฿100 per day (motor- **Transport**
bikes also available here). **Motorbike and jeep hire**: many places hire out jeeps, *360 km to*
motorbikes and scooters. Prices for motorbikes/scooters from ฿150-180 per day *Chiang Mai (274 km on*
(there are a couple of places at the southern end of Khunlum Praphat Rd), jeeps about *northern route),*
฿800-1,000 per day. **Car hire** *Avis*, airport, T620457, prices from ฿1,400 per day. *170 km to*
There is little point in listing companies – there are many, and guesthouses and trek- *Mae Sariang*
king companies are also in on the act. The **tuk-tuk** has also come to Mae Hong Son,
along with the **motorcycle taxi** (around ฿10-20 around town).

Long distance Air: airport is to the north of town on Niveshpishan Rd. It is only
about 1 km to town, so if staying at one of the central guesthouses it is easy enough to
walk (luggage allowing). The airport has an information counter and currency
exchange booth, and songthaews are also available for hire. Regular daily connections on Thai with Chiang Mai (35 mins) and Bangkok (2 hrs 10 mins).

Bus: station on Khunlum Praphat Rd, a short walk from town and most guesthouses.
There are 2 routes from Chiang Mai: the northern, more gruelling route via Pai (see
below), or the route described above, from the south, via Mae Sariang. Buses leave
through the day in both directions, (in total, 7 a day each way, most non-a/c, the first
via Pai at 0700 [฿48-100 to Pai, ฿94-180 to Chiang Mai]) and the first via Mae Sariang at
0600 [฿69-124 to Mae Sariang, ฿133-240 to Chiang Mai]). The trip to Pai takes 3-3½
hrs; to Mae Sariang, 4 hrs. For the journey all the way to Chiang Mai, the route via Pai
takes 8 hrs, via Mae Sariang 9½ hrs. Regular connections with Bangkok, 12½ hrs.

Directory **Airline offices** *Thai*, Singhanat Bamrung Rd, T611297. **Banks** Five in town, 3 with ATMs. *Thai Military Bank*, Khunlum Praphat (at intersection with Panit Wattana Rd). *Bangkok*, Khunlum Praphat Rd (0830-1900). *Bank of Ayodhya*, 61 Khunlum Praphat Rd. *Thai Farmers*, 78 Khunlum Praphat Rd. **Communications** Post Office: southern end of town, corner of Khunlum Praphat Rd and Soi 3, open 0830-1630 Mon to Fri and 0900-1200 Sat and Sun. **International Telephone service**: in new building behind Paa Dim Restaurant, 0830-1630 Mon to Sat. **Email**: at *Sunflower Café*, *Mae Hong Son Computer* (80 Khunlum Praphat Rd), *Reaun Pap Restaurant* and in an office over the bridge near the immigration office (the cheapest place). **Medical services** Clinic: Khunlum Praphat Rd. Hospital: at the eastern end of Singhanat Bamrung Rd. **Useful addresses** Immigration: Khunlum Praphat Rd (northern end of town, towards Pai). Tourist Police: 1 Rachathampitak Rd, T611812 (claim 24 hrs service).

Road to Pai

A stunning journey with magnificent views. This does not apply at the end of the dry season when fires cast a pall of smoke over the hills, obscuring the view. Some of the fires are intentionally lit to burn off paddy stubble or undergrowth; others are accidental, although the forest is adapted to periodic firing (it is a so-called fire-climax). The road winds through beautiful cultivated valleys and forest. Northwest of Pai is the **Shan** village of **Soppong**, a service centre providing for the needs of the surrounding hilltribe communities.

Soppong สบโป่ง

Colour map 1, grid A2

Soppong is a small way station between Pai and Mae Hong Son, about 44 km from Pai. Until it became a trekking centre there was almost nothing here bar the statutory school, clinic, bus stop, petrol station, grocery store and noodle shop. Now added to these are a handful of guesthouses. There is little reason to come here except to trek (and explore the surrounding countryside) – although this is a good place to escape to if nothing is what you want to do. There is a tourist 'office' – hardly an office, but there is a map of the area and several advertisements for guesthouses.

Excursions Guesthouses provide maps of the surrounding countryside and villages, with tracks marked. The main 'sight' hereabouts is **Lod Cave** (Tham Lod), about 10 km from town. The cave (in fact a series of three caves are accessible) has been used for habitation since prehistoric times and is a small part of what is presumed to be one of the largest cave systems in Northern Thailand. Guides hire out their services – and their lamps – to take visitors through the cave, which has a large stream running through it. Rafts are available to traverse the stream. To explore the accessible areas of the cave system takes around two hours. There is also a rather poor restaurant here. ■ *0800-1700 Mon-Sun.*

Mae Lanna is 6 km off the Soppong-Mae Hong Son Road, about 10 km along Route 1095 towards Mae Hong Son (after Phangmapha). The area offers limestone caves, good forest walks and stunning limestone scenery. There are hiking trails between Soppong and Mae Lanna, a quiet, highland shan village/town – guesthouses in Soppong provide sketch maps of the area. **E** *Mae Lanna Guesthouse* (closed July-August) is a good base from which to explore the surrounding countryside; the guesthouse is run by a French woman who is an excellent source of information and advice. An alternative place to stay is **E-F** *Top Hill*, not as well run or attractive but a good fall-back should the *Mae Lanna* be full. Even more remote (and basic) is the **F** *Wilderness Lodge*. This place is west of Phangmapha: get off the bus at Ban Nam Khong, turn off after Nam Khong Bridge. ■ *Getting there: to get to Mae Lanna, take a bus towards Mae Hong Son and get off at the turn-off for Mae Lanna (after Phongmapha); pick-ups run the 6 km (steeply) up to the village – or walk.*

There is excellent trekking from Soppong. Most of the guesthouses organize treks and this is one of the best bases hereabouts. Local villages include **Lisu**, **Black** and **Red Lahu**, and **Shan**. *T-Rex House* has set up *T-Rex Tours*, also known as *Wild and Exotic Thailand*, which markets tours in the UK with *Regent Travel UK*. It is the only company which boasts an eight day and a 15 day tour, which spans all three northern provinces (Mae Hong Son, Chiang Mai and Chiang Rai); more information on www.wild-exotic-thailand.com They also rent out quad bikes and have created some excellent dirt track routes through the (otherwise peaceful) surrounding countryside – noise pollution is making this unpopular with locals and visitors who have cherished the quiet. **NB** The Thai-Burmese border in this area is heavily mined and visitors should not hike without a guide. This applies particularly to Pang Ma Pha and Pai districts.

Trekking

As well as guesthouses either in, or close to, Soppong, there are also a number of places to stay to the northwest, around Mae Lanna. These are listed in the Mae Lanna excursion, above.

Sleeping
■ *on map, below*
Price codes:
see inside front cover

D *T-Rex House*, T617054, F617053. Run by Rudi and Ami, a Dutch/Thai couple. Spotless Western toilets, fans, reading lamps and hot showers, all powered by solar energy. Huts around a swimming pool in a quiet garden. There are also rooms in a stone farmhouse, which has a mini cinema for guests. Excellent restaurant (**cheap**) with large and diversely stocked bar. Trekking company run from here (see Trekking above). Quad bikes and motorbikes for hire. Recommended.

E *Cave Lodge*, a 1½-hr walk or ฿50 motorcycle journey from Soppong bus stop. This place is run by an Australian married to a Thai and has been highly recommended by visitors. Very peaceful location with bungalows and dormitory beds (**F**), increasingly popular travellers' haunt with attractive atmosphere, directions are posted at the bus stop in Soppong. Good information on excursions (including beautiful views from 'Big Knob', swimming in the local river) – the whole place can be a trifle damp in the wet season – and caving trips to the underground waterfall nearby, in a series of caves mapped by the owner of *Cave Lodge*, covering 9 km. Recommended. **E** *Jungle House*, 500 m out of Soppong towards Mae Hong Son, T617099. Attractive restaurant, another place with simple huts, hot water, nice garden and very friendly. They also organize treks. **E** *Charming House*, 1 km down a dirt track past the *Kemarin Guesthouse*. Very quiet and peaceful, several huts along a stream. **F** *Kemarin Garden*, a short way down a lane 200 m up the hill towards Pai. Four simple A frame bungalows, peaceful rural position with views over the hills, hot water showers. Huts and showers are surprisingly clean. Friendly management (but no English spoken). Recommended.

Thai massage and herbal sauna at some of the guesthouses, very relaxing after an exhausting trek.

Massage

Soppong

To Lod Cave (10 km) & Cave Lodge

To Mae Hong Son (66 km) & Mae Lanna

To Pai (44 km)

T-Rex House ■

Kemarin Guesthouse ■

Jungle House

Charming House

Not to scale

The Northern Region

Transport	**Bus** 6-7 buses each day (1 a/c) in each direction – west to Mae Hong Son (2 hrs), east
66 km to Mae Hong Son,	to Pai (1 hr) and Chiang Mai (5 hrs). **Motorbike/scooter hire** From shop close to the
44 km to Pai	bus stop and from *T-Rex House*.

Directory	**Banks** The nearest bank with exchange facilities is 1 hr away in Pai. **Communications** Post Office: by the *Lemon Hill Guesthouse*, towards Pai. **Telephone:** domestic calls can be made from the restaurant at the bus stop.

Pai ปาย

Colour map 1, grid A2

This small town lies in an upland valley between Mae Hong Son and Chiang Mai. The Pai River flows by the town and provides water for rice and vegetable cultivation. Although the last few years have seen considerable change as new guesthouses have opened, it is still charming and relatively unspoilt compared with places like Chiang Rai. It makes an excellent alternative base for trekking, or simply exploring alone on foot, bicycle or motorcycle.

The town has few sights as such – people come here to explore the surrounding area. There are two markets in town – the **talaat sot** (fresh market) on Rangsiyanon Road and the **talaat saeng thong araam** on Khetkelang Road. The finest monastery in town is Thai Yai-style **Wat Klang** near the bus station. A new monastery is **Wat Phrathat Mae Yen**, also known as the Wat on the Hill, about 1½ km east of town, on a hill. Most of the population of Pai are Shan and Thai, with a sprinkling of Muslims.

Excursions

Lisu, **Shan**, **Red Lahu** and **Kuomintang-Chinese** villages are all in the vicinity. There are also easy and attractive walks through the surrounding countryside. Most guesthouses provide rough maps of the surrounding countryside, detailing hilltribe villages, hot springs, caves, waterfalls and other sights. About 9 km from Soppong, after the Scenic Viewpoint rest area (Ban Nam Rin), is a guesthouse in the midst of a Lisu village. *Lisu Lodge* (E), run by a German/Lisu couple, is set in a beautiful natural setting, with caves, falls and more on the doorstep. Good German and Thai food, with basket weaving instruction on rainy afternoons.

Trekking

See Hilltribes & trekking, page 360

Many of the guesthouses run treks and there are plenty of companies offering a choice of treks and rafting trips. *Duang Trekking* (at *Duang Guesthouse*) offers basic trekking with all inclusive prices; *Karen Tours and Trekking* also offers elephant rides and rafting along with the treks; *PermChais* insists it offers non-tourist treks and will organize rafting and elephant safaris; *Back-Trax Tour and Trekking* organizes treks with Khun Chao, a TAT-registered guide and also offers Thai cookery courses and lessons in aromatherapy massage; *Lisu Tours and Trekking* has also been recommended. Average prices are in the region of ฿800-1,000 per day. One to four day treks are available. Shop around and talk to people who have recently returned. **NB** the Thai-Burmese border in this area is heavily mined and visitors should not hike without a guide. This applies particularly to Pang Ma Pha and Pai districts.

Tours

See also Tour operators below

Thai Adventure Rafting runs rafting expeditions down the Pai River (see Sport below). Elephant rides (they could hardly be described as 'treks') are also available from various companies (see Trekking above), including *Pai Elephant Camp Tours*, 5/3 Rungsiyanon Road, T699286, www.geocities.com/pai_tours Khun Thom is very helpful here and owns the elephant camp out of town towards the Hot Springs. Recommended elephant rides – you can even swim with them in the river or ride bare-back. She also runs a tour back to

The Northern Region

Chiang Mai in a truck, which includes a hotsprings visit at Pong Duat (about 63 km from Pai) and a visit to Mork Fah Waterfall (87 km from Pai). **NB** Many rafting companies only use their rafts once, then discard them. *Pai Elephant Camp Tours* re-use theirs.

C (for 4) *Pai Mountain Lodge*, 7 km northwest of town, T699068. For those wanting to 'get away from it all'. **C-D** *View Pai*, 143 Wiang Tai Rd, T699174. Shabby-looking and overpriced place, but fairly clean rooms. On the outskirts of town but with none of the out-of-town advantages, being situated on a main road and with no views from the rooms. **D** *Rim Pai Cottages*, 17 Moo 3, Wiang Tai, T699133. Good position on the river, small A-frame huts which are clean and cosy. Spotless Western toilets, a little over-priced but discounts available in the low season.

Sleeping
■ *on map, below*
Price codes:
see inside front cover

E *Duang*, 5 Rangsiyanon Rd, T699101. Opposite bus station, so noisy through the night. Clean and quiet, friendly English-speaking family-run guesthouse. Cheap, clean rooms with shared hot water showers, good restaurant (excellent coffee and French bread), trekking organized. Changes cash, bicycles for hire and maps provided. **E-F** *Peter and Vandee Huts*, east of town just past the turning for Mae Yen Waterfall, near the temple on the hill. Relaxing atmosphere, basic huts in shade of trees, set around pond, quiet location, shared toilets and shower room complete with foliage and tree inside it. Good food. **E-F** *Farmer's House*, on the road to Mae Yen Waterfall, 10 mins from Pai. Unshaded, quiet, basic huts with and without bathrooms, good food. **E** *Nunya's*, Rangsiyanon Rd, T699051. Seven clean rooms in 2-storey building set back from the road, upstairs rooms share hot water showers, those on the ground floor have attached clean Thai-style bathrooms, attractive small garden, well run.

The Northern Region

Pai

■ **Sleeping**
1 Big
2 Charlie's Place
3 Duang
4 Golden Huts
5 Nunya's
6 Rim Pai Cottages
7 Shan Guesthouse
8 Swan & Guy
9 View Pai

● **Eating**
1 All About Coffee
2 Be Bop
3 Butterfly Bakery
4 Duck Noodle Shop
5 Grandmother's Kitchen
6 Khao Soi Noodle Shop
7 Krazy Kitchen
8 Noodle shop
9 Own Home
10 Prick-Waan
11 River Corner

Treks organized through *Perm Chais Trekking*. **E** *Shan Guesthouse*, Rangsiyanon Rd. Located on the edge of town in a rather exposed position (but with great views), bungalows set in quiet location around a pond, with a Burmese pagoda-esque restaurant in the middle. Bungalows are raised off the ground and made of wood with 'leaf' roofs, good balconies. Seem to have trouble finding custom – probably because of the position. **E** *Swan and Guy*, 4 Rangsiyanon Rd, T/F699111. Excellent restaurant (see below), just a few rooms, really large 'suites' with bedroom, bathroom and sitting area, a little more expensive than other places but worth it, bathrooms with hot water showers are particularly notable (and the food). Recommended. Guy also arranges rafting expeditions on the Pai River (see Sport below). **E-F** *Charlie's Place*, 9 Rangsiyanon Rd (near the Krung Thai Bank). One of the larger places in town, with range of accommodation from dormitory beds to relatively sophisticated brick bungalows with attached bathrooms, all set in largish garden, good organization. Good trekking organized from here.

F *Big*, 70/1 Rangsiyanon Rd, T699080. Opposite the fresh market, rooms a little dark and dirty, with grubby Asian toilets. Look out for the wildlife in the courtyard, which includes a plastic zebra and kangaroo. **F** *Mountain Blue*, 1 km west of town, past hospital, nice bungalows around a pond, friendly. **F** *Golden Huts*, very quiet, beautiful out of the way location on the riverbank. Quiet and relaxing atmosphere, French owner provides a friendly service. Small but adequate restaurant with good food and great views. Recommended. **F** *Shan's*, out of town past police station. Clean rooms and good treks.

Eating

● *on map*
Price categories:
see inside front cover

Thai Cheap: *Prick-Waan Restaurant*, Chai Songkram Rd. Good Thai cuisine which tries not to pander to the sensibilities of the Western tastebud, more upmarket feel.

Western Mid-range: *Chez Swan*, 4 Rangsiyanon Rd. This is *the* place to eat – Guy is a Frenchman married to a Thai, and this is a little corner of France in Thailand. True to cultural stereotype, the food is excellent, the atmosphere appropriate: starched white tablecloths, wine, quiche, croque monsieur, crêpes, salads, steak and a few Thai dishes. Recommended (also open for breakfast). **Cheap**: *River Corner Restaurant*, newly opened in beautiful location on the river. Great food and views and friendly service. *Grandmother's Kitchen*, Chai Songkram Rd. Western food – normal traveller-type fodder. *Be Bop Restaurant*, Chai Songkram Rd. Thai and Western food, some live music. *Krazy Kitchen*, near the clinic. *Own Home Restaurant*, Ratdamrong Rd. Some Thai dishes, along with travellers' fare including tortillas, banana porridge, shakes, pizzas, moussaka and sandwiches. Food is good, although service can be semi-detached. **Seriously cheap**: *Duang's*, Rangsiyanon Rd. Good food. *Thai Yai*, Rangsiyanon Rd, northern end. Thai and international, good quiche, wholemeal bread etc, run by a Shan and his Scottish wife, books available to peruse. Recommended.

Bakeries *Butterfly Bakery*, Rangsiyanon Rd (not far from the fresh market). A number of coffee-come-pastry shops are on the main streets. **Cheap**: *All About Coffee*, next to *Prick-Waan*, is a quirky, arty café, with huge open chicken and cashew sandwiches and a large range of filter coffees and herbal teas.

Thai noodle shops Fed up with banana porridge and muesli? There are some very good noodle places in town (**seriously cheap**). By the post office on Khetkelang Rd is an excellent restaurant specializing in duck noodle soup. At the corner of Khetkelang and Chai Songkhram roads, one serves superb *Khao Soi* (spicy Northern noodles) – the *Nong Bear Restaurant*; the third good place is next to *Nunya's House* on Rangsiyanon Rd.

Night market Hardly a market as there is only a handful of stalls, but good pancakes and other food available.

Thai cooking classes At the *Sidewalk Kitchen*, Khetkelang Rd (near intersection with Chai Songkhram Rd).

Satang Bar, next to the bus stop. Sells Thai herbal whiskey (฿8 a shot), which is alleg- **Bars** edly medicinal, claiming to increase blood circulation, improve your health, increase bodily strength, relieve backache, aid sleep and also act as a poor man's Viagra. *Pai Corner Bar*, at crossroads of Raddamrong and Rangsiyanon roads. Snooker, darts, happy hour every Wed 1800-2000. *Mountain Blue Bar*, 1 km west of town, identifiable by its colourful façade. Live band most nights.

Traditional massage Opposite the *Rim Pai Cottages*, 68 Rachdamrong Rd, good **Massage** massage (฿120 per hour), friendly people, and at the Foundation of Shivaga Kommapaj and other places.

Books *Back Trax Tour and Trekking*, 67/1 Rungsiyanon Rd, rents, sells and **Shopping** exchanges English language books.

Duang Trekking, at the *Duang Guesthouse*. *Karen Tours and Trekking*, Rangsiyanon **Tour operators** Rd, opposite the market. *Perm Chais Trekking*, contact Nunyas or the office along *See also Tours above* Raddamrong Rd. *Back-Trax Tour and Trekking*, 67/1 Rungsiyanon Rd. *Lisu Tours and Trekking*, Rangsiyanon Rd, next to the market.

Rafting *Thai Adventure Rafting* arrange very good and professional 2-day expedi- **Sport** tions down the Pai River. They are run by Guy, a Frenchman, who with his Thai wife operates the *Chez Swan Restaurant* in Pai. The river is only high enough between Jul and Dec and a minimum of 4 people are required. For more information, contact Guy or Swan at the *Chez Swan* (see Sleeping).

Local Bicycle hire: ฿50 per day (mountain bikes) from the shop adjoining the **Transport** *Duang Guesthouse*, or from *Nunya's*. *Pai Tai Bike Society*, opposite the bus station, has *140 km to Chiang Mai,* information on routes and surrounding attractions. **Motorbike hire**: ฿150-200 per *110 km to Mae* day from several guesthouses and shops in town; eg *MS Bikes* opposite *Duang Guest- Hong Son* *house* at the top of Rangsiyanon Rd.

Long distance Bus: the bus stop is on Chai Songkhram Rd, near the centre of town. Most guesthouses are a short walk away. Four buses run to Mae Hong Son daily (3 hrs) and 4 to Chiang Mai (4 hrs). Also 5 connections a day to Fang (2½ hrs) via Mae Ma Lai. Some Fang buses continue to Tha Ton.

Banks *Krung Thai Bank*, Rangsiyanon Rd (the largest building in town and hard to miss). Open **Directory** 0830-1530 Mon-Fri. **Communications** Post Office: Khetkelang Rd. Overseas calls can be made from the office on Rangsiyanon Rd, not far from the fresh market. **Medical services** Clinic: open 1730-2030. Hospital: *Pai Hospital*, Chai Songkhram Rd (about 500 m from the town centre).

North to Kok River

Route 107 runs north from Chiang Mai to the former strategic town of Fang (152 km). From here a road winds eastwards over the mountains towards Chiang Rai. Few people stop in Fang; most merely pass through en route to Tha Ton, where boats and rafts can be hired to travel down the Kok River to Chiang Rai.

The Northern Region

Fang ฝาง

Phone code: 053
Colour map 1, grid A3

Fang was founded by King Mengrai in the 13th century, although its strategic location at the head of a valley means it has probably been an important trading and exchange settlement for considerably longer than seven centuries. The government has had some success in encouraging the predominantly Yao hilltribes to switch from opium production to other cash crops such as cabbages and potatoes – so-called crop substitution programmes. This, though, has not prevented Fang from remaining one of Thailand's key drug entrepôts. Opium, or refined heroin, passes from Burma into Thailand and to Fang, before being shipped on to other parts of the world. The valley land surrounding Fang is particularly fertile and is used for rice, fruit and vegetable cultivation. The Fang Oil Refinery, not far from the town on Route 109, also provides employment.

Tourists are a rarity in Fang; most visitors merely pass through en route to Tha Ton, where boats leave for the journey down the Kok River to Chiang Rai (see below). However, Fang is not without charm. Because it has attracted neither large numbers of tourists or great investment, the town has not suffered from crass re-development. There are a good smattering of **traditional wooden shophouses** in town. **Wat Jong Paen**, on Tha Phae Road at the northern edge of town, is Burmese in style.

Excursions & trekking

Chiang Dao Caves is a large cave complex, 90 km south of Fang off Route 107 towards Chiang Mai (see page 271). ■ *Getting there: take a bus to Chiang Mai and get off at the town of Chiang Dao. Songthaews take passengers the final 6 km to the caves.* **Hot springs** (*bor nam rawn*) can be found 12 km west of Fang, near Ban Muang Chom. ■ *Getting there: turn left shortly after leaving the town on the road north to Tha Ton.*

See Hilltribes and trekking, page 360. Treks can be organized through guesthouses in town, although there is a much wider choice in Tha Ton.

Sleeping
■ *on map*
Price codes:
see inside front cover

A-B *Angkhang Nature Resort*, 1/1 Moo 5 Baan Koom, Tambon Mae Ngon, T453515, F453520, angkhang@ amari.com, www.amari.com This place is around 40 km west of Fang, but to get to the resort it is necessary to drive 16 km south on Route 107 and then turn right on to Route 1249. The resort, which was developed under the auspices of the Royal Project Foundation, is situated high in the cool mountains, very close to the border with Burma and 25 km along Route 1249. It consists of 72 well appointed rooms with TV, IDD phones, hot water – and mountain bikes. A great place run by the Amari group and catering to those with thicker wallets. **B** *Chiang Dao Hill Resort*. Another place which is only really worth visiting for those with their own transport (or on a

Fang

To Tha Ton

Wat Jong Paen

Tha Phae Rd ■4 3■

Ⓢ ⓅPol

Wat Jedi Ngam
Market ○ ●JJ's Bakery
Rt 107

✉

🛏 Central Bus Station & Market
■1
○ Clock Tower

🚌 Minibuses to
Chiang Mai

■2

To Cheap Cheap Guesthouse,
Chiang Dao Caves & Chiang Mai

N

Not to scale

■ **Sleeping**
1 Chok Thani
2 New Poo Guesthouse
3 Uang Kham
4 Wiang Kaew

tour). Bavarian-style building on the main road north to Fang, 24 km from Chiang Dao and 52 km south of Fang. Comfortable rooms, hot water, overlooked by limestone pinnacles. **D-E** *Chok Thani*, 425 Chotana Rd, T451252, F451355. Some a/c, 'best' in town with clean if bare rooms. Functional, little more, just off the main road. **D** *Cheap Cheap Guesthouse*, 500 m off the main road towards the southern edge of the town (road to Chiang Mai), T453265. Its real name is Fang Academic Centre (FAC). Dorms for rent, and cheap cheap it is not – ฿200 for a dorm bed with fridge, TV and fan and cold water shower. Free laundry available. Food available if ordered in advance. Quiet location overlooking ricefields. **D** *Magic Home*, situated outside the town centre off Route 107 towards Chiang Mai. Dorm beds expensive (฿200), although dorms are clean and large. There are also more expensive rooms above the restaurant along the main road, with fan and toilet. **E** *New Poo Guesthouse*, off main road, just past *Chok Thani Hotel* down a dirt rack, T453210. Very small block with only 4 clean rooms, with fan and cold water shower and Thai toilet. Restaurant and snooker table, friendly management and quiet place. **E** *Uang Kham* (*Ueng Khum*), 227 Tha Phae Rd Soi 3, T451268. Clean bungalows, hot water. Recommended. **E** *Wiang Kaew*, just off Tha Phae Rd (over the bridge, north of the town centre). Simple but clean rooms, hot water, friendly place which has kept up standards long-term.

JJ's Bakery (opposite Wat Chedi Ngam, on the main road). Cakes, Thai and international. *Muang Fang* (on the main road, next to the Bangkok Bank), Thai. **Eating**

Bus Station is on the main road in the centre of town. Regular connections with Chiang Mai from the Chang Puak bus station on Chotana Road, 3 hrs. **Minibuses** run on the hour through the week between 0800 and 1600 from next to the hospital to Chiang Mai (฿80). **Songthaew**: regular connections with Tha Ton (40 mins). There are 2 routes to Chiang Rai: either take the songthaew from Fang to Mae Suai (40 mins), then catch a bus to Chiang Rai (95 km). Alternatively, take a songthaew from Tha Ton up to Doi Mae Salong, then to Mae Chan, then on to Chiang Rai (114 km). **Transport** *152 km to Chiang Mai*

Banks A number on the main road close to the clock tower. **Communications** Post Office: past the bus station, not far from the Bangkok Bank on the main road. **Directory**

Tha Ton ท่าตอน

Tha Ton lies on the Mae Kok and is a good starting point for trips on the Kok River to Chiang Rai, and for treks to the various hilltribe villages in the area. It is a pleasant little town with good accommodation and a friendly atmosphere. It also makes a good base for exploring this area of the north. Rafts travel downstream to Chiang Rai, while by road it is possible to head towards Doi Mae Salong, Mae Sai and Chiang Saen. *Phone code: 053* *Colour map 1, grid A3*

Wat Tha Ton overlooks the river, not far from the bridge. A stairway leads up to this schizophrenic monastery. On the hillside is a rather ersatz Chinese grotto, with gods, goddesses and fantastic animals including Kuan Yin, the monkey god and twining dragons. From this little piece of China, the stairway emerges in the compound of a classic, but rather ugly, modern Theravada Buddhist monastery. There is a restaurant, souvenir stall and more to show that Wat Tha Ton has truly embraced the pilgrim's dollar (or baht).

The **boat trip to Chiang Rai** takes four to five hours on a *long-tailed boat*, which is noisy and uncomfortable (฿200). A more relaxing form of transport is a gentle drift (at least in the dry season) on a bamboo raft. Most guesthouses will arrange raft trips and many will also combine the raft trip with a trek and/or elephant ride in various combinations, plus stops at hot springs, hill tribe villages and elephant camps. The rafts dock in Chiang Rai and the trip

The Northern Region

takes two days and a night, although motorized rafts complete the journey in a single day. The regular long-tail boat leaves at 1230, although they can be chartered at any time (maximum eight passengers, ฿1,600). The return boat from Chiang Rai departs at 1030.

NB At the end of 1997 a journalist reported that a group of Padaung (long-necked Karen) were being held against their wishes in a village on the Kok River, close to Tha Ton, and used as tourist attractions like exhibits in a human zoo. The journalist alleged collusion between the Padaung's owner, the Thai army and the Tourist Police. Since then further reports have argued that the Padaung are quite happy with the situation, that they receive a significant slice of the ฿250-300 paid by each visitor, and that they are much safer here than in a refugee camp closer to the Thai-Burma border. For more information on the Padaung, see page 306.

Trekking
See Hilltribes & trekking, page 360

The regular boat down the Kok River stops at riverside villages, from where it is possible to trek to hilltribe communities. **Louta**, 14 km east of Tha Ton and 1½ km off the main road between Tha Ton and Doi Mae Salong/Chiang Rai, is a well-off, developed Lisu village. (**E** *Asa's Guesthouse*, good food, a charming family-run house, attentive service. Recommended.) Other villages include **Tahamakeng** – one hour from Tha Ton (Lahu and Lisu villages within easy reach), **Ban Mai** – 45 minutes on from Tahamakeng (Lahu, Karen and Akha villages), and **Mae Salak** – further on still (Lahu, Lisu and Yao villages). Most guesthouses in Tha Ton will help you to organize these trekking or raft/boat trips, or take the scheduled daily boat from the pier. **Warning** In the past, trekkers have been robbed, but the TAT office in Chiang Rai inform us that there are now police checkpoints along the route, making it safer. Examples of pricing for treks are as follows: ฿1,500 for one night/two days including rafting. A one-day trip on an elephant will set you back ฿950, and a trip to Mae Sai and across the border into Burma costs ฿1,250 (including visa, car and guide).

Sleeping
■ *on map*
Price codes:
see inside front cover.
There is a good range of
accommodation here,
from basic guesthouses
through to comfortable
small hotels

AL *Mae Kok River Village Resort*, T459355, F459329, tiger@loxinfo.co.th This is the replacement for the now defunct *Mae Kok River Lodge*. River view, a/c, restaurant. The only place in Tha Ton with an (average) pool. Well run with lots of imaginative tours, from mountain biking to elephant trekking and rafting. Thai massage and herbal sauna. Quiet location on the river, away from town, restaurant on the banks of the Kok. Rooms are good but a trifle pricey. The hotel also arranges 6-day Thai coooking courses (US$240). Large garden. Some chalets around the pool, most in garden setting. **A** *Thaton River View Resort* (member of Comfort Inn group), T459289/373173, F459288. River view, a/c, restaurant. Small bungalows scattered along the riverbank. This is probably the most attractively positioned of all the places to stay in Tha Ton. It is on the river, at a confluence of the Mae Kok and a tributary, away from town and overlooking fields and mountains. Well run with friendly atmosphere. Rooms are comfortable and clean with satellite TV. Airy restaurant (**cheap**) with extensive Thai menu and a smattering of Western dishes, small library. Room rate includes buffet breakfast. Popular with tour groups – but don't be put off! **B** *Thaton Chalet*, 192/1 Mu 14, T373155, F373158. A/c, restaurant, 4 storeys, right by the bridge and overlooking the river with, as the name chalets, pretensions of chalet-ness. Rooms are clean and very comfortable with hot water showers (baths in the deluxe rooms), minibar and satellite TV. Riverside bar. **B-E** *Garden Home*, T373015. Away from the main bustle of places, this peaceful resort has good bungalows set in a large tree-filled orchard garden on the river's edge. Fan rooms are very clean, with spotless Thai toilets (Western toilets, a/c and hot water showers cost more), quiet and friendly, no restaurant. Note that the bungalows here range widely in price from guesthouse level up to hotel quality. Recommended.

D *Tha Ton Garden*. Easily confused with the nearby *Garden Home*. Riverside location, garden compound, well maintained, hot water and a/c. **D-E** *Apple Restaurant and Guesthouse*. There are 2 Apples. One, reminiscent of an Austrian ski chalet, has quite good clean fan rooms with bath, hot water and Western toilets. The airy restaurant downstairs has extensive menu of Western and Thai dishes, but management are unhelpful. The second Apple is the guesthouse about 100 m away. Peaceful, in large garden compound, but no river view. **D-E** *Thip's II*, 3½ km out of village on the Chiang Rai road (ask *Thip's I* for help in getting there). Situated in a farm with a nice garden on a hill, some rooms with hot water. This place was closed in mid-2000, but the manageress of Thip I was contemplating re-opening it should demand increase. **E** *Chankasem*, T459313. Near the pier, large restaurant overlooking the river. Rooms are spacious and clean, and have fan and shower. Tours and treks organized through *Tha Ton Tours*. **E** *Naam Waan Guesthouse*, close to the river and the centre of town. Rooms in a row in a long single storeyed structure, with attached bathrooms and hot water. No view. Adequate. **E** *Thip's Travellers House*, T459312, in front of police box, next to the bridge on the main road so traffic noise can be disturbing. Restaurant, basic, small but clean rooms with Asian toilets, in a compact garden courtyard. Mosquitoes are a problem, friendly and very popular place, rafting and trekking organized here. The manageress settled here when her policeman husband was transferred to Fang from Bangkok.

There are a number of attractive riverside restaurants, including: **Cheap** *Thaton Chalet Restaurant* is a riverside restaurant on the verandah of this hotel, serving Thai and Chinese food. **Seriously cheap** *Sonay Chainam Restaurant*, on the north side of the bridge by the riverside, serving Thai and European food. Average. *Khao Soi Restaurant*, friendly place right by the river and bridge, and next to *Thip's Travellers House* serving khao soi (of course) and the usual rice and noodle dishes. *Riverside Thai Restaurant*, a nice place to eat, open for breakfast, lunch and dinner. Thatched riverside affair with good fish dishes – watch out for mozzies in the evening.

Eating
● *on map, below*
Price categories:
see inside front cover

Northern Express Tours has been recommended as a helpful and friendly set-up which organizes trekking and raft trips. Situated just along from the Tourist Police Station. *Tha Ton Tours*, T/F373143, and *Thip Travel* (attached to *Thip's Travellers House*), T459312. Both arrange raft trips. For more imaginative but expensive tours, visit *Track of the Tiger*, based at the *Mae Kok River Village Resort* (see entry and map).

Tour operators

Local Songthaew: regular connections with Fang every 15 mins. **Bicycle hire**: from *Apple Guesthouse* and from *Thaton River View Resort*.

Transport
23 km to Fang

Long distance Bus: connections with Chiang Mai (4 hrs), or a minibus

Tha Ton

To Village

To Thip's II, Asa's Guesthouse, Mae Salong & Chiang Rai

River Kok

Check Point

To Chiang Rai

Wat Tha Ton

Pier o Taton Tour

To Chiang Mai & Fang

N

Not to scale

■ **Sleeping**
1 Apple Guesthouse
2 Apple Restaurant & Guesthouse
3 Chankasem
4 Garden Home
5 Mae Kok River Village Resort
6 Naam Waan Guesthouse
7 Thaton Chalet & Restaurant
8 Tha Ton Garden
9 Thaton River View Resort
10 Thip's Travellers House, Thip Travel & Khao Soi Restaurant

● **Eating**
1 Riverside Thai
2 Sonay Chainam

The Northern Region

Boat prices from Tha Ton

	Public boat	Private hire
Ban Mai	฿50	฿800
Mae Salak	฿65	฿500
Pha Tai	฿75	฿700
Jakue	฿90	฿900
Kok Noi	฿110	฿900
Pha Khang	฿110	฿1,300
Pha Kaew	฿160	฿1,300
Had Waudam	฿160	฿1,500
Ruam Mitr	฿185	฿1,500
Chiang Rai	฿200	฿1,600

NB Early 2000 prices quoted

to Fang which connects with more frequent buses to Chiang Mai (40 mins). Regular connections with Chiang Rai (2½ hrs), Mae Sai (1½ hrs), Chiang Saen (1½ hrs), Chiang Khong (2½ hrs) and Mae Salong (2½ hrs). It is also possible to get to and from Pai/Mae Hong Son without going through Chiang Mai: from Tha Ton, catch a bus through Fang heading for Chiang Mai and get off at Ban Mae Malai, at the junction with Route 1095. Then, pick up a bus heading for Pai/Mae Hong Son. Travelling in the other direction, simply remember to alight at the junction of routes 1095 and 107 and then catch one of the regular buses heading north to Fang. Finally, there are also regular connections with Bangkok, most leaving in the evening.

Boat: the regular boat to Chiang Rai departs at 1230 and takes 2½-3½ hrs, depending on the state of the river (฿200). Tha Ton Boat Office is open 0900-1500, T459427. Or hire the whole boat, seating up to 8 people, ฿1,600 (or slightly cheaper ฿1,400 if hired through one of the tour operators, see section above). See above for details on organizing a raft trip to Chiang Rai. Note that the pier in Chiang Rai has moved from close to the centre of town to a site around 2 km northwest, beyond the *Dusit Island Resort*; see map, page 328. **NB** Before leaving Tha Ton by boat, travellers must sign out at the tourist police box next to the pier.

Directory **Communications** Telephone Office: Ngam Muang Rd, near Wat Phra Kaeo. **Useful addresses** Tourist Police: emergency telephone number, T1155 (24 hrs).

Chiang Rai, Mekong and the Golden Triangle

Chiang Rai is the largest town in the far north of Thailand and a popular tourist centre. Route 118 is the most direct road from Chiang Mai (180 km), although buses from Bangkok and the south travel up Route 1 and through the town of Phayao. Chiang Rai has become Thailand's second-largest trekking centre, and is used as a base to explore the towns of the Golden Triangle and settlements on the Mekong River. Chiang Saen, 60 km northeast of Chiang Rai, was the capital of the Chiang Saen Kingdom and is situated on the banks of the Mekong. Travelling downstream for 70 km, the road reaches the small outpost of Chiang Khong. Meanwhile, 11 km upstream from Chiang Saen is Sop Ruak, at the apex of the Golden Triangle and a quickly expanding tourist centre. Mae Sai, upstream still further and 61 km north of Chiang Rai, is Thailand's most northerly town and a busy border trading-post with Burma. A new road runs off Route 110 to the hill town of Mae Salong, from where a poor track continues west to Tha Ton.

The new route to Chiang Rai cuts through forests and is fast and scenic. There are rather novel European-style country cottages along the way and some good resort-style hotels. The best is the *Felix Resort* (**A**), Suanthip Vana Resort, 49 Chiang Mai-Chiang Rai Rd (74 km from Chiang Rai, 12 km from Wiang Pa Pao), T2246984, F2446983, felixkt@loxinfo.com, www.felixhotels.com This is in a lovely location with spacious villas and a good pool; a great place to relax but not near anywhere. Mae Suai, with a hilltop monastery, is at the junction where roads lead south to Chiang Mai, north to Chiang Rai, west to Fang and southeast to Phayao. There is one reasonable guesthouse here (about 8 km north of Mae Suai), the **D-E** *Karen Guesthouse*, about 1 km north of Mae Suai on the road to Chiang Rai. Slightly more upmarket and a little further out of town is the *Harin Garden Resort*, with its own bakery and restaurant and reasonable villas.

Phayao พะเยา

Phone code: 054
Colour map 1, grid A3

Phayao is a relatively quiet and rarely visited town on the route up to Chiang Rai. It is attractively set on a lake and makes a worthwhile alternative place to stay on the route north to Chiang Rai. There is a sort of provincial esplanade, boats and pedalos for hire, and a profusion of foodstalls. Phayao became a provincial capital when a province of the same name was created in 1977, and still seems to be coming to terms with its new-found importance. Historically, the town appears to have been an important defensive site for many years, perhaps as far back as the Bronze Age. **Wat Si Khom Kham**, also known as Wat Phra Chao Ton Luang, is on the eastern banks of Phayao Lake and dates from 1491. The viharn contains an important 14 m-high and 16 m-wide Buddha image made in the 16th century; it is supposedly the largest Late Chiang Saen-style Buddha image in Northern Thailand. However, in recent years its origins have been obscured through an enthusiastic rebuilding programme. There is now a fantasyland of concrete animals and ogres to complement the more usual wat inhabitants. A festival is held here each May. Another 12th-century wat in the town is **Wat Luang Raja Santham**. For those who like to live dangerously, there are pedalos for hire on the lake – although you will probably end up swimming back to shore, as they are pretty dilapidated. There is a small wooden hut in the corner of the park on the lake side that proudly announces 'Tourist Information'. It is empty inside and very neglected out; a fitting symbol of Phayao's tourist industry.

A-B *Phayao Hotel*, 445 Phahonyothin Rd, T481970, F481973. A/c, large, comfortable hotel with 80 rooms, best in town. **D-E** *Tharn Thong*, 55-57 Donsanam Rd, T431302, F481256. A bare, airy hotel, with old but large and clean rooms. Rooms have shower and Thai toilets and face onto a concrete courtyard. Great value. **E** *Wattana*, 69 Donsanam Rd, T431203. Seemingly cleaner than its next door rival; rooms are pleasant with spotless Western toilets, fan and shower, also great value. **Sleeping**

Restaurants can be found on Chai Kwan Rd and Phahonyothin Rd. **Foodstalls and bars** There are lots of stalls on the lakeshore that provide mats and low tables on the grass. To get there, walk down Donsanam Rd and turn left. The small, well-kept park also has night stalls. **Eating**

Transport

*747 km to Bangkok,
142 km to Lampang,
93 km to Chiang Rai*

Bus The station is at the southern end of town, just off Donsanam Rd (on right-hand side when facing south – the lake is on your left). For people arriving in town, as you face the department store opposite, turn left onto Donsanam Rd and then left again, which takes you into the centre of town. Connections with Chiang Mai (3 hrs) and Chiang Rai, and with Bangkok's Northern bus terminal (10 hrs).

Directory

Banks Several along Donsanam Rd, all with exchange services. **Communications** There is a telecommunications centre opposite the Phayao Hospital (about 500 m south along Route 1), which provides an overseas calls service.

Chiang Rai เชียงราย

*Phone code: 053
Colour map 1, grid A3
Population: 40,000*

Given the ancient roots of Chiang Rai, the capital of Thailand's most northerly province, it is rather disappointingly short of sights of historical interest, with ugly shophouse architecture predominating. Even the local TAT office admits that the town itself has little to offer in the way of 'sights'. However, accommodation is of a high standard, and Chiang Rai makes a good base for trekking and visiting the towns and countryside to the north.

Ins and outs

Getting there
*See also Transport,
page 333*

Chiang Rai's newish airport is 8 km north of the city. There are daily connections with Bangkok and Chiang Mai, and some talk of flights to international destinations in the region. The bus station is slap in the centre of town (but a fair walk from most of the guesthouses), and there are regular connections with Bangkok, most northern towns including Chiang Mai and with assorted destinations in the Northeast and Central Plains. Scheduled boats ply the Kok River, upstream to Tha Ton and downstream to Chiang Khong.

Getting around

Chiang Rai is a sprawling town and, while walking is fine in the morning and evening, during the day many locals choose to travel by saamlor or songthaew. Most of the area's attractions lie in the surrounding countryside, and there are ample vehicle hire shops offering bicycles, cars, motorbikes and jeeps.

Tourist offices

TAT, 448/16 Singhaklai Rd (near the river, opposite Wat Phra Singh), T717433, F717434. Well-run office which opened in 1992, useful town maps and information on trekking and accommodation. Areas of responsibility are Chiang Rai, Phayao, Uttaradit, Phrae and Nan.

Background

Chiang Rai was founded in 1268 by King Mengrai, who later moved his capital here. The city became one of the key muang or city states within the Lanna Kingdom's sphere of control – until Lanna began to disintegrate in the 16th century. Although it is now Thailand's most northerly town, at the time of its foundation Chiang Rai represented the most southerly bulwark against the Mons. It was later conquered by the Burmese and only became part of Thailand again in 1786.

Today, Chiang Rai has ambitious plans for the future. Lying close to what has been termed the 'Golden Rectangle', linking Thailand with Laos, Myanmar and southern China, the city's politicians and businessmen hope to cash in on the opening up of the latter three countries. Always searching for catchy phrases to talk up a nascent idea, they even talk of the 'Five Chiangs strategy' – referring to the five towns of Chiang Tung (or Kengtung in Myanmar), Chiang Rung (in China), Chiang Thong (in Laos), and Chiang

Mai and Chiang Rai (both in Thailand). Roads linking the five are being planned and an EU-style free trade area discussed. Talk, as they say, is cheap; a mini-EU in this peripheral part of Asia seems a distant dream, despite a noticeable increase in cross-border activity.

Sights

The city's finest monastery is Wat Phra Kaeo, at the north end of Trairat Road. The wat was probably founded in the 13th century when it was known as Wat Pa-Year. Its change of name came about following divine intervention in 1434 when, local legend recounts, the stupa was struck by lightning to reveal the famous Emerald Buddha or *Phra Kaeo*, now in residence in Bangkok's Temple of the Emerald Buddha (see page 95). With this momentous discovery, the wat was renamed Wat Phra Kaeo and was elevated to the status of a royal wat in 1987. The finest structure here is the bot (straight ahead as you pass through the main gates on Trairat Road – the bai sema or boundary stones identifying it as the bot are rather hard to make out at first glance). It was built in Chiang Saen style and features accomplished woodcarving, a pair of fine nagas flanking the entrance way and, inside, a highly regarded 13th-century image of the Buddha calling the earth goddess to witness – in Indian Pala style. Presumably slightly peeved that the Phra Kaeo itself had been carted off to Bangkok, a rich local Chinese businessman – a Mr Lo – commissioned a Chinese artist to carve a replica image from Canadian jade. The work was undertaken in Beijing to mark the 90th birthday of the Princess Mother and she gave it the gargantuan name Phraphuttaratanakorn Nawutiwatsanusornmong-khon, or The Lord Buddha is the source of the Three Gems of Buddhism. The image was kept in the monastery's bot until a new building, specially designed to house it, had been completed and the image installed in a consecration ceremony held in September 1991. The Chiang Rai Phra Kaeo Shrine is behind the bot, with two ponds filled with turtles (set free by people to gain merit) in front of it.

Wat Phra Kaeo

Above Wat Phra Kaeo, perched at the top of a small hill, is Wat Ngam Muang, unremarkable save for the views it offers of the city and surrounding countryside. However, historically it is important, as the stupa here contains the ashes of the great King Mengrai (?-1317). The edifice is currently being renovated and will have a statue of the king placed in front of his *ku*.

Wat Ngam Muang

Further northwest still is Wat Phrathat Doi Chom Thong, again, and as its name indicates, built at the top of a small hill. The wat contains the city pillar (*lak muang*). **Wat Phra Singh** (dating from 1385) is an important teaching monastery on Singhaklai Road, in the north of town. Note the finely wrought animal medallions below the windows of the bot – rats, elephants, tigers,

Wat Phrathat Doi Chom Thong

The Northern Region

•••

Chiang Rai place names

Ban Du
บ้านดู่

Hill Tribe Education Center
ศูนย์พัฒนาการศึกษาชาวเขา

Wat Phrathat Doi Chom Thong
วัดพระธาตุดอยจอมทอง

Wat Phra Kaeo
วัดพระแก้ว

Wat Ngam Muang
วัดงามเมือง

Wat Phra Singh
วัดพระสิงห์

snakes and other beasts – and the gaudy but vivacious murals that decorate the interior. Also unusual is the Bodhi tree, surrounded by images of the Buddha in each of the principal mudras.

Wat Mung Muang South of Wat Phra Singh is Wat Mung Muang, notable largely for its corpulent image of the Buddha which projects above the monastery walls. The image is not at all Thai in style, but appears Chinese with its sausage-like fingers spinning the wheel of law. The area around Wat Mung Muang supports a **daily market** and in the mornings from 0600 or so, vegetable hawkers set up along the monastery walls, providing a wonderful contrast in colour and texture with the golden Buddha image. Songthaews, saamlors and tuk-tuks wait to transport market-goers back to their houses and villages. In the east of town, at the so-called *haa yaek* (five-way junction) on Phahonyothin Road, is the new **statue of King Mengrai**, Chiang Rai's most illustrious king.

Night Market Building on the success of Chiang Mai's night bazaar, Chiang Rai opened its own version off Phahonyothin Road a few years back. It has since expanded tremendously and sells the usual range of hilltribe handicrafts, carvings, china products, wooden boxes and picture frames; the Thai equivalent of beanie babies, catapults and so on. In many ways it is a nicer place to browse than the Chiang Mai Night Bazaar. It is more open, less frenetic, friendlier, and there is live music, open air restaurants and, it seems, a thicker sprinkling of Thais. It opens at nightfall.

Hilltribe Education Center The Population and Development Association's (PDA) Hilltribe Education Center, at 620/25 Thanalai Road, is one of the more interesting attractions in the town, with a small informative hill tribe museum and an audio-visual presentation on hilltribe life (open 1300-1330 Monday-Sunday, or on request, for a small fee, in English, Thai, French or Japanese). The PDA, better known for its family planning and AIDS work, is attempting to provide hilltribe communities with additional income-earning opportunities, as the pressures of commercial life increase. In 2000, building work next door was taking place; the new museum is to be six times the floor area of the existing room. Attached to the museum is a branch of the *Cabbages and Condoms* chain of restaurants (see **Eating**, below). ■ *0830-2000 Mon-Sun. Admission to museum ฿20, CRPDA@hotmail.com*

Excursions The towns of **Chiang Saen** (ancient capital of the kingdom of the same name), **Sop Ruak** (the Golden Triangle) and **Mae Sai** (border town with Burma) can all be visited as a day trip from Chiang Rai (see below).

Ban Du is a paper-making village, 8 km north of Chiang Rai off Route 110. Paper is produced from the bark of the *sa* tree, which is stripped off, air dried, soaked in water, boiled in caustic soda and finally beaten, before being made into paper. ■ *Getting there: by songthaew or bus travelling north on Route 110 (towards Mae Sai), or by tuk-tuk.*

Trekking
See Hilltribes & trekking, page 360 A two day/one night raft trip should cost about ฿800-1,100 per person, four day/three night trek about ฿1,500-2,000. Most treks are cheaper if organized through guesthouses and they are usually also more adventurous. The usual range of elephant rides and boat trips as part of a trek are also offered. Before embarking on a trek, it is worthwhile visiting the Hilltribe Education Center (see above). Tribes in the area include Karen, Lisu, Lahu and Akha. Trekking companies are concentrated around the *Wangcome Hotel* plaza area; most guesthouses also offer trekking services. For a listing, see below. The TAT office produces a list of companies with average prices and other useful advice.

Day tours to visit hilltribe villages, Sop Ruak and the Golden Triangle, Mae Sai, Mae Salong and Chiang Saen are organized by most of the tour/trekking companies listed below (₿600). Tours which include an elephant ride and boat trip, plus visits to hilltribe villages, cost about ₿700.

Tours
See also Tour operators below

Cruises on the Mekong *Mae Salong Tour*, 882 Phahonyothin Rd, T712515, F711011, runs various cruises on the Mekong that include Laos, China and Thailand in their itineraries.

Motorcycle tours These are becoming increasingly popular, and many guesthouses provide rental services and information on routes to take for a day's excursion.

Essentials

Accommodation in Chiang Rai is of a high standard. Guesthouses, particularly, are quiet, with large and generally clean rooms – a welcome change from some of the places in Chiang Mai. Most are concentrated in the quieter northern part of the city, some on the 'island' between both branches of the Kok River.

Sleeping
■ *on map, page 328*
Price codes:
see inside front cover

AL *Dusit Island*, 1129 Kraisorasit Rd, T715777, F715801, chiangrai@dusit.com A/c, restaurant, pool, overblown, fairly ostentatious hotel, just north of town on an 'island' in the river, set in lavish grounds. By far the best in Chiang Rai (but you pay for it), with 271 rooms and suites, and every facility including fitness centre, tennis courts and steam and sauna rooms (and some very enticing massage packages). Being located away from the city, it is rather detached from all the action. **A** *Inn Come*, 172/6 Ratbamrung Rd, 2 km south of town, close to *Little Duck Hotel*, T717850, F717855. A/c, restaurant, rather a hideous construction – little to recommend it and beginning to look tatty. **A** *Little Duck*, 4 Phahonyothin Rd, 2 km south of town, off main road to Chiang Mai, T715621, T02-691594, F715639. Price includes breakfast. A/c, restaurant, pool and its own department store. Large and impersonal but professionally run, with all amenities. **A** *Rim Kok Resort*, 6 Mu 4 Chiang Rai-Thaton Rd, 5 km from town, north of the river, T716445, F715859. A/c, restaurant, pool, lavish hotel in modern northern Thai style. Over 500 rooms, sports complex. **A** *Wiang Inn*, 893 Phahonyothin Rd, T711533, F711877. A/c, restaurant, small pool, the original 'luxury' hotel in town, renovated in 1992/93 and still holding its own. Fairly standard, but perfectly adequate rooms (with satellite TV), stylish lobby, competitively priced against the competition, central location but set back from the main road so comparatively peaceful, the buffet breakfast and lunch (with *dim sum*) are very good value. Recommended.
A-B *Wangcome*, 869/90 Premwipak Rd, T711800, F712973. A/c, restaurant (price includes breakfast), pool, very central, rather ugly high-rise block, with uninteresting though comfortable rooms.

C *Chiang Rai Inn*, 661 Uttarakit Rd, T/F712673. A/c hotel in modern interpretation of northern Thai architecture, large, spotless but plain rooms, immaculate bathrooms, hot water, comfortable, discounts available, good value. **C** *Golden Triangle Inn*, 590 Phahonyothin Rd, T711339, F713963. A/c, restaurant. This is a great little hotel on a tree-filled plot of land, rooms are clean and stylish (though rather overrun with mosquitoes), with hilltribe artefacts and an attention to detail which is rare at this level. Piping hot water in the bathrooms. Good treks, friendly atmosphere, breakfast included in room rate. Recommended. **C** *Sukniran*, 424/1 Banphaprakan Rd, T711055, F714701. Some a/c, good position close to clock tower, airy lobby and rooms facing a courtyard away from the main road, so not too noisy. **C** *YMCA*, 70 Phahonyothin Rd (the main highway, so some rooms are noisy), T713785, F714336. A/c, pool, clean and well kept, but some distance out of town towards Mae Sai, past the handicraft centre. **C-D** *Kijnakorn Guest House*, 24 Ruang Nakhon Rd, T744150. Set

The Northern Region

Chiang Rai

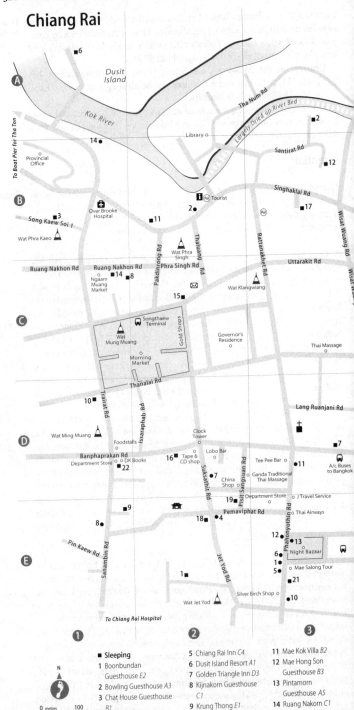

Dusit Island

Kok River

To Boat Pier for Tha Ton

Provincial Office

Library

Tha Num Rd

Longely Dried up River Bed

Santirat Rd

2

12

Singhaklai Rd

17

Tourist

2

11

Over Brooke Hospital

3

Song Kaew Soi 1

Wat Phra Kaeo

Wat Phra Singh

Pakdingnong Rd

Phra Singh Rd

Thaluang Rd

Rattanakhet Rd

Uttarakit Rd

Wisat Wuang Rd

Ruang Nakhon Rd

Ruang Nakhon Rd

14

8

Ngaam Muang Market

15

Wat Klangwiang

Wat Mung Muang

Songthaew Terminal

Gold Shops

Governor's Residence

Thai Massage

Morning Market

Thanalai Rd

Trairat Rd

10

Wat Ming Muang

Foodstalls

Banphaprakan Rd

Department Store

DK Books

22

Issaraphab Rd

16

Tape & CD shop

Clock Tower

Lobo Bar

Lang Ruanjani Rd

7

Tee Pee Bar

11

A/c Buses to Bangkok

Suksathit Rd

7

China Shop

Phisit Sangsue Rd

Ganda Traditional Thai Massage

Department Store

J Travel Service

9

Pemaviphat Rd

18

4

19

Thai Airways

8

Pin Kaew Rd

Sanambin Rd

Jet Yod Rd

1

12

Phahonyothin Rd

13

Night Bazaar

6

1

Mae Salong Tour

5

21

Silver Birch Shop

10

Wat Jet Yod

To Chiang Rai Hospital

6

14

3

1

2

3

N

0 metres 100

0 yards 100

■ **Sleeping**
1 Boonbundan Guesthouse *E2*
2 Bowling Guesthouse *A3*
3 Chat House Guesthouse *B1*
4 Chian Resort *A5*

5 Chiang Rai Inn *C4*
6 Dusit Island Resort *A1*
7 Golden Triangle Inn *D3*
8 Kijnakorn Guesthouse *C1*
9 Krung Thong *E1*
10 Lek House *D1*

11 Mae Kok Villa *B2*
12 Mae Hong Son Guesthouse *B3*
13 Pintamorn Guesthouse *A5*
14 Ruang Nakorn *C1*
15 Siriwattana *C2*

■4

■13 Soi Koh Kaew

Kao Loi Rd

Rong Khasat Rd

To Handicraft Centre, YMCA, Airport (8 km) & Mae Sai

Singhaklai Rd

Sriboonruang Rd

Wat Sriboonruang

Kong Yao Rd

20■

Uttarakit Rd

5■

King Mengrai's Monument

Nohng Boor Rd

To Highway 1232

PDA (Hill Tribe Museum & Centre)

●9   ●3

Nong Siijaeng Rd

Phahonyothin Rd

Asia Rd

Srikert Rd

Soi 1

Alliance Française

Soi 4

Soi 2

Wat Srigird

Phahonyothin Rd

Night Food Stalls

Market

Prasupsuk Rd

To Chiang Mai, Inn Come & Little Duck Hotels

4   **5**   **6**

away from the road down a tiny soi. This 'guesthouse' is more like a small hotel. Clean but bare and sterile rooms and bathrooms, some a/c. Slightly overpriced and lacks any memorable features. **C-E** *Boonbundan Guesthouse*, 1005/13 Jet Yod Rd, T717040, F712914. Some a/c, outdoor eating area, quiet leafy compound near centre of town. Professionally managed, good range of services, clean rooms with hot water although becoming shabby, wide range of rates. Recommended.

D *Thanapat Guesthouse*, 473/34 Singhaklai Rd, T/F712492. Some a/c, down a narrow soi not far from the TAT office. Large and very clean rooms (those facing the main road are rather noisy). Rather devoid of atmosphere, with the communal area in a car shelter. No English spoken. Range of services from trekking to bike hire. **D-F** *Chian House*, 172 Sriboonruang Rd (on the island), T713388. Pool, the cheapest place with a pool in town (fed by groundwater). Clean and friendly, if a bit concrete, more expensive rooms are a good size with hot water. The large bungalows are especially good value. Peaceful atmosphere and good food. Also organizes treks and tours and has an email service. **D-F** *Mae Kok Villa* (*Chiang Rai Youth Hostel*), 445 Singhaklai Rd, T711786. This former secondary school makes for an unusual hotel, the elegant though rather ramshackle main wooden building has dorm beds, while the bungalows in the big, leafy, riverside compound are large, if slightly murky, more expensive rooms with hot water (10% discount for ISIC cardholders). **D-F** *Pintamorn Guesthouse*, 199/1-3 Mu 21 Singhaklai Rd, T714161, F713317. Some a/c, run by a Hawaiian, who has given the guesthouse a distinctly 'Western' feel (rooms have names such as Ronald and Debbie), with Indian murals and posters of James Dean. Quiet and friendly guesthouse in a peaceful area of town. Rooms are large and well maintained, the 'VIP' room is a real bargain with a/c, hot water and a sitting area, all for ฿350. Other facilities include a pool table and bar, and trekking and motorbike and jeep rental can be arranged. A friendly place with lots of atmosphere and good value. Recommended.

E *Chat House*, 3/2 Trairat Soi Songkaew (near Wat Phra Kaeo), T711481. In a quiet, leafy compound down a narrow soi, and away from the main concentration of guesthouses. Smelly, damp rooms and attached bathrooms with hot showers (which may not work). A run down feel about the place, although friendly people and great potential. Dorm beds available, good food and satellite TV. Trekking and motorbike hire available. **E** *Siriwattana Hotel*, 458 Uttarakit Rd (by the GPO), T711466. Not many farangs stay in this hotel, but it is really not at all bad. Central location close to the market, but set back from the road so not too noisy. Steep steps lead up to rooms, with attached bathrooms showing signs of neglect. Not much English spoken. **E** *Tip House*, 1017/2 Jet Yod Rd, T716672. Central location, but set off main road. Single storey bungalow rooms, not in tip-top condition – tattered and box-like. **E-F** *Mae Hong Son*, 126 Singhaklai Rd, T715367. Run by a farang (Hans, a Dutchman), this friendly guesthouse is situated at the end of a very quiet soi. The traditional wooden house has clean rooms with shared bathrooms, also available are some newer, more expensive rooms with attached bathrooms but no a/c. Treks (recommended, with a great guide), jeep and motorbike hire, good source of information, peaceful, good food, good value. Recommended. **E-F** *The White House*, 789 Phahonyothin Rd, T713427. Set back off Chiang Rai's main road in a leafy compound. Rooms are dark and dirty, but the restaurant is cheerful and serves good food. **F** *Ya House*, down a soi at the western end of Banphaprakan Rd, T717090. Attractive wooden building and a quiet garden and reading library makes this a good place for backpackers to chill out. Some private hot water shower, and clean rooms, breakfast and evening food provided. **F** *Bowling Guest House*, 399 Singhaklai Rd, T712704. Small, quiet guesthouse, rooms are basic but clean, friendly management. **F** *Lek House*, 95 Thanalai Rd, T713337. Under new management since the last edition, and some renovation has taken place. Well organized, friendly place, with a bar and food and satellite TV. Hires motorbikes.

The greatest variety of restaurants is to be found in the streets around the *Wangcome Hotel*, from Mexican to French to cheap Thai and Chinese. For some reason, many of the tourist-oriented restaurants in Chiang Rai serve the same range of dishes – wiener schnitzel, lasagne, pizza, burgers, fried rice – as if every chef attended the same catering college. Having said that, the food is quite good here. In the evenings, the Night Bazaar off Phahonyothin Rd is good for stall food; there is an excellent range of places here where you can choose from spring rolls, wonton, pancakes, kebabs, noodles, rice dishes, even deep fried beetles and grubs – and then sit at a table and listen to live music – great atmosphere.

Eating

● on map, page 328
Price categories:
see inside front cover

Thai and Chinese Mid-range: *Chiangrai Island Restaurant*, 1129/1 Kraisorasit Rd (part of the *Dusit Island Hotel*). Northern Thai specialities, also serves international. *Haw Naliga*, 401/1-2 Banphaprakan Rd (west of *Ratburi* and *Phetburi* restaurants). Country setting, rather expensive but (usually) good food, although quality is highly variable – on a good day, excellent, and on a bad day execrable! **Cheap**: *Cabbages and Condoms*, 620/25 Thanalai Rd (attached to the Hilltribe Museum). Run by the PDA, a non-governmental organization, all proceeds go to charity. Good northern food including *laap* (spicy minced meat – really a northeastern delicacy), northern spicy sausage, duck curry and chicken in banana leaves. Eat inside or outdoors (rather noisy on the road), reasonably priced – free condoms. The restaurant will no doubt be moving into the new building next door – completion due in 2000. *Golden Triangle Café* (at *Golden Triangle Guesthouse*), 590 Phahonyothin Rd. Also serves international. Recommended. *Muang Thong*, Phahonyothin Rd (just south from the *Wiang Inn*). A serious restaurant where Chinese/Thai food is served, with little pretence on plastic plates. Especially good vegetable dishes, recommended by locals who make up the bulk of the clientele. *Tha Rua*, this place did overlook the river and pier, but because of the *Dusit Resort* development the river at this point has silted up and now the view is of a muddy river bed and a profusion of vegetation – the food is OK though. **Seriously cheap**: *Chum Cha*, Singhaklai Rd (next to TAT office). Clean, new place for coffee and ice-cream, with some simple noodle and rice dishes. *Mae Oui Khiaw* (no English sign), Sanambin Rd (opposite *Krung Thong Hotel*). Very well run Thai restaurant, open air, spotlessly clean, Northern Thai/Burmese specialities and a good range of unusual curries. Recommended. *Muang Man Café and Cocktail Lounge*, opposite Caltex station on Phahonyothin Rd. Also serves international food. *Phetburi*, Banphaprakan Rd, opposite *Sukniran Hotel*. Large selection of curries, eat in or takeaway, ฿15 per dish. *Ratburi*, Banphaprakan Rd, opposite *Sukniran Hotel*. Large selection of curries, eat in or takeaway, ฿15 per dish.

International Mid-range: *La Cantina*, Soi Punyodyana (near *Wangcome Hotel*, off Phahonyothin Rd by the clock tower). The manager and cook is an Italian so the food is pretty authentic, including some unusual regional dishes. *Napoli Pizza*, Phahonyothin Rd, reasonable pizzas, some average pasta dishes, friendly manager. **Cheap**: *Bierstube*, 897/6 Phahonyothin Rd. Reasonable German dishes and cold beer, as well as standard Thai fare. *Aye's Place*, Phahonyothin Rd, opposite entrance to *Wiang Inn*. Spacious restaurant open for breakfast (though not very early), lunch and dinner, extensive Thai and international menu. The baguettes are particularly good, the lasagne is only average. *Funny House Café*, Phahonyothin Rd, opposite Wiang Inn. German run, this diminutive place seems to be popular and has the same menu as many of the other 'international' restaurants on this strip. *Hungry Duck*, Phahonyothin Rd (opposite entrance to Night Market). Bar and restaurant serving burgers, lasagne and fish and chips. *Marco Polo Pizza*, Thanalai Rd, near PDA Museum. Popular with locals.

Stalls There are dozens of stalls at night around the Night Market off Phahonyothin Rd (by the bus terminal). There is a great *roti* man, who does stupendous banana,

The Northern Region

strawberry, orange and other pancakes – he usually sets up near the entrance to the Night Market. Other stalls on the alley leading from Phahonyothin Rd into the Night Market. Another group of stalls is to be found near Wat Ming Muang, at the intersection of Trairat and Banphaprakan roads.

Bars There are not many bars in Chiang Rai. On Phahonyothin Road, near the crossroads with Banphaprakan Rd, the *Tee Pee Bar* is worth visiting. Another lively place is down a narrow private soi off Phahonyothin Rd, near the clock tower – the *Lobo Bar*. *Easy House Bar and Restaurant*, Permaviphat Rd (opposite Wangcome Hotel), cocktails, beers, live music, self-consciously hip.

Entertainment **Music** Live music shows held periodically at the *Night Bazaar*, close to the bus terminal off Phahonyothin Rd.

Massage Several places in the network of streets near the Wangcome Hotel. Recommended is the *Ganda Traditional Thai Massage*, 869/59-63 Pisit Sangsuan Rd. The most luxurious place for a Thai Massage is the *Yogi massage and sauna centre*, at the *Dusit Inn* (฿900 for 2 hr massage and 30 min sauna). *Mue Thong Thai Massage*, *Inn Come Hotel*, 172/6 Ratbamrung Rd, T717850.

Shopping **Books** *Pho Thong Book Store*, Thanalai Rd (close to intersection with Trairat Rd). Mostly Thai language, but also some English books and magazines. *DK Book Store*, along Barnphaprakan Rd, sells guidebooks of the region in English.

China *Pisit Sangsuan*, Thai-decorated seconds for US and UK shops (Whittards), on sale here at rock bottom prices. Mugs, bowls, plates and teapots.

Department stores Corner of Banphraprakan and Sanambin roads. Also an a/c department store near the *Wangcome Hotel*, on the corner of Phahonyothin and Pemavipat roads.

Handicraft centres Out of town (eg *Chiang Rai Handicrafts Centre*, 3 km out on road to Chiang Saen). For more unusual woodcarvings and silverware, try *Silver Birch*, 891 Phahonyothin Rd, near *Wiang Inn*, more expensive but finely crafted. *Ego*, 869/81-82 (adjacent *Wangcome Hotel*), for Burmese and hilltribe antiques, beads, jewellery, carvings, textiles, reasonable prices. Recommended.

Hilltribe goods, silver, textiles, woodcarvings Many shops in town around the *Wangcome Hotel* plaza area and on Phahonyothin Rd. *Hilltribe Education Center*, at 620/25 Thanalai Rd sells genuine hilltribe textiles and other goods, all profits being returned to the communities.

Night Market There is a newish 'night bazaar' just off Phahonyothin Road, close to the bus terminal. The stalls and shops sell a range of goods, including hilltribe handicrafts, silverware, woodcarvings, T-shirts, clothes, pin cushions, Burmese bags and leatherware. Foodstalls and bars also open in the evening.

Tapes and CDs Chiang Rai is not the obvious place to come to buy tapes and CDs, but there is a great little music shop near the clock tower at the northern end of Jet Yod Rd.

Sport *Pintamorn Sportsclub*, 115/1-8 Wat Sriboonruang Rd. Sauna, exercise room and pool table.

Tour operators A number along Phahonyothin and Premwipak roads (a soi off Phahonyothin, near
See also Tours above the *Wangcome Hotel*). *Chiangrai Travel and Tour*, 869/95 Premwipak Rd, T713314, F713967. *Golden Triangle Tours*, 590 Phahonyothin Rd, T711339 (attached to the *Golden Triangle Hotel*). Recommended. *Maesalong Tour*, 882/4 Phahonyothin Rd, T712515 (treks come recommended, also organize river cruises and China and Lao tours). *Chiangrai Agency Centre*, 428/10 Banphaprakan Rd, T717274, F712211. *Far East North Tours Chiang Rai*, 402/1 Moo 13, Phahonyothin Rd, T715690,

F715691. *PDA*, 620/25 Thanalai Rd, T719167, F718869. Primarily a charity, working to improve the lot of the hilltribes, but they also have a trekking 'arm', guides tend to be more knowledgeable of hilltribe ways and speak the local dialects. Note that all profits from treks are ploughed back into the PDA's charity work. Treks also introduce clients to the PDA's community development projects, advance notice is recommended. *PD Tour*, 834/6 Phahonyothin Rd, T712829, F719041. Guesthouses which organize treks include: *Boonbundan, Bowling Guesthouse, Chat House, Chian House, Golden Triangle Inn, Mae Hong Son* (recommended), *Mae Kok Villa, Pintamorn, Thanapat Guesthouse* and *The White House* (see Sleeping above for full addresses).

Local Bicycle hire: ฿20-40 per day, from guesthouses. **Car hire**: from one of the many tour and travel companies around the *Wangcome Hotel*, or from *Budget*, based at the *Golden Triangle Inn*. **Jeep hire**: ฿800 per day from many guesthouses, eg *Bowling Guesthouse, Chian House, Pintamorn, Mae Hong Son Guesthouse* and from many tour companies. **Motorbike hire**: ฿150-200 per day, from most guesthouses and tour companies. **Saamlors, tuk-tuks** and **songthaews**: for longer trips. The local songthaew stand is near the morning market on Uttarakit Rd. Songthaews also run on set routes around the city (฿2).

Transport
See also Ins & outs, page 324; 197 km (new route), 334 km (old route) to Chiang Mai

Long distance Air: the new international airport is 8 km north of the city, just off the main Chiang Rai-Mae Sai highway. Regular connections with Chiang Mai (40 mins) and Bangkok (1 hr 25 mins). The runway has been lengthened to take wide-bodied jets, and there is some talk of the possibility of international connections in the near future with other Asian destinations. Angel Air flies twice a week to Luang Prabang.

Bus: central bus station is just off Phahonyothin Rd, T711224. Regular connections with Chiang Saen every 15 mins (1 hr 30 mins) and Mae Sai every 15 mins (1 hr 40 mins), Chiang Mai (3 hrs), Phayao (1 hr 40 mins), Phrae (4 hrs), Nan (6 hrs), Chiang Kham (2 hrs), Chiang Khong (3 hrs), Lampang (5 hrs), Phitsanulok (via Sukhothai) (6 hrs), Khon Kaen (12 hrs), Nakhon Ratchasima (13 hrs), Bangkok (12 hrs), Fang, Mae Suai, Nakhon Sawan, Sukhothai, Nakhon Phanom, Udon Thani and Pattaya. From Chiang Mai, buses taking the old route (*sai kao*) leave from the Old Lamphun Rd, near the Narawat Bridge; those on the new route (*sai mai*) leave from the Arcade bus station, northeast of the city on the 'Superhighway'. The old route goes via Lampang and Phayao (6 hrs); the new route takes Route 1019, via Doi Saket and Wiang Papao (hot springs) (4 hrs). A/c and VIP buses to Bangkok leave from the office on Phahonyothin Rd, opposite the *Golden Triangle Inn*.

Boat: long-tailed boats leave from the new pier to the northwest of town, around 2 km from the city centre. Follow Trairat Rd north, past the entrance to the *Dusit Island Resort*, to the T-junction with Winitchakun Rd. Turn right and continue past the golf course to the bridge over the Kok River. The pier is on the far side of the river. Boats for Tha Ton depart daily at 1030 (฿200). Boats can be chartered for ฿300 per hour or for ฿1,600 to Tha Ton, ฿500 to Rim Kok, ฿1,500 to Chiang Khong. A boat takes a maximum of 8 passengers, the pier is open 0700-1600 daily (see page 319).

Airline offices *Thai*, 870 Phahonyothin Rd, T711179. **Banks** Profusion of exchange booths and banks on Thanalai and Phahonyothin roads. Many are open 7 days a week and often into the evening. **Communications** Post Office: on Uttarakit Rd at the northern end of Suksathit Rd. An abundance of **internet** cafés in the area around the *Wangcome Hotel*, about ฿30 per hour. **Medical services** *Overbrook*, opposite *Chat House*, Trairat Rd, T711366. *Provincial*, on Sanambin Rd. *Chiang Rai Hospital*, Sathorn Payabarn Rd, T711403/711119. **Useful addresses** Tourist Police: Singhaklai Rd (below the TAT office, opposite Wat Phra Singh), T717779, and a booth at the Night Market. Or in an emergency call T1155 (24 hrs). **Police Station**: Rattanakhat Rd, T711444.

Directory

Chiang Saen เชียงแสน

Phone code: 053
Colour map 1, grid A3

Chiang Saen is an ancient capital on the banks of the Mekong River, the last village before the famed 'Golden Triangle'. It was probably established during the early years of this millennium and became the capital of the Chiang Saen Kingdom, founded in 1328 by King Saen Phu, the grandson of King Mengrai. Captured in the 16th century by the Burmese, the town became a Burmese stronghold in their constant wars with the Thais. It was not recaptured until Rama I sent an army here in 1803. Fearing that the Burmese might use the town to mount raids against his kingdom in the future, Rama I ordered it to be destroyed. Chiang Saen remained deserted for nearly 100 years. King Mongkut ordered the town re-populated, but it still feels as though it is only part-filled, its inhabitants rattling around in the area's illustrious history. The ancient city is a gazetted historic monument managed by the Thai Fine Arts Department, and in total there are 75 monasteries and other monuments inside the city walls and another 66 outside.

Sights Today, with the impressive town ramparts still very much in evidence, it is a charming one-street market town. The city walls run along three sides of the town and are pierced by five gates. The fourth 'wall' is formed by the Mekong River. Quiet, with wooden shophouses and a scattering of ruins lying haphazardly and untended amidst the undergrowth, it has so far managed to escape the uncontrolled tourist development evident in other towns in Northern Thailand. The **TAT** office, Phahonyothin Rd, opposite the National Museum, is attached to the sensitively designed Bureau for the Restoration and Conservation of the Historic City of Chiang Mai. ■ *0830-1630 Mon-Sun.*

In September 1992 a 120-tonne ship, with 60 Chinese delegates aboard, made the 385 km trip down the Mekong from Yunnan. Since then, links with China – as well as Laos – have developed apace. Cargo boats unload apples and other produce from China, and the market in Chiang Saen is stocked with low quality manufactured goods from the neighbouring countries. Anticipating a trade boom, the local authorities began constructing two new **piers** – one which was promptly partly washed away – and the grandly titled Lan Chang International Development company shares an office with the Yunnan Water Transportation Joint Operations Development Company on Rim Khong Road. The local big businessman has constructed a luxurious edifice for himself on the Mekong, a couple of kilometres south of town – demonstrating how much money there is around as people try to cash in on what has been termed the 'Golden Quadrangle' (Thailand, Burma, Laos and China).

The economic crisis in Thailand changed things somewhat. Before mid-1997 Thai tourists were rushing upriver to visit their ethnic brethren in Yunnan. With the crash of the baht in July 1997, the flow reversed: Thais stayed at home, no longer able to travel abroad, while Chinese tourists from Yunnan suddenly found a trip to Thailand within their financial grasp. With the recovery in Thailand's economy from 1999, the traditional flow began to reassert itself.

Chiang Saen place names

Wat Chom Cheung
วัดจอมเชิง

Wat Pa Sak
วัดป่าสัก

Wat Phrathat Chedi Luang
วัดพระธาตุเจดีย์หลวง

Wat Phrathat Chom Kitti
วัดพระธาตุจอมกิตติ

Wat Phrathat Pao Ngao
วัดพระธาตุเปางาว

The Northern Region

Entering the town from Chiang Rai, the ruins of **Wat Phrathat Chedi Luang** can be seen on the right-hand side shortly after passing through the city's ancient ramparts. Built by King Saen Phu in 1331, this wat was established as the main monastery in the city. The chedi, resting on an octagonal base, is 60 m tall, but has fallen into disrepair over the centuries and is now clothed in long grass. The viharn is in a similar state of decrepitude and is protected by a jury-rigged corrugated iron roof.

Just to the west of Wat Phrathat Chedi Luang is a small branch of the **National Museum**. It contains various Buddha images and other artefacts unearthed in the area, as well as a small display of hilltribe handicrafts including clothing and musical instruments. Among the Buddha images, the most significant are the so-called Chiang Saen style, with their oval faces and slender bodies. They are regarded by art historians as being among the first true 'Thai' works of art. ■ *0900-1200, 1300-1600 Wed-Sun, ฿10.*

West of the town, just outside the city ramparts, is the beautiful **Wat Pa Sak** or the 'Forest of Teak Wat' – so-called because of a wall of 300 teak trees, planted around the wat when it was founded. The monastery was founded in 1295 during the reign of Ramkhamhaeng of Sukhothai and actually predates the town. The unusual pyramid-shaped chedi, said to house a bone relic of the Lord Buddha, is the main building of interest here. Art historians see a combination of influences in the chedi: Pagan (Burma), Dvaravati, Sukhothai, even Srivijaya. The niches along the base contain alternating Devatas (heavenly beings) and standing Buddha images – poorly restored – the latter in the mudra of the Buddha 'Calling for Rain' (an attitude common in Laos but less so in Thailand). Much of the fine stucco work, save for fragments of nagas and garudas, has disappeared (some can be seen in the Chiang Saen Museum). The Spirit House at the entrance, by the ramparts, is also worth a little more than a glance. ■ *฿30.*

Two and a half kilometres north of Wat Pa Sak, following the ramparts and on a hill, is **Wat Phrathat Chom Kitti**, which may date from as early as the 10th century. A golden topped stupa is being restored, but there is little else save for the views of the river and surrounding countryside. **Wat Chom Cheung**, a small ruined chedi, lies close by on the same hill. If visiting by foot, the stairs start about 150 m from the city walls and come first to Wat Chom Cheung. A highly decorated new wat has recently been completed here.

The market

Strung out along the river bank, the market sells plenty of unnecessary plastic objects and is a good place to watch hilltribe people (Karen and Lua among others) browsing through the goods. Since trade with China and Laos has expanded, it is also possible to pick up cheap – but poorly made – products from 'across the water'.

Excursions

Wat Phrathat Pa Ngao lies 4 km from Chiang Saen, along the road which follows the Mekong downstream. Perched on a hill, it provides excellent views of the river and countryside. For **Sop Ruak** and the **Golden Triangle** take the same road upstream, 11 km from town (see below). ■ *Getting there: by songthaew or by long-tailed boat. Boats can be hired from the jetty below the Salathai Restaurant and will also take passengers to riverside villages. Bargain hard.*

Tours

There have been big plans over a number of years to exploit Chiang Saen's perceived strategic location on the Mekong, close to Laos, China and Burma. Hotels have been built on the banks of the Mekong in Sipsong Panna (Yunnan, China) to accommodate passengers. The journey upriver takes 8-10 hours, downriver about 6-8 hours. But Chiang Saen seems to have missed out on the project, and there is far more cross-border activity to the west in Mae Sai.

Chiang Saen

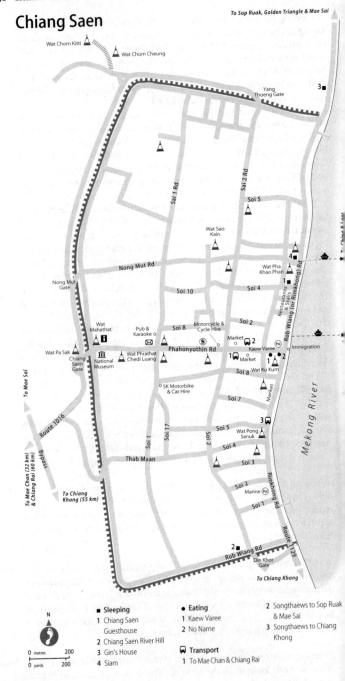

To Sop Ruak, Golden Triangle & Mae Sai

Wat Chom Kitti
Wat Chom Cheung

Yang Thoeng Gate

3

Sai 1 Rd

Sai 2 Rd

Soi 5

Wat Sao Kain

Nong Mut Rd

Nong Mut Gate

Soi 10

Soi 4

Wat Pha Khao Phan

4

1

Rob Wiang (or Rimkhong) Rd

Restaurants & Stalls

Soi 2

Motorcycle & Cycle Hire

Pub & Karaoke

Soi 8

Market

2

Phahonyothin Rd

Wat Mahathat

Kaew Varee

Immigration

Wat Pa Sak

Chiang Saen Gate

National Museum

Wat Phrathat Chedi Luang

Market

1

2

Wat Ku Kum

Soi 8

SK Motorbike & Car Hire

Soi 7

Market

Soi 5

Soi 17

Soi 1

Soi 2

3

Wat Pong Sanuk

To Mae Sai

Route 1016

Bypass

Soi 4

Thab Maan

Soi 3

To Mae Chan (32 km) & Chiang Rai (60 km)

To Chiang Khong (55 km)

Soi 2

Marine

Soi 1

Rimkhong Rd

Mekong River

Route 1129

2

Rob Wiang Rd

Din Khor Gate

To Chiang Khong

To Chiang Saen & Laos

To Laos

N

0 metres 200
0 yards 200

The Northern Region

For some reason, Chiang Saen seems to be yesterday's destination – never having 'made it' in the first place. Many of the guesthouses have closed and only the *Chiang Saen Guesthouse* seems to be doing a reasonable trade. Most people visit the city as a day trip from Mae Sai or Chiang Rai. This is a shame because the town is much more attractive and relaxed (which is maybe part of the reason!) than other places close by. However, a new, small and slightly more upmarket place has opened recently – the *Chiang Saen River Hill Hotel* – perhaps indicating that things will change.

Sleeping
■ *on map, opposite*
Price codes:
see inside front cover

B *Chiang Saen River Hill Hotel*, Phahonyothin Soi 2 (just inside the southern city walls), T650826, F650830, chiangsaen_office@cheerful.com A/c, restaurant. Best hotel in town with 60 rooms and 4 storeys. Nothing flash, but friendly management and comfortable rooms with attached showers (very clean), minibar and TV. **D** *Gin's House*, Rimkhong Rd. Around 500 m outside the northern city walls, on the road towards Sop Ruak and Mae Sai. Bungalows in a large compound, restaurant, bikes and motorbikes for rent. **E-F** *Chiang Saen Guesthouse*, Rimkhong Rd. Good restaurant for Thai food and breakfast. Cheaper rooms in the guesthouse are basic and not very clean, with a shared bathroom; they are also noisy, being close to the road and the river (long-tailed boats). The bungalow is a better option, with own bathroom, nice position, with views of the river and a pleasant garden. The American owner of the *Chiang Saen* is a keen naturalist and can offer advice on birdwatching and nature treks. Overall, the best place to stay but can be offhand. Recommended. **F** *Siam*, 234 Rimkhong Rd. Clean, good source of information, bicycles for hire. Recommended.

There are a number of cheap *kuaytiaw* stalls along the riverbank and on Phahonyothin Rd. The best restaurant is probably the *Riverside*, close to the *Chiang Saen Guesthouse*. Another clean and well run place, although it is currently nameless, is on the corner of Rob Wiang and Phahonyothin roads. It serves simple dishes, coffee, ice-cream etc. The *Chiang Saen Guesthouse* also does good breakfasts: banana pancakes, fruit, yoghurt and muesli. *Kaew Varee Restaurant*, Phahonyothin Rd, Thai and European dishes, ice-cream, open for breakfast, lunch and dinner. Further out of town towards Sop Ruak and the Golden Triangle are better riverside restaurants selling good Thai food, eg *Rim Khong* (2 km north of the city walls) and the *Mekong River Banks* (3 km).

Eating

Pub and Karaoke, Sai 1 Rd (off Phahonyothin Rd, not far from the Post Office). Reasonable place for a cold beer.

Bars

Long-tailed boats Can be hired from the river bank at the end of Phahonyothin Rd. A boat downstream to Chiang Khong should cost around ฿1,200-1,500 and can take 8 people (1 hr 20 mins). To Sop Ruak, upstream (30 mins), should cost ฿400 for a boat. **Motorbike and bicycle hire** From *SK Hire* on Soi 1 Rd and from a shop on Phahonyothin Rd close to Soi 2, ฿150 per day for a Honda Dream. **SK Hire** also has vehicles for hire. **Motorized saamlors** By the bus-stop for trips around the sights. **Bus** Regular connections with Chiang Rai, 1 hr 20 mins, Mae Sai, 1 hr, and Chiang Khong, 2 hrs.

Transport
32 km to Mae Chan,
60 km to Chiang Rai,
55 km to Chiang Khong

Banks *Siam Commercial*, 116 Phahonyothin Rd (exchange service). ATM on Phahonyothin Rd. **Communications** Post Office: Phahonyothin Rd.

Directory

Chiang Khong เชียงของ

Phone code: 053
Colour map 1, grid A4

This border settlement, situated on the south bank of the Mekong, is really more a collection of villages than a town: Ban Haad Khrai, Ban Sobsom and Ban Hua Wiang were all originally individual communities – and still keep their village monasteries. For such a small town, it has had a relatively high profile in Thai history. In the 1260s, King Mengrai extended control over the area and Chiang Khong became one of the Lanna Thai Kingdom's major principalities. Later, the town was captured by the Burmese.

Today, Chiang Khong owes its continued existence to legal and illicit trade with Laos: gems, agricultural products and livestock from Laos are traded for consumer goods and other luxuries. The traffic can be seen in action either at the pier end of Soi 5 or, to a greater degree, at Tha Rua Bak – 1 km or so north of town. For some years, while Thais and Laos could make the crossing to trade, foreigners had to stay firmly on the Thai side of the river. This has now changed and it is easy enough to arrange a visa and cross the Mekong to another country – and another world.

There is not much here, although its position on the Mekong and the relaxed atmosphere makes it an attractive spot to unwind. **Wat Luang**, in the centre of town, dates from the 13th century. An engraved plaque maintains that two hairs of the Buddha were interred in the chedi in 704 AD – a date which would seem to owe more to poor maths or over-optimism than to historical veracity. But it was reputedly restored by the ruler of Chiang Khong in 1881. The viharn sports some rather lurid murals. **Wat Phra Kaew**, a little further north, has two fine, red guardian lions at its entrance. Otherwise it is very ordinary, save for the *kutis* (monks quarters – small huts) along the inside of the front wall, which look like a row of assorted Wendy houses, and the *nagas* which curl their way up the entrance to the *viharn*, on the far side of the building.

Further south, at the track leading to the *Pla Buk Resort* at the grandly titled Economic Quadrangle Joint Development Corporation, is the town's *lak muang* or foundation pillar. Like Nong Khai and the other towns that line the Mekong in the Northeastern region, the rare – and delicious – *pla buk* catfish is caught here. It is sometimes possible to watch the fishermen catching a giant catfish on the riverbank to the south of town. If that is a no go, there are some pictures of stupendous *pla buk* in the restaurant of the *Ruan Thai Sophaphan Resort*.

Trekking See Hilltribes and trekking, page 360. There are hilltribe villages within reach of Chiang Khong, but the trekking industry here is relatively undeveloped. Ask at the guesthouses to see if a guide is available.

Visas for Laos Any tour company will organize visas; see Tour operators below. A photocopy of your passport is needed. The process normally takes about 24 hours, although visas cannot be arranged at weekends. The pier and Thai immigration are 1 km or so north of town, and long-tailed boats take people across for ฿20. The agent normally accompanies travellers and sees them through Lao immigration. Note that the visa situation for Laos is fluid. It is now possible to get a visa on arrival in Laos when crossing the Friendship Bridge near Nong Khai, in Northeast Thailand (see page 449). But for entry from Chiang Khong, advance visas are still necessary.

Sleeping
■ *on map, opposite*
Price codes:
see inside front cover

C *Plabuk Resort*, Tambon 122/1 Wiang Rd, T/F791281. A/c, restaurant open in the high season, hot water, this place is situated on the south edge of town on a large plot overlooking the Mekong. Rooms are bare, but clean and large, with small verandahs and attached bathrooms. There could have been more of an effort to create some

The Northern Region

Chiang Khong

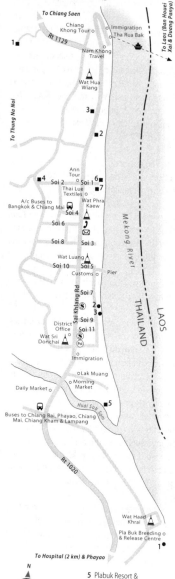

Sleeping
1 Baan Golden Triangle
2 Bamboo Riverside
3 Chiang Khong
4 Orchid Garden
  Guesthouse
5 Plabuk Resort &
  Restaurant
6 Ruan Thai Sophaphan
  Resort & Ban Tam
  Mi La Guesthouse
7 Wiang Kaew
  Guesthouse

Eating
1 Nang Nuan
2 Rimkhong
3 Rim Nam

sense of ambience, but it is quiet and peaceful. **C-D** *Baan Golden Triangle*, T791350. Positioned on top of a hill to the north of town, this is a stab at a 'back-to-nature' resort: wooden bungalows, garden, cartwheels. The rooms are fine, with attached bathrooms and hot water, great views too, over a tiny rice valley to the Mekong and Laos. **C-D** *Ruan Thai Sophaphan Resort*, Tambon Wiang Rd, T791023. Restaurant, big clean rooms with own bathroom and hot water, in a big wooden house with a large raised verandah. The upstairs rooms are better – down below is a little dark. There are also bungalows for 2-4 people, good river views, very friendly, self-service drinks, price negotiable out of season. Recommended. **D-E** *Ban Tam Mi La*, 8/1 Sai Klang Rd. Down a side street (northern end of town), T791234. Restaurant, cheaper rooms are very basic with mosquito net and shared bathroom, more expensive have own bathrooms, bungalows with river views. Attractive rambling garden along the riverside, good food, friendly and helpful, although some recent visitors have said that it is overpriced. **D-E** *Chiang Khong Hotel*, 68/1 Sai Khong Rd, T791182, F655647. Some a/c, Chiang Khong's original hotel and, although it is reasonably maintained, this place was designed before 'character' and 'atmosphere' figured in Thai architectural philosophy (some would say they still don't). It is plain, rather bare, and functional, but reasonable value. **D-F** *Orchid Garden Guest House*, 62 Ban Wiang Kaew Soi 2 (about 80 m off the main Sai Klang road). A friendly little guesthouse, run by young Thais with a laid back, slightly hip feel. Some bungalows with attached bathrooms, rooms in main house with shared facilities (upstairs is best) and some dormitory beds, quiet, and although it does not have the river close by, peaceful and relaxing – the dormitory beds are also the cheapest available. **F** *Bamboo Riverside*, Sai Khlang Rd. Balconies on riverbanks, clean, hot showers, friendly and full of information.

Eating
● *on map*

In theory, Chiang Khong would be a great place to eat river fish, but the range is rather disappointing. However, the position of the riverside restaurants compensates to some degree. In town, along the main road, there are a number of noodle and rice stalls. The more interesting places are along the river road, or down one of the sois leading to the Mekong. *Rimkhong*, in the centre, and *Rim Naam*, next door, are good value but the fish dishes are rather limited and hardly memorable. *Ruan Thai Saphaphan Resort* is also worth considering: very comfortable with wicker chairs, cold beer, a great view and good food. South of town, *Nang Nuan* is highly recommended by locals.

Shopping

Chiang Khong is not the obvious place to come shopping, but there is one decent place selling traditional textiles, woodcarvings, handicrafts and other items: *Thai Lue Textiles*, on the main road, just north of Wat Phra Kaew.

Tour operators

There are a growing number of tour companies in Chiang Khong. In town, *Ann Tour*, 6/1 Sai Klang Rd, T/F791218, is recommended. North of town, by the pier, there are the *Chiang Khong Tour* and *Nam Khong Travel*. They get most of their business arranging visas for Laos (see above), but can also provide transport and organize boat trips.

Transport
137 km to Chiang Rai,
55 km to Chiang Saen

Local Chiang Khong is small enough to explore on foot, but the town does have a rather quaint line in underpowered motorized rickshaws, which struggle gamely up anything which is not billiard table-flat. Tour companies provide cars with drivers for around ฿1,200 per day. Bicycles and motorbikes were not available for hire on our last visit, but with more people coming here to cash in on access to Laos this may have changed by the time this edition goes to press. **Long distance Bus**: hourly connections with Chiang Rai (3 hrs). A/c and non-a/c connections with Bangkok and Chiang Mai (6½ hrs), as well as Lampang and Phayao. A/c buses leave from the office on the main road near Wat Phra Kaew. Non a/c buses depart from the bus station, just over the Huai Sob Som on the south edge of town. Non-a/c buses for Chiang Saen leave from 0600, and take the attractive river road following the Mekong and the Thai-Lao border (2 hrs). **Songthaew**: regular connections with Chiang Saen and from there on to Sop Ruak, Mae Sai and Chiang Rai. Songthaews leave from the bus station on the southern edge of town, but can be flagged down as they make their way north through Chiang Khong. **Boat**: these can be chartered to make the journey to/from Chiang Saen (about ฿150 per head or ฿1,200-1,500 to charter an entire boat).

International connections to Laos It is possible for foreigners to cross into Laos from Chiang Khong, across the Mekong to Ban Houei Xai. Visas can be obtained in Chiang Khong from one of the tour operators that are mushrooming as travel to Laos becomes easier (see above for details). Long-tailed boats ferry passengers across the Mekong to Ban Houei Xai, from Tha Rua Bak (฿20).

Directory

Banks *Thai Farmers*, 416 Sai Khong Rd. *Siam Commercial*, Sai Khong Rd, opposite the district office, has a currency exchange service. **Communications** Post Office: on main road next to the army post. Telephone Office: in Post Office for international calls.

Sop Ruak and the Golden Triangle สบรวก

Phone code: 053
Colour map 1, grid A3

This small 'village', 11 km north of Chiang Saen at the apex of the Golden Triangle, where Burma, Laos and Thailand meet, has become a busy tourist spot – on the basis (largely unwarranted) of its association with drugs, intrigue and violence. A multitude of stalls line the road, selling hilltribe handicrafts and Burmese and Laotian goods. Two first-class hotels have been built to exploit the supposed romance of the place.

The '*Golden Triangle Paradise Resort*', to coin a phrase, was a luxury resort too far. A Thai investor leased 32 ha of land from the government of Burma and in the early 1990s began constructing a massive hotel and casino complex. This required some fancy footwork on the part both of the Thais and Burmese. In Thailand gambling is illegal, yet because the resort will not be on Thai soil, the government can turn a blind eye to the development. Equally, the Burmese, having leased the land out for 30 years, can claim that it is no business of theirs and therefore remain ideologically unsullied. A cunning way of exploiting the Thai, and especially the Sino-Thai, love of gambling. But relations between the investor and the Burmese government deteriorated, and though largely complete, the resort's opening has been postponed as border crossings have closed (it can be clearly seen from Sop Ruak) – a white elephant of truly gargantuan proportions. Some people suspected all along that it was designed to be a drug money laundering operation. At the end of 1996 the border post here was reopened, allowing construction work to be completed, and the casino opened in 1997 – just when many middle-class Thais found their disposable income evaporating in the wake of the devaluation of the baht and the collapse of the Thai economy. In mid-2000 there was a slightly disconcerting banner in Chiang Saen: 'Travelling out of Thailand for gambling not safety for yours life and properties Thai offices can not Thai care'.

Frankly, there is next-to-nothing to do or see in Sop Ruak, unless rows of tacky stalls hold any fascination. Indeed, it is remarkable that such a lot of commercial

Sop Ruak & the Golden Triangle

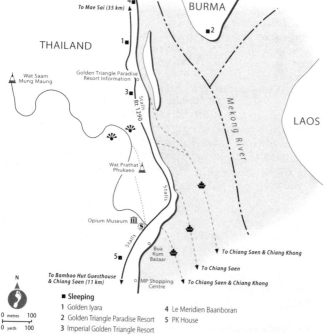

■ **Sleeping**

1 Golden Iyara
2 Golden Triangle Paradise Resort
3 Imperial Golden Triangle Resort
4 Le Meridien Baanboran
5 PK House

The Northern Region

activity can be supported on such a narrow base: a succession of maps and marble constructions inform visitors time and again that they are at the Golden Triangle where Thai, Lao and Burmese territory meet. For those searching for something else to experience, **Wat Prathat Phukaeo** provides good views of the Golden Triangle. A small but quite interesting **Opium Museum** is located close to the Km 30 marker. ■ *0700-1800 Mon-Sun, ฿20. Catch a songthaew for the 10-min ride to the much more interesting town of Chiang Saen.*

Excursions **Wanglao** lies 4 km west, towards Mae Sai, past *Le Meridien Baanboran Hotel*, and is a rice-farming community. It is sometimes possible to buy handicrafts here. *Songthaews* run through here, on the (longer) back route to Mae Sai.

Tours Boats can be chartered from the river bank opposite the Opium Museum for trips downstream to Chiang Saen (฿400 for five people, 30 minutes), or further on still to Chiang Khong (around ฿1,500-1,700, 1½ hours). Or they can be chartered just to pootle around the Golden Triangle area. Boats are also available from the river bank opposite the *Delta Golden Triangle Hotel*.

Sleeping
■ *on map*
Price codes:
see inside front cover

A little like Chiang Saen, Sop Ruak seems to have declined as a place that people want to visit. The 3 upmarket places have low occupancy rates and almost all the cheaper guesthouses have closed down. Most people come here on a day trip from Mae Sai or Chiang Rai. The Golden Triangle Paradise Resort (the Casino on the island in mid-stream) has an office on the main road through town, just north (upstream) from the Imperial Golden Triangle Resort.

AL *Le Meridien Baan Boran*, north of Sop Ruak, T784086, F784090. Pool, 'traditional' architecture taken to the limit, good service, wonderful evening views, a bit of a blot on the landscape for this timeless area of Thailand, but very well run and good facilities (including tennis and squash courts, gymnasium, pétanque and sauna). It is situated 1 km or so north of Sop Ruak, so is relatively peaceful. **A-B** *Imperial Golden Triangle Resort* (formerly the Delta Golden Triangle), 222 Golden Triangle, T784001, T02-6511113, F784006. A/c, restaurant, pool. It is rather a surprise coming upon a hotel like this in what should be a quiet corner of Thailand, 73 plush and tasteful rooms, well run and attractive but probably ill-conceived, as they seem to be having some difficulty finding the people to stay in the rooms – heavily discounted, especially in the low season. **A** *Golden Iyara Hotel*, at the northern end of Sop Ruak. The least attractive of the 3 upmarket hotels here. **C-F** *PK House*, main road, south end of stalls. Range of rooms from expensive dormitory beds (**E-F**), to rooms with attached hot showers (**C**), rather noisy as it is on the main road and it could hardly be described as charming, but it is the cheapest place to stay. **E** *Bamboo Hut Guesthouse*, a couple of kilometres downstream (south) from Sop Ruak and a little more than 6 km north of Chiang Saen.

Shopping Most people come to Sop Ruak for the shopping which, in its way, is interesting, but hardly spectacular. Goods from China, Laos and Burma, as well as hilltribe handicrafts, are on sale from countless stalls. The range of goods – and what vendors have decided people would wish to buy – is sometimes perplexing: crocheted hats, nylon hammocks, animal skulls, weaver bird nests. There are also some more expected things: gems, traditional textiles and T-shirts, for example. South of town is/was (in mid-2000 it looked distinctly abandoned) the massive and irredeemably monstrous *MP Shopping Centre*, for a/c browsing at your leisure.

Tour operators *Dits Travel*, *Baanboran Hotel*, T716678, F716680. Organizes tours to Burma.

The Northern Region

Local Boat hire: from the pier, for trips to Chiang Saen for ฿400 per boat and on to Chiang Khong (see Tours above for details). **Car hire**: from *Golden Triangle Hotel* (Avis). **Long distance Songthaew**: regular connections with Mae Sai, 40 mins, and Chiang Saen, 10 mins (฿10). Just flag one down on the road – they run through Sop Ruak about every 40 mins. **Boat**: from Chiang Saen (฿400 per boat).

Transport
11 km to Chiang Saen

Banks Two money changers by the Opium Museum, a *Thai Farmers Bank* and a small branch of the *Siam Commercial Bank*. Open 0900-1600 Mon-Sun.

Directory

Mae Sai   แม่สาย

Marking Thailand's northernmost point, Mae Sai is a busy trading centre with Burma, and has a rather clandestine and frenetic frontier atmosphere. The area around the bridge is the centre of activity, with stalls and shops selling gems and Burmese and Chinese goods, from knitted hats and Burmese marionettes to antiques and animal skulls. There are also an abundance of Burmese hawkers (selling Burmese coins and postage stamps) and beggars stretching about 1 km down the road, away from the border and towards Mae Chan.

Phone code: 053
Colour map 1, grid A3

The town of Mae Sai is rather drab, but the movement of myriad peoples across the border makes this an interesting place to visit. **Wat Phrathat Doi Wao** sits on a hill overlooking the town, off Phahonyothin Road, not far from the *Top North Hotel*. It is neither old nor beautiful and was reputedly built in the mid-1960s, in commemoration of a platoon of Burmese soldiers killed in action against a KMT force.

The border with Burma has recently opened to allow tourists, as well as Burmese and Thais, to cross the bridge that spans the river Sai and leads to the quiet Burmese town of **Tachilek**. Here, foreigners are free to roam for the day within a 5 km radius of the town, but not to stay overnight. The market is rather disappointing. The goods on sale are of poor quality and many of the stallholders appear to be Thai rather than Burmese in any case. (Border fee US$5, passports to be lodged with Thai customs, three photographs required, border open 0800-1800 Monday-Sunday.) The Burmese will also allow individuals and tour groups to travel the 167 km along a haphazardly upgraded road (6-8 hours) to **Kengtung**, known in Thailand as **Chiang Tung** (see page 346). They charge a fee of US$18 for a three night/four day visa and an additional transportation fee of US$10 at Tachilek (the trip into Burma does not count as an exit/re-entry for single entry Thai visas and the Thai immigration authorities keep hold of visi-

Excursions

tors' passports until they return). Visitors are also required to change US$100 into FECs at the official (and very low) rate of exchange. The 'visa' is either for a four day/three night or three day/two night visit, and all inclusive tours cost US$260 per person for a party of four for the three day/two night trip, or US$320 for four days and three nights. The long journey to Kengtung is through remote, wild forest, giving a good impression of what Northern Thailand must have been like 50 years ago. Kengtung itself is a historic Tai Yüan community, almost perfectly preserved. The town is a gem

• • • • • • • • • • • • • • • • • • • •
Mae Sai place names

Doi Tung

ดอยตุง

Kengtung

เชียงตุง

Luang Cave

ถ้ำหลวง

Mae Sai

แม่สาย

Tachilek

ท่าขี้เหล็ก

compared with raucous and fetid Mae Sai. **NB** Take a photocopy of your passport and Thai visa (there are photocopy shops close to the border). Only US dollars are accepted at the border. The border has periodically closed during periods of instability and tension in Burma. Tour companies, understandably, have been keen to encourage the Burmese government to free up their regulations and allow foreigners to venture further afield – and to stay longer. It has been suggested that tourists may also be given 'visas on arrival' to visit Mandalay. *Dits Travel* organizes tours to Burma (see page 342).

Luang Cave (Tham Luang) is an impressive cave, 3 km off Route 110 to Chiang Rai, 7 km from town, with large caverns and natural rock formations. After the initial large and impressive cavern, the passage narrows to lead – over the course of around a kilometre – to a series of smaller chambers. Guides with lamps wait outside to lead visitors – for a fee – through the system. ■ *Getting there: by regular songthaew to turn-off; ask for Tham loo-ang.*

Doi Tung is a 2,000 m-high hill village, almost 50 km south of Mae Sai. Travel south on Route 110 from Mae Sai for 22 km to Huai Klai and then turn off onto Route 1149. The road snakes its way past Akha, Lahu and KMT villages and former poppy fields, before reaching **Wat Phrathat Doi Tung**, a total of 24 km from the main road. The road is now surfaced to the summit – although it is still quite a stomach-churning journey and the road has a habit of deteriorating rapidly after heavy rain. The twin chedis on the summit are said to contain the left collarbone of the Buddha and to have been initially built by a king of Chiang Saen in the 10th century. The views from the wat are breathtaking. A few years ago the King's mother – who died in 1995 – built a palace here, a vast Austrian/Thai chalet with fantastic views over what was, at the time of construction, a devastated and deforested landscape. (Depending on who you talk to, the culprits were either shifting cultivators growing opium or big business interests logging protected land.) With the King's mother's influence, the hills around the palace were reforested. It is easiest to explore the area by rented motorbike. However, buses will drop passengers off at Ban Huai Khrai from where infrequent songthaews run to Doi Tung. To stay, there is **D-E** *Khwan Guesthouse*, A-frame huts, 2 km along Route 1149; **F** *Akha Guesthouse* (in the Akha village of Ban Pakha), 7 km along the road. Both are good sources of information on the surrounding area. We have been told that the *Akha Guesthouse* is officially closed but, unofficially, rooms are still available. **Caution**: this was a violent area until recently, with drug dealers, opium poppy cultivators and drug suppression units battling for control. Today, almost all opium cultivation has been displaced into neighbouring Burma, which is just a few kilometres away. Even so, it still has a reputation as being relatively lawless and travellers are not recommended to venture out after dark or off-track without a guide. ■ *Getting there: take a bus heading for Chiang Rai and ask to be let off in Ban Huai Klai, at the turn-off for Doi Tung. From there, songthaews run to Doi Tung. Now that the road is upgraded the songthaew service is rather more regular – but check on return journeys if you intend to make it back the same day.*

Tours A number of guesthouses, hotels and travel companies run tours to Burma (Kengtung – see above) and to some hilltribe areas of this region of Thailand (see Trekking below). For example, *Ananda Tour*, 22 Phahonyothin Road, T731038, F731749. *Mandalay Tour*, 382-83 Phahonyothin Road (next to Mandalay Shop). Or book in Bangkok with *Diethelm Travel*, Kian Gwan Building, 140/1 Wittayu Road, T2559150, F2560248. A three day/two night tour to Burma should cost around ฿6,500 or ฿8,000 for a four day/three night tour (minimum four persons). **Visas for Laos** These can be arranged in town either through one of the tour companies or through 'Kobra' Joe at the *KK Guesthouse*, Kkmaesai@chmai.loxinfo.co.th

See Hilltribes and trekking, page 360. Few trek from here; however, the *Mae Sai Plaza Guesthouse*, *Mae Sai Riverside* and the *Northern Guesthouse* all organize treks for about ฿300 per day.

Trekking

Most of Mae Sai's guesthouses are concentrated along Sawlongchong Rd which follows the Sai River and the Burmese border upstream (west). The exception is *Chad's House*. Sawlongchong Rd used to be quiet and relatively peaceful but there has been a good deal of new development and it is now rather dusty, noisy and busy. The guesthouses here are ramshackle affairs. In fact, it is almost as if all Thailand's incompetent builders and architects decided to descend on Mae Sai to make their living and pursue their craft. **A-B** *Wang Thong*, 299 Phahonyothin Rd, T733388, T02-2259298, F733399. A/c, restaurant (overrun by tour groups), pool, large new high-rise hotel with 150 rooms, rather over-the-top in terms of décor, small rooms. Set back from the road in the centre of town. **C-D** *Thai (Tai) Thong*, 6 Phahonyothin Rd, T731975, F731560. Some a/c, rooms are plain but clean and adequate, hot water and well priced. **C-D** *Top North*, 306 Phahonyothin Rd, T731955, F732331. Some a/c, from the outside this place doesn't look very promising, but in fact it is well run with large, clean rooms. They are even pretty quiet as the rooms are some way back from the main road over a river. Recommended. **C-F** *Northern Guesthouse*, 402 Tumphachom Rd, T731537, F2121122. Range of rooms on a large plot of land right by the Sai River. The best deals are the raised A-frame huts which are simple but have some charm, the more upmarket rooms – some with a/c, hot water, baths and views over to Burma – are not so competitively priced. All rather haphazard and badly built, but quite fun. **D** *Mae Sai Riverside*, Sawlomchong Rd (at end of road). Hot water.

E *KK (King Kobra) Guesthouse*, 35/5 Sawlomchong Rd, next door to *Mae Sai Plaza Guesthouse* restaurant, T/F733055. Rooms are a bit tatty, with beautiful murals on the economy room walls, but clean and attached bathrooms with hot water are fine. 'Kobra Joe' speaks very good English and runs trekking tours to the area west of Mae

Sleeping
■ *on map*
Price codes:
see inside front cover

The Northern Region

Mae Sai

BURMA

To Tachilek & Chiang Tung

Sai River

Thong Motorbike Rental

Sawlomchong Rd

Batman Motorbike

Pha Chom Cave

Wat Phrathat Doi Wao

Stalls

Sala Chao Phor Kum Kok Chinese Temple

Ananda Tour

Mandalay Shop
Mandalay Tour

Phahonyothin Rd

Songthaews to Sop Ruak (Golden Triangle) & Chiang Saen

To Chiang Saen

Market

Rt 110

Songthaews to Mae Chan & Chiang Rai

To Doi Tung

To Chad's House (400m), Post Office (1 km), Hospital (1¼ km),
Main Bus Station (5 km), Mae Chan (32 km) & Chiang Rai)

N

0 metres 100
0 yards 100

■ **Sleeping**
1 KK (King Kobra) Guesthouse
2 Mae Sai Plaza Guesthouse
3 Mae Sai Riverside
4 Northern Guesthouse
5 Thai (Tai) Thong
6 Top North
7 Wang Thong

Chan. He also organizes trips to Burma and can arrange visas for Laos. **E** *Mae Sai Plaza Guesthouse*, 386/3 Sawlomchong Rd, T732230. Good position overlooking river, with views to Burma from the verandahs of the huts that claw their way up the hillside like a small shanty town. Rooms with attached bathrooms and hot water, very popular, with good source of local information. Recommended. **E-F** *Chad's House*, 52/1 Phahonyothin Rd (1½ km from the bridge back towards Mae Chan and Chiang Rai, and about 50 m off the road). A friendly guesthouse run by a Shan family, dorm beds available, good source of information on surrounding countryside.

Eating　Restaurants in Mae Sai tend to be serious eating establishments with little character. There are numerous places along Phahonyothin Rd and the market area is good for stall food. There are also a number of riverside restaurants.

Shopping　Most people who come to Mae Sai come for the shopping. There are scores of stalls and shops selling Burmese, Chinese, Lao and Thai goods. The Burmese products are the most diverse and the best buys: puppets, cheroots, gemstones, 'antiques', lacquerware. **Gems** *Mandalay Shop*, 381/1-4 Phahonyothin Rd, for Burmese jade, sapphires and rubies (see page 501).

Transport
34 km to Mae Chan,
61 km to Chiang Rai,
906 km to Bangkok

Local Motorbike hire: many of the guesthouses that used to rent out motorbikes have stopped because of the number of accidents. However, there are still a couple of places hiring out bikes, and most guesthouses will find a machine if required. Prices start at ฿150 per day for a Honda Dream. *Thong Motorbike Rental*, Sawlongchong Rd. *Batman Motorbike*, Sawlongchong Rd. **Long distance Bus**: the main bus station is 5 km out of town, just off the main road running to Mae Chan and Chiang Rai. Songthaews and motorcycle taxis take passengers from town to the terminal and vice versa. Regular connections with Bangkok's Northern bus terminal (13-15 hrs), Chiang Mai (4¼-5 hrs), Chiang Rai (1 hr 20 mins), and Mae Chan. **Songthaew**: connections with Chiang Saen, Sop Ruak and the Golden Triangle, every 30-40 mins. Songthaews leave from Phahonyothin Rd near the centre of town. Songthaews for Mae Chan and Chiang Rai also leave from town, saving a journey out to the bus terminal.

Directory　**Banks** A number of banks with money-changing facilities, some open 0830-1700 Mon-Sun. *Thai Farmers*, 122/1 Phahonyothin Rd. *Krung Thai*, Phahonyothin Rd. *Bangkok Metropolitan Bank*, Phahonyothin Rd. **Communications** Post Office: Phahonyothin Rd (2 km from bridge towards Mae Chan). **Telephone Office:** next door to the Post Office.

Kengtung (Chiang Tung) 　 เชียงตุง

The Mae Sai-Tachilek border was previously only accessible for Thais and Burmese, but it has recently opened to foreigners. The Burmese government has officially sanctioned the border crossing to Tachilek, but the Thais have not, so your passport is not officially stamped as having left Thailand. The Burmese allow tour groups of up to 10 people to make the 167 km journey to Kengtung. The visa is only for a maximum of four days/three nights and is liable to change at a moment's notice. Visitors must leave the border before 1000 so they reach Kengtung by nightfall. The border is open 0600-1800 Monday-Sunday. It is obligatory to exchange US$100 into FECs on the border. For details on transport to Kengtung from Mae Sai, 167 km away, and entry formalities, see page 343.

The road to Kengtung is in bad condition – a four-wheel drive vehicle is advisable. However, the Thais are building a new road which is intended to eventually connect Thailand with China's Yunnan Province. It is the only way visitors can reach the otherwise inaccessible Burmese territory within the

Golden Triangle. The road, which winds precipitously through the mountain ravines on rock-cut shelves, is a major smuggling route, not only for heroin and opium, but for Chinese and Shan girls, many of whom end up in Bangkok brothels. James Pringle, one of the few Western journalists to have made the trip to Kengtung, reported seeing chain gangs of shackled prisoners breaking stones to be used for building the road to China. Some of the prisoners are reported to be students, arrested during the 1988 uprising. Pringle quotes a Burma specialist in Bangkok as saying: "The Burmese military is so out of touch with the real world it does not seem to realize it is doing anything wrong and is even allowing tourists to see this".

A smuggler's outpost, the city is often compared to Chiang Mai 50 years ago before it was hit by tourism. It is and was an important Shan stronghold. Next to the main hotel, originally named *The Kengtung*, is the site of an old Shan palace, demolished by the military in 1992 to build a car park. The central market, Kaad Luang, is worth visiting, and so too is the Shan Mahamyatmuni pagoda and Naung Tong Lake. The Buddha image, Maha Myat Muni, is the most sacred, but other important temples are the Sun Sali, Sun Taung and Sun Lwe. The town is a treasure trove of traditional architecture with old-style houses, with intricately designed wooden balconies so characteristic of Shan architecture.

There are just a handful to places to stay, all poor value for money compared with Thailand. The refurbished *Kyaingtong Hotel* (**B**) offers poor value for money, but is quite serviceable. The *Noi Yee Hotel* (**D**) is also expensive for dormitory-style accommodation.

Mae Salong (Santikhiri) แม่สลอง

Mae Salong is situated at an altitude of over 1,200 m, close to the border with Burma. After the Communist victory in China in 1949, remnants of the nationalist KMT (Kuomintang) sought refuge here and developed it as a base from which they would mount an invasion of China. This wish has long since faded into fantasy and the Thai authorities have attempted to integrate the exiled Chinese into the Thai mainstream. Many of the residents of Mae Salong do not speak Thai. However, these are generally not former KMT soldiers, but more recent immigrants from China. A paved road now leads to the town and is easily accessible.

Phone code:
Colour map 1, grid A3

Despite the attempts to Thai-ify Mae Salong, it still feels like a little corner of China. The hillsides are scattered with Japanese sakura trees, with beautiful pink blossom, whilst Chinese herbs and vegetables are grown in the surrounding countryside and sold at the morning market. Many of the inhabitants still speak Chinese, Yunnanese food is sold on the streets, and there are glimpses of China around every corner. One of the reasons why Mae Salong has remained so distinctive is because a significant proportion of the the KMT refugees who settled here became involved in opium production and trade (Khun Sa lived near here during the 1970s and the early years of the 1980s – see page 370). This put the inhabitants in conflict with the Thai authorities and created the conditions in which they were excluded from mainstream Thai society. Mae Salong's remoteness – at least until recently – also isolated the town from intensive interaction with other areas of the country.

It is also an alternative place to trek from. The **Morning Market** is worth a visit for early risers (0530-0800), as this is where hilltribe people come to sell their produce. **Wat Santakhiri** is situated in a great position, with views of the hills on the road up to the impressive shrine to the Princess mother. It is a Mahayana Buddhist monastery with images of Kuan Yin and Chinese-style salas.

Excursions

Pha Dua is a Yao village, 15 km from Mae Salong. It was founded by Yao tribespeople escaping from the Communist Pathet Lao Laos 45 years ago, and during the 1960s it became a centre for the trade in opium. With the opium trade curtailed by the government, the inhabitants have turned to food crops such as cabbages and strawberries, and to tourism, to earn a living. Handicrafts from Burma, Nan (in the eastern highlands) – even Nepal – are sold from small stalls, while women and children parade the streets in their traditional indigo costumes. You can get there on a tour or by songthaew.

Trekking See Hilltribes and trekking, page 360. Treks to Akha, Hmong, Shan and other hilltribe villages are arranged by the *Mae Salong Guest House* and the *Shin Sane Guest House*, among others (see Sleeping below). They also organize pony trekking to local hilltribe villages.

Sleeping
■ *on map*
Price codes:
see inside front cover.
Prices can be bargained
down in the low season

C-D *Mae Salong Resort*, set in a small village of its own, T765014, F765132. This is probably the best place to stay here, set up on the hill, with individual though basic bungalows set in a pine forest. Chinese/Thai restaurant and several stalls and shops sell trinkets and Chinese products (such as tea). **B** *Khumnaiphol Resort*, 58 Moo 18, about 1 km south of town, T712485, F716191. Expensive restaurant (**mid-range**), Thai-style bungalows with mattresses on the floor, attached bathrooms with hot water. Perched on the hillside with great views west and of Phra Borom That Chedi. Discounts for tours (minimum 10 people), friendly but overpriced. **B-C** *Mae Salong Villa*, just before Mae Salong, on road in from Chiang Rai, T765114, F765039. Hot water, good views, some bungalows and better value than the *Mae Salong Resort*. Large, barn-like Chinese restaurant attached, with views from the balcony. **C** *Mae Salong Central Hills Hotel*, set off the main road, with the bus stop out front. This Chinese hotel appears noisy at first glance; however, rooms are at the back and are clean and carpeted, with TV and telephone and wonderful views. **E** *Akha Guesthouse*, next door to *Shin Sane*, restaurant, outside is concrete, but the interior is all wood. Clean, basic, big rooms with shared bathrooms. A bit noisy but friendly management. Trekking organized by *Dan Hill Tribe Tours* from here. **D-E** *Golden Dragon Guesthouse*, T765009. Own bathroom with hot water and western toilets, clean and quiet rooms, no English spoken. **E-F** *Sinsane*. The older rooms in the wooden house are small, dark and not terribly clean, with outside (grubby) toilets, they are also very noisy being close to the road and a karaoke bar. The newer bungalows are clean and quiet and rooms have bathrooms with hot water. This is probably the cheapest accommodation in Mae Salong, there is a friendly atmosphere and the food is good.

Mae Salong

■ **Sleeping**
1 Golden Dragon Guesthou
2 Khumnaiphol Resort
3 Mae Salong Central Hills
4 Mae Salong Resort
5 Mae Salong Villa
6 Sinsane & Akha Guesthou

Mae Salong is a good place to eat Yunnanese (Southern Chinese) food. There are expensive restaurants at the *Mae Salong Villa* and *Mae Salong Resort*, and there is also a restaurant housed in a conservatory-type shelter on the roof of the *Mae Salong Central Hills Hotel*, next to the bus stop (fairly priced and great views). It is also worth sampling the excellent Chinese-style chicken noodle soup, which is sold in prodigious quantities from numerous roadside stalls.

Eating
Price categories: see inside front cover

Seriously cheap *Salima Restaurant* (100 m past *Shin Sane Guesthouse*, same side of the road). Recommended Muslim restaurant. *Mini*, 300 m past *Shin Sane* in direction of Tha Ton, friendly and good.

Songthaew Regular connections with Chiang Rai (1½ hrs); also morning songthaew connections along a rough road with Tha Ton (2 hrs); during the rainy season the road is sometimes closed. To get from Chiang Mai to Mae Salong, take the Mae Sai bus and get off at Ban Pasang (40 mins); from there catch a songthaew up the mountain to Mae Salong (1 hr). The last songthaew leaving from Mae Salong down to Ban Pasang is at 1700; buses on the Chiang Mai-Ban Pasang route run every 15 mins, 0600-1800.

Transport
68 km to Chiang Rai

Eastern highlands of the north

This is the least travelled of the main routes in the north. From Phrae, Route 101 runs northeastwards towards the border with Laos, and terminates at Nan, 340 km from Chiang Mai. This part of Thailand contains some of the finest forest in the country.

Phrae แพร่

Phrae is an attractive provincial capital that lies off the main tourist trail. The town is situated in a narrow rice valley on the banks of the Mae Yom River, flanked by mountains to the east and west. During the months of the cold season between December and February it becomes distinctly chilly at night and in the early morning, and the locals wrap themselves in sweaters and coats whilst waiting for the sun to take the chill out of the day.

Phone code: 054
Colour map 1, grid B3
Population: 25,000

Ins and outs

Phrae's small airport is 7 km southeast of town and there are daily connections with Bangkok. But most people get here by bus. The terminal is on the outskirts of town, 1 km from the centre, and there are connections with Bangkok, Chiang Mai, Nan and some other towns in the North. The nearest train station is at Den Chai, 24 km to the southwest.

Getting there
See also Transport, page 353

Phrae is not a large place. The main bus terminal is a 15 min walk from much of the accommodation and the town is pleasant enough to stroll around.

Getting around

History

Phrae was founded in the 12th century – when it was known as Wiang Kosai or Silk Cloth City – and is one of the oldest cities in Thailand. It still has its own 'royal' family and was an independent Thai *muang* (city state) until the early 16th century, when it was captured by an army from Ayutthaya. When Ayutthaya's power began to wane in the 18th century, Phrae – like many other northern principalities – came under the sway of the Burmese. It was finally incorporated into the Siamese state in the 19th century.

The Northern Region

Phrae's ancient roots can still be seen in the city walls and moat that separate the old city from the new commercial centre. On Charoen Muang Road, there are also a handful of attractive wooden Chinese shophouses – although the scourge of uncontrolled redevelopment is gradually gnawing away at the remnants of old Phrae. Although Phrae may have ancient roots, the province is best known in Thailand for the quality of its *morhom*, the rough blue garb of the Thai farmer. The morhom was popularized by the charismatic populist politician Chamlong Srimuang, the former governor of Bangkok and leader of the Palang Dharma (Buddhist Force) Party, and it has now become something of a fashion statement among the young of Bangkok (see Shopping, below).

Sights

Wats

Wat Chom Sawan is one of the most beautiful monasteries in this part of Thailand

The Burmese-style **Wat Chom Sawan** is on the edge of town, about 1 km northeast of the centre, on the road to Nan. It was commissioned by Rama V (1868-1910) and designed by a Burmese architect. Like most Burmese (Thai Yai) wats, the bot (ordination hall) and viharn (assembly hall) are consolidated in one elaborate, multi-roofed towering structure, with verandahs and side rooms. It has survived relatively unscathed: the wooden roof tiles have not been replaced by corrugated iron, and the rich original interior decoration of mirror tiles upon a deep red ground is also intact. Ask one of the monks to point out the rare Buddhist texts carved on sheets of ivory, and the bamboo and gold Buddha 'basket'. There is also a less remarkable collection of amulets, coins and betel boxes. At the front of the compound is a Burmese-style chedi, surrounded by 13 acolyte chedis. Built of brick and stucco, it has been allowed to gently weather into a mellow state of decrepit elegance. Near the chedi and along the east wall of the compound are some rather unfortunate caged boar, and rather more fortunate caged birds. ■ *Admission by donation.*

Wat Hua Khuang, within the city walls at the north edge of town, is notable only for its large, abandoned brick chedi.

Not far away at the north extension of Charoen Muang Road (and also within the city walls) is **Wat Sri Chum**. The interiors of the bot and viharn here are stark and rather beautiful, with seated and standing Buddha images in extremely high relief. Above the seated image, angels, again in relief, shower flowers down upon the Buddha.

Wat Luang is a few minutes' walk from Wat Sri Chum, near the city wall and moat. The wat was founded in the 12th century at about the same time as the city, although continuous renovation and expansion has tended to obscure its ancient origins. Particularly beautiful, however, is the Lanna Thai-style chedi, with its (admittedly rather crude) elephant caryatids and honorific

• •

Phrae place names

Ban Phrathap Jai
บ้านประทับใจ

Phae Muang Phi
แพะเมืองผี

Wat Chom Sawan
วัดจอมสวรรค์

Wat Hua Khuang
วัดหัวข่วง

Wat Luang
วัดหลวง

Wat Phrathat Chor Hae
วัดพระธาตุช่อแห

Wat Sri Chum
วัดศรีชุม

umbrellas. The wat also supports an impressive museum which the monks are happy to show visitors. In its varied collection (unfortunately with very little explanatory information in English) are valuable Buddha images, swords, coins, burial caskets, Buddhist texts, old photographs (one of a decapitation), betel boxes and jewellery. An old northern house with all the accessories of traditional life is also part of the collection. Finally, the wat is also notable for its fine well pavilion on the west wall and the individual monk's kutis, or cells, like small bungalows, along the south wall. ■ *Admission by donation.*

Ban Phrathap Jai is in the west suburbs of town. The tourist authorities are promoting this 'house' (in fact it was constructed in 1972 out of nine old teak houses) as one of the biggest teak Thai-style mansions in the country: it is disappointing in its ersatz atmosphere and crudity. The house is situated in a 'garden' of concrete animals and is really just a reason to attract visitors to the shops here, selling woodcarvings, 'antiques' and clothing. ■ *0800-1700 Mon-Sun, ฿20. Getting there: by saamlor (not more than ฿10) or walk the 2 km from the city centre.*

Excursions

Wat Phrathat Chor Hae is a hilltop wat 8 km southeast of town. It probably dates from the 12th to 13th centuries, and the 28 m-high chedi is said to contain a hair of the Lord Buddha, brought here by the Indian Emperor Asoka. The chedi is surrounded by a small cloister and linked to this is an ornate, high ceilinged, viharn, with bold murals depicting episodes from the Buddha's life. The name of the wat is the same as that of a particularly fine cloth woven by the people of the area and in which the chedi is shrouded each year. Also here at the foot of the hill are a number of souvenir stalls and a small, rather sad, **wildlife park** (the **Suan Sat Chor Hae**) (0700-1700 Monday-Sunday). ■ *Getting there: by songthaew from Charoen Muang Rd, near the intersection with Yantarakitkoson Rd, ฿10. NB There are few return songthaews in the afternoon, so it is best to make the trip in the morning.*

Muang Phi, or the City of Ghosts, is marketed as Thailand's Grand Canyon – which does little justice to the real thing. It is an area of strange eroded rock formations, about 15 km northeast of town. ■ *Getting there: turn right after 9 km off Route 101 to Nan, and onto Route 1134; the turning for the canyon is 6 km along Route 1134 and lies about 2 km off the road. It is easiest by chartered songthaew, as the area lies off the main highway (about ฿200) and going by public transport involves a change of vehicle and a 2 km walk. Alternatively, take a bus towards Nan and get off at the intersection with Route 1134, which is signposted to Muang Phi. From here, catch another songthaew (not regular) and get off after 6 km to walk the final 2 km or so to Muang Phi.*

See Hilltribes and trekking, page 360. Phrae has not built up much of a trekking infrastructure yet, although the elusive Mlabri tribe are accessible from town (see box, page 373). Ask at the *Mae Yom Palace Hotel* for information or travel to Nan where facilities are better developed (see below).

Tours & trekking

Essentials

A-B *Maeyom Palace*, 181/6 Yantarakitkoson Rd, T521028, F522904. A/c, restaurant, pool. Best hotel in town, situated 1 km from the town centre, large rooms and professional service, organizes tours to hilltribe villages and home industries, discounts available, especially in the low season, bikes for hire (฿100 per day).
A-B *Nakhon Phrae Tower*, 3 Muang Hit Rd, T521321, F521937. A monstrous hotel which towers over the city, good rooms, but no pool (as yet) and little 'northern'

Sleeping
■ *on map*
Price codes:
see inside front cover

ambience. **D** *Nakhon Palace*, 118 Rachdamnern Rd, T511122. Some a/c, ugly hotel sprawling across both sides of the street, average rooms, central. **D** *Pharadorn*, 177 Yantarakitkoson Rd, T511177. Some a/c, restaurant, karaoke bar, large concrete barn which doesn't look very enticing, but rooms are spacious, clean and well maintained, a/c rooms benefit from carpets and hot water, good value. Recommended. **D-E** *Thung Si Phaiboon*, Yantarakitkoson Rd (near intersection with Charoen Muang Rd), T511011. Some a/c, large, characterless and shabby rooms, Asian squat toilets rooms arranged in a 'U' around a courtyard, visitors sleeping in rooms on the street may be woken up by an early morning market. **E** *Ho Faa*, Charoen Muang Rd, T511140. Small, Chinese hotel near centre of town. **E** *Thepviman*, 226-228 Charoen Muang Rd, T511003. Typical Chinese hotel, friendly management.

Eating

● *on map*
Price categories:
see inside front cover.
There are several bars
on Rachdamnern Rd

Thai Mid-range: *Krua Yom Hom* (*Maeyom Palace Hotel*), Yantarakitkoson Rd. Expensive Thai, Chinese and European food, but live band and seafood barbecue in evening on terrace makes it worth it. **Seriously cheap**: *Arun Chai*, Charoen Muang Rd (opposite *Ho Faa Hotel*). Good food. *Barrahouse*, 45 Ban Mai Rd (1 km from town on road to Nan). Friendly owners, good food, clean and welcoming, coffee and ice-cream, along with usual Thai/Chinese dishes. *Cat* (*Maew*) 83 Charoen Muang Rd (near intersection with Rob Muang Rd). Good food in pleasant restaurant. Recommended. *Corner Road*, corner of Lak Muang and Khumderm roads. Also serves ice-cream, clean, friendly and pleasant atmosphere. *Luuk Kaew*, Yantarakitkoson Rd (opposite *Maeyom Palace Hotel*). Excellent Thai and Chinese food, succulent satay. Highly recommended. *Phet Pochana*, Yantarakitkoson Rd (next to the *Maeyom Palace Hotel*). Open-air restaurant, also serves Chinese dishes. *Ban Rai*, Yantarakitkoson Rd, large outdoor garden restaurant, 2 km out of town on road south.

Phrae

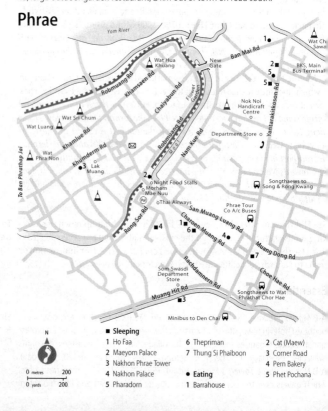

■ Sleeping

1 Ho Faa
2 Maeyom Palace
3 Nakhon Phrae Tower
4 Nakhon Palace
5 Pharadorn
6 Thepriman
7 Thung Si Phaiboon

● Eating

1 Barrahouse
2 Cat (Maew)
3 Corner Road
4 Pern Bakery
5 Phet Pochana

Bakery *Pern Bakery*, 347 Charoen Muang Rd. Cakes, pastries, coffee and ice-cream.

Traditional Thai massage *Maeyom Palace Hotel*, Yantarakitkoson Rd. **Massage**

Antiques *Ban Phrathap Jai*, see Sights above. **Clothing** Phrae is a centre of **Shopping** *morhom* production – the traditional blue garb of the Northern farmer. A simple tunic costs ฿60-100. Available all over town, but recommended is *Morhom Mae Nuu*, 60-62 Charoen Muang Rd. Another centre of production is the village of *Tung Hong*, 3 km northeast of town, on Route 101 to Nan. Getting there: by songthaew from the bus station on Tantharakitkoson Rd. **Handicrafts** *Nok Noi Handicraft Centre*, 6/3 Yantarakitkoson Trok [Soi] 2. Woodcarvings, some clothing, baskets, hats. *Ban Phrathap Jai house*. **Supermarket** *Yong Wattana*, Yantarakitkoson Rd.

Golf Small 9-hole course 2 km southeast of town, near the airport. Open to **Sport** non-members; it is said there are clubs for hire. **Swimming** At the *Maeyom Palace Hotel* (฿70).

Local **Songthaew** is the main form of local transport. Songthaews running north to **Transport** Song and Rong Kwang leave from outside the Piriyalai School on Yantarakitkoson Rd; *See also Ins & outs,* those running south to Den Chai (for the nearest train station) depart from *page 349;* Yantarakitkoson Rd near the intersection with Muang Hit Rd (by the petrol station). *627 km to Bangkok, 116 km to Nan*

Long distance **Air**: the airport is 7 km southeast of town. Daily connections on Thai with Bangkok (1 hr 20 mins). Thai lays on transport from town to the airport. Start-up airline PB Air are also negotiating for a licence to fly to Phrae.

Train: the nearest train station to Phrae is at Den Chai, 24 km southwest of town. Connections south to Bangkok (8½ hrs) and north to Chiang Mai (4½ hrs). Regular buses and songthaews from the train station to town; to get to Den Chai, pick up a bus on Yantarakitkoson Rd near the intersection with Muang Hit Rd (by the petrol station).

Bus: the terminal is 1 km northeast of the city centre off Yantarakitkoson Rd, opposite the *Maeyom Palace Hotel*. Regular connections with Bangkok's Northern bus terminal (8¼ hrs), Uttaradit, Chiang Mai and other towns in the north (hourly connections with Nan, 2-2½ hrs). A/c tour buses for Bangkok leave from *Phrae Tour's* offices at 141/6 Yantarakitkoson Rd at 2030 and 2100.

Airline offices *Thai*, Rachdamnern Rd, T511123. **Banks** Several on Charoen Muang Rd. **Directory** **Communications** Post Office: Charoen Muang Rd (in the old city), with telephone, telex and telegram facilities. **Telephone**: 163/2 Yantarakitkoson Rd.

Nan   น่าน

Nan is a province to be explored for its natural beauty, with teak forests (or today, *Phone code: 054* *rather, teak plantations), fertile valleys chequered with paddy fields, hilltribes* *Colour map 1, grid B4* *and fast-running rivers. It was not until 1931 that the central authorities man-* *Population: 30,000* *aged to overcome the area's inaccessibility and bring it under Bangkok's direct control. Even since then, there have been periods – most recently in the 1970s when Communist insurgency was a problem – when the army and the police have treated the province virtually as a no-go area. It still exudes an atmosphere of other-worldliness and isolation.*

Ins and outs

Getting there
See also Transport, page 359

There are daily air connections with Bangkok from Nan's small airport 5 km out of town, as well as flights 3 times a week to Chiang Mai and Phitsanulok. The town's 2 bus terminals, both on the outskirts, offer services to Bangkok, Chiang Mai and Chiang Rai, as well as a fair number of other destinations in the Northern and Central Plains regions.

Getting around

Nan is not a large town, and in the cool season – or in the cool of the day – walking is the best way to get around. Saamlors and songthaews provide local transport and it is also possible to hire bicycles and motorbikes.

History

Nan occupies a small valley in the far eastern highlands of the north – about 50 km from the border with Laos. It is thought the earliest settlers in the area came from the court of Laos in 1282. They established a town 70 km north of Nan, and from that point the Nan valley became an important centre. However, if local legend is to be believed, the Buddha himself was trekking here, picking out auspicious sites for wats, over 2,500 years ago. The 13th-century inscriptions of King Ramkhamhaeng of Sukhothai named Nan as one of the *muang* whose 'submission he received', although it would probably be more accurate to view the royal house of Nan ruling largely free from interference until the 15th century, when Lanna established suzerainty over Nan. Even then, the turbulent politics of the area, with the Burmese, Lao, Siamese and the partially independent muang of the area all vying with one another, coupled with Nan's remote location, afforded it considerable independence.

Sights

National Museum
An excellent museum, well worth visiting

The National Museum on Phakong Road, once the home of the Nan royal family, houses an impressive collection, including beautiful wood and bronze Buddha images, house models, ethnographic pieces, dioramas, ceramics, textiles, jewellery and musical instruments. The main piece is on the second floor: a 97 cm-long black elephant tusk which once belonged to the Nan royal family, and is reputed to have magical powers. Protected within a steel cage, it is clearly regarded as the most precious exhibit here, but pales into mediocrity next to the beautiful Buddha images and other works of art. All exhibits are well displayed and explained. ■ *0900-1200, 1300-1600 Wed-Sun. ฿30.*

Wat Phumin

Five minutes' walk from the National Museum on Phakong Road is Wat Phumin, one of Nan's artistic treasures. It was built in 1596, but has since been

• •

Nan place names

Doi Phu Kha National Park
อุทยานแห่งชาติดอยภูคา

Sao Din
เสาดิน

Tha Wang Pha
ท่าวังผา

Wat Chang Kham
วัดช้างค้ำวรวิหาร

Wat Nong Bua
วัดหนองบัว

Wat Phrathat Chae Haeng
วัดพระธาตุแช่แห้ง

Wat Phumin
วัดภูมินทร์

restored on numerous occasions – most extensively between 1865 and 1873. The unusual cruciform bot-cum-viharn (although it is surrounded by *bai sema*, the structure is both bot and viharn rolled into one) is supported by the coils of two magnificent nagas (mythical serpents). The head forms the buttress of the north entrance, and the tail the south. Inside, there are some of the finest murals to be found in the north. Painted at the end of the 19th century – probably in 1894 – they depict the tale of the Sihanadajataka (see box, page 356), but also illustrate aspects of northern Thai life: hunting, weaving, lovers, musicians, elephants and courtiers, along with bearded Europeans and steamships, the curses of hell, elephants, people being boiled alive, lovers, courtiers, catholic priests (for example, on the west wall), a starving farang clasping a tool for premasticating food (eastern wall, top), people with over-large testicles and starving men – a myriad of activity. Note the two life-size murals of a Burmese couple, both wearing lungyi (the Burmese sarong) – he has red circles and dancing monkeys tattooed on his chest to ward off evil. The naive style of the murals – large areas of empty space, figures of various sizes – distinguish them from the more sophisticated art of Bangkok. However, what the murals offer, uniquely, is a freshness of vision and gracefulness of style lacking in other works. Art historians do not know the identity of the man who created the murals. The assumption is that he was a Tai Lü man, meaning that he came from present-day southern Yunnan (China). The historian David Wyatt suggests that the scene of a tattooed and bare-chested man, whispering, apparently, into the ear of a beautiful girl, elegantly dressed, at the lowest level of the west wall, is in fact a self-portrait and that the girl is his lover. The unusual hair style of the man hints that he may be Tai Lü. Four Sukhothai-style gilded stucco Buddhas, each in an attitude of vanquishing Mara, face outwards towards the cardinal points. The carved doors of the building, with animals, birds and flowers, are also particularly fine.

Wat Chang Kham, next to the Sala Klang (provincial offices), features a chedi supported by elephant buttresses (caryatids), similar in inspiration to those at Si Satchanalai, Kamphaeng Phet and Sukhothai. The viharn was built in 1547 and contains three Sukhothai-style Buddha images, two walking and one standing. Also note the accomplished woodcarving on the façades of both the bot and the viharn, and the guardian singhas at the entrances to both. **Wat Phya Phu** – built in 1427 and since much restored – contains some examples of the post-classic Sukhothai Buddha image. The bronze walking Buddha, which is dated to 1426, shows the stylized features and the asymmetrical posture of the classic Sukhothai image; yet the robe is rigid, the face rounder. Many art historians regard such images as inferior, lacking the "grandeur and exultation of the classic Buddha image" (Stratton and Scott, 1981: 81).

Other wats in the town

    Wat Ming Muang, on Suriyaphong Road, contains the city of Nan's *lak muang* or city pillar, liberally draped in garlands. **Wat Hua Chang**, on the corner of Phakong and Mahaphrom roads, features an elegant two-storey stone and wood tripitaka or scripture library, a square-based chedi with four Buddhas in raised niches, each in the attitude of vanquishing Mara and a fine bot (with *bai sema*). **Wat Hua Wiang Tai** is on Sumonthewarat Road, just north of Anantavoraritdet Road. It is very gaudy, with nagas running along the top of the surrounding wall and bright vivacious murals painted on the exterior of the viharn. Other wats in the area include **Wat Suan Tan**, in Tambon Nai Wiang, which has a prang – unusual for the area – and a 15th century bronze Buddha image named Phra Chao Thong Thit. A fireworks display takes place at the wat during Songkran.

The Northern Region

The Northern Region

The murals of Wat Phumin and the theme of orphanhood

David Wyatt, an eminent Western historian of Thailand, published a small pamphlet on the murals of Wat Phumin as part of his wider work on the Nan Chronicle. The explanation below draws on his work and views.

The murals of Wat Phumin tell the tale of the Sihanada-jataka. In this story, the god Indra takes pity on a poor widow in the kingdom of Sisaket, descends to earth in the shape of a white elephant, and leaves behind his urine in one of his footprints. The widow drinks the urine and gives birth to a boy whom she names Khatthana. When Khatthana reaches adolescence he asks his mother about his father and on being told the story of the elephant sets out in search of him. This search takes Khatthana to strange lands and brings him into contact with many evil men and monsters. Eventually Indra hears of his son's search and again descends to earth in the guise of a white elephant. Then, before dying, Indra gives his son the source of his powers – his magical tusks. These he uses to forge a great empire. However, an enemy learns of the source of Khatthana's power, steals the tusks, and kills him. Following his father's death, one of Khatthana's sons sets out to retrieve the tusks, which he succeeds in doing, and uses their powers to bring his father back to life.

The question that concerns David Wyatt is why did the artist and his patron decide to illustrate this particular jataka tale? First, he argues that the decision was the patron's, not the artist's. Wat Phumin is an important temple with a long association with the royal family of Nan. The Nan Chronicle records the consecration of the four-sided mondop in which the murals are located as a great event. Their subject was not something to be taken lightly and it is likely that they were specifically commissioned.

Next, Wyatt argues that the leitmotif of the story is orphanhood, 'not so much the recurrent theme of children losing one or both parents – although there are numerous such cases – but rather the frequently repeated theme of Nan as a state being often, throughout its history, 'orphaned' (see page 823). The murals were painted shortly after an event which had catastrophic consequences for the power and prestige of the kingdom of Nan: an agreement between Siam and France in 1893, following which France took over control of Laos and with it half of the lands that came under the control of Nan. The murals depict numerous Westerners whom Wyatt takes to be Frenchmen: the five standing men on the wharf sport berets, a French flag flies behind the wall, and a French Roman Catholic priest kneels offering gifts (?). So the murals reflect contemporary events – the loss of Nan's power and influence – as well as representing a common theme through local history – orphanhood. "The Wat Phumin murals, I think, enable us to explore more deeply the thoughts and emotions of all those who were so deeply affected by the calamities of 1893; and with their help we can add to the pain felt by King Chulalongkorn the feelings of abandonment, despair, and quasi-orphanhood felt by the ruling line of Nan' (see page 824).

Source: Wyatt, David K. (1993) Temple murals as an historical source: the case of Wat Phumin, Nan, Chulalongkorn University Press: Bangkok. The small pamphlet is available from bookshops in Bangkok and is well worth buying if intending to visit Nan and Wat Phumin.

Excursions

Wat Phrathat Chae Haeng, 3 km southeast of town, was built in 1355. The 55 m-high, gold-sheeted chedi is Lao in style, and the bot has an interesting multi-tiered roof (a fair with fireworks and processions is held here on the full moon day of the first lunar month). Also notable are the fine pair of nagas that form the balustrade of the approach stairway to the monastery. ■ *Getting there: a 30 min walk across the Nan River and then east, or rent a bicycle/motorbike.*

Sao Din in Amphoe Na Noi lies about 30 km south of Nan, off Route 1026. It is a heavily eroded canyon – almost prehistoric in atmosphere – with tall earth pillars and deeply eroded earth, reminiscent of Muang Phi outside Phrae. ■ *Getting there: either catch a local bus to Amphoe Na Noi and then charter a motorcycle taxi, or charter a songthaew from town.*

Tha Wang Pha, an amphoe (district) capital 40 km to the north of Nan on Route 1080, is rather easier to get to. The town is famous for its Tai Lü weaving, much of which is produced in surrounding villages and then brought here for marketing. The Tai Lü were forced out of Yunnan in southern China by King Rama I (1782-1809). At the conclusion of the Thai-Burmese wars, they were settled in Nan province and turned to farming, and are now peacefully assimilated into the Thai population. But the Tai Lü have not lost all their cultural distinctiveness: they are skilled weavers and the women still wear a tubular *pha sin* of bright horizontal stripes and a short black jacket, decorated with multicoloured embroidered stripes and silver jewellery. Tai Lü textiles and jewellery are available in town. En route to Tha Wang Pha, about 35 km north of Nan, is the turn-off for **Ban Nong Bua** and the fine **Wat Nong Bua**. The monastery is Tai Lü in design and features fine murals, executed by the same Tai Lü artists who decorated Wat Phumin in Nan (see above). Tai Lü textiles are also available in this small town. ■ *Getting there: by regular local bus or songthaew from the stand on Sumonthewarat Rd, just north of Anantavoraritdet Rd. For Ban Nong Bua, get off at the fork before Tha Wang Pha and walk about 2 km (tell the conductor where you are going).*

Doi Phu Kha National Park, 40 km north of Nan, is a good day trip by motorbike. The park was gazetted quite recently, offers good trekking, and a range of hill peoples also live within its boundaries. **NB** The park is in the mountains, so it can get cold at night. Two government houses rent out rooms when no officials are staying. Pay by donation. There are also 14 bungalows with shared toilets (฿200 per night) and two campsites (one at headquarters and one at the Star Gazing Area (฿100 per night)). Blankets can be borrowed from headquarters for ฿20. There is no regular transport in the park and no restaurant. The cook at headquarters will prepare meals for you if you call (T6029844) ahead of arrival; breakfast (฿60), lunch (฿80), dinner (฿120). ■ *Getting there: catch a bus to Pua (1 hr); from Pua, songthaews run from 0800 to 1200 up to the Park HQ (฿20); outside those times they have to be chartered (฿350).*

Tours & trekking
See also Tour operators below

The best tour company in town is the *Phu Travel Service* (see Tour operators below). Mr Phu rents out bicycles and motorbikes and arranges tours to see the elusive Mlabri tribe (see box, page 373), the Doi Phu Kha National Park, provincial sites and boat tours up the Nan River. Prices from ฿600 per day upwards – his prices may seem steep, but many travellers told us he was good value for money. The *Dhevaraj, Nan Guesthouse, Doi Phukha* and *Nan Fah* also organize tours.

See Hilltribes and trekking, page 360. *Phu Travel Service* organizes treks into the surrounding area, including to see the Mlabri people; see box, page 373.

Essentials

Sleeping

■ *on map*
Price codes:
see inside front cover

A-B *City Park*, 99 Moo 4 Yantarakitkoson Rd, Tambon Tuu Tai, T710376. A/c, restaurant, large pool. New motel/resort-style hotel on a 10-acre plot outside town, all rooms have TV and minibar, peaceful and comfortable, but inconvenient for exploring the city. **C** *Dhevaraj*, 466 Sumonthewarat Rd, T710094. Some a/c, restaurant. Rather grubby Chinese hotel with the illusion it is something more. Rooms are tatty and characterless. Friendly management but overpriced. **C-D** *Nan Fah*, 438-440 Sumonthewarat Rd, T772640. Some a/c, known as the 'wooden hotel'. This place has a flavour of the Wild West about it. Rooms are large and bare and painted in flamboyant colours. Bathrooms have hot water and Western toilets, gift shop and tours arranged. **D-E** *Sukasem Hotel*, see map for location. Some a/c rooms, grubby and overpriced. **E** *Wiang Tai*, down the side street next to Wat Wiang Tai. Rooms are fairly small but adequately clean, with Thai squat toilets. Better value elsewhere, however. **E-F** *Doi Phukha Guesthouse*, 94/5 Sumonthewarat Soi 1, T771422. Very well-kept place, run by an extremely friendly family in a beautiful leafy compound. An old teak house has quiet, clean rooms with shared Western toilets, dorm beds also available (**F**), lots of trekking and excursion information, sells books and a good map of Nan, very friendly, good atmosphere. Recommended. The owner will organize tours if not too busy. **E-F** *Nan Guesthouse*, 57/16 Mahaphrom Rd, T771849. Clean and attractive, quiet location, not always very efficient, one visitor complained that food was sporadic and that it was run by children who spoke no English, but most guests seem to see this as part of the place's charm and report it to be very friendly. Thai and Western food served – good portions. Rents out bicycles (฿30 per day), some dorm beds, good information board.

Nan

To Wat Suan Tan & Airport (5 km)

Market

Anantavoraritidet Rd

Night
Food Stalls

Thai Payap
Development
Association

Kha Luang Rd

Mahawong Rd

Phakong Rd

Mahayod Rd

Wat Hua
Wiang Tai

Department Store
& Nan Silverware

Cinema &
Handicraft Centre

Market

Market & Local
Songthaews

Thai Payap
Development
Association

Wat Hua
Chang

Mahaphrom Rd

Thai Airways

Wat Chang
Kham

Sumonthewarat Rd

Phu Travel Service

Mahawong Rd

National
Museum

Suriyaphong Rd

Kha Luang Rd

Patana Paknua
Bridge

Wat Ming Muang
& Lak Muang

Phakong Rd

Nan River

Wat Phumin

N

0 metres 100
0 yards 100

■ Sleeping	● Eating	⌂ Transport
1 Dhevaraj	1 Chokchai	1 Buses to Chian
2 Doi Phukha Guesthouse	2 Laanchang Pub	Chiang Rai & P
3 Nan Fah	3 No Name Kwaytio Stall	2 BKS Terminal fe
4 Nan Guesthouse	4 Pizza	Phrae, Bangkok
5 Sukasem	5 Tanaya Kitchen	Phitsanulok &
	6 Siam	3 Songthaews to

Thai/Chinese Cheap: *Siam*, Sumonthewarat Rd (near the *Nan Fah Hotel*). Despite its dingy appearance, this is possibly the best restaurant in Nan, freshly cooked Thai and Chinese dishes, generous portions, efficient service – very well patronized by locals. **Seriously cheap**: *Chokchai*, Mahayod Rd. Good food in friendly surroundings. *No name*, 38/1 Suriyaphong Rd (next to Wat Ming Muang). Excellent spicy *kwaytio khao soi* (egg noodles in curry broth). *Tanaya Kitchen*, 75/23-24 Anantavoraritidet Rd, opposite Ayutthayan Bank. Cosy little wooden house with Thai and Chinese food and an extensive vegetarian menu.

Western Cheap: *Pizza Restaurant*, Sumonthewarat Rd. Serves Thai and Western food – hamburgers, salads, steaks and pizzas. One of the few places in town to go if the stomach cries out for Western food.

Foodstalls There is a small night market at the intersection of Phakong and Anantavoraritidet roads.

Laanchang, Sumonthewarat Rd. Wild ornamentation including leopard skins and hanging vines. Good place for an evening drink, occasional live music, serves Thai food (**cheap**), tours and treks, motorbikes for rent. *Pin Pub*, *Nan Fah Hotel*, live country music (which adds to the Wild West ambience) most nights and serves Thai food (**cheap**).

Mid Oct-mid Nov *Boat races*, at the end of the Buddhist Lent. These races are thought to have first started about a century ago, when they were part of the Songkran celebrations. Now they are associated with the robe-giving ceremony, kathin. These distinctive boats are hollowed out logs, painted in bright designs. There is a lively fair in the weeks before (and during) the races.

Department stores *Nara Department store*, Sumonthewarat Rd (north of inter-section with Anantaroraritdet Rd). **Handicrafts** *Ban Fai*, Kha Luang Rd. Basketry, textiles and woodcarving. There is also a shop in the *Nan Fah Hotel*, Sumonthewarat Rd, selling various handicrafts (textiles, silverwork and woodcarving) at reasonable prices. Recommended. *Thai Payap Development Association*, a co-op selling hilltribes' handicrafts, worth a visit. **Jewellery** *Nan Silverware*, corner of Sumonthewarat and Anantavoraritidet roads, for locally produced jewellery. **Supermarkets** *Big D Supermarket* along the Sumonthewarat Rd (opposite the Thai Payap Development Association).

See also Tours and trekking above. *Phu Travel Service*, 453/4 Sumonthewarat Rd, T710636.

Local Saamlors and **songthaews**. **Bicycles and motorbike hire**: from *Phu Travel Service*, *Oversea Shop*, *Nan*, and *Rob Muang guesthouses* and *Laanchang Pub*.

Long distance Air: the airport is on the northern edge of town (5 km from the centre). Connections on Thai with Bangkok daily at 1600 (2 hrs 10 mins), and 3 times a week with Chiang Mai and Phitsanulok. Start-up airline PB Air are also negotiating for a licence to fly here. **Bus**: Nan has 2 bus terminals. Buses for towns to the north and west, including Chiang Rai, Chiang Mai (9 hrs), Lamphun, Lampang, Phayao, Phrae and Den Chai, leave from the station off Anantaroraritdet Rd about 1 km west of the town centre. Buses serving destinations to the south, including Bangkok's Northern bus terminal (9½-10 hrs), Phitsanulok, Uttaradit, Nakhon Sawan, Kamphaeng Phet and Sukhothai, leave from the BKS terminal, 500 m to the north of the city centre on Kha Luang Rd. VIP and a/c buses serve all major destinations. **NB** Buses running north to Chiang Rai take 2 routes: either the shorter trip west and northwest on routes 1091

Sidebar (right margin):

Eating
● on map
Price categories:
see inside front cover

Bars

Festivals

Shopping

Tour operators

Transport
See also Ins & outs,
page 354;
749 km to Bangkok,
340 km to
Chiang Mai,
116 km to Phrae

The Northern Region

and 1251 to Phayao and then north to Chiang Rai, or by first running south to Phrae and then north to Phayao and Chiang Rai. All bus times and costs are displayed on information boards at the Nan and Doi Phukha Guesthouses, and the information officers at bus terminals also speak English.

Directory   **Airline offices** *Thai*, 34 Mahaphrom Rd, T710377. **Banks** *Thai Farmers* and *Bangkok* on Sumonthewarat Rd. **Communications** Post Office: Mahawong Rd (with international telephone, fax, telegram facilities). **Telephone centre:** 345/7 Sumonthewarat Rd. **Useful addresses** Immigration has moved to Thung Chang, 92 km north of Nan.

Hilltribes and trekking

A visit to a hilltribe village is one of the main reasons why people travel to the north of Thailand. The hilltribe population (Chao Khao in Thai – literally 'Mountain People') numbers about 800,000, or a little more than 1% of the total population of the country. However, these 800,000 people are far from homogenous: each hilltribe, and there are nine recognized by the government, has a different language, dress, religion, artistic heritage and culture. They meet their subsistence needs in different ways and often occupy different ecological niches. In some respects they are as far removed from one another as they are from the lowland Thais. As their name suggests, the hilltribes occupy the highland areas that fringe the Northern region, with the largest populations in the provinces of Chiang Mai (143,000), Chiang Rai (98,000), Mae Hong Son (83,000) and Tak (69,000). These figures are a few years old, but the relative balance between the provinces has not changed significantly. Although this guide follows the tradition of using the term 'hilltribe' to describe these diverse peoples, it is in many regards an unfortunate one. They are not tribes in the anthropological sense, derived as it is from the study of the peoples of Africa. And the word 'tribe' has uncomfortable, and inaccurate, connotations of 'primitive' and 'savage'.

Cultural extinction?   Much of the concern that has been focused upon the hilltribes dwells on their increasingly untenable position in a country where they occupy a distinctly subordinate position. Over a number of years, the Thai government has tried culturally and economically to assimilate the hilltribes into the Thai state (read, Tai state). Projects have attempted to settle them in *nikhom* (resettlement villages) and to 'instill a strong sense of Thai citizenship, obligation and faith in the institutions of Nation, Religion and Monarchy...' (Thai Army document). This desire on the part of the government is understandable, when one considers that the hilltribes occupy strategically-sensitive border areas.

There are a number of factors that have lent weight to this policy of resettlement and integration: the former strength of the Communist Party of Thailand (CPT), the narcotics problem (it has been estimated that as recently as 30 years ago, 45% of hilltribe households were engaged in the cultivation of the poppy), the more recent concern with the preservation of Thailand's few remaining forests, as well as the simple demographic reality that Thailand's population is growing. However, in many respects the most significant process encouraging change has been the commercialization of life among the hilltribes: as they have been inexorably drawn into the market economy, so their traditional subsistence systems and ethics have become increasingly obsolete. This process is voluntary, spontaneous and profound.

Although tourists may feel that they are somehow more culturally aware and sensitive than the next man or woman and therefore can watch and not influence, this is of course untrue. As people, and especially monetized Westerners, push their way into the last remaining remote areas of the north in an endless

The hilltribes of Thailand

Tribe	Population	Origins	Date of arrival in Thailand	Location (province)
Karen (Yang/Kariang)	270,000	Burma	C18th	Mae Hong Son
Hmong (Meo)	82,000	China	late C19th	Chiang Rai, Nan
Lahu (Mussur)	60,000	Yunnan (China)	late C19th	Chiang Mai Chiang Rai
Mien (Yao)	36,000	South China	mid C19th	Chiang Rai, Nan
Akha (Kaw)	33,000	Yunnan (China)	early C20th	Chiang Rai
Lisu (Lisaw)	25,000	Salween (China)	early C20th	Chiang Mai
Other tribal groups				
Htin	29,000	—	—	—
Lua	8,000	—	—	—
Khamu	7,000	—	—	—
Mlabri	138	—	—	—

NB These figures are early 1990s vintage; numbers have since increased.

quest for the 'real thing', they are helping to erode that for which they search. Not that the hilltribes could ever remain, or ever have been, isolated. There has always been contact and trade between the hilltribes and the lowland peoples. Their 'Westernization' or 'Thai-ization' is popularly seen as a 'bad thing'. This says more about our romantic image of the Rousseau-esque tribal peoples of the world than it does about the realities of life in the mountains. Certainly, it is impossible selectively to develop the hilltribe communities. If they are to have the benefits of schooling and medical care, then they must also receive – or come into contact with – all those other, and perhaps less desirable, facets of modern Thai life. And if culture is functional, as anthropologists would have us believe, then in so doing they are experiencing a process of cultural erosion. To dramatize slightly, they are on the road to cultural extinction.

Traditionally, most of the hilltribes practised slash and burn agriculture (see page 830), also known as swiddening or shifting cultivation. They would burn a small area of forest, cultivate it for a few years by planting rice, corn and other crops, and then, when the soil was exhausted, abandon the land until the vegetation had regenerated to replenish the soil. Some groups merely shifted fields in a 10-15 year rotation; others not only shifted fields but also their villages, relocating in a fresh area of forest when the land had become depleted of nutrients. To obtain salt, metal implements and other goods which could not be made or found in the hills, the tribal peoples would trade forest products such as resins and animal skins with the settled lowland Thais. This simplified picture of the hilltribe economy is being gradually eroded for a variety of reasons, the most significant being that today there is simply not enough land available in most areas to practise such an extensive system of agriculture.

Hilltribe economy & culture

The Northern Region

The Karen (or Kariang, Yang)

Origins The Karen, also known as the Kariang or Yang, are found along the Thai-Burmese border, concentrated in the Mae Hong Son region. They are the largest tribal group in Thailand, numbering about 270,000. Their origins are in Burma, where today many more are fighting a long-term and low-intensity war against the Burmese authorities for greater autonomy. The Karen started to infiltrate into Thailand in the 18th century and moved into areas occupied by the Lawa, possibly the oldest established tribe in Thailand. The evidence of this contact between the two groups can still be seen in the dress, ornamentation and implements of the Karen.

Economy & society The Karen are divided into two main sub-groups, the Sgaw and the Pwo. The Pwo make up about 20% of the total population and the Sgaw the remaining 80%. Most Karen live in mountain villages and practise shifting cultivation of the rotating field type (that is they move their fields, but not their villages). They prevent soil erosion on the steep slopes by taking care to maintain belts of forest growth between 'swiddens' or fields, by leaving saplings and tree roots to help bind the soil, and by not turning the soil before planting. When a community grows so large that the distance to the outer fields becomes excessive, a group of villagers establish a satellite village beyond the boundaries of the mother village. However, with the pressure on land and the incentive to commercialize production, this traditional pioneering strategy is often no longer possible. Karen are being forced to try and increase yields by developing irrigation, and some Karen have moved down into the valleys and taken-up settled agriculture, imitating the methods of the lowland Thais.

Karen houses are built on stilts out of bamboo, with thatched roofs. Animals are kept under the house at night for protection against wild animals and rustlers. Most houses have only one room and a spacious verandah. A household usually consists of a husband and wife plus their unmarried children. Should a man's wife die, he is not permitted to remarry until his children have left the home, as this would cause conflict with the spirits. Indeed, much of Karen life is dictated by the spirits. The most important is the 'Lord of Land and Water', who controls the productivity of the land and calls upon the rice spirit to grow. Also important is the matrilineal ancestor guardian spirit (*bga*).

The priest is the most revered individual in the village: he is the ritual leader and it is he who sets dates for the annual ceremonies. The post is an ancestral one and only changes when the priest dies – at which time the village must change location as well (although the distance may only be nominal). As the Karen have been incorporated into the Thai state, so increasing numbers have turned to Buddhism. The role of European missionaries in the highland areas also means that there are significant numbers of Christian Karen. A central Karen myth tells of a younger 'white brother' from across the water, who would arrive with the skills of writing given to him by God. This no doubt helped the missionaries enormously when they arrived, pasty-faced and clutching bibles. In most cases, however, while converting to Buddhism or Christianity, the Karen have at the same time maintained a healthy belief in their traditional spirits.

Material culture The Karen are prolific weavers. Weaving is done on simple backstrap looms and many Karen still spin their own thread. The upper garments worn by men, women and children are all made in the same way: two strips of material are folded in half, the fold running along the shoulder. They are then sewn together along the centre of the garment and down the sides, leaving holes for the head and arms. The stitching is not merely functional, it is an integral part of the design. Until girls marry, they wear only this garment, full length to just below their knees and made of white cotton. The Sgaw embroider a band of red or pink around their waists, the Pwo embroider red diamond patterns along the lower edge. Married women wear this garment as an over-blouse and they also wear a sarong. The over-blouse is considerably more elaborate than that of the girls: Job's-tear seeds (seeds from a grass) are woven into the design, or a pattern is woven around the border. Pwo women tend to embroider all over the blouse.

The sarong is made up of two strips of material, sewn horizontally and stitched together to make a tubular skirt. They are held up with a cord or metal belt and are worn knee or ankle-length, longer for formal occasions. The colour is predominantly red. The men's shirts are usually hip length, with elaborate embroidery. They wear sarongs or Thai peasant-style pants.

The Sgaw women and girls wear multiple strands of small beads, which hang from mid-chest to waist length, normally red, white or yellow. The Pwo wear them around their neck and to mid-chest length and they are mostly black. Their necklaces are made from old 'bullet coins', strung on braided red thread. Pwo women wear lots of bracelets of silver, copper, brass or aluminium. Sgaw are more moderate in their use of jewellery. All Karen wear silver cup-shaped earrings, which often have coloured tufts of wool attached.

The Hmong (or Meo)

Origins The Hmong, also known as the Meo, are the second largest tribal group in Thailand, numbering about 82,000. Although their origins are rather hazy, the Hmong themselves claim that they have their roots in the icy north. They had arrived in Laos by 1850 and by the end of the 19th century had migrated into the provinces of Chiang Rai and Nan. Today they are scattered right across the Northern region and have spread over a larger area than any other tribe, apart from the Karen.

Economy & society There are two sub-groups of the Hmong, the Blue and the White Hmong. The Hmong value their independence, and tend to live at high altitudes, away from other tribes. This independence, and their association with poppy cultivation, has meant that of all the hilltribes it is the Hmong who have been most severely persecuted by the Thai authorities. They are perceived to be a threat to the security of the state, a tribe that needs to be controlled and carefully watched. Like most hilltribes, they practise shifting cultivation, moving their villages when the surrounding land has been exhausted. The process of moving is stretched out over two seasons: an advance party finds a suitable site, builds temporary shelters, clears the land and plants rice, and only after the harvest do the rest of the inhabitants follow on.

Hmong villages tend not to be fenced, while their houses are built of wood or bamboo at ground level. Each house has a main living area and two or three sleeping rooms. The extended family is headed by the oldest male: he settles family disputes and has supreme authority over family affairs. Like the Karen, the Hmong too are spirit worshippers and believe in household spirits. Every house has an altar, where protection for the household is sought. Despite 21st-century pressures (particularly scarcity of land), they maintain a strong sense of identity. The children may be educated in Thai schools, but they invariably return to farming alongside their parents.

Material culture The Hmong are the only tribe in Thailand who make batik: indigo-dyed batik makes up the main panel of their skirts, with appliqué and embroidery added to it. The women also wear black leggings from their knees to their ankles, black jackets (with embroidery), and a black panel or 'apron', held in place with a cummerbund. Even the smallest children wear clothes of intricate design with exquisite needlework. Today much of the cloth is purchased from the market or from traders; traditionally it would have been woven by hand on a foot-treddle/back-strap loom.

The White Hmong tend to wear less elaborate clothing from day to day, saving it for special occasions only. Hmong men wear loose-fitting black trousers, black jackets (sometimes embroidered) and coloured or embroidered sashes.

The Hmong particularly value silver jewellery: it signifies wealth and a good life. Men, women and children wear silver: tiers of neck rings, heavy silver chains with lock-shaped pendants, earrings and pointed rings on every finger. All the family jewellery is brought out at New Year and is an impressive sight, symbolizing the wealth of the family.

Hilltribes

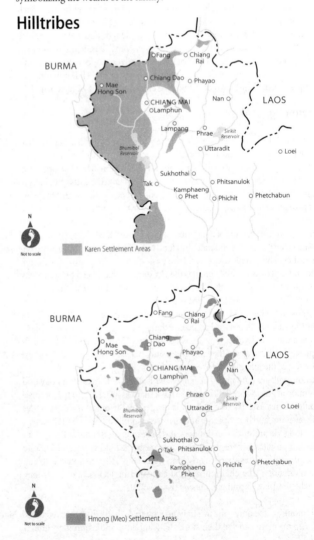

Even though the Hmong are perhaps the most independent of all the hilltribes, they too are being drawn into the 'modern' world. Some still grow the poppy at higher elevations, but the general shortage of land is forcing them to descend to lower altitudes, to take up irrigated rice farming, to grow cash crops, and to mix with the lowland Thais. This has led to conflicts between the Hmong and the lowlanders as they compete for the same resources – previously they would have been occupying quite different ecological niches.

The Lahu (or Mussur)

Origins The Lahu in Thailand are found along the Burmese border and number about 60,000. They originated in Yunnan (South China) and migrated from Burma into Thailand at the end of the 19th century. Today, the majority of Thai Lahu are found in the provinces of Chiang Mai and Chiang Rai. There are a number of Lahu sub-groups, each with slightly different traditions and clothing. The two dominant groups are the Black Lahu and the Yellow Lahu, which themselves are subdivided.

Economy & society Traditionally, the Lahu lived at relatively high elevations, 1,200 m or higher. Pressure on land and commercialization has encouraged most of these groups to move down the slopes, and most of these have now taken up irrigated rice farming in the small, high valleys that dissect the Northern region of Thailand.

Villages are about 30 houses strong, with about six people in each house. Their houses are built on stilts and consist of the main living area, a bedroom, a spirit altar and a fireplace. Houses are usually built of wood or bamboo, and thatch. The men are less dominant in the family hierarchy than in other tribes: they help around the home and share in the care of their children and livestock, as well as gathering water and firewood (the very epitome of a liberated male). A typical household is nuclear rather than extended, consisting of a man, his wife and their unmarried children. It is also not unusual for a married daughter and her husband and children to live in the household.

The Lahu believe in spirits, in the soul and in a God. Missionary work by Christians, and also by Buddhists, means that many Lahu villages are now ostensibly Christian or Buddhist. It is estimated that one-third of all Lahu live within Christian communities. But this does not mean that they have rejected their traditional beliefs: they have adopted new religions, while at the same time maintaining their animistic ones.

Material culture Because each Lahu group has distinct clothing and ornamentation, it is difficult to characterize a 'general' dress for the tribe as a whole. To simplify, Lahu dress is predominantly black or blue, with border designs of embroidery or appliqué. Some wear short jackets and sarongs, others wear longer jackets and leggings. Most of their cloth is now bought and machine-made; traditionally it would have been hand-woven. The jackets are held together with large, often elaborate, silver buckles. All Lahu make caps for their children and the cloth shoulder bag is also a characteristic Lahu accessory.

Ornamentation is similarly varied. The Lahu Nyi women wear wide silver bracelets, neck rings and earrings. The Lahu Sheh Leh wear large numbers of small white beads around their necks and silver bracelets. The Lahu Na wear engraved and moulded silver bracelets, and on special occasions heavy silver chains, bells and pendants. The Lahu Shi wear red and white beads around their necks and heavy silver earrings.

The Northern Region

☞ *The Hilltribe calendar*

	Karen	Hmong	Mien (Yao)
January	village ceremony	New Year festival	embroidering
February	site selection	scoring poppies	scoring poppies
March	clearing field	clearing field	clearing field
April	burning field	burning field	burning field
May	rice planting	rice planting	rice and maize planting
June	field spirit offering	weeding	weeding
July	field spirit offering	weeding	weeding
August	weeding	weeding	harvesting
September	rat trapping	poppy seeding	poppy seeding
October	rice harvest	thinning poppy field	rice harvest
November	rice harvest	rice harvest	rice harvest
December	rice threshing	New Year festival	rice threshing

Source: Tribal Research Institute, Chiang Mai University.

The Mien (or Yao)

Origins The Mien, or Yao, are unique among the hilltribes in that they have a tradition of writing based on Chinese characters. Mien legend has it that they came from 'across the sea' during the 14th century, although it is generally thought that their roots are in South China where they originated about 2,000 years ago. They first migrated into Thailand from Laos in the mid-19th century and they currently number about 36,000, mostly in the provinces of Chiang Rai and Nan, close to the Laotian border.

Economy & society The Mien village is not enclosed and is usually found on sloping ground. The houses are large, wooden affairs, as they need to accommodate an extended family of sometimes 20 or more members. They are built on the ground, not on stilts, and have one large living area and four or more bedrooms. As with other tribes, the construction of the house must be undertaken carefully. The house needs to be orientated appropriately, so that the spirits are not disturbed, and the ancestral altar installed on an auspicious day.

The Mien combine two religious beliefs: on the one hand they recognize and pay their dues to spirits and ancestors (informing them of family developments); on the other, they follow Taoism as it was practised in China in the 13th and 14th centuries. The Taoist rituals are expensive, and the Mien appear to spend a great deal of their lives struggling to save enough money to afford the various ceremonies, such as weddings, merit-making and death ceremonies. The Mien economy is based upon the shifting cultivation of dry rice, corn and small quantities of opium poppy.

Material culture The Mien women dress distinctively, with black turbans and red-ruffed tunics, making them easy to distinguish from the other hilltribes. All their clothes are made of black or indigo-dyed homespun cotton, which is then embroidered using distinctive cross-stitching. Their trousers are the most elaborate garments. Unusually, they sew from the back of the cloth and cannot see the

Akha	Lisu	Lahu
weaving	*New Year Festival*	*scoring poppies*
clearing fields	*Second New Year festival*	*New Year Festival*
burning field	*clearing field*	*burning field*
rice spirit ceremony	*burning field*	*field spirit house*
rice planting	*rice dibbling*	*rice planting*
weeding	*weeding*	*weeding*
weeding	*weeding*	*weeding*
swinging ceremony	*soul calling ceremony*	*weeding*
poppy seeding	*maize harvest*	*maize harvest*
rice harvest	*poppy seeding*	*field spirit offering*
rice harvest	*rice harvest*	*rice harvest*
New Year festival	*rice threshing*	*field spirit offering*

pattern they are making. The children wear embroidered caps, with red pom-poms on the top and by the ears. The men's dress is a simple indigo-dyed jacket and trousers, with little embroidery.

The Akha (or Kaw)

Origins The Akha, or Kaw, number about 33,000 in Thailand and are found in a relatively small area of the North, near Chiang Rai. They have their origins in Yunnan, southern China, and from there spread into Burma (where there are nearly 200,000) and rather later into Thailand. The first Akha village was not established in Thailand until the very beginning of the 20th century. They prefer to live along ridges, at about 1,000 m.

Economy & society The Akha are shifting cultivators, growing primarily dry rice on mountainsides but also a wide variety of vegetables. The cultivation of rice is bound up with myths and rituals: the rice plant is regarded as a sentient being, and the selection of the swidden, its clearance, the planting of the rice seed, the care of the growing plants, and finally the harvest of the rice, must all be done according to the Akha Way. Any offence to the rice soul must be rectified by ceremonies.

Akha villages are identified by their gates, a village swing and high-roofed houses on posts. They have no word for religion, but believe in the 'Akha Way'. They are able to recite the names of all their male ancestors (60 names or more) and they keep an ancestral altar in their homes, at which food is offered up at important times in the year such as New Year, during the village swing ceremony, and after the rice harvest.

At the upper and lower ends of the village are gates which are renewed every year. Visitors should walk through them in order to rid themselves of the spirit of the jungle. The gates are sacred and must not be defiled. Visitors must not touch the gates and should avoid going through them if they do not intend to enter a house in the village. A pair of wooden male and female carved figures are placed inside the entrance to signify that this is the realm of human beings. The two most important Akha festivals are the four-day Swinging Ceremony celebrated during August, and New Year when festivities also extend over four days.

Material culture Akha clothing is made of homespun blue-black cloth, which is appliquéd for decoration. Particularly characteristic of the Akha is their head-dress, which is adorned with jewellery. The basic clothing of an Akha woman is a head-dress, a jacket, a short skirt worn on her hips, with a sash and leggings worn from the ankle to below the knee. They wear their jewellery as an integral part of their clothing, mostly sewn to their head-dresses. Girls wear similar clothing to the women, except that they sport caps rather than the elaborate head-dress of the mature women. The change from girl's clothes to women's clothes occurs through four stages during adolescence. Unmarried girls can be identified by the small gourds tied to their waist and head-dress.

Hilltribes

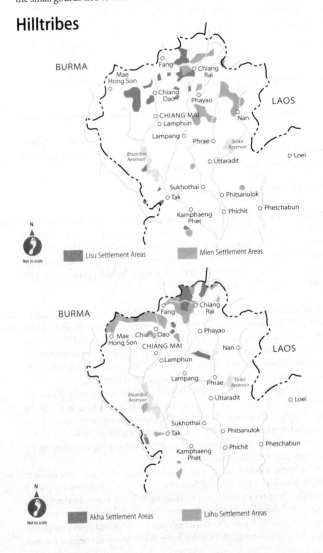

Men's clothing is much less elaborate. They wear loose-fitting Chinese-style black pants, and a black jacket which may be embroidered. Both men and women use cloth shoulder bags.

Today, the Akha are finding it increasingly difficult to follow the 'Akha Way'. Their complex rituals set them apart from both the lowland Thais and from the other hilltribes. There is no land, no game, and the modern world has little use or time for their ways. The conflicts and pressures which the Akha currently face, and their inability to reconcile the old with the new, is claimed by some to explain why the incidence of opium addiction among the Akha is so high.

The Lisu (or Lisaw)

The Lisu number some 25,000 in Thailand, and live in the mountainous region northwest of Chiang Mai. They probably originated in China, at the headwaters of the Salween River, and did not begin to settle in Thailand until the early 20th century.

Origins

The Lisu grow rice and vegetables for subsistence and opium for sale. Rice is grown at lower altitudes and the opium poppy at over 1,500 m. Villages are located so that the inhabitants can maintain some independence from the Thai authorities. At the same time they need to be relatively close to a market so that they can trade.

Economy & society

Lisu houses may be built either on the ground or raised above it: the former are more popular at higher altitudes as they are said to be warmer. The floors and walls are made from wood and bamboo, and the roof is thatched. The house is divided into a bedroom, a large living area, and also contains a guest platform. Within each house there will also be a fireplace and an ancestral altar.

Each village has a 'village guardian spirit shrine' which is located above the village, in a roofed pavilion that women are forbidden to enter. Local disputes are settled by a headman, and kinship is based upon patrilineal clans. As well as the village guardian, the Lisu worship Wu Sa – the creator – and a multitude of spirits of the forest, ancestors, trees, the sun, moon and everyday objects. Coupled with this, the Lisu fear possession by weretigers (*phi pheu*) and vampires (*phu seu*).

Lisu clothing is some of the most brightly coloured, and most distinctive, of all the hilltribes. They make up their clothes from machine-made cloth. The women wear long tunics – often bright blue, with red sleeves and pattern-work around the yoke – black knee-length pants and red leggings. A wide black sash is wound tightly round the waist. Looped around this at the back is a pair of tassels consisting of many tightly woven threads, with pompoms attached to the ends (sometimes as many as 500 strands in a pair of tassels). Turbans, again with coloured tassels attached, are worn for special occasions. The man's attire is simpler: a black jacket, blue or green trousers and black leggings.

Material culture

The most important ceremony is New Year (celebrated on the same day as the Chinese), when the villagers dress up in all their finery and partake in a series of rituals. At this time, the women wear copious amounts of silver jewellery: tunics with rows of silver buttons sewn onto them, and abundant heavy necklaces.

Visiting the hilltribes

There are a variety of ways to see the hilltribes, ranging from an easy visit of a single day, to a strenuous trek of a week. Although many will tell you that it is not possible to experience the 'real thing' unless you opt for the most exhausting and adventurous programme on offer, every encounter between a

The Northern Region

The Northern Region

Papaver Somniferum: the opium of the people

The hilltribes of Northern Thailand, and the very name the Golden Triangle, are synonymous in many people's minds with the cultivation of the opium poppy (Papaver somniferum L.). It is a favourite cash crop of the Lahu, Lisu, Mien and Hmong (the Karen and Akha only rarely grow it). The attractions of cultivating the poppy are clear: it is profitable, can be grown at high altitudes (above 1,500 m), has low bulk (important when there is no transport) and does not rot. This explains why, though cultivation has been banned in Thailand since 1959, it has only been since the 1980s that the Thai government, with US assistance, has significantly reduced the area cultivated. Today, most opium is grown in Burma and Laos, not in Thailand – although most is traded through the kingdom. A UN report estimated that 2,000 tonnes of opium are produced in Burma annually. A survey undertaken in Chiang Rai province in 1998 found just 1,000 rai (160 ha) under poppy cultivation – not even sufficient for opium consumption by the hill peoples themselves.

The opium poppy is usually grown as part of a rotation, alternating with maize. It is sown in September/October (the end of the wet season) and 'harvesting' stretches from the beginning of January through to the end of March. Harvesting occurs after the petals have dropped off the seed heads. The 'pod' is then carefully scoured with a sharp knife, from top to bottom, allowing the sap to ooze through and oxidize on the surface of the pod. The next day, the brown gum is scraped off, rolled into balls and wrapped in banana leaves. It is now ready for sale to the buyers who travel the hills.

Though a profitable crop, opium production has not benefited the hilltribes. In the government's eyes it has made them criminals, and opium addiction is widespread – among the Hmong it is thought to be about 30% of the population. Efforts to change the ways of the hilltribes have focused upon crop substitution programmes (encouraging farmers to cultivate crops such as cabbages) and simple intimidation.

When the infamous opium warlord Khun Sa surrendered to the Burmese authorities in January 1996, the price of the narcotic in Thailand shot through the roof. The price of heroin on the black market rose from ฿700-800 per vial (0.7-1.0 g) in 1995 to ฿6,000-10,000 in 1996. Prices rise dramatically along the marketing chain and as the product is further processed. The wholesale price of opium on the border in 1998 was ฿5,000-6,000 per joi (1 joi = 1.6 kg). The retail price in a local village is ฿10,000-12,000 per joi. For heroin, the figure is ฿200,000 per kg. However, since then it has been widely assumed that Khun Sa surrendered on his own terms and now lives in comparative luxury in Rangoon. US demands that he be extradited to stand trial in the US have been ignored. As former US Assistant-Secretary for Law Enforcement Affairs, Richard Gelbard, put it: "Burma's most important narco-traffickers are no longer holed up in jungle hideaways. They are buying real estate in Rangoon and Mandalay, investing in Burma's economy and openly courting military officials."

foreigner and a hilltribe community is artificial. As the Heisenberg principle has it, just by being there a visitor has a profound affect.

If you do not want to live rough, to spend five days tramping around the forests, or to spend your money on visiting the hilltribes, then opt for a **half day or day trip** by taxi, bus or hired motorcycle. The major towns of the North all have hilltribe communities within easy reach. On arrival you will probably be hounded by handicraft salespeople; you may well have to pay for any photographs that you take, but at least you will get a taste of a hilltribe village and their traditional costumes. You can also leave smug with the knowledge that you have not contributed much to the process of cultural erosion.

Ikat production

Ikat is a technique of patterning cloth characteristic of Southeast Asia, and is produced from the hills of Burma to the islands of Eastern Indonesia. The word comes from the Malay word mengikat, which means to bind or tie. Very simply, either the warp or the weft – and in one case both – are tied with material or fibre so that they resist the action of the dye. Hence the technique's name - resist dyeing. By dyeing, re-tying and dyeing again through a number of cycles, it is possible to build up complex patterns. Ikat is distinguishable by the bleeding of the dye, which inevitably occurs no matter how carefully and tightly the threads are tied; this gives the finished cloth a blurred effect. The earliest ikats so far found date from the 14th to 15th centuries.

To prepare the cloth for dyeing, the warp or weft is strung tight on a frame. Individual threads, or groups of threads, are then tied together with fibre and leaves. In some areas, wax is then smeared on top to help in the resist process. The main colour is usually dyed first, secondary colours later. With complex patterns (which are done from memory; plans are only required for new designs) and using natural dyes, it may take up to six months to produce a piece of cloth. Prices are correspondingly high, particularly for ritual cloths. Today, the pressures of the market place mean that it is more likely that cloth is produced using chemical dyes (which need only one short soaking, not multiple long ones as with some natural dyes), and design motifs have generally become larger and less complex. Traditionally, warp ikat used cotton (rarely silk) and weft ikat (silk). Silk in many areas has given way to cotton, and cotton sometimes to synthetic yarns. Double ikat, where (incredibly) both the warp and the weft are tied-dyed, is produced in only one spot in Southeast Asia: a village in eastern Bali.

Longer trips can either take the form of a two or three day excursion by bus, raft, boat and foot, or a trek of up to a week or more. The **excursions** are usually more comfortable, more highly organized, and do not venture far into the wilds of the North. They are easily booked through one of the many companies in Chiang Mai, Chiang Rai, Mae Hong Son and the other trekking towns of the region.

Trekking into the hills is undoubtedly the best way to see the hilltribes, however. To keep the adventure of trekking alive (or perhaps, the myth of adventure), most companies now promote 'non-touristic' trekking – if that is not a contradiction in terms. They guarantee a trek will not meet another trekking party. It is most important to try and get a knowledgeable guide who speaks good English, as well as the language(s) of the tribe(s) that are to be visited. He is your link with the hilltribes: he will warn you what not to do, tell you of their customs, rituals, economy and religion, and ensure your safety. Ask other tourists who have recently returned from treks about their experiences: a personal recommendation is hard to beat and they will also have the most up-to-date information. Sometimes an even better alternative is to hire a **private guide**, although this is obviously more expensive.

A final way to see the people of the hills is simply to **set off on your own**, either on foot or motorbike DIY trekking. This can be very rewarding – and is becoming increasingly popular – but it does have its risks: parts of the North are still fairly lawless and every year there are reports of hold-ups, even murders, of tourists. Remember, it's a jungle out there: take care preparing your trip and let someone know your schedule and itinerary. It is also easy to get lost, and unless you go prepared with the appropriate books, maps and other information, it is unlikely that you will gain much of an insight into hilltribe life. Most hilltribe villages will offer a place to sleep – usually in the headman's house; expect to pay about ฿50. The advantage – from the hill people's perspective – is that the money accrues to them,

The Northern Region

A Thai hilltribe clothing primer

Karen are among the best and most prolific of hilltribe weavers. Their traditional striped warp ikat, dyed in soft hues, is characteristically inter-sewn with job's seeds. Girls wear creamy white smocks with red stitching, whilst women wear coloured smocks and strings of beads. Their tunics are made up of two lengths of cloth, worn vertically, sewn together down the centre and sides, leaving a hole for the neck and the arms.

Hmong (Meo) produce exquisite embroidery made up of appliquéd layers of fabric of geometric shapes, worn by men, women and children. Some of the patternwork on their pleated skirts is achieved by batik (the only hilltribe to do this). Jackets are of black velvet or satinized cotton, with embroidered lapels. They wear black or white leggings and sashes to hold up their skirts. Hand weaving is a dying art among the Hmong.

Lahu (Mussur) groups traditionally wore a diverse array of clothing. All embroider, but many have now abandoned the use of traditional dress. Another common feature is the shoulder bag – primarily red in the case of the Lahu Nyi (the 'Red' Lahu), black among the Lahu Sheh Leh (and often tasselled), black with patchwork for the Lahu Na, and often striped in the case of the Lahu Shi.

Mien (Yao) embroidery is distinguished by cross-stitching on indigo fabric, worn as baggy trousers and turbans. They are one of the easiest of the hilltribes to identify because of their distinctive red-collared jackets. Virtually none of the cloth is hand woven – it is bought and then sometimes re-dyed before being decorated.

Akha are most easily distinguished by their elaborate head-dresses, made up of silver beads, coins and buttons. Akha cloth is limited to plain weave, dyed with indigo (after weaving) – and still often made from home-grown cotton. This is then decorated with embroidery, shells, buttons, silver and seeds. Akha patchwork is highly intricate work, involving the assembly of tiny pieces of cloth.

Lisu wear very brightly coloured clothing and (at festivals) lots of jewellery. Particularly notable are the green and blue kaftans with red sleeves, worn with baggy Chinese trousers and black turbans. Lisu weaving has virtually died out.

and does not line the pockets of some agent or trekking company. If you are intending to venture out on your own, it is a good idea to visit the **Hilltribe Research Center** at Chiang Mai University before you leave, and to get a map of the hilltribe areas (available from *DK Books*, 234 Tha Phae Road, Chiang Mai).

Practicalities of trekking

When to trek The best time to trek is during the cool, dry season, between October and February. In March and April, although it is still dry, temperatures can be uncomfortably high and the vegetation is parched. During the wet season, paths are muddy and walking can be difficult.

What to take Leave valuables behind in a bank safety deposit box. **NB** Trekkers who leave their credit cards for safekeeping in their guesthouses have sometimes found that a large bill awaits them on their return home. A safety deposit box hired at a bank is the safest way to leave your valuables.

Choosing a trekking company In Chiang Mai there are over 100 trekking companies, and many more in other trekking centres of the North. Check that the company is registered with the police and that they notify the Tourist Police before departure (as they are

The Mlabri: the spirits of the yellow leaves

The elusive Mlabri 'tribe' represent one of the few remaining groups of hunter-gatherers in Southeast Asia. They are also known as the Phi Tong Luang or 'Spirits of the Yellow Leaves', because when their shelters of rattan and banana leaves turn yellow, they take this as a sign from the spirits that it is time to move on. The destruction of Thailand's forests, even in this relatively inaccessible corner of the Kingdom, means that the Mlabri have been forced to lead more sedentary lives, turning to settled agriculture in place of hunting and gathering. Currently, it is thought that there are less than 150 Mlabri living in Thailand – in 1974, the ethnographer Gordon Young estimated that the population was a mere 50.

Traditionally, the Mlabri hunted using spears, but when stalking larger game, rather than throwing the weapon, they would brace it against the ground and allow the charging animal to impale

itself on the point. In this way, the Mlabri were able to kill the great saladang wild buffalo (Bos gaurus), as well as bears and tigers. Smaller game was more common, however, and this was supplemented with tubers, nuts, honey and other forest products to provide a balanced diet. Many of the Mlabri's traditions are already on the verge of extinction. Hunting and gathering is no longer a tenable livelihood in Thailand's denuded forests, the work of American missionaries has led to their conversion to Christianity, and disease and inter-marriage with other tribes is reducing their number. Perhaps this is no bad thing: as recently as the 1980s, a Mlabri was displayed in a cage in a Bangkok department store. Today, the problem is that the few Mlabri still alive, finding their forests impoverished, have been forced to become cheap labourers for groups such as the Hmong.

required to do). Shop around to get an idea of prices and try to get a personal recommendation from another tourist. Note that the best guides may move between companies or work for more than one.

Trekking companies should advise on what to take and many provide rucksacks, sleeping bags, first-aid kits and food. However, the following is a check list of items that might be useful: good walking shoes; bed sheet (blanket/sleeping bag in the cold season November-February); raincoat (July-October); insect repellent; toiletries (soap, toothpaste, toilet paper); small first-aid kit (including antiseptic, plasters, diarrhoea pills, salt tablets); sun protection (sun cream/sun hat); photocopy of passport (if venturing into border area); and water bottle (to cut down on the mountain of plastic bottles accumulating in the hills of the north).

Health precautions

By living in hilltribe villages, even if for only a few days, the health hazard is amplified significantly. Inoculation against hepatitis (gamma globulin) and protection against malaria are both strongly recommended. Particular dietary care should be exercised: do not drink unboiled or untreated water and avoid uncooked vegetables. Although the hilltribe population may look healthy, remember that the incidence of parasitic infection in most communities is not far off 100%.

The cost of a trek

It does not take long to work out the going price for a trek – just ask around. For a basic walking trek, costs are ฿250-500 per day, the cheaper end of the range relating to trekking companies that specialize in the backpacking market; if rafting and elephant rides are also included, the cost rises to ฿500-1,000 per day.

☞ ## Trekking areas of the North

Centres	Trekking areas	Tribes
Around Chiang Mai	North, west and southwest of the city. Rafting on the Mae Tang	Lisu, Akha, Karen, Lahu, Hmong and Shan.
Around Chiang Rai	Mainly along or near the Kok River and to the north in the vicinity of the Golden Triangle. Rafting on the Kok River.	Karen, Lisu, Akha, Hmong, Yao and Lahu.
Around Mae Hong Son	Most treks either run south to Mae Sariang or north and east to Pai. Rafting on the Pai River.	Karen, Lisu, Shan, Kaya, Hmong, Red Lahu and 'long-necked Karen' – more properly known as Padaung – as well as committee villages.
Eastern Highlands	West of Nan	Hmong, Karen, Yao, Akha, Lahu and the Mlabri or Yellow Leaves people.

Opium smoking For some, one of the attractions of trekking is the chance to smoke opium. It should be remembered that opium smoking, as well as opium cultivation, are illegal in Thailand. It is also not unusual for first-time users to experience adverse physical and psychological side-effects. **NB** Police regularly stop and search tourists who are motorcycle trekking. Be careful not to carry any illicit substances.

Trekking areas
See also box on opposite page The main trekking centres are in Chiang Mai, Chiang Rai and Mae Hong Son. There are also companies in Mae Sot, Mae Sariang, Pai, Soppong, Fang, Tha Ton, Chiang Saen, Sop Ruak, Mae Sai and Nan, and also in a handful of other places.

Donations Many trekking companies and some guesthouses take donations to help support the hill peoples, and in particular the many thousands of displaced refugees from Burma.

Books Boyes, Jon and Piraban S (1992) *A life apart: viewed from the hills*, Silkworm Books: Bangkok. This has been written with the trekker intentionally in mind. It is a series of hilltribe vignettes, written from the tribal people's perspective. In this respect the book is fine; where it fails is in providing a context for these vignettes. Here the authors over-generalize and sometimes provide misleading information. Take the book for the thumbnail sketches of life, not for background accuracy.

Guntamala, Ada and Kornvika Puapratum (1992) *Trekking through Northern Thailand*, Silkworm Books: Chiang Mai.

Lewis, Paul and Lewis, Elaine (1984) *Peoples of the Golden Triangle: six tribes in Thailand*, Thames and Hudson: London. Glossy coffee table book with a good supporting text. Too heavy to take on the road, but a good book for before or after.

McKinnon, John and Vienne, Bernard (1989) *Hill tribes today: problems in change*, White-Lotus/Orstom: Bangkok. This volume, though beginning to become rather dated in some respects, is accurate and informative. It also suffers from being a fairly hefty tome to lug around the hills.

Tapp, Nicholas (1986) *The Hmong of Thailand: opium people of the Golden Triangle*, report No 4, Anti-slavery Society: London.

Visiting the hilltribes: house rules

Etiquette and customs vary between the hilltribes. However, the following are general rules of good behaviour that should be adhered to whenever possible.

1. Dress modestly and avoid undressing/changing in public.

2. Ask permission before photographing anyone (old people and pregnant women often object to having their photograph taken). Be aware that hill people are unlikely to pose out of the kindness of their hearts – don't begrudge them the money; for many, tourism is their livelihood.

3. Ask permission before entering a house.

4. Do not touch or photograph village shrines.

5. Do not smoke opium.

6. Avoid sitting or stepping on door sills.

7. Avoid excessive displays of wealth and be sensitive when giving gifts (for children, pens are better than sweets).

8. Avoid introducing Western medicines.

Tapp, Nicholas (1989) *Sovereignty and rebellion: the White Hmong of Northern Thailand*, Oxford University Press: Singapore. Nick Tapp is an anthropologist at the University of Edinburgh. This book is intended mostly for an academic audience; it is interesting because it tries to challenge the established wisdom that the Hmong are a 'bad' tribe.

Guide Map of Chiang Rai, Bangkok Guides: Bangkok. *The Mae Kok River*, **Maps** Chang Puak: Bangkok; the Thai government also publishes 1:250,000 topographic sheet maps of every province, especially useful if venturing out without a guide.

The Northern Region

The Northeastern Region

6

The Northeastern Region

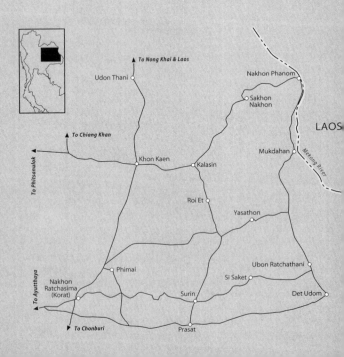

The Northeastern Region of Thailand, also known as the Isan region, is a massive sandstone plateau that undulates gently at between 100 m and 200 m above sea level. It covers 170,000 sq km, or one third of the total land area of the kingdom of Thailand, and also supports about a third of the total population, more than 20,000,000 people. Considering its size, the Northeast is surprisingly coherent from a geographical point of view: to the north and east it is bordered by the Mekong River, which forms the boundary between Thailand and Laos; and to the south and west by two ranges of mountains – the Phnom Dangrek and Phetchabun hills respectively.

Few visitors to Thailand (it is said, less than 1%) take the trouble to visit the Northeast, and those who do invariably merely visit Korat and the Khmer town of Phimai and one or two places on the Mekong River. This is understandable, in that tourist facilities are the least developed of any region in the country. But the people of the Khorat Plateau do have a charm lacking in the rest of Thailand. They are more laid back, more passive, more understanding. Even the countryside, so harsh at the end of the dry season in April and May when the heat is like a furnace, has its attractions: the neat mini-valleys with their chequer boards of paddy fields, the few remaining stands of dry dipterocarp savanna forest, the 1,500 m mountain Phu Kradung, the Mekong River, and the area's tradition of fine cotton and silk weaving. Furthermore, facilities are much improved from a few years ago and just about every provincial capital has a good hotel or two.

Background

The geographical features of the Northeastern region, and in particular the mountains to the south and west, have effectively isolated the Northeast from the rest of the country. This is clearly reflected in the poem *Nirat Nongkhai*, written during a military campaign of the 1870s, in which it took two months, 170 elephants, 500 oxen and many horses to proceed up the forested trail from Bangkok to Korat (Nakhon Ratchasima), on the southwest edge of the region. With his men dying all around him from malaria and food poisoning, and finding it difficult to procure supplies, the army's commander managed to miss the vital battle and returned to Bangkok having never confronted the enemy.

From books and from talking to people in Bangkok, it is easy to reach the conclusion that the Isan region has always been a marginal area. The environment is the harshest of anywhere in Thailand with sparse and intermittent rainfall, and the soils are some of the poorest in all Southeast Asia. WA Graham, a European visitor to Isan at the beginning of the 20th century, wrote that the Northeast was, in his opinion, 'one of the most miserable [regions] imaginable'. Warrington-Smyth, in the late 19th century, expressed similar sentiments when he wrote on leaving the region that he and his companions were 'thankful to wipe the whole Khorat plateau from our memories'.

The inhabitants of the area are also distinct from the rest of the country. They are Lao rather than Thai, and are culturally more closely affiliated with the people of Laos. They speak a dialect of Thai, Isan or Lao, dress differently and eat different food. This distinctiveness, coupled with the poverty of the area, played a part in making the Northeast one of the strongholds of the

Khmer sites of Northeast Thailand

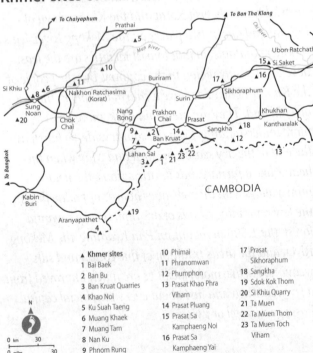

▲ Khmer sites	10 Phimai	17 Prasat
1 Bai Baek	11 Phranomwan	Sikhoraphum
2 Ban Bu	12 Phumphon	18 Sangkha
3 Ban Kruat Quarries	13 Prasat Khao Phra	19 Sdok Kok Thom
4 Khao Noi	Viharn	20 Si Khiu Quarry
5 Ku Suah Taeng	14 Prasat Pluang	21 Ta Muen
6 Muang Khaek	15 Prasat Sa	22 Ta Muen Thom
7 Muang Tam	Kamphaeng Noi	23 Ta Muen Toch
8 Nan Ku	16 Prasat Sa	Viharn
9 Phnom Rung	Kamphaeng Yai	

A Foot in the Door

★ The finest Khmer monuments outside Cambodia are here – Phnom Rung, Phimai, Muang Tam and Prasat Khao Phra Viharn (the last in Cambodia but accessible from Thailand) are the most impressive, but there are scores of others to be rooted out in otherwise forgotten corners of this region.

★ Khao Yai was Thailand's first national park. Other notable national parks in the area include Phu Kradung, Phu Reua, Kaeng Tana and Phu Wiang.

★ The Northeast's best-known festivals are the elephant round-up held near Surin

in November, the rocket festival in Yasothon in May, and the That Phanom temple fair held in January or February.

★ The Northeast is the centre of Thailand's silk weaving industry.

★ The prehistoric archaeological site of Ban Chiang outside Udon Thani and the truly weird Wat Khaek outside Nong Khai are worth a visit.

★ The Mekong towns stretching from Chiang Khan east to Nong Khai and then south to Nakhon Phanom, That Phanom, Mukdahan and Khong Chiam are good places to relax.

Communist Party of Thailand. Francis Cripps, who worked as a school teacher in Mahasarakham, writes:

> 'Mahasarakham?' they asked. 'Where is that? ... Oh! In the Northeast?' They looked at me with pity. Communist infiltrators, drought, hard, unpalatable glutinous rice – these were the hazards of life on the neglected ... northeastern plateau (1965:15).

Most of the population of the Northeast are farmers. They grow glutinous or 'sticky' rice (*khaaw niaw*) to meet their subsistence needs, and increasingly an assortment of upland cash crops such as cassava and kenaf (an inferior jute substitute) to earn an income. They have also traditionally migrated to Bangkok during the dry season to find work to boost their meagre incomes. Today, many thousands make the trip to the capital to work as tuk-tuk drivers, poultry slaughterers and servants. Some villages become so depopulated that they seem to consist of only the very old and the very young. Despite this migration, average incomes are only a third of those in other parts of Thailand, where the average wage for an agricultural labourer performing a back-breaking task such as transplanting rice is only ฿50 per day; in Bangkok the official minimum wage is over ฿150 per day.

With the heat, the poverty, the perceived threat of Communism, and the general backwardness of the Northeast, most other Thais steer well clear of the area. But, historically, the Khorat Plateau has played a very important role in the development not just of Thailand, but arguably of the whole of Southeast Asia. At Ban Chiang, a village to the east of Udon Thani, some of the world's earliest evidence of agriculture has been uncovered, dating back 5,000-7,000 years (see page 436). Later, the Khorat Plateau formed an integral part of the magnificent Khmer Empire based at Angkor, which flourished during the 12th-13th centuries. The still impressive ruins at Phimai, Phnom Rung and Muang Tham among other sites clearly show that the Northeast has not always been devoid of 'civilized' life, whatever those in Bangkok might like to think.

The most environmentally harsh area of this already marginal region is the appropriately named Tung Kula Rong Hai – the Weeping Plain. This covers the lower-central portion of the Northeast, including the provinces of Roi Et, Surin, Si Saket and Buri Ram. In 1998 geologists announced that they had found a huge underground aquifer underlying the provinces of Nakhon Ratchasima, Buriram and Surin, measuring 100 km by 10 km and containing 120,000,000 cu m of fresh water. They estimate that 40,000,000 cu m can be

The minor Khmer sites of the northeast

Prasat Khao Noi A small prasat in Prachinburi province, recently restored by the Fine Arts Department. The prasat consists of three prangs, of which the central example has been extensively restored. The carving here is very early – probably dating from the mid-seventh century (although the central prang is 11th century). The lintels have been removed and placed in the Prachinburi Museum.

Prasat Phum Phen Situated in the Sangkha District of Surin Province, this is relatively well-preserved for a seventh-century prasat, one of the oldest in Thailand. The square floor plan indicates that the prasat was probably built on to an earlier structure. Red paint found on some walls indicates that the interior was probably painted. The finest lintels found here are at the National Museum in Bangkok.

Prasat Nern Kuu and Prasat Muang Khaek Both these shrines are located in Song Nern District, Nakhon Ratchasima Province, 30 km west of Korat City. Both were built in the 10th century and are thought to have been religious centres linked to the ancient city of Khorakhapura. Prasat Nern Kuu consists of a small square cella enclosed within a wall. Prasat Muang Khaek was probably built around 940 AD. The main sandstone prang stands on a high brick base and is stylistically similar to the temples of the Chola period in India.

Prasat Sadok Kok Thom Located 33 km north of Aranyaprathet in Prachin Buri Province, it dates from the 11th century reign of Udayadityavarman and like other Khmer sites was 'caught up' in the Cambodian civil war. It only became open to Thai visitors in 1990. One gopura is in good condition, and there is also a collapsed prang and enclosing walls. An inscription here was instrumental in reconstructing the life of Jayavarman II.

Phrathat Narai Chengweng This small prasat is in Muang District, Sakhon Nakhon Province. Over the entrance to the porch on the east side is a carving of Indra riding Airavata. See page 460.

Prasat Yai He Nga Dates from the 12th century and is situated in Sangkhla District, Surin Province. Unusually, it consists of two prangs (three would be usual), with the main prang, for whatever reason, left unbuilt. It is in use by Buddhist monks.

Prang Ku Suan Taeng This comprises three prangs, built during the 12th century and located in the Puthai Song District of Buriram Province. The corbelled ceiling within the main, central prang is still in an excellent state of repair.

Prasat Ta Muan Toch This dates from the reign of Jayavarman VII and is situated in Ta Muan District, Surin Province. An inscription indicates that this prasat was built as a religious edifice attached to a hospital. The hospital was one of 102 built on Jayavarman VII's orders. Other inscriptions from the site list the nurses and doctors employed here and some of the drugs than they dispensed.

Prasat Ta Muan and Prasat Ban Bu These were both built under the orders of Jayavarman VII as resting places for travellers making the journey between Phimai and Angkor. The buildings at Ta Muan are better preserved than at Ban Bu.

Other Khmer sites noted in individual entries Prasat Phranomwan, Prasat Pluang, Prasat Phra Viharn, Prasat Na Kamphaeng Noi, Prasat Na Kamphaeng Yai, Prasat Sikhoraphum, Phnom Rung, Muang Tam, Phimai.

NB The above is only intended as a guide for those who wish to see some of the sites which are infrequently visited. The information comes mainly from secondary sources. Most of the above is a summary condensed from Smitthi Siribhadra and Elizabeth Moore's Palaces of the gods: Khmer art and architecture in Thailand, River Books: Bangkok.

extracted without environmental damage and experts hope that it will supply water for this otherwise water-short area.

The Northeast consists of 19 provinces, the two newest being created in 1993 when two districts were upgraded to provincial status: Amnat Charoen (previously part of Ubon Ratchathani) and Nong Bua Lamphu (previously part of Udon Thani). Travelling around the Northeast is relatively easy. During the Vietnam War the Thai government, with financial support from the US, built an impressive network of roads, in an attempt to keep the resurgence of Communism at bay. The opening of the Friendship Bridge in early 1994, the first bridge across the Mekong, linking Nong Khai in the Northeast with Vientiane, the capital of Laos, may presage greater tourist activity in this part of the country (and greater business activity). As Laos tentatively opens its doors to tourists, so the attraction of using the Northeast as a stepping stone to Laos will increase. There are various other bridge projects on the drawing board, and while the current economic crisis may bring a halt to them for the time being, there is a long term aim of integrating Laos and Thailand via the Northeast. Already international hotel chains have opened hotels in Nong Khai and Udon Thani. There is also optimism, perhaps unfounded, amongst the hoteliers of Ubon and the southeast of Isan that the forthcoming Ubon to Laos road will bring a tourist boom to this corner of Thailand.

Nakhon Ratchasima (Korat)
นครราชสีมา (โคราช)

Most visitors to the Northeastern region travel only as far as Nakhon Ratchasima, or Korat, possibly the largest town in the Northeast with around 250,000 inhabitants and the provincial capital of the province of the same name. An important and relatively prosperous commercial centre with more than its fair share of Thai yuppies, Korat is the main base for visiting the magnificent Khmer monuments of Phimai, Phnom Rung and Muang Tham.

Phone code: 044
Colour map 2, grid C2
Population: 250,000

Ins and outs

As one of Thailand's largest regional centres, Korat is well provided with transport links. The city's airport is 5 km south of town. Daily connections with Bangkok, 256 km away. There are 3 bus terminals serving Bangkok, as well as many other destinations in the North, Northeast and Central Plains. The railway station is west of the town centre and provides links with Bangkok and other destinations in the Northeast.

Getting there
See also Transport, page 392

Korat is a large town. A city bus system (bus maps available from the tourist office), along with a plentiful supply of tuk-tuks and saamlors, provide transportation.

Getting around

TAT, 2102-2104 Mittraphap Rd, on the western edge of town, is inconveniently located – although town bus No 2 runs out here - next door to the *Sima Thani Hotel*, T213666. Open 0830-1630 Mon-Sun. Areas of responsibility are Korat, Buri Ram, Susiu and Chaiyaphum. Good town maps available, along with a fair amount of other information of Korat and the Northeastern region. It is worth coming out here if you can find the time.

Tourist offices

The town

From Korat, Route 226 runs eastwards towards Ubon Ratchathani (311 km), and Route 2 northwards to Khon Kaen at the border with Laos (189 km) and Nong Khai (another 172 km). The Friendship Highway (Route 2), built with

American Aid during the Vietnam War, links Saraburi with Nakhon Ratchasima or Korat. People say that it is not really an Isan town at all, located as it is on the borders between the Central Plains and the Khorat Plateau. During the Vietnamese War, Korat supported an important US airbase and warplanes set out from here to bomb the routes that supplied the Communist Vietcong fighting in South Vietnam. The city was established when the older settlements of Sema and Khorakpura were merged under King Narai in the 17th century.

Sights

The older part of the town lies to the west, while the newer section is within the moat, to the east. Korat is usually only considered as a convenient jumping-off point for visits to the Khmer ruins of Phimai, Phnom Rung and Muang Tham. However, it does have some sights of interest. The remains of the town walls, and the moat that still embraces the city, date from the eighth to 10th centuries. More obvious are the town gates which have been rebuilt and make useful points of reference while exploring this large and rapidly expanding city.

For most Thais, and many foreigners, Korat is best known and remembered as the site of the *Royal Plaza Hotel* collapse. The hotel simply crumpled, killing

Nakhon Ratchasima (Korat)

To Khon Kaen, Phimai & Bus Terminal II

Rt 2

To Railway Station (300m), TAT Office, a/c Bus Station for Bangkok, Khao Yai National Park, Sima Thani Hotel, & Korat Doctor's Guesthouse

Suranari Rd

Burin Road

Mittraphap Rd

■13

Clock Tower

Wat Prok

Chumphon Rd

Wat Phaya

Bus Terminal I

Wat Muang

3■

Wat Sakae

Rachadamnern Rd

Wat Po

Suranari Rd

●4

11■

Buarong Rd

●1

Osaka Turkish Baths

10■

Phoklang Rd

■5 12●

8■

6●

Thusnee Thai Silk

Chumphon Gate Thao Suranari Sh

Motorbike Hire

Wat Chaeng Nai

Buarong Rd

Today Silk

Wat Bung

Jomsurangyaat Rd

■1 2● ✉

Klang Plaza II Shopping Centre

Wat Nong Bua Rong

Wat Sutchinda & Mahawirawong Museum

Sala Changw (Provincial H

N

0 metres 100
0 yards 100

To Race Course & Golf Course

■ **Sleeping**
1 Anachak
2 Asadang
3 Cathay
4 Chomsurang

5 Chumphon
6 Fah Thai
7 K Star
8 Pho Thong
9 Royal Princess Korat

10 Siri
11 Sripatana
12 Srivijaya
13 Thai

● **Eating**
1 Dok Som
2 Green House Garden
3 Phokaphan
4 SPK (Suan Phak)

137 people. The cause was poor design, incompetent construction, official corruption and greed; a tragically familiar concoction in Thailand.

Mahawirawong Museum

In the grounds of Wat Sutchinda just outside the city moat, on Rachdamnern Road, this museum houses a small collection of Khmer art which is now well organized and reasonably labelled. ■ *0930-1530 Wed-Sun, ฿10. (A ฿100 combination ticket gives access to the Museum as well as Prasat Phranomwan, Phimai and Muang Khaek, saving ฿40 if all are visited.)*

Thao Suranari Shrine

This shrine is in the centre of town, by the Chumphon Gate. This bronze monument erected in 1934 commemorates the revered wife of a provincial governor, popularly known as Khunying Mo, who in 1826 saved the town from an invading Lao army. Legend has it that she and some fellow prisoners plied the over-confident Lao soldiers with alcohol and then, having lulled them into a drunken stupor, slaughtered them. As a result, she has become something of a regional heroine and was given the title Thao Suranari, or Brave Lady. Local people come to pay their respects, wrap the statue in ribbons, rub gold leaf on to elephant statues given as gifts for wishes granted, and offer a whole range of other objects. Most evenings, traditional Isan (Northeastern) folk songs are performed at the shrine and in late March and early April a 10 day-long festival

The Northeastern Region

honours the heroine (see Festivals below). In the run-up to the November 1996 general election, aspiring MPs were bestowing rich offerings on the statue. Pairote Suwanchawee, standing for the New Aspirations Party, gave rice, flowers and fruit to the tune of ฿5,000. Liquor, chicken and a pig's head were not offered because, apparently, Thao Suranari would not appreciate such unclean offerings. But Chatichai Choonhaven of Chart Thai gave the whole 'set', worth ฿10,000, because, he argued, though Thao Suranari might not tuck into such morsels, she has lots of disciples who are not so principled.

Wat Sala Loi Just outside the northeast corner of the city moat is this modern wat, with an ubosoth resembling a Chinese junk. It was built in 1973 and is meant to symbolize a boat taking the faithful to nirvana. It is one of the few modern wats with any originality of design in Thailand (the great majority repeat the same visual themes) and it has won numerous architectural awards. The wat makes use of building materials supplied by local companies at Baan Dan Khwian (see Excursions below). A wat has been on this site for some time and the ashes of the local heroine Thao Suranari are interred here. ■ *Getting there: walk or take bus No 5.*

Markets A new **night market** is to be found on Manat Road, between Chumphon and Mahatthai roads, set up jointly by the Governor, the city authorities, the police and the TAT. There are lots of foodstalls here, as well as some clothes and handicraft stalls. The market is open every day from 1800. The **general market** is opposite Wat Sakae, on Suranari Road.

Excursions

Phimai See page 396. ■ *Getting there: regular departures on bus no 1305 from the terminal off Suranari Rd, ฿16 (1 hr). The last bus from Phimai back to Korat leaves at 1800.*

Prasat Phranomwan This wat is a smaller, inferior version of Phimai, which can be found about a third of the way between Korat and Phimai, next to a new monastery. It began life as a Hindu temple, and was only later converted for use as a Buddhist wat. The central prang and adjoining pavilion are enclosed within a galleried wall. When it was built is not certain: the carving on the lintels is early 11th century in style, yet the inscriptions refer to the Khmer King Yasovarman who ruled in 889. There are also art historians who believe that it was built largely during the early 10th century by another Cambodian king, Suryavarman I. The site is undergoing limited renovation, but the quality and the quantity of the carving does not begin to compare with either Phimai or Phanom Rung. Most of the lintels have been removed to museums; only the one over the north entrance to

● ●

Nakhon Ratchasima place names

Ban Dan Kwian	Phnom Rung
บ้านด่านเกวียน	ปราสาทหินพนมรุ้ง
Ban Prasat	Prasat Phranomwan
บ้านปราสาท	ปราสาทหินพนมวัน
Muang Tam	Wat Sala Loi
ปราสาทเมืองต่ำ	วัดศาลาลอย
Pak Thong Chai	
ปักธงชัย	

the main sanctuary remains. Buddhas (added at a later date) occupy the dilapidated niches. Originally, a wide moat surrounded the shrine, and to the east there is still a large baray or reservoir; both had cosmological significance in creating a model of the Hindu universe. ■ *Getting there: direct buses leave from Phonsaen Gate at 0700, 1000 and 1200 (฿7). Buses running towards Phimai pass the turn-off for Phranomwan; ask to be let off at Ban Saen Muang and either walk the 4 km to the monument or catch one of the irregular local songthaews. If driving, note that it is not yet signposted from Korat, although there is a sign if driving from the opposite direction (that is from Phimai). About 15 km from Korat driving north on Route 2, after crossing the flyover over the railway line and not far past the Korat A & M Institute of Technology, turn right. (Look out for the Shell garage on the right – the turning is shortly after this.) Drive 4 km through the villages of Saen Muang and Nong Bua to the site.*

This is a prehistoric site dating back about 5,000 years. The dig has been converted into an open air museum, much like Ban Chiang outside Udon Thani (see page 436). Indeed, there seem to be close cultural links between Ban Prasat and Ban Chiang. Similar high quality, red slipped and burnished trumpet-rimmed pots have been discovered at both sites. Rice was eaten as the subsistence crop, domestic animals raised, and the technology of bronze casting understood. The unearthing of sea shell ornaments also indicates communication with the coast. The examination of skeletons unearthed at the site reveals a high infant mortality rate, and a relatively short lifespan of only 34-36 years. ■ *Getting there: by bus towards Phimai. The site is 2 km off the main road and 45 km from Korat city, on the left-hand side, before the turning for Phimai. Ask for Ban Prasat.*

Ban Prasat

Lying 112 km southeast of Korat and 64 km south of Buri Ram, Phnom Rung gives a hint of what the less accessible Angkor Wat in Cambodia must be like. Indeed, it is thought to have been a stopping-off point on the road from Angkor to Phimai. Similar in layout to Phimai, both monuments are believed to have been the prototype for Angkor Wat.

Phnom Rung

The finest Khmer temple in Thailand. The most convenient way to visit Phnom Rung & Muang Tam is to go on a tour. See Tour operators below

Phnom Rung was built in sandstone and laterite over a period of 200 years between the 10th and early 13th centuries. It stands majestically at the top of Rainbow Hill, an inactive volcano overlooking the Thai-Cambodian border. The name Phnom Rung means 'Large Hill'. It was built on a grand scale – the approach is along a 160 m avenue of **pink sandstone pillars** (*nang riang*). A monumental staircase on five levels is reached via a five-headed **naga bridge**. Some of the nagas are particularly finely carved and well preserved and this 'bridge' is one of Thailand's Khmer treasures. The style indicates a date of the 12th century and their detail is superb: crowned heads studded with jewels, carefully carved scales and backbones, and magnificent rearing bodies. The naga bridge represented a symbolic division between the worlds of mortals and gods. From here the pilgrim climbed upwards via a **monumental staircase** to the sanctuary itself, a divine place of beauty and power.

Inscriptions found at Phnom Rung indicate that this area was controlled by a king who ruled autonomously from Angkor: King Narendraditya. The King was a relative of King Suryavarman II (1112-52) who occupied the throne at Angkor. Suryavarman used relatives such as Narendraditya to extend his influences into Northeast Thailand. After bringing the area under his control, it seems that Narendraditya retired from the cut and thrust of kingship to become an ascetic. Or at least that is what the inscriptions would have us believe. The King's son Hiranya took his place on the throne.

The **Prasat Phnom Rung (central Hindu sanctuary)** is of typical Khmer design, being symmetrical, of cruciform plan, with four gopuras leading to

The Northeastern Region

antechambers. It was probably built between 1050 and 1150, most likely by the Khmer King Suryavarman II. The outstanding stone carvings on the central prang illustrate scenes from the Ramayana, the Puranas and the Mahabharata. The Reclining Vishnu Lintel on the main east porch was discovered in the Art Institute of Chicago in 1973, and after repeated requests from the Fine Arts Department in Bangkok, it was returned to Thailand in 1988. It can now be seen in its original position. The pediment of this same eastern face portrays Siva cavorting in his dance of creation and destruction. The central hall of the shrine would probably have had a wooden floor – visitors now have to step down below ground level. The quality of the carving at Phnom Rung is regarded by some as being the finest of the Angkor period. Lunet de Lajonquiere, who first surveyed the site in 1907, wrote that "in plan, execution and decoration it is among the most perfect of its kind".

The oldest structures within the walls are the two brick *prasat* to the northeast of the central building, believed to have been built between 900 and 960 AD. The site was abandoned in the 13th century and was not acknowledged as a historical site by the Fine Arts Department until 1935. Renovation began in 1972 and was finally completed in 1988. It is now a national historical park. The Busabong Festival is held here every April. The only place to eat near the site is at the *Phnom Rung Park*, an assemblage of small restaurants and stalls serving cold drinks and good Isan food, including *kai yaang* (grilled chicken), *somtam* (spicy papaya salad) and sticky rice, along with standard Thai fare. ■ *0730-1800 Mon-Sun,* ฿*40.*

Transport Catch a bus towards Surin along Route 24 and get off at Ban Tako, 14 km beyond the district town of Nang Rong. In Nang Rong it is possible to stay at *Honey Inn*, 8/1 Soi Srikoon. The *Honey* is run by Mr Phaisan, a teacher, who will also help arrange tours in the area. From Ban Tako either take a motorcycle taxi (which wait at the intersection) to the site and back again (฿100) or a songthaew to Ban Dorn Nong Haen (฿5-10), and from there to the foot of the hill (some songthaews go straight to the foot of the hill). From here it is possible to walk. Alternatively, a bus from Ban Tako goes 6 km in the right direction (฿8) and a chartered songthaew for four people should cost about ฿200, with a 2 hr stop at the ruins. From Phnom Rung it is a short trip – 8 km – on to Muang Tam (see below), so it is worth paying a little extra if chartering a motorcycle taxi. An easier way to see the monument, and the others in the area, is simply to join a tour (see tours below). The route to the site is well signposted.

Phnom Rung

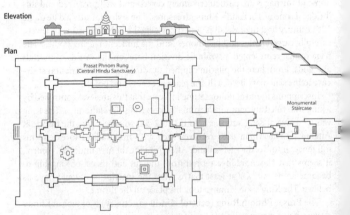

Elevation

Plan

Prasat Phnom Rung
(Central Hindu Sanctuary)

Monumental
Staircase

Muang Tam, or 'Temple of the Lower city', is found 8 km from Phnom Rung **Muang Tam**
and was built on a smaller, more intimate scale. This 10th-11th century Khmer
palace was completed by King Jayavarman V, although the absence of inscriptions makes exact dating impossible. It is thought to have been the palace of the
regional governor of the area. It is surrounded by colossal laterite walls pierced
by four gopuras, at the four points of the compass. Three still retain their
sculpted lintels. The carving of foliage and nagas across sandstone blocks
shows that the structure was built before any carving was undertaken. Only
after the blocks had been put in place were artists set to work. Nagas decorate
the L-shaped ponds which lie within the walls and surround the central courtyard and its five brick chedis, four of which have been rebuilt. These probably
symbolize the five-peaked Mount Meru. The nagas here are stylistically different from those at Phnom Rung: they are smooth-headed rather than adorned
with crowns, leading art historians to conclude that this prasat is earlier in date
by some 100-200 years. Many regard these nagas as unparalleled in their
beauty; lotuses are carved on some of their chests, jewels stream from their
mouths and garlands adorn them. The carving here also indicates that artists
were allowed considerable freedom. The same figures are portrayed in very
different ways on different lintels; for example, the rishis. Until 1990 Muang
Tham had a wonderfully dilapidated air; sandstone bas-relief lintels lay scattered alongside unworked blocks of stone. It is undergoing restoration by the
Fine Arts Department. ■ *0730-1800 Mon-Sun, ฿40. Getting there: catch a*
Surin bus to Prakhon Chai on Route 24. From there, songthaews leave for Muang
Tham. If the trip is to be combined with a visit to Phnom Rung, it is necessary to
charter a motorcycle taxi or hitch from Phnom Rung – there is no public transport
yet (see Phnom Rung, above, for details).

Fifteen kilometres to the southeast of Korat on Route 224, **Ban Dan Kwian** is a **Ban Dan Kwian**
one industry town. It seems that almost everyone is linked in one way or another
to its numerous ceramic and pottery factories. Rust-coloured clay – because of
its high iron content – from the local river is used to make vases, pots, wind
chimes, water jars, ceramic fish and other objects. Countless stalls and shops line
the main road. Unfortunately, most of the items for sale are too big to transport
home. There is also an exhibition of Asian carts and a tourist information centre
(on the right-hand side on entering the village from Korat). It is said the Ban Dan

The Northeastern Region

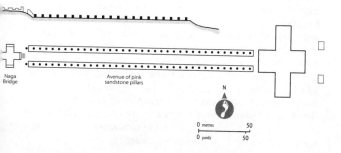

Naga
Bridge

Avenue of pink
sandstone pillars

N

0 metres 50
0 yards 50

Kwian specialized in pottery production because of its position on the road between Korat and Buri Ram. Travellers would stop here to buy storage jars and bowls for their journey. However, as imports of ceramics from China and products made in Bangkok became popular, so Ban Dan Kwian's rough pottery lost market share. Fortunately, just before it became moribund, two things happened. First, a new market emerged as sophisticated Thais and tourists looking for traditional folk pottery headed this way. And second, innovative local producers began to branch out away from functional items and into new products, designed to appeal to foreigners and the Thai nouveau riche. ■ *Getting there: take a songthaew towards Chokchai from the south city gates on Kamphaeng Songkhram and Chainarong roads, ₿6 (30 mins).*

Pak Thong Chai Thirty kilometres south on Route 304 and 2 km off the main road, Pak Thong Chai is a silk-weaving village with cloth for sale. It has become rather commercialized in recent years; a weaving centre has opened and cloth is now relatively expensive (recent visitors claim that it is cheaper to buy cloth in Bangkok). Four kilometres from Pak Thong Chai is **Wat Na Phrathat**, notable both for its rare early Rattanakosin murals in the *bot* (ordination hall) and the fine woodcarving over the doorway to the *hor trai*, or scripture library. There are a couple of basic (**E-F**) hotels on the main street in Pak Thong Chai. ■ *Getting to Pak Thong Chai: buses leave from Korat's bus station I off Bruin Rd every 30 mins, ₿11 (1 hr).*

Essentials

Sleeping
■ *on map, page 384*
Price codes:
see inside front cover

As an important commercial centre, Korat has a good stock of hotels; some 25 in total. Most, though, are geared to Thais, not farangs

AL *Royal Princess Korat*, T256629, F256601. A/c, restaurant, pool, 200-room hotel and the best in the city, tennis courts, situated north of town across the Takhong River off Suranari Rd and about 2 km from the town centre. **A** *Sima Thani*, Mittraphap Rd, T213100, F213121. West of town next to the TAT office, so not central. A/c, restaurants, pool, health club, early 1990s hotel with over 130 rooms. Quite good value, the only drawback being the out-of-town location. **B** *Chomsurang*, 2701/2 Mahatthai Rd, T257088, F252897. A/c, restaurant, pool, overpriced but comfortable, with good facilities. **B-C** *Siri*, 167-8 Phoklang Rd, T242831. Some a/c, centrally located, bare, but clean rooms and well priced. The staff are usually welcoming and based here is the *Veterans of Foreign Wars Café* – a legacy of the years when Korat was a US airforce base.

C *Anachak (Empire)*, 62/1 Jomsurangyaat Rd, T243825. A/c, restaurant, average. Convenient for a night's stopover. **C** *K Star*, 191 Assadang Rd, T257057. All mod cons with frills. Surgically clean business hotel. **C** *Sirivijaya*, 9-11 Buarong Rd, T242194. Some a/c, restaurant, good location. **C** *Sripatana*, 346 Suranari Rd, T242944. A/c, restaurant, pool, comfortable but characterless. **C** *Thai*, 646-650 Mittraphap Rd, T241613. A/c, clean rooms, ugly hotel. **D** *Chumphon*, 124 Phoklang Rd, T242453. Some a/c, not much obvious to recommend this place. **D** *Fah Thai*, 35-39 Phoklang Rd, T242533. Some a/c, must have been built by a prison architect, but rooms OK and it's central. **E** *Asadang*, 315 Assadang Rd, T242514. Some a/c, 40 rooms in medium-sized Chinese-style hotel. **E** *Cathay*, 3692/5-6 Rachdamnern Rd, T242889. 49 very plain rooms, many poorly maintained, but close to the bus station. **E** *Pho Thong*, Rachdamnern Rd. Almost in front of the Thao Suranari Shrine, own bathroom, quite clean, rooms on street are noisy but central location. **E-F** *Korat Doctor's Guesthouse*, 78 Suebsiri Rd Soi 4, T255846. West of centre, towards TAT, bus No 1 runs past the street leading to the guesthouse, Mukamontri Rd, guesthouse is on the left-hand side. Some a/c, mosquitoes can be a problem, rooms do not always have nets, clean, good value and an excellent source of information. Quiet and welcoming, with statements as to its homely atmosphere much in evidence. Recommended.

Thai/Chinese Mid-range: *The Emperor* (in the *Sima Thani*), Mittraphap Rd. Good Chinese restaurant, but now eclipsed by the *Seow Seow* in terms of quality; prices to match. **Cheap**: *Seow Seow* (pronounced *She She*), just off Mahathai Rd. Inexpensive Chinese restaurant that serves better food and is considerably cheaper. Huge menu, excellent service, seats 250 diners. Recommended. *Green House Garden*, 50-52 Jomsurangyaat Rd (next to the Post Office). Away from the road in a sheltered 'garden'. *SPK* (*Suan Phak*), 196 Chumphon Rd. Hangout for the Korat trendies, but good food, also serves cakes. Recommended. *Phokaphan*, Washara Sarit Rd. Recommended. **Seriously cheap**: *Dok Som Restaurant*, 130-142 Chumphon Rd, across the street from the *Pho Thong Hotel*. Very pleasant restaurant with covered terrace area, Thai and Western food. Recommended. *MD Restaurant*, Klang Plaza, Jomsurangyaat Rd. Lots of choice, good clean restaurant.

International *Veterans of Foreign Wars Café*, *Siri Hotel*, 167-8 Phoklang Rd. Restaurants serving a range of Western dishes along with simple Thai food, a good place for breakfast. *Pizza Hut*, next to the museum on Rachdamnern Rd.

Bakery *Ploi Bakery*, Chumphon Rd (near the Thao Surinari Shrine). Also serves Thai food. *Sweet Home Bakery*, Pho Klang Rd (next to *Fah Thai Hotel*).

Fast food *Dunkin Donuts*, Klang Plaza, Jomsurangyaat Rd. *KFC*, Klang Plaza, Jomsurangyaat Rd.

Ice cream *Swensen's Ice Cream*, Jomsurangyaat Rd (opposite Klang Plaza II).

Night market The night market on Manat Rd, open from 1800, has a good range of cheap Thai/Chinese cafés and excellent foodstalls. A number of bars and restaurants are to be found on Jomsurangyaat Rd. Good *kiaytiaw* restaurant, close to the corner of Buarong and Jomsurangyaat roads.

Eating
● on map, page 384
Price categories:
see inside front cover

Good Thai & Chinese
food to be found by the
west gates; near the
Thao Suranari Shrine,
for example

London Tavern, 176 Mahatthai Rd. Recently opened UK-style pub where local football fans congregate.

Bars

Mar-Apr *Tao Suranari Fair* (end of month), a 10-day fair commemorating the local heroine Tao Suranari who helped to defeat an invading Lao army (see above). Exhibitions, parades, bazaars, beauty contests, likay performances and the like, along with thousands of participants and onlookers, make this one of Thailand's most vibrant festivals.

Festivals

Books *DK Books*, Chumphon Rd (east of *lak muang*). **Handicrafts** The *Korat Craft Centre* is located behind the Sala Changwat (Provincial Hall). **Matmii** (hand-woven cloth): Korat is the centre for matmii, both silk and cotton (see box, page 433). There are a number of shops around the central square. *Thusnee Thai Silk*, 680 Rachdamnern Rd (opposite the Thao Suranari Shrine.) *Today Silk*, Rachdamnern Rd. *Klang Plaza Department Store*, Assadang Rd, and Klang Plaza 11 on Jomsurangyaat Rd.

Shopping

Swimming A number of hotels in Korat allow non-residents to use their swimming pools for a small fee. The *Sripatana Hotel* on Suranari Rd charges ฿50 per day for use of their swimming pool and the *Thep Nakhon* on Mittraphap Rd charges ฿60. The latter is the better pool. There are also a number of public pools in town including the Rama Swimming Pool on Mittraphap Rd. **Tennis** *Thot-saporn Court*, 1658 Mittraphap Rd, T251819, open 0900-2000 Mon-Sun, ฿25 per hr. The *Sima Thani Hotel* also has courts available. **Turkish baths** Korat has a reputation for its Turkish baths. Ask at the TAT office for the latest recommendations or try *Chao Phraya* on Jomsurangyaat Rd; or the *Osaka* at the intersection of Suranari and Phoklang roads.

Sport

Prayurakit, 40-44 Suranari Rd, T252114. *Hill Top Tour*, 516/4 Friendship Rd, Pak Chong, Korat, T311671. For organized tours of Khao Yai National Park. *Suphatthra*, 138 Chainarong Rd, T242758.

Tour operators

The Northeastern Region

Transport
See also Ins & outs, page 383; 256 km to Bangkok

Local Tuk-tuks (฿40-60) and saamlors. **Bus**: the TAT office supplies a map with bus routes marked. Buses cost ฿4-6 and are infrequent during rush hours. **Motorbike hire**: from *Virojyarnyon*, 554-556 Phoklang Rd, ฿150-200 per day.

Long distance Air: the airport is 5 km south of town on Route 304. Regular connections with Bangkok (daily), 30 mins. **Train**: the station is on Mukamontri Rd, in the west of town (T242044). Regular connections with Bangkok's Hualamphong station, 5-6 hrs, and also with Ubon, close to the border with Laos. **Road**: It is possible to travel from Korat to Pattaya and the east coast, avoiding the capital, by taking Routes 304, 33 and 317. **Bus**: the a/c bus terminal for Bangkok is on Mittraphap Rd, west of the town centre. Regular connections with Bangkok's new Northeastern bus terminal (4-5 hrs). There are 2 more long distance bus terminals for other destinations in Thailand. The more important is the new bus terminal II, which lies 2 km northwest of town on Route 2 to Khon Kaen and serves most Northeastern destinations, as well as Chantaburi and Pattaya. Bus terminal I off Burin Rd closer to the centre of town, serves Khon Kaen, Chiang Mai and Chiang Rai.

Directory

Airline offices *Thai*, 14 Manat Rd, T257211. **Banks** There are a number of banks offering foreign exchange services on Mittraphap and Chumphon roads. *Bangkok*, Jomsurangyaat Rd, close to the Post Office. **Communications Telecom centre**: Jomsurangyaat Rd, next to the Post Office. **Email** at the Internet Café next to Klang Plaza II. **Post Office**: main office on Assadang Rd, between Prachak and Manat roads; a more convenient branch is at 48 Jomsurangyaat Rd (next to the Klang Plaza II shopping centre). **Medical services** *Maharaj Hospital*, near the bus station on Suranari Rd, T254990. **Useful addresses** Police: Sanpasit Rd, T242010. **Tourist Police**: 2102-2104 Mittraphap Rd (on western edge of town, next to the TAT office; see Ins and outs above), T213333.

Khao Yai National Park and Pak Chong
อุทยานแห่งชาติเขาใหญ่

Phone code: 044
Colour map 2, grid C2

Khao Yai National Park, the first park to be founded in Thailand in 1962, is one of the country's finest. It covers an area of 2,168 sq km and encompasses the limestone Dangrek mountain range, a large area of rainforest, waterfalls and a surprisingly wide selection of wildlife. Visitors may be lucky enough to see Asiatic black bear, Javan mongoose, slow loris and tiger. Two notable species are the white-handed (or lar) gibbon and the pileated gibbon. There may be as many as 200 elephants in the park. Short trails are marked in the park; for longer hikes, a guide is usually needed. The 50 km of trails are the most extensive and best marked of any national park. The tourist office and visitors' centre at Khao Yai provide maps and organize guides on an intermittent basis. The centre is also probably the closest you will get to rare wildlife, but it is pickled or stuffed.

Kong Kaeo Waterfall is a short walk from the visitors' centre. Six kilometres east is the **Haew Suwat Waterfall** (three to four hours' walk). Waterfalls are at their best between June and November, wildlife is best seen during April and May, although August and September are good months to see the hornbills (of which there are four species here). Night time is good for animal observation, when you might be able to see sambar and barking deer, porcupine, gibbon, pig-tailed macaques, mongoose, civet cats and elephants. Spotlight safaris can be organized up until 2100, ฿300-600.

Unfortunately, because of the park's easy accessibility from Bangkok, it is overrun with visitors and its environmental integrity is at risk. In late 1992, for a time, the authorities actually forbade visitors to stay overnight, such was the pressure on wildlife. **Khao Yai Elephant Camp** is not the best place to see elephants; a collection of rather morose-looking elephants are chained to trees at the side of the road by the *Jungle House*. ■ *Rides are available 0800-1700 daily, for ฿600 per hr.* The **Khoa Luk Chang Bat Cave** lies 6 km from the park gate, 2 km up an unmade road. The cave is at the top of a limestone precipitous cliff. Access for the nimble is found at the base of a zip wire.

The closest town to the national park is Pak Chong. While there is some accommodation in the park itself, most of the commercial hotels and guest-houses are situated here and it is a good place to base yourself. There is little to see here, apart from the markets on the north side of Mittraphap Road.

Pak Chong

Jungle Adventure Tours, run by Tom and Maew from 63 Tedsabal, 16 Kongvaksin Road, had some bad press in the past, but on our last visit, despite an abrupt sales pitch, the tour offered convenience and was well-organized, albeit a bit pricey. A 1½ day tour costs ฿950 and it is run at a frantic pace. *KH Tours*, T515709, promises to show you 'bird with ear – mouse with wings', in their two day and slightly cheaper programme (฿650). Bikes for rent, ฿300 per day. Another outfit that has been recommended is *Khao Yai National Park and Wildlife Tours*, which operates out of *Khao Yai Garden Lodge* (see Sleeping below). A 1½ day tour is charged at ฿950 per person, but they also operate tours up to seven days long.

Tours
Numerous companies run organized tours to Khao Yai. A number are to be found in Pak Chong

Pak Chong or between Pak Chong and Khao Yai There are quite a few resort hotels, many not listed below, on the road from Pak Chong to Khao Yai. These are mostly frequented by Thais. **AL-A** *Landmark*, 151/1 Mittraphap Rd (2 km west of town), T280047. This is a new and pretty sophisticated hotel with a great pool. The rooms and the rest of the hotel are nothing special, but it's still a very comfortable place to stay. **AL** *Golden Valley Resort*, 188 Mu 5, T3350880, F2134330. A/c, restaurant, pool; another comparatively new luxury hotel situated out of town on the road to Khao Yai, with most facilities. **AL** *Juldis Khao Yai Resort*, Thannarat Rd, Km 17 Pak Chong (15-25 mins north of the northern gate to the park), T2352414, B2552480. A/c, restaurant, pool, tennis courts and golf available at this resort-style hotel, with both bungalows and larger blocks. **B-C** *Phuphaya*, 404/4 Mittraphap Rd, T313134. 56 rooms in this swish business hotel out on the east side of town. Pool and all facilities. **B-D** *Khao Yai Garden Lodge*, Km 7 Thanarat Rd, 7 km from Pak Chong, T313567, F312143, Khaoyaigarden@ hotmail.com Wide range of rooms from basic ones with shared facilities up to attractive suites with good views. Passive staff, but good facilities and tours available.

Sleeping
■ *on map*
Price codes:
see inside front cover

Accommodation listed here is in the national park, Pak Chong, or on the road to Khao Yai from Pak Chong

The Northeastern Region

Pak Chong

D *Phubade*, 781 Thetsaban Rd, T311979. 49 rooms in one of the few central hotels in town, otherwise known as Phubet, most mod cons but no frills. **E** *Happy Trails Tour and Guesthouse*, facing the train station in Pak Chong. Run by a Thai with good English who has returned from the US, simple rooms that could do with some sprucing up, but the owner is also a guide in the park so has a good knowledge of the area. **E** *Jungle Guest House*, 752/11 Kongwaksin Rd (off Soi 3), Pak Chong, T312877. A backpacker's haunt with enthusiastic staff and basic, rather overpriced rooms. They are also rather over-enthusiastic in pressing guests to use their tours. Popular.

Khao Yai B-D *National Park Lodges*, T7223579. To be booked at the National Park Accommodation Office, price includes bedding and bath facilities. Diverse range of accommodation from floor mats to individual bungalows. **F** *Ya Wachon Camp*, 2 km

Khao Yai National Park

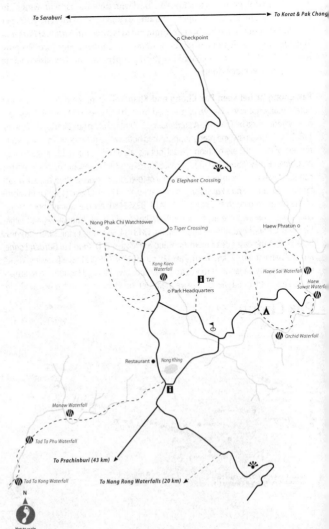

Trails in Khao Yai

Trail 1: Kong Kaew to Haew Suwat *Starts behind visitors' centre, marked in red, 6 km, 3-4 hours walking – transport back to headquarters should be arranged. One of the most popular trails, offering opportunities to observe gibbons.*

Trail 2: Kong Kaew to Elephant Salt Lick 2 *Starts behind visitors' centre, marked in blue, 6 km, 3-4 hours. Not well marked over grassland to salt lick – guide advisable. Frequented by elephants.*

Trail 3: Kong Kaew to Pha Kluai Mai *Starts behind visitors' centre, marked in yellow.*

Trail 4: Pha Kluai Mai to Haew Suwat *Starts on far side of campsite, marked in red, 3 km. Popular trail along Lam Takhong riverbank. Good trail for orchids and birdlife (blue-eared kingfishers, scarlet minivets, cormorant, hornbills – both wreathed and great). Probable sightings of gibbon, macaques and elephants.*

Trail 5: Haew Suwat to Khao Laem grassland *Starts across the Lam Takhong River from the parking area. Difficult trail to follow, not much wildlife but good views of Khao Laem mountain.*

Trail 6: Headquarters to Nong Phak Chi Watchtower *Starts across road from Wang Kong Kaew restaurant, south of Park Office, marked in red, 6 km round-trip. Popular and easy to follow until last 500 m. The tower makes a good viewing spot at dawn or dusk. White-headed gibbon, frequently seen. Clouded leopard has been seen occasionally, herds of wild pig, and even tiger.*

Trail 7: Headquarters to Wang Cham Pi *Starts same as 6, marked in blue, 4½ km round-trip, 2-3 hours, good for ornithologists, gibbons and macaques easily seen.*

Trail 8: Headquarters Looping Trail *Marked in yellow, 2½ km.*

Trail 9: Headquarters to Mo Singto *Marked in blue, begins 6, ends at a reservoir close to headquarters, 2 km. A favourite haunt for tigers.*

from park HQ. For the hardened traveller, dormitory accommodation and hard floors (bring your own bedding).

There is a campsite near the Kong Kaeo Waterfall, but no equipment for hire. Permission to camp must be obtained from the Park Office. There are 'rest areas' near Haew Suwat and Haew Narok waterfalls, providing drink and simple Thai food. **NB** Special permission is required from headquarters if trekkers want to spend the night at park outstations.

Camping

The best place to eat in Pak Chong is at the night market, which begins operation around 1700 and continues through to shortly before midnight. There are also a fair number of restaurants in town – this, after all, is on the main Bangkok-Korat highway. *Party House Restaurant*, quality food and also a good place for a cosy beer.

Eating
● *on maps*
Price categories:
see inside front cover

Train There are trains from Bangkok (3½-4 hrs) and Ayutthaya to Pak Chong, and onward to Ubon Ratchathani. **Road** The park turning is at the 165 km marker on Route 2, 200 km from Bangkok, 2-3 hrs by car. There are 2 entrances to the park. One from the north, near Pak Chong, the other from the south, near Prachinburi. Access from the south is mostly by hired or private vehicle; all buses go to the north entrance. Four buses leave Korat for Pak Chong in the morning (฿20), or it is possible to catch a Bangkok-bound bus and get off in Pak Chong. From Bangkok, take a bus (2½ hrs) or train to Pak Chong. There are numerous songthaews from Pak Chong to the park itself. Cars can also be hired – or there are tours available.

Transport

Phimai พิมาย

Phone code: 044
Colour map 2, grid C3

The ancient town of Phimai, northeast of Korat, lies on the Mun River – a tribu-tary of the Mekong and one of the Northeast's major waterways. The town itself is small and rather charming, with only two hotels, and has one major attraction to offer the visitor: the magnificent Khmer sanctuary of Phimai, around which the new town has grown.

Ins & outs
See also Transport, page 398

Getting there Hourly bus connections with Bangkok's Northeastern bus terminal and regular services to Korat. For buses north it is necessary to travel to Talat Khae, 10 km away. **Getting around** Phimai is a very small town. Saamlors are available and there are bicycles for hire from guesthouses. **Tourist offices** The *Bai Teiy Restaurant*, see Eating below, acts as an informal tourist information centre. The *Old Phimai Guest-house*, see Sleeping below, is probably a better source of information.

The site

The site was important even prior to the arrival of the Khmers; excavations have revealed burnished blackware pottery, from as early as 500 AD. The Mun River and one of its minor tributaries formed a natural defensive position, and the site also benefited from an extensive area of rich alluvium suitable for agri-culture. These twin advantages of security and nutrition meant that this area was probably occupied almost continuously for over seven centuries up to the establishment of the Khmer sanctuary, for which Phimai is known.

Dating from the reign of the Cambodian King Jayavarman VII (1181-1201), Phimai was built at the west edge of his Khmer Kingdom, on a Hindu site. A road ran the 240 km from his capital at Angkor to Phimai, via Muang Tham and Phnom Rung. Unlike other Khmer monuments which face east, Phimai faces southeast; probably so that it would face Angkor, although some scholars have postulated it was due to the influence of Funan, also to the south. The Chinese, who controlled maritime trade at the time, also had a cus-tom of southern orientation.

The original complex lay within a walled rectangle 1,000 m by 560 m, set on an artificial island. There are four gopuras, which have been placed in such a way that their entrances coincide with the sanctuary entrances. The south gate, **Victory Gate** or Pratu Chai, faces southeast and was built wide enough to accommodate an ele-phant. Shortly before the gate is the Khlang Ngoen, or Treasury, where important pilgrims were lodged. The discovery of grindstones here has also led some authorities to maintain it was used as a grain storehouse, possibly to prepare rit-ual offerings. From this gate, walk-ing towards the central prang along a raised path (the **ponds** would have been full), are two rest pavilions built by Jayavarman VII. Within the compound are three prangs: the largest, **Prang Prathan**, is made of white sandstone; those on either side are of laterite (**Prang Phromathat**) and red sandstone (**Prang Hin Daeng**). The Prang Phromathat originally held a statue

Plan of Phimai

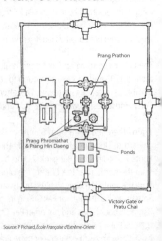

Source: P Pichard, École Française d'Extrême-Orient

of Jayavarman VII. The central, and largest, prang is a major departure for Khmer architecture. Though similar to Phnom Rung in plan, the elegant curving prang was something new entirely. It later probably became the model for the famous towers at Angkor.

Another unusual feature of Phimai is the predominance of Buddhist motifs in the carvings that adorn the temple. The lintel over the south gateway to the main sanctuary shows the Buddha meditating under a protective naga, the naga's coiled body lifting the Buddha above the swirling flood waters. Another scene, magnificently carved on the corridor leading into the south antecham-ber, depicts the Buddha vanquishing the evil forces of Mara. On the west side of the building is a lintel showing the Buddha preaching – both hands raised. The inspiration here seems to be Mon.

To the right of the gateway into the walled compound is a 'homeless lintels' park (leading one to speculate whether the Fine Arts Department have reas-sembled the stones in the right order), where the artistry of the Khmers can be examined at close quarters. The temple was dedicated to Mahayana Bud-dhism, yet Hindu motifs are clearly discernible. Indeed, the main entrance-way shows Siva dancing. On the lintel over the east porch of the main, central prang, is a carving showing the final victory of Krishna over the evil Kamsa. The carvings at Phimai are spectacular in their verve and skill. As Elizabeth Moore and Smitthi Siribhadra write:

The confidence and prosperity of Khmer culture reached its height during the 12th and 13th centuries. This is reflected at Phimai in the tensioned human figures; men and women who move amongst the riotous vegetation to fill the lintels surface.

Of particular interest to art historians is the design of the gateways with their petal-like decorations, similar to those at Angkor itself. As Phimai predates Angkor, there is speculation that it served as the prototype for Angkor Wat. The site has been restored by the Fine Arts Department and was officially opened in 1989. In 2000 a controversy surfaced regarding the Fine Arts Department's restoration of the site. Concerned that lichens were eroding the sandstone monument, they began to clean the stonework. Before long one prasat was a stark white in colour while the other remained in its more subdued state. Archaeologists and art historians attacked the Fine Art Deparment's work, claiming that it not only undermined the aesthetics of the site, but was also accelerating erosion by removing the protective lichens. ■ *0730-1800 Mon-Sun, ฿40*. An open-air **museum** on the edge of the town, just before the bridge, displays carved lintels and statues found in the area. An exhibition hall has recently opened with a well-displayed and labelled (in English) collection. ■ *0830-1630 Wed-Sun. Guidebook available, ฿60.*

On Route 206, just over the bridge which marks the edge of Phimai town, is Thailand's largest **banyan tree** at Sai Ngam. This is a good place for lunch; there are many foodstalls here. Walk the 2 km (travel northwest and do not fol-low the signs, or you will take a circuitous route through the backstreets) or catch a saamlor from Phimai (฿40 return).

D *International Youth Hostel*, the only one in the Northeast and the most characterful place to stay in town. The more expensive rooms are not that good value though. **D** *Phimai Hotel*, 305/1-2 Haruthairom Rd, T471689. Some a/c, comfortable but plain rooms. Front rooms are noisy, but it's good value. **E** *New Phimai Guest-house*, off Chomsudasadet Rd (opposite the *Old Phimai Guesthouse*). Reports are that this is also a good place to stay, although it has not built up the following of the old namesake. **E** *Old Phimai Guesthouse*, dormitory **F**, just off Chomsudasadet Rd,

Sleeping
■ *on map*
Price codes:
see inside front cover

The Northeastern Region

The Northeastern Region

T471918. Friendly, informative owner, attractive rooms, atmospheric, a much better place to stay than any in Korat (at the price). Recommended.

Eating
● *on map*
Price categories:
see inside front cover

The best food is served at the night market near the southeast corner of the prasat, open 1800-2400. Good Isan food is also available at the *Rot Niyom*, off Chomsudasadet Rd. *Sai Ngam* is a 'garden restaurant' further north still, near the ban-yan tree (hence the name). **Mid-range** *Rico Pizza*, Chomsudasadet Rd, close to the *Thai Farmers Bank*. High-quality home-made Italian and international food produced by an Italian. **Cheap** *Bai Teiy*, off Chomsudasadet Rd. Good range of Isaan and Chi-nese/Thai food and ice-cream. Recommended. *Rim Mun*, north of the city overlook-ing the river (as the name suggests). Eat Isaan food aboard a floating raft, reported to be safe as long as the irrigation canals are not flooded.

Festivals

Nov *Phimai Boat-races* (second weekend) held on the Phlaimat River, competition of decorated boats, various stalls.

Transport
See also Ins & outs,
page 396
54 km to Korat,
10 km to Thaket Khae
for buses north

Bicycle hire ₿25 per day from the *Old Phimai Guesthouse* (although machines are on their last legs) and from the *Bai Teiy Restaurant*. **Bus** Regular connections with Korat's main bus station on Suranari Rd 1½ hrs, last bus leaves Korat at 2000 and leaves Phimai at 1800. Hourly service to Bangkok between 0830 and 2300, 5 hrs. To travel north, take a local bus to Thalat Khae and then catch a bus travelling north.

Directory

Banks Currency exchange service opposite the entrance to the Phimai Historical Park. *Thai Farmers Bank*, Chomsudasadet Rd.

Phimai

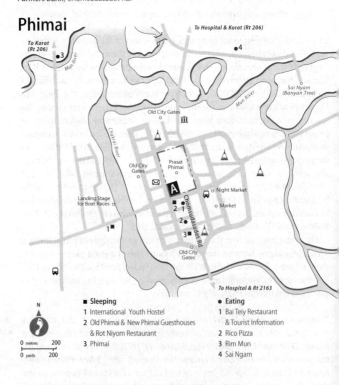

To Korat (Rt 206)
To Hospital & Korat (Rt 206)
To Korat (Rt 206)
Mun River
Chakrai River
Mun River
Sai Nyam (Banyan Tree)
Old City Gates
Old City Gates
Prasat Phimai
Night Market
Landing Stage for Boat Races
Market
Old City Gates
To Hospital & Rt 2163

N

0 metres 200
0 yards 200

■ **Sleeping**
1 International Youth Hostel
2 Old Phimai & New Phimai Guesthouses
& Rot Niyom Restaurant
3 Phimai

● **Eating**
1 Bai Teiy Restaurant
& Tourist Information
2 Rico Pizza
3 Rim Mun
4 Sai Ngam

The route east: Surin to Ubon

From Korat, Route 226 runs eastwards across the Tung Kula Rong Hai or the 'Weeping Plain'. This area came under the sway of the great Khmer Empire, and a number of towns can be used as bases to visit the lesser known Khmer monuments found here: Buri Ram, Surin and Si Saket in particular. Surin, 260 km from Korat, is famous for its yearly elephant round-up. Route 226 eventually reaches the city of Ubon Ratchathani, 311 km from Korat and a former US Airforce base. The town of Yasothon, 103 km northwest of Ubon, is renowned in Thailand for holding the most spectacular ngarn bang fai, or rocket festival, in the Kingdom.

Buri Ram   บุรีรัมย์

The province of Buri Ram contains the magnificent Khmer sanctuary of Phnom Rung (see page 387) and yet few people stay in the capital, preferring instead to travel from the larger city of Korat. The town – it's hard to call this provincial capital a city – is small, unassuming and, in all senses, provincial.

Phone code: 044
Colour map 2, grid C4
Population: 35,000

An **Isan Cultural Centre**, to preserve and develop the Northeast's distinctive Isan culture, has been opened at the Buri Ram teacher's college on Jira Road. The centre, housed in a new building designed to look like a Khmer prasat, supports a museum containing artefacts found in the province and beyond (for example, some Ban Chiang pottery), and also stages dance, music and drama performances, and exhibitions of folk art. So far the collection is small and most is labelled only in Thai. Opening hours are sporadic. The town's **fresh market** is off Soonthonthep Road, not far north of Buri Ram's largest wat, the peaceful but otherwise plain **Wat Klang**.

Phnom Rung, one of the finest Khmer sanctuaries in Thailand, is within easy reach of Buri Ram, 64 km south of the city (see page 387). ■ *Getting there: by bus from the station off Thani Rd towards Prakhon Chai. Get off at Ban Tako, before Prakhon Chai, and then see details on page 388. There are also several morning songthaews from Buri Ram's central market to Dong Nong Nae, which meet up with local songthaews that run direct to the ruins.*

Excursions

Muang Tam, 60 km south of Buri Ram, is also easily accessible and a visit here can be combined with one to Phanom Rung (see page 389). ■ *Getting there: take a bus from the station off Thani Rd to Prakhon Chai; from there, songthaews leave for Muang Tam.*

Khao Krudong is a 300 m volcanic cinder cone 8 km southeast of town. The hill, rising up from the surrounding rice plain, is a holy place and is crowned by a white 20 m-high statue of the Buddha. The views from the summit are best at sunset (although public transport is limited in the afternoon). ■ *Getting there: by songthaew in the morning from the station near the market, off Sriphet Rd.*

Unfortunately the swanky *Sang Rung Interpark*, which only opened a few years back, was standing forlorn and empty in 2000, one of the victims of Thailand's economic crisis. **B-C** *Buriram Plaza*, out of town on the road to Surin. A/c, restaurant and pool. **B-C** *Wongthong Hotel*, new(ish) hotel on the road towards the bus station off Jira Rd. A/c rooms have fridge and TV and there are hot water bathrooms; the best place to stay at present, and good value too. **B-D** *Buri Ram*, 148 Niwat Rd, T612504, F612147. Some a/c, 81 rooms in this plain hotel which has had a minor facelift, raising it from barely passable to passable. While it looks pretty dead, the place is reasonably clean and good value too. **C** *Thepnakorn*, Mu 3, Isan Rd (on edge of town, off continuation of Jira Rd), T613400, F613400. Reasonable, mid-range hotel. **C-D** *Grand*, 137 Niwat

Sleeping
■ *on map*
Price codes:
see inside front cover

The Northeastern Region

Rd, T611089. Some a/c, plain slab of a hotel with bare rooms, close to the railway station, a/c rooms with hot water – and a complimentary contraceptive. **C-D** *Thai*, 38/1 Romburi Rd, T611112, F612461. Some a/c, the best of the hotels in the town centre (which isn't, admittedly, saying much), all rooms with hot water, clean but plain and a safe bet given the limited competition in this category. Note that some rooms have no windows. **E** *Pracha Samakhi Hotel*, 147/9 Suthornthep Rd, T611198. 18 very basic rooms. **E-F** *Chai Charoen*, 114-116 Niwat Rd, T611559. No English sign identifies this place, directly outside railway station on the right, fan rooms with attached bath. Basic, but good value. **E-F** *Niwas*, 89/10-12 Niwat Rd, T611640. A dubious house of ill repute, with slothful management and an army of cockroaches.

Eating
■ *on map*
Price categories:
see inside front cover

Buri Ram is famous for its fiery papaya pok pok salad, similar to the more widely available Isan dish, somtam.

Mid-range *Phim Phit*, Thani Rd. A/c seafood restaurant selling freshwater and seawater fish, crabs and prawns; the freshwater fish is excellent. *Mr Suki*, off Thani Rd. Specializes in DIY suki dishes; however, the ambience is plastic and contrived and the food overpriced. **Cheap** *Beer House*, Romburi Rd. Open air bar and restaurant specializing in ice-cold beer and chargrilled seafood. Recommended. *Ploi*, Romburi Rd. Ice-creams, cakes and coffee in a/c coffee shop. **Seriously cheap** *Lung Chaan Restaurant*, Romburi Rd (near *Thai Hotel*). Excellent cheap Thai/Chinese food, with superb *kwaytio* and other simple dishes. *Nong Kai Restaurant*, Romburi Rd (south end). Pleasant shady open-air noodle house with excellent noodle soup specialities.

Festivals
Nov *Annual boat races at Satuk*, 40 km north of Buri Ram. The races take place on the Mun River, with contestants coming from all over Thailand to compete. The event opens with an elephant parade and festivities, beauty pageants and dancing fill the evenings. **Dec** *Kite festival* is held early in the month at Huai Chorakee Mak Reservoir, just south of Buri Ram. Processions of vehicles decorated with kites and a beauty pageant.

Buri Ram

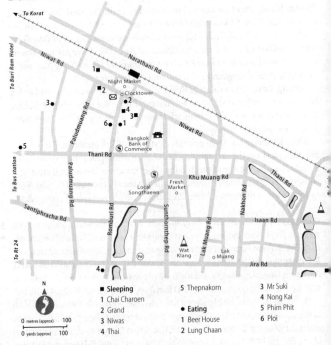

■ **Sleeping**	5 Thepnakorn	3 Mr Suki
1 Chai Charoen		4 Nong Kai
2 Grand	● **Eating**	5 Phim Phit
3 Niwas	1 Beer House	6 Ploi
4 Thai	2 Lung Chaan	

0 metres (approx) 100
0 yards (approx) 100

Handicrafts Buri Ram is known for silk and cotton cloth woven in Amphoe (district) **Shopping**
Phuttaisong and Amphoe Napho. Cloth available from shops on Romburi and Thani
roads. Distinctive Isan crafts including *matmii* ikat cloth and woven baskets.

Local Bus: pink town buses criss-cross the town, ฿5, any distance. **Tuk-tuks**: ฿10-20 **Transport**
around town. **Songthaew**: the terminal is near the market off Sriphet Rd.   *410 km to Bangkok*

Long distance Air: a new airport has recently opened in Buri Ram. Currently there
are 5 flights a week on Thai to Bangkok. **Train**: the station is at the end of Romburi Rd,
near the centre of town, connections with Bangkok's Hualamphong station and all
stops between Bangkok and Ubon Ratchathani. It's better to take the train as the rail
route is much more direct between Buri Ram and either Korat or Ubon. **Bus**: the station is on the east side of town off Bulamduan and Thani roads. Regular a/c and
non-a/c, connections with Bangkok's new Northeastern bus terminal (6½ hrs) and
with Pattaya, Chantaburi and Trat, as well as many towns in the Northeast including
Khon Kaen, Mahasarakham, Ubon, Si Saket and Surin.

Banks *Bangkok Bank of Commerce*, corner of Thani and Romburi roads. *Thai Farmers*, 132 **Directory**
Soonthouthep Rd. **Communications** Post Office: intersection of Romburi and Niwat roads, by
the railway station. Card phones available.

Surin   สุรินทร์

Surin is a silk-producing town, best known for its **Elephant round-up** held in the *Phone code: 045*
third week of November at the **Surin Sports Park**. The forested Thai/Cambodian *Colour map 2, grid C4*
border has long been the domain of a tribe of elephant catchers called the Suay. At *Population: 45,000*
the beginning of this century there were 100,000 domesticated elephants in Thai-
land, and the Suay were much in demand looking after the working population
and catching wild elephants. With the advent of other forms of transport the need
for elephants declined, and today there are only about 4,000 working elephants.
Contact the TAT in Bangkok for full information on the festival, see page 83.

During the festival, 40,000 people come to watch the Suay practise their
skills with at least 200 elephants. They take part in parades and mock battles.
There are also demonstrations of Thai dance and an unusual game of soccer
played by elephants and their mahouts. For the rest of the year Surin becomes a
backwater: the only reason to stay here is to visit the numerous Khmer temples
that are to be found in this south portion of the Northeast. The **Surin Museum**
on Chitbamrung Road displays many of the accessories used by the Suay to
capture wild elephants, including the magical talismen that are worn to protect
men from injury. ■ *Wed-Sun*.

Wooden shophouses are still to be found scattered around town. The
shophouse – shop-cum-garage on the ground floor, residential on the first floor –
is the most popular type of building in Thailand, and in many other parts of Southeast Asia. It is highly flexible and economical, as it combines home and business in
one structure. Even buildings constructed today follow the shophouse format.
One area where these traditional shophouses are to be found is in Surin's small
Chinatown, off Thetsabarn 1 Road. There is also a small Chinese temple here:
Mun Borisurin Samatkhi Kuson. A bustling **morning market** can be found
between Thetsabarn and Krungsi-Nai roads and a very small museum at the south
edge of town on Chitbamrung Road ■ *0830-1630 Mon-Fri*.

Ban Tha Klang is a settlement of Suay – the 'tribe' who tame and train ele- **Excursions**
phants – 58 km north of town. The Suay are said to have filtered into Thailand *See map on page 380*
from central Asia during the ninth and 10th centuries, and became the first *for location of the*
following sites

The Northeastern Region

people of the area to tame elephants for human use. The village is sometimes called Elephant Village because of the close association that the population have with the art and science of capturing and training pachyderms. Out of the official elephant round-up festival period, it is sometimes possible to see training in progress here. It is best to come here in the weeks just prior to the official round-up, when the villagers are intensively preparing for the festival. ■ *Getting there: by hourly bus from the terminal in town, 2 hrs.*

Prasat Sikhoraphum (aka Prasat Ban Ra-ngaeng) can be found at the 34 km marker from Surin to Si Saket, Route 226. Four small prangs sit on a laterite base, surrounding a larger central prang. A 12th-century Khmer temple, Sikhoraphum began life as a Hindu shrine. Later, during the 16th century, it was converted into a Lao Buddhist temple, which explains its hybrid architecture. Sadly, the Fine Arts Department seems to be renovating the complex in a rather heavy-handed manner. Even so, the central prang retains some beautiful carvings on the lintels (dancing Siva) and door jambs (door guardians and floral designs). The layout of the temple is unusual: four brick towers surrounded by a moat enclose a central, taller, prang. This is reminiscent of Pre Rup and Angkor Wat in Cambodia. ■ ฿20. *Getting there: by local bus going to Si Saket.*

Prasat Sa Kamphaeng Noi, another Khmer site, lies east of Sikhoraphum, 94 km from Surin on Route 2084 and 9 km before Si Saket. The ruins are in the compound of an active wat and consist of the remains of a Khmer stupa and library, surrounded by a laterite wall. Stylistically, it belongs to Jayavarman VII's reign (12th century), and it is thought that it may have been a healing house (*arokhaya sala*). It has been postulated that Jayavarman VII's building programme was so extensive that many structures were technically poorly built, explaining why some have collapsed. Prasat Sa Kamphaeng Noi falls into this category, and there is a visible difference in the quality of the stonework and masonry between here and the sister sanctuary of Prasat Sa Kamphaeng Yai (see below). The hospital is built of laterite and sandstone (for the *gopuras*) and there is a ritual laterite-lined bathing pool just outside the sanctuary. Also here, built on the Khmer *baray* (reservoir), is a modern naga bridge leading to a sala. It is not worth a major detour, but could be included in a tour of the Khmer temples of the area. ■ *Getting there: by local bus running to Si Saket; get off at the Km 94 marker, 9 km from Si Saket.*

Prasat Sa Kamphaeng Yai are more extensive Khmer ruins than Noi (above), and are also to be found in the compound of a wat. The discovery of artefacts, such as an accomplished bronze guardian figure, indicate that this was an important site. They lie 500 m off Route 226, just after crossing the railway line at the Km 74 marker. This shrine is said to have been built in the 11th century as a sanctuary probably dedicated to Siva, but was converted into a Buddhist temple in the 13th century. As a consequence, the fine carvings on

· ·

Surin place names

Ban Tha Klang
บ้านท่ากลาง

Chanrom
จันทร์รมย์

Khawao Sinrin
บ้านเขว้าสินรินทร์

Prasat Pluang
ปราสาทหินบ้านพลวง

Prasat Sa Kamphaeng Noi
ปราสาทหินวัดสระกำแพงน้อย

Prasat Sa Kamphaeng Yai
ปราสาทหินวัดสระกำแพงใหญ่

Prasat Sikhoraphum
ปราสาทศีขรภูมิ

Prasat Ta Muan Thom
ปราสาทตาเหมือนธม

the sandstone lintels and pediments show a mixture of religious subjects. An enormous gallery of laterite blocks, with a passageway and pierced by gopuras at the four cardinal points, surrounds the central stupas. The 'windows' in the gallery are stylistically similar to those at Phanom Rung and Prasat Phra Viharn, supporting the view that it was built in the early 11th century. These retain some beautiful carvings but have been rather unsympathetically restored, using modern angular bricks, which fail to blend in with the original laterite. The style of carving varies over the temple, indicating a long-term sequence of construction. ■ *Getting there: local bus going to Si Saket.*

Prasat Pluang is a well restored, neat prasat, 30 km south of Surin. Leave Surin on Route 214 and 2 km beyond the town of Prasat, after crossing Route 24, turn left. The monument is 500 m off the main road and is signposted. The prasat is raised up on a high laterite base. It is built in Baphuon style, and was probably constructed during the latter part of the 11th century. Excavations by the Fine Arts Department, which began in the 1970s, indicate that the temple was never completed. Two unfinished naga cornices were unearthed during excavations. Fine carvings adorn three of its four faces. On the east pediment, Krishna lifts the Wathana bull by the horns. ■ *0730-1800 Mon-Sun, ฿20. Getting there: catch a bus to Prasat. From the market place in Prasat, take a songthaew to Pluang village.*

Prasat Ta Muan Tot and **Prasat Ta Muan** lie just 100 m apart in Kab Choeng District, Surin Province, about 60 km due south of town on the Thai-Cambodian border. The site has only recently been opened to visitors; its position on the border made it of strategic value to the warring factions in Cambodia. Built in the 11th century during the reign of Khmer King Jayavarman VII, the prasats are situated on the road that linked Angkor in Cambodia with Phimai. These were once fine and extensive complexes, although they have been extensively damaged in recent years – largely during a period of occupation by Khmer Rouge troops. There are still said to be land mines in the area (these may have since been cleared), so it is best to stick to well-trodden paths. Prasat Ta Muan Tot was built as a hospital to minister to weary and sick travellers while Prasat Ta Muan was a chapel. There is an impressive 30 m-long staircase leading down into Cambodian territory, a central sanctuary, and associated minor prangs and buildings. This was clearly a major site, although archaeological work will need to continue for several more years before an idea of its extent is appreciated. It is worthwhile combining a trip here to a visit to Phnom Rung or Muang Tam, because it gives an excellent sense of how the latter ruins have been renovated. ■ *Getting there: not currently possible on public transport. However, the site is close to Phnom Rung and Muang Tam and could be included in a tour (see below) of these better known Khmer sites. Alternatively, hire a car or songthaew.*

Prasat Phra Viharn is a long excursion from Surin, but possible in a day on public transport. See page 410 for details on the site. ■ *Getting there: catch an early train or bus to Si Saket. From the bus station in Si Saket take a local bus to Kantharalak, and make it known you wish to go to Prasat Phra Viharn. The bus will stop at the Kantharalak before continuing on towards Phum Saron. The driver should drop you off at the intersection a few kilometres before reaching Phum Saron. From here it is necessary to hitch or take a motorcycle taxi. Alternatively, go on a tour (see Tours below) or hire a car or songthaew.*

Two silk-weaving villages lie within easy reach of Surin. Matmii silk and cotton ikat is made (see page 433) at **Khawao Sinrin**, 14 km north of town on Route 214 and at **Chanrom**, 9 km to the east on Route 2077. Villagers at Ban Khawao Sinrin also make silverware. ■ *Getting there: songthaews run to both villages from the market area off Thetsabarn 3 Rd (by the clock tower), but only in the mornings. However, songthaews can be hired for the journey.*

The superb Khmer sanctuary of **Phnom Rung** can be visited from there (see page 387). ■ *Getting there: the sanctuary is 83 km away, take bus no 274 to Ban Tako. From here either take a motorbike taxi (฿100 – worth it because they wait and then bring you back), or a songthaew to the Phanom Rung Resort at the foot of the hill (฿10); from the resort it is a 3 km walk, or hitch a lift.*

Tours

The Phetkasem Hotel organizes day trips and overnight tours to the Khmer monuments of the area, as well as to local silk weaving and Suay elephant training villages. *Mr Pirom* (see hotels) organizes tours to the temples at weekends, as well as tours of silk weaving villages in the area. Highly recommended.

Sleeping
■ *on map*
Price codes:
see inside front cover

During the Round-up, hotels in Surin become booked up & expensive

A *Tharin*, 60 Sirirat Rd, T514281, F511580. A/c, restaurant, pool, snooker and nightclubs, opened 1991, best in town, large high-rise hotel with over 200 rooms, one of the most comfortable places to stay in the Northeast, close to bus station on northeast side of town. **B-C** *Phetkasem*, 104 Chitbamrung Rd, T511274, F514041. A/c, restaurant, pool, 5-storey hotel with 162 rooms, rooms are good value, but now a little dated and frayed around the edges, 30% discounts available during the off-season. **C-D** *Memorial*, 646 Lak Muang Rd, T511288. Some a/c, restaurant, snooker hall. **C-D** *New Hotel*, 22 Tanasarn Rd, T511341, F511971. Some a/c, large hotel of 100 rooms with worn and dirty prison-like corridors, but rooms are suprisingly clean, no hot water and bolshy management, close to train station, hardly 'new'. **D-E** *Amarin*, 103 Thetsabarn 1 Rd, T511112. Large, basic hotel, friendly but no hot water, no character, rooms can be grubby. **D-E** *Saeng Thong*, 279-281 Tanasarn Rd, T512099. Some a/c, 125 rooms. **E-F** *Pirom's Guesthouse*, 242 Krungsi-Nai Rd. Basic rooms in a wooden house backing onto a small lake (mosquitoes a problem), but Mr Pirom is a mine of information and very friendly,

Surin

and the guesthouse is clean and well run. Mr Pirom will organize trips to Khmer sites and elsewhere at the weekends, the food is perhaps not as good value as the rooms, but nonetheless it is recommended. The construction of Mr Pirom's new guesthouse to the north of the railway line, about 1 km from the station, should now be completed. It promises to be a mock-Scandinavian affair, but if his current establishment is anything to go by, it should be well run and friendly. **E-F** *Thanachai*, 14 Thetsabarn 1 Rd, T511002. Poor and rather squalid rooms, the only plus point is the price.

Cheap *Samrap Ton Khruang*, Tat Mai Lang Rd. Good Thai and Lao food, and mediocre European, in sophisticated a/c restaurant, attractive décor and well run, good value for the ambience. Recommended. *Wai Waan*, Sanit Nikhom Rd. Steaks, pizzas and burgers in dark a/c bar-like atmosphere, also some average Thai food available. *Cocaa*, Soi Thetsabarn 2 Rd. This simple restaurant has Thai and Chinese dishes, with some excellent seafood. Recommended. **Seriously cheap** *Phailin Restaurant*, 174 Tanasarn Rd. Open-air restaurant with excellent cheap Thai and Lao food. **Foodstalls** Around the train station in the evening. The night market is also highly recommended; it has a wide range of food, good prices, great atmosphere.

Eating
● *on map*
Price categories:
see inside front cover

Bowling *Phetkasem Bowl*, near the *Phetkasem Hotel*, 104 Chitbamrung Rd. **Golf** The *Rim Khong* golf driving range is 2 km west of town on Route 226 towards Burram, just before the intersection with Route 214.

Sport

Nov *Elephant Round-up* (third week), see above.

Festivals

Silk Surin province is one of the centres of silk production in the Northeast, with villages in the area producing fine *matmii* silk and cotton ikat cloth (see page 433). See Excursions above on how to visit silk-weaving villages. There are a number of shops on Chitbamrung Rd near the bus station, eg *Surinat*, 361-363 Chitbamrung Rd, and *Nong Ying* (close to *Phetkasem Hotel*). In the same area are numerous tailors. There are also 2 shops selling silk and cotton cloth near the *Phetkasem Hotel*, *Net Craft* and *Mai Surin*. **Silverware** Silverware is also a traditional product of the area and many shops selling cloth also have small displays of local silverware. **Department stores** *Phetkasem Department Store*, Thetsabarn 1 Rd. *Surin Plaza*, large new a/c department store with restaurant and coffee bar and wide array of expensive imported goods.

Shopping

Local Bicycles: for hire from *Pirom's Guesthouse* (see Sleeping above), ฿30 per day. **Songthaews** to surrounding villages leave from the market area off Thetsabarn 3 Rd (near the clock tower), mostly in the morning. Drivers will also charter their vehicles out – expect to pay about ฿500 per day. Vehicles can be rented through the *Tharin Hotel*.

Transport
454 km to Bangkok,
260 km to Korat

Long distance Train: the station is at the north end of Tanasarn Rd, with a statue of 3 elephants outside. Regular connections with Bangkok's Hualamphong station (8 hrs), stops en route between Ubon and Bangkok. The overnight a/c express leaves Bangkok at 2100 and arrives in Surin at 0424. **NB** Tickets must be booked 2 weeks in advance for travel during Nov when the Elephant Round-up is under way. The TAT organize a special train during this period. **Bus**: the station is off Chitbamrung Rd. Regular a/c and non-a/c connections with Bangkok's new Northeastern bus terminal (6-7 hrs). Special a/c buses are laid on by tour companies and major hotels for the Elephant Round-up. Regular connections with Korat, Ubon and from other Northeastern towns, and also with Chiang Mai. A/c tour buses to Bangkok leave from the offices of Kitikarn Ratchasima near the Surin Plaza.

Banks *Thai Farmers*, 353 Tanasarn Rd. **Communications** Post Office: corner of Tanasarn and Thetsabarn 1 roads. **Medical services** Hospital: T511757. **Useful addresses** Police: Lak Muang Rd, T511007.

Directory

Si Saket ศรีสะเกษ

Phone code: 045
Colour map 2, grid C5
Population: 38,000

Si Saket is a good base from which to visit the lesser-known Khmer sites in the Lower Northeast (see page 382). The town is a small provincial capital with little to recommend it, except that it's quiet and almost no one comes here (which is a good enough reason to mosey on down). There is a daily **market** off Khukhan Road, down Chaisawat Road.

Excursions

Wat Prasat Sa Kamphaeng Noi (see page 402) is just over 8 km west of Si Saket, on Route 2084. ■ *Getting there: take a local bus from the bor kor sor station towards Surin and get off just after the 8 km marker; the site is signposted.*

Wat Prasat Sa Kamphaeng Yai (see page 402) is located in Ban (village) Sa Kamphaeng Yai on Route 226, about 40 km from Si Saket. ■ *Getting there: take a local bus running towards Surin.*

Prasat Sikhoraphum (see page 402) is located on Route 266, 34 km before reaching Surin and 69 km from Si Saket. ■ *Getting there: take a local bus running towards Surin.*

Prasat Phra Viharn lies just over the border in Cambodia and is also accessible as a day trip from Si Saket on public transport. See page 410 for details on the site. ■ *Getting there: from the bus station, take an early local bus to Kantharalak, and make it known you wish to go to Prasat Phra Viharn. The bus will stop at Kantharalak before continuing on towards Phum Saron. The driver should drop you off at the intersection a few kilometres before reaching Phum Saron. From here it is necessary to hitch or take a motorcycle taxi. Alternatively, hire a car for the day (ask at the Kessiri Hotel).*

Sleeping
■ *on map*
Price codes:
see inside front cover

B-C *Kessiri Hotel*, 1102-5 Khukhan Rd, T614007, F614008. A/c restaurant, pool, newish hotel which opened in 1994, surprisingly luxurious for a small town with 11th floor roof-top pool (although we understand that this is not even open to guests of the hotel!), satellite TV in lobby (not in rooms), coffee shop serving excellent food, with starched linen, marble foyer, spotless, co-operative and very friendly staff. Just a shame it isn't being maintained. Still a good place to base yourself. **C-E** *Phromphiman*, 849/1 Lak Muang Rd, T612677. Some a/c, not far from the railway line on the west side of town, unremarkable, comfortable enough. **D-E** *Si Saket Hotel*, 384/5 Si Saket Rd, T611846. Some a/c, the best budget hotel within easy reach of the railway station, although that is not much of a recommendation given the

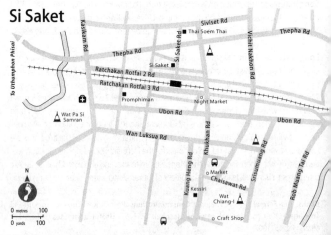

Si Saket

To Uthumphon Phisai

Kasikam Rd · Siviset Rd · Thai Soem Thai · Si Saket Rd · Vichit Nakhon Rd · Thepha Rd · Thepha Rd · Si Saket · Ratchakan Rotfai 2 Rd · Ratchakan Rotfai 3 Rd · Promphiman · Night Market · Ubon Rd · Ubon Rd · Wat Pa Si Samran · Wan Luksua Rd · Khukhan Rd · Srisumuang Rd · Rob Muang Tai Rd · Kuang Heng Rd · Market · Chaisawat Rd · Kessiri · Wat Chiang-I · Craft Shop

N

0 metres 100
0 yards 100

competition. **E** *Thai Soem Thai*, Si Saket Rd, T611458. 32 fan rooms in this featureless hotel, patronized mostly by truckers and travelling salesmen.

There is a collection of good Lao/Chinese/Thai restaurants strung out along Khukhan Rd. **Cheap** *Mr Hagen*, Ubon Rd. Small a/c restaurant serving a range of Western dishes; a pleasant stop-off and foot-rest. **Foodstalls** The night market off Ratchakan Rotfai 3 Rd is the best place for stall food.

Eating

Crafts There is a reasonable craft shop on a lane running off Khukhan Rd to the southeast of the *Kessiri Hotel* (see map), selling a range of products including Isan axe pillows.

Shopping

Train The station is in the centre of town on Kaanrotfai Rd. Regular connections with Bangkok's Hualamphong station and stations en route between Bangkok and Ubon. **Bus** The terminal (*bor kor sor*) is on the south side of town off Khukhan Rd. Regular connections with Bangkok's new Northeastern bus terminal (8-9 hrs) and with other Northeastern centres.

Transport
571 km to Bangkok

Banks *Thai Farmers Bank*, 1492/4 Khukhan Rd. **Communications** Post Office: Chaisawat Rd.

Directory

Ubon Ratchathani   อุบลราชธานี

The 'Royal city of the Lotus' is an important provincial capital on the Mun River. Like a number of other towns in the Northeast, Ubon was a US Airforce base during the Vietnam War and as a result houses a good selection of Western-style hotels, as well as bars and massage parlours. The money that filtered into the town during the war meant that it became one of the richest in the region: this can still be seen reflected in the impressive, although slowly decaying, public buildings. Like Udon Thani and Korat, there is still a small community of ex-GIs who have married local women and are living out their days in this corner of Thailand. When Bangkok and its surrounds were booming, some of the wealth filtered back to the Northeast and can still be seen in cities like Ubon: extravagant parties, Mercedes cars and lavish restaurants.

Phone code: 045
Colour map 2, grid C5
Population: 110,000

Ins and outs

The airport is a longish walk from the city centre. There are daily connections with Bangkok. However, most people arrive in Ubon by bus. There are frequent buses to Bangkok, around 8 hrs. The main bus terminal is north of town (too far to walk), but many tour buses drop off in the city centre. There are also connections with many other regional centres. Ubon's train station is south of town in Warin Chamrap. Connections with Bangkok and stops along the southern northeastern track. It is also possible to enter Laos from Ubon, via Chongmek.

Getting there
See also Transport,
page 415

Ubon is a large town. The TAT provide a map marking city bus routes. There are also lots of saamlors and tuk-tuks, as well as cars and motorbikes for hire.

Getting around

TAT, 264/1 Khuan Thani Rd (facing the Srikamol Hotel), T243770. Open Mon-Sun, 0830-1630. Provides a map of Ubon with bus routes and other handouts; a useful first stop, though not particularly switched on. Areas of responsibility are Ubon Ratchathani, Si Saket and Yasothon.

Tourist offices

The Northeastern Region

Sights

Museum There is a good archaeological, historical and cultural museum (the Ubon branch of the National Museum in Bangkok) on Khuan Thani Road. It is housed in a *panya*-style building, erected in 1918 as a palace for King Vajiravudh (Rama VI). The collection includes prehistoric artefacts collected in the province, as well as pieces from the historic period, including Khmer artefacts, and cultural pieces such as local textiles and musical instruments. The star of the collection is a large, bronze Dong-son drum. ■ *0900-1600 Wed-Sun, ₿30.*

Wat Phrathat Nong Bua This wat is 500 m west off Chayangkun Road travelling north to Nakhon Phanom, not far past the army base. It is a large white angular chedi built in 1957 to celebrate the 2,500th anniversary of the death of the Lord Buddha. It is said to be a copy of the Mahabodhi stupa in Bodhgaya, India. It is certainly unusual in the Thai context. Jataka reliefs and cloaked standing Buddhas in various stances are depicted on the outside of the chedi. ■ *Take town bus No 2 or 3, or go by tuk-tuk.*

Wat Thungsrimuang On Luang Road and named after the field (or *thung*) by the provincial hall, Wat Thungsrimuang is a short walk from the TAT office. It is notable for its red-stained wooden *hor trai* (or library) on stilts, in the middle of a stagnant pond. The library contains Buddhist texts and rare examples of Isan literature, but is usually locked. The monastery was built during the reign of Rama III (1824-51) and there is a fine late Ayutthayan-style bot, graciously decaying. The bot features murals depicting Northeastern country life and episodes from the life of the Buddha, but is usually firmly locked. The viharn, built more recently, contains garish and rather crude murals, and is usually open. Such is life.

Wat Supattanaram At the west end of Phromathep Road, Wat Supattanaram is pleasantly situated overlooking the Mun River. It was built in 1853 and supports monks of the Dharmayuthi sect. It is significant for its collection of lintels which surround the bot, commemorating the dead. One of the sandstone lintels is Khmer and is said to date from the seventh century. Also here is a massive, suspended wooden gong, said to be the largest in the country.

Hat Wat Tai This large sandbank in the middle of the Mun River is linked by a rope foot-bridge to Phonpaen Road. The residents of Ubon come here for picnics during the low water summer months, between March and May. Foodstalls set up in the evening and on weekends and it is possible to swim here. Take bus No 1, then walk south along Phonpaen Road.

There is a bustling **fruit and vegetable market** between the river and Phromathep Road, east of the bridge.

• •

Ubon Ratchathani place names

Kaeng Sapu	Sao Chaliang
แก่งสะพือ	**เสาเฉลียง**
Kaeng Tana National Park	Wat Pa Na Na Chat
อุทยานแห่งชาติแก่งตะนะ	**วัดป่านานาชาติ**
Pha Taem	Wat Phrathat Nong Bua
ผาแต้ม	**วัดพระธาตุหนองบัว**
Prasat Khao Phra Viharn	Wat Thungsrimuang
ปราสาทเขาพระวิหาร	**วัดทุ่งศรีเมือง**

Excursions

This busy town is 3 km south of Ubon over the Mun River. The main reasons **Warin Chamrap**
to come here are either to catch a public bus from one of the two bus terminals
in the town or to visit the train station. However, in so far as development has
been concentrated in Ubon, Warin still possesses some architectural charm
including a number of gently decaying wood, brick and stucco shophouses.
There is also a good mixed market near the main bus station (the *bor kor sor*).
■ *Getting there: town bus Nos 1, 2, 3, 6 and 7 all link Warin with Ubon.*

A series of rapids on the Mun River, 1 km outside the district town of **Kaeng Sapu**
Phibunmangsahan and about 45 km from Ubon, Kaeng Sapu do not compare
with the rapids at Kaeng Tana National Park (see below), but are much easier
to reach. Inner tubes can be hired to float downriver and there is a small market
with foodstalls and poor quality handicrafts. **Wat Sarakaew** is close by, with a
viharn showing some colonial influences. ■ *Getting there: take town bus Nos 1,*
3 or 6 to Warin Chamrap. From here buses run regularly to Phibunmangsahan, 1
hr. The rapids are 1 km from town; either walk or take a saamlor.

This is a sandstone cliff overlooking the Mekong River, which at this point cuts **Pha Taem**
through a wide and deep gorge, in Khong Chiam district, 98 km from Ubon *Views from this clifftop*
(along Route 2112 and then onto Route 2368). Ochre prehistoric paintings, *across the Mekong River*
about 3,000 years old, of figures, turtles, elephants, fish and geometric forms *to Laos are spectacular*
stretch for some 400 m along a cliff set high above the Mekong. A trail leads
down and then along the face of the cliff, past three groups of paintings now
protected (or, as the sign puts it, 'decidedly fenced') by rather unsightly barbed
wire. Two viewing towers allow the images to be viewed at eye level.

Two kilometres before the turn off for Pha Taem is **Sao Chaliang**, an area of
strange, heavily eroded sandstone rock formations. ■ *Getting there: it's rather*
difficult to reach on public transport. First take an Ubon town bus to Warin
Chamrap (No 1, 3 or 6), and from there to Khong Chiam via Phibun Mangsahan
(where accommodation is available, see below). There are also some direct buses to
Khong Chiam from Ubon. From Khong Chiam charter a tuk-tuk for the last 20 km
to the cliff (฿150 return). Chongmek Travellers *and* Takerng Tour *organize boat*
trips there (see Tours below), or hire a motorbike or car (see Transport below).

This national park, on the Mun River, lies about 75 km to the east of Ubon off **Kaeng Tana**
Route 217, where the park office is located. Alternatively, the park can be **National Park**
reached via Route 2222 which affords excellent views of the Kaeng Tana, a
series of rapids 2 km off Route 2222. The park covers 8,000 ha and was gazetted

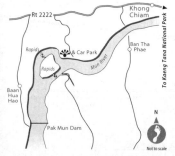

Kaeng Tana Rapids

in 1981. The Kaeng Tana – the
Tana rapids – after which the
park is named, are found at a
point where the Mun River
squeezes through a rocky outcrop before flowing into the
Mekong. In the dry season the
rocks present an almost lunar
landscape of giant ossified bones,
jumbled together into a heap of
eroded boulders. It is possible to
chicken leap across the river to
midstream. The controversial
Pak Mun Dam, completed in

The Northeastern Region

1994 and designed to generate hydropower and irrigate land, can be seen from the rapids. During the dry season it is possible to swim here, although the current is usually too strong for safe bathing in the wet season. Bungalow accommodation available or in Khong Chiam (see page 416). ■ *Getting there: easiest on a tour (see Tours below) or by private car/motorcycle (see Transport below). There is no easy way to reach the rapids on public transport. However, the nearest town is Khong Chiam. To get to Khong Chiam take town bus Nos 1, 3 or 6 to Warin Chamrap. From Warin, buses run to Khong Chiam, and from there motorcycle taxis may be available to Kaeng Tana.*

Prasat Khao Phra Viharn

A magnificent Khmer sanctuary, in one of the most spectacular positions of any monument in SE Asia

The 'Holy Monastery' of Prasat Khao Phra Viharn, known in Cambodian as *Preah Vihear*, lies south of Ubon, perched on a 500 m-high escarpment at the end of Route 221. It lies close to the border with Cambodia and there has been some discussion as to which side of the border it belongs; 30 years ago the international court in The Hague ruled that it lay inside Cambodian territory. However, from time to time the Thai authorities have apparently tried to challenge this ruling. Thai maps, for example, often mark the sanctuary as lying within Thai territory. In 1992 it opened to tourists for the first time for a number of years, with access from the Thai side of the border. However, in 1993 the Khmer Rouge took the temple and surrounding area, and it was not until 1998 that Cambodian government forces regained control. In August 1998 the wat was opened to tourists on a trial basis, under a bilateral agreement between the Thai and Cambodian armies. The Thai army has cleared a path through the mines and barbed wire to the Cambodian border. Admission details are provided below, but check with the TAT office in Ubon, Korat or in Bangkok before making the 150 km journey from Ubon (or from Surin or Si Saket, which are also a day's drive away). As Prasat Phra Viharn becomes more accessible, it is sure to become a required stop on any tour of the Northeast's Khmer heritage.

Built about 100 years before Angkor, it occupies a truly magnificent position at the top of a steep escarpment and overlooks the Khmer Rouge- controlled jungle of Cambodia. A hilltop location – whenever possible – was deemed important for all Khmer sanctuaries. In the case of Prasat Phra Viharn it was especially important, as this shrine was dedicated to Siva – the god whose abode was Mount Kailasa. The temple is orientated north-south along the escarpment, with a sheer drop on one side of 500 m to the Cambodian jungle below. In total, the walkways, courtyards and gates stretch 850 m along the escarpment, climbing 120 m in the process. In places the stairs are cut from the rock itself; elsewhere, they have been assembled from rock quarried and then

Prasat Khao Phra Viharn

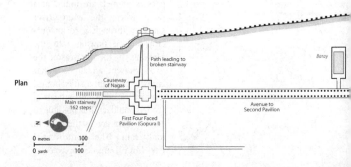

Elevation

Plan

carted to the site. Nagas carved from sandstone line the route upwards; stylistically they belong to the 11th century. In total, there are five *gopuras* or gateways, numbered I to V from the sanctuary outwards. Multiple nagas, kalas and kirtamukhas decorate these gateways and the balustrades, pediments and pillars that link them. At the final gateway, Gopura I, the pathway enters into a courtyard with a ruined prang within. The courtyard was encircled by a gallery, still intact on the east and west sides. Doors from here lead to two annexes – probably used for ritual purposes.

When Prasat Phra Viharn was built is not certain. Much seems to be linked to King Suryavarman I (1002-50), and it has been hypothesized that this was his personal temple. But there are also inscriptions from the reign of King Suryavarman II (1113-50), and he certainly seems to have commissioned parts of the second courtyard (between Gopuras I and II). With the death of Suryavarman II, Prasat Phra Viharn appears to have been abandoned and fell into disrepair. As Smitthi Siribhadra and Elizabeth Moore observe in their book *Palaces of the Gods*, it is difficult to imagine today the life and colour that filled Prasat Phra Viharn and the other Khmer temples: 'Ritual feasts and offerings included peacock feather fans with gold handles, rings with nine jewels, and golden bowls. The life of the court was filled with colour and music, for the temple also required offerings of dancers, flower receptacles, sacred cloths, incense and candles'. **NB** take your passport along in case officials at the border checkpoint want to see it. A stone stairway leads upwards through several sanctuaries to a shrine dedicated to Siva on the summit. The carvings are finely executed and particularly well preserved. Though the temple is on Cambodian territory, its position on the edge of an escarpment means that it is most easily approached from Thai territory. The site was closed between 1994 and 1996 due to fighting between the Khmer Rouge and forces of the State of Cambodia. However, it opened again at the end of December 1998, and with the effective demise of the Khmer Rouge as a fighting force should remain so. Nonetheless, check with the TAT office in Ubon, Korat or in Bangkok before leaving. ■ *0800-1530 Mon-Sun, ฿100. Getting there is difficult; it is quickest to catch a bus towards Kantharalak, halfway along Route 221 to the site, getting off at Phum Saron (tell the driver where you are going). From here it is necessary to hitch or take a motorcycle taxi. There are occasional songthaews travelling the road, but they don't always go the whole way, or hire a motorbike or car (see Local transport). There is a ฿100 crossing fee and then a new road, lined with shops, leads to the temple itself.*

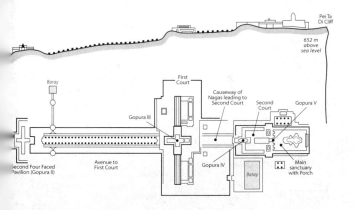

**Wat Pa
Na Na Chart** This is a forest wat 14 km from Ubon, on Route 226 towards Surin. The wat is a popular meditation retreat for *farangs* interested in Buddhism. The abbot is Canadian and most of the monks are non-Thais. English is the language of communication and both men and women are welcomed. ■ *Getting there: by local bus or songthaew running towards Surin from the station in Warin Chamrap to the south of town, over the Mun River. Get to Warin Chamrap by town buses nos 1, 2 or 6.*

Ubon Ratchathani

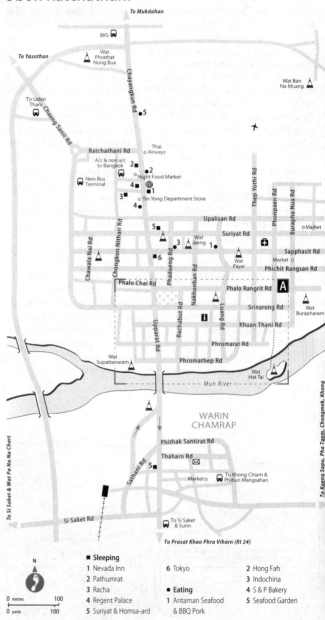

■ **Sleeping**
1 Nevada Inn
2 Pathumrat
3 Racha
4 Regent Palace
5 Suriyat & Homsa-ard

6 Tokyo

● **Eating**
1 Antaman Seafood
& BBQ Pork

2 Hong Fah
3 Indochina
4 S & P Bakery
5 Seafood Garden

N

0 metres 100
0 yards 100

Chongmek is a border town east of Ubon; see page 416 for details on negotiating the border. While most people are likely to come here in order to enter Laos, it is an interesting spot to visit in itself. There is a large Thai-Lao market selling food (including baguettes), baskets, clothes and basic manufactured goods, as well as some 'antiques' and wild animal products from Laos. It is also an important trans-shipment point for logs from Laos; a timber yard faces the market. Even those without entry visas for Laos are allowed to cross the Thai border and mosey around the market and duty-free shop in no man's land, between the two immigration posts. ■ *Getting there: catch town buses nos 1, 3 or 6 from Ubon Ratchathani to Warin Chamrap and then take a second bus from the station in Warin Chamrap (see map) to Phibun Mangsahan, 1 hr, about 45 km. From Phibun Mangsahan there are converted trucks (large songthaews) to Chongmek, 44 km away (1½ hrs).*

Takerng Tour organizes tours to the Kaeng Tana Rapids and Pha Taem (approximately ฿1,000 per person). *Chongmek Travellers* organize tours along the Mekong River, taking in a Blu village and the Pha Taem cave paintings, with a night in a fishing village. ฿1,340 per person, minimum three people for trip. Tours to Prasat Phra Viharn are also now available from companies in Ubon, assuming it is open; see above for the latest information. This also goes for the State Railways of Thailand, who offer a weekend trip to Prasat Phra Viharn leaving at 0925 on Saturday and returning 0535 on Monday, including accommodation in Ubon and all transport, T2256964, or visit the advance booking office at Hualamphong Station, Bangkok.

Chongmek
An official crossing point into Laos

Tours
See also Tour operators below

Essentials

Discounts of 20-30% at many hotels. There are limited good budget places here, so backpackers tend to bypass the city or stay in Khong Chiam; see page 416. **AL-A** *Pathumrat*, 337 Chayangkun Rd, T241501, F242313. North of town centre, near the market bus station, a/c, restaurant, pool, built during the Vietnam War to meet US military demand, it still exudes 1970s kitsch, some rooms have been modernized, and there is also a rather sterile new wing, but the *hong kao*, or old rooms, have character and atmosphere. **A-B** *Nevada Hotel*, 436/1 Chayagkul Rd, T313351-8, F313350. A/c, TV, some rooms with good views. Divides its karaoke goers into 'very' VIPs, VIPs and the normal karaoke rooms. Featureless restaurant, attached to a cinema complex with internet upstairs. **A-B** *Regent Palace*, 265-71 Chayangkun Rd, T255529, F255489. A/c, restaurant, newest hotel in town – with attached snooker club. Poorly maintained rooms are already looking worn and jaded. **A-B** *Tohsang Ubon*, 251 Phalo Chai Rd, T241925, F244814. A/c, large modern hotel with around 76 comfortable rooms, situated to the south of town. **B-C** *Srikamol*, 26 Ubonsak Rd, T255804, F243792. A/c, restaurant, ugly towerblock, featureless rooms. **C** *Montana Hotel*, 179/1 Uparat Rd, T261752. A/c, 40 comfortable rooms and friendly staff, central location close to town square, room rate includes breakfast.

Sleeping
■ *on maps, pages 412 & 414*
Price codes: see inside front cover

C-D *Krung Thong*, 24 Srinarong Rd, T241609, F242308. A/c, restaurant. **C-D** *Ratchathani*, 229 Khuan Thani Rd, T241136, F243561. Some a/c, featureless block in the centre of town near the TAT office, all rooms with TV and hot water, clean and generally well run, comfortable beds, rooms are competitively priced. **D** *Bodin*, 14 Phalo Chai Rd, T255777. Mostly frequented by Thais and there's not much to recommend it; the rooms seem overpriced. **D** *Pathumrat*, 337 Chayangkun (attached to the more lavish *Pathumrat*). A/c, stuck away round the back of the hotel, clean, dark rooms. **D-E** *Racha*, 149/21 Chayangkun, T254155. Some a/c, hot water in a/c rooms, plain and basic, fairly clean and friendly people. **D-E** *Suriyat*, 47/1-4 Suriyat Rd, T241144. Some a/c, grubby. **E** *Moon River Guesthouse*, 43-45 Sisaket 2 Rd, T322592. Situated in Warin, convenient for the station and bus routes (signposted at the

The Northeastern Region

station). Very helpful management and clean rooms with pleasant surroundings. Recommended, being the only budget place with any character around here. **E** *Si Isaan 1 and 2*, 220 Rachabut Rd, T254204. Some a/c and cheaper older rooms with fans and own bathrooms. Not a bad choice at this price and they also have a good location close to the river and night market. **E** *Tokyo*, 178 Upparat Rd, T241739. Some a/c, range of generally small rooms which have improved over the last few years. Rooms in the new block are better, although the beds are like breeze blocks, service is friendly. A small sign makes the hotel easy to miss; one of the better budget places. **F** *Homsa-ard*, 30 Suriyat Rd. Sa-ard means 'clean', but it isn't.

Eating
● *on map*
Price categories:
see inside front cover

Thai/Chinese Expensive: *Hong Fah Restaurant*, Chayangkun Rd (opposite *Pathumrat Hotel*). Expensive but excellent Chinese food in sophisticated a/c restaurant. **Cheap**: *Phon*, Yutthaphan Rd, opposite fire station. Thai and Chinese. Recommended. *Khai Di Restaurant*, 24/20 Sapphasit Rd (not far from Wat Jaeng). A rather grubby-looking place serving delicious *muhan* or barbecue suckling pig. Three Chinese restaurants on Khuan Thani Rd, close to *Ratchathani Hotel*, eg *Rim Mun 2*. Recommended.

Seafood Expensive: *Seafood Garden*, Chayangkun Rd (about 1 km north of the bus station on the opposite side of the road). Large seafood restaurant, barbecue fish and prawn specialities, a/c room, but tables on roof are by far the best in the evening. **Mid-range**: *Antaman Seafood*, Sapphasit Rd (opposite the Caltex garage, not far from Wat Jaeng). Barbecue seafood including *gung pao* (prawns), *maengda* (horseshoe crabs), sea and river fish and crabs.

Vietnamese Cheap: *Indochine Restaurant*, 168-170 Sapphasit Rd (not far from Wat Jaeng). Vietnamese food in basic but attractive restaurant, good value and great food, closes at 1800.

Vegetarian Cheap: *No name*, Khuan Thani Rd, 30 m west of the Chio Kee Restaurant. Clean and friendly cafeteria-style vegetarian restaurant, eat all you like.

Ubon Ratchathani centre

■ **Sleeping**	3 Montana &	5 Si Isaan
1 Bodin	Broaster Restaurant	6 Srikamol
2 Krung Thong	4 Ratchathani	7 Tohsang Ubon

Bakeries and breakfasts Cheap: *S & P Bakery Shoppe*, 207 Chayangkun Rd. Pastries, ice-cream and pizzas in pristine a/c western-style surroundings; a little piece of Bangkok in Ubon. *Jiaw Kii*, Khuan Thani Rd, a good place for breakfast with bacon and eggs, coffee and toast, as well as more usual Thai morning dishes.

Western Cheap: *Broaster Chicken and Pizza*, Upparat Rd. The name says it all really; new, brash a/c restaurant selling fried chicken, pizzas and fries etc.

Foodstalls Ubon has a profusion of foodstalls. A good range can be found on Chayangkun Rd, just south of the *Pathumrat Hotel*, including stalls selling *kanom* (sweets and pastries), seafood dishes and fruit drinks.

10 Pub, Khuan Thani Rd, opposite National Museum. *Ziggy Pub*, Upakit Rd. **Bars**

Golf Golf course at the airport. The **central park** becomes a sports emporium on **Sport** Sun – good to watch and even better to join in.

Jul *Candle Festival* (movable, for 5 days from the first day of the Buddhist Lent or **Festivals** *Khao Phansa*). Enormous sculpted beeswax candles are made by villagers from all over the province, and are ceremoniously paraded through the streets before being presented to the monks. The festival seems to have been introduced during the reign of Rama I. The Buddha is said to have remarked that the monk Anurudha, in one of his previous lives, led his people out of darkness using a candle – the festival celebrates the feat and is also associated with learning and enlightenment. Candles are given to the monks so that they have light to read the sacred texts during the Buddhist Lent.

Baskets On Luang Rd, near the intersection with Khuan Thai Rd, is a short strip of **Shopping** shops specializing in basketwork. **Department stores** *Ubon Plaza*, Uparat Rd. A/c department store and supermarket selling all necessities. *Ying Yong Department Store*, 143 Chayangkun Rd. **Handicrafts** *Phanchart*, 158 Rachabut Rd. Selection of antiques and northeastern handicrafts, including an excellent range of *matmii* silk (see page 433). *Peaceland*, Luang Rd. Provides a wide range of cultural artefacts and a few trinkets. **Silk** *Ketkaew*, 132 Rachabut Rd.

Chi Chi Tour, Chayangkun Rd, T241464. *Chongmek Travellers*, Srikamol Hotel, 26 Ubonsak **Tour operators** Rd, T255804. *Sakda Travel*, 150/1 Kartharalak, Warin, T323048. Thai agent. *Takerng Tour*, *See also Tours above* 425 Phromathep Rd, T255777. *Ubonsak Travel*, Chayangkun Rd, T311028.

Local **Car and motorbike hire**: car drivers often wait on Rachabut Rd and near the **Transport** TAT office. A car and driver for the day, including petrol, will cost about ฿800. *See also Ins & outs,* *Chaw Watana*, 39/8 Suriyat Rd, T242202 (฿250 for a motorbike, ฿1,000-1,200 for a *page 407;* car). There are several other car/motorbike rental places on Chayangkun Rd. *Chaw* *629 km to Bangkok,* *Watana* seems to hire out anything with wheels. **Town buses**: these follow 13 routes *311 km to Korat,* across town; pick up a useful map from the TAT office. **Saamlors and tuk-tuks** also *270 km to Nakhon* available (at break-neck speed), map from the TAT office (fare ฿3). *Phanom*

Long distance **Air**: airport on the north side of town. It is just about possible to walk into town with cool weather, a following breeze and light bags. A taxi service is available: ฿70 to the town centre, ฿120 to the railway station at Warin Chamrap. Bigger hotels pick up guests gratis. Regular daily connections with Bangkok, 1 hr.

Train: the station is south of the river in Warin Chamrap. Town buses nos 2 and 6 run into town. Regular connections with Bangkok's Hualamphong station (10 hrs) and all stations in between.

Bus: the recently renovated BKS station for non-a/c buses is some distance north of town, not far from Wat Nong Bua at the end of Chayangkun Rd. Get there by town, bus no 2 or 3. The station for a/c and non-a/c buses to Bangkok is at the back of the market on Chayangkun Rd, south of the *Pathumrat Hotel*. Regular connections with Bangkok's new Northeastern bus terminal (8 hrs), Nakhon Phanom (5½-7 hrs), and less frequently with other Northeastern towns – eg there are 2 bus companies who service Surin regularly (4 hrs); a/c and non-a/c tour buses to Bangkok also leave from Khuan Thani Rd, opposite the TAT Office; *Sahamit Tour* on Khuan Thani Rd near the National Museum, runs buses to Udon Thani via Mukdahan, That Phanom and Nakhon Phanom; *Sayan Tour*, near the *Ratchathani Hotel*, runs buses to Udon Thani via Yasothon, Roi Et, Mahasarakham and Khon Kaen. VIP buses to Bangkok leave from the station on the south side of the Mun River, north of Warin Chamrap on the left-hand side of the road, heading north. Night bus leaves at 2130, arriving in Bangkok at 0600. Reservations recommended.

International connections with Laos: it is possible to enter Laos east of Ubon at Chongmek (for details on Chongmek, see Excursions above). To get to Chongmek, take a bus from the station in Warin Chamrap (see map) to Phibun Mangsahan (1 hr, about 45 km). From Phibun Mangsahan there are converted trucks (large songthaews) to the border town of Chongmek, 44 km away (1½ hrs). The border customs posts are pretty relaxed and are open 0600-1800. After passing through the Lao border post (exchange facilities available for Thai baht and US dollars cash), there are trucks and share taxis waiting to whisk passengers to Muang Kao, along a recently upgraded road (1 hr). In mid-2000 a new bridge across the Mekong was completed, making the journey from the border to Pakse faster still.

Directory **Airline offices** *Thai*, 292/9 Chayangkun Rd, T254431. **Banks** *Bangkok*, 88 Chayangkun Rd. *Thai Farmers Bank*, 356/9 Phromathep Rd. *Siam Commercial*, Chayangkun Rd. *Thai Military*, 130 Chayangkun Rd. All have ATMs. **Communications** Post Office: corner of Srinarong and Luang Rd; telephone office at the back of the Post Office. Email next door and above the Nevada Hotel. **Internet café**: 322 Suriyat Rd and on Uparat Chayangkun and Srinarong roads. **Medical services** Hospital: *Rom Kao Hospital*, Upparat Rd (close to the Mun River), is said to be the best in the city. There is another hospital on Sapphasit Rd, T254906. **Useful addresses** Immigration: Phibun Mangsahan Rd, T441108 (in Phibun Mangsahan). **Tourist Police:** Corner of Srinarong and Upparat Roads, T243770.

Khong Chiam โขงเจียม

Phone code: 045
Colour map 2, grid C6

This attractive district town at Thailand's eastern-most point is situated on the Mekong River, close to the confluence of the Mun and Mekong, the so-called two-coloured river or Maenam Song Sii, because of the meeting of the red-brown Mekong and the deep blue Mun. Boats take visitors out to the point of confluence to view the ripple effect at close hand, which is best towards the end of the dry season in March to May. There is accommodation here and some excellent restaurants. Inner tubes can be hired to swim in the Mekong and it makes an alternative and much quieter place to stay than Ubon. It has also been reported that visitors can cross the Mekong to visit the town on the other bank for the day, although this cannot be used as an entry point to Laos. In addition, Khong Chiam can be used as a base to visit the other sights in this easternmost area of Thailand, see below. In the town a morning market operates between 0600 and 0830.

Pha Taem, **Kaeng Sapu** and **Kaeng Tana National Park** are all far closer to Khong Chiam than Ubon (see Excursions, Ubon). ■ *Getting there: regular songthaews/buses to Pha Taem and Kaeng Tana.*

The Thai-Lao border town of **Chongmek** (see page 413) is also easily reached from Khong Chiam. Chongmek is an important crossing point for

Laos and the Thai-Lao market is well worth a rummage. The shop opposite the post office is run by Nipon who speaks good English. ■ *Getting there: take the ferry across the Mun River to Tad Ton and from there to Chongmek.*

B *Rimkhong Resort*, close to Mekong River (as the name suggests). Luxurious big bungalows. **B-C** *Khong Chiam Marina Resort*, T361011. Range of bungalows some with a/c, good restaurant. **C** *Araya Resort*. A/c, hot water, fridge, large, attractive bungalows situated in a beautiful spot overlooking the river. **C-D** *Apple Guesthouse*, 267 Kaew Pradit Rd, T351160. Clean with attached showers, but the a/c rooms are a little on the cramped side, motorbikes and bicycles for hire, friendly owners. **C-E** *Khong Chiam Guesthouse*, T351160, F351074. Some a/c, private bathrooms, good source of information, motorcycle for hire. **E** *Pio Guesthouse*, Kaew Pradit Rd. On edge of town, close to the bus stop, good information but rooms are dirty, minimarket geared to farang tastes close by.

Sleeping

Cheap *Araya*, Santirat Rd, overlooking the Mekong, a beautiful and breezy place to eat, with Mekong River fish specialities including *yisok*. There are 4 karaoke restaurants. There are also several floating barges that double up as restaurants moored around the peninsula, which can hold hundreds of people. All serve similar Thai dishes (**cheap**) and there is little to choose between them – they make a pleasant place to sit and watch the sun go down.

Eating

Bus Catch town bus nos 1, 3 or 6 from Ubon Ratchathani to Warin Chamrap; and from there to Khong Chiam via Phibunmangsahan. There are also a/c bus connections with Bangkok's Northeastern bus terminal.

Transport

Banks *Krung Thai Bank*, Santirat Rd (exchange facilities available). **Communications** Post Office: store opposite the *Apple Guesthouse*. An international phone and fax is available here and also next door.

Directory

Yasothon ยโสธร

This small provincial capital is situated northwest of Ubon. Even by the standards of most of the Northeast, Thailand's tourist boom is a mere whisper in the wind. There are no remotely international hotels, nor even any traveller's guesthouses. All the more reason, some would say, to travel here. Other than the fact that no one comes here, there is really only one reason to visit the town: to see the famous **rocket festival**, or *bun bang fai*, which is held in its most extravagant form outside the *Sala Changwat* (Provincial Office) on the edge of town, on the road north towards Roi Et (Route 23). Once a regionwide festival, Yasothon has made it its own (see box).

Phone code: 045
Colour map 2, grid B5
Population: 34,000

In the centre of Yasothon, on Withdamrong Road, is a daily **market** which, though not geared to tourists, does sell functional handicrafts: Isan pillows and cushions, and baskets and woven sticky rice containers. **Wat Mahathat Yasothon**, just off the main road, is said to date from the foundation of the city. Its ancient roots are barely discernible amidst the new construction. The Phra That Phra Anon chedi, within the monastery's precincts, is said to date from the seventh century and contain the ashes of the Lord Buddha's first disciple, Phra Anon (better known outside Thailand as Ananda).

Ban Sri Thaan lies 20 km southeast of town off Route 202, towards Amphoe Amnaat Jeroen. The village is famous for its *mon khit* or traditional Isan axe pillows. These brightly coloured triangular cushions are made of cotton and traditionally stuffed with kapok. However, a few years ago the industry here

Excursions

began to suffer from a shortage of kapok as pillow production began to outstrip kapok supply. The producers' response was to turn to using the stuffing from old mattresses, a great example of ingenuity married with recycling.

■ *Getting there: take Route 202, southeast of town towards Amphoe Amnaat Jeroen. Between the Km 18 and 19 markers (before Bon Pa Tew), turn right towards Ban Sri Thaan. It is a further 3 km along the track. Buses from the station in town will drop people at the turn-off. Motorcycle/saamlors wait to take ferry visitors the last 3 km to the village.*

Sleeping
■ *on map*
Price codes:
see inside front cover

C-D *Yot Nakhon*, 143 Uthairamrit Rd, T711481/711122, F711476. Some a/c, large, featureless but comfortable enough, with, so it is claimed, a 24-hr coffee shop, a/c rooms have TV but no hot water. **D-F** *Surawit Watthana*, 128/1 Chaeng Sanit Rd, T711690. Fan rooms with attached bathrooms.

Festivals   **May** *Bun bang fai (skyrocket) festival*, celebrated most fervently here in Yasothon (see box, page 419).

Shopping   **Handicrafts**   Baskets from the market in the centre of town. Near the market on the main road, Chaeng Sanit Rd, is a handicraft shop selling axe pillows, Northeastern textiles and some baskets. Yasothon is renowned in Thailand for the quality of its triangular, colourful, axe cushions or *mon khit*. Most famous for making them is Ban Sri Thaan, 20 km away (see Excursions above).

Transport
103 km to Ubon

Air   There are no air connections with Yasothon. The nearest airports are in Ubon Ratchathani and Roi Et. The latter, marginally closer, opened in Mar 1999, and *PB Air* operates a thrice-weekly service with Bangkok. **Bus**   The bus station is at the northeastern edge of town, an easy walk from the centre. Non-a/c buses to Ubon, Udorn, Roi Et, Mahasarakham and Khon Kaen, as well as with Bangkok's Northeastern bus terminal (10 hrs). A/c buses leave from offices close to the station for Bangkok (10 hrs) and Ubon.

Directory   **Banks** *Thai Farmers Bank*, 289 Chaeng Sanit Rd.

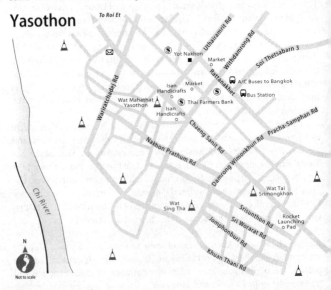

Yasothon

The Northeastern Region

Bun bang fai: the Northeast's sky rocket festival

Perhaps the Northeast's best known festival is the bun bang fai or skyrocket festival. This is celebrated across the region between May and June, at the end of the dry season, though it is most fervently in the town of Yasothon over the second weekend of May.

The festival was originally linked to animist beliefs, but through time it also became closely associated with Buddhism. The climax of the festival involves the firing of massive rockets into the air to ensure bountiful rain by propitiating the rain god Vassakarn (or, as some people maintain, Phya Thaen), who also has a penchant for fire. The rockets can be 4 m or more long and contain as much as 500 kg of gunpowder. As well as these bang jut rockets, there are also bang eh - rockets which are heavily and extravagantly decorated and are not fired, just for show. Traditionally the rockets were made of bamboo; now steel and plastic storm pipes are used such is the size of bang jut. Specialist rocket-makers commissioned months beforehand have taken over from the amateurs of the past.

The rockets are mounted on a bamboo scaffold and fired into the air with much cheering and shouting – and exchanging of money, as gambling has become part and parcel of the event. In 1992 there were 60 rockets fired, about a third to a half of which worked. The rocket which reaches the greatest height wins. The festival is preceded by a procession of monks, dancing troupes and musicians. There is even a beauty contest, Thida bang fai ko, or the Sparkling daughters of the skyrockets.

But like many festivals in Thailand, bun bang fai has been co-opted by the state and made a national event. In Yasothon, the provincial governor is closely involved in the celebrations, as are various government offices and army leaders. This means that it has been sanitized and made an official 'spectacle', for both tourists and Thais. Though it is still possible to see traditional bang fai in villages in the northeast, they too are changing or disappearing as the Yasothon event becomes definitive.

In the past, bun bang fai were local festivals, when neighbouring villages would take it in turns to bear the cost. The rockets were made by Buddhist monks who were the only people with the time and knowledge to build the gunpowder-packed rockets. It was far more lewd and wild than today. Men wearing phallic symbols would parade through the village, drunken groups would dance wildly imitating sexual intercourse, and young men and women would take the opportunity to meet and court. At the same time, young boys would be ordained and monks blessed. The governor of Yasothon has banned the use of phallic symbols, regarding them as unfitting for a national event, although he has had a more difficult time trying to outlaw drunkenness.

The heartland of the Khorat Plateau

Three provinces straddle the Chi River and lie in the middle of the Khorat Plateau: Mahasarakham, Roi Et and Kalasin. These are farming provinces off the tourist trail. They are en route to nowhere, yet encapsulate the culture and economy of the Northeast. They are centres of Northeastern culture and came under the influence of the great Khmer Empire, probably marking its most northerly extent in this part of Thailand. The roads are good and accommodation adequate.

Mahasarakham มหาสารคาม

Known locally as Sarakham, Mahasarakham is a quiet, provincial capital, situated right in the centre of the Khorat Plateau. There is a university, really a

Phone code 043
Colour map 2, grid B4

teacher training college, here and the town is known as a centre for North-eastern handicrafts and music, with the university and a new research institute, the **Research Institute of Northeastern Art and Culture**, acting as a focus for their development. The institute has a small permanent exhibition of textiles, basketry and other handicrafts, and sells a number of publications, mostly in Thai. It is located behind the main lecture building of the university. Ask for *Satapun Wichai Isan*. The university is 2 km west of town on the road to Khon Kaen. Ask for *mor saw war*. **Wat Mahachai** on Soi Atasaanwiset houses a collection of regional literature and works of art in the Northern Culture Museum, which is situated in the wat compound. The museum is often locked; such is the level of visitor demand. The wat is otherwise unremarkable.

There is a **daily fresh market** on the corner of Nakhon Sawan and Worayut roads, in the centre of town. The usual array of goods and foods; forest products like the *maeng da* beetle are also sold (see page 828). A night market operates every evening on Nakwichai Road; the best place to eat, see Eating below.

Excursions **Tambon Kwao**, 5 km east of Mahasarakham off Route 208 towards Roi Et, is a centre of pottery production. The turn-off for the village is 4 km along Route 208, and then 1 km down a laterite track. ■ *Getting there: take one of the regular local buses from the station on Somtawin Rd.*

Prang Ku is a late Khmer site, 12 km from town on the road to Roi Et. The site was a 'hospital' – a place of healing – at the Northern edge of the Khmer Empire. The prang is in a poor state of repair, with no decoration or carving, and rather rudimentarily reconstructed. Nearby is a large *baray* or reservoir. The site is also used to stage a small *bun bang fai* festival in May (the scaffold for the rockets is on the shores of the baray, see page 419). ■ *Getting there: take a bus from the station on Somtawin Rd running southeast towards Roi Et (Route 208) and get off just past the Km 12 marker. The prang is signposted and lies 1½ km off the main road on the left-hand side.*

Sleeping
■ *on map*
Price codes:
see inside front cover

C *Wasu*, 1096/4 Damnoen Nat Rd, T723075, F721290. Some a/c, restaurant, plain concrete hotel with nearly 100 equally plain and uninspired rooms, but clean enough. Restaurant has live music in the evening as Thai female crooners belt out badly performed songs for the benefit of Thai male visitors, an education in coffee shop culture if not in music, the 'no guns' notice on the door may worry some visitors. **E** *Pattana Hotel*, 1227/4-8 Somthawin Rd, T711473. Very grubby and barrack-like hotel close to the bus station, mostly used by bus and truck drivers. **E** *Suthorn Hotel*, 1157/1 Worayut Rd, T711201. Some a/c, small hotel in town centre with 30 rooms, a/c rooms have attached bathrooms, basic.

Eating
● *on map*
Price categories:
see inside front cover

Cheap *M and Y*, Nakhon Sawan Rd (about 1 km from town centre). Seafood restaurant, tables in garden, excellent chargrilled prawns. Recommended. *Nua Khaoli*, Somthawin Rd (near intersection with Padungwithi Rd). Cook-your-own on hot plates at each table, good food, clean and fun. Recommended. **Seriously cheap** *Jan Ngen*, Warayut Rd (corner with Nakwichai Rd). Wide selection of Thai dishes, a/c room. *Maeng Khian*, behind the bus station (*bor kor sor*). A/c restaurant in ranch house style with live music, Thai food, with good Isan specialities. *Somphort Pochana*, Somthawin Rd (near intersection with Warayut Rd).

● ●
Mahasarakham place names

Prang Ku
ปรางค์กู่

Tambon Kwao
ตำบลเขว้า

Good Chinese and Thai dishes, excellent value. There is a row of good restaurants, bars and bakeries on Nakhon Sawan Rd, about 1 km from the town centre near the turn-off for Kalasin; they mainly meet student demand from Mahasarakham University.

Night market or *Talaat tor rung*, on Nakwichai Rd, best place to eat in the evenings (0600-2100), selling Isan specialities like *kai yang* (barbecue chicken), *somtam* (hot papaya salad) and *laap* (minced meat with herbs), as well as rice and noodle dishes.

Feb *Bun Boek Fa and Red Cross Fair* (movable), week-long festival held in the grounds of the *Sala Changwat*, the provincial offices, on Nakhan Sawan Rd in the centre of town. Dances, beauty contest, silk weaving and local produce on sale. **May** *Bun bang fai* (movable), Northeast skyrocket festival (see box, page 419). A small example is held at Prang Ku, 12 km from town (see Excursions above). | **Festivals**

Handicrafts Small shop on Somthawin Rd, selling local baskets, pottery etc (see map for location). **Newspapers** English-language newspapers available from the stall in the market area on Nakhonsawan Rd. *Serm Thai*, Khlong Som Tha Rd (next to bus station), a/c department store with food centre. | **Shopping**

Air There are no air connections with Mahasarakham, but a new airport opened in Roi Et in Mar 1999 and *PB Air* operates a service to Bangkok 3 times a week. **Bus** The bus station for non-a/c buses is just south of the town centre on Somtawin Rd. Non-a/c buses leave regularly for Bangkok's Northeastern bus terminal (7 hrs) and other Northeastern towns. A/c buses leave from various offices around town for Bangkok (7 hrs), Ubon, Udon and elsewhere (see map). | **Transport** *475 km to Bangkok*

Banks *Thai Farmers Bank*, Worayut Rd. *Thai Military Bank*, Padongwithi Rd. Both with currency exchange. **Communications** Post Office: facing the clock tower on Nakhon Sawan Rd. | **Directory**

Mahasarakham

Not to scale

■ Sleeping
1 Wasu

4 Nua Khaoli
5 Somphort Pochana

● Eating
1 Jan Ngen
2 Maeng Khian
3 M & Y

🚌 Transport
1 A/c to Roi Et & Bangkok

2 A/c Night Buses to Bangkok
3 Chan Tour, A/c to Bangkok
4 A/c to Ubon & Udon
5 Non-a/c Bus Station

The Northeastern Region

Roi Et ร้อยเอ็ด

Phone code: 043
Colour map 2, grid B4
Population: 37,500

Roi Et is the capital of a province encompassing one of the poorest agricultural areas in Thailand. The Tung Kula Rong Hai is a large, dry, salty and infertile plain which covers much of the province, as well as parts of Mahasarakham, Buri Ram and Surin. The name means the 'Weeping Plain of the Kula', the Kula being a group of nomadic agriculturalists. Millions of baht have been invested in projects to improve the land and productivity of agriculture. Although there have been some successes, the incidence of circular migration – the movement of young men and women to Bangkok and elsewhere in a seasonal search for work – illustrates the inability of the land to support a population with rapidly rising needs and expectations.

Sights Roi Et is built around an artificial lake – the **Bung Phlan Chai**. The island in the centre, linked by footbridges, contains the town's *lak muang* or foundation pillar, protected by a sala. Also here is a large Sukhothai-style walking Buddha. This, and the moat which surrounds the city on three sides along with well-stocked gardens, makes Roi Et seem better planned and more airy than most other Thai towns. Paddle boats can be hired on the lake, and the island is a popular spot with locals for walking and feeding the fish.

Wat Klang Ming Muang is in the Northeast quarter of the city on Charoenphanit Road. The monastery is thought to pre-date the founding of the city and the bot, with its fine sweeping gables, was probably built in the Ayutthaya period (18th century). On the outside of the bot are a series of murals telling the life of the Buddha and the gathering of the 12 disciples or *devata*. In some areas rather badly decayed (they were last renovated in 1941), they are nonetheless bright and energetic. **Wat Phung Phralaan Chai** at the southwest corner of the lake is also ancient, but vigorous rebuilding has obliterated the old, excepting the *bai sema* or boundary stones which surround the new *bot*. The concrete high-relief morality tales which surround the three-storeyed, moated *mondop* are enjoyable. But Roi Et's most obvious 'sight' (if size is anything to go by) is the massive 59 m (sometimes 68 m, but who's counting?) **standing Buddha of Wat Buraphaphiram**, on the east side of town near Rop Muang Road. The Buddha is known as Phra Phutta Ratana Mongkhon Maha Mani. It is possible to climb up the side of the statue for a modestly exciting view over the town.

On Ploenchit Road is the **Mun Nithi Roi Et Chinese Temple**. In classic Chinese style, the ground floor is a trading business; the temple is on the first floor. Three altars face the room: to the left, one dedicated to the corpulent 'laughing' Buddha; in the centre, to the historic Buddha and various future Buddhas (or Bodhisattvas); to the right, to Kuan Yin or Quan Am, the Chinese Goddess of Mercy (see box). The pagoda pragmatically combines Theravada and Mahayana Buddhism (see page 793), and Daoism and Confucianism. Despite Thailand's large Chinese population – around 15% – it is relatively rare to see Chinese pagodas and temples. This is partly because the Chinese have assimilated so seamlessly into Thai society and become good Theravada Buddhists. Another reason is a wish to blend in, to reduce any chance of persecution. At times of economic nationalism –

Roi Et place names

Ku Kasingh

กู่กาสิงห์

Ku Phra Kona

กู่พระโกนา

Prasat Nong Ku

ปราสาทหนองกู่

The story of Quan Am

Quan Am was turned onto the streets by her husband for some unspecified wrongdoing and, dressed as a monk, took refuge in a monastery. There, a woman accused her of fathering, and then abandoning, her child. Accepting the blame (why, no one knows), she was again turned out onto the streets, only to return to the monastery much later when she was on *the point of death to confess her true identity. When the Emperor of China heard the tale, he made Quan Am the Guardian Spirit of Mother and Child, and couples without a son now pray to her. Quan Am's husband is sometimes depicted as a parakeet, with the Goddess usually holding her adopted son in one arm and standing on a lotus leaf (the symbol of purity).*

'Thailand for the Thais' – the Chinese have been discriminated against. Another, smaller, Chinese pagoda is the **Sala Chao Roi Et** on Phadungphanit Road, not far from the lake.

The **market** on and between Phadungphanit and Hai Sok roads sells Isan handicrafts and fresh foods, including insects. On the roadside, women market the ingredients for betel 'nut' (see page 825).

Prasat Kue or **Prang Kue** is a Khmer sanctuary tower about 10 km east of town. Few visitors come here and it has only recently begun to be excavated and researched. The site consists of an 11th-century three-tiered central prang, walled, with door niches and balustrade. Some carved lintels have been found and are on display, although there is talk of removing them to a museum. The prasat is in the grounds of Wat Sri Ratanaram. ■ *Getting there: take a bus from the station on Jaeng Sanit Rd. You need the Roi Et-Phontong road (the old Yasothon road). Get off at about the 8 km marker; Prasat Kue is off to the right, about 1 km.*

Excursions

Ku Kasingh is a second Khmer temple, rather more difficult to get to from Roi Et. The site consists of three prasat, raised on a single sandstone plinth. The whole is surrounded by walls and a moat, and is undergoing renovation by the Thai Fine Arts Department. From the style of carving of the lintels and the layout of the temple, it is thought to date from the 11th century, the Baphuon period. ■ *Getting there: the site is at Ban (village) Ku Kasingh in Amphoe (district) Kaset Wisai, almost into Surin province. Take Route 215 and then 214 south towards Sawannaphum and Surin – buses leave for Surin from the station on Jaeng Sanit Rd. The track to Ban Ku Kasingh and the Prasat are about 20 km south of Suwannaphum, on the right-hand side.*

Ku Phra Kona, a third Khmer sanctuary, is not far north of Ku Kasingh. Like Ku Kasingh it consists of three prangs, one of which has been remodelled (in 1928) into a tiered 'stupa', rather like Wat Phrathat Haripunjaya in Lamphun. A *baray*, or reservoir, 300 m from the site was probably linked by a naga bridge. The sanctuary is Baphuon in style and probably dates from the mid-11th century. ■ *Getting there: take Route 215 and then 214 south towards Suwannaphum and Surin – buses leave for Surin from the station on Jaeng Sanit Rd. Ku Phra Kona is at Ban Ku, about 12 km south of Suwannaphum.*

A *Roi Et Thani Hotel*, Santisuk Rd, T520387, F520401. This hotel is part of the Dusit group and opened in July 1995, with 167 rooms on 6 floors, a good pool, gym and business centre. It is undoubtedly the most luxurious place in the area and is also professionally run. **A-B** *Mai Thai*, 99 Haisok Rd, T511136, F512277. A/c, lavish hotel at northern edge of town with over 100 rooms, large coffee shop serving excellent food and illusions of grandeur, rooms are good value with hot water baths, TV and some with views. Plenty of nightlife here, with a nightclub, karaoke and snooker room.

Sleeping
■ *on map*
Price codes:
see inside front cover

The Northeastern Region

B-D *Phetcharat Hotel*, 66-80 Haisok Rd, T511741, F514078. North edge of town, a/c, restaurant, 3-storey hotel, good value a/c rooms, clean but bland.

D *Bungalow 99*, 102 Pracha-Thammarak Rd (Sunthornthep Rd), T511035. Some a/c, looks new and inviting, but rooms are disappointing. A/c rooms have hot water, all with small balconies, but poorly maintained. **D** *Khaen Khum*, 50-62 Rathakitkhaikhlaa, T511508. Some a/c with hot water, well managed and maintained, the best of the Chinese-style hotels in Roi Et. **D-E** *Bua Thong*, 40-46 Rathakitkhaikhlaa, T511142. Some a/c, best rooms on top floor where windows allow a breeze in, squat loos, no hot water, no frills but friendly. **D-E** *Phrae Thong*, 29 Ploenchit Rd, T511127. Some a/c, not very well maintained, squat loos, no hot water, but a/c rooms are cheap. **E** *Ban Chong*, 99-101 Suriyadej Bamrung Rd, T511235. Simple but good value and reasonably clean rooms with attached facilities.

Eating
● *on map*
Price categories:
see inside front cover

Excellent evening food market by the Post Office, from dusk until 2100, best choice of food in town including Isan specialities. There are also a collection of pleasant open-air garden restaurants situated around the central lake.

Festivals

May *Bun bang fai (skyrocket) festival*, celebrated most fervently in Yasothon (see page 419), but a more traditional example is held in the district town of Suwannaphum, south of Roi Et. Get there by regular bus from the station on Jaeng Sanit Rd.

Shopping

Department stores Roi Et Plaza, intersection of Santisuk and Ploenchit roads (near the Chinese temple). **Handicrafts** Roi Et is a centre for production of silk and cotton ikat cloth. It is sold by the *phun* and can range from ฿100 per phun for simple cotton cloth to ฿3,000 for a piece of finest quality silk. Go to *Jerinot*, 383 Phadungphanit Rd, or *Phaw Kaan Khaa* at 377-379 Phadungphanit Rd, to see a wide selection and to gauge prices. Also sold along this road and in market stalls are axe cushions, baskets, *khaens* (a Northeastern reed pipe) and other handicrafts.

Roi Et

■ Sleeping	
1 Ban Chong	5 Mai Thai
2 Bua Thong	6 Phetcharat
3 Bungalow 99	7 Phrae Thong
4 Khaen Khum	8 Roi Et Thani

The Northeastern Region

Air *PB Air*, a start-up domestic airline, fly 3 times a week to Bangkok from Roi Et's new airport. It is intended that Roi Et will become the hub for this portion of the Northeast, providing the most convenient flights for Mahasarakham, Kalasin, Mukdahan and Yasothon. **Bus** The main bus station is to the west of town, off Jaeng Sanit Rd (Route 23 towards Mahasarakham). Non-a/c buses to Bangkok (8 hrs), Kalasin, Khon Kaen, Ubon, Udorn, Nong Khai, Mahasarakham, Buriram, Surin and Korat. A/c bus connections with Bangkok's Northeastern terminal (8 hrs). The a/c bus terminal in Roi Et is at the southeast corner of town (see map).

Transport
512 km to Bangkok

Banks *Thai Farmers Bank*, 431 Phadungphanit Rd. *Thai Military Bank*, Ploenchit Rd (near intersection with Sukkasem Rd). **Communications Post Office:** Suriyadejbamrung Rd (at intersection with Santisuk Rd). **Telephone:** overseas calls can be made from the Post Office.

Directory

Kalasin กาฬสินธุ์

Kalasin is one of Thailand's smallest provinces and was once only an *amphoe*, or district. It still hardly exudes the ambience of even a Northeastern provincial capital. Although it may be a backwater today, the discovery of the Dvaravati site of Muang Fa Daed nearby (see Excursions below) indicates that, like other parts of the Northeast, this was a centre of activity in the early centuries of the first millennium AD.

Phone code: 043
Colour map 2, grid B4

There are not many, if any, notable sights in Kalasin. But it is a quiet, rather charming provincial capital. In the centre of town on Kalasin Road is a bronze statue of Thao Somphamit, who founded the city; he holds a kettle and clutches his sword. At the southern end of Somphamit Road, not far from the bus station, is a row of **travelling cinema companies**. They take films to out-of-the-way towns, bringing with them generators and a screen to enlighten villagers with the latest Kung Fu release. The spread of electricity and the television means the companies, like travelling dance troupes, are struggling for business. On the eastern edge of town, at the end of Kalasin Road, is a vibrant **open market** where villagers come to sell live fish, fruit and vegetables, and to buy clothes and other necessities.

Sights

Wat Klang, a large teaching wat on Kalasin Road, enshrines an impressive black Buddha image cast in bronze. During periods of drought, the image is carried in procession through the town to divine rain. Unfortunately, it is kept in the *bot*, which is usually locked. But the new rather gaudy *bot* does have some high relief concrete panels around it. These depict scenes from Northeastern country life – transplanting rice, spinning silk, playing the *khaen* and pounding rice. At the far end from the entrance on Kalasin Road, young chicks cry out *mae phom* (my mother!) as their mother's head is chopped off in a demeritous fashion. Also at Wat Klang is a footprint of the Buddha, again reputed to have considerable magical powers.

Wat Sribamruang, at the north edge of town off Somphamit Road, is more interesting. It contains a number of beautiful *bai sema* or boundary stones from Muang Fa Daed (see Excursions below).

Kalasin place names

Ban Phon
บ้านพล

Muang Fa Daed
เมืองฟ้าแดด

Muang Fa Daed is an ancient double-moated town, probably established in the eighth century AD, and one of the most important archaeological sites in the Northeast. Beautiful carved sandstone *bai sema*, or

Excursions

The Northeastern Region

boundary stones, have been unearthed (some of which can be seen at Wat Sribamruang in Kalasin town, see above), along with clay, and one bronze, pipes. The place is probably only of interest to budding archaeologists, as getting there is difficult. ■ *Getting there: the site is 19 km from Kalasin town. Take Route 214 south towards Roi Et for 13 km. Turn right at the Kamalasai School intersection and travel for another 6 km to the site. It is possible to take a bus to the intersection and then hire a motorized saamlor. Ask for* muang boraan *(ancient town), Muang Fa Daed.*

Ban Phon is a specialist weaving village 70 km northeast of Kalasin town. The Phu Thai people, a distinct cultural group within Isan, weave finely patterned silk cloth known as *phrae wa*. Their work is supported by the Queen Sirikit foundation. Cloth can be bought and the production process observed at the village. ■ *Getting there: catch a bus running towards the district town of Kham Muong from the station on Khaengsamrong Rd. The bus passes the turn off for the village. Ask for Ban Phon.*

Sleeping & eating
■ *on map*
Price codes:
see inside front cover

A-B *New Hotel*, not so new any more, built in 1995, this hotel is 1½ km out of town, over the Lam Pao River. Over 150 rooms, a/c, restaurant, pool, best in town, on an open field site. **C-D** *Suphak*, 81/7 Saenha Rd, T811315. Some a/c, restaurant, 52 rooms, coffee shop, plain rooms, some with hot water showers, echoing hallways, pre-dates the era of imaginative design in Thailand. **D-E** *Phaiboon*, 125/1-2 Somphamit Rd, T811661, F813346. Some a/c, hot water, rather plain barrack-like hotel in centre of town, OK for a stopover. **D-E** *Saithong Bungalow*, Somphamit Rd, T813348, F813346. Some a/c, completed early in 1994, these clean rooms have hot water and pristine bathrooms, TV in the a/c rooms, central location. **E-F** *Saithong Hotel*, Phirom Rd. Fans, rundown and dirty. **F** *Saengthong*, 100-102 Kalasin Rd, T811555. Grotty hotel with shared facilities. **Cheap** *Sairung*, off Kalasin Rd, east of town centre near the cinema. A/c ice-cream parlour and coffee shop.

Festivals

May *Bun bang far (skyrocket) festival* This festival, for which the Northeast is renowed, is usually associated with Yasothon (see box, page 419), but a more traditional

Kalasin

example is held annually at the district town of Kamalasai, 13 km south of Kalasin town. Get there by regular bus from the station on Khaengsamrong Rd.

Kalasin Plaza, Thetsabaan 23 Rd (set back). A/c shopping plaza. *English language newspapers* for sale on Thetsabaan 23 Rd, near Kalasin Plaza. **Shopping**

Air There are no air connections with Kalasin, but a new airport opened in Roi Et in Mar 1999 and *PB Air* operates a thrice-weekly service to Bangkok. **Bus** The bus terminal for a/c and non-a/c buses is on the southwestern edge of town, just off Khaengsamrong Rd. Regular connections with Bangkok's Northeastern bus terminal (8 hrs) and with other Northeastern centres. **Transport** *519 km to Bangkok*

Banks *Krung Thai*, intersection of Somphamit and Kalasin roads. **Communications** Post Office: Kalasin Rd (near the statue of Thao Somphamit). **Directory**

North from Korat to Udon Thani

From Korat, Route 2 runs north across the gently undulating plateau of the Isan region. West of here, near the Phetchabun mountains, is the sleepy town of Chaiyaphum. Khon Kaen, 189 km from Korat, is one of the largest cities in the Northeast. Route 12 winds westwards from here through the Phetchabun range of hills to Phitsanulok – where it links up with the Central Plains and the north – a nerve tingling journey along mountain roads; 117 km further north from Khon Kaen is Udon Thani, the site of a former US base and close to the important archaeological site of Ban Chiang. Continuing north for another 55 km, the road reaches Nong Khai.

Chaiyaphum ชัยภูมิ

This small provincial capital off the main tourist routes has few obvious attractions for the visitor. But those who truly want to avoid other tourists and sample provincial Northeastern Thai life might find this small corner of Thailand entertaining.

Phone code: 044
Colour map 4, grid B4
Population: 30,000

The name Chaiyaphum means site of victory, a reference to Pho Khun Lae's – the town's first governor – success in thwarting an attack from an invading Lao army during the reign of Rama III. He died in the battle and as a result has become something of a protector figure for Chaiyaphum and its inhabitants. A statue and shrine to his memory are situated 3 km west of town and a festival is held in his honour each January.

In the centre of town at Chaiyaphum's traffic circle is a statue of the founder of the city, **Phraya Phakdi Chumphon**. Rather more interesting is **Prasat Hin Prang Ku**, or simply **Prang Ku**, a 12th-century Khmer sanctuary tower 2 km east of the town centre on Bannakaan Road. Built of laterite blocks, it scarcely matches the Khmer monuments to be found elsewhere on the Khorat Plateau. What little carving there is, kala heads and a few lintels, is rather crude and provincial. Within the prang is a Dvaravati Buddha, highly revered by the townspeople. The statue is ritually bathed on the day of the full moon in April. Get there by saamlor, bicycle or walk. **Sights**

Chaiyaphum lies on the margins of the Khorat Plateau and the land around here is often planted to kenaf, an inferior jute substitute that is used to make rope and gunny bags. It is harvested during the winter months and bundles of the fibre can be seen soaking in the ponds that often line the main roads. The stalks are retted to remove the green part of the plant, leaving only the fibre.

The Northeastern Region

Unfortunately, this process also pollutes and deoxygenates the water, making the ponds and creeks useless for fish raising.

Excursions **Ban Khwao** is a village well known for the quality of its silk. Like Surin, Chaiyaphum and the surrounding area is a centre for silk production and weaving. Guesthouses will help arrange tours to silk weaving villages. Alternatively, simply catch a songthaew from Nornmuang Road (near the intersection with Tantawan Road), close to the centre of town, to Ban Khwao, 14 km west of Chaiyaphum (on Route 225).

Sleeping & **C-D** *Letnimit*, 14 Niwarat Rd, T811522, F822335. A/c, dull hotel opposite the bus sta-
eating tion, with equally dull rooms, interesting for the insight it offers into the Thai travelling
■ *on map* businessman. **C-D** *Sirichai*, Nornmuang Rd, T812848. Some a/c, another dull
Price codes: Sino-Thai hotel in the centre of town. **E** *Yin's Guesthouse*, off Niwarat Rd (directly
see inside front cover opposite the bus station, 150 m down a dirt track and facing a small lake). Partitioned rooms in raised wooden house, basic but friendly, run by a Norwegian and his Thai wife, bicycles lent gratis and tours to local silk-weaving villages arranged.

The best food in town is to be had at the **night market** on Taksin Rd. During the day, a good place for Isan specialities like *kai yaang* (grilled chicken) and *somtam* (spicy papaya salad) is the group of stalls on Bannakaan Rd, opposite the hospital. *Relax Beerhouse*, Nonthanakorn Rd (near the intersection with Bannakaan Rd), ice cold beer, relaxing as the name suggests.

Festivals **Jan** *Pho Khun Lae Festival* These celebrations are held in mid-Jan and celebrate the Pho Khun Laes victory over an invading Lao army. All the usual activities.

Transport **Bus** The BKS is on the northeast edge of
330 km to Bangkok town about 1 km from the centre. Regular bus connections with Bangkok's
Northeastern bus terminal (7 hrs), and
with Phitsanulok, Chiang Mai and towns
in the Northeast. A/c buses (VIP and standard) to Bangkok leave from the offices
of *Air Chaiyaphum* at 202/8-9
Nornmuang Rd, just to the north of the
Sirichai Hotel in the town centre. For a/c
buses to Chiang Mai and Ubon
Ratchathani, the terminal is on
Nornmuang Rd, south of the post office.

Chaiyaphum

Directory **Banks** Banks with exchange facilities are
located on Uthittham Rd (eg *Krung Thai*) and
Hot Thai Rd (eg *Thai Farmers Bank*).
Communications Post Office: intersection
of Bannakaan Rd and Nornmuang Rd
(telephone and fax facilities available).

Khon Kaen ขอนแก่น

Khon Kaen is a large commercial centre with, at least superficially, little charm. It supports the largest university in the Northeastern region and is an important administrative centre. Selected by the government as a 'growth pole' during the 1960s to help facilitate the development of the region, it was also home to a US airforce base during the Vietnam War. Partly in consequence, it has a good selection of hotels (more since built), cinemas, restaurants and bars. It is also growing and developing fast, with new hotels, cinemas, restaurants, shopping plazas and karaoke bars opening each year.

Phone code: 043
Colour map 2, grid B3
Population: 150,000

Ins and outs

Khon Kaen is the largest town in this part of the Northeast, and is well connected with Bangkok and other provincial centres. The airport is 6 km from town, with multiple daily connections to Bangkok. The railway station is on the edge of town, a 10-15 min walk to the centre, where there are many hotels. Train connections south to Bangkok and northeast to Nong Khai. The a/c and non-a/c bus terminals are both reasonably central, with bus services to Bangkok. Chiang Mai and many other destinations in the Northeast, North and Central Plains.

Getting there
See also Transport, page 434

Khon Kaen is a large town. Songthaews provide the main mode of public transport and run along 12 fixed routes (maps available from tourist office). There are also saamlors and tuk-tuks and local buses to out of town destinations.

Getting around

TAT, Prachasamoson Rd (near the *Rosesukon Hotel*), T244498, F244497. New and helpful branch of the TAT, with good maps and details on accommodation and attractions in and around Khon Kaen (with heavy emphasis on the dinosaurs; see Excursions below). Areas of responsibility are Khon Kaen, Mahasarakham, Roi Et and Kalasin.

Tourist offices

Sights

Because Khon Kaen is one of the principal transport hubs of the Northeast, tourists may find that they need to spend a night here en route elsewhere. There is little reason to spend more time than that as the town is not yet geared to tourist visitors. Indeed, given the town's size, it's surprising how little there is to moisten the excitement glands of the average tourist. Most foreigners who come here are on business.

However, Khon Kaen does support an excellent branch of the **National Museum** at the intersection of Kasikhon Thungsang and Lungsun Rachakhan roads, at the Northeast edge of the city. It contains, among other things, a good collection of Ban Chiang artefacts and beautiful Dvaravati boundary stones. ■ *0900-1200, 1300-1600 Wed-Sun, ฿10*. Also worthy of note is the **Bung Kaen Nakhon** at the southern edge of the city. This is a lake that expands and contracts according to the seasons, reaching a maximum extent at the peak of the rainy season of nearly 100 ha. On the northern shore of the *bung* (pond) is the Lao-style **Wat That**, with the characteristic lotus bud-shaped chedi of the Lao. The lake is used by local residents for evening walks and weekend picnics, and there are also a number of open air restaurants. Whether intentionally or ironically, the beach area here is locally known as Pattaya II.

The Northeastern Region

Excursions

Chonnabot

The villages around here are well known for the quality & variety of their matmii silk & cotton cloth

This is both a small town and a district near Khon Kaen. Much of the silk and cotton cloth from here is sent to Bangkok to be sold, for example at Chatuchak weekend market, but it is best bought here where it can also be seen being made. There is a handicraft centre where local cloth is sold, or lengths can be bought direct from weaving households – just wander through the village; looms can be seen under the houses. Note that cloth is bought by the *phun*. A normal sarong length will be about two *phun*, so prices will rarely relate to the whole piece of cloth. A difficulty is that English is not widely spoken, so it either takes a modest facility with the Thai language or skilful hand signals to secure a deal. Chonnabot town, the capital of the district, lies 12 km off Route 2, travelling south towards Korat (turn-off near Km 399 marker onto Route 2057).
■ *Getting there: take a local bus from the station on Prachasamoson Rd, 1 hr. Note that the last songthaew back to town leaves Chonnabot around 1600.*

Phu Wiang National Park

This area contains one of the world's largest dinosaur graveyards

Covering a little over 300 sq km, gazetted in 1991, this park lies around 85 km northwest of Khon Kaen and consists of a central plain encircled by low hills. However, it really sprung to modest fame a few years later when it was discovered that the area had one of the world's largest **dinosaur graveyards**. The first dinosaur fossils were unearthed here in 1978 and by 1991 nine sites had been uncovered. But Phu Wiang and Thailand entered the world dinosaur annals in 1996 when the remains of a new family of carnivorous thunder lizards were unearthed here, and were appropriately called *Siamotyrannus isanensis*. The importance of the find is that while the animals are considerably smaller than their well-known North American and Chinese cousins, the Thai tyrannosaur is much older – 120,000,000-130,000,000 years as opposed to 65,000,000-80,000,000 years. The dinosaur remains – and there is much more than just *Siamotyrannus isanensis* (for example, fossilized dinosaur footprints) – are concentrated in the northern portion of the park and it is possible to walk from dinosaur quarry to quarry.

Park essentials There was no accommodation in the park at the time of research, although park bungalows were under construction, T043-291393 for information. It is easiest to get here on a tour. By road, take the route from Khon Kaen towards Chumphae and turn right at the Km 48 marker onto Route 2038. Continue along this road for 38 km to the national park. It is also possible to get here by public transport: take a bus from the public bus terminal to Phu Wiang district town. From the town take a songthaew or tuk-tuk to the national park, about ฿200.

Phu Wiang National Park

- Viewing Pavilion
- Quarry 1
- Quarry 2 & Shellfish Cemetery
- Car Park
- Quarry 9
- Quarry 3
- Reservoir
- Car Park
- Reservoir
- Bungalows (under construction)
- Reservoir
- Toilets
- Check Point
- To Phu Wiang

0 metres 200
0 yards 200

- - - - Laterite Road (unsurface negotiable by vehicle)

Ban Kok Also known as **Tortoise Village**, Ban Kok is a sight that the TAT has recently begun to promote. A rather confused and confusing tale about tortoises means that they are regarded as sacred by the inhabitants of Ban Kok and surrounding villages. There are now said to be 2,000 of the animals (yellow tortoises or, in Thai, *khanaeng*) wandering about, unmolested, eating every piece of greenery in sight. Those who have hurt the tortoises have been afflicted with all sorts of strange maladies. Visitors to the village should respect the villagers' regard for the tortoises. ■ *Getting there: Ban Kok is 50 km from Khon Kaen. Take the Khon Kaen-Chumpae road past the airport and turn left at Ban Thum Then onto Route 2062. Continue along this road to the 40 km marker and turn onto an access road by the Shell petrol station. The village is a short distance off the main road. By public transport, take a bus from the public bus station in Khon Kaen to Mancha Kiri district town (there is said to be a bus at 0600 and a return bus at 1830); from here it is 4 km to Ban Kok.*

This is a recently renovated Khmer temple (10th century), about 80 km southeast of Khon Kaen. The four buildings that comprise the structure make it similar to the far better known Pimai – but smaller in scale. There is some sculpture. ■ *Getting there: take the main Khon Kaen-Korat highway (Route 2) and turn off at Ban Phai onto Route 23. After 23 km, turn off again onto Route 2297. This leads to the temple, which is situated at the entrance to a village.* **Prasat Puaynoi**

The Ubon Rat Reservoir lies about 50 km from Khon Kaen. It appears to the casual visitor to be an inland sea. There is a 'beach' here, with swimming, watersports, beach umbrellas and excellent fish; you could be on Phuket (well, almost). Vendors bring delicacies to your table; great for families (the water is not deep at the beach) and a wonderful day out. Not a farang in sight. Just before arriving at the beach is the small town of Ubon Rat, with a large hilltop Buddha overlooking the dam (441 steps to the top). The shrine beneath the Buddha has finely carved wooden shutters depicting scenes from the Buddha's life. ■ *Getting there: the dam and reservoir lie about 50 km northwest of Khon Kaen. Travel north on Highway 2 and turn left onto Route 2109 after about 28 km; the settlement of Ubon Rat is about 20 km along here.* **Ubon Rat Reservoir**

The Northeastern Region

Essentials

As one of the northeast's main commercial centres, Khon Kaen is well provided for with good and mid-range hotels. But there are no guesthouses to compare with those in other tourist areas, only cheap hotels, and many of those seem to be either distinctly unfriendly and/or geared to short-term customers. **Sleeping**
■ *on map, page 432*
Price codes:
see inside front cover

A *Hotel Sofitel Raja Orchid*, 9/9 Prachasamosorn Rd, T322155, F322150. A/c, restaurant, pool, health club and gym. Rather a monstrous hotel which opened in 1996 with several hundred rooms, but as Khon Kaen is hardly vying for World Heritage status this probably doesn't matter much. Efficient with a good range of facilities, occasionally provincial charm pushes the glitz aside and you realize that Khan Kaen does lie at the heart of Thailand's poorest region. The hotel's 3 restaurants cover just about the entire Asian region and offer Vietnamese, Chinese and Thai cuisine, as well as the requisite coffee shop. **B** *Charoen Thani Royal Princess*, 260 Sri Chand Rd, T220400, F220438. A/c, restaurant, pool with a great view of the city (open to non-residents), 320 rooms in high-rise block, a little piece of Bangkok in Khon Kaen, central location and good rates available, including discounts in the wet season. It is now looking a little jaded because the local tycoon who built the hotel during the years of boom has fallen on lean times. **B** *Kaen Inn*, 56 Klang Muang Rd, T237744, F239457. A/c, restaurant, well run but rather characterless, with all 'business' facilities. **B** *Khon Kaen*, 43/2 Phimphasut Rd, T237711, F242458. A/c, restaurant, geared to Thai businessmen with bars and massage parlours, comfortable – no more. **B** *Kosa*, 250-252 Srichand Rd,

T225014, F225013. A/c, restaurant, pool, the original 'Western' hotel, comfortable rooms, massage parlour, live music in the restaurant. Recommended. **B-C** *Rosesukon*, 1/10 Klang Muang Rd, T237797, F238579. A/c, comfortable modern hotel lacking in any character, barring the novel notion of placing slices of lemon in the men's urinals as an environmentally friendly form of air freshener.

C *Roma*, 50/2 Klang Muang Rd, T236276. Some a/c, the poor cousin to the *Khon Kaen*. Bare functional rooms in bare functional block which looks as though it has been made out of lego – but very reasonable for a/c and hot water and the best value place in town. Recommended. **D** *Kaen Nakorn*, 690 Sri Chand Rd, T224268. A/c, clean. **D** *Villa*, 79/1 Klang Muang Rd, T236640. A/c, massage parlour attached and certain amount of 'short term' business, hostile to Westerners. **D-E** *Sawatdi*, 177-9 Na Muang Rd, T221600. Some a/c. **E** *Saensamran*, 55-59 Klang Muang Rd, T239611. Rooms are dark and resemble a public toilet. **E** *Suksawad*, 2/2 Klang Muang Rd, T236472. Wooden building down soi off main road, so relatively quiet, rooms are shabby but clean, friendly, attached bathrooms, 3 min walk from the tourist office.

Eating
● *on map*
Price categories:
see inside front cover

The best selection of
cheaper Chinese/Thai
restaurants is on
Klang Muang Rd,
between the Kaen Inn
& Suksawad Hotel

Thai/Chinese Cheap: *Diamond Garden* (Beer Garden), Srichand Rd, near the Fairy Plaza. Thai. **Seriously cheap**: *Nong Lek*, 54/1-3 Klang Muang Rd. Well patronized Chinese restaurant, specialities including *khaaw na pet* (rice and duck) and seafood dishes. Recommended.

Vietnamese Cheap: *Krua We*, 1/1 Klang Muang Rd. Very good Vietnamese food as well as Isan specialities, served in attractive wooden house. Recommended.

Khon Kaen

Sleeping
1 Charoen Thani
  Royal Princess
2 Kaen Inn
3 Kaen Nakorn
4 Khon Kaen
5 Kosa
6 Roma
7 Rosesukon & Krua
  We Restaurant
8 Saensamran
9 Sawatdi
10 Sofitel Raja Orchid
11 Suksawad & Pizza
  & Bake Restaurant
12 Villa

Eating
1 Best Place
2 Parrot
3 Rachada

Matmii: Queen of cloths

Matmii cloth is perhaps the Northeast's most distinctive and best-known handicraft; some would say, work of art. It is a form of ikat, with the characteristic blurring of colours that is an inevitable product of the tie-dyeing process (see page 371).

Matmii can be made of either silk or cotton yarn. It is the silk cloths which are inevitably the finest and most expensive. The geometric designs are usually based on nature, snakes, flowers and birds, although these have become so abstracted in most cases as to be almost unrecognizable. However, cloth from Laos (or those made in Thailand, but imitating Lao designs) do sometimes clearly depict elephants, geese and other animals. Designs are handed down from mother to daughter and range from the simple sai fon (falling rain) design, where random sections of weft are tied, to the more complex mee gung and poon som. The less common pha kit is a supplementary weft ikat, although the designs are similar to those of matmii. Natural dyes derived from roots, insects and

earths are very rarely used today; almost all cloth is dyed using chemical dyes, which are cheaper, fix more easily and provide a wider range of colours to the weaver. There is, however, a movement to rediscover some of these natural dyes and promote their use again.

The resuscitation of the matmii weaving industry in the Northeast is closely associated with the work of Queen Sirikit. Until the mid-1970s, matmii production was in decline as cheaper and more colourful machine-made textiles, often made from synthetic yarn, became popular. But now wearing shirts and skirts made from matmii has become de rigueur in Bangkok, and tourist demand has also boosted the industry.

Matmii is usually sold by the phun, a length. A sarong length is usually two phun. Prices vary according to whether the cloth is silk or cotton and the complexity of the design. A simple cotton matmii may cost only ฿150 per phun; the finest silk ฿3,000 or more.

Western Cheap: *Best Place*, Klang Muang Rd (near *Kaen Inn*). Rather sanitized a/c restaurant, serving pizzas, burgers and other similar dishes. *Parrot*, 175 Sri Chand Rd. International. *Pizza and Bake*, Klang Muang Rd. Pizzas, burgers and various Thai dishes, good place for breakfast and Western food if needed.

Bakeries and ice-cream Seriously cheap: *Rachadaa*, corner of Na Muang and Prachasamoson roads. Ice-creams served at tables set in a small garden. *Sweet Home*, 79 Fairy Plaza, Srichand Rd. Ice-cream and bakery.

Foodstalls Usual array of foodstalls to be found on the streets. A good selection near the a/c bus terminal, off Sri Chand Rd.

Along with the high density of karaoke bars and massage parlours, there is also a cinema on Sri Chand Rd not far from the *Kosa Hotel*, which has a room where the soundtrack of English language films is piped. **Entertainment**

Late Nov to early Dec *Silk Fair and Phuk Siao (friendship) Festival* (movable). Wide variety of silks on sale and production processes demonstrated. People tie threads around each other's wrists to symbolize their friendship, known as *phuk siao* (*siao* means 'friend' in Lao). Folk culture performances. The festival is centred on the Sala Klang Changwat or Provincial Hall on the north side of town. **Festivals**

The Northeastern Region

Shopping

There is a general market area, opposite the bus station on Prachasamosorn Rd, & a larger market on Klang Muang Rd. Villagers hawk textiles on the street

Silk See also box, page 433. Good quality matmii silk and other traditional cloth can be found in Khon Kaen. *Heng Hguan Hiang*, 54/1-2 Klang Muang Rd (near intersection with Srichand Rd). Sells textiles, axe-pillows, Isan food and other handicrafts. *Prathamakant*, 79/2-3 Ruanrom Rd. Silk, cotton and handicrafts. *Rin Thai*, 412 Na Muang Rd, T221042. A long-established silk shop selling silk, cotton, local handicrafts, souvenirs and ready-to-wear clothes. Other local products include spicy pork sausages, which can be seen hanging in many shops. **Books** *Smart Books*, Klang Muang Rd. Some English books and a good range of stationery.

Sport

Swimming at the *Charoen Thani Hotel*, ₿50.

Tour operators

Northeast Travel Service, 87/56 Klang Muang Rd, T244792, F243238. At the a/c bus terminal. *Air Booking and Travel Centre Co*, 4 Srichand Rd, T244482.

Transport

See also Ins & outs, page 429;
450 km to Bangkok,
189 km to Korat,
207 km to Loei,
117 km to Udon

Local Saamlors and tuk-tuks. But the cheapest way around town is by songthaew. These coloured converted pick-ups run along 12 routes, fare ₿4. A list of the routes and stops can be picked up from the TAT office. **Car hire**: *R Rent Service*, T243543, ₿1500 per day.

Long distance **Air**: airport is 2 km off Route 12 to Phitsanulok, 6 km from town. Regular daily connections with Bangkok (55 mins) on *Thai*. **Train**: station on Station Rd in the southwest quarter of town. Regular connections with Bangkok's Hualamphong station (8 hrs), Korat and other stops en route north to Nong Khai. **Bus**: the vast non-a/c bus station is on Prachasamoson Rd; a/c buses leave from the terminal just off Klang Muang Rd. Regular connections with Bangkok's Northeastern bus terminal. Buses, both a/c and non-a/c, run to most other Northeastern towns and to Chiang Mai and Chiang Rai, and to Rayong (for Pattaya).

Directory

Airline offices *Thai*, 183/6 Maliwan Rd, T236523. **Banks** *Bangkok*, Sri Chand Rd (near the *Kosa Hotel*). *Siam Commercial*, 491 Sri Chand Rd. *Krung Thai*, 457-461 Srichand Rd. *Thai Farmers*, 145 Prachasamoson Rd. **Communications** Post Office: Klang Muang Rd (near the intersection with Sri Chand Rd), T221147. **Embassies and consulates** *Lao PDR Consulate*, 123 Photisan Rd, T223698. Tourist visas available for US$40, 1 hr service. Also provides leaflets detailing 'How to enter Laos/Vietnam'. *Vietnamese Consulate*, 65/6 Chatapadung Rd, T241586. **Medical services** Hospital, Sri Chand Rd, T236005. **Useful addresses** Police: Klang Muang Rd, T211162 (near Post Office).

West from the northeast to Phitsanulok

The route passes through the Phetchabun Mountains, descending (sometimes in hair-raising fashion) from the harsh terrain of the Northeast to the more fertile rice plains of the north. The land before the turn-off for Lom Sak (200 km from Khon Kaen, and 100 km from Phitsanulok and the usual bus route to Loei) is surely some of the most depressing in Thailand, at least for anyone with an environmental conscience. The forest has been decimated and all that remains is a wasteland of bare tree trunks and grassland. The area was a stronghold of the Communists until the early 1980s and has since been declared a national park: the Phu Hin Rongkla National Park (see page 203). It was partly in order to deprive the Communist rebels of a safe haven that the government allowed, some would say encouraged, the deforestation of the area.

Phetchabun เพชรบูรณ์

Phetchabun lies in the border lands that divide the Northeastern and Northern regions. Administratively it is part of the latter region, but in cultural and environmental terms it feels more like the Northeastern – hence its inclusion here in the Northeastern chapter. The town itself lies off the main route north and is rarely visited by foreign visitors, although it can be used as a base to visit the Si Thep Historical Park (see Excursions below). The town is located at the confluence of no less than five rivers, the most important of which is the Pasak River which here joins forces with the Kao, Ku, Taluk and Sala rivers. For a reason beyond the ken of most analysts, the aviation department opened an airport in Phetchabun in 2000. The answer is pretty simple: in the early 1990s the MP for the area was a deputy transport minister.

Phone code: 056
Colour map 2, grid B1

In town, **Wat Traiphum** on Phetcharat Road, within walking distance northeast of the town centre, contains a locally renowned Buddha image in Lopburi style. This image is said to have been found washed up on the banks of the Pasak River which flows through the town, at a spot opposite Wat Traiphum. The image was hauled up the river bank and installed in the wat. Some time later the image was found to have disappeared from the Wat, only to be rediscovered at the same spot on the Pasak River where it was originally recovered. Taking this as a sign that the image had incurable wanderlust (Buddha images are believed to have their own characters and predilections), each year the Phra Buddha Mahathammarat, as it is known, is paraded through town during the Sart Festival. The procession ends up at the very same spot on the Pasak River, for which the image has such an affinity. **Wat Mahathat** on Charoen Pattana Road, on the western edge of the centre of town, was established during the Sukhothai period (1238-1350) and was renovated by the Fine Arts Department in 1967.

Sights

The **Si Thep Historical Park** lies 107 km from town (see page 194). The **Phu Hin Rongkla National Park** lies partly within Phetchabun Province and is accessible from town (see page 203).

Excursions

A *Phu Kaew Princess*, T02-2384790, F2384797, for details and reservations. A new hotel in the Dusit group, about which we have few details. However, judging by their other hotels it should be very comfortable with most facilities. **D** *Burapha*, 308 Saraburi-Lomsak Rd, T721384. Some a/c, nearly 100 rooms, but rather inconveniently located to the north of the town centre on the main north-south highway. **E** *Sawatdii*, 54 Sankhumuang Rd, T721850. Some a/c, 24 rooms, central location. **E** *Siam*, 21 Sankhumuang Rd, T711301. Some a/c, 29 rooms, central location.

Sleeping

Air In 2000 a new airport was opened in Phetchabun, despite the lack of tourist or business interest in the immediate area. The airport is 28 km from town. Expect it to close when political winds and the balance of power changes. **Bus** The bus terminal, *bor kor sor*, is just off Sankhumuang Rd, to the south of the Sala River, within walking distance from the centre of town and most accommodation. Regular connections by both a/c and non-a/c buses with Bangkok and other regional centres in the North, Northeast and Central Plains.

Transport

Communications Post Office: Phra Buddhabat Rd (near the bridge over the Taluk River). **Telephone office:** Phetcharoen Rd (at the confluence of the Taluk and Ku rivers).

Directory

The Northeastern Region

Udon Thani อุดรธานี

Phone code: 042
Colour map 2, grid A3
Population: 115,000

Udon is a busy town with seemingly the greatest concentration of pedal saamlors in Thailand, which makes for hazardous driving. The northern quarter of the town contains government offices, with large, tree-filled compounds. Elsewhere the atmosphere is frenetic, or as close to frenetic as it is possible to get in this part of Thailand. The neatly kept palm-fringed roundabouts provide a tropical Riviera feel amidst the bustle; Udon has a reputation of being one of Thailand's cleanest provincial capitals. Most tourists only stay here because of its proximity to the outstanding prehistoric site at Ban Chiang. Like Khon Kaen, Udon was a boom town during the Vietnam War, so it retains reminders of that time, with massage parlours, bars, coffee shops and fully air-conditioned hotels. It is said that about 60 former US servicemen have married Thais and settled here. There is even a Udon branch of the US Veterans of Foreign Wars Association, along with a relay station of VoA (Voice of America), so the US-Udon link lives on.

The Northeastern Region

Ins and outs

Getting there
See also Transport, page 439

Udon is well connected partly because there was an important US airforce base here during the Vietnam War. The airport is 2 km out of town, with multiple daily flights to Bangkok. The train station is just to the east of the town centre, and there are services south to Bangkok and a stop further north to Nong Khai. Udon's 2 bus terminals, 1 central and the second slightly out of town, provide connections with Bangkok, Chiang Mai, Chiang Rai and most destinations in the Northeast.

Getting around

A profusion of saamlors provide the main mode of city transport, with buses and songthaews linking the town with local out of town destinations. Car hire is possible.

Tourist offices

TAT, Thesa Rd, facing Nong Prachak Silpakhorn, T325406, F325408. Open 0830-1630, limited resources but maps of Udon available.

Sights

In the northwestern quarter of town is **Nong Prachak Park**, a municipal park set around a large lake. There are a number of reasonable garden restaurants here and it is one of the more attractive places to come for an evening meal.

Excursions

Ban Chiang
One of the most important archaeological sites to be uncovered in SE Asia since the Second World War

Ban Chiang, 56 km east of Udon, was accidentally discovered by an American anthropology student, Stephen Young, in 1966. While walking in the village fields he fell over the root of a kapok tree and into history: all around him, protruding from the ground, were potsherds. Appreciating that his find might be significant, he sent the potsherds for analysis to the Fine Arts Department in Bangkok and then later to the University of Pennsylvania. Rumours of his finds spread and much of the area was then ransacked by the villagers, who sold the pieces they unearthed to collectors in Bangkok and abroad. Organized excavations only really commenced during the 1970s, when a Thai archaeologist, Pisit Charoenwongsa, and Chester Gorman, from Pennsylvania,

- -
Udon Thani place names

Ban Chiang

บ้านเชียง

Erawan Cave

ถ้ำเอราวัณ

Phu Phra Bat Historical Park

อุทยานประวัติศาสตร์ภูพระบาท

arrived to investigate the site (Gorman tragically died of cancer at the age of only 43 in 1981). Even though their task was compromised by the random digging of villagers and others, they still managed to unearth 18 tonnes of material in two years, including 5,000 bags of sherds and 123 burials.

The site spans a time period of over 5,000 years. Perhaps the greatest discovery is the bronzeware which has been dated to 3600 BC, thus pre-dating bronzeware found in the Middle East by 500 years. This shattered the belief that bronze metallurgy had developed in the Tigris and Euphrates basin about 3000 BC, and from there diffused to other parts of the world. The finds also indicated to archaeologists that they had been wrong about the relationship between China and Thailand; the oldest known bronzes from China only go back to 2000 BC, so bronze technology may well have gone from Thailand to China instead of vice versa, as had been previously believed. The site at Ban Chiang also provides evidence of an early development of agriculture. Again, it had previously been thought that settled agriculture evolved far later in Southeast Asia (which was regarded as a cultural backwater) than in China and the Middle East. Such a perspective can no longer be sustained following the excavations at Ban Chiang and elsewhere in the northeast (for example, Non Nok Tha and Ban Na Di).

Nevertheless, there is still heated debate among archaeologists about the dating and interpretation of many of the finds. In addition, despite these dramatic discoveries, little is known of the agricultural society which inhabited the site and which produced beautiful pots of burnt ochre 'swirl' design, sophisticated metalwork and jewellery. It was obviously not a hostile society, as the vast majority of the bronze artefacts discovered have been bangles, bracelets and anklets. The large number of infant burials (in jars) has also led archaeologists to speculate that the inhabitants led a precarious existence and possibly practised infanticide to stabilize population against food supply.

There are two burial pits at **Wat Pho Si Nai**, on the edge of the village of Ban Chiang. They have been left open for visitors to gain an idea of the process of excavation and the distribution of the finds; the first 'on site' museum in Thailand. At the other side of the village is a new, and excellent, orthodox museum. The Ban Chiang story is retold with clarity, displaying excellent models and many of the finds. The exhibition was put together with the help of the Smithsonian, Washington DC, and toured the US between 1982 and 1986. There is a guesthouse close to the museum, the **E** *Lakeside Sunrise Guesthouse*, T042-208167, with simple but clean rooms. ∎ *The site is open 1000-1600 Wed-Sun, ฿20. To cash in on the visitors to the site (tour buses now come here), the villagers of Ban Chiang, prevented from selling artefacts openly, market a range of handicrafts instead in shops around the museum. Getting there: after 50 km from Udon, turn left onto Route 2225 (signposted to the Ban Chiang Museum). The village is another 6 km along this road. Buses run direct to the village from the Udon bus station. Alternatively, take a bus going along Route 22 to Sakhon Nakhon and ask to be let off at Ban Chiang (just after the Km 50 marker). Tuk-tuk drivers hang around the junction to take visitors to the site.*

Erawan Cave

Tham Erawan – 'Elephant Cave' – is found 40 km west of Udon, about 2 km off Route 210, on the left-hand side of the road. The cave (as usual, linked to a wat, Wat Tham Erawan) is larger and more impressive than the usual selection of holes in the ground that pass as caves in Thailand. ∎ *Getting there: by bus en route to Loei.*

Phu Phra Bat Historical Park

Sixty kilometres north of the Erawan Caves, this sight has been almost continuously inhabited since prehistoric times (see page 451).

The Northeastern Region

Essentials

Sleeping
● *on map*
Price categories:
see inside front cover

A *Charoensri Grand Royal*, Prachak Rd (next to the main shopping complex, T343555, F3435502. A/c, a 250-room high-rise hotel, popular with royalty (hence the name change from *Charoensri* to *Charoensri Grand Royal* when they are in town), excellent Chinese restaurant (although unfortunately it now only really operates for parties). **A-B** *Napalai*, 572 Pracha-Raksa Rd, T347444, F347447, 2 km out of the city centre. A/c, restaurant, pool, good service and amenities, wonderful pool, excellent value. **B** *Ban Chiang*, Mukhamontri Rd, T327911, F223200. With 120 rooms, yet another mass-produced international standard hotel with nothing to recommend it. **B** *Charoen*, 549 Pho Sri Rd, T248155, F241093. A/c, restaurant, bar and nightclub, pool, Western-style, comfortable, good value, with newly opened wing offering high level of comfort at a higher price. For many years the best hotel in town, it has recently been eclipsed by 2 newer places (see above). **B** *Sleep Inn*, 14 Moo 1, Udon-Nongbualamphu Rd, T346223, F346514. Udon's very own airport hotel. New and efficient with 114 rooms, set in a garden plot with all mod cons, but really only useful for those looking for a place to stay before or after catching a flight close to the airport.

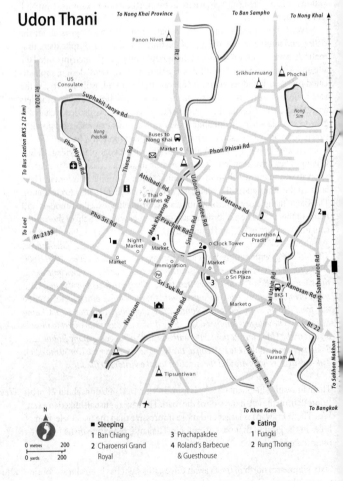

Udon Thani

■ Sleeping
1 Ban Chiang
2 Charoensri Grand Royal
3 Prachapakdee
4 Roland's Barbecue & Guesthouse

● Eating
1 Fungki
2 Rung Thong

C *Charoensri Palace*, 60 Pho Sri Rd, T242611, F222601. A/c, restaurant. **C** *Udon*, 81-89 Mak Khaeng Rd, T248160, F242782. A/c, central with 90 rooms, noisy and a little dishevelled, but friendly. **C-D** *Roland's Barbecue and Guesthouse*, off Sri Chom Chuen Rd. South of the city, short-term prices quoted, best avoided. **D** *Prachapakdee*, 156/8 Sulpakorn Rd, T221804. Functional rooms with clean attached bathrooms. Receptive staff, reasonable rates, in a convenient central location. **D-E** *Paradise*, 44/29 Pho Sri Rd, T221956. Some a/c, usefully located near the bus station, but little else to particularly recommended it. **D-E** *Thailand*, 4/1-6 Surakhon Rd, T221951. Some a/c. There are at least another 13 hotels at **D-E** grade, all basic with little obvious to distinguish between them. **E-F** *Srisawat*, 123 Prachak Rd. Rather seedy place with just 28 rooms, and noisy – but more atmospheric than most.

Fresh-baked 'baguettes' are available in Udon Thani; the bakeries here are some of the best in the country. Local specialities include shredded pork, or *muu yong*, and preserved meats.

Eating
● *on map*
Price categories:
see inside front cover

Thai/Chinese Mid-range: *Mayfair*, Charoen Hotel, 549 Pho Sri Rd. Perhaps the best Thai/Chinese restaurant in town, pricey for Northeast Thailand but worth a splash out. **Cheap**: *Rabeang Pochana*, 53 Suphakit Janya Rd (beside the lake). Locals continue to recommend this restaurant as the best in town. **Seriously cheap**: *Rung Thong*, Hor Nalikaa. A simple place facing onto the clock tower, which serves good, wholesome Thai and Chinese food at reasonable prices (not open in the evening).

There are some quite good garden restaurants around the lake in Nong Prachak Park

Indochinese Cheap: *Fungki Restaurant*, Pho Sri Rd. Excellent range of Thai/Indochinese food at a range of prices.

Buffet lunches Good value and excellent buffet lunches are available at both the *Charoen* and the *Charoensri Grand Royal* hotels, with the former probably just winning by a short head.

Western and fast food *Robinsons Plaza*, off Pho Sri Rd. For a choice of fast food chains: *KFC*, *Pizza Hut*, *Swensens*.

Robinson's Plaza, off Pho Sri Rd, has an abundance of shops, cafés and Western-style eating places.

Shopping

Most tour companies can arrange visas for Laos, but they are more expensive than in Bangkok. *Kannika Tour*, 36/9 Srisatha Rd, T241378, F241378. Tours in the Northeast and to Laos, Cambodia and Vietnam. *Aranya Tour*, 105 Mak Khaeng Rd, T243182. Also arranges visas for Indo-China. *Toy Ting*, 55/1-5 Thahaan Rd, T244771.

Tour operators

Local Car hire: *VIP Car Rent*, 824 Pho Sri Rd, T223758; *Parada Car Rent*, 78/1 Mak Khaeng Rd, T244147. **Taxi**: Mr Narong is based at the *Charoen Hotel*, T240887. He speaks no English, but is very reliable and charges ฿1,000 per day. Recommended.

Transport
See also Ins & outs, page 436;
560 km from Bangkok, 117 km from Khon Kaen, 306 km from Korat

Long distance Air: airport 2 km out of town off Route 2, south to Khon Kaen. Regular connections with Bangkok (1 hr), 4 times daily, on *Thai*. *Angel Airlines* now fly daily between Bangkok and Udon Thani, and also operates a thrice-weekly service between Chiang Mai and Udon.

Train: station is off Lang Sathanirotfai Rd. Regular connections with Bangkok's Hualamphong station (10 hrs) and all stops en route – Ayutthaya, Saraburi, Korat, Khon Kaen and on to Nong Khai.

The Northeastern Region

Bus: Udon has 2 main bus stations. BKS 2 is on the northwestern edge of town, about 2 km from the centre along Pho Sri Rd. Buses leave here for Chiang Mai and Chiang Rai in the North, Nakhon Phanom and Nong Khai in the Northeast, and Bangkok. There are buses to Phitsanulok, where there are connections to other destinations in the Central Plains and Northern region. Buses also run from the more central BKS 1 on Sai Uthit Rd, just off Pho Sri Rd. Destinations include Korat, Nakhon Phanom, Ubon, Khon Kaen, Roi Et, Sakhon Nakhon and Nong Khai, all in the Northeast, and Bangkok passengers can get to/from BKS 2 by yellow town buses (no 23) which run into the centre. A third smaller bus terminal is associated with the market, north of the centre on Udon-Dutsadee Rd. There are connections from here with Nong Khai.

Directory **Airline offices** *Thai*, 60 Mak Khaeng Rd, T246697. **Banks** *Bangkok Bank*, Pho Sri Rd. *Krung Thai*, 216 Mak Khaeng Rd. *Thai Farmers*, 236 Pho Sri Rd. **Communications** Post Office: Wattananuvong Rd (near the Provincial Governor's Office). **Embassies & consulates** *US Consulate*, 35/6 Suphakit Janya Rd, T244270 (northern section of town). **Medical services** Pho Niyom Rd, T222572. **Useful addresses** Police: Sri Suk Rd, T222285.

Nong Bua Lamphu

Nong Bua Lamphu is one of Thailand's newest provinces. It was formed from part of Udon Thani at the end of 1993 and, frankly, it shows. It feels as though this tiny town is just getting used to the idea of being a provincial capital; it is merely a junction on the road between Udon Thani and Loei. The only reason to stop here is for access to Phu Phan Kham National Park and the Erawan Caves (see page 442).

Sleeping & eating
Currently, there is a meagre choice of places to stay

F *Sawangchit*, 53 Wijarnrangsan Rd, T311349. Perched above a dining room, next to the *Thai Farmers Bank*. Shared facilities, shabby and basic, but lively atmosphere makes this an adequate stopover. **F** *Sri Somporn*, 68 Pho Chai Rd, T311048 (no English sign). Perhaps preferable to the *Sawangchit*, but it is a close call. It is slightly further from the centre, with cleaner rooms but bad mosquitoes. Basic facilities.

Nanseuy, serves various dishes. The owner, Amy, speaks English and will provide information on the surroundings. This makes a good place to take a break on the long Udon-Loei journey. There are also numerous stalls lining the busy streets.

Transport **Bus** from Udon Thani, (1 hr), from Loei, (2½ hrs). Buses can be caught from junction of Wisanudonk Rd and Route 210.

Directory **Airline offices** *Thai Airways* on Wisanudonk Rd. **Communications** Post Office: west side of lake next to telecom office (no international phone available).

Nong Bua Lamphu

To Loei

Supermarket
Market
Rt 210
To Udon Thani

Bus Stop
& Tuk Tuk
Stage

Naresuam Rd
Wisanudonk Rd

Sri Somporn
Po Chai Rd

Sawangchit
Supermarket
Wiriyothin
Wijarnrangsum Rd
Market

N

0 metres   200
0 yards   200

To Namseuy
Restaurant (400m)

To Thai Airways
Office (400m),
Chumphae
& Khon Kaen

£4000 worth of holiday vouchers to be won!

... that can be claimed against any exodus, Peregrine or Gecko's holiday, a choice of around 570 holidays that set industry standards for responsible tourism in 90 countries across seven continents.

exodus

The UK's leading adventurous travel company, with over 25 years' experience in running the most exciting holidays in 80 different countries. We have an unrivalled choice of trips, from a week exploring the hidden corners of Tuscany to a high altitude trek to Everest Base Camp or 3 months travelling across South America. If you want to do something a little different, chances are you'll find it in one of our brochures.

Peregrine

Australia's leading quality adventure travel company, Peregrine aims to explore some of the world's most interesting and inaccessible places. Providing exciting and enjoyable holidays that focus in some depth on the lifestyle, culture, history, wildlife, wilderness and landscapes of areas that are usually quite different to our own. There is an emphasis on the outdoors, using a variety of transport and staying in a range of accommodation, from comfortable hotels to tribal huts.

Gecko's

Gecko's holidays will get you to the best places with the minimum of hassle. They are designed for younger people who like independent travel but don't have the time to organise everything themselves. Be prepared to take the rough with the smooth, these holidays are for active people with a flexible approach to travel.

To enter the competition, simply tear out the postcard and return it to Exodus Travels, 9 Weir Road, London SW12 0LT. Or go to the competition page on www.exodus.co.uk and register online. Two draws will be made, Easter 2001 and Easter 2002, and the winner of each draw will receive £2000 in travel vouchers. The closing date for entry will be 1st March 2002. If you do not wish to receive further information about these holidays, please tick here. ☐ No purchase necessary. Plain paper entries should be sent to the above address. The prize value is non-transferable and there is no cash alternative. Winners must be over 18 years of age and must sign and adhere to operators' standard booking conditions. A list of prizewinners will be available for a period of one month from the draw by writing to the above address. For a full list of terms and conditions please write to the above address or visit our website.
To receive a brochure, please tick the relevant boxes below (maximum number of brochures 2) or telephone (44) 20 8772 3822.

exodus	Peregrine	Gecko's
☐ Walking & Trekking	☐ Himalaya	☐ Egypt, Jordan & Israel
☐ Discovery & Adventure	☐ China	☐ South America
☐ European Destinations	☐ South East Asia	☐ Africa
☐ Overland Journeys	☐ Antarctica	☐ South East Asia
☐ Biking Adventures	☐ Africa	☐ India
☐ Multi Activity	☐ Arctic	

Please give us your details:

Name: --

Address: --

Postcode: --

e-mail: --

Which footprint guide did you take this from?

----

exodus
The Different Holiday

(left margin) exodus The Different Holiday

(left margin) getaway tonight on www.exodus.co.uk

getaway tonight on

www.exodus.co.uk

exodus
The Different Holiday

exodus

9 Weir Road
LONDON
SW12 0BR

The northern Mekong River route

The Mekong River forms the border between Thailand and Laos for several 100 km in the Northeastern region. The Mekong River route begins for many at Loei, a provincial capital 50 km south of the Mekong and within easy reach of a number of fine national parks in the Phetchabun hills, including the popular Phu Kradung National Park. The riverside town of Chiang Khan provides a peaceful base with atmospheric accommodation. Travelling downstream, the beautiful river road passes through, in turn, Pak Chom (41 km from Chiang Khan), Sang Khom (another 63 km) and Si Chiangmai (a further 39 km), before reaching the provincial capital of Nong Khai (in total, 200 km from Chiang Khan). Nong Khai, with ferry access to Laos and the capital Vientiane, has become increasingly popular and two large hotels have recently opened. The town is one of the most attractive in the region, with French-style colonial architecture.

Loei เลย

This frontier settlement, known as Muang Loei, has dusty streets and seedy-looking shophouses, and is situated on the Loei River. Most tourists visit Loei either as a stop-off on the way to Chiang Khan (see Excursions below) or to sample the remarkable scenery of the area; there are no city sights as such. Loei, an important cotton growing area, is known for its warm cotton quilts, available in many shops around town.

Phone code: 042
Colour map 2, grid A2
Population: 25,000

Of all the provinces of the Northeast, Loei has managed to preserve the greatest proportion of its forests and the surrounding area was a haven for the Communist guerrillas until the early 1980s. There are a number of national parks in the province, of which the most famous is the **Phu Kradung National Park** (see Excursions below). Also accessible is the **Phu Hin Rongkla National Park**, an area formerly used as a sanctuary by the Communists, and the **Phu Reua National Park**.

Phu Kradung National Park is named after Phu Kradung or 'Bell Mountain', the highest point in the province of Loei at 1,571 m. The mountain is in fact a plateau which lies at between 1,200 m and 1,500 m. There are three explanations as to the origin of the mountain's name: one, and the most logical, is that it merely refers to the shape of the peak; the second is that it refers to the wild bulls (*krating*; the popular stimulant drink 'krating daeng' means 'red bull') which used to inhabit the area; and the third, and the more pleasing, is that on Buddhist holy days the noise of a bell can be heard issuing from the mountain. It is one of the coolest areas in Thailand; temperatures sometimes fall to near freezing-point from November to January, so come prepared. Loei, not coincidentally, is one of the centres for the production and sale of heavy cotton quilts. The park covers 348 sq km and supports a range of vegetation types: tropical evergreen forest, savanna forest and even some trees typical of temperate locations, for example oak and beech. Wild flowers are particularly prolific in the park – especially orchids. Mammals found in the park include wild pig, Asian wild dog and the white-handed gibbon, along with less frequently seen elephants, Asiatic black bears and sambar barking deer. There are at least 130 species of bird in the park. Residents include the brown hornbill, maroon oriole, large scimitar babbler and the snowy-browed flycatcher. There are nearly 50 km of marked trails for the keen trekker and naturalist. The park station at Sithan (at the foot of the mountain) has an Information Centre, restaurants and porters. For some time now there have been plans to construct a

Excursions
This park is one of the most beautiful in all Thailand

cable car up Phu Kradung, but they are encountering considerable protest from environmental and other groups.

Park essentials Tents can be hired (฿50) and camping is permitted at the summit (฿5). There are also cabins of various sizes and prices. Outside the national park is (**B**) *Phu Kradung House*, T811449, which has a large number of bungalows with hot water. Trekking maps are available and it is a strenuous 6 km hike up to the plateau itself, where the park HQ is situated. There is some basic accommodation (**E**), T02-5790529, and stalls selling food and basic necessities. Porters will carry luggage for ฿5 per kg. It is a very popular spot with Thais, so can be quite crowded at the weekends during the dry season, especially Dec to mid-Jan. The park is 82 km south of Loei, 8 km off Route 201 on Route 2019. Admission is ฿25. Gates open 0700-1500 Mon-Sun. **NB** The park is closed during the rainy season Jun-Aug. Best time to visit: Feb-Apr to see wild flowers, Nov-Dec to see the waterfalls at their best. Getting there: bus from Loei to Phu Kradung town, 1½ hrs (the Khon Kaen bus, leaving every 30 mins); from here there are motorcycles, songthaews and tuk-tuks to cover the final 8 km to the park office. From the south, catch a bus via Chumphae to Pa Nok Kao. From there, local buses leave for Phu Kradung town (8 km) and then motorcycles or charter cars are available for the trip to the park.

Phu Hin Rongkla National Park lies about 150 km southwest of Loei on Route 2113 to Phitsanulok. It was used as a base by the CPT in the 1970s and early 1980s and has become a sight, of sorts, as a result, see page 203 for more details. ■ *Getting there: catch one of the regular buses towards Phitsanulok via Nakhon Thai, and get off at Nakhon Thai (note that a/c buses usually go via Lom Sak and not via Nakhon Thai). From there, songthaews run to the park.*

Tham Paa Phu, a Buddhist meditation cave, is 11 km from town on the road to Tha Li. Kutis are arranged along a steep cliff; a peaceful place. ■ *Getting there: by bus towards Tha Li or by tuk-tuk.*

Erawan Caves are located 54 km east of Loei, 2 km off Route 210 running towards Udon Thani; see Udon Thani Excursions, page 437. ■ *Getting there: by bus en route to Udon.*

Tha Li and Chiang Khan are on the frontier with Laos, about 50 km north of Loei. For travellers searching for a 'Wild northeast' atmosphere (or as close as it is possible to get these days), both towns are worth visiting. Tha Li is a small district town, less than 10 km from the border with Laos. Now that relations between Thailand and Laos have improved, the amount of trade crossing the border here has escalated dramatically. In the past it was mainly smuggled; now most is legal, although there is also a black market in contraband from rare forest products to ganja. The Huang River marks the border between the two countries and Lao goods can either be bought at **Ban Paak Huay**, situated on the river, or in Tha Li 10 km away. Products for sale include cotton cloth, baskets, rough wrought metal goods and reed mats. The swimming at Ban Paak Huay is also said to be good. For information on places to stay in Chiang Khan, see page 445. There is also a simple but peaceful guesthouse in Ban Paak Huay – the **E** *OTS Guesthouse* – around 10 km from Tha Li. There has been talk of a guesthouse opening in Tha Li too. To get there take a songthaew from Loei.

Loei place names

Phu Hin Rongkla National Park

อุทยานแห่งชาติภูหินร่องกล้า

Phu Kradung National Park

อุทยานแห่งชาติภูกระดึง

Phu Reua National park

อุทยานแห่งชาติภูเรือ

Phu Reua National Park, literally 'Boat Mountain' National Park because of a cliff shaped like the bow of a junk, lies 1½ km outside the district town of Phu Rua, 50 km southwest of Loei. The highest point here approaches 1,500 m and temperatures can fall to below freezing. There is a good network of marked trails and some fantastic views over the lowlands from the higher ground and north to Laos. Eroded sandstone boulders perched on cliff edges give the park added natural presence. The road from Loei is reminiscent of Europe (Austria perhaps?), with its cultivation, pine trees and beautiful valleys. There are eight bungalows (**B-C**) at the visitors' centre and a camping ground part way up the mountain. It is necessary to book: T5790529/5794842. In addition, there are two 'back to nature' resorts, 2 km north of Phu Rua town, on the road to Loei. The **B** *Phu Rua Resort*, T899048, and the **B** *Phu Rua Chalet*, T899012. ■ *Getting there: regular buses from Loei to Nakhon Thai (Route 203), 1 hr. The turn-off for the park is at the Km 48 marker. A laterite road leads for 4 km to the park entrance.*

The **Phu Luang Wildlife Sanctuary** lies southwest of Loei and is one of the province's lesser visited protected areas. A recent visitor reports that it has excellent walks and 'quantities of animals'. Note that it is closed between June and September.

B-D *Royal Inn*, off Chumsai Rd, T812563. Plush renovation of average buildings, large rooms, all amenities and comfort. Quiet and good value. **C** *Meuang Fai*, Charoenrat Rd, by the Post Office, T811302, F812353. A/c, good sized and clean rooms, but looking a bit tatty. **C** *Udom*, 122/1 Charoenrat Rd. Some a/c, a little shabby but clean, hot water in all rooms from 1800, good showers. The most architecturally interesting (by Thai standards), but badly run. **C-D** *King*, 11/9-12 Chumsai Rd, T811701. Some a/c, restaurant, set around courtyard, characterless, but clean and well-managed. **C-E** *Phu Luang*, 55 Charoenrat Rd, T811532. Some a/c, comfortable bare rooms, hot water, TV, undistinguished Thai hotel, but OK as a base. **E-F** *Friendship Guesthouse*, 257/41 Soi Buncharoen Rd, T832408, north of wat, 200 m left off main road. Large rooms, shared facilities and huts on riverside. **E-F** *Muang Loei Guesthouse*, 103/31 Soi AD, 50 m off Ruamchai Rd (200 m from bus station, before Thai Military Bank). Sparse rooms in a new terraced house, professional management (when present), guttural locals. **E-F** *Sarai Thong*, 26/5 Ruamjit Rd, T811582. A sprawling place, 50-plus rooms, all with fans and attached shower, slightly seedy, but has the advantage of being quiet.

Sleeping
■ *on map, page 444*
Price codes:
see inside front cover

Thai/Chinese Cheap: *Green Garden Restaurant*, see map for location. Vegetarian food. *Saw Ahaan*, Nok Kaew Rd. Extensive Thai menu, attentive staff and pleasant open air setting. **Seriously cheap**: *Tong-O*, 64 Charoenrat Rd (opposite *Phu Luang Hotel*). A/c restaurant and bar ('beer house'), open 1600-0200, large menu of Thai dishes. *Luuk Chao Bu*, Sathorn Chiang Khan (near the clocktower). Good Thai dishes with generous portions. *Nang Nuan*, 68 Sathorn Chiang Khan Rd. Attractive, well run outdoor restaurant with *nua yaang* speciality – cook-it-yourself barbecue. Recommended.

Eating
● *on map, page 444*
Price categories:
see inside front cover

Bakeries and breakfast Cheap: *King Hotel Coffee Shop*, 11/9-12 Chumsai Rd. Good for ice-cream sundaes in a/c splendour. **Seriously cheap**: *Savita Bakery*, 139 Charoenrat Rd. Good breakfasts and Thai food. Cakes, coffee, ice-cream, plus all the usual dishes, efficiently served by staff dressed in red football shirts and baseball jackets.

Foodstalls The best place for stall food is at the night market on the corner of Ruamjai and Charoenrat roads.

Feb *Cotton Blossom Fair* (movable: early in the month), marks the end of the cool season. Cotton is in full bloom at this time. Cotton Blossom Beauty Queen contest,

Festivals

The Northeastern Region

processions, floats, local folk dancing and handicraft stalls. **Jun** *Phi Ta Khon* (movable: early in the month), similar to Halloween. The festival celebrates an obscure Buddhist legend in which Prince Vessandorn, the Buddha's last reincarnation, returns to his home city to be welcomed by his subjects. The homecoming is so enthusiastic that even the ghosts and spirits appear to witness the event. Locals dress in strange costumes and run around town evoking the spirits, while monks recount the tale from the scriptures.

Sport **Swimming** *Muang Loei Land Swimming Pool*, open 1000-2000 Mon-Sun, get there by tuk-tuk or by town bus/songthaew.

Transport **Motorized saamlor** ฿10-20 around town; songthaews for out of town trips.
558 km to Bangkok, **Air** There is an airport 5 km south of town, but it has had a rather chequered life. Over
147 km to Udon Thani, the last few years there has been some discussion of opening scheduled services to
206 km to Khon Kaen, Bangkok, but, as yet, nothing has materialized. **Bus** There is a new bus terminal on
287 km to Phitsanulok, Maliwan Rd, about 1 km south of town. The local equivalent of the tuk-tuk will trans-
48 km to Chiang Khan port passengers into town for ฿5, or take a blue songthaew for ฿3. Regular connections with Bangkok's Northeastern bus terminal (10 hrs), and with Udon Thani (4 hrs) and Khon Kaen. Connections with Phitsanulok (4 hrs), and from there on to Chiang Mai and other destinations in the north and central regions. Note that some buses travel via Lom Sak to Phitsanulok and others via Nathon Thai. For Chiang Khan (1 hr, ฿18) and other stops along the Mekong River route downstream (east), buses leave from the junction of Maliwan and Ruanchai roads.

Loei

Sleeping
1 Cotton Inn & Meuang Fai
2 Friendship Guesthouse
3 King
4 Muang Loei Guesthouse
5 Phu Luang
6 Royal Inn
7 Udom

Eating
1 Green Garden
2 Saw Ahaan
CR Charoen Rat

N Not to scale

Directory

Airline offices *Thai*, next to *Royal Inn Hotel*, T812344. **Banks** *Thai Farmers*, Ruamchai Rd. **Directory**
Siam Commercial, 3/8 Ruamchai Rd – both banks have exchange facilities.
Communications Post Office: Charoenrat Rd (southern end), telecom office on top floor.
Medical services Hospital: corner of Nok Kaew and Maliwan roads, T811806. **Useful addresses** Police: Phiphatmongkhon Rd, T811254.

Chiang Khan เชียงคาน

This is a place to visit for people who enjoy slow, lazy days watching a river, in this case the mighty Mekong, drifting by. There are no bars or discos here, few obvious sights, and accommodation, though characterful, is basic. The town marks the beginning (or end) of the Mekong River route. Chiang Khan is strung out for 2 km along the river and consists of just two parallel streets, linked by some 20 *sois*, or lanes. The riverfront road, Chai Khong Road, is quieter, with much of the original **wooden shophouse** architecture still standing; the inland road is the relatively busy Route 2186, linking Loei and Nong Khai.

Phone code: 042
Colour map 2, grid A2

The monasteries in town, like several settlements along the Mekong in this part of Thailand, show a French influence in their shuttered and colonnaded buildings. An example is **Wat Tha Khok** at the east edge of town near Soi 20 and overlooking the Mekong. The interior of the viharn displays some attractive murals. On the west edge of town, is **Wat Sri Khun Muang**. It is notable for its Lao-style chedi and the gaudy, vibrant murals on the exterior of the viharn. Other wats in town, all dating from the late-19th century, are **Wat Santi** and **Wat Pa Klang**. The oldest monastery is **Wat Mahathat**, where the bot is thought to date from the mid-17th century.

One of the most worthwhile things to do from Chiang Khan is simply to hire a bicycle or motorbike and journey through the surrounding countryside, sampling local life, stopping at villages en route. The best route runs upstream, crossing the Loei River and running west.

Excursions

Kaeng Kut Kou, a series of rapids, lie 4 km downstream from Chiang Khan. There is a park here with restaurants, souvenir shops and vendors selling spicy Isan food. It is also very popular; coachloads of Thai tourists stop off here. In the dry season it is possible to walk down to the river and eat at the riverside. Most hotels and guesthouses will arrange boat trips to the rapids, ฿150-250 for the journey, depending on the number of people. **NB** the rapids can be an anticlimax, more so in the wet season when the water is like a fast flowing river rather than a cataract. Most people visit the rapids as a day trip; however, there is accommodation available. The **E** *Cootcoo Resort*, T821248, has quiet huts on offer during the dry season only, but reports are that the **D** *See View Huts* are even better and more attractively positioned. More upmarket still is **C-D** *Chiang Khan Hill Resort*, T821285, which has bungalows near the rapids, but they are overrun by tourists visiting the rapids.

D *Nam*, 112 Chai Khong Rd (near Soi 4), T821295, F821342. Some a/c, elegant, French-style colonial house with wonderful teak floors and attractive riverside verandah, with views along the Mekong. **E** *Nong Sam*, 1¼ km west of town, T821457. English-run, quiet and atmospheric, with floral surroundings, spacious rooms, good home-cooked food and river views. Motorbikes for hire, ฿200, 0600-1800. **E** *Sook Somboon*, 243/3 Chai Khong Rd (opposite Soi 8), T821064. Wooden hotel overlooking the Mekong, attractive verandah restaurant built over the river, rooms with attached bathrooms are a little disappointing in comparison to the restaurant, overpriced. **E** *Ton Khong Guesthouse*, 299/3 Chai Khong Rd, T821187. Friendly and welcoming owners, but rooms are small. A bit noisy, but well situated place and an

Sleeping
■ *on map*
Price codes:
see inside front cover

Chiang Khan has a good selection of atmospheric guesthouses; hardly luxurious, but they make a change from the usual dull Thai hotels

The Northeastern Region

attractive building. Restaurant with food available all day. Boat trips on the Mekong organized, Thai massage available. **E-F** *Chiang Khan*, 282 Chai Khong Rd, T821023. Opposite end of town from the Loei bus stop, rather rundown, although riverside position helps (it also encourages mosquitoes). **F** *Poonsawat*, 251/2 Chai Khong Rd, Soi 9, T821114. Attractive wooden hotel, clean rooms, friendly management, shared bathrooms, small book collection to help while away the hours. Recommended. **F** *Zen*, 126/1 Chai Khong Rd, Soi 12, T821110. Traditional, stilted village house, converted into atmospheric guesthouse. Friendly, with an enthusiastic band of supporters, small library of books available, bicycles for hire (฿60 per day), river trips organized and traditional Thai herbal steam bath available.

Eating
● *on map*
Price categories:
see inside front cover

Isan food is excellent in Chiang Khan; a local speciality is live shrimps, fished straight from the Mekong River, served squirming in a spicy marinade of lemon and chilli (*kung ten*) – not for the faint-hearted or paid-up members of the SPS (Shrimp Protection Society). There are several riverside restaurants – the best places to eat, with views over the Mekong to Laos. **Seriously cheap** *Mekong Riverside*, Chai Khong Rd (opposite Soi 10). Quiet verandah, views over the Mekong, good food, especially fish dishes. *No Name*, Chai Khong Soi 9 (opposite *Poonsawat Hotel*). Very popular restaurant serving large portions of freshly wokked rice and noodle dishes. *Prachamit*, 263/2 Si Chiang Khan Rd (near Soi 9). Frequented by locals, no riverside position but good food. *Rabiang Rim Khong*, Chai Khong Rd (opposite Soi 10). Small restaurant overlooking Mekong, good food, generous portions. *Sook Somboon Hotel*, 243/3 Chai Khong Rd. Wonderful position overhanging the Mekong, excellent fish dishes, including succulent sweet and sour fish.

Massage

This massage is of the medicinal form, although more often than not given by untrained masseuses trying to earn a few extra baht. For a traditional Thai steam herbal bath, try the *Zen Guesthouse*, who claim they use ancient herbal mixes passed down through generations (ha!).

Shopping

Handicrafts *Thai Samakkhi*, 356 Chai Khong Rd (near Soi 12). Handicrafts, including local textiles. *Suankaan Phaap*, 101/1 Chai Khong Rd, between Sois 12 and 13. **Newspapers** *Bangkok Post* available in the afternoon from the supermarket on Chiang

Chiang Khan

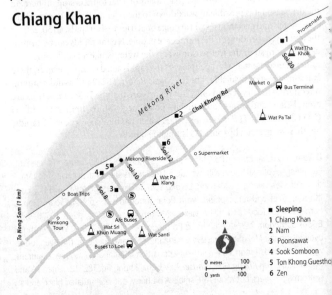

Sleeping
1 Chiang Khan
2 Nam
3 Poonsawat
4 Sook Somboon
5 Ton Khong Guesthouse
6 Zen

The Mekong: great river of Southeast Asia

The Mekong River is one of the 12 great rivers of the world. It stretches 4,500 km from its source on the Tibet Plateau in China to its mouth (or mouths) in the Mekong Delta of Vietnam. On 11 April 1995 a Franco-British Expedition announced that they had discovered the source of the Mekong: 5,000 m high, at the head of the Rup-sa pass, and miles from anywhere. Each year, the river empties 475,000,000,000 cu m of water into the South China Sea. Along its course it flows through Burma, Laos, Thailand, Cambodia and Vietnam, all of the countries that constitute mainland Southeast Asia, as well as China. In both a symbolic and a physical sense, then, it links the region. Bringing fertile silt to the land along its banks, but particularly to the Mekong Delta, the river contributes to Southeast Asia's agricultural wealth.

The first European to explore the Mekong River was the French naval officer Francis Garnier. His Mekong Expedition (1866-68) followed the great river upstream from its delta in Cochin China, and in the process 'discovered' the lost ruins of Angkor, tropical jungles, tribal groups, and much else besides. Of the 9,960 km that the expedition covered, 5,060 km were 'discovered' for the first time. The motivation for the trip was to find a southern route into the Heavenly Kingdom: China. In this they failed. The river is navigable only as far as the Lao-Cambodian border, where the Khone rapids make it impassable. Nonetheless, the report of the expedition is one of the finest of its genre.

Today the Mekong itself is perceived as a source of potential economic wealth, not just as a path to riches. The Mekong Secretariat was established in 1957 to harness the waters of the river for hydropower and irrigation. The Secretariat devised a grandiose plan, incorporating a succession of seven huge dams which would store 142,000,000,000 cu m of water, irrigate 4.3m ha of riceland, and generate 24,200MW of power. But the Vietnam War intervened to disrupt construction. Only Laos' Nam Ngum Dam, on a tributary of the Mekong, was ever built, and even though this generates only 150MW of power, electricity exports to Thailand are one of Laos' largest export earners. Now that the countries of mainland Southeast Asia are on friendly terms again, the Secretariat and its scheme have been given a new lease of life. But in the intervening years, fears about the environmental consequences of big dams have raised new questions. The Mekong Secretariat has moderated its plans and is now looking at less ambitious, and less contentious, ways to harness the Mekong River. Nonetheless, several new dams have been constructed on tributaries of the Mekong, and many more are at various stages of planning.

The Northeastern Region

Khan Rd. **Textiles** *Niyom Thai*, 246 Chai Khong Rd (near Soi 13). There are also several shops near the *Thai Farmers Bank* on Si Chiang Khan Rd.

Bicycle hire: from most guesthouses (฿60 per day). **Tuk-tuks**: for charter (฿10-20 around town). **Motorbike hire**: from *Zen Guesthouse* and *Nong Sam Guesthouse* (฿200-300 per day). **Bus**: buses from Loei stop at the western end of town; a 10 min walk to the main area of hotels and guesthouses, or take a tuk-tuk. Rather unreliable buses (in fact, converted trucks) travel to Loei (1 hr) and east towards Pak Chom, Sang Khom, Si Chiangmai, and on to Nong Khai. For Pak Chom, it may be quicker to join up with other travellers and hire a songthaew. A/c bus connections with Bangkok from the station on Soi 9 (inland from Si Chiang Khan Rd).

Transport
50 km to Loei,
41 km to Pak Chom,
103 km to Sang Khom

Banks *Thai Farmers* (exchange facilities), 444 Si Chiang Khan Rd. **Communications** Post Office: Chai Khong Rd (eastern edge of town). **Useful addresses** Immigration Office: next to Post Office. Visa extension possible.

Directory

Pak Chom

Phone code: 042
Colour map 2, grid A2

Pak Chom figured briefly in world affairs when it became the service centre for the huge Ban Winai Hmong refugee camp. The Hmong (see page 363) fought for the Royalists against the Communist Pathet Lao in Laos's civil war, and when the latter were finally victorious in 1975, hundreds of thousands fled across the border to Thailand to escape political persecution. Now, with improved relations between Laos and Thailand, the refugees have returned to their homes on the other side of the Mekong or have built new lives abroad, especially in the US, and the refugee camp has become history. One of the best accounts of this brief slice of history is Lynellyn D Long's *Ban Vinai: the refugee camp* (Columbia University Press: New York), which traces the lives of three refugee families. As a French Jesuit priest, who worked at the camp, explained to the author: "Before they had a life revolving around the seasons ... Here they cannot really work ... Here people make only dreams". This could be the epitaph for all refugees. Other than this tenuous link with recent events, Pak Chom has little to offer the traveller, although it is an attractive enough town of wooden shophouses. **F** *Pak Chom Guesthouse*, western edge of town (signposted), is basic but peaceful, with a good position near the river, good views and well run.

41 km to Chiang Khan,
63 km to Sang Khom

Transport Bus: green buses connect with towns to the east and blue buses to the west. Connections with Chiang Khan (1 hr) and Loei to the west and with Sang Khom (1½ hrs), Si Chiangmai and Nong Khai to the east.

Sang Khom สังคม

Phone code: 042
Colour map 2, grid A3

This place is little more than a village, but with four riverside guesthouses and attractive surrounding countryside, it has become a refuge for people wishing to escape from the stresses of life and the more popular tourist routes. As one visitor recently put it, "the only thing to worry about is finding something to worry about".

Two kilometres west of Sang Khom, on the road to Pak Chom, is **Wat Hai Sok**, beautifully positioned overlooking the Mekong. The bananas grown in the countryside around the town are highly regarded, and are cured, sweetened and then sold across the country as *kluay khai*.

Excursions

There are several **good walks** in the vicinity of Sang Khom. One of the most interesting is to the hilltop monastery on **Patakseua Cliffs**, which offers superb views over the Mekong to Laos. ■ *Getting there: walk east to the Km 81 marker (about 4 km) and then climb up to the monastery.*

Guesthouses arrange **boat and fishing trips** on the Mekong (฿50-60 per person). Inner tubes are also available from guesthouses to languidly float down the Mekong (out of the rainy season). Guesthouses have suggested itineraries for those intending to explore the surrounding **countryside**; best by bicycle or motorcycle.

One recent visitor has recommended the **Than Thip Falls**. The turn-off for the falls is a short distance east of Sang Khom between the Km 97 and 98 markers, and 3 km off the main road. The falls are enclosed by forest and there are a series of pools good for swimming. Another set of falls are the **Tharn Tong Falls**, 15 km from Sangkhom. For detailed information on directions to these two places, ask at one of the guesthouses.

This wat, superbly positioned on the Mekong, has great views up & downstream

Wat Hin Mak Peng is about 30 km east of Sangkhom. The former abbot of this monastery was the highly revered Phra Thute, so much so that the King of Thailand came to the cremation when he died in 1998. The audience hall is one of Thailand's finest. There is a museum devoted to Phra Thute's life. A peaceful, clean and beautiful place.

To stay here you need to be at one with nature; be prepared to share your hut and the bathroom with numerous other species. In 1992 the Mekong was so swollen with monsoon rains that 2 of the guesthouses lost bungalows as the bank collapsed; as the owners wryly said, their huts are now in Vietnam. **F** *Bouy*, Rim Khong Rd, 1 km west of the town 'centre', T/F441065. Nice bungalows overlooking the river. The attached restaurant serves good food in large portions. Probably the best choice here; it's a very relaxed place with friendly owners. Ideal for long-term stays. International phone and fax available. **F** *Mama's* (aka *TXK*), Rim Khong Rd. Basic bamboo huts overlooking the river, only a handful, although 'Mama', the maternal owner, has – as ever – big plans. **F** *River Huts*, this place has moved but is still good value and well run by a farang, with small library and good information. Also Thai traditional and herbal sauna.

Sleeping

Bicycle hire ฿50 per day. **Motorcycle hire** ฿250 per day, from *River Huts* guesthouse; the best way to explore the backroads. **Bus** Connections west to Loei via Chiang Khan, and east to Nong Khai via Si Chiangmai.

Transport
*104 km to Chiang Khan,
96 km to Nong Khai*

A small, rather dusty town, Si Chiangmai is best known as a centre of spring roll wrapper production, where not a lot else seems to be going on. Spring roll wrappers are made from rice flour and can be seen drying on racks in the sun in villages all around the town; ask at *Tim Guesthouse* if you would like to see the process. The main road is noisy and unattractive, but the riverside road is quiet and peaceful with restaurants built over the Mekong. The town's proximity to Laos is seen reflected in the baguettes, which are freshly baked each day. There is also a large Lao and Vietnamese population in town; the latter are said to control the spring roll wrapper industry hereabouts.

Si Chiangmai
*Phone code: 042
Colour map 2, grid A3*

Sleeping **C-D** *Maneerat Resort*, T451311. Very swish but seemingly woefully underoccupied, Thai cookery courses ran if there is demand. Nice restaurant with good views. **E-F** *Tim Guesthouse*, some dorm beds, attractive, quiet huts on the riverfront, with the front rooms being brighter and with better views. Swiss management, good source of information, motorcycles, bicycles and boats for hire. Western, Isan and Thai food available, as well as French liqueurs and custard in various flavours! Boat trips organized.

Transport **Bus**: regular connections with Nong Khai (45 mins) and Udon Thani. Less regular connections west along the river road to Loei, via Sang Khom and Chiang Khan.

40 km to Sang Khom

Nong Khai หนองคาย

In addition to the rather dubious excitement of being on the frontier with Laos, where not too far away at Ban Rom Klao the Thai and Lao armies fought a vicious minor battle during the late 1980s, Nong Khai is also a charming, quiet and laidback riverside town: the sort of place where jaded travellers get 'stuck' for several days, doing nothing but enjoying the romantic atmosphere of the place. Should that be too sedentary, there are a number of (admittedly largely unremarkable) wats to visit. From here, while supping on a cold beer, you can look across to Tha Dua in Laos and imagine the enormous and rare pla buk *catfish* (Pangasianodon gigas) *– weighing up to 340 kg – foraging on the river bed.*

*Phone code: 042
Colour map 2, grid A3
Population: 32,000*

Ins and outs

Nong Khai is situated at the end of Route 2, the Friendship Highway, and on the banks of the mighty Mekong River, which forms the border between Thailand and Laos. It is as far as it is possible to travel on the Northeastern rail line from Bangkok, although

Getting there
*See also Transport,
page 449*

there are plans to extend the track over the Friendship Bridge to Vientiane in Laos. Currently visitors to Laos have to cross the Mekong by road; visas are available on arrival in the country. The bus station is on the east side of town and there are connections with Bangkok and destinations in the Northeast.

Getting around Saamlors provide the main means of local transport; the town is strung out along the river, so it is quite a hike getting from one end to the other. Some guesthouses hire out bicycles and motorbikes. Local buses link Nong Khai with out of town destinations.

Background

The aforementioned fish was first described by Western science in 1930, although Thai and Lao villagers and fishermen were, of course, well aware of its existence way before then. The *pla buk* is unusual for a catfish in that it is vegetarian. It is also becoming increasingly rare, despite attempts at breeding and restocking, and fewer are reported to be making the journey upriver to China's Lake Tali to spawn. Although it may be said that the *pla buk* was only described by Western science in 1930, the English explorer and surveyor, James McCarthy, goes into considerable detail about the fish in his book *Surveying and exploring in Siam*, which was first published in 1900 and draws upon his travels in Siam and Laos between 1881 and 1893. He writes that he 'helped to take [a *pla buk* weighing] 130 lbs; it was 7 ft long and 4 ft 2 in round the body; the tail measured 1 ft 9 in. The fish had neither scales nor teeth, and was sold for 10 rupees.' He also notes that the roe of the fish, like its cousin the sturgeon, was considered a great delicacy, and when the Lao city of Luang Prabang was under Chinese suzerainty, part of the tribute was paid in *pla buk* roe.

Town development Nong Khai, over the space of just a handful of years, has changed from a quiet provincial town into a relatively sophisticated place. This development has been closely associated with the process of rapprochement between Bangkok and Vientiane. Laos, with some trepidation, has opened up to tourists and investors, and Nong Khai is on the front line – so to speak. The Australian-financed Friendship Bridge at Tambon Meechai, 2 km from town, the first bridge across the lower reaches of the Mekong River, was officially opened on 8 April 1994 (see box). To cope with the expected surge in arrivals, three major new hotels have opened: the *Nong Khai Holiday Inn*, the *Nong Khai Grand Thani* and the *Jommanee*. Check with the Lao Embassy in Bangkok for visas and whether the border is open (see page 453). Fortunately for the preservation of Nong Khai's charming core, much of the ugliest developments are concentrated along Highway 2 which leads to the bridge. But even the formerly quiet riverfront road, Rim Khong Road, has been redeveloped into a 'promenade' for tourists.

Sights

The influence of the French presence in Indochina can be seen reflected in the architecture of Meechai Road, which runs parallel with the river. Notable among the wats are the important teaching wat, **Wat Sisaket**, and, towards the east of town past the bus station, **Wat Pho Chai** – with its Lao-style viharn and venerated solid gold-headed Buddha (the body is bronze), looted from Vientiane by the future Rama I. The bot contains murals showing how the image is reputed to have got to Nong Khai: Rama I loaded the image onto a raft to cross the Mekong, but while negotiating the river the raft capsized and the image was lost. It then miraculously resurfaced (this is a common theme in the lost

Buddha image genre), to be retrieved and placed in Wat Pho Chai. (Or, less miraculously, it was dredged from the river 25 years after it was lost.) Unfortunately, at least as far as many visitors are concerned, the monastery has recently undergone a rather over-enthusiastic renovation programme, and is now bright, glittering and rather gross.

A third religious building, or rather what remains of it, is **Phrathat Nong Khai**, locally better known as **Phrathat Klang Nam** (Phrathat in the Middle of the River), because of its position submerged close to the centre of the Mekong's course. In Henri Mouhot's account of his trip up the middle and upper reaches of the Mekong in 1860, he wrote of this *that* when he remarked on arrival in 'Nong Kay' that a 'Buddhist tat or pyramidal landmark ... has been washed away from the shore, and now lies half submerged, like a wrecked ship'. The *that* is only visible during the dry season, when it emerges from the muddy river and is promptly bedecked with pennants. To see the *that*, walk (or take a saamlor) east along Meechai Road (downriver) for about 2½ km from the town centre, and turn off, left, down Soi Paa Phrao 3. The *that* should be visible from the riverbank, at the end of the Soi.

On the riverfront road, Rim Khong Road, there is a daily **market** where goods from Laos and beyond are on sale. Nong Khai also happens to be the logical place to start or end a tour of the Thai towns which line the Mekong River.

Excursions

Wat Phrathat Bang Phuan is 22 km southwest of Nong Khai. To get there, travel south down Route 2 towards Udon and turn right after 12 km onto Route 211 towards Si Chiang Mai. The wat is another 10 km along this road and is well signposted now that it has become a national historical sight. The wat contains an Indian-style stupa, similar (it is presumed) to the original Phra Pathom Chedi in Nakhon Pathom. Its exact date of construction is unknown, but it is believed to date from the early centuries AD. A newer chedi was built on the sight in 1559, which toppled over in 1970. In 1978 it was restored. As a result, the unrestored Lao chedis in this same compound are now of greater historical interest. The site is really only worth visiting en route to/from Udon or Nong Khai, and it doesn't begin to compare with other historical sights in the Northeast. However, with a rumoured 29 relics of the Buddha's chest enshrined here, it has considerable religious importance. ■ *Getting there: songthaew or bus running towards Si Chiang Mai, and state your destination. Alternatively, catch a bus going south on Route 2 and get off at the junction with Route 211; then catch a bus or songthaew west from here.*

Wat Phrathat Bang Phuan

Encompassing an area of 650 ha in the Phu Phan hills, the Phu Phra Bat Historical Park has been a site of almost continuous human habitation since prehistoric times. The area was clearly felt to be endowed with considerable religious significance. There are prehistoric cave paintings (sadly, some have been badly damaged by people lighting fires in the caves), Dvaravati boundary stones (seventh-10th centuries), Lopburi Bodhisattvas (10th-13th centuries), Lang Chan Buddha images (14th-18th centuries), and a stupa built in 1920 to shelter a Buddha footprint. The terrain consists of rocky outcrops, bare sandy soil and savanna forest, and it is easy to imagine why people for thousands of years have regarded the area as a magical place. The problem is that it is difficult to get to except by private car or motorcycle. But it is worth it for the peace. A new reception centre has been built, with a historical exhibition and a small café for drinks and simple food. Guides are also available here. It is now possible to get basic but good food at the entrance to the park. To see all the main sites allow at

Phu Phra Bat Historical Park

least three hours. The park is just about equidistant from Nong Khai and Udon Thani, almost 70 km. ■ *0830-1700 Mon-Sun. Getting there: catch a bus to Ban Phu (there is a very simple hotel here should visitors need to sleep over), the town where Routes 2020 and 2021 meet, a journey of about 2½ hrs. From there (it is signposted), the park is another 15 km by songthaew towards Ban Tiu (quicker to take a motorcycle taxi from here).*

Wat Phutthamamaka -samakhom

Also known as **Wat Khaek** ('Indian' Wat), the clumsily named Wat Phutthamamaka-samakhom was established in the late 1970s and lies 4½ km east of Nong Khai on Route 212 to Beung Kan. The sculpture park was set up by a Laotian artist named Luang Poo Boun Leua Sourirat, who died in 1996 at the age of 72. Luang Poo saw himself as part holy man, part artist and part sage. He studied under a Hindu rishi in Vietnam and formed his own synthesis of Buddhist and Hindu philosophy, which is displayed in his work here. He established a similar hideous concoction of concrete figurines near Tha Deua in Laos (not far from Vientiane), but was ejected from the country shortly after it became communist in 1975, probably on the grounds that he was simply too weird. A wealthy man, he bought a small slice of Thailand and started again.

Reflecting Luang Poo's beliefs, the wat promotes a strange mixture of Buddhist and Hindu beliefs and is dominated by a vast array of strange brick and cement statues. Some are clearly of Buddhist and Hindu inspiration; others are rather harder to interpret: for example, a life-size elephant being attacked by a large pack of dogs, four in a jeep, and some wearing sunglasses. This represents a Thai proverb; a man who is confident he has done no wrong need not worry about malicious rumour 'as an elephant does not care about barking dogs' (hence the apparent nonchalance of the elephant). The dogs, with their enlarged genitalia (representing their overblown egos), are Luang Poo Boun Leua Sourirat's critics. The 'Life and Death' grouping is especially interesting. The group are set within a walled enclosure, reached along a tunnel (symbolizing the birth process); at the end of the tunnel the visitor is confronted by a carved rock, topped with a lingam. Around the enclosure are arranged an assortment of figures: a baby, a business woman, soldier, beggar... The series concludes with two couples holding hands, one pair skeletonized and standing next to a coffin on a pyre. The meaning here seems pretty clear: dust to dust, and no loitering. Other figures in Wat Khaek include a giant seven-headed naga, an enormously corpulent Chinese, with some statues over 30 m high. The figures are arranged in a garden and music blares out from an equally large concrete-encrusted PA system. Even tour buses visit the wat, so well-known has its strange brand of Buddhism become. ■ *0830-1800, ₿10. Getting there: songthaew heading towards Beung Kan (Route 212) or by tuk-tuk. Turn right after the Km 4 marker, just past the St Paul Nongkhai School (signpost to Sala Kaeou), and it is 500 m off the main road. To cycle from town, it is best to take the riverside road as far as Wat Sirimahakatcha, then turn right and travel south past the school and through a wat compound.*

● ● ● ● ● ● ● ● ● ● ● ● ● ● ● ● ● ●
Nong Khai place names

Phu Phra Bat Historical Park

อุทยานประวัติศาสตร์ภูพระบาท

Wat Khaek

วัดแขก

Wat Phrathat Bang Phuan

วัดพระธาตุบังพวน

Wat Phu Tok

วัดภูทอก

Wat Phuttamamaka-samakhom

วัดพุทธมามกะสมาคม

Bridging the Mekong

In April 1994, King Bhumibol of Thailand and the President of Laos, accompanied by Prime Minister Chuan Leekpai of Thailand and Australia's Prime Minister Paul Keating, opened the first bridge to span the lower reaches of the Mekong River, linking Nong Khai in Northeast Thailand with Vientiane in Laos. The bridge had been a long time in coming. It was first mooted in the 1950s, but war in Indochina and hostility between Laos and Thailand scuppered plans until the late 1980s. Then, with the Cold War ending and growing rapprochement between the countries of Indo-China and Asean, the bridge, as they say, was suddenly an idea whose time had come.

The 1,200 m-long Friendship Bridge has been financed with US$30 mn of aid

from Australia. For landlocked Laos, it offers an easier route to Thailand and through Thailand to the sea. For Thailand, it offers an entrée into one of the least developed countries in the world, rich in natural resources and potential. While for Australia, it demonstrated the country's Asian credentials. The Thais would like to build one, and maybe two, further bridges, possibly at Mukdahan and Nakhon Pathom. The government of Laos is rather more circumspect, worrying that bridges not only bolster trade, but also bring consumerism, crime, prostitution and environmental degradation. (Nonetheless they have constructed a second bridge over the river at Pakse – where both banks are Lao territory.)

This wat is a very long day trip from Nong Khai, but may be an attractive proposition for those with time on their hands and the desire to see some more of the Isan region (see page 457). It is possible to stay the night at the wat and there are a couple of acceptable guesthouses in Seveli village. Camping is also permitted. ■ *Getting there: take a bus from Nong Khai to Beung Kan (2½ hrs). From Beung Kan, catch a songthaew to the village of Seveli (1 hr). From there, charter a tuk-tuk or motorcycle taxi to the wat, which is about 20 km away.*

Wat Phu Tok

Several companies and guesthouses organize tours to Laos, including *Pam Tour, International Meeting Place* guesthouse, *Frontier Guesthouse* and *Udom Rot Restaurant*. Currently it is not necessary to pre-arrange a visa before entering Laos. They are provided on arrival when crossing over the Friendship Bridge.

Tours to Laos
See also Tour operators below & page 164

Essentials

With the opening of the bridge into Laos, large hotels opened in Nong Khai, providing (almost) Bangkok-level opulence. Guesthouses in Nong Khai are also of a high standard. What seems to be missing are adequate mid-range places to stay.

Sleeping
■ *on map*
Price codes:
see inside front cover

AL *Holiday Inn Mekong Royal Nongkhai*, 222 Jomanee Rd, west of railway station out of town, T420024, F421280, www.holidayinnhotels.co.th A/c, restaurant, pool, tennis, 8-storey block, with nearly 200 rooms overlooking Mekong with all facilities, best in town. **A-B** *Nongkhai Grand Hotel I*, 589 Muu 5 Nong Khai Poanpisai Rd, 2 km east of town on Route 212, T420033, F412026. A/c, restaurant, pool, disco, 'luxury' hotel opened 1992, high-rise block on edge of town, all facilities. **C-E** *Phanthavee* (and across the road the *Phanthavee Bungalows*), 1241 Haisok Rd, T2202569. Some a/c, management is brusque and unfriendly; rooms are clean but otherwise unremarkable. **D** *Prajak Bungalows*, 1178 Prajak Rd, T2202116. A quiet place with good facilities for the price. Clean and well run.

The Northeastern Region

E *International Meeting Place*,1117 Soi Chuanjit, F412644. Run by a convivial Austra-lian, clean, small rooms in attractive wooden house, beer (ice cold) available in indus-trial quantities, bar atmosphere described as a dark, shell of a cave by one customer. Recommended. **E** *KC Guesthouse*, same entrance as *Mut Mee Guesthouse*, Kaeo Worawut Rd. Shared bathrooms, friendly place which is constantly passed by those bound for the popular *Mut Mee*. **E** *Mango Guesthouse*, Soi Watsri Chomchuen. Shared bathrooms, clean rooms, friendly and quiet. **E** *Poolsup*, 843 Meechai Rd, T2202031. Chinese-style hotel with perhaps the most hideous chair in the world in the 'foyer'; but don't be put off, the rooms are OK and the proprietress is charming – try her cool rainwater. **E** *Rimkhong Guesthouse*, Rimkhong Rd. Shared bathrooms, clean rooms with fans, friendly staff, wooden house with river views. Can be a little noisy due to the restaurant. **E** *Vientiane Guesthouse*, Meechai Rd, Soi Wat Naak, near the Post Office, T2202393. Clean wooden rooms, quiet. Recommended. **E-F** *Naina*, Phochai Rd. Concrete building, 6 rooms, shared bathroom, fan, clean, friendly, quiet. **E-F** *Sawasdee Guesthouse*, 402 Meechai Rd, T412602, F420259. Some a/c, old wooden house with inner courtyard brimming with plants, clean rooms and immacu-late bathrooms, help-yourself coffee, friendly, good source of information, fan, hot water. Recommended. **E-F** *Sukhaphon*, 823 Bamtoengjit Rd, T2202894. Old wooden hotel, worth staying here if the more popular guesthouses are full, rooms at the back are quieter. **E-F** *Tommy's*, 8 Peechai Rd (off Meechai Rd), on the river with clean rooms and cheap dorm beds – but rather neglected showers. **F** *Bamboo Guesthouse*, a little out of town to the west. Despite its name, there's no bamboo in sight. Not suitable for tall people due to low door frames. **F** *Mekhong Guesthouse*, 519 Rim Khong, T412320. Clean basic wooden rooms, on the river with a good verandah and informa-tion, but noisy from the road and the restaurant next door. Recommended. **F** *Mut Mee Guesthouse*, 1111/4 Kaeo Worawut Rd, F460717. Restaurant, large rooms and bungalows, nice garden by the river with hammocks, very friendly English man-agement, good source of information on Laos, bikes for rent, widely regarded as the best place in town. Recommended.

Nong Khai

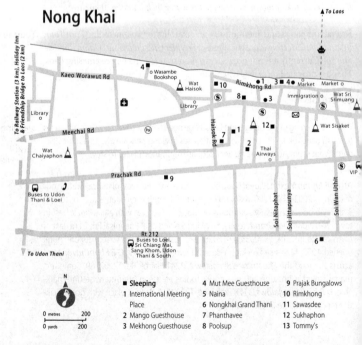

■ Sleeping	4 Mut Mee Guesthouse	9 Prajak Bungalows
1 International Meeting Place	5 Naina	10 Rimkhong
2 Mango Guesthouse	6 Nongkhai Grand Thani	11 Sawasdee
3 Mekhong Guesthouse	7 Phanthavee	12 Sukhaphon
	8 Poolsup	13 Tommy's

Thai Cheap: *Banya Pochana*, 295 Rim Khong Rd. Chinese, Thai and Lao food, fish dishes particularly good. *Steak House*, Meechai Rd (next to the *Sawasdee Guesthouse*), predictably selling steaks, taken from a variety of animals. *Khun Daeng*, 521 Rim Khong Rd (just west from *Udom Rot* and the Immigration office). Views over the Mekong River, seafood and Isan specialities which locals claim are excellent. *Udom Rot*, 193 Rim Khong Rd. Views over the Mekong River and a good place to watch the river traffic, seafood specialities and good Thai food, as well as some Lao and Vietnamese dishes. Recommended. *The Boat*, western end of Rim Khong Rd. Nice position on the river, but the ice-creams, sundaes and milkshakes are a little pricey. **Seriously cheap**: *Mut Mee*, Kaeo Worawut Rd. Wide trange of Thai and Western food, with delicious specialities such as pla shiu shii (fish with coconut and hot sauce). *Open air café* at intersection of Meechai and Haisok Rd.

Vietnamese Cheap: *Indochine*, 189/1 Meechai Rd. Serves good Vietnamese food including delicious Vietnamese-style spring rolls. Recommended.

Vegetarian Cheap: *The Fish*, vegetarian floating restaurant near to the *Mutmee Guesthouse*. Good range of dishes at reasonable prices.

Bakeries and coffee shops *Tukata Bakery and Restaurant*, Meechai Rd. Good cheap food including cakes and such like; a good place for breakfast. *The Coffee Shop*, Rim Khong Rd. Attractive rustic design.

Eating
● *on map*
Price categories:
see inside front cover

Arthit's Pub, Prajak Rd, a little further on from the Thai office. Live music.

Bars

Mar *Nong Khai Show* (2nd week). **May** *Rocket Festival*, or *ngarn bang fai* (2nd week) (see page 417). **Jul** *Candle Festival* (the beginning of the Buddhist Lent or Phansa) (see page 415). **Oct** *Boat races* on the Mekong (movable). Naga-powered canoes with up to 40 oarsmen race along the river, with a great deal of cheering and drinking from the onlookers that line the bank.

Festivals

Alternative Centre, next to the *Mut Mee Guesthouse* on Kaeo Worawut Rd. Daily yoga sessions; reiki, tai chi and astrology readings are some of the courses on offer.

Massage, yoga & tai chi

The best area to browse is down Rim Khong Rd, which (as the name suggests) runs along the river bank. Here Northeastern and Lao handicrafts are sold, together with Chinese, Soviet and East European goods. It is possible to come away with a (former) Soviet military watch, an Isan 'axe' pillow, and 'French' sandalwood soap made in Laos. For better quality handicrafts, visit *Village Weaver Handicrafts* at 786/1-2 Prajak Rd, a short distance on from the bus station. This outlet sells cloth, in particular mut mee, produced by a self help project which aims to provide women with an income earning activity and so prevent the city-ward drift of young people.

Shopping

● **Eating**
1 Boat
2 Steakhouse
3 Tukata Bakery
 & Restaurant
4 Udom Rot

Books The *Wasambe Bookshop*, near the *Mut Mee Guesthouse*, is an excellent bookshop and book exchange. It also has email and fax facilities.

Tour operators
See also Tours to Laos above

With the opening of the Friendship Bridge to Laos in Apr 1994, tour operators have multiplied and there are now more than 10, most of whom will arrange visas for Laos on the spot. It is worth shopping around for the best deal. *Udorn Business Travel* (Nong Khai branch), 447/10 Haisok Rd, T2202393. *Pam Tour*, 1112/1 Haisok Rd.

Transport
See also Ins & outs, page 449; 620 km to Bangkok, 55 km to Udon Thani, 204 km to Loei

Local Bicycle hire: from *Mut Mee Guesthouse*, ฿40 per day. **Motorcycle hire**: from the *International Meeting Place*, 1117 Soi Chuanjit (฿200 per day), and from the *Mut Mee Guesthouse*.

Long distance Air: there are no air connections with Nong Khai. The nearest airport is in Udon Thani and a shuttle bus takes passengers there.

Train: station is 3 km from town, west on Kaeo Worawut Rd. Regular connections with Bangkok's Hualamphong station (11 hrs) and all stops northeast: Ayutthaya, Saraburi, Korat, Khon Kaen and Udon.

Bus: BKS is on the east side of town on Praserm Rd, off Prajak Rd. Regular connections with Bangkok's Northeastern bus terminal (9-11 hrs) and Khon Kaen, Udon Thani and other Northeastern towns. There is also a service to Rayong on the eastern seaboard. Note that tuk-tuk drivers have taken to hounding farangs and charging exorbitant rates. Don't pay more than ฿20. VIP buses for Bangkok leave from 745 Prajak Rd. A/c buses from the corner of Haisok and Prajak roads. A/c buses also depart from the BKS station. **NB** There are lots of sharks about.

International connections with Laos The Friendship Bridge, over the Mekong River at Tambon Meechai, 2 km from town, opened in 1994 and now offers the first road link across the Mekong. The bridge is open 0800-1800 Mon-Sun. Visas are now available upon entry to Laos. The price had dropped to US$30 (payable in US dollars cash only) by early 1999 and may drop still further. No passport photographs are required. To get to the Friendship Bridge, take a tuk-tuk to the last bus stop before the bridge and from there catch a bus to Thai immigration.

Directory

Airline offices *Thai*, 453 Prachak Rd, T2202530. **Banks** *Bangkok*, 374 Sisaket Rd, *Krung Thai*, 102 Meechai Rd, *Thai Farmers*, 929 Meechai Rd are but a few. **Communications** Post Office: Meechai Rd (opposite Soi Prisnee); there is an international telephone office upstairs. **Email:** *Wasambe Bookshop* has email (wasambe@loxinfo.co.th), international phone and fax (F460717) available. **Embassies & consulates** For some time now there have been rumours of a Lao consulate opening in Nong Khai. So far this has not materialized. The closest Lao consulate is in Khon Kaen, although travel agents in Nong Khai will also arrange visas, for a fee (see Tour operators above). **Medical services** Hospital, Meechai Rd, T2202504. **Useful addresses** Immigration: Sisaket Rd, T2202154. **Police:** Meechai Rd, T2202020.

The southern Mekong River route

From Nong Khai, Route 212 follows the Mekong River eastwards, then southeastwards to the riverside town of Beung Kan (137 km) and from there to the provincial capital of Nakhon Phanom (another 175 km). An alternative route from Udon Thani (via Ban Chiang) would pass close to the provincial capital of Sakhon Nakhon. Continuing southwards from Nakhon Phanom on the river road for another 50 km, Route 212 reaches That Phanom, the site of one of the most revered chedis in Thailand: Wat That Phanom. This area is also a centre of traditional textile production, particularly around the town of Renu Nakhon – 15 km north of That Phanom. From That Phanom, Route 212 links up with the newly created provincial capital of Mukdahan (50 km south from That Phanom) and then, cutting away from the Mekong, with Ubon Ratchathani, a total of 267 km from Nakhon Phanom.

Beung Kan   บึงกาฬ

A much more scenic and adventurous way to reach Nakhon Phanom is by tak-ing the river road, Route 212, east from Nong Khai. This road follows the Mekong for nearly 320 km. The only logical place to break the journey is in the small and largely forgettable district town of Beung Kan, 137 km from Nong Khai and 175 km from Nakhon Phanom. There are regular connections with both places. Beung Kan is one of the more difficult Thai town names to pro-nounce: it's best to hold your nose to get the required nasal inflexion. There is a *Thai Farmers Bank* here.

Phone code: 042
Colour map 2, grid A4

Wat Phu Tok, also known as **Wat Chedi Ya Khiri Viharn**, is a cave wat situ-ated in an area of breathtaking limestone scenery, about 140 km east of Nong Khai. The wat was established by Phra Acaan Juen in 1968, and it is now a sprawling monastery with meditation grottoes, *kutis* (monks' cells) and *salas* spread among the honeycombed mountain. Phra Acaan Juen died a few years ago in a plane accident, while flying to Bangkok to celebrate Queen Sirikit's birthday. This episode, as well as the more recent accident in the south when one of the Queen's helicopters carrying a number of her retinue crashed killing all on board, has convinced some Thais that the Queen brings bad fortune.

Excursions

Climbing up the mountain is an exhausting business, but the views of the plain below make it all worthwhile; they are, quite simply, spectacular. The wat itself is at the foot of the hill. From here, vertiginous steps lead up through a series of levels, marked by shrines. Part way up the path divides: left is a bit of a scram-ble; right is spectacular and not for the faint-hearted, because the stairway (attached to the rock face) is 1.8 m wide with a fall of several hundred feet! At the end of this is an almost sheer rock face, with a rope to help those who might be considering putting their lives in the hands of some greater being and climbing the last 18 m. Back at ground level is a beautiful prang set on a small hill (accessi-ble), surrounded by a lake. It is possible to stay the night at the wat, although some recent visitors have reported that the monks are not terribly welcoming (take some donations if intending to stay). Visitors should also expect only very basic facilities. There are a couple of acceptable guesthouses in Seveli village and it is also possible to camp in the area. ■ *Getting there: take an early morning songthaew to the village of Siwilai (1 hr). From there, either charter a tuk-tuk or motorcycle taxi to the wat, which is about 20 km away, or there are a few public songthaews.*

Beung Kan

Mekong River Promenade
Thai Samak
● Restaurant
Meechai Rd
Samranit   Laundry
Prasatchai Rd
Neramit   Santisuk
Cinema ○   Market ○   A/c to Bangkok
Maesangkong Rd
Buses out of town
0 metres   200
0 yards   200
To Nong Khai (137 km) & Nakhon Phanom (175 km)

Ban Ahong is around 25 km west of Beung Kan on Route 212 (at the Km 115 marker) to Nong Khai. Close by is **Wat Paa Ahong** and its abbot and lone monk, Luang Phor Phraeng. The monas-tery is a strange oasis of shrubbery and plants. Luang Phor is renowned for his medicinal skills

The Northeastern Region

and is reputed to have magical powers of healing. It is possible to swim in the Mekong at this stretch of the river's course during the dry season. There is one guesthouse in Ban Ahong, the **F** *Hideaway Guesthouse*, a welcoming and peaceful place on the Mekong. ■ *Getting there: buses making the journey between Nong Khai and Bueng Kan all pass through Ban Ahong.*

Sleeping & eating
■ *on map, page 457*
Price codes: see inside front cover

Basic accommodation only, but all centrally located & with a certain provincial charm

F *Neramit*, Prasatchai Rd. Opposite the *Santisuk*, it boasts the only international phone in town. **F** *Samanmit*, Prasatchai Rd. **F** *Santisuk*, Prasatchai Rd. Some a/c, reasonable rooms at reasonable prices.

Cheap *Santisuk*, attached to the hotel of the same name; tasty food, but you may not be able to see it due to ambient lighting. *No Name*, tranquil open-air and indoor restaurant with pleasant views of the river, but an indifferent menu. **Foodstalls** There is a good *night market* situated near the a/c bus terminal on Bumrungrad Rd, plus the usual street-side Thai eating houses.

Nakhon Phanom   นครพนม

Phone code: 042
Colour map 3, grid B3
Population: 36,000

An unexciting ramshackle place, Nakhon Phanom does, however, have one plus point: it is situated on the Mekong River, with the mountains of Laos as a backdrop. Across the river is the Lao town of Thakhek and foreigners are permitted to enter Laos at this point. Like Nong Khai, sipping a beer or eating catfish curry overlooking the river does have a certain romantic appeal. But most people only visit Nakhon Phanom en route to Phra That Phanom Chedi, which is 50 km to the south and is the Northeast's most revered religious shrine (see That Phanom, below). Nakhon Phanom is the closest town with adequate hotels to the wat. Nakhon Phanom's limited sights include **Wat Sri Thep** on Srithep Road (which boasts a statue of Luang Pu Chan, a revered Northeastern holy man) and **Wat Mahathat** (with a lotus-bud chedi), at the southern end of Sunthon Vichit Road. The former monastery has some exuberant murals depicting episodes from the Buddha's life (the jataka tales); or simply wander along the riverfront, past handicraft shops and a Chinese temple. There is a morning market on the river. Just south of the *Grand View Hotel*, south of town, is an area of beach, **Hat Sai Tai Muang**, which local people use to lounge in the evening while stalls sell Thai snacks. During the dry season the exposed area of sand expands considerably. The **tourist office**, *TAT*, is housed in an attractive building on the corner of Salaklang and Suthorn Vichit roads. Areas of responsibility are Nakhon Phanom, Sakhon Nakhon and Mukdahan.

Excursions

Wat That Phanom (see page 462), the Northeast's holiest religious site, lies 50 km south of town. ■ *Getting there: regular buses from the station near the market.*

Renu Nakhon (see page 463) is a weaving centre 6½ km off the main highway (Route 212), on the way to That Phanom. ■ *Getting there: by bus from the station near the market.*

Wat Phrathat Narai Chengweng (Phrathat Naweng) is a Khmer prang dating from the 11th or 12th century. Despite being reconstructed in what appears to be a remarkably haphazard fashion (surely the Khmers, master builders, would have cut stone that fitted?), this small sanctuary is very satisfying. Lying in a peaceful wat compound, it displays finely carved lintels: the east lintel above the entrance to the sanctuary shows Siva dancing; the north face, Vishnu reclining on a naga. The wat is 88 km west of Nakhon Phanom on Route 22, at the junction with Route 223 (it is signposted). Walk through a green archway, and the wat is 500 m along a dirt track. There is a good, cheap Thai restaurant on the other side of the road from the wat, beyond the intersection on the way to Udon Thani (about 200 m). ■ *Getting there: take a bus travelling towards Sakhon Nakhon from the bus station near the market.*

Phrathat Choeng Chum, in the provincial capital of Sakhon Nakhon, is an important pilgrimage place for Thais; see page 433.

A-B *Nakhon Phanom River View*, 9 Nakhon Phanom-That Phanom Rd, T522333. A/c, restaurant, pool, fitness centre. This is a new 120-room hotel, situated on the river out of town towards That Phanom. It is, apparently, 'paradise on earth', and while it establishes its heavenly reputation is offering good discounts. **A** *Nam Khong Grand View*, 527 Sunthorn Vichit Rd, T513564, F511037. A/c, restaurant, pool, newish hotel with 114 impressive rooms, best in town with great views over the Mekong to Laos. **B-C** *Nakhon Phanom*, 403 Aphibarn Bancha Rd, T511455, F511071. A/c, restaurant, pool, rather shabby, best rooms in the new wing. **C-D** *River Inn*, 137 Sunthorn Vichit Rd, T511305. Some a/c, restaurant, nice position overlooking river, but overpriced, noisy rooms on the road side. **B-C** *Sri Thep*, 197 Sri Thep Rd, T511437, F511346. Some a/c, overpriced and past its best – rooms are stuffy and dark. **D-E** *First*, 16 Sri Thep Rd, T511253. Some a/c, rooms are rather mixed in terms of quality and cleanliness from acceptable to grubby. **E** *Chakkawan*, 676/12-13 Aphibarn Bancha Rd, T511298. A busman's holiday for a cockroach killer. **E** *Grand Hotel*, 210 Sri Thep Rd, T511526, F513788. Some a/c, a step up from the *First*, very clean and the best of the bunch in this category.

Sleeping

■ *on map*
Price codes:
see inside front cover

Because few travellers stop here, cheap accommodation is poor. Few places cater to travellers' needs

Nakhon Phanom

Sleeping ■
1 First
2 Grand
3 Nakhon Phanom
4 Nam Khong Grand View
5 River Inn
6 Sri Thep

There are numerous restaurants along the river road and they all serve the same broad range of dishes. Mekong catfish cooked in a variety of ways – curried, stir fried, deep fried, in soups – is a local speciality.

Eating

Cheap *Golden Giant Catfish*, Sunthorn Vichit Rd, this restaurant serves *pla buk*, the famed giant Mekong catfish, in a variety of guises. Recommended. *Nawt Laap Phet*, 464 Aphibarn Bancha Rd, this is an Isan restaurant serving Lao specialities including the usual grilled chicken and spicy salad, along with great *laap*. **Seriously cheap** *NKP Bakery*, by *Nakhon Phanom Hotel*.

Oct *Ok Phansa* (9-13th, end of Buddhist Lent), 4 day celebrations with *long-boat races*, and the launching of illuminated boats onto the Mekong.

Festivals

Swimming Non-residents can use the pool at the *Nam Khong Grand View* for ฿50. **Snooker** *Nakhon Phanom Hotel*, Aphibarn Bancha Rd.

Sport

Local Bus: the station for local buses and songthaews is near the market, opposite the *Nakhon Phanom Hotel*. **Songthaews** to That Phanom leave from the local bus station.

Transport
735 km to Bangkok, 242 km to Udon, 296 km to Nong Khai

The Northeastern Region

Long distance Air: There are daily connections on Thai with Bangkok. **Bus**: there is a relatively new bus terminal 2 km southwest of town. Take a tuk-tuk, locally known as skylabs (as they are in the Lao city of Savannakhet), after the piece of space hardware. Buses to That Phanom come back into town at the southern clock tower and then head south. Connections with Nong Khai via Sakhon Nakhon. If you wish to take the more interesting route which follows the Mekong, then take a bus to Beung Kan and change. Tour buses running south to Ubon leave every 2 hrs during the day from near the *Windsor Hotel* (4½ hrs). **International connections with Laos**: foreigners can cross the Mekong to Thakhek, using the ferry service linking the 2 settlements.

Directory **Banks** *Bangkok*, Srithep Rd. *Thai Farmers*, 439 Aphibarn Bancha Rd. **Communications Post Office**: Sunthorn Vichit Rd (northern end). **Telephone office**: off Fuang Nakhon Rd. **Medical services** Sunthorn Vichit Rd, T511422. **Useful addresses Immigration**: Sunthorn Vichit Rd, T51147. **Police**: Sunthorn Vichit Rd (northern end).

Sakhon Nakhon   สกลนคร

Phone code: 042
Colour map 2, grid A5
Population: 28,000

This ancient town was one of the Khmer Empire's more important provincial centres in the Northeast. It's now one of the region's smaller provincial capitals. Along with a revered monastery (see below), Sakhon Nakhon also has a reputation in Thailand as a centre of dog meat consumption. But most famously, Sakhon Nakhon is home to the second most sacred Lao-style stupa in Thailand: the **Phrathat Choeng Chum** (the most sacred is That Phanom). This 24 m-tall, white, angular, lotus bud chedi has become an important pilgrimage spot for Thais. The chedi is built over a laterite Khmer prang dating from the 11th or 12th century, and to reach the chedi it is necessary to walk through the viharn. The chedi is surrounded by ancient images of the Buddha captured during raids into Laos and Cambodia. Behind the stupa is an entrance through which pilgrims walk to make offerings to two revered Buddha images. The older, and finer, image is set behind a newer one, and is easy to miss. The wat next to Wat Prathat Choeng Chum is a popular teaching monastery.

Phrathat Narai Chengweng is another important chedi, situated 5 km west of town. Another important religious site in town is **Wat Pa Suthawat**, opposite the town hall. This is important not for any artistic merit, but because one of Thailand's most revered monks lived and died here: Phra Acaan Man Bhuritatto, better known as Luang Pho Man (1871-1949). A chapel in his memory has been constructed and his (few) possessions kept on display. ■ *0800-1800 Mon-Sun.*

The **Phu Thai** ethnic group inhabit the area around Sakhon Nakhon, and the Wax Castle festival is associated with them (see below). The 32 sq km **Nong Han Lake** is close to town beyond the beautiful and peaceful **Royal Park**. Boats can be hired to visit the islands on the lake (not as easy as it sounds, and needs to be done a day in advance), and it is a popular place at weekends. It is also said to be the largest natural inland water body in Thailand.

Excursions **Phrathat Narai Chenweng** is another important chedi, situated 5 km west of town in the village of Ban Thai. The 11th-century monastery was built as a Hindu shrine. The name *cheng weng* is Khmer for 'with long legs' and this is thought to refer to the carving of Vishnu on the northern pediment of the laterite prasat, still standing in the monastery's

---

Sakhon Nakhon place names

Phrathat Choeng Chum

พระธาตุเชิงชุม

Phrathat Narai Chengweng

พระธาตุนารายณ์เจงเวง

precincts. The four-armed Vishnu holds his head up with one hand while two of the other three hands hold a lotus and a baton. The prasat has several finely carved pediments and lintels. The eastern pediment shows a 12-armed (unusually, there are normally 10 in Thai representations), dancing Siva. The northern and eastern lintels depict Krishna. The southern lintel is in poor condition, but probably depicts a scene from the Ramayana. All are carved in Baphuon style. The northern side of the prasat has a false entrance through which a channel is cut, ending in the head of a makara; this would have drained lustral water used in ceremonies within the prasat. ■ *Getting there: by songthaew or local bus.*

Sleeping
■ *on map*
Price codes:
see inside front cover

A *Srisakol Thani Hotel*, T02-2384790, F2384797. A/c, restaurant, new hotel in the Dusit chain, the most comfortable place in town. **A** *JPK Mansion*, east of town centre, out of town. All facilities, but nothing to make it stand out from the crowd. **A-C** *MJ Hotel*, Kumuang Rd, located slightly outside town. The newest hotel in town, big and brash and certainly not beautiful, but the rooms are spacious, immaculate and good value. **C** *Dusit*, 1782-4 Yuwa Phattana Rd, T711198, F713115. Some a/c, swimming pool, not an up-country equivalent of the *Dusit Thani* in Bangkok, 102 rather average rooms. **C** *Imperial*, 1892 Suk Khasem Rd, T713320. Some a/c, 180 rooms and a snooker parlour, rooms in the new wing are considerably smarter, although the a/c rooms in the old wing are a good deal. **D-E** *Somkiat*, 1348/4 Kamchatphai, T711044. Some a/c, a central block with 22 additional bungalows, popular with travelling salesmen. Corridors more like a prison than a hotel, very stuffy. **E** *Araya 1*, 1432 Prempreeda Rd, T711224. Some a/c, 50 simple rooms. **E** *Araya 11*, cheapest in town and it shows – rundown, but sufficient for a night's stopover. Some rooms with bathrooms attached. **E-F** *Charoensuk*, 635 Charoen Muang Rd, T712916. Antiseptic smell, revelling in mediocrity.

Eating

For those seeking a new experience, just north of Sakhon Nakhon is a dog market which sells, slaughters and serves dog meat. **Thai/Chinese** *Sook Kasen*, Kamchatpai

Sakhon Nakhon

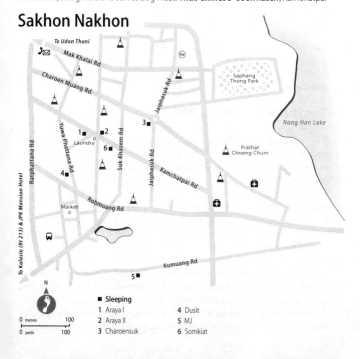

■ **Sleeping**
1 Araya I
2 Araya II
3 Charoensuk
4 Dusit
5 MJ
6 Somkiat

The Northeastern Region

Prathat Choeng Chum, Sakhon Nakhon

The Northeastern Region

Rd. Thai food. ***Best House Suki***, Prem Prida Rd. Excellent Isaan food served here, seafood specialities. **Foodstalls** There are 2 night markets in town. One is close to the *Charoensuk Hotel*, at the roundabout at the junction of Charoenmuang and Jaiphasuk rds. The other is at the intersection of Charoenmuang and Suk Khasem roads.

Festivals Oct *Wax Castle Ceremony*, celebrated at *Ok Phansa* (the end of the Buddhist lent), when elaborate and intricately detailed models of wats are moulded out of beeswax in order to gain merit. Images of the Buddha are placed inside these temporary edifices, and they are paraded through town accompanied by Northeastern music, singing and dancing. *Boat races* take place at Nong Han Lake at the same time.

Transport **Air** One flight a day on *Thai* to and from Bangkok. **Bus** Regular connections with
647 km to Bangkok Bangkok's Northeastern bus terminal (11 hrs) and with other Northeastern centres.

Directory **Airline offices** *Thai*, 1446 Yuwa Phattana Rd, T712259.

That Phanom   พระธาตุพนม

Phone code: 042   The small town of That Phanom is a quaint riverside settlement with one attrac-
Colour map 2, grid B5   tion: Wat That Phanom, the most revered temple in the Northeast and the second most revered by the people of Laos (the most revered being That Luang in Vientiane). The wat is dominated by an impressive 52 m white and gold Lao-style chedi. Around its square base, the chedi is decorated with carved brick slabs telling the stories of the five state rulers who are said to have built the original stupa in the ninth century. (Although legend has it that it was originally constructed in 535 BC to house a breastbone of the Buddha, eight years after his death.) Since then it has been restored no less than eight times, most recently in 1995 by the Thai Fine Arts Department. The most recent restoration but one, in 1977, followed the chedi's collapse after heavy rains in 1975. A legend said that should the chedi fall, then so too would the country of Laos; shortly afterwards, the Communist Pathet Lao took Luang Prabang and Vientiane, and ousted the American-backed government. The 1995 restoration gave thieves the opportunity, on 20 June, to climb the scaffolding and prise out the diamonds studded

into the finial. The perpetrators, one suspects, must be due to be consigned to the deepest of Buddhist hells, if they are not there already. The chedi is surrounded by seated Buddha images that the many hundreds of pilgrims have covered in gold leaf. During festivals and religious holidays, the wat is seething with people making offerings of flowers and incense.

On Monday and Thursday from around 0800 until 1200, a **Lao market** is held upstream from town when hoards of Laotians cross the Mekong to market their wares. They arrive laden with pigs, wild forest products and herbal remedies, returning home with cash and Thai consumer goods. The market winds down soon after midday, although the shops near the ferry pier sell excellent quality goods very cheaply every day of the week. Laotians and Thais spend the day being ferried back and forth across the river to trade, and the border here is now open for non-Thai and Laotian nationals too.

Renu Nakhon, a traditional weaving and embroidery centre, is almost 15 km northwest of That Phanom. Travel 8 km north on Route 212, and then left onto Route 2031 for another 6½ km (currently an unpaved road being improved). On market days (Wednesday) and fair days, the central wat of the village is home to hundreds of stalls selling a wide selection of local and Lao textiles (cotton and silk), as well as made-up garments and Isan axe pillows. Outside the wat compound, there are permanent shops selling a similar selection of cloth and local handicrafts throughout the week. Cloth is sold by the *phun* and there are about two *phun* in a sarong length. Prices quoted therefore do not usually relate to the piece. For simple cotton cloth, expect to pay ฿100-200 per *phun*; for the best silk, up to ฿3,000. ■ *Getting there: by bus from That Phanom (or Nakhon Phanom) to Renu Nakhon. If the bus drops you off at the junction of routes 212 and 2031, there are songthaews to ferry people the final 6½ km.*

Excursions

That Phanom

When the fair is on, it is difficult, often impossible, to find a room. No upmarket hotels here, so to be comfortable visitors will need to stay in Nakhon Phanom. There are 2 guesthouses in That Phanom mainly serving the needs of *farang* visitors, and 3 Thai-style hotels. There are also a couple of resort-style hotels a little out of the town centre.

C *That Phanom Resort*, south of the town, T541047. Some a/c, basic and boring rooms with the only plus that they are clean. **C-D** *Kaeng*

Sleeping
■ *on map*
Price codes:
see inside front cover

■ **Sleeping**
1 Chaiwan
2 Mr Pom's Guesthouse
3 Niyana's Guesthouse
4 Saeng Thong

N
Not to scale

Pho Resort, Highway 212 (3 km south of town), T541412. Some a/c, the better of Nakhon Phanom's 2 resort-style hotels, but even so this is hardly an example of rustic splendour – attractive gardens. **E-F** *Saeng Thong*, 34 Phanom Phanarak Rd. Small hotel with just 17 rooms, shabby, but at least it has some character. **E-F** *Chaiwan*, 34 Phanom Phanarak Rd. Another small hotel, marginally cleaner than the Saeng Thong and also quite characterful. **F** *Niyana's Guesthouse*, 288 Moo 2, Rimkhong Rd, T540588, upstream from town. Rooms in traditional country house, in peaceful leafy compound. Roof garden, large rooms with fans and nets, helpful and friendly owner, tours and motorbikes and bicycles for rent. Recommended. **E-F** *Mr Pom's Guesthouse*, Soi 2, pale green building. Clean and friendly place, keen to attract business away from other more popular places. Peaceful.

Eating Foodstalls and restaurants can be found on the riverfront and along Rachdamnern Rd; try the *That Phanom Pochana* or *Somkhane*, both fish restaurants close to the triumphal arch. Lao-style French fare is also available including good, strong fresh coffee and baguettes. The *night market* sells Thai dishes.

Festivals Jan/Feb *Phra That Phanom Chedi Homage-paying Fair* (full moon) – the Northeast's largest temple fair, when thousands of pilgrims converge on the wat and walk

Wat That Phanom

around the chedi in homage. Dancing, bands and other entertainments; perhaps the most vivid display of Northeastern regional identity. The entire town is engulfed by market stalls, selling a vast array of goods for the week of the festival, day and night.

Bus There is no bus terminal as such. Buses stop on Chaiyangkun Rd (the main Route 212, north to Nakhon Phanom and south to Ubon), an easy walk to the river and guesthouses. Regular connections with Nakhon Phanom, Mukdahan, Sakhon Nakhon, Udon Thani and Ubon Ratchatani. Buses for Bangkok leave from the southern end of Chayangkun Rd.

Transport
50 km to Nakhon Phanom

Banks *Thai Military*, on the main road into town (Route 212), north of Wat That Phanom (amongst others). **Communications** Post Office: north of the *Thai Military Bank*. No English spoken here, there is a phone available if you can make yourself understood. **Useful addresses** Immigration: Rachdamnern Rd, by the river, T541090.

Directory

Mukdahan   มุกดาหาร

The capital of one of Thailand's newer provinces, created in 1982, Mukdahan's greatest claim to fame is as the hometown of one of Thailand's best-known leaders, Field Marshal Sarit Thanarat (see page 757). Although Mukdahan is changing fast as one of the gateways to an emerging Laos, until recently many of the villages hereabouts were cut off from the outside world during the wet season. There are still a few old-style wooden houses, but they are fast disappearing.

Phone code: 042
Colour map 2, grid B5
Population: 29,000

   The town is situated on the Mekong River, and lies directly opposite the important Lao town of Savannakhet. There has been speculation that this will be the site of the second bridge of the lower reaches of the Mekong, the first being close to Nong Khai. It is like a quiet version of Nong Khai. For good views of the river and surrounding countryside, climb **Phu Manorom**, a small hill 5 km south of town. Take Route 2034 south towards Don Tan and after 2 km turn right. The summit is another 3 km from the turn-off.

   Because of its location, Mukdahan has become an important trading centre with goods from Laos, like gems, timber, cattle and agricultural commodities, being exchanged for Thai consumer goods. There is a Lao and Thai **market**, the so-called Talaat Indochine, held daily, along the river road running south from **Wat Si Mongkhon Tai**, which is situated opposite the pier where boats from Laos land. This wat is notable in that it was built in 1954 by Vietnamese settlers in the area and its origins are reflected in the abundance of statues of mythical creatures, unusual in the Thai context. It is best to get to the market in the morning. Along with Thai consumer goods, Lao silk and cotton cloth (see Shopping below), good French bread, china, 'axe' cushions, khaens (a local, bamboo pan pipe) and baskets are also sold. Near the pier and opposite Wat Si Mongkhon Tai is a Bodhi tree (*Ficus religiosa*). Traditional soothsayers often offer their advice here. The pier and riverside road is a good place to watch Mukdahan life go – slowly – by.

   Wat Sri Sumong, on Samran Chai Khong Road, the river road, is interesting for the colonial architectural elements reflected in the bot or ordination hall: the arches over the windows and the verandah. Between the bot and the more orthodox viharn is a small example of the distinctive Lao, lotus bud chedi. A little further north on the river road, **Wat Yod Kaew Sriwichai** also has Lao lotus bud chedis and a large, gold Buddha, in the mudra of spinning the Wheel of Law.

   The recently opened **Space Needle**, or **Hor Kaew Mukdahan**, is 2 km south of town. Looking rather like an air traffic control tower, the building houses a costume museum, a display of local artefacts, a gallery of Buddha images on the top floor, and a viewing gallery with exceptional views of Laos

The Northeastern Region

(and Savannakhet, on the opposite bank) and the river. The clothes in the costume museum are rather uncomfortably squeezed onto Western-sized mannequins. ■ *0800-1800, ₿20.*

Excursions **Phu Pha Thoep National Park** (also known as Mukdahan National Park) lies 15 km south of Mukdahan, off Route 2034. The park was gazetted in 1984 and covers a modest 54 sq km. The principal forest type here is dry dipterocarp savanna forest and there is a succession of oddly-shaped rock outcrops, easily accessible from park headquarters. The environment almost feels prehistoric, and fossils and finger paintings have been found amidst the boulders. Cut into the cliff face which rises above the headquarters is a cave packed with Buddha images, deposited here by villagers. There are no bungalows, but camping is permitted. ■ *Getting there: catch a songthaew travelling south towards Don Tan; the turning for the park is between the Km 14 and 15 markers and it is a 2 km walk from there to the park headquarters.*

Wat Phu Daan Tae contains a massive sitting Buddha made of brick and concrete, surrounded by acolytes. It can be seen clearly from Route 212, running south towards Ubon, about 50 km from town. ■ *Getting there: only worth stopping for the seriously committed. Take a bus running south towards Ubon.*

Tours There are four small tour offices opposite Wat Si Mongkhon Tai, at the north end of Samran Chai Khong Road: *TAR Tour, Mukdahan Tour (Thailand), Sompong Tour* and *Sakonpasa Department Store*. They are mainly oriented towards Thai tourists travelling to Laos and Vietnam. However, now that non-Thais can cross the border into Laos at this point, they have branched into providing services for *farangs*. Visa services and tours to Laos available.

Sleeping
■ *on map*
Price codes:
see inside front cover

A *Indochina Intercontinental*, Samut Sakdarak Rd, T611893, 1 km south of town centre. A/c, restaurant, 154 rooms in a riverside position. **A** *Mukdahan Grand*, 78 Song Nang Sathit, T630958, F612021. A/c, restaurant, comparatively plush but in a distinctly provincial manner, as evidenced in the local crooners, *Zubano Karaoke Bar* and *MG Snooker Club* – and some people would say all the more charming for it. Arguably the best hotel in town, though. **A-B** *Ploy Palace*, 1737/39 Song Nang Sathit, T612150. Competing to become the most upmarket hotel in town. All facilities including pool and conference hall. **C-D** *Mukdahan*, 8/8 Samut Sakdarak Rd, T611619, 500 m south of the town centre. Some a/c with hot water and TV, but no ambience, 4-storey hotel, quite new but already dilapidated at the edges, coffee shop with live music, friendly. **C-E** *Hua Nam*, 36 Samut Sakdarak Rd, T611137. Some a/c with TV and hot water, central location on corner with Song Nang Sathit Rd, looks from the outside like a cross between an American diner and a Chinese-style hotel, but rooms are large, clean and well maintained. Set around courtyard, so relatively quiet despite central crossroads location. Recommended. **D-E** *Hong Kong*, 161/1-2 Phithak Santirat Rd, T611123. Some a/c, Chinese-style hotel, quite well maintained, a/c rooms have hot water, central. **D-E** *Sansuk Bungalow*, 2 Phithak Santirat Rd, T611294. Some a/c, near the centre of town, clean rooms with friendly management, the best of a poor selection of cheaper accommodation.

• •
Mukdahan place names

Phu Manorom

ภูมโนรมย์

Phu Pha Thoep National Park

อุทยานแห่งชาติภูผาเทิบ

Wat Phu Daan Tae

วัดภูด่านแต้

Eating
• *on map*
Price categories:
see inside front cover

The best places to eat are along the river. Tables are set out on the pavement overlooking the Mekong and Laos. In the evening, with fairy light lit trees, and a gentle breeze, there can be few more attractive places to eat and drink. Riverside restaurants include the *River View*, *Sukhawadi* and *Phai Rim Khong*. **Mid-range** *Enjoy Restaurant*, 7/1 Samut Sakdarak Rd. Bright and cheerful restaurant with Lao specialities, a few Vietnamese dishes and river fish and prawns. **Cheap** *Phai Rim Khong* (*Riverside*), Samran Chai Khong Rd. A riverside restaurant to the south of town, serving good Thai dishes in attractive location with good views. *River View*, Samran Chai Khong Rd. Chalet-style restaurant with tables overlooking Mekong, average Thai and Lao food, spectacular setting. *Sukhawadi*, Samran Chai Khong. Mekong fish is best, but other Thai dishes available, great position on the river. **Seriously cheap** *No Name Restaurant*, Phithak Santirat Rd (on roundabout). Excellent cheap Thai dishes served from old wooden house.

Bakeries, breakfasts and ice-cream Seriously cheap: *Foremost*, 74/1 Samut Sakdarak Rd. Breakfast, ice-cream and coffee in a/c room. *Phit Bakery*, 709 Phithak Santirat. Good breakfasts, coffee, cakes and ice-creams, friendly. Recommended. *Bakery*, opposite the Ploy Palace Hotel, good cakes, coffee and ice-cream.

Mukdahan

To Indochina Intercontinental Hotel (500m), Phu Manorom & Space Needle (2 km)

N

0 metres   100
0 yards   100

■ **Sleeping**
1 Hong Kong
2 Hua Nam
3 Mukdahan

4 Mukdahan Grand

● **Eating**
1 Enjoy
2 Foremost
3 No name restaurant
4 Phai Rim Khong
5 Phit Bakery
6 River View
7 Sukhawadi

Foodstalls Seriously cheap: *Night market*, Song Nang Sathit Rd (western end, near the bus station). The best place for cheap Isan dishes and also for Vietnamese stall food.

Shopping **Antiques** *Sa-aat*, 77 Samut Sakdarak Rd. Small collection of antiques for sale including Chinese ceramics, old irons, Buddhist alms bowls and amulets. **Handicrafts** Mukdahan is a good place to buy Lao/Isan handicrafts like baskets, axe cushions and textiles. Cloth is usually sold by the *phun*; a sarong length is normally 2 *phun*, so when asking the price do not be surprised if the whole piece costs twice (or more) than the amount quoted. Cotton cloth is normally ฿100 per *phun*; silk costs several times more. The textiles with the elephant motif are distinctively Lao, although much of the cloth is now woven in Thailand, especially around Nong Khai. Textiles and other handicrafts can be bought in the daily riverside market (see Sights above). There are also permanent shops on Samut Sakdarak Rd.

Transport **Air** There are no air connections with Mukdahan, but a new airport opened in Roi Et in Mar 1999 and *PB Air* fly there from Bangkok 3 times a week. **Bus** The bus terminal (*bor kor sor*) for non-a/c and some a/c buses is at the western end of Song Nang Sathit Rd, about 2 km from the town

53 km S of That Phanom, 169 km N of Ubon

The Northeastern Region

centre (a ฿20 motor saamlor ride), or you may be dropped off at the junction of Muang Mai Rd and Route 212. Tuk-tuks wait here to extract from tourists rather more than their due. ฿20 is the usual rate into town. If you want to go to the bus terminal continue for 1 km south along Route 212 and it is on the right. Buses from here to Ubon, Nakhon Phanom and That Phanom, and some other northeastern towns, as well as Bangkok. A/c tour buses leave from close to Bangkok Bank on Song Nang Sathit Rd. Connections with Bangkok's Northeastern bus terminal (12 hrs), north to That Phanom and Nakhon Phanom (2 hrs), and south to Ubon Ratchathani (2½ hrs). Tour buses leave from *Sahamit Tours*, offices on Samut Sakdarak Rd, also close to the town centre.

International connections to Laos Ferries to Savannakhet and Laos leave from the pier near Wat Si Mongkhon Tai. Foreigners can cross from Thailand to Laos here. A second bridge across the Mekong (the first being near Nong Khai) had been agreed, although it looks as though the economic slump in the region has put it on the back burner for a while. The Thais are also considerably more enthusiastic than the Laotians.

Directory **Banks** *Bangkok Bank*, Song Nang Sathit Rd. *Thai Farmers*, Song Nang Sathit Rd. **Communications** Post Office: Phithak Santirat Rd (on the roundabout), be prepared for a steep ascent to the front desk. **Useful addresses** Immigration: Samran Chai Khong Rd, T611074.

The Eastern Region

7

The Eastern Region

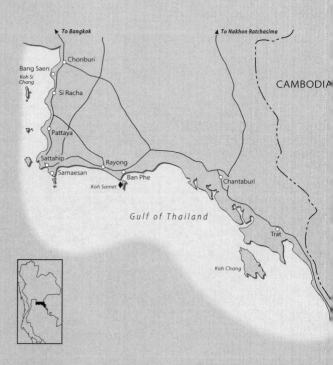

The Eastern region is sandwiched between the Gulf of Thailand to the south and the Damrek range of mountains to the north. It covers 37,507 sq km and stretches 400 km from Bangkok, southeast to Trat on the Cambodian border. It is similar to the Western region, in that it is small in area, without any focal city, and lacking a characteristic regional culture. It is also akin to the West in that, at least until not very long ago, the East was a relatively quiet and traditional area of fruit trees, gem mining and forests. It also had a flourishing fishing industry exploiting the waters of the Gulf of Thailand and serving the Bangkok market.

Although these activities have been overshadowed by recent developments, the deforestation of large swathes of land and a boom in tourism, there are still orchards between Rayong and Chantaburi, a multitude of fishing communities along the Gulf coast, and a major centre for gem mining at Chantaburi, where many of Thailand's finest sapphires are sourced.

Development and tourism

The east has been transformed since the 1960s. Illegal loggers have largely cleared the area of trees, and landless families from other parts of the kingdom – with the encouragement and support of Chinese middlemen – have moved in to plant the land to upland crops such as cassava and maize. As the forests were being replaced by crops, the beaches of the eastern Gulf were witnessing an extraordinary growth in tourism. This was focused on the famous (to some infamous) beach resort of Pattaya, about 150 km from Bangkok. Beginning as a resort for small numbers of Thais and farangs who wished to escape from the capital for weekend breaks, Pattaya developed into one of the key destinations for American GIs on leave during the Vietnam War. With the end of that war, Pattaya adroitly switched its attention to the international tourist market, attracting increasing numbers of men (and a few women). A Tourist Authority of Thailand survey revealed that over one-fifth of all tourists to Thailand visited the area of Pattaya and Chonburi. Assuming the survey is accurate (never a sensible assumption to make in Thailand), this would mean that well over a million international tourists visit this resort each year. When you add in domestic tourists, the numbers reach three million.

Although tourism is important to the economy of the east – and there is still room for further expansion – in recent years this has been superceded by its role as an overspill area for Bangkok. As Bangkok's infrastructure came under ever greater pressure, the government began looking for ways to ease the strain on the capital. In the early 1980s, it came up with the much vaunted Eastern Seaboard Development Project, a massive scheme which brought roads, ports, rail links, pipelines and gas separation plants to eastern Thailand – mostly concentrated along a corridor between the towns of Chonburi and Rayong.

Chonburi to Pattaya

Route 3 from Bangkok follows Thailand's eastern seaboard to the Cambodian border. The first 130 km (on the newish Highway 34) is a ribbon of development – effectively Bangkok's industrial overspill. Companies have moved here to escape the high land prices and congestion of the capital. As a result former sleepy towns like Chonburi and Si Racha have been engulfed. 147 km from Bangkok is the renowned beach resort of Pattaya, brash and brazen. Past Pattaya, Route 3 swings eastwards and passes through the town of Rayong (70 km from Pattaya), and then Ban Phe, where boats leave for the island of Koh Samet. Continuing on Route 3, Chantaburi is 109 km from Rayong, and Trat another 70 km on from here. Both towns are highly regarded for their fruit and gems. From the port of Laem Ngop, 17 km from Trat, boats leave for Koh Chang.

Chonburi ชลบุรี

Phone code: 038
Colour map 3, grid B4

Chonburi is the first significant town travelling southeast from Bangkok along Route 3. It is an important commercial centre with oyster farms and fruit processing and canning plants serving the sugarcane, cassava and coconut farms and plantations of the area. It also has a reputation as a battlefield for the Chinese mafia. There is not much of interest for the tourist in this dusty town. The oldest and most important wat in the province is **Wat Intharam**, which is near the old market. The wat, dating from the Ayutthaya Period, is unusual in that it has not been extensively restored. The bot contains an excellent series of

A foot in the door

★ The great bulk of visitors who travel to Thailand's Eastern region make for Pattaya, one of Thailand's most developed beach resorts. It isn't quaint, it isn't beautiful, it can hardly be described as an exemplar of environmentally friendly development, but people come here in droves and most leave with a smile on their face. It offers lots of bars, good restaurants, and a wide range of sports and activities.

★ For those who like their beach resorts a little more placid then Koh Samet and Koh Chang, both gazetted as national parks, will probably appeal rather more. Koh Chang particularly provides quiet, simple bungalow accommodation and time to read.
★ Chantaburi and Trat are provincial capitals not far from the Cambodian border. Chantaburi, famous throughout Thailand for the quality of its fruit, is the more attractive of the two.

formally structured murals with no sense of perspective dating from the late 18th century. Near the centre of town is **Wat Dhamma Nimitr**, which contains a 37-m high image of the Buddha in a boat and covered in gold mosaic. Not only is this Buddha image the largest in the region, it is also one of the few in the country with a maritime theme.

Sleeping There is a lot of accommodation in Chonburi, but it is rarely used by visitors to Thailand. This is an area of condominiums and time-share apartments for Bangkok's wealthy, get-aways for locals rather a holiday destination for foreigners. **B-C** *Sukjai Bungalow*, 17/32 Phayasatya Rd, T282255. Some a/c. **C** *Likhit*, 781 Chetchamnong Rd, T273810, F273811. Some a/c, restaurant.

Festivals **Oct** *Buffalo Races* (movable). Races and contests between buffalo and man.

Transport **Bus** Regular connections with Bangkok's Eastern bus terminal, Pattaya (67 km) and *80 km to Bangkok* other eastern destinations.

Bang Saen บางแสน

Phone code: 039
Colour map 3, grid B4

Bang Saen is a beach resort popular with middle-class Thais. It is crowded at the weekends but practically deserted during the week and has good seafood. The town is clearly attempting to become another Pattaya, although it is difficult to see how it will succeed. That said, it does have a Hotels and Tourism Training Institute, so it should provide skilled services – and the town is surprisingly clean. On Monkey Hill there is the **shrine of Chao Mae Khao Sammuk**, a Chinese girl who drowned herself in the 18th century after her parents refused to allow her to marry the man she loved. Now a Goddess, many Sino-Thais visit the shrine to improve their luck. The oyster beds for which the town is known can be seen from the hill. There is usually a welcome onshore breeze on the sandy palm-fringed beach. The **Ocean World Amusement Park** is on the Beach Road, T383096. ■ *Mon-Sun ฿150 adults, ฿100 children.*
There is a **Marine Science Museum** in Srinakarinwirot University.

Sleeping Like Chonburi, Bang Saen is mainly used by Bangkokians looking for a weekend away from the grime within easy reach of the capital. Overseas visitors rarely come here. **A-C** *Bang Saen Beach Resort*, 55-150 Beach Rd, T381675, B2536385. A/c, restaurant, pool, close to the action. **A-C** *Bang Saen Villa*, T282088, F311726. A/c, restaurant, pool, good views, well run and recommended attached restaurant. **C-D** *Saen Sabai Bungalow*, 153 Beach Rd, T381063, a/c, restaurant.

The Eastern Region

Transport
98 km to Bangkok

Road Bus: regular connections with Bangkok's Eastern Bus terminal (1½ hrs) and with Chonburi (18 km south) and Pattaya.

Directory   **Banks** *Siam Commercial*, 53/1 Bang Saen Rd.

Si Racha ศรีราชา

Si Racha, some 100 km from Bangkok, is the home of a locally famous hot chilli sauce (*nam prik Si Racha*), usually eaten with seafood, for which the town also has a reputation. The town has a profusion of seafood restaurants, the most enjoyable of which are built on jetties which protrude out to sea. Westerners usually visit Si Racha in order to reach the island of Koh Si Chang (see page 475), but the town does have character and is worth more than a cursory wander.

Sights   A short distance to the north of town is a small, gaudy but nevertheless enjoyable **Sino-Thai wat** built on a rocky islet – **Koh Loi** – connected to the mainland by a long causeway. The monastery commemorates a monk who spent many years on the rock and it boasts a footprint of the Buddha as well as an image of the Chinese Goddess of Mercy, Kuan Yin. On Choemchomphon Road, the waterfront road, and almost opposite Soi 16, is the **Jaw Phor Samut Dam Chinese temple** said to be 100 years old. Up the road towards the clock-tower at the southern end is a large covered **market**. However, perhaps the most enjoyable feature of Si Racha (and of Koh Si Chang) are the overpowered, chariot-like **motorized saamlors**. Purring along, with deep bucket seats and massive engines, the machines seem like outrageous modernized rickshaws. They cannot be a terribly efficient form of transport and it probably will not be long before they are elbowed out by the ubiquitous tuk-tuk – unless their macho appeal helps them to survive.

The Eastern Seaboard, and in particular the length of coast between Chonburi and Rayong, was selected in the 1980s as the overspill area for Bangkok's industry and as a result there has been an upsurge in activity around Si Racha. **Laem Chabang**, just the other side of Khao Nam Sap, a modest hill 10 km to the south of town, has been developed into a major deep-water port and can be seen from the road to Pattaya. Even closer to Si Racha, just a few kilometres south, is the Thai Oil refinery. So far, and surprisingly, Si Racha has maintained its poise amidst all this activity.

Excursions   Si Racha Tiger Farm is a little less than 10 km east of town, off route 3241. This really has a remarkable collection of tigers – well over 100 Bengal tigers at the last count – which appear to breed like rabbits. In addition to the tigers there is a scorpion zone and a crocodile farm as well as assorted camels, elephants and deer. ■ *Mon-Sun, 0800-1800, ฿250, ฿150 (children). Getting there: take a tuk-tuk from town.*

Sleeping   Like its restaurants, all the hotels mentioned below except the *Laemthong* are built over the sea – which makes a pleasant change from the usual featureless budget accommodation available in Thai towns. Many of these hotels are well run, clean and atmospheric affairs, most with great restaurants attached.

B-C *Grand Bungalow*, 9 Choemchomphon Soi 18, T312537. South end of town, range of bungalows built off a jetty. Better for larger groups or families

• •
Si Racha place names

Jaw Phor Samut Dam Chinese temple

วัดเจ้าพ่อสมุทรดำ

Laem Chabang

แหลมฉบัง

rather than couples. **B-C** *Laemthong Residence Hotel*, Sukhumvit Rd, T322888, F312651. A/c, restaurant, pool, tennis. Modern hotel lacking the character of the others listed here, but the closest thing to a starred establishment. Central location. **C-D** *Srivichai*, Choemchomphon Rd, Soi 8, T311212. Wooden hotel, much like the *Sri Wattana*, just a shade pricier, friendly, good attached restaurant, clean and classy. Recommended. **D-E** *Bungalow Sri Wattana*, Choemchomphon Rd, Soi 8, T311037. Wooden hotel constructed on a jetty, friendly and clean with great atmosphere and enthusiastic service. Good restaurant attached. Recommended. **D-E** *Samchai*, Choemchomphon Rd, Soi 10, T311134. Some a/c, wooden hotel, clean rooms, good atmosphere, great food. Recommended.

Eating

Si Racha is known for its seafood, which is generally excellent. Many restaurants are Chinese rather than Thai, or at least Sino-Thai. Mussels and oysters are particularly good, and many of the dishes come with Si Racha's famed chilli sauce. Price depends to a great extent on what type of seafood takes your fancy: grilled lobster is several times more expensive than a simple *pla kapong* dish. However all of the following are good. **Seafood** *Si Racha Seafood*, Choemchomphon Rd (near the bus stop). *Cherinot*, Choemchomphon Rd, Soi 14 (pier). *Jaw Sii*, 98 Choemchomphon Rd. *Hua Huat*, 102 Choemchomphon Rd. *Chua Li*, Choemchomphon Soi 10, most pricey of the seafood restaurants in town with an established, and well-deserved reputation for quality victuals.

Transport
105 km to Bangkok

Bus Connections every 30 mins or so with Bangkok's Eastern bus terminal as well as with Pattaya (29 km north) and Chonburi (24 km south). Songthaews for Naklua in Pattaya leave from close to the clock tower at regular intervals.

Train While just about everyone arrives here by bus, there are a handful of trains each day from Hualamphong station in Bangkok. Cheap, slow but considerably more attractive than the bus journey.

Boat Ferries for Si Racha depart from the pier at the end Jermjomphon Rd, Soi 14 (see Si Racha entry for details).

Directory

Banks *Bangkok Bank of Commerce*, Surasak Rd.

Koh Si Chang เกาะสีชัง

Koh Si Chang is a small island about 45 minutes ferry ride from Si Racha with a resident population of fewer than 5,000 people. Although it is quite feasible to visit the island as a day trip, there are hotels and camping facilities for those who might wish to stay longer.

Phone code: 038
Colour map 3, grid C4

Koh Si Chang used to be the trans-shipment point for both cargo and passenger vessels before the Chao Phraya River was dredged sufficiently to allow ships to reach Bangkok. Even though many vessels now bypass Si Racha, the surrounding water is still chock-a-block with ships at anchor (normally about 50, but sometimes as many as 100 ships), their cargoes being unloaded into smaller lighters and barges. The island's main trade is now as a service base for the freighter crews. Their visas often do not allow them to disembark, so all R & R is taken to them by the varied residents of Koh Si Chang. In the bay just out from the town can be seen a white ship – the *Phnom Penh* – previously a floating hotel but severely damaged by fire two years ago. Ever since then, the ship's crew have been confined, so it is said, to ship. The island also has a reputation as a sanctuary for criminals. The drugs trade is reportedly rife and corruption within the police force endemic. Reports of individual travellers being asked

The Eastern Region

for customary gifts of whisky and the like have been known. This is reportedly more of a problem in isolated spots like Tham Phang.

Sights

Don't come to Koh Si Chang expecting a tropical idyll.

At the northern edge of the town, set high up on a hill (a tiring walk to the top), there is a **Chinese temple – Chaw Por Khaw Yai**. With an assortment of variously decorated shrines and caves, and with views of the island and town, it makes a good first stop after docking at the jetty beneath the temple. A particular favourite with the Chinese at Chinese New Year, it is said that during the festivities, over 5,000 people visit the shrine each evening, more than doubling the island's population.

On the west side of the island is **Khaw Khad**, a popular weekend fishing spot for Bangkokians. Not far away to the south, and overlooking the town, is a **Buddhist retreat** set among limestone caves (unlit). A large, yellow, seated Buddha image looks out over the bay. On the east coast, south of the retreat, are the **ruins of a palace** built by Rama V. It was abandoned in 1893 when the French took control of the island during their confrontation with the Thais regarding each country's respective rights of suzerainty over Laos. Not much remains – in fact, most of the structure was dismantled and rebuilt in Bangkok. Rather eerie stairways, balustrades and an empty reservoir remain scattered across the rocky, frangipani-covered hillside – as if the palace had been vaporized. There has been some, limited re-building work but even so the only building of any size remaining is **Wat Atsadangnimit**. This monastery is still revered and attracts a surprising number of pilgrims largely because King Chulalongkorn used to meditate here. The Buddha image within the sanctuary is unusual in style if not remarkable in artistic accomplishment. ■ *0800-1800.*

The island also has a number of **beaches** and reasonable swimming and snorkelling. The quietest beach with the best coral and swimming is **Tham Phang** on the western side of the island (฿10 by tuk-tuk); easier to reach are **Tha Wang** (next to the palace) – a rocky beach and not suitable for swimming – and **Hat Sai Khao** (over the hill from the palace). At weekends the island becomes crowded with Thai day-trippers; it is more relaxed during the week. While it is possible to swim here, note that the waters are really pretty turbid and at certain times of year the currents can wash all sorts of trash onto the beach.

Sleeping

A-B *Si Chang Palace*, Atsadang Rd, T216276. A/c, restaurant, pool. The top of the pile on the island, this hideous building seems very out of place and is overpriced. Its redeeming feature is that is has great views (and a pool).

B-D *Si Phitsanu Bungalows*, Hat Tham, T216024. Some a/c, a range of rooms and bungalows available here with views over the sea, out of town not far from Hat Tham. **B-D** *Tew Phai*, T216084. Some a/c, restaurant (pricey), welcoming management and usually busy with activity, the best of the cheaper places to stay, but not as good as the hoardings suggest. A tout will meet you at the pier as you alight from your boat which goes a long way to explaining why it is so popular.

C-D *Benz*, T216091. Some a/c, unusual stone bungalows, clean and well kept, close to the sea. **D** *Green House*, T216024. Simple green rooms at the edge of the town, in a style reminiscent of 1960s Skegness. A good view, if it wasn't for the uncontrolled undergrowth.

Camping This is possible, but bring your own equipment; at weekends Thais from the mainland camp in large numbers.

Eating *Si Chang Palace Coffee Shop*, an a/c refuge offering a range of coffee and cakes.

The Eastern Region

Local There are a number of the massive motorized **saamlors** that are also found in Si Racha and Chonburi. Given that the roads (in reality, paths) only allow the drivers to attain a speed of about 30 km per hour, they must be among the most overpowered taxis in the world. A tour of all the sights should not be more than ฿150 – and in chariot-like splendour (the owner of No 38, Nerng, speaks reasonable English and distributes maps free of charge). **Transport**

Boat Regular daytime ferry service from Jermjomphon Rd, Soi 14 in Si Racha, 0900-1700 outward, 0630-1630 return, 40 mins, but frequently more, because of drop-offs to the many ships moored in the harbour (฿30). The more expensive hotels can be booked from the pier in Si Racha.

Banks *Thai Farmers*, 9-9/1-2 Coast Rd. **Directory**

Pattaya

Pattaya or 'Southwest wind' is argued by some to be Thailand's premier beach resort, yet only 25 years ago it was a little-known coastal village frequented by fishermen, farmers and a handful of Thai and farang weekenders.

Phone code: 038
Colour map 3, grid C4

Ins and outs

Pattaya is well connected with Bangkok. Most people arrive here by bus from the capital's Eastern bus terminal, and there are dozens of departures daily from VIP to economy. The road from Bangkok is good and fast and the journey takes about 2 hrs. There are even direct connections from Bangkok's Don Muang Airport. U-Tapao is the nearest airport to Pattaya but the only scheduled service is **Bankgkok Airways**' daily connection with Koh Samui. There is also a train station, although the service with Bangkok is limited.

Getting there
See also Transport, page 489

The town itself is simple to get around. It consists of one long straight seafront road running the length of the beach (Pattaya Beach Road), together with another parallel road just inland (Pattaya 2 Road). Linking the two there are innumerable sois (lanes) packed with bars, restaurants and hotels. The greatest concentration of restaurants and bars is at the south end of town. Local transport is abundant. Songthaews run regularly between all the tourist centres and there are also scores of people hiring out bikes, motorbikes and jeeps.

Getting around

TAT, 382/1 Beach Rd, T428750, F429113, has helpful staff and lots of information. Areas of responsibility are Pattaya and Samut Prakan. There are several free tourist magazines and maps available. Unlike some other areas of Thailand, obtaining information is easy.

Tourist offices

The resort

Pattaya began to metamorphose when the US navy set up shop at the nearby port of Sattahip (40 km further down the coast) and American sailors began to demand something more than just sand and sea. As the war in Vietnam escalated, so the influx of GIs on 'rest and recreation' also grew and Pattaya responded enthusiastically. (Not by chance, Pattaya was selected as an R & R destination for the UN peacekeeping forces in Cambodia in 1992-93 bringing the town the title 'city of peace'.) Today, it provides around 36,000 hotel rooms and supplies everything you could ever need from a beach holiday – except,

Around 3 m people are said to visit Pattaya each year

The Eastern Region

Pattaya

Related map
A Pattaya Beach,
page 483

0 metres 500
0 yards 500

N

■ Sleeping
1 Asia Pattaya
2 Central Wong Amat
3 Gardenia
4 Garden Lodge
5 Island View
6 Mermaid's Beach Resort
7 Pattaya Park Beach
8 Royal Cliff Beach
9 Sawasdee Palace
10 Sea Breeze
11 Silver Sand Villa
12 Sugar Hut

🚌 Buses
1 BKS non a/c to Bangkok
2 A/c bus to North & Northeast
3 A/c bus terminal
4 Bus to Sattahip
5 Sri Mongkhon Tour - buses to northeast
6 407 Pattana Tour - buses to Nong Khai

The Eastern Region

The Eastern Region

arguably, peace and quiet. Given its origins in the Vietnam War, it is hardly surprising that Pattaya's stock in trade is entertainment for unaccompanied men who arrive in droves, many of them on package tours. At any one time, about 4,000 girls are touting for work around the many bars and restaurants of Pattaya. In the past, most of Pattaya's tourists came from the US, Australasia and Western Europe. However over the last few years these traditional sources have been in decline while visitors from Eastern Europe and Russia have escalated. There are now even tourist magazines in Russian and most of the bars stock a good range of vodkas and the bar girls have a smattering of Russian.

While Pattaya's official population is a comparatively paltry 60,000, most people believe that at any one time there are between 200,000 and 300,000 staying in town, whether international tourists or migrant workers. This has inevitably led to environmental problems. Lack of treatment of polluted water has meant that the beaches are not as clean as they once were – and the waters offshore can have a coliform count that should make most people stick to their hotel swimming pools or baths. This applies particularly to South Pattaya Beach where swimming, as yet, is not recommended. However, in 1992, the government allocated US$42mn in an effort to clean up Pattaya's act and Pattaya is already Thailand's first provincial city to have a water treatment plant. South Pattaya Beach, according to the authorities, should (should being the operative word) be clean enough to swim off, now that new waste water works have been completed.

Indeed, Pattaya – according to official statements at least – is going out of its way to play down its go-go bar image and promote a 'family' resort profile. This is deemed to be good for business, and perhaps the only way that occupancy rates can be maintained when the sex industry in Thailand is coming under such scrutiny, both for health and social reasons. (In 1996 average occupancy rates barely touched 50%.) This emphasis on good ol' wholesome family fun is hard to reconcile with the reality. But still the effort continues. It was no coincidence that an international conference on 'sustainable tourism' was held in Jomtien, outside Pattaya, a few years ago. The conference produced the so-called Pattaya Protocol, a series of guidelines on how to promote culturally and environmentally sensitive tourism. As well as trying to entice families to come here, local planners are also trying to re-cast Pattaya as a conference and incentive break venue. But just when things look like they are improving, something comes along to makes a mess of all the efforts. In 1997 there was an algae bloom that made the water even less appealing than it usually is, and in July 1997 there was a blaze at the 16-storey *Royal Jomtien Resort*, with the death of 80 people. Most recently of all, in 2000 a British tourist was gored by an enraged elephant at the Nong Nooch Tropical Garden. She died in hospital shortly afterwards.

The busiest and noisiest area is at the southern end of town (South Pattaya or 'The Village'); from about Soi 11 to Soi Post Office (with Pattayaland 1, 2 and 3 being the gay areas of town), there must be one of the highest concentration of bars, discos, massage parlours, prostitutes and transvestites of any place in the world. Many people find this aspect of Pattaya repugnant. However, there

● ● ● ● ● ● ● ● ● ● ● ● ● ● ● ● ● ● ● ●
Pattaya place names
Bang Saray

บางเสร่

Elephant Village

หมู่บ้านช้าง

Khao Khieo 'Open Zoo'

สวนสัตว์เปิดเขาเขียว

Mini Siam

เมืองจำลอง

Nong Nooch Orchid Wonderland

สวนนงนุช

is no pretence here – either on the part of the hosts or their guests. This is a beach resort of the most lurid kind. **Warning** It is worth bearing in mind that whatever people might tell you, Thailand *does* have an **AIDS** problem, the most serious in Asia (see page 788).

Pattaya may be infamous in the west as a city of sin, but there is more to the resort than this popular perception might indicate. It is also a haven for watersports lovers: there is sailing, para-sailing, windsurfing, ski-boating, snorkelling, deep-sea fishing and scuba diving. And for the non-beach lover, there are trips to sapphire mines, orchid farms and elephant kraals as well as tennis, golf (the Siam Country Club has the best course in Thailand), bowling and a multitude of other sports. Pattaya is also remarkably good value. It is probably this, coupled with the range of activities and services on offer (and Pattaya's accessibility) which explains why – despite the bad press – the resort has so many repeat guests (25-50%). Indeed, Pattaya's negative press has been overdone; it is not the tourist hell-hole one might expect from some of the reports. It may be raucous and somewhat tarnished – but it is also a bargain.

Sights

Big Buddha There are few sights, as such, in Pattaya to compare with many other places in the Kingdom. However, many visitors do make their way to the **Big Buddha** on the hill at the southern end of the beach (see map page 478). There are good views over the resort from the vantage point and the monks based here are usually willing to talk to interested visitors. The main Buddha image is surrounded by smaller images representing each day of the week. In the evenings **South Pattaya Road** is entertaining to explore because it is closed off to traffic. It's the best time to check out the bars, shops and so on.

Jomtien Beach South of Pattaya Bay, past the Big Buddha on the hill, is the quieter **Jomtien Beach**, which is becoming more popular by the month. Here there are more hotels, restaurants and sports facilities as well as a slightly cleaner beach. One of the highlights of our most recent visit to Pattaya was a trip up the **Pattaya Park Tower**. Situated on the headland at Jomtien, this 240-m pinnacle provides spectacular views of the surrounding area, and for some extra excitement, it is possible to travel down the zip-wire from 170 m to ground level (see sports below). For ฿200, visitors travel to the top of the tower and get one ride down the zip wire. For another ฿300, a buffet meal is provided in the *Pinnacle Revolving Restaurant*. T251201 for more information.

Other things to do – and bear in mind that these are modest attractions to say the very most – include a visit to the verbosely named **Million Years Stone Park and Pattaya Crocodile Farm** at 22/2 Moo 1, Tambon Nong Pla Lai, Banglamong, T249347, where there are granite rock gardens, with fossils, bonsai trees and various rare animals. ■ *0900-1800*. Alternatively, you could try the **Siriporn Orchid Farm** at 235/14 Moo 5, Tambon Nong Prue, T429013, where there is an array of orchids on show (and for sale). ■ *Mon-Sun, 0800-1700, ฿10*. The **Bottle Museum** at 79/15 Moo 10, Sukhumvit Road, T422957, displays over 300 pieces of artwork, the result of 15 years hard labour by the Dutch sculptor Leter Bedelais. Finally, the **Ripleys Believe it or not Museum**, T710294, is on the third floor of the *Royal Garden Plaza*, easily identified by the red biplane stuck on the side of the building. It consists of a collection of curiosities, both originals and replica. All a bit tacky. ■ *Mon-Sun, 1000-2400, ฿150*.

Excursions

Mini Siam is a cultural and historical park where 80 of Thailand's most famous 'sights' – including, for example, Wat Phra Kaeo and the Bridge over the River Kwai – are recreated at a scale of 1:25. There are also replicas of some other sights including the Eiffel Tower and the Statue of Liberty. ■ *0700-2200. T421628 for details. Getting there: by tour or by songthaew; the park lies 3 km north of Pattaya Beach, on the Sukhumvit highway (Route 3) running to Bangkok, at the Km 143 marker.*

Khao Khieo 'Open Zoo' is a 500 ha forested area supporting 130 species of bird and 38 mammal (including a few leopards); there is also a wildlife education centre with museum, and the requisite waterfall (*Chanta Then*). There is no overnight accommodation. ■ *Daily 0800-1800. ฿20, ฿5 children, ฿20 for a car, T311561. Getting there: 30 km north on Route 3, turn inland near Bang Saen on Route 3144. The park lies close to Bang Phra Golf Course.*

The **Elephant Village** is near the Siam Country Club. ■ *฿300, show at 1430.* There is also elephant trekking available which lasts two hours and takes the intrepid pachyderm jockey into the surrounding bush (*฿700*). Contact *Tropicana Hotel* for booking, T428645-8, Ext Elephant Village Counter or T249174 after 1800.

The **Nong Nooch Tropical Garden** is a 200-ha park containing immaculate gardens with lakes (and boating), an orchid farm, family zoo, Thai handicraft demonstrations and a thrice-daily (1015, 1500 and 1545) 'cultural spectacular' with Thai dancing, Thai boxing and an elephant show, T429321 for details. In 2000 a British tourist was gored here by an enraged elephant and later died. It is similar to the 'Rose Garden' complex outside Bangkok and is rather artificial, though it serves a purpose for tourists visiting nowhere but Pattaya and is popular with children. Sleeping is available in traditional Thai cottages and there are a number of restaurants. But much better is Sunset Village, about 2 km fron Nong Nooch. Very quiet, with a small beach, good bungalows, pool and excellent seafood. Good for lunch or to stay the night. ■ *0900-1800, Mon-Sun. ฿20, ฿200 for the cultural show, or take a tour from Pattaya for ฿250, T238063. Getting there: most people arrive on a tour; the garden is 15 mins from Pattaya town 3 km off the main road at the Km 163 marker.*

Bang Saray is a fishing village 20 km south of Pattaya on Route 3, with seafood restaurants (notably the *Ruan Talay*) and a good base for game-fishing trips, which can be arranged at the *Fisherman's Inn, Fisherman's Lodge*, or the *Sea Sand Club*; a chartered boat costs about ฿2,500. **Sleeping B** *Fisherman's Lodge*, T436757. A/c, restaurant. **B** *Fisherman's Inn*, T436095. A/c, restaurant, pool, spacious grounds. **C** *Bang Saray Villa*, T436070. A/c, restaurant, pool. **C** *The Sea Sand Club*, T435163, F435166. A/c and facilities for windsurfing. Good seafood restaurants here. ■ *Getting there: by bus from Pattaya.*

When Pattaya gets too much, many people retire to one of the **Offshore Islands** for rest and recreation of a different kind. The largest island (and the only one with accommodation) is **Koh Larn**, with good snorkelling and scuba diving waters surrounding it. Glass-bottomed boats are available for touring the reef, as is the full array of watersports. The island even has an 18-hole golf course. **Sleeping** *Koh Larn Resort*, its office is at 183 Soi Post Office, T428422. **B** for bungalows, which include the boat fare and transfer to the bungalows.

The Eastern Region

■ *Getting there: the Resort office will organize boats, or tickets can be purchase from the booth next to the Sailing Club. Boats depart at 0930 and 1130, returnir at 1600, 45 mins (฿250). Boats can be chartered for ฿1,500 per day. A share sailing junk ฿250 (inclusive of lunch and coral reef viewing), or a chartered sailing junk costs ฿3,000 per day. 'Tours' to Koh Larn, have watersports organize by the travel agent.*

Further afield are the islands of **Koh Lin**, **Koh Sak** and **Koh Phai**, wher there is better coral but fewer facilities. Only charter-boats visit these island for double the price of Koh Larn.

Tours There are countless tours organized by the many travel agents in town: th standard long-distance trips are to Koh Samet, the sapphire mines nea Chantaburi, Ayutthaya and Bang Pa-In, Bangkok, the floating marke Kanchanaburi and the River Kwai Bridge (two days). There are also local tour to Nong Nooch village, the Elephant Village and Khao Khieo Open Zoo among others. Prices for day tours (meal included) range from ฿600-1,200

Essentials

Sleeping
■ *on map*
Price codes:
see inside front cover

Pattaya has the biggest selection of hotels in Thailand outside Bangkok (36,000 room at the last count), although there is little left here for the budget traveller, with room from ฿350 upwards. However, for those who are looking for places one notch u from budget places then there is lots to choose from and most are very good valu There are three distinct areas of accommodation. At the northern end of the beach the area of **Naklua**. This is the quieter end of town, although it still has its fair share clubs and bars with little attempt to disguise their raison d'être. **Pattaya beach** busier and gets noisier and more active from north to south. On round the headland **Jomtien**, with a better beach but less nightlife. All accommodation in our '**A**' rang has a/c, restaurant, pool, and prices are exclusive of tax. A continuing room gl means reduced rates (up to 50%) should be offered except at weekends and high sea son. The high season is Nov-Mar.

Naklua AL *Central Wong Amat*, 277-8 Moo 5, Naklua, T426990, F42859 www.centralgroup.com Set in 25 acres, choice of 100 or so deluxe rooms or 65 chal and bungalow rooms, business facilities, 2 pools (1 good sized laps pool), waterspor facilities, good position away from the main drag. **A** *Woodlands Resort*, 164/ Pattaya-Naklua Rd, T421707, F425663. On the edge of Pattaya and Naklua. This hot has tried to recreate a colonial lodge-type atmosphere – only partially successfully but it is quiet, leafy and airy with attractive rooms and pool and landscaped gardens.

B *Garden Lodge*, Naklua Rd, T429109, F421221. A/c, pool, bungalow rooms lookin onto mature gardens, quiet and excellent value. Recommended. **B** *Gardenia*, ne North Pattaya Rd, T426356, F426358. A/c, pool. **B** *Loma*, Soi Naklua 18, T42602 F421501. A/c, restaurant, pool. **B** *Sea View Resort*, Soi Naklua 18, T424825. A/c, restau rant, pool. **C** *Sawasdee Palace*, Naklua Rd (near Soi 16), T225651, F225616. A/c, poc Recommended. **C** *Sea Lodge*, Naklua Rd, T425128, F425129. A/c, pool.

Pattaya Beach L-AL *Dusit Resort*, 240 Beach Rd (north end), T425611, F42823 Health club, tennis, squash courts, children's pools, table tennis and a games roon watersports, clean, private beach, shopping arcade, disco, excellent hotel with 47 room, good service and all facilities. **L-AL** *Royal Cliff Beach*, 353 Moo 12 Cliff Beach, Sout Pattaya, T250421, F250511, www.royalcliffco.th A/c, restaurants, pool, every imagir able facility in this almost 1,000-room hotel, a great favourite with conference an incentive groups, but so large that it is hard not to be just one of the crowd. Set hig

The Eastern Region

Pattaya Beach

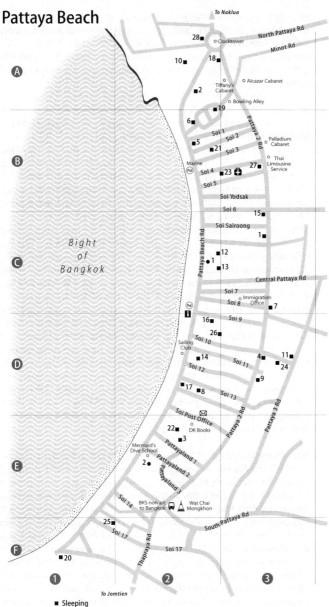

The Eastern Region

■ **Sleeping**

1 AA Pattaya C3
2 Amari Orchid Resort A2
3 ANZAC E2
4 Bay Breeze D3
5 Beach View B2
6 BJ's Guesthouse B2
7 Chris' Guesthouse C3
8 Caesar Palace D2
9 Diana Inn D3
10 Dusit Resort A2
11 Honey Inn D3

12 Merlin C2
13 Montien C2
14 Nautical Inn D2
15 Novotel Tropicana C3
16 Ocean View D2
17 Palm Garden D2
18 Palm Lodge A2
19 Regent Marina A2
20 Right Spot Inn F1
21 Royal Cruise B2
22 Royal Garden E2

23 Royal Night B3
24 Sawasdee Mansion
   & Guesthouse D3
25 Siam Bayshore F1
26 Siam Bayview D2
27 Thai Palace B3
28 Woodlands Resort A2

● **Eating**
1 Orient Express C2
2 Oslo E2

Related maps
Pattaya, page 478

up on the promontory at the south end of the beach, it is also rather gross with 9 res
taurants, 5 pools, fitness centre, tennis courts, 3-hole practice golf course and more
L-A *Royal Garden Resort*, 218 Moo 10, Pattaya 2 Rd, T428126, F429926. A/c, restau
rants, pool, tennis, 4-storey shopping mall with boutiques, handicrafts and fast-foo
outlets. Similar to McDonald's downstairs – tasteless, the same wherever you go an
nothing like the adverts.

AL *Montien*, Beach Rd, T428155, F423155, pattaya@montien.com   Central location
extensive mature gardens, still excellent hotel, despite its age and size. **AL-A** *Nov
Lodge*, Beach Rd (northern end), T420016, F429959. Large pool and gardens, tennis
simple (given the rates) rooms with balconies, central position. **AL-A** *Siam Bayshore*
Pattaya Beach Rd, T427272, F428730. A/c, restaurant, pool, 270-room hotel, made u
of rather sombre interlinking blocks, on large 20-acre plot of land at the southern en
of Pattaya Beach, set back from the beach, great swimming pools, tennis, separat
Garden Wing for families, with a playground and children's pool. **AL-A** *Siam Bayviev*
310/2 Moo 10 Pattaya 2 Rd, T423871, F423879. Rather ugly 270-room block, onl
some rooms with ocean views and balconies, small free-form pools, rather crampe
site. **A** *Amari Orchid Resort*, Beach Rd, North Pattaya, T428161, F42816Ṣ
www.amari.com   A/c, restaurants, Olympic-sized pool, tennis, mini-golf, watersport
230 room hotel on a tranquil 10 acre plot of lush landscaped gardens at the norther
end of the beach, away from most of the bars and discos. **A** *Merlin Pattaya*, Pattay
Beach Rd (near Central Pattaya Rd), T428755, F421673, B2557611. One of Pattaya'
original high-rise hotels with 360 rooms in 3 wings, a large compound, equally larg
pool, but rather impersonal. **A** *Novotel Tropicana*, 98 Pattaya 2 Rd, T428645, F42303
B2162278. Almost 200 rooms in this low-rise hotel which occupies a large plot in th
centre of town, rooms are unimaginative and the hotel rather impersonal, competi
tive rates. **A** *Regent Marina*, 463/31 North Pattaya Beach Rd, T429977, F42329€
B3902511. Situated in quiet northern end of town, well designed with excellent music
bar – the *Laser Pub*. **A** *Royal Cruise*, 499 Beach Rd, near Soi 2, T/F424242. Novel desig
– the hotel looks like a cruise liner (the 'first cruise on land', as they bill it) – rooms (c
'cabins') are average however, though rates are good and it offers a wide range c
facilities including sauna, gym and jacuzzi.

B *AA Pattaya*, 182-182/2 Beach Rd, Soi 13, T428656, F429057. In the midst of bar-lane
attractive fourth-floor pool, well-equipped rooms. Recommended. **B** *Bay Breeze*, 503/
Pattaya 2 Rd (near Soi 10), T428384, F429137. A/c, restaurant, pool, in the centre c
town, away from beach but rooms are large and well equipped, rather featureless bu
good value. **B** *Beach View*, 389 Beach Rd, near Soi 2, T422660, F422664. A/c, restauran
pool, one of Pattaya's older hotels, rooms are dated and the pool is small, but room rate
are keenly priced. **B** *Grand*, 103 Mu 10, Soi 14, T428249. A/c, friendly, good service
B *Ma Maison*, Soi 13 Beach Rd, T429318. A/c, pool. As the name suggests, it's Frenc
run. Rooms are arranged around a pool, restaurant serves excellent food. **B** *Nauti
cal Inn*, Soi 11 Beach Rd, T429890, F428116. A/c, restaurant, pool, older and now rathe
dated, low-rise hotel on large plot of land in the centre of town, large rooms are a littl
run-down, but has more character than most, with distinct seaside atmosphere
B *Ocean View*, Pattaya Beach Rd (near Soi 9), T428084, F424123. A/c, restaurant, poo
built over 20 years ago, which means rooms are a good size – if a touch dated and seedy ·
and the hotel benefits from a big compound in a prime position, good value
B *Palm Garden*, Pattaya 2 Rd (north end), T429386, F429188. A/c, restaurant, pool, room
have been redecorated to a high standard, but large compound, clean and well main
tained, good pool and excellent value. **B-C** *Palm Lodge*, North Pattaya Beach Rd (near So
6), T428779. Small hotel catering mainly for single male visitors, small pool, central, goo
room rates.

The bulk of the cheaper accommodation is at the southern end of the beach and is in our 'C' range; non a/c rooms are cheaper. **C** *BJ's Guesthouse*, 405 Beach Rd (northern end), T421148. A/c, good-value rooms in a small guesthouse above a restaurant. Unpredictable airconditioning. **C** *Caesar Palace*, Pattaya 2 Rd opposite Soi 8, T428607. A/c, restaurant, pool. **C** *Chris's Guesthouse*, Soi 12, Beach Rd, T429586, F422140. A/c, near centre of town down quiet soi in secluded courtyard, large, clean rooms, English management, friendly, the most welcoming place for backpackers. Recommended. **C** *Diana Inn*, 216/6-9 Pattaya 2 Rd, between Sois 11 and 12, T429675, F424566. A/c, restaurant, pool, on busy road but rooms have good facilities for price, modern, well-run, friendly and popular. Recommended. **C** *Honey Inn*, 529/2 Pattaya 2 Rd, Soi 10, T428117. A/c, restaurant, pool, large, clean rooms, small pool, frequented largely by single men – not a family hotel, but good value nonetheless, down quiet soi, away from beach. **C** *Right Spot Inn*, situated in south Pattaya. Clean and quiet with an excellent restaurant, there is no swimming pool but residents, provided they buy a drink, can use the pool at *Windy Inn* next door, central position and comes highly recommended by one multiple return visitor. **C** *Thai Palace*, 212 Pattaya 2 Rd, T423062, F427698. A/c, restaurant, small pool, central, rooms arranged around a courtyard, clean and competitively priced. **C-D** *Royal Night Hotel-bungalow*, 362/9 Pattaya Beach, Soi 5, T428038. Quiet hotel halfway down Soi 5, small shaded pool, good rooms, hot water, popular.

D *ANZAC*, 325 Pattayaland 1, T427822, F427823. A/c, restaurant, homely atmosphere with only 22 rooms, well run. **D** *Sawasdee Mansion and Guesthouse*, 502/1 Pattaya 2 Rd, Soi 10, T425360. Some a/c, one of the cheapest places in town, but don't expect a quaint bungalow on a palm lined beach ... this is a high-rise block down a built-up soi, but the rooms are clean, cool, serviceable and good.

Jomtien L *Ocean Marina Yacht Club*, 274/1-9 Moo 4, Sukhumvit Highway, T237310, F237325. Massive high-rise which is hard to miss, ostentatious hotel linked to the marina with choice of restaurants, a games deck with pool, tennis and squash courts, fitness centre, there is also a 25-m pool. Extensive business facilities. **L-A** *Asia*, 325 Cliff Rd, T250602, F250496, B2150808. Health club, tennis, golf, all facilities.

AL *Sugar Hut*, 391/18 Thaphraya Rd, on the way to Jomtien Beach, T251686, F251689. A/c, restaurant, 2 pools, overgrown gardens with rabbits and peacocks. Thai-style bungalows ('single' is adequate for 2 people), not on the beach, but very attractive grounds. Recommended. **A** *Ambassador City*, 21/10 Sukhumvit Rd, Km 55, Jomtien Beach, T255501, F255731, B2550444. Enormous. **A** *Pattaya Park*, 345 Jomtien Beach Rd (north end), T251201, F251209, B5110717. Watersports facilities (but you pay for them), ugly coffee bar, panoramic restaurant and bar charges ฿280 just to step inside. **A-B** *Silver Sand Villa*, 97 Moo 12, Jomtien Beach Rd, T231288, F231030. A/c, restaurant, pool, plain but reasonably sized rooms, large pool, on the beach.

B *Island View*, Cliff Rd, T250813, F250818, B2498941. A/c, restaurant, pool. **B** *Mermaid's Beach Resort*, 75/102 Moo 12 Nong Prue, Jomtien Beach Rd, T428755, F421673. A/c, restaurant, pool. **B** *Sea Breeze*, Jomtien Beach, T231057, F231059. A/c, restaurant, pool, good value.

Pattaya has the greatest choice of international cuisine outside Bangkok. This ranges from excellent 5-star restaurants, to European fast-food chains, to foodstalls on the beach or down the sois. Because so many of the guests are tourists, prices tend to be high by Thai standards – there aren't the locals to complain that a plate of fried rice shouldn't cost a king's ransom.

Eating
● *on map, page 483*
Price codes:
see inside front cover

The Eastern Region

Thai   Expensive: *PIC Kitchen*, Soi 5. 4 traditional Thai pavilions, Thai classical dancing in garden compound, good food. Recommended. *Somsak*, 436/24 Soi 1, North Pattaya. Recommended. *Ruen Thai*, Pattaya 2 Rd, opposite Soi Post Office. Very good Thai food and not excessively overpriced. Recommended. *Benjarong*, Royal Wing Royal Cliff Beach Hotel. *Deeprom*, 503 Moo 9 Central Pattaya Rd. Recommended *Kruatalay*, *Pattaya Park*, Jomtien beach, plus seafood. **Mid-range**: *Kiss*, Pattaya 2 Rd between sois 11 and 12 next to *Diana Inn*. Good range of Western and Thai food at low prices. An excellent place to watch the world go by.

Other Asian cuisine   Expensive: *Akamon*, 468/19 Pattaya 2 Rd. Best-known Japanese restaurant in town. *Alibaba*, 1/15-16 Central Pattaya Rd. Indian. *Arirang*, Soi 5 Beach Rd. Korean. *Empress*, *Dusit Resort*, large Chinese restaurant overlooking Pattaya Bay. Good dim sum lunches. *Koreano*, Soi 1 Beach Rd. Korean. *Narissa*, *Siam Bayview*, North Pattaya. Chinese, speciality Peking Duck. *White Orchid*, 110/3 South Pattaya Rd. Good Chinese food *Yamato*, Pattaya Beach Soi 13. Sushi bar (฿100) and sukiyaki, sashimi and tempura, all excellent. **Mid-range**: *Café India*, 183/9 Soi Post Office. *Mai Kai Supper Club*, Beach Rd. Polynesian, Haitian band. *Thang Long*, Soi 3 Beach Rd. Vietnamese.

International   Expensive: *Alt Heidelberg*, 273 Beach Rd. Roadside bistro, open 0900-0200, German cook and owner, German sausages, draught beer. *Buccaneer* Beach Rd. Seafood and steaks in rooftop restaurant above the *Nipa Lodge*. *El Toro Steakhouse*, 215 Pattaya 2 Rd. Top-quality steaks. *Green Bottle*, Pattaya 2 Rd (between Sois 10 and 11). Ersatz English pub with exposed 'beams', grills, seafood. *La Gritta*, Beach Rd (northern end past Soi 1). Some people maintain this restaurant serves the best Italian in town, pizzas, pasta dishes and seafood specialities. *Noble House*, Pattaya Beach Rd (near Soi 10). Italian, seafood and German dishes, good German breakfasts with fresh coffee. *Papa's*, 219 Soi Yamato. Range of international food including fondue, steaks and seafood. *Peppermill*, 16 Beach Rd, near Soi Post Office. First class French food. *Savai Swiss*, Pattaya 2 Rd, Soi 6. Swiss style, with international food. **Mid-range**: *Blue Parrot*, Pattayaland 2 Rd. Mexican. *Dream Bakery*, 485/3 Pattaya 2 Rd. English breakfasts, Thai. *Italiano Espresso*, 325/1 Beach Rd, South Pattaya. Traditional Italian food, and some Thai dishes. *Oslo*, 325/14 Pattayaland Soi 2 South Pattaya. Scandinavian style restaurant, with Scandinavian buffet and individual dishes. *Zum Wiener Schnitzel*, 98/7 Beach Rd. Traditional German and some Thai food, large helpings. **Cheap**: *Amsterdam*, Regent Marina Complex. Thai/German/English/breakfast. *Ice Café Berlin*, Pattaya 2 Rd. German. *Aussie Ken's Toast Shop*, 205/31 Pattaya 2 Rd. Fish and chips, sandwiches, cheap beer. *Bella Napoli*, Naklua Rd. Italian. *Pattaya Princess*, floating restaurant, pier at south end of Beach Rd.

Seafood   The best seafood is on Jomtien beach or at the southern end of Pattaya beach. **Expensive**: *Lobster Pot*, 228 Beach Rd, South Pattaya. On a pier over the water, known for very fresh seafood. **Mid-range**: *Nang Nual*, 214/10 Beach Rd, South Pattaya, on the waterfront. Recommended (there is another *Nang Nual* restaurant in Jomtien). *Seafood Palace*, on the pier, southern end of Beach Rd.

Bars   The majority of Pattaya's bars are concentrated at the south end of the beach between Beach Rd and Pattaya 2 Rd and there are hundreds to choose from. They are mostly open-air, lined with stools. The men-only bars are around Pattayaland Soi 3 and the Karaoke bars are along Pattaya 2 Rd.

Entertainment   Pattaya comes to life as dusk approaches – it is a beach version of Bangkok's Patpong. Music blares out from the many bars, discos and massage parlours which are mainly concentrated in South Pattaya, referred to as 'The Strip'.

The Eastern Region

Cabaret shows *Alcazar* and *Tiffany's*, both on Pattaya 2 Rd are the 2 biggest establishments in town. Shows at *Alcazar* are daily at 1830, 2000 and 2130, T428746 for reservations, ฿400. Although it might seem slightly odd visiting a cabaret show in Thailand, the acts are very professional and good value – nor are they anything like the acts in Patpong. This is family entertainment! There is also *Simon's*, on Pattayaland Soi 2 (1930 and 2130, ฿500)and the *Malibu Show* at the top end of Soi Post Office (all transvestite shows).

Disco Average admission ฿250, a selection are – *Marina Disco*, Regent Marina Hotel. *Captain's Club*, *Dusit Resort*. **Palladium**, 2nd Pattaya Beach Rd, just past *Big C Shopping Centre*, huge disco. **Spark**, southern end of Pattaya Beach. *Hollywood*, southern end of Pattaya Beach.

Badminton Soi 17. Open 1400-2400, 4 courts, ฿60 per hour, racquet hire ฿20, **Sport** shuttlecock ฿25. **Bowling** There are 3 bowling alleys in Pattaya. *Pattaya Bowl* (recommended), Tiffany Show Building, Pattaya 2 Rd. A/c, 20 lanes, open 1000-0200 Mon-Sun. *OD Bowl*, South Pattaya, *Royal Jomtien Hotel*, 8 lanes. **Bungee jumping** Near Jomtien Beach, *Kiwi Thai Bungee Jump* is said to be the highest in the world, T427555, open 1400-2100, Mon-Sun.

    Diving There are more than 10 dive shops in Pattaya, offering a range of services – dives from the offshore islands, instruction and equipment hire. A recommended and established centre is *Seafari*, Soi 5, T429253, run by an American couple. Cost for a day's diving to the nearby islands is ฿800 (group rate), to the outer islands and a wreck dive, ฿1,150. A day's introductory instruction costs ฿2,300, and a 4 day course, about ฿10,300. Dive shops include *Mermaid's Dive School* on Soi Mermaid, Jomtien Beach, T232219 and *Dave's Divers Den*, Pattaya-Naklua Rd, T420411 (NAUI). *Aquanauts*, 437/17 Soi Yodsak, *Seafari Sports Centre*, 359/2 Soi 5 Beach Rd.

    Fishing Panarak Park, en route to the Siam Country Club, freshwater lake. There are 4 or 5 game fishing operators in Pattaya. Fish commonly caught in local waters include shark, king mackerel, garoupa and marlin. Martin Henniker, at *Jenny's Hotel*, Soi Pattayaland 1, is recommended. *The Fisherman's Club*, Soi Yodsak (Soi 6) takes groups of 4-10 anglers and offer 3 different packages (including an overnight trip). The *Dusit Resort* organize angling contests. Angling equipment is available from Alan Ross at the *Pattaya Sports Supply* shop, opposite the *Regent Marina Hotel* (North Pattaya). For larger boat expeditions (30 or so anglers), expect to pay about ฿1,000, organized by Dieter at *Deutsches Haus*, Soi 4. **Fitness** *Royal Garden Spa & Fitness Club*, Royal Garden Restaurant, ฿30 million investment in the most luxurious spa in Pattaya. *Pattaya Fitness Centre* is near the *Regent Marina Complex*, North Pattaya. With weight-lifting facilities, gym and sauna, open 0800-2000 Mon-Sun. There is a *fitness park* on the road over the hill to Jomtien.

    Golf There are now 9 courses within 50 km of Pattaya. Green fees range between ฿250 and ฿1,000 during the week and ฿500 and ฿1,500 at the weekend. *Asia*, Asia Hotel, Jomtien. 9-hole course. Recommended. *Siam Country Club* is the closest to town, 20 mins from Pattaya, T428002. Restaurant and swimming pool available. Green fees ฿1,000, ฿150 caddy fee. *Royal Thai Navy Course*, near Sattahip, 35 mins from town, T428422. Slow and uneven greens but characterful. Green fees ฿250, ฿140 caddy fee. 2 other courses are the *Bangpra International* (one of the oldest courses in Thailand, accommodation and restaurant available, green fees ฿500, ฿150 caddy fee) and the *Panya Resort* (45 mins from town, large clubhouse with restaurant, green fees ฿800, ฿150 caddy fee), both near Chonburi. *Phoenix*, Sukhumvit Rd (15 km south of Pattaya). New course, 27 holes. Outings organized by *Cherry Tree Golf Tours* from the Red Lion Pub, South Pattaya, T422385 or by Mike Smith at *Caesars Bar*, Beach Rd – he's chairman of *Pattaya Sports Club*. 9-hole course behind the *Asia Pattaya Hotel*. Mini golf course, Naklua Rd, 500 m north of *Dusit Resort*. Rather further afield are: *Rayong Green Valley Country Club*, Ya Ra Rd, T603000-5, F614916. Green fees ฿700 weekdays, ฿1,200 weekends; and

The Eastern Region

the *Eastern Star Country Club*, Pala Rd, T602500, F602754. Green fees ฿250 weekdays, ฿400 weekends. *Green Way Driving Range*, Sukhumvit Highway, 2 km south of South Pattaya. *Aussie Ken's*, Pattaya 2 Rd. Computer golf simulator for up to 4 players.

Go-Kart *KR Go-Kart Pattaya*, 62/125 Moo 12 Thepprasit Rd, T3003479. Open 1000-1930, a 1.1 km circuit.

Helicopter Rides T535506. US$50 per person round trip to Koh Larn and Koh Sak, including the promise of 2 hrs funny time on Koh Sak. To charter for the hour, it will set you back US$1,500. **Jetskis** For hire, about ฿350 per 15 mins.

Motor racing *Bira International Circuit*, Km 14, Route 36. Races of Formula 3 cars, pick-ups and bikes held at weekends.

Paintball Next to Go-Kart track on Thepprasit Rd, T300608. ฿300 for a 2 hr game. Games begin at 1000 daily. **Parasailing**: near *Montien*, *Royal Cliff*, *Asia Pattaya* and *Wong Amat* hotels.

Riding *Pattaya Riding Club*, Highway 36 Km 11. Imported horses will canter until you are content in jungle and mountain surroundings. T3020814 for free transport. **Running** *Hash House Harriers* meet every Mon at 1600 at the *Hare House*, Soi Post Office.

Sailing Lasers, Hobie Cats and Prindles are available. *Royal Varuna Yacht Club* T428959. *Sundowner Sailing Services*, Ocean Marina, T423686. **Shooting** *Tiffany's* Pattaya 2 Rd, open 0900-2200 Mon-Sun, T421700. ฿120 range fee, range of rifles and handguns, rates charged per bullet. **Snooker** fees vary from ฿60 to ฿100 per hour. *Pattaya Bowl*, Pattaya 2 Rd, North Pattaya, open 1000-0200 Mon-Sun. T429466. Above *Mike's Department Store*, Beach Rd, is a small club with 5 tables. *JB Snooker Club*, *Jomtien Bayview Hotel*, open Mon-Sun 24 hrs, T425889. **Snorkelling** day trips to the offshore islands can be organized through the dive shops. **Speedboats** for rent, about ฿600 per hour. **Squash** *Cherry Tree*, on the *Siam Country Club* Rd, T423686, English run. **Swimming** there are now designated swimming 'zones' off Pattaya and Jomtien beaches. With the new waste-water treatment, it is hoped that the entire length of Pattaya Beach is now fit for swimming.

Tennis many hotels have courts. Instruction is often available, ฿100- ฿150 per hour.

Water scooters on the beach. **Water skiing** the water off Pattaya Beach is not particularly good for this, as it is rarely calm. However, an artificial freshwater lake has been created for waterskiers at Lake Land, T232690, south of Pattaya on Sukhumvit Road, restaurant by the lake. They specialize in cable skiing. **Water World** at *Pattaya Park Beach Resort*, between Pattaya and Jomtien beach. Admission ฿50 for adults, ฿30 for children. **Windsurfing** Many different schools – more than 20 in all. Best time to windsurf is from Oct to Jun.

Zip Wire Pattaya Tower, Jomtien Beach. A 170-m ride down a wire from the top of the tower to the ground. ฿200 for the experience, T251201.

Festivals Jan *Pattaya Carnival* is a purely commercial affair with floats, competitions and the like. Mar *Thai Music Festival*, the name of this festival really says it all, and it's not just Thai classical music but includes Thai country music, rock and roll, etc. Apr *Annual Pattaya Festival* celebrates nothing in particular but is a good excuse for a jamboree. Jul *Pattaya International Marathon*. This has expanded into a significant national sporting event and there are numerous other associated (and unassociated) attractions.

Shopping There are hundreds of market stalls and small shops on Pattaya 2 Road selling jewellery, fashion ware, handicrafts, leather goods, silk, fake watches and a good selection of shopping plazas where most western goods can be purchased.

Books *DK Books*, Pattaya Beach Rd, Soi Post Office. Best selection of books in Pattaya. *Asia Books*, Royal Garden Shopping Complex.

Department stores *Mike's*, Beach Rd. *Booneua Shopping Plaza*, South Pattaya Rd.

Gemstones/jewellery *World Gems*, Beach Rd. *Best Gems*, South Pattaya Rd. *Pattaya Lapidary*, Beach Rd.

Handicrafts *Northern Thai Handicrafts*, 215 Pattaya 2 Rd. *Shinawatra*, Pattaya 2 Rd.

Silk *Dada Thai Silk* (plus tailoring), 345 Beach Rd (southern end). *Shinawatra Thai Silk*, 78/13 Pattaya 2 Rd. *Fantasia* (hand-wrapped silk flowers). *Booneua Shopping Plaza*, South Pattaya Rd.

Supermarkets Plenty to choose from for Western food and pharmaceuticals (including *Boots The Chemist*).

Tailors *Royal Garden Boutique*, *Royal Garden Hotel*, Pattaya Beach Rd. *Princess Fashion*, *Complex Hotel*, 235/5 Beach Rd, South Pattaya. *Marco Custom Tailors*, opposite *Montien Pattaya*, 75/5-6 Pattaya 2 Rd.

For cheap airfares and tours to Indo-China, the best informed travel agent is *Exotissimo*, 183/19 Soi Post Office, T422788. Other travel agents include: *Lee Tours*, 183 Soi Post Office, T429738. *Malibu Travel*, 183 Soi Post Office, T423180. *Tour East*, 437/111 Soi Yodsak, T429708. *RTD Travel*, 370/11-12 Moo 9 Pattaya 2 Rd, T427539. **Tour operators**

PIC Kitchen, Soi 5. Wed 1930, ฿100. *Ruen Thai*, Pattaya 2 Rd, opposite Soi PO. Recommended. ฿120. **Traditional Thai dance**

Local Songthaews: are in abundance along Beach Road (for travelling south) and on Pattaya 2 Road (for travelling north), ฿5 for short trips around Pattaya Bay (although it is not uncommon for visitors to be charged ฿10), ฿10 between Naklua and Pattaya beach, ฿20 to Jomtien. To avoid being charged more than the standard fare, present the driver with the correct money and walk away (of course, prices may go up). Similarly, when boarding, just get in – even if it is empty – and do not attempt to negotiate the price, as the driver will expect you to hire the vehicle as a taxi. **Bicycle/motorbike/jeep/car hire**: along Beach Road (bargaining required), bicycles ฿100 per day or ฿20 per hour, jeeps ฿500-700 per day, motorbikes ฿150 per day for a small bike up to ฿600 for a larger machine. *Avis* at *Dusit Resort* (T425611) and the *Royal Cliff Beach Resort* (T250421). **NB** Jeeps are rarely insured. **Boat charter**: from along Beach Road. ฿700-1500 per day (seats 12 people). **Transport**
147 km S of Bangkok
See also Ins & outs, page 477

Long distance Air: There is an airport at U-Tapao, not far from Pattaya. This is gradually expanding and in 1997 it received its first international scheduled arrival for some years. There are daily connections on *Bangkok Airways* with Koh Samui, but none with Bangkok.

Train: The station is off the Sukhumvit Highway, 200 m north of the intersection with Central Pattaya Rd. There is a limited train service between Pattaya and Bangkok; running on weekends and holidays. The Bangkok-Pattaya train leaves at 0700, and the Pattaya-Bangkok at 1330, 3½ hrs.

Bus: a/c buses stop at the a/c bus terminal on North Pattaya Rd, near to the intersection with the Sukhumvit Highway. Songthaews take passengers to South Pattaya, past most of the Pattaya beach hotels (฿10) and to Jomtien beach (฿20) (as mentioned above, do not ask for price or this will be taken as an attempt to hire the taxi for yourself). Regular connections with Bangkok's Eastern bus terminal on Sukhumvit Soi Ekamai (Soi 63) 1¾-2½ hrs, ฿66 (0530-2100) or less frequent connections from the Northern bus terminal in Bangkok (*Mor Chit*), ฿67. There are also bus connection direct with Don Muang Airport.

The Eastern Region

THAI run a service from the airport to the *Royal Cliff Beach Resort*, ฿250 (pre-flight check-in available at *Royal Cliff*) and there is also a public bus leaving every 2 hrs, 0700-1700. Hotel and travel agencies in Bangkok run tour bus services to Pattaya. Non-a/c buses to Bangkok leave from the BKS stop in front of Wat Chai Mongkhon, near the intersection of Pattaya and South Pattaya roads. The main BKS terminal (non-a/c) for buses to other Eastern region destinations (for example Rayong, Sattahip, Si Racha) and beyond, is in Jomtien near the intersection of Beach Rd and Chaiyapruk Rd. If staying in Pattaya City, it is possible to stand on the Sukhumvit Highway and wave down the appropriate bus. Tour buses to the north (Chiang Mai, Mae Hong Son, Mae Sai, Phitsanulok, etc) leave from the station on the Sukhumvit Highway, near the intersection with Central Pattaya Rd. Nearby, buses also leave for Ubon (*Sri Mongkhon Tour*) and Nong Khai (*407 Pattana Tour*), both in the north-east. **Limousine service**: *THAI* operates a service from Don Muang airport, Bangkok to Pattaya. T423140 for bookings from Pattaya. A chauffeur-driven car from travel agencies in Bangkok should cost about ฿1,600.

Directory **Airline offices** *Bangkok Airways* office is on the 2nd floor, *Royal Garden Plaza*, 218 Beach Rd, T411965, F411965. *Thai*, T602192. *Kuwait Airways*, 218 Beach Rd, T410493. **Banks** There are countless exchange facilities both on the beach road and on the many sois running east-west, many stay open until 2200. **Communications** Internet café: *Royal Garden Shopping Complex*, top floor. ฿5 per minute (minimum ฿40). **Post Office**: Soi Post Office. **Safety deposit**: oversea service on Soi Post Office, ฿200 per month. **Telephone exchange service**: South Pattaya Rd, open 24 hrs. **Embassies & consulates** *Sweden*, 75/128-29, Moo 12, Jomtien Beach, T23163C **Medical services** Hospitals: *Pattaya International Clinic*, Soi 4, Beach Rd, T428374. *Pattaya Memorial Hospital*, 328/1 Central Pattaya Rd, T429422, 24-hr service. Dr Olivier Clinic, 20/23 Moo 10, South Pattaya Rd (opposite the Day-Night Hotel), T723521, F723522. Operated by an English-French-German speaking doctor, Dr Meyer. **Chemists**: *Nong Nooch Village Pharmacists*, plenty of drug stores on South Pattaya Rd. **Useful numbers** Tourist Police: T429371 or T1699 for 24-hr service and **Sea Rescue**: T433752 are to be found on Beach Rd, next to the TAT office.

Pattaya to Koh Samet

Coastal towns south of Pattaya

The beaches of Rayong All along the coast from U-Tapao Airport southeast past Ban Phe to Laem Mae Phim are resort-style hotels. The beaches here are scarcely memorable and there is very little accommodation of the budget variety. It is mostly Thais who come to stay here and because they tend to drive themselves it is hard to get about on public transport.

Sattahip สัตหีบ Sattahip is 20 km south of Pattaya and, like Pattaya, was also frequented by the US military. Now the port of Sattahip is the headquarters of the Thai navy which itself uses it as a vacation spot; many of the beautiful beaches are reserved for the military. It has recently been developed into an important commercial deep-sea port to take some of the pressure off Bangkok's stretched port facilities. The town has little to offer tourists: a modern and rather garish wat, a bustling market, and a few restaurants.

Samaesan แสมสาร Samaesan is a small, quiet and unspoilt fishing village, 52 km south of Pattaya. Offshore there are a number of beautiful islands: **Koh Ai Raet**, **Koh Samaesan**, **Koh Kham**, **Koh Chuang** and **Koh Chan**. It is possible to hire boats to visit the islands – enquiries can be made at the *Lam Samaesan Seafood Restaurant* (about ฿300). There is basic accommodation available in Samaesan. Boats to the islands also run from Ban Phe (see below), mostly at the weekend.

Rayong ระยอง

Rayong is famous, at least in the Thai context, for its *nam pla* (fish sauce) – made from a decomposed silver fish. This is usually mixed with chillies to produce the fiery *nam pla prik*. For most Thais: no *nam pla*, no eat, and in Thai elections it used to be common to find voters being 'bought' with free bottles of the watery sauce. (In recent elections cash has changed hands – the electorate have outgrown gifts of *nam pla*.) Rayong town does not have much to offer, except a few beaches, a 12 m-long reclining Buddha at **Wat Pa Pradu** which, unusually, reclines to its left and dates from the Ayutthaya Period. Also worth visiting is **Wat Khot Thimtharaam** on Thimtharaam Road. The monastery was built in 1464 and features some interesting murals. There is also a statue of Thailand's most famous poet – Sunthorn Phu (see page 492). However, few people stay long in Rayong; they just pass through on their way to the island of Koh Samet.

Phone code: 038
Colour map 3, grid C5

The area around Rayong has many orchards & is famed for its fruit, as well as its sea cucumbers

Sleeping

AL *Novotel Rim Pae Resort*, 4/5 Moo 3, Pae Klaeng Kram Rd, Chark Pong (roughly equidistant from Rayong and Ban Phe), T2371305/648008, F2364353/648002. A/c, restaurants, 4 pools, fitness centre, resort-style hotel with almost 200 rooms, very comfortable but not much to distinguish from all the other hotels of similar ilk. **A** *Palmeraie Princess*, Ban Phe-Mae Pim Rd, T638071, F638073. A/c, restaurant, pool, affiliated with the *Dusit Group* of hotels. **A** *Sinsiam Resort*, 235 Laem Mae-Pim, T2117026, B4373648. A/c, restaurant, pool. **B-E** *Otani*, 69 Sukhumvit Rd, T611112. Some a/c, large rooms but dirty. **C** *Rayong*, 65/1-3 Sukhumvit Rd, T611073. A/c, an ugly hotel with friendly staff, not much atmosphere but rooms are well priced. Good location for restaurants. **E** *Rayong International Youth Hostel*, 89/4 Moo 1, Mae Ramphung Beach Rd, T653374, B025137093. 100 m from the beach, nestled among a forest of high-rise hotels. 6 rooms with a total of 30 beds. Food available, but remote from other restaurants. Appears to be undergoing extensive expansion. They are not used to farangs, but recommended if you arrive in Rayong too late to cross to Koh Samet.

Festivals

May *Fruit Fair* (movable) local fruits, handicrafts on sale.

Transport
221 km to Bangkok
70 km to Pattaya

Car hire *Rayong Mahanakorn Co*, 74/3 Ratbamrang Rd, opposite Manora Massage Parlour. **Bus** Regular connections with Bangkok's Eastern bus terminal, Pattaya and other east-coast towns.

Directory

Banks *Thai Farmers*, Sukhumvit Rd. **Tourist offices** *TAT*, 153/4 Sukhumvit Rd, T655420. Covers Chantaburi too.

Ban Phe บ้านเพ

Once a small fishing village with a national reputation for its fish sauce, Ban Phe has become a way station for visitors heading for Koh Samet. It has many food and handicraft stalls, but few foreign tourists bother to stay any longer than it takes to catch the boat. In the vicinity of the village are a number of mediocre beaches lined with bungalows and resorts – **Hat Ban Phe**, **Hat Mae Ram Phung** (to the west), **Laem Mae Phim**, **Suan Son** and **Wang Kaew** (all to the east) which are largely frequented by Thai tourists.

Phone code: 038
Colour map 3, grid C5

Sleeping

Resort and bungalow developments line the 25 km of coast east and west of Ban Phe. Few foreign visitors stay either in the village or in the hotels around abouts – this is a resort geared to and patronized by Thais.

The Eastern Region

In Ban Phe D *Nual Napu*, east of the market, close to the pier for Koh Samet, T651668. Some a/c.

Outside Ban Phe AL *Rayong Resort*, 186 Moo 1, Ban Phe, T651000, F651007, www.rayongresort.com A/c, restaurant, pool, 167 room resort, on a cape with private beach, average rooms for the price. **B** *Diamond Phe*, 286/12 Ban Phe Rd, T615826. A/c, east of Ban Phe near the pier for Koh Samet, plain and rather kitsch but comfortable and convenient. **D-E** *TN Place*, close to the pier. Some a/c, reasonable for a stopover.

Transport **Bus** Regular connections direct from Bangkok's Eastern bus terminal and from Pattaya,
223 km to Bangkok 1 hr. Or via Rayong (20 km to the southeast), and then a songthaew to Ban Phe (฿10).

Directory **Banks** *Krung Thai*, a short distance west of the pier (if going to Samet it is a good idea to change money here as the rates are better than on the island). **Communications** Lenso Cardphone available here for international calls.

Koh Samet   เกาะสีชัง

Phone code: 038 *Koh Samet is a 6-km-long, lozenge-shaped island which used to be known as Koh*
Many of the hotels only *Kaeo Pisadan. Until the early 1980s it was home to a small community of fisher-*
have mobile numbers *men and was visited by a few intrepid travellers. The famous 19th-century Thai*
(prefixed with 01) *romantic poet Sunthorn Phu retired to this beautiful island and, inspired, pro-*
Colour map 3, grid C5 *ceeded to write his finest work, the epic Phra Aphaimani. The poem recounts the*
story of a prince, banished by his father to live with a sea-dwelling, bro-
ken-hearted giantess. Escaping to Koh Samet with the help of a mermaid, the
prince kills the pursuing giant with his magic flute and marries the mermaid.

Ins and outs

Getting there Koh Samet is, as the crow flies, the nearest to Bangkok of Thailand's many resort
See also Transport, islands. But unlike Koh Samui and Phuket there is no airport so it is necessary to bus to
page 497 Ban Phe, about 3½ hrs from Bangkok, and then take one of the regular boats out to the island, another 40 mins or so.

Getting around Koh Samet is only 6 km long so it is possible to explore the island on foot. Songthaews travel between the main beaches and there are also tracks negotiable by motorbike – which can be rented from a handful of places.

The best time to visit is between October and May; heavy rains can be a problem between July and September. However, during the rainy season rates are cut and the island is less crowded. It is best to visit during the week; at weekends it is very popular with Thais and this is particularly true during public holidays when it can be chocka with visitors camped out on just about every square foot of floor. Avoid these periods if possible.

The island

All visitors pay an It is unlikely Sunthorn Phu would find the necessary quiet today: over the past
entrance fee to visit decade, Koh Samet has become increasingly popular with young Thai holiday
Koh Samet (฿50 for makers and with foreign visitors. Because of its relative proximity to Bangkok
adults, ฿25 for children) (Ban Phe is only 223 km from the capital), it is particularly popular with Thais at the weekend and during public holidays, when the island is best avoided.

In 1981 Samet became part of the Khao Laem Ya National Park which also includes the neighbouring Kuti and Thalu islands as well as 100 sq km of surrounding sea (hence the admission fee). Authorities have ostensibly insisted that all accommodation remains limited to bungalows set back behind the tree line of the beach. This is difficult to reconcile with the scale and pattern of development that has occurred. The park authorities have periodically threatened to shut the island down on the basis that every bungalow owner is breaking the law. Indeed, they have actually closed the island to tourists on a couple of occasions, only to reopen it after protests from bungalow owners, many of whom were making a living on the island prior to 1981 when it was declared a national park. As the owner of the Wong Duan Resort said during one of the shut downs: "It is unfair. We fight, work hard, pay taxes and invest a lot of money ... the Forestry Department never invested anything. Now they are the owners and we are the encroachers." In March 2000 it was announced that after years and years of wrangling, the Royal Forestry Department and the bungalow operators were close to a deal. Apparently the operators are to sign over ownership of the land to the RFD and then the RFD has agreed to rent the land back to the operators on 10-, 20- or 30-year leases at a rental rate of ฿10-20 per rai (about ฿60-120 per hectare).

Like Phi Phi, the rubbish created by tourism is becoming an environmental threat on the island. It seems that however hard the park authorities, the TAT and the environmentalist pressure groups may try to protect Samet, they are fighting a losing battle; people continue to stay on the island in their thousands and yet more bungalows are being built.

Samet is a comparatively dry island (1,350 mm per year – Chantaburi 50 km away has rainfall of 3,164 mm per year) and therefore a good place to visit during the rainy season. However, between May and October there can be strong winds, and the seas are sometimes rough. The island's limited supply of fresh water was a constraint to tourist expansion for a number of years, now it is shipped in and most of the bungalows have a reasonable supply. In addition, malaria was quite prevalent but there is little or none left these days. Prophylactics are no longer recommended for the island but precautions – such as wearing long-sleeved shirts and trousers after sunset are nonetheless advisable.

Many visitors land at the main **Na Dan Pier** in the northeast of the island (but note that it is becoming more and more common for bungalow operators to run boats directly to their beaches from one or other of the piers in Ban Phe – see Road and Sea section below). There has been a settlement here for many years – while it is now a fishing settlement-come-tourist service centre, junks from China used to anchor here to be checked before the authorities would allow them to sail over the sandbar at the mouth of the Chao Phraya River and north to Bangkok. Along the beach here there is a collection of featureless bungalows. Unless you want to watch the boats come in (there is little else to do), head for one of the other bays.

Hat Sai Khao (Diamond Sand Beach) is a 10-minute walk from Na Dan Pier, and remains the most popular place to stay, perhaps because all other beaches must be reached by foot or boat. This was once a beautiful spot, but it has been disfigured by uncontrolled development. Shophouses, discos, bars and travel agents line the path from Na Dan to Hat Sai Khao and the beach itself. In front of the bungalow operations and resorts at the southern end of the beach are long lines of plastic tables sheltered from the sun and

Koh Samet place names

Ao Phrao

อ่าวพร้าว

Hat Sai Kaew

หาดทรายแก้ว

Na Dan

หน้าด่าน

Koh Samet

Sleeping

1 Ao Phai Hut *B2*
2 Ao Phrao Resort *B1*
3 Coconut House *B3*
4 Coral Beach *F1*
5 Jep's Inn & Restaurant *B2*
6 Laem Yai Resort *B3*
7 Lung Dam Hut *D1*
8 Malibu Golden Resort *D1*
9 Naga & Ao Hin Khok Post Office *B2*
10 Pia's Shop *D2*
11 Ploy Resort *B3*
12 Ploy Thalay *B3*
13 Sai Kaew Cabana *B3*
14 Sai Kaew Villa *B3*
15 Samet Cabana *D1*
16 Samet Villa *C2*
17 Samet Villa Resort *E1*
18 Sea Breeze *C2*
19 Sea Horse *D1*
20 Sea View *B3*
21 Silver Sand *C2*
22 Sinsamut *B3*
23 Tarn Tawan *D2*
24 Tok's Little Hut *B2*
25 Tubtim *C2*
26 Vongduern Villa *D1*
27 White Sand *B3*
28 Wonderland Resort *C*
29 Wong Duern Resort *L*

rain by vulgar, brightly coloured plastic roofing. In front of these lie deckchairs – five rows thick. In addition, jet-skis are a popular form of watersport. The northern end of the beach is very slightly less crowded and touristy. Despite the crowded, bustling atmosphere, the beach remains clean and it has a sandy bottom which makes it an excellent place to swim (especially for children). Just south along the coast from Hat Sai Khao is Ao Hin Khok where Koh Samet's one and only sight is to be found: a rather tatty statue depicting the tale of *Phra Aphaimani* (see above). A short distance further south still, just 1 km southwest from Hat Sai Khao, is **Ao Phai**, which is less developed and more peaceful. The bungalows here cater for *farang* rather than for Thai visitors. Two and a half kilometres from Ao Phai, past the smaller **Ao Tubtim**, **Ao Nuan** and **Ao Cho**, is **Ao Wong Duan**. This crescent-shaped bay has a number of more up-market resort developments. Consequently there is also a wider range of facilities: water-skiing, diving, boat trips, and windsurfing. Continuing south from Ao Wong Duan is **Ao Thian**, **Ao Wai** and **Ao Kiu Na Nok**. These are the most peaceful locations on Koh Samet, and the island's finest coral is also found off the southern tip of the island.

Ao Phrao, or Paradise Beach (2 km from Sai Kaew), is the only beach to have been developed (so far) on the west side of the island.

Hire a fishing boat (or go on a tour), take a picnic, and explore the **Kuti** and **Thalu islands**. *Excursions*

Small operators on many of the beaches organize boat trips to outlying islands such as Koh Kuti and Koh Thalu for fishing, diving and snorkelling. For example *Samet Villa* at Ao Phai run an adventure tour to Koh Mun Nok, Koh Mun Klang and Koh Mun Nai for ฿500 per person, trips to Thalu and Kuti for ฿300, and trips around the island for ฿200 per person. *Tours*

Essentials

Koh Samet mostly offers bungalow accommodation, although there are an increasing number of more sophisticated 'resorts' (at Wong Duan, Hat Sai Khao and Ao Phrao). Due to the cost for the bungalow operators of shipping in water and the proximity of the island to Bangkok, the cost of equivalent accommodation is higher than in other Thai beach resorts. This is particularly so in the high season when a very basic bungalow with attached bathroom may cost ฿450, or on public holidays when you may pay that much to rent a tent for the night. At low season, particularly Aug-Sep, prices can be bargained down. Only a selection of the bungalows is given below (at last count there were something like 50 developments – a lot for an island this size). The best source of information on whether standards are being maintained is recent visitors – ask those leaving the island. *Sleeping*
■ *on map*
Price codes:
see inside front cover

There is no mains electricity on the island so all the bungalow operations and resorts generate their own and electricity is only available at certain times of day (usually 1800 to 1000). Check before you book a room what hours electricity is available – some of them switch off at midnight – it can be very uncomfortable sleeping without a fan.

Hat Sai Khao (Diamond Sand Beach). Because there are so many shops, pubs and discos aligning the beach here, many of the bungalows look out onto the rear concrete walls of these establishments, so it's not the place to look for accommodation if you appreciate a seaview from your balcony. However, if you like to be where the action is, then this is the place to head for. Most of the bungalows are solid and uninspiring – take your pick from a number of different operators covering a wide range of budgets. All bungalows have attached restaurants. **AL** *Sai Kaew Villa*, T01-2186696. *Prices here vary enormously between high & low season*

A-D *Coconut House*, T01-651661. **B-D** *Diamond Hut* T01-3210814. **B-C** *Diamond Beach and Sea View*, T01-2390208. **D** *White Sand*, T01-321734. **C-D** *Ploy Thalay*, T01-2186109. **D-E** *Sinsamut*.

Ao Hin Khok D *Jep's Inn and Restaurant*, the restaurant here has a large range of dishes and is reputed to be very good. **E** *Tok's Little Hut*, T01-3230264. Used to be a favourite among the low budget travellers but following a change of ownership it is rumoured that standards of cleanliness have no longer been maintained. **E-F** *Naga*, T01-3532575, F01-3210732. English-run and friendly, offers home-baked cakes, bread and pastries. The only post office on Koh Samet is located here (Post Restante and satellite phone to Europe – expensive). Basic huts, some with fans, cheaper without, all have shared, if rather smelly, bathrooms.

Ao Phai C-E *Ao Phai Hut*, T01-3532644. Some a/c, friendly, clean operation, wooden huts higher up behind the tree line, mosquitoes prevalent. This place has a library and organizes minibuses to Pattaya. International phone available. **D** *Samet Villa*, T01-4948090. This clean and friendly Swiss-run establishment offers the best value accommodation on Samet, all rooms have fans and attached bathrooms and electricity is on round the clock (rare for Koh Samet). They organize a number of trips and excursions to neighbouring islands. Recommended. **D-E** *Silver Sand*, good value bungalows, popular restaurant offering wide range of dishes, large selection of recent videos, discos at the weekends. **E-F** *Sea Breeze*, T01-3211397. Bungalows are fairly cheap but are located facing the back wall of the restaurant and are fairly grotty inside and out, restaurant also poorly located set back from the sea beside the path. On the plus side, the seafood here is good and the staff friendly and helpful.

Ao Tubtim/Ao Phutsa D *Pudsa Bungalow*. **D** *Tubtim* more expensive huts have their own showers.

Ao Nuan D-E *Nuan Kitchen*, wooden huts with thatched roofs entered by crawling through a low door, no electricity (lamps are provided), all rooms have shared bathroom, there are lots of mosquitoes since the huts are higher up behind the treeline, but nets are provided, the food is reputed to be very good. This place certainly has more character than many of the concrete bungalows to be found on the island.

Ao Cho This bay, immediately north of Wong Duan features a couple of rather characterless operations with rather grotty concrete bungalows: **D** *Tarn Tawan*, has slightly better bungalows than *Wonderland* in a similar price bracket. **E** *Wonderland Resort*, T438409. Grotty bungalows and ugly glass-fronted building ruins any character this might ever have had – they do, however, organize trips around the island for ฿100 per person.

Ao Wong Duan This beach is becoming a close second to Hat Sai Khao in terms of shops, pubs, bars and nightlife, but the accommodation is not so cramped and it's not quite so crowded. Several of the guesthouses run boats to Ban Phe. **B-C** *Malibu Garden Resort*, T2185345. Offers a range of fairly solid and characterless bungalows situated (at time of writing) around a smelly, boggy patch. **B-C** *Wong Duern Resort*, T651777, F651819. Offers slightly nicer bungalows in the same price range in an attractive setting behind the tree line, restaurant offers a vast range of Thai and western dishes to suit all budgets. **A-C** *Vongduern Villa*, T651292. One of the most expensive resorts on the island with 2 VIP bungalows at the top end of their range even having hot water (very rare on Koh Samet), there are pool tables and the restaurant has its tables on rocks just beside the sea (or even in the sea at very high tides). **C-E** *Seahorse*, T01-3230049. Some a/c, friendly and popular with 2 restaurants and a travel agency but cheaper rooms in a longhouse aren't up to much. **E** *Samet Cabana*, basic dark wooden huts with shared bathroom. **E-F** *Pia's Shop*, behind the shop up the hill at the north end of the beach. Three bamboo huts with no electricity and shared bathroom, a good location for the low-budget traveller who would like a peaceful spot but doesn't want to be too far from the action.

Ao Thian – (Candlelight Beach) **E-F** *Lung Dam Hut*, T651810. Basic wooden and bamboo huts with grass roofs or you could try their treehouse just a few feet from the sea, only some of the huts have fans, some have own bath.

Ao Wai **B-C** *Samet Villa Resort*, bookable through the boat Phra Aphai at Ban Phe, T01-3211284. The only accommodation on this beach – good bungalows but quite expensive, very peaceful and attractive location, but lacks places to sit with views of the sea.

Ao Kiu Na Nok **B-D** *Coral Beach*, T652561. A range of rather grotty, overpriced huts and fan-cooled bungalows, the electricity goes off at midnight; food isn't up to much either.

Ao Phrao An altogether more peaceful experience on this side of the island, with the added bonus of sunsets. **A-B** *Ao Phrao Resort*, T651814. Once the most luxurious accommodation on the island, but unfortunately the management have got greedy and have crammed too many bungalows onto the plot, filling every available space. The only dive school on the island is located here. Regular boat service to Seree Ban Phe Pier in Ban Phe.

Camping Because the island is a national park, it is permissable to camp on any of the beaches. The best area is on the west coast, which means a walk on one of the many trails of not more than 3 km.

Eating Just about all the resorts and guesthouses on Koh Samet provide a selection of the usual Thai dishes and travellers' food, including fresh seafood. There are also one or two dedicated restaurants. The following places have a particular reputation for their food, but note that chefs move at the drop of a saucepan and one season's Michelin-starred guesthouse becomes the following season's greasy spoon. *Jep's Inn and Restaurant; Naga* (home-baked cakes, bread and pastries); *Sea Breeze* (good seafood); *Nuan Kitchen* (very good food); *Wong Duern Resort* (vast range of Thai and Western dishes); and the *Bamboo Restaurant* on Ao Cho – open through the day, reasonable food and one of the island's few restaurants).

Sports The major beaches offer sailing, windsurfing (฿150 per hour), scuba-diving, snorkelling, and water-skiing (฿500 per 15 mins) and jet-skiing (฿1,000 per hour). However, many of the bungalows display notices requesting visitors not to hire jet-skis because they are dangerous to swimmers (there have been 2 deaths already), damage the coral, and disrupt the peace. It is also not unheard of for those renting them to lose their deposits or have difficulty getting their passports back because the renter claims they have damaged the machine in some way. Ao Wong Duan has the best selection of watersports. The best snorkelling is to be found at Ao Wai, Ao Kiu Na Nok and Ao Phrao.

Tour operators *Citizen Travel*, Hat Sai Khao. *Citizen Travel 2*, Ao Phai. *CP Travel Service*, Hat Sai Khao. *Sea Horse Tours*, Wong Duan Beach, T01-2132849.

Transport
See also Ins & outs, page 492

Local Koh Samet is a small island and it is possible to walk just about everywhere. There are rough tracks, some suitable for songthaews, rather more negotiable by motorbike. There are also rocky paths that wind over the headlands that divide each

The Eastern Region

beach and which can only be negotiated on foot. **Songthaews**: are the main form of public transport, bouncing along the tracks that criss-cross the island. Rates are fairly expensive – from Na Dan it costs ฿15 per person to Hat Sai Khao, ฿20 to Ao Phai, ฿30 to Wong Duan or Ao Phrao, ฿40 to Ao Thian, and ฿50 to Ao Kiu Na Kok. It is also possible to charter songthaews; in fact, if a songthaew is not full the driver may insist that the passengers make up the fares to a full load. **Motorbike hire**: motorbikes can be hired from *Aladin* in Na Dan but this is expensive (฿100 per hour or ฿800 per day) and they disturb the peace (or what is left of it). The rental companies explain that because the roads are so bad their machines have a very short life expectancy. As Koh Samet is only 6 km long and 3 km wide, walking is always a possibility.

Road and sea Regular connections from Bangkok's Eastern bus terminal to Ban Phe, the departure point for the boat to Koh Samet. It is also possible to catch a bus to Rayong or Pattaya and then a connecting songthaew to Ban Phe. But if arriving in the late afternoon in Rayong it can be difficult to find a regular public songthaew making its way out to Ban Phe. Other than staying in Rayong for the night (see above for accommodation in Rayong) and catching a ฿15 songthaew the following morning, the only alternative is to charter a vehicle for the trip (฿150 upwards for the 22 km journey). A private car from Bangkok to Ban Phe should cost around ฿1,600 and take 3 hrs. There are regular boats to Na Dan from Ban Phe Pier throughout the day departing when full, 30-40 mins (฿40), with the last boat leaving at 1700. There are also many boats to various beaches from Nuanthip Pier and Seree Ban Phe Pier which lie just to the west of the main pier. Most of these boats are run by bungalow operators and they tend to cost ฿40- ฿50. You may also be charged ฿10 for a boat taxi to the beach at the island end. It is usually well worth catching one of these boats if you can find one going to your chosen destination you then avoid paying for the *songthaew* from Na Dan and also the park entry fee. Most boats dock at Na Dan or Ao Wong Duan. Some will also drop passengers off at Ao Phrao. Boats visit the southern beaches of Ao Thian, Ao Wai and Ao Kiu Na Nok less frequently – enquire before departure. Note that it may be difficult to find out which boat is going where; boat operators try hard to get visitors to stay at certain bungalows with which they are linked. It is best not to agree to stay anywhere until arrival on the island whereupon claims of cleanliness and luxury can be checked out. Travel agents on Khaosan Rd, Bangkok, also arrange transport to Samet, easier but slightly more expensive (and less fun?) than DIY.

Directory **Banks** The island has no banks, so for the best rates, change money on the mainland. Many of the bungalows and travel agents do offer a money changing service but take a 5% fee. The one exception is *Samet Villa* at Ao Phai which uses the mainland rates as published daily in the paper. **Communications** Post Office: situated inside *Naga Bungalows* at Hin Khok between Hat Sai Khao and Ao Phai (Poste Restante). Open 0830-1500 Mon-Fri, 0830-1200 Sat. **Telephone office:** between Hat Sai Khao and Na Dan (for overseas calls). It is also possible to make calls (including overseas calls) from many of the bungalows but rates may be more expensive. **Useful addresses** Police: Hat Sai Khao. Health centre: Koh Samet Health Centre, a small, public health unit, is situated on the road south from Na Dan to Hat Sai Khao [MARK ON MAP].

Chantaburi จันทบุรี

Phone code: 039
Colour map 3, grid C6

Chantaburi, or the 'city of the moon', has played a central role on several occasions as Thailand has faced external threats. With the fall of Ayutthaya to the marauding Burmese in 1767, King Taksin retreated here to regroup and rearm before venturing back to the Central Plains to confront the Burmese and establish a new capital. A century and a quarter later, Chantaburi was occupied by the French for over 10 years between 1893 and 1904, a period during which the future of Siam as an independent kingdom was seriously at threat.

Ins and outs

Chantaburi is a small provincial capital 330 km from Bangkok. There is no airport here, and the eastern train line doesn't reach this far, so the only public transport links are by bus. There are regular connections with Bangkok's Eastern bus terminal and also services to other eastern towns like Rayong and Pattaya and destinations in the Northeast such as Korat.

Getting there
See also Transport, page 503

Songthaews and local buses link Chantaburi with places nearby. Saamlors and tuk-tuks provide transport within the town.

Getting around

Sights

Chantaburi has built its wealth on rubies and sapphires – and especially the famous 'red' sapphire or Thapthim Siam (see box page 501). Many of the gem mines were developed during the 19th century by Shan people from Burma, who are regarded as being among the best miners in the world.

Muang Chan – as it is locally known – has a large Chinese and Vietnamese population, which is reflected in the general atmosphere of the town: narrower streets, shuttered wooden shophouses, Chinese temples and an air of industriousness. This atmosphere is most palpable along Rim Nam or Sukhaphiban Road which, as the name suggests, follows the right bank of the Chantaburi River. Old **shophouses**, some dating from the 19th century, house Chinese funeral supply and medicine shops. The active French-style **Catholic Cathedral** of the Immaculate Conception was built in 1880 and is the largest church in Thailand. Architecturally uninspiring (coloured beige and grey), it is significant merely for its presence. The interior though, is rather more interesting, Moorish pillars washed in cool colours, seashell chandeliers, and European stained glass. The Cathedral was built to serve the large number of Vietnamese Catholics who fled their homeland and settled here. On weekdays at 1600, children disgorge from the school near the Cathedral and an array of foodstalls miraculously appears in the compound, selling mouthwatering-looking snacks. The footbridge near the compound leads into the old part of town; the most interesting street architecture in the town is to be found in the road parallel to the river, westwards towards the main bridge. The Vietnamese part of town lies to the north of the cathedral, on the opposite side of the river.

It is Chantaburi's gems which attract most people's attention, but in addition, the province is highly regarded as a source of some of the best durians in Thailand, which flourish in the lush climate. The finest can cost several hundred baht (over a week's wages for an agricultural labourer), a fact which can seem astonishing to visitors who regard the fruit as repulsive - 'carrion in custard', as one Englishman is said to have remarked (see page 56).

• •

Chantaburi place names

Bo Rai

บ่อไร่

Catholic Cathedral

วิหารคาธอลิก

Khai Nern Wong

ค่ายเนินวง

Khao Ploi Waen

เขาพลอยแหวน

Nam Tok Krating

น้ำตกกระทิง

Nam Tok Pliu

น้ำตกพลิ้ว

Oasis Sea World

โอเอซีส ซีเวิลด์

The Eastern Region

Excursions

Khai Nern Wong Khai Nern Wong – a ruined fort – lies 4½ km southeast of town off Tha Chalaep Road. Take the turning towards Tha Mai, and walk or drive for another 200 m. The fort is not as well preserved as the official tourist literature suggests. King Taksin retreated here after Ayutthaya fell to the Burmese in 1767. With his army consisting mainly of Chinese, it is thought Taksin decided to flee to the region of his kingdom with the largest number of Chinese settlers. Consequently, he proceeded from Chonburi to Rayong and finally to Chantaburi. Even so, he had to wage a battle against the ruler of Chantaburi in June 1767 to secure his position. Within the precincts of the fort an **Underwater Archaeological Museum** has opened. This does not mean that visitors have to don scuba gear, but rather that the objects displayed have been recovered from wrecks lying in this part of the Gulf. Most of the pieces are earthenware pots and Sawankhalok china.

Khao Ploi Waen Khao Ploi Waen is a small hill 4 km past the fort. There is an active wat at the bottom of the hill and a Ceylonese-style chedi on the top, built during the reign of King Rama IV. It is a steep climb up steps to the top of the hill, where there are good views of the surrounding countryside with its orchards. The hill is pockmarked with gem mines, although they are all now abandoned and the vegetation has made a good job of covering up the evidence.

Khao Sa Bap National Park **Nam Tok Phui** is a waterfall located within the 16,800-ha **Khao Sa Bap National Park**, gazetted in 1975. It is to be found off Route 3, south towards Trat. After about 14 km, at Ban Plui, a left turn is signposted to the waterfall (there is a large, rather grand, Chinese temple close to the turn-off). Facing the waterfall are two chedis, the Alongkon Chedi and one commissioned by Rama V as a memorial to Princess Sunantha Kumareeratana in 1876. Park bungalow accommodation available, T5790529. ■ *Getting there: by minibus from the municipal market.*

Oasis Sea World Oasis Sea World is 25 km south of town off Route 3 near the small town of Laem Sing. The station covers 11 ha and was established to breed two species of dolphin – the humpbacked and Irrawaddy. Dolphin shows are performed at regular intervals through the day. ■ *Mon-Sun 0900-1800, ฿120 (adults), ฿60 (children). For information T399015.*

Kitchakut National Park **Nam Tok Krating**, another waterfall, can be found within the **Kitchakut National Park** (along with a few bat-filled caves), and is about 30 km north-west of town. The water is believed to have healing powers. The park is one of the smallest in the country, covering under 60 sq km, and was established in 1977. The falls are within hiking distance of the park headquarters. It is also possible to walk to the summit of the Phrabat Mountain, so-called because there is an impression of a footprint of the Buddha. Allow four hours to reach the top. There is accommodation available in the park near park HQ (B T5790529/5794842). ■ *Getting there: regular public songthaews run past the entrance to the park on Route 3249; from here it is a 15 min walk to the park HQ.*

Bo Rai Bo Rai is a gem mining area near the Cambodian border, with a gem market (see page 504).

Wat Khao Sukim Wat Khao Sukim, situated at Ban Khao Sukim 35 km northwest of Chantaburi is a famous wat – visited daily by hundreds who come to see Luang Pho Somchai, an elderly monk with mysterious powers and a nationwide reputation as a meditation teacher. The monastery is sited on the side of Sukim

The tears of the gods: rubies and sapphires

Major deposits of two of the world's most precious stones are found distributed right across mainland Southeast Asia: rubies and sapphires are mined in Thailand, Burma, Vietnam, Cambodia and Laos. The finest of all come from Burma, and especially from the renowned Mogok Stone Tract, which supports a town of 100,000 almost entirely upon the proceeds of the gem industry. Here peerless examples are unearthed, including the rare 'pigeon's blood' ruby. One Thai trader was reported saying that "Asking to see the pigeon's blood is like asking to see the face of God".

Although the Burmese government tries to keep a tight grip on the industry, many of the gems pass into the hands of Thai gem dealers, often with the connivance of the Thai army. Corruption, violence, murder, arson and blackmail are all part and parcel of the trade. Through fair means and foul, Bangkok has become the centre of the world's gem business and Thailand is the largest exporter of cut stones – indeed, it has a virtual monopoly of the sapphire trade. Thai buyers conclude deals with mines in Australia, Kenya, Sri Lanka, the USA – across the globe – and have a stranglehold on the business. Those who try to buck the system and bypass Bangkok risk having a contract taken out on their lives.

Rubies and sapphires are different colours of corundum, the crystalline form of aluminium oxide. Small quantities of various trace elements give the gems their colour; in the case of rubies, chromium and for blue sapphires, titanium. Sapphires are also found in a spectrum of other colours including green and yellow. Rubies are among the rarest of gems, and command prices four times higher than equivalent sized diamonds. The Burmese call the ruby ma naw ma ya or 'desire-fulfilling stones'.

The colour of sapphires can be changed through heat treatment (the most advanced form is called diffusion treatment) to 1,500-1,600°C (sapphires melt at 2,050°C). For example, relatively valueless colourless geuda sapphires from Sri Lanka, turn a brilliant blue or yellow after heating. The technique is an ancient one: Pliny the Elder described the heating of agate by Romans nearly 2,000 years ago, while the Arabs had developed heat treatment into almost a science by the 13th century. Today, almost all sapphires and rubies are heat treated. The most valued colour for sapphires is cornflower blue – dark, almost black, sapphires command a lower price. The value of a stone is based on the four 'C's: Colour, Clarity, Cut and Carat (1 carat = 200 mg). Note that almost all stones are heat treated to improve their colour. For information on buying gems in Thailand, see page 160.

The Eastern Region

mountain and a cable car runs up the side of the hill. Because so many gifts have been bestowed on the monastery by wealthy Thais there is now a **small museum** displaying the hoard. ■ *Getting there: take the 316 north out of Chantaburi, go west along Route 3, then north up the 3322.*

Essentials

A *Caribou*, 14 Chawana Uthit Rd, T323431. Recently built luxury hotel, pool, business facilities, 3 restaurants, Thai restaurant has live traditional Thai music most nights. **B** *Chantaburi Riverside*, 63 Moo 9, Chanthanimit 5 Rd, on the east bank of the Chantaburi River, north of town, T311726, F311726. A/c, restaurant, pool recently constructed, with Thai-style bungalows set in a tatty garden, all looking rather scruffy. Staff, however, are said to be friendly and helpful. **B** *KP Grand*, 35/200-201 Trirat Rd, T323201, F323214. 18 floors, so easy to spot, a/c, restaurant, newish hotel with all mod cons.

Sleeping
■ *on map, page 502*
Price codes:
see inside front cover

B-C *Eastern*, 899 Tha Chalaep Rd, T312218, F311985. Pool, all rooms have a/c, TV and bath tub – larger rooms also have fridges and are almost twice the price, smaller rooms are good value. **C** *KP Inn*, Trirat Rd, T311756. Very friendly but rather boring – all rooms have hot water and a/c, located directly opposite *KP Grand*. **C-D** *Mark's Travelodge*, 14 Raksakchamun Rd, T311531. A/c, own bathroom, spacious but quite far out. **D-E** *Kiatkachorn*, Tha Luang Rd, north side of town, T311212. Some a/c, boring bland exterior, not much better inside, noisy. **D** *Chantaburi*, 42/6 Tha Chalaep Rd, T311300. Some a/c, extremely grotty and very noisy, just about the only thing going for it is that it is central. **D-E** *Kasemsan Nung* , 98/1 Benchama Rachuthit Rd, T312340. Some a/c, large, clean rooms in big hotel, well run, but some rooms can be noisy. **D** *Siriwattana*, 51/3-4 Saritdet Rd, T328073. 5 clean rooms all with a/c, some with small balcony but room at back has no window, bright, friendly management, probably best value accommodation in town, located directly above *San Chandra Rice and Noodle House*. **D-E** *Muang Chan*, 257-259 Si Chan Rd, T312909. Noisy and characterless.

E *Arun Sawat*, 239 Sukha Phibal Rd, T311082. Situated in the most attractive part of town, small but clean rooms with homely atmosphere. **E** *Sukchai*, 28 Tha Chalaep Rd, T311292. Basic but relatively clean, central. **F** *Chantra River Hotel*, 248 Sukha Phibal Rd, T312310. Clean and friendly, shared bathroom, some rooms overlook river (located directly opposite *Arun Sawat*).

Chantaburi

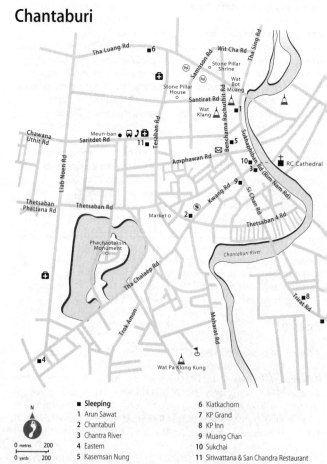

	Sleeping		
■	**Sleeping**	6	Kiatkachorn
1	Arun Sawat	7	KP Grand
2	Chantaburi	8	KP Inn
3	Chantra River	9	Muang Chan
4	Eastern	10	Sukchai
5	Kasemsan Nung	11	Siriwattana & San Chandra Restaurant

0 metres 200
0 yards 200

The Eastern Region

Most restaurants are on Tha Chalaep Rd. Where the road runs along the eastern side of King Taksin Lake, there is a profusion of pubs, bars and ice cream parlours – this is where Chantaburi's yuppies hang-out.

Eating
● on map
Price codes:
see inside front cover

Cheap *The Meun-ban* or 'Homely' restaurant is located directly next to the bus terminal and is probably the best low-budget restaurant in town. It offers a multitude of Thai dishes (including a huge vegetarian selection – something which it is not always easy to find in Thailand) and ice creams, at very low prices. The owners speak good English and are a helpful source of local information, it is also in an ideal location if you arrive tired and hungry after a long bus journey and need some refreshment. Recommended. *San Chandra (Chantaburi Rice and Noodle House)*, on Saritdet Rd, is another sparklingly clean and friendly restaurant offering delicious Thai food and ice creams, at the time of writing the menu is in Thai only but they are working on a translation – you can always point. Recommended.

Beware of *Chanthon Phochana* 98/1 Benchama Rachuthit Rd, the restaurant below the *Kasemsan I Hotel* – it serves unpleasant food at extortionate prices (there are no prices on the menu and farangs probably get charged more).

May or Jun *Fruit fair* (movable), celebrating local fruits such as durian, jackfruit, pomelo and rambutan; cultural shows, handicraft exhibitions.

Festivals

Gems and jewellery Si Chan Rd, or 'Gem Street' has the best selection of jewellery shops and gem stores. However you are unlikely to pick up a bargain. On Fri, Sat and Sun a gem street market operates along Krachang Lane.

Shopping

Rattan and basketwork Chantaburi is regarded as one of the centres of fine rattan work in Thailand. Available from numerous shops in town.

If coming from the northeast, it is possible to avoid the capital by taking routes 304, 33 and 317 south from Korat. The road descends from the Khorat plateau and follows the Thai/Cambodian border, through frequent checkpoints, south to Chantaburi.

Transport
330 km to Bangkok.
See also Ins & outs,
page 499

Bus Regular connections with Bangkok's Eastern bus terminal. Also buses from Pattaya, Rayong, Ban Phe and other eastern seaboard towns. If coming from Koh Samet, get a boat to Ban Phe, songthaew to Rayong (฿20) and then a bus to Chantaburi – buses leave every hour, the journey takes 2 hrs and costs ฿30. There are less regular bus connections with destinations in the Northeast including Korat.

Banks *Thai Farmers*, 103 Sirong Muang Rd. *Bangkok*, 50 Tha Chalaep Rd. **Communications** Post Office: at the intersection of Amphawan and Si Chan roads.

Directory

Chantaburi to Koh Chang

Trat ตราด

Trat is the provincial capital and the closest Thai town of any size to Cambodia. Like Chantaburi, it is a gem centre (see box, page 160). As the prospects of lasting peace in Cambodia get ever-so-slowly brighter, and as the government in Cambodia opts for Gorbachev-style policies of *perestroika*, so Chinese businessmen in Trat are getting increasingly excited about business prospects across the border. For a while, between 1894 and 1906, Trat was part of French Indo-China. But the French agreed to repatriate the town in exchange for the Thais giving up their traditional claims to western Cambodia.

Phone code: 039
Colour map 3, grid C6

The Eastern Region

Most people visit Trat en route to beautiful Koh Chang, and the emergence of Koh Chang as the latest in a long string of tropical Thai islands to entice the *farang* visitor has brought considerable business to the place. But truthfully, there is little to keep visitors in the town any longer than they need to catch a bus or boat onwards.

However, if your boat/bus connection means that you are stranded here, then there is a bustling **covered market** (attractively known in official literature as the 'Municipal Shopping Mall') in the centre of town on Sukhumvit Road. It offers a good selection of food and drink stalls. On the same road, north of the shopping mall, there is also an active **night market**. **Wat Buppharam**, also known as **Wat Plai Klong** dates from the late Ayutthaya Period. It is notable for its wooden viharn and monk's *kutis*, and is 2 km west of town, down the road opposite the shopping mall.

Excursions **Bo Rai** on the Cambodian border, used to be a really thriving gem market, cashing in on the supply of rubies from Cambodia as well as from local mines. However there are fewer and fewer high-quality gems being mined these days and so Bo Rai's significance has declined (it may also be that many of the gems are sold in Bangkok rather than through intermediaries in Bo Rai). While in the early 1990s there were several gem markets here, now there is just one – the **Khlong Yor Market** which operates during the morning. One unusual feature of the market is that it is the gem buyers who remain seated while the sellers walk around showing their wares. ■ *Getting there: songthaews leave from outside the market.*

An even better source of gems is over the border, in Cambodia. From 1991 for several years, thousands of Thais, after being taxed US$60 each by the Khmer Rouge, were penetrating the Cambodian jungles in search of their fortunes. One was quoted as saying, 'Over that mountain, a few days' walk away, you just stick your hands in the ground and the dirt is filled with precious stones'. Under pressure from the UN and the international community, the Thai government tried – or at least gave the impression of trying – to stop the flow of gems, so that the flow of funds to the Khmer Rouge would also stop. In this they were only partially successful. While Cambodia remains a tempting source of gems, the Khmer Rouge – thank goodness – are dead and buried.

Khlong Yai is the southernmost town on this eastern arm of Thailand and an important fishing port. The journey there is worthwhile for the dramatic scenery with the mountains of Cambodia rising to the east and the sea to the west. Khlong Yai is also a pretty and bustling little port, well worth the trip. There are several Cambodian markets and the seafood is excellent. **Sleeping** There is one hotel in Khlong Yai which, we understand, is serviceable. *Getting there: by songthaew from the back of the municipal market (฿25) or shared taxi from the front of the market (฿35 each).*

Sleeping
■ *on map*
Price codes:
see inside front cover

C-D *OK Bungalow*, down a narrow tree-lined road (no sign in English) on the left-hand side as you head east along the Wiwattana Rd, opposite the *Nam Chok* restaurant, T512657-8. This is a second branch of the *Muang Trat* and is the most up-market place to stay, it consists of a concrete line of bungalows, each separated from the next at ground level by a parking bay, the more expensive bungalows have hot water and a bath tub, most have a/c. **D-E** *Thai Rungrot*, 296 Sukhumvit Rd, T511141. Some a/c, north of town, to the right of Sukhumvit Rd, rather decrepit with boring rooms.

Trat place names

Khlong Yai

คลองใหญ่

Laem Ngop

แหลมงอบ

D *Muang Trat*, 4 Sukhumvit Rd, T511091. Some a/c, clean rooms, very centrally located on the south side of the lane which runs between the 2 markets – a fact which has put their restaurant out of business.

E-F *NP Guesthouse*, 1-3 Soi Luang Aet, Lak Muang Rd, T512564. Clean, friendly, well-run converted shophouse, with a bright little restaurant, shared bathroom, dorm beds. Recommended.

F *Foremost Guesthouse*, 49 Thoncharoen Rd, by the canal, last turn on the left off Sukhumvit Rd, towards Laem Ngop, T511923. First floor rooms, shared bathrooms, hot water, clean and friendly with lots of local information. Recommended.
F *Windy Guesthouse*, Thoncharoen Rd. Across the road from *Foremost*, owned by same family, slightly cheaper rooms, dorm beds available.

Trat

Sleeping
1 Coco's Guesthouse & Café
2 Foremost Guesthouse
3 Friendly Guesthouse
4 Garden Home Guesthouse
5 Jame's Guesthouse
6 Muang Trat
7 NP Guesthouse
8 OK Bungalow
9 Residang Guesthouse
10 Thai Rungrot
11 Trat Guesthouse
12 Trat Inn & Family Café
13 Windy Guesthouse

Eating
1 Jean Café
2 Max & Tick
3 Sang Fah

Transport
1 A/c buses to Bangkok
2 Non a/c Bus Station
3 Minibus & taxis to Laem Ngop
4 Buses to Chantaburi

The Eastern Region

The municipal market has a good range of stalls to choose from – good value and delicious. Other markets which sell food include the night market next to the a/c bus station. **Expensive**: *Suan Phu*, Ban Laem Hin, 10 km southeast of town. One of the best places to sample seafood in the region, with crab being the speciality (it is attached to a crab farm). Attractive seating area on piers out over the water. **Mid-range** *Max and Tick*, Soi Luang Aet, opposite the *NP Guesthouse*. A good place for breakfast, friendly owners who are a mine of local information. *Nam Chok*, corner of Soi Butnoi and Wiwatthana roads (off Thatmai Rd). Good local food served outdoors. *Sang Fah*, 156 Sukhumvit Rd. Thai food, extensive menu, especially seafood, a/c restaurant, quite good.

Jun *Rakham Fruit Fair* celebrates Trat's reputation as a fruit-growing centre.

Local Motorbike hire: from Soi Sukhumvit, just south of the municipal market and from *Windy Guesthouse* (they also have bicycles and may have canoes for exploring the canal).

Long distance Bus: a/c station is on Sukhumvit Rd, just north of the night market. Non-a/c buses leave from Wiwattana Rd, north, off Sukhumvit Rd. Regular connections with Bangkok's Eastern bus terminal 5½ hrs, Pattaya 3½ hrs, and with Chantaburi 1 hr 40 mins. **Songthaew**: to Laem Ngop from outside the municipal market on Sukhumvit Rd (฿15). **Shared taxi**: to Chantaburi 50 mins (฿30 each).

Eating
● on map
Price codes:
see inside front cover

Festivals

Transport
400 km to Bangkok

Boat from near the *Foremost Guesthouse*, boats leave very irregularly to Koh Kut and Koh Mak.

Directory **Banks** *Siam Commercial*, Sukhumvit Rd. *Thai Farmers*, 63 Sukhumvit Rd. *Thai Military*, Sukhumvit Rd. **Communications** Post Office: Tha Reua Jang Rd on northeast side of town. **Tourist offices** Found on Soi Sukhumvit, not far from the market; helpful and informative.

Laem Ngop   แหลมงอบ

Phone code: 039
Colour map 3, grid C6

This sleepy fishing village – in fact the district capital – has a long pier lined with boats, along with good seafood and a relaxed atmosphere. But this is unlikely to last: Laem Ngop is poised to explode into life as Koh Chang – an offshore island – becomes Thailand's next island beach resort to hit the big time (see below). At the time of writing, the town had a handful of guesthouses and some restaurants by the main pier in town. Two new piers, one rather prosaically called Koh Chang Centre Point, have been completed some distance outside town, to the northwest. There is a small tourist information centre in the Amphoe (district) Office, offering information on bungalows on Koh Chang and the other islands in the Marine National Park. The headquarters for the park are at Laem Ngop. Few people stay in Laem Ngop and almost everyone arrives here merely to catch the boat to Koh Chang.

Sleeping There are a number of guesthouses on the main road into the village. **D-E** *Laem Ngop Inn*, T597044. Some a/c. **D-E** *Paradise Inn*, T512831. Some a/c. **E** *PI*, large clean rooms, open high season only. **F** *Chut Kaew*, good source of information and comes recommended.

Tour operators *AD Tour*, by the pier, T2128014.

Transport *17 km to Trat* **Songthaew** From the stand outside the shopping mall, Sukhumvit Rd, in Trat (30 mins). Regular departures during daylight hours. After dark, songthaews must be chartered. **Boat** Regular boat departures for Koh Chang from the main pier in town; rather more intermittent from Koh Chang Centre Point outside town. For details, see Koh Chang entry, below.

Directory **Banks** Mobile exchange service at the pier. 0900-1600. **NB** exchange rates on Koh Chang are poor. **Medical services** *Malaria Centre* on main road, opposite *Laem Ngop Inn*. They give the latest information on malaria and can help with treatment. **Tourist offices** *TAT*, 100 Mu 1 Trat, Laem Ngop Rd, T597255. Areas of responsibility are Trat and the islands, including Koh Chang.

Koh Chang   เกาะช้าง

Phone code: 039
Colour map 3, grid C6

This – as yet – unspoilt island is Thailand's second largest (40 km long and 16 km wide) and is part of a Marine National Park which also includes another 50-odd islands and islets covering just over 650 sq km. Despite the 'protection' that its national park status should offer, Koh Chang is developing rapidly, with resorts and bungalows springing up virtually overnight along its shores.

Ins and outs

Getting there *See also Transport, page 512* To reach Koh Chang in a day from Bangkok means a very early bus – before 0800. Getting to Koh Chang is not easy – which probably explains why it has been slow to develop as a resort island. First of all it is necessary to get to Laem Ngop (see the previous entry), the departure point for boats to the island. From Bangkok catch a bus from the Eastern bus terminal to Trat (see page 505); from there, there are regular songthaews the 17 km to Laem Ngop. During the high season (Nov-May) boats leave every hour or so from Laem Ngop for Koh Chang. But during the low season departures are much more intermittent.

Getting around

Koh Chang's best beaches are on the western side of the island – **Hat Sai Khao** (white sand), **Hat Khlong Phrao** and, on the southern coast, **Hat Bang Bao**. These can be reached either by jeep taxi from Ao Sapparot (price ranging from ฿20- ฿40, depending upon destination, if you manage to fill up the taxi) or by boat from Laem Ngop. There is a dirt road up the east coast and down the west coast as far south as Ao Kai Bae. For destinations further south such as Hat Bang Bao you must either walk or get a boat – although if planned improvements to the track have progressed according to schedule then this section may also be open to road vehicles. The steep mountainous stretch between Ao Khlong Son and Hat Sai Khao is now paved and work is on-going so it may well be that more of the island's dirt roads are now surfaced. The intention is to create a paved ring road encircling the whole island, which should be completed by 2001, or thereabouts. In addition to songthaews there are also motorbikes (around ฿400 per day) and mountain bikes for hire. For walkers, there is a path crossing the middle of the island from Ban Khlong Phrao to Than Ma Yom but it is a strenuous day-long hike and locals recommend taking a guide.

Best to visit

For snorkelling and diving the best time to visit is between November and May, when visibility is at its best. This is also the best time to visit from the weather point of view. Koh Chang is a wet island with an annual rainfall of over 3,000 mm (the wettest month is August).

The area

Khlong Son, near Koh Chang's northern tip, is the largest settlement on the island. Even so, there's not much here: a health clinic, a few small noodle shops, a monastery, post office and school. Many of the other islands within the national park have villages, and a fair amount of land, particularly around the coast, has been cleared for agriculture – mostly coconut plantations. The park was only gazetted in 1982 and most of the people living within the parks boundaries were here many years beforehand. Even so, Koh Chang remains mainly undeveloped. But it is a matter of conjecture as to how long the island will remain uspoilt. Given the changes that have occurred elsewhere – Phuket, Samui and Samet – it is easy to be pessimistic about the environmental future of Koh Chang. Indeed, we are already receiving letters from people complaining of the rubbish. With no waste management system it doesn't take many visitors or guesthouses to create a serious refuse problem – and that is what appears to be emerging on Koh Chang's more popular beaches.

● ● ● ● ● ● ● ● ● ● ● ● ● ● ● ● ● ● ● ●

Koh Chang place names

Hat Bang Bao

หาดบางเบ้า

Hat Khlong Phrao

หาดคลองพร้าว

Hat Sai Khao

หาดทรายขาว

Than Ma Yom Waterfall

น้ำตกธารมะยม

Sights

Koh Chang is famed for its wild boar and the **Than Ma Yom Waterfall** – which is on the east side of the island. King Chulalongkorn (Rama V) visited this waterfall on no less than six occasions at the end of the 19th

Than Ma Yom Waterfall

The Eastern Region

century, so even given the Thai predilection for waterfalls of any size, it counts as an impressive one (in fact there are three falls). To prove the point, the king carved his initials (or had them carved), on a stone to mark one of his visits. Rama VI and VII also visited the falls, although it seems that they didn't get quite so far – they left their initials inscribed on stones at the nearest of the falls. The falls are accessible from either Ban Dan Mai or Thaan Ma Yom, both on the east coast and getting to the first of the cascades involves a walk of around one hour. It is around 4 km to the furthest of the three falls.

Khlong Phu Falls   More accessible from the west coast (which is where most people stay), and perhaps even more beautiful, are the **Khlong Phu Falls** at Ao Khlong Phrao. This waterfall can be reached by taxi or motorbike in 10 minutes from Hat Sai Khao. You can also travel to it from the road by elephant for ฿200 or for free by walking just 3 km. There is a good pool here for swimming as well as a restaurant and some bungalows. Because this is a national park it is also possible to camp.

The forest   Koh Chang is also likely to prove rewarding for naturalists. The **forest** here is some of the most species-rich in the country and while the island's coast may be undergoing development the rugged, mountainous interior is still largely

Koh Chang

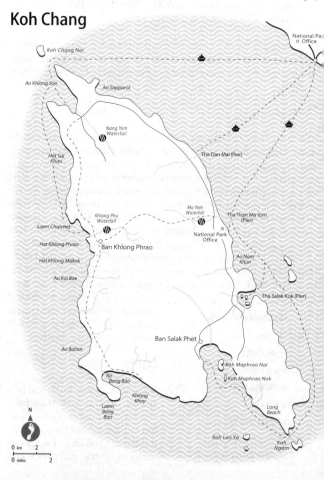

inaccessible and covered with virgin rainforest (around 70% is said to be forested). There is a good population of birds, including parrots, sunbirds, hornbills and trogons, as well as Koh Chang's well-known population of wild boar. While the waters around Koh Chang are clear there have been some reports of a deterioration in water quality connected with coastal gem mining on the mainland. Nonetheless, hard and especially soft corals are abundant. Fish are less numerous and varied than on the other side of the Gulf of Thailand or in the Andaman Sea.

NB Mosquitoes (carrying malaria) and sandflies are a problem on Koh Chang and surrounding islands, so insect repellent and anti-malarials are essential. Take a net if camping.

Other nearby islands

There are many other smaller islands near Koh Chang, which are also part of the Koh Chang National Park and which are likewise gradually being developed. These are mostly off the south coast, and are the best areas for snorkelling and diving.

Koh Kut

The next largest island after Koh Chang itself is **Koh Kut**. This island has lovely beaches, especially on the west side, and a number of small fishing villages linked by dirt roads. There is an impressive waterfall and the coral is also said to be good. However, mosquitoes are a problem. Koh Kut is not part of the national park and so there are almost no controls on development; the forest is being encroached upon by agriculture and developers are claiming the best pieces of shoreline. There are two resorts – the exclusive **AL** *Koh Kut Island Resort*, T039-511824 and **E-F** *Klong Chao Laguna*, basic huts near the waterfall. ■ *Getting there: two, sometimes more, boats per week leave from the pier on the Trat River in Trat (not Laem Ngop) for Koh Kut. During the high season (Nov-May) are on Mon at 1100 and Fri at 1400; day visitors from Koh Mak (see below) can make the trip on regular boats linking the two islands.*

Koh Mak

Koh Mak is the third largest island in the archipelago after Koh Chang and Koh Kut. It has been privately owned by a few wealthy local families and a little over half of the island has been cleared for coconut plantations. But there is still a reasonable area of forest and the coral is also good. The best beach is on the northwest shore. It is said that many of the prime pieces of shorefront have been sold to Bangkok-based developers, so it remains to be seen what happens to Koh Mak. Perhaps the economic downturn and the collapse of the property market will slow the pace of change. **Sleeping A-B** *Ban Laem Chan*, T01-9142593, F02-3982844. Seven wooden cottages with seaview, attached bathrooms and 'club house'. **A-B** *Koh Maak Resort*, reservations from Bangkok on T3196714 or from Trat on T3270220. **D** *Alternative House*, good bungalows in a pleasant location. **E-F** *Lazy Days*, basic huts. ■ *Getting there: boats leave daily for Laem Ngop for Koh Mak during the high season (Nov-May). Departures may be suspended during the low season.*

Koh Kut place names

Koh Khlum

เกาะคลุ้ม

Koh Kut

เกาะกูด

Koh Rang

เกาะรัง

Koh Kham

The tiny island of Koh Kham has two bungalows (**F**), tents and the **E** *Koh Kham Resort*. Boats leave from Laem

The Eastern Region

Ngop, 3½ hours (฿150). Koh Kham is well known for its swallows, nests and turtle eggs, as well as good coral and rock formations for divers.

Other islands with bungalows are **Koh Phrao**, **Koh Ngam**, **Koh Whai**, which has two bungalow operations **D-F** *Pakalang Resort*, **E-F** *Koh Whai Paradise*, T579131, **Koh Lao Ya** (with accommodation at the **A** *Lao Ya Resort*, T512552. A/c, hot water, half board compulsory, excellent restaurant; the ultimate place for 'getting away from it all'). **Koh Sai Khao** (**A** *Hat Sai Khao Resort*, T511429), and **Koh Khlum**.

Many of the more sophisticated bungalow operations on Koh Chang organize day trips to the islands during the high season (when the seas are calmer, the visibility greater and there is generally more demand). In the low season few boats go between these islands and either Koh Chang or the mainland and most of the accommodation closes down.

Essentials

Sleeping

Caution: there are many thefts on Koh Chang. If you're staying in a basic bamboo hut be sure not to leave valuables in it when you are not there, or near open windows when you are asleep
Price codes: see inside front cover

Rapid development means that the accommodation list below may date quickly. The best source of information is travellers returning from the island. Check the guest book at the *Foremost Guesthouse* in Trat. Almost all the accommodation is simple A-frames, with wood-slat walls, thatched roofs, communal showers and no protection against mosquitoes – although some establishments will provide netting. Longer-stay visitors should ask for a discount. During the high season (Nov-May) you can usually ask your boat driver to drop you at the beach of your choice. In the low season most boats land only at Ao Sapparot (or at Ban Dan Hao) – in which case the boat ticket will also include the songthaew journey from Ao Sapparot down the west coast to your destination if the seas are too rough for the boat to make it round there. Much of the accommodation closes during the low season so if you do find a boat willing to go to the west or south coasts check before you go that accommodation is open there – otherwise you may be faced with a night on the beach followed by a long walk the next day.

NB With the development of the tourist industry on Koh Chang prices are also increasing and particularly during the very busy months (Dec and Jan) prices may be much higher than you might expect for accommodation in that category (you may well pay ฿1,000 for a fairly smart bungalow with fan but no a/c and no hot water for example). Although there are now electric cables around the island, most places cannot afford the enormous connection fee and still generate their own electricity which means that electricity is restricted in many places and only available from 1800 to midnight or 0600, so if it is important to you to have a fan all night then check what time it goes off.

Ao Khlong Son Few people choose to stay here anymore but head instead for the beaches on the west or south coasts. There are only two operations still going here: **F** *Mannee*, rather run down but friendly and enthusiastic management. **D-E** *Premvadee*, some single rooms, and some larger bungalows with attached bathrooms.

Hat Sai Khao About 15 establishments here, all with similar facilities and prices – many provide mosquito nets. The water is very shallow. **B-C** *Phaloma Resort*, T01-3230164. German-Swiss-run operation on the southern tip of the bay, some bungalows with a view over the sea, again there is no beach here, the restaurant is very good if a little more expensive than average, small library, in the high season boat trips to Koh Yai, Rang and Khlum can be arranged, motorcycles can also be hired here. **C-D** *Mac Bungalow*, own bathrooms, quite nice bungalows. **D-E** *Ban Dung Rong Resort* T597184. **D-E** *Cookie*, south of Patthai, Hat Sai Khao. Efficiently run bungalows all with shower/WC in 3 rows at varying price, popular and cheap but closed in low season, long-stay discount. **D-E** *White Sand Beach Resort*, out of the way up at the northern end of the beach and rather run-down, some rooms with own bathroom.

E *Apple Bungalow*, slightly smarter huts than other places in this price category. **E** *Hat Sai Khao Bungalow*, featuring some of the smartest and most expensive bungalows on the beach, in addition to some basic bamboo huts, good associated restaurant. **E** *Sunsai Bungalow*, clean and good value, some with attached bathroom, but no beach here. **E-F** *Ya Kah Bungalow*, basic but characterful little huts, friendly management. **F** *KC Bungalow*, clean huts arranged along the sea front in a very good location, quiet but not too secluded. **F** *Rock Sand Bungalow*, a few basic huts situated higher up above the beach.

Hat Khlong Phrao This is the next beach, 5 km south of Hat Sai Khao, and 2 km long, spread out each side of the mouth of the Khlong Phrao canal – a beautiful beach but the water tends to be very shallow. **AL** *Koh Chang Resort*, T538054-9. A/c, expensive bungalows, probably overpriced. **B** *Khlong Prao Resort*, T597216. Rather tatty and overpriced bungalows set around a lagoon, plus a 2-storey block, beautiful beach, good for swimming. **C-E** *Chaiyachet Bungalow*, T21930458. Bungalows set in an attractive garden at the top end of the bay, 1½ km walk to the beach. **C-E** *Coconut Beach Bungalow*, T01-21930432. Wooden huts with shared bath, well built, mosquito nets provided, set above the beach, rather unfriendly management. **E** *Hobby Hut*, quite far back from the beach, attractive wooden bungalows and restaurant in pleasant setting in wood on bank of canal. **E-F** *PSS*, lovely, clean bamboo huts on beach, good food. Recommended. **E-F** *NP*, next operation south of *PSS* and the last on the beach, overpriced run-down huts.

Ao Khlong Makok There is almost no beach here at high tide and there are just a couple of bungalow operations which are virtually deserted in the low season. **D-F** *Chok Dee* and **D-F** *Mejic* both offer huts with attached and shared bathrooms and have restaurants attractively located on stilts above the sea.

Ao Kai Bae This is the southernmost beach on the west coast. The beach is beautiful but swimming is not so good as the bottom is very shallow and covered with rocks with dead coral in places. **A-E** *Sea View Resort*, T597143. Very comfortable bungalows set on a steep hill in a landscaped garden, very good value (particularly in the low season when prices tend to halve), they also have a number of cheap basic huts right on the beach. **B-E** *Siam Bay Bungalow*, south end of the beach. Bungalows on the hill with sea views. **C-E** *Kai Bae Hut Resort*, T21930452. Some a/c, good bungalows, restaurant, good food, small shop. Recommended. **C-F** *Kai Bae Beach*, rather tatty huts with grass roofs, not very friendly management. **D-F** *Coral Bungalow*, offers mountain bikes for hire for ฿30 per hour, telephone service, flight reconfirmation and has a TV and video selection. **E-F** *Kai Bae Garden*, located 500 m up from the beach and hence cheaper huts, there is also a shop here. **E-F** *Nang Nuan Bung*, located at the north end of the bay (no beach here). Small, wooden huts, rather close together, no mosquito nets, but the management are very friendly and the restaurant offers a good range of meat and seafood dishes. **E-F** *Poon*, huts on the beach, basic and rather run-down, but cheap.

There are lovely views out to the small islands dotted along the coast here

Ao Bang Bao This is a lovely beach on the south coast of the island. The bay dries out at low tide and it is virtually inaccessible in the low season when the accommodation tends to shut down. There are no regular boats here – you can either charter a fishing boat or walk from Hat Kai Bae (about 5 km). **C-D** *Nice Beach Bang Bao*, situated directly on the beach, concrete bungalows with attached bathroom placed quite far apart, attractive restaurant. **D-F** *Bang Bao Blue Wave*, 15 wooden bungalows situated in a small shady wood (with and without bathroom), friendly atmosphere. **D** *Bang Bao Beach*, 10 mins from the beach and village. **D-F** *Bang Bao Laguna*, located at the eastern end of the bay, wooden huts, friendly management. **E-F** *Tantawan Bungalow*, only 7 huts here.

The Eastern Region

Although there is a scattering of bungalow operations on the **East coast** very few people choose to stay here even in the high season. The only beach is at Sai Thong but the bungalow operation here had closed down at last check.

Tha Than Ma Yom D-E *Tha Than Ma Yom Bungalow*, overpriced, grotty huts on the opposite side of the road above the beach. **D-F** *Tha Than Ma Yom*, bungalows set above the sea in the woods.

Eating Guesthouses tend to serve an unchanging array of Thai and travellers' fare; restaurants and bars are appearing gradually and the gastronomy should improve. Grilled seafood is the best bet. *JJ Sabai Land* is on Khlong Phrao beach, Thai and Western food available. *Bubby Bong's*, south end of Ao Sai Khao, recently opened by 2 Californians, seafood, Thai food and burgers, an open-sided torch-lit hut – will inevitably become popular. *Patthai Bungalows*, run by *farang* lady, midway along Hat Sai Khao, serves home-made bread and excellent Lao filter coffee.

Cookie, south of *Patthai*, Hat Sai Khao, good selection of Thai and travellers' food, popular and cheap. *The Fisherman's*, between *Patthai* and *Cookie* on Hat Sai Khao, good fresh fish. *Thor's Palace*, on Hat Sai Khao, excellent restaurant of the variety where you sit on the floor at low, lamp-lit tables, very friendly management, popular, library.

Sport **Diving** There is a Swiss-run diving school, *Koh Chang Divers*, on Hat Sai Khao which offers PADI and snorkelling; no credit cards accepted. There is a second outfit on Ao Kai Bae, the *Seahorse Dive Centre*.

Transport
See also Ins & outs, page 506

To get to Koh Chang, take a bus to Trat (see Trat, page 503), a songthaew to Laem Ngop and then a boat to the island. When leaving the island it is advisable to get immediately into a songthaew to Trat (if that is where you want to go) rather than hanging around because if you miss the one which meets the boat you may have to wait hours for the next one or have to charter one. Details on getting to the smaller islands of Koh Mak and Koh Kut are given above.

Local No cars, but there are motorbike and jeep **taxis**. These are pretty expensive (about ฿20-฿40 per 5 km) The usual rule of not getting into an empty one without checking the price first in case you charter it applies of course. The high prices date back to the days when the roads were poor and the machines had a very short life-span but there is really no excuse for it now that the roads have been improved. **Motorbike hire**: from many of the guesthouses but, again, rates are high – ฿60 per hour, ฿400 per day. **Mountain bike hire**: some of the guesthouses now have mountain bikes for hire (around ฿100 per day).

Boat Boats leave daily for the various beaches from one of the three piers in Laem Ngop (฿50 and up). The main pier is right at the end of the road from Trat, before you fall into the sea. The other two piers are several kilometres west of Laem Ngop and service the more expensive resorts. Boats to Khlong Son Beach take 1 hr, to Than Ma Yom Pier 50 mins, to Dan Mai Pier 35 mins. During peak season (Nov-May) there are almost hourly departures, some to Than Ma Yom Pier (east coast), others to the west coast. From the island, there are boats from 0730 from Than Ma Yom Pier (pick-ups leave from Hat Sai Khao). Between Jun and Oct – the low season – boats are more irregular and some routes do not operate at all because of rough seas combined with limited demand. **NB** It is only possible to reach Koh Chang in a day from Bangkok by taking an early morning bus (first a/c bus 0700, non-a/c 0420). Beware of *Sea Horse*, who reputedly run minibuses to Laem Ngop and drive deliberately slowly to miss the last ferry, so that they get to choose where you stay (and take a commission).

Car ferry Car ferries leave from Koh Chang Centrepoint Pier, northwest of Laem Ngop, four times daily. Another vehicular ferry leaves from Laem Ngop's third pier, at Ao Thammachat on Route 3156 – five departures daily.

Directory

Banks There are no banks on Koh Chang, and rates are poor at the guesthouses that change money. **Communications** There is a telephone (overseas calls possible but at exorbitant rates), money exchange, stamps and letterbox and general grocery store at the southern end of Sai Khao beach. **Medical services** Doctors: in Ao Khlong Son and in Ao Khlong Phrao near *Hobby Hut*. For more serious injuries patients are transferred to Laem Ngop. **Tourist offices** There is an information centre on Sai Khao beach where boat trips, fishing and snorkelling can all be arranged. **Useful addresses** Police: there are 6 policemen permanently at the station in Khlong Son. Thefts should be reported immediately so that if there are suspects the next boat to the mainland can be intercepted by the mainland police.

The Eastern Region

The Eastern Region

The Western Region

The Western Region

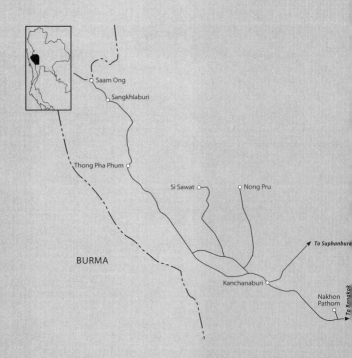

The Western Region stretches from the outskirts of Bangkok westwards to the frontier with Burma, and includes the historic city of Nakhon Pathom – with its imposing chedi – and Kanchanaburi, the site of the Bridge over the River Kwai. The total distance from Bangkok to Saam Ong (the Three Pagodas Pass), deep in the mountains that skirt the border between Thailand and Burma, is 370 km. Although Kanchanaburi is only 128 km from Bangkok, until quite recently the land beyond the town was forested and lawless. Guerrillas of the Communist Party of Thailand found sanctuary in the hills, and large expanses of the Western region were no-go areas for the Thai authorities. This has changed, and the region has now been extensively opened up for agriculture and tourism.

The region

For foreign visitors perhaps the most evocative name and sight in the Western region is the 'Bridge over the River Kwai'. This railway bridge, built by allied prisoners of war during the Second World War at great human cost, lies on the outskirts of the town of Kanchanaburi. The line was constructed under the orders of the Japanese to link Thailand with Burma and it is still possible to cross the bridge by train. However, the Western region has more to offer than just a 1940s vintage railway bridge (it isn't 1940s vintage in any case, having been largely rebuilt after the War). The town of Nakhon Pathom, 56 km from Bangkok, is the site of the largest chedi in Thailand – the 127 m-tall Phra Pathom Chedi. The town itself is one of the oldest in Thailand, dating back to the early centuries of the Christian era, and it later became a centre of the Dvaravati Kingdom. Further west, in the valleys that surround Kanchanaburi, a Danish prisoner-of-war working on the River Kwai Bridge found significant 4,000-year-old neolithic remains at Ban Kao. Close by are the ruins of the ancient Khmer city of Muang Singh. But the main reason why visitors take the trouble to travel west is to marvel at the scenery of the (fast disappearing) wilderness area beyond Kanchanaburi. This is especially true of the increasing numbers of Thai tourists aiming to escape from the pollution, noise and stress of Bangkok.

Route 323 runs west from Bangkok towards the Burmese border and the mountains of the Tenasserim range. Only 67 km from Bangkok is Nakhon Pathom – easily accessible as a day trip from the capital. The city may be the most ancient in Thailand, and at its heart is the largest chedi in the kingdom. Continuing northwest on Route 323 for another 55 km the road reaches the provincial capital of Kanchanaburi, site of the infamous Bridge over the River Kwai. The road from Bangkok to Kanchanaburi is not an attractive one; it is built up almost all the way. From here the road works upwards through secondary, degraded forest towards Burma. Saam Ong (or Three Pagodas Pass), 240 km from Kanchanaburi, marks the border.

Nakhon Pathom   นครปฐม

Phone code: 034
Colour map 3, grid B3
Population: 60,000

Nakhon Pathom, less than 70 km from Bangkok, is easily accessible on a day trip from the capital, whether by train or road, and makes a nifty getaway from the madness of the city. It is also possible to stop off here en route to places further west, like Kanchanaburi. While the Bangkok effect is noticeable even in Nakhon Pathom, the town does still have a provincial charm which makes it a refreshing counterpoint to the capital.

Sights
Nakhon Pathom is one of the oldest cities in Thailand, though there is little left to show for it

Some scholars believe that the great Indian Emperor Asoka dispatched two missionaries here from India in the third century BC to expound the teachings of Buddhism. It later became the centre of the Dvaravati Kingdom from the sixth to the 11th centuries (see page 743). The **Phra Pathom Chedi** is the largest in Thailand and dominates the heart of the town. The existing chedi was begun in 1853 at the instigation of King Mongkut (who visited its ruined predecessor while still a monk) and took 17 years to complete. The bell-shaped structure stands 127 m-high, encasing a much older, smaller Mon shrine (fourth century). This was added to in the Khmer period and subsequently sacked by the Burmese in 1057. A 19 m-high copy of the original can be seen on the outer platform to the east of the chedi. The new structure collapsed in a rainstorm and the present chedi was finally completed by King Chulalongkorn. The Thai habit of rebuilding over collapsed chedis is because, though the site remains holy irrespective of the

The Western Region

A Foot in the Door

★ *Kanchanaburi is the main draw of the Western region, with its infamous 'Bridge over the River Kwai', museums, river journeys, cave monasteries, and national parks.*

★ *Phra Pathom Chedi in Nakhon*

Pathom is Thailand's largest chedi standing 127 m high.

★ *Sangkhlaburi, close to the border with Burma, is interesting for its diverse inhabitants and wild surrounding countryside.*

condition of the monument, it is only by the act of building – of creating something new – that a monarch or benefactor accumulates religious merit.

The Phra Pathom Chedi is encrusted in gold and ochre tiles, supported by two ballustrades, and surrounded by a circular gallery. The inner walls of the gallery are inscribed in Pali with Buddhist teachings. The outer walls house 66 Buddha images in different positions. In addition to the chedi, the temple complex houses four viharns located at the cardinal points, and a bot to the south of the great stupa. The inner chamber of the east viharn, or **Viharn Luang**, displays a painting of the stupa depicting the original within it. The walls are covered with murals showing creatures and hermits paying homage to the chedi. The main entrance to the monastery is to the north, and the **Northern Viharn** contains a large standing Buddha which towers over visitors as they walk up the stairs towards the chedi. This image is known as **Phra Ruang Rojanarit**; it is a restored image, found by King Rama VI at Si Satchanalai while he was still a prince. At the base of the statue lie the ashes of the great king. The inner chamber of the Northern Viharn contains an image of the Buddha receiving gifts of a beehive and a jug of water from an elephant and a monkey. The bot was built during King Rama VII's reign and contains a Dvaravati-style Buddha image made of white stone, seated in a preaching position. ■ *0600-1800 Mon-Sun, ฿10.*

The Phra Pathom Chedi **National Museum** can be found just outside the south walls of the chedi and contains a good collection of Dvaravati sculpture and other works of art. ■ *0900-1200, 1300-1600 Wed-Sun, ฿20.* A second **museum** can be found near the east viharn; its collection is a hotch-potch of poorly displayed artefacts and mementoes including coins, shells, statues and amulets. ■ *0900-1200, 1300-1600 Wed-Sun.* A bustling **fruit market**, the Talaat Bon, is within easy walking distance to the north of the chedi. A speciality here is *khaaw lam*, sticky rice and beans cooked in bamboo.

Sanaam Chan Palace is to be found in a peaceful, leafy park about 10 minutes' saamlor ride west from the great chedi. The park is surrounded by a canal and contains a small zoo and playground. The palace was built by Rama VI, and is now used for government offices. It is of interest principally for its unusual interpretation of English Tudor, including a beamed and enclosed bridge crossing the moat. The park is surrounded by houses similar in style to those found in some of the colonial hill resorts of Southeast Asia.

The Western Region

• •
Nakhon Pathom place names

Phra Pathom Chedi
พระปฐมเจดีย์
Sanaam Chan Palace
พระราชวังสนามจันทร์

The **floating market** at **Damnoen Saduak** can be visited at the same time as a visit to Nakhon Pathom. ■ *Getting there: take a bus from the south side of the chedi, on Lung Phra Road (see page 121 for details).*

Excursions

The **Thai Human Imagery Museum** is also close to Nakhon Pathom, at Km 31 on the Pinklao-Nakhon Chaisri highway (see page 121).

Sleeping
■ on map
Price codes:
see inside front cover.
There are no particularly
attractive places
to stay here

A-B *Rose Garden Country Resort*, Km 32 marker, Phetkasem highway, Sampran, T321684, B2532276. A/c, cultural centre with traditional dancing and other shows, rather artificial. Rooms are OK, but the place is overpriced and showing its age. It is also some way out of town. **C** *Nakhon Inn*, 55 Rachwithi Rd, T251152, F532600. Restaurant, clean a/c rooms with satellite TV, room discounts available. Looks like the *Whale Hotel*, but is in a better state of repair, best in town with 70 rooms and some semblance of service. **C-D** *Whale*, 151/79 Rachwithi Rd, T251020. A stained concrete, dingy building and the a/c rooms are equally run-down. Expensive for the quality provided. Facilities include a karaoke bar, disco, golf driving range, snooker club, sauna. **D** *Mit Phaisan*, 120/30 Phayaphan Rd, T243122. Bright, though uncoordinated rooms, some a/c, with western bathrooms and Thai TV. Small restaurant (see Eating below). **E** *Mit Samphant*, 2/11 Lang Phra Rd, T252010. Basic, no windows, no expense lavished on décor, entrance through electrical shop, or in the side street. **E** *Siam*, 2/1-8 Rachdamnern Rd, T252230. Prison-like corridors, but the rooms, while basic, are clean with attached shower-rooms. Some a/c. Restaurant (see Eating below).

Eating
● on map
Price categories:
see inside front cover

There are a number of good Thai eateries around town and for those who might crave something rather culinarily closer to home, *Pizza Hut* and *Swensen's* have set up shop on the junction of Lang Phra and Phayaphan roads. **2** *Siam*, attached to the hotel of the same name. An a/c restaurant that tries a little too hard to be stylish, but it serves reasonably priced Thai food. **2** *Mit Phaisan*, attached to the hotel of the same name. Small restaurant serving the usual range of Thai dishes, well priced.

The **fruit market** (see above) is the best place for a snack or simple meal. Not only are there fruit sellers but also a range of stalls and carts selling Thai sweets, pastries and simple single-dish Thai meals.

Festivals
Sep *Food and Fruit Fair* (1st-7th), array of fruits grown in province, Thai and Chinese food preparation, floats and entertainment. **Nov** *Phra Pathom Chedi Fair* (over 7 days in Nov). The chedi is bathed in lights and food vendors, musicians, fortune tellers, monks and visitors throng the precincts and area around the chedi.

Nakhon Pathom

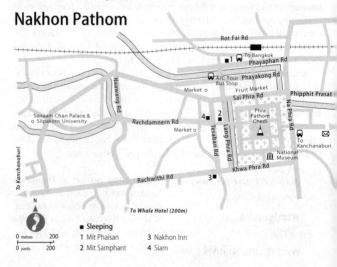

■ **Sleeping**
1 Mit Phaisan   3 Nakhon Inn
2 Mit Samphant   4 Siam

The Western Region

Train The station is to the north of the fruit market, an easy walk to/from the chedi.   **Transport**
Regular connections with Hualamphong station, Bangkok, 1 hr. Connections on to   *67 km to Bangkok*
Kanchanaburi and also to southern destinations including Phetburi, Hua Hin and
Surat Thani.

    Bus A/c buses stop to the north of the fruit market, an easy walk to the chedi. Reg-
ular a/c and non-a/c connections (every 15 mins) with Bangkok's Southern bus terminal, 1-2 hrs. Connections with Kanchanaburi.

Banks *First Bangkok City*, Sai Phra Rd (north of the chedi and fruit market). *Siam City*, Sai Phra Rd   **Directory**
(north of the chedi and fruit market). **Communications** Post Office: Tesaban Rd (running east
from the chedi).

Kanchanaburi   กาญจนบุรี

Famous for its proximity to the Bridge over the River Kwai and being close to the   *Phone code: 034*
Thai/Burmese border, this is an area of great natural beauty and is a good jump-   *Colour map 3, grid B3*
ing-off point for visits to national parks, trips on the River Kwai or excursions to   *Population: 45,000*
one of a number of waterfalls and caves. The province's wealth is derived from
gems mined at the Bo-Phloi mines, teak trading with Burma, sugar cane planta-
tions and tourism. It was from here that the Japanese set allied prisoners of war to
work on the construction of the notorious 'death railway', linking Thailand with
Burma during the Second World War (see box, page 524).

Ins and outs

There are regular connections by train with Nakhon Pathom and Bangkok. The jour-   **Getting there**
ney from Bangkok takes around 2½-3 hrs. Rather more people get here by bus and   *See also Transport,*
there are numerous daily departures from Bangkok (2 hrs on an a/c bus, rather longer   *page 533*
on a non-a/c bus). There are also bus connections with Nakhon Pathom (1½ hrs),
Suphanburi and onwards to Sangkhlaburi.

Bicycles, motorbikes and jeeps can all be hired in Kanchanaburi and offer the most   **Getting around**
flexible way to explore the surrounding countryside. Alternatively, saamlors provide
short-distance trips around town while tuk-tuks are handy for longer journeys. Rafts
and long-tail boats are available for charter on the river.

TAT, Saengchuto Rd, T511200 (walk south, towards Bangkok, from the market and   **Tourist offices**
bus station). A good first stop as it supplies up-to-date information on accommodation. Covers Kanchanaburi, Nakhon Pathom, Samut Sakhon and Samut Songkhram.

Background

The province of Kanchanaburi is becoming increasingly popular with Thai
tourists trying to 'get away from it all' and communing with nature. This is
reflected in the large number of resorts and jungle lodges that have been developed in recent years, which are dotted across the countryside, promising peace
and tranquility. The Bangkok equivalent of the yuppie can be seen frequenting
the many floating restaurants and discos found along the river. The tourist
office, TAT, claims that two million tourists visit Kanchanaburi each year, of
whom the great majority – about 1,700,000 – are Thai.

  As with so many tourist success stories, Kanchanaburi has its downside. In
this case, it is pollution from the 900-odd raft-based guesthouse and restaurant
operations. Almost none of the rafts has water treatment or waste disposal

The Western Region

systems. This was fine when there were just a handful of rafts and a few thousand tourists a year. Now the numbers are far greater and public health officials have detected a significant rise in water pollution. Of course, everyone blames everyone else. The raft operations claim that it is effluent and discharges from factories which are the problem, not them. This, frankly, is hard to believe.

Kanchanaburi itself was only established in the 1830s, although the ruins of Muang Singh (see Excursions, below) over 40 km to the west date from the Khmer period. On entering the town (called Muang Kan by most locals), visitors may notice the fish-shaped street signs. The fish in question is the *yisok*, a small freshwater fish found in the rivers of the province; it is the symbol of Kanchanaburi. Another slice of Thai fauna for which this area of Thailand is known is Kitti's hog-nosed bat. This bat – the smallest in the world, with a body the size of a bumble-bee – was discovered in 1973 by Dr Kitti Thonglongya in limestone caves near the River Kwai Bridge.

Sights

JEATH War Museum This museum (the letters in its name denoting the countries involved) can be found by the river, at the end of Wisuttharangsi Road, where there is a reconstruction of a prisoner of war camp and other war memorabilia. The most interesting element of the display are the photographs of life and work on the railway. The museum, which is more of a display than a museum, was established in 1977 and is run by the monks of Wat Chanasongkhram. As the museum's brochure explains, it has been constructed 'not for the maintenance of hatred among human beings but to warn and teach us the lesson of how terrible war is'. ■ 0830-1800 Mon-Sun, ฿30 (no photographs).

Kanchanaburi War Cemetery This cemetery, otherwise known as Don Rak, is about 1½ km from the centre of town on Saengchuto Road, travelling northwest. Immaculately maintained

● ●

Kanchanaburi place names

Ban Kao
บ้านเก่า

Bridge over the River Kwai
สะพานแม่น้ำแคว

Daowadung Caves
ถ้ำดาวดึงส์

Death Railway
ทางรถไฟสายมรณะ

Erawan National Park
อุทยานแห่งชาติเอราวัณ

Muang Singh Historical Park
อุทยานประวัติศาสตร์เมืองเก่า

Phrathat Caves
ถ้ำพระธาตุ

Phu Phra caves
ถ้ำภูพระ

Sai Yok National Park
อุทยานแห่งชาติไทรโยค

Tha Thungna Dam
ถ้ำพระธาตุ

Wat Tham Kao Noi
วัดถ้ำเขาน้อย

Wat Tham Kao Poon
วัดถ้ำเขาปูน

Wat Tham Kun Phaen
วัดถ้ำขุนแผน

Wat Tham Mongkorn Thong
วัดถ้ำมังกรทอง

Wat Tham Sua
วัดถ้ำเสือ

by the Commonwealth Cemeteries Commission, 6,982 Allied servicemen are buried here, most of whom died as prisoners of war whilst they built the Burma railway. ■ *0800-1700 Mon-Sun, or you can always look over the gates. Getting there: to get there, walk, hire a bicycle (฿20 a day) or take a saamlor.*

Situated 2 km south of town, this cemetery is small, peaceful and well kept, with the graves of 1,750 prisoners of war. ■ *Getting there: by boat from in front of the town gates, or by tuk-tuk or bicycle.* **Chungkai (UK) War Cemetery**

Situated 3-4 km north of the town on Saengchuto Road, the Bridge over the River Kwai (pronounced Kway in Thai, not Kwai) is architecturally unexciting and is of purely historical interest. The central span was destroyed by Allied bombing towards the end of the war, and has been rebuilt in a different style. Visitors can walk over the bridge, visit the **Second World War Museum** and **Art Gallery** (open: 0900-1630 Monday-Sunday, admission ฿30) or browse in the many souvenir stalls. The museum is an odd affair with some displays relating to the bridge and the prisoners of war who worked and died here, along with a collection of Thai weaponry and amulets, and a collection of astonishingly bad portraits of Thai kings (although, to be fair, no one knows what the early kings looked like, so these are more interesting for the insight they provide into the history of Thai dress). The museum was built and endowed by one family and provides a reasonable overview of Thai history. There is an old locomotive close to the bridge and several restaurants along the riverbank (and on the river). It is possible to ride an elephant on the other side of the bridge. ■ *A 10-min ride costs ฿50, for a longer 4 hr ride it costs ฿700 for 1 person, ฿1,200 for 2 people. Boats can be rented at the bridge. Getting there: take a saamlor, hire a bicycle, catch a songthaew or board the train which travels from the town's station to the bridge.* **Bridge over the River Kwai**

Muang Kan's **lak muang** (city pillar), encrusted in gold leaf and draped with flowers, can be seen in the middle of Lak Muang Road. Close by are the gates to Kanchanaburi town. Walking through the gates and turning right (north) is the old and most attractive part of town with wooden shophouses.

Excursions

Situated 5 km southwest of town, this wat is a few kilometres on from the Chungkai Cemetery. Early in 1996 the cave wat was the site of the murder by a Thai monk of British tourist Johanne Masheder (the cave where the murder took place is closed, permanently). The crime shook Thailand's religious establishment and the abbot of the monastery was suspended for neglect. Wat Tham Kao Poon is rather a gaudy temple with caves attached. Follow the arrows through the cave system. The tunnel is narrow in places and large individuals may find it a squeeze. The kitsch lighting is almost worth the visit in itself. There is a large Buddha image at the bottom of the system (and smaller ones elsewhere), as well as cells (*kutis*) in which monks can meditate. Intrepid explorers will find they emerge at the back of the hill. ■ *No entrance fee to the caves, but visitors are encouraged to make a contribution to the maintenance of the monastery (฿10-20). Getting there: hire a bicycle or tuk-tuk or charter a boat from in front of the town gates.* **Wat Tham Kao Poon**

Nestling in foothills, 5½ km south of town, is this unimpressive wat with a complex of unimpressive limestone caves attached. These are reached by walking up a long flight of stairs with dragons forming the balustrades. Inside, there are yet more meditation cells (there must be a great number of hermits in **Wat Tham Mongkorn Thong**

The Western Region

The death railway

The River Kwai will be forever associated with a small bridge and a bloody railway.

For the Japanese high command during the Second World War, the logic of building a rail link between Siam and Burma was clear. They lacked the merchant fleet to carry supplies to and from their fast-expanding empire, and it would cut almost 2,000 km off the journey from Japan to Rangoon. It was perceived to be crucial to the Japanese war effort. The problem was that the Japanese lacked the labour to construct the line through some of the wettest and most inhospitable land in the region. They estimated that, given their resources, it would take five to six years to finish. The solution to their dilemma was simple: to employ some of the 300,000 POWs who had so far been captured, most of whom were being unproductively incarcerated on Singapore.

Work began in June 1942. The Japanese engineer Fatamatsu chose a route which ran along the river valley of the Kwai Noi, a decision which has since been much criticized because of the harshness of the terrain. But the river was a useful artery of communication, and this allowed construction to begin simultaneously in a number of places, a

crucial factor when speed was of the essence. Most of the materials were locally sourced; there was simply not the fleet capacity to import materials and equipment from Japan. As a result, no less than 680 of the 688 bridges built were constructed of timber. Rails were pillaged from secondary tracks in Burma and Malaya, and bamboo and softwoods were extensively used in construction. In all, over 3,000,000 cu m of rock were shifted, 15 km of bridges built and 415 km of track laid. The workforce at its peak numbered 61,000 Allied POWs and an estimated 250,000 Asians. Work was hard; a prisoner, Naylor wrote:

"We started work the day after we arrived, carrying huge baulks of timber. It was the heaviest work I have ever known; the Japs drove us on and by nightfall I was so tired and sore that I could not eat my dinner and just crawled on to the bed and fell asleep. The next day was spent carrying stretchers of earth, also heavy work and incredibly monotonous. The hours were 0830 to 1930 with an hour for lunch."

The Japanese, but particularly the Korean overseers, adopted a harsh code of discipline – face-slapping, blows with rifle butts, standing erect for hours on end, and

Kanchanaburi), bats and bat-like smells (not recommended for the squeamish). The caves are narrow in places and visitors may have to crawl on their hands and knees. The exit is up a short steel ladder at the end of the cave system, halfway up the hill. Visitors are expected to make a small contribution before entering the caves. ■ *Getting there: rather difficult to reach by public transport; occasional buses from the bus station, or cross the river by ferryboat at Chukkadon Pier, or charter a tuk-tuk or songthaew.*

Death Railway & Hell Fire Pass At the end of the Second World War the Japanese – or rather their prisoners – had laid 415 km of track of possibly the most infamous stretch of line anywhere in the world. Of this, just 130 km of the **Death Railway** remain, from Nong Pradook station in the neighbouring province of Ratchaburi through to the small town of Nam Tok. From Kanchanaburi to Nam Tok the journey is some 77 scenically dramatic kilometres. The train stops at the ancient Khmer site of Muang Singh en route (see below). Construction has been underway on a 5-km extension to the line to take tourists to the waterfall (*nam tok*) itself. At this stage the line is close to the infamous 'Hellfire Pass'. Around 400 prisoners of war died while cutting the pass out of the limestone rock, 69 of them beaten to death by Japanese and Korean guards. The name for the pass is said to have been bestowed by one of the prisoners of war who, looking down on his solitary confinement for weeks in small cells made of mud and bamboo. The poor diet meant that the men were able to work at only half-pace, although it is notable that the Australians – who were both bigger and in better condition – before they arrived, were usually allotted to do the heavier work. By 1943, some of the men were in an appalling state. In Colonel Toosey's report of October 1945, he wrote:

'On one occasion a party of 60, mostly stretcher cases, were dumped off a train in a paddy field some two miles from the Camp in the pouring rain at 0300 hours. As a typical example I can remember one man who was so thin that he could be lifted easily in one arm. His hair was growing down his back and was full of maggots; his clothing consisted of a ragged pair of shorts soaked with dysentery excreta; he was lousy and covered with flies all the time. He was so weak that he was unable to lift his head to brush away the flies which were clustered on his eyes and on the sore places of his body. I forced the Japanese Staff to come and look at these parties, which could be smelt for some hundreds of yards, but with the exception of the Camp Comdt. they showed no signs of sympathy, and

sometimes merely laughed.' (Quoted in Davies, 1991:116).

The railway was finished in late 1943, the line from Nong Pladuk being linked with that from Burma on 17 October. For the POWs it was not the end, however; even after the Japanese capitulated on 10 August 1945, the men had to wait for some while before they were liberated. During this period of limbo, Allied officers were worried most about venereal disease, and Colonel Toosey radioed to Delhi for 10,000 condoms to be dropped by air – an incredible thought given the physical condition of the former POWs. In all, 16,000 allied prisoners lost their lives and Kanchanaburi contains the graves of 7,000 of the victims in two war cemeteries. Less well known are the 75,000 Asian forced labourers who also died constructing the railway. Their sufferings are not celebrated.

In August 1996 a plan was launched to rebuild the railway. Not only would this require great engineering expertise (it is said that 100 bridges spanned the deep gorges and rivers), but the proposal is deeply offensive to the relatives of those who lost their lives here; reportedly one man died for every sleeper laid.

The Western Region

comrades working below at night by the glow of numerous open fires, remarked that the sight was like 'the jaws of hell'. Australian Rod Beattie, with the support and financial assistance of the Australian government, has developed the pass as a memorial to those who died. He has cut a path to the pass and built a museum that opened in 1998. It is fascinating and informative. Clear, well-written wall panels surrounded by photographs, along with some reproduction objects, provide a very moving account of the cutting of the pass. There is also a good seven-minute introductory video. From here it is possible to walk a fair distance of the railway route (the rails no longer exist); stout shoes recommended. There are two routes: the full circuit is 4½ km-long and ends at Hellfire Pass itself; or the Konyu Cutting. ■ *There is no admission fee, but donations requested (most visitors leave ฿100). Getting there: 2 trains each way daily, leaving Kanchanaburi at 1045 and 1637, with return trains at 0525 and 1300, approximately 2 hrs. It is also possible to reach the pass by road. Take a bus travelling north on Route 323. Around 80 km from Kanchanaburi, on the left hand side of the road, is a Royal Thai Army farm (at the Km 66 marker). A track here leads through the farm and to a steep path that leads, after about 1 km, to the pass; it is signposted. If travelling by public bus, ask to be let off at the* suan thahaan *(army farm). Finally, and most easily, there are numerous organized tours to Hellfire Pass (see Tours below).*

Wat Tham Sua & Wat Tham Kao Noi Wat Tham Sua and Wat Tham Kao Noi lie 20 km southeast of Kanchanaburi. The main temple is a strange, pagoda-like affair perched on a hilly outcrop, and can be seen from afar. At the base of the hill is a Chinese temple, and a short walk further is the steep dragon-lined staircase that leads up the hill to the wat itself. The pagoda is a weird amalgam of Chinese and Thai, new and old (it contains modern steel windows topped with fluorescent lights). The view of the surrounding area is worth the climb. The wat also has a series of caves. The **Vajiralongkorn Dam** is not far away. ■ *Getting there: by hired motorbike or chartered tuk-tuk/songthaew.*

Phu Phra Caves & Wat Tham Kun Phaen Phu Phra caves and Wat Tham Kun Phaen are about 20 km north of town, just off Route 323 to Sangkhlaburi. The wat and its associated caves nestle in foothills which rise up towards Burma. Back on Route 323 is the **Kanchanaburi Cultural Centre**, with a collection of handicrafts, artefacts and historical exhibits. ■ *Getting there: by bus 8203 (tell the bus conductor where you want to get off), or hire a motorbike or songthaew/tuk-tuk.*

Ban Kao This neolithic site dating from around 2000 BC, 35 km from Kanchanaburi, was discovered by one of the Danish prisoners of war working on the death railway. It was not until 1961 that a Thai-Danish archaeological team confirmed the find and its significance. A small archaeological museum near to the site houses many of the bones and artefacts. ■ *0900-1600 Wed-Sun, ฿40. Getting there: hire a tuk-tuk/songthaew or a motorbike. It is also possible to take the train to Thakilen station and then walk or catch a motorcycle taxi the final 6 km to the site itself.* For non-archaeologists the museum is not particularly exciting, but it is en route to Muang Singh Historical Park, 8 km away.

Muang Singh Historical Park This ancient Khmer town, the 'city of lions', is situated on the banks of the Kwai Noi River – about 45 km west of Kanchanaburi town. It is not as complete or impressive as other archaeological sites in Thailand, but is peaceful and interesting to wander around. The site covers several square kilometres, but the main central prang and associated buildings are concentrated over a small area. The city is built of deep red laterite, and reached its apogee during the 12th-13th centuries when it flourished as a trading node linking Siam with the Indian Ocean. The city represents an artistic and strategic outlier of the great Cambodian Empire (perhaps the furthest west), and it is mentioned in inscriptions from the reign of the Khmer King Jayavarman VII. The moat and original outer walls can still be seen and some archaeologists have postulated that the remains provide evidence that an advanced system of water control was in use. On the inside of the north wall of the major shrine is a carving of a four-armed figure – probably Avalokitesvara Bodhisattva (the future Buddha). The discovery of a 160 cm-high stone statue of a Bodhisattva (now on display in the National Museum in Bangkok) indicates that the building was used as a Mahayana Buddhist shrine. Much of the stucco decoration that once covered the buildings has disappeared and no inscriptions have been discovered. Restaurants and refreshments are available close to the central ruins. ■ *0800-1700, Mon-Sun ฿4. Getting there: hire a tuk-tuk/songthaew or motorbike, or take the train to Thakilen station – it is about a 1½ km walk from here and is easy to find, or hitch a lift.*

Khao Phang & Sai Yok Noi waterfall Situated 60 km northwest of Kanchanaburi on Route 323, Khao Phang and Sai Yok Noi waterfall are only impressive in the wet season (July-September), and swimming in the pools below the falls is also best during this season. Close by are the **Vang Ba Dalh** caves. ■ *Getting there: take bus 8203 from Kanchanaburi* *town, 1 hr. Buses leave every 30 mins between 0645 and 1800. It is 1 km to the falls and 2 km to the caves (the sign for the falls is in Thai only, so follow signs to the cave which are in English).*

Sai Yok National Park lies 104 km northwest of Kanchanaburi. The park's main attraction is the **Sai Yok Yai waterfall**. Also near Sai Yok Yai are the **Daowadung Caves** (30 minutes north by boat from the falls and then a 3 km walk). The following places to stay are all near the waterfall: **A** *Panthawee Raft*, T512572, and **B** *See Pee Nong Raft*, T2156224, have a few rafts in the upmarket category. **B-E** *Kwai Noi Rafthouse*, T591075, has a small collection of floating rooms. **B-C** Ranthawee Raft, T51257, only has four rooms. **A-D** Rom Suk Saiyok Yai Raft, 231/3 Moo 7, T516130, has a wide range of rooms and camping facilities. ■ *Best time to visit: May-Dec. Getting there: boats can be hired from Pak Saeng pier in Tambon Tha Saaw, about 50 km north of Kanchanaburi town. A boat (maximum 10 people) to the park (including the Lawa caves and Sai Yok Yai waterfall), should cost about ฿1,200 per boat (seating 10-12 people) (or go on a tour) and the trip will take 2½ hrs upstream and 1½ hrs down. There are also buses from Kanchanaburi to the park, 1 hr.*

Sai Yok National Park
Tigers & elephants still inhabit this wild region of stunning scenery, stretching to the Burmese border

Sixty five kilometres north of Kanchanaburi is this park, which covers 550 sq km. It is an area of great natural beauty, with some impressive waterfalls, the Erawan Falls, which make this national park reputedly Thailand's most popular. The best time to visit is during the rainy season since the falls are not nearly as dramatic during the dry season. It is a 10 minute walk from the bus station to the park gates, another 15 minutes to the reception centre, and then a further 10 minutes to the first of the series of seven falls over 1½ km that constitute the **Erawan Falls**. The first level of the falls is the most popular with swimmers and picnickers. Level three is very beautiful, and level seven is well worth the steep climb. Refreshing pools await the trekker who makes the precarious climb to the top fall. The impressive **Phrathat Caves** are located about 10 km northwest of headquarters, a good hike or easy drive. An excellent place to see stalagtites and stalagmites in cavernous quantities. Ask at reception for directions.

Erawan National Park

Arguably the most striking waterfalls in this area are those at **Huay Khamin**, some way north of the Phrathat Caves. Situated 108 km from town to the west of the Srinakharin Reservoir, the falls are awkward to reach independently but tour companies will provide arranged trips. En route to Erawan the road passes the **Tha Thungna Dam**. Continuing north on Route 3199, past Erawan, the road reaches the **Srinakharind Dam** (named after the present Crown Princess of Thailand) and reservoir. This whole area has been at the centre of an intense environmental controversy over the construction of a third dam upriver from the Srinakharin Dam (which is just above the Erawan Falls). The proposed Nam Choan Dam would have flooded large areas of the Thung Yai and Huai Kha Khaeng wildlife sanctuaries, and destroyed rare stands of riverine tropical forest. The fact that public pressure ensured that the plans were shelved in 1989 represents the first significant victory for environmentalists in Thailand, and they are now a political force to be reckoned with. In 1992 the two sanctuaries were declared Southeast Asia's first Natural World Heritage Site by UNESCO, vindicating the environmentalists' stand.

There are some park bungalows that can be rented, although they tend to sleep large numbers so are not very appropriate for most visitors. However, it is possible to pitch a tent and staff will also sometimes find visitors somewhere to spend the night. There are two bungalow operations outside the park boundaries, before the entrance gates: the *Erawan Resort Guesthouse* and the *Phu Daeng Resort*. ■ *0600-1800 Mon-Sun, ฿25 for adults. Getting there: regular buses*

The Western Region

*(8170) every 50 mins from 0800 onwards from Kanchanaburi, 1½-2 hrs. **NB** The last bus back to Kanchanaburi leaves Erawan at 1600.*

Bo Phloi At the centre of one of Thailand's main gem-mining areas, 50 km north of town, is Bo Phloi. Here are some eight open-cast mines, extracting sapphires, onyx and semi-precious stones, and a number of polishing plants (see page 501). Displays of local production techniques are given. ■ *Getting there: bus 325 from Kanchanaburi bus station, 1½ hrs.*

Tham Than Lot Officially called the **Chalerm Rattanakosin National Park** (locals prefer the
National Park former name), this park lies around 100 km north of Kanchanaburi, past Bo Phloi and on along Route 398 past the town of **Nong Pru**. The park covers just 60 sq km, making it the smallest park in the province, and was established in 1980. (In 1982 its name was changed from Tham Than Lot to Chalerm Rattanakosin in commemoration of the bicentenery of the Chakri dynasty and the founding of Bangkok.)

The park encompasses a portion of the Tenasserim range of mountains that form the border between Thailand and Burma. Because of the park's small size it would be expected that wildlife would be limited. However, because this protected area abuts the much larger Srinakharin and Erawan national parks, the wildlife is surprisingly varied and includes small populations of Asiatic black bear, white-handed gibbon, elephant and serow, as well as smaller mammals and 68 species of bird from Indian pied hornbills to greater golden-backed woodpeckers. There is even talk that there may be tigers here. The highest peak is Khao Khampaeng, which rises to 1,260 m. Within easy walking of park HQ (where there is a visitors' centre) is **Than Lot Noi Cave**, after which the park was named. The cave reaches around 300 m into the mountain side. A trail leads from here for around 2 km to another cave, **Than Lot Yai**, where there is a small Buddhist shrine. The trail itself, which follows the course of the Kraphroi River, passes waterfalls and impressive stands of dipterocarps. The park is well worth a day trip for an escape away from the tourist route. There are bungalows in the park and it is also possible to camp. Alternatively, stay a night at the only hotel in the neighbouring town of Nong Pru (฿100 for fan and attached bathroom) – cheaper than staying in the park. ■ *Getting there: there are regular connections between Kanchanaburi and Nong Pru. The road to the park cuts off left from Route 3086 shortly before entering Nong Pru; the park entrance is 22 km from this turn-off. During the week it is usually necessary to charter a motorcycle or songthaew to the park, but at weekends there is a public service from Nong Pru.*

Tours There are a great many companies offering a similar choice of excursions: jungle trekking, elephant rides, bamboo rafting, visits to Hellfire Pass and various waterfalls. The most notable companies are listed under Tour operators, below. Enquiries about tours can be made at the TAT office, where there is also information on the very large number of resorts and basic raft huts in the province. In addition, hotels and guesthouses are a good source of information. In Bangkok virtually every hotel or tour office will be able to offer a day tour (or longer) to Kanchanaburi and surrounding sights.

Raft and boat trips, and motorized raft restaurants and discos are now very popular. At the weekends there can be hundreds of rafts blaring music of varying quality. In other words, don't expect a quiet drift with nothing but the sounds of birdsong and the gentle bubble of the water. Raft trips are not very easily organized oneself; it is probably better to go through a tour operator. The *River Kwai Village Hotel* organizes river tours to the Lawa Caves and Sai

Yok Yai Falls. The *BT Travel Co Ltd* organizes raft trips to the Chungkai Cemetery, together with fishing and swimming on the River Kwai Noi. They also arrange air-conditioned minibus tours to Muang Singh Historical Park, Ban Kao, Sai Yok Noi and elsewhere.

The State Railways of Thailand offer a worthwhile all-day tour from Bangkok to Kanchanaburi on weekends and holidays. The train leaves Thonburi station at 0615, stopping at Nakhon Pathom (40 minutes' stop) and the River Kwai Bridge (30 minutes' stop), and arriving at Nam Tok at 1130. A minibus service then goes to Khao Pang/Sai Yok Noi waterfall, the last bus leaving the falls for Nam Tok station at 1410. The train then leaves Nam Tok at 1430, arriving in Kanchanaburi at 1605 (45 minutes' stop to visit the prisoner of war cemetery) and returning to Bangkok at 1930. The State Railways also offer a number of other tours, with overnight stays, rafting and fishing. For details on all tours contact the Railway Advance Book Office at Hualamphong Station in Bangkok, T2256964. Advance booking recommended. A shorter train trip can be organized from Kanchanaburi to Nam Tok, leaving daily at 1030. Contact the *Train Travel Tour Company*, T561052, or Kanchanaburi Train Station, T511285.

Essentials

NB Disco boats on the river can cause noise pollution and the guesthouses on the river bear the brunt of the problem. However, the boats are only really active at weekends and usually stop no later than 2000.

Sleeping
■ *on map, page 530*
Price codes:
see inside front cover

AL-B *Felix River Kwai Hotel*, 9/1 Moo 3 Thamakhom, T515061, F515086. North of the bridge on the west bank of Kwai Yai River is this hotel, the most luxurious in town. With 255 rooms it is rather rambling, but it has all the facilities you'd expect from a first-class establishment. **A-B** *River Kwai*, 284/3-16 Saengchuto Rd, T511184, F511269. A/c, restaurant, pool, large unappealing and rather tatty hotel. Big discounts available during the week, popular with tour groups, large massage parlour next door indicative of the tone of the place. **C** *Mittapan Hotel*, 244, Moo 2 Saengchuto Rd, T515906. A little far from town, but it has a pool, restaurants and pleasant a/c rooms. **C-D** *MK*, Saengchuto Rd (opposite *River Kwai Hotel*, see above), T511184/511269, F511269. Clean, a/c motel-style rooms with good mosquito screens, TV and shower-room. Beauty salon, golf shop and laundry. **C-E** *Bamboo House*, 3-5 Soi Vietnam, Tha Makham, T512532. A quiet secluded spot with a range of accommodation from a/c wooden bungalows to floating bamboo huts with mattresses on the floor. Pleasant garden area.

D-E *Prasopsuk*, 677 Saengchuto Rd, T511777. Clean rooms with shower, TV and some with a/c. Good restaurant (see Eating below). **D** *Rick's Lodge*, 48/5 Rong Heeb Oil 2 Rd, T514831, F514831. Eleven rather unusual split-level A-frame huts with beds on top and sitting-room and bathroom below. Some rooms have river views. Expensive restaurant with magnificent views over mountains and jungle, serves Thai and European food. Organizes treks and tours, and Rick the owner is helpful. Recommended. **D** *VL*, 18/11 Saengchuto Rd, T513546. Some a/c, small restaurant, 3-storey block. Quiet, cool and secluded large rooms (with bathrooms) away from a busy road. Tasteful décor and breakfast is served in an attractive shady area. **D-E** *Sam's River Raft House*, Soi Rong Heeb Oil, Mae Nam Kwai Rd, T624231. Perhaps compensating for where *Sam's* other 2 ventures stumble, this new guesthouse is otherwise similar to its brothers but has good views across the river. **D-E** *Sam's House*, 14/1 Mae Nam Kwai Rd, T515956. Good wooden huts with toilets, and balconies on the mangrovesque edge of the Kwai – good value. Some a/c, though slightly let down by having no access to the river. Good restaurant (see Eating below). **D-E** *Sam's Place*,

The Western Region

Kanchanaburi

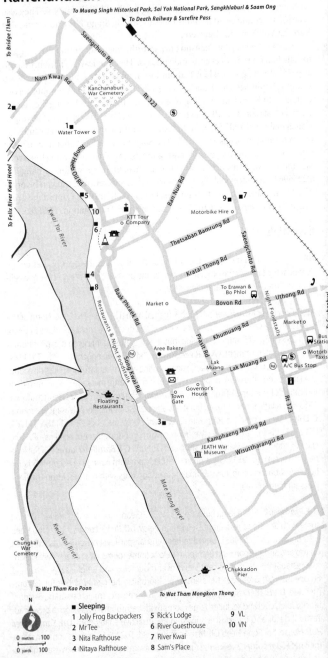

To Muang Singh Historical Park, Sai Yok National Park, Sangkhlaburi & Saam Ong

To Death Railway & Surefire Pass

To Bridge (1km)

Saengchuto Rd

Nam Kwai Rd

Kanchanaburi War Cemetery

Rt 323

Water Tower

To Felix River Kwai Hotel

Kwai Yai River

Rong Heeb Oil Rd

KTT Tour Company

Ban Nue Rd

Motorbike Hire

Thetsaban Bamrung Rd

Kratai Thong Rd

Saengchuto Rd

Restaurants & Night Foodstalls

Baak Phraek Rd

Market

To Erawan & Bo Phloi

Bovon Rd

Uthong Rd

Night Foodstalls

Market

Bus Station

Song Kwai Rd

Aree Bakery

Khumuang Rd

Prasit Rd

Lak Muang

Lak Muang Rd

Motorb Taxis

A/C Bus Stop

Floating Restaurants

Town Gate

Governor's House

Kamphaeng Muang Rd

JEATH War Museum

Wisuttharangsi Rd

Moe Klong River

Kwai Noi River

Chungkai War Cemetery

To Wat Tham Kao Poon

To Wat Tham Mongkorn Thong

Chukkadon Pier

N

0 metres 100
0 yards 100

■ Sleeping

1 Jolly Frog Backpackers	5 Rick's Lodge	9 VL
2 Mr Tee	6 River Guesthouse	10 VN
3 Nita Rafthouse	7 River Kwai	
4 Nitaya Rafthouse	8 Sam's Place	

The Western Region

7/3 Song Kwai Rd, T513971. Convenient central location next to the river. Large bamboo huts, some with a/c and some with good attached bathrooms. The tranquillity, however, has been somewhat disrupted by the major road bridge above the accommodation. Attractively designed, tours organized, very basic plumbing arrangements, floating restaurant next door has rather noisy crooners late into the night. Recommended. **D-E** *Sugar Cane*, 22 Soi Pakstan, Mae Nam Kwai Rd, T624520. With only 12 bamboo bungalows and no room for expansion, this secluded spot provides a retreat from the hordes while maintaining a good location. Spotlessly clean. Restaurant commands fantastic views over the river. Recommended.

E *Apple's Guesthouse (Krathom Thai)*, 293 Mae Nam Kwai Rd, T512017. This is an extremely good guesthouse, with very clean, comfortable mattresses and private showers. The proprietors, Apple and Noi, make every effort to be welcoming and helpful. Sadly, there is no direct access to the river, but plans to amend this are afoot. Very good restaurant (see Eating below). Recommended. **D-E** *Jolly Frog Backpackers*, 28 Mae Nam Kwai Rd, T514579. This popular well established guesthouse, with its attractive garden overlooking the river, is perhaps a little too large to be peaceful, but it has good travel and local tour information. It also offers a wide range of vegetarian, Thai and European food in an affordable restaurant. English and German speaking management, convivial atmosphere, canoes for rent. **E** *Mr Tee*, 12 Soi Laos, River Kwai Rd, north of town. Good, cleanish rooms in a 2-storey wooden block. Ground floor rooms have fans, some rooms have showers. Expensive restaurant, attractive quiet location on the river, good value. Recommended. **E-F** *C&C Guesthouse*, 265/2 Mae Nam Kwai Rd, Soi England, T624527-8. Pleasant accommodation, the cheapest rooms are in bamboo rafthouses, some with no fan, though a quick dip in the river provides a convenient cooling option. Tours available. Recommended. **E-F** *J Guesthouse*, 32/4 Rong Heeb Oil Rd, T620307. Novel huts constructed out of chipboard, quite clean, some have reasonable shower rooms and good views. Restaurant. **E-F** *Nita Rafthouse*, 27/1 Phakphrak Rd, T514521. Good restaurant (see Eating below). Small basic bamboo-lined rooms (some **F**), but very friendly owner with good English. All rooms float on the river and though close to the disco boats, guests are surprisingly untroubled. Boats, motorbike and bike for hire, videos at night. Recommended. **E-F** *Nitaya Rafthouse*, Song Kwai Rd (northern end), T513341. *Nitaya's* glory years were about 10 years ago, but now it seems to be in terminal decline, not helped by the construction of a flyover which obscures the entrance. Pleasant owner and pet boa constrictor. **D-F** *VN Guesthouse*, 44 Rong Heeb Oil 2 Rd, T514082. Next to the river with good views. Rooms clean but dark and bland. Communal washrooms are rather basic. Attractive, but quite expensive restaurant. **E-F** *J Guesthouse*, Rong Heeb Oil Rod (next to the *River Guesthouse*). On the river with floating raft houses and a good restaurant (though the beer is priced a little steeply!); run by a welcoming Thai couple, 16 clean rooms. **F** *River Guesthouse*, 42 Rong Heeb Oil Rd, T512491. Well laid out river complex with small bamboo huts, some with shower rooms, others without fans (cheapest rooms on the river with great views). Very popular traveller's hangout, some recent visitors have complained about the state of the toilet facilities, videos nightly. Tasty Thai restaurant.

Resorts

There are a large number of 'back to nature' resorts around Kanchanaburi. These are in the vicinity of the town; most cater for Thai tourists

A-B *Home Phu Toey*, 118 Moo 8, Tambon Thasao, T02-6211510. Near Sai Yok Waterfall, just north of Lawa Caves, a/c, restaurant, lake for swimming, accommodation in Thai-style huts, very attractive location. **A-B** *River Kwai Jungle House*, 96/1 Mu 3, Amphoe Sai Yok, 40 km from Kanchanaburi, near Muang Singh Historical Park, T561052. Rattan bungalows float on the river. **A** *Legacy River Kwai Resort*, 129 Moo 2, Tambon Klandoe, T213-9872-6, F515995, www.stcgroup-th.com/thlegacy, thlegacy@stcgroup-th.com. 154 log cabins and attractive position. A/c, TV, en suite etc. All facilities and interesting courses on macrobiotic diets, yoga, ayurvedic massage, and so on. **A** *River Kwai Village*, 74/12 Moo 4 Thasao Sai Yok, 70 km northwest of town, near Nam Tok, T634454, rkvh@bkk2000.com A/c, restaurant, pool, hotel and raft accommodation in remote setting. **B** *Kasem Island Resort*, 27 Chaichumphon Rd, T513359, F2556303. On an island on the Mae Klong, but close to the town centre and therefore accessible, restaurant, attractive, clean rafts.

Eating
Price categories: see inside front cover

Thai and Chinese Cheap: *Krathom Thais Restaurant*, 293 Mai Nam Kwai Rd (attached to *Apple's Guesthouse*), the enthusiastic cooks produce delicious Thai food here. *Nita's Rafthouse Restaurant*, 27/1 Phakpak Rd. Good Thai and Chinese food served in relaxed environs of an open-air raft, with cushions for seating. *Sugar Canes Restaurant*, 22 Soi Pakistan, Mae Nam Kwai Rd. Although the menu is limited, this restaurant has a beautiful view of the river. *The River Kwai Floating Restaurant*, right next to the famed bridge. This restaurant has a wide menu of mainly Thai and Chinese food. Its wood and thatch construction is far superior to the ugly concrete and plastic *River Kwai Restaurant*. **Seriously cheap**: *Woof*, Mae Nam Kwai Rd. An exclusively vegetarian restaurant serving mainly Thai food at reasonable prices. *The Brew House*, outstanding value for money. Tasty Thai food and cheap beer served at this friendly wood and thatch open-air establishment. Recommended.

Western food Cheap *Jolly Frogs Restaurant*, 28 Mae Nam Kwai Rd. A wide range of western and Thai grub with plenty of tourist information plastered on the walls. *Sams*, all of *Sams* establishments have restaurants producing delectable Thai food and some of the best western food available in town. *Prasopsuk Restaurant*, 677 Saengchuto Rd. A large, clean restaurant serving a wide range of dishes attached to the hotel of the same name.

Foodstalls Numerous stalls set up along the river in the evening, and there is also an excellent night market with a great range of food available in the vicinity of the bus station. Recommended.

Bakeries and breakfast *Aree Bakery*, Baak Phraek Rd. Delicious ice-creams and breakfasts. *Sii Fa Bakery*, by bus terminal, good range of pastries.

Bars
There are several karaoke joints along the riverfront

Apache Saloon, Saengchuto Rd, the hottest nightspot in town, decorated surprisingly enough like a kitsch wild west effort, complete with wagon wheels and stetsons. *Brew House Beer Garden*, Mae Nam Kwai Rd (Soi India Corner, near the King Naresuan statue), good value beer in a place run by a Thai who trained, of all places, in Bournemouth, southern England, and consequently plays an assortment of Cream, Led Zeppelin and 1970s soul; good food served too. No Name Bar, round the corner from the *Sugar Cane* guesthouse (Mae Nam Kwai Rd). Run by friendly British ex pats, frequented by tourists, serving huge portions of chips and good Thai food. Next door is the *Sports Bar*, nothing special on the culinary front, but BBC World News every day at 1700.

Festivals
Nov/Dec *River Kwai Bridge Week* (movable). The festival starts on the evening of the first day, with a religious ceremony conducted by dozens of monks. This is followed by a procession from the city Pillar Shrine to the bridge. The 45-min *son et lumière*, to commemorate the destruction of the original bridge by allied bombs in 1945, is very realistic. Other events include long boat races, exhibitions, steam train rides and cultural shows.

Shopping
Souvenir shops found near the bridge with the usual array of handicrafts. Bargain for purchases. Baak Phraek Rd is a pleasant road to walk down, with several clothes shops, tailors, kitchen and basketware shops.

Gemstones Blue sapphires, onyx and topaz are all mined at Bo Phloi, 50 km from Kanchanaburi. Good prices for them at shops near the bridge or in the market area of town.

Sport
Fishing On the Kwai River, Khao Laem and Srinakharin reservoirs. Travel agents will help organize expeditions.

West Tours, 21 Mae Nam Kwai Rd, T513654. *KSS* (*Kanchanaburi Trekking Tour Company*), corner of Rong Heeb Oil 2 Rd, T9228589. Branch at *Nitaya Rafthouse*, northern end of Song Kwai Rd. *AS Mixed Tours*, part of *Apple Guesthouse*, see Sleeping above. *C&Cs Guesthouse*, also runs tours, see Sleeping above. *Toi Tours*, 45/3 Rong Heeb Oil Rd, T8565523, F514209. An excellent source of local information. *RSP Jumbo*, 271/3 Saengchuto Rd, T512280. For a more culturally orientated, though expensive, tour.

Tour operators

Local Bicycles A good way to get around town and out to the bridge. Reliable bikes at ฿20 per day can be hired from *Green Bamboo* on the Mae Nam Kwai Rd, or ask at guesthouses. **Boat**: noisy long-tail boats roar up and down the river, tickets available at guesthouses. A more peaceful option is to hire canoes. *Safarino*, on the Mae Nam Kwai Rd, hires out canoes for ฿280 for 3 hrs. **Jeeps**: can be hired on Saengchuto Rd, beside TAT office and on Song Kwai Rd. **Motorbikes/scooters**: can be hired from *The Cash Shop* on Mae Nam Kwai Rd, ฿150 per day. **Saamlor**: charter for 2-3 hrs should cost about ฿100, for a trip to the Kwai bridge, JEATH museum and the cemetery. **Songthaews/tuk-tuks**: most useful for out-of-town trips. **Train**: it is possible to take a local train between Kanchanaburi and Nam Tok, getting off along the way.

Transport
See also Ins & outs, page 521
122 km NW of Bangkok

Long distance   Train: the station is 2 km northwest of town on Saengchuto Rd, not far from the cemetery, T511285. Regular connections with Nakhon Pathom and on to Hualampong Station. Weekends and holidays, special service (see Tours above). There is a left luggage office at the station.

Bus: non-a/c buses leave from the station in the market area, behind Saengchuto Rd. A/c buses leave from the corner of Saengchuto Rd, opposite Lak Muang Rd. Regular twice hourly connections with Bangkok's Southern bus terminal (a/c bus No 81), 2 hrs, or non-a/c bus, 3-4 hrs. Also connections with Nakhon Pathom from where there are buses to the floating market at Damnoen Saduak (see page 121).

Banks A number near the bus station, most with ATMs. *Bangkok*, 2 Uthong Rd. *Thai Farmers*, 160/80-2 Saengchuto Rd. *Thai Military*, 160/34 Saengchuto Rd. In more easy reach of the guesthouses is *The Corner Shop*, on Mae Nam Kwai Rd, also open at weekends. **Communications** Post Office: on the corner of Lak Muang Rd and Baak Phraek Rd (not far from Sathani Rot Fai Rd) – some distance out of town towards Bangkok. **Medical services** There is a hospital on Saengchuto Rd, close to Saengchuto Soi 20. **Useful addresses** Police: corner of Saengchuto and Lak Muang roads.

Directory

Sangkhlaburi and Saam Ong (Three Pagodas Pass)

The route to Sangkhlaburi (or 'Sangkhla', as it is known) and Saam Ong (Three Pagodas Pass) from Kanchanaburi, a total of some 200 km, follows the valley of the Kwai Noi, with the scenery becoming increasingly rugged towards Sangkhlaburi. The road passes through remnant forests and cultivated land, revealing deep red tropical soils planted to upland crops such as cassava, tamarind, mango and cotton. It then passes through the market town of Thong Pha Phum before continuing north, skirting the eastern edge of the massive Khao Laem reservoir. From here north, the road becomes increasingly windy and the landscape more mountainous and densely forested. For the last 40 km before Sangkhlaburi the road skirts the shore of the reservoir; a strange landscape of submerged (now dead) trees and what appear to be raft-houses. This upland area is home to several different ethnic groups: Karen, Mon and Burmese, as well as Thais.

The Western Region

Thong Pha Phum & Khao Laem Reservoir
Phone code: 034
Colour map 3, grid A2

A peaceful and unusual place to escape to, this small market town is situated in a beautiful position on the southern shores of the Khao Laem Reservoir, 74 km south of Sangkhlaburi. Many of the inhabitants of the town are Mon and Karen. Around Thong Pha Phum are a large number of lakeside resort hotels and raft operations, mainly geared to Thai weekenders from Bangkok. Comparatively few *farang* tourists make it up here – at least compared with Kanchanaburi – but this is changing as more and more people decide to explore further west. The Khao Laem Reservoir was created in 1983 when the Electricity Generating Authority of Thailand built the Khao Laem Dam and flooded the valley. About a dozen villages were inundated as a result. The trunks of trees killed when the valley was originally flooded still make navigation hazardous in the lake's shallows. It is still possible, however, to hire long-tail boats (although these can be rather expensive) and explore the lake, or go fishing and swimming. There are also numerous walks and trails to explore, and various waterfalls and caves.

Khao Laem National Park The Khao Laem National Park was gazetted in 1991 and covers almost 1,500 sq km. Unfortunately, by the time the authorities got around to slapping a protection order on the area, much of the forest, especially around the reservoir, had already been logged. However, the habitat is much better preserved, and richer, towards the northeast and the Thung Yai wildlife sanctuary which abuts Khao Laem. Because the park has been degraded, wildlife is thin. However, there are small populations of leopard, gibbon and macaque, as well as lesser mammals like civets and mongoose. The park headquarters are close to the main road (Route 323) to Sangkhlaburi. Thong Pha Phum has regular bus connections with Kanchanaburi's bus terminal (three hours) and onwards north to Sangkhlaburi.

■ *on map, page 536*
Price codes:
see inside front cover

Sleeping Thong Pha Phum: **C-E** *Somjaineuk*, T599067. New wing with a/c rooms and attached hot water bathrooms; older part of hotel with basic, but clean, rooms. **D-E** *Boonyong Bungalows*, T599049. Probably the best of the cheaper places to stay in Thong Pha Phum; set away from the road, some reasonable peaceful, clean a/c and fan rooms. **D-E** *Si Thong Pha Phum Bungalows*, T599058. Spacious bungalows, some with a/c.

On Khao Laem Reservoir: **AL-A** *Sam Anong Raft*, 438 Moo 1 Thongphaphum-Pilok Rd, T4039496. **A-C** *Ungkhana Raft*, 458 Moo 1 Thongphaphum-Pilok Rd, T599018. **A-C** *Wang Pai Chalet*, Thongphaphum-Pilok Rd, T2-2796189. Raft houses as well as terrestrial bungalows, basic and not very clean, possible to camp here too. **In Khao Laem National Park**: camping possible on a site 2-3 km from park HQ.

Sangkhlaburi

Colour map 3, grid A2

Sangkhlaburi is situated on the edge of the huge Khao Laem reservoir, which was created in 1983 with the damming of three rivers which used to feed the Khwae Noi River. The village is interesting for its diverse nationalities of Karen, Mon, Burmese, Indians, Pakistanis and Chinese. It is also a centre for wood and drugs smuggling and other illicit trading.

The **morning market** here provides a range of textiles and various Burmese goods. A 400 m **wooden bridge** across the lake, largely built by the Mon people, is said to be the longest in Thailand. It leads to a **Mon village** (Waeng Kha), which is interesting to walk around. The 8,000 inhabitants are mainly displaced Burmese who cannot get a Thai passport and can only work around Sangkhla.

From 1948 onwards refugees have fled Burma for the relative safety of Thailand. Most of them will never be allowed a visa or resident's permit. In 1982 the old town of Sangkhlaburi was flooded by the dam and these refugees were again left with no homes or land. The abbot of the flooded Wat Sam Prasop, the spires of which can be seen – so it is said – protruding above the lake waters during the dry season, was able to acquire land for a new wat and helped 500 households to re-establish themselves. However, these people are not wanted by the Thai government and there have been several raids by the army to round up Mon people without identity cards. At present, they are protected by the abbot, but he is now over 90 years old, so their future is uncertain.

The attraction of Saam Ong, which lies 20 km northwest of Sangkhlaburi, is its position on the border with Burma. This was the traditional invasion route for Burmese soldiers during the Ayutthayan Period (see pages 176 and 749). Although there is really nothing much to see here, the town does exude an illicit air and is a major smuggling point between Burma and Thailand. Relations between Thailand and Burma deteriorated markedly at the end of 1992, after Burmese troops occupied hill 491 on Thai territory. A serious conflict was only averted by the timely intervention of Thai King Bhumibol. The number of refugees who have been forced to settle in the area bears testament to the continuing harshness of the Burmese regime.

Wat Wang Wiwekaram is situated across the lake from Sangkhlaburi on a hill. It was built in 1982 to replace the old temple (Wat Sam Prasop), which was submerged as the waters of the reservoir rose and is revered by the Mons, Karens and Burmese, as well as by the Thais of the area. The wat is dominated by a chedi said to be modelled on the Mahabodhi stupa in Bodhgaya, India, and there are good views from the hill top. The new viharn, allegedly constructed with black market profits, is hardly subdued; it is a fine example of nouveau gauche temple architecture and decoration. To the east of the wat is a Burmese handicraft market, which is very busy at the weekends. Sarongs, silk, cloth, lacquerware, silver jewellery are all for sale. Avoid the 'gems' since they are almost certainly fake. To get to the monastery, walk across the wooden bridge.

Saam Ong (Three Pagodas Pass)

This is an unexciting spot with a tacky market in a makeshift shelter, which sells a few Burmese goods (teak, umghi, seed pearls) and a lot of Chinese imports. Avoid the 'gems', they will be fake. There is a tourist police office at the pass if you encounter problems. The pagodas, wrapped in red, saffron and white cloth, are truly unremarkable.

Phone code: 034
Colour map 3, grid A2

At the border, where posters declare 'Love your Motherland' and 'Respect the Law', visitors can pay a US$10 immigration fee to enter Burma and the village of **Payathonzu** (meaning Three Pagodas), which is more market than village. This fee, however, changes regularly, so you may find it to be anywhere

The border is open
0600-1800

The Western Region

• •

Sangkhlaburi place names

Ban Songkaria	Thung Yai Wildlife Sanctuary
บ้านซองกาเรีย	เขตรักษาพันธุ์สัตว์ป่าทุ่งใหญ่–
Daan Chedi Saam Ong	นเรศวร
ด่านเจดีย์สามองค์	
Kroeng Tho waterfall	Wang Bandan Cave
น้ำตกเกริงทอ	ถ้ำวังบ้านด่าน
	Wat Wang Wiwekaram
	วัดวังกวิเวการาม

between US$5 and US$18. At the time of writing it was no longer possible to pay in baht and you must also apply for an entrance permit (one passport photo needed) from the immigration office in Sangkhlaburi (see map, page 536). On the border lie the remains of the Burmese/Thai/Japanese railway. Motorbike taxis can transport you to the market area of Payathonzu (฿10 from the songthaew drop-off point). The market here is marginally more interesting than at Saam Ong, with a range of handicrafts, jewellery, jade, amulets, Burmese blankets, and an alarming amount of teak furniture. There is also a handful of Thai restaurants and noodle stalls and an Indian-run bakery. Beyond the village, there is another border post, beyond which visitors are

Around Sangkhlaburi

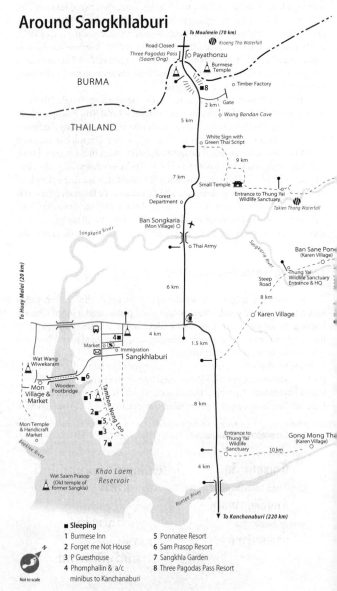

■ **Sleeping**
1 Burmese Inn
2 Forget me Not House
3 P Guesthouse
4 Phornphailin & a/c minibus to Kanchanaburi
5 Ponnatee Resort
6 Sam Prasop Resort
7 Sangkhla Garden
8 Three Pagodas Pass Resort

Not to scale

forbidden to go. Sometimes this area opens up to tourists and certainly the Thai and Burmese tourist organizations have plans on jointly developing the border area. Burmese restrictions may vary between 2 km and 20 km. **NB** It is inadvisable to cross the border anywhere other than at a check-point. Similarly, do not go beyond Payathonzu without permission of the Burmese army.

Over the last 10 years or so, control of this area has vacillated between the Burmese army and Mon and Karen rebels. At present it is firmly in the hands of the Burmese authorities, having been captured in February 1990, but note that this is still a lawless area of Burma. Some visitors may also be put off by the fact that the immigration fees go directly to the SPDC, the Burmese regime, and therefore help to support the military dictatorship which has made Burma one of the poorest economies and most repressed societies in the world. The democratically elected leader of Burma, Aung San Suu Kyi, currently under house arrest, has requested that tourists do not visit her country until the political situation has changed for the better. The only place to stay at Saam Ong is the *Three Pagodas Pass Resort*, see Sleeping below. ■ *Getting there: songthaews leave every 40 mins from the bus station, 30 mins (฿30). The last songthaew back to Sangkhlaburi leaves at about 1630; check on arrival.*

Excursions

Twelve kilometres beyond the border into Burma is **Kroeng Tho waterfall**, one of the best waterfalls in the area. It is rarely accessible to tourists, however, and at the time of research (mid-2000) local people were recommending that visitors avoid the area because of the security risk. The falls are similar to the Erawan Falls (see page 527), with impressive cascades. After a 40-minute walk alongside the river and the cascades - there are no trails - you reach the concrete walls of a reservoir, built by the Japanese during the Second World War. ■ *Getting there: when the waterfall is accessible, songthaews leave every 40 mins from Payathonzu, 30 mins.*

The Mon village of **Ban Songkaria** lies 6 km north from the turn-off to Three Pagodas Pass. It was once the headquarters for the Mon army. The airstrip on the right-hand side of the road opposite the village was originally used by the Thai Air Force. There has been talk of flights to Kanchanaburi and Bangkok, but nothing seems to have materialized.

One of the three local entrances to **Thung Yai Wildlife Sanctuary** lies 15 km northeast of Sangkhla, in the Karen village of Ban Sane Pong. Within the park is the **Takien Thong Waterfall**, with big pools for swimming. The falls lie 26 km from Sangkhla north of Ban Sane Pong, but are only accessible by taking the main road north for 13 km from the turn-off to Three Pagodas Pass, and then a right turn down a dirt road for 9 km, which is possible to drive down on motorbikes. Until recently this route was only negotiable during the dry season, but with the completion of a new all-weather road access should be year-round.

Wang Bandan Cave lies 18 km north from the turn off to Three Pagodas Pass, 2 km down a track to the right of the road. Monks used to live in the cave until just a few years ago, but (it is said) due to the effects of increasing tourism in the area, from both Thais and foreigners, they have moved to small houses at the bottom of the hill. The entrance and exit are different. There is no entrance fee, but the monks may try to charge ฿50 to guide visitors through the cave.

Tours

P Guesthouse and *Burmese Inn* both organize trips around Sangkhlaburi. Trips include visits to Karen village by boat, a two-hour elephant ride through the jungle, swimming and bamboo white-water rafting. The *Burmese Inn* may be able to organize a visit to a Karen camp. **NB** Malaria is common in this area, particularly in the jungle, so take precautions and try to avoid being bitten.

The Western Region

**Sleeping &
eating**

*There are many
inexpensive restaurants
around the Central
Market, some run by
Burmese serving good
Burmese food*

B *Three Pagodas Resort*, 1½ km before pass on right-hand side, T034-124159. Reasonably attractive wooden bungalows in a peaceful setting, restaurant, overpriced weekend resort for Thais. **B-C** *Forget Me Not House*, 85/1 Tambon Nong Loo, T595015, F595014. No restaurant. See also *Ponnatee Resort*. **B-D** *Ponnatee Resort*, 84/1 Tambon Nong Loo, T595134, F595270. Both *Forget Me Not House* and *Ponnatee Resort* are popular with Thais. They are next door to each other in a pleasant location just on the river. Rooms are clean and have either fan or a/c. Three and four person rooms available. **B-D** *Phornphailin* (formerly the *Sri Daeng*), in town, T595026. A/c and hot water, unattractive rooms and location. Lively karaoke bar. **C** *Sam Prasop Resort*, overlooking lake, by the wooden bridge, T595050. A/c, restaurant, individual bungalows, small rooms with bathroom, no English spoken. **C** *Sangkhla Garden*, overlooking lake, T595096. A/c, restaurant, geared for Thai tourists.

C-F *Burmese Inn*, 52/3 Tambon Nong Loo, T595556, F595146, burmese_inn@ access.inet.co.th Restaurant, which serves excellent Burmese curry, fan available, recently expanded and almost all rooms now have their own bathrooms, not as nice a position as *P Guesthouse*, but service and atmosphere better and friendlier, rooms quite basic (although the 5 bungalows and 7 other rooms have attached bathrooms), friendly Austrian owner (speaks English and German) and delightful Thai wife Meauw, who will organize tours, boat and motorbikes available for hire. Recommended.

F *P Guesthouse*, 81/1 Tambon Nong Loo, T595061, F595139. Good restaurant (with honesty system), very basic huts with wafer thin walls, mattresses on the floor, mandis outside, attractive position overlooking lake, well set up for travellers, helpful owner will organize tours and trekking (see Tours above), motorbikes (฿150 per day) and mountain bikes (฿100 per day), motorbike taxis to town, boat for hire ฿350 for up to 5 people for 2 hrs. A new restaurant has just been completed and, ultimately, more upmarket bungalows. We have, though, had the odd report of bookings going astray. Recommended.

Transport

*240 km to
Kanchanaburi,
335 km to Bangkok*

Local Motorbike taxis: ฿10 to almost everywhere, but ฿30 to the Mon monastery and market. They are to be found in town, by the bridge, or can be hailed along the road. **Long distance Bus**: regular connections on non-a/c bus with Kanchanaburi, 5-6 hrs, ฿80. **A/c minibus**: hourly connections with Kanchanaburi, 3½ hrs (฿105). Larger, more comfortable buses depart 3 times a day (฿125).

Directory

Banks There is a branch of the *Siam Commercial Bank* in town, which offers exchange services but no ATM. **Communications** Post Office: opposite 7-Eleven store. **Medical services** Hospital and malaria centre in town.

The Southern Region

9

The Southern Region

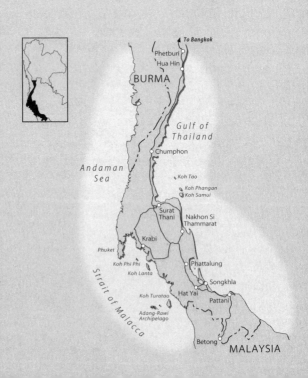

The South stretches over 1,000 km from Bangkok down to the border with Malaysia. Many visitors make a beeline for the beaches and the islands of this region and never leave – except to return home. Phuket and Koh Samui are internationally known. But there is more to the area than these and the coast is probably more suited to visitors with a yen for tropical seaside idylls than anywhere else in Thailand. Krabi, Koh Lanta, Cha-am, Hua Hin, Koh Phi Phi, Koh Tao and Koh Phangan are recognised by many. And there are scores of other, lesser-known places, where it is possible to forget about global warming, world poverty, and how to pay the mortgage for a week or two.

But the South is not just beaches and islands. Phetburi, Chaiya and Nakhon Si Thammarat are important historic towns; Khao Sam Roi Yod, Khao Sok, and the Surin and Similan islands are national parks with a good deal to offer from trekking to diving; Hat Yai – one of Thailand's ugliest towns – also offers some of the country's most divine Chinese cuisine; while monasteries like Wat Suan Mok and Wat Khao Tum provide meditation retreats for hassled farang. Moreover, Thailand's deep South, close to the border with Malaysia, is the country's Muslim heartland. Here monasteries are elbowed out by mosques and the food, dress and language take on a distinctly Malay feel.

Southern Peninsula: Phetburi to Chumphon

At its narrowest, this part of Thailand is only 20 km wide and only one road, the busy Route 4, links Bangkok with the South. The historic town of Phetburi, with perhaps the best-preserved Ayutthayan wats in Thailand, is 160 km south of Bangkok and can be visited as a day trip from the capital. Another 70 km south is Hua Hin, Thailand's original and premier beach resort, until it was eclipsed by Phuket and Pattaya. The route south is environmentally depressing: the forest has been almost totally extirpated, leaving only scrubland or degraded secondary forest.

Phetburi   เพชรบุรี

Phone code: 032
Colour map 3, grid C3

Phetburi (or Phetchaburi) is an historic provincial capital on the banks of the Phetburi River. The town is one of the oldest in Thailand and, because it was never sacked by the Burmese, is unusually intact. As Phetburi is only 160 km south of Bangkok (two hours by bus), it can be seen in a day from the capital.

Ins and outs

Getting there
See also Transport, page 547

Phetburi is just 160 km from Bangkok, so it is possible to visit the town on a day trip from the capital. Trains take 2½ hrs and the station is about 1½ km northwest of the town centre. The main bus terminal is about the same distance west of town, at the foot of Khao Wang, but the a/c bus terminal is more central, 500 m or so north of the centre. Buses take about 2 hrs from Bangkok. There are connections south to Cha-am, Hua Hin and onward.

Getting around

Phetburi – or at least its centre – is small enough to explore on foot. *Saamlors* are the main form of local transport.

History

Initially, its wealth and influence was based upon the working of the coastal salt pans found in the vicinity of the town, and which Thai chronicles record as being exploited as early as the 12th century. By the 16th century, Phetburi was supplying salt to most of Siam and the Malay Peninsula. It became particularly important during the Ayutthaya Period (14th century) and because the town was not sacked by the Burmese (as Ayutthaya was in 1767) its fine examples of Ayutthayan art and architecture are in good condition. Later, during the 19th century, Phetburi became a popular retreat for the Thai royal family, and they built a palace here. Because of its royal connections, Phetburi was *the* town to visit and to be seen in. Today, Phetburi is famous for its paid assassins who usually carry out their work from the backs of motorcycles with large-calibre pistols. Each time there is a national election, 15-20 politicians and their canvassers (so-called *hua khanen*) are killed. As in Chonburi, Thailand's other capital of crime, the police seem strangely unable to charge anyone.

Sights

Phetburi is littered with wats – below is a selection of some of the more interesting examples. Although it is possible to walk around these monasteries in

A Foot in the Door

★ The South is where most people come to laze on beaches, and there are scores to choose from. The most developed island is Phuket, where budget accommodation has been squeezed out. Hua Hin and Cha-am are smaller beach resorts on the mainland, but also with international-style places to stay. Koh Samui is one of Thailand's premier resorts but, unlike Phuket, still caters for backpackers. Beyond these, it is difficult to know where to begin: Koh Phi Phi, Koh Lanta, Koh Tao, Krabi, Chumphon, Khao Lak.

★ For diving, the best dive sites are the Surin and Similan Islands, the Ang Thong Marine National Park and the islands off Trang. Phuket and Koh Samui have the widest range of courses and dive companies to choose from.

★ Phetburi is the most interesting town in the South from a historical point of view, with its impressive collection of Ayutthaya-era monasteries.

★ Nakhon Si Thammarat is one of the cultural centres of the South, famed for its fine monastery – the biggest and most important in the South – and tradition of shadow puppetry.

half a day, travelling by saamlor is much less exhausting. Note that often the ordination halls (or *bots*) are locked; occasionally, if the abbot can be found, he may be persuaded to open them up.

Wat Phra Sri Ratana Mahathat

Situated in the heart of the town on Damnoenkasem Road, Wat Phra Sri Ratana Mahathat can be seen from a distance. It is dominated by five, much restored, Khmer-style white prangs, probably dating from the Ayutthaya Period (14th century). The largest is 42 m high. Inside the bot, richly decorated with murals, are three highly regarded Buddha images, ranged one in front of the other: **Luangpor Mahathat**, **Luangpor Ban Laem** and **Luangpor Lhao Takrao**. The principal image depicts the crowned Buddha. The complex makes an attractive cluster of buildings. Musicians and dancers are paid by those who want to give thanks for wishes granted.

Wat Yai Suwannaram

Across Chomrut Bridge and east along Pongsuriya Road is **Wat Yai Suwannaram**, on the right-hand side, within a spacious compound and a large pond. The wat was built during the Ayutthaya Period and then extensively restored in the reign of Rama V. The bot contains some particularly fine Ayutthayan murals showing celestial beings and, facing the principal Buddha image, Mara tempting the Buddha. Note the six-toed bronze Buddha image on the rear wall which is thought to be pre-Ayutthayan in date. Behind the bot is a large teak pavilion (*sala kan parian*) with three doorways at the front and two at the back. The front door panels have fine coloured-glass insets, while the (sword?) mark on the right-hand panel is said to have been made by a Burmese warrior en route to attack Ayutthaya. The wat also houses an elegant old wooden library. **Wat Boromvihan** and **Wat Trailok** are next to one another on the opposite side of the road, and a short distance to the east of Suwannaram. They are distinctive only for their wooden dormitories (or *kuti*), on stilts.

Wat Kamphaeng Laeng

South down Phokarong Road, and west a short distance along Phrasong Road, is **Wat Kamphaeng Laeng**. The five Khmer laterite prangs (one in very poor condition) – reminiscent of those in the northeast – have been dated to the 12th century. Little of the original stucco work remains, but they are nonetheless rather pleasing. Surrounded by thick laterite walls, the wat may have originally been a Hindu temple – a statue of a Hindu goddess was found here in 1956.

The Southern Region

Other wats West back towards the centre of town, and south down Matayawong Road are, in turn, **Wat Phra Song**, **Wat Laat** and **Wat Chi Phra Keut**, all on the left-hand side of the road. Just before reaching a bridge over Wat Ko Canal, is **Wat Ko Kaeo Sutharam**. The bot contains early 18th-century murals showing scenes from the Buddha's life and from Buddhist cosmology. The fact that the mural of the Buddha subduing Mara is on the rear wall, behind the principal Buddha image, has led to speculation that the entrance to the building was relocated at some time, possibly to gain access to a newly constructed road. The wat also houses interesting quarters for monks – long wooden buildings on stilts, similar to those at Wat Boromvihan.

Phra Nakhon Khiri At the west edge of the city is **Phra Nakhon Khiri**, popularly known as Khao Wang ('Palace on the Mountain'), and built in 1858 during the reign of Rama IV. Perched on the top of a 95-m-high hill, the palace represents an amalgam of Thai, Western and Chinese artistic styles. The hill complex is dotted with frangipani trees with three areas of architectural interest on the three peaks. On the west rise is the **royal palace** itself. This has recently been restored and is now a well-maintained museum, containing an eclectic mixture of artefacts collected by Ramas IV and V who regularly stayed here. The airy building, with good views over the surrounding plain, has a Mediterranean feel to it. ■ *Mon-Sun 0900-1600. ฿40.*

Also on this peak is the **Hor Chatchavan Viangchai**, an observatory tower which Rama IV used to further his astronomical studies. On the central rise of the hill is the **Phra That Chomphet**, a white stupa erected by Rama IV. On the east rise sits **Wat Maha Samanaram** (aka Wat Phra Kaeo). Within the bot there are mural paintings by Khrua In Khong, quite a well-known Thai painter. The wat dates from the Ayutthayan Period. (Watch out for the monkeys here. They seem innocent and friendly enough until you buy a bag of bananas or corn on the cob for ฿5. Sprawls between monkeys are quick to break out and, more often than not, the whole bag will be ripped from your hand. Just remember that they are wild animals!) A **cable car** (more a cable-tram than car) takes visitors up the west side of Khao Wang for ฿45 one way, ฿40 both ways. ■ *0800-1600.*

Foot of Khao Wang **Wat Sra-bua** at the foot of Khao Wang is late Ayutthayan in style. The *bot* exhibits some fine gables, pedestal and stucco work. Also at the foot of the hill, slightly south from Wat Sra-bua is the poorly maintained **Wat Phra Phuttha Saiyat**. Within the corrugated iron-roofed viharn is a notable 43 m-long brick

. . . .

Phetburi place names

Khao Luang Cave	Wat Phra Sri Ratana Mahathat
ถ้ำเขาหลวง	วัดพระศรีรัตนมหาธาตุ
Phra Nakhon Khiri	Wat Sra-bua
พระนครคีรี	วัดสระบัว
Wat Boromvihan	Wat Trailok
วัดบรมวิหาร	วัดไตรโลก
Wat Bun Thawi	Wat Yai Suwannaram
วัดบุญทวี	วัดใหญ่สุวรรณาราม
Wat Kamphaeng Laeng	
วัดกำแพงแลง	

The Southern Region

and plaster reclining Buddha dating from the mid-18th century. The image is unusual both in the moulding of the pillow, and in the manner in which the arm protrudes into the body of the building.

Excursions

Tham Khao Luang is on Route 3173, 3 km north from Phetburi. It offers stalactites, stupas and multitudes of second-rate Buddha images in various poses. This cave was frequently visited by Europeans who came to Phetburi in the 19th century. Mary Lovina Court (1886), an early example of the inquisitive but destructive Western tourist wrote: "At the mouth of the cave we found some curious rocks, and succeeded in breaking off several good specimens". She was also enchanted by the caves themselves in which, she records, there "are the greatest wonders". Mary Court ended her sojourn telling some Buddhist visitors about "the better God than the idols by which they had knelt". On the right hand side, at the entrance to the cave, is a monastery called **Wat Bun Thawi**, with attractive carved-wooden door panels. ■ *Getting there: by saamlor.*

Khao Luang Cave

See page 551 for more details on Kaeng Krachan National Park which lies around 50 km southwest of town. ■ *Getting there: buses from Phetburi run past the turn-off for Kaeng Krachan Dam (Route 3175). From here, there are occasional minibuses which take visitors to the dam and the park headquarters (another 8 km), or hitch a lift.*

Kaeng Krachan National Park

The Southern Region

Phetburi

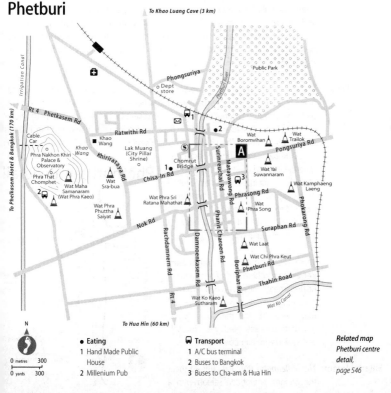

To Khao Luang Cave (3 km)

● **Eating**
1 Hand Made Public House
2 Millenium Pub

🚌 **Transport**
1 A/C bus terminal
2 Buses to Bangkok
3 Buses to Cha-am & Hua Hin

*Related map
Phetburi centre
detail,
page 546*

Essentials

Sleeping
■ *on map*
Price codes:
see inside front cover

Phetuburi has poor accommodation at the upper end – although there are one or two good budget places to stay – so for those wishing to spend more time viewing the town's wats, it is probably best to stay at Hua Hin, Cha-am, Nakhon Pathom or at the *Rose Garden Hotel* (see page 675).

A-C *Royal Diamond Hotel*, 555 Phetkasem Rd, T411061, F424310. Luxurious hotel compared to any others available in Phetburi, with a/c. The restaurant does a range of international food. Beer garden and pleasant, peaceful atmosphere.

C-D *Khao Wang*, 174/1-3 Ratwithi Rd, T425167, F410750. Some a/c, characterless overpriced rooms have attached bathrooms (with western toilet) and Thai TV but are rather tatty. The management are cold and generally unwelcoming and although there is a small restaurant at the edge of a snooker room it is very dark and unappealing. **D-E** *Phetkasem*, 86/1 Phetkasem Rd, T410973, F425581. Some a/c, clean rooms and friendly management, some rooms have hot water, there is no restaurant but it is located very close to some of the best eats in Phetburi (see Eating below). Best value place to stay in this category. **D-E** *Phet Chalet*, 7 km out of town on the Phetkasem Rd, T412748. Some a/c, noisy and isolated, no restaurant, attached bathrooms but no showers. **D-E** *Rabieng Guesthouse*, Damnoenkasem Rd, T425878, F410695. Well-decorated wood-panelled rooms with tiled floors. Great open-air seating area and clean communal facilities. Appealing restaurant overlooking the river (see Eating). Motorbikes can be rented here at ฿250 per day. Laundry service. Trekking and rafting tours in the National Parks are available. Recommended. **E** *Chom Klao*, on east bank of the river, T425398. Offers clean, quiet, and fair-sized rooms, though they are bare and unattractive. The rooms with views over the river are by far the best and have balcony areas. More expensive rooms have shower-rooms attached, ones without have basins. Friendly, helpful and informative management.

Eating
● *on map, below*
Price categories:
see inside front cover

Phetburi is well known for its desserts, including *khanom mo kaeng* (a hard custard made of mung bean, egg, coconut and sugar, baked over an open fire), *khao kriap* (a pastry with sesame, coconut and sugar) and excellent *kluai khai* (sweet bananas). There are several good restaurants along Phetkasem Rd, selling Phetburi desserts including: **Cheap** *Ban Khanom Thai* (literally, the 'Thai Sweet House', at No 130) and *Rotthip* (No 45/22). *Rabieng Restaurant Guesthouse*, Damnoenkasem Rd, attractively furnished riverside restaurant, serving a good range of Thai and Western food. Recommended. *Hand Made Public House*, Chisa-In Rd, is nicely decorated and serves a range of Thai and western food.

There is a small but excellent **night market** at the southern end of Surinreuchai Rd underneath the clock tower – you can get a range of delicious snacks here and may want to try the local '*patai*' (omelette/pancake fried with mussels and served with bamboo shoots).

Phetburi centre detail

Entertainment   *The Millennium Pub*, Ratwithi Rd (near the bridge). A wooden saloon with a

The Southern Region

western/Native American-Indian theme to it. Harley-Davidson posters alongside Manchester United and Liverpool banners; anything western goes. Every night a local Thai band plays live (so I was told). Does all the usual imported and local beers and whiskys. Accepts Visa and Mastercard. Open 5pm-1am every night.

Feb *Phra Nakhon Khiri Fair* (movable) *son et lumière* show.

Festivals

Local Saamlors: can be hired for about ฿100 per hour. **Motorbikes**: can be rented from *Rabieng Guesthouse* at ฿250 per day, and motorbike taxis cost about ฿20-30 per km.

Transport
See also Ins & outs, page 542
160 km S of Bangkok

Long distance Train: the station is 1,500 m northwest of town. Regular connections with Bangkok's Hualamphong station 2½ hrs, via Nakhon Pathom. Trains to Bangkok mostly leave Phetburi in the morning. Trains to Hua Hin, Surat Thani and southern destinations.
　Bus: regular a/c connections with Bangkok's Southern bus terminal near the Thonburi train station, 2 hrs; non-a/c buses from the new terminal on Phra Pinklao Road, 2 hrs. These buses arrive and leave from the new bus station behind Khao Wang near the 'cable car'. Songthaews meet the buses and take passengers into the town centre for ฿5. Also connections with Cha-am, Hua Hin and other southern destinations, between 6am and 6pm. These buses leave from the centre of town (see map).

Banks *Siam Commercial Bank* on Damnoenkasem Rd changes cash and TCs, and has an ATM. **Communications** Overseas calls can be made from the Post Office (on Ratwithi Rd).

Directory

Cha-am

■ Sleeping
1 Beach Garden
2 Cha-am Eurasia & Cha-am Cabana
3 Dusit Resort & Polo Club
4 Golden Sand
5 Regent Cha-am

N
Not to scale

Cha-am ชะอำ

Cha-am is reputed to have been a stopping place for King Naresuan's troops when they were travelling south. The name 'Cha-am' may have derived from the Thai word *cha-an*, meaning to clean the saddle. Cha-am is a beach resort with no town to speak of, some excellent hotels and a sizeable building programme of new hotels and condominiums for wealthy Bangkokians. A number of new hotels have opened on the seafront, offering more bungalows and simple rooms in the **B-C** price range, with a few in the **D** range. Unless you speak Thai, it will be difficult to make a phone booking, but it is highly likely that you'll find free rooms if you just show up. The town also has a good reputation for the quality of its seafood.
　Cha-am does not have the facilities of Pattaya or Phuket, but it is

Phone code: 032
Colour map 3, grid C3

Related map
A Cha-am detail, page 548

The Southern Region

easily accessible from Bangkok. It has become a popular weekend spot, so sizeable discounts are available during the week when most hotels are close to empty. At the weekend something of a transformation comes over this Jekyll & Hyde resort and it buzzes with life for 48 hours or so, before returning to its comatose state. You will need your Thai phrasebook or dictionary with you, as hand gestures and smiles alone will do little more than find you a room for the night in this town. There are a few locals who speak a little English. The **tourist office**, at 500/5 Phetkasem Road, T471005, is responsible for the areas of Cha-am and Prachuap Khiri Khan. There is a tourist information booth on the beach.

Excursions **Maruekkhathayawan Palace**, designed by an Italian and built by Rama VI in 1924 (the king is reputed to have also had a major hand in the design of the palace). The palace is made of teak and the name means 'Place of love and hope', which is rather charming. It is currently being renovated (and has been for the last 20 years) but consists of 16 pavilions in a very peaceful setting. ■ *0800-1600 Mon-Sun, admission is free although you are expected to leave a small gratuity for the shoe custodian. Getting there: by saamlor, or catch a bus heading for Hua Hin and walk 2 km from the turn-off.*

Sleeping
■ *on map*
Price codes:
see inside front cover

L-AL *Dusit Resort and Polo Club*, 1349 Phetkasem Rd, T520009, F520296, T02-2360450. A/c, restaurant, pool, large, stylish hotel block (300 rms), with horse-riding and polo 'motifs' throughout. Superb facilities including range of watersports, fitness centre, tennis courts, horse-riding and an enormous swimming pool, Thai arts and crafts demonstrations. **L-AL** *Golden Sand*, 853 Phetkasem Rd, T451200, F451209, T02-2598977. A/c, restaurant, pool, high-rise block with views onto the sea. Facilities including tennis, squash, watersports, fitness centre. **L-AL** *Regent*, 849/21 Phetkasem Rd, T451240, F471491, www.regent-chaam.com A/c, restaurants, pools, hotel and cottage accommodation on a 300-acre site, and every conceivable facility (squash, tennis, fitness centre, etc). **L-A** *Beach Garden*, 249/21 Phetkasem Rd, T508234, F508241, T02-2372615. A/c, restaurant, pool, right on the beach, 3-storey block and some cottage accommodation, facilities including watersports, tennis, fishing and a mini-golf course. **L-A** *Mark-land Plaza Hotel*, T433833, F433834. Luxury high-rise hotel with the works (pool, gym, etc). **L-A** *Methavalai*, 220 Ruamchit Rd, T471028, F471590, T02-6210600, BF2243960. A/c, good seafood and Thai restaurant, pool, some bungalows with several bedrooms – ideal for families – and a small area of

Cha-am detail

Snooker o Massage
Mini Mart
Naratip Rd
Buses to Bangkok
Ratphli Rd
Chaolai Rd
Ruamchit Rd
Not to scale

■ **Sleeping**

1	Anatachai	10	Rua Makam
2	Cha-am Guesthouse	11	Sam Resort
3	Cha-am Holiday Lodge	12	Santisuk
4	Cha-am Phaisiri	13	Savitree
5	Cha-am Villa	14	Som's Guesthouse
6	Kaenchan	15	Thipdharee
7	Mark-land Plaza	16	Thunya's Guesthous
8	Methavalai	17	Viwathana
9	Nirandorn	18	White

The Southern Region

private beach. **AL-A** *Cha-am Eurasia*, Klongtien Rd, T471327, F430397, T02-2586589. A/c, restaurant, pool. **AL-C** *Cha-am Holiday Lodge*, T471595. Rather grotty rooms, management speaks no English.

A *Cha-am Phaisiri*, T471047, 3-roomed bungalows, very average for this price range. **A-B** *Santisuk*, 263/3 Ruamchit Rd, T471212, T02-2511847. Range of accommodation, some a/c, 2 styles of accommodation – wooden cottages or a hotel block, both are good. **A-D** *Cha-am Villa*, 24/1 Ruamchit Rd, T471241, F471086. Nice rooms, friendly management, some a/c, good discounts during the week. Recommended. **B** *Thipdharee*, 274/34-35 Ruamchit Rd, T471879. Reasonable a/c rooms but rather boring. **B-C** *Kaenchan*, 241/3 Ruamchit Rd, T471314, F471531. Some a/c, small pool on the rooftop, range of accommodation. **B-D** *NP Place*, T471826, accommodation ranging from apartments with hot water and bath tub and a/c to bungalows with fan.

C *Anatachai*, T471980. Nice rooms with attached bathroom, TV and a/c, well run and competitively priced, ocean views. **C** *Golden Villa*, 248/13 Ruamchit Rd, T471881. A/c. **C** *Nirandorn*, T471893. Some a/c, wooden cottages. **C** *Pratarnchoke House*, 240/3 Ruamchit Rd, T471215. Range of rooms available here from simple fan-cooled through to more luxurious a/c rooms with attached bathrooms. **C** *Rua Makam*, T471073. Bland, boring, ugly, overpriced bungalows. **C** *Rung Aran Bungalow*, 236/26 Ruamchit Rd, T471226. A/c. **C** *Sam Resort*, 246/9 Ruamchit Rd, T471197. Reasonable rooms. **C** *Savitree*, 263/1 Ruamchit Rd, T434088. Rooms have TV and fridge but no hot water, perhaps rather overpriced. **C** *Viwathana*, 263/21 Ruamchit Rd, T471289. This hotel is one of the longer established with some simpler, fan-cooled wooden bungalows as well as a new brick-built block. All are set in a garden of sorts giving the place more character than most. The more expensive bungalows have 2 or 3 rooms and/or a/c – no restaurant or hot water – but good value for families. **C-D** *Cha-am Guest House*, T433400. Attached bathroom, some a/c, small balcony overlooking sea, no hot water, no restaurant. **C-D** *Jitravee*, 240/20 Ruamchit Rd, T471382. Clean rooms, friendly management, more expensive rooms have a/c, TV, fridge, room service, attached bathroom, cheaper rooms have clean, shared bathroom, some English spoken here. **C-D** *Thunya's Guesthouse*, T433504. Very nice rooms with attached bathrooms (western toilet and shower), TV, a/c, balcony, some have OK views over wooded area (rather than cement walls and roofs like much of the accommodation here). **D-E** *Som's Guesthouse*, 234/30 Ruamchit Rd, T433753. Nice clean rooms and one of the cheapest places to stay in Cha-am.

Eating Between the *Beach Garden* and the *Regent* there are several restaurants, notably *Family Shop* (**cheap**), on the beach, good barbecued fish. Plenty of seafood restaurants along Ruamchit Rd, mostly serving the same range of dishes, including such things as chilli crab and barbecued snapper with garlic.

Sport **Golf** *Springfields Royal Country Club*, designed by Jack Nicklaus, green fees ฿900 Mon - Fri, ฿1,400 at weekends. Caddy fee ฿170.

Transport **Road Bus**: regular connections with Bangkok's Southern bus terminal 2½ hrs, *25 km N of Hua Hin* Phetburi, Hua Hin and destinations south. Buses from Bangkok stop right on the beach but buses from Phetburi or Hua Hin stop on the Phetkasem Highway. Motorbike taxis from here to the beach cost ฿20 (avoid asking to be dropped at a hotel, as drivers try for ฿50 commission). To get to other southern destinations catch a bus to Hua Hin and change there.

Directory **Banks** *Bangkok Bank*, 241/41 Ruamchit Rd. **Communications Post Office**, Narathip Rd 400 m north of the Phetkasem Highway. Overseas calls can be made from here, also on Ruamchit Rd.

Hua Hin   หัวหิน

Phone code: 032
Colour map 3, grid C3

Thailand's first beach resort, Hua Hin has had an almost continuous royal connection since the late 19th century. In 1868, King Mongkut journeyed to Hua Hin to observe a total eclipse of the sun. In 1910, Prince Chakrabongse, brother of Rama VI, visited Hua Hin on a hunting trip and was so enchanted by the area that he built himself a villa. Sadly, today, Hua Hin has become a rather tawdry beach resort and the beach itself is an object lesson in what happens when people don't care.

Ins and outs

Getting there
See also Transport, page 556

Daily flights on Bangkok Airways to Bangkok and also connections with Koh Samui. The train station is on the western edge of town, within walking distance of the centre. The journey from Bangkok takes 4 hrs and there are connections onwards to all points south. It is presently a 3-hr drive from Bangkok, along a hazardous 2-lane highway (particularly bad over the last 80 km from Phetburi), jammed with *siplors* (10-wheel trucks). The bus terminal is reasonably central; regular connections with Bangkok and many southern towns.

Getting around

Hua Hin is an increasingly compact beach resort and many of the hotels, restaurants and places of interest (such as they are) are within walking distance of one another. But there is also a good supply of public transport. Songthaews run along fixed routes; there are taxis and saamlors; and bicycles, motorbikes and cars are all available for hire.

Tourist offices

The local tourist office is at 114 Phetkasem Rd, T512120. ■ *Mon-Sun 0830-1630.*

History

The first of the royal palaces was built by Prince Naris, son of Rama V – Saen Samran House. In the early 1920's, King Vajiravudh (Rama VI) – no doubt influenced by his brother Chakrabongse – began work on a teakwood palace, 'Deer Park'. The final stamp of royal approval came in the late 1920s, when King Phrajadipok (Rama VII) built another palace, which he named **Klai Kangwon**, literally 'Far From Worries' (not open to the public except when a permit has been obtained from the Royal Household in advance – a good hotel should be able to arrange this). It was designed by one of Prince Naris' sons. The name could not have been more inappropriate: the king was staying at Klai Kangwon in 1932 when he was dislodged from the throne by a *coup d'état*. In late 2000 it was reported that the king of Thailand, fed up with polluted Bangkok, was spending more and more time at his other royal palaces and especially at his Hua Hin home. You can tell when he is in residence by the presence of one or two Thai navy frigates moored offshore.

Early guidebooks, reminiscent of English seaside towns, named the resort Hua Hin-on-Sea. *Hua* (head) *Hin* (rock) refers to a stone outcrop at the end of the fine white-sand beach. The resort used to promote itself as the 'Queen of Tranquility'. Until the 1980s, it was a forgotten backwater of an earlier, and less frenetic, tourist era. However, in the last few years the constant influx of tourists have livened up the atmosphere considerably. With massage parlours, tourist shops selling the usual paraphernalia, and numerous western restaurants and bars lining the streets, it's hard to get a moment's peace in this town. The old-world charm that was once Hua Hin's great selling point has been lost. As Hua Hin is billed as a beach resort, people come here expecting – this is Thailand after all – a beautiful tropical beach. Don't be fooled. It's filthy. The *Melia Hua Hin Hotel* has initiated a 'Save the Hua Hin Beach Environment' campaign but there's a lot of work to do.

The famous **Railway Hotel** was built in 1923 by a Thai prince, Purachatra, who headed the State Railways of Thailand. It became Thailand's premier seaside hotel, but by the 1960s had fallen into rather glorious disrepair. It experienced a short burst of stardom when the building played the role of the Phnom Penh Hotel in the film *Killing Fields*, but it still seemed destined to rot into oblivion. Saved by privatization, it was renovated and substantially expanded in 1986 and is now an excellent five-star hotel. Unfortunately, it has been renamed, and goes under the unromantic name of the *Sofitel Central*. At the other end of Damnoenkasem Road from the Railway Hotel, on the opposite side of the main highway, is the **Railway Station** itself. The station has a rather quaint Royal Waiting Room on the platform.

Sights

Khao Takiab (or Chopstick Hill), south of town, is a dirty, unremarkable hill with a large standing Buddha facing the sea. As Hua Hin expands, so this area is also developing. At present, it resembles a building site. Nearby is **Khao Krilat**, a rock covered in assorted shrines, stupas, ponds, salas and Buddha images. To get there, take a local bus from Dechanuchit Road.

Kaeng Krachan National Park, 63 km northwest of Hua Hin, is Thailand's largest protected area covering 2,915 sq km. It was gazetted in 1981. It is said to support significant populations of large mammal species – elephant, tiger, leopard, gibbon, the Malayan pangolin – and birds, in particular, hornbills, minivets, pheasants and bee-eaters. Endangered species include the wooly-necked stork and the plain-pouched hornbill. (Few visitors see many, if any, of these animals, though.) Extensive trails lead through undisturbed forest and past a succession of waterfalls (the best being Pa La-U), to hot springs and a Karen village. Guides are advisable and cost ฿500 per day, though many of them don't speak English, so make sure you meet the guide who will be taking you before paying your money. The Tenasserim Mountain range cuts through the park, the highest peak stands at 1,207 m. Phanoen Thung Mountain offers superb views of the surrounding countryside (warm clothes are needed for the chilly mornings). It is a six-hour hike to the summit. En route to Pa La-U, 27 km from Hua Hin and close to Nongphlab village, are three caves: **Dao**, **Lablae** and **Kailon**, which contain the usual array of stalactites and stalagmites. Guides with lanterns will take visitors through the caves for ฿30. Boat trips can be made on the reservoir. Until recently, entrance to the park was only ฿20, but was suddenly increased to ฿200 with another charge of ฿200 for the Pa La-U waterfalls. Due to this dramatic increase, a number of tour operators have decided to boycott the park, in the hope they'll drop the price. **Sleeping** Bungalows are available at headquarters (฿750-1,000 per bungalow, which sleeps 5-6 people), but you must bring all necessities with you (eg blankets, food and water). ■ *Getting there: take a minibus from the station on Srasong Road to the village of Fa Prathan, 53 km (฿15). For the caves, take the same bus but get off at Nongphlab village (฿10) and ask at the police station for directions – the caves are a 45 mins to 1 hr walk away. Tours are also available (see below).*

Excursions

Khao Sam Roi Yod National Park, about 45 km south of Hua Hin, is one of the best-managed protected areas in the country (see page 557).

The Southern Region

Tours
See also Tour operators below

Companies run day tours to the Sam Roi Yod (around ฿850-900) and Kaeng Krachan National Parks (around ฿1,000), and to the Pa La-U waterfall, with lunch (see above). A number of other tours are available, including the usual 'adventure' tours (rafting, trekking, elephant rides), day trips to Burma ($5 immigration fee, and a chance to extend your visa for another 30 days) and the Tennaserrim mountain range, as well as diving, snorkelling, and fishing excursions. Many tour companies in Hua Hin offer such tours at competitive prices.

Essentials

Sleeping
■ *on map*
Price codes: see inside front cover

L *Chiva Som International Health Resort*, 73/4 Phetkasem Rd, T536536, F511154, chivasom@ksc9.th.com A/c, restaurant, pool, this is a luxury health resort (*Chiva-Som* means 'Haven of Life'), set in 3 ha of land, with a large spa building housing a spacious gym, Roman bath, enormous jacuzzi, circular steam room and dance studio. There is also an outdoor freshwater pool. With health consultants, hydrotherapy and lots of herbal tea and healthy food, this is the place to come to lose weight or firm up those buttocks without feeling that life is too miserable. All for a considerable price, but at least one leaves feeling good about oneself, a truly pampering kind of hotel. **L-AL** *Melia Hua Hin*, 33 Naresdamri Rd, T511612, F511135, T02-2713435, BF2713689, www.solmelia.com A/c, restaurants, pool with water slide and jacuzzi, ugly high-rise hotel with all facilities, all rooms have sea views. **L-AL** *Royal Garden Resort*, 107/1 Phetkasem Rd, T511881, F512422, T02-4760021, BF4601805, www.royal-garden.com A/c, restaurant, pool, to complement the even larger L-shaped block, good sports facilities including tennis, fitness centre, watersports. There's also a mini-zoo and shopping arcade. Recommended. **L-AL** *Sofitel Central* (previously, the *Railway Hotel*), 1 Damnoenkasem Rd, T512021, F511014, T02-5411463, BF5411464, www.sofitel.com A/c, restaurant, pool, Hua Hin's original premier hotel. Both maintain excellent levels of service and enjoy an excellent position on the beach, and while the new rooms are small they are well appointed. In addition the seafood restaurant here – with a French chef – is truly worth seeking out. Recommended. **L-A** *Hua-Hin Grand Hotel and Plaza*, 222/2 Petchakasem Rd, T511391, F511765, T02-2547675, BF2547675, www.huahingrand.co.th Large swimming pool, all mod cons, spacious rooms, fully equipped meeting rooms, shopping plaza, restaurants and bars, 24-hr coffeeshop.

AL *Royal Garden Tower*, 43/1 Phetkasem Rd, T512412, F512417, T02-2558822. A/c, suites only. **AL** *Royal Garden Village*, 45 Phetkasem Rd, T512412, F520259, T02-2518659. A/c, restaurant, pool, teak pavilions set around a pool, good sports facilities but no beach to speak of. **AL-A** *City Beach Resort*, 16 Damnoenkasem Rd, T512870, F512488, www.citybeach.co.th A/c, restaurant, pool, pub with live music and karaoke, conference halls available for booking, central, unattractive interior. **AL-A** *Sailom*, 29 Phetkasem Rd, south of the centre, T511890, F512047, T02-3922109, BF3902799. A/c, restaurant, pool. **A** *Mercure Hotel*, 1 Damnoenkasem Rd, T512036, F511014. A/c, restaurant, pool, 41 villas in garden compound. This hotel benefits from access to the good facilities at the *Sofitel Central* next door. **A** *Sport Villa*, 10/95 Phetkasem Rd, 3 km south of town, T511453. A/c, restaurant, large pool, sauna. **A-B** *Hua Hin Highland Resort*, 4/15 Ban Samophrong, north of town, T2112579, T02-2800750. A/c, popular with golfers. **A-B** *Sirin*, Damnoenkasem Rd, T511150, F513571. A/c, quiet despite being central, standard, over-priced. **A-C** *Chanchai*, 117/1-18 Phetkasem Rd, T511461, F532376, banchanchay@hotmailcom Bungalows on the beach, a/c, satellite TV, telephones in rooms, slightly outside the ruckus of central Hua Hin, quieter beach.

B *Ban Boosarin*, 8/8 Poonsuk Rd, T512076, F512089. A/c, comfortable rooms and reliable and friendly management. Recommended. **B** *Fu Lay*, 110/1 Naresdamri Rd,

T513670, F530320, www.huahinguide.com/guesthouses/fulay (an enquiry form can be filled out from here). A/c, small hotel, clean and friendly, sea view. They also have a cheaper guesthouse across the road (T513145, F530320). Recommended. **B** *PP Villa*, T533785, F511216. A/c, restaurant, pool, recently upgraded with the addition of a pool and the construction of an adjacent hotel under the same management, the *Puang Pen Hotel* (also in our **B** category). *Fresh Inn*, 132 Naresdamri Rd, T511389. A/c, restaurant, the *Melia* blots out any sea view it may once have had but the rooms are

Hua Hin

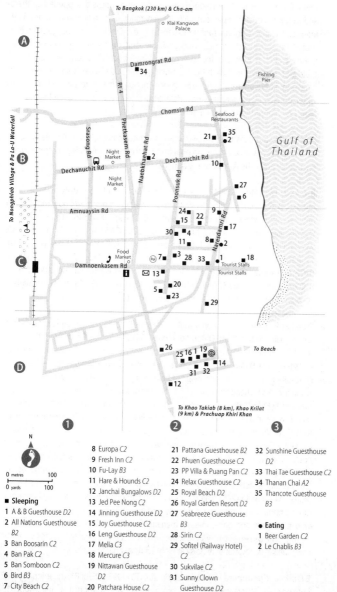

The Southern Region

■ Sleeping
1 A & B Guesthouse *D2*
2 All Nations Guesthouse *B2*
3 Ban Boosarin *C2*
4 Ban Pak *C2*
5 Ban Somboon *C2*
6 Bird *B3*
7 City Beach *C2*
8 Europa *C2*
9 Fresh Inn *C2*
10 Fu-Lay *B3*
11 Hare & Hounds *C2*
12 Janchai Bungalows *D2*
13 Jed Pee Nong *C2*
14 Jinning Guesthouse *D2*
15 Joy Guesthouse *C2*
16 Leng Guesthouse *D2*
17 Melia *C3*
18 Mercure *C3*
19 Nittawan Guesthouse *D2*
20 Patchara House *C2*
21 Pattana Guesthouse *B2*
22 Phuen Guesthouse *C2*
23 PP Villa & Puang Pan *C2*
24 Relax Guesthouse *C2*
25 Royal Beach *D2*
26 Royal Garden Resort *D2*
27 Seabreeze Guesthouse *B3*
28 Sirin *C2*
29 Sofitel (Railway Hotel) *C2*
30 Sukvilae *C2*
31 Sunny Clown Guesthouse *D2*
32 Sunshine Guesthouse *D2*
33 Thai Tae Guesthouse *C2*
34 Thanan Chai *A2*
35 Thancote Guesthouse *B3*

● Eating
1 Beer Garden *C2*
2 Le Chablis *B3*

good and it is well priced. **B-C** *Jed Pee Nong*, 17 Damnoenkasem Rd, T512381, F532063. Uninviting pool surrounded by uprising buildings, some a/c, breakfast included, clean, boring and popular. Rooms in the older block are run down and over-priced for what they offer. The newer blocks are better. **B-D** *Thanan Chai*, 11 Damrongrat Rd, T511755. Some a/c, north of centre, but quite good value. **C** *Patchara House*, Naresdamri Rd, T511787. Some a/c, clean, friendly, room service, hot water, TV, pleasant restaurant. Recommended.

Guesthouses   A new area of slightly more expensive guesthouses has sprung up just south of the town. The area is called Soi Thipurai after the first guesthouse that opened up there, and all tuk-tuk drivers know it as such. It's very much its own little community, with internet facilities (though slightly expensive), restaurants in all the guesthouses, motorbike and bicycle rental, tours available, and even a fashion house for tailor-made clothes. Everyone speaks very good English and the people are very hospitable and friendly. The beach here is much quieter and cleaner than the noisy and harassing atmosphere at the main beach in Hua Hin. There are still the same watersports available, jetskis, windsurfs, etc, but at least you're not hassled so much. A highly recommended area for a quiet retreat.

All the following guesthouses have similar spacious rooms with a/c, hot water, satellite TV, and access to a swimming pool (though the beach might be a better option). Prices may enter the **A** price range during high season.

B-C *A&B*, T532340, F512711, www.travel.to/A&B Friendly Swedish management, minibar. **B-C** *Jinning Beach*, T513950, F532597, www.jinningbeachguesthouse.com Minibar and video channel available. **B-C** *Leng*, T513546, F532095, leng@workmail.com Minibar and fridges in rooms. **B-C** *Nilawan*, T512751, F533630, www.travel.to/nilawanhouse Internet service and coffeeshop. **B-C** *Royal Beach*, T532210, royalbeach@hotmail.com Minibar and video channel available. **B-C** *Sunny Clown*, T512936, F533368, sunnyclown@mail.tele.dk Restaurant area. **B-C** *Sunshine*, T515309, Cell661-8662352, sunshineguesthouse@yahoo.com Slightly cheaper than the others, and fridges in some rooms.

These are concentrated around Naresdamri Rd, one road in from the beach; some residents rent out rooms in their homes

D *Ban Pak*, T511653. Fair rooms with wooden ceilings and comfortable chairs, some a/c, no balcony but clean. **D** *Ban Somboon*, T501338. Rooms OK but slightly on the small side, all have attached shower rooms with hot water and TVs, attractive restaurant and sitting area. **D** *Bird*, T511630. Rooms on wooden platform on stilts above the beach, no restaurant but you can get breakfast here, sitting area with views over the sea, more ambience and character than most. **D** *Kanokporn*, Damnoenkasem Rd. Recommended. **D** *Pala-U*, Naresdamri Rd. A/c, clean rooms with attached bathrooms, laundry service, well run by a German and his Thai wife. Recommended. **D** *Seabreeze*, next door to *Bird Guesthouse* with a similar set up – again no restaurant but drinks and snacks available. Rooms are OK, those with sea view are slightly more expensive – which might not be worth it as at low tide the beach is less than appealing. **D** *Thai Tae*, 8 bungalows on wooden stilts – fair size, some a/c. **D** *Thancote*, T513677. Some a/c, seafood restaurant, friendly owners. There is no reception area, but the owners can be found in the restaurant. **D-E** *Joy*, T512967. Fair rooms if a little bit boring, some have own bathroom, nice communal sitting area and balcony upstairs, lively bar and restaurant downstairs with pool table and darts, friendly management. **D-E** *Sukvilae*, T513523. Range of rooms, some cement, some wood, some own bath, some a/c and hot water, OK rooms, communal balcony, but very noisy at night with beer garden below.

E *Pattana Guesthouse*, 52 Naretdamri Rd, T513393, F530081, huahinpattana@hotmail.com Attractive location down a small alley, making it a quiet spot. 13

twin-bedded rooms with fans in 2 original Thai teakwood buildings set around a flower-filled compound, some rooms with own bathrooms. 50 m from the beach, breakfast and dinner available, email and internet service. **E** *All Nations*, Dechanuchit Rd, T512747, F530474, gary@infonews.co.th Email facilities, shared bathrooms, own balcony, clean and friendly. One of the cheapest in Hua Hin. **E** *Europa*, 158 Naresdamri Rd, T513235. Restaurant (international food), own bathroom. **E** *Forum*, Soi off Naresdamri Rd. Some private bathrooms. **E** *Hare & Hounds*, 8/5-7 Soi Kanjanomai, T533757, mags118@hotmail.com Small, simple, clean rooms, communal showers. **E** *Phuen*, Soi off Naresdamri Rd, T512344. Old wooden house, quiet, but rather small rooms all with own bathroom, fax and phone services, 24-hr coffee house. **E** *Relax*, 6 Soi Binthabart, T513585, located down a small quiet alley, nice rooms all with own bathroom, smaller rooms are cheaper, communal balcony at front.

Try the central market for breakfast. Good seafood is widely available particularly at the northern end of Naresdamri Rd. Most of the fish comes straight from the boats which land their catch at the pier at the northern end of the bay. There is also a concentration of restaurants and bars geared to farang visitors along Naresdamri surrounding lanes.

Eating
● *on map*
Price categories:
see inside front cover

Seafood   Very expensive: *Sofitel Hotel Seafood Restaurant*, 1 Damnoenkasem Rd, the seafood restaurant in this refurbished hotel is probably the best in Hua Hin. Don't expect the usual range of Thai dishes; the chef is French. **Expensive**: *Meekaruna*, 26/1 Naresdamri Rd. Small pavilion. Recommended. *Seangthai*, Naresdamri Rd. Also serves Thai, large open-air restaurant on the seafront and long established by Hua Hin standards. Regular visitors maintain that it remains one of the better seafood restaurants. *Tappikaew House*, 7 Naebkaehat Rd. Attractive Thai restaurant, indoor and outdoor eating by the sea. *Charlie's Seafood*, Naresdamri Rd. Also serves Thai. *Charoen Pochana*, Naresdamri Rd. Also serves Thai. *Europa*, Naresdamri Rd. Also serves International and Thai. *Supharos*, 69/2-3 Phetkasem Rd. Also serves Chinese. *Tharachan*, Phetkasem Rd. Also serves Thai.

Chinese   Chinese restaurants are to be found around the junction of Phetkasem and Naebkhaehat roads.

Indian   *Moti Mahal*, Naresdamri Rd. Reasonable Indian restaurant serving the usual dishes.

International   Expensive: *Le Chablis*, 33 Naresdamri Road. Highly recommended French (and Thai) cuisine, the restaurant was run by a Thai-French couple but since the death of the husband in 1998 the wife has successfully continued the enterprise. First-class and very reasonable food (and wine). Recommended. **Mid-range**: *Lo Stivale*, 132 Naresdamri Rd. The best Italian restaurant in town. Recommended. *Beer Garden*, Naresdamri Rd. Mostly serves western dishes from steaks to grilled chicken with a sprinkling of Thai dishes – a popular watering spot. *La Villa*, Poonsuk Rd, pizzas, pasta and other Italian dishes, nothing remarkable but pleasant surroundings.

Foodstalls   There is an excellent new *Food Market* opposite the Town Hall on Damnoenkasem Rd. The night market just off Phetkasem Rd does the usual selection of cheap Thai food as well as seafood that is so fresh that they have to tie the crabs' and lobsters' pincers shut.

The most distinctive buy is a locally produced printed cotton called *pha khommaphat*. The usual tourist shops can be found lining most streets in the town. There are also a

Shopping

The Southern Region

number of tailors shops that have opened recently, guaranteeing any style you want, made-to-fit within 3-4 days.

Night market Dechanuchit Rd, close to the bus station. Open dusk-2200; it sells a range of goods including Tibetan jewellery, paper dragons, T-shirts, cassettes, watches and silk scarves. **Seashell souvenirs** To be avoided. **Shopping centre** 1/9 Srasong Rd.

Sport   **Golf** *Royal Hua Hin Golf Course*, designed in 1926 by a Scottish engineer working on the Royal Siamese Railway, is the oldest in Thailand and recently upgraded. Open to the public Mon-Sun 0600-1800. Green fees ฿1,000 at the weekend and ฿600 during the week (per 9 holes). Caddies available ฿100. 19 holes. **Minigolf** Phetkasem Road, T511585 (south of town), open Mon-Sun 0900-2300 ฿60-100 per person. 3 more golf courses are under construction. **Snooker** Parlours in town. **Watersports and horse riding** Along the beach.

Tour operators   Concentrated on Damnoenkasem and Phetkasem roads. *Ken Diamond Company Ltd*, 162/6 Naresdamri Rd, T513863, F513863. *Thip's Top Tours*, 162/4 Naresdamri Rd, T532488, F532488, thiptop@loxinfo.co.th *Western Tours Hua Hin*, 11 Damnoenkasem Rd, T512560. *Pran Tour*, 1st flr, *Siriphetkasem Hotel*, Srasong Rd, T511654. *Hua Hin Travel*, *The Royal Garden Resort*.

Transport   **Local Bicycle hire**: ฿100 per day (on Damnoenkasem and Phetkasem roads). **Bus**: sta-
See also Ins & outs,   tion on Dechanuchit Rd. Buses to Khao Krilas or Khao Takiab every 20 mins, ฿10. **Car**
page 550   **hire**: jeeps ฿800-1,000 per day (on Damnoenkasem and Phetkasem roads). **Motorbike**
230 km S of Bangkok   **hire**: ฿200 per day upwards (on Damnoenkasem and Phetkasem roads). **Saamlor**: ฿20-40 around town, ฿150 for a sightseeing tour. **Songthaew**: run set routes around town and out to Khao Takiab, ฿10. **Taxis**: run prescribed routes for set fares, taxi stand on Phetkasem Rd, opposite *Chatchai Hotel*. Taxis can be hired for the day for ฿400 plus petrol. Motorcycle taxis (identified by 'taxi' sign) will take you wherever you want to go.

Long distance Air: Bangkok Airways, T5352498, daily connections with Bangkok at 1900, 35 mins.

Train: the station is on Damnoenkasem Rd, T511073. Regular connections with Bang-kok's Hualamphong station (same train as to Phetburi) 3½-4 hrs. Day excursions run on weekends, leaving Hualamphong at 0615, arriving Hua Hin at 1130, departing from Hua Hin at 1630, arriving Bangkok 2030. Regular connections with Phetburi 1 hr.

Bus: station is on Srasong Rd, next to the Chatchai market, T511654. Regular a/c con-nections with Bangkok's Southern bus terminal near the Thonburi train station 3½ hrs; non-a/c buses leave from the new terminal on Phra Pinklao Rd 3½ hrs. Also con-nections with Phetburi, Cha-am and other southern destinations. Overnight VIP buses to Phuket available (11 hrs). **Taxi**: 3 hrs from Bangkok (about ฿1,600-1,800).

Directory   **Airline offices** *Bangkok Airways*, 114/17 Phetkasem Rd, T532113, F532115. **Banks** Currency exchange booths along Phetkasem Rd. **Communications Email** service: at the post office and internet cafés around town. **Overseas telephone office**: Damnoenkasem Rd. **Post Office**: 21 Damnoenkasem Rd. **Medical services** 511-743 Phetkasem Rd, T511743 (4 km downtown). **Useful addresses** Police station: Damnoenkasem Rd, T511027.

Khao Sam Roi Yod National Park

Khao Sam Roi Yod National Park (Mountain of Three Hundred Peaks), lies about 45 km south of Hua Hin, east off Route 4. It was declared Thailand's third national park and first marine park in 1966. The park occupies an area of limestone hills surrounded by salt-water flats, and borders the Gulf of Thailand. Its freshwater marshes provide 11 different categories of wetland habitat (as much as the Red River Delta in Vietnam which covers an area nearly 200 times greater). A haven for water birds, the area has been extensively developed (and exploited) as a centre of prawn and fish farming limiting the marshland available to the waterbirds who breed here. The park has the advantage of being relatively small – it covers just 98 sq km – with readily accessible sights: wildlife (including the rare and shy serow), forest walks, caves (**Phraya Nakhon**, close to Ban Bang Pu beach, with two large sinkholes where the roof collapsed a century ago, and a pavilion which was built in 1896 for the visit of King Rama V and Sai Cave, which contains impressive stalactites and stalagmites and 'petrified waterfall', created from dripping water) and quiet beaches. At least 237 species of land and water-birds have been recorded – including painted storks, herons, egrets and many different waders. Boats can be hired from local fishermen, organized at Park headquarters, to visit caves and beaches (฿200-700). Boat trips usually sight

Colour map 3, grid C3

The plains of Sam Roi Yod were also used as the location for Pol Pot's Killing Fields in the film of the same name

The Southern Region

Khao Sam Roi Yod National Park

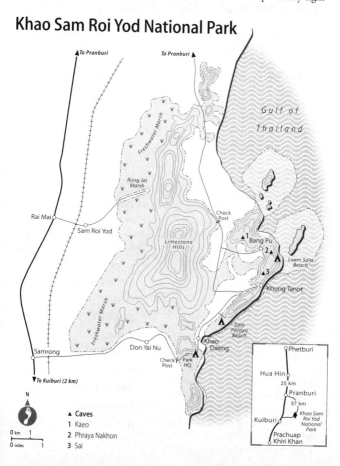

schools of dolphin. The biggest challenge facing the park – which supports a remarkable range of habitats for such a small area – is encroachment by private shrimp ponds; more than a third of the park area was cleared for fish and shrimp farming in 1992. Ironically, most of the prawn farms are now deserted, due to prawn disease. The soil was highly acidic which caused bacteria to flourish and oxygen to reduce in the ponds. Money is now needed to restore the farms back to parkland – this may be received if the park becomes a world conservation site. The park now distributes a very useful guide with comprehensive details on fauna and flora and other natural sights in the park. Available at the park HQ.
■ *Getting there: by bus or train from Hua Hin or Bangkok to Pranburi. From Pranburi charter a songthaew (฿250) or a motorcycle taxi (฿150) to the park HQ. NB Be sure you are taken to Khao Sam Roi Yod National Park, and not Khao Sam Roi Yod village. For Laem Sala Beach (located within the park), there are regular songthaews from Pranburi market to Bang Pu village between 0600 and 1600, ฿20.*

Sleeping **B-D** Bungalows T02-5614292 ext 747, either for hire in their entirety or per couple (฿100 per person per night) and a camping ground (tents for hire are in worn state). You can also pitch your own tent here for around ฿20. Bungalows are available at both the park HQ and at Laem Sala Beach. **NB** Take mosquito repellent.

Prachuap Khiri Khan   ประจวบคีรีขันธ์

Phone code: 032
Colour map 3, grid C3

Prachuap Khiri Khan is a small and peaceful resort with a long cres-cent-shaped beach. The town is more popular with Thais than with farangs and it has a reputation for good seafood. An exhausting climb up **Khao Chong Krachok**, the 'Mountain with the Mirror' (past armies of preening monkeys), is rewarded with fine views of the surrounding countryside and bay. At the summit there is an unremarkable shrine containing yet another footprint of the Buddha. There is a good **night market** at the corner of Phitakchat and Kong-Kiat roads. The **tourist office** is on Sarathip Road.

Excursions **Ao Manao** is an attractive bay 5 km south of town with a rather disappointing beach and lots of day trippers. However there is one place to stay here which makes it is an alternative to sleeping in Prachuap. **Sleeping** *Sawadii Khan Wing*, T02-611017. Small cottages, well maintained, sea views, attached bathrooms, some large bungalows available for families. The management here is poor and lacking in initiative but the rooms are OK. ■ *Getting there: easiest by motorbike taxi (฿20-30). Alternatively, take the tourist road train (which looks like something from Disneyland). This goes regularly between Ao Manao and town and can be flagged down on the beach ฿15. To explore nearby (largely deserted) beaches, hire a motorbike and drive the small roads between Prachuap and Ban Saphan.*

Tours Informal tours can be organized with *Mr Pinit*, who can often be found on the beach, or can be contacted on T550059. He has motorbikes and will take you to wats, caves, waterfalls, or nearby islands. If you need any information on the local surroundings, for example times and prices for the National Parks, he's recom-mended as the guru of all in the area, and speaks very good English.

Prachuap Khiri Khan names

Ao Manao

อ่าวมะนาว

Bang Saphan

บางสะพาน

Huai Yang waterfall

น้ำตกห้วยยาง

Khao Chong Krachok

เขาช่องกระจก

At weekends, accommodation is hard to find, with the influx of Thais. During the week, room rates can be negotiated down.

AL-B *Hat Thong*, 7 Susuk Rd, T601050, F601057. A/c, restaurant (good Thai buffet lunch Mon-Fri), comfortable, overlooking the sea, good value, best in town. **A-D** *Thaedsaban Bungalows*, T611204. Solid concrete bungalows on stilts across the road from the beach, own bathroom, squat toilet, no TV, no hot water, some a/c. **C-D** *Golden Beach*, located 200 m south of *Happy Inn*, T601626. Similar prices and set-up but rooms are smaller, some a/c. **C-D** *Happy Inn*, located 500 m north of Khao Chong Krachock, T602082. Quite nice bungalows with TV and bathroom with squat

Sleeping

■ *on map*
Price codes:
see inside front cover

Watch out for wild monkeys who live on Khao Chong Krachok, as they sometimes try to raid the bungalows

Prachuap Khiri Khan

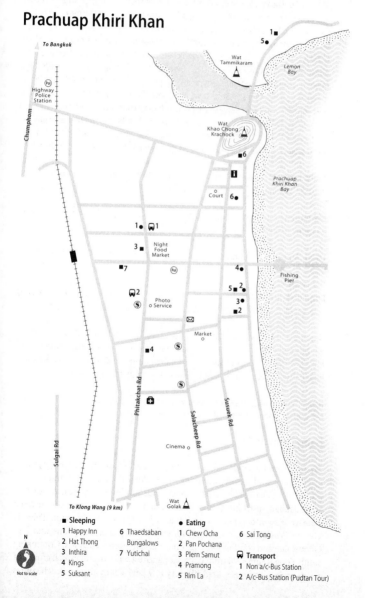

The Southern Region

■ **Sleeping**
1 Happy Inn
2 Hat Thong
3 Inthira
4 Kings
5 Suksant
6 Thaedsaban Bungalows
7 Yutichai

● **Eating**
1 Chew Ocha
2 Pan Pochana
3 Plern Samut
4 Pramong
5 Rim La
6 Sai Tong

🚌 **Transport**
1 Non a/c-Bus Station
2 A/c-Bus Station (Pudtan Tour)

N
Not to scale

toilet attached, some a/c. Just across the road from the beach, beside the river. **C-D** *Suksant*, T611145. Average rooms with TV, some with a/c but no hot water, rather seedy in the evenings. **D** *Kings*, 800/3 Phithakchat Rd, T611170. Fan rooms only. **D-E** *Prachuap Suk Hotel*, T611019, F601711. Simple but clean rooms with some fan, some a/c. **E** *Inthira*, T611013, Kong-Kiat Rd, T611013. Noisy and not very nice. **E** *Yutichai*, 35 Kong-Kiat Rd, T611055. OK rooms with own bathroom and fans.

Eating
● *on map*
Price categories:
see inside front cover

Prachuap is famous for its seafood and there are a number of excellent restaurants (as well as some more average ones) in the centre of town and along the seafront.

Mid-range *Laplong Seafood*, also north of the river, south of *Prenkoon*. Offers an extensive range of seafood, probably the best selection in town (with a few meat dishes too), reasonably priced and friendly service. *Shiew Ocha I*, located near the non-a/c bus station. Offers a good range of Thai and Chinese dishes (including a fair amount of seafood). *Shiew Ocha II*, on the seafront towards the north of the town. Good range of seafood and meat dishes. *Plern Samut*, on the seafront near the *Had Thong Hotel*, large range of seafood and other meat dishes. *Mong Lai*, 2½ km north of Laplong on the north end of the bay below the mountain. Country-style restaurant, well known for its spicy dishes. *Pan Pochana*, in the centre of town. Only offers a small selection. *Pheuenkoon*, located north of the river on the seafront. Offers a good selection of seafood and other dishes. *Pramong*, is on the seafront beside the pier but only offers a small selection of prawn, chicken and pork dishes and is reputed more for the heavy drinkers that frequent it than the quality of the food.

Night markets One in the centre of town, near the police station and another in front of the Bangkok Bank on Salacheep Rd.

Shopping Prachuap is best known for its printed cotton, known as *pha khommaphat*, although it's better to buy this in Hua Hin.

Transport
323 km to Bangkok
93 km S of Hua Hin

Local Motorized saamlor: Prachuap has its own distinctive form of tuk-tuk – motorcycles with sidecars and benchseats.

Long distance Train: the station is on the west side of town, regular connections with Bangkok's Hualamphong station 5 hrs, Hua Hin and destinations south.

Bus: the station is on Phithakchat Rd, regular a/c connections with Bangkok's Southern bus terminal near the Thonburi train station, 5 hrs; non-a/c buses leave from in front of the *Inthira Hotel*, but thse go to Chumphon, not to Bangkok. They leave every hour between 0600 and midday, but in low season there may be fewer.

Directory **Banks** The Government Savings Bank just off Salacheep Rd on the way to the pier cashes TCs and has an ATM. **Communications** Post Office: around the corner from *Hat Thong Hotel*.

Bang Saphan

Phone code: 032
Colour map 4, grid A2

There are several beaches along this strip of coast at Bang Saphan, 60 km south of Prachuap, and they are beginning to develop into small beach resort areas, geared as much to Thais as to foreigners. Hat Somboon is the nearest beach to Bang Saphan, just 1 km away. The position is attractive enough although the sand very soon degenerates into mud below the low water mark. There is **C** *Nipa Beach Bungalows*, air conditioning, hot water, telephone and TV. Good value and comfortable. Next door is *Slab*. Recommended. Continuing south along Route 3374 from Bang Saphan are a series of other small groups of resorts and guesthouses – all still very low key. Tonthonglang Beach comes recommended by one recent visitor; there are a small number of cheaper places to stay here. Around 5 km further south is a ferry link to the off-shore island of Koh Talu where there is one bungalow resort.

Chumphon ชุมพร

Phone code: 077
Colour map 4, grid A2

Considered the 'gateway to the south', this is where the southern highway divides, one route running west and then south on Route 4 to Ranong, Phuket and the Andaman Sea side of the Peninsula; the other, south on Route 41 to Surat Thani, Koh Samui, Nakhon Si Thammarat and the waters of the Gulf of Thailand. In his book *Surveying and exploring in Siam*, published in 1900, James McCarthy writes of 'Champawn' marking the beginning of the Malay Peninsula. Though a group of French engineers had already visited the area with a view to digging a canal through the Kra Isthmus, it was clearly a little place: the "harbour was full of rocks covered with oysters. The usual cocoa-nut palms and grass shanties marked the position of the village".

At the end of 1988, Typhoon Gay tore its way through Chumphon province, causing extensive flooding and the death of more than 300 villagers. The positive side of the disaster was that it led to a ban on all logging in Thailand; deforestation was perceived to be to blame for the severe flooding.

Chumphon is 8 km off Route 4/41. There is not much to see, but there are some good beaches nearby and it can be used as an access point for Koh Tao (see the end of **Transport**, below). The **tourist information centre**, in front of the railway station, is not very informative.

Pak Nam Chumphon lies 11 km southeast of Chumphon (on Route 4901), on the coast, at the mouth of the Chumphon River. This is a big fishing village with boats for hire to the nearby islands where swiftlets build their nests for the Chinese speciality, bird's nest soup – *yanwo*, in Chinese. Many concessionaires are accompanied by bodyguards; visitors should seek permission before venturing to the nest sites. Islands include Koh Phrao, Koh Lanka Chiu and Koh Rang Nok. ■ *Getting there: songthaews from opposite the morning market on the southern side of town.*

Excursions

Diving, jungle treks, boat trips to caves can all be organized through a guest-house or travel agent here. *Infinity*, 68/2 Tha Taphao Rd, can help with boats to Koh Tao from Paknam and will arrange day tours. For example they organize one-day trips to Yai Ai Beach (a 3-km-long beach 45 km north of Chumphon) and the nearby Koh Khai, both of which are very good for snorkelling, for ฿600. Two-day trips cost ฿1,000 (including camping on the beach). At the time of writing there is no accommodation on the beach but there are plans to build a hotel here as soon as the Chumphon airport has been opened. *Infinity*, 68/2 Tha Taphao Rd, also organize a one-day tour to **Rubror Cave**, on the hill near Wat Thep Charoen a kilometre from Chumphon, containing stalactites and stalagmites, **Phitsadarn Cave** and **Thung Wua Laen Beach** for ฿400. The *Chumphon Guesthouse* organizes one-day tours to Hat Sai Ri, Thung Wua Laen Beach, and both caves for ฿450 including lunch (leave 0900, arrive back 1800). *Mayazees Resthouse* rents out motorcycles for ฿150 per day if you would prefer to go out and explore the area on your own.

Tours

B *Janson Chumphon*, off 188-65 Saladaeng Rd, T502520, F503403. A/c, restaurant, pool, newest in town. Fairly clean, well-equipped a/c rooms. Restaurant serves a wide range of Thai food. Discotheque attached. **C** *Pharadorn Inn*, 180/12 Pharadorn Rd, T511598. A/c, restaurant, pool, A/c rooms furnished with attractive bamboo furniture.

Sleeping
■ *on map*
Price codes:
see inside front cover

The restaurant offers a wide range of reasonably priced food. **C** *Tha Taphao*, 66/1 Tha Taphao Rd, T511479, F502479. Large a/c rooms with cable TV; some also have a fridge. Attractive restaurant.

D *Sri Chumphon*, Saladaeng Rd. Hotel is not a very beautiful building, but it is comfortable to stay. These words are emblazoned on a window outside the hotel and sum the place up nicely. Clean rooms, some have a/c and TV, coffee shop. **D** *Suriwong*, 125/27-29 Saladaeng Rd, T511203. Somewhat dingy rooms, some a/c, TV but Thai channels only. **D** *Mayazee's Resthouse*, 111/35-36 Soi Bangkok Bank, Saladen Rd, Tha Taphao, T504452. Bright, clean, comfortable and welcoming guesthouse. Rooms are brightly decorated and spotlessly clean. Some have a/c, some have a small balcony. Spacious sitting area upstairs and down. Free drinking water, tea and coffee provided. Every effort is made to make the guest feel at home. Highly recommended. **D-E** *Sri Taifa*, 73-75 Saladaeng Rd, T511063. The a/c rooms are much nicer that the fan rooms which are quite dirty and unappealing. The entrance is through a bustling restaurant.

E *Ekawin Guesthouse* , 5/3 Krom Luang Chumphon Rd, T501821. The most expensive room has a private shower-room, but it is dark as it has, as yet, no window. The other rooms have basins and they are all very clean. The service is friendly and some food is served. Good tour information provided. Recommended. **E** *Chumphon Guesthouse* (otherwise known as *Maio Guesthouse*) located on 2 different sites on and close to the Krong Luam Chumphon Rd, T501242. Bright, clean, cosy rooms with wood-panelled

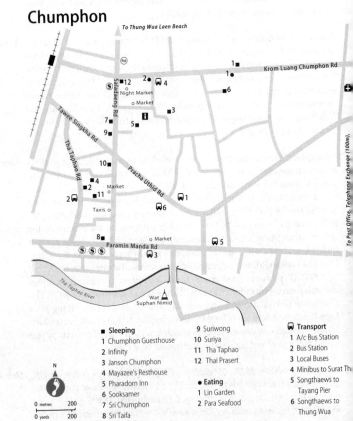

Chumphon

To Thung Wua Laen Beach

Krom Luang Chumphon Rd

Saladaeng Rd
Tawee Singkha Rd
Tha Taphao Rd
Pracha Uthid Rd
Paramin Manda Rd
Tha Taphao River

Wat Suphan Nimid

N

0 metres 200
0 yards 200

■ **Sleeping**
1 Chumphon Guesthouse
2 Infinity
3 Janson Chumphon
4 Mayazee's Resthouse
5 Pharadorn Inn
6 Sooksamer
7 Sri Chumphon
8 Sri Taifa
9 Suriwong
10 Suriya
11 Tha Taphao
12 Thai Prasert

● **Eating**
1 Lin Garden
2 Para Seafood

🚌 **Transport**
1 A/c Bus Station
2 Bus Station
3 Local Buses
4 Minibus to Surat Th
5 Songthaews to Tayang Pier
6 Songthaews to Thung Wua

To Post Office, Telephone Exchange (100m).

floors, homely atmosphere, friendly and helpful management who speak good English. If you book the boat trip to Koh Tao from here they only charge ฿30 rather than ฿50 for the taxi to the ferry. **E** *Suriya*, 25/24-5 Saladaeng Rd, T511144. Rooms are a little tatty, but clean enough. Squat loos. Recommended. **E-F** *Infinity*, 68/2 Tha Taphao Rd, T501937. Only 3 rooms, one larger with balcony, 2 smaller with no windows – all have fans, very basic but clean, shared bathrooms. Very friendly and helpful management, but it closes at 2230 and you cannot get in (or out) between then and 0730. Good travel service offered here, some food served. **E-F** *Sooksamer* (or *Pat's Place*), 118/4 Suksamer Rd. Thai and European food, friendly, clean rooms, English-speaking owner, good source of information. Recommended. **E-F** *Thai Prasert*, OK rooms with fan, some have own bathroom, but not as nice as *Chumphon* and *Mayazees* guesthouses.

There are 2 **night markets** on Krom Luang Chumphon Rd and on Tha Taphao Rd. There are also several restaurants on Tha Taphao and Saladaeng roads and on the Krom Luang Chumphon Rd. *Lin Garden* and *Para Seafood* have been recommended.

Eating
● *on map*

Air A new airport has recently opened in Chumphon and start-up domestic airline *PB Air* operate a service to Bangkok. **Train** Station at west end of Kram Luang Chumphon Rd. Regular connections with Bangkok's Hualamphong station, 7½-9 hrs and all stops south.

Transport
500 km S of Bangkok
121 km N of Rayong

Bus Terminal on Tha Taphao Rd, not far from the night market. Regular a/c connections with Bangkok's Southern bus terminal near the Thonburi train station, 7 hrs; non-a/c buses leave from the new terminal on Phra Pinklao Rd, 7 hrs. Also connections with all destinations south.

Getting to Koh Tao (see page 688) By boat from the pier 10 km southeast of town. There is a slow midnight boat which takes 6 hrs and costs ฿200 (taxi to the pier from town usually costs ฿50 but if you book through *Chumphon Guesthouse* they only charge ฿30 for the taxi). There is a speedboat at 0800 which arrives at 0940 and costs ฿400 (plus taxi). There is also a slower, larger speedboat at 0730 for ฿400 which takes 2½ hrs. Tickets for these boats can be bought at all the travel agents in town.

Banks *Thai Farmers' Bank*, Saladaeng Rd. **Communications** Post Office: this has recently moved to new premises on the Paramin Manda Rd about 1 km out of town on the left-hand side. Telephone Office: for overseas calls slightly further on the right.

Directory

Beaches around Chumphon

Pharadon Phap Beach, 1 km south of Pak Nam on the Chumphon estuary: **A-B** *Porn Sawan Hotel Resort*, has 60 bungalows, a/c, restaurant, pool, tennis.

Hat Thung Wua Lean, 18 km north of Chumphon, is beautiful, probably the best beach in the area. There are a number of hotels and bungalow operations here: **B-C** *Chumphon Cabana Resort*, T501990, has some nicely decorated a/c bungalows set in attractive gardens and two hotel blocks all with a/c and hot water. The newer buildings have all been designed on energy-saving principles in keeping with the owner's environmental concerns. The resort has all the usual facilities including a pool, a very peaceful location and a great view of the beach from the restaurant and some of the bungalows. Down sides are that the food served at the restaurant is very bland, and sometimes there is an unpleasant smell from the drains in some of the rooms in the hotel blocks. **B-C** *Chuan Phun*, has 40 rooms in an apartment block, all with a/c, hot water and TV, rooms at the back with no sea view are slightly cheaper. **B-C** *Kray Rim Lae*, has nice a/c bungalows of varying sizes. **B-D** *View Sea Food*, has

Sleeping
There are a number of good beaches around Chumphon, most of them with accommodation

nice bungalows. **C-D** *Clean Wave*, has some a/c and some cheaper fan-cooled bungalows. **C-E** *Sea Beach*, only has fan-cooled bungalows at varying prices depending upon the size. ■ *Getting there: catch a bus from the market in Chumphon for ฿30.*

Hat Sai Ri is 3 km south of Hat Pharadon and close to Koh Thong Luang – there is good snorkelling in the area. There is also a shrine to His Royal Highness Prince Chumphon, the so-styled father of the Royal Thai Navy. The **D** *Tung Makham* offers good bungalows with fan and attached bathroom, and organizes snorkelling trips (15 mins by speedboat) to Thong Luang. To get to this beach get a songthaew (฿20) from opposite *Infinity Travel* or from the post office.

Amphoe Thung Tako (Sunny Beach) is located 50 km south of Chumphon. **B-C** *Chumphon Sunny Beach Resort*, T2811234. Has fan-cooled and a/c bungalows. ■ *Getting there: get a bus from the bus station in Chumphon.*

Amphoe Lang Suan is 62 km south of Chumphon. There are reports of two beautiful caves in the area – Tham Khao Ngoen and Tham Khao Kriep – although we have not been able to confirm this. The district is also locally renowned for the quality of its fruit. **C-E** *Tawat Hotel*, T541341. A hotel with 100 rooms, some with fan and some a/c. **D-E** *Chumphon 99 Bay Resort*, T541481. Bungalows. **D-E** *Jane Resort*, T541330. A smaller hotel than *Tawat* and with slightly cheaper rooms (fan-cooled only). ■ *Getting there: get a bus from the bus station in Chumphon.*

The West Coast: Chumphon to Phuket

Ranong   ระนอง

Phone code: 077
Colour map 4, grid B2

Ranong province is the first southern province bordering the Indian Ocean and Thailand's rainiest (often in excess of 5,000 mm per year), narrowest and least populated. Kra Buri, 58 km north of Ranong, is the point where the Kra Isthmus is also at its narrowest, and there has been debate for centuries about the benefits of digging a canal across the Isthmus, so linking the Gulf of Thailand with the Andaman Sea. The name Ranong is derived from *rae* (tin) *nong* (rich), and the town was established in the late 18th century by a family from Hokkien, China. Ranong has a predominantly Sino-Thai population. In town there are a number of attractive 19th-century Chinese-style houses. There is a small **tourist office** on Kamlungsab Road.

Sights

Surrounded by forested mountains, Ranong is a scenic place to stay for a day or two. However, there is little to keep the demanding visitor here for much longer than this. It is a small and unpretentious provincial capital, an important administrative centre but hardly a place endowed with natural beauty or historical or artistic significance.

Geo-thermal mineral water springs
The water is not too hot to touch, but hot enough to cook an egg in

The town contains **geo-thermal mineral water springs** (65°C) at **Wat Tapotharam**, 2 km east of the town and behind the *Jansom Thara Hotel*. The hot water bubbles up into concrete tubs named *bor mae*, *bor por* and *bor luuk saaw* – mother, father and daughter pools respectively. The springs provide the *Jansom Thara Hotel* with thermal water for hot baths and a giant jacuzzi. There is a small park with a cable bridge over the river, a number of bathing pools (sometimes empty of water), and a second-rate animal garden. The wat is rather dull, containing a footprint of the Buddha. ■ *Getting there: by songthaew along Route 2; ask for 'bor naam rawn' (hot water well).*

Port of Ranong lies 3 km from town. Each morning the dock seethes with activity as Thai and Burmese fishing boats unload their catches. Boats can be hired at a pontoon next to the dock, to tour the bustling harbour and look across the Kra River estuary to the Burmese border (approximately ฿300). For those who wish to actually step ashore in Burma, then it is possible to visit Kawthoung (see below). **NB** Border officials can be touchy, carry your passport with you. Ranong is an important point of contact between Burma and Thailand. Not only is there considerable trade, but many Burmese, in search of higher wages, cross the estuary to work.

Surin and **Similan Islands**: boats sail from Ranong Port, see page 604.

There are a number of notable **beaches** and **islands** in the neighbourhood of Ranong, many within the limits of the **Laem Son National Park**, such as Hat Bang Baen, Koh Payam, Koh Nam Noi, Koh Kam Yai, Koh Chang and Koh Kam Tok. The islands are only easily accessible in the high season, between November and April. The park was gazetted in 1983 and covers a little over 300 sq km. The water here is not terribly clear – the park and the islands effectively lie at the outer limits of the Kra River estuary – so don't expect coral and excellent visibility. Mangroves fringe many of the islands and because of the high rainfall in the area the natural vegetation is tropical rainforest. While the islands may not have great water, or great beaches for that matter, they do have good birdlife (there are around 47 bird species in the park) and because there is no electricity it is peaceful and relaxed (some of the bungalows have generators). The only time to visit is between November and April; outside this period the guesthouses shut and the long-tailed boats stop operating. ■ *Getting there: long-tail boats run from Ranong Port out to Koh Chang around 3 or 4 times a day, in the morning. There is no fixed fare – it depends how many people are travelling. Return boats tend to leave Koh Chang in the afternoon.*

Sleeping on the islands   There are around 10 bungalow operations on **Koh Chang**. Some can be booked through *Ranong Travel* in town. **E** *Koh Chang Resort* offers wooden huts, some with attached bathroom and has a restaurant. Snorkelling and fishing can be organized from here.   **E** *Rasta Baby* , T833077. Small group of

Ranong

bungalows on north side of island, laid-back atmosphere in line with its name. **E** *Sunset*, this small operation offers clean bungalows and a friendly atmosphere. **E** *Chang Thong* and *Phung Thong* are next door to each other, just 5 mins walk from the pier. **F** *Sabai Jai*, probably the best value and one of the best-run places on the island. Clean and with good, home-cooked food, dorm beds available as well as range of bungalows. **B** *Andaman Peace Bungalows* on **Hat Bang Baen** is in an idyllic spot although the bungalows need some attention. They come with fan and fridge.

Sleeping
■ *on map*
Price codes:
see inside front cover

A-B *Jansom Thara*, 2/10 Phetkasem Rd, Bang Rin, F821821, T02-4242050. A/c, restaurant, pool, international-style hotel, the bath-water comes straight from the thermal springs. Check in before 1600 to enjoy the thermal baths in your room. Lovely views from most of the rooms (many of which have balconies). **A-B** *Jansom Thara Resort* (out of town), Paknam Ranong, T821611, T02-4242050. A/c, restaurant, pool, overlooks Kra River estuary.

B *Eiffel Inn*, 6 km out of town, T823271-2. Comfortable bungalows (and some rooms in apartment block), coffee shop, room service, rooms have a/c, hot water, TV, fridge, friendly but rather spoilt by a hideous misrepresentation of the Eiffel Tower sitting in the car park. Room maintenance sometimes leaves a little to be desired, so it's worth checking out your room first. **B-C** *Spa Inn*, 25/1 Phetkasem Rd, T811715. All rooms have hot water, bath tub, a/c and are comfortable with wall-to-wall carpeting. Slightly more expensive ones come with TV and fridge.

C-D *Ranong Inn*, 29/9 Petchkasem Rd, T822777. Most rooms have balconies overflowing with flowers, OK rooms, carpeted, some have a/c, swimming pool.

D *Ranong Guesthouse*, T833369. Some a/c, all have TV and attached bathrooms (Asian toilet) but no hot water. Spacious, clean and light rooms. Good value but rather stern management. **D-E** *Asia*, 39/9 Ruangrat Rd, T811113. Some a/c, clean rooms, well located hotel but can be noisy. Rooms are adequate and staff seem reasonably tuned in. **D-E** *Sin Ranong*, 26/23-4 Ruangrat Rd, T811454. Adequate.

E *Rattanasin*, corner of Ruangrat and Luwang roads, T811242. Large rooms with attached bathrooms (Asian toilet), some a/c, central location but noisy and watch out for the cockroaches.

Eating

In the centre of town on Ruangrat Rd the excellent **cheap** *J&T Food and Ice*, serves a range of delicious but very reasonably priced Thai food and ice-creams, very popular place with locals and farangs alike, friendly owners. Recommended. *Somboon Restaurant*, opposite the *Jansom Thara Hotel*, serves delicious Thai and Chinese seafood much of which is displayed in tanks in front so it should be pretty fresh.

Shopping

Batik Shop on Thawi Sinkha Rd.

Tour operators

Ranong Travel, 37 Ruangrat Rd is probably a better source of information than the tourist information office. They can book bungalows on Koh Chang (see Excursions), arrange fishing trips, and advise on visiting Burma.

Transport
600 km to Bangkok

Air The airport is 20 km south of town. *Bangkok Airways* fly once a day to and from Bangkok, leaving Ranong at 0900. **Road Bus**: The road journey from the north is arduous – 8 hrs – the last half of which is through mountains; not good for travel sickness sufferers. Consider taking the train from Bangkok to Chumphon and the bus from there (which takes the same amount of time). The bus terminal is on the edge of town, near the *Jansom Thara Hotel*. Regular a/c and non-a/c connections with Bangkok's Southern bus terminal near the Thonburi railway station. Also connections with

Chumphon, Surat Thani and Phuket (304 km south). For private coach companies T2816939 or 2817011.

Airline offices *Bangkok Airways*, 50/18 Mool, Phetkasem Highway, T835096, F835097. **Banks** On Tha Muang Rd there are branches of the *Bank of Ayudya*, *Thai Military Bank*, *Thai Farmers Bank* and *Siam Commercial Bank*, all with ATMs and/or exchange facilities. **Communications** Post Office: Chon Rao Rd, near the junction with Dap Khadi Rd. There is also a Poste Restante service. The **telephone office** is on Ruangrat Rd. **Medical services** Hospital: situated at the junction of Permphon and Kamlungsab roads (currently being extended).

Directory

Takua Pa to Khao Lak

The western coastline is lined with beaches, but many are quite hard to get to. The **Bang Sak Beach** area lies just south of Takua Pa off the main road to Phuket. Although at least one resort has been operating for about ten years, this area has only just begun to draw the attention of tourism operations targetting non-Thai tourists. The beaches in the area are mostly gently sloping with pale yellow-to-white sands lined with casuarinas and backed with beach forest and some swamp forest. Unlike the Khao Lak area further south there are no hills as a backdrop to the resorts, but the isolation of many of these beaches, miles from anywhere, is an attraction in itself for those who want to escape completely. Bang Sak beach itself is a Thai tourism spot popular with local picnickers and well served with small seafood restaurants. It is too out of the way to be tacky, however, but it does look as though this will be the next area to take off in terms of tourism development.

Takua Pa, no more than an hour's drive from Bang Niang, and considerably less from Bang Sak, was once the centre of Phangnga province. Once a nationally important centre of tin mining, Takua Pa has lost much of its financial power since the collapse of the tin market in 1983, but it is a friendly place to wander, and the main shopping and administrative centre for this part of Phangnga province. The town has a charming, rambling layout and some lovely old streets with Sino-Portugese buildings.

Prathong Island has one resort well known for its environmental focus: the *Golden Buddha Beach Resort*. The Chelon Institute carries out research on sea turtles at Prathong Island with the assistance of this resort, and also accepts volunteers. See details on the resort in the accommodation section below. **Khor Khao Island** further south has one newly opened resort. This island lies in a beautiful bay with views to the hills of Ranong and nearby islands to the north and west.

Takua Pa & Bang Sak
Phone code: 076
Colour map 4, grid B1

There are several islands off the Phangnga coast near Takua Pa

There is a stretch of **coral reef** lying off shore between *Sun Splendour Lodge* and *Bang Sak Beach Resort*, about 1 km north of *Bang Sak Beach Resort* which is revealed at low tide. The nearby village is a Moken community (also known as the Chao Le) who have settled in this area but continue to practice fishing with traditional fishing gear.

Several **national parks**, are within easy reach of this area including the Similan and Surin Marine National Parks, Khao Lak-Lam Ru National Park, Khao Sok (see page 575), and Sri Phang Nga National Parks.

Excursions

Information on tours can be found at almost every resort.

Tours

L-A *Bang Sak Beach Resort*, about 15 mins drive from Takua Pa bus terminal, or 1-2 hrs from Phuket International Airport, T446520, F446520, annemathuros@hotmail.com Just opened, this is a delightful resort right on the beach with comfortable cottages built in

Sleeping
■ *on map*
Price codes:
see inside front cover

The Southern Region

local style from natural materials, and equipped with all the facilities television). A wooden walkway leads through some natural forest which has been left intact in various places in the grounds. Some of the cottages are tucked away in these forest patches. Two restaurants serve seafood dishes in Thai and international style. Facilities also include a mineral spa, massage, aromatherapy, body and beauty treatments, and a Thai cooking class. Nice pool with a deck, mini golf, petanque and a children's playground are all available and there will be a souvenir shop. Recommended. There is a new luxury development under construction at Laem Pakarang (Coral Cape).

AL-B *Similana Resort*, off the main Takua Pa – Phuket road, just a bit further south of the Bang Sak area, signposted down a dirt road. T420166-8, www.losthorizonsasia.com/simitxthtm Perched on a rocky hillside overlooking a private bay, the resort is beautifully – and thoughtfully – laid out. The bungalows and tree houses are particularly attractive with high ceilings, wood furnishings and window seats. The hotel block has forest views and large balconies (and baths). Tree houses, in fact they are bungalows on high stilts, are at beach level. Two restaurants serving Thai, Italian and northern European food. Facilities include pool and recreation room, massage services, reflexology, gift shop, jeep rental and tours to the Similans and other national parks in the area. Very friendly and helpful staff. Limousine services from Phuket International Airport are available. Recommended, but the number of steps and narrow paths might make it difficult for those unsteady on their feet. **A-B** *Theptharo Lagoon Beach Resort*, Off the main Takua Pa-Phuket road follow the signs to the resort from Ban Khuk Khak village. T420151-5, www.khao-lak.com/theptharo Large, smart concrete bungalows with traditional shingle roofs, Thai-style furnishings (the doubles are quite romantic with four-poster beds), balconies and sunken baths (some with a view!). All a/c. Set in landcaped gardens overlooking the sea. All facilities including a pool. The setting is attractive but the resort is new and the garden looks rather sparse. **A-C** *Sun Splendor Lodge*, in Thai this is called the 'Tap Tawan Resort'. Down the same road as the *Bangsak Beach Resort* on the road leading to Tap Tim Beach off the main Takua Pa-Phuket road, this resort is located on a small sandy headland with very shallow waters on the beaches. Chalet-style accommodation (all with a/c) in open grounds, with a small pool. Larger chalets sleep four in two double beds (in the same large room). Rooms are simply furnished. The restaurant serves Thai food only. Friendly staff. There are fan rooms above the reception and restaurant building. These are better value than the a/c rooms. **B** *Golden Buddha Beach Resort*, www.losthorizons.com/asia A full-board rate of an additional ฿550 is also available. Located on Prathong Island off the Phangnga coast, the *Golden Buddha Beach Resort* supports a turtle conservation project run by the Chelon Institute on the same beach as the resort. Volunteers for the project are accommodated at the resort. Biologists can get reduced rates if they want to work on the project (see the website for more details). Reports from those who have visited the resort describe it as 'idyllic' and 'paradise'. Accommodation is in one-bedroom bungalows. 5-day, 4-night tours of the area with accommodation at the resort can be pre-booked from overseas.

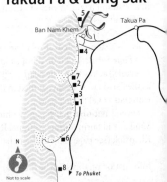

Takua Pa & Bang Sak

Not to scale

■ **Sleeping**
1 Bangsak Inn
2 Bangsak Beach Resort
3 Bangsak Resort
4 Diamond Beach Resort
5 Koh Khor Khao Resort
6 Similana Resort
7 Sun Splendor Lodge
8 Theptharo Lagoon Beach Resort

C-D *Bangsak Resort*, about 1 km on from the *Bangsak Inn* down the winding beach road and within sight of the *Bangsak Beach Resort*. A mixture of old and new fan bungalows in gardens. The new bungalows are quite nice, in a coconut plantation, the old bungalows are rather run-down and in regimental gardens with little charm. Nice beach and walking distance to several local seafood restaurants. Not bad value (for the new bungalows) if you don't mind being miles from anywhere. **D** *Diamond Beach Resort*, about 5 km out of Takua Pa down the road leading to the Khor Khao Pier, and Nam Khem fishing village, there is a turn-off to the left and a dirt road leads to the Diamond Beach Resort. T01-9584916. Very basic concrete bungalows in an open setting with some Casuarina trees. Closed during the low season. Looks very run-down. About 500 m from the nearest beach. The beach is quite pleasant, but nothing special for the area and there are no facilities, e.g. restaurants or other refreshments, nearby. **D** *Koh Khor Khao Resort*, past the turn-off to *Diamond Beach Resort*, the road winds through a fishing village to the pier to Koh Khor Khao. Boats can be taken to the resort for ฿10 per person each way, and ฿400 return for a vehicle. The resort is closed from May to Oct. T01-2292303, 593176. The resort can be contacted at the office at the entrance to the road to Nam Khem Fishing Village on the main Takua Pa-Phuket road. Fan rooms only. **D-E** *Bangsak Inn*, Take the road down to Bang Sak Beach off the main Takua Pa-Phuket road, there is a T-junction at the beach and *Bangsak Inn* is about 100 m down the road to the right just across the road from the beach. T422476 after 1700. Dingy, dirty rooms with ceiling fan on very low ceilings. Not recommended.

Road Bus: some a/c and non-a/c connections between the Southern terminal in Bangkok and Takua Pa (12 hrs). From Krabi and Phangnga, take a bus towards Phuket and change at Kochloi to a bus running north to Takua Pa. From Phuket take a local bus to Takua Pa. Local buses and songthaews provide transport between smaller communities.

Transport
Takua Pa is 134 km N of Phuket & 54 km N of Khao Lak

Khao Lak   เขาหลัก

The Khao Lak area is a relatively recent discovery for visitors to Thailand, popular with Germans (which may account for the generally high standard of cleanliness at virtually all the resorts!). It stretches from just south of the Khao Lak-Lam Ru National Park, north to the Bang Niang beach. There is a string of resorts along a series of shallow, secluded beaches, roughly midway between Takua Pa (30 km north) and Thai Muang (30 km south), 80 km north of Phuket on the Andaman Sea coast. From north to south the beaches are: Chong Fah, Bang Niang, Nang Thong and Khao Lak. There is a small **tourist information** stand on the beach, between *Nang Thong Bay Resort* and *Garden Beach Resort*, staffed by people with an extensive knowledge of the area. They will organize tours to any of the places mentioned in **Excursions** below. ■ *0900-1100, 1600-1800.*

Phone code: 076
Colour map 4, grid C1

Khao Lak Beach itself is actually quite small, separated from the longer Nang Thong Beach by a small rocky headland where some more resort development is currently taking place. South of Khao Lak lies the National Park headquarters on another forested rocky headland. There are small beaches here which you can get to from the National Park headquarters and *Khao Lak Nature Resort*. South of the National Park is the *Poseidon Bungalow Resort* which also has its own beach. To date, Khao Lak beach is targetting the upper end of the Khao Lak market, particularly people looking for peace and quiet. The beach is very clean and bungalow-resorts are generally equipped with all the facilities.

Nang Thong Beach has a wider range of accommodation and facilities, although it is still fairly pricey. Budget accommodation is usually set back a little way from the beach. There are several beach restaurants and bars at the northern end. The main strip of small bars and restaurants that used to run through the middle of the beach is being evicted from what is government land, ostensibly so that the local government can create a park in this area.

After another small headland, there is **Bang Niang Beach** which runs into Chong Fah Beach. Bang Niang Beach has a mixture of accommodation (from budget to tourist class), some small shops and two dive shops (*Sea Dragon* and *High Class Adventure* both have booking offices here). There isn't a real sense of identity to Bang Niang yet, and it is uncertain which way tourism is likely to develop along here, but apparently a huge 600-room hotel is planned for the area in the next year, and this could change the beach considerably.

Chong Fah Beach has a stronger backpacker/budget feel with fairly long-stay visitors in several bungalow outfits. There are the tourist-class resorts too, but these do not really affect the overall character of the beach. Somewhat incongruous mixed clientele: many come for the quiet but there are also some who are attracted by the raucous Full Moon Parties (complete with booming bass which can be heard for a couple of kilometres) which are held at the far northern end of the beach.

Excursions   **Waterfalls**, there are several along the coast, two of them are **Chong Fah** (5 km north) and **Lampee** (20 km south). ■ *Getting there: the easiest way is by hired motorbike, ฿200 per day (see Local transport).*

Coral reef, an interesting half-day trip is to a local reef, 45 minutes by long-tail boat. Charges are about ฿300 for snorkelling equipment and ฿1,000 for diving, which includes equipment and two dives.

Turtle releases are held every Mar as the highlight of an annual district festival   **Turtle Beach**, at the Khao Lampee-Had Thai Muang National Park, is a 20 km-long stretch of beach where turtles, including the giant leatherback, come ashore at night to nest from November to February (entrance fee ฿20). Young turtles can be seen hatching from March to July. Hawksbill and Olive Ridley turtles are currently being raised in ponds near the park headquarters.

Khao Sok National Park is within fairly easy reach of Khao Lak – and many tour companies offer trips to the park (see page 575).

Khao Lak-Lam Ru National Park stretches from a small bay just south of the main Khao Lak tourism area, inland up into the hills. There is a tiered waterfall with walks from the main path at the top of the hill, and forest rangers can take trekkers through the hills. However, the level of English spoken leaves rather a lot to be desired and trails are not regularly maintained so it can be fairly heavy-going.

Khao Lampee-Had Thai Muang National Park is a relatively small national park, covering an area of 72 square km, and comprising two distinct geographical areas: the Thai Muang Beach area and the Khao Lampee area. The western portion, Thai Muang Beach, has 14 km of undisturbed beach lined with casuarina trees. The park continues inland for about 1 km and includes mangrove forest along the edge of the sea inlet, some swamp forest (*pa samet*) and freshwater lagoons from the old mine works from which Thai Muang derives its name (Muang in this case means mine). The

• •

Khao Lak place names

Chongfa
ช่องฟ้า

Lumpee
ลำพี

Turtle Beach
หาดเต่า

eastern portion, inland, covers several waterfalls and surrounding forested hills. There is an office in the Khao Lampee area, but the park headquarters are based in the Thai Muang area near the entrance. Accommodation is available in four fan-cooled bungalows in the Thai Muang part of the park. Prices range from ฿800 for a bungalow which can accommodate 6 people, to ฿1,000 for a bungalow which can accommodate 10 people. Bookings can be made at the central Forestry Department office in Bangkok (Reservations office, Marine National Parks Division, Royal Forest Department, Chatuchak, Bangkok, 10900 – T02-5797047-8) or at the park headquarters in Thai Muang. The bungalows may not be available while they are being improved, however, so it is best to have a back-up alternative if you do wish to stay here. Camping is allowed and food and drinks can be purchased at the canteen.

Dusit Hot Spring Beach lies south of the Thai Muang National Park and can be reached from the main Phuket-Takua Pa road (Petchkasem Road) by following the signs to Na Tai Beach and then taking the turn off to the Dusit Hot Spring Beach. The hot springs are being developed into a spa-type resort, with separate hot mineral spas for men and women set in gardens. Bungalow-type accommodation is under construction. For details contact T581360.

Tours Information on tours can be found at almost every resort. Tours to the **Similan Islands** (see page 604) are organized by *Poseidon Bungalows* and by *Khao Lak Bungalows*. A three-day trip costs around ฿3,500, including transport, accommodation and all food. They will also organize diving and snorkelling trips. *Poseidon Bungalows* will shortly be organizing five-day trips to the **Surin Islands** (see page 605). The *Thai Dive Company*, T571434, have an office in Thai Muang and will organize transport from Phuket. This is a British-managed company, with a friendly and professional manner. They are well equipped and supply excellent food. Diving companies can be found at the *Khao Lak Laguna Resort* (*Sea Dragon* and *Phuket*) and *Khao Lak Bayfront* (*Kon Tiki*), and at offices in Nang Thong and Chong Fah for the other two dive companies. *Garden Beach Resort* organize snorkelling and fishing trips (฿300 per day including meals) and trips to waterfalls (฿250-450 per day). Peter and Mani, of the *Khao Lak Restaurant* organize walking jungle trips (฿450 per day, including food), boat tours around Phangnga Bay, diving to Similan and Surin.

Sleeping
■ *on maps*
Price code:
see inside front cover

Chong Fah Beach is reached by taking the signposted road off the main Phuket-Takua Pa Highway (Route 4 to Ranong). Once you get to the beach, the resorts are off to the right down a dirt track. **B-D** *Barn Soraya Bungalows, Restaurant and Pub*, 55 Moo 5, Petchkasem Rd, Khukkhak, T420192-4, baansoraya@yahoo.com Just past the *Chong Fah Beach Resort*, this is a small concrete block next to, but not facing the sea, with 6 well-appointed fan and a/c bungalows (the a/c bungalows are more expensive). Clean and comfortable with a small balcony by the door. Koen (the owner) and his wife and mother-in-law are all very friendly and happy to help guests. Fishing tours can be arranged from a small stall at the front. Koen plans to open a restaurant and pub which will play jazz-type music and serve a mixture of western and Thai food. At the far northern end of the beach right next to the mouth of a small river, a new bungalow outfit, the **Wunder Resort**, is under construction. Adjacent to *Wunder* is **C-D** *Mai's Quiet Zone Bungalows*, 53 Moo 5 Banbangniang, T420196 F420197. Bungalows vary in size and charm. One room comes complete with kitchen for a longer stay. All fan, all equipped with mosquito nets. Doug and Mai are the friendly owners and relatively long-term residents at Chong Fah. They will rent motorbikes, jeep and bicycles and arrange elephant trekking, airport taxi, and boats to go fishing or snorkelling. Apparently the Full Moon Parties up the beach can be pretty noisy on the one night in the month they occur (cheaper in the low season or for long lets).

A-C *Bang Niang Beach Resort*, T420171-5, F420176, bangniangresort@png.a-net.net.th Set about 500 m back from the sea behind the *Chong Fah Beach Resort*, this is a small hotel-style resort with fan and a/c concrete bungalows arranged in a round with a swimming pool in the middle and a small garden. Rooms are spacious and clean. A/c rooms are all to be equipped with TV, fridge and minibar. Restaurant serves Thai, Chinese and Western food. Discounts available for low season. *Pascha Resort*, just along from the *Bang Niang Beach Resort* are a series of sea-facing wood and brick bungalows belonging to the *Pascha Resort*. The bungalows look well constructed and the garden is pleasant. About a 2 min walk to the sea. The view could be blocked by future development. **A-D** *Chong Fah Beach Resort*, 6 Moo 5 Kukkak, Petchkasem Rd, Takua Pa, T420056-9, F420055. Simple but very clean rooms with fan and bathroom, excellent Thai and international food, friendly staff. More expensive, spacious, and well-equipped a/c bungalows with large balcony, fridge, TV and hot water also available – rather characterless and in a very sparse garden of sorts. **C-E** *Coconut*, T420256 T01-9264567, which is just before *Pascha*, is something a bit different from the usual resort; staying at *Coconut* is more like staying in a home-stay. Acharn Pat Junkaew, the owner and retired teacher of the Phuket Teachers' College, wants to introduce visitors to the traditional lifestyles of Thailand's past. Three of the five rooms are in his house. Two "rooms" are reconstructions of traditional Thai houses from the Yaw Island in the Songkhla Lagoon (Songkhla Province). One is wood and the other bamboo. These houses are the best value, set in what feels like their own kitchen gardens. The accommodation is very simple with mosquito nets and basic bathrooms. He and his wife are both charming and will go out of their way to introduce guests to southern Thailand. *Coconut* comes complete with dogs, cats and chickens! No luxury, but lots of atmosphere. Recommended. **D-C** *Gerd & Noi's Sabai Bungalows*, T(01)2292197 the first bungalow outfit on your left as you come into the main area of Chong Fah Beach. A row of simple bamboo bungalows facing the sea but set back about 200 m. You can book dive trips through *High Class Adventure Diving* from their office at this bungalow outfit.

Bang Niang Beach can be reached by taking the road to Chong Fah Beach (Had Chong Fah) and then taking the dirt road off to the left, about 500 m off the main Phuket-Takua Pa Highway. The first resort you come to on the right hand side is **B-C** *The Beach Resort*, 48 Moo 5 Kukkak, Takua Pa, Phangnga 82190 T420103-6 F420107. Raised concrete bungalows in a garden plot about 2 mins walk from the beach. Fan and a/c accommodation. All rooms have hot water showers. Swimming pool due to open in late 2000. New, clean, spacious. Friendly management. Restaurant serving Thai and western food. Hotel-style facilities including laundry service, gift shop, room service, airport pick-up (฿ 800 one way). Good value especially in low season. Motorbikes are available for rental for ฿250 a day. Next door in a small row of shops is an office for *High Class Adventure Diving*. **A-B** *Palm Andaman Beach Resort*, 59 Moo 5, Tambol Kukkak, Takua Pa, Phangnga 82190, T420185-8, F420189 Large a/c bamboo cottages

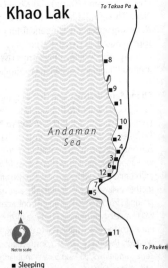

Khao Lak

Andaman Sea

To Takua Pa

To Phuket

Not to scale

■ **Sleeping**
1 Chong Fah Beach Resort
2 Khao Lak Andaman Beach Resort
3 Khao Lak Bay Front Resort
4 Khao Lak Laguna Resort
5 Khao Lak Nature Resort
6 Khao Lak Palm Beach
7 Khao Lak Resort
8 Khao Lak Tropicana Resc
9 Mai's Quiet Zone
10 Palm Andaman Beach Resort
11 Poseidon Bungalows
12 Sunset Resort

with airy bathrooms and an interior garden. For some reason the bamboo has been painted grey on the outside which makes the cottages look as though they are built from unpainted concrete. Generous sea-facing hardwood balconies on all bungalows. A pleasant quiet setting with a good restaurant, beach bar and soon-to-be completed pool. **C-D** *Paradise Bungalow and Restaurant*, T420184, 420254, 01-2709849, just across from the *Palm Andaman Beach Resort*, several bamboo bungalows on the beach. Larger bungalows at the front are more expensive. Very simply decorated, bathrooms are very basic. Not particularly good value. Friendly staff. Prices are negotiable for long-lets and during low season.

Nang Thong Beach is reached by taking the road signposted Nang Thong Beach just after the Khao Lak area. The *Khao Lak Laguna Resort* and *Barn Khao Lak Resort* can be reached directly from the main road, and the road marking Nang Thong Beach is just after these resorts. This area is rapidly developing so it is worthwhile taking a look around to see if there are any new resorts. These will often give good discounts as they may not yet have a regular clientele or tour bookings. Along Highway 4 just near the turn-off to Nang Thong Beach you will also find the greatest accumulation of shops, internet facilities, and some new restaurant developments in the Khao Lak area. **A-B** *Khao Lak Tropicana Beach Resort*, T420231-40, F420240, www.khaolak-tropicana.com About 2 km along from *Nang Thong Beach* signs for the *Khao Lak Tropicana Beach Resort* direct you down a short surfaced road to the sprawling, 82-bungalow resort. Set back from the sea (the land beside the sea is owned by the government) the resort is not very imaginatively laid out and rather over-priced for average rooms. Small pool, restaurant. Can arrange tours. **A-C** *Barn Khao Lak Resort* is along from Khao Lak Laguna Resort and next to Nang Thong Bay Resort. Access is from the main road down a short dirt road. T420199, F420198, www.baankhaolak.com 28 modern, 'mimimalist'-style rooms in architect-designed bungalows. Rooms are quite sparse in decoration but pleasant and airy as are the bathrooms. A/c prices are higher than fan rooms but all rooms come with both options. If you want to pay fan rates tell the desk and they will lock the air-conditioning off. Restaurant, pool. Good value for the area. **B** *Khao Lak Laguna Resort*, 1 km south of town at the far southern end of Nang Thong Beach accessible from the main road, T420200, F431297. A real resort with shops, barbers, etc. Very nice and spotlessly clean rooms. **B-C** *Khao Lak Andaman Beach Resort*, the northernmost resort on Nang Thong Beach, next to *Khao Lak Bungalows*, T420134-5. A huge resort with a rather boring regimented layout: rows on rows of bungalows all of the same design and facing the same way. Inside the bungalows are clean and spacious if rather boring, and a/c, hot showers etc, are all of a high standard. Restaurant is on the beach. **B-C** *Khao Lak Bungalows*, next door to the *Garden Beach Resort* at the northern end of Nang Thong Beach. Take the road signposted Nang Thong Beach and turn right at the T-junction, *Khao Lak Bungalows* is about 500 m down the road. T420145. Small beachfront restaurant, traditional Thai-style bungalows, set in jungly garden, some luxury bungalows, and family apartments. Older bungalows are a bit faded but better designed than the newer bungalows. Both fan and a/c available. The owners, Gerd and Noi, organize exotic trips (quite expensive), such as a cave tour and snorkelling/diving trips to the Similan Islands. **B-C** *Nang Thong Bay Resort I*, Km 60 Hat Nang Thong, T420088-9, F420090. Large, 2-storey restaurant with extensive menu serving European and Thai food (recommended), good-value breakfasts. 60 rooms all with bathrooms, some a/c, some fans, the manageress Yoy speaks excellent English and is very helpful. Onward bus tickets can be booked from here. **B-C** *Nang Thong Bay Resort II*, T420078-9, F420080. Take the Hat Nang Thong (Nang Thong Beach) exit off the main Phuket-Takua Pa road and turn left at the T-junction. An excellently run, if unimaginatively titled, resort. A lovely place to stay with large and immaculately kept rooms. Extensive menu in the restaurant and the beach is a stone's skim away. Quieter than *Nang Thong Bay Resort I* (the elder sister resort). **B-D** *Khao Lak Green Beach Resort*

Take the road signposted Nang Thong Beach and turn right at the T-junction, this is the first resort on the left-hand side. T420043-7, F420047. Three styles of bungalows in well-shaded gardens (with fan or with a/c). The rooms are comfortable and clean and the staff friendly and helpful. Good restaurant serving mainly Thai dishes with some European favourites at the beach, and lots of picnic tables. **C-D** *Garden Beach Resort*, a few minutes walk north of *Nang Thong Bay Resort I*, T7231179. Extensive menu at beachfront restaurant, mainly Thai food, but a few European favourites, all rooms have fans and attached bathroom. The bungalows closest to the beach, where guests are lulled to sleep by the sound of the waves, are more expensive. Onward bus and air tickets bookable here (see **Tours**). Rather too many bungalows, not particularly attractive design. **NB** may close from May to Oct. **C-D** *Krathom Khaolak Resort and Restaurant*, on the main Takua Pa-Phuket Rd just beyond the turn-off to Nang Thong Beach as you travel north. T420149, phutesuan@hotmail.com   A nice bamboo, wood and brick restaurant and 9 clean, cosy bungalows tastefully decorated with local materials. The bungalows are set in a coconut plantation. The beach can be reached by walking through the plantation. Managed by a doctor and his son, the doctor also runs a small clinic (Dr Seree's clinic) for tourists. Friendly, helpful owners. Recommended.

■ *on map*
Price codes:
see inside front cover

Khao Lak Beach   L-A *Khao Lak Palm Beach Resort*, 26/10 Moo 7, T. Khuk Khak, adjacent to the *Khaolak Sunset Resort* on the main road from Phuket to Takua Pa, T420099-102, F420095, www.khaolakpalmbeach.com   Large, comfortable bungalows in gardens with all facilities, the attached bathrooms have step-down tiled baths and showers. Pool and restaurant overlooking the beach. The resort faces due west and is in a lovely quiet location to sit and watch the sun set. Standard rooms are probably better value than the suites, the living room of which is rather sparsely furnished. Friendly and helpful staff. **AL-A** *Khao Lak Bay Front Resort* next to the *Khao Lak Palm Beach Resort*, T420111-17, F420118, khaolak@cscoms.com   Thai-style furnishings and bungalows, well equipped, all with a/c. More expensive rooms have a sea view. Beachside pool and bar. Restaurant serves Thai, Chinese, Vietnamese and European dishes. Can arrange tours in the area. *Kon Tiki Diving* has an office in a shop on the premises. Facing due West on a quiet beach. The resort looks into some splendid forest on its northern side, but it's anybody's guess how long this will last now that it has been cleared on all sides and if there is more resort development. **A-C** *Khao Lak Sunset Resort*, 26/7 Moo 7, T. Khuk Khak, A. Takuapa, at the southern end of the the Khao Lak Beach area, T420075-77, F420147, khaolaksunset @hotmail.com   The more expensive rooms have beautiful views over the sea, but the management is a little haphazard for the price. Fan rooms are set back in a separate building near the road. Beachfront restaurant.

B-C *Khao Lak Nature Resort*, past *Poseidon Bungalows*, and just before the entrance to the National Park Headquarters as you travel north from Phuket. The reception is in the main restaurant (Thai and Chinese) building. T420179-81, F420182, nature_resort@hotmail.com   Very new and sensitively laid out. This resort is right next to the boundary with the Khao Lak-Lam Ru National Park. 40 bungalows have been arranged so as to avoid felling any trees and are spread out up into the forest on the hill. There is a bar with a view over the bay to the west, and a steep walk down some steps to a private beach. A swimming pool and deck have been built at the top of the hill with mosquito screening for the pool! A/c rooms are available but are less appealing than the fan rooms as they can become a bit musty in the damp of the forest. All rooms have excellent mosquito screening and nice bathrooms (hot water only with the a/c rooms). Very friendly and helpful owner with an interest in the environment. Transport from Phuket airport and other transport centres can be arranged. The resort has a small open-air meeting room for the use of groups. Recommended. **C-D** *Poseidon Bungalows*, 1/6 Tambon Lam Kaen, Mu 2, Amphoe Thai Muang, T443258. 5 km south of main Khao Lak area, range of rooms, some with bathrooms and beachfronts. Restaurant built out over the sea on stilts, Thai and European food. The bungalows are situated in a sheltered bay with a secluded beach, surrounded by jungle and rubber plantations. The owners are very friendly and are a mine of local information, they can organize day and longer trips to local places of interest, boat trips and snorkelling, including a live-aboard to the Similans dedicated to snorkellers. Closes from May to Oct. Recommended.

D *Phu Khao Lak*, T420140 situated on the opposite side of the road to the beach. As a result this resort is cheaper. Closed in the wet season. **D-E** *Khao Lak Resort*, Km 58 Si Takua Pa Rd, T721061. Coming from the south, through Khao Lak National Park, this is the first set of bungalows, some rooms have attached bathrooms, others are very basic. Unattractive resort, fallen into disrepair, only open in high season.

Several good restaurants attached to the bungalows, see above. A row of **foodstalls** can be found next to the Information Stand, on the beach. **Cheap** *Khao Lak Restaurant*, on the main road, Thai, International and American breakfast (see Tours above). Restaurants in the Ruen Mai complex on the main road to Takua Pa in the Nang Thong area. Tiny bar/snack shop on the beach run by Thai fishermen – no English spoken. **Eating**

There are bars at most of the larger bungalow establishments and at Ruen Mai on the main road to Takua Pa in the Nang Thong area. Beach bars can be found next to *Khao Lak Green Beach Resort*, and on the beach at Bang Niang and the northern end of Chong Fah. A 'sunset' bar on the promotory overlooking the whole Khao Lak area is to be found at the *Khao Lak Nature Resort*. **Bars**

Diving The *Sea Dragon*, *Phuket Dive* and *Kon Tiki* all offer diving to the Similan and Surin Islands. They have offices near and in various resorts along the coast from Khao Lak to Chong Fah. The Swiss-run *Kon Tiki*, Laguna Centre is a well organised dive shop and comes recommended. **Sport**

Local Jeeps: for hire from *Nang Thong Resort* and from *Garden Beach Resort*, ฿800 per day. **Motorbikes**: for hire from *Nang Thong Resort* and from *Garden Beach Resort* and from *Khao Lak Restaurant*, ฿200 per day. **Transport**

80 km N of Phuket

Long distance Bus: some a/c and non-a/c connections with the Southern terminal in Bangkok. Departs 1900, about 13 hrs. From Krabi and Phangnga, take a bus towards Phuket and change at Kochloi to a bus running north towards Takua Pa and Ranong. From Phuket take a local bus to Takua Pa or an a/c bus towards Ranong. Be careful – it is easy to miss this place, there is no actual sign on the roadside, but there are signs for the guesthouses. It is a 5 min walk from the road through a rubber plantation to the beach. Many buses now travel on a new road which bypasses Khao Lak and goes straight to Phangnga town, and then on to Phuket. Check that your bus passes through Khao Lak/Takua Pa/Ranong. Different bus companies have different routes.

Banks At *Nang Thong Resort*. **Communications** Internet: services can be found in the Nang Thong area and at certain resorts (eg *Khao Lak Sunset*). **Post Office**: the nearest Post Office is at Lam Kaen, a small village 5 km south of Khao Lak. Banks, shops and post offices can also be found in Takua Pa and Thai Muang, both 30 km north and south of Khao Lak respectively. **Directory**

Khao Sok National Park

Khao Sok National Park is bordered by the Sri Phangnga National Park to the west, the Khao Phanom National Park to the south, and the Khlong Saen and Khlong Nakkha Wildlife Sanctuaries to the north. It is part of the largest

Colour map 4, grid B1
Phone code: 076

The Southern Region

protected area in Southern Thailand. The closest town is Takua Pa but many companies from Phuket, Phangnga, Krabi and Surat operate day and overnight tours. (Try to take an overnight tour, as otherwise it's a long drive with little time to explore the national park and not really worth the money.)

With its dramatic limestone karst mountains (the tallest reaches over 900 m), low mountains covered with evergreen forest, streams and waterfalls, and a large reservoir and dam, Khao Sok has it all. The impressive scenery alone would be a good enough reason to visit, but Khao Sok also has an exceptionally large number of fauna. The list of 48 confirmed species of mammals include: wild elephants, tigers, barking deer, langur, macaques, civets, bears, gibbons and clouded leopards. Of the 184 confirmed bird species, perhaps the most dramatic include: the rhinoceros hornbill, the great hornbill, the Malayan peacock pheasant and the crested serpent-eagle. The plants to be found there are also of considerable interest. If you visit between December and February, the Rafflesia Kerri Meijer (found only in Khao Sok) is in flower. This parasitic flower (it depends on low-lying lianas) has an 80-cm bloom which smells of rotting flesh!

In the centre of the park is the Rachabrapah Reservoir. Near the dam there is a longhouse of sorts, and several houseboats. Tours can be taken to the dam area for day trips or for overnight stays. Visitors to Khao Sok should, of course, be aware that one has to be extremely lucky or very experienced to see wild animals, particularly in evergreen forest such as is found in the south of Thailand. However, for Khao Sok, the best location for animal spotting is near the reservoir where grassland at the edge of the reservoir attract animals. If you really want to get into the forest, it is probably a good idea to take an overnight tour into the park with an experienced guide. Tours are available from virtually all the various bungalows near the park. Park rangers will also act as guides. Have a chat with your intended guide before you make up your mind to go so you can be sure you feel comfortable about the level of English (or other languages) they speak, familiarity with the park, and general knowledge of the environment and wildlife. Expect to pay from ฿300 per person for a guide to take you on a day trek, and around ฿2,000 per person for an overnight trip to the reservoir (this includes accommodation and all meals. **NB** prices will vary depending on how many people are in the group). In addition to camping, canoeing and walking tours, you can take elephant treks at Khao Sok. The routes taken must be outside the park, however, as elephant trekking is not permitted within the confines of the national park.

Sleeping
Price codes:
see inside front cover

There is a well-developed tourism business centred on Khao Sok, and visitors have a considerable degree of choice in how they travel to the park and where they stay. There are several bungalow operations near the park headquarters and new operations seem to be sprouting up every year in the general area. Prices range from around ฿200 to about ฿800. Particularly noteworthy are *Art's Riverview Lodge, Khao Sok Rainforest Resort,* and *Our Jungle House.* **Art's Riverview Lodge** F421614, or write to Art's Riverview Jungle Lodge PO Box 28, Takua Pa, has a range of rooms some built like Thai houses with several rooms together, all have simple bathrooms, mosquito nets, etc. The only lighting provided is in the form of candles. The reception area and restaurant is right beside the river near a swimming hole. *Our Jungle House,* T01-8939583, F421706, our_jungle_house@hotmail.com is also right on a river bend with several styles of accommodation. The Thai managers are very friendly and helpful and the setting is peaceful and inviting with the central Thai-style house and restaurant set in a large park-like garden. The *Khao Sok Rainforest Resort,* the first resort on the left as you go down the entrance to the park, is located right next to the forest (most other bungalows are off to the right as you go towards the entrance and are near orchards and fields). This provides excellent opportunities to see birds and other wildlife from your room!

Further afield, the **B-C** *Khao Sok Riverside Cottages,* Km 106.5 (Highway 401), T01-2293750, F075-612544, is a simple but stylish alternative. About 2.5 km down a dirt road off the main Takua Pa-Phun Phin road, east of the National Park Headquarters, there are several wooden and bamboo cottages dispersed through an area of forest on a small hill beside a bend in the river. The restaurant, right beside the river, serves very good, simple Thai food. Cottages with twin beds are slightly larger and more expensive than doubles (prices include breakfast). The cottages are delightful, built using traditional materials, with lots of windows, spacious balconies and clean bright bathrooms. The manager and designer of the resort, Khun Daycho, is the president of the local conservation group. *Khao Sok Riverside Cottages* run walking tours and elephant trekking to forest adjacent to the resort (not actually in the National Park) and also do overnight camping and day visits to the lake.

Tours are run from most tourism centres from Phangnga, Phuket, Krabi and Surat Thani. **Transport** Or take a local bus from Takua Pa to Phun Phin near Surat Thani, and ask the driver to stop at the Khao Sok National Park (*oo-tayaan-haeng-chart-khao-sok*). Bungalow operators wait to whisk you off to their establishment, or you can walk. If you decide to walk take a small pack as it's quite a hike to some bungalows! Incidentally the drive from Takua Pa to Panom (about halfway between Takua Pa and Surat) is very scenic with views of dramatic limestone karst, forested mountains and valleys.

Phuket Island   เกาะภูเก็ต

Phuket, Thailand's premier resort island, lies on the west coast of the Kra Isthmus   Phone code: 076
in the warm Andaman Sea and is connected to the mainland by the 700 m-long   Colour map 4, grid C1
Sarasin causeway. The name Phuket is derived from the Malay word bukit,
meaning hill, and it is Thailand's only island to have provincial status. Known as
the 'Pearl of Thailand' because of its shape, it measures 21 km at its widest point,
and is 48 km long. With a land area of 550 sq km, it is about the same size as Singapore – making it Thailand's largest island.

Ins and outs

Phuket is nearly 900 km south of Bangkok. Even so, it is well connected and getting to **Getting there** the island is easy – especially if you are willing to pay for the air fare. Phuket Interna- *See also Transport,* tional Airport is in the north of the island, about 30 km from Phuket Town, but rather *page* closer to many of the main beaches and hotels. There are international connections with Hong Kong, Kuala Lumpur, Singapore, Penang, Taipei and Tokyo, as well as Munich and Dusseldorf. There are multiple daily connections on THAI with Bangkok as well as connections with Koh Samui (on Bangkok Airways), Chiang Mai and Hat Yai. The southern railway line doesn't come to the island. However it is possible to take a train to Phun Phin near Surat Thani and then catch a connecting bus. The main bus terminal is in Phuket Town and there are regular connections with Bangkok (a long 14 hrs) as well as destinations in the South.

Buses run from Phuket Town to all the beaches at regular intervals from 0600 to 1800. **Getting around** There are also numerous places to hire cars and motorbikes as well as mini vans that can be used as meterless taxis.

The Southern Region

History

Phuket was first 'discovered' by Arab and Indian navigators around the end of the ninth century, although it is said to have been marked on charts as far back as the first century. The first Europeans (Dutch pearl traders), arrived in the 16th century. **Phuket Town**, the island's capital in the southeast, was built in the middle of the last century to replace Thalang, which had been destroyed by the Burmese in 1800.

Historically, the province derived much of its wealth from tin production. Phuket was first mentioned as a major source of tin in the mid-16th century (when it was known as Junkceylon). Such was the wealth generated that Phuket Town was probably the first place in all Thailand to have paved roads and cars, around 1910. The inhabitants of Phuket are still among the wealthiest in Thailand, a fact reflected in the richly endowed temples. This does not mean, though, that there are not poor people on Phuket. Indeed, in 1995, strike action by employees at one of the island's hotels was agreed – the first time, apparently, in Phuket's history – because wages were felt to be too low to sustain a reasonable standard of living. The population of the province has risen from 6,000 in the early 1900s, to 140,000, with five times that number of visitors every year.

Phuket offers little in the way of sights of historical interest, but much of natural beauty, although the wild elephants, rhinos and tigers which once roamed the island have long since been killed. There are national parks, long sandy beaches (particularly on the west coast), good snorkelling and diving, peaceful coconut groves and rubber plantations, and some traditional (well, -ish) villages. Phuket seems big enough to absorb large numbers of tourists and still maintain a semblance of 'tradition' in some areas – although Thai and farang tourism activists would dispute this vehemently.

Sights

South of
Phuket Town

There are a handful of historical and cultural sights around the island. South of Phuket Town, down Sakdidej Road which becomes Route 4023, in the grounds of the *Cape Panwa Sheraton Hotel*, is **Panwa House**, a fine example of Sino-Portuguese architecture. At the tip of Panwa Cape is the **Marine Biological Research Centre and Aquarium**. The air-conditioned aquarium is well laid out, with a moderate collection of salt and fresh water fish, lobsters, molluscs and turtles. ■ *0830-1600 Mon-Sun, ฿20, T391128*. Getting there: there are regular public songthaews every hour (฿10) from the market area on Ranong Rd to the Aquarium. It is possible to charter **long-tailed boats** from here to **Koh Hii** (฿600) and **Koh Mai Ton** (฿1200) or to go fishing (฿1200).

Six kilometres south of Phuket Town, just north of Chalong Junction, is the ostentatious **Wat Chalong**, best known for its gold-leaf encrusted statues of the previous abbots, Luang Pho Chaem and Luang Pho Chuang. The former was highly respected for his medical skills, which proved to be particularly valuable when Phuket's Chinese miners revolted in 1876. The halving of the

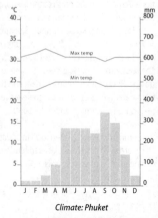

Climate: Phuket

international price of tin coupled with Bangkok's attempt to extract excessive taxes from the province raised the ire of the Chinese. Some 2,000 gathered around the governor's house, and when they failed to take the building turned their attention to the less well-defended villages. The spree of killing and looting was only finally brought to an end at Wat Chalong.

North of Phuket Town

Twelve kilometres north from Phuket Town on Route 402, towards the airport, is the village of **Tha Rua**. At the crossroads there is a statue of two female warriors: **Muk** and **Chan**. These sisters helped to repel an army of Burmese invaders in 1785 by dressing up all the women of the town as men, so fooling the Burmese. Rama I awarded them titles for their deeds, and they are celebrated in bronze, swords drawn. The statue was erected in 1966 and Thais rub gold-leaf on its base as a sign of respect and to gain merit. The **Thalang National Museum** is just east of this crossroads on Route 4027. It has a well-presented collection, displaying various facets of Phuket's history and culture. ■ *0900-1600, Wed-Sat ฿30*. Also in Thalang is the extraordinary **Wat Phranang Sang**. Designed as if the architect did not know what he was building, this monastery is surrounded by a modern crenellated castle wall. Inside the wall, a statue of the Chinese goddess Kuan Yin, encircled by a dragon, stands in front of a particularly gaudy bot (ordination hall). This place is worth visiting – if in Thalang anyway – for its highly syncretic interpretation of Theravada Buddhism.

Continuing north on Route 402, just beyond the district town of Thalang, is **Wat Phra Thong**, surrounded by life-sized concrete animals. The wat contains a buried Buddha image, with just its head protruding from the ground, covered in gold-leaf. Legend has it that shortly after a boy had tethered his buffalo to a post, they both fell mysteriously ill. On excavating the post, villagers discovered this golden Buddha. It is believed that anyone trying to disinter the image will meet with a disaster – Burmese invaders attempted to do so in 1785 and they were attacked by a swarm of hornets. There is also a museum here with a bizarre and motley collection: Chinese porcelain, an old typewriter, sea shells, mouldering books, faded photographs, animal heads and, in the centre of the room, an old gramophone with a 78 of Victor Sylvester singing *Why did she fall for the leader of the band?* on the turntable.

Fantasea

To the west of Thalang is Kamela Beach, where Phuket's most recent attraction is staged. Fantasea, a US$100 mn extravaganza, has won Best Tourist Attraction 2000; a theme park/Las Vagas-style show. With a cast of 150, 30 elephants in a 3,000-seat theatre and dining for 4,000, this is entertainment on a grand scale. ■ *Park operates from 1730-0200 except Tue. www.phuket_fantasea.com*

• •

Phuket Island place names

Bang Pae Waterfall
น้ำตกบางแพ

Khao Phra Thaeo Wildlife Park
อุทยานสัตว์ป่าเขาพระแทว

Thalang National Museum
พิพิธภัณฑสถานแห่งชาติถลาง

Tha Rua
ท่าเรือ

Wat Chalong
วัดบุญทวี

Wat Phranang Sang
วัดพระนางสร้าง

Wat Phra Thong
วัดพระทอง

The Southern Region

Phuket Island

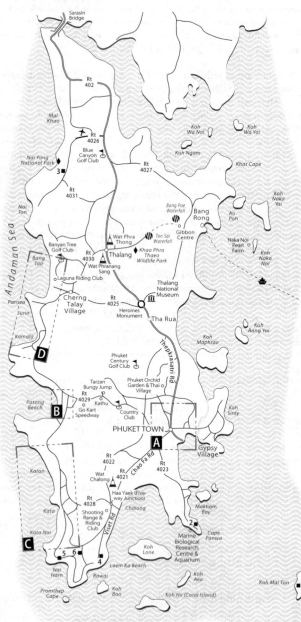

The Southern Region

N

0 km 2
0 miles 2

Related maps

■ **Sleeping**

1 Mai Ton Resort
2 Panwa House & Cape
   Panwa Sheraton Hotel
3 Pearl Village
4 Phuket Island Resort
5 Phuket Yacht Club
6 Rawai Garden Resort

Sea, water and weather conditions on Phuket

November-April *Fair seas with morning breezes of 15-20 knots, lessening as the day wears on. Winds increasing during March and April. Water conditions and visibility best during these months.*
May-October *Moderate winds and seas.*

Squalls becoming more common from June. Seas can be rough and water conditions and visibility suffer accordingly. Stiff currents and rip tides on the West Coast – observe warning flags and ask about conditions daily.

Khao Phra Thaeo Wildlife Park lies 20 km from Phuket Town. Turn east off the main road in Thalang and follow signs for Ton Sai Waterfall. This beautiful, peaceful road winds through stands of rubber trees and degraded forest. The park supports wild boar and monkeys and represents the last remnant of the island's natural forest ecosystem. The **Ton Sai Waterfall** is located within the park, but is really only worth a visit during the rainy season; even then the falls are a bit of a disappointment. There are bungalows and a lakeside restaurant here, and a number of hiking routes. Visitors can paddle in the upper pool. ■ *0600-1800*.

    The road east from the waterfall becomes rough and can only be negotiated on foot or by motorbike. This track leads to **Bang Pae Waterfall**. Alternatively, the falls can be approached from the other direction, by turning off Route 4027 and driving 1 km along a dirt track. There is a beautiful lake, refreshment stands, forest trails, and bathing pools. ■ *0600-1800*. Just south of the waterfall is a **Gibbon Centre**; a rehabilitation centre for these endangered animals funded from the US and apparently the only such initiative in Southeast Asia. Follow signs off Route 4027. Also off Route 4027, at **Ao Poh**, there is a long wooden jetty where boat tours leave for Naka Noi Island and Pearl Farm – Thailand's largest (see below).

Khao Phra Thaeo Wildlife Park

Most people do not go to Phuket for history or culture. They go for **beaches**, and in this respect the island is hard to beat. Its size, and the length of its beaches means that it is still possible to find a peaceful spot to sunbathe. The best beaches are on the west coast, although the resort of Patong is far from peaceful. The east coast is rocky and fringed with mangroves and the beaches are poor for swimming. There are now some excellent luxury hotels on Phuket; the island is no longer a haven for backpackers – most have moved on to cheaper locations such as Phi Phi, Samui and Lanta. That said, it is still possible (just) to stay relatively cheaply on Phuket.

Beaches
Details of the various beaches are given after the section on Phuket Town

In order to explore some of the sights mentioned above, it is best to hire a motorbike or jeep for the day. A suggested route might run north from Phuket Town or east from Patong to Tha Rua, the Heroines' Monument and the National Museum at Thalang. Take a side trip to Ton Sai Waterfall and the National Park, then continue north on Route 402, before turning left for Nai Yang Beach and National Park. Crossing Route 402, drive east through rubber plantations, taking in Bang Pae Waterfall, before returning to the main road at the Heroines' Monument. A half to one day trip.

Tour by motorbike or jeep

Koh Yao Noi and **Koh Yao Yai** are two largish islands to the east of Phuket Island. They remain untouched by the tourist industry and hold a scattering of fishing villages. There is good diving off the islands and many dive shops run expeditions out here. ■ *Getting there: boats leave from the village of Ban Rong.*

Excursions

Full-day tours to **Phi Phi** (see page 627) are organized by *Aloha Tour*, *Cruise Centre*, *Pee Pee Hydrocraft* (฿750), *Silver Queen*, and *Songserm Travel* (who

Tours

The Southern Region

operate a large catamaran called the *King Cruiser*). Day trips to Phi Phi are also available on the *Andaman Queen*, T215261, leaving at 0830 (฿750-950).

Similan Islands (see page 604). Full-day tours leave from Chalong or Patong beaches. *Phuket Travel and Tour Co* and *Songserm Travel* (T222570), organize tours for about ฿1,500, which includes a tour of the reef in a glass bottomed boat, lunch, and dinner on the boat back to Phuket. Many other tour companies in Phuket Town and on Patong Beach organize similar tours.

Phangnga Bay (see page 607). A day trip costs about ฿650.

Coral Island (Koh Hii) Full-day tours include swimming, snorkelling and fishing. Regular boats leave from Chalong Bay, 0930, ฿50 per person one way. Chartered boats leave from Chalong, Rawai and Laem Ka, ฿600 per person including hotel transfer, lunch, snorkelling equipment, etc, T218060, F381957.

Naka Noi Island and the Pearl Farm Boats leave from Ao Poh, in the northeast of the island, for the 15-minute-trip at 1030 daily. Tours, including admission to the Pearl Farm and a 'demonstration,' cost ฿500, T219870 for information. ■ *Pearl Farm open Mon-Sun 0900-1530.* Accommodation available at bungalow resort. **NB** Ensure your visit is to Naka Noi, rather than Naka Yai, where the 'Pearl Farm' seems to be a fake.

Tour by glass-bottomed boat Two-hour cruises in the Andaman Sea, ฿300 (or on a chartered basis for ฿5,000 per two hours).

Nature tours There is not much 'nature' left on Phuket but nonetheless *Phuket Nature Tours*, 5/15 Chao Fah Road, T225522, F215126, have managed to climb on board the eco-tourism bandwagon and offer tours to forests, rice fields, villages, plantations, secluded beaches and so on. *Siam Safari* offer *Eco Nature Tours*, T213881, F210972; a similar set up to the above. *Etc Asia*, www.ultimate -asia.com also offer nature and other tours.

Diving The warm, clear water off Phuket is rich in marine life, and affords excellent diving opportunities. Dive centres – over 25 of them – will normally offer introductory courses for those who have never dived before, leading to one of the internationally recognized certificates (such as PADI and NAUI). For an open water course the cost is about ฿8,000-10,000. The course stretches over four days, beginning in a hotel pool and ending on a reef. A simple introductory dive, fully supervised, will cost ฿1,500-2,000 (one dive) to ฿2,000-2,500 (two dives). For those with diving experience there are a range of tours from single day, two-dive outings to dive spots like Koh Phi Phi, Koh Raja Yai and Koh Raja Noi (both due south of Phuket), and Shark Point (off to the east of Phuket); to one-week expeditions to offshore islands such as the Similan and Surin Islands. Prices vary, but a day-trip to Phi Phi with two dives should cost about ฿2,500-3,000 per person, and to the Similans about ฿3,000-3,500 per person. Four days and three nights, around ฿11,000-12,000 (eight dives) and five days and four nights about ฿14,000 (10 dives). Snorkelling is good on the outer islands; the waters around Phuket Island itself are mediocre. It is best to catch one of the boat tours to Phi Phi Island for the day and snorkel on either side of the land bridge that separates the two halves of Phi Phi Don (see page 628). But even here, development has reduced the clarity of the waters. For the best snorkelling and diving it is necessary to go to the Similan Islands.

Best time to visit The driest months are November-April, which also have the most sunshine. May to October are wetter with more chance of overcast conditions, although daily sunshine still averages five to eight hours.

Phuket's festival of mortification

The Chinese Vegetarian Festival or Ngan Kin Jeh is said to have its origins about 150 years ago when a Chinese opera troupe's visit to the island coincided with a terrible plague. The artistes decided it was in some way connected with their pre-performance rituals and they sent one of the cast back to China to light and bring to Phuket a vast jos stick. In this way, the Nine Emperor Gods of China might be invited to Phuket in order to cure the population of the plague. They succeeded, so it is said, and today's festival commemorates the event.

To open the proceedings, participants light candles and lanterns to invite the Nine Emperor Gods to return to Phuket. The first four days of the festival are comparatively peaceful and ordinary – as festivals go. It is during the last five days that events, for most foreigners, turn really weird. Each of the five Chinese temples or pagodas of Phuket Town in turn arranges a procession. Devotees show their commitment and the power of the Nine Emperor Gods by piercing their cheeks, tongues and various other parts of their anatomy. The processions end in a large field where razor ladders, caldrons of boiling oil, and pits of red-hot embers await the supplicants. Most appear to get off relatively lightly, although in some years tourists – possibly excessively carried away with the festivities – also try their hand (or their feet, or their cheeks) at such mortifications, and end up severely injured.

On the ninth day, a crowd of thousands converge on Saphan Hin to the south of Phuket Town (see page 586), and offerings are cast into the sea, thereby allowing the Nine Emperor Gods to return to their heavenly abode, and many of the participants to return home and eat a meal of meat.

Essentials

Sleeping
Phuket has literally hundreds of places to stay, largely at the upper price end. See individual areas for listings. **NB** During the low season (Jun-Oct) room rates may be as little as half the high season price. All rates quoted are high season. It is recommended that visitors book hotel rooms during high season (particularly at Christmas and New Year).

Cookery courses
Thai cookery courses At the Boathouse Inn Cookery School, Kata Beach, T2514707 (see Kata Beach accommodation for full address).

Festivals
March Thao Thep Kasattri and Thao Sisunthon Fair (13th). An annual fair held to celebrate the the 2 female warriors, better known as Muk and Chan, who helped repel an army of Burmese invaders in 1785 (see page 579).

April Fish Releasing Festival timed to coincide with Songkran or Thai new year (see page 603). Baby turtles are released at several of Phuket's beaches.

May Seafood Festival not much of a festival; more of a tourism PR junket which is meant to celebrate Phuket's wealth of seafood. Lots of carved ice-sculptures, piles of lobsters and mussels, and so on.

July Marathon (2nd week).

October Chinese Vegetarian Festival or Ngan Kin Jeh (movable), lasts 9 days and marks the beginning of Taoist lent. No meat is eaten, alcohol consumed nor sex indulged in (in order to cleanse the soul) and men pierce their cheeks or tongues with long spears and other sharp objects and walk over hot coals and (supposedly) feel no pain. The festival is celebrated elsewhere, but most enthusiastically in Phuket, and especially at Wat Jui Tui on Ranong Rd in Phuket Town (see box). This must be one of the star attractions of a visit to Phuket. Visitors are made to feel welcome and to take part in the event.

Diving in Phuket

Diving in Phuket is regarded as top quality because of the combination of number of dive shops (over 25), the professionalism of the instructors, the range of dive sites, and the variety of other entertainment and facilities from excellent hotels to superb food.

__Dive sites within easy reach of Phuket__ Shark point and __Koh Dok Mai__ are one hour and 1½ hours east of Phuket Island. As the name of the former indicates, this site is known for its sharks and has been declared a marine sanctuary. Koh Dok Mai offers a good wall dive. Depth: 10-27 m; visibility: fair to excellent. The twin Rajah islands (Rajah Yai and Rajah Noi – Big and Little Rajah) lie due south of Phuket, about 1½-2 hours

by boat. Raja Noi attracts large schools of skipjack tuna and barracuda and Rajah Yai is known for the clarity of its water. There are hard and soft corals and steep drop-offs. Depth: 10-35 m; visibility: good to excellent. Less good, but better for non-divers and snorkelling is __Coral Island__, 40 minutes by boat south of Phuket. The __Phi Phi Islands__ are another popular dive site. See page 627 for further details.

__Dive sites further afield__ Perhaps the finest diving, however, is to be found off the __Surin and Similan Islands__ in the Andaman Sea, to the west of Phuket. Diving here requires an overnight stay, but many dive shops organize trips. See page 604 for further details on the two groups of islands.

November *Phuket Travel Fair* (1st). Another ersatz PR event designed to raise Phuket's tourism profile. More activity than during May's Seafood festival though.
December *King's Cup Regatta* (5th). Yachting competition in the Andaman Sea, timed to coincide with the King's birthday (the King is a yachtsman of international repute). The event attracts competitors from across the world.

Sport Canoeing *Sea Canoe* (who also operate from Krabi and Phi Phi), and *Andaman Sea Kayak*, hire out specially designed 2-man canoes to explore the grottoes, capes and bays that line Phuket's coast but which are often not accessible by road. Day trips cost about ฿2,500-3,000; 6-day expeditions, all inclusive, ฿24,000. For *Sea Canoe* T/F212172. *Andaman Sea Kayak*, T235353, F235353. *Santana Canoeing*, 92/18 Sawatdirak Rd, Patong, T340360. River canoeing through the jungle as well as sea canoeing.

Diving centres The greatest concentration of diving companies is to be found along Patong Beach Rd, on Kata and Karon beaches, at Ao Chalong and in Phuket Town. **Phuket Town**: *Phuket Aquatic Safaris*, 62/9 Rasada Centre, Rasada Rd, T216562. *Andaman Sea Diving*, 3rd Flr, Tian Sin Bldg, 54 Phuket Rd, T215766. **Patong**, all on the Beach Rd: *Ocean Divers*, Patong Beach Hotel, T321166, or T341273, F340625. *Scuba Cats*, Beach Rd, T293120. *Pioneer Diving Asia*, Patong Beach, T342508. *Santana*, Sawatdirak Rd, T294220. *Andaman Divers*, T321155. *Fantasea Divers*, T340088, F340309 (instructors for English, French, German and Japanese); *South East Asia*, T340406 (instructors for English, French, Swedish, Italian and German). **Kata/Karon**: *Siam Diving Centre*, Kata-Karon Beach, T330936 (instructors for English and Swedish); *Kon Tiki*, T396312. *Marina Cottage*, Kata Beach, T381625. *Phuket International Diving Centre* (*PIDC*), *Le Meridien*, Karon Noi Beach, T321480. **Chalong**: *Sea Bees Diving*, T381765.

Fishing *Big Game Fishing*, Phuket Sport Fishing Centre, Patong Beach, T214713, F330680. *Ao Chalong Game Fishing*, Chalong Beach, T280996. **Golf** *Blue Canyon*, to the north of the island, near the airport, T327440, F327449. The most expensive, but also the best course on the island. *Phuket Country Club*, Route 4029 to Patong, T321025, F321721. *Phuket Century*, in the middle of the island, T321929, F321928. *Banyan Tree*, part of the Laguna Phuket Complex, a new course, so it needs time to 'mature', T324350, F324351. *Thai Muang Beach*, north of Phuket on the coast, T571533, F571214. Part of a new complex with hotel, sports facilities, etc. **Paintball** *Asia 'Top Gun'*, Ao Chalong Shooting Range, Kata Rd, T381667. Open Mon-Sun 0900-1800, ฿275 for 25 round game.

Riding *Laguna Riding Club*, Bang Tao Bay, just before Phuket Laguna complex, T324009. Open Mon-Sun. *Phuket Riding Club*, south of Chalong Circle on Viset Road, T288213. Open Mon-Sun 0700-1100 and 1400-1830. *Crazy Horse Club*, look out for signs near Nai Harn Bay from Rawai, open 0800-1700, ride through jungle or on the beach. **Swimming** swimming and snorkelling are safe from Nov to Apr when the sea is calm. But during the monsoon between May and Oct, there can be strong surf and undertows – especially after storms. Swimmers should check the beaches for red flags, which indicate whether conditions are dangerous. **Sailing** Phuket is an important sailing centre and many boats pick up and drop off crew here. The *Kanda Bakery*, 31-33 Rasada Road, in Phuket Town have a notice board advertising crewing opportunities.

Local Bus: for Patong, Kamala, Surin, Makham Bay, Nai Yang, Kata, Karon, Nai Harn, Rawai, Thalang and Chalong buses leave every 30 mins between 0600 and 1800 from the market on Ranong Rd in Phuket Town. Fares range from ฿20 to whatever the ticket collector thinks he can get away with. **Car hire**: jeeps can be hired from small outfits along most beaches, expect to pay ฿600-1,200 per day, depending on age of car, etc. **Avis** has an office opposite Phuket airport, T311358 and desks at various hotels including *Le Meridien*, the *Holiday Inn*, the *Phuket Cabana* (all on Patong Beach), the *Dusit Laguna* (on Bang Tao Beach) and the *Metropole* (in Phuket Town) (฿1,200 per day, ฿7,200 per week). **Hertz** has a desk at the airport, T311162, and at the *Patong Merlin* and *Tara Patong*; prices are similar to Avis. There are other local companies down Rasada Rd in Phuket Town (see Phuket Town). **Long-tailed boat**: these can be hired to visit reefs and the more isolated coves, ฿600-1200 per day. **Motorbike hire**: as above, ฿150-350 per day. There are also several places on Rasada Rd in Phuket Town. Note that not all places insist on taking your passport as a deposit/collateral and it is best not to let it out of your hands. **Motorbike taxi**: men (and a few women) with red vests will whisk passengers almost anywhere for a minimum of ฿10. They congregate at intersections. **Small minibuses**: can be chartered for journeys around the island. Karon to town – ฿130, town to airport – ฿250, Patong to town – ฿130.

Long distance Air: the airport is to the north of the island, 30 km from Phuket Town. For flight reservations, T211195 (domestic) and T212855 (international) on Phuket, and T2800070 in Bangkok. Regular domestic connections on Thai with Bangkok, 1 hr 15 mins, Chiang Mai 2 hrs, Hat Yai 55 mins, Nakhon Si Thammarat 1 hr 40 mins, Surat Thani 35 mins and Trang 40 mins. Bangkok Airways also run daily connections with Koh Samui 50 mins. **International connections** with Hong Kong, Penang and KL (Malaysia), Singapore, Taipei, Tokyo and Munich and Dusseldorf. Airlines include ANA, Bangkok Airways, Dragonair, MAS, Qantas, Thai and Tradewinds. **Airport facilities**: café, left luggage (open 0700-2030, ฿25 per day), Thai reconfirmation desk, *Hertz* car rental, tourist information counter, currency exchange, and hotel information. **Transport to town**: Thai Airways appear to have a virtual monopoly on transport from the airport and prices are not cheap (unless being picked up by your hotel). There are 2 ways to avoid the ฿70 fare into Phuket Town. One is to walk the 3 km to the main north-south road, Route 402, and pick up a public bus or songthaew there. Alternatively, walk out of the airport gate and wait for a motorcycle taxi dropping someone off (฿30). (They cannot pick up fares at the airport itself). Motorcycle taxis wait at the intersection with Route 402 to ferry people to the terminal (฿30); it's getting from the airport to Route 402 which is more difficult. Thai run a minibus service into Phuket Town for ฿70 (from Phuket Town to the airport, the minibus leaves from the Thai

Transport

See also Ins & outs, page 577

890 km S of Bangkok

The Southern Region

office, 78 Ranong Rd), they also have a taxi and limousine service to town. Buses take passengers to Patong, Kata and Karon beaches for ฿100, or by private taxi for ฿400.

Train: there is no rail service to Phuket. However, some visitors take the train to Phun Phin, outside Surat Thani (usually the overnight train), where buses wait to take passengers on to Phuket 6 hrs (see page 655).

Bus: station (*bor ko sor* – BKS) is on Phangnga Rd in Phuket town, T211480. Tickets bought here are cheaper than through travel agents. The information desk here usually stocks a timetable and fare list produced by the TAT detailing all departures as well as local transport. Regular a/c and non-a/c connections with Bangkok's Southern bus terminal 14 hrs. A/c tour buses also ply this route. In Bangkok many depart from Khaosan Rd where substantial numbers of guesthouses are concentrated. Regular morning connections with Hat Yai 8 hrs, Trang 6 hrs, Surat Thani 6 hrs and Satun 7 hrs. Regular connections with Phangnga 2 hrs, Takua Pa 3 hrs, Ranong 6 hrs and Krabi 4 hrs. Note that buses leave for the beaches from the market area from around 0600 – although the taxi drivers may try to convince you otherwise! **Taxi**: taxis will leave when they are full (usually with 5 passengers). For Surat Thani, they leave from the coffee shop opposite the Pearl Cinema on Phangnga Rd (฿150 per person).

Phuket Town   เมืองภูเก็ต

Sights

Phone code: 076
Directory assistance
& overseas phone
service: 100
Colour map 4, grid C1

Phuket Town is interesting for its **Sino-Portuguese architecture** (similar to that of Penang and Macao), dating back 100-130 years. Wealthy Chinese tin barons built spacious colonial-style residences set in large grounds to celebrate their success. The best examples are along Thalang, Yaowarat, Ranong and Damrong roads and include the Chartered Bank (the first foreign bank to establish offices in Thailand), the Thai Airways office on Ranong Road opposite the market, and the Sala Phuket on Damrong Road. Less grand, but nonetheless elegant, are the turn-of-the-century shophouses on, for example, Thalang Road. There is some talk of renovation, in an attempt to preserve these deteriorating buildings but an appreciation of the architectural wealth that still exists in Phuket Town appears to be only slowly developing. There are **night markets** on Ong Sim Phai and Tilok Uthit 1 roads.

Khao Rang, a hill overlooking Phuket Town, can either be reached by foot (a longish climb), or by songthaew or tuk-tuk. It is a public park, with fitness track, and affords a good view of the island and countryside to the southwest. Other views of the island are obscured by trees (chartered tuk-tuk ฿50 round trip).

Koh Sire/Siray – or Sire Island – is connected to Phuket by a short bridge. There is not much to see here; fishing boats unload their catches (turn right immediately after crossing the bridge) and there is a village of sea gypsies (or *chao talay*) and fishermen who embrace animist beliefs. They are thought to be descended from Andaman/Nicobar islanders to the west of Phuket (chartered tuk-tuk ฿60 round-trip).

Saphan Hin, a small promontory to the south of town, is a place where Thais congregate in the evening. With the on-shore breeze, array of street sellers, and a wonderful spirit house, it is worth the trip. It is just a shame the beach is like a rubbish tip.

The **Crocodile Farm and Elephant Land** is on Chana Charoen Road. It is run down and poorly managed and would offend the sensibilities of those with any love for crocodilians. . ■ *Mon-Sun 0900-1800. Daily shows at 1230 and 1530. ฿200.* The **Snake Farm** is on Thepkrasatri Road, just north of the turn-off to Patong. Snake-leather goods for sale. ■ *Snake shows from*

1100-2400. Another very touristy affair is the **Phuket Orchid Garden and Thai Village** with the usual assortment of cultural shows with dancing, Thai boxing and handicraft displays, elephant rides and an orchid garden. Pretty forgettable, overall. ■ *Show times at 1100 and 1730, ฿230. Getting there: the centre is off Thepkrasatri Rd, just north of town, T214860 for further details.*

The **tourist office**, *TAT*, 73-75 Phuket Rd, T212213, F213582, is good for specific local questions and problems relating to Phuket and Phangnga. They provide useful town maps and transport details. A free monthly magazine is also produced for visitors, *Travel and Style Phuket*. It is financed by advertising, so don't expect too much critical comment. Nonetheless it does contain some useful background information. More critical in its comment is the *Phuket Gazette*, a monthly tabloid newspaper (English language), produced for, and by, farang residents and visitors (฿20). There is also a good, free colour map of Phuket and the beaches with most hotels and other places of interest marked, distributed by *Thaiways Magazine*.

Travel agents in town will organize full or half-day tours to Phangnga Bay, Phi Phi Island, Coral Island, the pearl farm, or scuba-diving around Phuket Town.

Tours

Hotels in town are rather uninspired; most people avoid staying here and head straight for the beaches, although those on business or needing to catch an early morning bus connection might need to spend a night here.

Sleeping
■ *on map*
Price codes:
see inside front cover

AL *Metropole*, 1 Montri Rd, T215050, F215990. A/c, restaurant, pool, ostentatious hotel with pretensions of grandeur. Massive and impersonal with rather heavy, over-elaborate decor. **AL** *Novotel Royal Phuket City*, T233333, F233335 opposite the main bus station in town. Swimming pool, business centre, gym but no beach and no holiday atmosphere. Expensive but up to 50% discount in the wet season, this place is surprisingly tacky for such a large establishment. **AL-A** *Thavorn Grand Plaza*, 40/5 Chana Charoen Rd, T222240, F222284. A/c, restaurants, 2 pools, 125 rooms, large high-rise hotel geared to businessmen not to holiday-makers, located away from town centre. **AL-B** *City*, Thepkrasatri Rd, T216910, F213554, B2535768. A/c, restaurant, pool, ugly high-rise block near centre of town. **AL-B** *Pearl*, 42 Montri Rd, T211044, F212911, B2601022. A/c, Chinese rooftop restaurant, pool, small attractive garden, clean rooms. **AL-B** *Phuket Merlin*, 158/1 Yaowarat Rd, T212866, F216429. A/c, restaurant, pool, clean, comfortable high-rise block, free shuttle bus to Patong Beach throughout the day. 35% discount available in the wet season. Overstaffed. **A** *Phuket Garden*, 40/12 Bangkok Rd, T216900, F216909. A/c, restaurant, helpful staff, the suite rooms are good value. **A** *Phuket Island Pavilion*, 133 Satool Rd, T210444, F210458. Very nice rooms with a different layout to most places. Superior rooms are sumptuous. Swimming pool and all facilities. Outdoor reception at the bottom of this circular sky-rise.

B-C *Sinthavi*, 89 Phangnga Rd, T211186, F211400. Clean, fair rooms, but typically slow staff. Restaurant and bakery attached. **C** *Daeng Plaza*, 57 Phuket Rd, T216428. A/c, restaurant, a multi-storeyed hotel in the centre of town with 75 rooms and helpful staff, despite their lack of English. Not much to recommend this place unless somewhere to rest one's head is all that is required. **C-D** *Thavorn*, 74 Rasada Rd, T211333, F215559, A/c, restaurant, pool, central and dull but good-value rooms. Cheesy historical feel, the staff are about as active as some of the exhibits in the attached museum. Some attempts to develop a sense of style, for example the attached *Collector Pub and Restaurant* is really rather stylish and tasteful, but it sits incongruously next to the gloomy lobby where Thai female coffee shop crooners in tight sequined dresses congregate at night, overall this is probably the best hotel in this price bracket. **C- D** *Imperial*, 51 Phuket Rd, T212894, F213155. Co-operative

The Southern Region

staff, good clean rooms at realistic rates. **C-D** *Downtown Inn*, 56/16-19 Ranong Rd, T216884. A/c. Probably a brothel but clean and reasonable rooms.

D *Nara Mansion*, 15/1 Soi Mongkon, Yaowarat Rd, T259238. Cheap and reasonable rooms, but the management didn't even seem to realize they were running a hotel. Some a/c. **D** *Talang Guesthouse*, Krabi Rd, T215892. Welcoming rooms, helpful owner, good rates. **D-E** *On On*, 19 Phangnga Rd, T211154. Attractive hotel dating from 1929 situated in the heart of town. Clean and comfortable a/c rooms with attached cold-water showers can sometimes be rather gloomy, fan rooms a bargain. This place has real

Phuket Town

- **■ Sleeping**
- 1 City
- 2 Daeng Plaza
- 3 Downtown Inn
- 4 Imperial
- 5 Laemthong
- 6 Metropole
- 7 Nara Mansion
- 8 Novotel Royal
  Phuket City
- 9 On On
- 10 Pearl
- 11 Pengman
- 12 Phuket Garden
- 13 Phuket Inn
- 14 Phuket Island Pavilion
- 15 Phuket Merlin
- 16 Siam

- 17 Silver
- 18 Sinthavi
- 19 Siri
- 20 Talang Guesthouse
- 21 Thavorn Grand Plaza
- 22 Thavorn Hotel
- 23 Wasana Guesthouse

- **● Eating**
- 1 Bondeli Café
- 2 Kanda Bakery
- 3 Koh Lao Luat Mu
- 4 Lai-An Lao
- 5 Mae Porn
- 6 Thiptawan House
- 7 Vegetarian
- 8 Venus

- **🚍 Transport**
- 1 Long distance bus
  terminal to
  destinations beyond
  Phuket (Bor Kor Sor)
- 2 Local buses to
  beaches, Thalong,
  Sarasin Bridge &
  turn off for
  airport

- **▲ Other**
- 1 Ocean Shopping Mall
- 2 Rasada Shopping
  Centre
- 3 Suriyadet Circle

Related maps
Phuket Island,
page 580
Patong Beach,
page 593
Karon & Kata Beaches,
page 597
Bang Tao,
Pansea & Kamala
Beaches, page 602

The Southern Region

character, attached a/c coffee shop and good restaurant plus tour desk. Recommended. **D-E** *Wasana Guesthouse*, 159 Ranong Rd, T211754. Central location just by the fresh market, bargain basement a/c rooms with attached shower rooms, cavernous lobby looking a little like an extremely grubby operating theatre, rooms are clean enough though, and friendly at our last visit. **E** *Siam*, 13-15 Phuket Rd, T212328. Noisy location but clean rooms. **E** *Pengman*, Phang-nga Rd, near the *On-On Hotel*. Noisy small rooms but OK for the money and its location is convenient. **F** *Laemthong*, 24-26 Soi Romanee, Thalang Rd, T212310. Very basic rooms in attractive old street.

Thai Expensive: *Ka Jok See*, 26 Takua Pa Rd, T217903. Excellent Thai restaurant, booking is essential. The success of the restaurant is leading to some pretty sharp pricing policies, but nonetheless we have had comments from customers who believe the atmosphere, character, style, and first-rate cuisine make it worth paying the extra few hundred baht. *Krua-Thai*, 62/7 Rasada Centre. Clean restaurant with well-presented food. Recommended. *Lucky Seafood*, 66/1 Phuket Rd. Saphan Hin, seafood, large restaurant with Chinese/Thai food, not central. *Phuket Seafood*, 66/2 Phuket Rd. Saphan Hin, seafood, large, Chinese/Thai restaurant, not central. *Tunk-Kao*, Khao Rang. Seafood, good views over town from here, food is reasonable. **Mid-range**: *Thiptawan House*, Takua Pa Rd. Good, well-priced Thai food in a/c restaurant. Recommended. *Phuket View*, Khao Rang. Seafood, good position on Rang Hill with views overlooking Phuket Town, average food. *Sip Gaeng*, Yaowarat Rd. Translates as '10 curries'. **Cheap**: *Mae Porn*, 50-52 Phangnga Rd. Excellent food available from this unprepossessing corner restaurant, including ice creams, shakes, Thai dishes and seafood specialities, a/c room available. Recommended.

Other Asian cuisines Expensive: *Lai-An Lao*, 58 Rasada Rd. Chinese restaurant with seafood specialities. Recommended. *Venus Chinese Restaurant*, next to *Mae Porn Restaurant*, classy establishment serving a variety of Chinese and Thai dishes. **Mid-range**: *Vegetarian Restaurant*, Ranong Rd. Respectable place with a good choice of veggie dishes. *Kaw Yam and Bakery*, 11/1 Thung Kha Rd. *Erawan*, 41/34 Montri Rd. Seafood, Chinese. *Omar E Khyam*, 54/1 Montri Rd. Indian.

International Expensive: *Bondeli Café*, Rasada Rd (corner of Phuket Rd). A/c café and boulangerie with good pastries and savouries including pizzas and quiche, sophisticated place for a coffee (excellent – probably the best in town) and cool off. **Mid-range:** *Kanda Bakery*, 31-33 Rasada Rd. Spotlessly clean a/c restaurant with art deco undertones, serves breakfast, Thai and international dishes and good cakes like cinnamon rolls, croissant and chocolate brownies. Recommended. *Le Café*, Rasada Centre. Elegant café serving burgers, steaks, sandwiches, cappucino and milkshakes. *Le Glacier*, 43/3 Rasada Centre. Ice creams, coffee and drinks. *Suthep Roast Chicken*, 480 Phuket Rd.

Fast food In the *Ocean Shopping Mall* – which has been closed for renovation since 1998 but presumably will re-open at some point – there was (and should be again) *McDonalds, Burger King, Pizza Hut, KFC, Svensons, Mister Donut*, enough for even the most dedicated fast foodie.

Foodstalls The best place to browse on the street is around the market on Ranong Rd. Here, roadside stalls serve such delicacies as deep fried chicken feet, *khao niaw mamuang* (sticky rice and mango – when in season), grilled bananas, squid and *kanom* (Thai sweets). A very good and cheap restaurant close by is *Koh Lao Luat Mu* (name only in Thai), on the circle linking Ranong and Rasada roads, which serves tasty noodle and rice dishes. Alternatively, *Khai Muk*, Rasada Rd (opposite the *Thavorn Hotel*) serves superb *kuaytiaw* (noodle soup).

Eating
● *on map*
Price categories:
see inside front cover

The Southern Region

Entertainment

Cinema 4 cinemas renting headphones with English dialogue. *The Pearl* is on corner of Montri and Phangnga roads, 3 shows daily at 1230, 1900 and 2130. Some shows with the English soundtrack (ask at ticket office).

Cultural shows *Orchid Garden and Thai Village*, 2 km off Thepkrasatri Rd, T214860. Sword fighting, Thai boxing, Thai Classical dancing, folk dances, almost 1 ha of orchid gardens, handicraft centre and elephants. Open 1000-2200. Daily cultural shows 1100-1200 and 1730-1830.

Discos Most discos run from 2100-0200. *Marina Club* at the *Phuket Merlin*, 158/1 Yaowarat Rd. *The Wave* at the *Pearl Hotel*, Montri Rd. *Diamond Club* at the *Thavorn Hotel*, Rasada Rd (cover charge ฿50 for women, ฿70 for men).

Shopping

Most souvenirs found here can be bought more cheaply elsewhere in Thailand, and if travelling back to Bangkok, it is best to wait. Best buys are pearls and gold jewellery.

Antiques *Ban Boran Antiques*, 39 Yaowarat Rd (near the circle), recently moved from old shop on Rasada Rd, this is arguably the best antique shop on Phuket; interesting pieces from Thailand and Burma especially, well-priced, charming service. *Antiques House*, Rasada Centre, central location, limited stock of Thai and other Asian antiques. *Puk Antiques*, Phangnga Rd (close to *On On Hotel*); *Chan's Antiques*, Thepkrasatri Rd, just south of the Heroines Monument, not many 'antiques', but a selection of Thai artefacts.

Books *Seng Ho Phuket Co*, 2/14-16 Montri Rd. *The Books*, Phuket Rd, a few English language and German books and magazines, coffee bar.

Department stores *Rasada Centre*, Rasada Rd, or *Ocean Shopping Mall*, opposite the *Metropole Hotel* facing the clocktower has been closed since 1998 for renovation but should re-open. Further down the road is the *Ocean Plaza* shopping centre which is very good.

Handicrafts *Cheewa Thai Crafts Centre*, 250/1 Thepkrasatri Rd. *Dam Dam*, Rasada Rd (near the fountain circle), interesting selection. From numerous stalls at the *Rasada Centre*, Rasada Rd.

Jewellery There are a number of shops on Montri and Rasada roads, designs tend to be 'Asian'.

Pewterware *Phuket Pewter Centre*, 52 Phuket Rd.

Silk *Silk Master*, Thepkrasatri Rd, just north of turn-off to Patong Beach. Hand-weaving demonstrations, huge range of silk products, tailor-made clothes, leather goods, 'antiques', pots.

Tailors There are a number of tailors and fabric shops on Yaowarat Rd, near the circle. Clothes can be copied and made up in as little as a day.

Textiles *Ban Boran Textiles*, 51 Yaowarat Rd. Modern Thai and hilltribe textiles and some other handicrafts.

Sport

Bowling *Pearl*, behind Pearl theatre, Phangnga Rd. **Diving** See page 584. **Game fishing** *Phuket Tourist Centre*, 125/7 Phangnga Rd, T211849. *Andaman Queen Tour*, 44 Phuket Rd, T211276, F215261. **Golf** See page 595. **Jogging** Fitness Park on Khao Rang. **Shooting range** Indoor and outdoor, snooker club and restaurant, at 82/2 Patak Rd (west of Chalong 5-way intersection). ■ *Open Mon-Sun 0900-1800.* **Snooker** *Nimit Snooker Club*, 53/57 Nimit 1 Rd, T213202. ■ *Open 0900-late, VIP table ฿120 per hour, standard ฿50 per hour.* **Thai boxing** Every Fri at 2000 (tickets available from 1600), unfriendly place. The stadium is on South Phuket Rd (Saphan Hin). ฿350 (overpriced).

Tour operators

There are several around Rasada Rd and the Rasada centre, and along Phuket Rd. See the introduction to Phuket (page 581), for a full background on the tours available. Among the companies in Phuket Town are: *Dits Travel*, 11 Sakdidej Rd, T212848, F213934. *Songserm Travel*, 51-53 Satool Rd, Phuket Town, T222570. *Silver Queen*,

1/10 Thung Kha Rd, T214056, they also have a desk at the *Patong Merlin Hotel*. *Aloha Tour*, Chalong Bay, T216726. *Cruise Centre*, Rawai Beach, T381793.

Local Car hire: Pure Car Rent, 75 Rasada Rd, T211002 ฿900 per day. **Phuket Hori-** **Transport** zon Car Rent, 235/4 Yaowarat Rd, T215200. **Avis**, *Metropole Hotel*, 1 Montri Road, T215050, ฿950 per day. **Motorbike hire**: from the same places and many others from ฿150 per day. **Tuk-Tuk**: ฿7 within town, ฿10 from town to suburbs.

Long distance See page 585 for information on transport beyond Phuket. The bus terminal is just off Phangnga Rd.

Airline offices *Bangkok Airways*, 158/2-3 Yaowarat Rd, T212341. *Dragonair*, 37/52 Montri Rd **Directory** (from Hong Kong). *Malaysia Airlines*, Merlin Hotel, T216675. *SilkAir*, 183/103 Phangnga Rd, T213891, F213887. *Thai*, 41/33 Montri Rd, T212400. *Thai* (domestic), 78 Ranong Rd, T211195. *Tradewinds*, 95/20 Phuket Rd, T213891 (from Singapore). **Banks** Along Rasada, Phuket, Phangnga and Thepkrasatri roads there are branches of all the major banks, all with ATMs and currency exchange. **Communications** Post Office: Montri Rd (at the corner of Thalang Rd). Telephone centre: 122/2 Phangnga Rd, open 24 hrs. Overseas telephone and fax also available from the post office in town. **Medical services** *Mission*, Thepkasatri Rd, T212386. *Wachira*, Yaowarat Rd, T211114. *Bangkok Phuket Hospital*, Yangyok Uthit Rd, T254421. **Places of worship** Christian Church: Chao Fa Rd, Sun service at 1030. **Useful addresses** American Express agent: *Sea Tour*, 95/4 Phuket Rd, T216979. Immigration office: South Phuket Rd (close to Saphan Hin). Ask for the boxing stadium; the office is next door. T212108. **24 hrs petrol station**: Esso, Thepkasatri Rd. **Tourist Police** Emergency call, T219878 (till 1630), then Police on T212115. Police station on corner of Phuket and Phangnga roads.

Phuket's beaches

The beach areas listed below begin with the principal resort of Patong, followed by the beaches south of Patong from Karon and anti-clockwise to Chalong. Finally, there is a section on the less-visited beaches of the west coast, north of Patong.

Patong Beach   หาดป่าตอง

The most developed beach on Phuket is the 3 km-long **Patong**, 15 km due west *Phone code: 076* of Phuket Town. It began to metamorphose from a hippy paradise into a com- mercial centre during the 1970s. It is the Pattaya of the south, with a mass of *Looking down the main* neon signs advertising the many hotels, massage parlours, restaurants, straight *drag, Patong could be* bars, gay bars, nightclubs, clothes stalls and discos. The cheap accommoda- *anywhere: south of* tion has now been almost entirely displaced to remoter parts of the island *France, the west coast of* although cheaper places do exist, especially on Rat Uthit Road. Sadly, there is *the US ... there is little* little indication that any thought has been given to the overall planning of the *sense of 'Thai-ness' here* area: individual hotels and restaurants can be excellent, but the whole ensem- ble is a shambles; enormous, impersonal skyscraper hotels tower over rather more attractive two-storey guesthouses. Developers bypass planning restric- tions by offering 'gifts' to the appropriate officials. In an article published in the London *Sunday Times* in 1996, Mark Ottaway lamented that "Many commen- tators, myself included, spent much of the last decade agonizing as to whether it was 'going the way of Pattaya'", adding that "the omens get worse with every visit". One thing cannot be denied though: Patong generates a great deal of for- eign exchange.

Having said all this, Patong seems popular with families these days and is less frenetic than Pattaya, with the sex tourism scene not really in evidence. It also offers the widest selection of watersports on Phuket and in spite of the hotel development, it is still possible to snorkel on the reef at the southern end of the bay. Patong could not, in any sense, be described as peaceful, but it is the best place to stay if you are looking for a nightlife. The beach is also safe for children, as the seabed shelves gently and the water is generally calm. The beach at the northern end of the bay is quiet but rocky; at the southern end also quiet but sandy and better for swimming.

Tours Express boats leave Patong for day trips to the Similan Islands (see page 604), or to Phi Phi (see page 628). *Thai Tour Patong Beach*, T213275, organize two-hour tours in a glass-bottomed boat to view the coral reef. Daily departures from Patong Beach at 1000, 1200, 1400 and 1600 (฿300).

Sleeping There are dozens of hotels on Patong and new ones still under construction; the fol-
■ *on map* lowing is only a small selection. Most hotels are situated on Patong Beach Rd (also
Price codes: known as Thaweewong Rd), but there are also quite a few on Rat Uthit Rd. Most hotels
see inside front cover are situated south of Sawatdirak Rd.

AL *Amari Coral Beach Resort*, 104 Trai Trang Rd, T340106, F340115, coralbea@
loxinfo.co.th www.amari.com On secluded promontory at southern end of beach,
200 a/c rooms, all with balconies, restaurants, pools, fitness centre, tennis courts,
private beach and a recently opened health spa – one of the more peaceful places
here. **AL** *Andaman Sea View*, 2 Thaweewong Rd, T341300, F340103, info@
seaviewphuket.com, www.seaviewphuket.com A/c, restaurant, pool, attractive
hotel at southern end of the bay, facing onto a section of beach which is less cluttered and busy than elsewhere on Patong. This, by Patong standards, is a classy
hotel, well designed, good pool, attentive service. Recommended.
AL *Club Andaman*, 77/1 Patong Beach Rd, T340530, F340527, B2701627. A/c, restaurant, pool, large new block and some older thatched cottages, set in large spacious grounds. Fitness centre, tennis courts, watersports, children's games room.
AL *Merlin*, 99/2 Song Roi Pee Rd, T340037, F340394, B2532536. A/c, restaurant, 3
sculptured pools and a children's pool, large 4-storey hotel, quite attractively laid
out with well-designed, spacious rooms. Nice garden, watersports, fitness club.
Rather out on a limb, away from the activity of Patong. **AL** *Seapearl Beach*, 42/30
Beach Rd, T341901, F341122, seapearl@ phuket.ksc.co.th, at the southern end of
the beach. Pool, mini shopping centre. A relative newcomer, 60 rooms with rather
ostentatious decor, pleasantly low-rise, right on the beach and most rooms have a
seaview. **AL-A** *Diamond Cliff Resort*, 61/9 Kalim Beach, T340510, F340507,
B2455815. A/c, restaurant, pool, northern end of Patong, large impressive resort on
side of hill but not much beach immediately in front of hotel, tennis courts,
mini-golf, health club. **AL-A** *Holiday Inn*,52 Patong Beach Rd, T340608, F340435,
B2554260. A/c, restaurants, pool very close to the main road, making it rather public
to passers by. Ugly concrete hotel block on the beach, popular with tour groups.
Tennis, watersports, gym, golf driving range, diving centre. **AL** *Patong Beach Hotel*,
124 Patong Beach Rd, T340301, F340541, B2612986, patong@sun.phuket.ksc.co.th
A fairly ugly 11-storey block situated in the middle of Patong beach, several restaurants to choose from, free form pool, jacuzzi, fitness centre, health club, bars and
disco – a happening place. **A** *Patong Bay Garden Resort*, 61/13 Patong Beach Rd,
T340297. A/c, restaurant, small pool, 2-storey Spanish-style hotel, 60 rather small
rooms but intimate atmosphere and it has the advantage of being on the beach.
A *Patong Beach Bungalows*, 96/1 Patong Beach Rd, T340117, F340213. A/c, restaurant, small pool, a 35 room strip of rather small and damp bungalows, not particularly attractive, but it's right on the beach which explains why the rooms here go for
a premium. There are better and cheaper places to stay – but they don't have a
beach front position. **A** *Phuket Cabana*, 41 Patong Beach Rd, T340138, F340178,
B2782239. A/c, open-air café, small pool for size of hotel (about 140 rooms),

wooden cabins quite well laid out in leafy winding paths, rather close together, but hotel is in a good location by the beach and has a longer pedigree than most and something approaching an intimate atmosphere. **A-B** *Le Jardin*, Na Nai Rd, T340391, F344182. Pool, restaurant, obviously aimed at the French tourists but not noticeably hostile to other nationalities. **A-B** *Neptuna*, 82/49-50 Rat Uthit Rd, T340824, F340627. A/c, restaurant, tiny pool, 2-storey small hotel, a bit cramped. **C** *Sand Inn*, 93/35 Rat Uthit Rd, T340275, F340273. Very pleasant rooms, well run, good restaurant downstairs.

B *Bel-Aire Mansion*, 76 Beach Rd, T340280. Superb rooms, great location but perhaps a little noisy. Located 20 m from the beach and for this price, a bargain. Recommended. **B** *K Hotel*, 82/47 Rat Uthit Rd, T340832, F340124. Some a/c, restaurant, decent-sized pool for a low-key hotel, well-maintained compound, quiet 2-storey hotel with 40 rooms, largely German clientele, quite expensive. Recommended. **B** *Patong Villa*, 85/3 Patong Beach Rd, T340132, F340133. Centre of beach, restaurant, pool. **B** *Safari Beach*, 83/12 Patong Beach Rd, T340230, F340231. A/c, restaurant attached, small pool, small 2 and 3-storey hotel set around pool in leafy compound just north of Soi Bangla, peaceful, considering how central it is. **B** *Thara Patong*, 81 Patong Beach Rd, T340135, F340446, B3214989. A/c, restaurant, attractive pool, 3-storey hotel with 130 rooms, good value.

Patong Beach

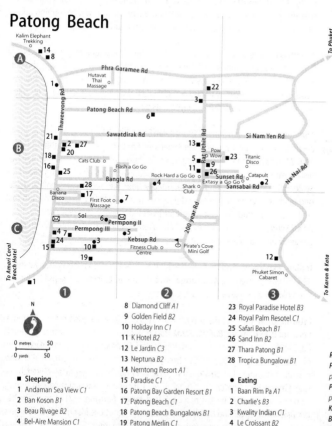

Related maps
Phuket Island, page 580
Phuket Town, page 588
Karon & Kata Beaches, page 597
Bang Tao, Pansea & Kamala Beaches, page 602

The Southern Region

B *Tropica Bungalow Hotel*, 94/4 Patong Beach Rd, T341463, F340206. A/c, *Malee's Seafood Restaurant* in front of hotel, small pool, very leafy compound set back from road, quite dark rooms, but it's central, quiet and good value for the middle of town.

C *Capricorn*, 82/29 Rat Uthit Rd, T340390, F295468. Private bathroom. **C** *Nerntong Resort*, Kalim Beach, T340572, F340571. A/c, restaurant, pool, north of Patong and away from the beach, attractive for its seclusion. **C** *Paradise*, 93 Patong Beach Rd, T340172. Southern end, a/c. **C** *PS 2 Bungalow*, Rat Uthit Rd, T342207, F290034. (Good) restaurant, some a/c, 60 rooms, newer (and more expensive, with hot water) ones in a block, older in individual bungalows, this hotel is looking a little jaded now although the newer rooms are in reasonable condition, the guesthouse is located about 10 mins walk from the beach on a large garden plot so rooms are quiet, remains popular, motorcycles for hire. **C-D** *Beau Rivage*, 77/15-17 Rat Uthit Rd, T340725. Some a/c, large rooms – some suites – with clean bathrooms, spacious and good value although like the other hotels on Rat Uthit Rd it is some way from the beach. **D** *Ban Koson*, 81/3 Patong Beach Rd, T340135. Near Soi Post Office. **D** *Club Oasis*, 86/4 Patong Beach Rd, T293076. Near Soi Post Office. **D** *Golden Field*, Patong Beach Rd, T340375. **D** *Jeep I*, 81/7 Bangla Rd, T340264. Huts in a grassy compound. **D** *Jeep II*, 38/8 Rat Uthit Rd, T340100. Centre of beach. **D** *Royal Palm Resotel*, 86/4 Patong Beach, T340141. Near Soi Post Office. **D** *White*, 81/4 Rat Uthit Rd. Quiet guesthouse down a narrow lane running off Rat Uthit Rd, attractive garden, clean rooms. Recommended.

Eating
● *on map*
Price categories:
see inside front cover

*There is lots of choice
for fast food along
the Beach Rd. Fruit
stalls are at northern
end of Rat Uthit Rd*

As with accommodation, there is a huge selection of restaurants selling all types of food; seafood is recommended. Though it may sound less than Holmsian, the best way to find somewhere to suit your palate and wallet is to wander around until you strike lucky. Places are easy to find at night when the neon lights spring to life. Most restaurants have their menus displayed outside.

Thai Expensive: *Baan Rim Pa*, 100/7 Kalim Beach Rd, T340789. Open terrace, on cliff overlooking bay, great position but expensive. *Krua Thai*, 99/61 Rat Uthit Rd (south end). *Malee's Seafood*, 94/4 Patong Beach Rd. Also serves Chinese and International dishes. *No 4 Seafood*, Bangla Rd. Seafood. *Patong Seafood*, 98/2 Patong Beach Rd. Seafood, basic but good. **Mid-range**: *Hungry Tiger*, intersection of Bangla and Second roads, Thai as well as western dishes, one recent visitor reported with relish that "they have the guts to serve [the food] unmoderated ... hot really means hot!". *Sabai Sabai*, Soi Post Office, it may not be a terribly original name, but this small restaurant serves good and well-priced Thai food.

Indian Expensive: *Shalimar*, 89/59 Soi Post Office. Seafood specialities. *Kashmir*, 83-50 Patong Beach Rd. **Mid-range**: *Kwality Indian Cuisine*, Soi Kepsab. This is a good place if you need a curry fast, good choice.

International Many of the sois off Patong Beach Rd sell a good range of international food. **Expensive**: *Buffalo Steak House*, 94/25-26 Soi Patong Resort, off Bangla Rd, T340855. Scandinavian fare with lots of beef. *Da Maurizio*, on Kalim Beach, north of Patong, opposite *Diamond Cliff Hotel*, T344079. Italian food in attractive setting, booking recommended. *La Mousson*, Sawatdirak Rd. Quite sophisticated French cuisine. *Patong Beer Garden*, by *K Hotel*, 82/47 Rat Uthit Rd. Attractive garden setting, Viennese food cooked by Austrian chef. **Mid-range**: *Babylon*, 93/12 Bangla Rd. Italian. *Blackbeard's*, behind *Holiday Inn*, on site of Pirates Cove Minigolf. Great burgers, good for families, reasonable prices. *Charlie's Restaurant*, Soi Sansabai. Thai and Tex-Mex. Barbecue every Fri from 2100. Good bar. *Grillhutte*, 85 Patong Beach Rd. Sauerkraut and mash. Huge menu and German beer. *Lai Mai*, 86/15 Patong Beach Rd.

Great Western breakfasts. *Le Croissant*, Soi Bangla. Thai/European restaurant/bakery. Good selection. *Mon Bijou*, 72/5 Rat Uthit Rd. German. *Lisa's Scandinavian Restaurant*, Soi Permpong. Easy to find, plenty of choice and good value. *Rock Hard Café*, 82/51 Bangla Rd. Garden, steaks, pizzas. *Vecchio Venezia*, Bangla Rd. Pizza. *Waikiki Dive Café*, Soi Patong Resort. Food and pool and internet. A cool place to chill out, open until 0200, more a bar than a restaurant.

Bars

Bars in Patong are concentrated along Rat Uthit Rd and Bangla Rd. The latter is throbbing with activity in the evening with dozens of bars catering for all nationalities and persuasions. *Black and White*, 70/123 Paradise Complex. *Bounty Bar*, Bangla Road. *Captain Hook's*, 70/142 Paradise Complex. *Maxim's*, Rat Uthit Road. *Oasis*, off Bangla Road. *Stardust a go-go*, *Extasy*, *Titanic*, *Fawlty Towers*, all on Soi Sunset, Rat Uthit Road.

Entertainment

Cabaret *Phuket Simon Cabaret*, Patong Rd, T342114, shows at 1930 and 2130. A tourist trap, but very professional transvestite show.

Cultural shows A Thai-style house on the hill before Patong Beach provides Thai boxing, classical dance, sword fighting. 2 shows a night, with Thai dinner, T7230841.

Discos *Banana* at *Patong Beach Hotel*, **Deep Sea Video Theque** at *Phuket Arcadia Hotel* and at *Le Crocodile*. *Tin Mine 21* in *Royal Paradise Hotel*, Rat Uthit Road. *Shark Club*, Soi Bangla, popular, brand new place with state-of-the-art audio visuals. Largest club in Patong.

House of Horror T293123. Asia's biggest Horror House. *Daily 1700-0200*.

Music *Le Crocodile*, just off Bangla Rd, and at many of the bars. Also the usual assortment of massage parlours, straight and gay bars, and revues.

Traditional Thai massage From countless (usually untrained) women on the beach or from *Hide Away*, 47/4 Na Nai Rd, Patong Beach, T340591, or *Hutavat Thai Massage*, 45/11-12 Phra Baramee Rd, Patong Beach, T342427. **First Foot Massage**, Soi Bangla, T340027.

Shopping

All the usual tourist goods available here: T-shirts, sandals, mediocre handicrafts, sea-shells (unfortunately). Stalls line Patong Beach Rd and several sois off here. *Centre Point* is a covered market area on Rat Uthit Rd. There are several **jewellery** shops in the centre of Patong Beach Rd.

Sport

Bungy jumping *Jungle Bungee Jump*, on Route 4029 into Patong. ■ *Mon-Sun 0900-1800*, T321351. *Catapult*, Soi Sunset, run by the same group. ■ *2000-2400*. **Crazy golf** *Pirate's Cove*, behind *Holiday Inn*, two 18-hole courses ฿150, good restaurant attached (*Blackbeards* – see above). **Diving** Centres are concentrated along Patong Beach Rd. Trips range from 1-day tours to Phi Phi Island, to week-long expeditions to the Similan Islands National Park and the Surin Islands. See general diving section on page 584 for listings. **Elephant trekking** *Kalim Elephant Trekking*, Kalim Beach, T290056. ■ *0800-1000*. **Fitness** The *Fitness Club Centre* T340608, with aerobics, sauna and body building is in the *Holiday Inn* on Patong Beach. ■ *Mon-Sat 0900-2100, Sun 1200-2100. Daily, weekly and monthly membership is available.* **Game fishing** Quite a few operators along Patong Beach Rd. Expect to pay about ฿1,500-2,000 per day. **Go-Kart racing** *Go-Kart speedway*, track on left, at the bottom of the hill leading to Patong (Route 4029), T321949. ■ *Mon-Sun 1000-2100*. **Golf** *Phuket Country Club*, on main road between Phuket Town and Patong, T213383, 18-hole, ฿150. ■ *0800-1800*. Caddy ฿100. **Watersports** A wide range: windsurfing, waterskiing, sailing, diving, snorkelling, deep-sea fishing. Ask at your hotel or at one of the sports shops along Patong Beach Rd.

Tour operators

Magnum Travel, Patong Beach Rd, T381840. *Travel Company*, 89/71 Patong Beach Rd, T321292.

Transport
15 km W of town

Local Jeep and motorbike hire: from outlets along Patong Beach Rd. Motorbikes on Rat Uthit Rd. *Avis* has desks at the *Holiday Inn* (T340608) and *Phuket Cabana Hotel* (T340138), *Hertz* is at the *Merlin* (T340037).

Road Chartered tuk-tuk: ฿130 one way, from Patong to town or vice versa. **Songthaews/minibuses**: regular departures from Ranong Rd, by the market in Phuket Town (฿10).

Directory

Banks Banks and currency exchange booths are concentrated on Patong Beach Rd (Thaweewong Rd). **Communications** Post Office: Patong Beach Rd (the beachfront road), near Soi Permpong Pattana (aka Soi Post Office). International telephone service next door to the Post Office on Patong Beach Rd. Open 0800-2300. **Medical services** *Kathu Hospital* on Rat Uthit Rd. **Useful addresses** Tourist Police: on Patong Beach Rd.

Karon and Kata Beaches   หาดกะรนและหาดกะตะ

Phone code: 076

The horseshoe-shaped Karon and Kata Beaches south of Patong are divided by a narrow rocky outcrop. Karon started tourist life as a haven for backpackers; it is now well developed, with a range of hotels and bungalows and a wide selection of restaurants. But the density of building is much less than at Patong. Hotels are more widely spread, the atmosphere is more relaxed, less frenetic. Karon's major drawback, perhaps, is the beach which is exposed, offering almost no shade from trees. At crab-eye level it must seem an inhospitable expanse of baking sand. Most hotels are also set some distance away from the beach, so that reaching the sea requires a walk across scrubland and a road. Nonetheless, there are good mid-range places to stay on Karon, and the slower moving pace of life here will appeal to many.

Kata consists of two beaches: **Kata Yai** (Big Kata) and **Kata Noi** (Little Kata), divided by a cliff. Kata Noi is dominated by the *Amari Kata Thani Hotel*, although there are a few bungalows here. The snorkelling is good around Koh Pu, the island in the middle of the bay, and at the south end of Kata Noi. Kata Yai is a sprawling mass of development: hotels, souvenir shops and roadside restaurants abound. It has no real charm – although it does provide excellent facilities for the holidaymaker.

Sleeping
■ *on map*
Price codes:
see inside front cover

In Karon AL *Arcadia*, T396038, F396136, Bangkok T2640291. Centre of beach, a/c, restaurant, pool, modern, overbearing high-rise with countless rooms, all overlooking the sea, health club, tennis, watersports, set back, away from the beach. **AL** *Le Meridien* , T340480, F340479, Bangkok T6532201. A/c, restaurants, pools, nightclub, plenty of entertainment including fitness centre, tennis, squash, mini-golf, watersports, very private and secluded with large landscaped pool to complement this massive 470-room L-shaped block. **AL** *Thavorn Palm Beach*, 128/10 Moo 3, T396090, F396555, Bangkok T2475150. A/c, 5 restaurants, 5 pools, squash, tennis, snooker, a large hotel facing the beach with all facilities but not much style, it has outgrown itself. **AL-A** *Islandia Park Resort*, T396200, F396491, B5136756. A/c, restaurant, pool, high-rise block, all rooms facing sea, new and plush (for how long?). **A** *Felix Karon View Point* (*Swissôtel*), 4/8 Patak Rd, T396666, F396853. A/c, restaurant, pool smallish, low-rise hotel with 125 rooms at the northern end of Karon Beach, the style of the place is more Spanish than Thai, but nonetheless it is more attractive than most, small pool, away from the beach, inland from the road. **A** *Karon Beach Resort*, 5/2 Moo 3 Patak Rd, T330006, F330529, katagrp@loxinfo.co.th A/c, restaurant, simple laps pool, right on the beach at the Southern end of the bay, slightly frayed interior, all rooms with balconies overlooking beach, owned by the Kata Group, the managing director is an English woman. **A** *Karon Villa Royal Wing*, T396139, F396122, B2516615. Centre of beach, a/c, restaurant, pool. **A** *Marina Cottage*, PO Box 143, southern end of beach, T381625/330493, F381516. A/c, 2 good restaurants, beautiful secluded pool, individual cottages in lush grounds, no private beach, *Marina Divers* here, tours and boat trips organized. Recommended. **A** *Phuket Island View*, T396452, F396632. Southern end of beach, a/c, restaurant, pool. **A** *Sand Resort*, T212901. A/c, restaurant, simple bungalows, clean, small rooms. **A** *South Sea Resort*, 36/12 Moo 1, Patak Rd, T396611, F396618. A/c, restaurant, pool, nearly 100 rooms in this hotel which is almost Wild West in design, attractive central pool, good range of facilities, location in a relatively quiet spot at the north end of the bay, set away from the beach, rooms are unremarkable with little local feel, good balconies. **A-B** *Kharon Inn*, T330530, F330128. A/c, restaurant, pool, some 60 bungalows and 40 more modern rooms in a low-rise block on large plot, small pool, overall feels rather dated but not unattractively so.

B-C *Shady Bungalow*, T330677. Well located on the beach but slightly cramped with so many other places in operation in this small space at the southern end of Kata. **B-C** *Phuket Ocean Resort*, 9/1 Moo 1, Karon Beach, T396176, F396470, B7320608. A/c, restaurant, pool, a rather ramshackle affair with older bungalows and newer rooms in tiered blocks on the hillside, position is at the quieter, northern end of the bay, away from the beach, good mid-range place to stay, no pretensions, comfortable.

C *Karon Guesthouse*, T396860, F396117. A decent, very average mid-range place. **C-D** *Lumi and Yai Bungalow*, northern end of beach, T396096. 15 reasonable rooms, well located for access to both Karon/Kata and Patong. **C-D** *Kata Noi Club Bungalow*, T330194. Isolated position on this lovely beach and at a reasonable price, well managed. **C-D** *Kata Noi Riviera Bungalow*, T330726. Similar rates to *Kata Noi Club* and likewise benefitting from being relatively alone on the beach. **C-E** *My Friend*, northern end of beach, T396344. Simple huts within easy reach of the beach. **D** *Happy Hut*, 121/2 Kata-Karon Beach, T330230. Small, clean and green. **D** *Karon Sea View* (next to *Sand Resort*), T396798. Good value

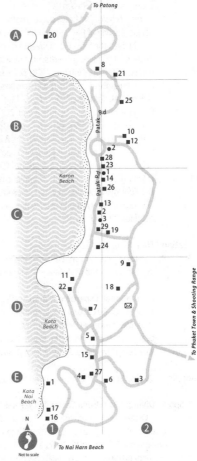

Karon & Kata Beaches

Not to scale

To Patong

To Phuket Town & Shooting Range

To Nai Harn Beach

N

■ **Sleeping**
1 Amari Kata Thani *E1*
2 Arcadia *C1*
3 Bell Guesthouse *E2*
4 Boathouse Inn *E1*
5 Club Med *D1*
6 Cool Breeze *E2*
7 Fantasy Hill *D1*
8 Felix Karon View Point *A1*
9 Happy Hut *D2*
10 Islandia Park Resort *B2*
11 Karon Beach Resort *D1*
12 Karon Guesthouse *B2*
13 Karon Sea View *C1*
14 Karon Villa & Karon Villa Royal Wing *C2*
15 Kata Beach Resort *E1*
16 Kata Noi Club *E1*
17 Kata Noi Riviera *E1*

18 Kata Tropicana *D2*
19 Kharon Inn *C2*
20 Le Meridien *A1*
21 Lumi & Yai Bungalow *A2*
22 Marina Cottage *D1*
23 My Friend *B2*
24 Phuket Island View *C1*
25 Phuket Ocean Resort *B2*
26 Sand Resort *C2*
27 Shady Bungalow *E1*
28 South Sea Resort *B2*
29 Thavorn Palm Beach *C1*

● **Eating**
1 Al Dente *C2*
2 Little Mermaid *B2*
3 Old Siam *C1*

The Southern Region

chalets. **E** *Bell Guesthouse*, T330111. One of the cheapest places to stay in Karon/Kata, but away from the beach.

In Kata (All with restaurant, pool and a/c.) **L-AL** *Boathouse Inn*, T330015, F330561. Southern end of beach, a/c, several restaurants (good seafood), pool, attractive high-end choice, big hotel, but retains the feel of a small hotel. Very well run, large central jacuzzi, one of the best and most refined places to stay on Phuket, small touches delight even the most world-weary expense account traveller, there is also the added excitement of a Thai cookery school here for those who wish to leave knowing how to handle a chilli. **AL** *Club Med*, T285225, F330461, B2540742. Centre of beach, looking rather threadbare, superb sports activities, large piece of private beach, excellent for children. **AL** *Kata Beach Resort*, 5/2 Mue 2 Patak Rd, T330530, F330128, B9394062, katagrp@ loxinfo.co.th Southern end, 262 rooms in L-shaped block set around a free-form pool, run by an English lady married to a Thai, this is an efficiently run hotel, paired with *Karon Beach Resort* and *Kharon Inn*. **A** *Amari Kata Thani*, Kata Noi Beach, T330127, B2675213. A/c, restaurants, unexciting pools, large average hotel, popular with package holidays, but lovely beach. **A** *Mansion*, T381565. A/c, restaurant, quiet area of beach. **D** *Kata Tropicana*, T330141. Simple chalets, friendly and clean. Recommended. **D-E** *Fantasy Hill*, between Karon and Kata, T330106. Rather noisy. **E** *Cool Breeze*, Kata Noi, T330484. Very good value, with excellent restaurant (which is in the guesthouse but doesn't belong to it).

Eating
● *on map*
Price categories:
see inside front cover

Thai *Ruan Thep*, southern end of beach. *Old Siam*, T396090. Traditional Thai food in traditional Thai atmosphere. Great position on the beach with indoor and terrace dining. Expensive, and while farangs may not realise that it is overpriced, most Thais do.

International Expensive: *Maxim*, seafood, southern end of Karon. *Hayashi*, T381710. Japanese. *Co Co Cabana*, pizza, northern end of Karon. *Gustos* and *No 2* near *Kata Thani Hotel*. **Mid-range**: *Al Dente*, T396569, Italian fare. *Gung Café*, next to the *Boathouse*, Kata beach. Al fresco dining on the beach. Thai and seafood. *Little Mermaid*, T396628. Good value, extensive menu. *Swiss Bakery*, *Western Inn*, Recommended.

Shopping

Books *Good Earth*, second-hand book shop next to the *Rose Inn*.

Sport

Diving *Siam Diving Centre*, 121/9 Patak Rd, southern end of Karon Beach, T330936. – Organize diving expeditions to the Similan Islands. *Marina Divers*, southern end of Karon Beach, T330272, F330516. PADI certified courses, very professional set-up. Recommended; and *PIDC Divers* at *Le Meridien Hotel*, T321479. **Horse riding** Next to shooting range, T381667. ฿600 per hour. ■ *0700-1200, 1300-1830*. **Shooting range** *Phuket Shooting Range*, 82/2 Patak Road, T381667. Off Route 4028 between Kata and Chalong. ■ *Mon-Sun 1000-1800*.

Transport
20 km to Phuket Town

Local Car hire: *Avis* has a desk at the Phuket *Arcadia* (T381038), *Le Meridien* (T340480) and *Kata Beach Resort* (T381530). *Hertz* has a desk at the *Thavorn Palm Beach* (T381034). **Minibus**: chartered minibus to/from town, ฿130; **Songthaews**: to both Karon and Kata leave regularly from the Ranong Rd Market, Phuket Town (฿15).

**Nai Harn &
Promthep Cape**
Phone code: 076

Nai Harn, 18 km southwest of Phuket Town, is one of the island's most beautiful locations, with spectacular sunsets. It is now possible to stay here in luxury at the *Phuket Yacht Club* (built, illegally, on protected land). During the monsoon season between May and October, the surf and currents can be particularly vicious and care should be taken when swimming. From Nai Harn it is possible to walk to **Promthep Cape**, the best place to view the sunset. Walk out to the cape itself or simply look down on the surrounding sea and coastline from the road, for a spectacular view. Near the highest point there is a shrine covered in gold leaf and surrounded by wooden elephants.

Sleeping **L** *Le Royal Meridien Phuket Yacht Club*, T381156, F381164, T02-2545435, info@phuket-yachtclub.com A/c, restaurants, pool, lovely position on hill, overlooking Nai Harn and Promthep Cape, well run with109 luxurious rooms, secluded. Spacious and recently refurbished rooms have large secluded balconies with sea views, massive bathrooms. Excellent food, fitness club, tennis courts, lovely beach, the hotel was built contravening environmental laws but as money can move mountains in Thailand, little could or can be done. **AL** *Nai Harn Villa*, 14/29 Wiset Rd, T381595, F381961. Overpriced but well run. There are better-value places elsewhere. **AL-C** *Jungle Beach*, T381108. Some a/c, pool, remote, attractive position, has a long and pretty good track record – a lot of local farangs swear by it – although there are reports that it is on a slow slide. **C** *Nai Harn Beach Resort*, 14/29 Moo 21 Wiset Rd, T381810. Some a/c, good rooms for the price. Clean and well kept. **D** *Ao Saen*, T288306. On the beach. **E** *New Sunset Bungalow*, 93/1 Moo 6, clean bungalows in nice setting.

Sport **Riding**: *Crazy Horse Club*, rides on the beach or along mountain trails (฿300 per hour). Other 'sports' available here include: Waterskiing, windsurfing, mini-golf, herbal sauna.

To the north of Promthep Cape, up the eastern side of the island the first beach is Rawai, 14 km from Phuket Town. This crescent-shaped beach is now relatively developed although not to the same degree, nor in the same style, as Patong or Karon. It is patronized by Thai tourists rather than foreigners and as a result has a quite different atmosphere. There is a small market selling assorted handicrafts and various snacks. The bay is sheltered from the monsoon and it is safe to swim throughout the year. But the beach is rather dirty and it is rocky. At Rawai there is a 'sea gypsy' tribal village, **Chao Le**.

Rawai
Phone code: 076

Excursions **Koh Kaew Pisadarn** can be seen from Promthep Cape and is a short 15-minute ride by boat from Rawai Beach. The island is the site of not one, not two, but an amazing three footprints of the Buddha. Two of the footprints are located among the boulders and stone on the upper shore; the third is situated just below the low watermark. For many years important Buddhist festivals were celebrated here because of the island's supposed spiritual power and significance; then, about 40 years ago, these religious pilgrimages stopped. Sam Fang, who researched a story on the island for the *Bangkok Post*, discovered a tragedy had occurred about this time. A storm had sunk some rowing boats making the trip out to the island, and locals assumed that a resident sea serpent, angered by the visits, was involved. When a series of attempts were made to construct images of the Buddha on the island between 1952 and 1967, these were continually thwarted by bad weather and high seas. In this way there developed a belief that the island was in some way cursed. Only in 1994 were attempts at erecting a Buddha image renewed. The 1½ m-high standing image cast in concrete is on the northeastern side of the island, overlooking Promthep Cape, and about a 10-minute walk along a laid path from the boat landing. The image is surrounded by two protective nagas that slither over the top of the encircling balustrade. The footprints themselves are located on the shore beneath the Buddha; steps lead down to them. In 1995 the celebration of Loi Krathong at Koh Kaew Pisadarn was reintroduced. ■ *Getting there: by long-tailed boat from Rawai Beach. Negotiate with one of the boat-owners, take a picnic, and arrange to be picked up at a convenient time.*

The Southern Region

Sleeping and eating AL-A *Phuket Island Resort*, T381010, F381018, T02-2525320. A/c, restaurant, pool, luxurious hotel with almost every conceivable facility. Well run by helpful staff. **C** *Salaloi Resort*, 52/2 Wiset Rd, T381370. Some a/c, well established, good restaurant, cheaper rooms are good value. **C** *Rawai Resort*, T381298. A/c, restaurant. **D** *Rawai Garden Resort*, T381292. Restaurant, small affair but pleasant. **D** *Pornmae*, T381300.

Sport Diving: equipment can be hired from the *Phuket Island Resort*. **Paintball**: *Top Gun*, 82/2 Patak Rd, T381667.

Laem Ka & Chalong beaches The next beaches up the east coast are **Laem Ka Beach** and **Chalong**. Ao Chalong is 1 km off the main road. There is not much here for the sun and sea-worshipper and the beach is rather dirty. Offshore tin-dredging is said to have ruined the beach. Boats can be caught to the offshore islands for game fishing, snorkelling and scuba diving from Chalong's long pier, and there is a small collection of good seafood restaurants. The rest of the east coast has not been developed for tourists as the coast is rocky. *Aloha Tours* (T381220) and the *Chalong Bay Boat Centre* (T381852) are both on Wisit Rd. *Ao Chalong* arrange trips to Phi Phi, Coral, and Raja Islands as well as fishing and diving expeditions.

Price codes: see inside front cover **Sleeping and eating B-C** *Laem Ka Beach Inn*, T381305. Restaurant. **B-C** *Phuket Fishing Lodge*, T281003, F281007. Easier to reach than some of the other places to stay. Fair rooms but not overly receptive reception. **B-C** *Wichit Bungalow*, 16/1 Wiset Rd, T381342. To the south of Chalong bay. Nice area, but a bit out of the way. **B-D** *Atlas Resort*, 14 Wiset Rd, T381279, F381279. Isolated from the other establishments and in the middle of the long beach. Reasonable rooms, fair prices. **C** *Boomerang Bungalow*, T281068, F381690. Not on the beach but the price doesn't reflect its inferior position. Not bad, nonetheless. **E-F** *Ao Chalong Bungalow*, T282175. Restaurant. **Expensive**: *Kan Eang Seafood*, on the beach, excellent selection of seafood. Recommended. *Ruan Thai Seafood*.

Sport Golf: 18-hole mini-golf course (open 1000-2300 Mon-Sun) left of the narrow road to Ao Chalong from the main road. Herbal sauna, sailing centre and dive shop (see dive section, page 584).

Cape Panwa The Marine Research Centre and aquarium are to be found on this remote point (see page 578), as well as Panwa House, in the grounds of the only significant hotel here – the *Cape Panwa Sheraton*. Boat trips to nearby islands leave from the cape.

Sleeping and eating AL-A *Cape Panwa Sheraton*, T391123, F391117, B2339560. Beautifully secluded, some bungalows for families, tennis courts, fitness centre, electric train down to the private beach, coral reef 40 m off-shore. This hotel plays on the fact that Leo of *The Beach* fame stayed here but we have had reports from disgruntled guests who have complained of cockroaches and half-baked service.
  Koh Tapao Yai, a small island off the cape is home to a couple of hotels, the **A** *Tapao Yai Island Resort*, T391217, all facilities and **B** *Phuket Paradise Resort*, T391217, F214917, B3941949. *Yaun Yen* (200 m from the aquarium), reasonable food, seafood is best.

Koh Lone & Koh Mai Ton *Phone code: 076* There are places to stay on several of the islands off the east and southeast coasts of Phuket. All the resorts here play on the desert island getaway theme. These places may be hard to reach in the monsoon season. Koh Mai Ton, for instance, is a private island 9 km southeast of Phuket with very little on it except the

Mai Ton Resort. This fits the bill for those truly 'deserted tropical island' holidays, except the Resort seems rather out of place with mock-classical pillars by the pool and rooms that could be on any tropical island. All a bit pretentious.

Sleeping **Koh Lone**: **B** *Lone Pavilion*, T381374. A/c, restaurant. **C** *Lone Island Resort*, T211253. **Koh Mai Ton**: **L** *Mai Ton Resort*, T214954, F214959, maiton@ksc.th.com A/c, restaurants, pools, 75 individual Thai pavilions with wooden floors and separate sitting-room, good sports facilities and beautiful white-sand beaches.

Other islands: **Koh Hii** **AL-A** *Coral Island Resort*, T281060, F381957. **Koh Raya Yai** *Raya Andaman Resort*, T381710, F381713. **Koh Sire** **D** *Sire Resort*, T221894. **Koh Taphao Yai** **B** *Phuket Paradise Resort*, T391217, F214917.

North from Patong เหนือหาดป่าตอง

Travelling north from Patong, there remain some beautiful unspoilt beaches. This part of Phuket's shoreline has virtually no cheap accommodation but a number of exclusive hotels.

A *Thavorn Beach Village*, 6/2 Moo 6, Nakalay-Patong Beach (between Kamala and Patong beaches, on the Kao Phanthurat Pass, 5 km from Patong), T340436, F340384. Attractively designed Thai-style villas, with 4 rooms each (2 ground floor, two first) many with poolside verandas, large lagoon-like pool. A secluded spot on an almost private beach (rocky at low tide).

Sleeping

Kamala Beach is 10 km north of Patong and the road to this still quiet bay has recently been surfaced and upgraded – although sections may remain rough. The beach is rather bare, with little shade, but the (Muslim) village has a nice atmosphere, with its own post office, telephone service, police station, health centre, dive centres (*Seahawk Divers* and *Thai Dive*), tour operator and travel agent and vehicle rental outfits. Indeed, visitors wishing a quiet and relaxing holiday need never leave Kamala – except to get home again. How long Kamala will remain a quiet corner of Phuket is a moot point. Land speculators have made their mark and development is underway.

Kamala Beach
Phone code: 076

As many of the local people here are Muslim, topless bathing is regarded as beyond the pale & will offend

Sleeping **AL** *Kamala Bay Terrace Resort*, 16/12 Moo 6, Tambon Kamala, T279801, F279818, T02-6426107, room@kamala.co.th, www.kamalabay.com A/c, restaurants, disappointingly small pool, tennis, built on hillside overlooking the sea, quieter location than most with virtually its own private beach, but rooms unremarkable for the price and a bit of an eyesore to boot. **AL** *Kamala Beach Estate*, T324111, F324115. **A** *Phuket Kamala Resort*, T324396. Right on the beach, a big complex but this doesn't seem to spoil the relaxed ambience. **C** *Bird Beach Bungalow*, quiet and relatively cheap but not very exciting. **C-D** *Maya's House* and *Yada's Cottage* are 2 small bungalow operations on Kamala Beach, little to choose between them, although the garden at *Yada's* is more mature and luxuriant, these are clean, simple bungalows on a quiet beach.

■ *on map, page 602*
Price codes:
see inside front cover

Eating There are a number of reasonable restaurants on Kamala. Along with the usual seafood places. **Expensive-mid-range**: *White Orchid* serves French cuisine and *Paul's Place* (at the southern end and overlooking the bay), T324111. An excellent restaurant serving good Thai food (with a marine flavour – try the fried pomfret with garlic).

Entertainment *Phuket Fantasea*, a ฿3.3 billion entertainment complex, is currently being built near Kamala Beach, to be completed by 1999. It will inevitably lure tourists to this as yet relatively undeveloped area.

The Southern Region

Surin Beach
Phone code: 076

Lined with casuarina trees and open-air restaurants, patronized mostly by Thais. The seabed shelves away steeply from the shoreline and swimming can be dangerous. Small golfcourse and no hotels on the beach. Surin Beach is particularly dirty.

■ *on maps*
Price codes:
see inside front cover

Sleeping Pansea Beach is a tiny beach just north of Surin with two exclusive hotels on it: **L** *Amanpuri Resort*, 118/1 Pansea Beach, T324333, F324100, T02-2870026, a/c, restaurant, pool, more expensive rooms are beautifully designed Thai pavilions, with attention to every detail. Superb facilities include private yacht, watersports, tennis and squash courts, fitness centre, private beach, library, undoubtedly the best on Phuket but not recommended for small children, because of many steps around the resort. For a place of such style the food is mediocre – the surroundings, style and service incomparable. **L-AL** *Chedi Phuket* (formerly the *Pansea Resort*), T324017, F324252, T02-2374792, south of *Amanpuri*, a/c, restaurant, pool, exclusive resort with range of traditional Thai cottages to sleep from 2-10 people, superb facilities, including all watersports, cinema, library, games room, secluded beach. *Hertz* have a desk here. High season surcharge that itself is more than the price of many rooms on the island.

Bang Tao, Pansea & Kamala Beaches

Eating The Thai restaurant (**Very expensive**) at the *Amanpuri* is considered one of the best on the island (and the setting is sensational), at least 48 hrs advanced booking needed during peak season (T324394).

Bang Tao (Laguna)
Phone code: 076

■ *on map*
Price codes:
see inside front cover

Development on Bang Tao Bay is in two distinct areas. To the north is the *Laguna Phuket*, a complex consisting of four **L-AL** hotels built around a lagoon. Free tuk-tuks and boats link the hotels and guests are able to use all the facilities. Excellent range of watersports and good provision for children – all facilities free. The recently opened Canal Village offers 40 or so shops and a lagoon-side café, serving satay. The adjoining bakery serves good pastries and cakes. To the south of the *Laguna Phuket* (and quite a long way round by road) there is a smattering of other places to stay.

Sleeping L *Banyan Tree*, T324374, F324375, banyan@samart.co.th, banyantree.com A/c, restaurant, pool, excellent, elegant hotel with all facilities and superb service. *The Allamanda*, T324359, F324360, www.lagunaphuket.com/allamanda The most recent addition to the Laguna Phuket, situated behind the *Sheraton Grande*, half the rooms look east over the *Banyan Tree Golf Club*,

Related maps
Phuket Island,
page 580
Phuket Town, page 588
Patong Beach,
page 593
Karon & Kata Beaches,
page 597

■ **Sleeping**
1 Allamanda
2 Amanpuri Resort
3 Bangtao Lagoon
Bungalows
4 Banyan Tree
5 Bird Beach Bungalow
6 Chedi Phuket (Pansea Resort)
7 Dusit Laguna
8 Kamala Bay Terrace

9 Kamala Beach Estate
10 Laguna Beach Resort
11 Phuket Kamala Resort
12 Royal Park Resort & Lanna Resort
13 Sheraton Grande Laguna

● **Eating**
1 Paul's Place

The Southern Region

pools, restaurants, a large scale resort. **L-AL** *Dusit Laguna*, T324320, F324174, T02-2384790. A/c, restaurants, attractive pool, the quietest and most refined of the *Laguna Phuket* complex. Excellent service, immaculate gardens, beautifully laid out unimposing hotel, tennis courts, watersports and a Children's Corner. **Avis** have a desk here. **L-AL** *Laguna Beach Resort*, Bang Tao Beach, T324352, F324353, www.lagunabeach-resort.com A/c, restaurants, pool, 250 rooms in low-rise blocks on an 8-ha (20-acre) site. This hotel has a sports emphasis: the pools are simply spectacular: a sort of marine Angkor – Raiders of the Lost Ark affair with spouting statues, caves and slides, there is also tennis, diving, squash, golf driving, etc, good for children and those with a penchant for activity/sports-filled holidays. **L-AL** *Sheraton Grande Laguna*, T324101, F324108, T02-2366543. A/c, 5 restaurants (with a good choice of cuisine), interesting design in the 'Chess Bar', large pool with interlinked sections, including a sandy 'beach' and a sunken bar, rather impersonal accommodation some of which is out on stilts on the lagoon, tennis courts, health centre, massage, children's corner. **A** *Lanna Resort*, T212553, F222502. 4 bungalows sleeping 2 to 6 people each, Thai style, 10 mins from beach, no a/c, but secluded with space, rather overpriced. **A** *Royal Park Travelodge Resort*, Southern end of the beach, T324021, F324243, T02-5411524. A/c, several restaurants, pool, large 3-storey hotel, with watersports, tennis, fitness room, gift shops.

B-D *Bangtao Lagoon Bungalow*, 72/3 Moo 3, Tambon Cherng Talay, T324260, F324168. Some a/c, small pool, a rather haphazard bungalow development in a comparatively isolated position. Range of chalets from simple (and rather worn) fan bungalows to 'deluxe' a/c affairs, the latter are small and featureless, but very clean, family cottages also available, all set within a large coconut and casuarina grove 100 m from a rubbish-strewn beach. This resort doesn't really feel as though it is on Bang Tao, as access is much further south.

Shopping *Canal Village*, shops including *Jim Thompson's*, several gem stores, clothing and handicrafts. All quite pricey and exclusive. Another 'arcade' of shops is opening up just after the turn-off from Cherng Talay to the Laguna Complex.

Sport Golf: the 18-hole *Banyan Tree Golf Club* is situated here, with driving range attached, on Wed nights, a 9-hole tournament takes place, T324350, F324351.

Between Bang Tao and Nai Yang is the isolated beach of Nai Ton which consists of little more than a handful of drinks stalls, where deck-chairs and umbrellas can be hired. However, the track leading to the beach is in the process of being improved and the rate of development may soon accelerate. So the drinks stalls may soon be joined by other more grandiose developments. South of Nai Ton is an exquisite cove, most easily accessible by boat. **B-C** *Nai Thon Beach Resort* is the only place to stay here and apparently only open in the high season, T213928, F222361.

Nai Ton
Phone code: 076

Nai Yang is the northernmost beach and part of the **Nai Yang National Park**. It is close to the airport and 37 km from Phuket Town (entrance ฿5 for car). The park encompasses Nai Yang and Mai Khao beaches, which together measure 9 km, making it the longest stretch of beach on the island. The area was declared a national park in 1981 to protect the turtles which lay their eggs here from November to March. Eggs are collected by the Fisheries Department and young turtles are released around about the second week of April each year (check on the date as it changes from year to year), on 'Turtle Release Festival Day'. Not as exciting as it may sound. The north end of the beach (where there is good snorkelling on the reef) is peaceful and secluded, with the only accommodation being in the National

Nai Yang
Phone code: 076

The Southern Region

Park bungalows. ■ *The Visitors Centre is open Mon-Sat 0830-1630. Further south, there is more activity, with a range of luxury hotels and bungalows.*

Sleeping and eating **AL** *Crown Nai Yang Suite Hotel*, T327420, F327323. A/c, restaurant, pool. **AL** *Pearl Village*, T327006, F327338, T02-2601022. A/c, restaurant, attractive pool, well run, friendly management, beautiful gardens, facilities including tennis courts, horse riding, elephant riding, good for families. Recommended. **B-D** *National Park bungalows*, T327047. **C-E** *Garden Cottage*, T327293, F327292. 2 mins from the airport, cottage-style guesthouse, friendly owner who is willing to show you the island. **Camping**: available in the National Park (฿60). There are several seafood places, for example *Nai Yang Seafood*.

Transport 30 km from Phuket Town. **Bus**: from the market on Ranong Rd in Phuket Town.

Directory **Banks**: mobile exchange van.

Koh Similan   เกาะสิมิลัน

Colour map 4, grid A1

Avoid taking too much luggage, as visitors must transfer from ferry to precarious long-tailed boat mid-ocean

The **Similan Islands National Park** consists of nine islands. They lie 80 km northwest of Phuket and are some of the most beautiful, unspoilt tropical idylls to be found in Southeast Asia. The water surrounding the archipelago supports a wealth of marine life and is considered one the best diving locations in the world as well as a good place for anglers. A particular feature of the islands is the huge granite boulders. These same boulders litter the sea-bed and make for interesting peaks and caves for scuba divers. On the west side of the islands the currents have kept the boulders 'clean', whilst on the east, they have been buried by sand.

Koh Miang houses the park office and some dormitory and camping accommodation. Koh Hu Yong, the southernmost island is the most popular diving location. From some 16,000 tourists in 1994, the numbers visiting the Similan Islands has risen to over 25,000. Anchor damage and the dumping of rubbish is a big problem here, although buoys have now been moored and some people say that the rubbish situation is slowly improving.

The best time to visit is December to April. The west monsoon makes the islands virtually inaccessible during the rest of the year; be warned that boats have been known to capsize at this time. Also, be warned that transport away from the islands is unpredictable and you might find yourself stranded here, rapidly running out of money. At the end of March/beginning of April, underwater visibility is not good, but this is the best time to see manta rays and whale sharks.

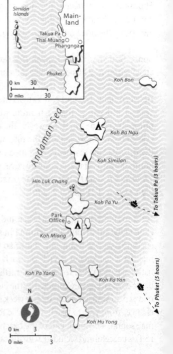

Similan Islands

The Southern Region

See page 582 for details on diving. Most dive companies in Phuket offer tours to the Similan Islands (see page 584). Hotels in Khao Lak (see page 616), organize boat and dive trips to Similan. **Tours**

Bungalows are available on Koh Ba Ngu (**E-F**). There are also some bungalows and a restaurant on Koh Pa Yang. Reservations can be made at the Similan National Park Office, Thai Muang, or at Tap Lamu Pier (T411914). There are several (overpriced) huts on Koh Miang, but no fans, no mosquito nets and uncooperative kitchen staff, very limited menu and poor overpriced food. **Sleeping**

Camping On Koh Ba Ngu, Koh Similan and Koh Miang. Bring your own tent, although there are some battered tents available on Koh Miang. ฿20.

Boat Boats leave from Ao Chalong and Patong Beach (T222570, *Songserm Travel*) every Sat, Thu, and Tue from Dec-Apr, Phuket 6-10 hrs. Vessels also depart from Thap Lamu pier, 20 km north of Thai Muang, 3-5 hrs. Finally, boats leave from Ranong, a busy deep-sea fishing port. Although it is possible to visit the Similan Islands independently, it can be an expensive and/or time-consuming business; it is far easier to book onto a tour (see above). **Transport** *40 km offshore*

Useful addresses For information on weather conditions T2580437. **Directory**

Koh Surin   เกาะสุรินทร์

Five islands make up this Marine National Park, just south of the Burmese border, and 53 km off the mainland. The two main islands are **Koh Surin Tai** and **Koh Surin Nua** (South and North Surin respectively), separated by a narrow strait which can be waded at low tide. Both islands are hilly, with few inhabitants; a small community of Chao Le fishermen live on Koh Surin Tai. The diving and snorkelling is good here and the coral reefs are said to be the most diverse in Thailand. Dr Thon Thamrongnawasawat, a marine biologist, has established an underwater nature trail with markers and underwater information pamphlets sealed in plastic. However, overfishing has led some people to maintain that diving is now better around the Similan Islands. Novices will still find the experience both exhilarating and enchanting. The National Park office is at Ao Mae Yai, on the southwest side of Koh Surin Nua.

The best time to visit is December to March. For information on weather conditions T2580437. **NB** Koh Surin Tai may close to visitors during the full moon each March, when the Chao Le hold an important festival.

At **Ao Mai Yai**, southwest side of Koh Surin Nua, 3 dormitories, ฿1,500 (for whole dormitory), T411545 for details. There is also a bungalow that sleeps 6, ฿600. **Camping** On south side of island, there is a campground, ฿80 for a tent for 2 people. Food is supplied at the bungalow, ฿250 per day for 3 set meals. **Sleeping & eating**

Long-tailed boats can be hired, ฿400 for 4 hrs. **Boats** Leave from Patong or Rawai on Phuket (10 hrs), from Ranong (through the *Jansom Thara Hotel*) or from the pier at Ban Hin Lat, 1 km west of Khuraburi 4-5 hrs (฿500). **Transport**

The Southern Region

Phuket to Satun

Phangnga   พังงา

The drive to Phangnga from Phuket passes through impressive limestone scenery. En route, it is possible to watch rubber being processed by smallholders. Not long ago, over-mature rubber trees (those more than 25 years old) were cut down and processed into charcoal. Today, due to the efforts of an enterprising Taiwanese businessman, a rubber-wood furniture industry has developed. As the road nears Phangnga, there are a number of roads down to the coast, from where tours to Phangnga Bay depart. At these junctions, men frantically beckon potential customers.

Sights
Phone code: 076
Colour map 4, grid C1

Phangnga itself is a bit of a one-horse town – or at least a one-road town – though spectacularly located in the midst of limestone crags. Due to the limestone geology, there are a number of caves in the vicinity. Just at the outskirts of town on Route 4 towards Phuket, on the left-hand side, are the **Sinakharin Gardens**, visible from the road. Within the gardens is **Tham Luu Sii**, a watery, sun-filled cave which would be beautiful if it were not for the concrete pathways. At the entrance to the cave sits Luu Sii, the cave guardian, under an umbrella. **Tham Phung Chang** is a little closer into town on the other side of the road, within the precincts of **Wat Phraphat Phrachim Khet**. There is a spring and Buddha images in this unremarkable cave, and a small pool where

Phangnga Bay

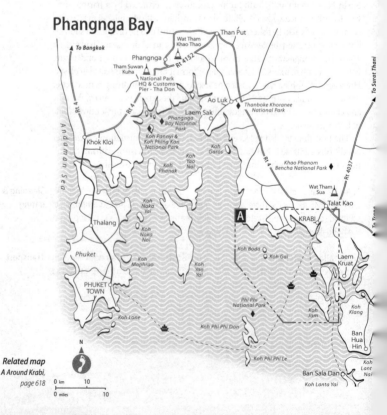

Related map
A Around Krabi,
page 618

0 km   10

0 miles   10

local boys swim. The wat itself is probably more interesting, with its fine position against the limestone cliff and set within a large compound. To get to the wat and cave, take a songthaew from town. About 300 m past the traffic lights (themselves past the *Lak Muang 2 Hotel*) is the arched entrance to the wat.

In the centre of town, behind the *Ratanaphong Hotel* is the fresh produce **market** while along the main street near the *Thaweesuk Hotel* are some remaining examples of the **Chinese shophouses** that used to line the street.

Phangnga Bay is best known as the location for the James Bond movie *The Man with the Golden Gun*. Limestone rocks tower out of the sea (some as high as 100 m) and boats can be hired to tour the area from Tha Don, the Phangnga customs pier (see Tours, below). ■ *Park entrance fee: ฿5. Best time to visit: Nov-Apr. Long-tailed boats can be chartered from the pier for a trip around the sights of Phangnga Bay for about ฿350-450 although it is cheaper to take a tour (see Tours, below). Bungalows are available at the headquarters of the National Park (which incorporates the Bay). Getting there: take a songthaew to the pier (฿10) from Phangnga town. 7 km along Route 4 there is a turning to the left (Route 4144 – signposted Phangnga Bay and the Ao Phangnga National Park Headquarters), and the pier is another 3 km down this road.*

Tham Suwan Kuha is 12 km from Phangnga on Route 4 to Phuket. A turning to the right leads to this airy cave temple. It is popular with Thais and is full of Buddha images, the largest of which is a poorly proportioned reclining Buddha. Stairs lead up to a series of tunnels, containing some impressive natural rock formations. King Chulalongkorn visited the cave in 1890 and his initials are carved into the rock. The cave is associated with a wat, Wat Suwan Kuha or Wat Tham. ■ *฿10. Getting there: take a bus travelling southwest along Route 4 towards Phuket.*

Wat Tham Khao Thao is 12 km from Phangnga on Route 4152 to Krabi, on the left-hand side of the road, under a cliff wall. There are views of the surrounding plain which can be seen from a stairway being built up the cliff-face. The road here passes through nipa palm which then becomes an area of mangrove. Aquaculture is an important sideline industry, and tiger prawns are raised in the brackish waters of the mangroves and in purpose-built ponds. ■ *Getting there: take a bus along Route 4152 towards Krabi.*

Excursions

The standard tour of **Phangnga Bay** winds through mangrove swamps and nipa palm, past striking limestone cliffs, before arriving at **Tham Lod** – not really a cave at all, but a tunnel cut into the limestone, through which boats can pass. From Tham Lod, the route skirts past the Muslim fishing village of **Koh Pannyi** with its turquoise green mosque (and seafood restaurants), and then reaches the 'highlight' of the trip: **James Bond Island**, or **Koh Phing Kan** or, sometimes, **Koh Tapoo**. Greatly overrated, the 'famous' overhanging rock, like a chisel, seems much smaller than it should be, and the beach and cave are littered with trinket-stalls and other tourists. Close to Koh Pannyi are some **ancient cave paintings** of dolphins and other creatures (rather disappointing). There are two main tour companies in town, *Sayan* and *Kean*. Both advertise widely: at the bus terminal, in the *Thaweesuk* and *Ratanaphong* hotels. Both companies run very similar tours and charge the same – ฿300 for half day, ฿600 for full day. The tours are

Tours

Phangnga place names

Phangnga Bay
อ่าวพังงา

Tham Suwan Kuha
ถ้ำสุวรรณคูหา

Wat Tham Khao Thao
วัดถ้ำเขาเต่า

The Southern Region

worthwhile and good value – and for an extra ฿250 *Sayan Tour* will put you up in a Muslim village for the night and provide a seafood dinner.

Canoeing and jungle tours are organized by the environmental tour company *Green Spirit*, T411521.

Sleeping
■ *on map*
Price codes:
see inside front cover

A *Phangnga Bay Resort*, 20 Thadon Rd (out of town, near the customs pier), T412067, F412057, B2162882. A/c, restaurant, pool, mostly tour groups, modern, overpriced but excellent views. **B** *Phangnga Valley Resort*, 5/5 Phetkasem Rd, T412201, F411201. Restaurant, just before the turn-off for Phangnga from Route 4, about 6 km or so from the town centre, lovely setting, 15 bungalows. **C-D** *Lak Muang 2*, 540 Phetkasem Rd, T412218, F411500. Some a/c, restaurant, pool, good value rooms with hot water tubs, carpets and TVs, but featureless and located 2 km or so from the bus station and the centre of town, note that rooms facing onto the road are very noisy. **D-E** *Ratanaphong*, 111 Phetkasem Rd, T411247. Some a/c, in town centre, friendly with clean, though unremarkable and noisy, rooms, good and popular restaurant. **E** *Lak Muang 1*, 1/2 Phetkasem Rd, T412486, F411512. Some a/c, restaurant. **E** *Thaweesuk*, 79 Phetkasem Rd, T411686. Clean rooms of variable size, strange, rather elusive management, good information but not unlike sleeping in a prison. **E** *Rak Phangnga*, on the main street in town, cheap but rather drab interior and noisy due to its location.

Eating

Cafés on Phetkasem Rd, near the market, sell the usual array of Thai dishes; including excellent *khaaw man kai* (chicken and rice) and *khaaw mu daeng* (red pork and rice). Try the rather dark but very popular *Kha Muu Restaurant* opposite the *Thaweesuk Hotel*. There are several coffee houses across from the *Thaweesuk*.

Mid-range *Duang Seafood*, 122 Phetkasem Rd (opposite Bank of Ayudhya). Excellent seafood restaurant, Chinese specialities. **Cheap** *Khru Thai* (Thai Teacher), Phetkasem Rd (opposite the Post Office). Clean and cheap place, local civil servants eat here and the dishes are openly displayed making selection easy.

Transport
100 km to Phuket
93 km to Krabi
879 km to Bangkok

Local Ancient, cramped **songthaews** constantly ply the main road – rather slowly (฿5). **Motorbike hire**: from the *Thaweesuk Hotel*. **Road Bus**: the bus station is on Phetkasem Rd, near the centre of town and a short walk from the *Thaweesuk* and *Lak Muang 1* hotels. Motorcycle taxis wait to take passengers further afield and regular songthaews run up and down the main road (฿5). Buses from Bangkok's Southern bus terminal, 15 hrs; T434119 for a/c bus information and T4345557 for non-a/c bus information. 3 VIP buses leave in the evenings for Bangkok. Regular connections with Phuket's bus terminal on Phangnga Rd, 2 hrs and with Krabi, 2 hrs. Also buses to Ranong, Takua Pa, Hat Yai and Trang.

Phangnga

To Takua Pa

Khao Wong

Phetkasem Rd

Market

Immigration Office

Wat Phraphat Prachim Khet

To Phuket & Sinathorin Gardens

N

Not to scale

■ **Sleeping**
1 Lak Muang 1
2 Lak Muang 2
3 Phangnga Valley Resort

4 Phang Nga Bay Resort
5 Rak Phang-nga
6 Ratanaphong
7 Thaweesuk

Directory

Banks Mostly on the main street, Phetkasem Rd. **Communications** Post Office: on Phetkasem Rd, 2 km from centre on main road entering town from Phuket. Overseas telephone service.

Krabi   กระบี่

Phone code: 075
Colour map 4, grid B3

From Phangnga to Krabi, the road passes mangrove swamps and nipa palm, more dramatic karst formations and impressive stands of tropical forest.

Krabi is a small provincial capital, situated on the banks of the Krabi River, close to where it discharges into the Andaman Sea. Formerly Krabi's economy was based squarely on agriculture and fishing; but since the mid to late-1980s tourism has grown by leaps and bounds so that today it probably contributes more to the town's – and possibly the province's – economy than any other single activity. This transformation is all too evident.

The town is visited by tourists largely because it is a jumping-off point for **Phi Phi Island** (see page 627), **Koh Lanta** (see page 631), **Ao Nang** and **Rai Leh** (see page 616). Many people find they need to spend a night here, and the guesthouses and hotels, not to mention the multitude of tour agents and restaurants, have sprouted to serve this community. While Krabi town itself does not contain much to keep a visitor here, the rising cost of accommodation in beach-side areas and on nearby islands is leading increasing numbers of visitors to choose to stay in Krabi and day-trip to the many attractions the province as a whole has to offer. There is a **general market** on Srisawat and Sukhon roads, and a **night market** close to the Chao Fah Pier. The Promenade, on the river front is a pleasant place to walk in the evenings.

There is a small *TAT* **tourist office** on Uttarakit Road and a newer office near Chao Fah Pier on Khong Kha Road. Both are helpful. ■ *0830-1630 Mon-Sun.* Many other places also advertise themselves as offering 'tourist information'; be aware that this is not done for altruistic reasons but in order to sell tours, tickets and rooms. A very useful locally produced guidebook is the *Krabi Holiday Guide* by Ken Scott (฿40). It provides far more information on Krabi, Ao Nang, Phra Nang, Raileh, Phi Phi and Koh Lanta and the smaller neighbouring islands than we can offer here. Good maps of Krabi and the surrounding area can be obtained from numerous shops and tour agents around town.

Wat Tham Sua or the Tiger Cave Temple (see map page 606), is 3 km northeast of town just past Talat Kao down a track on the left and has dozens of *kutis* (monastic cells) set into the limestone cliff. Walk behind the ridge where the bot is situated to find a network of limestone caves, which eventually lead back to the entrance. There is also a steep staircase on the left; 1270 steps leading to the top of a karst hill with fantastic views of the area and some meditation areas for the monks. An exhausting climb, this is best reserved for cool weather and cooler times of day. ■ *Getting there: Wat Tham Sua is east along Route 4. Take a red songthaew from Phattana Rd, in town to Route 4. From here either walk along Route 4 to the Cave Temple or take a motorcycle taxi (about ฿10). Walk to the cave from the main road.*

Excursions

The caves of **Tham Phi Hua To** and **Tham Lod** can be reached by boat from a pier just down the road from Hat Nopparat Thara (take the first left as you exit towards Khlong Muang), or you can take one of many tours by boat or canoe to the same caves. Phi Hua To cave is so named because of the large prehistoric human skulls found there. *Phi* means ghost or spirit, *Hua* means head, and *To* means large. Tham Lod is in fact a tunnel through the limestone karst through which you can travel by boat. The boat ride to these caves passes mangroves and limestone karst outcrops – a good day or half-day trip.

Butterfly World just established as a butterfly zoo, this small locally operated natural history centre is in landscaped gardens on the road leading to Ao Nang from Krabi approximately 3 km out of the municipality. Also a souvenir shop. ■ *Getting there: white songthaews from Krabi municipality from Phattana or Maharat Rd. (฿10).*

Susaan Hoi literally 'shell cemetery', lies 20 km southwest of Krabi, near the village of Laem Pho (not far from Ao Nang Beach). See page 618 for location and more information. ■ *Getting there: white songthaews from Krabi from the corner of Phattana and Maharat Rd, or from the pier every hour (฿20).*

Thanboke Khoranee National Park is a beautiful, cool and peaceful forest grove with emerald rock pools, streams and walkways. Swimming is permitted in the upper pool. Near the pool there is a small nature trail leading up into the limestone cliffs (sturdy shoes are advised). ■ *Getting there: take Route 4 back towards Phangnga; turn left down Route 4039 for Ao Luk, after 45 km. Two kilometres down this road there is a sign for the gardens, to the left. By public transport, take a songthaew from Krabi Town to Ao Luk, and then walk or catch a local songthaew.*

Laem Sak juts out from the mainland just North of Ao Luk and makes a good trip before or after a visit to the Thanboke Khoranee National Park. Turn left as you come out of the park and continue on Route 4039 into the town of Ao Luk and beyond down a small road to the end of the peninsula. There is a good seafood restaurant to the left, down a steep slope, near the fishing pier. Views back towards the mainland are impressive with a wall of limestone karst in the distance fringed by mangroves. Out to sea and to the west are a group of rocky islands. The fishing pier is a hive of activity and the restaurant serves excellent seafood and is a good place to watch the fishing boats pass by. ■ *Getting there: take Route 4 back towards Phangnga; turn left down Route 4039 and continue on through the town and along the winding road along the peninsula.*

It is easy to get stranded if you have not made arrangements to get back because not very many people visit the park

Khao Phanom Bencha National Park provides a magnificent backdrop to the town, with the peak rising more than 600 m above the surrounding land. Near the national park entrance is the lovely **Huai To Waterfall**. The drive to the waterfall is very pleasant with a distinctly rural feel, and the area around the park entrance has some lovely trees and open grassland which makes for a good picnic spot. Park rangers can take people on treks up to the peak and across down to a waterfall on the other side. To date, however, tourists seem to miss Khao Phanom Bencha park so the level of English spoken by park rangers can vary – check that you feel comfortable with any potential guide before setting out. The trek takes more than one day as the climb is quite steep. ■ *Getting there: motorcycle or other transport out on the main road going towards Trang (past Talat Kao). The turn-off comes before the exit for Wat Tham Sua.*

Khao Nor Chu Chi lowland forest, the **Crystal Pool and Hot Springs** are all located in Khlong Thom district to the south of Krabi province. Khao Nor Chu Chi has a forest trail and bungalow-style accommodation that was initiated as part of an ecotourism project aimed at conserving the seriously endangered Gurney's Pitta, a bird believed to be extinct but found recently by the well-known ornithologists Philip Round and Uthai Treesucon. Sadly, local influence has led to so much encroachment and plans for infrastructure development for tourism in this area that the project to support conservation of the Gurney's Pitta is generally considered to have been a failure.

The Crystal Pool is so called because of the exceptional clarity of the water and its emerald colour. In fact the colour derives from mineral deposits which can be seen through the water. The pool is quite shallow and the water very bouyant. However while the pool may look attractive enough, the deposits feel rather crunchy and not particularly pleasant under foot and the slopes leading into the pool are very slippery. Fun to swim in if you have no nerves about the water, but probably not recommended for nervous swimmers as it can be quite a struggle to get out of the pool once in!

A visit to **hot springs** on a hot day may seem rather odd, but the temperature of the water is quite comfortable and it's a relaxing place to spend some time in amidst the trees. ■ *Getting to Khao Nor Chu Chi lowland forest, the Crystal Pool and the Hot Springs: tours can be arranged from most tour offices in town. For self-drive, the turn-off to Khao Nor Chu Chi is just after the major intersection in Khlong Thom town. It is marked. That said, once you get on to the road to the crystal pool and hot springs, signposting tends to deteriorate and it can be quite an adventure getting to the final destination (be it hot springs, lowland forest or crystal pool).*

Ao Nang and **Nopparat Thara Beaches** See page 617 for details. ■ *Getting there: white songthaews leave regularly from 0600 to 1800 from Maharat and Phattana roads stopping at both Nopparat Thara and Ao Nang (฿30).*

Most tour companies operate daily and overnight tours around Phangnga Bay (see page 607), often incorporating a visit to Wat Tham Suwan Kuha and other local sights. Also available are river trips, birdwatching, tours to national parks and reserves (including Khao Nor Chu Chi lowland forest and crystal pool, Khao Phanom Bencha and Khao Sok), motorcycle treks and sea canoeing.

Tours

In Krabi, the word guesthouse often means neither a warm, family welcome nor a homely atmosphere – with a few exceptions, hotels and guesthouses are very ordinary. Few people want to stay in town more than the single night . As a result, perhaps, most rooms are very plain and functional. Some newer guesthouses do have a bit more style, and it appears there is a shift in markets now with more backpackers spending time in Krabi town to avoid the high cost of accommodation on the beaches. The guesthouses on Ruen-Ruedee Rd are generally cramped and stuffy; those up the hill and elsewhere in the town are a little more spacious. Note that prices during the high season can be double the rates for the low season.

Sleeping
■ *on map, page 612*
Price codes:
see inside front cover

A *Krabi Meritime Hotel* [sic], T620028-46, F620047 Krabi town's first luxury hotel, it is located about 2 km from town, off the road towards the bus station. Built overlooking the mangroves and limestone karst, they run a ferry service to a private beach and club. Expensive, and there have been complaints about poor service. They have another, newer, better-run hotel at Ao Nang, the *Ao Nang Pakasai Resort*.
B-C *Boon Siam Hotel*, 27 Chao Khun Rd, T632511-5 F632510. One of the newest hotels in the town, the rooms are all a/c (with hot water) spacious and comfortable. A bit far out of the town, but still within walking distance of the centre (it's not a large town). Good value – the best in this price range. **B-C** *Grand Mansion*, 289/1 Uttarakit Rd, T611371. Some a/c, clean with good-sized rooms and spotless bathrooms. The main drawback is that this 4-storey hotel is 2 km or so from the centre of town, on the road towards the bus station. **C** *Thai*, 7 Issara Rd, T6111474, F620564. Some a/c, large hotel with 150 rooms, grotty corridors but the rooms are fine, large and clean with reasonable bathrooms, an acceptable mid-range place in need of a character transplant. **C-D** *Chao Fah Valley Resort*, 50 Chao Fah Rd, T612499. Some a/c, this used to have attractive, clean and well-maintained wood and rattan bungalows but a recent visitor reports that it is sinking into decreptitude. The bathrooms are none too clean and food is best avoided. **C-D** *City Hotel*, 15/2-3 Sukhon Rd, T621280, F621301. Some a/c, 3-storey hotel for which we have received good reports, rooms are clean with attached bathrooms and friendly service, faces onto one of the quieter streets in town. Better value than the *Thai*.

D *Europa Café and Guesthouse*, 1/9 Soi Ruamjit Rd, T620407. Under Thai and Danish management, the *Europa Café* has five rooms above the restaurant. All rooms are nicely decorated, and clean, but the smallest rooms are rather dark as they don't have a window. Shared bathroom with hot water. The restaurant, which is decorated a bit like a pub (and features many photographs including one of Leonardo di Caprio during his stay in Krabi), serves good-quality northern European food (imported meats and cheeses). Henrich and Tip are good sources of local information – both speak excellent English and German, and Danish of course. The guesthouse closes at 2300 so guests have to be back by that time. **D** *Hollywood*, 26 Issara Road, T620508. Large-ish restaurant and bar serving western and Thai food in a shop house dressed

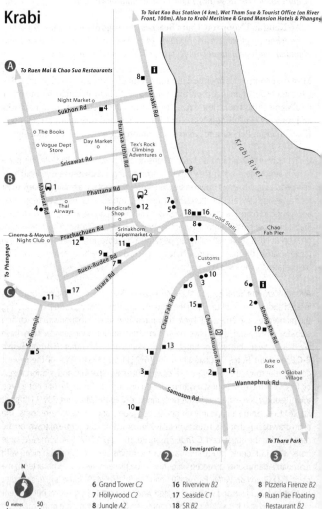

Krabi

To Talat Kao Bus Station (4 km), Wat Tham Sua & Tourist Office (on River Front, 100m). Also to Krabi Maritime & Grand Mansion Hotels & Phangnga

A To Ruen Mai & Chao Sua Restaurants

Night Market

Sukhon Rd

The Books

Vogue Dept Store

Day Market

Srisawat Rd

Tex's Rock Climbing Adventures

B

Maharat Rd

Phruksa Uthit Rd

Phattana Rd

Thai Airways

Handicraft Shop

Srinakhorn Supermarket

Uttarakit Rd

Krabi River

Food Stalls

Chao Fah Pier

Cinema & Mayura Night Club

Prachachuen Rd

Ruen-Rudee Rd

Issara Rd

Customs

Chao Fah Rd

Chamai Anuson Rd

C

To Phangnga

Soi Ruamit

To Immigration

Samoson Rd

Juke Box

Global Village

Wannaphruk Rd

Khong Kha Rd

To Thara Park

D

N

0 metres 50
0 yards 50

■ Sleeping
1 Bai Fern *D2*
2 Cha *D2*
3 Chao Fah Valley Resort *D2*
4 City *A1*
5 Europa Guesthouse & Café *D1*

6 Grand Tower *C2*
7 Hollywood *C2*
8 Jungle *A2*
9 KL House *C1*
10 KR Mansion *D2*
11 May & Mark's Guesthouse & Restaurant *C2*
12 NC *C1*
13 New Wave Guesthouse & Bar *C2*
14 PAN Guesthouse *D3*
15 PS Tour & Guesthouse *C2*

16 Riverview *B2*
17 Seaside *C1*
18 SR *B2*
19 Star Guesthouse *C3*

● Eating
1 Azzurra Pizzeria *C2*
2 Chawan *C3*
3 Chok Dee *C2*
4 Dalah Coffee *B1*
5 GoHoy *B2*
6 Kwan *C3*
7 Lisa Bakery *B2*

8 Pizzeria Firenze *B2*
9 Ruan Pae Floating Restaurant *B2*
10 Sea House *C2*
11 Smile *C1*
12 Viva *B2*

🚌 Transport
1 White Songthaews to Ao Nang & Nopparat Thara *B1*,
2 Minibus to Talat Kao

up to look like a log cabin. Friendly staff but service can be a bit slow. Upstairs there are 10 rooms, all with shared bathrooms (separate male and female). Rooms are large, well-furnished, cool and very clean with ceiling fans, some rooms have a nice view. **D** *KR Mansion*, 52/1 Chao Fah Rd, T612761, F612545. Some a/c, well-priced restaurant, clean, bright and airy rooms, friendly staff, roof-top balcony for an evening beer and good views, videos shown nightly. This place is at the quieter top end of town, a 10 min walk from most of the bars and restaurants, one criticism we have received is that they can be rather pushy with their overpriced tours and tickets. Apparently, however, security at this guesthouse leaves rather a lot to be desired. There have been complaints of thefts from the rooms. **D** *Rai Leh Hotel* 28 Maharaj Road Soi 5, T613031-2 F613046. Very new. Simple rooms in a rabbit warren of a building. Not all rooms have windows. Very friendly service and not a bad place for the price, but located in a street with a lot of bars and karaoke places; this may not be the most comfortable place for a single woman to stay. **D** *Star Guesthouse* Chao Fah Rd, (opposite the market), T611721. A charming wooden guesthouse over the top of a small convenience store and tour office, the rooms (7) are tiny, leaving little space for more than a bed, but there is a pleasant balcony with tables and chairs overlooking the night market and the river. Separate bathrooms are downstairs near a small bar area in a garden at the back. Recommended. **D-E** *Bai Fern Guesthouse*, 24/1 Chao Fah Rd, T611254. Attached shower, clean fan rooms all with balcony. **D-E** *PAN Guesthouse*, 182 Uttarakit Road, near the Post Office, T612555/612041. More expensive rooms have own bathroom. Set in garden on hill with a restaurant, tour office and car rental at the front. Rooms are very simple and the garden is not very well maintained, but it's not a bad choice for Krabi town. **D-F** *Grand Tower*, 73/1 Uttarakit Rd, T611741. Good restaurant, a large guesthouse which, though not exactly towering, does have 5 floors, rooms are bare but clean, some with attached showers, videos are shown nightly in the ground-floor restaurant-cum-meeting area, and there is also a roof-top balcony to sit out in the evenings. Good travel agency attached. As with *KR Mansion*, there have been some complaints of poor security.

E *Ano Guest House* Just off *Maharaj Rd*, mostly caters to a Thai clientele. Quite old and a bit jaded, but the rooms are clean and well-kept, and adequate with bathrooms en suite (but partition walls only). **E** *KL House*, 24-32 Ruen-Ruedee Rd, T612511. Warren of a place above a tour office, small rather stuffy rooms with shared bathrooms, their claim of 'spacious and luxurious' rooms should be viewed as taking poetic license to extremes. **E** *NC Guesthouse* Prachachuen Rd. Large, smart rooms, restaurant downstairs. Central location and amenable staff. **E** *Siboya*, T611258, F630039. Wooden building brightly painted with a small café downstairs, souvenir shop and agent for the *Siboya Island Bungalow Resort* on Siboya Island. Rooms are priced depending on whether or not they have a window. Share bathroom. Clean, simple. **E** *SR Guesthouse*, Khong Kha Rd (next door to *River View Guest House*). Big, clean rooms with shared bathroom, hospitable owners, great value. Downstairs there is a large second-hand bookstore. **E-F** *New Wave Bar and Guest House*, 25-1/2 Chao Fah Rd. Simple accommodation in 3 rooms of a wooden house with a common area and a west-facing balcony overlooking one of the greener parts of town. The New Wave Bar is in the garden adjacent to the Guest House (advertisements for full moon parties suggest the guest house may be rather noisy when the season is in full swing). Run by an English woman, Emma, and her Thai boyfriend, both very friendly. **E-F** *PS Guest House*, 71/1 Uttarakit Rd T620480. Small guesthouse with just 4 rooms. Clean with shared bathroom. Quite dark and very simple, but friendly and helpful owners. Room rates depend on the size. **E-F** *River View Guesthouse* Khong Kha Rd. Only 4 rooms with views of the river, above the Thammachart Tour Company and Restaurant, but clean, decent and good value – and with a friendly owner (Acharn Lek), who speaks excellent English and will (for a fee) act as translator should anyone need assistance in legal affairs. The *Thammachart Restaurant* specializes in vegetarian food, although they also serve non-vegetarian dishes. **F** *Cha*, Chao Fah Rd, T611141. Restaurant, basic huts set in garden compound on the main road but set back. Dirty but friendly, motorbike and jeep hire. **F** *Jungle Tours & Guesthouse*, Uttarakit Rd. Restaurant serving basic meals, shared bathroom facilities, tiny, dark rooms but comfy beds and very friendly family owners, tickets and tours sold.

Eating
● *on map*
Price categories:
see inside front cover

Thai Expensive: *Ruan Pae*, Uttarakit Rd (floating restaurant). Attractive location but overpriced and very mediocre food.

Expensive-mid-range: *Ruen Mai*, on Maharaj Rd well beyond the *Vogue Department Store* up the hill on the left-hand side as you leave the town. Excellent Thai food in a quiet garden setting. Popular with locals, with good English-language menu and helpful staff. Has a number of southern specialities. Fish dishes are particularly good, as are the salads (yam). *Chao Sua*, on Maharaj Rd, along the road from the *Ruen Mai* (the sign, with a leopard on it, is in Thai). The restaurant itself has a rambling slightly chaotic feel and service can be highly variable. Serves excellent Thai food. Barbecued seafood and virtually anything that is fried are especially good. A very original menu with lots of house specialities, for example, the Chao Sua eggs are delicious. They also have an English-language menu.

International Expensive: *Azzurra*, Uttarakit Rd just passed the police box. Pretty good pizza and pasta. Nice fresh coffee. There is a branch in Ao Nang. *Europa Café*, 1/9 Soi Ruamjit Rd, T620407. Serves tasty Northern European food with imported ingredients. A favourite with locals and local expats. *Pizzeria Firenze*, Khong Kha Rd. Usual mix of Thai and Italian dishes, nothing culinarily notable. *Viva*, Phruksa-Uthit Rd between Pattana and Issara roads. Serves a range of European, Italian and Thai food and good fresh coffee (Lavazza). Looks set to become quite a hang-out for travellers, but the music can be very loud and the food is nothing special. **Mid-range**: *Go Hoy*, Uttarakit Rd at the junction with Issara Rd. One of the oldest restaurants in the town, they have been operating for over 50 years, the restaurant has changed along with the rest of Krabi. The building used to be built entirely from wood standing above water. Behind the restaurant along what is now Maharaj Rd was forest. Go Hoy serves jok (rice porridge) in the morning and Hainanese chicken, red pork and other basics for the rest of the day. Closed for the evening. Friendly, very informal, service and a good range of food on an English-language menu. They do vegetarian dishes too. *May and Mark's Restaurant*, Ruen-Ruedee Rd. Good information, friendly atmosphere and good food, home-made bread, Mexican and Italian dishes, Thai food, excellent fresh coffee, breakfasts and all the usual from banana porridge to pizza. **Mid-range-cheap**: *Chawan*, serves Thai food and the usual western dishes (sandwiches, spaghetti, etc). The Thai food comes in generous portions for a reasonable price – caters to a western palate. *Chok Dee*, Chao Fah Rd. Reasonable prices, some dishes are really delicious, and very good value prices for the quality and quantity of food. The owner has two televisions with cable and video – good selection of movies. It can get a bit loud, but the owner is responsive if you can't hear a movie or you want the sound turned down. Friendly management and staff. *Kwan Coffee Corner*, 75 Uttarakit Rd. Fresh coffee, sandwiches, milk shakes, ice creams, cheap and tasty Thai food, good breakfasts of fruit and muesli, almost everything even if as they put it, "coffee is not your cup of tea". Recommended. There are several other places on Khong Kha Rd by the pier.

Cheap: *Dalah Coffee* Maharaj Rd, on the other side of the road to *Vogue*, next to the access to the forest temple and across from a doctor's clinic. Serves fresh coffee, tea and ice cream in a pleasant, clean coffee shop with a small 'garden' down the side of the shop. Popular with locals, the owner and his wife both speak reasonable English

Sea House, Chao Fah Rd. Reasonable prices, menu includes freshly ground coffee. *Smile*, opposite Soi Ruanjit on Issara Rd. Shiny new place with outdoor seating, serving fast food (as well as non-fast), ice cream and coffee.

Bakeries *Lisa Bakery*, 120-123 Uttarakit Road. For rather synthetic cakes and reasonable croissants. *May & Mark's Restaurant*, Ruen Rudee Rd. Home made bread: sourdough, rye and whole wheat. Fresh bread is also available from the *Pizza Firenze* and *Chawan* near the pier.

Foodstalls A **night market** sets up in the early evening on Khlong Kha Road, along the Krabi River, good seafood dishes. Tasty ice cream from the ice cream stall, and good Thai desserts from the dessert stall furthermost up the hill. Stall food is also available from the **fresh market** between Srisawat and Sukhon roads, and from scattered places along Uttarakit Rd, facing onto the Krabi River. The *Vogue Department Store* on Maharat Rd also has an a/c 'food court' on the 3rd floor with dishes only marginally more expensive than out on the street.

Toyaiman, 228 Uttarakit Rd (on the hill). *Juke Box Pub* and *Global Village* both on **Bars** Khong Kha Rd. The latter is probably the better of the 2.

Boat races on the river, very noisy. *Berg Fa Andaman Festival* in the gardens beyond the **Festivals** pier in Nov (coinciding with *Loy Krathong*) – a showcase for traditional dancing and singing from around Thailand, sadly there is little information in English available at the festival. Also features local handicrafts from the Andaman region.

Books *The Books*, 78-80 Maharat Rd (next to *Vogue Department Store*). Many of the **Shopping** guesthouses and tour companies also run book exchanges. **Department stores** *Vogue Department Store*, Maharat Rd. **Supermarkets** *Sri Nakhorn*, opposite the *Thai Hotel*. **Clothes and tailoring** There is a tailor on the corner of Issara and Khong Kha roads. Lots of clothes stores on Phattana, Prachachuen and Uttarakit roads mostly selling beach wear. **Souvenirs** *Khun B Souvenir*, and other souvenir shops on Khong Kha and Uttarakit Rd sell a range of souvenirs from all around Thailand and Southeast Asia; *Hot & Spicy* on Prachachuen Rd, sells handicrafts mostly from the Northern region, and *Thai Silver* opposite *Thai Hotel* sells silverware mostly from Nakhon Sri Thammarat.

Game fishing *Phi Phi Marine Travel Co* can arrange expeditions to catch marlin, **Sport** sailfish, barracuda and tuna.

Concentrated on Uttarakit and Ruen-Ruedee roads and close to the Chao Fah Pier. **Tour operators** Guesthouses often double up as tour companies and travel agents. There are so many tour and travel companies/agents, and information is so freely and widely available, that it is not necessary to list outfits here. Prices and schedules are all openly posted and a 30-min walk around town will reveal all. We have, though, received negative reports regarding the professionalism of *Pee Pee Sea Tour*, 35 Issara Rd, and *Krabi Happy Tours*, KR Mansion Hotel. **Rock climbing** *Tex's Rock Climbing Adventure* has an office and shop in Krabi town, on Uttarakit Rd, at the back of *Jam Travel*, as well as at Rai Leh East.

Local Motorbike hire: many of the guesthouses and tour companies hire out **Transport** scooters and motorbikes, ฿150 – 200 per day. **Songthaews**: drive through town, *93 km to Phangnga* stopping at various places such as Phattana Rd, in front of *Travel & Tour*, for Ao Phra *180 km to Phuket* Nang and in front of the foodstalls on Uttarakit Rd for Noppharat Thara Beach. They *867 km to Bangkok* also run regularly to the bus station at Talaat Kao, 5 km from town.

The Southern Region

Long distance Air: Krabi airport is located about 8 km out of town on the road towards Trang. THAI and PB Air operate daily flights (for about ฿4,200 return). It is usually possible to get hotels/resorts to arrange a pick-up. Alternatively, PB Air will arrange a pick-up (from their flights) if you call their office in town (T622048-9). There is usually a songthaew waiting for incoming flights. Alternatively, regular connections with Phuket, and from there take a bus to Krabi.

Train: some people take the train (usually the overnight sleeper) to Phun Phin (Surat Thani) where the train is met by buses for the 3-hr journey to Krabi. Buses drop travellers at the tourist office in Krabi, where bookings for the islands can be made. Alternatively travel to Trang or Nakhon Si Thammarat.

Bus: station is 5 km out of town, in Talat Kao (Old Market), close to the intersection of Uttarakit Rd and Route 4. Red songthaews regularly run between the bus station and town (฿5). Motorcycle taxis also wait to ferry bus passengers into town. Numerous evening a/c, VIP and non-a/c connections with Bangkok's Southern bus terminal, 16 hrs. Regular a/c and non-a/c connections with Phuket via Phangnga, 3 hrs and 1½ hrs respectively. Morning buses to Koh Samui, via Surat Thani with ferry connection, 6 or 7 hrs by *Songserm Travel's* express boat. Regular connections with Surat Thani (3 hrs) and Trang, a/c minibuses to Hat Yai. Tickets and information about bus connection (both public buses and private tour buses) available from countless travel agents. **Taxi**: to Trang 2 hrs (฿150). For Ao Nang and Nopparat Thara take a white songthaew from Phattana Rd (฿15).

International connections with Malaysia and Singapore: by a/c minibus to Singapore, Kuala Lumpur and Penang (departs 0700 and 1200, 7-11 hrs, ฿300). Buses stop in Hat Yai, for passports to be checked. Some travel agents charge ฿10 'border service' – avoid paying if possible.

Train and road Combination tickets from Bangkok via Surat Thani. Travel agents will book tickets.

Boat all boats leave from Chao Fah Pier. Daily boats to Phi Phi 0930 and 1430, returning 0900 and 1300, 1½ hrs (฿150). Express boats to Phi Phi 1030 and 1430, (may be more frequent in the high season) returning 0900 and 1300, 1 hr. Daily boat to Koh Lanta at 1330, returning 0800, 2½ hrs (฿150). Also boats to Phra Nang. Every Tue and Thu at 0830 express boats from Makham Bay, Phuket 3½ hrs, stopping at Phi Phi, 1½ hrs en route. To Phuket, the boat leaves at 1300 on Tue and Thu.

Directory **Banks** Branches of all major banks with ATMs. **Communications** Internet: lots of services available around the town, especially on Uttarakit Rd, Chao Fah Rd (towards the pier) and around *Hollywood*. Prices per minute vary. Connections are still quite slow in Krabi. **Post Office**: Uttarakit Rd (half way up the hill, not far from the Customs Pier). It has a Poste Restante counter. International telephone: quite a way out of the town on the way to the Krabi Meritime Hotel. Alternatively, look for services in some tour offices on Uttarakit Rd. **Useful addresses** Immigration office: Uttarakit Rd, a little way up from the post office on the same side of the road. The office will extend visas for an extra 30 days (฿500) and provide 14-day visas (free) for people arriving by sail boat. They can also provide re-entry permits for those travelling on longer-stay visas. Open 0830-1200, 1300-1630, Mon-Fri. **NB** Photocopies can be made at a couple of shops just across the road from the Immigration office in the row of wooden shophouses.

Ao Nang อ่าวนาง   and Nopparat Thara นพรัตน์ธารา

Phone code: 075   The beaches at Ao Nang and Nopparat Thara lie 18 km and 22 km respectively to the west of Krabi town. Many of the local people in the area are not Buddhist but Muslim Thais and it is noticeable, for example, that pork is rarely on the menu of restaurants hereabouts. (It should also be noted that as for most places in Thailand, but especially with respect to Muslim communities, topless sunbathing is very definitely frowned upon in the area). The road to the coast winds for 15 km past spectacular limestone cliffs, a large reclining Buddha, rubber stands and verdant forest. Arriving at the coast in the evening, with the setting sun turning the limestone cliffs of Ao Nang a rich orange, and the sea interspersed with precipitous limestone crags, is a wonderful sight.

Ao Nang provides a range of accommodation and facilities including diving, windsurfing, fishing and tours to the surrounding islands. It is still quite relaxed, with a relatively peaceful atmosphere, although sometimes the noise of the long-tail boats plying back and forth to Rai Leh and nearby islands can be disturbing. The sandy, gently shelving beach is being eroded at one end by run-off from the beach road, but the beach is good for swimming out of the monsoon season with calm waters, and beautiful limestone scenery. The surrounding beaches, coves, caves and grottoes provide good trekking and boat trip destinations. Note that between June and October the monsoon makes swimming risky and many bungalows shut down for the season. Excellent seafood available here.

Three kilometres northwest of Ao Nang, **Nopparat Thara Beach** is a long sandy beach, popular with Thai picnickers and part of the **Had Nopparat Thara – Phi Phi Islands National Marine Park**, although you'd never guess that looking at the Ao Nang end of the beach where accommodation, bars and stalls are rapidly moving in. There is a visitors' centre here with a small exhibition and a multitude of foodstalls. ■ *0830-1630*. At low tide it is possible to walk out to some of the islands in the bay. In the opposite direction, beyond the limestone crags, is **Phra Nang** and the beaches (and accommodation) of **Rai Leh** – accessible only by long-tailed boat (see below).

Fossil Shell Beach or *Susaan Hoi* lies 5 km east of Ao Nang. Great slabs of what looks like concrete are littered along the shoreline but on closer inspection turn out to be countless fossilized freshwater shells, laid-down 75 million years ago. It is one of only three such cemeteries in the world; the others are in the USA and Japan. **Sleeping C** *Dawn of Happiness Resort*, PO Box 35, Krabi 81000, T612730. This is a guesthouse with a difference, good traditional bungalows, environmentally and culturally sensitive, library, hammocks, trips to local monasteries, isolated position in Ao Nam Mao, close to Susaan Hoi. *Sea and Sand Bungalows*, up the road from the *Dawn of Happiness Resort* down a small dirt road. Set back from the beach which is about a two-minute walk past a shrimp nursery and through another resort. Simple bungalows, but furnished with a bit of care, some a/c, cheaper with fan. The owners are in a partnership to build a three-storey resort with bungalows in the land between this bungalow resort and the sea. *Holyland Bungalows*, between Ao Nang and the Fossil Shell Beach down a dirt road through rubber plantations in a stunning location at the far end of Ao Nam Mao next to the limestone crags that fringe Rai Leh. The layout of the bungalows, sadly, makes little use of its wonderful location. There are some bamboo bungalows with better views and location overlooking the bay, but most are concrete and set back in sparse gardens. A couple of motorbikes can be rented at ฿200 per day.

Khlong Muang and around Krabi the *Green Earth Botanical Garden Co Ltd* operated by Mr Gift (of Gift's Bungalows that used to be on the beach at Ao Nang) operates tours between Hat Nopparat Thara via boat and land ending up with a tour of the botanical gardens and including lunch. He also operates small group mountain bike tours of the province and walking tours up the highest peak in Krabi province. Equipment is well maintained, and staff are

Excursions

Time your visit to coincide with low tide when more of the pavement is exposed

The Southern Region

friendly and helpful. Prices range from ฿900-฿1,200 per person, usually including a meal. Contact: T637190 or T637190.

Koh Boda (see map page 606) is 30 minutes by boat from Ao Phra Nang. It is a haven for snorkellers, with wonderfully clear water. Round-trip excursions last five hours. There are bungalows available on the island for ฿350, book through the *Krabi Resort* (T611389 or B2518094). The bungalows are a good size, restaurant, 'Western' loos, not particularly friendly staff. Camping is

Around Krabi

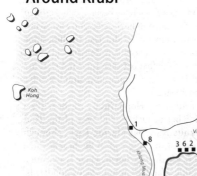
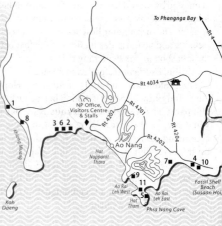

Related maps
Ao Nang,
page 623
Krabi, page 612

0 km   2
0 miles   2

■ Sleeping

1 Andaman Holiday Resort	5 Dusit	9 Rai Leh Village
2 Andaman Inn	6 Emerald	10 Sea & Sand Bungalows
3 Bamboo	7 Holyland Bungalows	11 Sunrise Bungalows
4 Dawn of Happiness	8 Pine Bungalow	

possible on the island (฿50). The nearby **Koh Gai** is also a 30 minutes boat trip from Ao Phra Nang.

Koh Phi Phi is accessible as a day trip from Ao Nang (see page 627). Arrange a ticket for the boat trip through your guesthouse. The boat departs from Ao Nang at 0900 returning at 1630.

Phra Nang and **Rai Leh** are also easily accessible. Long-tailed boats leave regularly from the beach opposite *Sea Canoe*, 15 minutes (฿50).

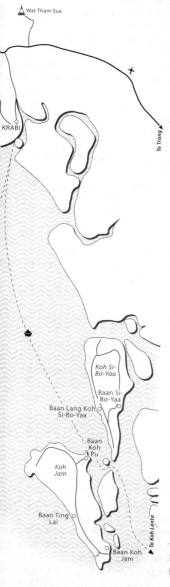

Accommodation in Ao Nang is currently in a state of flux. Guesthouses and bungalows are appearing further and further inland, while more expensive hotels are being developed nearer the beach. Some of the old favourites in the centre of the beach area have had to move on as the owners of the land have terminated contracts and this central area is now becoming dominated by shops, restaurants and bars. Behind these developments there are some rooms available, but it's rather over-crowded. Some new hotels have been developed up in the hills overlooking Hat Nopparat Thara – most are fairly pricey, and this is the location of Ao Nang's two luxury resorts (the *Ao Nang Pakasai Resort* and the *Thai Village Resort*. It's difficult to see where development of this area is going. The Hat Nopparat Thara beach area is changing rapidly from a quiet, undeveloped and beautiful beach to, frankly, a rather tacky beach front. Sadly, the forested hills have also been targeted by large-scale developers, even though apparently these were once designated as reserve forest (in this case it's tempting to say, 'what's new?').

Ao Nang L-AL *Ao Nang Pakasai Resort*, 88 Moo 3, Ao Nang, T637777, F637637, yoonpk@loxinfo.co.th A new plush resort, up a small road off the main road running between Hat Nopparat Thara and Ao Nang. Complete with vanishing-edge pool with a great sea view. Rooms are spacious and offer pretty much everything you'd expect for the price. Huge range of rooms with some incredibly expensive suites. One restaurant and a pool bar. Also offers cookery classes and bicycle rental. **L-AL (promotional rate)** *Thai Village Resort*. A huge hotel up in the forest with views over Nopparat Thara beach and bay.

Sleeping
■ on map, page 623
Price codes:
see inside front cover

High-season (Nov-May) room rates may be as much as double (or more) the low-season (Jun-Oct) rates

The Southern Region

Although a new resort is being constructed opposite, this does not obscure views of the bay from the rooms at the Thai Village. Built in central Thai style but without any special charm and with rather large paved areas throughout the resort. There are three large swimming pools including a pool bar, and also a children's pool. Expensive, luxury resort with all the extras. Still, expensive at the upper bracket price given that this is not a beach-front property.

AL (high)-A (low) *Lai Thai Resort*, 25/1 Moo 2, Ao-Nang T637281 F637282, info@laithai-resort.com, http://laithai-resort.com/ About 1 km from the beach, but with a shuttle service for free. Family-run resort with great views of the mountains at the back of Ao Nang. The swimming pool (black-tiled) is one of the best in Ao Nang. Friendly owners (Robert and his Thai wife). Rooms are spacious, well decorated and very comfortable. Restaurant and bar have good ambiance and a range of food including Mexican. **A** *Krabi Resort* (office in Krabi at 53-57 Phattana Rd, T611389, T02-2089165). At northwest end of the beach, a/c, restaurant overlooking the sea, nice pool, some bungalows, rooms are some of the best available on Ao Nang, large and airy, with satellite TV and baths. In need of refurbishment but a good location and friendly staff. Apparently the bungalows are better than the hotel rooms. **A-B** *Ao Nang Villa*, 133 Ao Nang Rd, southeast end of the beach, T/F637270. A/c, restaurant, pool, a range of rooms here, the most expensive are in a 3-storey block built around a swimming pool (small for the size of hotel), there are also bungalows with attached bathrooms, both a/c and fan. Excellent views from upper-floor rooms in new block. Could do with better maintenance and cleaning. **A (high)-B (low)** *AP Resort*, T637342. Very pleasant proprietor, simple, decent rooms, but rather overpriced, also have a travel desk and email facilities. **A (high)-B (low)** *Arcadian Villa*, 264/1 Moo 2, Ao Nang, T637837. Five concrete bungalows by the side of the road near the Ao Nang School, quite a distance (over 2 km) from the sea. Sensibly they are facing in towards the coconut plantation behind. Twin beds in all rooms, very new, very clean and well-equipped with satellite TV, a/c, fridge. Pleasant location, but a bit pricey for somewhere this far from the beach. **A (high)-B (low)** *Ao Nang Beach Resort*, T637766-9, F637812. Hotel style accommodation in a block along the seafront. The entrance is set back from the front but the hotel lives up to its claim that many of the rooms have excellent sea views. Clean, standard type of rooms, central location. **A-B** *Beach Terrace*, 154 Moo 2, Ao Nang, TB7220060, FB7220061. A/c, there are really 2 hotels here: one is a 6-storey block rather incongruously sited on a beach where most places are just a single storey tall; the second 'hotel' is a series of large, solidly made concrete bungalows. At these prices you don't really get very much: comfortable enough rooms with superb views from the upper floors of the block, but a down-at-heel coffee shop that would look average in a hotel charging half these rates, and not even a swimming pool. **A (high)-B (low)** *Frito Misto Villa*, T637692, F637691, frittomisto1@hotmail.com Italian-owned time-share property that rents out apartments and rooms to guests when the owners are not in residence. Up on the hill away from the beach in a quiet location, with pool and good facilities (excellent bathrooms with bidets no less!). Variable decorations. A bit far from everything, but represent pretty good value for the facilities. **A (high)-B (low)** *Krabi Nopparat Resort*, 83 Moo 3, Ao Nang T637632-3 F637634 Small two-storey blocks facing towards the sea. Upper rooms have balcony and are separate. Lower rooms have balcony and are connecting. Simply furnished, a/c, hot water, satellite TV, telephone. There are two rows of rooms close together. The front row has views of the sea. The back row has views of the front row! Behind the resort there is a small lawn overlooking the *khlong* and the mangroves. **A (high)-B (low)** *Ocean Garden View Resort*, T637527-31, F637211. Large new development with several two-storey blocks of rooms on the hillside back from the main road. Located next to the Ocean Mart, just up from the *Phranang Inn*. Rooms are well equipped and comfortable with balconies.

All rooms have views of the sea, rooms at the back, higher up the hill have the best views. Pool under construction. Not a bad choice for the price, but the steps are quite steep up the hill. **A (high)-C (low)** *BB Bungalows*, T637542-3, F637304. Both fan and a/c available. Older cottages here are now showing their age and the attached bathrooms with Asian toilets are rather grotty, newer bungalows much better – large and solidly built, but constructed too close together and overpriced for what they offer. **A (high)-D (low)** *Ao Nang Paradise Resort*, T637650-1, F637652, aonangparadise @hotmail.com, continuing down the road from the *Lai Thai Resort* and near the older boxing stadium, this is a new bungalow resort with a very welcoming reception area and good lighting throughout. Good views of the mountains with coconut palms in the foreground. Bungalows are well designed with lots of natural light and some nice decorative features.

B *Ban Ao Nang Resort*, 31/3 Moo 2, Ao Nang, T7220258, F612914, TB7220258. A/c, 3-storey modern block with balconies overlooking the sea. Rooms have satellite TV and fridge, solid wooden floors, large bathrooms with hot-water showers. This place is competitively priced and the rooms are better than those at most of the more expensive resorts. **B** *Phra Nang Inn*, PO Box 25, T637130, F637134. A/c, restaurant, small pool, older wing of hotel is on one side of the road, a new 3-storey concrete structure faced in wood to try and make it more 'natural' on the other. Rooms are mediocre at this price, although the views in the evening from the top floor of the new wing are spectacular. **B-C** *Ao Nang Thara Lodge*, T7230517, F3916245. Between Ao Nang and Nopparat Thara, good restaurant, own bathroom, but generally looking pretty jaded. Views are obscured by the trees in front of the bungalows, water garden, friendly management. **B (high)-C (low)** *BB Inn Hotel*, T627148, F637147. A new hotel block owned and operated by the same owner as the *BB Bungalows*, and adjacent to them. Rooms are spacious and clean with tiled floors but tacky decor. Well equipped with baths, small TV, fridge. **B-C** *Hill Side Village*, 168/10 Moo 2 Ao Nang, T637604, Leem@loxinfo.co.th Opposite the *Lai Thai Resort*. Recently converted concrete row of rooms. Rooms come in sets of two (double at back, twin at front) and would make good family rooms. Rooms to the back are smaller and cheaper, with shower only and no hot water. Rooms at the front are twin beds with a bath and hot water. All rooms come with a/c, TV (satellite), and a fridge. Restaurant serves the usual international favourites. **B-D** *Krabi Seaview Resort* (Krabi office at 171-173 Uttarakit Rd, T611648). Some a/c, solidly built brick A-frame bungalows with zinc roofs, looking almost alpine, set around a rather unattractive pond. Attached bathrooms, there are also some much cheaper cottages set back further away from the road, with good views over the treetops and out to sea. **B-D** *Peace Laguna Resort*, 193 Moo 2, T611972, T02-7231005. Some a/c, this is one of the more attractive and better designed of the mid-range places, virtually in the shadow of the limestone crag that dominates the southeastern end of Ao Nang. Solid brick and tile-roofed bungalows built around a large pond and off the road so much quieter than many other places, all bungalows with hot-water in bathrooms, cheaper cottages with fan, a path leads down to Ao Nang Beach allowing guests to avoid the road. **B (high)-D (low)** *Sea of Love*, T637204. Trendy bar and restaurant with accommodation in 4 rooms in rustic style behind. If you can get over the embarrassment of staying somewhere called the 'Sea of Love', this is a good choice – rooms are all different, nicely designed with a bit of style, and though the back area is quite closely packed the feel is villagey rather than over-crowded.

C *Ao Nang Palm Hill Valley*, up and across the road from the *Lai Thai Resort* there are several concrete bungalows in mature gardens. Variable state of repair. Tours are offered at the front desk. **C** *Ao Nang Royal Resort*, T7231071. Group of 15-odd a/c bungalows built in a circle around a concrete pond. Rooms are functional, they have no view (the hotel is set back from the beach), but are some of the best-value, a/c rooms available here (especially good rates in the low season), bathrooms with hot-water showers, a good place to stay if intending to remain out during the day and just want somewhere cool to sleep at night. **C** *Dutch Mansion*, 249/2 Moo 2, Ao Nang, T01-3968152. Newly renovated and decorated rooms in a shophouse. Rooms are huge, all with a/c, warm water, TV and fridge. Very clean. Simply furnished. Rooms vary so ask to see a few if you can. Some rooms at the back have little natural light, but these are probably quieter as they are away from the road. Good value. **C** *Lavinia House*, good clean rooms in the centre of the beach at the back, behind the shops. **C-D** *Ao Nang Blue Bayou Bungalow*, T637558. About a third of the way along the road between Ao Nang and the National Parks offices, the *Blue Bayou Bungalows* used to be the only accommodation (even development) on Hat Nopparat Thara beach. Now obscured behind the *Rim Leh Seafood Restaurant*, these basic fan or a/c bungalows, no hot water, are looking very run-down. Friendly staff. Tours available from the front desk. They have their own restaurant. **C (high)-D (low)** *Ao Nang Mountain Paradise*, 26/11 Moo 2, Ao Nang, T637659, 9 rooms in bungalow-style accommodation (identical to *Ao Nang Garden Home Resort* in style). Ceiling fan with some a/c, hot water. Simply furnished but clean, in a quiet location down a dirt road near the *Lai Thai Resort* with good views of the limestone mountains. Friendly management. Well-priced basic breakfasts are available at the tiny restaurant/office at the front. **C-D** *Leela Valley*, 262/1 Ao Nang T635673. Some simple bamboo bungalows on the ground and some smarter fan and a/c houses on tall stilts with balconies, set in spacious grounds rather lacking in shade. Good views of the mountains. Rooms are clean. Discounts are given for long lets. Quite a distance from the sea, but excellent value. **C-D** *Seagull Huts*, next to *Lai Thai Resort*. Brick and wood bungalows with the limestone karst mountains in the background. About 50 m off the main road. Fan rooms. Basic.

D *Ao Nang Ban Lae*, T7220243. Reasonable and adequate. **D** *Ao Nang Garden Home Resort* , T637586 Bungalow style is almost identical to the *Ao Nang Mountain Paradise* which is just down the road, but these are raised above the ground and have nice wooden bannisters to the balconies. No hot water. Serves only coffee for breakfast. **D** *Rainbow Restaurant and Bungalows*, 248 Moo 2, Ao Nang, T/F637336 About 1.5 km away from the beach, after the turn-off from the Fossil Shell Beach. Bungalows are up on the hill. Very simple with shared bathrooms (clean). Quiet location. The owners have found a sensible solution to the problem of the distance to the beach by providing residents with the free use of a bicycle each. Bicycles can also be hired for ฿100 per day. **D** *Phra Nang Place*, Laem Nang, T512172, F612251. On private plantation, catch a boat from Ao Nang or Krabi, restaurant, quiet location and well designed. **D-E** *Ao Nang Beach Bungalows*, near the centre of the beach, thatched bamboo bungalows spaced widely enough apart so as not to be oppressive, attractive garden setting. **D-E** *Ao Nang Village*, simple tidy rooms and only 5 mins from the beach despite being the last on the row. **D-E** *Jungle Hut Bungalows*, simple, rustic, split bamboo huts up the road, away from the beach, these are among the cheapest bungalows on Ao Nang.

E *Green Park*, 13/1 Mu 2. Some of the cheapest bungalows available here, but showing their age, they are also some of the quietest, set back from the road and virtually in the middle of a forest, there are no views and although the basic cottages have good verandas the trees shade out most of the sun, more expensive cottages have simple attached shower rooms.

Guesthouses There is a line of older guesthouses (*Orchid, Dream Garden House, Mountain View, Nong Eed House* and *Penny's*) on one side of the road to the Fossil

Shell Beach; they all offer traditional second- and third-storey rooms in our **E** category. *Nong Eed House* has a block of new rooms at the back, but at our last visit the staff were anything but friendly. Penny's has also made some changes and upgraded accommodation (http://phket.loxinfo.co.th/~johneyre, Pennys@loxinfo.co.th, T637295). The rooms are clean and quite large, usually with shared bathrooms. In the low season rates are in our **F** category, rising to **E** in the high season.

Nopparat Thara B-C The headquarters of the *Nopparat Thara and Phi Phi Islands National Park* has some bungalows and camping facilities, T5790529. **D** *Emerald Bungalow*, Don Son Beach, T611944. Catch a boat from Nopparat Thara pier across the estuary, westwards, this place is very peaceful with large, fan bungalows, to get here follow instructions as per *Bamboo*. **D-E** *Andaman Inn*, T612728. 35 rooms and some basic

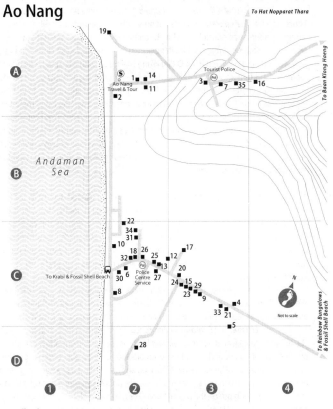

Ao Nang

To Hat Nopparat Thara

The Southern Region

■ **Sleeping**

1 Ao Nang Ban Lae Guesthouse A2	**12** BB Bungalows C2
2 Ao Nang Beach Bungalow A2	**13** BB Inn C2
3 Ao Nang Pakasai Resort A3	**14** Beach Terrace A2
4 Ao Nang Palm Hill Valley C3	**15** Dream Garden House & Tour C3
5 Ao Nang Paradise Resort C3	**16** Frito Misto Villa A4
6 Ao Nang Royal Resort C2	**17** Green Park C3
7 Ao Nang Thara Lodge A3	**18** Jinda C2
8 Ao Nang Villa C2	**19** Krabi Resort A2
9 Ao Nang Village C3	**20** Krabi Seaview Resort C3
10 AP Resort C2	**21** Lai Thai Resort C3
11 Ban Ao Nang A2	**22** Lavinia House C2
	23 Mountain View C3

24 Nong Eed House C3
25 Ocean Garden View Resort C2
26 One C2
27 Orchid C2
28 Peace Laguna Resort D2
29 Penny's C3
30 Phra Nang Inn C2
31 PK Mansion C2
32 Sea Beer C2
33 Seagull Huts C3
34 Sea World C2
35 Thai Village Resort A3

huts. **E-F** *Bamboo*, on round the coast from Noppharat Thara over the river, restaurant (good food), shared facilities, very basic, friendly staff. Recommended. **E-F** *Nature Restaurant and Bungalow*, very basic place run by friendly young Thais, the most remote place on the beach. To get there, take a bus from Krabi to the National Park office; the staff from *Bamboo* will pick you up from here (5 mins boat trip over river).

Khlong Muang L-AL *Andaman Holiday Resort*, T7220207, T02-7111942. Large resort which extends right down to the beach in a peaceful and isolated spot. Pool is a bit under-sized for the number of rooms. Rooms vary, with the more expensive villas representing better value. Over-priced for what it is. Service at the restaurant is lacking professionalism given the price of the rooms and the food. **C** *Green Earth Botanical Garden Co, Ltd.* Two rooms in the main building. Rooms are nicely, if simply furnished with twin beds and a fan, and the setting is delightful in nearly an acre of tropical gardens. This is operated by Mr Gift of *Gift's Restaurant and Bakery*. Also operates various tours (see **Tours**), teaches Thai cookery, and runs this nursery/botanical garden. Mr Gift ascribes to strong environmental principles, and keeps things very low impact and peaceful. Recommended. Both *Klai Wang* and Mr Gift's place are for those looking for something very peaceful and off-the-beaten track. **D** *Klai Wang* Thai house with two simply-decorated rooms and a bathroom set in a lovely garden near a waterfall and a couple of fish ponds. A couple of kilometres from the sea, the house is right by the stream running down from the waterfall. Friendly owner who will take visitors on a trek up past fields and mountain forest to a cave (for a fair price). Vegetables served at the restaurant are organic, grown in a small plot opposite the accommodation. He rents the whole house for ฿500 a night. Recommended. **E** *Pine Bungalow* (Krabi T612192). Basic grass huts with mosquito nets, friendly staff, Asian toilets, cold water, boat trips to nearby islands arranged, dirt road all the way there. Recommended.

Eating
Price categories: see inside front cover

As one would expect, the best food available at Ao Nang is seafood. Almost all the restaurants along the beach front road, and then lining the path northwest towards the *Krabi Resort*, serve BBQ fish, chilli crab, steamed crab, prawns and so on. There is little to choose between these restaurants. Most lay their catches out on ice for customers to peruse – snapper, shark, pomfret, tiger prawns and glistening crabs. Evening is certainly the best time to eat, drink and relax, with the sun illuminating the cliffs and a breeze taking the heat off the day.

There are also some places serving more specialist dishes. For example, *Wanna's Place*, Beach Front Rd. Produces Swiss cuisine – veal escalopes, rösti and chicken and also serves wine; there are three good Italian restaurants: *Azzurra*, which has a branch in Krabi town, *La Luna* and *Fantasia Mediterranea*. All three are on the beach-front road. The 'Italian' restaurant on the corner near *Krabi Resort* is using an old sign and menu from a previous establishment and should not even pretend to be capable of cooking Italian food, even if pizza is on the menu! Their Thai food isn't bad. There is also a German garden restaurant next door to the *Baan Lae* guesthouse. *The Roof Restaurant* attractive building and setting although not on the beach. Good extensive menu. Note: All the land on the beachfront road at Ao Nang is rented, not owned, by the shops and restaurants.

Bars Plenty to choose from but they tend to open and close with great frequency. Try the *Full Moon House* on the beach front, and *Hotaru* next to *Ao Nang Thara Lodge*. *The Luna Beach Bar* on Hat Nopparat Thara has a good location but a scary reputation with reports of regular fights.

Shopping Shops open on the beach front during the evening selling garments, leather goods and other products made specifically for the tourist market. There's little unusual on sale – except for batik 'paintings', usually illustrating marine scenes, which are produced from small workshops here.

Canoe trips *Sea Canoe*, T212252, F212172, anurak@hotmail.com, or Anurak @seacanoe.com), run out of an office next to the *Phra Nang Inn*, provide small-scale sea canoeing trips (self-paddle), exploring the overhanging cliffs and caves, and the rocky coastline of Phra Nang, Rai Leh and nearby islands (see www.seacanoe.com). Also see **Sea World Kayaking** (T637334, F637334) and **Sea Kayak Krabi** (T630270), both on the front. It seems fairly difficult to choose between these companies. *Sea Canoe* has some strong environmental policies, including restrictions on the number of people per trip, and no foam or plastic-packaged lunches. The best thing is probably to spend some time chatting to your prospective guide to see if you like the way they operate and whether you are happy with the level of English they speak. **Diving** *Seafan Divers* (NAUI and PADI certification) by the *Phra Nang Inn*. *Calypso* (PADI certification), also near the *Phra Nang Inn*. **Phra Nang Divers** near the new guesthouses. *Aqua Vision Diving* next to *Beach Bungalows*. *Ao Nang Divers* (PADI Certification) at *Krabi Seaview Resort*. **Rock-climbing** *King Climbers* has an office down towards *Phra Nang Inn*. **Muay Thai** there is a new and well-supported stadium for Thai boxing in the Ao Nang area. The old one, just recently closed, was next to *Ao Nang Paradise*. The new and much larger stadium which attracts national standard boxers is set back from Hat Nopparat Thara beach by about 300 m.

Ao Nang Ban Lae Travel (close to *Krabi Resort*). *AP Travel* very helpful and friendly.

Local Jeep hire (฿800-1,200 per day) and **motorbike hire** (฿250 per day) from travel agents and guesthouses.

Road Songthaew: regular white songthaew connections with Krabi town 30 mins (฿20). From Krabi town, songthaews leave from Phattana Rd, opposite the *New Hotel* and travel to Ao Nang via Nopparat Thara Beach. For the return trip, songthaews leave from the eastern end of the Beach road, opposite *Sea Canoe*. The service runs regularly 0600-1800.

Boat Regular long-tailed boats to Rai Leh during the high season (Oct-May), 15 mins (฿50). The *Ao Nang Princess* links Ao Nang with Rai Leh and Koh Phi Phi daily during the high season, 2 hrs (฿150). Tour agents and some guesthouses (for example *Gift's*) advertise crewing jobs on sail boats to Malaysia and Singapore.

Banks Mobile exchange booths along Ao Nang beachfront and a more permanent place next to the *Phra Nang Inn*, run by the Siam City Bank. Thai Military Bank booth next to *AP Resort*, open daily 1000-1730. During low season (Jun-Oct) exchange booths may not open. **Communications** Fax and overseas telephone facilities available from numerous tour and travel agents along the beachfront road. **Useful addresses** Police station: half way along the beach road – really just a police booth. **Tourist Police** near the *Ao Nang Pakasai Resort* and another general police box near the *Phra Nang Inn*.

Rai Leh ไร่เล   and Phra Nang พระนาง

Phra Nang is the peninsular to the south of Ao Nang. There are no roads on Phra Nang, which makes it a beautifully secluded place to stay. The point consists of **Rai Leh West** and **Hat Tham** on the west side and **Rai Leh East** on the east. The best beach is on the west side – a truly picture postcard affair. The beach on the east coast is poor. There is good snorkelling and swimming in archetypal crystal-clear water. The limestone rock formations are spectacular, and there are interesting caves with stalagmites and stalactites to explore. At the southern extremity of the bay is a mountain cave dedicated to the goddess of the area – Phra Nang. There's a walkway from Rai Leh east through to Hat

Tham (there are no accommodation or restaurants on Hat Tham). On the walkway, there is a sign to an inland lagoon, a tough 15-minute climb (good views from the top). There are several climbing schools (see **Sport**, below, for details) and the tower karst formations offer some truly outstanding climbing opportunities – as well as spectacular views.

Like Phi Phi (see page 627), a very similar place in a variety of ways, Rai Leh is suffering from being too popular. Development will need to be carefully controlled if tourists and tourism are not to overrun this scenically glorious site.

Sleeping
■ *on map, page 618*
Price codes:
see inside front cover

There is not much to distinguish between the various lower-end bungalow operations at Rai Leh. Most offer a range of bungalows from older, smaller, more run-down and cheaper cottages to larger and more sophisticated places. Unfortunately, some owners have crammed too many structures onto too small an area, and others have grown too large (with 40 or more cottages) and service has consequently suffered. All places to stay have their own restaurants, bars and often minimarts, tour desks and international phone facilities. Many also have an exchange service.

Rai Leh West A beautiful beach, but huts have been built too closely together, making for overcrowded conditions and very basic (but not cheap) accommodation. To get there, take a boat from Ao Nang. Boats to Phi Phi stop at Rai Leh West. **AL-B** *Lanka Daeng*, T01-4644338, rbclub@phuket.ksc.co.th Off on its own section of beach (at the opposite end to the *Premier Rayavadee*) this has to be one of the most stylish places to stay at Rai Leh. Traditional Thai-style houses have been built and sold on as holiday homes. Their owners now let them out whenever they are not in residence. Fully equipped with kitchens and bathrooms but no a/c. Electricity goes off after midnight. Prices vary depending on the size. Houses are available for 2 people or more. **A-B** *Railey Village Bungalows*, T2284366. Large outfit with a range of bungalows with attached bathrooms arranged in a strip running inland, pleasant rooms in attractive grounds. A/c is more expensive. Book exchange, masks and fins for hire, traditional Thai massage, western-style toilets. **A** *Sand Sea Bungalows*, T611944. 60-odd a/c bungalows, has grown too large to offer much in the way of personal service, reasonable range of facilities. **A-C** *Rai Leh Bay Bungalows*, T611789. Restaurant, the cheaper rooms are hot and somewhat dingy, but a/c ones are better.

Rai Leh East **B-C** *Diamond Cave*, only a few rooms on a hill next to a huge limestone outcrop. Solidly built and clean bungalows. **C** *Sunrise*, standard bungalows, restaurant serves mediocre food. Movies played at the restaurant every night. **C** *Viewpoint*, T2304619. Friendly, well run, clean and well-maintained rooms. Good restaurant. The least accessible of all the places to stay at the far end of Rai Leh East, but some of the best bungalows available, especially given the rates. **D-E** *Coco Bungalows*, T612915. Very basic and natural bungalows made of split bamboo and roofed with thatch, small operation so has the personal touch that other larger places now lack. Excellent food. **D-E** *Yaya*, T611585. 6 rooms set in 2-storey (some higher) groups. Wooden constructions, different and aesthetically pleasing! Friendly place to stay, but if you're the shy retiring type this may not be for you as it is quite loud. Also offers camping but at ฿200 a night per person this is fairly pricey. One of the few places that offer fresh coffee in the morning. Bit of a hang-out for rock climbers (and coffee addicts).

Phra Nang headland **L** *Premier Rayavadee*, 67 Moo 5 Susaan Hoi Rd, T620740, F620630. A/c, restaurant, pool, luxurious isolated get-away with 75 villas and suites set in 10 ha (26 acres) of gardens, beautiful pool and romantic sitting rooms with grand bathrooms, access is by boat, the *Premier's* attempt to 'protect the environment' means that no motorized watersports are allowed. No longer a part of the Dusit group, but still very expensive. The quality of the food has been criticised (given the price) and there is a long-standing campaign by one outspoken activist concerning the location (she asserts the hotel has been built within the limits of the national park).

Ton Sai Bay has a few bungalow operations accessible after a walk across to the beach. **C** *Dream Valley*, T01-4646479. Simple bamboo bungalows with fans and en suite bathrooms. **C** *Andaman Nature*, simple bamboo bungalows. **D** *Ton Sai Hut*, T075-637092, simple bungalows with shared bathrooms. Most of these close during the low season. This beach is a favourite spot for the rock climbers, and is also reasonably quiet compared with Rai Leh West.

Canoeing Kayaks available to explore the limestone grottoes off the Phra Nang headland. **Diving and snorkelling** Most guesthouses hire out masks and flippers and many places now have their own dive operations. *Baby Shark Divers*, based at *Sunrise Bay Bungalows* (NAUI certification). *Phra Nang Divers* has an office in Ao Nang (in the row of shophouses near the *Phra Nang Inn*). They offer introductory courses as well as more advanced dives at sites like Koh Boda. **Rock climbing** This is now one of the best-known and most popular attractions to the Rai Leh area. Professional farang and Thai climbers will instruct novices on Phra Nang's limestone cliff faces and their equipment and safety record are both said to be excellent. Most operations are based on Rai Leh East. These include *Tex Rock Climbing* (www.thaibiz.com/texsrockclimbing/), *Phra Nang Rock Climbers,* and *King Climbers*. There are several other places operating out of resorts. See www.simonfoley.com/climbing/krabi.htm for a personal take on climbing in Rai Leh and lots of travel information. Half-day introductory climbing courses should costs ฿500, ฿1,000 for a full-day course and ฿3,000 for a three-day course. All prices are per person. **Sport**

Boat Regular long-tailed boats from Ao Nang Beach, southeastern end, throughout the day during the high season from Nov to May, 15 mins (฿20). From Krabi town long-tailed boats leave through the day from the pier, 45 mins (฿50 (if there are enough passengers at any one time, otherwise you can wait for more passengers or take the whole boat for an agreed sum). The *Ao Nang Princess* links Phi Phi, Ao Nang and Rai Leh during the high season, 2 hrs (฿150). Note that the sea can be rough between Jun and Oct which is one reason why there are no boats between Ao Nang and Rai Leh at this time. **Transport**

Banks It is possible to change money at Rai Leh but rates are poor. Better to change money before arriving in Krabi. **Directory**

Koh Phi Phi   เกาะพีพี

Koh Phi Phi consists of two beautiful islands – Phi Phi Le and Phi Phi Don. All accommodation is on the larger Phi Phi Don. Shaped like an anvil and fringed by sheer limestone cliffs and golden beaches, it offers good swimming, snorkelling and diving.

Phone code: 075
Colour map 4, grid C2

Ins and outs

The only way to get to Phi Phi is by boat. There are daily connections with Krabi, 1 hr on an express boat and 1½ hrs on the normal service. Boats also run from the beaches of Ao Nang and Rai Leh close to Krabi, 2 hrs. There are boats from Koh Lanta (1 hr) and Koh Tarutao and finally from various spots on Phuket (1-1½ hrs). The quickest way of getting to Phi Phi from Bangkok is to fly to Phuket and catch a boat from there. **Getting there**
See also Transport, page 631

The Southern Region

Getting around There are no roads on Phi Phi Don, so the only way to get around the island – which is a National Park – is on foot. However long-tailed boats can be hired from the village to explore the nearby sister island of Phi Phi Le and the coastal waters around Phi Phi Don.

The island

The western arm has no tourist accommodation on it. Boats dock at the 'neck' – **Ton Sai Bay** – near the village of the same name. Formerly, a quiet Muslim fishing community, it is now almost entirely geared to the demands of tourists, with restaurants, dive schools, tour companies, currency exchanges, laundry services and souvenir shops. Unfortunately, the island is too small to absorb the number of visitors that flock here; evident in the piles of rubbish and the worrying statistic that 80% of the fresh water wells are contaminated with faeces. Some attempts are now being taken to combat this deterioration of the environment. Funds have been allotted to improve rubbish disposal and water supply, and to reduce noise pollution by encouraging long-tailed boat operators to fit mufflers to their exhausts. On our last visit we got a sense that development had peaked – only one resort was expanding – and that the guesthouses and resorts had begun to clean up their acts. The rubbish situation, for example, appears to have improved.

The best snorkelling on the island is at **Hat Yao** (Long Beach). **NB** It is possible to travel to Koh Phi Phi all year round but during the rainy season (October-May), the boat trip can be very rough and not for the faint-hearted.

Phi Phi Le is a National Park, entirely girdled by sheer cliffs, where swiftlets nest (see box). It is not possible to stay on Phi Phi Le but it can be visited by boat. Most boat excursions include a visit to the **Viking Cave**, which contains prehistoric paintings of what look like Viking longboats, and the cliffs where birds' nests are harvested for bird's nest soup.

Excursions Hire a **long-tailed boat** from the village, or from your resort to take a **trip around the island**. Boats seat eight people, half-day trip, ฿500 per boat.

It is possible to climb to one of the **viewpoints** on the island by walking east from the village. The ascent takes about 30 minutes. A walk to Long Beach along the beach, or on the track, takes about 20 minutes.

Tours A day trip snorkelling around the island is well worthwhile (฿300 per person, including lunch, snorkels and fins).

Phi Phi Le There are regular trips to see the cliff formations, the Viking Cave, Lo Samah Bay and Maya Bay (about ฿140 per person). Maya Bay was used in the filming of *The Beach* starring Leonardo DiCaprio (see box, page 634).

Sleeping
■ *on map*
Price codes:
see inside front cover

Hotels and bungalows are poor value for money in comparison to other beach resorts in Thailand. Most accommodation is clustered on the central 'neck' of the anvil, close to Ton Sai village, on both the north and south shores. Rooms get very booked up during peak season at Christmas and New Year and people have had to sleep on the beach or restaurant floors. Prices fluctuate enormously, depending on the season, prices quoted are high-season prices.

Ton Sai Bay A *Ton Sai Village*, contact *Phi Phi Marine Travel*, 201 Uttarakit Rd, Krabi, T/F612132, T02-2557600. A/c, pool, best hotel on this side of the island, it consists of nearly 250 a/c rooms with hot-water bathrooms, satellite TV and minibar, overpriced. **A** *Phi Phi*, T611233, F2303138. A/c, hot water, restaurant, big hotel right in the middle of things, but considering the price facilities are limited. **A-B** *Island Cabana*, T620634, F612132. The old *Cabana* remains with reasonable rooms at the lower rate, and the new

Koh Phi Phi

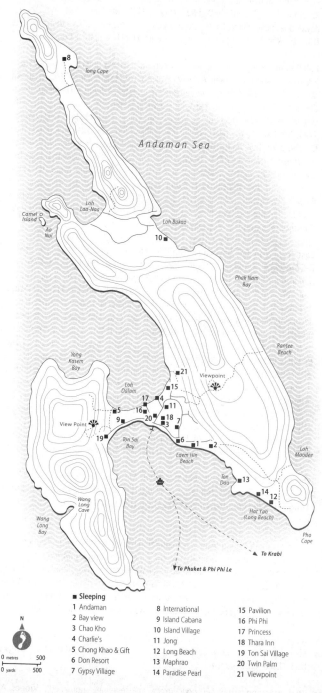

The Southern Region

extension is immaculate. Good staff and excellent rooms, pool and other facilities. Recommended. **C-E** *Phi Phi Don Resort*, T2284252. Stone bungalows on the beach, newer ones built behind, limited electricity supply, some rooms have mosquito nets. **D-E** *Chao Kho*, T611313. Slow staff but a nice stretch of beach, small bungalows.

Loh Dalam Facing north, this beach is clean and relatively quiet and is gently shelving, so is suitable for children. **A** *Phi Phi Princess*, T612188, F620615. A/c, restaurant, satellite TV, individual bungalows, rather close together. **A-B** *Phi Phi Pavilion*, next to *Charlie's*, T/F620633. Friendly management, well-maintained bungalows right on the beach, up to 50% discount in low season. Breakfast included. **C-D** *Charlie's*, T7230495. Close to the beach, clean, reasonable rooms, OK restaurant, good value. **C-E** *Thara Inn*, built on the back of the hill, the more expensive rooms are your best bet, cheaper rooms are grotty. **D** *Jong*, restaurant, only 6 rooms, all with double bed and fan, friendly management, open high season only. **D-E** *Chong Khao*, noisy location next to the generator. **D-E** *Gift*, noisy location next to the generator. **E** *Phi Phi Viewpoint*, T722011 or in Krabi T611318, F611541. Built on the side of the hill, wooden bungalows with good views, indifferent management. **E** *Twin Palm Guesthouse*, spacious rooms, reasonable value.

East from Ton Sai Bay Laem Hin: beautiful fine sand and tree-lined beach: **B-C** *Bay View Resort*, T7231144. Restaurant, private bathroom. **C-E** *Phi Phi Andaman*, T7231073. Large number of small huts in uniform rows, 3 standards of room, all have mosquito nets, some have fans and own bathrooms. **D** *Gypsy Village* (behind *Phi Phi Don Resort*), big stone bungalows, quieter and cleaner than most here. Recommended. **Ton Dao Beach**: **D-E** *Maphrao*, restaurant, quiet, private beach, bungalows set on a shaded hill, 3 grades of accommodation, the most expensive have own bathrooms, 24-hr electricity and fans, all rooms have mosquito nets. **Long Beach (Hat Yao)**: a long-tailed boat ride from Ton Sai (₿20-30 per person, one way, ₿50-100 at night time). Good-value accommodation on a lovely beach, away from all the bustle of Ton Sai. Good snorkelling off shore here. **C-F** *Paradise*, T7230484. Big restaurant, quiet, 80 bungalows with a range of rooms all with own bathrooms, the cheaper ones have limited electricity and no fan, the more expensive ones are spacious, tours organized to Phi Phi Le, etc, snorkels and fins for hire, videos, boats to Ton Sai. Recommended. **D-E** *Phi Phi Long Beach*, good food, some private bathrooms, salt water showers in dry season, simple but OK, unfriendly staff.

On the East coast Loh Bakao: **A** *Phi Phi Island Village*, T2111907 or T02-2770704. Set alone to the north of the island, some a/c overpriced. **Laem Tong**: **AL-B** *Phi Phi International* T7231250, T02-9828080. To the north of the island, good diving and snorkelling.

Eating

Price categories: see inside front cover

There are about 5 good seafood restaurants in the village, all with similar menus. All display (and barbecue) their catch on the street. **Mid-range** *Captain's*, good Thai food and Western breakfasts. *Malinda* for steaks. *Mama*, French, friendly, popular and excellent food. Recommended. *Patcharee Seafood*. Recommended. *Pizza House*, Italian, French bakery sells delicious croissants. *Top Ten* for burgers. **Cheap** *PP Bakery* good selection of pastries and sweet things with restaurant area as well.

Bars & nightclubs

A number of bars are to be found on the track from Ton Sai to the northern shore. Many show latest video releases. *Crazy Bar* is the loudest. *Lazy Bar* is the most laid back. **Disco** *Casa Blanca*.

Massage **Thai massage** ₿100 per hour (many masseurs are untrained). **Videos** At bungalows.

Second-hand books for sale or to rent on track from Ton Sai to the northern shore. **Shopping**

Boxing 'Stadium' occasionally holds fights on national holidays. **Diving** There have **Sport**
been worries expressed that Phi Phi's frantic development has degraded the marine
environment. A 1995 report by one diver maintained that this was not so. Pollution is
minimal, and animal life flourishing. There are about 12 dive schools on the island and
rates are very competitive. *SSI (Scuba School International)*, which offers a 5-day certificate course, has been recommended. Alternatively, book up with one of the many
dive centres on Phuket. Areas of interest for divers include the Bida Islands, south of
Phi Phi Le, where the variety of coral is impressive. There is a 50 m underwater tunnel
here for more experienced divers. Wrecks can be found behind Mosquito Island. The
best visibility is from Dec-Apr (25-40 m). **Game fishing** Can be organized in the village. Prices are normally ฿1,600 per day for a long-tailed boat and 2 lines. Lunch
included. **Kayaking** *Phi Phi Viewpoint Resort* rents out kayaks for ฿400 for 8 hrs or
฿100 per hour. A good way to visit deserted bays. **Paddle boats** For rent for ฿100
per hour from the northern shore. **Paragliding** ฿500 a time. **Rock climbing** The
limestone cliffs here are known internationally. Sometimes there are climbers available to give tuition on the Ton Sai cliffs. **Snorkelling** Snorkels and fins can be hired
from most bungalows or in the village (฿50 per day). **Walking** To the viewpoint
(drinks available here) or around the island. See map for marked paths. **Waterskiing**
Off the north shore. **Yacht charter** *Top Ten Burger Bar* for information. Yachts sail to
Phangnga Bay, Similan Islands and Andaman Islands in high season.

There are several agents in Ton Sai, all charging similar prices and able to organize all **Tour operators**
sorts of tickets.

Boat Connections from the Chao Fah Pier in Krabi at 0930 and 1430, 1½ hrs, or 1 hr **Transport**
for the express boats which leave at 1030 and 1430. Return boats from Phi Phi to Krabi *See also Ins & outs,*
depart at 0900 and 1300 for both the normal and express services. Daily connections *page 627*
with Ao Nang and Rai Leh on the *Ao Nang Princess*, 2 hrs. There are also boat connec- *Phi Phi lies between*
tions with Koh Lanta 1 hr and Koh Tarutao. Connections with Phuket from Patong, *Krabi & Phuket & can be*
Siray and Chalong (*Aloha Tours*, T381215) 2 hrs. The 'King Cruiser', run by *Ferryline* and *reached from both*
Songserm (51-53 Satool Rd, Phuket Town, T222570) makes 2 trips a day from Makham
Bay 1½ hrs. There is also an express boat from Tien Sin on Phuket (on the *Andaman
Queen*, T215261) at about 0830, 1 hr 20 mins.

Banks there is a small branch of Krung Thai Bank with exchange facilities open daily 0830-1530 **Directory**
in between Ton Sai and Loh Dalam. **Communications** Stamps can be bought, and letters can be
posted in the postboxes in the village. **Medical services** Rescue unit and first aid: next to *Phi
Phi Andaman*.

Koh Lanta   เกาะลันตา

Koh Lanta is actually a group of islands, the three largest of which are Koh *Phone code: 075*
Lanta Yai (which is the one with the resorts), Koh Lanta Noi and Koh Klang. It *Colour map 4, grid C2*
is one of the more recent beach developments in Southern Thailand, but, like
so many other islands and beaches in Thailand has had to contend with a very *This is somewhere*
rapid expansion in business. Land speculation is rife, with one *rai* (0.15 ha, 0.4 *where you can truly 'get*
acre) of prime land with resort potential worth about ฿1-2 mn. Locals are *away from it all'*
being encouraged not to sell out to speculators and efforts are being made to
prevent the island from becoming another Phi Phi, where rapid and uncontrolled growth has led to problems. Even with this laudable attempt to control
and manage development, it is all too clear that bungalow owners are free to
build whatever they like, just about anywhere they like.

The Southern Region

Sharks' fin

Throughout Asia, wherever there are large populations of Chinese, sharks' fin soup is on the menu of the more expensive or traditional restaurants. For those tempted to partake, be aware however, that the shark is a little understood animal with important and complex interactions with key marine systems such as coral reefs. Sharks are critical to maintaining a natural balance in reef systems. Take away the sharks, and parrot fish and other fish which graze on coral increase, leading to excessive grazing and later destruction of the reef system.

Shark fisheries have been increasing dramatically as demand not only for shark fins, but also for other shark products, rises year by year. In 1994, 182,000 million tonnes of sharks were brought to shore by the fisheries sector. This does not include the millions of sharks thrown away into the sea after being caught accidentally during fishing for more lucrative commercial species such as blue tuna. The real total catch is estimated to be as much as twice as great as the statistics show.

Nowadays, sharks are usually stripped of their fins before being discarded in the oceans, and there is a growing fisheries sector focusing on sharks. The biology of the shark, unlike other fish, does not lend itself to large-range exploitation. Sharks are at the very top of the food chain. They live for a long time and produce few young, most of which will survive to adulthood. This is vastly different from most commercial fisheries where the catch species produce many young, most of which die, and live for only a few years. Furthermore, little is known about many shark species which are highly migratory. We do not, therefore, know the impact of this increase in fishing of sharks for products, such as the fins. We cannot even say whether any species of shark is currently threatened by this fishing activity, but past experience in shark fisheries does not bode well. To date every fishery directed at sharks has quickly collapsed as the shark populations have been decimated.

Until we know more about shark fisheries and understand the impacts of our desires for shark products, please take the precautionary approach and stay clear of sharks' fin soup. In June 2000, responding to passenger concern, Thai Airways took sharks' fin soup off its in-flight menu.
(Statistics taken from the 1997 TRAFFIC South East Asia report on species in danger: Managing Shark Fisheries: Opportunities for International Conservation, by Michael L Weber and Sonja V Fordham)

Various developments are underway: electrification is being extended, phone links are being improved and rubbish collection is being stepped up. In addition, there are plans to surface more of the island's tracks to improve accessibility. Koh Lanta is recognized by the Thai government as a 'site of natural beauty' and a portion of the south of the island has recently been gazetted and designated as a National Park. This should keep this part of the island, at least, relatively untouched.

The beaches on the west, particularly to the north, are sandy and safe for swimming. There are boat trips to neighbouring islands for snorkelling and there are attractive forest and cliff-top trails, but little else. There is also a sizeable sea gypsy village to the southeast of the island, where the inhabitants continue with a lifestyle they have maintained for generations. It is said that they have no wish to become yet another 'tourist attraction' – the appalling experiences of the sea gypsies of Phuket may be at the forefront of their minds in apparently rejecting the tourist dollar.

Tham Khao Mai Kaeo is a series of caves, situated in the middle of the island; follow the signs to the supernatural caves. The best way to visit them is by hired motorbike, but they are not that easy to find so ask for directions at your hotel or guesthouse. The old administrative centre and port on Koh Lanta, now known as 'Ban Koh Lanta' is slowly developing its own tourism niche. With stunning views across to the islands and mainland to the east of the island, and most of its original old wooden shophouse/fishing houses still standing, the small town has a certain charm. Local entrepeneurs are beginning to open galleries and souvenir shops, and there are plans in the offing to start offering accommodation and cultural activities. This is also where many of the islands internet services can be found. *Lanta Orchid Nursery*, close to Lanta Long Beach Bungalows, orchid farm and exhibition, open November to mid-April daily, ฿30 adults, ฿20 children.

All bungalows offer day trips to Trang's Andaman Islands (see page 643), ฿350 per person or ฿600 per boat including lunch and snorkelling gear. (Note that it is a long trip – three hours each way – and some people find the noise unbearable for just an hour or two's snorkelling.) A ferry leaves Sala Dan at 0830 for the day-trip to Phi Phi, ฿240 per person. Fishing trips are organized by *La Creperie*, ฿450 per day, ฿1,200 for two days (which includes camping on a deserted island with food provided). Encourage your boatman to anchor at a buoy, not using an anchor – as this damages the coral.

Tours

Most bungalow operations are scattered down the west coast of Koh Lanta Yai and usually offer free pick-up from the pier at Sala Dan. Travel agents and tour companies in Krabi and Ao Nang advertise accommodation on Koh Lanta so it is possible to get a pretty good idea of the various places before arriving. With very few exceptions the bungalow operations are much of a muchness. The choice is basically between simple concrete bungalows (some with a/c) and bamboo or wood bungalows (usually fan). Some resorts have been nicknamed 'army camps' or 'chicken farms' for the unimaginative and over-crowded layout. This is particularly true of resorts at Ao Khlong Dao. However, this is the main area where bungalows are open year round. In most other places, bungalows close during the wet season. Further up the coast, there are some new and more interesting resorts, and the whole area is much less crowded and has a gentle peaceful atmosphere (although there are regular parties during the high season). Note that like other beaches and islands hereabouts there is considerable variation between high-season (roughly, Nov-May) and low-season (Jun-Oct) rates. Expect to pay half the high-season rate during low season. The attraction of visiting in the low season is that the island is virtually deserted and room rates are very competitive. Agents in Krabi and Ao Nang will provide information of which places are open.

Sleeping
■ *on map*
Price codes:
see inside front cover

Ao Khlong Dao A (high)-C (low) *Lanta Andaman Resort*, towards the south is the first real hotel on Koh Lanta. The 2-storey building is not very pretty, and although there is a pool, the very ordinary rooms are over-priced for what they are. Note also that prices rise by a third during the high season and during peak months another ฿600 is added to the bill. Games room, snooker, restaurant. **B-C** *Sayang Beach*, T01-4766357, situated just south of the *Lanta Villa*. This operation is run by a local lady called Tukta and they have taken care to protect the environment while constructing their bungalows (unlike many). Excellent food with fresh fish nightly. Large bugalows; no a/c. **C-E** *Diamond Sand Inn*, T2284473. Some a/c. Spotless big rooms and huge attached bathrooms. Limited electricity supply, but this is the only negative thing to say about this place. The restaurant is good, with nice views and the proprietors are extremely welcoming and amiable. Very competitive rates in the low season, reflected in the price range quoted here. Recommended. **C-E** *Lanta Sea House*, T2284160. Well kept plot, with casuarina trees and tidy garden, 2 grades of room, both are clean and well

The Southern Region

Life's a Beach

During 1998 and early 1999 Phi Phi attracted more column inches of media attention than you would expect for a tiny island. The reason: Leonardo DiCaprio came head-to-head with environmental correctness.

Towards the end of the year, 20th Century Fox began filming The Beach, based on Alex Garland's novel, having selected DiCaprio as the bankable heart-throb and Phi Phi as a suitably sun-drenched island. (In fact Phi Phi Le, just to the south of the main island, Phi Phi Don.) But there were three problems – not enough atmospheric palm trees, too much scrubby grass, and lumpy sand dunes. Easy: ship in 92 trees, turf out the grass and bulldoze the dunes. But Phi Phi is also part of a National Park, so when Thailand's environmental movement got wind of what was going on they realised they were onto an environmental winner. Environmental lawyers, local people and activists joined forces to bring the devastation to the wider world. "In a society which shuns confrontation except in the heat of the moment," opponents said as they took the film company to court to prevent filming, "this is an unprecedented step taken in desperation".

In response to an increasingly hysterical and effective anti-Leo campaign, producer Andrew McDonald said that he had sought and received permission from the National Parks' office and had made a payment of US$100,000. He also made a commitment to return everything to its natural state on completion of filming. "We are being picked on", he complained to The Nation, "because we are a big studio name and because Leonardo DiCaprio is involved". He said that before filming could begin the crew had to remove six tons of rubbish from Maya Beach. He also asked why similar attention has not been brought to bear on the conflagration of restaurants and bungalow operations, the piles of rubbish, the constant coming-and-going of boats, the pillaging of the reefs... He has a point. Phi Phi – still a beautiful island – is a mess; over-crowded and over-developed.

supplied, the more expensive have spacious balconies and their own bathroom. Very good value in the low season (reflected in the price grading here). Recommended. **C-E Lanta Villa**, T/F611944. Another place which has declined in quality over the last couple of years. Range of rooms from simple A-frame bungalows with attached shower rooms to larger and more sophisticated Thai-style, red-roofed cottages with wood floors, and large tiled bathrooms. However the bungalows are too close together and during the high season it is crowded and noisy. Credit cards accepted. **C-F Kaw Kwang Beach Bungalow**, restaurant, lovely beach with safe swimming, double rooms with fans, some very cheap and basic wooden huts available. Closed in low season. **D Lanta Royal**, impersonally large restaurant, large, rather bare rooms with unattractive cement floors. This is one of the larger places on the island with over 50 cottages, as a result, perhaps, it lacks the family atmosphere of the smaller outfits but does have a range of facilities. **D-E Deer Neck Cabana**, T7230623. Northern end of Koh Lanta, on the promontory, the beach here is rather muddy, but the sea bed shelves very gently making it a good place for children to play and paddle but hopeless for proper swimming and snorkelling. A better beach lies a short walk across the neck of the promontory. The bungalows are good for the price and the management are very friendly and helpful, excellent restaurant with Thai and western food, good value. Recommended. **D-E Golden Bay**, clean, own bathroom, electricity, some simple wood and bamboo huts, some concrete. Very good value (especially in the low season when it is down to **F** for a good room). Friendly, helpful owners and an easy place to get to. **D-E Lanta Garden Home**, a small number of A-frame basic huts and some wooden bungalows on stilts, shady plot. New resorts in this area include the **Lanta Island Cabana** which has a curious restaurant designed to look like a large boat and a row of simple, solidly built wooden bungalows, the *Lanta Island Resort* which definitely falls into the army camp category, and the fairly ordinary *Merry Beach Bungalows* and *Cha Ba*. All are fairly close together just up from the *Lanta Villa*.

Ao Phra-Ae (a lovely beach) **AL (high)-B (low)** *Lanta Resotel*, Bungalow development that definitely falls into the 'army camp' or 'chicken farm' (for 'hatching tourist eggs') categories. Large solidly built wooden bungalows with a/c and all hotel amenities. It advertises itself as a home rather than a hotel, but the regimented layout of row on row of bungalows with no gardens to speak of, and plans to add another 50 bungalows belies the publicity material. **A-D** *Wang Thong Resort*, lies about 250 m from the beach and is set in amongst trees and along the banks of a canal. The thatched bamboo and wood bungalows on high stilts that are on the left-hand side (looking towards the beach) are lovely. Nicely spaced out and with a secluded natural feeling to the layout, there are lots of walkways between the bungalows and small wooden bridges over the water. These are all fan only. On the right-hand side are newer houses currently under construction. Also set in amongst the trees, the 2-bedroom affairs are ideal for families, with a cooking space under the house and a spacious deck beside the bedrooms. These are also fan only. The only blots on the landscape are the blocks of a/c rooms at the front on the right-hand side. These are totally out of character with the rest of the resort, being made of concrete and hideous red-tiled walls. One can only hope the owner sees sense and redesigns them, soon! **C** *Rapala Long Beach*, small swimming pool, rather out of place, pretentious, new resort, hexagonal bungalows with small triangular shower rooms and a rocky beach. Closed in the low season. **C-E** *Relax Bay Tropicana*, 1 Moo 2, T02-7220089, T/F620618. Restaurant, 48 large wooden bungalows raised high off the ground and scattered through beachside grove of trees, every effort has been taken to keep this development *au naturel* and the beach and location are very quiet, all rooms have glass and/or mosquito panels in the windows, fans and shower rooms in the open-air adjoining. **D** *Last Horizon Resort*, 175 Moo 2, Baan Phu Klom Beach, T01-2283625, last_horizon@hotmail.com Opened in late 1999, 25 stone bungalows in a coconut grove with attached showers, 24-hr electricity, restaurant and beach bar. Friendly management, motorbikes for hire, tours arranged. The only downside is that the beach here is only suitable for swimming at high tide. Recommended. **E** *Lanta Long Beach*, bamboo huts with mosquito nets provided. Also a number of smaller huts. **E-F** *Lanta Palm Beach*, T7230528. Adequate restaurant, small rather shabby huts rather close together, some electricity, all with bathrooms, tents ฿30, free taxi service to Sala Dan.

From *Lanta Palm Beach* onwards to Hat Khlong Khuang there are several new bungalow operations. With the exception of *Wang Thong* which has a lot of charm, and *Lanta Resotel* which has none, these are all very similar. Either they are concrete bungalows (usually over-crowded) or bamboo bungalows (often with a bit more space). In most cases, they are set back a little from the beach in coconut plantations or in gardens just off the road. Any of these would probably be a pleasant enough place to stay, but none have any special qualities to distinguish from the rest. All fall under our **C-D** price range and all close during the low season. The list includes: *Tamrin Resort*, *Lanta Emerald Bungalow*, *Lanta Riviera*, *Lanta New Beach Bungalows*, *Baan Gayee*, and the *Good Day Resort*, but no doubt there will soon be more names to add!

Hat Khlong Khoang C (high)- E (low) *Lanta Coconut Green Field*, pleasant bamboo bungalows in a coconut plantation by a rocky shore. Friendly staff and peaceful setting. Restaurant with movie showings. **D (high)-E (low)** *Bee Bee*, a 'village'-like set-up of unusual-looking bamboo bungalows set just back from the beach in a coconut plantation. Some with two levels and all with bamboo bathrooms! Charming and different from its neighbours. Closed during the low season. **D-F** *Lantas Lodge Bungalows*, restaurant,

Koh Lanta

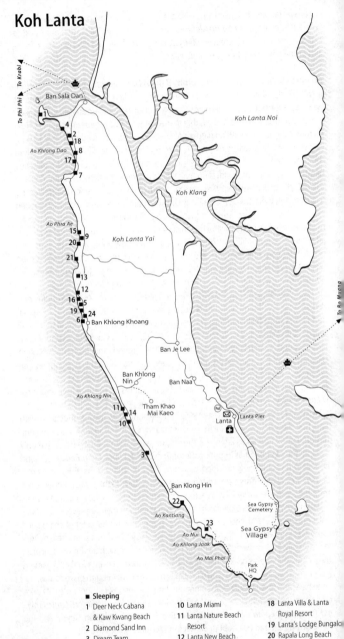

■ **Sleeping**

1 Deer Neck Cabana
   & Kaw Kwang Beach
2 Diamond Sand Inn
3 Dream Team
4 Golden Bay Cottages
5 Lanta Emerald Bungalow
6 Lanta Coral Beach
7 Lanta Garden Home
8 Lanta Island Resort
9 Lanta Long Beach

10 Lanta Miami
11 Lanta Nature Beach
    Resort
12 Lanta New Beach
13 Lanta New Beach
    Bungalows
14 Lanta Paradise
15 Lanta Palm Beach
16 Lanta Riviera
17 Lanta Sea House

18 Lanta Villa & Lanta
    Royal Resort
19 Lanta's Lodge Bungalow
20 Rapala Long Beach
    Resort
21 Relax Bay Tropicana
22 Seasun
23 Waterfall Bay Resort
24 Where Else

lovely beach, 'A' frames, some wooden huts and tents, very attractive plot amongst coconut trees, electricity in restaurant only, good fish on menu. **E** *Lanta Riviera Bungalow*, 121 Moo 1, Saladan Koh Lanta. Bungalows with fan and attached shower, quiet and relaxed atmosphere and friendly staff, lovely clean beach. Recommended. **E** *Where Else*, 14 spacious bamboo and wooden bungalows with semi-outdoor bathrooms. Friendly owner, good views from the rooms on the southern side. The restaurant is known on the island for its Indian and vegetarian dishes as well as its Thai food. Recommended.

Ao Khlong Nin A-E *Lanta Miami*, T2284506. A/c and fan available. Family-run, all rooms come with attached bathrooms. Rooms are quite closely packed. Snorkelling organized from here. **B-C** *Lanta Coral Beach*, New bungalow resort. Concrete bungalows in rows in a garden. Rocky shore but with some areas where swimming is safe. Staff are not very friendly. Restaurant and tour desk. **C-E** *Lanta Nature Beach Resort*, good bungalows, friendly and helpful owners. One of the better places on this beach. Good discounts in the off season, reflected in the price range quoted here. **B (high)-D (low)** *Lanta Paradise*, T7230530. Not such a pleasant beach, all beds have mosquito nets and fans. Some new bungalows are behind the road away from the beach. Tour desk. Motorbike rental available. **D-E** *Dream Team*, good restaurant using their own home-grown produce, wooden huts with fans and night time electricity, lovely gardens but facing a rocky beach.

Ao Kantiang B-E *Lanta Marine Park Resort*, T3970793 A new resort set up high on the hill overlooking Ao Kantiang with great views of the bay from the bungalows in the front. Several styles of bungalows – the small bamboo bungalows set back from the view are the cheapest. The larger concrete bungalows with views from the balconies are the most expensive. Rooms are spacious and comfortable. The walk up to the bungalows will keep you fit! Between Ao Kantiang and Ao Khlong Jaak is another very pleasant bay with white sands and a small stream. Here the only resort is the **C-E** *Same Same But Different*, 9 rooms built in amongst the trees on the bay with a restaurant and bar on the beach, and a rest area with hammocks swinging in the sea breezes. Nicely laid out with a bit of style, this does more than live up to its name. Same owner as the *Ruen Mai* restaurant in Krabi town (another location where not a tree has been felled!); if the restaurant is as good as *Ruen Mai*, Koh Lanta will be very well served. Recommended. **E** *Kan Tiang Bay View Resort*, 2 rows of basic bamboo bungalows with mosquito nets. Restaurant, tour desk, and motorbike rental. **E** *Seasun*, T7230497. Rather grotty concrete and some bamboo huts, one wooden bungalow up a 20-ft staircase with great views, very pretty and remote cove, not such good snorkelling, friendly Muslim owners.

Ao Khlong Jaak B-D *Waterfall Bay Resort*, T2284014, Krabi 612084. Adjacent to the national park, in a small but lovely bay with a couple of waterfalls within easy walking distance. Large A-frame bungalows, some with 2 storeys and attractive balconies, attached shower rooms. Very quiet and peaceful and close to the national park. The owner, Khun Areeya, has a strong conservation ethic and is an excellent cook (of both Indian and Thai food). She is happy to teach Thai cookery to anyone with an interest. The staff is very friendly and extremely good with children. Open all year round, but it is best to book in advance from Oct to Mar. **D-E** *Khlong Jaak Bungalows*, simple bamboo bungalow resort. Closed in the low season.

All the guesthouses provide restaurants with similar menus; Thai and European food **Eating** with lots of seafood and fruit. *Danny's*, southern end of Khlong Dao beach. Huge menu of seafood, Thai and international, Sun evening Thai buffets are very popular. In Sala Dan there are some small cafés. 3 restaurants overlook the bay between Lanta Yai and Lanta Noi (rather windy): *Seaview 1* (aka *Monkey in the Back*), slow service, good seafood, no electricity, cheap. *Seaview 2*, larger menu, Thai and seafood, friendly, cheap. *Swiss Bakery*, Sala Dan, good pastries and coffee. *Same Same but Different*, just down from Waterfall Bay, the owner runs the *Ruen Mai* restaurant in Krabi town. This is an excellent restaurant and reportedly the cook at *Same Same but Different* has been brought over from the *Ruen Mai*, so the food should be good! *Where Else*, cooks Indian and vegetarian as well as Thai food.

Bars   *Reggae*, *First* and *Bongo*, Khlong Dao beach. **Sun Moon Music and Beer Bar**, *Dream Team* bungalows, Ao Khlong Nin.

Shopping   Only basic supplies available in Sala Dan and Lanta (on southeast coast). *Minimart* on Khlong Dao beach open in high season.

Sport   **Diving**   Several schools in Sala Dan (some with German spoken); check equipment before signing on. *Atlantis*, *Aquarius Diving* and *Koh Lanta Diving Centre* are both to be found in Sala Dan. **Pool tables** In Sala Dan, opposite *Sea View 1*. **Snorkelling** Known locally as 'snorking'. Most guesthouses hire out equipment at about ฿30 per day, although the quality is varied.

Tour operators   *Makaira Tour Centre*, 18 Moo 1 Sala Dan. *Sala Dan Travel Centre*, *O & M Travel*, *IC Travel*, are all in Sala Dan. Most bungalows can also make travel arrangements.

Transport   **Local Long-tailed boats hire**: from bungalows for ฿600 per day. **Motorbike hire**: from bungalows for ฿250 per day or ฿40 per hour, or in Sala Dan. **Mountain bike hire**: from bungalows for ฿130 per day. **Pick-up trucks**: some ply the island, ฿100 to end of the island, others serve individual bungalows only. **NB** The laterite roads are rough.

Long distance Boat: boats leave from Sala Dan on the northern tip of the island, and from Lanta Pier on the southeast coast. Connections with Chao Fah Pier in Krabi, 2 hrs via Koh Jam (฿150). Departures vary, but usually one departure each day at 1300, Krabi to Lanta, 0900 and 1300 Lanta to Krabi. **NB** there is no ferry from Krabi to Lanta (and vice versa), in the wet season. Instead, a minibus runs from Chao Fah Pier and via 2 short car ferries across Lanta Noi and to Ban Sala Dan (2 hrs) (฿150). There are also boat connections with Ban Hua Hin, on southern tip of Koh Klang. Songthaews from Krabi go to Ban Hua Hin (฿25). In the high season, there is one boat a day from Phi Phi at 1300, 1 hr ฿150 one way. Guesthouse owners hassle mercilessly for your custom on this trip.

Directory   **Banks** Siam City Bank Exchange in Sala Dan; you cant miss it, it's bright red. **Communications** Post Office: Lanta Pier. **Medical services** Health centre: in Sala Dan. Hospital: Lanta Pier. **Useful addresses** Police: Sala Dan.

Koh Jam   There are only three bungalow operations on the tiny island of Koh Jam. **E** *Joy Bungalow*, T01-7230502. 30 bungalows; good food, good location. Two newer, but not necessarily better, operations are: **E** *New Bungalows*, T01-4644230 which has simple wooden bungalows and a restaurant, and **D** *Andaman Bungalows*, T01-4646500 basic A-frame bungalows with tiled floors. The boat from Krabi to Koh Lanta goes via Koh Jam (see above) 1 hour 30 minutes, ฿150. There are also connections with Koh Phi Phi and with Laem Kruat, on the mainland.

Koh Bubu   Koh Bubu is a tiny island in the Lanta group of Koh Lanta Yai. There is one bungalow establishment here, with 13 thatched bungalows (**D-E**), restaurant and little else except sea and solitude. People who have stayed here report returning to the mainland completely relaxed and detached from the world they left behind. There are regular vans from Krabi to Bo Muang village pier, then take a boat to Samsan Pier on the east coast of Lanta Yai (฿100), and finally on to Bubu by chartered For a long-tailed boat (฿150-200), contact *Thammachart*, Khong Kha Rd, Krabi. There is a free ferry service from Lanta Pier to Bubu (one a day).

Trang ตรัง

Phone code: 075
Colour map 4, grid C3

Trang is an important port and commercial centre but is a fairly nondescript, Chinese town. It is famous for its char-grilled pork, sweet cakes and as the birthplace of Prime Minister Chuan Leekpai. The town was established as a trading centre in the first century AD, and flourished between the 7th and 12th centuries. Its importance rested on its role as a relay point for communications between the east coast of Thailand and Palembang (Srivijaya) in Sumatra. It was then known as Krung Thani and later as Trangkhapura, the 'City of Waves'. The name was shortened in the 19th century to Trang.

The arrival of the Teochew (Chinese) community in the latter half of the 19th century was a boon to the local economy which, until the introduction of rubber from Malaysia, was reliant on tin mining. Trang's rubber plantations were the first in Thailand (the first tree was planted just south of the city) and its former ruler, Phraya Rasdanupradit Mahitsara Phakdi, is credited with encouraging the spread of its cultivation. There is a statue of him 1 km out of town on the Phattalung road. Rubber smallholdings and plantations are still the biggest money-earner in the region.

Trang has retained the atmosphere of a Chinese immigrant community with some good Chinese restaurants and several Chinese shrines. The **Kwan Tee Hun shrine**, dedicated to a bearded war god, is in Ban Bang Rok, 3 km north of Trang on Route 4. Clearly, to keep tourists in Trang for longer than it takes to catch a minibus to Pakmeng for the boat to Trang's offshore islands requires a sight or two. The **Trang Aquarium**, within the Rajamangala Institute, should now be open. **Prime Minister Chuan Leekpai's house** (ask locally for directions) has also become a pilgrimage spot of sorts and is open to visitors.

There is a temporary **tourist office** at the Railway Station and plans to build a TAT office. ■ *Best time to visit Jan-Apr, out of the monsoon season.*

Beaches around Trang Trang's embryonic tourism industry has so far escaped the hard sell of Phuket and Pattaya – excellent news for nature-lovers, reef-divers and explorers. The strip of coast running south from Pakmeng (38 km west from Trang) round to Kantang, boasts some of the south's best beaches.

Excursions
For Trang's Andaman Islands, see page 643

Pakmeng and Chang Lang beaches are the most accessible – 40 km west of Trang town. The sea is poor here for swimming, but it's a nice place to walk.

Trang place names

Chang Lang

หาดฉางหลาง

Khao Chong Forest Park

อุทยานป่าเขาช่อง

Pakmeng

ปากเหม่ง

Sleeping Pakmeng: B-C *Pakmeng Resort*, T218940. Turn left after reaching the main seafront and continue on towards the national park. The resort is on the left and is well marked. Wooden bungalows with attached bathroom and fan, excellent restaurant. Newer a/c bungalows have a bit more style about them and are slightly pricier. The resort backs onto the main *khlong* leading to the river. Motorbikes (฿250 per day) and

The Southern Region

bicycles (฿70 per day) for rent. **B** *Le Trang Resort*, T274027-8 F274029. A new bunga-low resort just up from the pier. The restaurant is well known and serves good sea-food. The bungalows are in a very pleasant garden with some seating. Well built, and well equipped but quite small for the price and there is no hot water. Sea canoes can be rented for ฿150 per hour and guides are available on request. There are mangroves and small islands along the shore so it is possible to use the canoes even in the mon-soon season. The resort will also arrange camping on the nearby islands, complete with picnic and mobile phone should anything go wrong! Very enthusiastic owner. **D** *no name* – look for the Mittweida sign, T230200. Associated with the *Thai Jin Resort* in Trang muncipality, the bungalows are behind a café near the many seafood stalls along Pak Meng beach. Simple bamboo rooms, very well-equipped and nicely deco-rated. **Chang Lang**: **C** *Chang Lang Resort*, well signposted and with a very grand entrance, the resort itself is rather run down. Adequate bungalows but nothing spe-cial for the price. **D** *Chang Lang Sea Sand Resort*, T213611 is on the main road to the national park. Unattractive concrete bungalows with sparse furnishings to say the very least. Not recommended.

To the north, down the road from Sikao is **Hua Hin**, which also has a good beach and is famed for its *hoi tapao* – sweet-fleshed oysters. Unfortunately the oyster season climaxes in November – the peak of the wet season. Hua Hin Bay is dotted with limestone outcrop islets. Other beaches to the south include **Hat San**, **Hat Yong Ling**, **Hat Yao** and **Hat Chao Mai**; private ventures are not permitted at any of the beaches within the national park (ie Hat Chao Mai, Hat Yong Ling and Hat San). Hat Yao has a very good restaurant (**Mid-range**: *Hat Yao Seafood*) which is open-fronted and looks out onto the beach. **Sleeping**: **C-E** *Barn Chom Talay – Seaview Guest House*, dormitory room and bunga-lows all clean. The bungalows are nicely furnished. The daughter of the owners speaks excellent English. Also offer every type of tour including kayak rental, trips to the nearby caves, and boat tours to the islands. A pleasant out-of-the-way place to stay. Recommended. There are also impressive caves near the village, known for their layered curtain stalactites. The beaches and many of the offshore islands fall under the jurisdiction of the 230 sq km **Hat Chao Mai National Park**. Accommodation available at park headquarters (6 km outside Chao Mai); **D** bungalows; there is no restaurant here – you can buy food from a very small shop in Chao Mai village. Further south of Kantang, in Amphoe Palien, is Hat Samran. ■ *Getting there: taxis to Pakmeng, Chao Mai, Katang and Palien leave from outside Trang's Diamond Department Store, near the railway station.*

Tours **High season only (October-April)**: *Trang Travel*, for trips to Trang's Andaman Islands. The company runs a boat and offers day-long excursions for a minimum of four, visiting islands and reefs on request, for ฿500-600 (including lunch and snorkelling equipment).

Sleeping Most of Trang's hotels are on Phraram VI Rd, between the clock tower and the railway
■ *on map* station. More recently a number of high-rise luxury hotels have sprung up slightly fur-
Price codes: ther out of town. **A** *Thamrin Thara*, 69/8 Huay Yod Rd, T223223. 285 rooms. Considered
see inside front cover to be the No 1 hotel in town. The double rooms are more expensive than twins. Service is generally unresponsive: catering to local bigwigs at the expense of other guests. The hotel seems to have infrastructure problems with the boiler breaking down on more than one occasion (and no discount for no hot water). Unimpressive. **A** *Trang Plaza*, 132 Phattalung Rd, T226-90210. 2 km out of town, 2 restaurants, swimming pool. **A-B** *Clarion MP Resort*, 184 Phattalung Rd, T214230, F211177. 15 km out of town, res-taurant, swimming pool, tennis, gym, golf driving range, 250-odd rooms.

C *Thumrin*, Thumrin Square, T211011, F218057. Some a/c, restaurant, OK but some signs of disrepair. Abundant staff. **C** *Trang*, 134 Visetkul Rd (clock tower intersection), T218157, F218451. Some a/c, restaurant, large rooms, some with balconies. More expensive rooms have TV and hot water.

D *Koteng*, 77-79 Phraram VI Rd, T218622. Some a/c, restaurant, friendly owners. Reasonable rooms; probably the best of the cheaper places. **D** *Queen's*, Visetkul Rd, T218229, F210414. Some a/c, no restaurant, large hotel with average rooms and attached bathrooms, hot water and western toilet. Clean but uninspiring. **D-E** *Wattana*, 127/3-4 Phraram VI Rd, T218184. Reasonable rooms, more expensive ones have a/c and TV, all have attached bathroom, some with hot water and western toilet, restaurant. Unimpressive management. **E** *Petch*, T218002. Good value, large, cheap rooms, some have attached bathroom with squat toilet, restaurant, friendly.

Trang's barbecued pork is delicious and one of the town's few claims to national fame. It is made from a traditional recipe brought here by the town's immigrant Chinese community and is usually served with dim sum. It is the speciality of several Chinese restaurants in town.

Thai Cheap: *Sritrang Bakery*, Phattalung Rd. Desserts are a speciality. *Trokpla Seafood*, Trokpla Soi, Rama VI Rd. Excellent Thai and Chinese food on the 3rd floor of *Diamond Department Store*.

Eating
*Price categories:
see inside front cover*

Trang

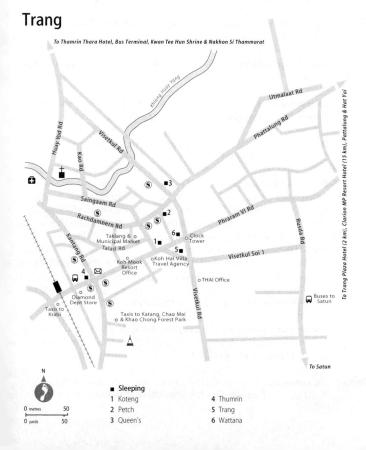

The Southern Region

■ Sleeping

1 Koteng	4 Thumrin
2 Petch	5 Trang
3 Queen's	6 Wattana

Chinese Mid-range: *Thumrin Coffee Shop*, 99 Thumrin Square. Extensive menu. **Cheap**: *Jan Jan*, Thaklang Rd. Barbecued pork. *Ko Choi*, Wienkapang Rd. Also serves Thai. *Ko Lan*, Huai Yod Rd. Trang-style barbecued pork. *Koyao*, Huai Yod Rd. Vast menu.

International Cheap: *Hoa*, at the front of *Diamond Department Store*, coffee shop and bar. *Queen's Hotel restaurant*, Visetkul Rd. Good American breakfast. *Sin Oh Cha*, next to railway station (opposite *Diamond Department Store*), coffee shop.

Foodstalls Two night markets offer good food, one is on Visetkul Rd, north of clock tower, the other is in the square in front of the railway station.

Festivals   **October** *Vegetarian Festival* (movable). 9-day-long festival in which a strict vegetarian diet is observed to purify the body. Mediums pierce their cheeks and tongues with spears and walk on hot coals. On the sixth day a procession makes its way around town, in which everyone dresses in traditional costumes. The same event occurs in Phuket.

Shopping   Best buys include locally woven cotton and wicker work and sponge cake!

Markets Thaklang and Municipal Markets are next door to each other in the centre of town, off Rachdamnern Rd; they are a good place to browse for local goods.

Sport   **Snorkelling** Equipment for hire from *Trang Travel*, Thumrin Square.

Tour operators   *Trang Travel*, Thumrin Square, T219598/9, F218057. *KK Tour & Travel*, opposite the railway station, T211198.

Transport
828 km to Bangkok
317 km to Phuket
163 km to Hat Yai

Local Motorbike hire: at corner of Municipal market on Rachdamnern Rd, ฿200 per day.

Long distance Air: the airport is 7 km from town. Daily connections on Thai with Bangkok 2 hrs 10 mins (฿2,005), connections to Bangkok only.

Train: the station is at the end of Phraram VI Rd. 2 daily connections with Bangkok (15½ hrs) at 1344 and 1820.

Bus: buses to most places leave from the bus terminal 1 km out of town on the Huay Yat road (get there by , ฿7-10) – the exception are the buses to Satun which leave from the terminal on Rusda Rd. Buses to Satun leave from Jermpanya Rd. Overnight connections with Bangkok 12 hrs and regular connections with Satun (2 hrs), Hat Yai (2 hrs), Phuket (฿62), Krabi (฿30), Phattalung (฿15) and Nakhon Si Thammarat (฿30). **Shared taxi**: to Nakhon Si Thammarat and Surat Thani leave from Huai Yod Rd (near junction with Rachdamnern Rd), taxis to Krabi leave from the railway station, taxis to Phattalung and Hat Yai leave from Phattalung Rd (opposite the police station), and to Satun they leave from Jermpanya Rd. Phuket (฿150), Krabi (฿50), Nakhon Si Thammarat (฿60), Hat Yai (฿50), Satun (฿50), Phattalung (฿30).

International connections with Langkawi, Malaysia: 4 ferries daily from Satun and Langkawi Island (at 0845, 1200, 1530 and 1700). Get a local bus to Satun (they take 1 hr 10 mins and cost ฿200).

Directory   **Airline offices** *Thai*, 199 Visetkul Rd (not in the centre of town), T218066. **Banks** Banks are clustered along Phraram VI Rd. **Communications** General Post Office and Telegraph Office: Jermpanya Rd.

Trang's Andaman Islands   หมู่เกาะของตรังในทะเลอันดามัน

Trang's Andaman Islands number 47 in total, spread out to the south of Koh *Colour map 4, grid C2*
Lanta. Few tourists – relatively speaking – visit the islands, although their
beauty, rich birdlife, and the clear waters that surround them make future
development highly likely. **NB** There are no ferries to Trang's Andaman
Islands in the rainy season, although long-tailed boats can be taken by those
with the money and the courage. It is only advisable, though, in calm seas –
check the weather forecast service, T02-3994012/3 (nationwide).

Although **Koh Ngai (Hai)** forms the southernmost part of Krabi province,
and is most easily reached from Pakmeng in Trang province, 16 km away, it is
also possible to get there from Koh Phi Phi and Koh Lanta. This 5 sq km island
is cloaked in jungle and fringed with glorious beaches. A coral reef sweeps
down the eastern side, ending in two big rocks, between which rips a strong
current – but the coral around these rocks is magnificent.Koh Ngai is used as
the jumping-off point for trips to the other islands.

Koh Chuak and **Koh Waen** (between Koh Hai and Koh Mook) are also
snorkellers' havens – the latter is the best reef for seafan corals.

On the western side of **Koh Mook** is the **Emerald Cave** or Tham Morakot – *According to local*
known locally as Tham Nam – which can only be entered by boat (or fearless *fishermen, a colony of*
swimmers) at low tide, through a narrow opening. After the blackness of the *mermaids lives off the*
80-m-long passage it opens into daylight again at a circular pool of emerald *east coast of Koh Mook*
water ringed with powdery white sand and a backdrop of precipitous cliffs.
The cave was only discovered during a helicopter survey not very long ago and
– as is the way with these things – is thought to have been a pirates' lair. **Be
warned**, you can only leave the pool at low tide. The island's west coast has
white beaches backed by high cliffs where swallows nest. There are also beautiful beaches on the east coast facing the craggy mainland.

Koh Kradan, most of which falls within the bounds of the Chao Mai
National Park, is regarded as the most beautiful of Trang's islands, with splendid beaches and fine coral, particularly on the east side. Two Japanese war-
ships sunk during the Second World War lie off the shore and are popular dive
spots. The areas not encompassed by the National Park are a mixture of rubber
smallholdings and coconut groves. The island – bar the park area – is privately
owned having been bought by Mon Sakunmethanon in 1985 for ฿5 million.

Koh Talibong (Libong), which is part of the Petra Islands group to the south,
is renowned for its oysters and birdlife. The Juhoi Cape and the eastern third of
the island is a major stopping-off point for migratory birds, and in March and
April the island is an ornithologist's El Dorado. Typical visitors, on their way
back to northern latitudes, include brown-headed gulls, crab plovers, four species of terns, waders, curlews, godwits, redshanks, greenshanks, reef egrets and
black-necked storks. From October to March the island is famed for its unique

The Southern Region

• •

Trang's Andaman Islands

Koh Chuak

เกาะเชือก

Koh Hai (Ngai)

เกาะไหง

Koh Kradan

เกาะกระดาน

Koh Mook

เกาะมุก

Koh Talibong (Libong)

เกาะลิบง

Koh Waen

เกาะแหวน

Hoi Chakteen oysters. The rare manatee (*Manatus senegalensis*) and the green turtle also inhabit the waters off the island. The best coral reef is off the southwest coast, directly opposite the *Libong Beach Resort*. Snorkelling equipment is available from the resort who also provide fishing gear. Libong's main town is Ban Hin Kao, where the daily ferry from Kantang docks. Motorcycle taxis take visitors along rough trails to the island's beaches and villages. There is one hotel on the island (see **Sleeping**) and no nightlife. The population is almost exclusively Muslim, and alcohol is not widely available.

Koh Sukorn (Muu), **Koh Petra**, **Koh Lao Lieng (Nua** and **Tai)** are also part of the Petra Islands group, off Palien, 47 km south of Trang and can be reached from there or Kantang. **Koh Sukorn** (locally known as Koh Muu – or Pig Island) is, rather ironically, inhabited by Muslims. Apart from its golden powder-sand beaches, its main claim to fame are the mouth-watering water melons that are grown here (March/April).

Dolphins can often be seen offshore **Koh Petra** and **Koh Lao Lieng** have sheer cliffs which are the domain of the birds' nest collectors who risk life and limb for swiftlet saliva. The islands have excellent sandy beaches on their east coasts and impressive reefs which are exposed at low tide.

Trang's Andaman Islands

■ **Sleeping**
1 Koh Ngai Resort   3 Koh Mook Resort   5 Libong Beach Resort
2 Koh Ngai Villa   4 Kradan Island Resort

anuary-April. The weather is unsuitable for island-hopping from May-December and although it is sometimes still possible to charter boats out of season, it can be expensive and risky: the seas are rough, the water is cloudy and you may be stranded by a squall.

Best time to visit

Koh Ngai B *Koh Ngai Resort*, southeastern corner of the island, with its own magnificent private beach. More up-market than *Koh Ngai Villa*, chalets have fans and private balconies, they can be booked through the Trang office, 205 Sam-Yaek Mohwith, 210317 (or on the island T211045). See www.asiatravel.com/thailand/prepaidhotels/kohngairesort/ **D** *Koh Ngai Villa* is half way up the eastern side of the island, facing the reef, contact Koh *Ngai Villa Travel Agency* in Trang, T210495. 15 grass-roofed chalets equipped with mosquito nets, restaurant, tents also available (฿150).

Sleeping & eating
■ *on map*
Price codes:
see inside front cover

Koh Mook D-E *Koh Mook Resort*, only accommodation on the island, fantastic views (see map, page 644), office, 25/36 Sathani Rd, Trang, T211367.

Koh Kradan B-C *Kradan Island Resort*, only accommodation on the island, restaurant, rather expensive for the quality of accommodation provided (60 rooms). Recent visitors have been disappointed as the resort is run down with poor rooms at this price. However, the staff are friendly and enthusiastic and the island is wonderful. Tents are available for ฿150. Rooms can be booked at 25/36 Sathani Rd, T211367, Trang, or by phoning T02-3920635, BF3911315. The Trang office also run a daily boat service to the island (฿240 return).

Koh Talibong (Libong) C *Libong Beach Resort*, Ban Lan Khao, T210013, or in Trang, 214676. Large open-fronted restaurant with about 15 basic bungalows set in a coconut grove facing onto a sandy beach, 5 km from the main town Ban Hin Khao, opened in 1993, the *Conservation of Wildlife Committee* on Libong Island also have a free guesthouse at Laem Juhol on the east coast, the guesthouse must be booked in advance, and food is not available, letters can be addressed to the secretary at the Libong Regional Department, PO Box 5, Kantang, Trang 92110 (T251932).

Koh Sukhorn south of Talibong C *Koh Sukhorn Resort*, T219679. 50 rooms.

Diving *Rainbow Divers*, in the *Koh Ngai Resort*, T211045, run by a German couple, they offer PADI courses and excursions around the island, open from mid-Nov until the end of Apr.

Sport

Boat Boats leave from Pakmeng, about 25 km west of Trang. Mini-buses leave from the junction of Huay Yod and Kantang roads in Trang (฿30 one way). Boats from Pakmeng to Koh Hai 45 mins (฿150 one way, ฿1,000-฿1,500 day charter), that is boats are the same price for all 3 destinations; to Koh Mook 1 hr; to Koh Kradan 1½ hrs. *Kradan Island Resort* operates a hovercraft which takes a maximum of 5 people (฿600 return).

Transport

For Koh Talibong (Libong) it is cheaper and faster to take a taxi the 24 km from Trang to Kantang (฿10-15). From there a ferry leaves daily at 1200 for Koh Talibong's 'capital' of Ban Hin Khao. From there motorcycles take visitors the 5 km to the only hotel, the *Libong Beach Resort*. *Trang Travel*, opposite the *Thumrin Hotel* in Trang, also operates a boat which can be chartered to any of the islands. For those with less time on their hands, they offer day excursions (see Tours, Trang).

The islands can be reached from several small ports and fishing villages along the Trang coast, the main ones being Pakmeng and Kantang (24 km from Trang) – both ฿10 taxi ride from Trang – Chao Mai and Palien. It is also possible to charter boats with the Muslim fishermen who live on the islands.

The Southern Region

Satun ระนอง

Colour map 5, grid B2 Surrounded by mountains, Satun is cut off from the Malaysian Peninsula and the eastern side of the Kra Isthmus. Few tourists include Satun on their itinerary. Instead they make a bee-line for Ban Pak Bara 60 km or so north of town and catch a boat to the Turatao Islands (see page 648). But perhaps Satun deserves a few more visitors.

The province seems to have spent the last century searching for an identity separate from that of its neighbours. In the early years of this century it was administered as part of Kedah in Malaysia. In 1909, following a treaty between Thailand and Britain, it came under the authority of Phuket. Fifteen years later it found itself being administered from Nakhon Si Thammarat and it was not until 1932 that it managed to carve out an independent niche for itself when it was awarded provincial status by Bangkok.

The town is very Malay in feel and around two-thirds of the population are thought to be Muslim. The town's main mosque – the **Mesjid Bombang** – is a modern affair built in 1979 on Satunthani Road. More interesting perhaps are the preserved **Chinese shophouses** on Buriwanit Road. They are thought to be around 150 years old and fortunately the town's authorities slapped a preservation order on the buildings before they could be torn down to be replaced by something more hideous. **Ku Den's Mansion** on Satunthani Road also dates from the last century. It was originally the governor's residence but has been developed into the **Satun National Museum** (opened in May 2000).

Excursions **Thale Ban National Park** lies 40 km from Satun, bordering Malaysia, and was gazetted in 1980 after four years of wrangling and threats from local so-called *ithiphon muut*, or 'dark influences'. It is a comparatively small park, covering just over 100 sq km and in 1994 was visited by 14,000 people. How it got its name is the source of some dispute. Some people believe it is derived from the Malay words *loet roe ban*, meaning sinking ground; others that it is derived from the Thai word *thale*, meaning sea. The lake that lies at the core of the park covers some 30 ha, between two mountains, Khao Chin to the east at 720 m and Khao Wangpra to the west. A hiking trail leads from the park HQ to the summit of Khao Chin where it is possible to camp. (Tents available for hire from park HQ.) There are also waterfalls and caves; the most frequently visited waterfall is Ya Roi, situated 5 km north of the park HQ and accessible by vehicles. The falls here plunge through nine levels; at the fifth is a good pool for swimming. En route to Ya Roi is a modest cave: Ton Din. The park has a large bird population: hawks, hornbills, falcons and many migratory birds. Animal residents include dusky leaf monkeys, white-handed gibbon, lesser mousedeer, wild boar and, it is said, the Sumatran rhinoceros. Forest trails lead from the HQ and it is not unusual to see hornbills, langurs, macaques, even wild pigs. The round trip takes about four hours. Best time to visit: between December and April when rainfall in this wet area (2,662 mm per year) is at its least. **Sleeping** 10 bungalows for rent around the lake, sleeping between eight and 15. There is also a Thai restaurant and an information centre at the park HQ. **Camping**: tents available for hire from park HQ. ■ *Getting there: 37 km from Satun, 90 km from Hat Yai. Take Highway 4, 406 and 4184 to the park. By public transport catch a songthaew from Samantha Prasit Rd (by the pier) to Wang Prajan. From here there are occasional songthaews the last few kilometres, or take a motorcycle taxi.*

Tours *Charan Tour* runs boat tours every day to the islands between October and May. Lunch and snorkelling equipment are provided.

B-C *Sinkiat Thani*, Buri Wanit Rd, T721055, F721059. A hotel with a modicum of style, large, well kept rooms and great views from the upper floors, Satun's No 1 hotel. Low-season discounts. **C** *Wangmai*, 43 Satunthani Rd, T711607. A/c, restaurant, a well-run place with good facilities and clean rooms, quite acceptable and well priced. **C-D** *Satunthani*, 90 Satunthani Rd, T711010. Some a/c, restaurant, OK but slow service. **E** *Rain Tong*, Samantha Prasit Rd (at the western end, by the river). Simple but clean rooms with attached bathrooms and cold-water showers.

Sleeping
Price codes:
see inside front cover

Cheap *Kualuang*, Satuntanee Phiman. Best in a group of small Thai restaurants. *Banburee*, Buriwanit Rd. 1 of 2 places with English signs. Modern establishment situated behind the *Sinkiat Thani*. Thai food. *Suhana*, Buriwanit Rd. The other English-signed place on Buriwanit Rd, behind the mosque. Muslim food. *Smile*, round the corner from the *Wangmai Hotel* on Satuntanee Phiman Rd. Fast-food, budget prices. *The Baker's*, on Satuntanee Phiman, the main street into town, pastries, ice cream and soft drinks, budget. Pretty much opposite the Sinkiat Thani are several small restaurants serving Malay food and a *roti* shop selling banana, egg and plain *roti* in the mornings.

Eating
Price categories:
see inside front cover

Foodstalls Night market with stalls serving Thai and Malay dishes on Satun Thani Soi 3. There is a plentiful supply of roadside food joints – particularly on Samantha Prasit Rd. All serve cheap rice and noodle dishes.

Cinema On Satun Thani Rd, just past the *Satun Thani Hotel*. **Discos** The most popular disco in town is at the *Wangmai Hotel*.

Entertainment

Charan Tour, 19/6 Satunthani Rd, T711453, F711982. *Satun Travel Ferry Service* (part of *Charan Tour*), Satunthani Rd, opposite *Wangmai Hotel*.

Tour operators

Local Motorbike taxis: from outside Thai Farmers Bank, near the market and from outside *Satunthani Hotel* on Satunthani Rd. **Long distance Bus**: overnight connections with Bangkok 15 hrs. Buses for Bangkok leave from Sarit Phuminaraot Rd. Regular connections with Hat Yai and Trang from opposite the wat on Buriwanit Rd. **Taxi**: Hat Yai from Bureevanith Rd, Trang from taxi rank next to Chinese temple. **Boat**: it is possible to charter a boat from Satun to Koh Turatao, but it is a lot cheaper to bus it up to Ban Pak Bara and take one of the regular boats from there (see page 651).

Transport
1,065 km to Bangkok

Boat Ferries leave from Satun and dock at one of 2 places, depending on the tide. If the tide is sufficiently high, boats arrive/leave from the jetty at the end of Samanta Prasit Rd. At low water boats dock at Tammalang Pier, south of Satun. Songthaews run to the pier from Buriwanit Rd. There are connections with Langkawi and Kuala Perlis. Daily ferries to Langkawi. Tickets can be purchased in advance from *Charan Tour*.

Transport to Malaysia

Banks *Thai Military*, Buriwanit Rd (across from Hat Yai taxi rank on Buriwanit Rd). *Thai Farmers*, opposite the market. There are now branches of all the major banks, located on either Buriwanit or Satun Thani roads. **Communications Internet**: near the Sinkiat Hotel on Satunthani Rd is an e-café *Satun Cybernet* which offers internet connections for ฿30 per hour. **Post Office**: Samantha Prasit Rd (near intersection with Satun Thani Rd). **Telephone Office**: attached to the GPO. **Useful Addresses** The new(ish) Immigration Office is at the end of Buriwanit Rd.

Directory

The Southern Region

Turatao National Park and the Adang-Rawi Archipelago

Turatao National Park
Colour map 5, grid C4

To Bu cliff, just behind the park headquarters on Ao Phante, has good views & is the spot for sunset romantics

Turatao was Thailand's first marine national park, created in 1974. It is made up of 51 islands, the main ones being Turatao, Adang, Rawi, Lipe, Klang, Dong and Lek. The park is divided into two main areas: the Turatao Archipelago and the Adang-Rawi Archipelago. This is one of Thailand's best preserved marine areas with excellent coral reefs, beaches and wildlife. Don't, though, expect luxurious living: this is for visitors who can do without mini-bars, watersports, satellite TV and air-conditioning.

The mountainous island of **Turatao** is the largest of the islands, 26 km long and 11 km wide and covering an area of 151 sq km. A mountainous spine runs north-south down the centre of the island, with its highest point reaching 708 m. The interior remains largely forested, cloaked in dense semi-evergreen rain forest. The main beaches are Ao Moh Lai, Hin Ngam, Ao Phante, Ao Chak and Ao Son, mostly on the west of the island which has long sweeps of sandy beach punctuated by headlands and areas of mangrove. Ao Son, for example, is a 3 km-long stretch of sand fringed with casuarina trees. (Much of the mangrove was cut for charcoal during the early 1960s before the national park was finally gazetted in 1974.) The prison at Ao Talo U-Dang, in the south, was established in 1936 and was once used as a concentration camp for Thailand's political prisoners; the graveyard, charcoal furnaces and a fish fermentation plant are still there. The other main camp was at Ao Talo Wao on the east side of the island and was used for high-security criminals. A road, built by inmates, connects the two camps. It is said that high-class political prisoners were segregated from the lowlier criminals, and the latter had to wait upon the former. The prisons have been partially restored as historical monuments but there are no plans to reactivate them – today the only people living on the island are the park wardens.

Turatao National Park

Koh Lamai

Koh Bulon-Leh
Koh Bulon Don
Langu

Koh Bulon Maipai
Koh Khao Yai
Ban Pak Bara

Andaman Sea

Koh Bulon Rang

Dang Cave

Tarun Cave

Satun

Marine Park Offices
Koh Bitsi

Koh Rawi

Koh Adang

Koh Turatao
Than Nak That Waterfalls

Koh Bula (Koh Hin) Ngam
Koh Butong

Koh Khai

Koh Lipe

N

Koh Lankawi (Malaysia)

0 km   10
0 miles   10

Coconut plantations still exist on Turatao but the forests have barely been touched, providing a natural habitat for lemur, wild boar, macaques and mouse deer. Crocodiles are said to inhabit Khlong Phante and there is a large cave on the Choraka (crocodile) water system known as Crocodile Cave (bring a flashlight). There are also many species of birds on the islands, including colonies of swiftlets found in the numerous limestone caves – mainly on Koh Lo Tong (to the south of Turatao) and Koh Ta Kieng (to the northeast). Large tracts of mangrove forest are found here, especially along Khlong Phante Malacca on Turatao. The islands are also known for their trilobite fossils, 400 to 500 million years old, found not just on Turatao but all over the national park.

Many of the islands' caves have been used by pirates for centuries but some are still unexplored

While the waters around Turatao are home to four species of turtle – the Pacific Ridleys, green, hawksbill and leatherback – and dugongs, whales and dolphins are also occasionally seen, the sea is clearer further west in the waters of the Adang-Rawi archipelago (see below).

Adang and **Rawi** lie 43 km west of Turatao and are the main islands in the archipelago of the same name. They offer a stark contrast to Turatao. While Turatao is composed of limestone and sandstone, the rugged hills of Adang and Rawi are granite. Adang's highest mountain rises to 703 m while Rawi's is 463 m in height. Koh Adang is almost entirely forested and there is a trail that leads up to the summit, for good views over Koh Lipe and the Andaman Sea. The main beaches on Adang are Khai, Laem Son, Ao Lo Lae Lae and Lo Lipa, and Sai Khao on Rawi.

Adang-Rawi archipelago

Koh Lipe is the flattest island in the group and has the largest settlement in the archipelago, of Chao Le fisherpeople (some 900 people), who were the original inhabitants of the islands. They have their own unique culture, language and peculiar architectural style. The Chao Le hold a traditional ceremony called *pla juk* twice a year. A miniature boat is built out of *rakam* and *teenped* wood by the villagers. Once the boat is completed, offerings are placed in it, and the Chao Le dance until dawn and then launch the boat out to sea, loaded with the village's communal bad luck. The prisoners originally incarcerated on Turatao have been moved to Koh Lipe where they now complete their sentences. It was only in 1940 that Koh Lipe officially became Thai territory – up to then it was none too clear whether the Chao Le here were putative Malaysians or Thais. Locals maintain that the Thai authorities encouraged them to plant coconut trees to show that they had settled, presumably on the basis that occupation is as good as ownership. Paths criss-cross this small island and the main beach here, unfortunately named Pattaya Beach, is miles more attractive than it more famous namesake to the east. Most accommodation in the Turatao archipelago is concentrated on Koh Lipe and, unusually for an island in a national park, the local Chao Le have been granted land onwership rights. Inevitably, though, these are being gradually taken up by powerful Bangkok-based interests. By early 2000 there were five resorts with a total of some 200 bungalows.

Koh Lipe is a stunning island, a true tropical idyll

Koh Hin Ngam is southwest of Adang and is known for its

● ● ● ● ● ● ● ● ● ● ● ● ● ● ● ● ● ● ●

Adang-Rawi place names

Koh Bulon

เกาะบุหลัน

Koh Bulon-Leh

เกาะบุหลันเล

Koh Hin Ngam

เกาะหินงาม

Koh Khai

เกาะไข่

Koh Lipe

เกาะหลีเป๊ะ

The Southern Region

strange-shaped stones found on the beaches. **Koh Khai** has white powdery sand beaches and some excellent diving.

Koh Bulon and **Koh Bulon-Leh** are less than 20 km north of Koh Turatao and about the same distance west of Ban Pak Bara. While they are part of the same archipelago as Turatao the islands are outside the boundaries of the Turatao National Park. The two islands have developed into quiet beach resorts with simple bungalow accommodation. There are a number of small fishing villages inhabited by so-called Sea Gypsies or Chao Le in the northern part of Koh Bulon-Leh. While development here is still low-key, land speculation began during the 1990s and investors are no doubt hoping that the island will develop.

Whales, dolphins & turtles are common here

Despite dynamite-fishing in some areas, the island waters still have reasonable coral, and provide some of the best **dive sites** in Thailand – particularly around the natural stone arch on Koh Khai. Adang Island has magnificent coral reefs.

Best time to visit November to April, coolest months are November and December. Park is officially closed May-October, but it is still possible to get there – services run providing the weather is OK. Bulon Leh island is accessible year round.

Tours For tours to Turatao, see Satun, page 646, *Tarutao Travel*, T781284, 781360 in La-Ngu town (on the way to Pak Bara Pier), and *Udom Tour* in Pak Bara itself (the office is round the back near the National Park's office – Khun Udom is a licensed tour guide, local to the area, and with a good knowledge of the islands, etc.) T01-8974765.

Sleeping Accommodation is restricted to Koh Turatao, Koh Adang and and Koh Lipe. On the former two islands the accommodation is Forestry Department (ie government) run; Koh Lipe is the only island where the private sector has a presence. As a result it is on Koh Lipe where resorts are best.

Turatao Book through the National Parks' office in Bangkok T02-5790529 or T074-711383 (the Pak Bara office). There is also a National Parks office at Ban Pak Bara pier. Accommodation is in the north and west of Turatao. *Tabag Bungalows*, on northern tip of Turatao, 2 rooms **B**, one room **C** - rooms accommodate 4 people. **D** *Bamboo house*. **F** per person *'Longhouse'* dormitory. **Camping** Hired tent ฿60, own tent ฿10. Best spots for camping are on Ao Jak and Ao San.

Adang Accommodation is at Laem Son. *Bamboo longhouse* with 10 rooms, each accommodating 4 people at **F** per person. There is also a simple restaurant. The island essentially closes down during the rainy season.

Lipe Five bungalow operations (**B-D**) are in enthusiastic competition. A few years ago these were mainly operated by the indigenous Chao Le, but more commercially astute outsiders are beginning to muscle in on the tourism industry. The accommodation is basic – it is best to check bungalows out before deciding where to stay. There are no telephones on the island, so advance booking is impossible.

Bulon-Leh E-F *Pansand Resort*, T7220279, or *First Andaman Travel*, in

Koh Bulon Leh

Panka Yai Bay
Panka Noi Bay
Nose Cave
Bulon Leh School
Pansand Resort ■
Bat Cave
Ao Muang
N
Not to scale

Trang, T218035, F211010. A-frame bungalow accommodation with attached bathrooms along with dormitories. Good watersports. They also organize camping, snorkelling and boat trips. There are also around 5 or 6 other, smaller bungalow operations on the island all in our **E-F** price categories.

Ban Pak Bara E-F *Andrew's* and a number of bungalow operations strung out along the beach (**E-F**). Some of these are moving a little up-market. The **D-E** *Diamond Beach* offers bungalows with sea views, and the **C** *Bara Resort* has a/c bungalows with hot water, also right on the beach. About 20-30 mins drive from Pak Bara Pier, near Langu town (free transportation is provided) is the **D** *Panyong Country Club Resort*, T781230, a grand name for quite a simple set-up – a new(ish) development with simple wooden bungalows and a restaurant in a garden overlooking Nipa palms, mangroves and some marshland. It's about 200-m walk to a beach on a shallow bay. The beach is nothing special although the views are nice, and the resort is quiet.

Camping *Charan Tours* can organize tent hire (see page 646).

Eating Guesthouses all offer food, but of the basic single-dish Thai variety with little choice. Fish is usually the best bet. **Koh Lipe** The best restaurant on the island is run by Mrs Supenit, who also has a few bungalows. Here seafood dishes are divine.

Sport **Snorkelling** Equipment for hire on Adang. Some of the best spots for coral in the park are: northwest of Koh Rang Nok, northwest of Turatao, southeast of Koh Rawi, around Koh Klang between Turatao and Adang, and off Koh Kra off Koh Lipe's east coast.

Transport Koh Turatao lies off the coast 30 km south of Ban Pak Bara; Koh Adang, Rawi and Lipe are another 40 km out into the Andaman Sea; while Koh Bulon-Leh is 20 km due west of Ban Pak Bara. Ferries leave and dock at Ban Pak Bara which is about 60 km north of Satun.

Local Boats: for hire from Turatao and Adang. ฿350 to go between the 2 islands. ฿200 to Crocodile Cave from Turatao.

Boat Ferries and boats for all the islands leave from Ban Pak Bara, 62 km north of Satun. Boats to **Koh Turatao** at 1030 and 1400 from Nov-May, 2 hrs (฿100 one way). They dock at Ao Phante Malaka on the island's west coast. The return leg from Turatao departs at 0900 and 1400. It is often too rough between May and Oct for ferries to operate, and the park is officially closed in any case. However boats can, in fact, be chartered at the discretion of their captains throughout the year (฿800 plus). Boats to **Koh Adang**, **Lipeh** and **Rawi** are less frequent. Ferries leave every Tue, Thu and Sat during the season at 1030 for these 3 islands. The ferries stop at Turatao on the way out and then continue on. Boats can also be chartered from Turatao. **Koh Bulon** is visited once a day by boat from Ban Pak Bara (฿100); the boat leaves at 1400 and takes 1½ hrs; Koh Bulon-Leh can only be reached by long-tail boat from Koh Bulon. Boats travel on from Koh Bulon to Koh Adang, Koh Turatao and Koh Lipe. Long-tailed boat charters from Ban Pak Bara to Koh Bulon cost ฿700-1000 per boat. **NB** Beware of travelling to any of these islands during bad weather; it is dangerous and a number of boats have foundered.

To get to Ban Pak Bara **Road** **Bus**: from the market in Satun, or from in front of Plaza Market, Hat Yai during the tourist season. Hat Yai is 158 km east of Ban Pak Bara. There are also regular buses from Trang (100 km north) to Ban Pak Bara. Buses from Satun, Ban Pak Bara connect with ferries. **Taxi**: to Langu (from Satun) and then a songthaew to Ban Pak Bara. There are also taxi connections with Trang. **Accommodation in Ban Pak Bara**: not really recommended except as a last resort but there are several guesthouses – mostly of the short-stay variety – strung out along the beach road. A much more salubrious alternative is the *Pak Nam*

The Southern Region

Resort, T074-781129, on Koh Kebang, a 15-min long-tailed taxi ride from Ban Pak Bara pier. The accommodation ranges from bungalows to A-frame huts, all with fan and attached bathroom. Excellent restaurant but the water here is dirty.

The East Coast: Chumphon to Phattalung

Surat Thani   เขาหลัก

Phone code: 077
Colour map 4, grid B2

Surat Thani or 'City of the Good People' is a provincial capital and the jumping-off point for Koh Samui. During the 1970s, the Communist Party of Thailand was active in the area, the guerrillas being disillusioned ethnic Tais, not Malays as further south. Although the town has an interesting river front worth a visit, its main purpose serves as a transportation hub; either to Koh Samui, Koh Phangan or Koh Tao, or south to Krabi. **Suan Sattarana Park** lies south of town, on the river. Boats can be hired for trips on the river (฿200 for up to six people). The better journey is upstream. There is a big **Chinese temple** and an attractive old viharn in the compound of **Wat Sai**, both on Thi Lek Road, near the *Seree Hotel*. The town brightens up considerably during the *Chak Phra Festival* in September or October (see below).

The **tourist office**, *TAT*, 5 Talat Mai Rd, T288818, F282828, near *Wang Tai Hotel*, southwest of the town centre, is a good source of information for less-frequented sights in the province. Areas of responsibility are Surat Thani, Chumphon and Ranong.

Chaiya

Lying 50 km north of Surat Thani on Route 41, this city was an important outpost of the Sumatran-based Srivijayan Empire and dates from the late seventh century – making it one of the most ancient settlements in Thailand. The Mahayana Buddhist empire of Srivijaya dominated Sumatra, the Malay Peninsula, and parts of Thailand and Java between the seventh and 13th centuries. It had cultural and commercial links with Dvaravati, Cambodia, north and south India and particularly Java. The syncretic art of this civilization clearly reveals these links. Chaiya today is a pleasant, clean town with many old wooden houses.

Wat Phra
Boromthat
Chaiya

Two kilometres outside Chaiya, 1 km from the Chaiya railway station, stands **Wat Phra Boromthat Chaiya**, one of the most revered temples in Thailand. Within the wat compound, the central *chedi* is strongly reminiscent of the eighth-century *candis* of Central Java, square in plan with four porches and rising in tiers topped with miniature *chedis*. The *chedi* is constructed of brick and vegetable mortar and is thought to be 1,200 years old. Even though it was extensively restored in 1901 and again in 1930, its Srivijayan origins are still evident. A small **museum** nearby exhibits relics found in the vicinity which have not been 'acquired' by the National Museum in Bangkok. ■ *Wed-Sun, 0900-1200, 1300-1600* ฿20. Another architectural link with Srivijaya can be seen at **Wat Kaeo**, which contains a recently restored sanctuary reminiscent of Cham structures of the ninth century (Hoa-lai type, South Vietnam), but again with Javanese overtones (with particular links to Candi Kalasan on the Prambanan Plain). Just outside Chaiya is the village of Poomriang, where visitors can watch silk being woven. **Sleeping** There is just one hotel in Chaiya, the (**E**) *Udornlarb*, located near the market, T431123, just 11 large, clean rooms. ■ *Getting there: trains from Surat Thani's Phun Phin station north-wards stop at Chaiya (40 mins). Regular buses from Surat Thani to Chaiya from Talat Kaset Nung (1). Regular songthaews ('taxis') from close to Talat Kaset Song (2) (฿30).*

Also known as **Wat Suan Mokkh** or, in full, **Wat Suan Mokkhabalarama**, this popular forest Wat (*wat pa*) which has become an international Buddhist retreat, lies 50 km north of Surat Thani on Route 41. The monastery was founded by one of Thailand's most revered monks, the late Buddhadasa Bhikkhu, on a peaceful plot of land covering around 50 ha of fields and forest. Since he died in 1993 the monastery has been run by monks who have continued to teach his reformist philosophy of eschewing consumerism and promoting simplicity and purity. (Buddhadasa Bhikku developed and refined the study of Buddhist economics and he follows a long tradition in Thailand of scholar-monks.) Ten-day *anapanasati* meditation courses are held here beginning on the first day of each month; pick up a leaflet from Surat Thani's TAT office or telephone Khun Supit on T02-4682857. Enrolment onto the course takes place on the last day of the month, on a first-come first-served basis and the full course costs ฿900. For those who are considering taking the course, bear in mind that students sleep on straw mats, are woken to a cacophony of animal noises at 0400, bathe in a communal pool, and are expected to help with chores around the monastery. But the course does include tasty rice and vegetable meals twice a day at 0800 and 1300. No alcohol, drugs or tobacco are permitted and the sexes tend to be segregated. If intending to visit the monastery or enrol on a course, it is worth bringing a torch and mosquito repellant (or buy these at the shop by the main entrance). ■ *Getting there: by bus from Talat Kaset Nung (1); the road passes the wat (1 hr). The town of Chaiya is closer to the monastery, so if arriving by train direct from Bangkok alight here and catch a songthaew to Wat Suon Mok.*

Wat Suan Mok
Courses for Westerners are run with the assistance of a number of foreign monks & novices

This is south of Surat Thani on Route 401, towards Nakhon Si Thammarat, 2 km off the main road. The only monkey capable of being trained to pick coconuts is the pig-tailed macaque (or *ling kung* in Thai). The male is usually trained, as the female is smaller and not so strong; strength is needed to break off the stem of the coconut. The training can start when the animals are eight months old. The course lasts three to five months, and when fully trained, the monkeys can pick as many as 800 coconuts in a day and will work for 12-15 years. "Working monkeys are very cheap – they cost no more than ฿10 a day but make millions of baht a year", Somphon Saekhow, founder of a coconut-collecting school. ■ *Getting there: take a songthaew or bus from Surat Thani heading towards Nakhon Si Thammarat, on Talat Mai Rd, which becomes Route 401. The turning to the centre is on the right-hand side, just over the Thathong Bridge, past a wat and school. The centre is 2 km down this road.* **NB** *There were rumours that the centre was due to close down; check at the TAT office before leaving.*

Monkey training centre

The Southern Region

• • • • • • • • • • • • • • • • • • • •
Surat Thani place names

Chaiya
ไชยา

Wat Kaeo
วัดแก้ว

Wat Phra Boromthat Chaiya
วัดพระบรมธาตุไชยา

Wat Suan Mok
วัดสวนโมก

For some reason, it seems that all Surat Thani's hotel owners must have sat down over a few cases of Singhas and decided to name their hotels so

Sleeping
■ *on map*
Price codes:
see inside front cover

as to confuse their guests. So, before venturing out into the night, make sure you know whether you are staying at the *Wang Tai*, the *Muang Tai*, the *Thai*, the *Thai Thani*, the *Siam Thani*, or the *Siam Thara*. The choice in our **D** category is enormous.

A *Southern Star* (formerly the *Thanawat*), 253 Chonkasem Rd, T216414, F216427. The most luxurious hotel in the centre of town. The rooms are tastefully decorated and are well equipped with satellite TV and minibar. There are 3 restaurants, one on the 16th floor which commands great views over the city. For those looking for nightlife, the *Southern Star* is also home to the largest discotheque in the south. **A** *Wang Tai*, 1 Talat Mai Rd, T283020, F283020, T02-2537947. A/c, restaurant, pool, top hotel in town (southwest of town centre).

C *Siam Thani*, 180 Surat-Phun Phin Rd, T273081, F282169. A/c, restaurant, pool, tennis. **C** *Siam Thara*, 1/144 Donnok Rd, T273740, F282169. A/c, restaurant. **C-D** *In Town Hotel*. Near the *Bandon Hotel*. The matter-of-fact name says it all: clean functional rooms, some a/c, with satellite TV and hot water. **C-D** *Lamphoo Bungalow*, Tapi River Island, T272495. Some a/c, restaurant, for a change of scene, this accommodation is a little more unusual. **C-D** *Tapi*, 100 Chonkasem Rd, T272675. Large clean rooms, some a/c, with large shower rooms. An improvement on others in this price bracket as the rooms have Thai TV, drinking water and hot water showers.

D *Thairungruang*, T286351, F286353. Some a/c, characterless hotel with dark, forbidding corridors but rooms are clean and have large windows. Attached shower rooms with western toilet. **D** *Grand City*, 428/6-10 Na Muang Rd, T272960. Very tatty hotel,

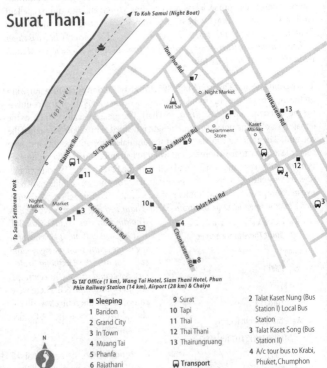

Surat Thani

To Koh Samui (Night Boat)

Tapi River

Bandon Rd
Si Chaiya Rd
Na Muang Rd
Ton Pho Rd
Mitkasem Rd
Talat Mai Rd
Chonkasem Rd
Permjit Pracha Rd

Wat Sai
Night Market
Department Store
Kaset Market
Night Market
Market

To Suan Sattarana Park

To TAT Office (1 km), Wang Tai Hotel, Siam Thani Hotel, Phun Phin Railway Station (14 km), Airport (28 km) & Chaiya

N
0 metres 200
0 yards 200

■ **Sleeping**
1 Bandon
2 Grand City
3 In Town
4 Muang Tai
5 Phanfa
6 Rajathani
7 Seree
8 Southern Star
9 Surat
10 Tapi
11 Thai
12 Thai Thani
13 Thairungruang

🚌 **Transport**
1 Buses to Songserm's Express Boat Pier
2 Talat Kaset Nung (Bus Station I) Local Bus Station
3 Talat Kaset Song (Bus Station II)
4 A/c tour bus to Krabi, Phuket, Chumphon (Office opposite)

fan cooled rooms with squat loos. Some a/c. Overpriced. **D** *Muang Tai*, 390-392 Talat Mai Rd, T272559. The large rooms could be cleaner but some are a/c and all have attached Western bathroom. **D** *Rajathani*, 293/96-99 Talat Kaset, T273584. Reasonably clean rooms, TV, some a/c, attached bathroom with squat toilet. **D** *Seree*, 2/2-5 Ton Pho Rd, T273193. The rooms are clean, but the décor is somewhat tasteless. Most have attached shower rooms with a western toilet. The cheapest is much dirtier and only has a squat toilet. Coffee shop. **D** *Thai Thani*, 442/306-8 Talat Mai Rd, T272977. Large, cleanish rooms with attached shower rooms, some a/c. **D** *Surat*, 496 Na Muang Rd, T272287. Overpriced hotel. The rooms are not particularly clean and the communal facilities are grotty. Some a/c. **D** *Bandon*, Na Muang Rd, T272167. Clean tiled rooms, some a/c, all with private shower rooms. Best value in town. **D** *Thai*, 24/4-6 Si Chaiya Rd, T272932. Large clean rooms, squat loos, management speaks no English. **E** *Phanfa*, 247/2-5 Namuang Rd, T272287. These large, cleanish rooms with attached shower rooms are the cheapest in town.

Mid-range *Suan Isaan*, near Donnok Rd, in a small *soi*. Large traditional Thai house, northeastern Thai food, menu in Thai but excellent food. Recommended. *Kampan*, Pakdee Rd, Thai. There is a good **bakery** next to the *Tapi Hotel* on Chonkasem Rd. **Cheap** *J Home*, near corner of Chonkasem and Na Muang roads. A/c café, English menus. *Malisas*, in the Night Market, for coffee, beer, ice cream.

Eating
Price categories: see inside front cover

Foodstalls On Ton Pho Rd (delicious mussel omelettes near to intersection with Na Muang Rd). Plentiful supply of fruit and *kanom* stalls along the waterfront. Market next to the local bus terminal (Talat Kaset 1). Good **Night Market** on Na Muang Rd, and on Ton Pho Rd and vicinity, road down to Si Chaiya Rd from Na Muang Rd. **Breakfast**: Good European breakfast in little café opposite the pier.

Aug *Rambutan Fair* (movable). **Oct-Nov** *Chak Phra Festival* (movable) marks the end of the 3-month Buddhist Rains Retreat and the return to earth of the Buddha. Processions of Buddha images and boat races on the Tapi River, in long boats manned by up to 50 oarsmen. Gifts are offered to monks as this is also *kathin*, celebrated across Buddhist Thailand.

Festivals

Available at the *Seree Hotel* (฿80 per hour).

Massage

Department Stores *Jula Department Store*, Vithi That Rd. *Sahathai Department Store*, Na Muang Rd. **Jewellery** At shops near corner of Chonkasem and Na Muang roads.

Shopping

Swimming Non-residents can use the pools at the *Wang Tai* or the *Siam Thani Hotel*.

Sport

Phantip, 442/24-25 Talat Mai Rd, T272230, opposite *Thai Thani Hotel*. *Songserm Travel Centre Co Ltd*, opposite night boat pier, T285124. *Samui Tour*, 326/12 Talat Mai Rd, T282352. *Samui Ferry Co*, T423026. *Ferry Phangan Co*, 10 Chonkasem Rd, T286461. Other agents organizing bus transport are to be found on Bandon, Chonkasem and Na Muang roads.

Tour operators

Local Songthaews: known as 'taxis'. Suzuki vans, bus. **Motorbike hire**: shop next to *Samui Tours* on Talat Mai Rd (฿350-750 per day).

Transport
644 km S of Bangkok

Long distance Air: the airport is 27 km south of town on Phetkasem Rd, T200605. Twice daily connections with Bangkok on Thai (1 hr).

Train: the station is at Phun Phin, 14 km west of Surat Thani (T311213) local buses go into town stopping at the Talat Kaset Nung (1) terminal. Regular connections

The Southern Region

with Hualamphong station, Bangkok (11-13 hrs). The 1830 train is the most convenient for catching a ferry to Koh Samui. Trains out of Phun Phin are often full: advance booking can be made at *Phantip* travel agency on Talat Mai Rd. *Songserm Travel Service*, Koh Samui also arrange reservations. Regular connections with Hua Hin, Trang, Yala, Hat Yai and Sungei Golok. Buses meet the train for the transfer to the various ferry terminals for Koh Samui, Phangan and Tao (see page 661). An international express leaves for Butterworth at 0155 (11 hrs) from where it continues on to Kuala Lumpur and Singapore.

Bus: the 2 stations in Surat Thani are within easy walking distance of one another – Talat Kaset Nung (1) is for local buses (for example Krabi) and Talat Kaset Song (2) for longer-distance journeys. **NB** Bus services are sometimes badly organized, with overbooked buses and combination tickets being no guarantee of follow-on services. A good supply of patience is sometimes required. Regular a/c connections with Southern bus terminal in Thonburi (Bangkok), 11 hrs; non-a/c connections with the new terminal on Phra Pinklao Rd (11 hrs). Also buses to Narathiwat (6 hrs), Trang (3 hrs), Phuket (6 hrs), Nakhon Si Thammarat (2½ hrs), Krabi (3½ hrs) and Hat Yai (5 hrs) and on to Kuala Lumpur and Singapore. Note that the border at Sungei Golok closes at 1700; not all buses (and despite protestations to the contrary) make it there before then so be prepared to spend a night in Sungei Golok. **Private tour companies** run bus services to/from Bangkok (10 hrs) (฿285-440) and Krabi 3-4 hrs (฿80) (see travel agents for listing). The advantage of taking a tour bus from here to Krabi is that they go all the way into Krabi town, to the Chao Fah Pier, rather than stopping at the bus station, out of town. Tour buses to Bangkok go from opposite the Phangan Ferry Office on Chonkasem Rd. **A/c minibus**: for some destinations there are very few buses but minibuses leave for most places regularly from the bus terminal and cost approximately 50% more than the a/c bus. **Taxi**: terminal next to bus terminal. Taxis to Trang 3 hrs (฿110), Nakhon 2 hrs (฿60), Krabi 2 hrs (฿150), Hat Yai 3½ hrs (฿150), Phuket 4 hrs (฿150), Phangnga 4 hrs (฿150).

Hovercraft: a service leaves from Tha Thong Pier, 5 km from Surat Thani at 0730 and 1030, 1½ hrs (฿350), it docks at Na Thon Pier, Koh Samui. For more details on transport to and from Koh Samui, see page 661.

Directory **Airline offices** *Thai*, 3/27-28 Karunrat Rd, T273710. **Banks** Several currency exchanges on Na Muang and Chonkasem roads. An exchange van operates from 0630-1800 across the street from the Koh Samui/Koh Phangan boat pier. **Communications** Main Post Office: near corner of Talat Mai and Chonkasem roads. **Branch Post Office**: on corner of Na Muang and Chonkasem roads (check letters are franked in your presence). **Telephone service**: for overseas calls on Don Nok Rd. **Medical services** *Bandon Hospital*, Na Muang Rd. **Useful addresses** Tourist Police: Na Muang Rd, T272095.

Koh Samui   เกาะสมุย

Phone code: 077
Colour map 4, grid B3

Koh Samui is the third largest of Thailand's islands, after Phuket and Koh Chang. Over the last decade tourism has exploded and now that it is accessible by air, the island is making the transition from a backpacker's haven to a sophisticated beach resort. Unlike Phuket, it does still cater for the budget traveller, with a great variety of bungalows scattered around its shores. The following sections have been organized by beach, beginning at Nathon (Samui's 'capital') and working clockwise around the island.

Sea, water and weather conditions on Koh Samui

March-October Light winds (averaging 5 knots), calm seas, the driest period of the year but downpours can still occur. Water visibility is good. This is the period of the southwest monsoon and though generally calm, Bophut and Mae Nam beaches can be windy, with choppy conditions offshore. Chaweng is normally calm even when Bophut and Mae Nam are rough.

October-February The northeast monsoon brings rain and stronger winds, averaging 10-15 knots but with gusts of 30 knots on some days. Sea conditions are sometimes rough and water visibility is generally poor although Koh Tao (see page 688) offers good year-round diving.

Ins and outs

Flying is the easiest and quickest option. It is relatively inexpensive and hassle free, landing you in the northeastern corner of the island after a flight from Bangkok of little more than an hour. The airport – really an airfield, with just a strip and a few airport buildings – is privately owned by Bangkok Airways. There are multiple daily connections with Bangkok and flights to U-Tapao (near Pattaya) and Phuket. There are also daily international connections with Singapore. The alternative to flying is to take a ferry. Most leave from one of Surat Thani's piers and the journey takes about 2 hrs. See page 662 for further details on the list of possibilities. Surat Thani can be reached either by bus from Bangkok or by train to Phun Phin, 14 km from Surat Thani. The alternative to travelling from Surat Thani is to catch the boat from Chumphon to Koh Tao, and from there to Koh Samui via Koh Phangan. But this is a much longer sea journey and only really makes sense if intending to stop off on Koh Tao.

Getting there
See also Transport, page 661

Koh Samui is a large island – well over 20 km both long and wide. Beaches and hotels and guesthouses can be found on just about every stretch of coastline although the two most popular and developed beaches are both on the east coast, Chaweng and Lamai. The main town of Nathon, where most of the ferries dock, is on the west side of the island. A ring road follows the coast along the north, east and south sides of the island, but runs inland cutting off the southwestern corner. Songthaews run around the island during daylight hours and can be flagged down anywhere. The destination is displayed on the front. From dusk the service becomes increasingly intermittent. There are scores of places renting out motorbikes and jeeps but note that the accident rate on Koh Samui is horrendously high (see page 661).

Getting around

There is no TAT representation on Koh Samui – the nearest **tourist office** is at 5 Talat Mai Road, Surat Thani, T288818. However, since Koh Samui is such a well-developed and popular tourist destination, stacks of information is available. Several tourist magazines are distributed free of charge: *Samui* (www.go-siam.com), *What's on Samui, Samui Guide* and *Samui Welcome* (samuiwelcom.com). Free maps include *Samui Guide Map, Green Map* and *Guide Map to Samui*. Pick them up from the Koh Samui information desk at Don Muang Airport, from Koh Samui Airport, or from hotel lobbies and shops across the island.

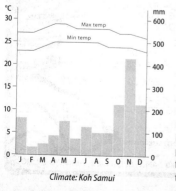

Climate: Koh Samui

The Southern Region

The Southern Region

Sights

Koh Samui is the largest in an archipelago of 80 islands, six of which are inhabited. It is 25 km long and 21 km wide. About 40,000 people live here, many of whom are fishermen-turned hoteliers. The number of annual visitors is many times this figure. The first foreign tourists began stepping ashore on Samui in the mid-1960s and early 1970s. At that time there were no hotels, no electricity (except generator-supplied), no telephones, no surfaced roads – nothing, it seems, but an over-abundance of coconuts. This is still evident because, apart from tourism, the mainstay of the economy is coconuts; two million are exported to Bangkok each month. Monkeys are taught to scale the trees and pluck down the ripe nuts; even this traditional industry has cashed in on tourism – visitors can watch the monkeys at work and also visit the coconut fibre factory, about 5 km from the Hin Lad Waterfall. (A monkey training centre has been established outside Surat Thani, see page 653.)

The island's main attractions are its wonderful beaches; most people head straight there, where they remain until they leave. However, if boredom sets in, there are motorbikes or jeeps for hire to explore inland. Two-thirds of the island is forested and hilly with some impressive (in the wet season) waterfalls – **Hin Lad Waterfall** and wat are 3 km south of Nathon and can be reached from the town on foot, or by road 1 km off Route 4169. It's a 45-minute walk from the vehicle parking area. **Na Muang Waterfall**, in the centre of the island has a 30-m drop (and a good pool for swimming). Songthaews leave for the

Koh Samui

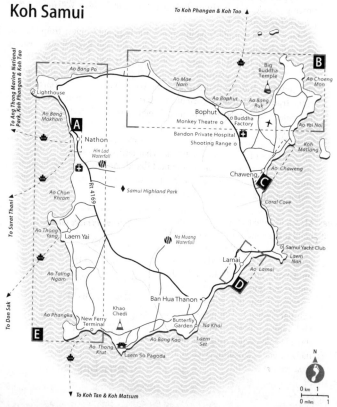

The Southern Region

waterfall from Nathon. This being the only fall on the island which is accessible by paved road makes it overpopulated at weekends and holidays. The sign to **Samui Highland Park** is just before the 3-km marker, south of Nathon. From here, it is a two-hour climb to the highest ridge, through rubber plantations (the route can be confusing, so ask directions). There are good views of the south and west coasts from the top. The **Temple of the Big Buddha** sits on an island linked to the mainland by a short causeway, near Bophut Beach. This unremarkable, rather featureless modern seated image is 12 m high. In recent years, the site has been smartened up and made into a 'proper' tourist attraction; there are now 50 or so trinket stalls at the entrance and several foodstalls. It has become a popular spot on the motorbike touring trail. There is a '**Monkey Theatre**' just south of Bophut, which holds several shows daily, displaying Thai sword fighting and Thai dancing, followed by monkey baiting. All rather unpleasant and tacky. ■ *Overpriced at ฿150, and ฿50 for children, T245140.* There is a **Cultural Hall** and small museum near Ban Lamai and a group of phallic rock formations, known as **Grandfather and Grandmother Rocks** (or, less obtusely, the **Genital Rocks**), at the south end of Lamai Beach, with the usual array of touristy shops leading up to it. The signpost marks them 'Wonderful rocks'. The **Samui Butterfly Garden** is set on the side of the hill behind *Laem Set Inn*. It features a screened butterfly garden with a limited collection of butterflies, a display of (dead) insects, moths and butterflies, a few beehives, a hillside observatory, observation platforms for views of the coast, a glass-bottomed boat for viewing a coral reef and a restaurant. **NB** Their boats emit appalling fumes and could be considered a health hazard. They are in the process of building some bungalows here too. ■ *0930-1800, ฿50 (adult), ฿20 (child). T424020-2.*

Many of Koh Samui's inhabitants are not Thai, but Chinese from Hainan who settled on the island between 150 and 200 years ago. So far as most visitors are concerned, this little nugget of history will remain hidden; the Chinese across Thailand have assimilated to such a degree that they are almost invisible. However, evidence of this immigration of Hainanese can be seen reflected in the **traditional architecture** of the island. Houses, though they may also incorporate Indian, Thai and Khmer elements, are based on Hainanese prototypes. The use of fretwork to decorate balconies and windows; the tiled, pitched roofs; the decoration of the eaves – elements such as these make the older houses of Samui distinctive in Thai terms. The sadness is that it is unlikely that many will survive the next decade or two. They are being torn down to make way for more modern structures, or renovated and extended in such a way that their origins are obscured.

Best time to visit March to June is hot and fine with a good breeze and only the occasional thunderstorm. At this time of year good discounts can be had on accommodation. June to October is also sunny and hot, with short showers. The 'worst' time of year is October to February, when the monsoon breaks and rain is more frequent. Note, though, that even during this period daily hours of sunshine average five to seven hours.

Koh Samui place names

Hin Lad Waterfall
น้ำตกหินลาด

Na Muang Waterfall
น้ำตกหน้าเมือง

Samui Highland Park
สมุยไฮแลนด์

Temple of the Big Buddha
วัดพระใหญ่

Road madness on Samui

By some measures, Thailand has the world's highest death rate on the roads. Koh Samui has the highest rate in Thailand and accidents, fatal and otherwise, are certainly horrifyingly common. There are several reasons for this state of affairs:

narrow roads
poorly maintained vehicles and machines
visitors unused to driving on the left
visitors unused to driving in Thailand
locals driving without lights
visitors driving drunk or on drugs

*It means that visitors should be especially careful when driving on the island and also make sure that they test their motorbike (particularly) or car before completing a rental agreement. It is also advised that people **do not leave their passports** as collateral. Should there be an accident, it leaves the renter of the vehicle at the mercy of its owner. For more details on driving in Thailand, see page 47.*

Essentials

There are well over 300 registered bungalows and hotels providing over 6,000 rooms (with yet more under construction); the choice is overwhelming. For nightlife, the two most popular beaches are still Lamai and Chaweng, both on the east side of the island. They also have the longest stretches of uninterrupted beach, with good swimming and watersports. Mae Nam and Bophut, on the north shore, are also becoming popular, with good watersports. For a quieter scene, there are some remote bungalows down the west shore, although it is best to hire a vehicle, as many of them are off the main road. Some of these bungalows have their own generators, so electricity may only be available in the evenings. The advantage of staying on this side of the island is to see the spectacular sunsets. The list of places to stay is not comprehensive; bungalows survive on reputation and it is often best to stay somewhere which has been personally recommended. **NB** Accommodation prices tend to soar during the peak months. Bargain during the off-season; a reduction of up to 50% is possible.

Sleeping

See each beach for details. **NB** Jet skis/propellor skis are a cause of loss of life and limb annually. Extreme caution is advised.

Sport

The easiest way to get to Koh Samui is by air. The overland journey can be rather arduous, with an overnight bus (or train) to Surat Thani, another bus to the ferry and then the crossing to the island, but is considerably cheaper. It is possible to buy 'combination' bus/ferry tickets from any travel agent in Khaosan Rd (Bangkok), prices vary so it's worth shopping around, they should cost about ฿260.

Transport
See also Ins & outs, page 657
84 km NE of Surat Thani

Local Hitching: is quite easy. **Motorbike and jeep hire**: cheaper from the town of Nathon than on the beaches. Jeep hire is ฿600-900 per day without insurance (see box, page 661 for cautions). **Motorbike taxis**: available from the port. **Songthaews**: the most common form of transport, songthaews visit all the island's beaches during daylight hours. Their final destination is usually written on the front of the vehicle and they stop anywhere (prices start at ฿20 per person). From Nathon, songthaews travel in a clockwise direction to Chaweng and anti-clockwise to Lamai. After 2100, songthaews are thin on the ground and expensive.

Long distance Air: the airport is in the northeast of the island. This is a private airport, and Bangkok Airways is a private airline, which accounts for the grossly inflated airport departure tax (₿500 from Koh Samui, only ₿30 from Bangkok). *Airport facilities*: hotel reservation (**NB** this is owned by Bangkok Airways and attempts are made to divert clients to *Samui Palm Beach* – owned by the airline), reconfirmation of flights, restaurant. *Hertz* car rental, money changer. **Transport to town or beach**: a/c minibus to Bo Phut, Mae Nam, Chaweng, Choeng Mon, Lamai and Big Buddha. Again prices are enormously inflated, but Bangkok Airways have a monopoly. The alternative is to walk out onto the road, but it is a 1 km walk and tricky with luggage. Multiple daily connections with Bangkok, 1 hr 10 mins. Bangkok Airways also fly to Phuket twice a day, 50 mins, and to U-Tapao (Pattaya) and Krabi, once a day. T02-2534014 (Bangkok) and T272610 (Koh Samui) for reservations. Thai flies to Surat Thani, 1 hr, with a connecting limousine and boat service (see Surat Thani entry).

Train: from Bangkok's Hualamphong station to Phun Phin, outside Surat Thani, 10-12 hrs. The State Railway runs a rail/bus/ferry service from Bangkok to Koh Samui 18 hrs. This needs to be booked 2-3 days in advance. Note that it is not necessary to buy a combination ticket; buses from all the ferry companies meet trains to transfer passengers to the various ferry terminals.

Bus: to Surat Thani, from Bangkok's Southern bus terminal, a/c buses leave between 2000 and 2200, 12 hrs. See page 656 for further details.

Boat The listings below may seem confusing, but because of the number of tourists visiting Koh Samui, the transport system is well organized and it is difficult to go wrong. Options are:

1. *Songserm Travel* run 3 **express passenger boats** daily during the peak season (Nov-May), leaving Surat Thani 0730, 1200 and 1400, and leaving Koh Samui at 0730, 1230 and 1500, 2 hrs. These boats usually dock at Tha Thong Pier, 6 km east of Surat Thani and at Nathon Pier, on Koh Samui. To reach Tha Thong Pier, take a bus from Ban Don Rd, on the riverfront in Surat Thani. On leaving Koh Samui, a/c buses meet the 0730 express boat for transfers to Phuket, Krabi, Hat Yai and Penang. T02-2529654 (Bangkok) for more information. **NB** *Songserm* tend to overload their boats and not provide sufficient lifejackets.

2. **The slow overnight boat** leaves from the pier in Surat Thani (otherwise known as Ban Don) at 2300, 6-7 hrs and docks at the pier in Nathon.

3. **The vehicle and passenger ferry** (known as the 'Express ferry') leaves from Don Sak, 60 km from Surat Thani. Travellers arriving by train at Phun Phin will be transferred to Don Sak. Buses from Surat Thani to Don Sak leave 1½ hrs before ferry departs either from *Samui Tour*, Talat Mai Rd or from *Phuntip Tour*, Talat Kaset I. The ferry docks at Tong Yang, south of Nathon. 8 ferries leave Samui and Surat Thani daily, more on public holidays and peak periods, 1½ hrs. T282352 in Surat Thani for more information. Songthaews run from Tong Yang to Nathon and the beaches. There is also a *Songserm* car ferry from the mainland port of Khanom which docks in downtown Nathon at the new dock there. If you are coming from Surat Thani, the only advantage this port has over Don Sak is the fact that they will take bookings for cars – a great advantage during peak periods.

Hovercraft: a service leaves from Tha Thong Pier, 5 km from Surat Thani at 0730 and 1030, 1½ hrs (₿350); it docks at Na Thon Pier, Koh Samui.

Directory **Communications** Internet There are internet cafés in all the beach resort areas. **Telephone**: Calls are much cheaper if made at the post office. High street 'booths' are 3-4 times more expensive. International calls can also be made from many hotels and travel agents. **Medical services** Koh Samui has three hospitals. The Samui International Hospital in Chaweng, Bandon International Hospital in Bo Phut and a government-run hospital in Nathon. All three offer a 24-hr emergency clinic and the Samui International Hospital also has a dental clinic. Note that if someone is involved in a serious accident it is best to transport the injured person to the hospital; the ambulance service can be very slow. A reasonable level of English is spoken. **Useful addresses** Tourist Police: T421281 or T1699 for emergency.

Nathon   หน้าทอน

Nathon is Koh Samui's capital, where the ferry docks. It is a town geared to tourists, with travel agents, exchange booths, clothes stalls, bars, and restaurants supplying travellers' food. Nathon consists of three roads running parallel to the seafront, with two main roads at either end linking them together.

Phone code: 077
Colour map 4, grid B3

Ang Thong (or 'Golden Basin') **Marine National Park** is made up of 40 islands lying northwest of Koh Samui, featuring limestone massifs, tropical rainforests and beaches. Particular features are **Mae Koh** (a beautiful beach) and **Thale Nai** (an emerald saltwater lake), both on **Koh Mae Koh** and **Koh Sam Sao**, which has a coral reef and a huge rock arch as well as a hill providing good views of the surrounding islands. The area is the major spawning ground of the short-bodied mackerel, a popular eating fish in Thailand. There is also good snorkelling (the main attraction), swimming and walking. The park's headquarters are on Koh Wua Talap. It is best to visit between late March and October, when visibility is at its best. **Sleeping** Available on Koh Wua Talap (T286025 or T02-5790529), five guesthouses sleep 10-20 people each, ฿600-1,000 per guesthouse, tents available for rent (฿50). ■ *Getting there: daily tour from Nathon pier, leaving at about 0800 (฿240). It is possible to leave the tour, stay on Koh Wua Talap and rejoin it several days later at no extra charge (make sure you tell the ferry driver which day you want to be picked up). The boat returns to Nathon at about 1700.*

Excursions

   Koh Phangan Passenger boats travel from Bophut Pier (north of the island) to Koh Phangan, leaving at about 0930, 40 minutes (see page 679).

Day trips to **Ang Thong Marine National Park** for snorkelling, fishing and diving leave Nathon at 0830 and return at 1700 (฿300). There are also day tours around the island (฿380, including lunch). Book with *Samui Holiday Tour*, 112/2 Chonvithi Road, T421043 or at *Highway Travel Booking*, 11/11 Taweraj Pakdi Road, T421285 (opposite the pier). *Songserm* organize day tours to Koh Phangan, two to three boats each day, 30 minutes (฿60).

Tours

Few people stay in Nathon, for obvious reasons. **C-D** *Palace*, seafront road, T421079, F421080. A/c, clean, adequate and well-maintained rooms, hot water.

Sleeping

There are plenty of places to eat here, particularly good are the 'coffee shop' patisseries – there are a couple off the main road and some on the seafront.
   Thai Mid-range: *Koh Kaeo*, on seafront, best Thai food in Nathon. Good noodle and rice restaurant almost opposite the pier.
   International Mid-range: *Fountain*, Angthong Rd. Italian proprietor (and food). Recommended. *Sunset House*, south end of town overlooking the sea, good Thai and international food. *Tang's*, near market at south end of main road, pizza, pasta, sandwiches and pastries. **Cheap**: *New York Deli and Grill*, near market at southern end of main road, pizza, seafood, pasta, breakfast, rather dirty. *RT Bakery*, corner of main road and Watana Rd. Excellent breakfasts, rolls and croissants. *Bird in the Hand*, north end

Eating
● *on map*
Price categories:
see inside front cover

The Southern Region

of town, on east/west road remains popular. *El Pirata*, near *Bird in the Hand*, Spanish. *Golden Lion*, opposite *El Pirata*, European/seafood.

Seafood   On seafront road.

Bars   *Eden*, main road. Open 1600-0300. There are a number of other bars near the *Bird in the Hand* restaurant, at north end of town.

Massage   Thai traditional massage at north end of seafront road.

Shopping   Nathon remains the centre for shopping on the island. It is worth a visit to browse through the stalls and take a walk down the main road, past the fresh market on the left and on down to the 'hardware' market on the right. The stalls provide the usual array of T-shirts, tapes, watches, handicrafts, etc. As usual, remember to bargain hard. The inner road – Angthong Rd – is worth walking down too.

Book Exchange   On northern east/west road.

Handicrafts   Several shops on the main east/west road to the south of town selling puppets, etc.

Shoemaker   On the main east/west road to the south of town.

Silk and jewellery shop   On the seafront road.

Supermarket   *Giant*, sells English, German and French newspapers as well as good range of European food.

Tattoo artist   On southeast/west road.

T-shirt shop   *Samui Seven Seas*, 2 shops on Angthong Rd, for the best designs on the island.

Sport   **Scuba diving**   There are a number of different dive schools on the island. *Swiss Dive Centre* (41 Na-Amphur Rd), *Matlang Divers* (67 Watana Rd), *Koh Samui Divers* (64 Nathon Pier) and *Pro Divers* all have shops in town, as well as having small offices on the various beaches. Most of the schools have English-speaking instructors. A 5-day PADI course should cost about ฿7,000-8,000. A 1-day trip for those with certification, including 2 dives and food, costs about ฿1,200-1,800, depending on the dive destination. A trip to one of the islands, 2 nights/3 days, for about 6 dives, will cost around ฿4,000. The best time for diving is Apr and the best water is to be found around Koh Tao, Tan, Matsum and the Marine Park. Visibility is obviously variable, depending on the weather. Most of the schools also organize advanced open-water courses, rescue and first aid.

Shooting range   Route 4169 just south of Monkey Theatre, near the airport, open 0900-1800, T425370. **Thai boxing**   At north end of town.

Related map
Koh Samui, page 659

Nathon   To Chaweng & Airport

Dumrong Town Hall

Book Exchange

Express Boats to Koh Phangan

Express & Night Boats to Surat Thani

Restaurants

Angthong Rd

Gulf of Thailand

Stalls

Stalls

T-shirt Stalls

Palace

Dive Samui

Fresh Market

Bangkok Airways

Handicrafts

Hardware Market

N

0 metres   100
0 yards   100

● **Eating**
1 Bird in the Hand   4 Sunset House
2 Fountain   5 Tang's Bakery
3 RT Bakery

There are many travel agents cluttered along the seafront (particularly around the pier) and main roads, providing air/train/bus bookings and reconfirmation of flights. For example, *Songserm*, 64/1-2 Nathon Pier, Chonvithi Rd, T420163 seems efficient; they organize joint train and express boat tickets from Bangkok, via Surat Thani and on to Koh Phangan.

Tour operators

Local For details on local transport, see page 661. Motorbikes and jeeps can be hired in Nathon and songthaews travel from here to all the beaches – destinations written on the front of each vehicle. **Boat charter**: for visiting some of the islands in the Marine National Park, T425360 and ask for Khun Lek.

Transport

Airline offices *Bangkok Airways*, 72/1 Chonvithi Rd, T420133, F421297, or at the airport, T425012, F425010. **Banks** Exchange booths along the seafront and main roads. Open Mon-Sun, 0830-1700 or 1800. **Communications** Post Office: to the north of the pier, international telephone and poste restante service. **Medical services** Clinic and dentist: on main road in town. Hospitals: in the event of an accident *Bandon International Hospital* is the best hospital on the island. It is located near the airport, almost opposite the Shooting Range, T425382/245236, F425342, 24-hr emergency service. The government hospital outside Nathon is not well equipped to handle foreign tourists. *Doctor Pongsak* is probably the best doctor on the island (outside the hospitals), he is to be found at the *Lamai Clinic*, T424219, F424218, near the Boxing Stadium. His English is fluent. **Places of worship** Catholic Church: 0830 and 1830. **Useful addresses** British Consular representative at *Laem Set Inn*, T424393. **Immigration office**: on main road next to the police station. A 2-month tourist visa can be extended here by 30 days for ฿550. **Tourist police**: 3 km south of town T421245, just past turning to Hin Lad Waterfall.

Directory

Sleeping **C-D** *Sunbeam*, only bungalow here, quiet location, clean, friendly, private beach, some private bathrooms. Recommended.

Bang Bo

Mae Nam   แม่น้ำ

A quiet, clean beach, good for swimming and a good atmosphere. There is a post office, currency exchange and health centre here, as well as a bookshop for rental or exchange of books. Motorbike hire is available on the beach.

L *Santiburi*, 12/12 Moo 1 Tambon Mae Nam, T425031, F425040, santiburi @dusit.com (part of the Dusit group of hotels). A/c, restaurant, pool, superb new resort of beautifully furnished Thai-style villas and suites, watersports, sauna, tennis and squash courts, situated on a quiet stretch of beach so there's also some degree of privacy. **AL** *Seafan*, T/F421350. A/c, pool, restaurant, overpriced but lovely wooden bungalows on stilts, whirlpool, attractive gardens, watersports facilities. **A** *Chaiya Rai*, T425290, F425290. A/c, restaurant, pool, price includes breakfast, excellent service, large, clean and well-maintained bungalows. Recommended.

Sleeping
■ *on map, page 666*
*Price codes:
see inside front cover*

D *Co-Co Palm*, quiet, nice garden. Recommended. **D** *Naplarn*, off beach, big, clean rooms, own bathroom. Recommended. **D** *Palm Point Village*, T425095. 15 mins walk from Mae Nam village, this place has bungalows on the beach (quiet and peaceful here), the more expensive with attached showers (cold water) and balcony, good food, motorbikes for hire. Recommended. **D** *Rainbow*, bungalows close together, some private bathrooms. **D-F** *Koseng II*, T425252 and T427106. Friendly and popular in ideal quiet location, excellent food, bungalows ranging from very basic to much more comfortable to suit all budgets. **E** *OK Village*, T427189, off the beach, restaurant, own bathroom. Recommended. **E** *Shady Shack*, T425392, restaurant, recently refurbished, clean, some private bathrooms, very friendly people, good value.

Chez Tom for French and Thai food. *Golden Dream*, east end of Mae Nam, for pizzas, pasta and Thai food in a traditional raised Thai house.

Eating

The Southern Region

Bophut บ่อผุด

Colour map 4, grid B3 Bophut is one of the few places on the island where there are still traditional wooden Samui houses with Chinese lettering above the doors side-by-side with modern tourist accommodation. Unsurprisingly, it has grown increasingly popular in the last few years and there are now currency exchanges, bookshops, restaurants and good watersports facilities, yet none of these has really spoilt the ambience. The beach itself is rather straight and lacks the sweeping expanse of Chaweng, or the quiet intimacy of Laem Set, yet the place maintains a friendly village atmosphere. A daily passenger boat leaves here for Koh Phangan (Hat Rin West), at 1030 and 1530, 50 minutes (฿30), see page 679. There are no clubs in Bophut so the nightlife is less noisy (or less fun, depending on your viewpoint), than Chaweng or Lamai but the restaurant scene is popular and vibrant. For those in need of the club scene, there is a nightly taxi service from the various hotels into Chaweng and Lamai, leaving Bophut at 2000 and returning 0300-0400 (฿50).

Excursions *Bophut Guesthouse* offers fishing, snorkelling and sightseeing charters.

Sleeping
■ *on map*
Price codes:
see inside front cover

AL *Euphoria*, 101/3 Bophut Bay, T425100, F425107, euphoria@loxinfo.co.th A/c, restaurant, pool. A rather impersonal hotel with 124 rooms in an unattractive 3-storey block. The facilities, however, are comprehensive and include tennis and squash courts, a pool, a putting green and a variety of watersports. **A** *Samui Palm Beach*, 175/3 Thaveerat-Pakdee Rd, T425494 F425358, spbresot@samart.co.th Well-designed a/c bungalows facing the sea and some cheaper accommodation with no sea view. There is a good pool and an international and Thai restaurant. **A-B** *World*, T/F425355/427202, world@sawadee.com Fan and a/c bungalows. The a/c accommodation is particularly appealing, as the rooms are spacious and wood panelled. There is a large pool and a beach restaurant that serves Thai and Western food.

B *The Lodge*, 91/1 Moo 1, Bophut, T425337, F425336. This small, appealing hotel has a number of well-decorated a/c rooms, all of which have satellite TV, a minibar, and en suite bathroom. While there is no restaurant, there is a bar that serves basic Western food. **B** *Nara Garden* T425364, F425292. A/c, restaurant, small pool. This well-run resort provides a U-shaped group of attractive rooms with decking walkways, good discounts available, simple but clean and professionally run. **B** *Peace*, T425357, F425343. Offers basic fan bungalows, with attached shower-room, to very nicely

North coast

To Koh Phangan & Koh Tao

Ao Choeng Mon

Ao Mae Nam

Big Buddha

Ao Bang Ruk

Ao Bophut

Bophut

Buddha Factory

Ao Yai Noi

Monkey Theatre

To Airport

Related maps
Koh Samui, page 659
Nathon, page 664
Chaweng Beach,
page 671
Lamai Beach, page 674
West Coast,
page 678

0 km 1
0 miles 1

■ **Sleeping**
1 Boat house
2 Chaiya Rai
3 Koseng II

4 Mae Nam Resort
5 Naplarn
6 OK Village
7 Palm Point Village

8 Samui Palm Beach
9 Sandy Resort
10 Santiburi
11 Seafan

12 Shady Sha
13 White Hou
14 World

decorated a/c bungalows. The fan rooms are overpriced. There is a beachside restaurant that serves Thai, international and seafood. **B-C** *Smile*, T425361, F425239. There is a choice of either a/c, or fan bungalows. Both are kept quite clean, but they are small and crammed far too close together. Large pool on the roadside, so a little public. The fan accommodation is good value. Beachside restaurant (see Eating, below). **B-D** *New Boon*, T421362. Some a/c, new but already scruffy, no hot water. **B-D** *Ziggy Stardust*, T/F245354. These clean fan and a/c Thai-style bungalows are excellently laid out in a mature tropical garden. The staff are helpful and friendly and there is a good beachside restaurant (see Eating, below). Recommended. **C** *Sandy Resort*, 177/1 Bophut Beach. T425353, F425325, sandy@sawadee.com Accommodation ranges from fan-cooled bungalows to a/c rooms in a somewhat ugly 2-storey building. There are 2 restaurants, one of which is on the beach.

D *Salathai*, quiet and clean with fan rooms. Expensive restaurant (but good food). **D-F** *Calm Beach Resort*, T425357, run down but quiet, no mosquito nets for cheapest bungalows. **E-F** *Oasis*, near pier for boats to Hat Rin (Koh Phangan), rooms in private house. **F** *Boon*, tiny wooden huts with Samui-style detailing. Shared washing facilities. Run by the shop on the opposite side of the road.

Eating
Price categories: see inside front cover

Unlike Chaweng and Lamai, Bophut is small enough to cater for the demand for seafood without having to import produce from elsewhere. There are, therefore, a number of restaurants that set up elaborate seafood displays. Inevitably, the choice on offer varies from day to day.

Expensive *La Sirene*, a delightful little restaurant that is run by a friendly Frenchman. The seafood is fresh and locally caught, and the coffee is excellent. French and Thai food offered. Recommended. **Mid-range** *Bird in the Hand*, Thai and Western food in an attractive building that has good views across the bay. *Smile*, offers a wide variety of seafood. *Ziggy Stardust*, in one of the best positions on the beach with great views over to Big Buddha Beach. Thai and seafood.

Bars & clubs

Paris London Bar. A stylish bar that invites people to view the beautiful sunset with a cocktail. *Rasta Baby*. The loudest place on Bophut is towards the western end of the beach and out of earshot of most places.

Shopping

There are a number of shops along the main road of Bophut. There is a good bookshop, selling books in German, English and French, and a few shops selling gifts, clothes and produce from around Thailand, Laos and Cambodia.

Sport

Fishing Organized by *Bophut Guesthouse*. **Snorkelling** Organized by *Bophut Guesthouse*. **Watersports** Windsurfing and waterskiing (฿150), sailing (฿300) and jet skis (฿350-800). High speed 30-ft boat available from Bophut Pier.

Transport

Local As with most of the more remote beaches on Samui, the songthaews that are allotted for the beach run rather infrequently. It is possible to charter them, and there are always motorcycle taxis around.

Directory

Banks There are no major banks in Bophut, but there are several bank booths and tour agencies that change money.

Big Buddha or Bang Ruk พระใหญ่หรือบางรัก

A small bay which has become increasingly popular, despite being near the road. Accommodation is rather cramped and it also tends to be rather noisy, as the bungalows are squashed between the beach and the road. However, the beach is quiet and palm-fringed and the water is good between May and September, but gets choppy during October to February when it is unsuitable for swimming. See page 660 for details on the Big Buddha.

Sleeping
■ *on map, page 666*
Price codes:
see inside front cover

A-B *Farn Bay Resort*, T273920, F286276. Some a/c, restaurant, small pool, videos, breakfast included, hot water, tiled-roof bungalows on a small casuarina and palm tree plot, rather too close together, but well-run establishment, may be overpriced. **A-B** *Nara Lodge*, T421364, B2482094. A/c, restaurant, pool, tennis court, videos, some hot water, motel-style accommodation, US manager, popular with families. **C** *Ocean View*, T425439, ovsamui@yahoo.com Some a/c, concrete and wooden bungalows, some rather small. **C-D** *Beach House*, T245124, F245123. Some a/c and hot water, small restaurant, small operation on the beach, quite quaint but overpriced. **C-D** *Big Buddha Bungalows*, T425282. Some a/c, restaurant, large, comfortable rooms, good value, popular. **C-D** *Phongphetch Servotel*, T245100, F425148, this needs to be mentioned as an example of appallingly misplaced architectural design – it's a horror and should never have passed the regulators. **D** *Champ Bungalows*, some a/c, friendly, diving school. **D-E** *LA Resort*, some a/c, friendly staff, excellent food, clean, comfortable, good-value bungalows, very popular bar by the beach. Recommended. **E** *Kinaree*, small huts rather close together and very unfriendly, but good food. **E** *Sunset Song*, T421363, average rooms, private bathroom.

Eating *Crowded House*, good food, pool table, video and bar.

Sport **Diving** *Swiss Dive Resort*. **Sailing, fishing and snorkelling** Organized by *Asian Yacht Charter*.

Choeng Mon   เชิงมน

At the northeasternmost part of the island, this is arguably the prettiest bay on Samui. The crescent of extremely fine white sand has an island at the most eastern end, attached to the mainland by a sandbar, traversible at low tide. While in places it is rocky underfoot in the centre of the bay, the sand continues well out to sea. The beach does not have any nightlife to speak of; everything grinds to a halt well before midnight. Prior to this, however, the restaurant scene is pretty lively, particularly in the centre of the beach where bamboo tables with oil lamps reach right down to the bonfires near the water's edge. Occasionally fire jugglers are hired to provide entertainment. The beach is most popular with couples and families.

Sleeping
■ *on map, page 666*
Price codes:
see inside front cover

L *Tongsai Bay*, western end, T425041, F425460, T02-2619000, www.tongsaibay.co.th A/c, restaurant, pool. Attractive bungalows scattered across a hillside coconut plantation, and overlooking their own private bay. Watersports, tennis courts and gym. The best bungalows are the newer ones which are very appealing and well designed. The rooms in the older block near the swimming pool are rather public and less attractive. The hotel's USP is its open-air bathtubs. Food in the main restaurant is excellent, particularly the buffet breakfast which is stupendous. There are two further restaurants, one a beachside bar and café and a rather more sophisticated place for dinner (disappointing on our last visit). Overall an excellent place with friendly and professional management and staff. Recommended. **L** *The White House*, centre of the beach, 59/3 Moo 5, T245315, F245318, www.whitehouse.kohsamui.net Set in a delightful shady tropical garden, this is a small collection of large white houses with Thai-style architectural detailing. There's a small museum which residents may view on request in a traditional Ayutthayan wooden house which is over 70 years old.

The hotel also has the standard pool, jacuzzi and restaurants. Overall, a highly refined place. Recommended.

AL *Boat House* (Imperial Group), eastern end, T425041, F425460, T02-2619000, www.imperialhotels.com A/c, restaurant, pool, 34 converted teak rice barges make for unusual suites, 182 other rooms in 3-storey ranch-style-comes-to-Thailand blocks, with limited views, watersports available, boat-shaped pool adds to the theme-park feel of the place. **B-D** *Island View*, eastern end, 24/9 Moo 5, T245031, F425081. Some a/c in concrete bungalows, cheaper rooms are made of wood and have small verandah areas and squat loos. **B-E** *O Soleil*, T425232. Some a/c rooms with hot water. Even the cheapest rooms here are solidly built and bamboo lined with mosi-screens on the windows and attached (and clean) private shower rooms. Single rooms are available even more cheaply for solo travellers. Good restaurant. Recommended.

C *Chat Kaeo*, centre of the beach, some a/c. White concrete villas with roof terraces set back from the sea. Fan cooled huts are wooden and situated towards the seafront. Unfriendly staff and slightly overpriced. **C** *PS Villas*, towards the western end, T425160. Large wooden constructions with uninspired décor. A double and single bed in every room. Some a/c. **C-D** *Sun Sand*, just beyond the headland at the eastern end T425404, F421322. A/c, restaurant. The first bungalows on Choeng Mon, these well-spaced bungalows are spacious with solid wood floors, bamboo-lined walls and ceilings, and large windows on all sides facing the sea. On the hill overlooking the bay the bungalows are linked by winding wooden slatted walkways (it's a steep descent to the beach). The position at the end of the beach and the distance between the rooms also mean that it has more privacy than most.

Choeng Mon is blessed with a number of excellent eateries. This is a selection of the best.

Eating
Price categories:
see inside front cover

Mid-range *Bong Go*, centre of the beach. Especially good as a night-time venue, as it is the best value of the restaurants in the centre of the beach. It also serves reasonably priced breakfasts. Recommended. *Honey Seafood Restaurant and Bar*, at the most easterly tip of the beach. Great seafood. Recommended. *Jeanys Kitchen*, eastern end. Very small, with only 2 tables but decorated in a homely manner and rather appealing. *Otto's Pub and Restaurant*, centre of the beach. Thai food and a Thai interpretation of pizza and pasta dishes. Also offers a range of alcoholic beverages. *Phayorm Park Restaurant* and *Shadows Restaurant and Bar*, centre of the beach. A range of Thai and Western dishes. **Cheap** *O Soleil*, towards the western end. Offers the best value for money, particularly good is the curry fried rice. Recommended.

Local Car hire: *Avis*, *Imperial Tongsai*, T425015. **Songthaew**: Choeng Mon is off the main Samui road and songthaews officially designated to serve this beach may come only once an hour. There is a songthaew station at the far eastern side of the town, behind the beach.

Transport

Chaweng   อ่าวเฉวง

This is the biggest beach on the island, split into three areas – north, central and Chaweng Noi. **Chaweng Noi** is to the south, round a headland and has three of the most expensive hotels on the island. **Central Chaweng** is a vast sweep of sand with lovely water for swimming and a proliferation of bungalows, restaurants and bars. The town that has grown up here is entirely geared towards tourists and in recent years it has become swamped. Along the incredibly uneven track, there are dozens of Pattaya-like bars, discos, clubs, tourist agencies, and watersports facilities and for those trying to find a secluded spot,

The Southern Region

this area is best avoided. In comparison to the other beaches on the island it is very crowded.

Chaweng contains a rather jarring combination of international hotels and basic bungalows. This gives it an unusual feel, and enables visitors staying in US$150-a-night hotels to cross the road and have a full American breakfast for under US$2. Compared with Lamai, Chaweng is slightly more up-market and a little cleaner.

NB Many of the hotels, particularly those in the centre of the beach, are affected by the noise pollution coming from the discotheques, often until as late as five or six in the morning

Sleeping
■ *on map, page 671*
Price codes:
see inside front cover

L *Central Samui Beach Resort*, T230500, F422385, www.centralgroup.com An elegant, if expensive, low-rise Greek temple comes to the Orient-style block resort with good facilities. The accommodation is wood panelled and set in a palm grove. Large pool, health centre and a very good restaurant. **L** *Poppies*, T422419, F422420. A/c, restaurant, pool, following their success on Bali, *Poppies* have built on this tiny plot. Beautifully designed to maximize space, these Thai-style houses have open-air bathrooms (familiar to anyone who has visited Ubud, in Bali), and set in a tropical garden with water running through it. An excellent and very popular open-air restaurant (see **Eating**), but small pool. Though very refined, it is overpriced for the facilities on offer.

AL *Amari Palm Reef* (north end), T422015, F422394, reservations@ palmreef.amari.com This hotel is built on two sides of the main road through Chaweng. The original part of the hotel is on the seaward side of the road. Rooms here are in blocks, in a garden compound. There is also a rather public swimming pool, right next to the beach. All slightly cramped. On the other side of the road are the newer Thai-style bungalows and duplexes. There is a quieter, more secluded pool here. Restaurant is average. Facilities include a tennis court, dive centre and massage. **AL** *Baan Samui Resort*, 14/7 Moo 2, T230965, F422412, bansamui @loxinfo.co.th A rather awkward resort with an ugly 3-storey building at the front. The accommodation is clean and the facilities include a good pool and restaurant, but the Spanish stucco and tiling make it feel slightly out of place. There is no sense of Thai-ness and its overpriced. **AL** *Beachcomber*, 3/5 Moo 2, T422041, F422388, www.kohsamuinet/ beachcomber A popular luxury resort, often frequented by tour groups. 60 rooms in a 3-storey block, children's pool and jacuzzi; this could be on a tropical beach resort anywhere in the world. **AL** *Blue Lagoon* northern end, T422037, F422401, www.kohsamuinet/ blue-lagoon A/c, international restaurant, large and attractive pool, well-designed accommodation with 60 rooms in 2-storey Thai-style blocks. Recommended. **AL** *Chaweng Regent*, 155/4 Chaweng Beach, T422389, F422222, admin@chawengregent.com, www.chawengregent.com A/c, good restaurant (seafood speciality, Thai and European), large pool, 137 wooden Thai-style cottages linked by decking, rather close together, attractive but overpriced and rather big and impersonal, no shade by the pool. **AL** *Imperial* southern end, T422020, F422396. A/c, restaurant, saltwater and freshwater pools. The first 5-star hotel on the island, rooms are in a large 5-storey Tuscan style block. **AL** *Chaweng Buri Resort*, 14/6 Moo 2, T230349, F422466, info @chawengburi.com, www.chawengburi.com Reasonably attractive a/c bungalows set in a garden. There is a restaurant and a pool, but the place is rather anonymous. **AL-A** *The Fair House (The President Samui)*, 4/3 Moo 3, T422255, F422373, fairhouse@sawadee.com Some a/c, restaurant, pool. Down a lengthy track from the road. A variety of rooms in attractive garden setting. The more expensive rooms are light and airy, while the bungalows have privacy as they do not fall into the common trap of being packed together. The cheaper rooms, however, are a little tatty. Its main advantage is that it's right on the beach. **AL-C** *Samui Resotel* (previously *Munchies*), T422374, F422421, resotel@sawadee.com A wide range of

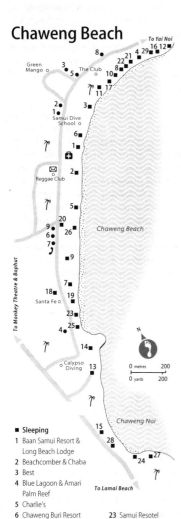

Chaweng Beach

To Yai Noi

Green Mango

The Club

Samui Dive School

Reggae Club

Chaweng Beach

To Monkey Theatre & Bophut

Santa Fe

Calypso Diving

Chaweng Noi

To Lamai Beach

N

0 metres 200
0 yards 200

■ Sleeping

1 Baan Samui Resort & Long Beach Lodge
2 Beachcomber & Chaba
3 Best
4 Blue Lagoon & Amari Palm Reef
5 Charlie's
6 Chaweng Buri Resort
7 Chaweng Cabana
8 Chaweng Regent & The Island
9 Chaweng Resort
10 Chaweng Villa
11 Coconut Grove
12 Coral Bay Resort
13 Fair House
14 First
15 Imperial
16 Matlang Resort & Matlang Divers
17 Montien House
18 Parrot
19 Poppies & Joy
20 Princess Village & Village
21 Samui Cabana
22 Samui Natien

23 Samui Resotel
24 Samui Yacht Club
25 Sans Souci Samui
26 Tradewinds
27 Tropicana Beach
28 Victorian
29 Villa Flora

● Eating

1 Café Thai
2 Chez Andy
3 Crystal
4 Eden Seafood
5 La Taverna
6 Magic Light
7 Oriental Gallery
8 Rainbow
9 Wild Orchid & Chaweng Arcade

accommodation from fan rooms to luxurious suites; all of them are well decorated. They are, predictably, too close to one another, but this place emerges as being better than most as it has a pleasant beachside restaurant and live music. **A** *Chaweng Cabana*, T422377, F42137. Not to be confused with *Samui Cabana*. This is yet another resort where the good a/c bungalows are constructed with little space to breathe. International restaurant and pool. **A** *Chaweng Resort*,T422247, F421378. A/c bungalows, decent pool and restaurant, attractive gardens. **A** *Coral Bay Resort*, T422223, F422392, north of Chaweng Beach (Yai Noi Bay). A/c, restaurant, pool, good a/c bungalows in a spacious setting. The beach is not good for swimming or sunbathing and it is very overpriced for the services provided. **A** *First*, T422327, F422243. As implied by its name, this was the first resort to appear on Chaweng Beach and the a/c bungalows are clean and nicely laid out. There is a restaurant, but no pool – a big minus when most other places in this price bracket do. **A** *The Princess Village*, northern end of beach, T422216, F422382, princess@sawadee.com Tries hard to disconnect the guests from the less-attractive side of Western culture, by deliberately not having televisions in the transplanted traditional Ayutthayan-style houses which are set in a strikingly attractive tropical garden. Unlike most places, the houses are not built too close together. It is the most unusual luxury resort along the beach and perhaps the most appealing. There is a good beachside restaurant. Recommended. **A** *Sans Souci Samui*, T422044, F422045. Small, personal resort with only 13 rooms set in a nice garden. **A** *Tradewinds*, T230602, F231247. A very appealing resort, as the 21 excellent bungalows are set out in an attractive part of the beach. As a result of its size, it is an intimate place and is relatively peaceful at

The Southern Region

Related maps
Koh Samui, page 659
Nathon, page 664
North Coast, page 666
Lamai Beach, page 674
West Coast, page 678

night. There is a beachside bar and restaurant and a pool. **A** *Tropicana Beach*, T412408. Rather characterless resort with restaurant and pool, but good, clean rooms. **A** *Victorian*, Chaweng Noi Beach, T422011, F422111, T02-4245392. Southern end, a/c, restaurant, small pool, 2/3-storey ugly 'Victorian' building, too many rooms in too small a space. **A** *Villa Flora*, T281535, T02-2517646. A/c, restaurant, unattractive resort, split into two by a busy road, with 2 pools, one of which is far too public for comfort. Most of the accommodation is on the non-beach side of the road.

B *Blue Horizon Bungalows*, 210/Moo 4, T422426. A small place to stay with good clean bungalows. The a/c accommodation is better value than the fan rooms. Restaurant. **B** *Central Bay*, T422118, a huge new resort owned by *Central Department Store*, it's a miracle they don't contravene the height restrictions – or do they? **B** *Chaweng Villa*. T231123, F231124, www.kohsamui.net/ chawengvilla Each large, wood- floored, a/c bungalow has its own balcony. Those nearer the beach are more expensive. Beachside restaurant with BBQs each evening. Friendly management. **B** *The Island*, T424202. A/c, restaurant, north end of beach, some a/c, good restaurant, bathrooms, individual huts right on the beach, attractive garden, run by farang, bar open after 2200, ideal for 'trendy backpackers'. **B** *Montien House* northern end of beach, T422169. Some a/c, restaurant on the beach. Too many bungalows, but they are large and clean and laid out in a pleasant shady garden. For the services provided, however, it is overpriced. **B** *Samui Yacht Club*, T422225, F421378, south end of Chaweng, just before headland. A/c, restaurant, pool, traditional-style thatched attractive bungalows set in coconut plantation, fitness centre, private beach. **B** *Village*, T422216, F422382. Some a/c, restaurant, Thai-style bungalows, simpler version of the *Princess Village*, yet similarly attractive. **B-C** *Chaweng Gardens*, T422265, F422265. Some a/c, bungalows close together but well designed. **B-C** *Samui Natien Resort*, T422405, F422309, natien@loxinfo.co.th Accommodation ranges from fan cooled to a/c bungalows. Clean, but a little basic for the price. **B-D** *Best*. A very popular resort towards the north end of the beach with a large range of accommodation from basic guesthouse rooms to a/c hotel rooms – all attractively decorated. Pool and a rather expensive restaurant. **B-D** *Long Beach Lodge*, T/F422372. Some a/c, very large coconut- studded plot for so few bungalows (20), laid back and peaceful, bungalows are a reasonable size, a/c rooms good value. Recommended.

C-D *Matlang Resort*, T422172. Some a/c, restaurant, small brick bungalows with rattan roofs, quite nice garden, secluded spot but rather dirty. **D** *Coconut Grove*. The wood and concrete bungalows are too close together once again and are rather bland. At the beach end of the resort there is *Plonkers Bar,* which succinctly describes the type of person that would choose to drink here. **D** *Lucky Mother* (north end), T230931, friendly, clean, excellent food, some private bathrooms. Recommended. **D** *Parrot*, T231221, F422347. Some a/c, 20 bungalows in wonderful overgrown jungle, on 'wrong' side of the road, but it's quiet and unusual. The rooms are well designed, spacious, comfortable and good value. There is no restaurant but there are plenty nearby. Friendly owner. Recommended. **D** *Samui Cabana*, T421405. Well-laid-out huts at the north end of the beach, some a/c. Good value. **D** *Tropic Tree Resort*, T230998. Basic rustic bungalows with fan, clean and right on the beach, good restaurant, friendly welcome. **D-E** *Charlie's*, T422343, F422482. Divided into 3 main compounds, each with separate restaurants, though the menu is the same. The accommodation is very simple, the cheapest being in clean fan-cooled wooden huts with thatched roofs. Shared washing facilities of variable cleanliness. No electricity between 1000 and 1800. This is certainly the place to stay if you are a first time solo traveller and need some reassurance as to how easy it is to meet people. **D-E** *Joy*, T421376, F421376. Attractive Spanish-style bungalows in mature colourful garden, rooms are small. A good cheap place to stay.

Chaweng offers a range of international restaurants as well as plenty of seafood. **Expensive** *Chez Andy Restaurant*, 164/2 Chaweng Beach Rd, T8916148. A popular grill house, though it is a little impersonal and expensive. *Eden*, attractive thatched pavilions, excellent seafood, rather tacky décor. *La Taverna* serves good range of Italian food, though the prices are inflated. *Magic Light*, near the Chaweng Arcade, a Swiss-owned restaurant serving a wide range of European cuisine as well as some Thai food, pizzas and seafood. Bakery attached. *Mama Roma*. T230649. Another Italian restaurant notable for its very good pizzas. *Poppies*, T422419, an excellent Thai and international restaurant, perhaps the best on the beach. *Spice Island*, T23500 ext 4950. Part of the *Central Samui Resort*. Sit either in the a/c or the relaxing beachside part of the restaurant and try good BBQ food and a wide range of excellent, and sophisticated, Thai dishes. *Tropic Tree Resort*, lovely restaurant on the beach.

Mid-range *Betelnut*, Soi Colibri, near *Central Hotel*, T413370. Californian chef serves up great food in this exclusive but friendly place. *Café Thai*, 164/9 Chaweng Beach, T231096. Offers a wide range of good Thai and French food at reasonable prices. *Caffé e Cucina*, opposite *OP Bungalows*. A new Pizzeria run by Angelo from Rome. Good Italian food, friendly and excellent value. Recommended. *Crystal Restaurant*. A wide choice of Thai food on offer. *Gringo's Canting*, near Centre Point. Mexican food. *The Island*, north end of beach, part of *The Island Hotel*, seafood, Thai, pasta and even Australian steaks and lamb. *Munchies*, popular seafood restaurant which spills onto the beach, live music. *Oriental Gallery*, T/F422200, a very atmospheric restaurant with books on Oriental and Southeast Asian art available to buy or simply read over a meal. Refined décor and elegant garden furniture associated with an exclusive antique shop. An oasis on a busy road. Recommended. *Osteria*, T230057, Chaweng Arcade 1st Floor. Italian. *Rainbow* (off the main drag, across the road from *Chaweng Villa* and *Montien House* at north end of beach), a restaurant which aims to serve good food without the usual tourist accompaniments of TV, video and music. *Wild Orchid*. Next to the *Oriental Gallery*. Specializes in more unusual Thai dishes.

Bakery *Will Wait Bakery* T231152, for excellent pastries and breakfast.

Most of the bars are at the northern end of the strip. *The Reggae Club* is popular, as is *Santa Fe* and *The Cotton Club*. Other clubs on the strip include *Bananas*, *Black Cat*, *Eden*, *Green Mango* and *Mao*. *The Club* is a particularly good place, with good music, and no prostitutes. All are on the road parallel to the beach. *Sound Shaft*, open disco, not very popular with its neighbours.

There is a wide range of shops along the beach road, where most things can be bought. Many places remain open until late. There are the usual array of tourist shops, beachware, T-shirts, jewellery, handicrafts. *Sawang Optical*, 168/5 Chaweng Beach Rd, for a large range of frames and a professional service. *Sawang Watch*, 168/5 Chaweng Beach Rd, for range of Swatch watches.

Diving *Koh Samui Divers*, T421465, are to be found on the beach. *Matlang Divers* are at *Matlang Resort*. *Samui International Diving School* is at the Malibu Beach Club, T422386/413050, F231242, info@planet-scuba.net *Calypso Diving*, southern end of beach, T422437, info@calypso-diving.com **Hash House Harriers** Monthly runs from Red Fox, Lamai Night Plaza, T236371 for details. **Snorkelling** Masks and fins can be hired from most bungalows. **Speedboats** Can be rented for ฿1,200 per hour. **Watersports** Include windsurfing, catamaran sailing (฿440 per hour), waterskiing (฿200 per session), jet skis (฿400 per hour), jet scooters (฿400 per hour), parasailing (฿400 per 10 minutes fly). *Chaweng Cabana* has good watersports. Many luxury hotels offer such services.

Eating
● *on map, page 671*
Price categories:
see inside front cover

**Bars &
nightclubs**

Shopping

Sport

The Southern Region

Tour operators There are dozens of these along Chaweng Beach Rd.

Transport **Local** **Car hire**: *Avis*, *Imperial Hotel*, T422020. **Minibus**: there is an a/c minibus that leaves from the northern end of the beach and goes to the airport, 6 times a day (฿40). **Motorbike taxis**: Motorcycle taxis will take you anywhere for a price. Rough costs are: to Lamai ฿100, Bophut ฿80, Choeng Mon ฿130, airport ฿130 and waterfall ฿15.

Directory **Banks** Money-changing facilities are strung out all along Chaweng Beach Rd. The bank booths are worth seeking out for their substantially lower rates of commission. **Medical services** **Clinic:** There are a couple of clinics along the road and the Samui International Clinic is nearby. German and English spoken. As it is a private clinic, the service provided is pricey. One on road into Chaweng from Route 4169, one near the *Thai Restaurant*. **Places of worship** Catholic Church: on the main road. Service at 1030.

Between Chaweng and Lamai

There is not much beach along this stretch of coast but some snorkelling off the rocky shore. Snorkelling is best at Coral Cove, between Chaweng and Lamai or at Yai Noi, north of Chawen.g

Sleeping **A** *Samui Yacht Club*, T422225, F422400. A/c, restaurant, pool, health centre, children's room, peaceful bay, small pool but good-sized bungalows, mature jungled garden, good value. **A** *Coral Cave Chalet*, T422260, F422496. A/c, restaurant, small pool, lovely chalets on hillside, linked by decking walkways, steps down to very small private beach with little sand but some snorkelling offshore, well run tropical ambience. Recommended. **B** *Silver Beach*, T422478, F422479, a/c, restaurant, 20 clean but quite basic rooms, rather close together, lovely little bay, quiet, relaxing atmosphere with friendly management.

Lamai อ่าวละไม

Koh Samui's 'second' beach is 5 km long and has a large assortment of accommodation. Much of the lower grade accommodation is so bad that it has not been included in this listing. Rates are similar to Chaweng, but the

Related maps
Koh Samui, page 659
Nathon, page 664
North Coast, page 666
Chaweng Beach, page 671
West Coast, page 678

Lamai Beach

To Chaweng Beach

Ban Lamai Cultural Hall

Easy Divers

Clinic

Clinic

Bars

Lamai Morning Market

Rt. 4169

Lamai Beach

Pongpornrat Rd

Doi Thai

To Butterfly Garden & Namuang Waterfall

Shops
Tourist

Shops

Hinyai & Hinta Rocks

N

0 metres 200
0 yards 200

■ **Sleeping**
1 Aloha
2 Coconut Beach
3 Galaxy
4 Lamai Coconut Resort
5 Lamai Inn 99
6 Magic Resort
7 Marina Villa
8 Pavilion
9 Platuna
10 Rocky
11 Rose Garden
12 Royal Blue Lagoon
13 Samui Laguna Resort
14 Samui Park Resort
15 Samui Residence
16 Sea Breeze
17 Sea Garden
18 Spa Resort
19 Suan Thale
20 Wanchai Villa
21 Weekender Bungalow
22 Weekender Resort
23 Whitesand

supporting 'tourist village' has developed rapidly and is somewhat dishevelled looking. However, the beach itself is still nice. The renowned **'grandmother'** (*Hinyai* and *Hinta*) and **'grandfather'** rocks are to be found just south of here (signpost to 'Wonderful rocks').

The first edition of the *Greater Samui Magazine* in 1995 attempted to paint Lamai as some sort of traditional village getaway with nightlife attachments when the editors wrote: "This second most popular of Samui's beaches offers a combination of plentiful accommodation, nightlife and picturesque village scenes ... Visitors are charmed by the open market and the old monastery". Such a vision of Lamai is really stretching credulity a little too far. Depending who you talk to, or who you are, this is either a rather tawdry, down-market Pattaya, or an idiosyncratic, slightly hip and colourful Hua Hin. It is not particularly peaceful; nor could it be described as picturesque. It can be a lot of fun though, and some people love it.

Companies along the main road parallel to the beach, for trips around the islands, fishing and snorkelling.

Tours

AL-A *The Pavilion*, T424420, F424029. 52 large, round, a/c bamboo and wood huts with verandahs and comfortable teak chairs. There is an attractive small pool, a gift shop, tour information and a restaurant serving Thai and Western food. **A** *Aloha*, T424418, F424419, www.sawadee.com.samui/aloha Well-designed a/c rooms in this relaxing resort. There is a good pool and the restaurant offers a wide range of good seafood, though it is not locally caught. Tours can be booked here. **A** *P&P Resort*. The bungalows are well appointed and the ones nearer the beach more expensive. There is a good restaurant, with a large choice of seafood. **A** *Royal Blue Lagoon*, T424086, F424195. Not to be confused with the other 2 *Blue Lagoons*, this is the first and the best. A family-run affair, the accommodation is in attractive Thai-style bungalows set in lush gardens in a striking position on Laem Nan headland at the northern end of Lamai. There is a private beach and a freshwater pool. The restaurant (see Eating, below) is one of the most appealing on the island, as it has stunning views of Lamai Bay. Recommended. **A** *Samui Laguna Resort*, T424215, F424371. A/c rooms are in an ugly 3-storey block, but there are some pleasant a/c wood and concrete bungalows, each with a verandah. Small pool. **A** *Samui Park Resort*, T/F424008. A/c, restaurant with good views, pool. The rooms are clean and spacious but they are in a rather ugly 3-storey block; popular with Thais. **A-B** *Galaxy Resort*, 124/61 Moo 3. T424441. The teak bungalows are too close together for comfort and while they are clean and fully equipped, the décor is somewhat reminiscent of the seventies. **A-B** *Weekender Resort*, T424429, F424011. This pleasant resort has 3 types of accommodation, in a/c bungalows, an ugly 3-storey block, and Thai-style houses. All of them are good and clean, but they do tend to get swamped by tour groups.

Sleeping
■ *on map*
Price codes:
see inside front cover

B-C *Marina Villa* T424426. The reasonably furnished, fan and a/c huts on stilts are far too close together to create a relaxed atmosphere. **B-D** *Rocky* T418367, F418366, rockie@surat.loxinfo.co.th This is another long-time resort dating from around 1980. Each of the bungalows has a verandah. The well-placed restaurant commands beautiful views. Videos shown nightly. **B-D** *Sea Breeze*, 124/3 Moo 3, T424258. One of the oldest places on the island. The accommodation ranges from basic fan rooms to comfortable a/c bungalows with hot water. The restaurant serves Thai and Western food at reasonable prices and the staff are very friendly. **C** *Lamai Coconut Resort*, next to the *Weekender Resort*, T232169. The a/c bungalows are basic, but nevertheless attractively decorated and the management are friendly. The restaurant serves a range of Thai food (**3**). **C** *Lamai Inn 99*, T424427. Rather dull rooms. Some a/c and some with fridge and TV. Thai restaurant. **C-D** *Rose Garden* northern end, T424115. Some a/c bungalows with shower-rooms attached. Rather

The Southern Region

badly laid out in a rose garden that has seen better days. Restaurant. **C-D** *Samui Residence*, large peaceful plot (for Lamai), with good-sized bungalows – less regimented than most and therefore more attractive, rustic feel, plot leads down to beach. The bungalows, some a/c, are good and clean. **C-E** *Coconut Beach*, T434209, shabby, some attached bathrooms. **C-E** *Spa Resort*, T230855, F424126, www.surat.loxinfo.co.th/-thespa As far as health resorts go this is excellent as the services provided are very good value and the staff are very welcoming. Run by an American and his Thai wife, with sauna, steam room and excellent bungalows with attached bathrooms.

D *Magic Resort*, T424229, no a/c, twin row of small bungalows, some thatched, on long thin plot running down to the beach, very average. **D** *Platuna*, T424138. More expensive rooms have bathrooms attached, no hot water, fan, 10 solidly built bungalows, rather crammed onto a small plot next to a canal, good restaurant attached, quiet end of Lamai. **D** *Sea Garden Bungalows*, T424238. A small resort with just a handful of huts in a coconut grove that leads down to the beach. A bit too central to be quiet but appealing nevertheless. Bikes for hire. **D** *Weekender Bungalows*, T424417. Not the same management as the more up-market *Weekender Resort* opposite, simple cheap bungalows behind a supermarket run by the same woman, on inland side of road, stuffy and no breeze, so can be very hot. **D-E** *Suan Thale*, T424230. Some a/c, restaurant, rooms in bungalow 'blocks', largish plot, reasonable rooms with a bit more atmosphere than most. **E** *Animal House*, average rooms, attached bathroom. **E** *Green Banana*, Laem Nan headland, north of Lamai, very small A-frame huts and some larger bungalows in a large plot, quiet and peaceful spot, away from the nightlife of Lamai. **E** *Whitesand*, T424298, large, clean bungalows on beachfront, attached bathroom. **E-F** *Wanchai Villa*, T424296, 3 km south of Lamai. Rather out of the way but motorbikes available for hire, simple bungalows, shared facilities, very friendly owners and the restaurant serves excellent food, quiet and good value.

Eating
Price categories: see inside front cover

There are several seafood restaurants along the Lamai beach road offering a wide choice such as the *L'Auberge* and the *Rimklong*. Prices vary enormously and there is nowhere particularly good and cheap. Below is a just a selection of the better places to eat.

International cuisine Widely available along the road parallel to the beach in restaurants such as *Il Tempo*. **Expensive**: *Sala Thai* T233180. Serves good Thai food, seafood, steaks and Italian. It is, however, far too expensive. *Papas*, a popular restaurant serving pasta and Thai food, and is particularly well known for its steaks. *The Spa*. Serves a wide range of vegetarian and Thai food, though it is expensive. *Rimklong*, *L'Auberge*, *Toms Bakery* and *Milan*. A popular breakfast joint is the *Will Wait Bakery*, with delicious pastries and croissant.

Bars Most are located down the sois which link the main road and the beach. *Flamingo Mix* (large dancefloor), and *Time Spaceadrome*. *Samui Arms 2*, near *Brauhaus* disco. English pub with darts, pool, quizzes and large screens for watching football.

Entertainment **Buffalo fighting** In the stadium at the north end (ask at hotel for date of next fight). **Massage** On the beach. **Spa** The *Spa Resort*, T230855, F424126, www.spasamui.com, offers 'exotic rejuvenation', anything from Herbal Steam Room to a 'Liver Flush Fast', prices seem quite reasonable, they are to be found next to the *Weekender Villa* at the north end of the beach.

Videos At many of the bungalows.

Shopping Jewellery, beachware and clothing boutiques along the main road, attractive sarongs in little boutique at entrance to *Thai House Inn*.

Diving *Matlang Divers* are based at *Aloha*. **Swiss Dive Centre** are at *Weekender*. **Pro** **Sport**
Divers is based at *Rocky Bungalows*. *Easy Divers*, near *Lamai Resort* (north end of
beach), T231190, F424244, www.thaidive.com German, English and Swedish spoken. **Fishing** T231190, tackle for rent or sale. **Watersports** Waterskiing (฿300), jet
skis, windsurfing, parasailing (฿500), snorkelling at southern end of the beach. **Thai**
boxing Classes available.

Companies along the main road organize ticket reservations. **Tour operators**

Local Jeep and motorbike hire: widely available. **Songthaews**: to Nathon (฿15). **Transport**

Banks Currency exchanges are to be found along the main road parallel to the beach. **Directory**
Communications Post Office: south end of main road. **Medical services** *Lamai Clinic*, T424219,
F424218, near the Boxing Stadium. Doctor Pongsak here is excellent and speaks fluent English.

The South Coast

The small beaches that line the south coast from Ban Hua Thanon west to Thong
Krut are quieter and less developed, with only a handful of hotels and bungalows.

Ban Hua Thanon is an attractive rambling village with wooden shophouses **Ban Hua**
and *kwaytio* stalls – and the only Muslim community on Koh Samui. The fore- **Thanon**
bears of the inhabitants come from Pattani in Thailand's far south. The village
is quiet and rarely visited by tourists. North of the village are a couple of restaurants – one seafood, one northeastern Thai.

A *Samui Orchid*, T424017, F424019, a/c, restaurant, large pool, some older bunga- **Na Khai**
lows and a new three-floor 'apartment' block, secluded resort amongst coconut
grove, rocky beach, off the beaten track. **B-D** *Samui Maria Resort*, T433394, F424024,
some a/c, basic restaurant, large pool, snooker and outdoor multi-gym, concrete a/c
bungalows built in regimental line, featureless resort with bare garden, basic rooms
and dirty beach. **E** *Cosy Resort*, about 12 small bamboo bungalows in a rather tatty
coconut grove, very basic rooms with nets and shower rooms, rather dirty but lots of
space on the compound, very quiet place to stay, dirty beach (bought by *Samui Maria*
Resort, who will be expanding); **E** *Hi He Resort*, T424340, next to *Cosy*, five very basic
bungalows in a quiet, peaceful coconut grove, Mr He speaks English and has been
trained at Wat Po in the art of acupuncture. Mrs He is a good cook.

AL-A *Laem Set Inn*, 110 Mu 2, Hua Thanon, T424393, F424394, www.laemset.com **Laem Set**
Some a/c, restaurant, pool. This is an exclusive, secluded resort in an attractive compound, with a range of accommodation, run by an Englishman. Several private a/c
'suites' with small pools attached, all commanding beautiful views of the South China
Sea; many of the buildings are reconstructed wooden Samui houses. A more recent
addition is a brick-built villa with several well-designed (but small) rooms, and adjoining
bunk-bed rooms. All rooms are more expensive than comparable accommodation elsewhere on the island, but the owner believes his set-up is unique, providing a very different experience to the big, rather sterile alternatives in this price bracket. Room rate
includes use of mountain bikes, kayaks pedal boats, masks and snorkels. This is an ideal
place for families, with day nursery and baby-sitting facilities (hourly rates charged),
children's and toddler's playground. The food is excellent and well priced (lunchtime
meals are popular with non-residents). The staff are delightful and offer a homely welcome. Cookery courses are held in May and Sep in custom-built training kitchens at the
Inn. Jeep for rent. Recommended. **AL** *The Butterfly Garden*, T424020. The rooms are
decorated in an elegant Japanese style, and very well equipped. Nevertheless, they are

The Southern Region

crammed far too closely together in the tropical garden setting. The international restaurant has an unimaginative menu, the snorkelling equipment is expensive to hire. Too expensive for the services on offer. Price includes American breakfast.

Bang Kao
A quiet but not very attractive beach

D *Waikiki*, average rooms. **E** *River Garden*, T424035, attached bathroom. Between Bang Kao and Thong Krut, the Laem So Pagoda overlooks the sea. It has recently been smartened up and is worth visiting if you're passing. It houses the remains of a monk, whose diocese included the Hainanese community on Koh Tan.

Thong Krut

Ferries go daily from Thong Krut to Koh Tan and Koh Matsum and there are several tour companies here who organize fishing and snorkelling trips, T423117. There is an excellent Thai restaurant here. It has no name in English but is recognizable by the red mailbox outside the front. It has some of the best genuine Thai food on the island. **E** *Thong Krut Bungalow*, rather close to the road but very quiet, friendly and unspoilt. Recommended.

Koh Tan

This island lies due south of Thong Krut and is about 3 km long and 2 km wide. It was first colonized by Hainanese; there is a Chinese cemetery with those first colonizers' graves on the island. There are three small villages and four bungalow developments on the island which, though undeveloped, is not blessed with spotless beaches and crystal-clear waters – as one might suppose. Still, it is quiet and just about away from it all. **E** *Tan Village Bungalow*, T9684131. Rather bare compound studded with bungalows within a stone's throw of the sea. **E** *Koh Tan Resort*, T233342. Large bungalows on the beach, with clean attached shower rooms, some attempt at a garden, the owner is rather camp but the accommodation is good value.

Koh Matsum

This is a sorry sight – all the coconut trees have been stripped by a beetle, leaving a desolate landscape of bare tree trunks. The Butterfly Garden have opened bungalows here, but it's not really worth the visit. The *Laem Set Inn* organize barbecues, but the place is full of dumped rubbish and not very appealing.

The West Coast

Like the south coast, the western coastline south of Nathon is undeveloped, with secluded coves and beautiful sunsets. Phangka, near the southwest tip of the island has good

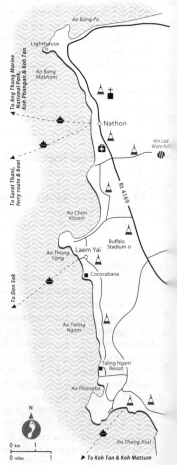

West coast

snorkelling in the quiet waters of a small bay; Thong Yang, further north, is an isolated strip of beach, relatively untouched by the frantic developments underway elsewhere. The vehicle ferry from Don Sak, on the mainland, docks here. Chon Khram is the last bay before Nathon.

L-AL *Ban Taling Ngam Resort*, T423019. A/c, restaurants, 2 pools, in an isolated position, built on the side of the hill, Thai-style houses spill down to the shore, very plush but somehow rather out of place here, the suites, tennis courts and one of the pools and restaurant are down by the beach – a steep climb down, or for the less energetic, there are buggies provided. The beach is disappointing, with dirty water and the lower pool is small for the size of the resort.

Sleeping

Phangka **D** *Cococabana*, T423174, north of Phangka, just before vehicle ferry. Friendly, quiet, some bathrooms. **D-E** *Pearl Bay*. Some attached bathrooms. **D-E** *Sea Gull* T423091. Some attached bathrooms. **E** *Emerald Cove*. Clean, attached bathrooms. Recommended. **F** *Gems House* T423006. Clean, attached bathroom. Recommended. **Chon Khram** **B-E** *International*, T423366. Some a/c, range of bungalows, some hot water. **D-E** *Lipa Lodge*, friendly.

Koh Phangan   เกาะพงัน

Koh Phangan (pronounced Pa-ngan), is Koh Samui's younger sister and is at an earlier stage in the tourist development cycle. Bungalows are generally basic and tourist facilities less extensive. Fishing and coconut production remain mainstays of the economy, and villages still have a traditional air – although tourism is now by far the island's largest single industry.

Phone code: 077
Colour map 4, grid B3

Ins and outs

There is no airport on Koh Phangan and everyone arrives by boat. There are daily ferries from Don Sak Pier and Bandon near Surat Thani on the mainland (a 4-6-hr journey, depending on the service) and also from the larger, neighbouring island of Koh Samui. The quickest way to Koh Phangan is to fly from Bangkok to Koh Samui (see page 661) and then to catch one of the express boats from Samui to Koh Phangan (a 40-min journey). This saves on the long bus or train journey south from the capital. Alternatively, it is possible to fly to Surat Thani. If also intending to travel to Koh Tao then it may make sense to catch a boat from Chumphon to Koh Tao; there are regular ferries between Koh Tao and Koh Phangnan (1½ hrs).

Getting there

Koh Phangan stretches 15 km north to south and 10 km east to west. The main settlement is Thong Sala and there is a limited network of poor roads and tracks served by songthaews. For off-the-road beaches it is often easiest to travel by long-tailed boat. Motorbikes are available for hire and so too are mountain bikes. In many instances walking is the best option.

Getting around

The island

The pace of development on the island has been extremely rapid. The number of bungalows increased from a mere eight in 1983 to 146 in 1990. In 1993 the five-storey *Phangan Central Hotel* opened in Thong Sala marking the arrival of big money on the island. Though still relatively unspoilt, more and more travellers are passing Koh Phangan by and continuing on to the next, and yet more geographically remote island of Koh Tao.

These tropical islands that fringe the coast are liable to change more rapidly than any other tourist destination in Thailand

The main village of Koh Phangan is the port of **Thong Sala** where most boats from Koh Samui, Surat Thani, and Koh Tao dock. Thong Sala has a branch of the Siam City Bank, telephone and fax facilities, a post office and telegraph service (poste restante), travel and tour agents, a small supermarket, dive shops, photo processing, motorbike hire, and a second-hand bookstore. The greatest concentration of bungalows is at Hat Rin on the southern 'foot' of the island-and the place where the infamous Full Moon Parties are held.

Sights

It is a good idea to buy one of the maps of the island available in town

Koh Phangan offers 'natural' sights such as waterfalls, forests, coral, and viewpoints but little of historical or cultural interest. The best way to explore the island is on foot, following one of the many tracks that link the various villages and beaches, which cannot be negotiated by songthaew or (sometimes) by motorbike. Most roads are unpaved and poor, although improvement work is underway (as it has been for many years!). Even the longest hike is an easy day's walk.

Waterfalls **Phaeng Waterfall** is to be found in the interior of the island, about 4½ km from Thong Sala and 2 km from the village of Maduawan. The walk east to Hat

Koh Phangan

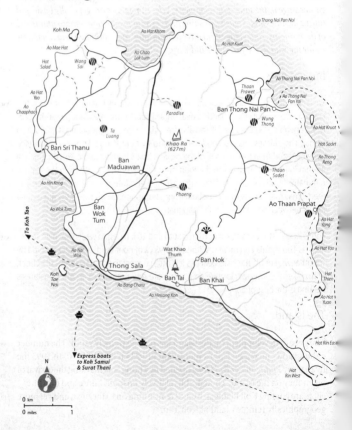

Full Moon Parties

The Full Moon Parties, which have been going since 1990, are now accompanied by Half and Black Moon Parties ... oh, and of course, Saturday Night Parties. On Full Moon night, if you are not planning to party till dawn, it is advisable to stay elsewhere, unless you feel you can sleep to the boom of the bass from the beach. Up to 10,000 people turn up on Hat Rin East every month to dance and watch the jugglers, fire eaters and fireworks displays.

Tips for the party

Be aware that the musical choice is restricted to techno, trance, drum and bass, dance and reggae.
Don't bring valuables with you; if safety

deposit boxes are an option at your bungalows it is worth leaving your passport and credit cards there, otherwise secrete them in a discrete place in your bungalow.
Do not eat or drink anything that is offered by strangers.
Don't take drugs. It's not worth the risk. At almost every party plain clothes policemen take a number of Westerners down to the jail from where they will only be released on bail if they can pay the ฿50,000 fine. Otherwise they will be held for five to six weeks prior to trial.
Follow the above advice and you should have a fantastic time.

Sadet runs parallel to a river along which are three waterfalls and the carved initials of several Thai kings who visited here, including King Chulalongkorn (Rama V) who was so enamoured that he reportedly came here on 10 occasions between 1888 and 1909, and the present King Bhumibol (Rama IX) in 1962. These can be reached on foot or on mountain bikes. Other waterfalls include **Ta Luang** and **Wang Sai** in the northwest corner, **Paradise** in the north (and near the *Paradise Resort*), and **Thaan Prawet** and **Wung Thong** in the northeast corner. The highest point is **Khao Ra** (627 m). A path runs to the summit although visitors have reported that the trail is indistinct and a guide is necessary. Outside Ban Tai, on the coast and to the east of Thong Sala, is **Wat Khao Tum** and the **Vipassana Meditation Centre**. There are views from the hill-top wat to Samui and the Ang Thong Islands. Ten-day meditation courses are held every month with 20-day courses and three-month retreats also available (all in English). All-in fees are ฿1,600 for ten days. Write to: Wat Khao Tum, Koh Phangan, Surat Thani, Thailand, for more information. It is possible to walk on a trail from Hat Rin up the east coast to Hat Sadet and then on to Thong Nai Pan, where four-wheel drive vehicles offer a daily service to Thong Sala, depending on the weather (฿60).

Except for Hat Rin, the beaches are uncrowded although not quite as beautiful as those on Koh Samui. The water is good for snorkelling, particularly during the dry season when clarity is at its best.

Boats leave from Thong Sala for the Ang Thong Marine National Park (see page 663).

Excursions

Besides the *Phangan Central Hotel* in Thong Sala, there are no big hotels. It is also worth noting that many of the bungalows are without frills; that is they have neither fans – or attached shower rooms. Still, they are mainly located right on the seafront, so they receive they sea breezes and not having standing water in your room means you get fewer mosquitoes. In addition, communal facilities tend to be more frequently cleaned. In general, expect to pay in our **F** range for a hut with shared bathroom, **D-E** for a bungalow with private bathroom. The higher of the price ranges given for most of the accommodation indicates an attached bathroom. Hat Rin is more expensive than other beaches. During the high season (Dec-Feb and Jul-Sep), prices are 50% higher than in

Sleeping
Price codes:
see inside front cover

The Southern Region

the low season: bargain if bungalows seem empty. The bungalows are listed below in order, running anti-clockwise round the island from the capital, Thong Sala.

Thong Sala (pronounced Tong-sala) **AL-A** *Phangan Central Hotel*, T377068, F377032. The only five-star hotel on the island. Some a/c rooms overlooking the sea, opened in 1993, this 5-storey hotel offers TVs and fridges. **B-C** *Phangan Chai Hotel*, 45/65 Mu 1, T377068, F377032. Price varies with the view – the more expensive look out on to the sea, the others on to the garden. All are a/c, with a fridge, shower and a western toilet. The choice of décor, however, leaves something to be desired. **D** *Kao Guest House*, 210/9-10 Thongsala-Chaloklum Rd, T238061. Some a/c, travel agency attached. Main door is locked at 2300. **D** *Buakhao Inn*, some a/c, A very small hotel. **D** *Blackhouse*. Another very small guesthouse. **E** *Sea Mew*. Behind the windy wood and thatch frontage of the restaurant is a concrete terrace of very clean, well-maintained tiled rooms, each with a mattress on the floor and a good fan. Squat toilet and shower room attached. **E** *Shady Nook*. A guesthouse with just 3 rooms, clean, comfortable but basic, useful if taking the early morning ferry.

From Thong Sala to Ban Tai: Bang Charu and Hinsong Kon This stretch of beach is unpopular with visitors due to its proximity to Thong Sala and as a result accommodation is good value. The beach shelves gently and is good for children, but the water is a little murky. Bungalows are well spread out and quiet: **B-C** *First Villa*, T/F377225, firstvilla@kohphangan.com, kohphangan.com/firstvilla Garishly decorated but clean a/c and fan rooms along the beach front in a pleasant tropical garden. Overpriced. **D-F** *Charm Beach Resort*. The bungalows are well laid out and the most expensive are a/c. The cheap rooms, which are bamboo and thatch huts, are particularly good value, but often full. The restaurant serves Thai and European food. **E-F** *Phangan Villa*, T377083. Rooms with or without attached bathroom. Free horse riding. **F** *Liberty Bungalows*, T238171. Very quiet as the owner doesn't solicit custom at the pier. Clean and comfortable rooms with attached shower rooms.

From Ban Tai to Ban Khai and just beyond Some snorkelling, good swimming, generally quiet and secluded. The beach may not be so good as at Hat Rin, but this is more than made up for by cheaper accommodation and less noise. **B-F** *Chokana Resort*, T238085. A huge choice of rooms, from basic huts with an outside shower, to very smart, rather glamorous, round a/c bungalows. **E** *Mac's Bay Resort*, a very popular spot with basic huts. Food available. Slightly better than most, well run and clean. The more expensive rooms are large and have attached shower rooms. There is a restaurant with a wide menu and nightly videos. Money exchange and an international collect-call service. **E-F** *Triangle Lodge*, F421263. Some rooms beginning to look slightly dilapidated, but they all have hammocks and access to a western toilet. The restaurant is appealing as it has a wide and imaginative menu with tasty interpretations of Western dishes and the staff are friendly. **D-E** *Dream Land Bungalow*. The 2 cheaper rooms are made of wood and have hammocks, while the villas are rather small and not particularly appealing. Nightly BBQ on the beach, and the restaurant offers Thai food. **E** *Phangan Lodge*, T01-2701075. This very laid back place has unusual and brightly coloured triangular huts. **E-F** *Bantai Beach*. The cheapest rooms have no fan, while the most expensive are board huts on the beach and have attached shower rooms. The restaurant serves cheap food. **E-F** *Lee's Garden*, T238150, basic huts set in a garden, good food, quiet, well-run.

THE place for parties, noise & activity (full moon parties are particularly popular, see box page 681)

Hat Rin is at the southeastern tip of Koh Phangan. The best, and most popular beaches are to be found here, with some good snorkelling. It also has the greatest concentration of bungalows which are packed close together (except on the hillsides). A hair-raising, twisting, winding road has been built from

Thongsala along which songthaew drivers either turn up their music really loud, or toot their horns every 5 seconds to warn oncoming drivers. The more restful alternative is to catch a boat here – boats run from both Thong Sala and Ban Khai to Hat Rin. A boat leaves Hat Rin for Thong Sala at about 1030, 45 minutes (฿40), where it meets up with boats to Koh Samui and Surat Thani. The 'East' beach is more attractive – it is cleaned every morning and there are waves. The 'West' beach is dirtier and is almost non-existent at high tide; accommodation is slightly cheaper here. The two beaches are less than 10 minutes walk apart and are both wonderfully quiet until about 1300, as most people are sleeping off the night's excesses. At night the noise from generators and the bars can be overpowering.

Hat Rin West

On the whole the accommodation here is rather unappealing but it is cheaper than in Hat Rin East. The restaurants also have a habit of closing down in the off season. However, this isn't really a problem as it's only a few minutes to the centre of Hat Rin where there is plenty of choice. The bungalows from *Sun Beach* to *Rainbow Bungalows* are on the worst stretch of the beach with rotting and vandalized accommodation due to a chronic lack of attention. Expect to be charged over the odds (**E**) for a grotty little hut. **C-F** *Family House*, this recently upgraded place has accommodation ranging from basic huts to a/c bungalows. **D-E** *Charung Bungalow*, simple bungalows with attached shower room and fan. They also have 24-hr electricity. Hammocks in front of every room. Restaurant has Thai cushions and mats on the floor. **D-E** *Friendly*, clean, and with a higher standard than most. **D-E** *Palm Beach*, some bungalows with attached shower rooms, on the side of the small headland which is less affected by litter, popular. **D-F** *Crystal Palace*. Still one of the crummier options. While the bungalows themselves are fine and those near the front are flower bedecked, the site itself looks like a bomb's hit it. Litter has gathered on this part of the beach, thanks to a rocky outcrop which stops it being washed further down the beach. No effort is made to keep the actual grounds clean either. **E** *Hatrin Village*, fan, own shower and toilet, hammocks. **E** *Neptune*, probably the best kept of the bungalows in Hat Rin West – not that there is masses of competition. The huts are bamboo, some with thatched roofs and there is a fairly pleasant stretch of beach immediately in front.

Hat Rin East

A-D *Pha-ngan Bay Shore Resort*, T7250661. Cheapest rooms have shared washing facilities, the most expensive are a/c and kept very clean. Films are shown nightly. Hammocks on the verandahs of some rooms. **B-E** *Sea View Hat Rin Resort* , T01-7250599. Huge range of rooms from very simple huts with shared washing facilities, to a/c bungalows with 2 double beds. **C-E** *Palita Lodge*, T01-2135445. All rooms are fan cooled and the cheapest have shared shower rooms. The restaurant is given over to a food festival every full moon when a wide range of Thai food is available. They also provide travel services. **D** *Mountain View Resort*. On the hillside at the most northerly end of the beach, overlooking the bay. All the bungalows have attached shower rooms with squat loos and fans. Restaurant and rather appealing bar. **D** *Paradise*, T01-7250661. The originators of the full moon party, the management of this set up run what are now, slightly tatty bungalows with attached shower rooms. But on the plus side, these are set in a pleasant garden and can accommodate up to 4 people in 2 double beds. **D-E** *Serenity*. Some rooms with attached shower rooms. As the name suggests this is one of the more peaceful locations in Hat Rin with rooms perched on rocks just the other side of the cape. **D-E** *Tommy's Resort*, T01-2293327. Some bungalows have attached shower rooms. Those without are tatty board constructions crammed in behind the others.

Hat Thien to Thaan Sadet

E *Haad Tien Resort*, T01-2293919, koh phangan.com/haadtien/ There is no road access to this peaceful resort which is 15 mins from Hat Rin by boat. The wood and bamboo bungalows all have attached shower rooms and verandah areas. **E-F** *Sanctuary*. A quiet and appealing little place, only accessible by boat.

Thong Nai Pan This is a relatively quiet double bay (Noi and Yai) with fine white-sand beaches and excellent snorkelling; it is said to have been Rama V's favourite beach on the island. The journey by truck from Thong Sala takes almost an hour and the road is very muddy in the rainy season, but it does take you through untouched jungle and so is quite an experience. It is also possible to get a boat from Hat Rin here. **A-B** *Panviman Resort*, T377048, F377154, kohphangan.com/panviman.html Mediterranean-style villas or large, airy rooms in the hotel block. Their taxi service will collect you from the pier at Thong Sala. Impressively huge thatch-roofed restaurant. **C-F** *White Sand*. Offers a range of accommodation, but the cheapest huts are particularly good value. The food is tasty and very reasonably priced, and the staff are friendly. Recommended.

Thong Nai **C-F** *Nice Beach Bungalows*. The cheapest rooms do not have a fan or a shower room.
Pan Noi The most expensive are large, concrete and tiled bungalows with western toilets, but they are rather unappealing. Motorbikes and jeeps are available for rent. Restaurant.

Thong Nai **E** *Star Huts*. By far the largest, and certainly the most popular place on the beach. The
Pan Yai bamboo huts with thatched roofs are attractive, though built too close together. The good restaurant serves Thai and Western food (cheap). It is well managed and efforts are made to keep the beach clean. The owner does not appreciate guests indulging in the use of illicit substances. Good information about the island available. Recommended. **D-E** *Tong Ta Pong*. A range of wooden bungalows set either on a hillside, or on the beach. Some have attached shower rooms. The restaurant has an almost Mediterranean feel with its terracotta floor tiles and mosaics. The food is also good and very reasonably priced. **E** *Central Cottage*, T238447. Attractive bamboo huts with wood shutters and thatched roofs. They have a tiled shower room, a western toilet, and a verandah. The restaurant offers Thai food (cheap).

Hat Kuat 5 km northwest of Thong Nai Pan, Hat Kuat it is even more isolated, with a beautiful beach. However, standards have fallen in recent years and bungalows are not as well maintained as they used to be. It has also developed a reputation for being a bit of an English ghetto. To get there take a taxi boat from Chao Lok Lum; the journey lasts about 10 mins. **E-F** *Bottle Beach*, wooden bungalows under coconut palms, very peaceful. **E-F** *OD Bungalows*, northern end, bungalows built perched on boulders, with bamboo walkways, superb views and sunsets, basic.

Chao Lok Lum This is a deep, sheltered bay on Koh Phangan's north coast. There is now an excellent road from Thong Sala to here, daily songthaews leave the pier at Thong Sala at 1230, 20 mins (฿50), or by taxi (฿70 per person). It is gradually developing into a quiet, comparatively refined, beach resort area. In the village of Ban Chao Lok Lum, there are bikes and diving equipment for rent. **E** *Paradise*, inland from the coast, very friendly with swimming at a nearby waterfall. Recommended. **E** *Wattana Resort*, the larger rooms have balconies on 2 sides with hammocks and mosquito screens. The cheaper rooms are large, but very basic, though they have mosquito nets. **F** *Try Thong*, attached shower, friendly management, good food, quiet.

Hat Salad & **D-F** *Island View Cabana*. One of the oldest places on the island, it is set in a particu-
Ao Mae Hat larly wide part of the beach where a sand bar stretches out to an offshore island which
This is one of the provides good snorkelling. The accommodation is in fairly simple huts, some of which
most peaceful parts have attached shower rooms with western toilets. The restaurant has a wide menu
of the island & has and serves good, cheap food, and there is a pool table (฿60 per hour). This is a
the cheapest well-organized place and popular. Recommended. **E-F** *Crystal Island*. There are 12
accommodation

bungalows here set on a hill overlooking Ban Maehat and the more expensive have attached shower rooms. **F** *My Way Bungalows*. Bamboo bungalows with thatched roofs and hammocks, but no fan. The electricity stops at 2300. Clean, tiled communal shower room. The restaurant serves good, cheap Thai cuisine. **F** *Salad Huts*. Bamboo huts with hammocks. The communal facilities are clean, but the restaurant is over-priced. Electricity until 2200. **F** *Maehat Bungalows*. The more expensive rooms have attached shower rooms. The communal facilities are clean. Friendly management. Electricity between 1800 and midnight. **F** *Maehaad Bay Resort*. A variety of accommodation, crowded in together. Very small bamboo and thatch huts, and the slightly larger ones are concrete. **F** *Wang Sai Resort*. In a beautiful setting behind a stream feeding into the sea, the 18 attractive bungalows, some of which are perched on boulders, are clean and well maintained, though from most it is not possible to see the sea. Snorkelling equipment is available to hire, and there is a book exchange. The restaurant serves Thai and Western food (cheap). Electricity from 1800 until 2300.

An attractive, clean beach on the west coast with good swimming and snorkelling. 20 mins by songthaew from Thong Sala. Bungalows are spread out and quiet. **D-E** *Sea Board Bungalows*. The accommodation is board-lined and has mosquito screens, with attached tiled shower rooms and western toilets. There is a travel agent attached with overseas call facility. Good snorkelling equipment for hire. Restaurant. **F** *Sandy Bay*. Some rooms have attached shower rooms. The bungalows are kept clean and all have verandah areas with hammocks. It has the best restaurant on the beach which mainly serves Thai food (cheap). Recommended. **B-E** *Hat Yao*. Accommodation ranges from basic huts to a/c bungalows. All have attached tiled shower rooms with western toilets. There are hammocks in front of every room. **F** *Blue Coral*. Very basic bungalows without fans, though some have a shower. The restaurant offers Thai and Western food (cheap). **E** *Ibiza*. A strange, and rather unfriendly atmosphere pervades this establishment. **F** *Benja Waan Bungalows*. There are only 10 bamboo huts with thatched roofs here, some without fans. Each is set on a hillside and overlooks the bay and has a hammock. The restaurant serves Thai and Western food (cheap). **C-D** *Dream Hill Bungalows*. Rather drab bungalows lined with grey board, but each has its own verandah with great views. The restaurant serves a wide range of food at reasonable prices, snorkelling equipment is available for hire, and there is an overseas call facility. **D-F** *Silver Beach*. A rather haphazard range of materials has been used to build these bungalows. They all have tiled shower rooms and fans, though with a squat toilet. The restaurant serves Thai and Western food (cheap).

Hat Yao

E *Great Bay Resort*. Rather characterless bungalows with attached shower rooms. Restaurant offering Thai and Western food. **E** *Haad Chaophao*. Bungalows set in pleasant garden, with attached shower rooms. Restaurant offering Thai and farang food. Electricity until midnight. **E** *Seaflower*. Prices vary with distance from the beach. Run by a Canadian-Thai couple, this offers well-laid-out wooden bungalows, with high peaked thatched roofs set in a mature, shady garden. The management run camping expeditions and organize snorkelling (their equipment is free for guests), fishing, cliff diving and caving trips. Restaurant with an interesting menu. Recommended. **E** *Seethanu Bungalow*. Basic fan bungalows, some with attached shower rooms. The restaurant has attractive Thai cushions and mats and offers good Thai food. **E** *Jungle Huts*. 2 rows of large and airy huts made of board, timber and thatch with attached shower rooms. On the large verandahs there are hammocks. Restaurant specializes in cocktails, of which they have 38 varieties.

Ao Chaophao

This is a long but rather narrow strip of sand. 15 mins by songthaew from Thong Sala. Behind the beach is a freshwater lake fringed by pine trees which is ideal for swimming. **D-E** *Laem Son*. Family-run bungalows, the more expensive of which have

Ao Sri Thanu
A peaceful spot to spend a few days

The Southern Region

western loos and attached shower rooms. **D-E** *Loyfa Bungalows*. There is a range bungalows on the sunset side of the hillside overlooking Ao Sri Thanu. Most have hammocks. **E** *Laem Son Bay Bungalows*. Family-run establishment with fan bungalows of varying size along the beach front. Signs request that guests should eat at their restaurant which offers Thai and some Western food (cheap). 24-hr electricity. **F** *Nantakarn Resort*. Well-maintained concrete bungalows. Free use of snorkelling equipment. Good food and great shakes. **F** *Seaview Rainbow*. Small resort with wooden huts with attached shower rooms; fan cooled.

Ban Wok Tum North of Thong Sala and south of Ban Sri Thanu; the beaches here are average and swimming is poor because the seabed shelves gently. Accommodation is good value: **E** *Siripun*, south of Wok Tum, popular bungalows, fans, swimming ok; **E-F** *Charn*; **E-F** *Lipstick*, north of Wok Tum, quiet location, rocky swimming, some fans in rooms. **F** *Chuenjit Garden*, positioned above the beach, good food. **F** *Cookies*, basic. **F** *Kiet*, excellent food, average bungalows but good value on beach, Italian-managed. **F** *OK*, friendly, short distance off the beach.

Ao Hin Kong to Ao Nai Wok North of Thong Sala and south of Ban Sri Thanu; the beaches here aren't particularly striking and swimming is difficult as the seabed shelves so gently. Accommodation is correspondingly good value. **C-E** *Siripun*. All rooms have attached shower rooms, some are a/c. They range from small bamboo huts to large concrete villas. **D-E** *Sea Scene*. The more expensive rooms are characterless concrete bungalows. However the cheapest rooms are charming, solidly built wood and bamboo constructions with thatched roofs, a verandah area and hammocks. **E** *Darin*. The fairly large bungalows are lined up along the seafront. They have bamboo weave walls and thatched roofs, roomy verandahs, and tiled shower rooms are attached to some of them. **E-F** *Bounty Bungalows*. Clean and attractive board huts with tiled shower rooms. Snorkelling gear available. Does not yet have 24-hr electricity. **E-F** *Cookies*. Very attractive bamboo bungalows set in a pleasant garden. Those without attached shower rooms are particularly good value with their seafront location and verandahs with hammocks screened by large boulders. Less private are the communal showers which are open topped and in clear view of the bungalow on the hill behind. The helpings at the restaurant are slightly thin (cheap). **E-F** *Lipstick Cabana*. A friendly, family-run establishment, the simple huts have attached shower rooms but no fans. They are set in a shady garden with views over the tidal Ao Hin Kong. **E-F** *OK Bungalows*, T84280. Set in a shady garden, fairly large but basic bamboo bungalows, some of which have attached shower rooms.

Eating Most visitors eat at their bungalows and some serve excellent, and cheap, seafood. Most of the cheaper bungalows serve standard meals of rice and noodles. However there are also increasing numbers of restaurants and cafés in virtually every village and hamlet. Word-of-mouth recommendations are the best guide; new ones are opening all the time, and old ones deteriorate. **Cheap** *Mr Chin* at Thong Sala Pier sells good food.

Bars In Hat Rin and Thong Sala. Nightlife starts around 2200.

Entertainment **Videos** At some of the bars or guesthouses.

Massage At most beaches (฿60-80 per hour).

Shopping **Batik art and paintings** The biggest range is available from *Thongsala Batik* 79/10-12 Thong Sala Town, T/F238401.

Sport **Diving** For the trained diver, the west coast offers the best diving with hard coral reefs at depths up to about 20 m. There are also some islets which offer small wall soft coral and filter corals along with large shoals of fish. Dive trips are also available to further sites such as Koh Wao Yai in the north of the Ang Thong Marine National Park, or Hin Bai (Sail Rock). Here the dives are deeper. *Chang Diving School* are based on Hat Rin East. They do courses and trips on a daily basis. T01-8213127, F377028, kohphangan.com/ChangDiving *Phangan Divers* are also based in Hat Rin, near the pier on the west side, T01-9584857. *Chaloklum Diving School* is based in Chao Lok Lum Village or contactable through *Wang Sai Resort*. *NAS German Diving School*, PO Box 13, Thong Sala (behind *Phangan Central Hotel*), T377136. *NAS* offers PADI certificated courses as well as canoe rental and snorkelling trips. **Fishing** *Ang Thong Island Tours*, Thong Sala. **Gym and Thai boxing** *Haadrin Jungle Gym*, www://kohphangan.com A fully equipped gym run by a Canadian and a Kiwi offering Thai boxing courses as well as aerobics, yoga and other training and courses. At Thong Sala, boxers from Bangkok and elsewhere fight every 2-3 weeks, especially on holidays. ฿50 and ฿100 tickets. **Snorkelling** There is coral to found off most beaches, except for those on the east coast. Particularly good are those in Mae Hat where corals are just a few meters below the surface.

Tour operators

Mr Chin, Thong Sala Pier, T377010, F377039. *Songserm Travel Co*, 35/1 Talat Thong Sala, T377045.

Transport

Local The roads remain poor on Phangan. There is a concrete road from Thong Sala to Ban Khai but the stretch from Ban Khai to Hat Rin is hilly and impassable for anything but a 4-wheel drive vehicle during the rainy season. **Boat**: long-tailed boats take passengers from Thong Sala and Ban Kai piers to Hat Rin, Thong Nai Pan, Hat Yao and Hat Kuat. Expect to pay about ฿150 per person from Thong Sala to Thong Nai Pan – bargain hard. Boat charter is about ฿500. **Motorcycle hire**: in Thong Sala and from the more popular beaches. Some of the guesthouses also hire out motorbikes. Expect to pay ฿150 per day upwards. **Songthaews**: run from the pier to any of the bays served by road. A trip to Hat Rin is ฿50, to Thong Nai Pan, ฿80. The cost to the other bays depends on how many people are going with you. **Mountain Bikes**: the most appealing area in which to ride bikes is in the south and west of the island, which are fairly flat. Well-maintained imported bikes can be hired from the *Phangan Batik Shop* in Thong Sala for ฿160 per day. They also provide a local bike trail map. Open 1000 to 2000. **Walking**: is the best way to see the island.

Long distance Train: the State Railways of Thailand run a train/bus/ferry service to Koh Phangan from Bangkok's Hualamphong Station (฿459-489).

Boat: all boats dock at the pier at Thong Sala.
   1. A ferry leaves daily from Don Sak Pier, Surat Thani, at 0915, 3¾ hrs (฿105-125). Buses leave Surat Thani at 0745 to take passengers to Don Sak Pier. The night boat leaves Koh Phangan for Surat Thani at 2100. A night boat leaves from the pier at Bandon, Surat Thani at 2300 (and from Phangan at 2100), 6 hrs (฿70-90). Day boats depart from Koh Phangan at 0615 and 1230 (4 hrs). Contact Ferry Phangan, on corner of Bandon and Chonkasem roads in Surat Thani, T286461, or in Thong Sala, Phangan, T377028.
   2. An express boat leaves twice a day from Don Sak Pier, Surat Thani, at 0730 and 1330 (and from Phangan at 0615 and 1300), 3¼ hrs (฿145). Buses from Surat Thani, from the airport, and from Phun Phin Railway Station connect with these boats.
   From Nathon on Koh Samui, express boats leave at 1000 and 1600 (and from Phangan to Samui at 0615, 1230 and 1600), 40 mins (฿60). A boat also leaves from Bophut, on Samui and lands at Hat Rin East, 1 hr (฿50). From Hat Rin Pier to Bophut, boats leave at 0930, 1130 and 1430. *Songserm* ferries link Koh Phangan with Koh Tao, departing daily at 1000 and 1230 (leaving Koh Tao at 0900) 1½ hrs (฿150). From Koh Tao there are ferries to Chumphon (see page 694).

The Southern Region

Directory **Banks** *Siam City Bank* (currency exchange centre), south end of Thong Sala, open 0830-1800. There is a currency exchange on Hat Rin. There is as yet no ATM machine on the island but major credit cards can be used to withdraw money at the bank. **Communications** Internet *Phangan Batik Internet Service* is in Thong Sala. They charge ฿4 per minute with a minimum time of 15 mins. **International telephone and fax service:** Thong Sala. **Post Office:** at the far eastern end of the sea front road. The post office is open 0830-1630, Mon-Fri and until 1230 on Sat. **Medical services** The main hospital is 3 km north towards Ban Hin Kong but there are also a number of smaller clinics in Hat Rin and Thong Sala. **Useful addresses** Police: 2 km down the road from Thong Sala towards Chao Lok Lum.

Koh Tao   เกาะเต่า

Phone code: 077 (but numbers prefixed by '01' are mobile phones & will not require this code) Colour map 4, grid B3

The name Koh Tao, literally translated as turtle island, relates to the shape of the island rather than to the wildlife in the surrounding seas. While your chances of spotting a turtle may be slim, the waters around Koh Tao are still reputed to offer some of the best diving and snorkelling sites in the Gulf of Thailand. Bleaching of the coral through exposure to unusually high water temperatures and storm damage in 1997 means the shallow coral beds are less spectacular than in the past, but they are still swarming with large and brightly coloured fish and their habitat is expected to recover.

Avoid bringing any plastic bottles or tin cans to the island as these are very difficult to dispose of

The easy accessibility of interesting marine life at depths available to beginners, the fairly gentle currents and the relatively low costs all contribute to making Koh Tao a particularly good place to learn to dive. The presence of giant manta rays and whale sharks (plankton feeders which can reach 6 m in length) means that even more experienced divers will find something of interest here. With these attractions in its favour, Koh Tao's reputation as a good, low-cost dive centre has grown rapidly, and in the space of just 10 years the island has made the transition from out-of-the-way backwater to mainstream destination. Improved transport links with the mainland have also made the island more accessible to the short-stay tourist, and so it is no surprise that the former economic mainstay of coconuts has now been eclipsed by the still-expanding tourist trade. Already, the number of rooms for tourists outnumbers the Thais resident on the island. Sensibly, though, as on Koh Samui, there are height restrictions on new buildings and this, in conjunction with the poor infrastructure, means the 'palm tree horizon' has not yet been blotted by multi-storey monstrosities.

While most people come here for the swimming, snorkelling and diving – as well as beach life in general – the fact that most paths are vehicle-unfriendly makes the island walker-friendly and there are some good trails to explore. Land-based wildlife includes monitor lizards, fruit bats and various non-venomous snakes. If planning to go on walks it is worth purchasing V Honsombud's *Guide Map of Koh Phangan & Koh Tao*.

Excursions **Koh Nang Yuan** lies off the northwest coast of Koh Tao and is surrounded by crystal clear water. Once a detention centre for political prisoners, the three islands that make up this mini-archipelago are surrounded by wonderful coral and are linked by sandbars at low tide. There is one bungalow complex, the **C-D** *Koh Nangyuan Dive Resort*, T2295085, F2295212, marion@kscl15.th.com

● ●

Koh Tao place names

Ban Mae Hat

บ้านแม่หาด

Hat Sai Ri

หาดทรายรี

Koh Nang Yuan

เกาะนางยวน

Snorkelling trips around the island Taxi boats around the island cost around ฿200 per person for a day trip with stops for snorkelling. ■ *Getting there: there is a daily boat at 1030 (฿60) from Ban Hat Sai Ri. A return boat leaves Koh Nangyuan at 1530.*

The densest areas of accommodation are Hat Sai Ri and Chalok Ban Kao. These offer some degree of nightlife and easy access to the dive schools. On the other hand, if you are looking for a greater sense of remoteness, the other bays are more secluded. This has largely been due to the poor quality of the roads which makes them considerably more difficult to reach without a bit of a trek or the use of taxi boats.

Despite the rapid rate of bungalow construction it remains difficult for non-divers to find empty, cheap accommodation unassisted during the high season. If you don't want to risk having to hike around with a heavy backpack for several hours in search of free rooms, the simplest option is to follow a tout from the pier. You can always move out the following day, but try and book the next place in advance. Alternatively, make your way straight to one of the more remote bays where places are often less booked out, but be warned that if they are full you may have to walk further to locate a final resting place. If diving, you should head straight for the dive shops around the pier where they will find you a place to stay in affiliated accommodation – often at a subsidised rate on the days when you are diving.

Twenty-four hour electricity is the exception rather than the rule on Koh Tao, although the relevant authorities are now beginning to make noises about bringing in a more comprehensive service. While being sent off to your room with just an oil lamp and glorious silence from the television adds to the romance of the place for many people, for those staying a shorter time, the lack of a fan overnight, particularly in the warmer months, can be rather trying.

The other unusual point about accommodation in Koh Tao is the early check out times. These reflect the need to free up rooms for those arriving on the early boats from the mainland. Finally, it is not unknown for guests to be evicted from their bungalows if they have not been spending enough in the restaurant so it is worth enquiring if there is a minimum expenditure before checking in. Most guesthouses have restaurants attached to them, but see also listings under 'Eating' on page 693.

Sleeping
Price codes:
see inside front cover

Koh Tao

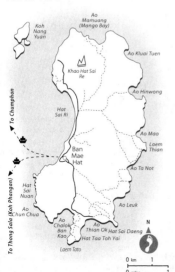

Around Ban Mae Hat (west coast) This is the beach either side of the harbour with easiest access to the facilities in town.

To the south of the pier A-D *Sensi Paradise* T2293645. A great range of rooms, the cheapest of which are very overpriced having neither fans nor private shower rooms. Nor are they particularly attractive. At the other end of the price range, however, the buildings are very sensitively designed wooden affairs with traditional Thai architectural features. The garden in which it is set is also richly planted and the small bay behind the resort is truly idyllic. They also operate an

The Southern Region

Related map
Ban Mae Hat, page 690

environmental policy. **B-D** *Koh Tao Royal Resort*. Smart, well-maintained wood and bamboo bungalows. Some a/c. Friendly staff and a lively restaurant. 24-hr electricity. **D-E** *CL Bungalows*. Simple bamboo huts with thatched roofs. Those set back from the beach are the smallest and cheapest and have shared toilet and shower facilities. Those on the beach are larger, with roomy verandahs. 24-hr electricity.

■ *on map, page 690*
To the north of the pier **B-C** *Beach Club* T01-2101808. Very attractive, airy rooms with high bamboo-lined ceilings, some with a/c. Recommended. **C** *Crystal* T2294643, F2293828. Cement bungalows with rather garish décor but clean and tiled bathrooms. In high season reserved exclusively for divers.

Hat Sai Ri (west coast) The longest stretch of uninterrupted beach on the island. **B** *Sunset Buri Resort*, T377171. Swimming pool. Only the most expensive rooms have a/c. Offers a good deal on snorkelling equipment. The restaurant serves rather meagre helpings. **B-D** *AC Resort*, T377197. Well-maintained bungalows on the 'wrong' side of the road with mosquito screens on the windows and nets over the beds. Tiled shower rooms, fan, verandah and 24-hr electricity. **C-D** *SB Cabana*. Fan-cooled chalet-style huts with a sea front restaurant. **C-D** *Seashell Resort*, T01-2293152. Attractive wood and bamboo huts with spacious verandahs. Travel agency attached. Roasted rice with shrimp and pineapple is reportedly among the best dishes at the restaurant. Plans to build some a/c rooms. **C-E** *O-Chai*. Same management as *Pranee's*. The cheapest rooms don't have fans, the largest are very smart wooden chalets. Electricity until midnight.

D *AC Two Resort*. On the landward side of the road, private shower room, fan, verandah and 24-hr electricity. **D** *Bow Thong Beach*. The last place on the beach and well-spaced bungalows, so quite private and quieter than most. Squat loos only. Electricity until midnight. **D** *Pranee's Bungalows*. A small resort with wooden bungalows set in a coconut grove. Snorkelling gear and kayaks for hire. 24-hr electricity. **D** *Sai Ree Huts*, T01-2293152. Bamboo weave and timber bungalows with hammocks and a swing on the beach. **D** *Sairee Cottage*. A well-established resort with the more expensive rooms situated on the beach front. Relaxed and friendly with a volleyball net in the garden. Western loos in all rooms, spacious verandahs. The restaurant serves reasonably priced food and does cheap cocktails. **D** *Simple Life Villa*. A mixture of concrete and wooden bungalows. Electricity cut off at midnight. **D-E** *Blue Wind*. Small and friendly set up. The cheaper rooms have shared shower rooms. Basic wood bungalows nestled in a beautiful mature garden. Recommended. **D-E** *New Way*. Peaceful, calm-ing atmosphere. Basic wooden huts with palm frond roofs. Very reasonably priced restaurant with a number of tasty

Related map
Koh Tao, page 689

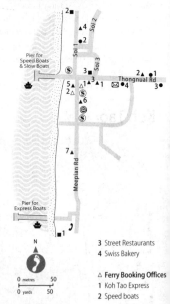

Ban Mae Hat

3 Street Restaurants
4 Swiss Bakery

△ **Ferry Booking Offices**
1 Koh Tao Express
2 Speed boats

■ **Sleeping**
1 Beach Club
2 Sensi Paradise
3 Crystal & Dive School

● **Eating**
1 Farango
2 Far Out Cafe

▲ **Dive Schools**
1 Buddha View
2 Carabao
3 Koh Tao Divers
4 Master Divers
5 Nangyuan
6 Scuba Junction
7 Sea Rover

Environmental problems on Koh Tao

The lack of a decent waste disposal system is threatening the sustainability of Koh Tao's promotional image as an example of a pristine tropical island getaway. While recycling of plastic bottles does occur, the refund to the bottle collector of just ฿3 per kilo makes it so uneconomic to transport them to the plant on the mainland that it is not widely practised. Instead bottles are burnt or dumped in the sea. For this reason some resorts only provide glass bottles – and where they do not, it may be worth requesting them, if only to bring home the fact that there is a demand for glass over plastic. Rubbish is also accumulating on beaches which are not privately owned. Sadly, although the diving schools promote their environmental credentials, they have as yet failed to organize regular, systematic clearance of the beaches, either by hired labour or by dive students in return for discounts on their courses, as goes on elsewhere.

The water shortage is another major problem. There is no surface water on Koh Tao. The sudden growth in population on the island has lead to excessive ground water extraction for shower and toilet facilities and pumping is now at a rate significantly higher than that of replenishment. As a result, the water-table has dropped markedly in recent years. If demand continues to escalate there is an imminent danger that salt water incursion will occur, contaminating the fresh water supplies. For this reason, several bungalows have signs in their shower facilities reminding guests not to be wasteful of water.

---

vegetarian dishes on the menu. Recommended. **D-E** *Suthep*, F377196. Run by an English-Thai couple, the cats have gone but the restaurant has been refurbished and produces excellent, tasty Thai and Western dishes. Films at the restaurant at 2000 every night. Library hires out a good range of books for ฿20 a day. Small bar on the beach serves drinks at cheaper rates at sunset. **D-F** *Ban's Diving Resort*, T01-2293181. In peak season the accommodation in this large resort is reserved exclusively for divers. More rooms are being added some of which will be a/c (and slightly more expensive). 24-hr electricity.

E-F *Queen Resort, Tommy's Dive Resort* and *View Cliff*. Owned by the same family and offering identical deals and prices. A mixture of clean concrete, wood and bamboo huts, some a/c, allied to the *VL Dive school*. Cheapest rooms are in *Tommy's Resort*, above the office. **F** *Scuba Junction*, T377169. Has just 6 newly built bungalows, exclusively for the use of divers. Shared shower room.

Cliff at the northern end of Sai Ri Beach D-F *CFT*. Views over to Koh Nang Yuan, rather isolated and very quiet. Very cheap rooms with shared shower facilities. Electricity until midnight. **E** *Golden Cape*. Small and very basic huts with thatched roofs. Mainly inhabited by long-term residents. Restaurant with views over the hillside. **E** *Silver Cliff*. Several rooms have great views out to sea. No fans in the cheaper room and tank and bucket rather than shower facilities. Hammocks on all verandahs. Slightly pricey food and with a sign reading 'Please eat here'. **E** *Sun Lord*. This guesthouse is only accessible by an unconvincing track through the jungle. Nevertheless, it commands fantastic views and the cheapest rooms made of bamboo and without shower room are perched precariously on huge granite boulders. Beneath them there is good coral, perfect for snorkelling. **E-F** *Sun Sea*. Cheaper rooms have clean shared shower rooms with squat loos. Most room have great views out to sea. Signs request your patronage at mealtimes. **F** *Eden*. Shared shower rooms and no fan. Very laid back. Set in a tropical garden on the landward side of the main road. Electricity until midnight. Some rooms with Western loos.

The Southern Region

Ao Mamuang (north coast) No tracks or roads lead to this bay so it remains solely accessible by boat. **F** *Coral Cove*, peaceful and well managed. Recommended. **F** *Mango Bay*. Secluded.

Ao Hinwong (east coast) A very peaceful bay with no beach to speak of but you can swim off the rocks. A taxi from the pier (฿50) will normally stop 1 km short of the bay itself from where the road deteriorates making it difficult for vehicles to pass. The accommodation consists of very simple huts with shared washing facilities and no electricity in the rooms. **F** *Green Tree Resort*. All rooms have shared toilet facilities. For ฿100 the resort will provide you with snorkelling gear whenever it is required for the duration of your stay. **F** *Hin Wong Bungalows*. Well spaced and clean wooden huts with verandahs overlooking the sea. Plenty of windows to let in the sea breeze, reasonably priced restaurant, snorkelling equipment for hire, friendly staff.

Ao Mao and Laem Thian (east coast) **F** *Laem Thian*. **F** *Sunrise*.

Ao Ta Not (east coast) A poor road serves the bay but vehicles brave the conditions to pick up guests from the ferry. **C-E** *Ta Not Bay Resort*, T01-9704703. Cheaper rooms have shared shower rooms, electricity until midnight. **C-F** *Poseidon*, T01-2294495, F377196. Cheaper rooms with shared shower rooms. Overseas call service. Taxis leave the resort twice a day for the pier (฿50). Electricity until 0600. **D-E** *Mountain Reef Resort*. A family-run resort which will take guests out fishing for their dinner. Taxi boats to the pier can be arranged here costing ฿50 (around 30 mins). **E** *Bamboo Huts*. Simple bamboo and thatch huts.

Ao Leuk (east coast) This beach shelves more steeply than most of the others around Koh Tao and so is good for swimming and has some of the best snorkelling on the island. This does mean groups visit from elsewhere, but on the whole this is a very quiet beach. Both the establishments here are very small and simple and neither have fans in the rooms. **D-E** *Leuk Bungalows*. Simple wood bungalows. Cheaper rooms have shared shower rooms. You can get a boat to the pier from here for ฿100, restaurant. **E** *Nice Moon*, F01-2293828. Just a couple of hundred metres south of the beach itself on cliffs overlooking the bay. Snorkelling equipment is free to guests. Kiet who runs the place in conjunction with his mother is friendly and informative and the restaurant serves delicious Thai food. Recommended.

Hat Taa Toh Yai (south coast) Easy access from Chalok Ban Kao. **C-E** *Tah Toh Lagoon Resort*, T01-2294486. Very good deals available for divers and in high season the resort is reserved exclusively for their use. The cheapest rooms for non-divers are those above the office which have fans, although the electricity only runs until midnight. Some 'luxury' bungalows have been added recently.

Ao Thian Ok (south coast) **E** *Rocky Bungalows*, only bungalows in bay. Basic but well spaced out and friendly with reasonably priced food.

Ao Chalok Ban Kao (south coast) This large bay has the highest concentration of diving resorts. **A** *Ko Tao Cottage Dive Resort* T377198, F01-7250751. The first up-market resort on the island. **C-D** *Laemklong*. Wooden huts on stilts with good views out to sea from roomy verandahs. Squat loos, electricity until midnight. Travel agency attached offering the normal services. **D** *Porn Resort*, T377744. Spacious rooms in either wood or concrete. Both are rather unusual, with the rooms of concrete including sections of massive granite boulders as part of the walls and the rooms of wood having bathroom walls made of glass bottles set in concrete giving a rather quaint stained glass effect. Recommended. **D** *Sunshine*. Attractive wood bungalows lined with bamboo weave with tiled bathrooms and western loos. Electricity until 0200. **D** *Sunshine 1*. Bad value for money, no water, very noisy restaurant and rude staff. **D-F** *Big Bubble Dive Resort*. Don't be confused by the separate signs for *Taraporn Bar and Restaurant, Haraporn Bungalows* and *View Point Bungalows* – they all operate as a whole. The large bamboo and thatch rooms are clean and pleasant with great views, the cheapest have shared shower rooms. Particularly good bargains available for those diving with the school. Recommended. **E** *Big Fish Dive Resort*, T377832, www.bigfishresort.com Accommodation is reserved solely for divers during high season. Electricity until 0600. Large, clean wooden bungalows with squat loos. **F** *Carabao Dive Resort*, T/F377898. Rather scruffy board huts, some with fans. The shared washing facilities are clean but very basic having only squat loos and tank and bucket showers. Electricity until midnight. Free for open-water certificate students. **F** *Buddha View Dive Resort*, 45 Moo 3, T2294693, F2293948. Clean, well-maintained painted timber, bamboo or thatch bungalows with mosquito screens on the windows and verandahs, or rooms in a rather characterless hotel block all with 24-hr electricity. A/c class rooms. Free water skiing for divers.

Hat Sai Nuan Really a series of small beaches but widely known by their collective name. **D-E** *Siam Cookies*. Attractive bamboo huts. Rooms don't have fans. Cheaper rooms share very clean and well-maintained shower rooms. **D-F** *Char Bungalows*. Friendly family-run bungalows in which the cheapest rooms have shared shower rooms and no fans. Electricity until 2300. Snorkelling equipment is free to guests. Squat loos. **E-F** *Taa Thong Bungalows*. On the headland so views of the sea on both sides. Simple wood and bamboo huts with large verandahs, well placed to make the most of sea breezes. Recommended.

Around Ban Mae Hat (west coast) Mid-range: *Farango* Thongnual Rd, an Italian restaurant which serves excellent pizzas. Now offers a delivery service. *Swiss Bakery* Thongnual Rd. Makes western-style bread. **Cheap**: *Far Out Café*, Thongnual Soi 2. Small friendly café serving a decent breakfast and a wide range of sandwiches. *Pon Bakery*, next to *Sairee Cottage*, rye, granary and sour dough bread sold.

Eating
● *on map, page 690*
Price categories:
see inside front cover

Cliff at the northern end of Sai Ri Beach Mid-range: *AC Seafood*, centre of the beach. Large complex with impressive fresh seafood displays. *DD Hut Seafood Restaurant*. Films shown nightly. *Gelmo Bistro*, opposite the *Blue Wind Bakery*. An up-market (ish) place for more sophisticated soirées. *Flower Restaurant*, centre of the beach. Quieter alternative to *ACs*, allied to *AC Two*. *Suthep Restaurant*, centre of the beach. Western specials served every 3rd day. Does great mashed potato, also toad in the hole, and Marmite sandwiches. Popular with long-term Western residents on the island. Good value. Stops serving at 2200. **Cheap**: *Blue Wind Bakery*, towards the northern end of the beach. Specializes in breads and desserts and does reasonable sandwiches. Now also offers fresh pasta including stuffed speciality pastas with basil, sun-dried tomato and mushroom-fillings. Upstairs, videos are shown at around 1930 if requested. *New Way Restaurant*, towards the northern end of the beach. Very good Thai food at reasonable prices and cheap drinks. Has a number of tasty vegetarian dishes on the menu. Recommended.

Ao Ta Not (east coast) Mid-range: *Poseidon*. A good range of vegetarian dishes on the menu.

Ao Chalok Ban Kao (south coast) Mid-range: *New Heaven*, rather a climb, at the top of the hill. A bit pricey but very good food. Only open in the evenings. *Taraporn Bar & Restaurant*, across the slatted walkway at the most westerly end of the beach. There are hammocks and cushions and mat floor seating at this restaurant on stilts above the sea. A great

The Southern Region

venue. **Sunshine Dive School**, has a BBQ evening buffet every night with baked potatoes, garlic bread, calamari, kebabs, salad and some rice dishes. **Cheap**: *Viewpoint Restaurant*, beyond the *Bubble Dive Resort* at the eastern end of the beach. Wide menu of Thai and some Western food. Also perched just above the sea. A very laid-back restaurant serving very reasonably priced food in comparison to most others on the beach.

Bars & clubs At night the bars on Sai Ri Beach do quite a brisk trade. **Acs** is probably the most developed club here. The ambience at **Venus** (Sai Ri Beach) is more intimate. It is on a smaller scale and the owners have deliberately avoided using imported building materials. On the other main beach on the island (Ao Chalok Ban Kao), the **Museum Bar** is the main night spot. A number of smaller bars are also growing up on both these beaches. **The Watering Hole**, Sai Rai Beach. Wooden bar, very sociable, some food, good ambience and live music from time to time. **Babaloo**, Ao Chalok Ban Kao. Excellent bar set in the rocks and decorated with sculptures, open from 2100.

Meditation **Two View** runs yoga courses, fasting and colonic irrigation and does past life sessions.
retreats On top of the prices for the courses you have to pay ฿50 a night for a basic hut; alternatively you can opt to sleep in the nearby caves if you have your own sleeping mat and bag. ■ *Getting there: the retreat is a 1 hr hike off the main road (from where it is clearly signed), along a steep but clearly marked track. It is best to start out in the early morning.* 5-day courses based in **New Way Bungalows** (Hat Sai Ri) are run most weeks on the subject of *Tian Chi Kung* by an Australian teacher who trained in China.

Shopping **Unwanted possessions** **Mr J** has a well-signed shop to the south of the pier which buys and sells second-hand goods from books to boots. He also accepts used batteries which he recycles.

Sport **Diving** is big on Koh Tao with the number of dive shops now exceeding well over 20. All
Diving is possible all dive schools have come to an arrangement where they charge exactly the same amount
year round on Koh Tao for an open water course (฿7,800). What varies are the sizes of the groups and the additional perks you will receive such as a free dive or free or subsidised accommodation. A discover scuba dive is about (฿800) and a fun dive for qualified divers is (฿600). All schools will accept credit card payment. If you are considering diving but want to watch the divers in action before making the investment, many of the dive schools are prepared to take you out to dive sites with their groups. You only pay for the snorkelling equipment. **Snorkelling equipment hire:** many of the guesthouses hire out their own equipment, but this is frequently of low quality. The most reliable gear is that hired from the dive shops. You generally pay (฿50) for the mask and snorkel and a further (฿50) for fins.

Transport **Local Kayak hire:** ฿150 per hour from *Seashell Resort*. ฿300 per day from *Pranee's*
59 km N of *Bungalows*. ฿250 per day or ฿80 per hour from *Laemklong Bungalows* on Ao Chalok
Koh Samui Kao. **Bicycle hire:** at the northern end of Sairee Beach a former dive instructor has set
47 km N of up shop offering mountain bikes for ฿150 per day from the back of her bungalow.
Koh Phangan **Motorbike hire:** ฿200 per day from *Seashell Resort* and *Pranee's Bungalows*. **NB** Unless you are a very experienced dirt bike rider this is not really an advisable form of transport as reaching any of the isolated bays involves going along very narrow, twisting, bumpy trails. **Long-tailed boats**: link the beaches, ฿20-50. **Songthaews**: during daylight hours cost ฿20 to anywhere on the island. After dark, ฿100.

Boats There is an overnight boat to Surat Thani which leaves at 0800 and arrives at around 2000 the following morning. (฿250). The speed boat to Chumphon costs ฿400, the express boat ฿300 and the slow night boat ฿200. The speed boat to Koh Phangan costs ฿300, the express boat ฿200 and the slow boat ฿150. The speed boat to Koh Samui is ฿400, the express boat ฿300 and the slow boat ฿200. There are also boats to Koh Tao running from the places listed above. In the monsoon season it is worth leaving a couple of spare days to get back on to the mainland as boats are occasionally cancelled. It is really only worth booking all-in-one (boat, bus and train) tickets on Thai holidays and during the high season.

Banks The only bank booth is the *Siam Commercial* at the end of the pier which is open Mon-Fri 1100-1400. It will not accept money transfers but does change travellers cheques with the lowest commission on the island. Two money changers in Ban Mae Hat offer visa advances but demand a heavy 7% commission. They are open from 0900-2000. Some dive shops will also sometimes provide cash back on credit cards for an additional 5%. **Communications** Internet: *Scuba Junction* offers the facility to send messages but it is apparently less keen to let you read those which have been sent to your account. *Koh Tao Cottages* will let you read your incoming mail for ฿50 and send replies for an additional ฿50 (for 15 mins). *Banana Rock*, on Ao Chalok Ban Kao, offers email at ฿1 per minute. **Overseas telephone** facilities are easily available on Sai Ri Beach, Ao Chalok Ban Kao and Ban Mae Hat. If you are on Tanot Bay you will have to go to *Poseidon Bungalows*. There are no telephone connections (bar mobile) from the other bays. Telephone calls are expensive. **NB** The phone lines on Koh Tao remain temperamental and are liable to go down at any time. **Post Office:** Thongnual Rd, straight up from the pier.

Directory

Nakhon Si Thammarat   นครศรีธรรมราช

Nakhon Si Thammarat ('the Glorious city of the Dead' or Nagara Sri Dhammaraja, 'the city of the Sacred Dharma Kings'), has masqueraded under many different aliases: Marco Polo referred to it as Lo-Kag, the Portuguese called it Ligor – thought to have been its original name – while to the Chinese it was Tung Ma-ling. Today, it is the second biggest city in the south and most people know it simply as Nakhon, or Nakhon Si.

Phone code: 075
Colour map 4, grid c3

Ins and outs

Nakhon, as it is locally known, although it may not be a very popular tourist destination is a provincial capital and therefore well connected. There is an airport north of town with daily flights to Bangkok. Nakhon lies on the main north-south railway line linking Bangkok with points south and the station is within easy walking distance of the town centre. The main bus station is about 1 km west of town, with connections to Bangkok and most destinations in the south. There are also minibus and share taxi services to many destinations in the south.

Getting there
See also Transport, page 702

The centre of Nakhon is comparatively compact, and navigable on foot. But for sights on the edge of town – like Wat Phra Mahathat – it is necessary to catch a public *songthaew*, or a *saamlor* or motorcycle taxi. The *songthaew* is the cheapest option.

Getting around

TAT, is at Sanam Na Muang, Rachdamnern Rd, T346516. The staff here produce a helpful pamphlet and hand out sheets of information on latest bus and taxi prices. A useful first stop. ■ *Mon-Sun, 0830-1630.* (Close by is the unremarkable city pillar or *lak muang* contained within a concrete monstrosity.)

Tourist offices

History

Nakhon was at its most powerful and important during King Thammasokarat's reign in the 13th century, when it was busily trading with south India and Ceylon. But as Sukhothai and then Ayutthaya grew in influence, the city went into a gradual decline. During the 17th century, King Narai's principal concubine banished the bright young poet, Si Phrat, to

The Southern Region

Nakhon. Here he continued to compose risqué rhymes about the women of the governor's court. His youthful impertinence lost him his head.

Nakhon used to have the dubious honour of being regarded as one of the crime capitals of Thailand – a position it had held, apparently, since the 13th century. Locals maintain that the city has now cleaned up its act and Nakhon is probably best known today for its prawn farms and nielloware industry (see page 817). The shop where the industry started some 50 years ago still stands on Sitama Road and production techniques are demonstrated on Si Thammasok I Road. Elsewhere, other than in a few handicraft shops on Tha Chang Road, nielloware is a rather illusive commodity, although the National Museum has some examples on display.

Sights

Wat Phra Mahathat A 2 km-long wall formerly enclosed the old city and its wats – only a couple of fragments of this remain (the most impressive section is opposite the town jail on Rachdamnern Road). Wat Phra Mahathat, 2 km south of town on Rachdamnern Road, is the oldest temple in town and the biggest in South Thailand – as well as being one of the region's most important. The wat dates from 757 AD, and was originally a Srivijayan Mahayana Buddhist shrine. The 77 m-high stupa, *Phra Boromathat* – a copy of the Mahathupa in Ceylon – was built early in the 13th century to hold relics of the Buddha from Ceylon. However, the wat underwent extensive restoration in the Ayutthayan Period and endured further alterations in 1990. The *chedi's* square base, its voluptuous body and towering spire are all Ceylonese-inspired. Below the spire is a small square platform decorated with bas-reliefs in gold of monks circumambulating (*pradaksina*) the monument. The spire itself is said to be topped with 962 kg of gold, while the base is surrounded by small stupas. The covered cloisters at its base contain many recently restored Buddha images all in the image of subduing Mara. Also here is the *Vihara Bodhi Langka*, a jumbled treasure-trove of a museum. It contains a large collection of archaeological artefacts, donated jewellery, bodhi trees, Buddhas, and a collection of sixth to 13th-century Dvaravati sculpture – some of the latter are particularly fine. The mural at the bottom of the stairs tells the story of the early life of the Buddha, while the doorway at the top is decorated with figures of Vishnu and Phrom dating from the Sukhothai Period. ■ *The cloisters are open Mon-Sun 0830-1200 and 1300-1630. ฿5.*

Phra Viharn Luang The nearby Phra Viharn Luang (to the left of the main entrance to the stupa) is an impressive building – with an intricately painted and decorated ceiling – dating from the 18th century. The best time to visit the monastery is in October during the Tenth Lunar Month Festival when Wat Mahathat becomes a hive of activity: foodstalls, travelling cinemas, shadow-puppet masters, the local

• •

Nakhon Si Thammarat names

Khanom beach	Nai Phlao beach
หาดขนอม	หาดนายเพลา
Khao Luang National Park	Wat Phra Mahathat
อุทยานแห่งชาติเขาหลวง	วัดพระมหาธาตุ
Khao Wang Thong Cave	Wat Wang Tawan Tok
ถ้ำเขาวังทอง	วัดวังตะวันตก

mafia, businessmen in their Mercedes, monks, and handicraft sellers all set up shop – making the wat endlessly interesting.

Not far from Wat Mahathat is the puppet workshop of Nakhon's most famous *nang thalung* master – Khun Suchart Subsin. His workshop is signposted off the main road near the Chinese temple (hard to miss) and as well as giving shows (see **Entertainment**) and selling examples of his work starting at ฿50 or so for a simple elephant the compound itself is interesting and peaceful with craftsmen hammering out puppets under thatched awnings.

Puppet workshop

Nakhon Si Thammarat

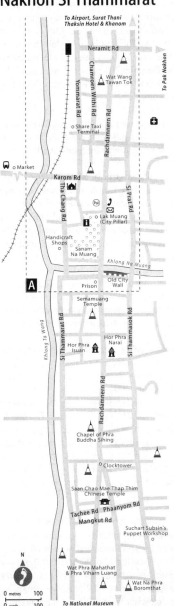

To Airport, Surat Thani
Thaksin Hotel & Khanom

Neramit Rd

Yommarat Rd

Chamoen Withi Rd

Wat Wang
Tawan Tok

Rachdamnern Rd

To Pak Nakhon

o Share Taxi
Terminal

Market

Karom Rd

Tha Chang Rd

Si Prat Rd

o Lak Muang
(City Pillar)

Handicraft
Shops

Sanam
Na Muang

Khlong Na Muang

Old City
Wall

Prison

Khlong To Wang

Semamuang
Temple

Si Thammarat Rd

Si Thammasok Rd

Hor Phra
Isuan

Hor Phra
Narai

Rachdamnern Rd

Chapel of Phra
Buddha Sihing

Clocktower

Saan Chao Mae Thap Thim
Chinese Temple

Tachee Rd Phaanyom Rd

Mangkut Rd

Suchart Subsin's
Puppet Workshop

N

Wat Phra Mahathat
& Phra Vihan Luang

Wat Na Phra
Boromthat

0 metres   100
0 yards   100

To National Museum

Also on Rachdamnern Road, about 700 m or so beyond Wat Mahathat, the Nakhon branch of the National Museum is one of the town's most worthwhile sights. The impressive collection includes many interesting Indian-influenced pieces as well as rare pieces from the Dvaravati and later Ayutthaya Periods. Some exhibits are labelled in English. The section on art in South Thailand explains and charts the development of the unusual local Phra Phutthasihing (or Buddha Sihing) style of Buddha image, which was popular locally in the 16th century. Also in this section is the oldest Vishnu statue in Southeast Asian art (holding a conch shell on his hip) dating from the fifth century. The museum has sections on folk arts and crafts and local everyday implements. To the right of the entrance hall, in the prehistory section, stand two large Dongson bronze kettle drums – two of only 12 found in the country. The one decorated with four ornamental frogs is the biggest ever found in Thailand. ■ *0900-1200, 1300-1600 Wed-Sun, ฿10. Getting there: the museum is a long 2-km walk from most of the hotels; catch one of the numerous blue songthaews running along Rachdamnern Rd and ask for 'Pipitipan Nakhon Si Thammarat' (฿4).*

The Nakhon Si Thammarat National Museum

*Related map
A Nakhon Si
Thammarat centre,
page 699*

The Southern Region

Wat Wang Tawan Tok Back in the centre of town is Wat Wang Tawan Tok, across Rachdamnern Roa from the bookshop. It has, at the far side of its sprawling compound, a souther Thai-style wooden house, built between 1888 and 1901. Originally the hous (which is really three houses in one) was constructed without nails – it has sinc been poorly repaired using them. The door panels, window frames and gables, a rather weather-beaten now, were once intricately carved but it is still infinite more appealing than the concrete shophouses going up all over Thailand.

Chapel of Phra Buddha Sihing The Chapel of Phra Buddha Sihing, sandwiched between two large provincia office buildings just before Rachdamnern Road splits in two, may contain on of Thailand's most important Buddha images. During the 13th century a image, magically created, was shipped to Thailand from Ceylon (hence th name – Sihing for the Sinhalese people). The Nakhon statue, like the other tw images that claim to be the Phra Buddha Sihing (one in Bangkok, see page 97 and one in Chiang Mai, Northern Thailand), is not Ceylonese in style at all; conforms with the Thai style of the peninsula.

Market A worthwhile early morning walk is west across the bridge along Karom Roa to the **Morning Market** (about 1 km). This gets going early, but by 0630 c 0700 it is feverish with activity. It is almost entirely a fresh food market.

Thai Traditional Medicine Centre On the outskirts of the city, after Wat Mahathat is the small Wat Mechai. Whil the temple is fairly ordinary, at one end of the temple grounds is a recentl established centre for traditional medicine, including massage. If you want traditional massage, the cost is about ฿120 per hour (if you'd like longer yo will need to say first). You can also take a course in massage, paying by th hour, and learn more about traditional herbal medicine (there is a small gar den of medicinal plants at the front).

Sleeping
■ *on map*
Price codes:
see inside front cover
Although recent additions and upgrades have improved the standard of accommoda tion in Nakhon it must still have some of the grimmest hotels in Thailand. At the to level, it is well served with a decent 5-star hotel, and the middle range now has a coupl of hotels worthy of a mention, but as for the rest, there is little to choose between them.

A *Twin Lotus Hotel* (used to be the Southern BM), on the outskirts of the town centre opened in 1995, 410 a/c rooms with TV and minibars, and a reasonably sized swim ming pool, fitness centre, etc. The usual services expected for a 5-star hotel for what i quite a reasonable price (including a good buffet-style breakfast). A well-run anc well-maintained hotel, and the staff are friendly, but the hotel is too large to offer a personal service. **B-C** *Grand Park Hotel*, 1204/79 Pak Nakhon Rd, T317666-7 F317674. Opposite the Nakhon Garden Inn – a bit of a block architecturally, it doesn' really live up to its grand name, but clean, adequate rooms, centrally located, with lot of parking. A/c hot water, TV, mini-bar. One of the better hotels in this category **B-C** *Taksin*, 1584/23 Si Prat Rd, T342790, F342794. A/c, another pretty mediocre hote – even gruesome. Hideous block, kitsch rooms, massage parlour, karaoke bar anc disco for those in need.

C-D *Montien*, 1509/40 Yommarat Rd, T341908, F345561. Some a/c, from the outside this looks like a combination fire and health hazard, inside the rooms may come as a pleasant surprise by comparison, with attached bathrooms and western toilets, anc more expensive ones with TV and hot water – but it is still pretty grim. **C-D** *Thai*, 1375 Rachdamnern Rd, T341509, F344858. Some a/c, restaurant, formerly the best hotel in a rather mediocre bunch, it still has the advantage of a central location over the new comer, *Twin Lotus Hotel*, but otherwise there is little to recommend it, the front part is

Nakhon Si Thammarat centre

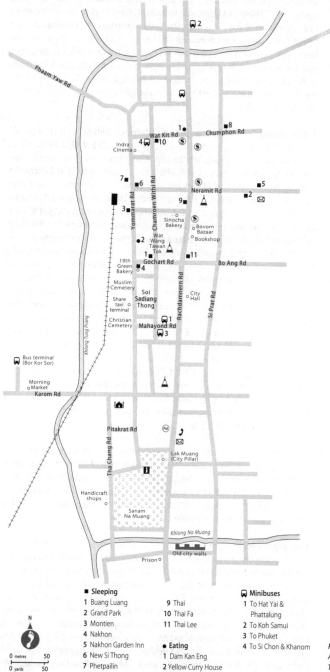

The Southern Region

■ Sleeping
1 Buang Luang
2 Grand Park
3 Montien
4 Nakhon
5 Nakhon Garden Inn
6 New Si Thong
7 Phetpailin
8 Taksin
9 Thai
10 Thai Fa
11 Thai Lee

● Eating
1 Dam Kan Eng
2 Yellow Curry House
(Kaeng San)

🚐 Minibuses
1 To Hat Yai &
   Phattalung
2 To Koh Samui
3 To Phuket
4 To Si Chon & Khanom

Related map
A Nakhon Si
Thammarat,
page 697

cheaper while the rear annex is a touch more up-market, still pretty grim with requisite karaoke bar, ancient massage parlour and disco. **D** *Nakhon Garden Inn*, 1/4 Pak Nakhon Rd, T344831, F342926. A/c, restaurant, friendly staff, one of the nicest mid-range places to stay – a rustic feel for Nakhon, with two brick buildings on either side of a large garden compound with clean rooms and hot water. The rooms have been nicely decorated in keeping with the rustic feel – rather dark, but good value and something a bit different from most of the places in the city centre. The rooms come with coupons for a 50% discount for breakfast. Souvenirs from Khiriwong (tie-dye clothing in natural dyes) and Cha-ouad district (basketry) are sold at the front desk. Recommended.

D-E *Bua Luang*, 1487/19 Sai Luang Muang, Chamroen Withi Rd, T341518, F342977. Some a/c, large clean rooms, popular with businessmen. **D-E** *Nakhon Hotel*, 1477/5 Yommarat Rd, T356318. Some a/c, the best of the Chinese-style hotels in this category, more expensive rooms come with a/c, hot water and TV. **D-E** *Phetpailin*, 1835/38-39 Yommarat Rd, T341896, F343943. Some a/c, right by the railway station, over 100 rooms in this ugly block, the sort of hotel where men clean out their ears in the lobby with surgical equipment. **D-E** *Sakol Hotel*, on Pak Nakhon Rd, just after the turn in to the road. The sign is in Thai only, but the hotel is very easy to find. It is a large pale blue building that looks a little like a school, set back a couple of hundred metres from the road, and lying behind a large green wooden house in a garden (incidentally, this house is about a 100 years old and gives a good idea of a traditional urban home of a wealthy family of the time). Although very simply furnished, and with the most basic of bathrooms (but there are sit-down toilets), *Sakol Hotel* looks good for its 50 or so years! Both ceiling fan and a/c are available. The rooms upstairs are better than those on the ground floor as they have a private balcony on the way out to the bathroom. Very friendly management. **E** *Thai Lee*, 1128 Rachdamnern Rd, T356948. Large, bright, clean rooms with fan and attached bathroom (western toilet), friendly management, best-value accommodation in the lower end of the market. **E-F** *New Si Thong*, 1547/2-3 Yommarat Rd, T356702. Much like the *Thai Fa*, a Chinese hotel with bare very functional rooms, sometimes dirty. **E-F** *Thai Fa*, 1751 Chamroen Withi Rd, T356727. Chinese-style hotel, bare rooms but reasonably clean, and a good size with attached bathrooms (squat toilet), though not very private as the top metre of the partition is wire mesh only.

Eating
● *on map*
Price categories:
see inside front cover

Prawns are Nakhon's speciality – farms abound in the area. Good seafood (including saltwater prawns) at reasonable prices is served in most of the town's restaurants. Roadside stalls sometimes sell a Nakhon speciality: small prawns in their shells, deep fried in a spicy batter and served as a sort of prawn pattie. The *Bovorn* Bazaar in the centre of town off Rachdamnern Rd is a good place to start in any hunt for food: it has restaurants, stalls, a bakery, a bar and a coffee shop.

Thai Expensive: *Rim Nam*, Jaturong Ratsami Rd. This restaurant is reputedly the best place for southern curries and seafood. It is about 2 km out of town. **Mid-range**: *Dam Kan Eng*, intersection of Wat Kit and Rachdamnern roads. Very good Sino-Thai restaurant which locals believe serve some of the best food in town, seafood is especially good. *Dang Ah*, 74 Rachdamnern Rd. Excellent sea-fresh tandoori prawns, also serves Chinese. Recommended. *Lakorn*, at the back of Bovorn Bazaar off Rachdamnern Rd. Only restaurant in Nakhon with an Indian rubber tree growing through the middle of it, pleasant eating spot, with open verandahs, art work, wicker chairs and a reasonable line in seafood dishes. Recommended. *Pak Nakhon*, 10 km out of town on Pak Nakhon Rd. Highly recommended for seafood, also serves Chinese. *Yellow Curry House*, 1467 Yommarat Rd. This place is recommended by the local culinary élite, seafood specialities and also some oddities (to the western palate), like red ants.

International Mid-range: *A & A Restaurant*, a/c restaurant just down the road from the Nakhorn Garden Inn and marked with flags boasting fresh coffee. Serves Thai-style toasted bread with jam, marmalade, condensed milk, sugar, etc, excellent fresh coffee, and very tasty Thai food. They also do western breakfasts for a very reasonable price. *Hao Coffee Shop*, in Bovorn Bazaar, off Rachdamnern Rd. Attempt at creating some ambience: charmingly decorated with antiques and assorted oddities. Try the *Kuay Tioaw Si Khrong Moo* (pork rib noodle soup) and the fried minced chicken noodles. At the front of the shop you can buy herbal products from the Khiriwong village, including a mangosteen soap and shampoo!

Bakeries Nakhon has tens of bakeries, some of them really very good. *Ligos*, on corner of Rachdamnern Rd and Bovorn Bazaar, has a good selection of pastries and doughnuts; perhaps even better is *Sinocha* (sign only in Thai), down the narrow alleyway by the *Thai Hotel*. It sells danish pastries, doughnuts and more sickly concoctions as well as a good range of dim sum. Recommended. Another a/c bakery is the *19th Green* on Yommarat Rd which does a good line in gaudy cakes. *A & A Restaurant*, on Pak Nakhon Rd has some excellent cookies of various kinds and serves bread, steamed or toasted, with jam, marmalade, condensed milk, etc. *Nom Sod and Bakery*, at the front of Bovorn Bazaar, has a sign in Thai only, but is pretty easy to spot right at the front, a/c and serving fresh milk, Thai-style toast and steamed bread with jam, condensed milk, etc.

Foodstalls *Nam Cha Rim Tang* is a stall in the *Bovorn Bazaar*, which sets up in the early evening and produces exceedingly good banana rotis. Lining Rachdamnern Rd, along the wall of the playing fields for nearly a kilometre (up to *Dang Ah* restaurant) there are countless stalls selling *som tam*, a chilli-hot papaya salad from Thailand's northeastern region usually served with BBQ chicken or *kai yaang*.

Rock Bar and Grill, *Bovorn Bazaar*, Rachdamnern Rd. A western-style open-air bar with cold beer and a small menu. **Bars**

Shadow plays Most of the plays relate tales from the Ramakien (see page 98) and the *jataka* tales. Narrators sing in ear-piercing falsetto accompanied by a band comprised of *tab* (drums), *pi* (flute), *mong* (bass gong), *saw* (fiddle) and *ching* (miniature cymbals). There are 2 sizes of puppets. *Nang yai* (large puppets) which may be 2 m tall, and *nang lek* (small puppets) (see page 813). Shows and demonstrations of how the puppets are made can be seen at the workshop of Suchart Subsin, 110/18 Si Thammasok *Soi* 3 (take the road opposite Wat Phra Mahathat, turn left – there's a small pond at the top of the *soi* where Suchart Subsin is signposted – and walk 50 m), T346394. This group have undertaken several royal performances. **Entertainment**

Feb *Hae Pha Khun That* (20th-29th) 3 day event when homage is paid to locally enshrined relics of the Buddha. **Festivals**

Sep-Oct *Tenth Lunar Month Festival* (movable). A 10-day celebration, the climax of which is the colourful procession down Rachdamnern Rd to Wat Phra Mahathat; *Chak Phra Pak Tai* (movable) centred around Wat Mahathat, includes performances of *nang thalung* (shadow plays) and *lakhon* (classical dance). This is a southern Thai festival also held in Songkhla and Surat Thani.

Nakhon is the centre of the South Thai handicrafts industry. Nielloware, *yan liphao* basketry (woven from strands of vine of the same name), shadow puppets, Thai silk brocades and *pak yok* weaving are local specialities. **Shopping**

Books *Suun Nangsuu Nakhon*, Rachdamnern Rd close to *Bovorn Bazaar* has a small selection of English books plus articles on the surrounding area and sells day-old English-language newspapers.

Clothes An array of cheap clothes stalls down the alleyway behind the *Thai Hotel*.

Handicrafts Shops on Tha Chang Rd, notably the *Thai Handicraft Centre* (in the lime green tradition at wooden house on the far side of the road behind the tourist office), *Nabin House* and *Manat Shop*. With the exception of the *Thai Handicraft Centre* silverware predominates. Odds and ends can also be picked up in the market in front of Wat Phra Mahathat.

Nielloware Original shop on Chakrapetch Rd. A few handicraft shops on Tha Chang Rd also sell it.

Shadow puppets From the craftsmen at *Suchart House*, Si Thammasok Rd, Soi 3 (see above) and stalls around Wat Phra Mahathat.

Yan liphao Best at *Tha Rua Village*, 10 km out of town on Route 408 or shops on Tha Chang Rd.

Sports **Thai boxing** Every Sun 2100 in the stadium, Rachdamnern Rd. ฿40.

Transport
See also Ins & outs,
page 695
800 km S of Bangkok

Local Songthaew: from one end of town to the other (฿4). **Saamlor**: the old pedal *saamlor* is still in evidence though it is gradually being pushed out by the noisier and more frightening **motorcycle taxi** of which there seem to be hundreds.

Long distance Air: airport lies north of town. Connections with Bangkok (daily), 1 hr 55 mins.

Train: station on Yommarat Rd. Overnight connections with Bangkok. Most south-bound trains stop at the junction of Khao Chum Thong, 30 km west of Nakhon, from where one must take a bus or taxi. Two trains go into Nakhon itself, the Rapid No 47, which leaves Bangkok's Hualamphong station at 1735 and arrives at Nakhon the next day at 0840, and the Express No 15, which leaves Bangkok at 1915 and arrives at 0930.

Bus: the bus station (*bor kor sor*) for non-a/c connections is about 1 km out of town over the bridge on Karom Rd, west of the mosque. Most people pick up a bus as it works its way through town though. The TAT office produces a useful sheet giving the latest information on bus and share taxi fares and times. Overnight connections with Bangkok's Southern bus terminal 12 hrs. Regular connections with Krabi (3 hrs), Surat Thani (2½-3 hrs), Hat Yai (3½ hrs), Phuket (7 hrs), Trang (3 hrs), Phattalung, Songkhla and with other southern towns. A number of **minibus** services are also operating to destinations in the south including Hat Yai, Phuket, Krabi, Trang and Surat Thani. They tend to be marginally quicker and slightly more expensive than a/c coaches. See the map for locations but check beforehand as their 'patches' seem to change from time to time. **Share taxi**: as in Malaysia, this is a popular way of travelling long distance in the south. The share taxi terminal is on Yommarat Rd. Prices are fixed (they are listed on a board at the terminal) and most large centres in the south are served from here including Hat Yai, Phuket, Krabi, Trang, Surat Thani, Phattalung and Songkhla.

Directory **Airline offices** *THAI*, 1612 Rachdamnern Rd, T342491 and T343874. **Banks** *Bangkok*, 1747 Rachdamnern Rd. *Bank of Ayudhya*, 1366/1-3 Rachdamnern Rd. *Thai Farmers*, 1360 Rachdamnern Rd. *Siam Commercial*, 1166 Rachdamnern Rd. **Communications Internet**: Internet cafés can be found opposite the *Twin Lotus Hotel* and in the area around Bovorn Bazaar. **Post Office**: Rachdamnern Rd (opposite the police station). There is also a small post office opposite the *Nakhon Garden Inn* on Pak Nakhon Rd. **Telephone office**: attached to the post office on Rachdamnern Rd, overseas calls available.

Beaches north of Nakhon Si Thammarat

Beaches around Nakhon are unattractive, with filthy water. But 80 km north, near Khanom district, there are some secluded stretches of shoreline: **Khanom beach** (2 km from the village), **Nai Phlao beach** nearby, and a couple of other bays opening up to development. This area is predominantly visited by Thai tourists. The recent economic crisis has seriously affected the tourism business in this area with quite a few of the older operations looking very run-down. Newer operations seem also to be targeting western tourists who are beginning to look towards the mainland in this area for reasonably priced peace and quiet, and convenience they have failed to find in Samui.

A-B *Khanom Golden Beach Hotel*, T326690, F529225, khanom@nksrat.ksc.co.th Hotel block with pool and all amenities (snooker room, children's room), tour desk, restaurant, and rental of windsurf boards, sailing dinghies, bicycles, etc. Friendly and professional staff. Rooms are rather characterless but clean and comfortable. The

Sleeping
■ *on map*
Price codes:
see inside front cover

Beaches north of Nakhon Si Thammarat

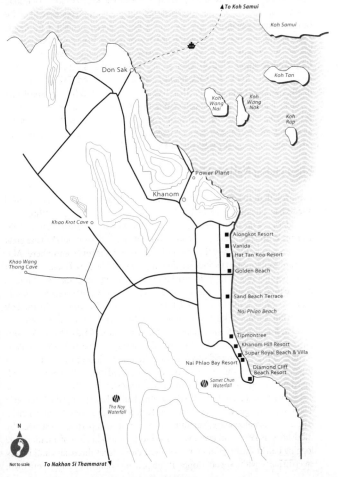

The Southern Region

larger suites (prices not listed here) are very spacious and well equipped. The honeymoon suite (completely pink) comes with chaise longue and heart-shaped pillows. Also offer tours to the Southern Archipelago National Park. **A-B** *Supar Royal Beach Hotel*, T529039, hotel block under same management as the *Supar Villa*. Clean rooms, tiled floors, every room has a view of the sea but the rooms are generally pretty characterless. **A-C** *Alongkot Resort*, T529119, boring layout with tacky rooms and overpriced, and for those who like heavy industry there is an industrial port just down to the right! ors, every room has a view of the sea but the rooms are generally pretty characterless. **A-C** *Nai Phlao Bay Resort*, T529039. A/c, restaurant, large resort, quite pricey for what it is. Impersonal service. **B-C** *Khanab Nam Diamond Cliff Resort*, T529144. A/c, restaurant, pool, no hot water. A good location with views over the bay, cottage-style accommodation, but very run-down and with generally unfriendly staff. No beach access. The restaurant is exorbitantly expensive given the quality and quantity of food. **B-C** *Khanom Hill Resort*, overlooking the bay, fairly standard bungalows. A/c and fan available. The views are obscured by the large, private, Thai-style holiday home which occupies the prime place in the grounds. **B-C** *Supar Villa*, T529237. A/c, restaurant. **B-D** *Sand Beach Terrace Resort*, Huge range of clean, well-maintained rooms, some with a/c and some with fan, including some 'house-style' accommodation with several rooms for rent separately or as a set. Friendly staff, good-value food including western-style breakfasts. Nicely laid out grounds with places to sit on the beach. Gently sloping and safe swimming beach. Recommended. **C** *GB Resort*, T529253, A-frame bungalows on the beach with mature trees providing plenty of shade. A/c rooms come with hot water and a fridge. Tiny bathrooms. **C** *Tipmontree Resort*, T528147, large comfortable bungalows with basic amenities on pretty beach front. Laid-back, friendly staff. **C** *Vanida Resort*, T326329, Spacious rooms, very basic bathrooms, TV (Thai channels only). Okay. **C-D** *Had Tan Koo Resort*, T529039, Bungalow accommodation, quite old but well kept and clean. Fan only. ■ *Getting there: regular buses from Nakhon (฿20), a/c micro buses (฿60) leave from Wat Kit Rd, near the Thai Fa Hotel (see map, page 699). The beaches are situated about 8 km off the main road; turn at the 80-km marker.*

Khao Luang National Park

Colour map 4, grid B3 Lying less than 10 km west of Nakhon, the Khao Luang National Park is named after Khao Luang, a peak of 1,835 m – the highest in the south. Within the boundaries of the mountainous, 570-sq-km national park are three waterfalls. **Karom Waterfall** which lies 30 km from Nakhon, off Route 4015, has a great location with views over the lowlands. There is a Visitors Centre here. Also here are cool forest trails and fast-flowing streams. The park is said to support small populations of tiger, leopard and elephant, although many naturalists believe they are on the verge of extinction here. ■ *Getting there: take a bus to Lansaka (then walk 3 km to falls) or charter a minibus direct.* **Phrom Lok Waterfall** is about 25 km from Nakhon, off Route 4132. ■ *Getting there: take a minibus from Nakhon and motorbike taxis can be hired for ฿10 for the last very pleasant 8-km trip to the falls.* However, the most spectacular of the waterfalls is **Krung Ching** – 'waterfall of a hundred thousand raindrops' – 70 km out of town, and a 4-km walk from the park's accommodation. The 1,835-m climb up **Khao Luang** starts from Khiriwong village, 23 km from Nakhon, off Route 4015. The mountain is the highest in South Thailand and part of the Nakhon Si Thammarat range, running from Koh Samui south through Surat Thani to Satun. The scenic village, surrounded by forest, was partially destroyed by mudslides in 1988 – an event which led to the introduction of a nationwide logging ban at the beginning of 1989. The climb takes three days and is very steep in parts, with over 60° slopes. If you plan on doing this walk on your own, there is no accommodation, so it is necessary to carry your own equipment and food. Dr Buncha Pongpanit, the owner of *Saun Sangsan Nakhon Bookstore*, Rachdamnern Road (close to Bovern Bazaar) will sometimes organize climbs for tourists. The villagers at Khiriwong village can organise trips up the mountain, but do not speak English. Alternatively, TVS-REST (T02-6910437-9, F02-6902796), a Thai not-for-profit involved in community development, offers tours and visits to Khiriwong village, with activities and accommodation at the village and with treks into the forest. See www.ecotour.in.th/indexen.html The tour leaves from Bangkok and costs ฿3,600. Tours to Krung Ching waterfall, including white-water rafting, and other tours in the province can be organised at: *Krung Ching Tours* and other tour companies in the city of Nakhon Sri Thammarat. ■ *Getting there: Mazda songthaews leave Nakhon for Kiriwong every 15 mins or so (฿15).*

Phattalung   พัทลุง

Phone code: 074
Colour map 4, grid C3

The 'town of the hollow hill,' is so named because of the cave systems in its limestone hills (Khao Hua Taek to the west and Khao Ok Thalu to the east). In fact the town enjoys a rather beautiful position surrounded by rugged, tree-clothed, limestone outcrops (although one is being insensitively quarried for road-building material leaving a vivid scar visible for miles around).

But Phattalung's main claim to fame is as the place where *nang thalung*, Thai shadow plays, originated; records mention them as far back as the 15th century. *Nang* means leather and *thalung* probably derives from Phattalung. That said, *nang thalung* was almost certainly not 'invented' in Thailand: it is thought to have reached Siam from Java (where *wayang kulit* have been shadow dancing for centuries), possibly via Cambodia. The more popular Thai *khon* dances developed from it, supplanting the *nang thalung* everywhere except in the south. Performances of this traditional form of theatre can still be seen in Phattalung (only during festivals) and in Nakhon Si Thammarat. Performances begin around midnight – emphasizing the artform's links with the spirit world – and end at about 0400.

Phattalung is a very quiet provincial capital. Perhaps being sandwiched between Hat Yai to the south and Nakhon Si Thammarat to the north – two of Thailand's largest cities – has drained it of its commercial life blood. Anyway, here there are no a/c shopping malls, no glitzy hotels – even karaoke bars are pretty thin on the ground. It's easy to explore on foot. The tourist office, on Ramet Road (near the intersection with Kanasan Road), is not really a tourist office, but more like a handicraft shop which provides limited information.

• •

Phattalung place names

Lam Pam

ลำปำ

Wat Kao

วังเก่า

Wat Mai

วังใหม่

Wat Wang

วัดวัง

Sights

Wat Kuhasawan, to the west side of town on the road to Tha Miram, is associated with a large cave, **Tham Kuhasawan**, containing images of monks and the Buddha. Steps lead around the cave to the top of the mountain, from where there is a good view of the surrounding countryside. On the second set of steps is a statue to commemorate a hermit who lived in the cave. **Tham Malai Cave** is 3 km north of Phattalung – take a boat from behind the railway station to get there.

The Southern Region

Excursions   **Wat Wang** is 6 km east of the town, on the road to Lam Pam, and is thought to be several hundred years old. The original *chedi* lies in front of the wat, while the closed *bot* contains unrestored murals dating back 200 years. ■ *Getting there: motorbike taxis (₿20 return) from outside the post office or a songthaew from the same spot.*

Wang Kao and **Wang Mai**, the Old and New palaces respectively, lie about 8 km east of Phattalung in Tambon Lam Pam. Originally there were four palaces (the third and fourth being the Suan Dok and Central palaces), but two fell into disrepair and their sites have been redeveloped. The Old and New palaces however have been extensively restored by the Fine Arts Department, the work beginning in 1988. The buildings were constructed between 1866 and 1868 and became the residences of Phraya Apaiborirak, after whom the road from town towards the palaces is named (it is Rame-Apaiborirak Road). The structures consist of a number of traditional raised wooden houses, roofed with unglazed terracotta tiles, and linked together into a single living unit. ■ *Getting there: by songthaew or motorcycle taxi from outside the Post Office.*

The **Thale Noi Waterbird Sanctuary** is 39 km northeast of Phattalung at the northernmost end of the Thale Sap Songkhla, where the water is fresh (towards its southern end it is saline). The sanctuary supports nearly 200 species of bird (100 of which are waterfowl) and becomes an ornithological paradise between January and April when the migrants stop here. The best way to see the birdlife (jacanas, crakes, egrets, teal ...) is by hiring a boat to venture along the waterways (₿150 per hour). There is a viewing platform on the lake and several hundred families live in stilted houses along its shores. **Sleeping** D *Forestry Department* bungalow on the lake. ■ *Getting there: the*

Phattalung

To Nakhon Si Thammarat

To Tham Malai Cave

Entrance to Wat Kuhasawan

Khuha-Sawan Rd

Shrine

Nivat Rd

Taxis to Nakhon Si Thammarat

Boom Ice Cream

Pian Plaza   Night Market

Pian Yin Dii Rd

English Language Newspapers

Taxis to Lam Pam

To Tourist Office

Ramet Rd

Dissara-Sakharin Rd

Pracha Bamrung Rd

To Bus Station

N

0 metres   50
0 yards   50

■ **Sleeping**
1 Hor Fah
2 Phattalung
3 Phattalung Thai

🚌 **Transport**
1 Buses to Thale Noi & Nakhon Si Thammarat
2 Songthaews to Thale Noi
3 Buses to Hat Yai (a/c)

turn-off for the sanctuary is 20 km north of Phattalung along Route 41. Here turn right onto Route 4187 (it is signposted), for another 19 km. Songthaews leave from close to the train station off Nivat Rd for Thale Noi (see map).

Phattalung's handful of hotels have improved considerably over the last few years and 2 at least offer clean and functional rooms. The only catch is that hotels here charge almost twice as much for rooms with 2 beds as they do for those with a double bed. **C-D** *Hor Fah*, 28-30 Khuha-Sawan Rd, T611645, F613380. Some a/c, 6-storey hotel with good views from the upper rooms, the rooms are fine, surprisingly good in fact given first lobby impressions – clean and bright – but perhaps a little overpriced. **C-D** *Phattalung Thai Hotel*, 14/1-5 Dissara-Sakharin Rd, T611636. Some a/c, very reasonable rooms, clean with good bathrooms and showers, friendly management, marginally the better bet in this category. **E-F** *Phattalung Hotel*, Ramet Rd (opposite Thai Farmers Bank). Hard to spot and best missed, a grim place but the cheapest rooms in town.

Sleeping
■ *on map*
Price codes:
see inside front cover

Thai Cheap: *Klert Beer*, 6/4 Dissara-Sakharin, just down from *Thai Hotel*. Phattalung's best attempt at ambience, simple but good menu – including seafood. *Lam Pam Resort*, Lam Pam, good menu with lots of seafood. *Boom*, in front of the railway station, for sundaes and cold drinks. **Foodstalls** Perhaps the best place to eat in town is from one of the stalls that set up near and in the *Pian Plaza*, on Pian Yin Dii Rd.

Eating

Books English-language newspapers available from the store opposite the *Pian Plaza* on Pian Yin Dii Rd.

Shopping

Local Motorbike taxis (₿10) and **songthaews** from Ramet Rd, next to the post office.

Transport
888 km to Bangkok
110 km to Hat Yai

Long distance Train: station between the canal and Nivat Rd. Overnight connections with Bangkok, 15 hrs and regular connections with all stops on Bangkok-Butterworth route, Sungei Golok 5 hrs, Hat Yai 1 hr 20 mins, Yala 3 hrs 20 mins and Surat Thani 4 hrs.

Bus: buses leave from between the market place and the railway station. Overnight connections with Bangkok 12 hrs; also connections with Nakhon Si Thammarat 3 hrs, Hat Yai 1½ hrs and other southern towns. **Share taxi**: for Nakhon Si Thammarat leave from the road in front of the train station, 2½ hrs, ₿50. There are also share taxis to Trang.

Banks *Bangkok Bank*, Ramet Rd. *Thai Farmers*, Ramet Rd (main road through town). **Communications Post Office:** off Ramet Rd, not far from the railway station.

Directory

Hat Yai หาดใหญ่

Hat Yai has become a 'rest and relaxation' centre for Malaysians and Singaporeans. Many come for the shopping, and Hat Yai has a seemingly inexhaustible supply of gold shops and air-conditioned shopping centres. It must also be admitted – although the TAT office tries desperately to counter these slurs against Hat Yai's probity – that many Malaysians come to sample the city's 'barbershop' and ancient massage industries. For all its sins, Hat Yai is the unofficial capital of the south and the region's largest city with around 150,000 inhabitants. The local tourist office is doing its best to change the city's image to a more wholesome one. In this it may be fighting a losing battle.

Phone code: 074
Colour map 5, grid C5

The Southern Region

Ins and outs

Getting there
See also Transport, page 714

Hat Yai is the South's largest city and lies nearly 1,000 km south of Bangkok. The airport is 12 km from town and there are regular domestic connections with Bangkok and Phuket and international flights to Singapore and Kuala Lumpur. The train station is on the western edge of the city centre. There are connections with Bangkok and destinations to the south including Butterworth and Kuala Lumpur (Malaysia), and Singapore. The main bus terminal has a rather inconvenient out-of-town location but there are also many tour bus companies with centrally situated offices. Buses of all levels of luxury travel to Bangkok, destinations in the south, and even to towns in the north like Chiang Mai. Because so many visitors to Hat Yai are from south of the border, buses to destinations in Malaysia and Singapore are also very frequent. For connections to Hat Yai's sister town of Songkhla catch one of the striped green buses that leave from the clock tower every 7 mins through the day.

Getting around

Hat Yai is a large and busy city. *Songthaews* provide the main form of local public transport along with a good number of tuk-tuks and taxis. There are also several car hire outlets in town.

Tourist offices

TAT, 1/1 Soi 2, Niphat Uthit 3 Rd, T243747, F245986, covers the Songkhla, Hat Yai and Satun area. The office is 30 m off Niphat Uthit 3 Rd. Grit Wattanapruek is very helpful and keen but he does have his work cut out for him – with respect to Hat Yai at least.

Sights

On the plus side, Hat Yai does have numerous, excellent restaurants to choose from, and some of the best Chinese and Malay food to be had in Thailand. But beyond its cuisine and one or two good clubs and bars, there is little to love in Hat Yai.

Hat Yai's paucity of anything culturally interesting is exemplified by **Wat Hat Yai Nai**, which, for the town's top sight, is mediocre. The wat is 3 km west of Hat Yai, off Phetkasem Road (before U-Taphao Bridge), and houses the world's third longest reclining Buddha (35 m tip to toe) – *Phra Phuttah-atmongkol*. This spectacularly hideous statue now resides in a massive new concrete viharn. It is occasionally possible to climb inside the Buddha for an inspection of his lungs, but the temple authorities now seem to have restricted access to this breathtaking pleasure. At the exit to the compound, next to a merry-go-round of 10 rotating monks, a jaunty banner reads: 'May the triple gems always be with you'. *Songthaews* running past the wat leave from the *hor nalikaa* (clock tower) on Phetkasem Road (฿5).

For those who really want to scrape the sights barrel there is an amusing **Chinese temple** on Niphat Uthit 3 Road, just north of the *Hat Yai Central Hotel*. **Wat Lian Kao Ko** is jauntily painted in bright colours and outside its gates on the pavement sit ladies selling wild birds that visitors can buy and set free to accumulate merit. It is scarcely significant in any artistic or architectural sense, but the vast incense sticks and the doors painted with giant and fearsome warriors are entertaining. Another promoted sight is **bullfighting** (see Entertainment, below).

Essentials

Sleeping
■ *on maps, pages 709 & 712*
Price codes: see inside front cover

Hat Yai has a huge collection of hotels – around 100 – and there are new ones springing up all the time. Recently built establishments tend to be much cleaner, and are often good value for money. The town's hotel industry has a symbiotic relationship with its booming 'hairdressing' industry. For those venturing into barbershop country in pursuit of a room for the night, there is a general rule of thumb: if a TV costs an extra ฿200, it's likely there are pornographic films on the in-house video. The distinction between 'Thai Traditional Massage' (ubiquitous throughout Thailand) and 'Ancient Massage' (ubiquitous throughout Hat Yai and the south) should also be noted. Ancient masseuses usually belong to the oldest profession. Many of them are located around Tanrattanakorn

Hat Yai

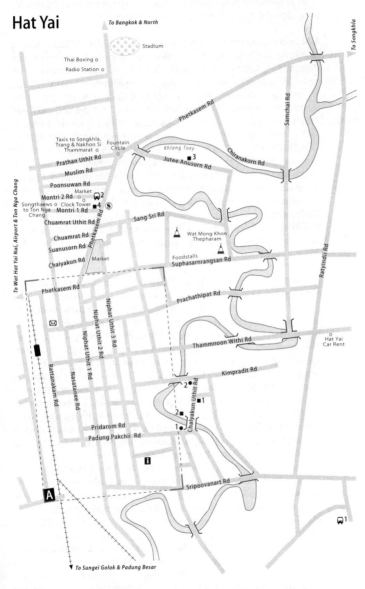

The Southern Region

■ Sleeping	**● Eating**	**🚌 Transport**
1 Daiichi	1 Isan Garden	1 City terminal
2 Garden Home	2 Seafood Court	2 Buses to Songkhla, Phattalung,
3 JB		Nakhon Si Thammarat,
4 Sorrasilp Guesthouse		Pattani, Yala etc

Related map
Hat Yai detail,
page 712

and Phaduangpakdi roads. Hotels with clocks showing Malaysian or Singapore time in the lobbies cater for Malaysian and Singaporean clientele. Those with garish and ugly grandfather clocks indicate a Sino-Thai commercial interest in the establishment. Not far away, on the other side of the fetid *khlong* however, is Boss Square around which there are a number of smart, clean hotels and restaurants. Where Hat Yai gets poor marks on the accommodation stakes is in regard to its budget accommodation which is limited, almost uniformly characterless, and often grubby.

A-AL *Central Sukhontha*, 3 Sanehanusorn Rd, T352222, F352223, CENTEL @ksc.th.com A/c, restaurant, pool, this place is run by the *Central Department Store* chain and is attached to their Hat Yai branch. One of the most luxurious places to stay in the city with a business centre and gym. **A** *JB*, 99 Jutee-Anusorn Rd, T234300, F234328. A/c, restaurant, pool, health club, tennis courts and 400-odd rooms, the Ritz of Hat Yai, but not central, situated about 1½ km north of the town centre. **A-B** *BP Grand Tower*, 74 Sanehanusorn Rd, T239051, F239767. A/c, restaurant, pool, a large new addition to Hat Yai's hotels. Across the road is its even more up-market sister hotel the *BP Grand Suite*, (T355155, F354528). **A-B** *Daiichi*, 29 Chaiyakun Uthit 4 Rd, T230724, F231315. A/c, restaurant, enormous, glitzy hotel, catering for conventions, small but smart rooms, reasonable value for money. **A-B** *Grand Plaza*, 24/1 Sanehanusorn Rd, T234340, F230050. A/c, restaurant, pool, better than many in town and recently expanded and given a new frontage to trick people into thinking it's a 1990s construction, older rooms are cheaper. **A-B** *Regency*, 23 Prachathipat Rd, T234400, F234102. A/c, restaurants, a notch above many of the other hotels in price and facilities but even so can't throw off the impression that it's just another very ordinary Hat Yai hostel with plastic trees in the lobby and an over-enthusiastic use of marble.

B *Asian*, 55 Niphat Uthit Rd, T353400, F234890. A/c, yet another addition to Hat Yai's mid-range hotels, has the advantage of being new, so rooms are in good condition, the staff are keen, and the décor is not too overwhelming. **B** *Diamond Plaza*, 62 Niphat Uthit 3 Rd, T230130, F239824. A/c, restaurant, this was the best hotel in this bracket in Hat Yai, but while it has declined in quality other new and better hotels have opened. It is now rather down-at-heel and overpriced given the competition, but still quite acceptable – and it has a pool. **B** *Florida*, 8 Sripoovanart Rd, at the southern end of Niphat Uthit 2 Rd, T234555, F234553. A/c, restaurant, situated on a large plot of land, average rooms and with the usual array of facilities including a club with local talent on show (vocal) and an ancient massage parlour. **B** *Hat Yai Central*, 180-181 Niphat Uthit 3 Rd, T230000, F230990. Another Hat Yai hotel almost indistinguishable from every other, it has the requisite karaoke bar, massage parlour (rather amusingly named the *Tum Rub Massage*), and snooker club, and 250 acceptable but scarcely memorable rooms. **B** *Hat Yai Rama*, 9/5 Sripoonvanart Rd, T230222, F234560. A/c, restaurant, this is one of the kitschest hotels in Hat Yai, which for Hat Yai is saying a great deal. The *Slubpetch* restaurant could do with being rechristened but the hotel is quite good value and the staff, apparently realizing that if they don't try no one will stay, are friendly and welcoming. **B** *Kosit*, 199 Niphat Uthit Rd, T234366, F232365. A/c, restaurant, club with crooners, massage, barber shop plus 200 rooms which were clearly decorated by someone who was either just beginning their career or who lacked any intuitive feel for the art of interior design. **B** *Lee Gardens*, 1 Lee Pattana Rd, T234422, F251888. A/c, restaurant, currently the best of the places in the competitive ฿600-900 price bracket, newly refurbished, rooms are cheaper in the old wing which dates back to the mid-1980s but even there the rooms have been well maintained and are surprisingly pleasant. **B** *Lee Gardens Plaza*, 29 Prachatipat Rd, T261111, F353555. A/c, restaurant, pool, health centre (under development). A large hotel which feels like it mostly caters to tours. Rooms don't feel very cosy, but the bathrooms are well designed and the hotel provides all the amenities one would expect for the price. 2 non-smoking floors are provided. Great views from the upper levels (especially the larger suites which have a wall of windows), but rather impersonal service. Like the *Central Sukhontha* (opposite) it is located above a shopping mall. Part of the Lee Gardens Group. **B** *Siam City*, 25-35 Niphat Uthit 2 Rd, T353111, F231060. A/c, restaurant, snooker club, karaoke bar, massage parlour, a new place with 200 rooms, central location and reasonable rooms and at the time of writing comparatively clean and glitzy. Character and charm? Forget it. **B** *VL Hotel*, 1-7 Niphat Uthit Rd, T352201, F352210. A/c, mid-range hotel, much like all the others. **B-C** *Indra*, 94 Thammnoon Withi Rd, T245896. Some a/c, one of Hat Yai's more venerable establishments, now given a coat of lime green paint, rooms could do with some improvement too, lacklustre but central and perhaps the finest bevy of sequined crooners in Southern Thailand. **B-C** *Sakura*, 185/1 Niphat Uthit 3 Rd, T246688, F235936. A/c, restaurant, clean, reasonable and very popular.

C *Garden Home*, 51/2 Hoi Mook Rd, T234444, F232283. A/c, restaurant (sometimes), plush and well looked after modern hotel, built around waterfall garden. Rooms at the front have small balconies, all are well appointed and excellent value for money. The only downside is that this modest stab at Rome-comes-to-the-jungle overlooks a canal with scarcely a thing alive in it. Recommended. **C** *Rajthani*, 1 Thammnoon Withi Rd, T231020. A/c, restaurant, station hotel, so convenient for transit stop-overs although rooms are average. There is a small steam locomotive outside the front. **C-D** *Laem Thong*, 46 Thammnoon Withi Rd, T244433, F237574. Some a/c, clean old Chinese hotel, fan rooms are particularly good value. Recommended. **D-E** *Ladda Guesthouse*, 13-15 Thammnoon Withi Rd, T220233. Some a/c, convenient for station, rooms are small but very clean with good attached bathrooms, well run, the best place in this bracket. Recommended. **D-E** *Louise Guesthouse*, 21-23 Thammnoon Withi Rd, T220966, F232259. A/c, convenient for station, close to the *Ladda Guesthouse* and almost as good, clean rooms keenly priced. Recommended. **D-E** *Sorrasilp*, 251/7-8 Phetkasem Rd, T232635. Some a/c, reasonable place right by the *hor nalikaa* or clock tower, so great for picking up an early morning bus. **D-E** *Wangnoi*, 114/1 Sangchan Rd, T245729. A/c, clean, good value, but short on windows.

E-F *Cathay Guesthouse*, corner of Thammnoon Withi and Niphat Uthit 2 roads, T243815. Centrally located and well run with friendly management although it could not be said that operating-theatre levels of cleanliness are achieved. Even so, it has become one of the busiest travellers' places to stay with good information and services for those on a tight budget. Rooms are a little dingy but have attached squat loos, it is situated above a tour company's offices, dorm beds available.

Hat Yai's saving grace is its cuisine. There are excellent Chinese, Malay and Thai restaurants. The city is particularly noted for its seafood (including shark's fin) and birds' nests. Many of the restaurants exist to meet the culinary predilections of the thousands of visitors from south of the border. Snacking from the roadside stalls is an entertaining way to dine – everything from saté to deep fried battered sea crabs in their shells (*bu thalae thort*).

Eating
● *on maps,*
pages 709 & 712
Price categories:
see inside front cover

Thai Expensive: *Thuay Thor Jor Chaam*, Niphat Uthit 3 Rd (just south from *Hat Yai Central Hotel*). Clean a/c restaurant serving fried rice, chicken rice, noodles, plus speciality coffees. **Mid-range**: *Isan Garden*, Padungpakdee Rd (opposite *Ambassador Hotel*). Isan food in open-air restaurant next to the stinking *khlong*. *Nai Yaaw*, corner of Thammnoon Withi and Niphat Uthit 3 roads. Very popular Sino-Thai restaurant, it may look rather chaotic but the food is tremendous. *Pee Lik 59*, across from *Sakura Hotel* on junction of Niyomrat Rd and Niphat Uthit 3 Rd. Barbecued seafood in a large (and very popular) open-air restaurant. Recommended. **Cheap**: *Mae Thip*, 187-188 Niphat Uthit 3

Rd. Clean and airy place with good Thai food as well as some Malay favourites like saté, succulent BBQ seafood available. Recommended. *A&A*, Niphat Uthit 2 Rd (on intersection with Pridarom Rd). Good little 'hawker centre' with Sino-Thai favourites as well as some Malay dishes including *rojak penang*, clean. *On Oiam*, 186 Niphat Uthit 2 Rd.

Hat Yai detail

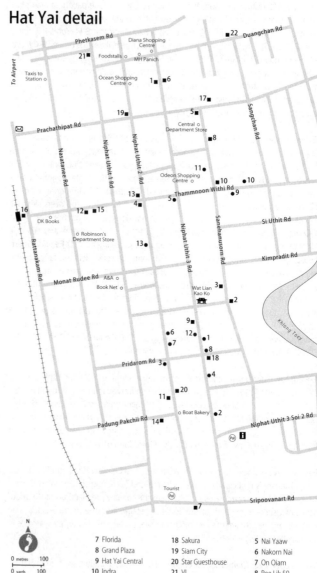

Related map
Hat Yai, page 709

N

0 metres 100
0 yards 100

■ **Sleeping**
1 Asian
2 BP Grand Tower
3 BP Grand Suite
4 Cathay Guesthouse
5 Central Sukhontha
6 Diamond Plaza
7 Florida
8 Grand Plaza
9 Hat Yai Central
10 Indra
11 Kosit
12 Ladda Guesthouse
13 Laem Thong
14 Lee Gardens
15 Louise Guesthouse
16 Rajthani
17 Regency & Rang Nok Restaurant
18 Sakura
19 Siam City
20 Star Guesthouse
21 VL
22 Wangnoi

● **Eating**
1 Dim Sum Restaurants
2 Kaan Waelaa Bar & Restaurant
3 Kor Pochana
4 Mae Thip
5 Nai Yaaw
6 Nakorn Nai
7 On Oiam
8 Pee Lik 59
9 Post
10 Sugar Rock Bar & Restaurant
11 Thalae Seafood
12 Thuay Thor Jor Chaam
13 Wardee Musling

Simple restaurant selling very good (and firey) Thai curries in clean surroundings, the dishes are displayed and customers point and select. Recommended.

International Mid-range: *Post Restaurant*, Thammnoon Withi Rd (opposite the *Indra Hotel*). A hangout, a/c, wicker chairs, steaks, salads and sandwiches, cold beer, some Thai food and laser discs. *Sometime*, Hat Yai Garden Home Hotel, 51/2 Hoi Mook Rd. Reasonably priced menu with a good selection of seafood. *Sugar Rock*, 114 Thammnoon Witfaranghi Rd (30 m east from the *Indra Hotel*). A/c restaurant with music, steaks, salads and sandwiches, also serves breakfast, draught beer available. **Cheap**: *Boat Bakery*, 190/11 Niphat Uthit 2. Cakes, ice creams and soft drinks, breakfasts also served. *Nakorn Nai*, 167 Niphat Uthit 2. Good breakfasts, salads, sandwiches, pasta and pizza as well as a reasonable selection of Thai food in an attractive setting.

Chinese Expensive: *Rang Nok*, Prachathipat Rd (close to the *Regency Hotel*). Specializing in bird's nest and shark's fin dishes, also other seafood dishes. **Mid-range**: *Thalae/Seafood*, Sanehanusorn Rd (not far from the *Indra Hotel* in the *Pahurat Shopping Centre*). This little open-air place serves excellent seafood – lobster, crab and tiger prawns, shark's fin – the name is only in Thai and Chinese but it is worth checking out.

Malay There is a concentration of restaurants serving Malay (Muslim) food to the hordes of Malaysians who come to Hat Yai on Niphat Uthit 2 Rd, especially between Pridarom and Thammnoon Withi roads. Recommended is *Wardee Musling Restoran* at 121 Niphat Uthit 2 Rd (just south of Thammnoon Withi Rd), which serves excellent *rojak* and *rotis*.

Dim Sum *Dim sum* or Chinese 'dumplings' are good in Hat Yai. There is a row of dim sum shops north of the *Sakura Hotel* on Niphat Uthit 3 Rd.

Fast food *KFC* and *Dunkin' Donuts* in the *Diana Shopping Centre* on the corners of Niphat Uthit 3 and Duangchan roads. There is another branch of *KFC*, as well as a *Burger King* and a *Mister Donut* in *Robinson's Department Store* on Nasathani Rd.

Foodstalls Suphasarnrangsan Rd, Chee Kim Yong Complex, Hat Yai municipal market. There is a good little group of stalls operating on the corner of Duangchan and Niphat Uthit 2 roads, serving simple Sino-Thai dishes like *khao muu daeng* (red pork and rice), *khao man kai* (chicken and rice), and *khao naa pet* (duck and rice). The newly opened *Robinson's Department Store* on Nasathani Rd has an a/c food court. For cheap(ish) seafood try the open-air food court just over the pungent *khlong* on Kimpradit Rd.

Bars & nightclubs

Kaan Waelaa, Niphat Uthit 3 Rd (a little north from the TAT office). Looks rather like an antique shop and the sign is only in Thai, live music in the evenings and some food, atmospheric. The *Post Restaurant* on Thammnoon Withi Rd (opposite the *Indra Hotel*) is also a popular watering hole with farangs, it has draught beer, laser discs, shows football and serves food. *Grand Laser House*, Grand Plaza Hotel, 24/1 Sanehanusarn Rd. Popular with Hat Yai's young and active.

Disco *New York Club*, Manhattan Palace, 29 Lamai Songkroh 4 Rd. *Royal*, 106 Prachathipat Rd.

Nightclubs In many of the major hotels, such as the *Nora, Lee Gardens, Emperor, Kosit*. There are karaoke bars on every street and 'sexy shows' in several hotels and hairdressing outlets.

Entertainment

Bullfights Held once a month, on the first Sat of the month (contact TAT for information). Fights (and gambling), take place continuously from 0900 to 1600. The local tourist office recommend that visitors check the venue with them as it changes from

The Southern Region

time to time. Recently fights were being held near the Nern Khua Thong Garden, about 8-9 km from town en route to the airport. To get there, take a *songthaew* from the *hor nalikaa* (clock tower) on Phetkasem Rd. ■ ฿*100-200*.

Cinema With English-speaking soundproof-rooms – *Plaza* on Phetkasem Rd, *Chalerm Thai* on Suphasarnrangsan Rd and *Diana 2* in the *Diana Department Store* on Niphat Uthit 3 Rd.

Shopping The principal shopping areas are concentrated around Niphat Uthit 1, 2 and 3 roads, Sanehanusorn Rd and the Plaza Market. The narrow *sois* between these roads are packed with stalls. As the main reason why Malaysians and Singaporeans come here is to shop, the city is rather overloaded with gold and jewellery shops and shopping centres.

Batik A good place for batik and other textiles and some made-up garments is *MH Panich* on Duangchan Rd.

Books *Praevittaya Bookshop*, 124/1 Niphat Uthit 3. Regional and international English-language magazines available. *DK Books*, 2/4-5 Thammnoon Withi Rd, west end, for English-language books, maps and magazines; there is also a book department on the top floor of the *Central Department Store* on Sanehanusorn Rd. *Book Net*, Niphat Uthit 2 (opposite Thai Airways), English-language newspapers and some – mostly travel – books.

Gold and jewellery Acres of them on Thammnoon Withi Rd.

Markets The main market area is at the southern end of Phetkasem Rd – piles of clothes, fruit, leather goods, batik, torches, toys, etc.

Shopping centres and department stores *Diana Shopping Centre*, Duangchan and Niphat Uthit 3 roads. *Central Department Store*, Sanehanusorn Rd. *Odeon Shopping Centre*, Thammnoon Withi Rd. *Robinson's Department Store*, Nasathani Rd. *Ocean Shopping Town*, Niphat Uthit 3 Rd.

Sport **Golf** The best course near Hat Yai is the *Hat Yai Exclusive Golf Course*. They have an office in town at 120 Jutee Anusorn Rd (opposite the *JB Hotel*), T/F234921, T243179, green fees are ฿600 for 18 holes, Mon-Fri, ฿800 on Sat and Sun with a discount after 1530. Clubs (฿300), shoes (฿100) and caddies (฿150) all available. *Kho Hong Golf Course*, 4 km northeast of town on Route 407, 9 holes. Green fees ฿200 Mon-Fri, ฿400 Sat and Sun, caddy fee ฿50, T211500-3 ext 549 for reservations. **Thai boxing** Competitions held every Sat from 1400-1700, just north of the sports stadium on Niphat Songkhroh Rd. ■฿*30-40*.

Tour operators There are scores of tour and travel agents mostly operating tours to Songkhla and surrounding sights. Most are concentrated along Niphat Uthit 1, 2 and 3 roads and on Thammnoon Withi Rd.

Transport

See also Ins & outs, page 708
933 km to Bangkok
480 km to Phuket
209 km to Nakhon Si Thammarat

Local Car hire: *Hat Yai Car Rent*, 189 Thammnoon Withi Rd (opposite *Nora Hotel*), T234591. *Avis*, Ground Floor, *Dusit JB Hotel*, 99 Jutee-Anusorn Rd, T234300. *Jutee Car Rent*, 59/2 Jutee-Anusorn Rd, T239447. Cheapest car rental in town with prices starting at around ฿1,500. **Share taxis**: for Songkhla and Satun the taxi stand is on Prathan Uthit Rd, between the *President Hotel* and the *Siam Nakharind Department Store* (฿20 per person during the day, ฿25 at night, 7 people per taxi). **Tuk-tuks** and **songthaews** around town cost ฿5-10, bargain for longer distances. Just flag one down and say where you are going.

Long distance Air: Hat Yai airport is 12 km west of town (T244145, 244521). *Transport to town*: Thai Airways operate a minibus to and from their office on Niphat Uthit 2 Rd (฿50). Taxis operating on a voucher system cost ฿180 to Hat Yai or ฿250 to Songkhla. *Songthaews* run past the airport and terminate at the *hor nalikaa* (clock tower) on Phetkasem Rd. There is a tourist information desk at the airport (not always manned), as well as a Post Office and restaurant. Regular daily connections with

Bangkok 1 hr 25 mins and Phuket 40 mins on THAI. At the airport there is a notice with a checklist of identifying characteristics of a 'hippy'. For reference, they are: 1. A person who wears just a singlet without underwear; 2. A person who wears skirts that are not respectable; 3. A person who wears any type of slippers or wooden sandals except when these are part of a national costume; 4. A person who wears silk pants that do not look respectable; 5. A person who has long hair that appears untidy and dirty; 6. A person who is dressed in an impure and dirty-looking manner. In theory, anyone with any of these characteristics can be prevented from entering the country.

Train: station on Ratakan Rd. Overnight connections with Bangkok, 16-19 hrs. Regular connections with Phattalung, Yala, Sungei Golok and Surat Thani.

Bus: the main a/c bus terminal is inconveniently located some way out of town to the northeast on Shotikun Rd. Partly as a result, most people book tickets through one of the many private tour companies concentrated along Niphat Uthit 2 and 3 roads. Non-a/c buses to most destinations in the south including Pattani, Yala, Nakhon Si Thammarat, Krabi, Surat Thani, etc can be picked up at the municipal market on Montri I and Phetkasem roads, better known as the *hor nalikaa* or clock tower which is within walking distance of the town centre. For Songkhla, green striped buses (no 1871) leave every 7 mins from the clock tower, 0600-1930 (฿9). They can also be flagged down on their way out of town. Overnight connections with Bangkok 14 hrs. Also regular connections with Phuket 6 hrs, Krabi 4 hrs, Koh Samui (including ferry), Nakhon Si Thammarat 2 hrs, Satun 1 hr, Sungei Golok 4 hrs, Surat Thani 4 hrs, Songkhla 30 mins. A/c **tour buses** and **mini vans** operated by private tour companies run to destinations in southern Thailand (Phuket, Krabi, Surat Thani), to Bangkok, and to Northern Thailand. There are also combined bus/boat tickets available to Koh Samui and Koh Phangan. Many of the companies have offices on Niphat Uthit 2 and Niphat Uthit 3 roads. **Taxi**: see map for positions of taxi ranks.

Air Daily connections with Singapore (1 hr 20 mins) on THAI and Silk Air. Regular connections with Kuala Lumpur on **MAS** and Silk Air. **Train** Daily connections with Padang Besar (on the Malaysian border), Butterworth, 4 hrs, Kuala Lumpur and Singapore. **Road Bus**: there are several travel agencies on Niphat Uthit 2 and 3 roads offering packages by bus south to Butterworth, Kuala Lumpur, Langkawi, Singapore and elsewhere on the Malay Peninsular, most going via Padang Besar. For long-distance journeys south it is more comfortable to take the bus to Padang Besar, 1 hr and change on to the train south down the west coast of Peninsular Malaysia and on to Singapore (see above). But there are through buses to Butterworth (for Penang), Kuala Lumpur 13 hrs and Singapore 17 hrs. There are also Malaysian shared taxis from Padang Besar. **Taxi**: to Penang leave from the railway station. **Taxi agents** include: *Asia Tours*, 85 Niphat Uthit 2 Rd, T232147. *Magic Tour*, 93/1 Niphat Uthit 2 Rd (*Cathay Hotel*), T234535.

Transport to Malaysia & Singapore

Airline offices *SilkAir*, Chaiyong Building, 7-15 Jutee Uthit Rd, T238901, F238903. *THAI*, 166/4 Niphat Uthit 2 Rd, T245851. *MAS*, Lee Garden Hotel, Thammnoon Withi Rd, T243729. **Banks** There are multitudes of banks and money changers in Hat Yai, many on Niphat Uthit 1 Rd and Niphat Uthit 3 Rd. *Thai Farmers*, 188 Phetkasem Rd. *Bangkok*, 37 Niphat Uthit 2 Rd, open until 1900 or 2000. Large hotels have money changers. **Communications** Post Office: the GPO is on Niphat Songkroh Rd, some way from the centre of town going north towards the stadium; there is also a more convenient branch office on Rattakarn Rd. Telephone centre: Phangnga Rd. Numerous shops offer IDD services. The main telephone office is by the GPO on Niphat Songkhroh Rd, some distance from the centre. Internet: *Cyber-in-Town*, Niphat Uthit 2 Rd, south of Ocean Shopping Centre, ฿40 per hour. **Medical services** Hat Yai Hospital, Rattakarn Rd, T243016. **Useful addresses** Immigration: Nasathanee Rd. Police: T243021/243333 or T1699. Tourist Police: 1/1 Soi 2, Niphat Uthit 3, T246733. Also tourist police office on Sripoonvanart, just set back from the road down an alley and 50 m or so from the *Florida Hotel*, and a tourist police booth on Sanehanusorn Rd, near the *Meridian Shopping Centre*.

Directory

The Southern Region

Songkhla   สงขลา

Phone code: 074
Colour map 5, grid B5
Songkhla, known historically as Singora, is situated on a spit of land between the Gulf of Thailand and the mouth of a huge lake – the Thale Sap Songkhla. This is Thailand's largest – and probably most polluted – body of inland water – 80 km long and 20 km wide. Although it is a freshwater lake, the water is quite salty closer to the Gulf. The lake used to be a fertile fishing ground but catches are now small due to extensive dumping of effluent.

Ins and outs

Getting there
See also Transport, page 723

Songkhla is off the main transport routes – although it is not too difficult to get here. The rail line was closed some years ago and the nearest airport is at Hat Yai, about 40 km west. But there are direct buses to Bangkok and some other destinations in the south and the transport hub of Hat Yai is also very well connected, with buses leaving for the city every 7 mins through the day.

Getting around

Songkhla is a small and pedestrian-friendly town. There are also public *songthaews* which scoot around town and visit outlying destinations.

Songkhla

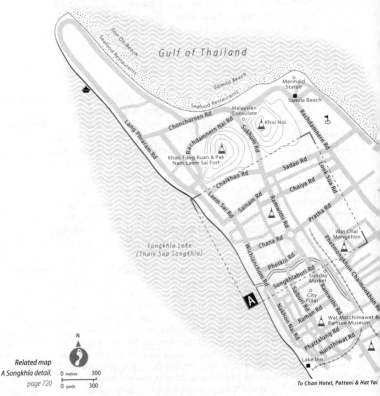

Related map
A Songkhla detail, page 720

N

0 metres 300
0 yards   300

To Chan Hotel, Pattani & Hat Yai

History

The city's early history is as murky as its lake, but like Nakhon Si Thammarat, it was incorporated into the Srivijayan Empire (eighth to 13th century). Unfortunately, little remains of this period apart from a number of small Srivijayan bronze images unearthed at nearby Sating Phra. Songkhla was mentioned in 1769 when a Chinese merchant, Yienghoa, petitioned the king for licences to collect birds' nests from Koh Siand and Koh Ha in the east of the province. The present city was built in 1836 by Phraya Vichian Khiri, the governor of Songkhla during the reign of Rama III. Later, Chinese immigrants flooded into South Thailand hoping to make their fortunes from tin mining. Their descendants settled in Songkhla, and the town retains its Chinese atmosphere. Songkhla is the provincial capital, although its sister city Hat Yai is the main commercial centre. There is a sizeable expatriate population here, mainly oil-workers servicing the offshore platforms in the gulf.

Sights

Although the port is unsuitable for big ships and has gone into decline, the **waterfront** on the inland sea side still bustles with activity as fishermen unload their catch in the early morning and evenings. Fish – fresh, frozen, fermented and sun-dried – is one of Songkhla's major exports. The fish-packing factories along the road to Hat Yai bear malodorous witness to the scale of the fish industry. The town itself is a mixture of Chinese, Malay and Thai styles. The town's oldest thoroughfare is Nakhon Nai Road where many old Southern-style Chinese shophouses still stand. **Waterfront**

The town is surrounded on three sides by water, but swimming is only possible (or advisable) on the seaward side. The focal point of the main beach, Laem Samila (or Samila Beach), is a pouting bronze mermaid, opposite the *BP Samila Hotel*. Further up the peninsula is Son On Beach, lined with seafood restaurants. The two offshore islands, Koh Nu and Koh Maew (Mouse and Cat Island respectively) are both uninhabited.

Most visitors to the province of Songkhla stay in Hat Yai rather than Songkhla. Yet Songkhla is a much nicer town. There is more to see, it is more attractive with its Sino-Thai architecture and less frenetic atmosphere, and the accommodation, especially at the lower end, is better. With beaches within walking distance and a coastal feel, Songkhla is the better option for anyone who is not too bothered about shopping, sharks' fin soup, or massage parlours (for which Hat Yai wins hands down).

● ●

Songkhla place names

Chana

จะนะ

Folklore Museum

พิพิธภัณฑ์ศิลปพื้นบ้าน

Khu Khut Waterfowl Park

อุทยานนกน้ำคูขุด

Thale Sap Songkhla

ทะเลสาบสงขลา

Wat Pakho

วัดพะโคะ

Wat Matchimawat (also called **Wat Klang**), a little way south of the centre of town on Saiburi Road, is 400 years old and the largest temple in Songkhla. The **Partsee Museum** within the complex has a chaotic display of disparate items: from human skulls to Buddha statues, stuffed snakes and coins. Nothing is labelled and the museum is badly lit. ■ *0900-1700 Wed-Sun* . The *bot* is said to contain some interesting 19th-century frescoes, representing the arrival of European navigators in the South China Sea, although it is **Wat Matchimawat & Partsee Museum** usually locked. On Nang Ngam Road, not far from Wat Matchimawat stands the **city pillar** (*lak muang*).

Wat Chai Mongkhon The other main wat in Songkhla is Wat Chai Mongkhon, known for its Buddha relic from Ceylon, which is buried somewhere in the main golden *chedi*. In front of the *chedi* is the monastery's unusual squat viharn. Although the doors are often locked, it is usually possible to peek through the windows to see the wat's pride and joy: a reclining Buddha protected behind a glass screen.

Songkhla National Museum The Songkhla branch of the National Museum is housed in an 1870's Sino-Thai-style building, built as a private residence for the influential Phraya Sunthranuraksa family. Phraya Sunthranuraksa was governor of Nakhon Si Thammarat province in the latter years of the 19th century. It is situated between Rong Muang and Chana roads with the main entrance on Wichianchom Road. On the ground floor there is a good prehistory section including a collection of primitive jewellery along with bronze cannon, swords and spears, a whale skeleton and various assorted pieces of farm equipment. Upstairs is a large collection of southern religious art (including some rare Srivijayan pieces), as well as furniture (including King Mongkut's bed) and various household items. The museum is a joy partly because of the charming building with its airy rooms, balconies, flaking plaster work and polished wooden upper floors, and partly because of the highly eclectic collection that it contains. The museum staff have even provided some informative material in English which is more than can be said of many provincial museums in Thailand. ■ *0900-1200, 1300-1600 Wed-Sun, ฿10.*

The old city wall Opposite the museum on Chana Road are some remains of the **city wall**, built in 1839 by Phraya Vichian Khiri, then governor of Songkhla. A little way east of here is a modest, traditional Thai stilt house. This was the birth place of Songkhla's most famous son – the 16th Prime Minister of Thailand, Prem Tinsulanond. In many ways he was the architect of Thailand's 'miracle', bringing political and economic stability to a country which had been chronically unstable. A picture of the eminent man – who is still alive and very influential, being perhaps the King's favourite politician – stands at the top of the wooden stairs. Prem's legacy is also recorded in concrete in the **Tinsulanond Bridge** which completes the road link up the east coast, spanning the Thale Sap via Koh Yo; it was completed in 1986 and is 2.6 km long.

Docks Although it is not billed as a sight by the TAT, the **docks** just to the west of the museum and old city walls are well worth a wander. Here trawlers unload their catches and stock up with ice before putting to sea once more.

Khao Noi & Khao Tung Kuan The north end of the peninsula is dominated by two hills. On the top of **Khao Noi** there is an old *chedi* and a small topiary garden affording panoramic views of the town. **Khao Tung Kuan**, to the west of Khao Noi, is littered with shrines which were restored during the reign of Rama IV. The *chedi* at the top of the hill was built by King Mongkut in 1866. **Pak Nam Laem Sai Fort** is on the side of the hill, on Laem Sai Road. It dates from the early 19th century.

Excursions

Koh Yo Koh Yo is a small island near the outlet of Songkhla's interior 'sea', the Thale Sap Songkhla. Or it was an island until the **Tinsulanond Bridge** (really more of an elevated causeway) was completed which uses the island as a convenient staging post. Koh Yo is still well worth visiting though. At its southern end, and visible from the highway, is the attractive **Wat Laem Po**. Travelling north, the eastern shoreline is dotted with seafood restaurants while at the northern end of the island is the **Institute of Southern Thai Studies** with its excellent little **Folklore Museum** (or *Khatichon Wittaya Museum*). It has a permanent exhibition of southern arts and culture and also mounts occasional shadow play shows. The museum has a reasonable collection of books and other material on southern Thai culture. Apparently it is possible to stay at the Institute, but it should be borne in mind that the gates to the Institute are closed at 1700 and it could be pretty lonely up on the hill ■ *Mon-Sun, 0830-1700, ฿50, T311187-8*. Also on the northern end of the island is Koh Yo's second monastery, **Wat Khao Bo**. The cages which float just offshore are used to raise and fatten sea bass. An added attraction of Koh Yo is the island's small cotton weaving industry. *Phaa Khao Yo* are woven from cotton on traditional looms and available from the market on the island either in lengths or made up into shirts and skirts. The local Tambon Council for Koh Yo has engaged in some small-scale and culturally focused tourism. Visit their office to rent a bicycle and obtain a map and you can take a cultural cycling tour of the island. The map is excellent, giving deitails of restaurants around the island as well as some of the island sights. Eight sites are marked with signposts giving some information about what you can see there. Sites include an old house, a woman's weaving group (complete with looms), and a fruit orchard. The southernmost route around the island is a very pleasant cycling route, albeit without a proper trail, passing several lovely old Koh Yo-style houses, complete with terracotta tiles, along the island coast. The Tambon Council can also organise boat trips around the island. For further information email: kohyaw@hotmail.com or look at http://www.thai.to/ web/kohyaw The staff at the Tambon Council office are very friendly, but English is not particularly strong. **Sleeping** Most places providing accommodation on Koh Yo will quote hourly as opposed to nightly rates and are generally not to be recommended. ■ *Getting there: although the island is accessible by road the best way to get here is by boat from the market wharf in town.*

Koh Yo

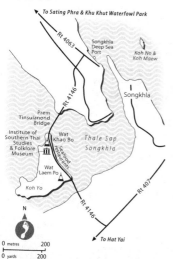

Thirty kilometres from Songkhla, north of the district town of Sating Phra the **Khu Khut Waterfowl Park** has a huge migratory bird population between December and April; over 140 species have been recorded. The park is comparatively small, covering around 500 sq km but the park office is well organized and has pamphlets and organizes boat outings. The best time to visit is early in the morning. ■ *Getting there: boats can be hired from Khu Khut village (฿100-200). Regular buses from Songkhla to Sating Phra and from there a motorcycle taxi.*

Khu Khut Waterfowl Park

The Southern Region

Essentials

Sleeping
■ *on map*
Price codes:
see inside front cover

Unlike its sister city Hat Yai, Songkhla has a good selection of budget accommodation, generally well maintained, clean and friendly. It does not have the multitudes of mid-range places to stay which throng Hat Yai, but in many respects even here Songkhla offers a better deal.

A *BP Samila Beach Hotel*, Samila Beach, T440222 F440442. Located right on the beach front and with a large free-form pool, this is Songkhla's top hotel. Operated by the BP Group (from Hat Yai), with comfortable rooms and lovely views over the sea. The pool is open to the public (for ฿60 per day for an adult) and fortunately, is large enough to take the crowds of children in the afternoons and at weekends. **A** *Hat Kaeo Princess*, 5 km north of town, towards Khu Khut Waterfowl Park, on the Sathingphra Strait, T331059, F331058. A/c, restaurant, pool, situated on a lagoon, rooms and bungalows available, recently taken over by the Dusit group. **A** *The Pavilion*, 17 Pratha Rd, T441850, F323716. A/c, restaurant, used to be Songkhla's most sophisticated hotel and it does have more élan than most places in Hat Yai, but now out-competed by the newer, better-equipped and better-positioned *BP Samila Beach Hotel*. It has the requisite karaoke bar and snooker club but these are low key and generally restrained, central location, well run, and not too large. **A-B** *Green World Palace*, 99 Samakkeesuk Rd, just off Saiburi Soi 7, T437900-8 F437899. Well equipped and reasonably priced with good views over the lake from the west side. The top floor is a bit more pricey and also has views of the sea. A/c, pool, minibar, well-run with friendly staff. Popular with long-staying oil workers. Karaoke, etc,

Songkhla detail

■ Sleeping		● Eating
1 Amsterdam Guesthouse	6 Pavilion	1 Jazz Pub & Restaurant
2 Arom Guesthouse	7 Queen Hotel	2 Kuaytiaw
3 Choke Dee	8 Royal Crown	3 Raan Phonphun
4 Holland House	9 Sansabai	4 Sip Muun
5 Narai	10 Songkhla	
	11 Sooksomboon II	

but very low-key. The pool is crowded out with children in the evenings and at weekends. Sometimes gives promotional rates of half the standard rates. Out of the centre, but the hotel offers free transport to and from anywhere in the town. **B** *Royal Crown Hotel*, 38 Sai Ngam Rd, T312174, F321027. A/c, restaurant, a nice, little hotel down a quiet road with comfortable rooms and enthusiastic staff, but looking rather tired.

C *Lake Inn*, 301-303 Nakhon Nok Rd, T314823, F314843. A/c, restaurant, refurbished in 1991 and well appointed, the more expensive front rooms (recommended) have great views of the lake, looking out over the wharf where the fishing boats put in. **C** *Songkhla Palace*, Rachaphat Institute, Songkhla, T443013. A/c, clean, well maintained. This hotel is owned and operated by the Rachaphat Institute partly to provide training opportunities for students majoring in tourism. Very reliable, but located well outside the main part of town and somewhat lonely at night. **C-D** *Nang Ngam Hotel*, 42 Nang Ngam Rd, T313913 or 01-8481162. Right in the heart of the old Chinese part of town on one of the best eating streets in Songkhla this newly, and tastefully, renovated hotel is more than half a century old. Rooms have been decorated in keeping with the style of the hotel, but with a/c. Sadly, upstairs the owner has used carpets rather than opt for the more traditional polished wood. All rooms have shared bathrooms but these are spotless and well equipped. Nice details throughout, including a small garden in a courtyard. Without a doubt the star in the firmament at this price range (discounts for long lets are also available). The hotel also offers tours of the city in a plush tuk-tuk. Recommended. **C-D** *Queen*, 20 Saiburi Rd, T311138, F313252. A/c, a rather characterless place and certainly no match for the other hotels and guesthouses in town, cheaper rooms have no windows. **C-D** *Sansabai*, 1 Phetkiri Rd, T311106. Some a/c, clean, but overpriced. **D** *Abritus Guesthouse*, 28/16 Ramwithi Rd, T326047, abritus_th @yahoo.com Centrally located within walking distance of the Pavilion and the sea (a longish walk), family-operated by a Bulgarian family and very friendly. Clean. Must be popular as it has been full at every visit! Serve good breakfasts with fresh coffee. Recommended. **D** *Chan*, 469 Saiburi Rd, T311903. Some a/c, restaurant, south of town. **D** *Sooksomboon II*, 14-18 Saiburi Rd, T323808. Some a/c, restaurant, old hotel with wooden and tile flooring and fan-cooled rooms, and a plush new a/c annex, excellent value, with spotless, spacious, very comfortable rooms. Recommended.

E *Amsterdam Guesthouse*, 15/3 Rong Muang Rd, T314890. The best of the cheaper places to stay, clean and bright rooms, well maintained with attractive sitting area on the ground floor, quiet and attractive, as the name suggests, it is run by a Dutch woman. Recommended. **E** *Choke Dee*, 14/19 Wichianchom Rd, T311158. A/c, restaurant, refurbished in 1991 and well appointed, the more expensive front rooms (recommended) have great views of the lake, looking out over the wharf where the fishing boats put in. **E** *Holland House*, 27 Rong Muang Rd. Rooms in a small, wooden house, previously a private residence, well maintained and quite acceptable. **E** *Narai*, 14 Chaikhao Rd, T311078. Rooms basic but clean and large, only a few with attached bath, small, friendly, family-run hotel on the north side of town in a quiet leafy area and overlooked by Khao Tung Kuan, peaceful and relaxing place to spend a few days. **E** *Songkhla Hotel*, 68-70 Wichianchom Rd. Rooms are light and airy and generally pretty clean, the hotel is on a busy road so it can be noisy, but the house is a traditional one with wooden floors and some character. **E-F** *Arom Guesthouse*, Rong Muang Rd. Next door to the rather more popular *Amsterdam Guesthouse*, this place, though, has cheaper dormitory beds (**F**) and bicycles and motorcycles for rent.

Mid-range *Chay Khao*, Nang Ngam Rd, just along from *E&P's Bakery* bakery products are more Thai-style than in *E&P's* and only serves instant coffee. Does western-style breakfasts and serves alcohol and some basic Thai meals throughout the day. A very nice renovation and pleasant decor in a pale yellow and cream bringing

Eating
● *on map*
Price categories:
see inside front cover

The Southern Region

out the details of this lovely wooden building. Friendly management. *Chinatown*, Nang Ngam Rd, a stylish renovation in the old Chinese part of town serving very tasty Thai food. The main restaurant is a/c, but you can also sit out in a garden at the back. Recommended. *Isan*, Srisuda Rd. The name of this little restaurant serving spicy northeastern Thai food is not in English but it is opposite the *Paradise Beer Garden* and is worth visiting if you like chillis. *Jazz Pub and Restaurant*, Pratha Rd (opposite the *Pavilion Hotel*). A/c restaurant and bar patronized by the farangs who live in Songkhla. *Raan Phonphun*, Srisuda Rd. A/c Thai restaurant serving good spicy salads, *laap* (minced meat, Isan style), fish like *plaa chon* and frog).

Cheap *Aray*, corner of Srisuda and Chaiya roads. Ice creams and some other simple dishes. *E&P's Bakery*, Nang Ngam Rd, the best of three in terms of coffee and bakeries. A/c, excellent fresh coffee (best in Songkhla), and very good cakes (especially the baked cheesecake and the apple pie). Open from 1100 to 2100. Recommended. *Kuaytiaw*, intersection of Nakhon Nai and Songkhlaburi roads. Some of the best noodles in town served on the ground floor of this old Sino-Thai house. Recommended. *Open Bakery*, Pratha Rd (at intersection with Srisuda Rd). Cakes and sandwiches served in an open-air cafeteria-style restaurant, cakes are rather sickly but OK for a coffee and rest. *Sip Muun*, Wichianchom Rd (10 m north of the *Songkhla Hotel*). This is a very well-run, open-air Thai restaurant (the name, which is not in English, means Ten Thousand), with good Thai salads and seafood, all freshly cooked out front. Recommended.

Seafood A string of restaurants on Son On Beach all offer excellent fresh seafood. There is another group of seafood restaurants on Samila Beach.

Traditional Chinese Food Nang Ngam Rd has a plethora of old Chinese restaurants serving excellent traditional favourites. Hainanese chicken (*khao man kai*), red pork (*khao moo daeng*), various noodle soups, and rice porridge and there is one shop that sells some of the best *jok* with pork in Thailand – just ask for the jok shop it is so well known no one will have any problem pointing you in the right direction – only open in the morning. Another excellent restaurant has no sign in English – it's about halfway down the Nang Ngam section with the *Nang Ngam Hotel* but on the other side and has lots of old wooden chairs and tables and ceiling fans (it's also usually full which is another indicator of the quality of the food). The *tom yam haeng* is excellent and something a little different.

Foodstalls The main concentration is around the Post Office on Wichianchom Rd. Foodstalls also set up on Samila Beach, and in the area in front of the old train station. An unusual place to find a foodstall is in the grounds to the Chinese school on Nang Ngam Rd. The stall is set up with tables under the stage used for Chinese theatre. Needless to say eating under the stage isn't really an option for anyone over 5 ft 5 ins, and there are also seats 'outside'. The stall has been operating in the same place for over 80 years with the recipes passed on from mother to daughter. They are now on to their third generation. Excellent pork meatballs which you can have with soup, or separate in a bowl with a sauce, chicken (you might want to indicate if you don't want the feet, etc). Recommended.

Bars There are a number of watering holes down quiet Srisuda Rd which has become something of a farang enclave. *Auntie's Bar* is an a/c place with some food, the *Paradise Beer Garden* a little further north really speaks for itself while the *Lucky Pub*, at the corner of Chaiya Rd is a noisier place to drink. Turning east onto Sai Ngam Rd are 2 small open-air bars, very popular with oil workers, the *Jungle Bar* and *Parlang*. *Laguna Terrace*, *Lake Inn*, 301 Nakhon Nok Rd. Roof-top bar, good views.

Sep-Oc *Chinese Lunar Festival* (movable), Thais of Chinese origin make offerings to the moon or Queen of the Heavens. Festivities include lion and dragon dances, lantern processions, folk entertainment.

The main shopping areas are along Nakhon Nai and Nang Ngam roads. **Markets** Central Market, on Nakhon Nai Rd, opposite the Post Office. Sunday market near the main bus and taxi stand. **Textiles** Songkhla is known for *phaa kaw yor* woven cotton, made on Koh Yo in the middle of the lake. Available in shops along Nang Ngam and Nakhon Nai roads.

Golf *Songkhla Golf Course*, 9-hole beachside course next to the *Samila Hotel*. Clubs for hire. Green fees, ฿100. **Watersports** *Watersports Centre* on Samila Beach, near the golf course, hires out rowing boats, paddle boats, speedboats and jet skis.

Piya Tours, 51 Platha Rd, T313770.

See also Ins & outs, page 716
950 km S of Bangkok, 30 km to Hat Yai

Songthaews ฿5 around town. There are always several around the bus station.

Air Nearest airport at Hat Yai (see page 714). **Train** Nearest station is at Hat Yai (see page 715). The rail line to Songkhla is now overgrown and the old station reeks of urine – though it still stands near the centre of town. **Bus** Buses for Hat Yai leave every 10 mins or so from Saiburi Rd, opposite Wat Chaeng (฿9). Overnight connections with Bangkok, 13 hrs. Regular connections with Nakhon Si Thammarat, 2½ hrs. **Taxi** Share taxis to Songkhla leave from Wichianchom Rd. **Boat** Ferries across the lake leave from Lang Phraram Rd, north of town. There is a boat which travels to Bangkok, 14 hrs.

Banks *Bangkok Bank* and *Bank of Ayutthaya* are on Wichianchom Rd, near the market. The *Thai Farmers Bank* at the intersection of Chana and Ramwithi roads has an exchange desk. *Thai Military* on corner of Nakhon Nok and Ramwithi roads. **Communications** Post Office: opposite the market on Wichianchom Rd, nearby telephone office for international calls. **Embassies & consulates** *Malaysian Consulate*, 4 Sukhum Rd, T311062. **Medical services** 161 Ramwithi Rd, T311494. **Useful addresses** Police: there is a small police box on Wichianchom Rd, near the post office and market.

Pattani ปัตตานี

Pattani province, once a semi-autonomous Malay-speaking sultanate, and an important trading port in Southeast Asia since well before the sixteenth century, is the heartland of Malay-Muslim South Thailand – although there are a lot of Thai-speaking Muslims here too. Unlike the Chinese, the Malays of South Thailand are not recent immigrants. Their descendants settled on the lower Kra Isthmus centuries ago, yet they have never willingly assimilated into modern Thailand. Few have found their way into local or central government and school children prefer to drop out after primary education rather than continue their studies in the Thai medium.

Pattani is strongly Muslim and the big mosque, **Matsayit Klang**, is a key place of interest. It is quite a beautiful mosque, located on Yarang Road, 200 m from the bus stop and is considered to be the central mosque for the three provinces of Narathiwat, Pattani and Yala. Worth a visit is the **Chao Mae Lim Kor Niew Shrine**. Centred around a cashew nut tree (apparently moved from the site where Chao Mae Lim Kor Niew hanged herself), and around figures of this tragic figure (now revered as a goddess) carved out of cashew nut wood this shrine is a major focus of pilgrimage for Malaysian, Thai and Singaporean ethnic

Chinese. Fairly gaudy and mostly modern, it is the major tourist location for Pattani's current tourism market. Ceremonies to pay respect to the goddess are held every year during the 3rd month of the lunar calendar (about two weeks after Chinese New Year). During this time the main statue of the goddess is paraded around the streets. The street in which the shrine is located is the oldest in the town of Pattani and contains some lovely examples of Sino-Thai architecture. If you walk down towards the river, there is also a pleasant walk along the river front where there are also some beautiful examples of traditional architecture and picturesque sights of boats on the river. There is also an interesting Chinese clan house **Muun Nithi Chao Ong Sua**. In any case, Pattani is a very picturesque town, particularly along the river, where the **harbour** is choked with gaily painted fishing vessels including the *ko-lae* for which Pattani is famous.

Excursions   For excursions from Pattani, see page 726.

Sleeping   For a provincial capital, Pattani is remarkably devoid of hotels and guesthouses. There is
■ *on map*   just one up-market hotel – the *CS Pattani*. That said, this has to be one of the nicest (if not
Price codes: THE nicest) of this class of hotel in the whole of this part of the southern region of Thailand.
see inside front cover

B *CS Pattani Hotel*, 299 M4, Nongjik Rd, a little out of town on the same road as the Provincial Hall. T335093-4, F331620, cspatani@cscoms.com Established by a 4th generation wealthy business Chinese-Pattani family and associated with the sports club and restaurant next door (all facilities are available to guests including

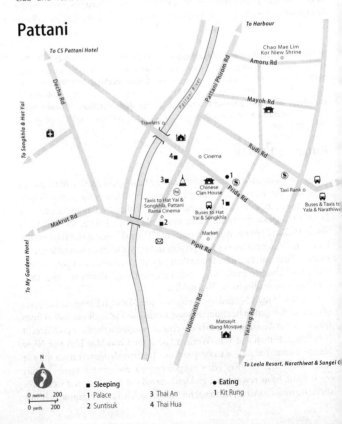

Pattani

■ **Sleeping**
1 Palace
2 Suntisuk
3 Thai An
4 Thai Hua

● **Eating**
1 Kit Rung

badminton courts, two pools, sauna, etc). The *CS Pattani* has been designed and is operated with love and care. The friendly, western-educated, owner and manager is frequently on hand to welcome guests. Rooms are spacious and well designed (the corner doubles are beautiful with lots of light), and suites are very spacious. All the amenities you could ask for and some extra details to leave you feeling very well-cared for. The design of the hotel draws much from the southern heritage – staff are dressed in traditional southern-style uniforms, and southern music is softly played in the elevators and corridors! The details even extend to the excellent buffet break-fast included in the price. Highly recommended. **B-D** *My Gardens*, 8/28 Charoenpradit Rd, west of town, T348933, F348200. Some a/c, restaurant, a good hotel with clean and spacious rooms – it is about 1 km out of town though. **C** *Leela Resort*, 52 km south of Pattani (10 km from Chana), T7120144. Some a/c. **D-E** *Palace Hotel*, 190 Prida Rd (behind the *Chong Ar Restaurant*), T349039. Some a/c, the closest thing Pattani has to luxury in the centre of town, large attached restaurant, rooms are OK. **E** *Suntisuk*, 1/16 Pipit Rd, T349122. The best of the cheaper Chinese hotels, attached bathrooms, some rooms with TV, friendly owner and central. **E** *Thai An*, 67 Pattani Phirom Rd, T348267. Basic.

Thai Mid-range: *Diana* (opposite *My Gardens Hotel*), opens 1800, seafood special-ity. *River*, Rong-Ang Rd (road straight down from clock tower to the river). Set on a bend in the river, very picturesque, excellent Thai menu. Recommended by locals. **Cheap**: *Black Coffee*, on the roundabout by the clock tower. Good selection of cof-fees, menu in Thai. *Kit Rung*, Prida Rd (next to the Bangkok Bank). **Eating**

Chinese Mid-range: *Chong Ar*, 190 Prida Rd. Large selection of dishes at this large restaurant attached to the *Palace Hotel*. *Pailin* (*My Gardens Hotel* restaurant), also serves seafood. *Pornthip*, 9/38 Watanatham Rd, T348123. Large fancy restaurant with a huge menu with all the expensive specialities, prices quoted are for parties of 6-10, so no need to panic, open 1000-0200.

Foodstalls There is a row of good *kuaytiaw* shops on Pipit Rd not far from the bridge.

Music *Black Coffee*, by the clock tower, band in the evenings. *Pornthip*, see Eating above, live Chinese pop band. **Entertainment**

Golf There is a golf driving range around 3 km out of town on the road to Hat Yai/Songkhla. **Sport**

March *Chao Mae Lim Kornaeo* (2nd weekend) fire-walking festival. **Festivals**

Local Songthaews: ฿5 around town. **Transport**
1,149 km to Bangkok
115 km to Hat Yai
105 km to Songkhla

Long distance Air: there is a Thai office in town, and an airport about 15 km out of town on the way to Hat Yai and Songkhla but in 1999 Thai were still operating no ser-vice, having suspended it in 1994. **Bus**: buses leave from the intersection of Rudi/Ramkomud/ Yarang roads. Overnight connections with Bangkok's Southern bus terminal on Pinklao-Nakhon Chaisi Rd, 15 hrs. Regular connections with Narathiwat and Hat Yai. **Taxis**: most taxis leave from stands near the bus stops on Yarang Rd, taxis to Hat Yai leave from near the bridge.

Airline offices *THAI*, 8 Prida Rd, T394149. **Banks** Bank with currency exchange on Rudi Rd, not far from intersection with Yarang Rd. *Bangkok Bank*, corner of Prida and Udomwithi roads. **Communications** Internet: Several cafés and computer shops on the road leading up the Prince of Songkhla University, Pattani campus. **Post Office**: Pipit Rd (not far from the bridge). **Directory**

The Southern Region

Muslims in a Buddhist world

The far south of Thailand is more Muslim than Buddhist and successive governments' failure to integrate the Muslim population into the mainstream has created animosity – and fuelled a long-running separatist movement. In the early 1970s a separatist group, the United Pattani Freedom Movement (bankrolled by Colonel Gadaffi), sprang up in defiance of heavy-handed Thai bureaucracy. A decade later their rebellion had all but died out, but the seeds of alienation remain today. In recent years the King has tried to make Muslims feel more a part of

the Thai nation – by presenting awards for Koranic studies and meeting with Muslim leaders. However, Malay Muslims remain unenthusiastic celebrants of wate festivals and other Buddhist holidays which dominate the Thai calendar. At the end of 1997 a bomb damaged the bridge over the Pattani River and two weeks late another bomb was planted at a police station, injuring three officers. Right at the end of December a fire broke out at a school in the province. In each instance, Muslim separatists were thought to have been at work.

Excursions from Pattani

Matsayit Kreu Se
The oldest mosque in the area, Matsayit Kreu Se lies 8 km east of Pattani, o Route 42 in the village of Ban Kreu Se. The mosque was built in 1578 by Lim T Khieng, a Chinese immigrant who married a local Pattani woman and con verted to Islam. His betrothal was not received enthusiastically by his family and on hearing the news his sister travelled from China to dissuade him an encourage him to return to the fold. Unable to persuade him to return, it i reported that his sister (Chao Mae Lim Kor Niew) hanged herself from cashew nut tree but not before cursing the mosque so that it could never b completed (a shrine to the tragic figure is in town – see above). Its brick wal and arches are still standing in a well-tended garden and the mosque is in us today. Locals say that after 400 years, plans are afoot to finish its construction but would-be contractors risk being struck by lightning: this is said to be th fate awaiting those who try. Though the story is quaint the mosque is unre markable. ■ *Getting there: bus to Narathiwat.*

Yarang Ancient Town
Located in Tambon Wat of Yarang district, Yarang Ancient Town is believe to be the site of the ancient city of Lankasuka which is referred to in tradin documents of the period. This major archaeological site of the South consist of at least two sites in Ban Wat and Ban Prawae townships. Occupation at th larger and more important settlement at Ban Wat dates back to the 6th-8t centuries. Unfortunately, the Fine Arts Department has only a limited budge and there is not as much interpretation of the information available on this sit as one might wish. Many of the artefacts found here have been moved to th Songkhla National Museum, some are also to be found in the museum at th Prince of Songkhla University campus in Pattani. ■ *Getting there: bus t Yarang and songthaew or motorcycle taxi to the old town (*muang borahn*).*

Wat Chang Hai Rasburanaram
This is another temple with an ancient legend and a venerable past. Apparentl the temple was established when Governor Gaemdam of Saiburi wanted t build a city for his sister, Jehsiti. He made a wish and sent off two elephants t find a suitably propitious location for the new city followed by the Governor his sister and their entourage. The elephants came to the spot where Wa Chang Hai is located (hence the name *chang hai* or bestowed by elephants) an circled the area three times. Unfortunately, the setting didn't please Jehsiti an

Splitting the birds' nests

A curiosity on the same street as the Mae Lim Ko Nieow shrine in Pattani is a Chinese shophouse with two clear entrance ways. The house has been divided through a feud over the lucrative dividends from collecting birds' nests. Apparently, the swiftlets that produce edible nests have been nesting in this house for a couple of generations, and collection of the nests produces a very considerable income (up to ฿400,000 baht per month!). A family feud at the current generation has resulted in the house being physically divided. Only the level with the birds' nests is left complete and there is only one staircase up to this level. Every month the two sides of the family make an appointment to meet and collect the nests together – this being the only way they feel confident of not being cheated.

another site was eventually chosen and named Pattani (originally at Krue Se). However, on the Governor's return he passed the place the elephants chose and decided to build a temple. After his return to Saiburi, he invited Somdej Prakoh, or Luang Pu Thuad (of Wat Pakho fame in Songkhla) to be the abbot of this new temple. Before Luang Pu Tuad passed away at Saiburi, he gave instructions that he be cremated at Chang Hai temple. A stupa was subsequently built here to enshrine his remains. This is considered a major site of pilgrimage for southern Buddhists and is the venue where annual rituals are carried out to bless the remains of this most revered southern monk. Most of the temple buildings are fairly new, but the *Wat Chang Hai Vocational Training Centre* is quite interesting and a good place to look for local handicrafts. ■ *Getting there: take route from Pattani to Khok Pho district. The turn-off to the temple is about 30 km from Pattani and then a further 1 km up the road.*

Wat Chang Hai Vocational Training Centre just down the road from the Chang Hai temple was set up by a former governor of Pattani in response to suggestions from Her Majesty the Queen. Local people are trained in the production of handicrafts and arts such as silk-weaving, basketry, embroidery, the manufacture of *kris*, engraving of the *kris hilt*, and the manufacture of *korlae* boats and miniature boats. All these can be purchased at the centre and on occasion you can see them being made there too. Unfortunately, this centre has not taken off as a major tourist destination and the stock and number of activities being carried out at any one time varies enormously. ■ *Getting there: take route 409 to Khok Pho district. The turn-off to the temple is about 30 km from Pattani and then little way up the road to Wat Chang Hai.*

The Folk Studies Museum (*Pipitapan katichonwittaya*) is in the grounds of the Prince of Songkhla University Pattani Campus. There are actually two museums. The first, in the temple-like building, contains a mixed collection of artefacts donated to the museum by a famous monk (things used by the monk are held on the first floor up the stairs). Of most interest are the pieces of traditional Pattani cloth which has not been woven for about a century. Unfortunately there are almost no labels in either English or Thai anywhere in the museum and the only explanatory information on the fabric is in a Thai pamphlet. Behind this museum is the modern building housing the folk studies collection. Not the best of these types of collections in the South (the Institute of Folk Studies in Songkhla province is more extensive and better laid out) but there are some lovely pictures of the traditional Malay-style houses of this part of the South. Unfortunately these are about the only exhibits with no English labels at all! The museum also contains a Chinese gravestone believed to be the oldest in Southeast Asia and demonstrating the long links between Pattani's

Folk Studies Museum

port and the Chinese trading communities in this area. ■ *Getting there* *songthaews and taxis, ask for 'mahawitiyalai songkhla-nakarin' and then for th* *'pipitipan' when you get into the grounds.*

Beaches

There are some lovely beaches all along the coast from the north near Songkhla down to Saiburi district

Laem Ta Chee, Ta Chee peninsular, lies just beyond Pattani town and can b reached by boat taxi from the pier in the town, or by driving the 30 km along it length (it might be possible to negotiate with a *songthaew* driver to take yo there, but otherwise self-drive is pretty much the only option). No accommo dation to date, and not a huge amount to do, but this is still an interesting view point for the sea and the mainland.

It should be borne in mind that the deep south is not the place for strippin off to sunbathe. Most local visitors will be dressed in at least a T-shirt an shorts when they enter the water; anything less would be regarded as deeply shocking and indecent. **Rachadapisek** lies around 13 km west of town. Stall are set up under the casuarina trees and at weekends demurely attired local frolic carefully. About the same distance east of town is **Talo Kapo Beach** - more a fishing village than a resort, but the beach is OK and there are variou vendors and stall keepers, especially at weekends. **Khae Khae Beach** is one o the prettiest beaches along the coast, with yellow sand and some lovely rock formations in a small bay with a hilly backdrop, about 30 km to the south of the main town. A local favourite is **Wasukri Beach** about 80 km from Pattan town on highway 42. This is a long stretch of white sand with casuarina trees and a gently sloping beach good for swimming. Gradually, small bungalow operations are setting up along the coast north and south of Pattani – most o these cater to middle-class Thais, with air-conditioning, a small restaurant etc. Prices are mostly in the **B-D** range. As individual bungalow operations are somewhat isolated from anything else, this may be a better option for those with their own transport rather than for travellers dependent on local buses. I you do want to take local transport, most beaches to the north (and bungalow operations) can be reached by taking the Pattani-Songkhla bus or the Pattani-Hat Yai bus and getting off when you see a sign to a bungalow.

Narathiwat   นราธิวาส

Phone code: 073
Colour map 5, grid C6

Narathiwat is an Islamic stronghold and has one of the biggest mosques in southern Thailand. There is also a **Muslim fishing village – Ban Thon** jus beyond the market to the north of the town, where they still use the brightly painted *kor lae* – traditional fishing boats with curved bows and tails. Today the *kor lae* is an endangered species: diesel-powered Darwinism dictates tha long-tails do it better. Across the bridge from the Muslim village is a pleasan beach area known as of Hat Narathat, rather like Samila Beach at Songkhla There are several small outdoor restaurants serving seafood and it is a popula spot with locals and visiting Malaysians.

The town's two main **mosques** are a contrast in architectural styles. At the northern edge of town, close to the Muslim fishing village, is a new mosque built in modern style, while in the centre of town, near the clock tower, is the wooden **Mesjid Klang** or Central Mosque built over 100 years ago. No prizes for guessing which is the more appealing.

Excursions

Wat Khao Kong is 6 km southwest of town. The centre piece of this monastery is a 25 m-high seated golden (but bronze) Buddha image (Phra Buddha Taksir Ming Mongkol) – making it the largest seated image in Thailand – built on a small hill. It is more than 15 m from knee to knee and decorated with gold mosaic tiles. ■ *Getting there: songthaew (฿5).*

Taksin Palace is the Royal Summer Palace on Manao Bay, 8 km south of Narathiwat, off the main Narathiwat-Tak Bai Road. The palace is worth a visit for its beautifully kept gardens right on the coast. There is also a small zoo here, and a handicraft centre under the SUPPORT project (an income-generation project under the patronage of Her Majesty the Queen). Products in the handicraft centre may seem a little on the pricey side when compared with similar products to be found around Thailand, but the quality of the workmanship is truly excellent. The palace itself is modern and not of great interest. ■ *0800-1200, 1300-1630 Mon-Sun, except when the King or Queen are in residence (usually between Aug and Sep). Getting there: songthaew (฿8).*

Hala Bala Wildlife Sanctuary lies adjacent to one of the larger forested areas in Malaysia and covers parts of Narathiwat and Yala province. The proximity to forests in Malaysia means that although covering only a small area, it is exceptionally rich in plant and animal species. Several hornbills, including the rhinoceros hornbill can be found in this sanctuary. Access to Hala Bala can be either from Betong district in Yala or Waeng district in Narathiwat. Prospective visitors interested in going to the sanctuary to study the wildlife there (eg birdwatchers) are requested to contact the sanctuary office in advance (Hala Bala Wildlife Sanctuary, PO Box 3, Amphur Waeng, Narathiwat 96120).

The **Sirindhorn Peat Swamp Forest Nature Study and Research Centre** is located on the way to Sungei Golok from Tak Bai and is located at the edge of one of the few remaining areas of freshwater peat forest (Pa Pru) in Thailand. Bird species found in the forest include Malaysian blue flycatcher, rufous-tailed shama, red-crowned barbet and the rare garnet pitta. The small mouse deer can also be seen on occasion. An English-language handbook is available at the centre providing information on the history and ecology of the forest. A board walk nature trail has been laid out through the forest with the entrance just behind the visitors centre. Various nature interpretation signs have been posted along the trail and there is a tower which bird watchers can use for observation purposes. ■ *0800-1600, T01-7150159. Getting there: from Sungei Golok on Route 4057 to Tak Bai, at Km 5 turn at the Chawanant intersection, head along this route for approximately 5 km and you will reach the centre.*

Talo Mano or Wadi Al-Hussein Mosque a beautiful wooden mosque in Amphur Ba Jo, is known in places as the '200-year-old mosque' or the '300-year-old mosque'. Some literature gives the date of foundation as AD 1624, while others argue it was built in AD 1769. The entire building was built without the use of nails or screws. The design and decoration of the mosque incorporates Chinese-, Malay- and Thai-style reliefs carved in wood. ■ *Getting there: take Route 42 from Narathiwat to Pattani, and take the exit for Ban Beu Ra Ngair.*

Beaches There are several good beaches and a handful of resorts between Narathiwat and Tak Bai. Few Westerners stop off in these places – they are mostly used by Malaysians. The beaches are deserted and safe for swimming, although it's not the cleanest stretch of sand in Thailand. **Sleeping C-D** *Panon Resort*, T514749, 3 km from Taksin Palace (signposted off the main road). This resort has beach-front chalets, a golf driving range (of all things!), and large gardenc. A/c, restaurant, concrete bungalows and chalets, cheaper motel-style rooms a bit like factory units. ■ *Getting there: songthaew (฿10).*

Ao Manao (or Lime Bay) is another stretch of beach, this with

* *

Narathiwat place names

Taksin Palace

พระตำหนักทักษิณราชนิเวศน์

Wat Khao Kong

วัดเขากง

a national parks office, considered to be the most beautiful in the area by most natives of Narathiwat. It is a long bay with yellow sand, lined with casuarinas and some picturesque rocks at each end. **Sleeping C-D** *Ao Manao Resort*, small bungalows and rooms in a hotel block. Plain but adequate. No hot water in any of the rooms. Fan and a/c. ■ *Getting there: songthaew (₿10).* The bay is about 3 km out of the provincial town off the route south to Tak Bai.

Sleeping
■ *on map*
Price codes: see
inside front cover

Most of the hotels are strung out along and just off Pichit Bamrung Rd. **B** *Royal Princess Narathiwat*, 228 Pichit Bamrung Rd, T515041, F515040, rsvnctr @dusit.com This 117-room hotel opened in 1997. Plush carpets and solid doors herald your entry into sumptuous if predictable rooms. The service is good and the price (in the off season, at the low end of our banding) is superb. There is a pleasant pool, which can also be used by non-residents. **C** *Tanyong*, 16/1 Sophaphisai Rd, T511477, F511834. A/c, restaurant, once the best hotel in town, the Tanyong hasn't yet adjusted to the idea of competition, clean and well appointed but overpriced and rather noisy. The snooker club, disco and massage parlour give the game away.

C-D *Ban Burong*, T511027. A pleasant building on the river, only 3 rooms – apparently all with views. The owner runs a visa extension service for people spending more than a couple of months in Thailand. Canoes, bicycles and motorbikes are available for rent. Just opposite is a small bakery that does various plain and creamy cakes, ice cream, cold drinks, *salapao* (delicious), and some very nice 'butterscotch' buns – well priced too!

D *Pacific*, 42/1-2 Warakhamphiphit Rd, T511076. Some a/c, restaurant, cheerless rooms but good value. **D-E** *Rex*, 6/1-2 Chamroonnara Rd, T511134, F511190. A/c, restaurant, clean, airy and well-kept rooms. **D-E** *Yaowarat*, 131 Pichit Bamrung Rd, T511148, F511320. A/c, Chinese-run and characteristically clean, tidy – and rather characterless. **E** *Cathay*, 275 Pupha Pakdi Rd, T511014. Another Chinese warehouse-like hotel, lazy management, lacklustre but adequate rooms. **E** *Narathiwat*, 341 Pupha Pakdi Rd, T511063. Attractive wooden building on waterfront, shared bathrooms with Asian toilets. Building has charm but rooms are dreary. **E-F** *Bang Nara*, 274 Pupha Pakdi Rd, T511036. Clean and large rooms.

Eating
● *on map*
Price categories:
see inside front covert

Thai Mid-range: *Mangkornthong*, Chinese and Thai on the river with plenty of seafood. Popular with local business people. Good views and plentiful servings of well-cooked food. **Cheap**: *Boonthong*, 55 Sophapisai Rd. *Run Thai*, Satilraya Rd. *Chittawat*, opposite the

Narathiwat

Food stalls

Muslim Fishing Village

To Airport

Buses to Pattani (North end of Town)

Pichit Bamrung Rd

Puphapakdi Rd

Market

Motorbike Taxis

o Customs

Sophaphisai Rd

Bang Nara River

Chamroonnara Rd

7■

8■   5■   ●2

Ⓢ Ⓢ Ⓢ 1■

Motorbike Taxis

6■ ●1

Ⓢ

Night Market

o Thai Airways

Ⓢ

Clock Tower o

■3

●2

Mesjid Klang

Ⓢ

4■

Warakhamphiphit Rd

✉

To Pattani

To Taksin Palace & Tak Bai (30 km)

N

0 metres 100
0 yards   100

■ Sleeping	
1 Bang Nara	7 Tanyong
2 Cathay	8 Yaowarat
3 Narathiwat	
4 Pacific	● Eating
5 Rex	1 Makanan Isla
6 Royal Princess	2 Mangkornthc

Cathay Hotel on Pupha Pakdi Rd. More of a bakery with a sitting area, but good for light snacks and refreshments. *Makanan Islam*, Pichit Bamrung Rd. Muslim delicacies, quite cheap but nothing extravagant.

International Mid-range: *Nida Foodland*, Sophapisai Rd. Chinese. *Rimnam*, 3 km down Tak Bai Rd, T511559. The town's most sophisticated restaurant patronized by the high society of Narathiwat, it's a longish hike out of town on the road south, but worth the trouble, seafood and curries. **Cheap**: *Smerp*, opposite *Yaowarat* on Chamroonnara Rd. Foremost ice creams and cold drinks. *Tanyong Hotel*, 16/1 Sophapisai Rd. Set-meal rates, huge restaurant, band at night.

Seafood Line of scruffy seafood stalls along the beach just to the north of town. **Mid-range**: *Bang Nara*, Tak Bai Rd (by the bridge). A little out of town, but excellent seafood and views over the mosquito-infested river. **Cheap**: *Nasir*, Pichit Bamrung Rd. Also serves Thai and Malay food.

May *Jao Mae To-Mo Fair*. **September** *Narathiwat Fair* (3rd week), *Kor lae* boat racing takes place on the Bang Nara River. Dove cooing contests and sale of local produce. **Festivals**

Swimming Non-residents can use the pool at the *Royal Princess Narathiwat*, 228 Pichit Bamrung Rd. **Sport**

Local Songthaews and motorbike taxis from opposite the market. **Transport**
1,315 km to Bangkok

Long distance Air: airport north of town. Thai operate a minibus for passengers to and from their office in the centre of town. Daily connections with Bangkok via Phuket.
    Bus: buses leave from near the Muslim fishing village and from Pichit Bamrung Rd. Overnight connections with Bangkok 17 hrs. Regular connections with Hat Yai, Pattani, Yala and Sungei Golok. **Taxi**: from Pichit Bamrung Rd.

Airline offices *Thai*, 322-324 Phupha Pakdi Rd, T511161. **Banks** *Thai Farmers*, Phupha Pakdi **Directory**
Rd, beyond Thai Airlines office. There are also branches of other major banks in the centre of town.
Communications Internet: computer shops providing internet services can be found in the shophouses just across from the *Royal Princess Hotel* (friendly owner who speaks some English and can give information about places to visit in Narathiwat), and down Jitpatima Rd. **Post Office**: Pichit Bamrung Rd (south of the clock tower). **Telephone Office**: international calls can be placed at the telephone office attached to the GPO on Pichit Bamrung Rd.

Tak Bai and Ta Ba   ตากใบ

Tak Bai is the first village on the road south from Narathiwat; its major attraction is *Colour map 5, grid C6*
Wat Chonthala Singh, the last bastion of Thai Buddhist culture before the Malaysian border. When Malaya's British colonial administration laid claim to the former Thai provinces that are now the states of Perlis and Kedah (to the west), at the beginning of the century, they had their eyes on Narathiwat too. Rama V defiantly built this strategically important wat to stake Siam's territorial claim to the area.
    Within its sprawling compound are a collection of sadly dilapidated wooden buildings in the beautiful and distinctive southern style. The monks, workmen and everyone else in and around the wat enclave speak Thai – nearly everyone else in Tak Bai speaks Malay. The wat is signposted off the road in Tak Bai (to get there, go straight through the market and turn left) and sits in a picturesque spot on the riverbank. Just down from the temple is a wooden walkway which leads out to Koh Yao – a small island with some fishing villages. This area has been settled for over a hundred years. A peaceful place for a stroll with attractive views.

Peculiar to this region is the longkorn, a golf-ball-sized fruit

Two kilometres down the road from Tak Bai is the small port town of **Ta Ba**, where passenger and car ferries ply the river to and from Malaysia. Ta Ba has an exciting, colourful **market**, with what must be some of the juiciest, tastiest fruit in Southeast Asia – particularly during the mango and durian seasons. *Taba Tours*, Takbai-Taba Rd (next to *Taba Plaza Hotel*) sells express bus and train tickets (from Sungei Golok).

Sleeping

All the hotels are on the road to Narathiwat, about 1 km from the port of Ta Ba

Taba Plaza, 7/20 Takbai-Taba Rd, T581234. A/c, restaurant. **C** *Takbai Lagoon Resort*, 311/2 Moo 7 Tambon Che Hey (signposted on main road), T581478, tlagoon @cscoms.com A/c, restaurant, same price as *Taba Plaza*, but better. Canoes and bicycles for rent here. **C-D** *Masaya Resort*, 58/7 Muangmai Rd, T581125. Some a/c, restaurant, clean and best of the 3. **D** *Pornphet*, 58/22 Takbai Rd, T581331. Some a/c, restaurant. Off the main road. Now looking slightly jaded, but its OK if you want to stay in Tak Bai.

Transport

39 km to Narathiwat

Bus Buses leave from pier by Ta Ba market and pick up passengers in Tak Bai. Regular connections with Narathiwat and Sungei Golok. **Taxi**: from pier by Ta Ba market.

Transport to Malaysia

Ta Ba is a little-used but speedy crossing-point between Thailand and Malaysia, as taxi and bus stands on both sides are adjacent to the ferry. The disadvantage is that Ta Ba is not well connected with other towns in Thailand, although it is easy enough to get to Sungei Golok (just 32 km to the west) for the train north.

Boat: the border is open Mon-Sun 0700-1600 (Thai time). Passenger ferry crossing from next to Ta Ba market and bus stop. If crossing with a car it is necessary to go through the customs section in a large compound next door. Regular crossings from Ta Ba to Pengkalan Kubor, Malaysia. On the Malaysian side, there are regular buses from Pengkalan Kubor to Kota Bahru.

Directory

Banks Bank next to the *Taba Plaza Hotel* with exchange facilities. *Krung Thai* in Tak Bai and *Thai Military Bank* in Ta Ba.

Yala ยะลา

Phone code: 073
Colour map 5, grid C5

Yala is the capital of the only landlocked province on the Kra Isthmus. Conspicuously prosperous, much of its wealth has been built on the rubber industry. The town has a bit of a split personality. South of the railway line it feels very Chinese. The buildings show southern-Chinese influences, particularly in their roof styles, the hotels are run by Sino-Thais, and many of the restaurants serve Chinese food – and, like the shops, use Chinese as well as Thai characters in their names. North of the railway line, on Sirias Road, is the notably muslim **Central Mosque** – a modern brick-and-concrete affair – as well as Malay-style houses (sadly, though, being demolished with enthusiasm), Muslim food, demure women in headscarves, and men in sarongs wearing the white skull cap indicating they have made the Haj to Mecca.

Wat Phutaphoom on Pipitpakdi Road has a highly visible, albeit unremarkable, standing Buddha in its extensive grounds. Not far away on Phutphumvithi Road is the Chinese **Mair Lim Niao** temple. **Chuang Phuak Park**, to the north of the railway station, is a popular spot with locals, offering a large man-made lake with boats for hire. Founded as a provincial

Yala place names

Bang Lang Dam
เขื่อนบางลาง

Than To National Park
อุทยานแห่งชาติธารโต

capital in 1933, the city is well laid out with broad avenues and leafy parks and has received the accolade of being voted the 'cleanest city in Thailand' on several occasions.

Bang Lang Dam lies 12 km off the Yala-Betong road, 10 km south of Ban Nang Sata. The road twists up through the hills to two small villages, Ban Santi 1 and 2 on the far side of the lake. There is a very picturesque drive overlooking the lake, which is dotted with tiny islands. **Than To National Park** is another 3 km further down the Yala-Betong Road. **Sleeping** E Bungalows by the lake, run by the Electricity Generating Authority of Thailand (EGAT), T213699, reservations essential as it is a popular venue for conferences; the road to the bungalows is to the right up a very steep hill just after the entrance barrier, restaurant, pool and tennis courts. ■ *Getting there: songthaew from the railway station.*

Excursions

Wat Khuha (also known as **Wat Khuha Phimuk** or, popularly, **Wat Naa Tham**) – one of the most important monuments in the south – is signposted off the Yala-Hat Yai road (Route 409 to the provincial town of Yaha), 8 km northwest of town on the left-hand side. It is around a kilometre walk to the cave temple from the main road – the limestone outcrop gives the game away. A small museum by the entrance to the **cave temple** exhibits some of the Srivijayan finds from the area: votive tablets, manuscripts and small bronze figures. Wat Khuha was assumed by archaeologists to have been an important religious centre in the south during the Srivijaya Period from the seventh to 13th century. The 25-m reclining Buddha – Phra Phutthasaiyat – is in the main cave sanctuary of this pleasant cave temple. Its sprawling interior is dramatically lit by shafts of light. The statue has been restored and is believed to have an older Bodhisattva figure inside. The original image dates from 757 AD, and was commissioned by the Srivijayan King of Palembang (Sumatra). There are a couple of other cave temples to explore nearby – take the path along the bottom of the rock face. The caves are huge and well illuminated but not especially interesting. There are several other caves in the area including **Tham Sumphao Thong**, signposted in Thai off the road about 3 km back towards the city. Notable here are, reportedly, a collection of Srivijayan murals although murals in their original state (that is untouched-up) would never have survived this long. ■ *Getting there: songthaew from the railway station.*

Ban Sakai, home to some of Thailand's few remaining so-styled 'hunter-gatherers' (they scarcely count as such today) is accessible from Yala but really only by hired vehicle (see page 736 for more details).

B *Chang Lee*, Sirirot Rd, T211223, F211773. A/c, restaurant, 16-storey hotel and Yala's pride and joy – although it is hard to see why. It opened in 1995 and while Yala's great and good may congregate here – and the rooms are very comfortable – service is slow and unenthusiastic. This is surpsiring because just a few years ago the staff seemed to be bubbling over with pride that they were working in such a cosmopolitan place. Now they are thin on the ground and seemingly keen to avoid contact with guests! **B-C** *Yala Rama*, 21 Sribamrung Rd, T212563, F214532. A/c, restaurant, until 1995 this was the best hotel in town, rooms are comfortable, with satellite TV and are very well priced, facilities include the requisite disco, Karaoke bar, massage parlour and snooker club. Although it's been eclipsed by the *Chang Lee* as Yala's No 1 spot, it is still very acceptable, a lot cheaper and friendly.

D-E *Cola Hotel*, Kotchasani 1 Rd, T212208. Some a/c, rather a dingy place with what seems like a regular turn around of short-stay customers. **D-E** *Saensuk*, *Muang Thong* and *Metro*, Ratakit Rd. Three Chinese hotels with very little to choose between them, in fact they seem to be competing in a cunning look-like-your-neighbour

Sleeping
■ *on map, page 734*
Price codes:
see inside front cover

competition. Reasonable food served downstairs in each, average rooms bordering on the grubby upstairs. How you find the rooms seems to depend on the day of the week or the month of the year but the *Metro* got our vote at the last visit. **D-E** *Sri Yala*, 16-22 Chaicharat Rd, T212170. Some a/c, restaurant. Fair rooms but the prices are not competitive. **D-E** *Thepwimarn*, 31-37 Sribamrung Rd, T212400. Some a/c, restaurant, basic and rambling, rooms are fine and it is probably the best place to stay at this price. It is not, however, a palace of deity nor pleasant as territory heavenly, as they claim, although for wishful thinking the management deserve top marks.

E *Hua Ann*, Sirirot Rd, T212989. A classic Chinese hotel with 40-odd rooms, feels more like a converted warehouse than a hotel, rooms are OK with attached bathrooms. Popular with travelling salesmen, which just about sums it up – a bed for the night, nothing more, the management, though, appealingly bill their hotel as the hotel 'which makes you feel at home but with a service which makes you feel like a king'! **E-F** *Aun Aun Hotel*, 32-36 Pipitpakdi Rd, T212216. Typical Chinese affair, sombre but clean rooms. Good for budget travellers. **E-F** *Phan Far Hotel*, Sirirot Rd, right next door to *Hua Ann* and very similar in price and standard – nothing to choose between them. **E-F** *Daan Naman*, Phutphumvithi Rd. Central location and a rather fetching lime green colour scheme, but otherwise nothing to recommended it – except price perhaps.

Eating
● *on map*
Price categories:
see inside front cover

Mid-range *Ai Hiang* (name only in Thai and Chinese), corner of Phutphumvithi and Kotchasani 3 roads. Excellent little Chinese restaurant, it looks very average, but the food is good and prepared and cooked in a bank of woks for all to see. Recommended. *Luuk Ket*, Pipitpakdi Rd. A/c restaurant, good for ice creams and a cool off, also serves regular Thai dishes like fried rice of mediocre quality. *Yala Rama Coffee Shop*, 21

Yala centre

■ Sleeping
1 Aun Aun
2 Chang Lee
3 Cola
4 Daan Naman
5 Hua Ann
6 Metro
7 Muang Thong
8 Phan Far
9 Saensuk
10 Sri Yala
11 Thepwimarn
12 Yala Rama

● Eating
1 Ai Hiang
2 Fast Food Joint
3 Luuk Ket
4 Seafood Restaurant

🚌 Transport
1 To Hat Yai
2 To Pattani
3 Bus Station

Sribamrung Rd. Reasonable Thai buffet and international food. *Unnamed seafood restaurant* (see map for location), seafood cooked before you in this open, corner side restaurant. *Thai fast-food joint* (see map for location), burgers, chicken, etc – a Western incursion, virtually the only gastronomic one in the town.

Wild West, Rotfai Rd. Folk music in the evenings.

Entertainment

Feb *Chinese New Year* (movable) celebrated enthusiastically by Yala's large population of Sino-Thais. **Mar** *Dove competition* (1st weekend), and ASEAN competition, with exhibitions. **May/Jun** *Yala city pillar* celebrations (movable) in honour of the town's guardian spirit, Jao Paw Lak Muang. Traditional southern Thai entertainment such as shadow puppet performances. A great time to be in the city if you are interested in southern Thai culture.

Festivals

Books *Bookshop*, Sribamrung Rd (close to the *Yala Rama Hotel*), sells mostly Thai-language books but does also carry English-language newspapers.

Shopping

Air There is no airport at Yala – the nearest is outside Pattani. However, there is a Thai Airways office in town, on Pipitpakdi Rd. **Train** Station on northeast side of town. Overnight connections with Bangkok and other stops north. Also regular connections with Hat Yai and Sungei Golok.

Transport
1,153 km to Bangkok
178 km to Hat Yai

Bus Pattani buses leave from Pattani Rd on the far side of the railway track. Buses to all other destinations leave from the mini *bor kor sor* just southeast of the railway station, not far from the *Yala Rama Hotel*. Regular connections with Bangkok 16 hrs, Hat Yai 3 hrs, Songkhla 3 hrs, Pattani 2 hrs, Phetburi, Prachuap Khiri Khan, Phattalung, and Sungei Golok. Betong buses (mini Mercedes) leave mornings only. No buses to Narathiwat. **Taxi**: from along the road in front of the railway station – ask for the exact spot. **Share taxis** to Betong, Pattani, Hat Yai, and Songkhla each laying claim to a different piece of pavement.

Airline offices *THAI*, Pipitpakdi Rd (close to Bangkok Bank of Commerce). **Banks** *Bangkok Bank of Commerce*, Pipitpakdi Rd. *First Bangkok City Bank*, Pipitpakdi Rd. *Thai Military Bank*, Sirirot Rd. **Communications** Post Office: Sirirot Rd (100 m south of the *Chang Lee Hotel*). Telephone Office: international calls can be made from the Post Office on Sirirot Rd, or from the Telecom Office about 1-2 km out on Pipitpakdi Rd.

Directory

Betong   เบตง

After the magnificent mountain drive from Yala which winds up through dramatic limestone hills, Betong is a disappointing, ugly town, full of barbershops, massage parlours and hotels catering for Malaysians on cross-border weekends and 'business trips'. The only reason to come here is to leave it – to cross the border; it is a dreary town.

Phone code: 073
Colour map 5, grid C5

Until 1990, when Chin Peng's Communist Party of Malaya came out of the jungle and the rebels laid down their arms, Betong's forested hills concealed his HQ and acted as the base for guerrillas heading south down the peninsula. Joint Malaysian-Thai army patrols regularly mounted search-and-destroy missions against the CPM base, known ominously as 'Target One'. The Communists made this as difficult as possible by seeding trails with anti-personnel mines, which they are now being made to clear in joint Thai-Malaysian-CPM operations. Now that this subversive excitement is history, Betong's only claim to fame – other than its sex industry – is an **enormous postbox** which is said to be the biggest in the world, but is actually disappointingly diminutive.

The Southern Region

Excursions

Betong Hot Springs are situated 10 km from town; drive 3 km north on the road to Yala and then turn right onto a dirt track for a further 7 km. The big steaming pool is rather dirty, although the smaller pool is cleaner. The springs are in a pleasant setting surrounded by hills. There are several stalls catering mainly for elderly Chinese tour groups hoping for a cure or second lease of life. ■ *Getting there: hire a saamlor from Betong (฿100 upwards).*

Highland Friendship Village (Pityamit One) is 10 km up the road from the hot springs and is a former jungle base camp belonging to the Marxist-Leninist faction of the Communist Party of Malaya, which fought the Malaysian and Thai armies from here for nearly 30 years. Even the intelligence services of both armies were unaware of the existence of the camp until after the communists laid down their arms in 1989. At the entrance, there is now a 4 m-high statue of four white doves in the middle of a fountain. (This is the emblem of the village – the former guerrillas themselves refer to them as 'peace pigeons'; literature from one Betong hotel misguidedly refers to the statue as 'a seagull memorial'). The camp's residents sell souvenirs to tourists and host guided tours of the old jungle camp itself, which is a 10-minute walk up the hillside to the right of the main entrance. Exhibits are carefully labelled; they include uniforms and other regalia and memorabilia of the former People's Liberation Army of Malaya. Camp facilities are on show – including the kitchen area which had an ingenious flue, constructed so as to suck up the smoke and embers and release them on the other side of the hill enabling the camp's location to remain a secret. The pride of the camp, however, is its network of subterranean tunnels in which the comrades once sheltered from Malaysian mortars and Thai patrols. They took 50 cadres three months to dig, working round the clock in shifts. There are eating and sleeping areas and a radio communications room 10 m underground. Other nearby camps had similar tunnel systems, but they have not yet been opened to the public as their environs are still strewn with boobytraps. **Sleeping** *Friendship Resort*, Pityamit One, fan, food available at hot springs, clean little white rooms in two modern bungalows on hillside overlooking village, modestly furnished but a pleasant alternative to staying in Betong. ■ *Getting there: as with hot springs, hire saamlor/taxi from Betong (฿150-200).*

Ban Sakai is home to a community of formerly semi-nomadic Sakai 'aboriginals'. Turn left near a bridge off the main Betong-Yala road between the Km 66 and Km 67 markers. The road follows the river up the valley for 4 km; Ban Sakai is signposted from the main village. In Malaysia, the Sakai are called *orang asli* (indigenous man); the Thais are less polite, referring to them as *ngao* – or 'rambutans', as the fruit has a not dissimilar hairstyle. This is one of the few remaining groups of Sakai in Thailand, although they are largely settled now. Most work as tappers in the local rubber holdings. ■ *Getting there: take Yala buses and walk 4 km from the main road.*

Sleeping
■ *on map*
Price codes:
see inside front cover

Although most of Betong's hotels cater for the sex industry, a number of more sophisticated hotels have recently opened, the best of which is the *Merlin*. Prices are mainly quoted in Malaysian ringgit. **B** *Merlin*, 33 Chayachaowalit Rd, T230222, F231357. A/c, restaurant, pool, superb value for money, very high standard of rooms with wide range of facilities including fitness centre, snooker club, sauna and disco. Recommended. **B** *Penthouse Resort*, 68/1 Rattanasatien Rd, T231501, F230879. A/c, restaurant, smaller rooms than *Merlin*, but well-kept in

••••••••••••••••••••••••••••

Betong place names

Ban Sakai
บ้านซาไก

Betong Hot Springs
น้ำพุร้อนเบตง

lush garden surrounds, good range of facilities. **B-D** *Sri Betong*, Thammwithi Rd, T230188. 3 buildings with different rates (newest rooms are most expensive). Rates are also divided into Fri-Sat and Sun-Thu. Notwithstanding the feeling that this hotel has more than its fair share of short-stay visitors, it has decent rooms. **C-D** *Cathay*, 17-21 Chantarothai Rd, T230999. A/c, restaurant, formerly top hotel in town, newly spruced up to keep pace with recent arrivals, reasonably clean, spacious rooms, facilities include barber shop and disco, ticketing agent. Good value. **C-D** *Khong Kha*, 1 Thammwithi Rd, T230441. Some a/c, restaurant, poor. **D** *Fortuna*, 50-58 Pakdidamrong Rd, T231180. A/c, restaurant, reasonable value, best of lower bracket. **E** *Fa Un Rong*, 113/1-2 Chantarothai Rd, T231403. Another hotel which is passable but where Malaysians enjoying Thai womanhood are common. A sign on the desk warns that only condom users are well served.

Chinese Several restaurants around town. **Cheap**: *New Restaurant*, on the road in front of the clock tower, is the best, standard Chinese fare, serves *dim sum* for breakfast. Plenty more restaurants along Sukhayang Rd. **Malay and Chinese stalls** Behind the *Cathay Hotel*   **Eating**

Bus Daily connection with Yala from the road in front of the clock tower. **Taxi**: to Yala, 4 hrs from the road in front of the clock tower.   **Transport**

The border post is 8 km out of town but it is only a short stroll across to Malaysia and there are plenty of taxis waiting the other side. It is marked by an old boundary stone emblazoned with a quaint colonial map of Malaya. **Taxi**: from Betong to the border post (฿80 for the whole taxi) or *saamlor* (฿10). From the Malaysian side of the border post to Keroh (M$1). From Keroh to Sungai Petani (M$25).   **Transport to Malaysia**

Banks *Thai Farmers* and *Thai Military* opposite Esso station. Other banks are to be found on Sukhayang Rd and around the clock tower   **Directory**

Betong

To Hot Springs, Highland Friendship Village, Ban Sakai & Yala

Sukhayang Rd

Veeraphan Rd

To Wat Phutthathiwat & Hospital

Penthouse Resort

Tesachinda Rd

New

Tanta Veera Rd

Rattanasatien Rd

Saritdech Rd

Chantarothai Rd

Jirajinda Rd

Samon Ta Rai Rd

Rattanakit Rd

To border (8 km)

Customs

Immigration

Soi Fa Unrung

Fa Un Rong

Sukhayang Rd

Clock Tower

Sri Betong

Chayachaowalit Rd

Merlin

Pakdidamrong Rd

Khong Kha

Fortuna

Amarit Rd

Thammwithi Rd

Public Park

N

Not to scale

Sungei Golok   สุไหงโกลก

Phone code: 073
Colour map 5, grid C6

This border town is the jumping-off point for the east coast of Malaysia and is another unattractive southern Thai town catering for Malaysian 'business travellers'. The border crossing connects with Rantau Panjang. The *Tourist centre service*, Asia 18 Rd, next to immigration post on the bridge, T612126, F615230, covers the areas of Narathiwat, Yala and Pattani. They are helpful, with plenty of maps and information.

Sleeping
■ *on map*
Price codes:
see inside front cover

Most of the hotels are around Charoenkhet Rd. Many are used by Malaysians on short stays. Hotels accept Thai baht or Malaysian ringgit.

B *Genting*, 250 Asia 18 Rd, T613231, F611259. A/c, restaurant, featureless block, good-sized pool. Very good value and well run. **B** *Grand Garden*, 66 Soi 3 Prachawiwat Rd, T613600. A/c, restaurant, small pool with waterfall, featureless rooms. **B-C** *Marina*, 173 Charoenkhet Soi 3, T613881, F613385. A/c, restaurant, pool. The cheaper rooms are well priced, clean and presentable.

C *City*, 28-32 Sariwong Rd, T613521. Rambling, unsightly block, fair rooms, well kept. Central location in town. **C** *Intertower*, 160-166 Prachawiwat Rd, T612700, F613400. A/c, restaurant. Fair rooms but dull. **C** *Tara Regent*, 45 Charoenkhet Soi Phuthon, T611801, F613385. Some a/c, restaurant. Rooms are a bit dingy but tidy; not as good value as others in this price bracket. **C** *Venice Palace*, 22 Cheunmanka Rd, T613700, F612418. Friendly staff, a/c rooms have hot water and are clean and smart. Good value at this price. **C-D** *Plaza*, 2 Thetpathom Rd, T611875, F613402. Interesting lime green colour scheme in the rooms but otherwise, superb. Clean rooms with hot water, TV, fridge and a/c. Very good value. Well used by tours and business groups. **D** *Valentine*,

Sungei Golok

■ Sleeping			● Eating
1 City	4 Intertower	7 Tara Regent	1 Angel Bakery
2 Genting	5 Marina	8 Valentine	2 Ramli
3 Grand Garden	6 Plaza	9 Venice Palace	

The Southern Region

2/1 Waman Amnoey Rd, T611229, F611929. Some a/c, rooms are OK but no hot water. Hospitable welcome.

There is a plethora of other hotels in the **D-E** brackets. None of them is anything special, some are easier to spot than others. Rooms have no mod cons. It is worth paying an extra ฿100-200 and get a decent (if uninspired) room.

Angel Bakery, Waman Amnoey Rd (opposite *Valentine Hotel*). Good sweet pastries and other snacks. *Ramli Restaurant*, Charoenkhet Soi 3, Muslim cuisine. There are plenty of other roadside places to eat.

Eating
● *on map*

Malaysian batik Available in shops all around town.

Shopping

Motorcycle taxi From town over the border (฿10-20). **Train** Station on Asia 18 Rd (the road to the border). Overnight connections with Bangkok. Connections to Yala, Hat Yai, Phattalung, Nakhon Si Thammarat. **Bus** Station on Bussayapan Rd (near *An An Hotel*). Overnight connections with Bangkok 18 hrs. Regular connections with Surat Thani 10 hrs, Hat Yai 4 hrs, Narathiwat 1 hr. **Taxi**: Tak Bai, Narathiwat, Pattani, Yala, Hat Yai.

Transport
1,220 km to Bangkok

Border open Mon-Sun, 0500-1700 Thai time. This is the main crossing-point on the east side of the peninsula, as Sungei Golok is well connected with other towns by train and bus (฿40 by train to Hat Yai). But the bus stop and railway station in Sungei Golok are at least 1 km from Golok Bridge (the crossing-point), so it is necessary to hire a motorbike or trishaw to go from the railway station or bus stop across the bridge.
    Road Bus: Rantau Panjang's bus stand is 1 km from Golok Bridge. Regular connections with Kota Bahru. **Taxi**: taxi stand in Rantau Panjang is opposite Golok Bridge. **Share taxis** to almost anywhere in Malaysia including Kota Bahru, Kuala Lumpur, Butterworth and Alor Star.

Transport to Malaysia

Communications Post Office: off Bussayapan Rd.

Directory

The Southern Region

Background

10

Background

History

Prehistory

See also box, page 744

Research since the end of the Second World War has shown Thailand to be a 'hearth' – or core area – in Southeast Asian prehistory. Discoveries at archaeological sites such as Ban Chiang (see page 436) and Non Nok Tha in the northeast, Spirit Cave in the north, and Ban Kao (see page 526) in the west have revealed evidence of early agriculture (possibly, 7000 BC) – particularly rice cultivation – pottery (3500 BC) and metallurgy (2500 BC). Although heated arguments over the significance and the dating of the finds continue, there is no doubt that important technologies were being developed and disseminated from an early date. These finds have altered the view of this part of the world from being a 'receptacle' for outside influences to being an area of innovation in its own right.

Today, the population of Thailand is made up of Tai-speaking peoples. For long it has been thought that the Tai migrated from southern China about 2,000 years ago, filtering down the valleys and along the river courses that cut north-south down the country. These migrants settled in the valleys of North Thailand, on the Khorat Plateau, and in parts of the lower Chao Phraya basin. Even at this early date there was a clear division between hill and lowland people. The lowland Tai mastered the art of wet rice cultivation (see page 821), supporting large populations and enabling powerful states and impressive civilizations to evolve. In the highlands, people worked with the forest, living in small itinerant groups, eking out a living through shifting cultivation (see page 830) or hunting and gathering. In exchange for metal implements, salt and pottery, the hill peoples would trade natural forest products: honey, resins such as lac, wild animal skins, ivory and herbs. Even today, lowland 'civilized' Thais view the forest (*pa*) as a wild place (*thuan*), inhabited by spirits and hill peoples. This is reflected in the words used to denote 'civilized' lowland Thais – *Khon Muang*, People of the Town – and 'barbaric' upland people – *Khon Pa*, People of the Forest.

Mon, Srivijayan and Khmer influences

Dvaravati
See also box, page 745

Before the Tais emerged as the dominant force in the 13th century, Thailand was dominated by Mon and Khmer peoples. The Mon kingdom of Dvaravati was centred close to Bangkok, with cities at modern day Uthong and Nakhon Pathom. Dvaravati relics have also been found in the north and northeast, along what are presumed to have been the trade routes between Burma east to Cambodia, north to Chiang Mai and northeast to the Khorat Plateau and Laos. The Dvaravati Kingdom lasted from the sixth to the 11th centuries. Only the tiny Mon kingdom of Haripunjaya, with its capital at Lamphun in the north, managed to survive annexation by the powerful Khmer Empire and remained independent until the 13th century. The state of Dvaravati was an artistic and political outlier of the Mon Empire of Burma. Unfortunately, virtually nothing of the architecture of the Dvaravati period remains. Buildings were constructed of laterite blocks, faced with stucco (a mixture of sand and lime) and, apparently, bound together with vegetable glue. In Thailand, only the stupa of Wat Kukut outside Lamphun gives an indication of Dvaravati architecture (it was last rebuilt in 1218, see page 254). Dvaravati sculpture is much better represented and the National Gallery in Bangkok has some fine examples. The sculptors of the period drew their inspiration from India's late-Gupta cave temples, rendering human form almost supernaturally.

Srivijaya

The powerful Srivijayan Empire, with its capital at Palembang in Sumatra, extended its control over south Thailand from the seventh to the 13th centuries. Inscriptions

Background

Thailand's Prehistory (11,000 BP–1,500 BP)

11,000 BP	Evidence of hunter-gatherers (Spirit Cave, Northern Thailand)
8,000 BP	Earliest excavated pottery in Thailand (Spirit Cave)
5,500 BP	Rice chaff associated with human habitation, probably wild (Banyan Valley Cave, Northern Thailand)
5,000 BP	Evidence from Northeast Thailand of the origins of agriculture and domestication of animals (pig, dog, chicken, cattle)
5,000 BP	Beautiful cord-marked pottery excavated (Ban Chiang, Northeast Thailand)
4,000-3,500 BP	Early evidence of bronze metallurgy (Ban Chiang)
3,000 BP	Cave and cliff paintings (Pha Taem, Northeast Thailand)
2,500 BP	Silk impressions in bronzeware (Ban Na Di)
2,300 BP	Iron-ware (Ban Na Di)
2,000 BP	Red-on-buff pottery (Ban Chiang)
1,500 BP	Moated settlements (Northeast Thailand)

NB Some of the dates above are contested, especially for such things as the origins of agriculture and the domestication of animals. BP = Before the Present.

and sculptures dating from the Srivijayan period have been found near the modern Thai towns of Chaiya and Sating Phra in Surat Thani, and Songkhla provinces. They reveal an eclectic mixture of Indian, Javanese, Mon and Khmer artistic influences, and incorporate both Hindu and Mahayana Buddhist iconography. Probably the best examples of what little remains of Srivijayan architecture in Thailand are Phra Boromthat and a sanctuary at Wat Kaeo, both in Chaiya (see page 652).

The Khmer Of all the external empires to impinge on Thailand before the rise of the Tai, the most influential was the Khmer. Thailand lay on the fringes of the Angkorian Kingdom, but nonetheless many Thai towns are Khmer in origin: That Phanom, Sakhon Nakhon and Phimai in the northeast; Lopburi, Suphanburi and Ratburi in the lower central plain; and Phitsanulok, Sawankhalok and Sukhothai in the upper central plain.

The period of Khmer inspiration is referred to as 'Lopburi', after the Central Thai town of the same name which was a Khmer stronghold. The peak of the Khmer period in Thailand lasted from the 11th to the 13th centuries, corresponding with the flowering of the Angkorian period in Cambodia. However, antiquities have been found that date back as far as the seventh and eighth century AD. The most impressive architectural remains are to be found in the Northeastern region: Phimai, not far from Nakhon Ratchasima (Korat) (see page 396), and Muang Tham (page 389) and Phnom Rung (page 387), both south of Buriram. As Cambodia's treasures are still relatively expensive and hard to get to, these 'temple cities' are a substitute, giving some idea of the economic power and artistic brilliance of the Khmer period. There are also many lesser Khmer ruins scattered over the Northeastern region, many barely researched, and these offer worthwhile forays for those with a real interest in Thailand's historical and archaeological past.

The Tai

The Tai did not begin to exert their dominance over modern Thailand until the 12th-13th centuries. By then they had taken control of Lamphun in the north, founded Chiang Mai, established the Sukhothai Kingdom in the Yom River valley, and gained control of the southern peninsula. From the 13th century onwards, the history of Thailand becomes a history of the Tai people.

Background

The Dvaravati, Srivijaya and Khmer empires in Thailand (6th-14th centuries)

Dvaravati	**6th-11th centuries (west, central and Northern Thailand)**
	661 AD (19 February), Haripunchaya reputed to have been founded at Lamphun in Northern Thailand by a group of Buddhist holy men.
	late 7th century: Queen Chamadevi, a daughter of the ruler of Lopburi, becomes queen of the Mon (Dvaravati) kingdom of Haripunchaya.
Srivijaya	**7th-13th centuries (Southern Thailand)**
	7th century: evidence of a thriving Buddhist entrepôt based at Palembang in Sumatra, with a presence in southern Thailand.
	13th-14th centuries: Srivijaya loses its control of the Malay peninsula and southern Thailand to the young and vigorous Tai states of Sukhothai and, later, Ayutthaya.
Khmer	**9th-13th centuries (Northeast and central Thailand)**
	889-900 AD: reign of Yasovarman I. He expands the Khmer empire onto the Khorat Plateau of Northeast Thailand.
	1001-1002: reign of Udayadityavarman, who mounts an invasion of Haripunjaya following an attack by Haripunjaya on the Khmer town of Lopburi.
	12th century: Lopburi is regarded by Angkor as Syam – ie Siam.
	1113-1150: reign of Suryavarman II.
	1181-1219?: reign of the great Jayavarman VII, who develops the Angkorian communications system, helping to hold together his vast empire. Lopburi is firmly incorporated into the Khmer Empire.
	1220-1243: reign of Indravarman II.

An important unit of organization among the Tai was the *muang*. Today, muang is usually translated as 'town'. But it means much more than this, and to an extent defies translation. The muang was a unit of control, and denoted those people who came under the sway of a *chao* or lord. In a region where people were scarce but land was abundant, the key to power was to control manpower, and thereby to turn forest into riceland. At the beginning of the 13th century, some Tai lords began to extend their control over neighbouring muang, forging kingdoms of considerable power. In this way, the Tai began to make a history of their own, rather than merely to be a part of history.

In Northern Thailand, various Tai chiefs began to expand at the expense of the Mon. The most powerful of these men was **King Mengrai**, born in October 1239 at Chiang Saen, a fortified town on the Mekong. It is said that Mengrai, concerned that the constant warring and squabbling between the lords of the north was harming the population, took it upon himself to unite the region under one king. That, inevitably, was himself. Entranced by the legendary wealth of Haripunjaya, Mengrai spent almost a decade hatching a plot to capture this powerful prize. He sent one of his scribes – Ai Fa – to ingratiate himself with the King of Haripunjaya, and having done this encouraged the scribe to sow seeds of discontent. By 1280, the king of Haripunjaya was alienated from his court and people, and in 1281, Mengrai attacked with a huge army and took the city without great trouble. Mengrai then set about uniting his expansive, new kingdom. This was helped to a significant degree by the propagation of Ceylonese Theravada Buddhism, which transcended tribal affiliations and helped to create a new identity of Northern Thai. The Lanna (literally, 'Million Ricefields') Thai Kingdom created by Mengrai was to remain the dominant power in the north until the mid-16th century, and was not truly incorporated into the Thai state until the 19th century.

Chiang Mai or Lanna Thai
See also box, page 746

Background

Lanna Thai (1239-1660)

1239	King Mengrai, the founder of the Lanna Kingdom, is born in Chiang Saen
1259	Mengrai becomes ruler of Chiang Saen, succeeding his father
1262	Mengrai founds Chiang Rai
1281	After years of preparation, Mengrai takes the Haripunchaya kingdom based at Lamphun
1289	Mengrai takes Pegu, and extends his empire into Burma
1292	Mengrai establishes Chiang Mai as his new capital
1317	Mengrai dies and the Lanna kingdom enters a period of instability
1355	King Ku Na of Lanna brings some stability and direction back to the kingdom; he is a fine scholar and a cultured man
1369	King Ku Na invites a monk from Sukhothai to establish a monastery in Chiang Mai
1404-5	Lanna is invaded by a large Chinese army from Yunnan; they are repulsed after the king raises an army said to be 300,000-strong
1442-43	Ayuthaya sends an army against Lanna and the principality of Nan revolts against Lanna domination. In time, Lanna defeats both
1456-57	The beginning of a long period of conflict between Lanna and Ayuthaya over control of the upper Central Plains and lower North, which continues until about 1486
1478-79	A Vietnamese army from Luang Prabang (Laos) tries to take Nan, and is repulsed
1526	The death of King Muang Kaeo marks the beginning of the decline of Lanna
1546	Lanna comes under the suzerainty of Lane Xang (Laos)
1564-1660	Lanna is controlled over much of the period by Burma, whose king puts a series of puppet rulers on the throne of Lanna
1595	Kings of Lane Xang and Nan try to oust the Burmese from Lanna, but fail
1660	King Narai takes Chiang Mai and Lampang, but is eventually repulsed by a Burmese army

In 1296, Mengrai built a new capital which he named Chiang Mai – or 'New Town' (see page 256). The art of this era is called Chiang Saen and dates from the 11th century. It is still in evidence throughout the north – in Chiang Saen, Chiang Mai, Lamphun and Lampang – and shows strong stylistic links with Indian schools of art (see page 804).

Sukhothai

See also box opposite South of Chiang Mai, at the point where the rivers of the north spill out onto the wide and fertile Central Plains, a second Thai kingdom was evolving during the 13th century: the Sukhothai Kingdom. Its most famous king was **Ramkhamhaeng** (?1279-98) or 'Rama the Brave', who gained his name – so it is said – after defeating an enemy general in single-handed elephant combat at the age of 19. When Ramkhamhaeng ascended to the throne in 1275, Sukhothai was a relatively small kingdom occupying part of the upper Central Plain. When he died in 1298, extensive swathes of land came under the King of Sukhothai's control, and only King Mengrai of Lanna and King Ngam Muang of Phayao could be regarded as his equals. But King Ramkhamhaeng is remembered as much for his artistic achievements as for his raw power. Under Khmer tutelage, he is said to have devised the Thai writing system and also made a number of administrative reforms. The inscription No 1 from his reign is regarded as the first work of Thai literature, and contains the famous lines:

Sukhothai (1240-1321)

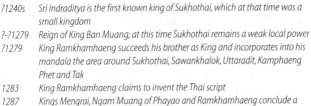

?1240s	Sri Indraditya is the first known king of Sukhothai, which at that time was a small kingdom
?-?1279	Reign of King Ban Muang; at this time Sukhothai remains a weak local power
?1279	King Ramkhamhaeng succeeds his brother as King and incorporates into his mandala the area around Sukhothai, Sawankhalok, Uttaradit, Kamphaeng Phet and Tak
1283	King Ramkhamhaeng claims to invent the Thai script
1287	Kings Mengrai, Ngam Muang of Phayao and Ramkhamhaeng conclude a strategic alliance
1292	Inscription No 1 of Sukhothai
1294	King Ramkhamhaeng mounts a military campaign in the south, near Phetburi
1298	King Ramkhamhaeng dies
1298	Lo Thai (r. 1298-1346 or 1347) is crowned king and his father's empire begins to decline
1319	Sukhothai territories in Pegu (Burma) are lost
1321	Tak becomes a tributary state of Lanna and Sukhothai declines in influence to become a small principality among many competing states

In the time of King Ramkhamhaeng, this land of Sukhothai is thriving. In the water there is fish, in the fields there is rice. The lord of the realm does not levy toll on his subjects for travelling the roads; they lead their cattle to trade or ride their horses to sell; whoever wants to trade in elephants does so; whoever wants to trade in horses, does so; whoever wants to trade in silver and gold, does so. When any commoner or man of rank dies, his estate – his elephants, wives, children, granaries, rice, retainers and groves of areca and betel – is left in its entirety to his son. ... When [the King] sees someone's rice he does not covet it, when he sees someone's wealth he does not get angry ... He has hung a bell in the opening of the gate over there: if any commoner in the land has a grievance which sickens his belly and gripes his heart, and which he wants to make known to his ruler and lord, it is easy; he goes and strikes the bell which the King has hung there; King Ramkhamhaeng, the ruler of the kingdom, hears the call; he goes and questions the man, examines the case, and decides it justly for him. So the people of this muang [city/state] of Sukhothai praise him.

Every Thai schoolchild is taught to memorize the opening lines of the inscription, ones which seemingly just about every book on Thailand also repeats: *Nai naam mii plaa, nai naa mii khao*: 'in the water there are fish, in the fields there is rice'.

Although the kingdom of Sukhothai owed a significant cultural and artistic debt to the Khmers, by the 13th century the Tais of Sukhothai were beginning to explore and develop their own interpretations of politics, art and life. The kingdom promoted Theravada Buddhism, sponsoring missionary monks to spread the word. For many Thais today, the Sukhothai period – which lasted a mere 200 years – represents the apogee, the finest flowering of Thai brilliance. A visit to the ruins of Sukhothai or its sister city of Si Satchanalai reinforces this (see pages 208-227).

Ayutthaya

In the middle of the 14th century, Sukhothai's influence began to be challenged by another Thai kingdom, Ayutthaya. Located over 300 km south on the Chao Phraya River, Ayutthaya was the successor to the Mon kingdom of Lavo (Lopburi). It seems that from the 11th century, Tais began to settle in the area and were peacefully incorporated into the Mon state, where they gradually gained influence. Finally, in

From the 14th century

Background

☞ Ayutthaya (1314-1767)

1314	Birth of U Thong, reputed to have been the founder of Ayutthaya
1351	Ayutthaya is established and U Thong – renamed King Ramathibodi – ascends to the throne
1390	King Ramesuan captures Chiang Mai
1409-24	Reign of King Intharacha
1424	Following King Intharacha's death, his two elder sons contest a duel on elephant back for the throne – both die from their injuries, allowing a third son to accede
1431-32	King Borommaracha II takes and then sacks Angkor in Cambodia
1448-88	Reign of King Boromtrailokant, best known for his administrative and legal reforms
1507-15	Drawn out war between Ayutthaya and Lanna
1549	Burmese invade and are repulsed
1555	Naresuan, later to free Ayutthaya from the yoke of the Burmese, is born
1558	Burmese take Chiang Mai
1564	Burmese invade Ayutthaya
1569	Burmese take the city of Ayutthaya and put their own puppet ruler, Maha Thammaracha, on the throne. The Burmese period lasts until 1593
1570-87	Cambodians forces invade Ayutthaya on six occasions in 18 years
1585-87	Naresuan defies and defeats the Burmese occupiers on two occasions
1593	The Burmese send a massive army to defeat Naresuan, and are vanquished at Nong Sarai. Ayutthaya is restored as an independent kingdom
1608	Siam sends its first diplomatic mission to Europe and trade relations, especially with the Dutch, grow
1662	King Narai mounts an invasion of Burma
1664	Trading treaty concluded with the Dutch
1687	A large French diplomatic mission arrives in Ayutthaya
1688	Narai's death leads to the Ayutthaya 'Revolution' and the execution of Constantine Phaulcon. Links with Europe and Western traders and emissaries are cut
1733-58	Reign of King Boromtrailokant, marking the apogee of Ayutthaya's power
1760	Burmese forces beseige Ayutthaya, but retreat
1766-67	Burmese forces, after defeating Chiang Mai and other northern towns, beseige, capture and sack Ayutthaya, marking the end of the Ayutthaya period

1350, a Tai lord took control of the area and founded a new capital at the confluence of the Pa Sak, Lopburi and Chao Phraya rivers. He called the city Ayutthaya – after the sacred town of Ayodhya in the Hindu epic, the Ramayana. This kingdom would subsequently be known as Siam. From 1350, Ayutthaya began to extend its power south as far as Nakhon Si Thammarat, and east to Cambodia, raiding Angkor in the late 14th century and taking the city in 1432. The palace at Angkor was looted by the Thai forces and the Khmers abandoned their capital, fleeing eastwards towards present-day Phnom Penh. Although Sukhothai and Ayutthaya initially vied with one another for supremacy, Ayutthaya proved the more powerful. In 1438, King Boromraja II placed his seven-year-old son, Ramesuan (later to become King Boromtrailokant), on the throne, signalling the end of Sukhothai as an independent power.

During the Ayutthayan period, the basis of Thai common law was introduced by King Ramathibodi (1351-69), who drew upon the Indian Code of Manu, while the powerful King Boromtrailokant (1448-88) centralized the administration of his huge kingdom and introduced various other civil, economic and military reforms. Perhaps

Penis balls and sexual roles in historical Southeast Asia

One notable feature of Thai – and more widely, Southeast Asian – society is the relative autonomy of women. This is most clearly illustrated in sexual relations. As the historian Anthony Reid writes in his book Southeast Asia in the Age of Commerce 1450-1680: 'Southeast Asian literature of the period leaves us in little doubt that women took a very active part in courtship and lovemaking, and demanded as much as they gave by way of sexual and emotional gratification'. He then goes on to describe the various ways – often involving painful surgery – that men would try to satisfy their partners. Metal pins, for example, were inserted into the penis, and wheels, studs and spurs attached as accessories to increase the female's pleasure. Alternatively, metal balls or bells, sometimes made of gold or ivory, would be inserted beneath the skin of the penis. Numerous early European visitors expressed their astonishment at the practice. Tome Pires, the 16th-century Portuguese apothecary, observed that Pegu lords in Burma 'wear as many as nine gold ones [penis bells], with beautiful treble, contralto and tenor tones, the size of the Alvares plums in our country; and those who are too poor...have them in lead...Malay women rejoice greatly when the Pegu men come to their country... [because of] their sweet harmony'. Whereas, in Africa, genital surgery was, and is, often intended to suppress pleasure for women or increase it for men, in Southeast Asia the reverse was the case. The surgery described above was also widely practised – in Burma, Siam, Makassar, among the Torajans of Sulawesi, and Java.

the most important was the *sakdi naa* system, in which an individual's social position was related to the size of his landholdings. The heir apparent controlled 16,000 ha, the highest official 1,600 ha, and the lowest commoner 4 ha. A code of conduct for royalty was also introduced, with punishments again linked to position: princes of high rank who had violated the law were to be bound by gold fetters, those of lower rank by silver. The execution of a member of the royal family was, it has been said, carried out by placing them in a sack and either beating them to death with scented sandalwood clubs or having them trampled by white elephants. Even kicking a palace door would, in theory, lead to the amputation of the offending foot.

By King Boromtrailokant's reign, Ayutthaya had extended its control over 500,000 sq km, and the capital had a population of 150,000. Although the art of Ayutthaya is not as 'pure' as that of Sukhothai, the city impressed 16th and 17th century European visitors. The German surgeon Christopher Fryke remarked that 'there is not a finer City in all India'. Perhaps it was the tiger and elephant fights which excited the Europeans so much. The elephants (regarded as noble and representing the state) were expected to win by tossing the tiger (regarded as wild and representing disorder) repeatedly into the air. The fact that the tigers were often tied to a stake or attacked by several elephants at once must have lengthened the odds against them. (In Vietnam it was reported that tigers sometimes had their claws removed and jaws sewn together.) Despite the undoubted might of Ayutthaya and the absolute power that lay within each monarch's grasp, kings were not, in the main, able to name their successors. Blood was not an effective guarantee to kingship and a strong competitor could easily usurp a rival, even though he might – on paper – have a better claim to the throne. As a result, the history of Ayutthaya is peppered with court intrigues, bloody succession struggles and rival claims.

During this period, the fortunes of the Ayutthayan Kingdom were bound up with those of Burma. Over a 220-year period, the Burmese invaded on no less than six occasions. The first time was in 1548 when the Burmese king of Pegu, Tabengshweti, encircled the capital. King Mahachakrapat only survived the ensuing battle when

The 16th-18th centuries
See also box above

Background

The early Chakri period (1767-1855)

1767	Ayutthaya sacked and capital moves to Thonburi
1769-70	Taksin begins to piece Siam back together when he takes control of Cambodia, Phitsanulok, Nakhon Si Thammarat and Fang
1782	Rama I relocates capital from Thonburi to Bangkok
1785	Burmese mount a huge invasion force, which is eventually repulsed
1787	Burmese invade Lanna; also repulsed
1788-89	The Pali-language Buddhist Tripitaka is re-written in definitive style
1800	Threat from Burma is ended and Siam becomes the leading power in the area
1805	As part of his modernization programme, Rama I gives a committee of judges the job of reforming the Siamese legal code. They produce the Three Seals Laws
1812	Growing friction between Siam and Vietnam
1813	Siamese suzerainty of Cambodia ends, with Vietnam filling the void
1821	John Crawfurd visits Siam on behalf of the governor-general of British India
1825	John Burney is sent as British emissary to Siam
1826	The commercial and diplomatic Burney Treaty is signed
1827	King Anou of Laos invades Northeastern Siam; his forces are eventually decimated and Vientiane is sacked by the Siamese army
1829	Anou is captured and dies in captivity in Bangkok
1833-34	A Siamese and Lao army invades Cambodia; it is defeated by Vietnamese forces and Cambodia falls within the Vietnamese sphere of influence
1855	Signing of the Bowring Treaty

one of his wives drove her elephant in front of an approaching warrior. Elephants figured heavily in war and diplomacy during the Ayutthayan period: Tabengshweti justified his invasion by pointing out that he had no white elephants, the holiest of beasts (the Buddha's last reincarnation before his enlightenment was as a white elephant). The Ayutthayan king meanwhile had a whole stable of them, and was not willing to part with even one. Although this attack failed, in 1569, King Bayinnaung mounted another invasion and plundered the city, making Ayutthaya a vassal state. When the Burmese withdrew to Pegu, they left a ravaged countryside devoid of people, and large areas of riceland returned to scrub and forest. But a mere 15 years later, Prince Naresuan re-established Thai sovereignty, and began to lay the foundations for a new golden age in which Ayutthaya would be more powerful and prosperous than ever before (see page 176).

The 17th century The 17th century saw a period of intense commercial contact with the Dutch, English and French. In 1608, Ayutthaya sent a diplomatic mission to the Netherlands and in 1664 a trading treaty was concluded with the Dutch. Even as early as the 17th century, Thailand had a flourishing prostitution industry. In the 1680s an official was given a monopoly of prostitution in the capital; he used 600 women to generate considerable state revenues. The kings of Ayutthaya also made considerable use of foreigners as advisers and ministers at the court. The most influential such family was founded by two Persian brothers, who arrived at the beginning of the 17th century. However, the best known was the Greek adventurer Constantine Phaulcon, who began his life in the East as a mere cabin boy with the East India Company and rose to become one of King Narai's (1656-88) closest advisers and one of the kingdom's most influential officials before being executed in 1688 (see page 193). He was implicated in a plot with the French against King Narai and his execution heralded 100 years of relative isolation as the Thais became wary of, and avoided close relations with, the West.

Background

The height of Ayutthaya's power and glory is often associated with the reign of King Boromkot (literally, 'the King in the urn [awaiting cremation]', as he was the last sovereign to be honoured in this way). Boromkot ruled from 1733 to 1758 and he fulfilled many of the imagined pre-requisites of a great king: he promoted Buddhism and ruled effectively over a vast swathe of territory. But, in retrospect, signs of imperial senility were beginning to materialize even as Ayutthaya's glory was approaching its zenith. In particular, King Boromkot's sons began to exert their ambitions. Prince Senaphithak, the eldest, went so far as to have some of the king's officials flogged; in retaliation, one of the aggrieved officials revealed that the prince had been having an affair with one of Boromkot's three queens. He admitted to the liaison and was flogged to death, along with his lover.

The feud with Burma was renewed in 1760 when the Burmese King Alaungpaya invaded Thailand. His attack was repulsed after one of the seige guns exploded, seriously injuring the Burmese king. He died soon afterwards during the arduous march back to Pegu. Three years later his successor, King Hsinbyushin, raised a vast army and took Chiang Mai, Lamphun and Luang Prabang (Laos). By 1765, the Burmese were ready to mount a second assault on Ayutthaya. Armies approached from the north and west and at the beginning of 1766 met up outside the city, from where they laid seige to the capital. King Suriyamarin offered to surrender, but King Hsinbyushin would hear nothing of it. The city fell after a year, in 1767. David Wyatt writes:

> The Burmese wrought awful desolation. They raped, pillaged and plundered and led tens of thousands of captives away to Burma. They put the torch to everything flammable and even hacked at images of the Buddha for the gold with which they were coated. King Suriyamarin is said to have fled the city in a small boat and starved to death 10 days later.

The city was too damaged to be renovated for a second time, and the focus of the Thai state moved southwards once again – to Thonburi, and from there to Bangkok.

Bangkok and the Rattanakosin period

After the sacking of Ayutthaya, **General Taksin** moved the capital 74 km south to Thonburi, on the other bank of the Chao Pharaya River from modern day Bangkok. Taksin's original name was Sin. Proving himself an adept administrator, he was appointed Lord of Tak (a city in the upper Central Plain), or Phraya Tak. Hence his name Tak-sin. From Thonburi, Taksin successfully fought successive Burmese invasions, until the stress caused his mental health to deteriorate to the extent that he was forced to abdicate in 1782. A European visitor wrote in a letter that 'He [Taksin] passed all his time in prayer, fasting, and meditation, in order by these means to be able to fly through the air'. He became madder by the month and on 6 April 1782 a group of rebels marched on Thonburi, captured the king and asked one of Taksin's generals, Chao Phya Chakri, to assume the throne. The day that Chao Phya Chakri became King Ramatobodi, 6 April, remains a public holiday in Thailand – Chakri Day – and marks the beginning of the current Chakri Dynasty. Worried about the continuing Burmese threat, Rama I (as Chao Phya Chakri is known) moved his capital to the opposite, and safer, bank of the Chao Phraya River, founded Bangkok and began the process of consolidating his kingdom. By the end of the century, the Burmese threat had dissipated, and the Siamese were once again in a position to lead the Tai world.

During **Rama II's** reign (1809-24), a new threat emerged to replace the Burmese: that of the Europeans. In 1821, the English East India Company sent John Crawfurd as an envoy to Siam to open up trading relations. Although the king and his court remained unreservedly opposed to unfettered trade, Crawfurd's visit served to impress upon those more prescient Siamese where the challenges of the 19th century would lie.

Rama II's death and succession illustrates the dangers inherent in having a claim to the throne of Siam, even in the 19th century. The court chronicles record that in 1824 Prince Mongkut was ordained as a monk because the death of a royal white elephant indicated it was an 'ill-omened time'. Historians believe that Rama II, realizing his death was imminent, wished to protect the young prince by bundling him off to a monastery, where the robes of a monk might protect him from court intrigues.

Rama III's reign (1824-51) saw an invasion by an army led by the Lao King Anou. In 1827, Anou took Nakhon Ratchasima on the edge of the Central Plain and was within striking distance of Bangkok before being defeated. After their victory, the Siamese marched on Vientiane, plundering the city and subjugating the surrounding countryside. In 1829, King Anou himself was captured and transported to Bangkok, where he was displayed to the public in a cage. Anou died shortly after this humiliation – some say of shame, others say of self-administered poison. Before he died he is said to have laid a curse on the Chakri dynasty, swearing that never again would a Chakri king set foot on Lao soil. None has, and when the present king Bhumibol attended the opening of the Thai-Lao Friendship bridge over the Mekong in 1994, he did so from a sand bar in the middle of the river. There were also ructions at the court in Bangkok: in 1848 Prince Rakrannaret was found guilty of bribery and corruption and, just for good measure, homosexuality and treason as well. Rama III had him beaten to death with sandalwood clubs, in time-honoured Thai fashion.

The 19th century was a dangerous time for Siam. Southeast Asia was being methodically divided between Britain, France and Holland as they scrambled for colonial territories. The same fate might have befallen Siam, had it not been blessed with two brilliant kings: King Mongkut (Rama IV – 1851-68) and King Chulalongkorn (Rama V – 1868-1910).

Mongkut was a brilliant scholar. He learnt English and Latin and when he sat his oral Pali examination, performed brilliantly. Indeed, his 27 years in a monastery allowed him to study the religious texts to such depth that he concluded that all Siamese ordinations were invalid. He established a new sect based upon the stricter Mon teachings, an order which became known as the *Thammayutika* or 'Ordering Adhering to the Dharma'. To distinguish themselves from those 'fallen' monks who made up most of the Sangha, they wore their robes with both shoulders covered. Mongkut derisively called the main Thai order – the *Mahanikai* – the 'Order of Long-standing Habit'.

But Mongkut was not an other-wordly monk with scholarly inclinations. He was a rational, pragmatic man who well appreciated the economic and military might of the Europeans. He recognized that if his kingdom was to survive he would have to accept and acquiesce to the colonial powers, rather than try to resist them. He did not accede to the throne until he was 47, and it is said that during his monastic studies he came to realize that if China, the Middle Kingdom, had to bow to Western pressure, then he would have to do the same.

He set about modernizing his country, along with the support of other modern-thinking princes. He established a modern ship-building industry, trained his troops in European methods and studied Western medicine. Most importantly, in 1855, he signed the **Bowring Treaty** with Britain, giving British merchants access to the Siamese market, and setting in train a process of agricultural commercialization and the clearing of the vast Central Plains for rice cultivation. As David Wyatt writes: 'At the stroke of a pen, old Siam faced the thrust of a surging economic and political power with which they were unprepared to contend or compete'. Mongkut's meeting with Bowring illustrates the lengths to which he went to meet the West on its own terms: he received the British envoy and offered him port and cigars from his own hand, an unheard of action in Thai circles.

It would seem that King Mongkut and **Sir John Bowring** were men of like mind. Both were scholars who believed in the power of rational argument. Bowring was a close friend of the philosophers Jeremy Bentham and John Stuart Mill, and he wrote a number of articles for the *Westminster Review*. He was a radical reformer, in favour of free trade and prison reform and bitterly opposed to slavery. He was a member of the House of Commons for six years, governor of Hong Kong, and Her Majesty's Consul in Canton (China). He was a remarkable man, just as Mongkut was a remarkable man, and his achievements during a long 80-year life were enough to satisfy a dozen ambitious men. It seems that Bowring used a mixture of veiled military force and rational argument to encourage Mongkut to sign the Bowring Treaty, perhaps the single most important treaty in Thailand's history. Bowring's account of his visit, the two volume *The kingdom and people of Siam*, published in 1857, is a remarkably perceptive work, especially given the brevity of Bowring's visit to Siam. As David Wyatt writes in a reprint of the work (Oxford University Press, 1977), the book is undoubtedly 'the finest account of Thailand at the middle of the 19th century, when it stood on the threshold of revolutionary change'.

Unfortunately, in the West, Mongkut is not known for the skilful diplomacy which kept at bay expansionist nations considerably more powerful than his own, but for his characterization in the film *The King and I* (in which he is played by Yul Brynner). Poorly adapted from Anna Leonowens' own distorted accounts of her period as governess in the Siamese court, both the book and the film offend the Thai people. According to contemporary accounts, Mrs Leonowens was a bad tempered lady obviously given to flights of fantasy. She never became a trusted confidant of King Mongkut, who scarcely needed her limited skills, and there is certainly no evidence to indicate that he was attracted to her sexually. It appears that she was plain in appearance.

King Mongkut died on 1 October 1868 and was succeeded by his 15-year-old son **Chulalongkorn**. However, for the next decade a regent controlled affairs of state, and it was not until 1873, when Chulalongkorn was crowned for a second time, that he could begin to mould the country according to his own vision. The young king quickly showed himself to be a reformer like his father – for in essence Mongkut had only just begun the process of modernization. Chulalongkorn set about updating the monarchy by establishing ministries and ending the practice of prostration. He also accelerated the process of economic development by constructing roads, railways, schools and hospitals. The opium trade was regulated, court procedures streamlined and slavery finally completely abolished in 1905. Although a number of princes were sent abroad to study – Prince Rajebuidirekrit went to Oxford – Chulalongkorn had to also rely on foreign advisors to help him undertake these reforms. In total he employed 549 foreigners – the largest number being British, but also Dutch, Germans, French and Belgians. Chulalongkorn even held fancy dress parties at New Year and visited Europe twice. These visits included trips to the poor East End of London and showed Chulalongkorn that for all the power of Britain and France, they were still unable to raise the living standards of a large part of the population much above subsistence levels.

These reforms were not introduced without difficulty. The *Hua Boran* – or 'The Ancients' – as the King derogatorily called them, strongly resisted the changes and in late December 1874 Prince Wichaichan attempted to take the royal palace and usurp the king. The plot was thwarted at the last possible moment, but it impressed upon Chulalongkorn that reform could only come slowly. Realizing he had run ahead of many of his subjects in his zeal for change, he reversed some of his earlier reforms, and toned-down others. Nevertheless, Siam remained on the path of modernization – albeit progressing at a rather slower pace. As during Mongkut's reign, Chulalongkorn also managed to keep the colonial powers at bay. Although the king himself played a large part in placating the Europeans by skilful diplomacy

Background

☞ The reign of King Chulalongkorn (1868-1910)

1868	King Mongkut dies on 1 October. Fifteen year-old Chulalongkorn becomes king, but the appointment of a regent to guide the 'boy' king limits his powers
1873	Chulalongkorn is 'crowned' for a second time in November
1873-74	Chulalongkorn's reforming zeal riles the Hua Boraan or 'the Ancients', the Siamese old guard
1874-75	The Front Palace Crisis almost brings down the king as the Ancients resist Chulalongkorn's reforms – which he is forced to tone down
1874	Anglo-Siamese treaty establishes a system of bi-national courts to deal with issues involving nationals of the two countries
1874-80	King sends a royal commissioner to Chiang Mai and the city is gradually brought under Bangkok's control
Early 1880s	The King's power is strengthened as the old guard begin to die and Chulalongkorn is able to put his own men in place
1885	Major Siamese expedition sent to Laos to establish stonger links and pre-empt French expansionist intentions
1886	French challenge Siamese claims over Laos
1887	Prince Devawongse attends the celebrations marking Queen Victoria's 50th year on the throne of Great Britain; he also looks into European systems of government, with the aim of reforming Siam's administration
1888	New administrative system is introduced, which extends Bangkok's power to the outer provinces
1892	The administrative reforms are extended and a new system of ministries is introduced
1893	The French encroach on and take control of Laos; Chulalongkorn has no choice but to sign a treaty giving up claim to the lands east of the Mekong, following the decisive Pak Naam incident
1905	Slavery outlawed
1909	Siamese rights to the Malayan states of Kelantan, Perlis, Terengganu and Kedah are relinquished to the British
1910	Chulalongkorn dies on 24 October

Background

and by presenting an image of urbane sophistication, he was helped in this respect by a brilliant minister of foreign affairs, Prince Devawongse (1858-1923), who controlled Siam's foreign relations for 38 years.

The fundamental weakness of the Siamese state, in the face of the European powers, was illustrated in the dispute with France over Laos. Despite attempts by Prince Devawongse to manufacture a compromise, the French forced Siam to cede Laos to France in 1893 and to pay compensation – even though they had little claim to the territory. As it is said, power grows out of the barrel of a gun, and Chulalongkorn could not compete with France in military might. After this humiliating climbdown, the king essentially retired from public life, broken in spirit and health. In 1909, the British chipped away at more of Siam's territory, gaining rights of suzerainty over the Malay states of Kelantan, Terengganu, Kedah and Perlis. In total, Siam relinquished nearly 500,000 sq km of territory to maintain the integrity of the core of the kingdom. King Chulalongkorn died on 24 October 1910, sending the whole nation into deep and genuine mourning.

The 20th century The kings that were to follow Mongkut and Chulalongkorn could not have been expected to have had such illustrious, brilliant reigns. Absolute kingship was becoming increasingly incompatible with the demands of the modern world, and the kings of Thailand were resisting the inevitable. Rama VI, **King Vajiravudh** (1910-25), was educated at Oxford and Sandhurst Military Academy and seemed well prepared for kingship. However, he squandered much of the wealth built up by Chulalongkorn and ruled in a rather heavy-handed, uncoordinated style. He did try to inculcate a sense of 'nation' with his slogan 'nation, religion, king', but seemed more interested in Western theatre and literature than in guiding Siam through a difficult period in its history. He died at the age of only 44, leaving an empty treasury.

Like his older brother, **King Prajadhipok** (Rama VII – 1925-35), was educated in Europe: at Eton, the Woolwich Military Academy and at the Ecole Superieure de Guerre in France. But he never expected to become king and was thrust onto the throne at a time of great strain. Certainly, he was more careful with the resources that his treasury had to offer, but could do little to prevent the country being seriously affected by the Great Depression of the 1930s. The price of rice, the country's principal export, declined by two-thirds and over the same two-year period (1930-32) land values in Bangkok fell by 80%. The economy was in crisis and the government appeared to have no idea how to cope. In February 1932, King Prajadhipok told a group of military officers:

> The financial war is a very hard one indeed. Even experts contradict one another until they become hoarse. Each offers a different suggestion. I myself know nothing at all about finances, and all I can do is listen to the opinions of others and choose the best. I have never experienced such a hardship; therefore if I have made a mistake I really deserve to be excused by the officials and people of Siam.

The people, both the peasantry and the middle class, were dissatisfied by the course of events and with their declining economic position. But neither group was sufficiently united to mount a threat to the King and his government. Nevertheless, Prajadhipok was worried: there was a prophesy linked to Rama I's younger sister Princess Narinthewi, which predicted that the Chakri Dynasty would survive for 150 years and end on 6 April 1932.

The date itself passed without incident, but just 12 weeks later on 24 June a clique of soldiers and civilians staged a **coup d'état**, while the king was holidaying at the seaside resort of Hua Hin. This episode is often called the Revolution of 1932, but it was not in any sense a revolution involving a large rump of the people. It was orchestrated by a small élite, essentially for the elite. The king accepted the terms offered to him, writing:

The Revolution of 1932

Background

> I have received the letter in which you invite me to return to Bangkok as a constitutional monarch. For the sake of peace; and in order to save useless bloodshed; to avoid confusion and loss to the country; and, more, because I have already considered making this change myself, I am willing to co-operate in the establishment of a constitution under which I am willing to serve.

However, King Prajadhipok had great difficulty adapting to his lesser role and, falling out with the military, he abdicated in favour of his young nephew, Prince Ananda Mahidol, in 1935. The prince at the time was only 10 years old, and at school in Switzerland, so the newly created National Assembly appointed two princes to act as regents. From this point, until after the Second World War, the monarchy was only partially operative. Ananda was out of the country for most of the time, and the civilian government took centre stage. Ananda was not to physically reoccupy the throne until December 1945 and just six months later he was found dead in bed, a bullet through his head. The circumstances behind his death have never been satisfactorily explained and it remains a subject on which Thais are not openly permitted to speculate. Books investigating the death are still banned in Thailand.

While the monarchy receded from view, the civilian government was going through the intrigues and power struggles which were to become such a feature of the future politics of the country. The two key men at this time were the army officer Phibun Songkhram and the left-wing idealist lawyer Pridi Panomyong. Between them they managed to dominate Thai politics until 1957.

When **Prime Minister Pridi Panomyong** tried to introduce a socialist economic programme in 1933, pushing for the state control of the means of production, he was forced into exile in Europe. This is often seen as the beginning of the tradition of authoritarian, right-wing rule in Thailand, although to be fair, Pridi's vision of economic and political reform was poorly thought through and rather romantic. Nonetheless, with Pridi in Paris – at least for a while – it gave the more conservative elements in the government the chance to promulgate an anti-communist law, and thereby to usher in a period of ultra-nationalism. Anti-Chinese propaganda became more shrill, with some government positions being reserved for ethnic Tais. In 1938 the populist writer Luang Wichit compared the Chinese in Siam with the Jews in Germany, and thought that Hitler's policies might be worth considering for his own country.

This shift in policy can be linked to the influence of one man: **Luang Phibun Songkhram**. Born of humble parents in 1897, he worked his way up through the army ranks and then into politics. He became Prime Minister in 1938 and his enduring influence makes him the most significant figure in 20th century Thai politics. Under his direction, Siam became more militaristic, xenophobic, as well as 'religiously' nationalistic, avidly pursuing the reconversion of Siamese Christians back to Buddhism. As if to underline these developments, in 1939 Siam adopted a new name: Thailand. Phibun justified this change on the grounds that it would indicate that the country was controlled by Thais and not by the Chinese or any other group.

Second World War & post-war Thailand

During the Second World War, Phibun Songkhram sided with the Japanese who he felt sure would win. He saw the war as an opportunity to take back some of the territories lost to the French (particularly) and the British. In 1940, Thai forces invaded Laos and Western Cambodia. A year later, the Japanese used the kingdom as a launching pad for their assaults on the British in Malaya and Burma. Thailand had little choice but to declare war on the Allies and to agree a military alliance with Japan in December 1941. As allies of the Japanese, Phibun's ambassadors were instructed to declare war on Britain and the United States. However, the ambassador in Washington, Seni Pramoj, refused to deliver the declaration (he considered it illegal) and Thailand never formally declared war on the USA. In Thailand itself, Pridi, who had returned as regent to the young monarch King Ananda, helped to organize the Thai resistance – the Free Thai Movement. They received help from the US Office of Strategic Services (OSS) and the British Force 136, and also from many Thais. As the tide of the war turned in favour of the allies, so Prime Minister Phibun was forced to resign. He spent a short time in gaol in Japan, but was allowed to return to Thailand in 1947.

After the war, Seni Pramoj, Thailand's ambassador in the USA, became Prime Minister. He was soon followed by Pridi Panomyong as Prime Minister, who had gathered a good deal of support due to the role he played during the conflict. However, in 1946 King Ananda was mysteriously found shot dead in his royal apartments and Pridi was implicated in a plot. He was forced to resign, so enabling Phibun to become Prime Minister once again – a post he kept until 1957. Phibun's fervent anti-Communism quickly gained support in the USA, who contributed generous amounts of aid as the country became a front-line state in the battle against the 'red tide' that seemed to be engulfing Asia. Phibun's closest brush with death occurred in June 1951. He was leading a ceremony on board a dredge, the *Manhattan*, when he was taken prisoner during a military coup and transferred to the Thai navy flagship *Sri Ayutthaya*. The airforce and army stayed loyal to Phibun,

Thai, Siamese or Tai?

Is a Thai a Tai? And is this the same as a Siamese? Sometimes. Thai here is used to mean a national of Thailand. Prior to the Second World War, Thailand was known as Siam, a name by which Europeans had referred to the kingdom from the 16th century. However, in 1939 Prime Minister Phibun Songkhram decided a change was in order, largely because he wished to disassociate his country from the past, but also because of his xenophobia towards the Chinese community. The name he chose is a more direct translation of the Thai term prathet Thai, and firmly established Thailand as the 'country of the Tais'. Nonetheless, because the change is associated with the right-wing Phibun government, some academics still refuse to use the name and talk, rather pointlessly, of Siam.

Tai here is used to refer to the Tai-speaking peoples who are found not just in Thailand, but also in Burma, Laos and southern China. Some Thais are not Tai (for example, the Malay-speaking Thais of the south), while many Tais are not Thais. As David Wyatt writes in his Thailand: A Short History:

'The modern Thai may or may not be descended by blood from the late-arriving Tai. He or she may instead be the descendant of still earlier Mon or Khmer inhabitants of the region, or of much later Chinese or Indian immigrants. Only over many centuries has a 'Thai' culture, a civilization and identity emerged as the product of interaction between Tai and indigenous and immigrant cultures.'

A slightly different issue is the question of what makes a Thai a Thai. In other words, what are the defining characteristics of Thai-ness. This is shaky ground, dotted with metaphorical minefields. Ethnicity is noted on every Thai's identity card, but there is no system governing the categories applied. A person with 'Chinese' parents is counted a 'Thai', yet a Muslim Thai from the south is counted a 'Muslim', not a Thai. Some would say that there is method in this muddle, and that being a Theravada Buddhist is a critical component of being counted a true 'Thai'. Rather less contentious is an uncritical love of the King. All schoolchildren are taught that Thai-ness is encapsulated in three symbols, 'King, Nation, Religion', and this goes much of the way to explaining what the average Thai views as representative of being a Thai.

---

and planes bombed the ship. As it sank, the Prime Minister was able to swim to safety. The attempted coup resulted in 1,200 dead – mostly civilians. For the navy, it has meant that ever since it has been treated as the junior member of the armed forces, receiving far less resources than the army and airforce.

Prime Minister Phibun Songkhram was deposed following a coup d'état in 1957, and was replaced by **General Sarit Thanarat**. General Sarit established the National Economic Development Board (now the National Economic and Social Development Board) and introduced Thailand's first five-year national development plan in 1961. He was a tough, uncompromising leader, and following his death in 1963 was replaced by another General – **Thanom Kitticachorn**. With the war in Indochina escalating, Thanom allowed US planes to be based in Thailand, from where they flew bombing sorties over the Lao panhandle and Vietnam. In 1969 a general election was held, which Thanom won, but as the political situation in Thailand deteriorated, so Prime Minister Thanom declared martial law. However, unlike his predecessors Sarit and Phibun, Thanom could not count on the loyalty of all elements within the armed forces, and although he tried to take the strongman – or nak laeng – approach, his administration always had a frailty about it. In addition, historian David Wyatt argues that developments in Thai society – particularly an emergent middle-class and an increasingly combative body of students – made controlling the country from the centre rather harder than it had been over the previous decades.

Background

Thailand enters the modern period (1911-46)

1910	King Chulalongkorn dies, Vajiravudh accedes to the throne
1911	Wild Tiger Corp established
1912	Attempted coup against the king is thwarted
1917	A small force of Siamese soldiers is sent to Europe to fight with the Allies in the First World War
1919-20	Appalling rice harvest and other economic problems lead to severe economic difficulties
1925	King Vajiravudh dies at the age of only 44 on 26 November
1927	King Prajadhipok (educated at Eton and the Woolwich Military Academy) writes a paper on 'Democracy in Siam', and also appoints an advisory council to deliberate on government reform
1930-32	Great Depression hits Siam
1932	The Revolution of 24 June, and Siam becomes a constitutional monarchy. Phraya Mano becomes the first Prime Minister
1935	King Prajadiphok abdicates on 2 March. King Ananda Mahidol comes to the throne aged just 10. Two princes rule while he is finishing his schooling in Switzerland.
1938	Phibun Songkram becomes PM and introduces nationalistic and anti-Chinese policies
1939	Phibun changes the country's name from Siam to Thailand
1940	Thai forces invade Laos and Cambodia following the German defeat of France
1941	Japanese forces invade Thailand, and Bangkok is forced to agree a military alliance with Japan in December
1944	Phibun is forced to resign with the Japanese on the verge of defeat
1945	King Ananda Mahidol returns to Thailand to take his throne
1946	King Ananda Mahidol is killed in mysterious circumstances. King Bhumibol Adulyadej comes to the throne

It was Thailand's students who precipitated probably the single most tumultuous event since the Revolution of 1932. The student body felt that Thanom had back-tracked and restricted the evolution of a more open political system in the country. In June 1973 they began to demonstrate against the government, printing highly critical pamphlets and calling for the resignation of Thanom. A series of demonstrations, often centred on Sanaam Luang near the radical Thammasat University and the Grand Palace, brought crowds of up to 500,000 onto the streets. During the demonstrations, Thanom lost the support of the army: the Commander-in-Chief, General Krit Sivara, was unwilling to send his troops out to quell the disturbances, while Thanom, apparently, was quite willing to kill thousands if necessary. With the army unwilling to confront the students, and with the King – crucially – also apparently siding with Thanom's army opponents, he was forced to resign from the premiership and fled the country.

David Wyatt writes of the **October revolution**:

In many important respects, the events of October 1973 deserved far more the name revolution than either the events of 1932 or the authoritarian program of Sarit. They brought about an end to one-man, authoritarian rule; and if they did not bring an end to the military role in politics, then they at least signaled a new consciousness of the necessity of sharing political power more widely than had ever been the case in the past.

The October revolution ushered in a period of **turbulent democratic government** in Thailand, the first such period in the country's history. It was an exciting time: radical scholars could openly speak and publish, students could challenge the establishment, labour unions could organize and demonstrate, and leftist politicians could make their views known. But it was also a period of political instability. While there had been just five prime ministers between 1948 and 1973, the three years following 1973 saw the rapid coming and going of another four: Sanya Dharmasakti (October 1973-February 1975), Seni Pramoj (February-March 1975), Kukrit Pramoj (March 1975-January 1976) and Seni Pramoj (April-October 1976). This instability was reinforced by the feeling among the middle classes that the students were pushing things too far. The fall of Vietnam, Cambodia and Laos to Communism left many Thais wondering whether they would be the next 'domino' to topple. This gave an opening for rightist groups to garner support, and anti-Communist organizations like the Red Gaurs and the Village Scouts gained in influence and began, with the support and connivance of the police, to harrass and sometimes to murder left-wingers. 'Violence, vituperation, and incivility', as Wyatt writes, 'were now a part of public life as they never had been before in Thailand'.

This was the background that led the army to feel impelled to step in once again. However, the trigger for the **appalling events of October 1976** was the return of former Prime Minister Thanom from exile, who joined the sangha and became a monk. Installed in a Bangkok monastery, Thanom was visited by members of the royal family. The students took this as royal recognition of a man who had led the country into violence and to the edge of civil war. Demonstrations broke out in Bangkok, again centred on Sanaam Luang and the nearby Democracy Monument. This time, though, the students were not able to face down the forces of the Right. Newspapers printed pictures apparently showing the Crown Prince being burnt in effigy by students at Thammasat, and right wing groups, along with the police and the army, advanced on the university on 6 October. Details of the hours that followed are hazy. However, it seems clear that an orgy of killing ensued. With the situation rapidly deteriorating, the army stepped in and imposed martial law. Tanin Kraivixien was installed as Prime Minister, to be replaced the following year by Kriangsak Chomanan.

In 1996, on the **20th anniversary** of the massacre, newspapers in Thailand were filled with the reminiscences of those from both sides who were involved. The bones of the tragic episode were picked over exhaustively and the still grieving parents of some of those who were murdered or 'disappeared' were interviewed. Such was the coverage of the event – far more detailed and honest than anything at the time – that it was almost as if the Thai nation were engaged in a collective catharsis, cauterizing the wounds of 20 years earlier. Yet in a way the debate over the massacre said as much about the present as the past. Kasian Tejapira, one of the student leaders involved, and by 1996 a university lecturer, suggested that the anniversary was an opportunity "to redefine the meaning of Thai identity – one that is anti-elitist and not conservative; one that was put down at Thammasat 20 years ago". The former student activists are now in positions of power and influence. Some are wealthy businessmen, others university lecturers, while more still are involved in politics. Most seem to have retained their commitment to building a more just society. It must be somewhat depressing for them to find the students of today more interested in fashions and consumer goods than in social justice. In a way that – in microcosm – is the problem with Thailand's political culture: too much money and too few ethics.

The 1976 massacre was a shot in the arm for the **Communist Party of Thailand (CPT)**. Left-wing intellectuals and many students, feeling that they could no longer influence events through the political system, fled to the jungle and joined the CPT. The victories of the Communists in neighbouring Indochina also reinforced the

Jit Poumisak's radical history

Most histories of Thailand tell a conservative tale: of peasants working in the fields, protected by the merit of a benevolent king. Indeed, many Thai historians seem to go out of their way to paint a picture of Thailand's history, which is notable for its conservativism. It is no accident that perhaps the greatest early Thai historian, Damrong Rajanubhab, was himself a Chakri prince. Throughout the 19th century and the first half of the 20th century, Thai scholars eschewed radicalism and perpetuated a conservative view of Thai history.

In 1957 this cosy world was disrupted by the publication (in Thai) of Jit Poumisak's The real face of Thai feudalism today. The book turned Thai history on its head. For the first time, it presented a picture of Thailand where feudalism, and not just benevolent monarchs, reigned; where the masses were engaged in a struggle against oppressive rulers; where history was interpreted through economics; and where the social system governed relations between classes. It was Thailand's history with a Marxian visage.

Jit's reinterpretation of Thai history was, at least in the Thai context, astounding for its daring. Religion and culture were recast as the agents through which kings maintained their positions of power. Peasants – the great mass of the population – became pawns manipulated in the interests of the ruling classes, their impoverished position both maintained and justified in terms of religion and culture.

Jit's work was not received particularly warmly by Thailand's elite. In 1958 the book was banned and Jit was imprisoned for sedition. In 1973 it was republished during Thailand's experiment in democracy, only to be banned again in 1977, as the forces of dictatorship gained the upper hand. In 1979 it was reprinted for a third time as the threat of Communism receded and remains in print, required reading by every student of Thai history.

During the brief phase of democratic politics between 1973 and 1976, Jit became a central figure in the Left's struggle against the Right. Students read his works and seminars were arranged to discuss his life and thoughts. Jit became an emblem of – and an emblem for – the Left. By all accounts he was a brilliant scholar with a highly original mind.

His radical inclinations first became evident in 1953 when he was appointed editor of the Chulalongkorn University Yearbook. But just before the book went to press, the university authorities tried to halt its publication, claiming it was seditious. A university assembly was called to discuss the affair and some 3,000 students attended. Jit made an impassioned and eloquent speech defending his editorial role, but just as the audience seemed to be swinging in his favour a group of engineering students rushed the stage and knocked Jit unconscious.

From that moment on, Jit was on the outside. He continued to enrage the authorities with his radical writings. He was arrested and interrogated by the police. He moved closer to the Communist Party of Thailand – although he was not made a member until after his death. The final break with the establishment came in 1965, when he left Bangkok and fled to the jungle to join in the Communist Party of Thailand's struggle against the government. Less than a year later, in May 1966, he was shot and killed in Sakhon Nakhon province in the Northeastern region. Accounts differ on who shot him. However, it seems that a local headman killed him, possibly as he and a fellow insurgent stopped to barter for supplies. According to one source, a hand was cut from the corpse and sent to Bangkok for identification.

Background

sense that ultimately the CPT would emerge victorious. By the late 1970s the ranks of the party had swelled to around 14,000 armed guerrillas, who controlled large areas of the northeast, north and south. However, with the ascendancy of Prem Tinsulanond to the premiership in 1980 and a rapidly changing global political environment, the CPT fragmented and quickly lost support. Its leaders were divided between support for China and the Cambodian Khmer Rouge on the one hand, and the Soviet Union and Vietnam on the other. When the government announced an amnesty in 1980, many of the students who had fled into the forests and hills following the riots of 1973 returned to mainstream politics, exhausted and disenchanted with revolutionary life. In true Thai style, they were largely forgiven and re-integrated into society. But those who died on Sanaam Luang and in the streets leading off it have never been acknowledged, and in many cases their parents were never informed that they had been killed. Nor were they allowed to collect their children's bodies. As the Thai historian Thongchai Winichakul lamented on the 20th anniversary of the massacre in 1996, this shows the extent to which Thai society still values national stability over individual rights: "Life is more significant than the nation".

Prem Tinsulanond presided over the most stable period in Thai politics since the end of the Second World War. He finally resigned in 1988, and by then Thailand – or so most people thought – was beginning to outgrow the habit of military intervention in civilian politics. Chatichai Choonhaven replaced Prem after general elections in 1988, by which time the country was felt to be more stable and economically prosperous than at any time in recent memory. During his reign, the present King Bhumibol has played a crucial role in maintaining social stability, while the political system has been in turmoil. He is highly revered by his subjects, and has considerable power to change the course of events. There are essentially two views on the role of the king in contemporary Thailand. The general view is that he has influence far beyond that which his constitutional position strictly permits, but that he is careful not to overexercise that power and only intervenes at times of crisis. The king, in short, is his own man and acts in the best interests of the Thai people. The alternative view is that after his coronation, influential courtiers and generals tried to diminish the power of the king by making him a semi-divine figurehead and surrounding him in protocol. The king became a tool used by right-wing dictators and the army to justify their authoritarian ways. (For further background on the King, see the box on page 765.)

The widely held belief that the Thai political system had come of age proved ill-founded. In February 1991, with Prime Minister Chatichai daring to challenge the armed forces in various ways, General Suchinda Kraprayoon led a coup d'état which toppled the civilian government. Thailand has now had 17 coups or attempted coups since 1945, and over the 67 years since the original coup of 1932, army strongmen have been in power for no less than 49 years.

Modern Thailand

As Thailand entered the 21st century and the third millennium, the country was also, rather shakily, recovering from the deepest contraction of the economy since the 1930s. Until July 1997, everything was hunky dory in Thailand. Or that, at least, is what the World Bank and most business people and pundits thought. The Kingdom's economy was expanding at close to double-digit rates and the country was being showered with strings of congratulatory epithets. It was a 'miracle' economy, an Asian 'tiger' or 'dragon' ready to pounce on an unsuspecting world. Thailand has become the 'Cinderella' of Southeast Asia – a beautiful woman long disguised beneath shabby clothes – and academics and journalists were writing

Modern Thailand (1946-present)

1946	King Bhumibol accedes to the throne
1951	Attempted coup by the Navy against PM Phibun Songkhram (he became PM again) is thwarted by the army and airforce
1957	Sarit Thanarat become PM; he ushers in the era of modern development, known as samai pattana
1961	Publication of the first of Thailand's Five Year Development Plans
1963	Thanom Kitticachorn replaces Sarit as PM following Sarit's death
1964	US military aircraft are based on Thai soil. Operations increase as the Vietnam War escalates
1967	Thailand becomes a founder member of the Association of Southeast Asian Nations (ASEAN), following the signing of the Bangkok Treaty in the Thai capital
1967	Bangkok agrees to send a ground combat unit to support the USA in South Vietnam
1968	45,000 US personnel in Thailand and 600+ aircraft
1973	Massive demonstrations at Thammasat University in support of democracy leads to the resignation of Thanom
1973-76	Period of turbulent democratic government
1976	Massacre of students at Thammasat University in Bangkok as the military step in again. A shot in the arm for the CPT
late 1970s	CPT has 14,000 men and women under arms
1980	Prem Tinsulanond becomes PM
mid-1980s	CPT a spent force. Thailand enters its period of rapid economic growth
1988	Democratic elections, Chatichai Choonhaven becomes PM
1991	Suchinda Kraprayoon leads a succesful coup against Chatichai's administration
1992	Massacre of anti-dictatorship demonstrators in Sanaam Luang
1992	Democratic elections
1997	Baht is devalued and Thailand's economic crisis begins
2000	Thaksin Shinawatra is elected prime minister

books with glowing titles like *Thailand's Boom* (1996), *Thailand's Turn: Profile of a New Dragon* (1992) and *Thailand's Macro-economic Miracle* (1996). Wealth was growing, poverty falling and Bangkok was chock-full of designer shops, meeting the consumer needs of a growing – and increasingly hedonistic – middle-class.

Then everything went horribly wrong. The local currency, the baht, went into freefall, the stockmarket crashed, unemployment more than doubled, and the economy contracted. Bankrupt business people, the *nouveau pauvre*, cashed in their Mercedes, and wives were put on strict spending diets. Almost overnight, apparently prescient commentators, who had remained strangely silent during the years of growth, were offering their own interpretations of Thailand's fall from economic grace. A distinct whiff of schadenfreude filled the air. Epithet writers went back to their computers and came up with titles like the 'Asian contagion', the 'Asian mirage', 'Frozen miracles' and 'Tigers lose their grip'. In Thailand itself, locals began to talk of the *Thaitanic* as it sank faster than the doomed liner.

It is tempting to think that Thailand will never be the same again. The economy's malaise, which became evident in May 1997, quickly developed into a full-scale crisis. Prime Minister Chaovalit Yongchaiyut tried to sound convincing in the face of a collapsing currency and a contracting economy, but before the year was out so was he. While his government was on the verge of collapse, Parliament embraced a new constitution aimed at cleaning up Thailand's notoriously corrupt political system. Chuan Leekpai was appointed 1998's second prime minister, and he, in turn, appointed the year's fourth finance minister. Politicians now have to reveal their assets – financial, that is – and there are pressure groups pressing for good governance and greater accountability. As this book went to press, the newly elected prime minister, Thaksin Shinawatra, was facing the prospect of a five-year ban from politics for filing a false asset declaration (see below).

Notwithstanding the slowdown associated with the economic crisis, the rapid pace of change has brought with it social, economic and environmental tensions and conflicts. Bangkok is overstretched, its transport system on the verge of collapse, and around one million people live in slum conditions in the capital. Deforestation is such that the government felt impelled to impose a nationwide logging ban at the beginning of 1989, and national parks are poached and encroached. In the poor Northeastern region, incomes have stagnated, causing social tensions to become more acute and millions to migrate to the capital each dry season, in a desperate search for work. In the Central Plains, the country's rice bowl, land is now so scarce that some households are being forced to give up farming altogether. While in the North, AIDS has cut a scythe of death through some villages where scarcely a household has not been touched by the disease.

In the 1970s some scholars suggested that the country could be encapsulated by reference to the 'four Rs': rice, rivers, religion and royalty. Today, computer parts, jewellery and garments all exceed rice in terms of export value. Highways have replaced rivers as arteries of communication and religion has become so commercialized that Thais have coined a word to describe it: *Buddhapanich*. Only the King has stood head and shoulders above the fray, the one thread of continuity in a country changing and re-inventing itself with bewildering speed.

'Traditional' Thai life is becoming the stuff of history as modernity engulfs people and places. But just as the recent past becomes sepia-tinted, so the future becomes less compelling. Even before the crisis, some economists worried that Thailand's miracle had run its course. The country's green movement laments the environmental costs of economic growth, and sociologists highlight the wasted youth, the drug culture and the underclass as evidence of the corrosive social effects of modernization. Tourism has brought its own problems – 80% of freshwater wells in the Phi Phi National Park are contaminated because of the sheer numbers using the island's limited services. Some educated Thais also blame tourists for the explosion of the sex industry and the proliferation of AIDS (see page 69). Where Thailand is headed as it continues its roller coaster ride is as much a mystery as a challenge.

Politics

From Bangkok's high rise offices and glitzy hotels, it is all too easy to forget that in 1992 the Thai army fired on unarmed demonstrators protesting against General Suchinda Kraprayoon's military dictatorship. Well over 100 students and others were killed. Parliamentary democracy in Thailand is new and fragile and not only have there been 16 constitutions inflicted on the people of Thailand since 1932, but these have been interspersed with 18 coup d'états. It seems that never a year goes by without mutterings of army intervention – although the army top brass have studiously distanced themselves from such rumours in recent years.

The last decade of the 20th century was a pretty eventful one for Thailand. In February 1991, **General Suchinda Kraprayoon** staged a bloodless coup d'état and ousted the democratically elected government of Prime Minister Chatichai Choonhavan. At the end of the year, egged on by two generals-turned-politicians – Chamlong Srimuang and Chaovalit Yongchaiyut – 100,000 people gathered in

From massacre to crisis: 1991-97

Bangkok to protest against a Suchinda and military-imposed constitution. Elections in March 1992 produced no clear winner and General Suchinda tearfully agreed to become premier – something he had previously promised he would not do. Chamlong Srimuang took this as his cue to call his supporters onto the streets and announced he was going on hunger strike. Tens of thousands of people gathered around the Parliament buildings and Sanaam Luang, near the Grand Palace. Suchinda buckled under this weight of public outrage and appeared to agree to their demands. But Suchinda went back on his word, and in response tens of thousands of demonstrators returned to the streets. Suchinda called in the army and scores of people were killed.

Three days after the confrontation between the army and the demonstrators, **King Bhumibol** ordered both Suchinda and opposition leader Chamlong – who had to be released from gaol for the meeting – to his palace. There, television cameras were waiting to witness Suchinda's global, public humiliation. He and Chamlong prostrated themselves on the floor while the king lectured them, asking rhetorically: "What is the use of victory when the winner stands on wreckage?" Immediately afterwards, the army and the demonstrators withdrew from the streets. On Friday, Suchinda offered his resignation to the King, and on Saturday, less than one week after the killing began, Suchinda Kraprayoon fled the country. In a televised address, Suchinda accepted responsibility for the deaths.

After the riots of May 1992, and General Suchinda's humiliating climbdown, Anand Panyarachun was appointed interim prime minister. New elections were set for September, which the Democrat Party won. **Chuan Leekpai was appointed 1992's fourth prime minister**. Chuan, a mild-mannered Southerner from a poor background – his father was a fish vendor in Trang – gained his law degree while living as a novice monk in a monastery. Never one for flashiness and quick fixes, Chuan became known as Chuan Chuengcha – or Chuan the slowmover. He may have been slow but his government lasted more than 2½ years, making it the longest serving elected government in Thai history, before he was forced to resign over a land scandal.

The Chart Thai Party, led by 62-year-old **Banharn Silpa-Archa**, won the election – or at least the largest number of seats – and formed a coalition government of seven parties. Bangkok's intelligentsia were horrified. Like Chuan, Banharn came from a poor background and was very much a self-made man. But in almost all other respects, Banharn and Chuan could not have been more different. Banharn's Chart Thai was closely associated with the military junta and was viewed as incorrigibly corrupt. As British political scientist Duncan McCargo explained: 'there's no movement for [true] democracy. There's nothing but the money, and the results [of the election] bear that out'. Two Chart Thai candidates in the elections were even accused of involvement in the narcotics trade. Thanong Wongwan was indicted in California with drug trafficking, where he was reportedly known as 'Thai Tony', and the party's deputy leader Vatana Asavahame had a visa request turned down by the US authorities on similar grounds. Banharn was even accused of plagiarism in his Masters thesis, which is said to bear a striking similarity to a paper by his academic advisor – who Banharn appointed to his cabinet.

While the press may have hated Banharn – *The Nation* stated that 'the only way for 1996 to be a good year is for the Banharn government to go' – he survived because he was an arch populist politician. He used to step from his limousine and order local officials to mend roads, provide electricity, or improve health services. Here was a man getting things done, sweeping away red tape, and putting the interests of ordinary people first. But while Banharn might have been able to ignore the press, he couldn't ignore the King. In late summer 1995, Banharn's government found itself explicitly criticized by the palace when the King highlighted

King Bhumibol and the Monarchy

Although Thailand has been a constitutional monarchy since the Revolution of 1932, King Bhumibol Adulyadej and the Royal Family have an influence that far exceeds their formal, constitutional, powers. It seems that the leaders of the Revolution shied away from emasculating the monarchy, and decided to keep the king at the centre of the Thai social and political universe. Nonetheless, the only truly active king since 1932 has been the present one, King Bhumibol, who acceded to the throne in 1945 and in 1995 celebrated 50 years as Sovereign.

King Bhumibol Adulyadej – the name means Strength of the Land, Incomparable Power – has virtually single-handedly resurrected the Thai monarchy. The King was born in the USA, where his father was a doctor in Boston. He graduated in engineering from Lausanne, Switzerland and speaks English and French. He is a skilled jazz saxophonist (he has played with Benny Goodman) and an accomplished yachtsman (he won a gold medal at the Asian Games).

After returning from his studies abroad to become King he entered the monkhood, and since then has continuously demonstrated his concern for the welfare of his people. The King and his Queen, Sirikit, travel the country overseeing development projects which they finance, visiting remote villages and taking a keen interest in the poor. The King has also largely managed to maintain his independence from the hurly-burly of Thai politics. When he has intervened, he has done so with great effect. In October 1973, after the riots at Thammasat University, he requested that Prime Minister Thanom, along with his henchmen Praphat and Narong, leave the country to stem the tide of civil disorder. They obeyed. In a repeat of the events of 1973, in May 1992, the King called Prime Minister General Suchinda Kraprayoon to his palace where, recorded on television, he was publicly – though not overtly – humiliated for ordering the army to quell demonstrations against his premiership. Three days later, Suchinda had resigned and left the country.

The undoubted love and respect that virtually all Thais hold for their King raises the question of the future and whether the monarchy can remain a stabilizing force. The suitability of his eldest son Crown Prince Vajiralongkorn has been questioned, while his eldest daughter Crown Princess Sirindhorn is respected and loved almost as much as the King himself. In January 1993, Vajiralongkorn – in an unprecedented move – lashed out at his critics. He was quoted in the Bangkok Post as saying: '[They say] I act as a powerful chao poh [Godfather] providing protection for sleazy business ... Do I look like a chao poh type? The money I spend is earned honestly. I do not want to touch money earned illegally or through the suffering of others.' Thais worried about the succession are comforted by a legend that the Chakri Dynasty would only have nine monarchs: King Bhumibol is the ninth.

Visitors should avoid any open criticism of the Royal Family: lèse majesté is still an offence in Thailand, punishable by up to 15 years in prison. In early 1995 Frenchman Lech Tomacz Kisielwicz uttered an expletive on a Thai Airways flight, apparently directed at fellow passenger Thai Princess Soamswali and her daughter. On arrival at Don Muang Airport he found himself arrested and then incarcerated, before being released on bail. In cinemas, the national anthem is played before the film and the audience – including foreigners – are expected to stand. In towns in the countryside, at 0800 every morning, the national anthem is relayed over PA systems, and pedestrians are again expected to stop what they are doing and stand to attention. It is in ways like this that the continuing influential role of the monarchy becomes clear.

Background

Thailand's flag: nation, religion, monarchy

Thailand's flag was introduced in 1917 by Rama VI, anxious to present a 'modern'-style flag to the world following Siam's joining with the Allies in the First World War. It consists of horizontal stripes of red, white and blue. The two outer red stripes represent the Thai nation, the two white stripes, religion, and the inner blue band symbolizes the monarchy. The three stripes therefore represent the three pillars of society: nation, religion and monarchy. Thailand's athletes wear red, white and blue strip, and the colours have become the Kingdom's unofficial national colours. Before 1917, Thailand's flag was a white elephant, symbolizing the monarchy, on a red background, symbolizing courage. The elephant motif was added by Rama II (1809-24); before then the flag was plain red.

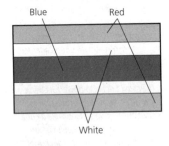

Blue   Red

White

government failures to address Bangkok's infrastructural mess and its shortcomings in dealing with serious flooding. Ministers, the King said, only "talk, talk, talk and argue, argue, argue". Taking the King's cue, the great and the good including businessmen, influential civil servants, four former Bank of Thailand governors, opposition politicians (of course), even his own daughter, demanded that he step down. On 21 September 1996 Banharn announced his resignation. The King dissolved parliament.

The **elections of 17 November 1996** were close, with **Chaovalit Yongchaiyudh's** New Aspirations Party (NAP) just managing to win the largest number of seats, and after the usual bickering and horse-trading he managed to stitch together a six-party coalition controlling 221 seats in the 393-seat House of Representatives. Chaovalit, a canny 64-year-old former army commander-in-chief, never completely managed to hide his ambition to become premier. He was an old-style patronage politician who depended on his links with the army and on handing out lucrative concessions to his supporters. "Transparency", as Democrat MP Surin Pitsuwan was quoted as saying in August 1996, "is not in his dictionary".

In retrospect, the mid-1990s were a **watershed in contemporary Thailand's history**. On 18 July 1995 the Princess Mother (the King's mother) died. After the King she was probably the most revered person in the country. Born a commoner and trained as a nurse, she married a prince. Their two sons, Mahidol and Bhumipol, unexpectedly became kings (Mahidol for only a short time before his tragic death). Her funeral in 1996 was a grandiose affair and her death has been likened to that of Britain's Princess Diana. Even Bangkok's massage parlours closed as a mark of respect. 1996 also saw the 50th anniversary of King Bhumibol's accession to the throne and the country threw a massive party to celebrate the event. The celebrations were as much a mark of Thailand's coming of age as of the King's golden jubilee. No expense was spared by the newly self-confident Tiger Thailand. Both events – the Princess Mother's funeral and the King's jubilee – were, for those so inclined, omens. The night before the funeral there was an unseasonable rainstorm; and during the procession of royal boats on the Chao Phraya it also poured. The King's boat was washed off course and had to be rescued by the navy. As it turned out, 1996 was the last year when money was no object.

Chaovalit was, in a sense, unlucky to take over the reins of government when he did. Economic conditions were a cause for concern in the country in late 1996, but no one – scholar or pundit – predicted the economic meltdown that was just a few months away. He appointed the well-respected Amnuay Virawan as Finance Minister. But the collapse of the baht, the Bangkok stock market, the property and finance sectors, and a haemorrhaging loss of domestic and international confidence created conditions that were impossible to manage. Even so, his performance was hardly memorable. As *The Economist* tartly put it, 'he dithered when decisions were needed, bumbled when clear words might have helped, and smiled benignly while the economy got worse'. The central bank spent a staggering US$10bn trying to defend the baht's peg to the US dollar, and interest rates were raised to 1,300% for offshore borrowers in an ultimately futile attempt to keep the speculators at bay. The baht was allowed to float on 2 July, ending 13 years during which it had been pegged to the US dollar. Two cabinet reshuffles during August did little to stem the criticism of Chaovalit and his administration, and there was talk of military intervention – though the army commander-in-chief quickly distanced himself from any such suggestion. In September, Chaovalit used his promised support for a vote on a new constitution (see below) to defeat a no-confidence motion. Even so, the end of Chaovalit's administration was in sight. On 7 November, **Chaovalit resigned** as Prime Minister after less than a year in power.

Economic crisis: 1997-2000

Following Chaovalit's resignation, Chuan Leekpai, leader of the Democrat Party, stitched together a new seven-party, 208-person coalition and became Prime Minister for the second time. Given talk of military intervention a few months earlier, it was a relief to many that Thailand had achieved a peaceful change of government. The key question, however, was whether Chuan could do any better than Chaovalit, particularly given the mixed make-up of his coalition government. Chuan and his finance minister, Tarrin Nimmanahaeminda – the year's fourth – vigorously implemented the IMF's rescue package and even managed to negotiate a slight loosening of the terms of the package.

The economic crisis enabled a coterie of young, reform-minded politicians to gain high office – like urbane, US-educated foreign minister Surin Pitsuwan. Fed up with coups and corruption, and backed by an increasingly assertive middle-class, these politicians are committed to change. As Chuan's special assistant, Bunaraj Smutharaks, explained to journalist Michael Vatikiotis, "If we don't seize this opportunity to instigate change, the future generations will see this [economic] crisis as a lost opportunity" (FEER, 30.6.98).

Under Chuan's leadership, Thailand became a role model for the IMF and foreign investors applauded the government's attempts to put things in order. The difficulty that Chuan faced throughout his second period as premier was that what began as just an economic 'blip' took far longer to work itself out – and in particular to have an impact on Thailand's poor. Particularly galling for Chuan must have been those who argued that he, the poorest Prime Minister in Thailand's history, was anti-poor. As it turned out, Chuan's adherence to the IMF line lost him the election at the beginning of 2001 (see below).

A characteristic of Chuan's coalition government was that while it continued to gather plaudits from foreigners, it was at the receiving end of considerable criticism domestically. This was largely, it seems, because of the widely held feeling that Thailand was in hock to the IMF and foreigners more generally. With foreign

Background

companies buying up Thai companies at 'fire sale' prices, and the IMF apparently dictating domestic economic policy, it became easy for opposition politicians and journalists to depict the Chuan government as having sold Thailand down the river.

Old wine in new bottles? Thaksin takes over, 2001- The beginning of January 2001 saw the election of Thaksin Shinawatra and the Thai Rak Thai party, in a landslide victory over Chuan Leekpai and the Democrats. Thaksin won for two reasons: first, he made grand promises and second, his opponent, Chuan, was stuck with the charge that he had sold the country out to the IMF and foreign business interests. A good dose of populism won the day.

While Thaksin may have won almost half of the popular vote – virtually unprecedented in Thai terms – he nonetheless formed a coalition by linking up with General Chaovalit Yongchaiyut's New Aspirations Party and the Chart Thai party. How he will perform – and how long he will last – is anyone's guess.

Thaksin's strengths are also his weaknesses. He brings to government a business-mind and a business approach – critical for a country still struggling to recover from an economic crisis that hit way back in mid-1997. The fear is that cronyism will also increase. Thaksin is under considerable pressure to roll-back the constitutional and financial reforms encouraged by the IMF. And Thaksin's resounding majority probably means that these changes can be pushed through parliament without too much trouble.

There is little doubt that Thaksin has promised a great deal: a grant of one million baht (US\$23,200) to each of Thailand's 70,000 villages; a debt moratorium for some classes of farmer; cheap medical care; and more. A stimulus to the economy may do it some good in the short term. Critics worry what the long-term implications of such profligacy might be. There was also one other question mark that hung over Thaksin's premiership as this book went to press. In late 2000 the Constitutional Court found him guilty of concealing his assets (now required of all politicians under the new constitution, see below). If this ruling is upheld, he would be barred from politics for five years.

Getting to grips with the Thai political system Thai politics has traditionally been a game of money, not of ideas. In rural and provincial constituencies – and that means over 90% of constituencies – candidates are expected to buy their votes. The Thai Farmers Bank estimated that ฿17bn was spent on the 1995 election, while the figure for the November 1996 elections – widely thought to have been one of the dirtiest in Thai election history (quite a claim) – was estimated to be between ฿20bn and ฿30bn, or a staggering US\$800m-US\$1.2 bn. Bank of Thailand figures show that an unusually high sum of money was transferred out of commercial banks during the election period – the assumption being that a significant slice was withdrawn for vote buying. Various reforms to the electoral process introduced under Chuan's leadership were directed at stamping out corruption. But while they may have dealt with some of the more blatant vote buying, it seems that one form of corruption has simply been replaced by another (see below).

Until the reforms of 1997, it was common for whole villages to be bought. In the 1995 elections villages cost ฿30,000 to ฿50,000 and up-country bank branches ran out of ฿100 notes as they were pressed into hundreds of thousands of eager hands. No wonder Banharn, the leader of the Chart Thai Party which won the largest number of seats in the 1995 election, earned himself the nickname 'Mr ATM' (Mr Automatic Teller Machine): all one had to do was key in the right series of digits and out spewed crisp ฿100 notes. In 1996, Gordon Fairclough of the *Far Eastern Economic Review* accompanied the Northeast MP Newin Chidchob while he pressed the flesh in Buriram. Fairclough wrote that the MP 'paused to talk to a young girl' and then 'handed her a crisp ฿20 note, and she got her first lesson in what politics is all about'. Boonyok Hankla, an elder in a village in Lampang province in the north, explained the farmers' electoral logic to Gordon Fairclough in simple terms: "The MP gets what he wants, and we get what we want." Another farmer in Lampang, 59-year-old Jai Manefan, added: "They're generous with us, so we have to give something in return. I don't think that's really vote buying, do you?"

In Bangkok, ideas and integrity have always counted for much more. It is this divide in the electoral environment which accounts for the fact that few parties have managed to bridge the gap between the rural and urban electorates (or rather between Bangkok and the rest of the country). The tale of Thailand's electoral history over the last two decades or so has been a tale of two constituencies. This is worrying to the extent that the billions invested in buying votes in the Northeast has to be recouped – and that can only be done through corruption.

Nor has it just been a case of the votes of constituents being bought; candidates have also traditionally put themselves up for sale. The notion of being a committed Democrat or Chart Thai politician was – and remains – rare. ฿10m or US$400,000 was said to have been the going rate to encourage a politician to switch allegiances in 1995, and it was probably rather more in the 1996 contest. And as up-country voters tend to vote for characters, not for parties or policies, candidates usually take their supporters with them when they indulge in a spot of party-hopping.

The Thai political system, then, has always been something of an anomaly. It is widely thought to be 'fair': PollWatch, an independent organization with around 50,000 workers, watches out for fraud and intimidation during the vote itself; newspapers are notably free and free-wheeling compared with those in some neighbouring countries; and the army, at least during the last few elections, has kept well out of the way. Yet elections in Thailand are still about power, wealth and muscle. The association of truly vast sums of money with the democratic process means that so-called *ithiphon muut* or 'dark influences' are always close at hand. Godfathers who have lavished millions on a candidate or party expect their reward after their chosen ones have won. Money politics rules and violence is not far from the surface.

But while this approach to politics may have been acceptable from the 1950s until the 1970s, by the 1980s there were calls for greater accountability and transparency, and an end to money politics. By the 1990s these had become more insistent still and in late 1997 a new constitution was passed which, it was hoped, would bring a new (more upright) tone to Thai politics.

Parliamentary & political reform

On 27 September 1997 parliament approved a **new constitution** by a massive margin. Two weeks later the King signed the new constitution into law. The constitution, which was months in the drafting, had its origins in the widespread belief that the only way to change Thai politics was to radically reform the political system. The new constitution, it was hoped, would set the Kingdom off on a new democratic path where money politics might be replaced by debate.

The new constitution contains various innovations which, on paper at least, should clean up the country's sordid political system: there is a new constitutional court, a parliamentary ombudsman and a national Counter Corruption Commission, for example. In addition, the constitution recognizes citizens' rights, strengthens civil liberties, allows for greater political participation, includes a provision encouraging greater freedom of information, and guarantees the freedom of the press. The constitution is the first really concerted attempt to address the issue of money politics (which explains why so many MPs initially resisted it). There is a new national election commission as well as a directly elected upper house. Under the new constitution, some MPs are elected to single-member constituencies, while others are drawn from party slates and elected by proportional representation. All MPs need to have, at a minimum, a university degree. Another new step is that all Cabinet ministers have to make public financial statements listing their assets.

Background

But while there is no doubt that this constitution goes further than any previous one, it is worth remembering that it is not Thailand's first stab at designing an effective constitution. It is the country's 16th. The question then, after it was signed into law by the King, was whether the new constitution would be any more successful than the many others that litter Thailand's political history.

The opening test of the new constitution came in the elections to Thailand's new 200-seat Senate in March 2000. This was the first time the Upper House had been elected since 1932. There were reports of widespread vote buying (the Bank of Thailand revealed that 20 billion baht was withdrawn from banks in the days leading up to the election). Many commentators expected the new Election Commission to allow tainted victories to go through on the nod, particularly if those standing had links with powerful and well-established political dynasties. As it turned out, the watchdog proved itself to have teeth: the victories of 78 senatorial candidates were annulled on the basis of fraud or suspected fraud and re-elections called. Later in the year, in March, another new body created under the auspices of the new constitution, the National Counter Corruption Commission (NCCC), forced Interior Minister Sanan Kachornprasart to resign his position after it was revealed that he had falsified documents. These actions are remarkable when one considers that in the 68 years between the end of absolute monarchy and 2000, just one Thai politician has been tried and convicted for corruption.

Former Prime Minister, privy councillor and Thai worthy, Anand Panyarachun, said in an interview in the *Far Eastern Economic Review* in April 2000: 'It's the beginning of the end of Thailand's old political culture. The checks and balances enshrined in the new constitution are no longer just concepts on paper – they are coming to life in implementation' (FEER, 13.4.00). But while it would be nice to think that Thailand is entering a new era of democratic politics, there are still many politicians who will continue with the old ways of doing things, and many voters who are happy to oblige them. Take the pattern of fraudulent elections in the March 2000 poll for the Senate. The Election Commission disqualified just two of the 18 victors in Bangkok, but 76 out of 182 in the provinces.

The views of the pessimists would seem to have been vindicated in the most recent election of all: the general election of 6 January 2001.

The election was dirty, even with the electoral reforms pushed through by the outgoing Chuan government. Indeed, there were those who maintained that it was the dirtiest ever – which is saying something in the context of Thailand's electoral history. However, it was dirty, but dirty in new ways: the nature of corruption may have changed. Senator Kraisak Choonhavan was quoted as saying the day following the poll that: "With the new rules, political parties have figured out it's cheaper and easier to buy election commissioners rather than voters". Critics suggested that while the Election Commission may have showed its teeth in the Senate elections of 2000, it shied away from doing so in the general elections of 2001. There were more than 1,000 accusations of fraud, but the commission demanded new polls in just 62 out of 400 constituencies. As the *Far Eastern Economic Review* put it: 'Perhaps it was inevitable, culturally and politically, that the many sharp reforms enshrined in the new constitution would be measured by a degree of compromise' (8.2.2001).

Getting to grips with corruption On just about every and any measure of corruption, Thailand figures high. And while there have been many attempts to 'stamp out' corruption, none has seriously addressed the issue. Most have been hypocritical attempts by massively corrupt politicians to garner cuedos and, perhaps, a handful of votes. But the economic crisis, as they say, concentrated minds. Many people believe that corruption was at least a contributory cause in the crisis. As a result, and for the first time, some serious steps were taken to address the problem of corruption. This is not to say that Thailand has become another Singapore.

A question much debated in the bars of Bangkok is why is Thailand so corrupt? Putting aside for one moment the fact that Thailand is clearly not unique in being corrupt, there are various arguments that do the rounds. Some people point to the fact that Thailand is a 'soft' state without the rigid rules that apply in countries like Singapore. Being soft and fuzzy means that people can argue that corruption is really not that bad – just part of the cultural landscape. Others highlight the low salaries paid to civil servants and others in public service. In 1996 a civil servant with C3 rank and a BA degree received a salary of ฿6,360 (US$250) per month, at the prevailing exchange rate. Civil servants' salaries are pitched low because everyone knows that they benefit from corruption. The logic becomes circular: civil servants are paid little because they are corrupt/they are corrupt because their salaries are so low. Suthichai Yoon, a commentator for *The Nation*, described in 1998 how senior officers in the Police Department set targets for the number of motorists who have to be fined. For each fine, the policeman on the beat receives 20%, the rest being passed up the ladder to line the pockets of more senior officers. To meet the targets, innocent motorists are framed.

Thai bureaucracy, like that in the other countries of Southeast Asia, is a many-headed hydra. Becoming a civil servant, or in Thai *kharatchakan* (literally 'servant of the crown'), brings with it considerable prestige, a certain amount of power, a great deal of job security and a limited salary. One way that bureaucrats have overcome the last of these is by *kin muang* – literally 'eating the country' – extracting from the land and its people far more than their own meagre salaries. Of course, there are also many committed government officials who act in what they perceive to be the best interests of the population whom they (in theory) serve.

In spite of King Chulalongkorn's reforms of the civil service at the turn of the century, the relationship between bureaucrats and the people is still a 'top-down' one in which the official talks and the people listen. To a large extent, this is just a reflection of Thai social relations, and the pervasive superior-inferior/patron-client ties. In general, petty officials are recruited locally. They will usually have been educated to secondary school level and have little chance of advancing to the higher echelons of the civil service. More senior officials are university-educated and often have their roots (and hearts) in Bangkok. A challenge for the bureaucracy today is that Thailand's rapid economic growth during the 1980s and much of the 1990s dramatically widened wage differentials between the public and private sectors. With a decline in the prestige associated with joining the civil service and becoming a *kharatchakan*, fewer talented young Thais are being enticed into the bureaucracy.

The bureaucracy

Traditionally, young men gained a limited education when they entered the monkhood. A system of secular education was not introduced until the reign of King Chulalongkorn, who called on the expertise of many monks and employed them as teachers. When compulsory, universal primary school education was inaugurated in 1921 and was for a period of four years (to *bor sii*). Since 1978, all children have had to undergo six years of primary education (to *bor hok*). In 1996 the government extended the period of compulsory education to nine years. Primary school education is free, but school uniforms and stationery must be paid for, and many farmers also complain when their children are not around to look after the buffalo and undertake other farm chores. Even a child of six is an economic resource in the countryside. Some Thais question whether the conservative, urban-orientated and Western-based curriculum is really relevant to those who spend their lives in agriculture, and say a more vocational curriculum should be introduced. Nonetheless, the system as it currently stands has contributed towards the achievement of a literacy rate which exceeds 90%.

Education

Background

The Saudi Gem Scam: Thailand in the dock

More foreign visitors are duped by buying fake or undervalued gems than in any other way in Thailand (see page 160). The Kingdom's embassies have even taken to inserting a leaflet into every visa applicant's passport, warning them of the dangers. Still it continues. But no tourist has been tricked like the Saudi Prince Faisal Fahd Abdulaziz. The Saudi Gem Affair is simply astounding.

This story begins in 1989 when a Thai contract worker, employed as a cleaner by the Saudi Prince Faisal Fahd Abdulaziz in Riyadh, stole 90 kg of jewellery – valued at US$20 mn – from his employer. Among the gems was the priceless 70-carat Blue Diamond. Kriangkrai Techamong fled the country and buried the gems in his back garden. A year later the police tracked down Kriangkrai and unearthed the stolen gems. It is at this point that the story changes from one of simple thieving – albeit on a monumental scale – to duplicity, intrigue and corruption at the highest level, and murder. The gems were displayed by the proud and successful policemen, filmed for television, and photographed for the newspapers. They were then flown back to Saudi Arabia. Unfortunately, when the Prince looked through the cache he realized that over half the pieces were missing. Later, others were confirmed as poor fakes.

As some of the missing gems were identified in the newspaper and television coverage of the haul, and as others had reportedly been seen adorning the necks and wrists of police generals' wives, the Saudis reacted with fury. They withdrew their ambassador and halted the issuing of all new visas for Thai contract labourers. As there were an estimated 250,000 such workers in Saudi Arabia in 1989,

sending back US$340 mn in remittances, while there are now just 20,000 sending a comparative pittance, this was a huge blow not just to Thailand's international image, but also to the country's foreign exchange earnings. The Saudis also stopped their nationals travelling to Thailand as tourists. In 1988 nearly 55,000 Saudi Arabian tourists arrived in the Kingdom. In 1992 this had dropped precipitously to under 3,000. Just to make absolutely sure that the Thai authorities knew that they meant business, the Saudis also appointed Mohammed Said Khoja as special envoy, charged with the sole task of untangling the mess. He has been constantly on the job since March 1990 (his initial posting was for three months), and by the beginning of 1995 had had dealings with five prime ministers, five interior ministers and six foreign ministers. Soon, it seems, he will have negotiated with virtually all the Great and the Good in Thailand.

It was not until August 1994 that the debacle turned nasty. A Thai gems dealer and jeweller, Santi Srithanakhan, was said to have knowledge of the whereabouts of the missing gems. A short time later his wife and son were found battered to death on the unfortunately named 'Friendship' Highway, north of Bangkok. To begin with, the police said it was murder; then it became an accident; then, when the impossibility of such injuries being sustained in an accident became clear, it reverted to murder. A witness is said to have turned up the radio of his pick-up to drown the screams of the woman and her child as they were battered to death with a steel pipe.

Most commentators believed that the police were closely involved in not just the

Secondary school education is divided into two periods of three years each: lower and upper secondary school. At both levels fees are levied. Most secondary school students live in urban areas. It is rare for a rural Thai to progress as far, and even rarer for them to gain entrance to higher education. Of Thailand's institutes of higher education, more than half are located in Bangkok and they graduate 70% of students. The most prestigious is Chulalongkorn University, followed by the more stealing of the gems, but also in the double murder and the cover-up. The image and reputation of the police, flawed at the best of times, was becoming as fissured as the Grand Canyon. To date, six people have been murdered as a result of the affair: three Saudi diplomats (in February 1990), a Saudi businessman (later in February 1990), and now Santi's wife and son. Some people have put the number of deaths linked with the case as high as 15. Said Khoja refers to the scandal as a 'farce', The Nation newspaper as 'delayed and twisted justice' which 'would expose Thailand's law-enforcement and political institutions to almost unendurable embarrassment'. In all cases, the feeling is that the case goes to the very top. People are simply too scared of the implications of the truth to have the truth revealed.

But the Thais, and in particular the Thai police, did not count on the relentless Said Khoja nor on the willingness of the Saudi government to put the immense resources of that Kingdom behind the case. It seems that everyone except some sections of the police – and perhaps some sections of the government – would like the truth revealed. The Thai public, in particular, are sick of the corruption that pervades their police and worry about the battered reputation of their country. Every Thai knew that the police were corrupt; few thought their law enforcement officers would stoop this deep in the filth – 'Staggering greed', as the journalist Terry McCarthy has put it. One positive thing to come out of the affair is a shake-up of the police. It seems that there is a concerted effort to make sure that things are done differently now – not just for Saudi princes, but for every Thai citizen too. Prime Minister Chuan Leekpai himself said

in an interview at the end of 1994: "Although we can't make everybody equally rich, we can at least ensure that there is equality before the law". Perhaps this is too much to hope for.

Gradually the truth appears to be coming out. So far eight police officers have been indicted, including two generals. But it is still not clear whether those at the top of the tree will be brought to book – the sums of money involved, the power of some of those implicated, and the iniquities of the judicial and police systems make it equally likely that some of the guilty parties will get off scot-free. The world of the rich and powerful in Thailand, as Terry McCarthy has explained, "is a world of cynical, grasping people whose money can paper over any crime and whose connections and influence make them virtually untouchable". To speed up the process, Said Khoja has threatened to reveal the names of the 'top' people he thinks are involved. He is protected by four bodyguards and always carries a gun. Ordinary Thais only hope that this time, in trying to outwit the Saudi government, the duplicitous big names have tried to cross a bridge too far.

It's more than 10 years on, the gems are still missing, the murderers are at large, and Thai-Saudi relations remain stymied. In December 1998 Saudi Arabia pulled out of the Asian Games – hosted by Thailand – in protest at the authorities' failure to solve the case. Evidence that this long-running dispute may be coming to an end surfaced in February 2000, when Thai and Saudi officials held their highest level meeting (coinciding with the UNCTAD conference in Bangkok) since relations were downgraded in 1991.

Background

radical Thammasat University. Businessmen complain that the country trains too many students in the arts, and not enough in the sciences and engineering. Many Thais feel that a humanities degree is superior to one in the sciences or engineering (see page 780 for further discussion of Thailand's educational deficiencies).

The fear that some Thais at least do not take education seriously was, seemingly, illustrated in the middle of 1994 when the Director General of the Department of

More generals than tanks

The army is one of Thailand's key institutions. It has been at the centre of political and economic power since the 'revolution' of 1932, mounting 18 coups since that date. There are currently 200,000 men in uniform. But, with the threat of internal insurrection from the Communist Party of Thailand (CPT) and the external threat from Vietnam now both virtually extinguished, it is becoming harder to justify such a large army. The austerity measures forced upon the government by the economic downturn have also caused analysts to reconsider the size and role of the armed forces in modern Thailand. In fact, the case for slimming-down the armed forces was recognized by General Wimol Wongwanich when he took over as supreme commander in 1992.

But most remarkable of all in the make-up of Thailand's army is the number of generals. In 1998 there were 2,646 generals in the armed forces – considerably more than the number of tanks the army could muster. Of these top brass, 700 are in 'inactive posts' – a euphemism for doing nothing – and the army has traditionally been viewed as a job for life by those passing through the prestigious

Chulachomklao Military Academy.

This view of Thailand's military as top heavy and sclerotic has been gradually changing. In 1998 Prime Minister Chuan Leekpai announced that the number of generals would be slashed by 75% over a period of 10 years. This will be achieved by leaving posts vacated by retiring generals unfilled, unless they happen to be command posts. In addition, the military academy will recruit fewer young men to train as officers – 150 a year as opposed to 400-500 previously. Nonetheless, with the military continuing to take 15-20% of the national budget, and with many officers still seeing the military as the sole, legitimate defender of King and Nation, it will remain a key and powerful institution.

So, what do all these generals do? Well, it seems, just about anything but train men and mug up on the latest hardware and tactics. The Thai press write of 'Golfing generals', and it is generally accepted that when they are not playing golf these hardened military men without any assignment are usually running their own businesses. But it may be coming to an end: in April 2000 it was announced that generals without assignment would be put on committee work.

Education, Banchong Pongsastra, took the decision to give all schools the 19 July off. This happened to be the day that the World Cup final was broadcast live to Thailand at 0230-0530. Banchong explained his decision to a sometimes incredulous press, by stating that "It's better to let the students and teachers watch the game in peace rather than expect them to come in late and fall asleep in class."

The press & media

Newspapers The first newspapers to appear in Thailand were published by American missionaries. The *Bangkok Recorder* (in Thai) appeared each month between 1844 and 1845, while the *Bangkok Daily Advertiser* (in English) appeared between 1868 and 1878. Today there are numerous daily and weekly publications, serving a variety of markets. The widest-selling Thai language newspapers are *Sayam Rat* and *Thai Rat*, the latter with a circulation of around 750,000 and a readership of as much as 10 times that. *Matichon*, with a far smaller circulation, is regarded as the leading 'serious' Thai language newspaper. Of the English language press, the two most respected newspapers are the *Bangkok Post* and *The Nation*, both enjoying a high reputation for their reporting.

As would be expected, newspapers are widely read in the cities, less so in the countryside – although many villages now have 'libraries' where magazines and newspapers are available. Towards the end of 1994, after he was accused of a rather cavalier approach to the facts in his newspaper column, Thai opposition MP Kasem

Disaster and death

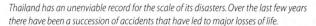

Thailand has an unenviable record for the scale of its disasters. Over the last few years there have been a succession of accidents that have led to major losses of life.

September 1990	*A lorry carrying gas cylinders collides with a tuk-tuk on Bangkok's expressway and bursts into flames. Death toll: 91.*
February 1991	*A lorry carrying dynamite explodes near Phangnga, in the Southern region, while onlookers gather around. Death toll: 171.*
March 1992	*A ferry transporting Buddhist pilgrims to Si Racha, in the Eastern region, sinks after colliding with an oil tanker. Death toll: 119.*
May 1993	*A fire at a toy factory outside Bangkok causes mayhem due to blocked escape exits. Death toll: 189.*
August 1993	*A hotel collapses in Korat, northeast region. Death toll: 120.*
February 1994	*A ferry carrying Burmese workers back to Burma from Thailand capsizes. Death toll: about 200.*
June 1995	*A crowded ferry jetty on the Chao Phraya River in Bangkok collapses. Death toll: 28.*
July 1997	*A fire blazes through a hotel on Jomtien Beach, Pattaya. Death toll: 80.*

Thailand also scores highly in terms of traffic accidents and homicides. In 1987, 4,636 people died in traffic accidents; by 1994 the official figure for the number of deaths on the country's roads was 18,000. More surprising perhaps is that 4,542 were murdered in 1995 (down from a horrific 10,661 in 1982) in Thailand. This translates into a homicide rate of 7.6/100,000; the figure for the USA – in many people's mind the murder 'capital' of the world – is 8.6/100,000, while England's is just 1.2/100,000 and Germany's 4.5. It should be added that it is extremely rare for a tourist to be murdered.

Malasiri commented that "My constituents don't read newspapers. They use them for rolling their cigarettes." Thailand's press is one of the least controlled in Southeast Asia and the only area where no hint of controversy is permitted is concerning the monarchy. Everyone and everything else is fair game, and the Thai newspapers can make the British tabloids appear tame by comparison.

The role of the media in exposing the excesses of politicians was illustrated in their battle with Banharn Silpa-Archa's administration during 1995 and 1996. Right from the start of his premiership the media, in Banharn's view, had it in for him. Headlines trumpeted allegations of 'Graft', 'Nepotism' and 'Godfather Government'. To some extent, changes in Thai society have been encouraging the media to alter their reporting ways. Middle-class Thais are expecting more investigative journalism and more challenging pieces. Journalists have also embraced the notion that they have a role to play rooting out corruption and graft – digging the dirt, so to speak. Not that this means there is a whole raft of Pulitzer Prize winners emerging from smoke-filled rooms.

Radio and television Traditionally it has been the print media that has contested the government view of events. Radio and television, by comparison, have been tightly controlled. The military monitors all terrestrial radio frequencies and actually controls about a third of the country's 500-odd radio stations. Indeed, until the early 1990s identical news broadcasts were transmitted on all Thailand's stations simultaneously. This cosy situation – at least from the military's point of view – began to break down during the democracy demonstrations of 1991. People listened into overseas Thai language broadcasts, particularly from the BBC, and watched the CNN view of events. As radio and television journalists realized they

Background

were being manipulated by the authorities and were in danger of losing their credibility, they began to defy the military and tell the news as they saw it. Since then, radio stations particularly have built upon this new found independence and though broadcasts might not always be particularly professional or edifying, at least more than one version of events is being put about.

Though radio may have broken out, television remains tightly controlled. Up to July 1996, of the country's five television networks, two were owned by a state-run corporation, two by the military, and one by the government's Public Relations Department. In view of this, it is hardly surprising that Thai television tends to broadcast a judicious mix of government propaganda, crass comedies and dubbed martial arts films. Recognizing that there is ample room for a good independent station, a number of corporations have been trying to break this stranglehold, and on 1 July 1996 Thailand's first independent TV channel, ITV, began transmitting.

Economy

The end of a miracle The final years of the 20th century are ones that most Thais would choose to forget. In the early part of the 1990s Thailand was the fastest growing economy in the world. By the end of the 1990s the economy was in free fall. The economy contracted by nearly 10% in 1998 and the country experienced the worst recession since the 1930s. The death of the Asian Miracle, and of the Asian century, can be dated from the collapse of the Thai baht in mid-1997. This volte-face in Thailand's economic fortunes is reflected in a book written by two of the country's most influential academics. In 1996, at the height of the miracle, Chris Baker and Pasuk Phongpaichit published a book with the title *Thailand's Boom!* Two years later they released a new edition. They called it *Thailand's Boom ... and Bust!* Their latest volume is just entitled *Thailand's Crisis*. While the crisis is now over, people will be picking over the economic and political tea leaves for years to come.

Explaining the crisis Even though Thailand's economic crisis is now old news, it is still unclear what exactly led to the country's economic meltdown. As with so many things, it was probably a coincidence of factors. For some, it can be linked to the operation of the global economy. Amnuay Virawan, the first of 1997's four finance ministers, claimed that 'We are facing a major threat from very greedy people' as he identified currency speculators as the cause of the run on the Thai baht (*The Economist*, 25.5.97). A meeting of nine Asian foreign ministers at the end of July 1997 led to a joint communique, which noted the 'well-coordinated efforts [of speculators] to destabilize ASEAN currencies for self-serving purposes', and in particular George Soros. 'For Thailand to blame Mr Soros' *The Economist* argued, 'is rather like condemning an undertaker for burying a suicide.' This was echoed by Professor Paul Krugman, who told reporters in September 1997 that "the only way Asia's growth could stop is if it ... starts looking for conspiracies" (*Financial Times*, 19.9.97).

While the more colourful conspiracy theories of Malaysia's Prime Minister Mahathir Mohamad and others can be rejected, there is some credence in the claim that foreign investors took to the lifeboats in droves, thereby accentuating the crisis. Take the flows of private capital into Indonesia, Malaysia, the Philippines, South Korea and Thailand. In 1996, the year before the Asian crisis, these flows amounted to US$93bn. In 1997 this was reversed and there was an outflow of private capital to the tune of US$12bn. This led some people in Thailand – including the King – to call for a de-linking from the global economy and a promotion of protectionist policies. In this explanatory schema, Thailand's economic problems are seen to lie in the dependency and vulnerability that has arisen because of the process of export-oriented, foreign investment-driven industrialization.

So where are the roots of Thailand's economic crisis to be found? Some look back to the late 1980s and early 1990s, when the government of Chatichai Choonhaven was spectacularly corrupt and venal, even by Thai standards. In Thailand, as in Asia more generally, many have seen the origins of the crisis lying in the close links that evolved between government and business. This so-called **'crony capitalism'** – or less pejoratively, state-led development – has meant that investment decisions have been based on 'know who' rather than 'know how'. Billions of dollars of cheap money were speculatively invested, and much of that contributed to Thailand's massive burden of bad debts. 'In country after country', Nayan Chanda wrote at the beginning of 1998, 'corruption and crony capitalism had weakened solid economies built on years of hard work and prudent investment'. The size of the debt was masked by a financial system which was far from transparent and by a political system which endeavoured to maintain the fiction of financial probity.

In retrospect it is clear that this could not go on forever. As the scale of the bad debts became evident, so **foreign investors took fright**. Currency speculators attacked the baht, forcing the central Bank of Thailand to spend some US$10bn defending the currency. The revelation that Thailand's banks and finance companies were shouldering massive bad debts (perhaps 10–20% of total debt, against 1% in the US) led to a haemorrhaging loss of domestic and international confidence. Because businesses had grown used to stable exchange rates (the baht had been pegged to the US dollar for 13 years), they had not hedged their currency bets and many companies became insolvent as they saw their US dollar debts more than double in local currency terms.

To prevent a complete loss of confidence, the **IMF** decided to extend US$17bn in emergency loans to Thailand in August 1997 – massive at the time, but a fraction of the sums later extended to Indonesia (US$40bn) and South Korea (US$55bn). The IMF's rescue package demanded wide-ranging reforms of the financial sector, with a view to making it both more transparent and more accountable.

The government tried various additional ways of solving – or at least ameliorating – the crisis. At the beginning of 1998, for example, the government launched a 'Sell Dollar' programme as part of its 'Thais Helping Thais' campaign. The Gold Traders Association, meanwhile, encouraged people to hand over gold in exchange for bonds – with a maturity period of three to five years – to assist the government in supporting the baht. With the aim of collecting one kilo of gold per shop, the target was to stockpile, in total, some 10,000 kg. While these efforts were laudable in bringing Thais together during a period of national crisis, their actual economic effects were limited.

Ever since the collapse of the Thai baht in 1997, the government has been concerned, above all else, to get the economy back on track. The fact that almost four years on from the onset of the crisis, growth is still sluggish, highlights the challenge that still remains.

Dealing with the crisis

A significant part of the reforms insisted upon by the IMF, in exchange for loans of US$17 bn, involved the finance and banking sectors. In March 1999 the Senate approved a Corporatization Bill which has smoothed the privatization of state owned businesses, and in the following month a new bankruptcy bill was also approved by the Senate. For the first time, domestic banks are now majority foreign owned – such as the Thai Danu Bank, Nakornthon Bank, Radanasin Bank and the Bank of Asia – something that would have been unthinkable before the crisis. The presence of foreign companies in the domestic banking scene has shaken up the hide-bound and rather stuffy atmosphere that used to exist. Even family-owned local banks realize that they now have to compete against international players, even in their (previously) protected domestic market.

However, while Thailand's banking sector may be very different post-crisis than it was pre-crisis, many analysts continue to argue that the reason why Thailand's recovery has been so slow in coming is because of the failure of some banks

Background

comprehensively to restructure their bad debts. Many companies, it seems, are merely tinkering with their deep-seated problems. In their report on Thailand in 2000, the ADB warned: "If this situation continues and high non-performing loan ratios persist, it could jeopardise the much hoped for recovery in private investment and again put bank capital at risk". These sentiments were echoed in the 2000 annual report of the Bank for International Settlements.

The new government of Thaksin Shinawatra unveiled his grand plan to deal with debt and insolvency on 24 February 2001: an Asset Management Company. Some 1.2 trillion baht in assets will come under the control of the AMC. Thaksin is clearly hoping that a centralized AMC will manage bad loans better than the current system. He is presenting it as a means to push through necessary corporate restructuring and bank reform; critics see it as a means to protect poorly managed companies. But the economic crisis was not just a crisis for financiers and capitalists: The little people got burnt too.

The human impact "It was the rich who benefited from the boom … but we, the poor, pay the price of the crisis. Even our limited access to schools and health is now beginning to disappear. We fear for our children's future. What is the justice in having to send our children to the garbage site every day to support the family?", said Khun Bunjan, a community leader from the slums of Khon Kaen, North East Thailand.

With the focus on the massive loan package from the IMF, failing companies and plunging exchange rates, there was a tendency in the international press to ignore the **human costs** of Thailand's economic crisis.

Migrants from rural areas who found work in Bangkok and other towns drifted back to their villages as employment opportunities dried up. International migrants in their hundreds of thousands faced the prospect of expulsion, including over 600,000 Burmese along with 300-400,000 assorted migrants from Laos, Cambodia, Vietnam and China. For Thais who had lost their jobs, the effects of the crisis were just as great. Urban work financed the rising expectations of rural households, buying consumer goods, paying for school fees, and subsidizing agricultural modernization. This source of funds, on which many households had become dependent, evaporated as the crisis bit.

The **effects of the economic crisis** were visible in numerous small and large ways. Taxi drivers in Bangkok found their regular customers switching to public transport. In provincial towns people began to walk to work and the shops, rather than take a *saam lor*. Travelling salesmen found that with less disposable income there was no market for their wares. The turnover of small village shopkeepers tumbled as fellow villagers cut back on their outlays. Factory workers returning to their farms displaced landless wage labourers, who hitherto had filled the labour void. Without a social security system to speak of, and with the 'moral' community economy of old fractured by years of modernization, there were few places for these people to turn. Households whose regular incomes had disappeared were forced to pawn their motorbikes, bicycles and televisions to meet their immediate, essential needs.

Humans are, of course, cunning creatures, and this particularly applies to the poor and the near poor. Pushed out of formal work, many found **opportunities in the informal sector**. For example, in 1998, to the casual observer at least, there seemed to be more noodle carts and hawkers on the streets of Bangkok. The rural, agricultural sector also absorbed many of those displaced from urban areas. In his 70th birthday speech, the King suggested that returning to a self-sufficient, subsistence-oriented, farm-based economy might be the answer to the crisis. "Whether or not we are a tiger is unimportant", he said. "The important thing is for the economy to be able to support our people", adding "We need to go back so that we can go forward" (*Thai Development Newsletter* 33, July-December 1997). But not everyone hit by the economic retrenchment was able – or willing – to go 'back to the farm'. Many younger workers, particularly, are not enamoured with the agricultural way of life, while others find that their bolt-hole in the countryside has been undermined by years of neglect.

Between the late 1980s and 1997, Thailand's economy grew faster than almost any country on earth. This rapid growth was accompanied by a huge inflow of foreign investment, the rapid expansion of the industrial sector and fundamental structural change – and a boom in the sale of such luxury items as Mercedes' cars, mobile phones and golf clubs.

Growth, modernization & inequality

In 1993 the World Bank published a study which tried to make sense of the Asian economic success story, with the snappy title *The East Asian Miracle: Economic Growth and Public Policy*. The report was commissioned because Asia's – including Thailand's – unprecedented rate of economic growth demanded an explanation so that other, less fortunate, regions of the world might also embark on this road to fortune. Although the World Bank study began by pointing out that there is no 'recipe' for success, it did highlight a number of critical elements which countries and governments needed, in their view, to get right. As the World Bank put it, the so-called High Performing Asian Economies, or HPAEs, 'achieved high growth by getting the basics right'. These basics included: investment in physical and human capital; allowing the market to determine prices; and creating a business-friendly environment. In retrospect, the report was notable more for what it didn't say than what it did. However, to be fair, even critics of the report never envisaged an economic meltdown. Their concern was with the negative side-effects of the type of fast-track industrialization that Thailand was 'enjoying'. In their view – and they were just a minority and of more radical persuasion – Thailand was an example not of development, but of 'mal-development'. Or as some put it at the time, of 'modernization without development'.

Most glaring of all has been the **unequal distribution** of the country's breakneck economic growth. In 1981 Thailand was already an unequal society: the richest 10% of the population earned 17 times more than the poorest 10%. By 1992 they earned 38 times more. The figures are just as startling in terms of quintiles: in 1975 the richest 20% grabbed 49% of the income cake; in 1995 they absorbed 63%. Over the same period the poorest 20% saw their share of income halve from a paltry 6% to a derisory 3%.

At the beginning of 1997 the Assembly of the Poor (see box opposite), a congregation of over 10,000 poor villagers with a range of grievances, descended on Bangkok and began a drawn-out sit-in outside Government House. Initially the government tried to ignore the demonstration. But as the months ticked by and the make-shift shelters took on the air of a permanent camp, so more senior ministers tried to settle the affair. Bangkokians with a social conscience began to make donations of cash, food and things like electric fans. The demonstrators vowed to remain until their demands had been met. The main issue concerned land, and in particular those villagers alienated from their land due to dam construction or because they were designated as living on protected forest land. However, the demonstration also highlighted a new

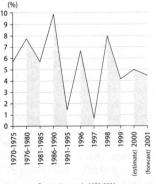

Economic growth, 1970-2001

Seen but not heard: the Assembly of the Poor

For two years a tidy, tent village of plastic sheets and bamboo has incongruously faced Government House in Bangkok. This is the voice of the Assembly of the Poor. Nearly 500 people, mainly from the poor northeast, live here to protest their loss of livelihood and ancestral lands to dam and forestry-related projects.

Each tent has a cardboard sign stating the village of origin of the people who live there and the project that has displaced them: Pha Taem National Park, Nong Phue Yai village; Lam Dome Yai Dam, Ubon Thani; Pak Moon village and dam... Many of the disputes are more than a decade old, but all result from state-led commercialization of agriculture and industrialization. A typical example is the case of the Pak Moon dam. Sixteen villages, representing over 3,000 families, are allied to the Assembly of the Poor. Many more depend on the 700 km-long Moon River for subsistence farming and fishing. The dam has changed all this, in return producing only 40 MW of electricity.

The Assembly members' experience of forest and dam projects has been forced eviction from communal land for logging, plantations and national parks; disrupted fishing stocks and farming patterns; and small markets shut down for large commercial buildings without notice. In some cases, compensation, relocation or consultation rights have been granted; in others nothing. The Assembly of the Poor insists this is an unacceptable trade off for homes flooded, habitats destroyed and a way of life lost.

On 16th-17th July 2000, during Buddhist Lent celebrations, 200 desperate Isan villagers 'stormed' Government House, and were captured by TV being beaten by the police. The following week the Cabinet unveiled plans to deal with the Assembly demands. In response, Isan villagers began a 'mass fast' in the name of Buddhism until meaningful resolutions were agreed and long-term grievances addressed. The decision by Pak Moon to drop compensation claims in return for 'letting the Isan bloodstream run free' is a significant development. Phra Paisarn, a respected monk living with the poor, hoped the mass fast would 'unlock people's hearts'. He and others saw it as a spiritual act and a means to cut through public apathy, especially on issues concerning the rural poor. Phra Paisarn is under threat of being de-robed for mixing religion with politics. His stance is that the Buddhist precept of right action permits – indeed enjoins – him to redress environmental degradation and social injustice.

For more information, visit their website: www.geocities.com/munriver_2000 Or contact Friends of the People: fop@asiaaccess.net.th

concern for 'social justice', a concept which hitherto had never courted much attention in Thailand.

Although it is the inequity of Thailand's growth which grabbed the headlines before the crisis, there were some economists – even then – who pointed to what they regarded as more fundamental weaknesses in the Kingdom's economic development. Thailand's growth has been based upon foreign technology and capital. Thailand is not a Taiwan or South Korea, with a creative, innovative, class of industrialists. Indeed, **education** – or rather the lack of it – is highlighted by most economists as one of the major constraints facing the Kingdom. Only one in five workers has anything more than primary level education, and a mere fraction enter higher education. In 1996, Thai newspapers highlighted the absence of inventors in the Kingdom, noting the small number of copyright applications lodged each year. In listing famous Thai inventions, close to the top of the list was the long-tailed boat – hardly on a par with penicillin or the integrated circuit. And it's not just the lack of Nobel prizewinners. Thailand's growth is also retarded by such basic shortcomings as a woefully poor facility with foreign languages.

Background

Incidence of poverty in Thailand, by region, % (1975-98)

	1975	1981	1988	1992	1995	1998
North	33	22	21	14	11.2	9.0
Northeast	45	36	35	22	19.4	23.2
Centre	13	14	16	13	6.3	7.7
South	31	20	22	12	11.5	14.8
Bangkok	8	4	3	2	0.6	0.6
Thailand	**30**	**23**	**22**	**18**	**11.4**	**12.9**

One of Thailand's key challenges is how to boost and improve education. More children enter secondary school in Indonesia and the Philippines than they do in Thailand, despite the fact that Thailand is considerably wealthier on a per capita income basis. While close to 100% of Thais of the relevant age group attend primary school, the figure for upper secondary school is 35% and for higher education, 20%. In the countryside, just 10-15% continue their education after primary school. On average, a Thai completes 5.3 years of formal education – hardly the foundations for building a modern, 'thinking' economy. Part of the reason may be cultural, but probably more important is the money that the government allots to education – just 4% of GDP, the lowest in the region. Without the skills that come from education, some commentators find it hard to see how the country can continue to entice foreign companies to invest.

The education ministry has a particular reputation for graft and corruption in a political system where graft and corruption are commonplace. It is the ministry's failure to get to grips with the country's crying need for a decent education system that has given impetus to calls for fundamental reform. In November 1998 a National Education Bill was passed, decentralizing control to schools and universities. This is supposed to free schools and colleges from the dead hand of the ministry, and make education more relevant and more responsive to the needs of parents and pupils. As one Western consultant remarked to journalist Michael Vatikiotis: "The ministry's inflexibility has kept the national curriculum consistently six or seven years behind the economy's needs" (FEER, 8.10.98). But for many Thais these changes are a generation too late. Somphob Promyen, with six years of education, remarked to Gordon Fairclough of the *Far Eastern Economic Review*: "I can't move up [from being a department store salesman], I just don't have enough education. These days, a ninth grade education is not enough. Sometimes I feel like I have no future."

Planning Thailand's miracle

Thailand embarked on its current path to development in the late 1950s, when General Sarit Thanarat became Prime Minister after a coup d'état and decided to abandon the preceding policy of economic nationalism. Government intervention in the economy was reduced, foreign investment welcomed, and a national development plan drawn up. Even the Thai term for 'development' – *kanpattana* – only came into widespread use at this time and Thais talk of *samay pattana* – the 'development era' – following Sarit's change of economic tack around four decades ago.

Since 1961 the National Economic and Social Development Board (NESDB) has published a series of Five-Year Economic and Social Development Plans. Most commentators, however, see these as little more than paper plans – wish lists that reflect the concerns of the day. Governments appear to rarely take any notice of them in formulating their economic policies and it would seem that the economy succeeded in the 1980s and 1990s not so much because of the government, but in spite of it. It is also true – and this has been particularly true recently – that plans have often been overtaken by events.

Background

Since the 1950s, there has seen a rapid expansion of the industrial and service sectors, and a relative decline of agriculture. Today, agriculture contributes just 11% of GDP (1998), while manufacturing alone contributes over 30%. Rice, the main export for hundreds of years, is exceeded in value terms by textiles, electronics and tourism. In 1995 Thailand sold more frozen shrimps than it did rice. (Even so, the country remains the world's largest exporter of rice.) Although the economy has diversified significantly, government statistics still show that marginally more than 50% of the labour force are employed in agriculture. (This figure is slightly dubious because many Thais work in both agriculture and non-agriculture, keeping one metaphorical foot on the factory floor and the other in the paddy field.) The slow growth of the agricultural sector compared with industry has meant that inequalities between town and country have widened.

Discrepancies between rural & urban areas The yawning expectation gap between what rural areas have to offer and what young Thais (especially) want has led to a massive migration of men and women from the countryside to the towns and cities, and especially to Bangkok. Young men and women, enticed by the culture of consumerism which has infiltrated the most remote villages and frustrated by the lack of opportunities at home, have, to coin a phrase, got on their bikes. They work as tuk-tuk and saamlor drivers, labourers on building sites and in textile mills, domestic servants, and as prostitutes. Each month they remit money back to their families, saving up so they can afford to send their children to secondary school, buy a television, or extend their house.

Even before the crisis, whether the Thai economy could continue to absorb this army of 'surplus' labour – somewhere between one and two million temporary migrants flood into the capital each dry season – was a key challenge. **Rural industrialization** is one solution that is being tried. In effect, this means relocating industries such as textiles, shoemaking and gem cutting to rural areas, thereby employing people in the countryside and stemming the flow of migrants to Bangkok. There have been some notable successes: North East Textile in Nakhon Ratchasima, for example. On the face of it, it appears that everyone 'wins': rural people can live cheaply at home and benefit from wages that are not too much lower than in Bangkok; Bangkok does not suffer from the added congestion and infrastructural strain that each migrant creates; companies can save in lower wages, land and overhead costs; and the government can feel smug that it is helping to reduce poverty and under-production in the countryside. As Banjob Kaewsra, a 23-year-old worker at North East Textile, was quoted as saying in an article in the *Far Eastern Economic Review*: "Working here is better [than in Bangkok]. Wages aren't much lower and the cost of living is far less. Besides, it's home." The trouble is that this all sounds rather familiar. Successive Thai governments have been trying to decentralize economic activity since the first Five-Year Development Plan was introduced in 1961, and the yawning gap between Bangkok and the rest of the kingdom has yawned wider ever since. But perhaps this is an idea whose time has come: Bangkok is evermore congested and the growing middle-class now realize that there is a large section of the population who simply have not benefited from the Kingdom's (formerly) rapid economic growth. With people being laid off in the cities, there is even greater reason to promote opportunities in rural areas.

Although Thailand's townspeople lead more comfortable lives than their country cousins, Thai farmers are relatively well-off, indeed rich, compared with those in India, Bangladesh or on Java, Indonesia. Thai farmers usually own their land – although tenancy is a problem in some areas, especially in the Central region and parts of the North – nutrition is reasonable, and agricultural surpluses are the norm rather than the exception. Some farmers and intellectuals complain that the incorporation of rural Thailand into the national and international cash economies has meant that they have become vulnerable to fluctuations in the

Banking on buffaloes

One popular way of helping poor farmers in Thailand is through establishing what are known as 'buffalo banks'. Buffalo are usually necessary for the cultivation of rice, but are too expensive for many poor farmers to buy. So projects like the Thailand Lahu Baptist Convention, which works with the Lahu in the northern changwats of Chiang Rai, Chiang Mai, Lampang, Tak and Mae Hong Son, loan pregnant female buffalo to households.

The offspring from these buffalo are then lent to other needy households, the loan having to be repaid (at 1% interest) over four to six years. In some projects the animals are given to the households free-of-charge; in other cases the family keeps the calf and the mature animal is lent to another household. In all cases, the idea is to enable poor farmers to gain access to a resource – a buffalo – which would otherwise be beyond their means.

global market – and they plead for a return to 'traditional' life. Most farmers, however, have embraced the cash economy with alacrity and seem unimpressed by such protestations.

Tourism in Thailand

Looking at the experience of the 1990s emphasizes the fickleness of the tourist industry. In 1990, Thailand was the place where everyone wanted to go and where every tour operator and hotel owner was making money. On the basis of the growth in the number of arrivals from the late 1980s, analysts and the Tourist Authority of Thailand (TAT) projected that arrivals would just keep on growing. Instead, arrivals stagnated. This was a shock for those who saw investing in tourist facilities as a sure thing. Hotel occupancy rates dropped to 50% or lower, and hoteliers resorted to slashing their room rates to encourage custom. The problem was that over-optimism fuelled over-construction, which led, in turn, to over-capacity.

Why this should happen to a country with so much to offer is a lesson in the uncertainties of the tourist industry. But to understand what happened, one has to look back to the early 1990s. First of all there were the domestic political problems that sullied the smiling face of Thailand, the coup d'état of 1991 and the widely reported massacre of demonstrators in 1992. Rather harder to pin down is Thailand's poor PR. By the mid-1980s, the Kingdom was perceived to be yesterday's destination. People had moved on to Indonesia, Vietnam and elsewhere. Among 'travellers' or 'backpackers', Thailand had become spoilt. Among family holidaymakers, Thailand's AIDS crisis (see page 788) had become a cause for concern and among those looking for pristine beaches and a clean environment, overdevelopment in places like Pattaya and Phuket had turned them away. All in all, the Tourist Authority of Thailand had an image problem. It invented a new word – *wattanathammachaat*, or 'culture and nature' – to try and cash in on the eco-tourism bandwagon, but it took, nonetheless, almost a decade for Thailand's tourist industry to recover a semblance of vitality.

Rather ironically it was Thailand's economic crisis which really put some fizz back into the tourist industry. Even before the economic crisis, the growth in the number of foreign tourists appeared to have picked up. In 1995, an encouraging 6.95m tourists visited the country and in 1996, coinciding with the Tourist Authority of Thailand's PR effort connected with the 50th anniversary of King Bhumibol's accession to the throne, 7.2m. But with the collapse in the value of the Thai baht, so the country became – overnight – incredibly good value for money. 1998 saw a record 7.8m tourists visit the country, coinciding with the new 'Amazing Thailand' campaign, and numbers have remained buoyant through 1999 and 2000. The campaign saw a number of particularly tacky attempts to entice visitors to different corners of the country: the world's biggest ever omelette, largest plate of fried rice,

Background

longest beach party, and such like. In Nakhon Pathom the world's tallest joss stick collapsed in November 1998, tragically killing five people.

Notwithstanding such tragi-comic disasters, it seems that Thailand is once again fashionable. There are other factors which have played a role too. Indonesia is beset with political problems and communal violence; Indonesia, Malaysia and Singapore have had the 'haze' to contend with; and the Philippines has had kidnappings of tourists and a long-running insurgency. The result is that many people who might have intended to visit one of these countries opted for Thailand instead.

Culture

Women in Thai society

Although the logic of Buddhism relegates women to a subordinate position, women in Thailand have considerable influence. In the rural North and Northeast, land is usually inherited by the female members of a household, and husbands reside with their wives. It is common to find the wife controlling the finances in a family, determining where and how much fertilizer to buy, and even giving her husband an 'allowance'. This has been noted for centuries: in 1433 the Chinese Muslim traveller Ma Huan recorded: 'It is their [Siamese] custom that all affairs are managed by their wives ... all trading transactions great and small'. Although in public the role of the man is accentuated, in private, equality of the sexes or the reverse is more usually the case. In the fields, ploughing is usually done by men, but other tasks are equally shared – and often women do more than their fair share.

The relative strength of the woman's role even extends to sexual relations. Ma Huan's 15th-century account of Siam noted how men would have penis balls inserted under their foreskin to increase their partner's pleasure: 'If it is the king ... or a great chief or a wealthy man, they use gold to make hollow beads, inside which a grain of sand is placed ... They make a tinkling sound, and this is regarded as beautiful'.

The contrast between the subordinate position of women in Thai society and their much more influential underlying role is a recurring theme. This would seem to lend credence to the old Thai adage that the two front legs of an elephant are male and the two rear legs, female – the implication being that men lead the way and women follow. Female traders and businesswomen, for instance, are well represented – indeed, there are thought to be more female than male traders. But at the same time, their influential role in private enterprise arises partly because they are largely excluded from high office in the public sector. As a result, ambitious women are forced to enter the private sector. Politics is an almost exclusively male domain. It took 17 years from when women were granted equal political rights to men in 1932 for the first female MP to enter Parliament. In the November 1996 elections, the male/female balance in Parliament was 371 to 22. In the 53 cabinets between 1932 and 1996, only 11 women have held ministerial posts (three of them, twice). Even at the village level, women are under-represented. In 1996, of 65,873 village heads, just 6,375 were village head 'women'.

19th Century mural of a Thai woman wearing a pha sin; note the stylized 'axe' cushion in the background

The few women who do become MPs, Juree Vichit-Vadakan writes, 'are perceived to be mere decorative flowers to brighten and lighten the atmosphere' (*Bangkok Post*, 25.3.97). They are not expected to contribute much to the political process and are not taken seriously by their male counterparts. Thai family law also reveals a streak of discrimination: Thai men are permitted to demand a divorce if their wives have but one affair; Thai women can only request a divorce if their husband honours another woman as his wife – he can have as many affairs as he likes.

In previously booming Thailand, *mia noi* became *de rigeur*, and having a mistress was rather like having a limited edition Mercedes with a badge showing membership of the Royal Bangkok Sports Club. When it comes to *mia noi*, there is an unwritten set of rules over how they are to be treated, rules that are accepted by both errant husbands and their (first) wives. It is only when these rules are transgressed that all hell breaks loose. *Mia noi* get BMWs; first wives get rather staider Mercedes, probably with a chauffeur thrown in for good measure. The *mia noi* will drive herself, wearing Armani sunglasses and perhaps a Versace suit. *Mia noi* are to be enjoyed in (semi) private. They can be taken for discreet weekends up country, or out to dinner, but they must not attend official functions and should not grace the society pages arm-in-arm with their men. As long as the men and their *mia noi* stick to the rules, then things seem to work just fine.

The collapse in the Thai economy has clearly changed things. For most men, there's simply not as much money to throw around on luxuries like minor wives. However, the *mia noi* of senior politicians may have benefited from the rules introduced in late 1997 that require cabinet ministers to declare their assets (see page 769). Apparently, some politicians, rather than have their improbably extensive holdings exposed to the glare of publicity, have transferred cars, houses and other baubles to their minor wives. Even first wives have got something out of the new asset-revealing measures. Former Prime Minister Chaovalit Yongchaiyut, who resigned at the end of 1997, valued his own assets at ฿17m; his wife's amounted to ฿124m.

Not every woman in Thailand becomes a *mia noi*, of course. In fact it has been argued that education and a career have put many middle-class Thai women off marriage of any sort, whether as first or second wives. They are reluctant to 'marry down' to secure a partner and instead develop their careers and gain social status in that way. While women do face discrimination, Thai society does give them the social space to acquire status on their own, independent of a husband. Some Thai women sense a change in the role and position of women in Thailand, especially in politics. In the 1998 local government elections, nearly 1,500 women were voted in as village heads. This may be just 2½% of the total, but to have a women as a village head was hitherto almost unheard of. Moreover, in the municipal and provincial council elections of early 2000, the proportion of women winning seats reached 10% of the total, double the figure for the previous elections.

The oldest industry in Thailand: prostitution

Embarrassingly for many Thais, their country is synonymous in many foreigners' minds with prostitution and sex tourism, and now with AIDS. That prostitution is big business cannot be denied: various estimates put the numbers of women employed in the industry at between 120,000 and two million, in some 60,000 brothels. Estimating the numbers of commercial sex workers (CSWs) is difficult, but a survey by the Thai Red Cross and Mahidol University plumped for a figure at the lower end of this range – between 120,000 and 200,000.

Despite the ubiquitousness of the prostitute in Thai life, the government has often appeared blind to the scale of the industry. This is clear in one official estimate of the numbers of prostitutes and brothels in the Kingdom: 67,067 and 5,754 respectively. Part of the problem is admitting to the problem in a society where these things are usually left unsaid. As US-based Thai author Somtow Sucharitkul explained: "The main difference between American and Thai sexuality is that in America you can only talk about it but can't do it, but in Thailand you can't talk about it, you can only do it."

Although the growth of prostitution is usually associated with the arrival of large numbers of GIs on 'Rest & Recreation' during the Vietnam War, and after that with the growth of sex tourism, it is an ancient industry here, just as it is in most countries. In the 1680s, for example, an official was granted a licence to run the prostitution monopoly in Ayuthaya, using 600 women who had been captured and enslaved.

Prostitution has been illegal since 1960. Until the introduction of a new legal code in 1996, only the pimp and the prostitute were liable for prosecution. The act made it a crime to 'promiscuously [render] sexual services for renumeration', and police interpreted this as applying only to the provider of such services, not the recipient. With the new 1996 Act, customers are now also liable for prosecution if the prostitute is under 18 years of age.

The scale of the prostitution industry in Thailand indicates that the police turn a blind eye and at the same time no doubt gain financial reward. There is a brothel or 'tea house' in every town, no matter how small. Farmers are trucked in from the countryside, and it has been the norm in many universities for male 'freshers' (first year undergraduates) to be taken to a brothel by the older students as part of their initiation into university life. One survey recorded that 95% of all men over 21 had slept with a prostitute; another put the figure at 75%. Girls in these 'tea houses' are paid ฿30-50 per customer, and Pamela DaGrossa writes: 'The women I interviewed told me that prostitutes in these brothels [for Thais] are not required to participate in the actual sex act in any way except for lying on their backs. The men expect and receive no more. It is even rumoured that some more experienced prostitutes read newspapers while they 'work''.

In the North and Northeast, families have been known to 'sell' their daughters (and occasionally their sons) for between ฿10,000 and ฿30,000. But for families mired in poverty, and for daughters who are expected to help their parents, this is not seen as reprehensible. One father, in Phayao Province in the north, explained to the Thai journalist Sanitsuda Ekachai: "I didn't sell my daughter ... she saw me suffer, she saw the family suffer, and she wanted to help". Some people maintain that the subordinate role of women in Buddhism means that there is less stigma attached to becoming a prostitute. In some villages, having a daughter who has 'gone South', as it is euphemistically termed, is viewed as a good thing. The benefits are clear. Sanitsuda Ekachai continues: "Riam has given her father more than a house, a television set, a refrigerator and a stereo. She has made him someone in the village. He was once a landless peasant, one of those who sat in the back row at village meetings. Now he sits at the front ..."

During the 1990s, with the wide availability of alternative employment in garment and electronics factories for girls with nimble fingers, and the heightened awareness of the dangers of prostitution following successive public health campaigns, the flow of girls from rural Thailand began to diminish. To fill the void, the flesh trade looked to Thailand's 500,000-strong hilltribe population and to neighbouring countries for women. It has been estimated that there are 30,000 Burmese women in Thai brothels, with 10,000 new recruits joining their ranks each year. Asia Watch believes there is "clear evidence of direct official involvement in every stage of the trafficking process". There are also women working in the trade from Yunnan (South China), Laos and Cambodia.

A disturbing development is the apparent spread of **child prostitution** and the attraction of paedophiles to Thailand, where under-age girls and boys are more available than in Western countries – and where the risks of getting caught are perceived to be less. (Foreign paedophiles also seem to think that having sex with children is also safe in terms of the associated AIDS risk. The medical evidence does not bear this out.) There has been a spate of 'outings' of foreign paedophiles, who have found their names splashed across the national and international media. The police have also become more assiduous in tracking down paedophiles and

Keeping abreast of volleyball in Thailand

The members of the crack men's volleyball team at the National Games, held in June 1996, stood out from the rest of the contestants. For a start, they wore lipstick. Closer inspection revealed that some also sported breasts, while off the field they wore high-heeled shoes and ladies' clothing. Even so, this slight, almost diminutive team of sports[men] from the northern Thai province of Lamphun trounced the more macho sides and won the gold medal. But when it came to selecting the national team a month later, not one of their number was included. Peeved that their efforts had not been recognized, the transvestites of Zone 5 decided to accuse the national volleyball

body of sexual discrimination. They pointed out that while some of them might have breasts, they all still had penises. Although the national governing body did not admit as much, it seems they were worried that opponents in the international arena might snigger behind their hairy hands at Thailand's effeminate spikers, while there were also fears of a breakdown in locker room discipline.

In 2000 a film of the story was released – Satree lex. The film did well for a Thai production. As director Yongyut Thongkongtoon said: "This film breaks all the rules. There is no hero or heroine. Most of the lead characters are gay. And, you know, gays are a no-no, a taboo subject in Thai films."

bringing them to court. For example, a man from British Guyana – arrested in Khon Kaen in 1993 – was sentenced to 10 years in jail, and a Frenchman – arrested in Bangkok in the same year – was incarcerated for four years. In the last decade there has been an increase in co-operation between the Thai police and overseas forces, especially in Europe. In 1993 a Swedish man – who was arrested in Pattaya, but then fled the country after being released on bail was rearrested in Sweden and convicted by a Swedish court in 1995. Under Thai law, sex with a child under 15 is illegal and penalties for the sexual abuse of children range from four to 20 years. If the child is under 13, the sentence can be extended to life.

As with adult prostitutes, how many children are involved in the commercial sex industry is a source of considerable dispute. The police estimated in 1990 that there were 100,000 under-age prostitutes in the Kingdom. The Ministry of Public Health in 1993 put the figure at 13,000-15,000; while Sanphasit Koompraphant, the director of the Centre for the Protection of Children's Rights, quoted a figure of 800,000. This latter estimate seems to be grossly inflated, and designed more to impress on people the seriousness of the issue than to be based on any accurate survey. It would mean that nearly one in five girls aged seven to 15 are engaged in prostitution, or one in 10 boys and girls.

The difficulty of dealing effectively with the problem is that the police are, in some cases, in league with those who traffic in under-age prostitutes. Their modest salaries makes them easy targets for corruption, and they are paid to overlook brothels where child sex occurs. In addition, as Thailand develops and local children become less available (Thailand's economic growth and generally improving standard of living means that fewer parents have to resort to such drastic action – although the economic crisis may reverse this in the short-term), so under-age prostitutes from neighbouring countries, especially Burma, are filling the void. Some are little more than sex slaves; sold into prostitution and living illegally in Thailand, they have little choice but to do exactly as the brothel owner or pimp requires until they have worked off their indemnity. Pressured by poverty at home and living outside the law, it is these children who are most at risk. There is also the question of where the main problem lies. Much of the media attention has been on foreign paedophiles. But the police are the first to admit that, in terms of numbers, Thai men and their activities are more of a problem.

Background

The following NGOs are working to minimize child prostitution in Thailand: Centre for the Protection of Chidren's Rights (CPCR), T02-4121196/4120739; Friends of Women Foundation, T02-2797158; Task Force to Fight Against Child Exploitation (FACE), T02-5095782.

Prime Minister Chuan Leekpai, during his first shot at the premiership, tried to clean up the prostitution business. There has been discussion of legalizing the industry so that it can be more effectively regulated, and the police have been entrusted with a crackdown on establishments. In places like the southern Thai town of Hat Yai, where the tourist industry is largely based on prostitution (there isn't much else in the place to attract the discerning visitor), this has brought wails of anguish from local businessmen. There are also some new laws on the books: it is now, for example, illegal for men to have sex with women and girls aged under 18 years old, and parents selling their children will also face prosecution. Fines and terms of imprisonment have also been increased substantially. The problem for the government is that prostitution is so widely accepted and so ingrained into the Thai way of life that combating commercial sex work requires a national change of attitude. In 1993, 313 foreign nationals were convicted in Thailand under anti-prostitution laws, and the Thai government is pressing hard for tour operators and foreign governments to take action. In particular, the government has been hoping that more Western countries will introduce legislation that will make it a crime in their own countries for tourists to commit child sex offences in Thailand (or anywhere else). Such legislation is already on the statute books in Australia, Germany and Sweden. However, the increasing role of women from neighbouring countries in Thailand's commercial sex industry makes the problem yet more intractable. These women are 'doubly illegal': they are working in an outlawed industry, and are illegal immigrants to boot. In addition, the police are often involved in the industry in one way or another. Recently, a British national convicted of child sex offences was released after allegedly paying a bribe of ฿410,000. The Royal Thai Embassy in London, in a Fact Sheet on child prostitution in Thailand, stated that 'this sort of corruption cannot and will not be tolerated'. Perhaps not, but the problem remains.

The modern scourge: AIDS

Thailand has a massive, and growing, AIDS crisis on its hands – the worst in Asia. The first person to be tested HIV positive in Thailand was in 1984; by the end of 1995 there were thought to be around 800,000 people infected with the virus, and by the end of the century this had risen to well over one million. By that time some 400,000 Thais had died of AIDS.

The spread of AIDS in Thailand has been explosive. It seems, as Tim Brown and Peter Xenos of the East-West Population Institute in Hawaii describe, to have gone through five overlapping phases. To begin with, in the mid-1980s, it afflicted homosexual and bisexual men; by the end of the 1980s it had spread to the intravenous drug-using population; in the early 1990s high levels of infection were being reported among female sex workers; shortly afterwards, there was a marked increase in infection among the wives and girlfriends of men who frequented brothels; and, most recently of all, babies born to women with AIDS have been identified as carrying the virus.

Thailand's first AIDS case, reported in 1984, was a homosexual student who had returned from study in the USA. For the next two years, almost all cases in Thailand involved either homosexual or bisexual men. But between November 1987 and August 1988, methodone treatment centres for drug addicts in Bangkok found, to their horror, that the presence of the HIV virus in blood samples rose from 0% to 30% – this constituted the second 'wave' in Thailand's AIDS crisis.

Partly in response, a nationwide system for ascertaining levels of HIV infection by province was introduced in 1989 – known as Sentinel Surveillance. The data from this study shed light on the third wave: they indicate that by December 1993, levels of infection among sex workers had reached 30%. More recent still, HIV infection levels among wives and girlfriends have risen and this is feeding into the fifth and most recent phase: the infection of babies. In June 1993, 1.8% of women visiting pre-natal clinics tested HIV positive and by 1995, 5,000 HIV-infected children were being born each year.

What makes the pattern of spread of AIDS in Thailand so worrying is that it seems that it will not be largely confined to the homosexual and drug-using populations, as AIDS has in Europe and North America. By the early 1990s, 2% of the reproductive-age population in Thailand were infected – a catastrophic rate of spread. Also extraordinary is the geographical dispersal of the disease. A staggering 15% of army conscripts from the North – mostly country people – tested HIV positive in the mid-1990s. This reflects the prevalence of prostitution, and the mobility of Thais. Now that girls from neighbouring countries – Burma, Laos, Cambodia and southern China – are being attracted or forced into the industry, the disease is being spread across international borders. (More recent figures on HIV-infection rates among army conscripts have shown a steady fall, reflecting the success of the country's AIDS-awareness campaign.)

The cause of Thailand's AIDS epidemic does not lie with the tourist industry, but with the culture of prostitution in the country. It is a way of life. It seems that the pattern of sexuality in the Kingdom has also contributed to the tragedy. Thai women are still expected to be virgins on marriage; at the same time, most Thai men expect, and are expected, to have had sexual relations. Nick Ford and Sirinan Kittisuksathit surveyed 1,469 young women in Bangkok and found that 91% had never had sexual relations. By contrast, only 37% of the 564 young men interviewed remained virgins. This means that very large numbers of men are looking for sex from comparatively small numbers of women – a scenario in which the spread of AIDS is likely to be rampant. It has been estimated that some 80% of Thai men have paid for sex with a prostitute by the time they reach their mid-20s. Compounding this, studies have further shown that a high proportion of prostitutes have other sexually transmitted diseases (which dramatically increases the likelihood of HIV infection), while men also like to change prostitutes regularly.

Initially, the Thai government played down the problem, fearing that it would harm the tourist industry – the country's largest foreign exchange earner. After all, they reasoned, 70% of visitors are male (1992 was designated 'Ladies Visit Thailand Year'); could this be only by chance? But soon it was realized that the problem was of crisis proportions and skirting around the issue in the interests of international public relations was no longer an option. This heralded the introduction of perhaps the largest and most innovative anti-AIDS programme in Southeast Asia. The charismatic Mechai Viravaidhya, the former head of Thailand's family planning programme, was put in charge of the anti-AIDS campaign and the Prime Minister himself chaired the National AIDS Committee. (Mechai's success in promoting birth control is reflected in the fact that condoms in Thailand are known as 'mechais'.) The National AIDS committee launched a '100% condom campaign' in April 1991, threatening to shut down brothels that did not comply. The government assisted this effort by providing 60 million free condoms a year. Experts claim Mechai's success in raising AIDS consciousness in Thailand is unparalleled in the developing world. As Sidney Westley wrote in a paper published in July 1999: 'Between 1990 and 1993, the proportion of men reporting any pre-marital or extra-marital sex in the previous year fell from 28% to 15%. The proportion reporting a visit to a sex worker fell from 22% to 10%, and the proportion reporting condom use in commercial sex increased from 36% to 71%.' That's quite some success rate.

Background

As a result of Mechai's efforts, condom use has changed from being very rare to being the norm. Close to 90% of prostitutes now use condoms and one side-effect has been that the prevalence of male sexually-transmitted diseases has slumped from over 200,000 per year at the end of the 1980s to around 20,000 by 1995. Even so, the future cost to Thai society of treating large numbers of terminally ill AIDS patients is huge. In addition, AIDS is unusual in that it characteristically strikes the young, decimating the population of producers of the future. It also leave thousands of orphans, who either need to be cared for by their grandparents, or the state. The World Health Organisation has estimated that Thailand will have suffered an AIDS-related loss of US$11bn by 2000, while Mechai Viravaidhya stated in the later 1990s that he believed – contentiously – that the epidemic would cut the Kingdom's GDP by one fifth.

Minorities in Thailand

Chinese Anything between 9% and 15% of the population of Thailand is thought to be Sino-Thai (depending on how 'Chinese' is defined). Hundreds of thousands emigrated from China during the 19th and early 20th centuries, escaping the poverty and lack of opportunity in their homeland. In Thailand they found a society and a religion which was inclusive rather than exclusive. Forced to learn Thai to communicate with the ruling classes (rather than English, French or Dutch, as in neighbouring colonial countries), they were relatively quickly and easily assimilated into Thai society. They took Thai names, married Thai women, converted to Buddhism – although they were not required to renounce ancestor worship – and learnt Thai: in short, they became Thai. As elsewhere in the region, these Chinese immigrants proved to be remarkably adept at moneymaking and today control a disproportionate slice of businesses.

While the Chinese are well integrated into Thai society, compared with other countries in the region like Malaysia and Indonesia, there have been times when the Chinese have felt the hot breath of Tai nationalism. In 1914 King Rama VI wrote an essay under the *nom de plume* Atsawaphaahu, entitled *The Jews of the East*, blaming many of his country's problems on the Chinese. During Phibun Songkram's premiership between 1938 and 1944, anti-Chinese xenophobia was also pronounced and was a major reason why, in 1939, the country's name was changed from Siam to Thailand. This was to be a country of the Tais, and not any other ethnic group . Even today, it is common for government documents to maintain that the plight of the farmer is due to the unscrupulous practices of Chinese traders and moneylenders.

Although the Chinese have been well assimilated into the fabric of the nation, Bangkok still supports a large Chinatown. Here, the Chinese language can be heard spoken, shop signs are in Chinese, and Chinese cultural and religious traits are clearly in evidence.

Some commentators report a resurgence of pride in being Chinese. While from the 1930s through to the 1980s the Chinese wished in the most part to be invisible, wealth has brought confidence and Sino-Thais are once more learning the 'mother' tongue (Mandarin), praying to Mahayanist and Taoist deities like Kuan Im (Kuan Yin), and travelling to China to discover their roots. Partly, this makes good economic sense. Trade with China is booming and China is the great emerging economic (and military) powerhouse in the Asia-Pacific. To be able to converse in Mandarin and draw on family links with the homeland is perceived to be good for business. There are dangers in this rediscovered love of China, however: Thailand's past shows periods of xenophobia when Sino-Thais have been persecuted and their businesses burnt, and most are quick to add that their allegiances are to Thailand.

Of the various minority ethnic and religious groups in Thailand, the Thai Malays and Thai Muslims have often felt most alienated from the Thai nation. Not only do many in the southern four provinces of the country – Yala, Narathiwat, Pattani and Satun – speak Malay rather than Thai, but the great majority (about 80%) are also Muslim rather than Buddhist. The fact that the government has sometimes been rather heavy-handed in its approach to their welfare and citizenship gave great impetus to the growth of the Communist Party of Thailand (CPT) in the South, during the 1960s and 1970s. Pattani was only incorporated into the Thai state at the beginning of the 20th century, and even then just loosely. It was not until the 1930s that the government in Bangkok began to try and Thai-ify the far south, and many of the problems that remain evident today in relations between Tai-Thais and Thai-Malays can be dated from that period.

Relations are far better today, but it is still true that few Thai Muslims have been recruited into the civil service or army, and schools in the south still give lessons in Thai and present an essentially 'Tai' view of the country. (It is for this reason that the majority of Muslim parents still choose to send their children to private Islamic *pondok* schools, even though it means paying fees.) The Islamic revival in Southeast Asia has brought the issue of Muslim disaffection in the south to the fore once again.

King Bhumibol has done more than most to incorporate the Thai Malays into the fabric of the nation. He presents awards for Koranic study and regularly visits the region, staying in his newly-built palace at Narathiwat. Certainly things seemed to have cooled down a little since the 1980s, and today most Thai Muslims, rather than calling for a separate state, are using the political system to raise their profile and make their voices heard. The difficulty is that the acceptance that they should work within the system to achieve change has been accompanied by the spread of orthodox, conservative Islam. Unlike the Chinese, Thai Muslims are unwilling to compromise over matters of faith and simply blend in with the mass.

In April 1997 the Thai army clashed with armed separatists linked with the Barisan Revolusi Nasional (BRN), in Narathiwat province. While few people believe that the BRN, or other similar groups, represent a threat to the integrity of the Thai state, clashes like this demonstrate that the task of integrating the far south into the mainstream of Thai political life is still to be completed.

Thai Malays

The largest, and least visible, 'minority' group in Thailand are the Lao of the Northeastern region, who constitute nearly a third of the total population of the country. The region and its people are also referred to as 'Isan' (meaning northeastern) and they are often regarded by Central Thais as being the equivalent of country bumpkins. Their linguistic and cultural distinctiveness, and the patronizing attitude of the central authorities, led considerable numbers of the population in the Northeast, as in the South, to support the CPT during the 1960s and 1970s. The murder, by the police, of prominent Northeastern politicians during this period also did little to help integrate Northeasterners into the fabric of Thailand. Although the situation has since stabilized, and separatist sentiments are much reduced, the Northeast is still the poorest and least developed part of the country, with the highest incidence of poverty, malnutrition and child mortality. As a result, the government invests considerable resources trying to develop the area.

Lao

Thailand's assorted hilltribes, concentrated in the North and West, number over 500,000 people. For more background information, see page 40.

Hilltribes

Thailand's relative economic prosperity, coupled with the wars that have afflicted neighbouring countries, have brought in waves of refugees to the Kingdom in recent years. Following the victory of Communist forces in Cambodia and Laos in

Refugees

Background

the mid-1970s, many thousands fled to the safety of Thailand. Those escaping the atrocities of the Khmer Rouge – over 300,000 – settled in refugee camps along the southern rim of the Northeastern region and have since been repatriated. The several hundred thousand Lao who crossed the Mekong River as the Pathet Lao took control of Laos took shelter in temporary refugee camps along the northern sweep of the Northeast. These camps too have been closed and their former inmates largely resettled in the USA, Australia, France and Canada.

More recently, the crushing of the democracy movement in Burma in 1988 caused several tens of thousands of Burmese to flee to Thailand. They continue to live in camps along the Thai-Burmese border, from Prachuap Khiri Khan in the south to Mae Hong Son in the North. In September 1998 there were an estimated 88,000 Karen refugees alone living in Thailand, most in camps strung out along the border in the vicinity of Mae Sot. There were also 13,500 Karenni and 9,000 Mon refugees. Guesthouses in Mae Sot, and also in Sangkhlaburi, often collect clothes and medicines for distribution to the refugee camps. These Karen refugees are now proving a bit of an embarrassment to the Thai army. Since 1997, Burma has been a fellow member of Asean – which has, as one of its cardinal principles, non-interference in members' affairs – and the army has proved powerless to stop Burmese forces from attacking the camps more or less at will.

However, these political refugees, fleeing persecution – or the fear of persecution – in their own countries, have been joined since the late 1980s by a new army of economic refugees. In 1997 there were an estimated one million illegal migrant workers in Thailand, most of them (around 75%) from Burma, but with large numbers also from China, Laos, Cambodia and Vietnam, and smaller populations from India, Bangladesh and Pakistan. There are probably more illegal labour migrants and refugees in Thailand than there are hill peoples, making them the largest 'minority' group in the country.

In mid-1996 the government announced that it would permit illegal migrants already in the country (but not new arrivals) to work for two years before their repatriation. At the end of the three-month amnesty that was granted to allow illegal immigrants to register, the Immigration Department had compiled a list 342,000 names-long. The reason for this strange policy decision was that Thailand, at that time, was woefully short of cheap labour: rapid economic growth had priced many Thai workers out of the lower paid, unskilled manual jobs, and illegal labour migrants from neighbouring Myanmar, Cambodia and Laos were seen as a neat (and cheap) way to fill the gap. Jobs in road maintenance, sugar cane cutting, construction, food packing and freezing, for example, were characteristically filled by immigrants willing to take so-called 3-D jobs (dangerous, dirty and demeaning – sometimes, for good measure, difficult, too). By the mid-1990s, with rising incomes and a proliferation of job opportunities, many Thais were shying away from such work.

With the economic crisis, the logic of the government's decision was undermined. In 1997 and 1998, Thais were being laid off as factories shut down. Immigrant workers, in their turn, were displaced as the sensibilities of Thais over what they did eased in the face of economic necessity. The result was that tens of thousands of Burmese found themselves living in camps on the Thai-Burmese border, waiting for repatriation. But while the crisis certainly made life hard for Thailand's economic migrants, many continued to fill the least attractive jobs. In August 1998 the government agreed to allow 95,000 foreign workers to remain in the country for another year, because rice millers had been complaining that they could not find enough Thais to do the back-breaking work. There is little doubt that many thousands of Burmese workers remain in Thailand, many illegally, often taking on the jobs which are too dirty, dangerous and poorly paid to attract the average Thai.

Religion

The Thai census records that 94% of the population is Buddhist. In Thailand's case, this means Theravada Buddhism, also known as Hinayana Buddhism. Of the other 6% of the population, 3.9% are Muslim (living predominantly in the south of the country), 1.7% Confucianist (mostly Sino-Thais living in Bangkok) and 0.6% Christian (mostly hilltribe people living in the north). Though the king is designated the protector of all religions, the constitution stipulates that he must be a Buddhist.

Theravada Buddhism was introduced into Southeast Asia in the 13th century, when monks trained in Ceylon (Sri Lanka) returned actively to spread the word. As a universal and a popular religion, it quickly gained converts and spread rapidly amongst the Tai. Theravada Buddhism, from the Pali word *thera* ('elders'), means the 'way of the elders' and is distinct from the dominant Buddhism practised in India, Mahayana Buddhism or the 'Greater Vehicle'. The sacred language of Theravada Buddhism is Pali rather than Sanskrit, Bodhisattvas (future Buddhas) are not given much attention, and emphasis is placed upon a precise and 'fundamental' interpretation of the Buddha's teachings, as they were originally recorded.

Theravada Buddhism
For a general account of Buddhism see box, page 794

Buddhism, as it is practised in Thailand, is not the 'other-worldly' religion of Western conception. Ultimate salvation – enlightenment, or *nirvana* – is a distant goal for most people. Thai Buddhists pursue the Law of Karma, the reduction of suffering. Meritorious acts are undertaken and demeritorious ones avoided so that life, and more particularly future life, might be improved. Outside many wats it is common to see caged birds or turtles being sold: these are purchased and set free, and in this way the liberator gains merit. 'Karma' (act or deed, from Pali – *kamma*) is often thought in the West to mean 'fate'. It does not. It is true that previous karma determines a person's position in society, but there is still room for individual action – and a person is ultimately responsible for that action. It is the law of cause and effect.

It is important to draw a distinction between 'academic' Buddhism, as it tends to be understood in the West, and 'popular' Buddhism, as it is practised in Thailand. In Thailand, Buddhism is a 'syncretic' religion: it incorporates elements of Brahmanism, animism and ancestor worship. Amulets are worn to protect against harm and are often sold in temple compounds (see page 101). Brahmanistic 'spirit' houses can be found outside most buildings (see box above). In the countryside, farmers have what they consider to be a healthy regard for the spirits (*phi*) and demons that inhabit the rivers, trees and forests. Astrologers are widely consulted by urban and rural dwellers alike. Even former prime minister, Chaovalit Yongchaiyudh, employed a monk to knock his head with a wooden mallet for good luck. It is these aspects of Thai Buddhism which help to provide worldly assurance, and they are perceived to be complementary, not in contradiction, with Buddhist teachings. But Thai Buddhism is not homogeneous. There are deep scriptural and practical divisions between 'progressive' monks and the *sangha* (the monkhood) hierarchy, for example.

Virtually every village in Thailand has its wat. There is no English equivalent of the Thai word. It is usually translated as either monastery or temple, although neither is correct. It is easiest to get around this problem by simply calling them wats.

The wat & the life of a monk

While secularization has undoubtedly undermined the role of Buddhism to some extent (see below), and therefore the place of the wat, they still remain the focus of any community. The wat serves as a place of worship, education, meeting and healing. Without a wat, a village cannot be viewed as a 'complete' community, and in 1997 there were 30,102 scattered across the country, supporting a population of around 300,000 monks and novices. The figures for the latter are for non-Lent; during Lent the population of monks and novices increases by over 100,000, as people are ordained for the Buddhist Rains Retreat that runs from July to October.

In Siddhartha's footsteps: a short history of Buddhism

Buddhism was founded by Siddhartha Gautama, a prince of the Sakya tribe of Nepal, who probably lived between 563 and 483 BC. He achieved enlightenment and the word buddha means 'fully enlightened one', or 'one who has woken up'. Siddhartha Gautama is known by a number of titles. In the west, he is usually referred to as The Buddha, ie the historic Buddha (but not just Buddha); more common in Southeast Asia is the title Sakyamuni, or Sage of the Sakyas (referring to his tribal origins).

Over the centuries, the life of the Buddha has become part legend, and the Jataka tales which recount his various lives are colourful and convoluted. But central to any Buddhist's belief is that he was born under a sal tree, that he achieved enlightenment under a bodhi tree in the Bodh Gaya Gardens, that he preached the First Sermon at Sarnath, and that he died at Kusinagara (all in India or Nepal).

The Buddha was born at Lumbini (in present-day Nepal), as Queen Maya was on her way to her parents' home. She had had a very auspicious dream before the child's birth of being impregnated by an elephant, whereupon a sage prophesied that Siddhartha would become either a great king or a great spiritual leader. His father, being keen that the first option of the prophesy be fulfilled, brought him up in all the princely skills – at which Siddhartha excelled – and ensured that he only saw beautiful things, not the harsher elements of life.

Despite his father's efforts, Siddhartha saw four things while travelling between palaces: a helpless old man, a very sick man, a corpse being carried by lamenting relatives, and an ascetic, calm and serene man as he begged for food. The young prince renounced his princely origins and left home to study under a series of spiritual teachers. He finally discovered the path to enlightenment at the Bodh Gaya Gardens in India. He then proclaimed his thoughts to a small group of disciples at Sarnath, near Benares, and continued to preach and attract followers until he died at the age of 81 at Kusinagara.

In the First Sermon at the deer park in Sarnath, the Buddha preached the Four Truths, which are still considered the root of Buddhist belief and practical experience: suffering exists; there is a cause of suffering; suffering can be ended; and to end suffering it is necessary to follow the 'Noble Eightfold Path' – namely, right speech, livelihood, action, effort, mindfulness, concentration, opinion and intention.

Soon after the Buddha began preaching, a monastic order – the Sangha – was established. As the monkhood evolved in India, it also began to fragment into different sects. An important change was the belief that the Buddha was transcendent: he had never been born, nor had he died; he had always existed and his life on earth had been mere illusion. The emergence of these new concepts helped to turn what up until then was an ethical code of conduct into a religion. It eventually led to the appearance of a new Buddhist movement, Mahayana Buddhism, which split from the more traditional Theravada 'sect'.

Despite the division of Buddhism into two sects, the central tenets of the religion are common to both. Specifically, the principles pertaining to the Four Noble Truths, the Noble Eightfold Path, the Dependent Origination, the Law of Karma, and nirvana. In addition, the principles of non-violence and tolerance are also embraced by both sects. In essence, the differences between the two are of emphasis and interpretation. Theravada Buddhism is strictly based on the original Pali Canon, while the Mahayana tradition stems from later Sanskrit texts. Mahayana Buddhism also allows a broader and more varied interpretation of the doctrine. Other important differences are that while the Theravada tradition is more 'intellectual' and self-obsessed, with an emphasis upon the attaining of wisdom and insight for oneself, Mahayana Buddhism stresses devotion and compassion towards others.

House of spirits

It does not take long for a first-time visitor to Thailand to notice the miniature houses, often elaborately decorated, that sit in the corner of most house compounds. Private homes, luxury hotels and international banks do not seem to be without them; the more grandiose the building, the more luxurious their miniature alter ego. The house outside the World Trade Centre is one of the most ostentatious. Some look like gaudy miniature Thai wats made from cement and gilded; other, more traditional examples are attractively-weathered wooden houses. *Phi* – spirits – are also apparently not adverse to living in Corboisier-eque modern affairs, like the angular house outside the Pan Pacific Hotel at the end of Silom and Surawong roads.

These *san phra phum* or 'spirit houses' are home to the resident spirit or *phra phum* of the compound, who has the power to help in emergencies but also to wreak havoc should the spirit not be contented. Small models of the guardian spirit and his retainers, moulded from plaster, usually occupy the building. The spirit occupies the inner room of the abode, and is usually represented as a figure holding a sword or fly whisk in the right hand and a book in the left. The book is a death register. Around the house on the raised platform (the spirit house should be at or above eye level) are arranged the retainers: servants, animals and entertainers. Sunday is traditionally designated house cleaning day.

Usually the spirit house will occupy one corner of the house compound – the shadow of the main house should never fall on the spirit house. This would court disaster and entice the spirit to move from its residence into the main house. But the art of placing the spirit house goes much further than just keeping it out of the shadow of the main house and is akin to the Chinese art of geomancy or feng shui. Often, when misfortune strikes a family, one of their first actions is to refurbish and move the spirit house. In the normal run of events though, the spirit merely needs placating with food, incense, flowers, candles and other offerings. Each has its own character and tastes: one family, facing serious difficulties, employed a *mor du* ('seeing doctor', a medium) to be told that, as their spirit was a Muslim, he had been offended by being offered pork. The family changed the spirit's diet and the difficulties melted away. Guests who stay the night should ideally ask the spirit for permission and then visit the shrine again before leaving.

Large wats may have up to 600 monks and novices, but most in the countryside will have less than 10, many only one or two.

The wat represents the mental heart of each community, and most young men at some point in their lives will become ordained as monks, usually during the Buddhist Rains Retreat. Previously, this period represented the only opportunity for a young man to gain an education and to learn how to read. The surprisingly high literacy rate in Thailand before universal education was introduced (although some would maintain that this was hardly *functional* literacy) is explained by the presence of temple education.

The wat does not date as far back as one might imagine. Originally, there were no wats, as monks were wandering ascetics. It seems that although the word 'wat' was in use in the 14th century, these were probably just shrines, and were not monasteries. By the late 18th century, the wat had certainly metamorphosed into a monastery, so sometime in the intervening four centuries, shrine and monastery had united into a whole.

Royal wats, or *wat luang* – of which there are only 186 in the country – can usually be identified by the use of the prefixes *Rat, Raja* or *Racha* in their names. (Different ways of transliterating Thai into English arrive at slightly different spellings of the prefix.) This indicates royal patronage. Wats that contain important relics also have the prefix *Maha* or Great – as in Wat Mahathat. Community wats make up the rest and number about 30,000. Although wats vary a great deal in size and complexity, there is a traditional layout to which most conform (see box, page 808).

It seems that wats are often short-lived. Even great wats, if they lose their patronage, are deserted by their monks and fall into ruin. Unlike Christian churches, they depend on constant support from the laity; the wat owns no land or wealth, and must depend on gifts of food to feed the monks and money to repair and expand the fabric of its buildings.

Today, **ordination into the monkhood** is seen as an opportunity to study the Buddhist scriptures, to prepare for a responsible moral life – to become 'ripe'. Farmers sometimes still say that just as a girl who cannot weave is 'raw' (*dip*) and not yet 'ripe' (*suk*) for marriage, so the same is true of a man who has not entered the monkhood. An equally important reason for a man to become ordained is so that he can accumulate merit for his family, particularly for his mother, who as a woman cannot become ordained. The government still allows civil servants to take leave, on full pay, to enter the monkhood for three months. Women gain merit by making offerings of food each morning to the monks and by performing other meritorious deeds. They can also become nuns. In 1399, the Queen of Sukhothai prayed that through such actions she might be fortunate enough to be 'reborn as a male'. Lectures on Buddhism and meditation classes are held at the World Fellowship of Buddhists in Bangkok (see page 153).

For Thais from poor backgrounds – or at least male Thais from poor backgrounds – the monkhood may be the only way that they can continue their education beyond primary level. In 1995 there were almost 87,000 novice monks in monasteries in Thailand; many come from poor, rural families. In light of this, there is clearly an incentive for youngsters to join the monkhood not for spiritual reasons, but for pecuniary and educational ones. This is beginning to worry some in the Buddhist hierarchy who would like to think that novices join primarily to become monks, not to become educated. It is a drain on their resources – the government only pays 20% of the costs of educating these novices – and in some instances may pollute the atmosphere of the *wat*. In addition, it means that the quality of monks is probably lower than many in the Buddhist hierarchy would wish. The Venerable Phra Dhammakittiwong, the abbot of Wat Rachaorot and a member of the Supreme Sangha Council, was quoted in 1997 saying, quite plainly, that the problem with Thai Buddhism is that "people who are considered bright and smart do not want to become monks" (*The Nation*, 20.7.97). Nonetheless, there have been some notable successes of this form of education: Prime Minister Chuan Leekpai, who comes from a poor southern family, studied law for six years while a novice.

Another problem which has emerged in recent years is that of empty wats. It was estimated in 1997 that of the 30,000 wats in the country, over 5,000 stood empty. Often people give alms to build new monasteries, as this is the main means of gaining merit. But Thailand is not producing enough monks to man these new monasteries, with the result that around 15% stand empty. This has led some Buddhist scholars to question the assumption that building more wats is good for Thai society. In mid-1998 the Sangha Supreme Council took the unprecedented step of ordering monasteries to stop all new, non-essential construction work. The overt reason was to pare down costs in the face of the economic crisis; an additional reason was probably the belief that construction had got out of hand as monasteries vied with each other in the size and opulence of their buildings.

As Thailand has modernized, so there have appeared new Buddhist 'sects' designed to appeal to the middle-class, sophisticated, urban Thai. The **Thammakai movement**, for example, counts among its supporters large numbers of students, businessmen, politicians and members of the military. Juliane Schober maintains that the movement has garnered support from these groups because it has managed to appeal to those people who are experiencing 'disenchantment with modern Thai society, but [are] reluctant to forego the benefits of modernization'. 'Through effective use of modern media, marketing, fund raising strategies, and mass appeal of religious consumerism', the author suggests, 'it offers its followers concrete methods for attaining spiritual enlightenment in this life and membership in a pristine Buddhist community that promises to restore the nation's moral life, individual peace, and material success.' During 1998 the Thammakai movement was criticized for its unorthodox money-raising activities – getting supporters to solicit door-to-door – and in November the Education Ministry ordered an investigation of its activities by the Supreme Sangha Council. The movement is trying to raise US$360m to build a massive chedi, but claims of miracles are raising suspicions that the hard sell has gone too far. The movement has even won a business management prize. But as defenders point out, miracles and claims that generous donors will be rewarded in heaven is common to many Thai monasteries. What really bugs the opposition is that the Thammakai movement is so successful.

Another movement with a rather different philosophy is **Santi Asoke**. This movement rejects consumerism and materialism in all its guises, and enjoins its members to 'eat less, use little, work a lot, and save the rest for society'. Both Santi Asoke and Thammakai have come in for a great deal of scrutiny and have been criticized for their recruiting methods and their fundamentalist positions. They are indicative, in the eyes of some Thais, of a crisis in Thai Buddhism.

The intrusion of modern life and mores into the *wat* has created considerable tensions for the *sangha* in Thailand, reflected in a growing number of scandals. At the beginning of 1995 a monk, Phra Sayan, took the law into his own hands when he beheaded his abbot, Chamnong, for having sexual relations with a woman. He explained his actions in the context of a very popular Chinese television series about the legendary Song Dynasty magistrate Judge Pao, who rights wrongs and fights for the little person, by explaining: "Judge Pao used to say, 'Even if the emperor commits crimes, he should be punished just like ordinary people.' So there was no excuse for the abbot." Perhaps most remarkably of all, one monk was caught having sex with a corpse.

A crisis in Thai Buddhism?

More recently, in late December, 2000, Abbot Wanchai Oonsap was captured on camera dressed as an army colonel, disguised behind dark glasses and underneath a wig, with a bevy of girls in tow and an assortment of pornographic videos and empty bottles of spirits in the house where he was living it up. Earlier, Phra Pativetviset was found at a karaoke bar where the girls pronounced him a real 'party animal'. Other monks, in recent months, have been implicated in drug dealing, rape and murder – one was even caught having sex under a crematorium.

The wider problem concerns how monk superstars deal with their fame and fortune. While monks are technically prohibited from handling money, the exigencies of modern life mean that most cannot avoid it. This, in turn, opens monks up to a whole series of temptations that their predecessors, living in rural monasteries and supported by poor rural communities, never faced.

In short, keeping the Buddhist precepts is far harder in Thailand at the end of the millennium. Many Thais lament the visible signs of worldly wealth that monks display. It is this gradual erosion of the ideals that monks should embrace, rather than the odd lurid scandal, which is the more important. Many monks come from poor backgrounds and few are well educated. The temptations are all too clear in a society where a newly wealthy laity see the lavish support of individual monks and their monasteries as a means to accumulate merit. Thais talk with distaste of *Buddhapanich* – commercialized Buddhism – where amulets are sold for US$20,000 and monks attain the status and trappings of rock stars. It was reported in 1995 that

Background

one wat had earned a business school marketing award. The abbot of Wat Bon Rai in Northern Thailand, Luang Poh Koon, gave away nearly ฿64 mn in 1994. The reason why he managed to generate such staggering sums is because people believe he can bring wealth and health. Each morning his monastery throngs with people, itching to hand over cash in the hope that it will be a wise investment. It is thought that he takes US$1,000 a day in this manner. Taken together, Thailand's monasteries have a turnover of billions of baht; individual monks have personal bank accounts running into millions. It is this concern for money, in a religion where monks take a vow of poverty, which critics find particularly worrying.

Most of these stories of greed, commercialism and sexual peccadillos rarely make the leap from the Thai to the international media. However, the murder in January 1996 of Johanne Masheder, a British tourist, by a monk at Wat Tham Kao Poon (a cave wat), outside the town of Kanchanaburi in western Thailand, led Western journalists to look more closely at Buddhism in Thailand. In court it was revealed that the monk, Yodchart Suaphoo, was a former member of the Thai underworld and had already served time for rape. How could he have possibly been allowed to join the monkhood, many foreigners wondered. Yet taking the saffron robes of the monk has been a traditional way for men to make up for past crimes. Dictators, hit-and-run drivers, drug addicts hoping to dry out, even murderers, have all found sanctuary in Thailand's monasteries. As Police Colonel Vorathep Mathwaj, head of the Investigation Division of the Immigration police, put it: "This does not look good for Thailand and our monkhood". A month after his arrest, Yodchart was sentenced to death by firing squad after a one-day trial. He pleaded to be taken to the mouth of the cave and shot right away, but his wish was not granted. His death sentence was later commuted to life – as is usual in Thailand.

The Sangha Council, which is supposed to police the monkhood, has, at times, seemed perplexed as to what to do. In July 1998, for example, they found Phra Khru Sopitsutkhun, the abbot of Wat Sanam Chang in Chachoengsao, not guilty of bringing Buddhism into bad repute with his murals of naked men and women, his image of the Buddha in the so-called Superman mudra – arms outstretched and foot planted firmly on a globe – and his sale of lustral water. The *Bangkok Post* deplored the Council's unwillingness to confront unsavoury commercialism within the sangha, and viewed the case of Wat Sanam Chang as an example of "Buddhism gone horribly wrong" (*Bangkok Post*, 22.7.98).

Sulak Sivaraksa, one of Thailand's most respected scholars and critics, has suggested that there is a "crisis at the core of organized Thai Buddhism". In his view, Buddhism has simply failed to adapt in line with wider changes in economy and society. It evolved as a religion suited to a country where there was a feudal court system and where most people were subsistence farmers. Now most people live in the cash economy and work in modern sectors of the economy. These views are not restricted to those outside the monkhood. Prayudh Payutto, perhaps Thailand's greatest living monk-scholar, was quoted in 1996 as saying "More and more monks are living luxurious lives", adding that they "are no longer keeping to the letter or to the spirit of the rules [the 227 precepts]". Even more dramatically, Sompong Rachano, the director of the Religious Affairs' Buddhist Monastery Division, stated in 1997 that "Not many Buddhist monks can adhere to the 227 Buddhist precepts, few can discuss the teachings of the Buddha with lay people and fewer still – perhaps one in a thousand – have the ability to deliver a sermon before a congregation" (*The Nation*, 20.7.97).

Islam While Thailand is often portrayed as a 'Buddhist Kingdom', the provinces of the far south are majority Muslim. This is because these provinces have, historically, come under the cultural influence of the former sultanates of the Malay peninsula.

Language

According to the Thai census, 97% of the population of Thailand speak Thai – the national language. However, it would be more accurate to say that 97% of the population speak one of several related 'Tai' dialects.

See also words & phrases, page 837

The Thai language is an amalgam of Mon and Khmer, and the ancient Indian languages, Pali and Sanskrit. It has also been influenced by various Chinese dialects and by Malay. There remains strong academic disagreement as to whether it should be seen as primarily a language of the Sino-Tibetan group, or more closely linked to Austronesian languages. It is usually accepted that the Thai writing system was devised by King Ramkhamhaeng in 1283, who modelled it on an Indian system using Khmer characters (although see page 211). The modern Thai alphabet contains 44 consonants, 24 vowels and four diacritical tone marks. Words often show links with other languages, particularly technical words. For example, *praisani*/post office (Sanskrit), *khipanawut*/guided missile (Pali) and *supermarket*/supermarket (English). There is also a royal court language (*rachasap*) with a specialized vocabulary, as well as a vocabulary to be used when talking to monks.

The usual view of Thailand is one of homogeneity in language terms. Even long-term residents and those who speak Thai will observe that the Kingdom is almost mono-lingual. But, as William Smalley – a linguistics professor at Bethel College and a former missionary linguist in Vietnam, Laos and Thailand – explains in his book *Linguistic Diversity and National Unity: Language Ecology in Thailand* (University of Chicago Press: Chicago, 1994), there are over 80 languages spoken in Thailand and great diversity in linguistic terms. What is interesting is that despite this great diversity, language has not become a divisive and politicized issue. There are those in the Northeast and the South who argue the case for a greater recognition of regional languages – Lao (or Isan) and Pak Tai respectively – but so-called Standard Thai is still perceived to be the language of *all* Thais. Thus, the view of Thailand being a country of 'one' language, though it may in academic terms be incorrect, in functional and political terms is broadly accurate. Thailand is a country with a united sense of itself, yet with a fragmented linguistic pattern. Successive governments have contributed to this by portraying the country as culturally homogenous and assuming that everyone who speaks one of a number of Tai dialects speaks Thai. William Smalley illustrates this diversity by giving the example of a teacher from the Northeast:

> *A high school teacher in the provincial capital of Surin in Northeast Thailand speaks the Northern Khmer language of the area to her neighbors and in many other informal situations around town. She learned it by living and working in the city for several years. On the other hand, she speaks Lao with her husband, a government official, because that is his mother tongue. She learned it (and met him) when she was in training as a teacher in the Lao-speaking area of the Northeast. She teaches in Standard Thai, which she herself learned in school. She talks to her children in Lao or Northern Khmer or Standard Thai, as seems appropriate at the time. When she returns to her home village, an hour's ride by bus to the east of Surin, she speaks Kuy, her own native language, the language of her parents, the language in which she grew up (Smalley 1994:1).*

Thailand's four main regional languages are Lao (spoken in the Northeast), Kham Muang ('language of the principalities', spoken in the North), Thai Klang (spoken in the Central region) and Pak Tai ('southern tongue', spoken in the South). These four languages, and Standard Thai, are spoken by the following proportions of the total population: Thai Klang (27%), Lao (23%), Standard Thai (20%), Kam Muang (9%), Pak Tai (8%). **NB** Thai Klang (Central Thai) is not the same as Standard Thai.

Background

Thai, like many languages, has borrowed extensively from the English language. However, Thai has always pillaged other languages – particularly Chinese, Khmer, Pali and Sanskrit. Sometimes there are different words for pieces of modern technology which span this divide. For example, anyone being taught formal Thai will learn that the word for television is *thoorathat*. This is constructed from two classical words meaning 'far away' and 'view'. However, saying *thoorathat* is a little like saying gramophone in English, and may elicit a giggle. Most Thais now talk about the *thii wii*, clearly borrowed from the English. There are many other Thai words with English borrowings: *thek* from discotheque, *piknik* from picnic, *chut* from suit (for a set of something), and so on.

Literature

The first piece of Thai literature is recognized as being King Ramkhamhaeng's inscription No 1 of 1292 (see page 747). The *Suphasit Phra Ruang* ('The maxims of King Ruang'), perhaps written by King Ramkhamhaeng himself, is regarded as the first piece of Thai poetry of the genre, known as *suphasit*. It shows clear links with earlier Pali works and with Indian-Buddhist religious texts, and an adaptation of the original can be seen carved in marble at Wat Pho in Bangkok (see page 93).

Another important early piece of prose is the *Traiphum Phra Ruang* or the 'Three worlds of Phraruang', probably written by King Li Thai in the mid-14th century. The work investigates the Three Buddhist realms – earth, heaven and hell – and also offers advice on how a *cakravartin* – a Universal Monarch – should govern.

The literary arts flourished during the Ayutthayan period, particular poetry. Five forms of verse evolved during this period, and they are still in use today – *chan*, *kap*, *khlong*, *klon* and *rai*. The first two are Indian in origin, the last three are Thai. Each has strict rules of rhyme and structure.

The genre of poetry known as *nirat* reached its height during the reign of King Narai (1656-88). These are long narrative poems, written in *khlong* form, usually describing a journey. They have proved useful to historians and other scholars in their attempts to reconstruct Thai life. The poem *Khlong Kamsuan Siprat* is regarded as the masterpiece of this genre. Unfortunately, many of the manuscripts of these Ayutthayan works were lost when the Burmese sacked the city in 1767.

During the Rattanakosin period, focused on Bangkok/Thonburi, the first piece of Thai prose fiction was written – a historical romance written by Chao Phraya Phra Khlang. The first full version of the Ramakien was also produced in *klon* verse form (see page 98). The acknowledged poetic genius of the period was Sunthorn Phu (1786-1855) – who the Thais think of as their Shakespeare – whose masterpiece is the 30,000 line romance *Phra Aphaimani* (see page 492).

The Revolution of 1932 led to a transformation in Thai literature. The first novel to be received with acclaim was Prince Arkartdamkeung Rapheephat's *Lakhon haeng chiwit* ('The circus of life'), published in 1929 (which has been translated into English – see below). Sadly, this gifted novelist died at the age of 27. Two other talented novelists were the commoner Si Burapha, whose masterpiece is *Songkhram chiwit* ('War of life') (1932), and the female writer Dokmai Sot, whose publications include *Phu dii* ('The good person') (1937). The works of Dokmai Sot, like those of Prince Akat, deal with the theme of the clash of Thai and Western cultures. Their works are particularly pertinent today, when many educated Thais are re-examining their cultural roots.

Since the Second World War, second rate love/romance writing has flourished. The plots vary only marginally from book to book: love triangles, jealousy, macho men, faithful women... This dismal outpouring is partly balanced by a handful of quality works. Notable are those of Kukrit Pramoj, a journalist and former Prime Minister, whose most famous and best work is *Si phaen din* ('The four reigns') (1953).

Background

This traces the history of a noble family from the late-19th century to the end of the Second World War – a sort of Barbara Cartland à la Thailand.

During the political turmoil from the 1950s through to the present day, but particularly from 1973 to 1976, literature began to be used more explicitly as a tool of political commentary and criticism. *Phai daeng* ('Red Bamboo') (1954) is a carefully constructed anti-communist novel by Kukrit Pramoj, while the poems of Angkhan Kanlayanaphong became favourites of the radical student movement of the 1970s. Many of the more radical novelists were gaoled during the 1950s, of whom the most talented was probably Si Burapha. He, and the other radical novelists' and poets' work, represent a genre of socialist realism in which the country's afflictions are put down to capitalism and right-wing politics. But perhaps the most successful of Thai novels are those that deal with the trials and tribulations of rural life: Kamphoon Boontawee's *Luuk Isan* ('Child of the Northeast') (1976) and Khammaan Khonkai's *Khru ban nok* ('The Rural Teacher'), later made into the film *The Teacher of Mad Dog Swamp*.

Increasing numbers of Thai novels and short stories are being translated into English. In particular, TMC (Thai Modern Classics) are publishing a number of what their editorial team regard as the best works of Thai literature. (Some Thai literature scholars have been offended that a farang was chosen to head the editorial board and to play a leading role in identifying those novels and short stories worthy of the 'classic' label.) By mid-1995 three volumes had come out: Arkartdamkeung Rapheephat's *The Circus of Life*, Sila Khoamchai's *The Path of the Tiger*, and an anthology of pieces from 20 Thai novels. All are very competitively priced and more have been published since then.

Thai literature available in English

Pira Sudham (1988) *Monsoon Country*, Shire Books: Bangkok. Pira Sudham (1987) *People of Esarn*, Shire Books: Bangkok. Pira Sudham (1983) *Siamese Drama*, Shire Books: Bangkok. Pira Sudham (1993) *Pira Sudham's Best*, Shire Books: Bangkok. (*Monsoon Country* has also been translated into French.) All four of these books are widely available in Bangkok and essentially have the same tale to tell: one of country life in the poor Northeastern region. Pira comes from a rural background and won a scholarship to study English in New Zealand; he has since become a bit of a gadfly in farang circles. However, it is intriguing that his books have not been translated into Thai and his main admirers remain farangs and not Thais; indeed, many Thais find his rather romantic view of rural life somewhat unconvincing. His books are all rather similar in style and content; there is little here to identify Pira as one of the greats of Thai literature, but they are worth reading nonetheless – although some of his views should be viewed with scepticism.

Kampoon Boontawee (1988) *A Child of the Northeast* [*Luuk Isan*], Duang Kamol: Bangkok. This novel covers a year in the life of a village in the Northeast in the 1930s. It centres on the experiences of an eight-year-old boy, Koon, and concentrates on the sheer struggle to make ends meet in a capricious land. The image here of traditional life could be usefully set against Pira Sudham's more golden view of the past. The original Thai version of the book won the 1976 Best Novel of the Year award and is highly recommended.

Sanitsuda Ekachai (1990) *Behind the Smile: Voices of Thailand*, Thai Development Support Committee: Bangkok. This is not a novel, but a series of vignettes of contemporary Thai life, written in English by a *Bangkok Post* reporter. They are well-written, perceptive and stimulating, providing a realistic view of the pressures, aspirations and opportunities facing ordinary people in Thailand. A more recent, more expensive and considerably glossier book, by the same author, is *Seeds of Hope*: *Local Initiatives in Thailand* (1994) which also focuses on the theme of development, but with an emphasis on self-help and the work of NGOs.

Background

Khammaan Khonkhai (1992) *The Teacher of Mad Dog Swamp*, Silkworm Books: Bangkok. Another book about life in the Northeast, this centres upon the experiences of a diligent young teacher who, on graduation, is sent to an up-country primary school. Almost inevitably, his concern for the people of the area results in him being labelled a communist. The book provides an excellent insight into the concerns of villagers and also incorporates a political plot. It was originally published in Thai as *Khru Ban Nok* – or *Rural Teacher* – in 1978; the author was brought up in the Northeast and also trained as a teacher, and is semi-autobiographical.

Botan (1991) *Letters from Thailand*, Duang Kamol Books: Bangkok.

Siburapha (1990) *Behind the painting and other stories*, OUP: Singapore. These short stories, only recently translated into English by David Smyth – who teaches Thai at the School of Oriental and African Studies in London – are written by an author who is regarded as one of the 'greats' of modern Thai literature. He was at the forefront of the transformation of Thai literature into a modern genre, and was also an influential social and political activist.

Khamsing Srinawk (1991) *The Politician and Other Stories*, OUP: Singapore. This volume consists of 12 short stories. The author comes from a farming background and the stories largely describe the difficulties that rural households are facing in coming to terms with modernization.

Nikorn Rayawa (1992) *High Banks, Heavy Logs*, Penguin. Story of a woodcarver in Northern Thailand and his struggle against change, and the declining moral and artistic standards that are seen to accompany that change.

Kukrit Pramoj (1953) *The Four Reigns* [*Si phaen din*], DK Books: Bangkok. This novel, one of the most famous written in Thai, is a historical saga recounting the experiences of a nobel Thai family through the reign of four kings from the late-19th century. Written by a former prime minister of the country, some view it as a masterpiece of Thai literature; others may simply see it as a historical novel in the Cartland/Cookson mould. Entertaining, but hardly high art.

NB *DK Books* sell the widest selection of Thai works in English although branches of *Asia Books* are also worth trying (see Bangkok and Chiang Mai, Shopping, for addresses).

Art and architecture

The various periods of Thai art and architecture were characterized by their own distinctive styles. For illustrations, see the Buddha images on page 811.

One of the problems with reconstructing the artistic heritage of any Southeast Asian civilization is that most buildings were built of wood. Wood was abundant, but it also rotted quickly in the warm and humid climate. Although there can be no doubt that fine buildings made of wood were constructed by the various kingdoms of Thailand, much of the art that remains – and on which our appreciation is built – is made of stone, brick or bronze. There are few wooden buildings more than a century or so old.

Dvaravati style
c6th-11th centuries

The Dvaravati Kingdom is rather an enigma to art historians. Theravada Buddhist objects have been unearthed in various parts of the Central Plains which date from the sixth century onwards, among them coins with the inscription 'the merit of the king of Dvaravati'. The capital of this kingdom was probably Nakhon Pathom, west of Bangkok, and it is thought that the inhabitants were Mon in origin, and also spoke Mon. The kingdom covered much of Lower Burma and Central Thailand, and may have been influential from as early as the third century to as late as the 13th.

Dvaravati Buddha images show stylistic similarities with Indian Gupta and post-Gupta images (4th-8th centuries), and with pre-Pala (also Indian) images

(8th-11th centuries). Most are carved in stone, with only small images cast in bronze. Standing images tend to be presented in the attitude of vitarkamudra (see page 810), and later carvings show more strongly indigenous facial features: a flatter face, prominent eyes, and thick nose and lips. Fragments of red paint have been discovered on some images, leading art historians to believe that the carvings would originally have been painted.

Also characteristic of Dvaravati art are terracotta sculptures – some intricately carved (such as those found at Nakhon Pathom and exhibited in the museum there) – carved bas-reliefs and stone Wheels of Law. As well as Nakhon Pathom, Dvaravati art has also been discovered at Uthong in Suphanburi province, and Muang Fa Daed in Kalasin (Northeastern region). But perhaps the finest and most complete remnants of the Dvaravati tradition are found in the Northern town of Lamphun, formerly Haripunjaya (see below).

Haripunjaya style
7th-13th centuries

It seems that during the seventh century the Dvaravati-influenced inhabitants of Lopburi (Lavo) migrated north to found a new city: Haripunjaya, now called Lamphun (see page 253). Although the art of this Mon outlier was influenced by the Indian Pala tradition, as well as by Khmer styles, it maintained its independence long after the rest of the Dvaravati Kingdom had been subsumed by the stronger Tai kingdoms. Indeed, it was not until the late-13th century that Haripunjaya was conquered by the Tais, and as a result is probably the oldest preserved city in Thailand.

Srivijaya
8th-13th centuries

The Srivijayan Empire was a powerful maritime empire which extended from Java northwards into Thailand, and had its capital at Palembang in Sumatra. Like Dvaravati art, Srivijayan art was also heavily influenced by Indian traditions, in particular Gupta, post-Gupta and Pala-Sena. It seems likely that this part of Thailand was on the trade route between India and China, and as a result local artists were well aware of Indian styles. A problem with characterizing the art of this period – which spanned five centuries – is that it is very varied.

Srivijaya was a Mahayana Buddhist Empire, and numerous Avalokitesvara Bodhisattvas have been found, in both stone and bronze, at Chaiya (see page 652). Some of these are wonderfully carved, and particularly notable is the supremely modelled bronze Avalokitesvara (eighth century, 63 cm high), unearthed at Chaiya and now housed in the National Museum in Bangkok. In fact, so much Srivijayan art has been discovered around this town that some experts went so far as to argue that Chaiya, and not Palembang, was the capital of Srivijaya. Unfortunately, however, there are few architectural remnants from the period. Two exceptions are Wat Phra Boromthat and Wat Kaeo, both at Chaiya (see page 652).

Khmer-style Prang

Background

Khmer or Lopburi style
7th-14th centuries

Khmer art has been found in the Eastern, Central and Northeastern regions of the country, and is closely linked to the art and architecture of Cambodia. It is usually referred to as Lopburi style, because the town of Lopburi in the Central Plains is assumed to have been a centre of the Khmer Empire in Thailand (see page 190). The art is Mahayana Buddhist in inspiration and stylistic changes mirror those in Cambodia. In Thailand, the period of Khmer artistic influence begins with the reign of Suryavarman I (1002-50) and includes Muang Tham, Prasat Phranomwan and the beginnings of Phanom Rung; Phimai, the most visited of the Khmer Shrines, was built during the reign of the great King Jayavarman VII (1181-1217).

Lopburi Buddhas are authoritative, with flat, square faces, eyebrows that form almost a straight line, and a protuberance on the crown of the head signifying enlightenment. They are the first Buddhas to be portrayed in regal attire, as the Khmers believed that the king, as a *deva raja* (god king), was himself divine. They were carved in stone or cast in bronze. Sadly, many of the finer Khmer pieces have been smuggled abroad. Khmer temples in Thailand abound and some are among the most magnificent such structures in Southeast Asia. The biggest are those of the Northeastern region, including Phimai, Muang Tham and Phanom Rung, although Khmer architecture is also to be found as far afield as Lopburi and at Muang Kao outside Kanchanaburi.

Chiang Saen or Chiang Mai style
c11th-18th centuries

This period marks the beginning of Tai art. Earlier works were derivative, being essentially the art of empires and kingdoms whose centres of power lay beyond the country – like Cambodia (Khmer), Sumatra (Srivijaya) and Burma (Mon/Dvaravati). There are generally thought to be two styles within this Northern tradition: the Chiang Saen and Chiang Mai (or Later Chiang Saen) schools. The Chiang Saen style, in which the Buddha is portrayed with a round face, arched eyebrows and prominent chin, is stylistically linked to Pala art of India. Nevertheless, local artists incorporated their own vision and produced unique and beautiful images. The earliest date from around the 11th century and their classification refers to the ancient town of Chiang Saen, situated on the Mekong in Northern Thailand, where many of the finest pieces have been found. The second style is known as Later Chiang Saen or, less confusingly, Chiang Mai. The influence of Sukhothai can be seen in the works from this period: oval face, more slender body and with the robe over the left shoulder. Images date from the mid-14th century.

Buddha images from both of the Northern periods were carved in stone or semi-precious stone, and cast in bronze. The most famous Buddha of all, the Emerald Buddha housed in Wat Phra Kaeo, Bangkok, may have been carved in Northern Thailand during the Late Chiang Saen/Chiang Mai period, although this is not known for certain.

Architecturally, the Northern school began to make a pronounced contribution from the time of the founding of the city of Chiang Mai in 1296. Perhaps the finest example from this period – indeed, some people regard the buildings that make up the complex as the finest in all Thailand – is the incomparable Wat Lampang Luang, outside the town of Lampang in the North (see page 248).

Stupa

1 Umbrella spire
2 Shaft
3 Harmika
4 Bell
5 Mouldings
6 Base or plinth
7 Platform

The Sukhothai Buddha is one of the first representations of the Ceylonese Buddha in Siam, the prototypes being from Anuradhapura, Sri Lanka (Ceylon). The Buddha is usually represented in the round, either seated cross-legged in the attitude of subduing Mara; or the languid, one-foot forward standing position, with one hand raised, in the attitude of giving protection as the enlightened one descends from the Tavatimsa Heaven. Most were cast in bronze, as Thailand is noticeably lacking in good stone. Some art historians have also argued that Sukhothai artists disliked the violence of chiselling stone, maintaining that as peaceful Thais and good Buddhists they would have preferred the art of modelling bronze. This is fanciful in the extreme.

For the seated Buddha, the surfaces are smooth and curved, with an oval head and elongated features, small hair curls, arched eyebrows and a hooked nose. The classic, enigmatic Sukhothai smile is often said to convey inner contentment. The head is topped by a tall flame-like motif or *ketumula*. The shoulders are broad and the waist is narrow. The length of cloth hanging over the left shoulder drops quite a long way down to the navel, and terminates in a notched design.

The graceful walking Buddha – perhaps the greatest single artistic innovation of the Sukhothai period – features rather strange projecting heels (which follows the ancient writings describing the Buddha's physical appearance). Toes are all the same length and the soles of his feet are flat. The figure is almost androgynous in appearance – this was Buddha depicted having achieved enlightenment, which meant that sexual characteristics no longer existed. The finest examples were produced in the decades immediately prior to Ayutthaya conquering the city in 1438. Steve van Beek and Luca Tettoni write in *The Arts of Thailand*:

> *Sukhothai sculpture suggests a figure in the process of dematerializing, half way between solid and vapour. He doesn't walk so much as float. He doesn't sit, he levitates, and belies his masculine nature which should be hard and inflexible. Even his diaphanous robes … portray a Buddha which has already shed the trappings of this world.*

The initial influence upon Sukhothai art and architecture was from Cambodia. Khmer influence can be seen reflected, for example, in the distinctive 'prang' towers of the period (see illustration, page 803). Subsequent stupas can be classified into three styles. First, there is the Ceylonese bell-shaped stupa (see illustration, page 804). This is characterized by a square base surrounded by caryatids, above which is another base with niches containing Buddha images. Wat Chang Lom, in Si Satchanalai, is a good example. The second style of stupa is the lotus bud chedi, examples of which can be found at Wat Mahathat and Wat Trapang Ngoen in Sukhothai, Wat Chedi Jet Thaew in Si Satchanalai, and also in Kamphaeng Phet, Tak, Phitsanulok and Chiang Mai. The third style of stupa constructed during this period is believed to be derived from Srivijayan prototypes, although the links are not well established. It is, however, very distinctive, consisting of a square base, above which is a square main body, superimposed with pedestals, containing niches within which are standing Buddha images. Above the

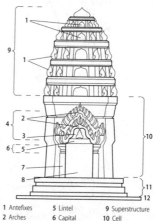

1 Antefixes	5 Lintel	9 Superstructure
2 Arches	6 Capital	10 Cell
3 Tympanum	7 Pilaster	11 Base
4 Pediment	8 Niche or door	12 Platform

13th-century Khmer Sanctuary Tower After Stratton & Scott, 1981

main body are bell-shaped *andas* of reducing size. Examples of this style can be found on the corner stupas at Wat Mahathat and some subsidiary stupas at Wat Chedi Jet Thaew (Si Satchanalai). Mention should be made of the mondop, built in place of the stupa on a square plan and always containing a large Buddha image. A good example is Wat Sri Chum (Sukhothai). It is said that the stupa 'evolved' as the Buddha lay dying. One of the disciples, Ananda, asked how they might remember the Enlightened One after his death, to which the Buddha replied it was the

Archaeological sites

doctrine, not himself, that should be remembered. As this reply was clearly unsatisfactory to his distraught followers, the Buddha added that after cremation a relic of his body might be placed within a mound of earth – which, over time, became the stupa.

Both the art and architecture of this period can be split into four sub-periods spanning the years from 1350 to 1767, when Ayutthaya was sacked by the Burmese.

As far as Ayutthayan Buddha images are concerned, for much of the time the artists of the city drew upon the works of other kingdoms for inspiration. To begin with, Uthong Buddhas were popular (themselves drawing upon Khmer prototypes). Then, from the mid-15th century, Sukhothai styles became highly influential – although the images produced looked rather lifeless and are hardly comparable with the originals. In the mid-16th century, when Cambodia came under Thai control, Ayutthayan artists looked to, and imitated, Khmer sculpture (identifiable by the double lips and indistinct moustache). Finally, in the Late Ayutthayan period, a home-grown but rather fussy style arose, with the Buddha often portrayed crowned.

The first of the four sub-periods of Ayutthayan architecture commenced in 1350 and may have been influenced by the prang of Wat Phra Sri Ratana Mahathat in Lopburi, though prangs at Ayutthaya are slightly taller. The second period (1488-1629) is dominated by the round Ceylonese-style stupa, the major example of this being Wat Phra Sri Samphet. During the third period (the first half of the 17th century), the King sent architects to Cambodia to study the architectural characteristics of the Khmer monuments. As a result, the prang became fashionable again – Wat Watthanaram and Wat Chumphon (Bang Pa-In) were built at this time. The final period was from 1732 until the sacking of Ayutthaya by the Burmese in 1767. The many-rabbeted chedis were popular during this period, although less new building was constructed as King Boromkot was more interested in restoring existing buildings. Most of the viharns and ubosoths have long since perished. What remains dates mainly from the Late Ayutthayan period.

The Bangkok or Rattanakosin period dates from the founding of the Chakri Dynasty in 1782. But, initially at least, the need for Buddha images was met not by making new ones, but by recovering old ones. King Rama I ordered that images be collected from around his devastated kingdom and brought to Bangkok. About 1,200 in all were recovered in this way, and they were then distributed to the various wats (see, for example, the fine array at Wat Pho, page 93).

It is generally accepted that the Buddhas produced during the Bangkok era are, in the main, inferior compared with the images of earlier periods. In particular, art historians characterize them as 'lifeless'. Initially, they followed the Uthong and Ayutthayan traditions. King Mongkut (1851-68) did 'commission' a new style: these Buddhas are more lively in style, with carefully carved robes. But Mongkut's new-style Buddha did not catch on, and more often than not old images were merely copied.

Architecturally, there is a similar aping of the past rather than the development of any new styles. During the first three reigns (1782-1851), the prang (eg Wat Rakhang, see page 111; and Wat Arun, page 109) and redented chedi (eg Wat Pho, see page 93) were popular, as were Ayutthayan-style viharns and ubosoths. There are, admittedly, one or two new developments, but these were peripheral to the mainstream of architecture. During the third reign, for example, the influence of Chinese art becomes quite pronounced. Other 'oddities' include the early 20th-century Wat Nivet Thamaprawat at Bang Pa-in, which is Gothic in inspiration (see page 174), and Wat Benchamabophit in Bangkok, which is a fusion of Eastern and Western styles (see page 114). In general, Rattanakosin wat buildings are airier and less ornate than those of Ayutthaya.

Ayutthayan style
Mid 14th-mid 18th centuries

Bangkok style
Late 18th-20th centuries

Background

The Thai Wat

*Wats are usually separated from the secular world by **two walls**. Between these outer and inner walls are found the **monks quarters** or dormitories (kutis), perhaps a **bell tower** (hor rakang) that is used to toll the hours and to warn of danger and, in larger complexes, schools and other administrative buildings. Traditionally, the kutis were placed on the south side of the wat. It was believed that if the monks slept directly in front of the principal Buddha image, they would die young; if they slept to the left, they would become ill; and if they slept behind it, there would be discord in the community of monks. This section of the compound is known as the* sanghavasa, *or* sanghawat *(ie for the Sangha – the monkhood).*

*The inner wall, which in bigger wats often takes the form of a **gallery** or cloister (phra rabieng) lined with Buddha images, represents the division between the worldly and the holy, the sacred and the profane. It is used as a quiet place for meditation. This part of the wat compound is known as the* buddhavasa, *or* phutthawat *(ie for the Buddha). Within the inner courtyard, the holiest building is the **ordination hall**, or* ubosoth, *often shortened to just **bot**. This building is reserved for monks only. It is built on consecrated ground, and has a ring of eight stone tablets or boundary markers (bai sema), sometimes contained in mini-pavilions, arranged around it at the cardinal and subcardinal points. These bai sema are shaped like stylized leaves of the bodhi tree, and often carved with representations of Vishnu, Siva, Brahma or Indra, or of nagas. Buried in the ground beneath the bai sema are* luuk nimit – *stone spheres – and sometimes gold and jewellery. The bai sema mark the limit of earthly power – within the stones, not even a king can issue orders.*

The bot is characteristically a large, rectangular building with high walls and multiple sloping roofs, covered in glazed clay tiles (or wood tiles, in the North). At each end of the roof are chofaa, or 'bunches of sky', which represent garuda grasping two nagas in its talons. Inside, often through elaborately carved and inlaid doors, is a Buddha image. There may also be numerous subsidiary images. The inside walls of the bot may be decorated with murals depicting the

Background

Thai murals   Like sculptural art in Thailand, paintings – usually murals – were devotional works. They were meant to serve as meditation aids, and therefore tended to follow established 'scripts' that any pilgrim could 'read' with ease. These scripts were primarily based on the *Ramakien* (see page 98), the *jataka* tales and the *Traiphum* (*The Three Worlds*). Most such murals are found, appropriately, on the interior walls of bots and viharns. Unfortunately, there are no murals to compete in antiquity with carvings in stone, although they were certainly produced during the Sukhothai period and probably much earlier. The use of paint on dry walls (frescoes are painted onto wet plaster and survive much better) made the works susceptible to damp and heat. None has survived that pre-dates the Ayutthaya period and only a handful are more than 150 years old.

The sequence of the murals tend to follow a particular pattern: beneath the windows on the long walls are episodes from the Buddha's life; behind the principal Buddha image, the Three Worlds – heaven, earth and hell (see illustration page 812); and on the end wall facing the Buddha, the contest with Mara. But, in amongst these established themes, the artist was free to incorporate scenes from everyday life, animals, plants, and local tales and myths. These are often the most entertaining sections. All were portrayed without perspective using simple lines and blocks of uniform colour, with no use of shadow and shading.

Modern Thai   Few visitors – or residents for that matter – see much but crudity in modern Thai
architecture   buildings: Elegant wooden shophouses are torn down to make way for the worst in

Jataka tales, or scenes from Buddhist and Hindu cosmology. Like the Buddha image, these murals are meant to serve as meditation aids. It is customary for pilgrims to remove their shoes on entering any Buddhist building (or private house for that matter), although in state ceremonies, officials in uniform are not required to do so.

The other main building within the inner courtyard is the **assembly hall**, or **viharn**, but not all wats have one, and some may have more than one. Architecturally, this is often indistinguishable from the bot. It contains the wat's principal Buddha images. The main difference between the bot and viharn is that the latter does not stand on consecrated ground, and can be identified by the absence of any bai sema – stone tablets – set around it. The viharn is for general use and, unlike the bot, is rarely locked. Both bot and viharn are supposed to face water, because the Buddha himself was facing a river when he achieved enlightenment under the bodhi tree. If there is no natural body of water, the monks may dig a pond. In the late Ayutthayan period,

the curved lines of the bot and viharn were designed to symbolize a boat.

Also found in the inner courtyard may be a number of other structures. Among the more common are **chedis**, bell-shaped **relic chambers** with tapering spires. In larger wats these can be built on a massive scale (such as the one at Nakhon Pathom, see page 518), and contain holy relics of the Buddha himself. More often, chedis are smaller affairs containing the ashes of royalty, monks or pious lay people. A rarer Khmer architectural feature sometimes found in Thai wats is the **prang**, also a relic chamber (see page 803). The best known of these angular corn-cob-shaped towers is the one at Wat Arun in Bangkok (see page 803).

Another rarer feature is the **library** or scripture repository (hor trai), usually a small, tall-sided building where the Buddhist scriptures can be stored safely, high off the ground. Salas are open-sided **rest pavilions**, which can be found anywhere in the wat compound; the sala kan parian or **study hall** is the largest and most impressive of these and is almost like a bot or viharn without walls. Here the monks say their prayers at noon.

Background

Wat Suwannaram (Bangkok)

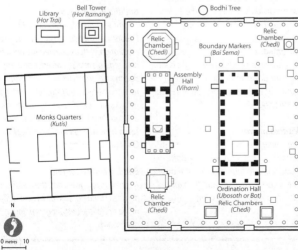

Mudras and the Buddha image

An artist producing an image of the Buddha does not try to create an original piece of art; he or she is trying to be faithful to a tradition which can be traced back over centuries. It is important to appreciate that the Buddha image is not merely a work of art, but an object of – and for – worship. Sanskrit poetry even sets down the characteristics of the Buddha – albeit in rather unlikely terms: legs like a deer, arms like an elephant's trunk, a chin like a mango stone and hair like the stings of scorpions. The Pali texts of Theravada Buddhism add the 108 auspicious signs, long toes and fingers of equal length, body like a banyan tree and eyelashes like a cow's. The Buddha can be represented either sitting, lying (indicating paranirvana) or standing, and (in Thailand) occasionally walking. He is often represented standing on an open lotus flower: the Buddha was born into an impure world, and likewise the lotus germinates in mud, but rises above the filth to flower. Each image will be represented in a particular mudra or 'attitude', of which there are 40. The most common are:

Abhayamudra
Dispelling fear or giving protection; right hand (sometimes both hands) raised, palm outwards, usually with the Buddha in a standing position.

Varamudra
Giving blessing or charity; the right hand pointing downwards, the palm facing outwards, with the Buddha either seated or standing.

Vitarkamudra
Preaching mudra; the ends of the thumb and index finger of the right hand touch to form a circle, symbolizing the Wheel of Law. The Buddha can either be seated or standing.

Dharmacakramudra
'Spinning the Wheel of Law'; a preaching mudra symbolizing the teaching of the first sermon. The hands are held in front of the chest, thumbs and index fingers of both joined, one facing inwards and one outwards.

Bhumisparcamudra
'Calling the earth goddess to witness' or 'touching the earth'; the right hand rests on the right knee, with the tips of the fingers 'touching ground', thus calling the earth goddess Dharani/Thoranee to witness his enlightenment and victory over Mara, the king of demons. The Buddha is always seated.

Dhyanamudra
Meditation; both hands resting open, palms upwards, in the lap, right over left.

Other points of note:
Vajrasana
Yogic posture of meditation; cross-legged, both soles of the feet visible.

Virasana
Yogic posture of meditation; cross-legged, but with the right leg on top of the left, covering the left foot (also known as paryankasana).

Buddha under Naga
A common image in Khmer art; the Buddha is shown seated in an attitude of meditation, with a cobra rearing up over his head. This refers to an episode in the Buddha's life when he was meditating: a rain storm broke and Nagaraja, the king of the nagas (snakes), curled up under the Buddha (seven coils) and then used his seven-headed hood to protect the Holy One from the falling rain.

Buddha calling for rain
A common image in Laos; the Buddha is depicted standing, both arms held stiffly at the side of the body, fingers pointing downwards.

Background

Bhumisparcamudra – calling the earth goddess to witness. Sukhothai period, 13th-14th century.

Dhyanamudra – meditation. Sukhothai period, 13th-14th century.

Abhayamudra – dispelling fear or giving protection. Lopburi Buddha, Khmer style, 12th century.

Vitarkamudra – preaching, 'spinning the Wheel of Law'. Dvaravati Buddha, 7th-8th century, seated in the 'European' manner.

Abhayamudra – dispelling fear or giving protection; subduing Mara position. Lopburi Buddha, Khmer style, 13th century.

The Buddha – 'Calling for rain'.

Background

concrete crassness; office buildings are erected with apparently not a shred of thought as to their effects on the surrounding environment; multi-storeyed condominiums are built with abandon and bad taste. This is tragic, given the beauty and environmental common sense that informed traditional designs; much like Singapore, in a few years' time the Thais may be frantically putting back what they have so recently pulled down. But there are Thai architects who are attempting to develop a modern Thai architecture that does not merely ape the worst in Western designs, and there are some notable new buildings.

In wat architecture, there is a move away from the gaudy, rather over-worked (to Western eyes) traditions of the Bangkok period, towards a sparer, almost ascetic vision. Bright colours have been replaced by expanses of white and subdued hues; the hectic angles of tradition, with simpler geometric shapes. Monasteries like Wat Sala Loi, in Nakhon Ratchasima (Korat) in the Northeast, and Wat Dhammakaya in Pathum Thani province, keep decoration to a minimum. Wirot Srisuro, of Khon Kaen University and the architect of Wat Sala Loi, explained to the *Bangkok Post*: "Buddhism teaches us to follow the middle path, to avoid extravagance. Our buildings should reflect this thinking by staying simple." Although Ajaan Wirot's work and that of other modernists has attracted great attention – much of it negative – far more monasteries are being built in traditional style, but with cement and concrete blocks replacing brick and stucco.

Punishment in the eight Buddhist hells, commonly found on murals behind the principal Buddha image in the bot. Adapted from Hallet, Holt (1890) A Thousand Miles on an Elephant in the Shan States, William Blackwood,

Background

In retrospect, the mid-1990s were a **watershed in contemporary Thailand's history**. On 18 July 1995, the Princess Mother (the King's mother) died. After the King, she was probably the most revered person in the country. Born a commoner and trained as a nurse, she married a prince. Their two sons, Mahidol and Bhumipol, unexpectedly became kings (Mahidol for only a short time before his tragic death). Her funeral in 1996 was a grandiose affair and her death has been likened to that of Britain's Princess Diana. Even Bangkok's massage parlours closed as a mark of respect. 1996 also saw the 50th anniversary of King Bhumibol's accession to the throne and the country threw a massive party to celebrate the event. The celebrations were as much a mark of Thailand's coming of age as of the King's golden jubilee. No expense was spared by the newly self-confident Tiger Thailand. Both events – the Princess Mother's funeral and the King's jubilee – were, for those so inclined, omens. The night before the funeral there was an unseasonable rain storm; and during the procession of royal boats on the Chao Phraya, it also poured. The King's boat was washed off course and had to be rescued by the navy. As it turned out, 1996 was the last year when money was no object.

Dance, drama and music

The great Indian epic, the Ramayana (in Thai known as the Ramakien, see page 98), has been an important influence on all Thai arts, but most clearly in dance and drama such as *nang* and *nang thalung* (shadow plays, see page 817), *khon* (masked dramas) and *lakhon* (classical dance dramas). Also important is the *likay* (folk drama).

Dance

Lakhon These dance dramas are known to have been performed in the 17th century, and probably evolved from Javanese prototypes. They became very popular not just in the court, but also in the countryside and among the common people. Consisting of three main forms, they draw upon the Jatakas (tales of the former lives of the historic Buddha), the Ramakien, and upon local fables, legends and myths, for their subject matter. Performers wear intricate costumes based on ancient dress, and character parts – such as demons and yogis – wear masks. In genuine lakhon, all performers – bar clowns – are played by women. A chorus sing the parts, not the actors.

Drama

Khon masked drama evolved in the royal court of Siam, although its roots lie in folk dances of the countryside. Performers don elaborate jewelled costumes, men wearing masks and women crowns or gilded head-dresses. Music accompanies the dance, and words and songs are performed by an off-stage chorus. Many of the dances are interpretations of traditional myths, and performers are expected to begin their training at an early age.

The **ramwong** is a dance often performed at ceremonies and originates from the central region. The **fawn** is a similar Northern dance. Slow, graceful, synchronized dancing, accompanied by drums and symbols – in which hand movements are used to evoke meaning – characterize the dance. Ungainly Westerners are often encouraged to perform these dances, to the obvious amusement of Thais.

It is thought that **likay** evolved from Muslim Malay religious performances. It was adopted by the Thais and in time became primarily a comedy folk art enjoyed by common people, with singing and dancing. In recent years, likay artists have begun to incorporate political jibes into their repertoires. Cultured people in Bangkok used to look upon likay as rough and unsophisticated, although in recent years it has gained greater recognition as an art form.

Nang shadow plays, with characters beautifully engraved on leather, are frequently performed at cremation ceremonies, particularly in the South (see page 701). There are usually 10 puppeteers in a nang troupe, who wear traditional

Background

👉 *Muay Thai: kick boxing*

Along with Siamese cats and inaccurate films, Thailand is known in the West for muay Thai – *literally Thai boxing* – or 'kick boxing'. This art of self-defence is first mentioned in the Burmese chronicles of 1411. King Naresuan (1590-1605), one of Thailand's greatest monarchs, made muay Thai a compulsory element of military training and gradually it developed into a sport. Today it is Thailand's most popular sport and is one of the few ways that a poor country boy can turn his rags into riches. It is no coincidence that most of Thailand's best boxers have come from the harsh and impoverished Northeastern region, which seems to turn out a never-ending stream of tough, determined young men.

A boy will begin training at the age of six or seven; he will be fighting by the age of 10, and competing in professional bouts at 16. Few boxers continue beyond the age of 25. In the countryside, boys herding buffalo will kick trees to hone their skills and learn to transcend pain, all with the intention of using their strength and agility to fight their way out of poverty. Trainers from Bangkok send scouts up-country to tour the provinces, in search of boys with potential.

In muay Thai, any part of the body can be used to strike an opponent, except the head. Gloves were only introduced in the 1930s; before then, fists were wrapped in horse hide and studded with shell or glass fragments set in glue. Fatalities were common, and for a time in the 1920s muay Thai was officially banned. Today, fights are staged much like boxing in the West: they are held in a ring, with gloves, and consist of five three-minute rounds, with two-minute rest periods between each round. Before beginning, the boxers prostrate themselves on the canvas while an orchestra of drums and symbols raises the tension. The opponents wai to each corner before the music stops, and the fight begins. Punching is rare – far more effective are the kicks and vicious elbow stabs. The intensity of many contests make Western heavyweight boxing seem slow and ponderous. As Doug Lansky, who sent us an amusing email, commented:

"These kickboxers may have been small, but I wouldn't want to step into a ring with any of them. They are kicking machines. Apparently, defense has not been introduced in this sport. It was like watching a battery commercial where two robots go at it until the cheaper battery runs out of power, or in this case, one of the fighters runs out of blood."

costume and are often made-up. The narrator (usually the oldest member of the troupe) offers some help with the story line, while a traditional phipat band provides musical accompaniment. Nang was probably introduced into Thailand from Java during the early Ayutthaya period. *Nang thalung* puppets are smaller, more finely carved, and usually have articulated arms (see page 817). In both cases, the figures 'perform' in front of – or behind – a screen, usually enacting stories from the Ramakien. Like likay, nang and nang thalung have, in the past, been looked down upon as rather crude, unsophisticated arts.

Unfortunately for those who are trying to preserve traditional Thai arts – among them the Thai Royal Family – they are gradually, but steadily, losing their popular appeal. Although tourists may expect and hope to witness a performance, most Thais, both urban and rural, would rather watch the TV or go to the movies.

Music Thai traditional music is a blending of musical elements from a number of cultures, namely Chinese, Indian and Khmer. This applies not just to the instruments, but also to the melodies. Although Thai music can therefore be seen to be derivative, it nonetheless developed into a distinctive form that is regarded as belonging to the 'high' musical cultures of Southeast Asia. In the past, talented young musicians would become attached to the king's court or that of a nobleman, and would there receive training from established musicians. Musicians and composers independent of such patronage were rare, and public guilds seldom lasted very long.

With the ending of the absolute monarchy in 1932, the role of the nobility in supporting musicians began to die. Traditional music became viewed as 'un-modern' and performances were actively discouraged by the authorities. It has only been in about the last 25 years that an interest in traditional Thai music has re-emerged. But because of the years of neglect, the pool of talented musicians is very small.

Although court music may have withered, folk music remained popular and vibrant throughout this period – and perhaps nowhere more so than in the Northeastern region of the country. Here *mor lam* singers are renowned, and in some cases they have become national celebrities. Accompanied by the haunting sound of the *khaen* (bamboo pipes) and singing 'songs from the ricefields' about rural poverty and unrequited love, they are among the most traditional of performers.

Textiles

Thai traditional textiles have experienced something of a rebirth since the end of the Second World War, with the support of the Royal Family, NGOs and the *Jim Thompson Thai Silk Company*. In 1947, Jim Thompson – an American resident in Bangkok – sent a sample of Thai silk to the editor of *Vogue* in New York. Then a near moribund industry, today it produces over 10,000,000 m of silk a year. In the past, cloth was made from silk, cotton or hemp. Because of a shortage of such natural yarns, it is common today to find cloth being woven from synthetic yarn. Likewise, chemical aniline dyes are used in place of natural animal and vegetable dyes although there has been a revival of interest in vegetable dyes, (particularly on cotton) in recent years. Among the most distinctive of Thai textiles is *matmii* cloth, produced using the ikat dyeing technique (see below). The dyed yarn is then woven into cloth using plain weave, float weave, supplementary weft and tapestry weave techniques. In the North, hill peoples also produce appliqué cloth.

Silk weaving appears to be of considerable antiquity in Thailand. Excavations at Ban Chiang in the Northeast (see page 237) have revealed silk threads, in association with artifacts dated to 1,000-2,000 BC. If this is corroborated by other evidence (it remains contested), then the accepted view that the technology of sericulture filtered south from China will have to be revised. According to legend, the origins of sericulture date back to 4,000 BC, when China's first emperor noticed that the leaves of the mulberry trees in his garden were being eaten at a prodigious rate by a small grub. Having eaten their fill, the voracious grubs spun cocoons of fine thread. Lei Zu, a concubine, collected the cocoons and dropped some into boiling water, whereupon they unravelled into long lengths of fine, but strong, thread.

The silk 'worm' lives for just 20 days, and 35,000 hatch from 30 g of eggs. In their short lives, this number of worms consume mulberry leaves (fresh, preferably young) three times a day, or 680 kg in under three weeks. Laid out on circular bamboo trays, the noise of 35,000 tiny jaws chomping their way through barrow-loads of leaves is like a gentle rustling sound. Susceptible to cold, disease, pest attack and all manner of other threats, the worms must be lovingly cultivated if they are to live long enough to weave their cocoons of silk. After they have formed cocoons – a process which takes around 36 hours – the worm metamorphoses into the silk moth. This gives the silk reelers just 10 days before the moth chews its way out of the cocoon, destroying the silk thread in the process. The cocoons are dropped into boiling water, killing the forming moth, and then unreeled, often by hand. A single cocoon can yield a thread between 200 and 1,500 m long, and about 12,500 cocoons are needed to produce 1 kg of silk yarn.

Background

Clothing The *pha sin* is an ankle length tubular piece of cloth, made up of three pieces and worn by women. The waistband (*hua sin*) is usually plain, the main body of the skirt (known as the *pha sin*) plain or decorated, while the lower hem (*dtin sin*) may be intricately woven. Traditionally, the pha sin was worn with a blouse or shawl (*pha sabai*), although it is common today to see women wearing T-shirts with the pha sin.

The *pha sarong* is the male equivalent of the pha sin and is now a rare sight. As the name suggests, it is a tubular piece of cloth which is folded at the front and secured with a belt. It is worn with either a Western-style shirt or a *prarachatan* (a tight-collared long-sleeved shirt).

Cloth *Matmii* ikat (see page 371) – woven cotton cloth – is characteristic of the Northeastern region. Designs are invariably geometric and it is very unusual to find a piece which has not been dyed using chemicals. Designs are handed down by mothers to their daughters and encompass a broad range from simple *sai fon* ('falling rain') designs, where random sections of weft are tied, to the more complex *mee gung* and *poom som*. The less common *pha kit* is a supplementary weft ikat, although the designs are similar to those found in matmii. The characteristic 'axe cushions' – or *mawn kwan* – of the Northeast are usually made from this cloth, which is thick and loosely woven. These cushions are traditionally given to monks (usually at the end of the Buddhist Rains Retreat) to rest upon. *Pha fai* is a simple cotton cloth, in blue or white and sometimes simply decorated, made for everyday use and also as part of the burial ceremony, when a white length of pha fai is draped over the coffin. Centres of weaving in the Northeast include: Khon Kaen, Udon Thani, Renu Nakhon (outside That Phanom), Surin, and Pak Thong Chai (outside Korat).

Except for the hilltribe textiles (see page 372), weaving in the North and Central regions is far less diverse than that of the Northeast. Indeed, most of the cloth that is handwoven is produced in Lao (ie Northeastern) villages that have been relocated to this part of the country. Distinctive pha sin are woven by the Thai Lu of Phrae and Nan, featuring brightly coloured horizontal stripes interspersed with triangular designs. Centres of weaving in the North include: Pasang and San Kampaeng (both outside Chiang Mai), and Nan and Phrae.

The textiles of the South exhibit links with those of Malaysia and Sumatra. In general, the handwoven textile tradition is weak in this part of the country. *Pha yok* is similar to *songket* (a Malay cloth), consisting of cotton or silk interwoven with gold or silver yarns. *Han karok* is a technique in which two-coloured twisted thread is woven. Centres of production in the South include villages around Trang and in the Songkhla Lake area.

Recommended reading Conway, Susan (1992) *Thai Textiles*, British Museum Press: London. A richly illustrated book with informative text, placing Thai textiles in the context of Thai society and history.

Crafts

Mother-of-pearl The method used to produce mother-of-pearl in Thailand differs from that in China and Vietnam. The 'pearl' is from the turban shell, from which pieces are cut and sanded to a thickness of 1 mm. These are then glued to a wooden panel and the gaps between the design filled with layers of lac (a resin), before being highly polished. This art form reached its peak during the 17th and 18th centuries. Masterpieces include the doors at Wat Pho, Wat Phra Kaeo and Wat Benchamabophit (all in Bangkok), and the footprint of the Buddha at Wat Phra Singh in Chiang Mai. In Vietnam and China, the wood is chiselled-out and the mother-of-pearl cut to fit the incisions.

To produce nielloware, a dark amalgam of lead, copper and silver metals is rubbed into etched silver. The craft was introduced to Nakhon Si Thammarat (see page 695) from India and then spread north. It is used to decorate trays, betel boxes, vases, cigarette cases and other small objects.

Nielloware

Khon masks depict characters from the Ramakien (the Thai Ramayana) and are made from plaster moulds. Layers of paper are pasted over the mould, glued, and then coated in lac. The masks are then painted and decorated.

Khon masks

In the production of lacquerware, three layers of lacquer from the sumac tree (*Gluta usitata*) are brushed onto a wood or wicker base, and each layer polished with charcoal. Then a fourth layer of lac is added, and once more highly polished with charcoal. After drying, the piece is inscribed with a sharp instrument and then soaked in a red dye for two to three days. The polished black part of the surface resists the dye, while the inscribed areas take it. Because this traditional method is so time-consuming, artists today tend to paint the design on to the lacquer. The art dates from the mid-Ayutthaya period and was possibly introduced by visiting Japanese artists. Some of the finest examples of lacquerware are to be found at Bangkok's Suan Pakkard Palace (see page 114).

Lacquerware

Kite-flying has been a popular pastime in Thailand, certainly from the Sukhothai period (where it is described in the chronicles). During the Ayutthaya period, an imperial edict forbade kite-flying over the Royal Palace, while La Loubère's journal (1688) records that it was a favourite sport of noblemen. Today it is most common to see competitions between 'chula' (formerly 'kula') and 'pukpao', at Sanaam Luang in Bangkok (see page 99). The chula kite is large – over 2 m in length – while the diamond-shaped pukpao is far smaller and more agile. The frame is made from bamboo (*sisuk* variety), cut before the onset of the rains and, preferably, left to mature. The bamboo is then split and the paper skin attached, according to a long-established system.

Kites

Nang yai puppets, literally 'large skin', are carved from buffalo or cow hide and may be over 2 m in height. Though they can be skilfully decorated, nang yai are mechanically simple: there are no moving parts. Interestingly, some characters require particular types of hide. For example, a Rishi must be cut from the skin of a cow or bull that has been struck by lightning or died after a snakebite, or from a cow that has died calving. After curing and stretching the hide on a frame, the figure is carved out and then painted (if it is to be used for night performances, it is painted black).

Puppets

    Nang thalung are smaller than nang yai and are related to Javanese prototypes. They are more complex and have even stranger hide requirements than the nang yai: traditionally, key characters such as Rishi and Isavara need to be made from the soles of a dead (luckily) nang thalung puppet master. If master puppeteers are thin on the ground, then an animal which has died a violent death is acceptable. For the clown character, a small piece of skin from the sexual organ of a master puppeteer (again dead) should be attached to the lower lip of the puppet. One arm of the figure is usually articulated by a rod, enabling the puppet master to provide some additional expression to the character.

Background

Land and environment

Geography

Thailand covers an area of 500,000 sq km (about the size of France) and had a population in 1998 of 61.5 million, which is growing at 1½% per year. It shares its borders with Burma, Laos, Cambodia and Malaysia. Administratively, the country is divided into five main regions: the North, Northeast, Central Plains, South and the Bangkok Metropolitan Region. Two smaller, additional regions are also sometimes identified: the East and West. Each of these seven regions has its own distinctive geographical character.

The **Central region** is Thailand's 'rice bowl', encompassing the wide and fertile Central Plains: this is the economic and cultural heartland of the Thai (or Tai) nation. The construction of dams, and the spread of irrigation in the region, has enabled Thailand to become, and remain, the world's largest rice exporter. Yet most farms remain small, family-owned affairs. Towards the southern extremity of the Central Plains lies the **Bangkok Metropolitan Region**. With an official population of 5.6 million (1998), it is many times larger than Thailand's second city and is the country's economic and political hub. Indeed, it has outgrown its administrative borders and the population of the entire urban agglomeration is nearer to 10 million. Bangkok supports both the greatest density of businesses, as well as the key institutions of government.

The **North** is Thailand's largest region, and includes the Kingdom's second city of Chiang Mai. It is a mountainous region with narrow river valleys, and supports most of the minority hilltribes. The area was not incorporated fully into the Thai state until the 19th century. Doi Pha Hom Pok, the country's highest peak at 2,300 m, is located in Chiang Mai Province.

The **Northeast** or '**Isan**' is the second largest, and poorest, region of Thailand. It is also known as the Khorat Plateau and is environmentally harsh. The people of the Northeast speak a dialect of Thai – *Lao* – and they are culturally distinct in terms of food, dress and ritual. Most are rice farmers living in approaching 29,000 villages.

Just south of the Northeast, sandwiched between the sea and the Damrek range of hills, is the **Eastern region**. This has become an overspill area for Bangkok, with businesses moving to take advantage of cheaper land and less congested infrastructure. The Eastern region also contains the renowned seaside resort of Pattaya.

To the west of the Central Plains and Bangkok is the **Western region**. Until recently this was a relatively undeveloped, mountainous and largely forested area. But over the past 10-20 years, pioneer agriculturalists and logging companies have moved into the West, clearing large tracts of forest, and planting the land with cash crops such as sugar-cane and cassava. Despite these developments, the beautiful mountains which rise up towards the border with Burma remain relatively unspoilt. Towns here have a 'frontier' atmosphere.

Thailand's seventh region is the **South**, which stretches 1,150 km south to the border with Malaysia. The far south has more in common with island Southeast Asia than mainland Southeast Asia; the climate is tropical, many of the inhabitants are Malay, Islam is the main religion, and rubber is the dominant crop. Most visitors travel to the South to visit the beach resorts of Koh Samui, Phuket, Koh Phi Phi, Hua Hin and Koh Phangan.

Below the region, there are a series of further administrative subdivisions. First, the *changwat*, or province, of which there are 76, each with a governor at its head. Below the province is the *amphoe*, or district, numbering 811 in all, each headed by a *nai amphoe*, or district officer. Then comes the *tambon*, a 'commune' of villages, of which there are 7,409, each with a *kamnan* in charge. And finally, the lowest level of administration is the *mubaan* – the village – of which there are 67,581, each headed by a democratically elected *phuuyaibaan*, or village head. **NB** All figures are for 1997.

Background

Climate

Thailand lies within the humid tropics and remains hot throughout the year. Mean temperatures vary between 24°C in the far north to 29°C in the Central region, while rainfall ranges from 1,200 mm in parts of the Northeast to over 4,000 mm in some parts of the South (eg Ranong) and East (eg Khlong Yai, Chantaburi). Far more important than these mean annual figures are seasonal fluctuations in rainfall and,

For best time to visit, see page 20

Provinces

BURMA

LAOS

VIENTIANE

Chiang Rai

Mae Hong Son

Chiang Mai

Phayao

Nan

Lamphun

Lampang

Phrae

Uttaradit

Nong Khai

Nakhon Phanom

Loei

Nong Bua Lamphu

Udon Thani

Sakon Nakhon

Sukhothai

Tak

Phitsanulok

Phetchabun

Khon Kaen

Kalasin

Mukdahan

Kamphaeng Phet

Phichit

Chaiyaphum

Maha Sarakham

Roi Et

Yasothon

Amnat Charoen

Nakhon Sawan

Uthai Thani

Chai Nat

Lopburi

Nakhon Ratchasima

Buri Ram

Surin

Si Saket

Ubon Ratchathani

Suphanburi

Saraburi

Kanchanaburi

Phachin Buri

Sa Kaeo

Chachoengsao

Ratchaburi

Chonburi

Rayong

Chantaburi

Trat

Phetburi

CAMBODIA

PHNOM PENH

VIETNAM

Prachuap Khiri Khan

Gulf of Thailand

Chumphon

Ranong

Phangnga

Surat Thani

Nakhon Si Thammarat

Krabi

Phuket

Trang

Phatthalung

Andaman Sea

Satun

Songkhla

Pattani

Yala

Narathiwat

MALAYSIA

Mekong River

1 Bangkok
2 Samut Prakan
3 Samut Sakhon
4 Samut Songkhram
5 Nakhon Pathom
6 Nonthaburi
7 Pathum Thani
8 Nakhon Nayok
9 Ayutthaya
10 Ang Thong
11 Sing Buri

N

0 km   100
0 miles   100

Background

Temperature and rainfall: selected towns

Town	Region	Height above sea level	Annual Temp, °C Max	Min	Av	Average Rainfall, mm	% rain falling, May -Oct
Bangkok	C	3m	39.9	9.9	28.1	1418	86%
Lopburi	C	14m	41.8	8.4	28.1	1239	87%
Chiang Mai	N	314m	41.5	6.0	25.8	1268	89%
Mae Hong Son	N	417m	42.0	6.0	26.2	1256	92%
Korat	NE	189m	43.4	4.9	27.1	1197	82%
Udon Thani	NE	181m	43.9	2.5	26.8	1367	88%
Kanchanaburi	W	29m	43.5	5.5	27.8	984	81%
Chantaburi	E	5m	40.8	8.9	27.2	3164	89%
Sattahip	E	56m	40.5	12.3	29.0	1366	65%
Nakhon Si Thammarat	S	7m	37.7	17.1	27.4	2491	39%
Narathiwat	S	4m	36.4	17.1	27.0	2644	41%

See individual climate charts for details on temperatures and rainfalls.

to a lesser extent, temperature. With the exception of the southern isthmus, which receives rainfall throughout the year, Thailand has a dry season which stretches from November to April, corresponding with the period of the northeast monsoon, and a wet season from May to October, corresponding with the southwest monsoon.

The distinction between the dry and the rainy seasons is most pronounced in the Northeast, where as much as 98% of rain falls between April and October. Nonetheless, like the English, Thai's talk endlessly about the weather. The seasons – and this means rain – determine the very pattern of life in the region. Rice cultivation, and its associated festivals, is dependent in most areas on the arrival of the rains, and religious ceremonies are timed to coincide with the seasons. Kampoon Boontawee, in his novel *Luuk Isan* (Child of the Northeast) about village life in the Northeastern region of Thailand, writes: 'When Koon and Jundi and their fathers arrived at the *phuyaiban's* [headman's] house, the men were talking about what they always talked about – the lack of rain and the lack of food in the village'.

The dry season can be divided into two: cool and hot. During the cool season in the North, which extends from December to February, it can become distinctly chilly, with temperatures falling to as low as 7°C at night. The hot season runs between March and May and temperatures may exceed 40°C, before the cooling rains arrive towards the end of the period. But for much of the time, and in most places, it is hot whatever the month. The French diplomat La Loubère, who visited Thailand in the 17th century, was convinced that the hot climate 'effiminated the courage', and noticed that the mere sight of a sword would put 100 Thais to flight. Westerners attributed a whole range of presumed character traits to the hot climate – as they did in many other tropical countries.

Seasons **Hot season** March-May, dry with temperatures 27°C-35°C, but sometimes in the 40s for extended periods.

Wet or rainy season June-October, wet with lower temperatures (due to the cooling effect of the rain and increased cloud cover) 24°C-32°C, but higher humidity.

Cool season December-February, when conditions are at their most pleasant, with little rain and temperatures ranging from 18°C to 32°C.

Seasons in the South Similar weather to that of the Malay peninsula, with hot, humid and sunny weather most of the year. Chance of rain at any time, although more likely during the period of the two monsoons, May-October (particularly on west side of the peninsula) and November-April (particularly on east coast).

Water for life: wet rice cultivation

Rice probably spread into Southeast Asia from a core area, which spanned the highlands from Assam (India) to north Vietnam. Some of the earliest evidence of agriculture in the world has been uncovered in and around the village of Ban Chiang in Northeastern Thailand, and also from Bac-son in north Vietnam. However, archaeologists are far from agreed about the dating and significance of the evidence. Some believe that rice may have been cultivated as early as 7,000 BC; others say it dates back no further than 3,000-2,000 BC.

By the time the first Europeans arrived in the 15th century, the crop was well-established as the staple for the region. Today, other staples are frowned upon, being widely regarded as 'poor man's food'. The importance of rice can be seen reflected in the degree to which culture and crop have become intermeshed, and in the mythology and ceremony associated with its cultivation. The American anthropologist DeYoung, who worked in a village in Central Thailand in the late 1950s, writes that the farmer:

> reverences the crop he grows as a sentient being; he marks its stages of growth by ceremonies; and he propitiates the spirit of the soil in which it grows and the good or evil spirits that may help or harm it. He considers rice to possess a life spirit (kwan) and to grow much as a human being grows; when it bears grain, it has become 'pregnant' like a mother, and the rice is the seed or child of the Rice Goddess.

Wet rice, more than any other staple crop, is dependent on an ample and constant supply of water. The links between rice and water, wealth and poverty, and abundance and famine are clear. Throughout the region, there are numerous rituals and songs which honour the 'gift of water' and dwell upon the vagaries of the monsoon. Water-throwing festivals, designed to induce abundant rainfall, are widespread, and if they do not have the desired effect villagers will often resort to magic. The struggle to ensure a constant supply of water can also be seen reflected in the sophisticated *müang fai*, traditional irrigation systems of Northern Thailand. Less obvious, but no less ingenious and complex, is that farmers without the benefits of irrigation have also developed sophisticated cultivation strategies designed to maintain production through flood and drought.

While rice remains Thailand's key crop and a marker of Thai-ness, it does not occupy the central position in life and livelihood that it once did. Young people, increasingly, wish to avoid the drudgery of farming which has become, through the twin effects of education and the media, a low status occupation. Anyone spending time in the Northern region or the Central Plains may notice uncultivated land, effectively abandoned because there is no one to farm it. (An alternative explanation is that it has been purchased for speculative reasons.) Many farmers have sold their buffalo and bought rotavators – known as *kwai lek* or iron buffalo – because they plough the land more quickly and don't have to be fed, grazed and bedded. Broadcasting has replaced transplanting in some areas because it saves time. There are even cases of weekend farmers who travel up from Bangkok on Saturdays to keep their farms ticking over. Today, it is not uncommon for rural households to earn 50% or more of their income from non-farm sources. In the countryside, older Thais sometimes lament this loss of subsistence innocence, but the young, of course, will have nothing of it. The future, so far as they are concerned, does not lie in farming.

Background

The cycle of wet rice cultivation

There are an estimated 120,000 rice varieties. Rice seed – either selected from the previous harvest or, more commonly, purchased from a dealer or agricultural extension office – is soaked overnight, before being sown into a carefully prepared nursery bed. Today, farmers are likely to plant one of the Modern Varieties or MVs, bred for their high yields.

The nursery bed into which the seeds are broadcast (scattered) is often a farmer's best land, with the most stable water supply. After a month the seedlings are uprooted and taken out to the paddy fields. These will also have been ploughed, puddled and harrowed, turning the heavy clay soil into a saturated slime. Traditionally, buffalo and cattle would have performed the task; today, rotavators, and even tractors, are becoming more common. The seedlings are transplanted into the mud in clumps. Before transplanting, the tops of the seedlings are twisted off (this helps to increase yield) and then they are pushed into the soil in neat rows. The work is back-breaking and it is not unusual to find labourers – both men and women – receiving a premium – either a bonus on top of the usual daily wage or a free meal at midday, to which marijuana is sometimes added to ease the pain.

After transplanting, it is essential that the water supply is carefully controlled. The key to high yields is a constant flow of water, regulated to take account of the growth of the rice plant. In 'rain-fed' systems, where the farmer relies on rainfall to water the crop, he has to hope that it will be neither too much nor too little. Elaborate ceremonies are performed to appease the rice goddess and to ensure bountiful rainfall.

In areas where rice is grown in irrigated conditions, farmers need not concern themselves with the daily pattern of rainfall, and in such areas two or even three crops can be grown each year. But such systems need to be carefully managed, and it is usual for one man to be in charge of irrigation. In Northern Thailand he is known as the hua naa muang fai. He decides when water should be released, organizes labour to repair dykes and dams and to clear channels, and decides which fields should receive the water first.

Traditionally, while waiting for the rice to mature, a farmer would do little except weed the crop from time to time. He and his family might move out of the village and live in a field hut, to keep a close eye on the maturing rice. Today, farmers also apply chemical fertilizers and pesticides to protect the crop and ensure maximum yield. After 90-130 days, the crop should be ready for harvesting.

Harvesting also demands intensive labour. Traditionally, farmers in a village would secure their harvesters through systems of reciprocal labour exchange; now it is more likely for a harvester to be paid in cash. After harvesting, the rice is threshed, sometimes out in the field, and then brought back to the village to be stored in a rice barn or sold. It is only at the end of the harvest, with the rice safely stored in the barn, that the festivals begin. As Thai farmers used to say, having rice in the barn is like having money in the bank.

Today, rice agriculture in Thailand has moved on for many farmers. Modern varieties are grown in place of traditional rices. Broadcasting has replaced transplanting in many areas. Land preparation is by tractor rather than buffalo. Threshing is mechanized. Even combine harvesters are common. More to the point, rice agriculture for many farmers is no longer a way of life; it is business.

Flora and fauna

It has been estimated that Thailand supports 18,000 species of plant, 6,000 insect species, 1,000 kinds of bird, and 300 species of mammal. Even so, it is difficult not to escape the conclusion that the Kingdom's flora and fauna are woefully depleted. As recently as 1950, over half the country's land area was forested. Today, barely a day goes by before yet another scandal with an environmental tinge is revealed in the newspapers. This concern for the environment, though, is comparatively recent, dating only from 1973. In that year, an army helicopter crashed, and as investigators picked over the wreckage they discovered not just the bodies of the crew and passengers, but also the corpses of several protected wild animals. It became clear that the human victims – prominent army officers – had been illegally hunting in the Thung Yai Naresuan Wildlife Sanctuary. A public scandal ensued and the environmental movement in Thailand was born. Today, the environment has become big business. This, as Jonathan Rigg has written in *Counting the Costs: Economic Growth and Environmental Change in Thailand* (Singapore: ISEAS, 1995), is rather ironic because in many people's eyes it has been big business which has created the problems in the first place. At a simplistic level, the costs of Thailand's modernization are reflected in an environment which is both diminished and degraded. Now that Thais are becoming wealthy, the 'growth at all costs' cry is being replaced by a widening concern that economic development should not be pursued to the detriment of the environment. In other words, 'sustainable development' has come to Thailand. Young Thai trendies are buying Green Cotton's unbleached and undyed clothes, and Lever Brothers Thailand are marketing eco-friendly products. Environmental awareness has become a fashion statement, and commercial companies realize, of course, that there is money in fashion.

People & land

An Indian king is reported to have said to a man boasting about the extent of the lands ruled by the King of Siam: "It is true, I admit, that they are greater in extent than mine, but then the King of Golconda [in India] is a king of men, while your king is only king of forests and mosquitoes".

Thailand was relatively land-rich compared with India and China. In 1687, La Loubère estimated the Kingdom's total population to be 1.9 million, and in 1822 John Crawfurd believed it to be less than 2.8 million. (Today the figure is more than 60 million.) Forests and wildlife abounded, and the inhabitants at times had great trouble maintaining their small areas of 'civilized space'. Even today, the Thai word for 'forest' – *paa* – implies 'wild' and 'uncivilized'.

The wealth of forest resources meant that most buildings – even those of the richest nobles and merchants – were usually constructed of wood, bamboo and other forest products. The only exception to this rule was in the construction of religious edifices. For these, stone and brick were used, no doubt signifying the permanence of faith, and the impermanence of humans. Today, the building skills of the early Thai civilizations can be seen reflected, for example, in the temples of Sukhothai and Ayutthaya. In most cases the temples stand stark and isolated, which accentuates their visual impact. However, when they were built they would have been surrounded by wooden houses, shops, and the bustle and infrastructure of an ancient ceremonial city. These have now rotted away in the region's humid climate, leaving a religious skeleton of monastic building and chedis.

The abundance of land in Thailand, and in Southeast Asia more widely, during historical times meant that people were very highly valued. A king's wealth was not measured in terms of the size of his kingdom, but the number of people that came under his control. Land was not 'owned' in the usual sense; ownership was transitory and related to utilization. When a farmer stopped cultivating a piece of land it would revert to the ownership of the king, but ultimately to God. The value of people becomes clear in the art of warfare in the region. In general, the objective was not to gain land, but to capture prisoners, who could then be carried off to become slaves on the victorious king's land. This principle held true for the great kingdoms of Burma, Siam and Cambodia, and the remotest tribes of Borneo. At times entire villages would be transported into captivity. Battles rarely led to many casualties. There was much noise, but little action, and the French envoy Simon de la Loubère,

Thailand's orchids: a blooming business

Thailand's forests, wetlands and grasslands support over 1,000 varieties of orchid (there are between 17,000 and 30,000 species worldwide, and another 30,000 registered hybrids), and the country has become Southeast Asia's largest exporter of the blooms. In 1991, flower exports – mostly orchids – earned US$80m. The industry began in the 1950s, but only really expanded in the mid-1980s as orchid farms were established around Bangkok. Of the various genuses, the most popular is Dendrobium, which is particularly suited to Thailand's seasonal climate and has the added attraction of blooming throughout the year.

Over half of Thailand's orchid exports go to Japan – where customers have a particular predilection for pink and purple blooms – 20-25% to Europe, and 15-20% to the USA. A problem that has prevented an even more dramatic increase in exports is a lack of air-freight space. But even with such healthy growth, there are fears that a change of fashion in Japan might undermine the market. The price of the popular pink Sonia dendrobium has already declined from ฿5-6 to ฿2-3 per bloom. An area of the economy which has bloomed even faster than orchids is that of artificial flower production. In 1996, exports of plastic and silk flowers and foliage totalled nearly US$70 mn.

in his 17th-century account of Siam, wrote: 'Kill not is the order, which the King of Siam gives his troops, when he sends them into the field'.

Flora Thailand's dominant natural vegetation is **tropical forest**. In the south, parts of the west, and in pockets such as Chanthaburi province in the east, this means 'jungle' or tropical rain forest – the sort of stuff that Tarzan would swing through if he happened to be Asian. Tigers, elephants, banteng (wild ox), sambar (deer) and tapirs still roam the lowland forests, although not in great numbers. Thailand's forests have been depleted to a greater extent than in any other country in Southeast Asia (with the one exception of Singapore, which doesn't really count). In 1938, 70% of Thailand's land area was forested; by 1961 this had been reduced to just over 50%. Today, natural forest cover accounts for only a little more than 15% of the land area and projections indicate that by 2010 this will have declined to less than 10%. The Royal Forestry Department still insists on a figure of over 20% and puts the area of National Reserve Forest at 40% – despite the fact that over large areas not a single tree remains standing, and even a cursory glance at satellite images will show both figures to be palpably fraudulent.

The causes of this spectacular, and depressing, **destruction of Thailand's forests** are numerous: simple population growth (in 1911, the Kingdom had a population of just eight million, today it is over 60 million), commercial logging, commercialization and the spread of cash cropping, and dam construction. Cronyism and corruption, which is part and parcel of logging across the region, has also marred the management of Thailand's forests. In late 1988, such was the public outcry after floods in the South killed 300 people – and whose severity was linked in the public imagination to deforestation – that a nationwide logging ban was introduced in January 1989. Few doubt, though, that deforestation continues. 'The Forestry Department', Nok Nguak (a pseudonym) argued in the *Bangkok Post*, 'can be described at best as ineffective and at worst as one of the main culprits in the destruction of our forests' (*Bangkok Post*, 24.3.98). In February 1998 it was revealed that a logging mafia, in league with the Royal Forestry Department (RFD), had been instrumental in the logging of protected forest in the Salween area near Mae Hong Son, in Northern Thailand. After the revelation of a ฿5 mn bribe, *The Nation* opined that the RFD was 'hopelessly corrupt'.

The universal stimulant – the betel nut

In more remote areas of Thailand it is not uncommon to meet men and women whose teeth are stained black, and gums red, by continuous chewing of the 'betel nut'. This, though, is a misnomer. The betel 'nut' is not chewed at all: the three crucial ingredients that make up a betel 'wad' are the nut of the areca palm (Areca catechu), the leaf or catkin of the betel vine (Piper betel), and lime. When these three ingredients are combined with saliva, they act as a mild stimulant. Other ingredients (people have their own recipes) are tobacco, gambier, various spices and the gum of Acacia catechu. The habit, though also common in South Asia and parts of China, seems to have evolved in Southeast Asia, and it is mentioned in the very earliest chronicles. The lacquer betel boxes of Thailand illustrate the importance of chewing betel in social intercourse. Galvao, in his journal of 1544, noted: 'They use it so continuously that they never take it from their mouths; therefore these people can be said to go around always ruminating'. Among Westernized Southeast Asians, the habit is frowned upon: the disfigurement and ageing that it causes, and the stained walls and floors that result from the constant spitting, are regarded as distasteful products of an earlier age.

The tropical rain forests of Thailand, although not comparable with those of Malaysia and Indonesia, have a high diversity of species, exceeding 100 per hectare in some areas. In total, it is estimated that Thailand supports 20,000-25,000 species of plant.

In the North and the Northeast the vegetation is adapted to a climate, with a dry season that may stretch over six months. For this reason, the forests are less species-rich than the forests of the south. In many cases they are also highly degraded due to encroachment by loggers and farmers. Other sub-types of tropical forest in Thailand include semi-evergreen forest (in the Peninsula and North, along the border with Burma), dry evergreen forest (in the wetter parts of the Northeast and the North), ixed deciduous and dry dipterocarp savanna forest (mostly in the Northeast and parts of the northern Central Plains).

Fauna

Thailand's fauna is even more threatened than its forests. Of the Kingdom's 282 species of mammal, 40 are endangered and 14 are critically endangered. For its birds, the picture is equally gloomy: 190 endangered species out of 928, with 38 critically endangered. While for the country's reptiles and amphibians, there are 37 endangered species out of 405, of which seven are on the critical list. A century ago, wild elephants and tigers roamed the Bang Kapi area east of Bangkok – now it is overrun with shopping malls. It was only in 1960 that a law was enacted protecting wild animals, and even today it doesn't take an investigative journalist to find endangered – and protected – animals for sale, whether whole (and alive) or in bits.

Thailand supports a rich and varied fauna, partly because it lies on the boundary between several zoogeographic regions: the Indochinese, Indian and Sundaic (Malesia). It also lies on a crossroads between North and South, acting as a waystation for animals dispersing north from the Sundaic islands, and south from the Asian mainland. The problem in trying to maintain the country's biodiversity (both floral and faunal) is that most of its national parks and wildlife sanctuaries are thought to be too small to be sustainable. A single male tiger, for example, needs about 50 sq km of forest to survive; some of Thailand's parks cover less than 100 sq km.

Mammals

During the 1980s, some of Thailand's endangered species of mammal disappeared entirely. The Javan and Sumatran rhinoceros, the kouprey (Bos sauveli, the largest cattle in the world), the wild water buffalo and Eld's deer (Cervus eldi) are probably all extinct in Thailand, or on the verge of extinction. The world's last Schomburgk's

Protected species

Clouded leopard
Dugong
Eld's deer
Fea's muntjak
Freshwater giant ray
Goral
Gurney's pitta
Javan rhinoceros
Kouprey
Malayan tapir
Princess Sirindhorn's white-eyed river
  martin
Sarus crane
Schomburgk's deer
Serow
Sumatra rhinoceros
Wild buffalo

NB *These are protected species gazetted under Thailand's Wildlife Conservation Act (1992), last amended in mid-1996. Some of the species are extinct within Thailand or throughout their range.*

deer (*Cervus schomburgki*) was kept as a pet in the grounds of a Buddhist monastery in Samut Sakhon province before, reputedly, being clubbed to death by a drunk in 1938.

The reasons for this pattern of extermination are not difficult to fathom: destruction of habitat and over-hunting (see below). Thailand does have national legislation protecting rare species from hunting, capturing and trade, but too often the legislation is ignored and even officials have actively flouted the law, sometimes hunting in national parks. Of Thailand's 282 species of mammal, 40 are listed in the International Union for the Conservation of Nature and Natural Resources' (IUCNs) Red List of Endangered Species. These include the pileated gibbon (*Hylobates pileatus*), the clouded leopard (*Neofelis nebulosa*), the Malayan tapir (*Tapirus indicus*) and the tiger (*Panthera tigris*). Indeed, almost all Thailand's large mammals are in danger of extinction in the country.

Birds Birdlife in Thailand is also under severe pressure. Birds' habitats are being destroyed, pollution is increasing, and hunting is barely controlled. Even in Thailand's national parks, a lack of resources and widespread corruption mean that bird populations are under threat.

Over the last three decades or so, 80% of Thailand's forests have disappeared – and with them, many bird habitats. Birds are also hunted by farmers for food and virtually any size and shape of bird is considered fair game. The rarer and more colourful species are hunted by collectors for the bird trade – for which Thailand is a centre. It is not unusual to walk in the countryside and neither see nor hear a bird of any type. Three of Thailand's birds are listed by the IUCN as threatened with extinction: the giant ibis (*Pseudibis gigantea*), the Chinese egret (*Egretta eulophotes*), and the white-winged wood duck (*Cairina scutulata*); many others have had their populations decimated.

In total, Thailand has 928 species of bird – more than double the number found in Europe – which account for a tenth of the world's species. This richness of birdlife is due to the varied nature of Thailand's habitats and the country's position at the junction of three zoological realms. The country is also an important wintering area for migrant birds from the northern latitudes.

Reptiles & amphibians Thailand supports an impressive and varied population of snakes, lizards and other assorted cold-blooded creatures. In total there are 298 reptile and 107 amphibian species, of which 37 are regarded as endangered. The closest most people come to a snake (at least knowingly) is at Bangkok's Red Cross Snake Farm, or at the snake farm near the floating market in Thonburi. If bitten, see page 70.

The large **non-venomous** pythons are active around dusk and kill their prey by constriction. The reticulated python (*Python reticulatus*) can grow to a length of 15 m and, although non-venomous, their bite is powerful. Other smaller pythons include the blood python (*Python curtus*) and rock python (*Python molurus bivittatus*).

Elephants have nowhere to go

According to the local office of the World Wide Fund for Nature, there are 2,705 domesticated elephants in Thailand and 1,975 wild animals. But the trained elephants and their mahouts are out of a job and out of luck. With the imposition of a logging ban in 1989, their traditional work in the forests of the country all but dried up. Some took the rather degrading alternative option of working in tourist-oriented elephant 'camps', where the stately pachyderms are forced to play football and harmonicas. But there is a limit to the tourist potential of the elephant, and many of these down-on-their-luck animals and mahouts took to begging for food. As it is Bangkok where most of the money is to be found, it was Bangkok where elephants gravitated. Because the elephant is the holiest of beasts, Buddhists can make merit by buying sugar cane and bananas for the animals. It was in this way that the mahouts managed to feed their mounts – at an estimated cost of ฿2-3,000 a month.

But in 2000 the governor of Bangkok banned elephants from the city. The mahouts saw the hands of environmentalists in this ban - and in particular, foreign environmentalists. It was suggested that Roger Lohanan, of the Thai Society for the Prevention of Cruelty to Animals, and Solaida Salwala, of the Asian Elephant Lovers Foundation, had been instrumental in convincing the governor

that elephants are not designed for city life. There were reports of elephants being hit by cars, having their feet lacerated by nails and broken glass, and going beserk in the heat and fumes. Mahouts were accused of cruelty, and of furthering their own interests at the expense of the elephants. The mahouts reacted furiously, accusing the elephant lovers of ignorance. One mahout, 60-year-old Ta Jongjaingam, even asked "Why do they let the Burmese and Khmers stay [in Bangkok] – but not our elephants?". As is usual with these things in Thailand, lots of slightly crazed people (and some sensible ones) wrote letters to the newspapers, arguing one way or the other.

Some people have pointed out that even before the logging ban, life was not always a bed of bananas for the elephants. There have been reports that they were fed on amphetamines to keep them working, and when they became too ill or exhausted they were simply sold – often to be slaughtered. An elephant trunk is said to be worth ฿40,000 and the genitals ฿15-20,000; a good pair of tusks considerably more than this. Unfortunately, Thailand is really not in a position to support a large number of elephants any longer. There is neither the work, the space, nor the interest. Even wild elephants are becoming a pest in some areas, as they venture out of national park areas and destroy crops.

Background

Stories about reticulated pythons swallowing people are usually difficult to substantiate. One report in a Calcutta newspaper in 1927 stated that a Burmese salesman, Maung Chit Chine, had been swallowed while on a hunting trip; his partners found his hat and the snake, asleep, nearby. They killed the python and cut it open to reveal Maung's body inside. A more recent story – and this one is easier to confirm – comes from Malaysia. On Wednesday 6 September 1995, a rubber tapper was found in the process of being swallowed by a 7 m-long python near the town of Semagat, about 150 km south-east of Kuala Lumpur. The unfortunate victim's brother found the snake at its repast and called the police, who shot the creature. It was, though, too late. The snake – which weighed 140 kg – had crushed Ee Heng Chuan, who had suffered multiple fractures. Fang marks on Heng Chuan's legs led the authorities to suspect that the rubber tapper had been caught while he was resting, possibly asleep. Trapped within the snake's powerful coils – its body measured 30 cm in diameter – Heng Chuan would have found it impossible to escape. This episode, it should be added, was exceptional and led to the python (not just this one, the species in general) receiving a good deal of largely unjustified bad

The forest in the market

A walk around almost any up-country market will reveal not just an abundance of familiar fruits, vegetables, fish, meats and consumer goods, but also a range of 'forest products'. Grubs, beetles, frogs, roots and turtles are sold – usually for the pot. Among the various insects, the most common is the large maeng da, a beetle which may be 5 cm long. Maeng da are caught at night: nets are strung up and powerful lights used to attract the insects. But because of extensive deforestation, maeng da have become a luxury item; a single beetle costs ฿6 or more. They are deep fried and usually served with chilli. The name maeng da is also the Thai term for pimp, and for the prehistoric horseshoe crab. In all three cases the reason is the same: the male of the species latches on to the female and allows her to carry and support him.

press. As Kiew Bong Heang, Associate Professor of Zoology at the Universiti Malaya remarked, the python is "a nice creature if it's not eating you".

Some of the most beautiful non-venomous snakes in Thailand are the racers (genus Elaphe and Gonyosoma). They live in a variety of habitats, and because they are diurnal are often seen. The visually striking, gold-coloured copperhead racer (*Elephe radiata*) can grow to a length of 2 m and lives in open grasslands; the bright green, red-tailed racer (*Gonyosoma oxycephalum*) lives in trees. It can also grow to 2 m and is easily identified by its brown tail. Other snakes found in Thailand include the rat snakes (genus Zaocys and Ptyas), the beautiful whip-like bronzebacks (genus Dendrelaphis), and the keelbacks (sub-family Natricinae).

But it is the dread – often misplaced – of the **venomous species** which make them the most fascinating of snakes. There are two types: the front-fanged (more venomous) and back-fanged (mildly venomous) snakes. The latter include whip snakes (genus Ahaetulla and Dryophiops), water snakes (sub-family Homalopsinae) and cat snakes (genus Boiga). The former include cobras, the best known of which is the king cobra (*Ophiophagus hannah*), common Chinese cobra (*Naja naja atra*) and the monocled cobra (*Naja naja kaouthia*). The king cobra is said to be the longest venomous snake in the world; it has been known to reach lengths of up to 6 m. It is also among the most dangerous due to its aggressive nature. One specimen shot in the mountains of Nakhon Si Thammarat in 1924 measured 5.6 m. Their venom is a very powerful neurotoxin, and victims can be dead within half an hour. It has even been claimed that elephants have died after being bitten, the snake puncturing the soft skin at the tip of the trunk. King cobras are found throughout the country, in most habitats. It should be emphasized that despite their aggressiveness, few people die from cobra bites in Thailand.

The venom of **sea snakes** (family *Hydrophiidae*) is even more powerful than that of cobras, and the common sea snake's (*Enhydrina schistosa*) is said to be the most toxic of any snake. Fortunately, sea snakes are not particularly aggressive, and it is rare for swimmers to be bitten. Twenty-two species have been found in the waters of Southeast Asia, and all bar one (*Laticauda colubrina*, which lays its eggs in rock crevices) produce their young live. They grow to a length of 2 m and feed on fish.

Snakes of the viper family (*Viperidae*) grow to a length of 1 m, and the kraits (genus Bungarus) to 2 m. Vipers are easily identifiable by their arrow-shaped heads. The vipers' long fangs, their position at the front of the mouth, and their aggressiveness, makes them more dangerous than other more poisonous species. The Malayan pit viper (*Agkistrodon rhodostoma*) and Pope's pit viper (*Trimeresurus popeiorum*) are both highly irritable. Kraits, though possessing a toxic venom which has been known to kill, are of sleepy temperament and rarely attack unless provoked. The banded krait (*Bungarus fasciatus*), with its black and yellow striped body, is very distinctive.

The 'Siamese' Cat

There were, originally, 23 breeds of cat that came from Thailand. Of these, only one is regarded by cat fanciers as the Siamese Cat – the Korat or Si Sawat. The original 23 breeds are described in the Cat Book Poems, a 14th-century manuscript including paintings and verse now housed in Bangkok's National Library. Of the 23, 17 were regarded as good luck cats, and the remaining six as cats of ill fortune. Today, however, only six of the original 23 breeds remain and, fortunately, all are good luck cats.

Korat (officially, Nakhon Ratchasima) is a large town in Thailand's Northeastern region, and the original name of the Siamese cat is said to have arisen when King Rama V (1868-1910) asked a court official where a particularly beautiful cat came from, to be told 'Korat'. Certainly, Western visitors to this part of the Northeast remarked on the breed's existence at the beginning of the 20th century.

It was not, however, until 1959 that the first confirmed pair of Korats were imported into the US. Today the Korat is more usually called Si Sawat, a reference to the cat's colour (silver-blue). The sawat is a grey-green non-edible fruit; sawat also happens to mean good fortune. Why the Si Sawat is associated with good luck is not clear. It has been said that its colour is symbolic of silver, signifying good fortune. Others have argued that the colour is akin to rain clouds, indicating a bountiful rice crop. Even the colour of the cat's eyes have been likened to the colour of ripening rice. A pair of Si Sawats given to a bride before marriage is said to bring good fortune to the partnership. Other than the Korat's distinctive colour, it is also unique in that its hair does not float off when it is stroked, making the animal particularly suitable for those with a cat allergy.

For further information, contact: Rose Meldrum, President, Korat Cat Fanciers' Association Inc, 6408 Shinnwood Road, Wilmington, NC 28409, USA; or The Cat Fanciers' Association Inc, PO Box 1005, Manasquan NJ 08736-1005, USA.

A rather different, and less dangerous – at least in its current form – reptile is *Siamotyrannus isanensis*, a tyrannosaur beloved of school children (and some grown ups) around the world. On 19 June 1996, Thai and French palaeontologists announced the discovery of a 7 m-long tyrannosaur. This may not be the largest member of the family – 'rex' is twice the size – but it is the oldest, predating the next most senior by 20 million years. It is also Thailand's very own dinosaur (see page 430).

Insects

Insects are not usually at the top of a visitor's agenda to Thailand. But, as with the Kingdom's birds and flora, the country also has a particularly rich insect population due to its position at a crossroads between different, and varied, zoogeographic zones. There are over 1,400 species of butterfly and moth (*Lepidoptera*), including one of the world's largest moths, the giant atlas (*Attacus atlas*) which has a wing span of up to 28 cm. Beetles are even more numerous, although how numerous is not known: one single sq km of the Thung Yai-Huai Kha Khaeng area was found to support 10,000 species alone.

Marine life

Thailand's coastline abuts onto both the Indian Ocean (Andaman Sea) and the South China Sea (Gulf of Thailand), and therefore has marine flora and fauna characteristic of both regions. In the Gulf, 850 species of open-water fish have been identified including tuna, of which Thailand is the world's largest exporter (although most are now caught outside Thailand's waters). In the Andaman Sea, game fish such as blue and black marlin, barracuda, sailfish and various sharks are all present.

Among sea mammals, Thailand's shores provide nesting sites for four species of **sea turtle**: the huge leatherback, green, Ridley's and the hawksbill turtle. The latter is

Fields in the forest – shifting cultivation

Shifting cultivation, also known as slash-and-burn agriculture or swiddening, as well as by a variety of local terms, was one of Thailand's characteristic farming systems and remains important in some areas. It is a low-intensity form of agriculture, in which land is cleared from the forest through burning, cultivated for a few years, and then left to regenerate over 10-30 years. It takes many forms, but an important distinction can be made between shifting field systems, where fields are rotated but the settlement remains permanently sited, and migratory systems, where the shifting cultivators shift both field (swidden) and settlement. The land is usually only rudimentarily cleared, tree stumps being left in the ground, and seeds sown in holes made by punching the soil with a dibble stick.

For many years, shifting cultivators were regarded as 'primitives' who followed an essentially primitive form of agriculture, and their methods were contrasted unfavourably with 'advanced' settled rice farmers. There are still many government officials in Thailand who continue to adhere to this mistaken belief, arguing that shifting cultivators are the principal cause of forest loss and soil erosion. They are, therefore, painted as the villains in the country's environmental crisis, neatly sidestepping the considerably more

detrimental impact that commercial logging has had on Thailand's forest resources.

Shifting cultivators have an intimate knowledge of the land, plants and animals on which they depend. One study of a Dayak tribe, the Kantu' of Kalimantan (Borneo), discovered that households were cultivating an average of 17 rice varieties and 21 other food crops each year, in a highly complex system. Even more remarkably, Harold Conklin's classic 1957 study of the Hanunóo of the Philippines – a study which is a benchmark for such work even today – found that the Hanunóo identified 40 types and subtypes of rocks and minerals, when classifying different soils. The shifting agricultural systems are usually also highly productive in labour terms, allowing far more leisure time than farmers using permanent field systems.

But shifting cultivation contains the seeds of its own extinction. Extensive, and geared to low population densities, it is coming under pressure in a region where land is becoming an increasingly scarce resource, where patterns of life are dictated by an urban-based élite, and where populations are pressing on the means of subsistence. Today, in Thailand, there are few shifting cultivators still practising their traditional techniques.

now very rare, while a fifth species, the loggerhead turtle, has disappeared from Thailand's shores and waters. Other marine mammals include several species of sea snake (see above), the saltwater crocodile (which may now be extinct), three species of dolphin, and the dugong or sea cow.

Coral reefs probably contain a richer profusion of life than any other ecosystem – even exceeding the tropical rainforest in terms of species diversity. Those in Thailand's Andaman Sea are among the finest in the region – and maritime parks like the Surin and Similan islands have been gazetted to help protect these delicate habitats. Although the country's reefs remain under-researched, 210 species of hard coral and 108 coral reef fish have so far been identified in the Andaman Sea. Literally tens of thousands of other marine organisms, including soft corals, crustacea, echinoderms and worms, would have to be added to this list to build up a true picture of the ecosystem's diversity.

But like the rest of Thailand's natural heritage, life under the sea is also threatened. Collin Piprell and Ashley J Boyd vividly recount this story in their book *Thailand's Coral Reefs: Nature under Threat* (see Recommended reading below). Some reefs have been virtually wiped out by human depredations – for example, that off Koh Larn near Pattaya. Fish stocks in the Gulf of Thailand are seriously depleted and the destruction of mangroves along both the eastern and western seaboards has seriously eroded the main breeding grounds for many fish. Untreated effluent and raw sewage are dumped into the Gulf and, because it is an almost enclosed body of water, this tends to become concentrated. Marine biologists have identified some instances of sex-changes in shellfish communities – apparently because of the build-up of toxic compounds.

It has to be acknowledged that although tourism in some areas of Thailand has an interest in maintaining the sanctity of the marine environment, it has also been a major cause of destruction. Anchors, rubbish and sewerage, the thrashing fins of novice divers, and the selfish grabbing hands of collectors of shells, all contribute to the gradual erosion of the habitat that tourists come to experience. Other sources of destruction have less or nothing to do with tourism: the accumulation of toxic chemicals, Thailand's voracious fishermen, cyanide and dynamite fishing, the trade in aquarium fish, and collection and sale of certain species for their use in traditional Chinese medicines. The Kingdom is, for example, the world's largest exporter of seahorses. Around 15 tonnes of the dried creatures are exported each year, mostly to Taiwan and Hong Kong, where their crushed bodies are believed to be an aphrodisiac and a cure for certain respiratory ailments. Like the Kingdom's forests, there are fears that within a decade there might be little left for the discerning diver to enjoy.

Boonsong Lekagul and JA McNeely (1988) *Mammals of Thailand*, Association for the Conservation of Wildlife. For keen ornithologists, Boonsong Lekagul and Edward Cronin's (1974) *Bird guide of Thailand*, Association for the Conservation of Wildlife: Bangkok; a newer publication is Boonsong Lekagul and Philip Round's (1991) *The Birds of Thailand*, Sahakarn Bhaet: Bangkok. Boonsong Lekagul et al's (1977) *Fieldguide to the Butterflies of Thailand*, Association for the Conservation of Wildlife: Bangkok. Available from most large bookshops in Bangkok. Collin Piprell and Ashley J Boyd's (1995) *Thailand's Coral Reefs: Nature under Threat* (Bangkok: White Lotus) is a well-illustrated plea for the conservation of the Kingdom's reefs.

Recommended reading

National parks

In 1961 Khao Yai became Thailand's first national park – although King Ramkhamhaeng of Sukhothai created a royal reserve in the 13th century, and the grounds of Buddhist wats have always provided havens for wildlife. By late 1995 there were 81 parks covering over 41,000 sq km spread throughout the kingdom, encompassing all the principal ecological zones – and more have been gazetted since. Including Thailand's 35 wildlife sanctuaries (which cover another 29,000 sq km), and 48 non-hunting areas, nearly 15% of Thailand's land area is protected in some way. Though impressive on paper, this does not mean that there are some 70,000 sq km of protected forest, grassland, swamp and sea. Settled and shifting agriculturalists live in many parks, illegal logging is widespread (though better controlled today than in the 1980s), and poaching continues to be a problem. Poor pay, lack of manpower and corruption, all contribute to the difficulties of maintaining the integrity of these 'protected' areas. Park rangers, for example, are provided with no uniform or equipment and are paid only ฿70 per day – hardly conditions or a salary on which to build commitment or motivation. Even so, 40 park wardens have been murdered doing their job.

There has been an increase of late in public awareness towards wildlife and the environment. Certainly, there have been some notable successes: the logging ban of 1990, the shelving of the plan to build the Nam Choan dam in the contiguous Huai Kha Khaeng and Tha Thungna Wildlife Sanctuaries (see page 527), and – without being patronizing – a far wider concern for the environment amongst average Thais. But the battle is far from won. Loggers, poachers and tree plantation companies wield enormous financial and political power. In 1990, such was the exasperation of Sueb Makasathien, the highly regarded director of the incomparable Huai Kha Khaeng Wildlife Sanctuary, that he committed suicide. It is generally agreed that Sueb killed himself because he was unable to prevent corrupt officials, loggers and poachers from degrading his park – 2,400 sq km of the finest forest in all Southeast Asia. (Sueb was hoping to get the sanctuary accepted as a World Heritage area by UNESCO.) Tourism has also left its mark on the parks. Khao

National parks

Yai is now so popular as a weekend trip from Bangkok that its capacity has been exceeded, while coastal and island marine parks suffer from refuse-littered beaches and campsites.

In 1993 the Tourist Authority of Thailand (TAT) suggested that they take over control of some of Thailand's national parks from the National Parks Division of the Royal Forestry Department. Environmentalists, perhaps unsurprisingly, were outraged. Having promoted, in their eyes, the ruination of some of the Kingdom's finest coastal areas, here was the TAT intending to do the same to the few areas of wilderness left. But to be fair, the TAT also had a case: many of the parks are woefully poorly protected, and the money from tourism could have helped fund a better parks service. Koh Samet and Koh Phi Phi, both national parks, are – illegally – covered with bungalow developments. Khao Yai, Thailand's first park, has hotels and golf courses within its area. The Thaplan National Park in the Northeast is extensively logged by army-backed interests. The national parks, as they stand, are being ruined by poor management; the question is whether the TAT might provide better management.

National park facilities

Most national parks have a park office with wardens (often not English-speaking), bungalows and dormitories for hire, camping grounds and trails (not always well-marked). Bungalows in the more popular parks – Khao Yai, Phu Kradung, Doi Inthanon, Nam Nao, Doi Suthep and Erawan – are often booked-up, so advance booking is recommended. For reservations contact: Reservation Office, National Parks Division, Royal Forestry Department, Phanhonyothin Road, Bangkhen, Bangkok, T02-5794842/5790529/5614292; or telephone park offices given in the relevant sections of this guide.

Recommended reading

Gray, D, Piprell, C and Graham, M (1994) *National Parks of Thailand*, Industrial Finance Corporation of Thailand: Bangkok.

Background

Footnotes

11

Footnotes

Words & phrases

Thai is a tonal language with five tones: mid tone (no mark), high tone (´), low tone (`), falling tone (^), and rising tone (ˇ). Tones are used to distinguish between words which are otherwise the same. For example, 'see' pronounced with a low tone means 'four'; with a rising tone, it means 'colour'. Thai is not written in Roman script but using an alphabet derived from Khmer. The Romanization given below is only intended to help in pronouncing Thai words. There is no accepted method of Romanization and some of the sounds in Thai cannot be accurately reproduced using Roman script.

Polite particles

At the end of sentences males use the polite particle 'krúp', and females, 'kâ' or 'ká'.

Learning Thai

The list of words and phrases below is only very rudimentary. For anyone serious about learning Thai it is best to buy a dedicated Thai language text book or to enrol on a Thai course. Recommended among the various 'teach yourself Thai' books is: Somsong Buasai and David Smyth's (1990) *Thai in a Week*, Hodder & Stoughton: London. A useful mini-dictionary is the Hugo *Thai phrase book* (1990). For those interested in learning to read and write Thai, the best 'teach yourself' course is the *Linguaphone* course.

General words & phrases

Yes/no
  chái/mâi chái, or: *krúp(kâ)/mâi krúp(kâ)*
Thank you/no thank you
  kòrp-kOOn/mâi ao kòrp-kOOn
Hello, good morning, goodbye
  sa-wùt dee krúp(kâ)
What is your name? My name is...
  Koon chêu a-rai krúp (kâ)? Pǒm chêu...
Excuse me, sorry!
  kǒr-tôht krúp(kâ)
Can/do you speak English?
  KOON pôot pah-sǎh ung-grìt
a little, a bit *nít-nòy*
Where's the... *yòo têe-nǎi...*
How much is... *tâo-rài...*
Pardon? *a-rai ná?*
I don't understand
  pǒm (chún) mâi kao jái
How are you? Not very well
  sa-bai dee mái? Mâi sa-bai

At hotels

What is the charge each night?
  kâh hôrng wun la tâo-rài?
Is the room air conditioned?
  hôrng dtìt air rěu bplào?
Can I see the room first please?
  kǒr doo hôrng gòrn dâi mái?
Does the room have hot water?
  hôrng mii náhm rórn mái?
Does the room have a bathroom?
  hôrng mii hôrng náhm mái?
Can I have the bill please?
  kǒr bin nòy dâi mái?

Travelling

Where is the train station?
  sa-tǎhn-nee rót fai yòo têe-nǎi?
Where is the bus station?
  sa-tǎhn-nee rót may yòo têe-nǎi?
How much to go to...?
  bpai...tâo-rài?
That's expensive
  pairng bpai nòy
What time does the bus/train leave for...?
  rót may/rót fai bpai...òrk gèe mohng?
Is it far? *glai mái?*
Turn left/turn right
  lée-o sái / lée-o kwǎh
Go straight on
  ler-ee bpai èek
It's straight ahead
  yòo dtrong nâh

At restaurants

Can I see a menu?
  kǒr doo may-noo nòy?
Can I have...?/ I would like...? *Kǒr...*
Is it very (hot) spicy?
  pèt mâhk mái?
I am hungry *pǒm (chún) hěw*
Breakfast *ah-hǎhn cháo*
Lunch *ah-hǎhn glanhg wun*

Time & days

in the morning	*dtorn cháo*
in the afternoon	*dtorn bài*
in the evening	*dtorn yen*
today	*wun née*
tomorrow	*prÔOng née*
yesterday	*mêu-a wahn née*
Monday	*wun jun*
Tuesday	*wun ung-kahn*
Wednesday	*wun pÓOt*
Thursday	*wun pá-réu-hùt*
Friday	*wun sÒOk*
Saturday	*wun săo*
Sunday	*wun ah-tít*

Numbers

1	*nèung*
2	*sŏrng*
3	*săhm*
4	*sèe*
5	*hâa*
6	*hòk*
7	*jèt*
8	*bpàirt*
9	*gâo*
10	*sìp*
11	*sìp-et*
12	*sìp-sŏrng...etc*
20	*yêe-sìp*
21	*yêe-sìp-et*
22	*yêe-sìp-sŏrng...etc*
30	*săhm-sìp*
100	*(nèung) róy*
101	*(nèung) róy-nèung*
150	*(nèung) róy-hâh-sìp*
200	*sŏrng róy...etc*
1,000	*(nèung) pun*
10,000	*mèun*
100,000	*săirn*
1,000,000	*láhn*

Basic vocabulary

airport	*sa-năhm bin*
bank	*ta-nah-kahn*
bathroom	*hôrng náhm*
beach	*hàht*
beautiful	*sŏo-ay*
big	*yài*
boat	*reu-a*
bus	*rót may*
bus station	*sa-tăh-nee rót may*
buy	*séu*
chemist	*ráhn kai yah*
clean	*sa-àht*
closed	*bpìt*
cold	*yen*
day	*wun*
delicious	*a-ròy*
dirty	*sòk-ga-bpròk*
doctor	*mor*
eat	*gin (kâo)*
embassy	*sa-tăhn tôot*
excellent	*yêe-um*
expensive	*pairng*
food	*ah-hăhn*
fruit	*pŏn-la-mái*
hospital	*rohng pa-yah-bahn*
hot (temp)	*rórn*
hot (spicy)	*pèt*
hotel	*rôhng rairm*
island	*gòr*
market	*dta-làht*
medicine	*yah*
open	*bpèrt*
police	*dtum-ròo-ut*
police station	*sa-tăh-nee*
	dtum-ròo-ut
post office	*bprai-sa-nee*
restaurant	*ráhn ah-hăhn*
road	*thanon*
room	*hôrng*
shop	*ráhn*
sick (ill)	*mâi sa-bai*
silk	*măi*
small	*lék*
stop	*yÒOt*
taxi	*táirk-sêe*
that	*nún*
this	*née*
ticket	*dtŏo-a*
toilet	*hôrng náhm*
town	*meu-ung*
train station	*sa-tăh-nee rót fai*
very	*mâhk*
water	*náhm*
what	*a-rai*

Glossary

A

Amitabha
the Buddha of the Past (see Avalokitsvara)

Amphoe
district; administrative division below the province (see page 818)

Amulet
protective medallion (see page 101)

Ao
bay

Arhat
a person who has perfected himself; images of former monks are sometimes carved into arhat

Avadana
Buddhist narrative, telling of the deeds of saintly souls

Avalokitsvara
also known as Amitabha and Lokeshvara, the name literally means 'World Lord'; he is the compassionate male Bodhisattva, the saviour of Mahayana Buddhism, and represents the central force of creation in the universe; usually portrayed with a lotus and water flask

B

Bai sema
boundary stones marking consecrated ground around a Buddhist bot (see page 808)

Ban
village; shortened from muban

Baray
man-made lake or reservoir

Batik
a form of resist dyeing

Bhikku
Buddhist monk

Bodhi
the tree under which the Buddha achieved enlightenment (*Ficus religiosa*)

Bodhisattva
a future Buddha. In Mahayana Buddhism, someone who has attained enlightenment, but who postpones nirvana to help others reach it.

Bot
Buddhist ordination hall, of rectangular plan, identifiable by the boundary stones placed around it; an abbreviation of ubosoth (see page 808)

Brahma
the Creator, one of the gods of the Hindu trinity, usually represented with four faces, and often mounted on a hamsa

Brahmin
a Hindu priest

Bun
to make merit

C

Caryatid
elephants, often used as buttressing decorations

Celadon
pottery ware with blue/green to grey glaze (see page 158)

Chakri
the current royal dynasty in Thailand. They have reigned since 1782

Champa
rival empire of the Khmers, of Hindu culture, based in present-day Vietnam

Changwat
province (see page 818)

Chao
title for Lao and Thai kings

Chat
honorific umbrella or royal multi-tiered parasol

Chedi
from the Sanskrit *cetiya* (Pali, *caitya*), meaning memorial. Usually a religious monument (often bell-shaped), containing relics of the Buddha or other

holy remains. Used interchangeably with stupa (see page 804)

Chofa
'sky tassel' on the roof of wat buildings

CPT
Communist Party of Thailand

D

Deva
a Hindu-derived male god

Devata
a Hindu-derived goddess

Dharma
the Buddhist law

Dipterocarp
family of trees (*Dipterocarpaceae*), characteristic of Southeast Asia's forests

Dvarapala
guardian figure, usually placed at the entrance to a temple

F

Farang
Westerner

G

Ganesh
elephant-headed son of Siva

Garuda
mythical divine bird, with predatory beak and claws, and human body; the king of birds, enemy of naga and mount of Vishnu

Gautama
the historic Buddha

Geomancy
the art of divination by lines and figures

Gopura
crowned or covered gate, entrance to a religious area

H

Hamsa
sacred goose, Brahma's mount; in Buddhism it represents the flight of the doctrine

Hang yaaw
long-tailed boat, used on canals

Harmika
box-like part of a Burmese stupa that often acts as a reliquary casket

Hat
beach

Hinayana
'Lesser Vehicle', major Buddhist sect in Southeast Asia, usually termed Theravada Buddhism (see page 793)

Hong
swan

Hor kong
a pavilion built on stilts, where the monastery drum is kept

Hor takang
bell tower (see page 808)

Hor tray/trai
library where manuscripts are stored in a Thai monastery (see page 808)

Hti
'umbrella' surmounting Burmese temples, often encrusted with jewels

I

Ikat
tie-dyeing method of patterning cloth (see page 371)

Indra
the Vedic god of the heavens, weather and war; usually mounted on a three-headed elephant

J

Jataka(s)
the birth stories of the Buddha; they normally number 547, although an additional three were added in Burma for reasons of symmetry in mural painting and sculpture; the last 10 are the most important

K

Kala (makara)
literally 'death' or 'black'; a demon ordered to consume itself; often sculpted with grinning face and bulging eyes over entranceway to act as a door guardian; also known as kirtamukha

Kathin/krathin
a one-month period during the eighth lunar month, when lay people present new robes and other gifts to monks

Ketumula
flame-like motif above the Buddha head

Khao
mountain
Khlong
canal
Khruang
amulet (see page 101)
Kinaree
half-human, half-bird, usually depicted as a heavenly musician
Kirtamukha
see kala
Koh
island
Koutdi
see kuti
Krating
wild bull, most commonly seen on bottles of *Red Bull* (Krating Daeng) stimulant drink
Krishna
incarnation of Vishnu
Kuti
living quarters of Buddhist monks in a monastery complex

Laem
cape (as in bay)
Lakhon
traditional Thai classical music
Lak muang
city pillar
Laterite
bright red tropical soil/stone, commonly used in construction of Khmer monuments
Linga
phallic symbol and one of the forms of Siva. Embedded in a pedestal, shaped to allow drainage of lustral water poured over it; the linga typically has a succession of cross sections: from square at the base, through octagonal, to round. These symbolize, in order, the trinity of Brahma, Vishnu and Siva
Lintel
a load-bearing stone spanning a doorway; often heavily carved
Lokeshvara
see Avalokitsvara

Mahabharata
a Hindu epic text, written about 2,000 years ago
Mahayana
'Greater Vehicle', major Buddhist sect (see page 793)
Maitreya
the future Buddha
Makara
a mythological aquatic reptile, somewhat like a crocodile and sometimes with an elephant's trunk; often found along with the kala framing doorways
Mandala
a focus for meditation; a representation of the cosmos
Mara
personification of evil and tempter of the Buddha
Matmii
Northeastern Thai cotton ikat (see page 433)
Meru
sacred or cosmic mountain at the centre of the world in Hindu-Buddhist cosmology; home of the gods (see page 212)
Mon
race and kingdom of southern Burma and central Thailand, from 7th-11th century
Mondop
from the sanskrit, *mandapa*. A cube-shaped building, often topped with a cone-like structure, used to contain an object of worship like a footprint of the Buddha
Muang
'town' in Thai, but also sometimes 'municipality' or 'district'
Muban
village, usually shortened to ban
Mudra
symbolic gesture of the hands of the Buddha (see page 810)

N

Naga
benevolent mythical water serpent, enemy of Garuda

Footnotes

Naga makara
fusion of naga and makara
Nalagiri
the elephant let loose to attack the Buddha, who calmed him
Namtok
waterfall
Nandi/nandin
bull, mount of Siva
Nang thalung
shadow play/puppets (see page 817)
Nikhom
resettlement village
Nirvana
release from the cycle of suffering in Buddhist belief; 'enlightenment'

Pa kama
Lao men's all-purpose cloth, usually woven with checked pattern
paddy/padi
unhulled rice
Pali
the sacred language of Theravada Buddhism
Parvati
consort of Siva
Pha sin
tubular piece of cloth, similar to sarong
Phi
spirit
Phnom/phanom
Khmer for hill/mountain
Phra sinh
see pha sin
Pradaksina
pilgrims' clockwise circumambulation of holy structure
Prah
sacred
Prang
form of stupa built in Khmer style, shaped like a corncob (see page 803)
Prasada
stepped pyramid (see prasat)
Prasat
residence of a king or of the gods (sanctuary tower), from the Indian prasada (see page 805)

Quan Am
Chinese goddess (Kuan-yin) of mercy (see page 423)

Rai
unit of measurement, 1 ha = 6.25 rai
Rama
incarnation of Vishnu, hero of the Indian epic, the *Ramayana*
Ramakien
Thai version of the *Ramayana* (see page 98)
Ramayana
Hindu romantic epic, known as *Ramakien* in Thailand (see page 98)

Saamlor
three-wheeled bicycle taxi
Sakyamuni
the historic Buddha
Sal
the Indian sal tree (*Shorea robusta*), under which the historic Buddha was born
Sala
open pavilion
Sangha
the Buddhist order of monks
Sawankhalok
type of ceramic (see page 223)
Singha
mythical guardian lion
Siva
the Destroyer, one of the three gods of the Hindu trinity; the sacred linga was worshipped as a symbol of Siva
Sofa
see dok sofa
Songthaew
'two rows': pick-up truck with benches along either side
Sravasti
the miracle at Sravasti, when the Buddha subdues the heretics in front of a mango tree
Stele
inscribed stone panel

Stucco

plaster, often heavily moulded

Stupa

chedi (see page 804)

Talaat

market

Tambon

a commune of villages

Tam bun

see bun

Tavatimsa

heaven of the 33 gods, at the summit of Mount Meru

Tazaungs

small pavilions, found within Burmese temple complexes

Tham

cave

Thanon

street in Thai

That

shrine housing Buddhist relics, a spire or dome-like edifice commemorating the Buddha's life or the funerary temple for royalty; peculiar to parts of Northeastern Thailand, as well as Laos

Thein

Burmese ordination hall (see page 808 for Thai equivalent)

Theravada

'Way of the Elders'; major Buddhist sect, also known as Hinayana Buddhism ('Lesser Vehicle') (see page 793)

Traiphum

the three worlds of Buddhist cosmology – heaven, hell and earth

Trimurti

the Hindu trinity of gods: Brahma, the Creator, Vishnu the Preserver and Siva the Destroyer

Tripitaka

Theravada Buddhism's Pali canon

Tuk-tuk

motorized three-wheeled taxi

Tukata

doll

Ubosoth

see bot

Urna

the dot or curl on the Buddha's forehead, one of the distinctive physical marks of the Enlightened One

Usnisa

the Buddha's top knot or 'wisdom bump', one of the physical marks of the Enlightened One

Vahana

'vehicle', a mythical beast, upon which a deva or god rides

Viharn

from Sanskrit *vihara*, an assembly hall in a Buddhist monastery; may contain Buddha images and is similar in style to the bot (see page 808)

Vishnu

the Protector, one of the gods of the Hindu trinity, generally with four arms holding a disc, conch shell, ball and club

Wai

Thai greeting, with hands held together at chin height as if in prayer

Wat

Buddhist 'monastery', with religious and other buildings (see page 808)

Zayat

prayer pavilion found in Burmese temple complexes

Zedi

Burmese term for a stupa

Food glossary

a-haan food
ba-mii egg noodles
bia beer
chaa tea
check bin/bill cheque
chorn spoon
gaeng curry
gaeng chud soup
jaan plate
kaafae (ron) coffee (hot)
kaew glass
kai chicken
kap klaem snacks to be eaten when drinking
khaaw/khao rice
khaaw niaw sticky rice
khaaw tom rice gruel
khai egg
khai dao fried egg
khanom sweet, dessert or cake
khanom cake cake
khanom pang bread
khanom pang ping toast
khing ginger
khuan scramble
khuat bottle
kin to eat
kleua salt
krueng kieng side dishes
kung crab
kwaytio noodle soup, white noodles
lao liquor
man root vegetable
man farang potatoes
manaaw lemon
mekong Thai whisky

mit knife
muu pork
nam chaa tea
nam kheng ice
nam kuat bottled water
nam manaaw soda lime soda
nam plaa fish sauce
nam plaa prik fish sauce with chilli
nam plaaw plain water
nam som orange juice
nam taan sugar
nam tom boiled water
nom milk
nua meat (usually beef)
phak vegetables
phat to stir fry
phet hot (chilli)
phon lamai fruit
pla fish
priaw sour
priaw waan sweet and sour
prik hot chilli
raan a-haan restaurant
ratnaa in gravy
rawn hot (temperature)
sa-te satay
sorm fork
talaat market
thao mai luai morning glory
thua nut/bean
tom to boil
tort to deep fry
waan sweet
yam salad
yen cold

Fares and timetables

Average distances and flying time on domestic routes

ROUTE	DISTANCE (km)	FLYING TIME (outbound)
From Bangkok to:		
Chiang Mai	567	1 hr 5 mins
Chiang Rai	667	1 hr 25 mins
Hat Yai	776	1 hr 25 mins
Khon Kaen	370	55 mins
Lampang	500	1 hr
Nakhon Ratchasima	187	40 mins
Nakhon Si Thammarat	611	1 hr 55 mins
Phitsanulok (ATR)	324	1 hr 5 mins
Phrae	470	1 hr 20 mins
Phuket	693	1 hr 15 mins
Trang	720	2 hrs 5 mins
Sakon Nakhon	522	1 hr 35 mins
Surat Thani	555	1 hr 5 mins
Ubon Ratchathani	482	1 hr 5 mins
Udon Thani	453	1 hr
From Chiang Mai to:		
Chiang Rai	154	40 mins
Mae Hong Son (ATR)	119	30 mins/40 mins
Mae Sot	239	50 mins
Nan	191	45 mins
Phuket	1,187	2 hrs 5 mins
From Nakhon Si Thammarat to:		
Surat Thani	117	35 mins
From Nan to:		
Phrae	89	30 mins
From Phitsanulok to:		
Lampang	185	35 mins
Nan	231	55 mins
Mae Sot	188	45 mins
From Phuket to:		
Hat Yai (ATR)	265	44 mins/55 mins
Surat Thani	146	35 mins
Trang	160	40 mins
Narathiwat	419	1 hr 15 mins
From Surat Thani to:		
Nakhon Si Thammarat	117	35 mins

Footnotes

Sample domestic air fares

ROUTE	FARE (baht)*

Thai Airways

Bangkok to:

Buriram	1,030
Chiang Mai	1,870
Hat Yai	2,585
Khon Kaen	1,200
Krabi	2,120
Lampang	1,650
Mae Sot	1,595
Nakhon Phanom	1,820
Nakhon Ratchasima	630
Nakhon Si Thammarat	2,005
Nan	1,735
Narathiwat	2,920
Phetchabun	1,005
Phitsanulok	1,080
Phrae	1,500
Phuket	2,270
Sakon Nakhon	1,735
Surat Thani	2,025
Trang	2,275
Ubon Ratchathani	1,595
Ubon Thani	1,485
Chiang Mai to:	
Chiang Rai	475
Mae Hong Son	390
Mae Sot	735
Nan	575
Phuket	3,920

ROUTE	FARE (baht)*

Bangkok Airways

Bangkok to:

Samui	3,150
Ranong	2,280
Sukhothai	1,790
Chiang Mai to:	
Sukhothai	830
Koh Samui to:	
Krabi	1,770
Pattaya (U-tapao)	2,155
Phuket	1,720

Early 2001 fares quoted, one-way economy (return fares are double).
See www.thaiair.com for latest fare information and seat availability for Thai Airways,
and www.bangkokair.com for Bangkok Airways.

State railways of Thailand: sample routes and fares

ROUTE	TIME	DISTANCE (km)	FARE (Baht)* 1st Class	2nd Class	3rd Class
Bangkok north to:					
Don Muang	45 mins	22	21	11	5
Ayutthaya	1½ hrs	71	66	35	15
Lopburi	2½ hrs	133	123	64	28
Nakhon Sawan	4 hrs	246	218	110	48
Phitsanulok	5-6 hrs	389	324	159	69
Uttaradit	8 hrs	485	394	190	82
Den Chai	8 hrs	534	431	207	90
Nakhon Lampang	11¾ hrs	642	512	244	106
Lamphun	8½ hrs	729	575	273	118
Chiang Mai	11-13 hrs	751	593	281	121
Bangkok northeast to:					
Nakhon Ratchasima	5 hrs	264	230	115	50
Surin	8 hrs	420	346	169	73
Si Saket	9½ hrs	515	416	201	87
Ubon Ratchathani	10 hrs	575	460	221	95
Bua Yai Jn	5 hrs	346	294	145	63
Ban Phai	8 hrs	408	338	165	71
Khon Kaen	8 hrs	450	368	179	77
Udon Thani	9½ hrs	569	457	219	95
Nong Khai	11 hrs	624	497	238	103
Bangkok east to:					
Chachoeng Sao Jn	1½ hrs	61	57	30	13
Prachin Buri	3 hrs	122	115	59	26
Kabin Buri	3½ hrs	161	149	76	33
Aranyaprathet	4½ hrs	255	222	111	48
Chonburi	2¾ hrs	108	102	53	23
Pattaya	3¾ hrs	155	140	72	31
Bangkok south to:					
Nakhon Pathom	1½ hrs	64	60	31	14
Kanchanaburi	2½ hrs	133	123	64	28
Rachaburi	2 hrs	117	110	57	25
Phetburi	3 hrs	167	153	78	34
Hua Hin	4 hrs 10 mins	229	202	102	44
Prachuap Khiri Khan	5 hrs	318	272	135	58
Chumphon	7¾ hrs	485	394	190	82
Surat Thani	11 hrs	651	519	248	107
Thung Song Jn	12 hrs	773	608	288	124
Trang	15 hrs	845	660	311	135
Nakhon Si Thammarat	15 hrs	832	652	308	133
Phatthalung	15 hrs	862	675	318	137
Hat Yai	16 hrs	945	734	345	149

Footnotes

ROUTE	TIME	DISTANCE (km)	FARE (Baht)*		
			1st Class	2nd Class	3rd Class
Bangkok south to:					
Pattani	-	1,025	793	372	161
Yala	-	1,055	815	382	165
Tanyong Mat	-	1,116	863	404	174
Sungai Kolok	-	1,159	893	417	180
Padang Besar	-	990	767	360	156

* Early 2001 fares quoted. Supplementary charges which apply for express trains, rapid trains, special express trains, a/c services and sleepers are not included. See www.srt.motc.go.th for latest information.

Buses in Thailand: sample routes and fares

ROUTE	DISTANCE (km)	HOURS	FARE (Baht)		
			VIP	A/C	Non-A/C
Bangkok north to:					
Ayutthaya	75	1½	-	45	32
Lopburi	155	-	-	67	48
Kampaeng Phet	358	-	-	147	105
Phitsanulok	368	5½	230	163	108
Mae Sot	423	-	-	272	151
Sukhothai	440	7	-	191	160
Lampang	610	9	490	370	176
Chiang Mai	713	9¾	570	369	207
Chiang Rai	849	12	-	506	241
Chiang Khong	875	12¾	525	371	250
Chiang Saen	909	-	730	469	261
Mae Hong Son	928	12½	-	509	283
Nan	677	10½	445	319	214
Bangkok northeast to:					
Korat	256	4-5	-	139	77
Chaiyaphum	330	-	-	176	98
Surin	451	6¾	-	195	108
Loei	558	-	-	227	162
Udon Thani	561	8¾	-	241	162
Ubon Ratchathani	679	10	400	290	195
Khon Kaen	444	7	416	360	129
Nong Khai	614	9	492	372	177
Nakhon Phanom	735	-	585	376	209
Bangkok south to:					
Nakhon Pathom	56	1	-	28	15
Phetburi	160	2	-	-	51
Hua Hin	201	3½	-	92	61
Chumphon	500	7	268	190	136
Surat Thani	668	11	350	285	158
Nakhon Si thammarat	800	12	640	410	230
Phangnga	879	15	625	401	224
Phuket	891	14	570	378	254
Krabi	867	14	655	421	234
Trang	862	14	685	439	246
Hat Yai	954	15	625	428	289
Songkhla	1,004	16	500	425	286
Yala	1,153	16	865	555	310
Sungai Golok	1,266	18	-	533	282

ROUTE	DISTANCE (km)	HOURS	VIP	FARE (Baht) A/C	Non-A/C
Bangkok east to:					
Chonburi	80	-	-	47	26
Pattaya	136	-	-	66	37
Ban Phe	196	-	-	90	50
Chantaburi	239	-	-	129	92
Trat	317	-	-	158	113
Chiang Mai to:					
Bangkok	720	10	-	369	287
Nan	348	6	-	-	160
Phrae	190	3	-	180	140
Phayao	160	3	-	160	83
Mae Sai	337	6	-	194	151
Chiang Khong	337	6	-	194	151
Mae Sot	393	6	-	207	-
Phitsanulok (old route)	431	6	-	227	176
Phitsanulok (new route)	389	6	-	-	114
Sukhothai	373	5	-	196	153
Khon Kaen	774	12	-	414	322
Chiang Rai	194	3	-	119	92
Mae Hong Son (old route)	355	8	-	239	-
Mae Hong Son (new route)	250	7	-	-	93
Pai	137	4	-	-	51
Udon Thani	712	12	-	480	287

NB

1. *Times are for travelling by a/c bus; non-a/c buses are slower.*

2. *Early 2000 fares quoted; note that fares have increased and they also vary between services (for example, there is more than one type of a/c service). These should only be taken as indicative.*

3. *VIP coaches have fewer seats (just eight rows) and seats that can recline further; VIP coaches are not available on all routes, and most travel on overnight journeys only.*

Index

Note: Colour map references are given in italics. Thus 'Ayutthaya *M2C1*' will be found on colour map 2, grid C1

Shorts

Footnotes

Maps

Will you help us?

We try as hard as we can to make each Footprint Handbook as up-to-date and accurate as possible but, of course, things always change. Many people email or write to us – with corrections, new information, or simply comments. If you want to let us know about your experiences and adventures – be they good, bad or ugly – then don't delay; we're dying to hear from you. And please try to include all the relevant details and juicy bits. Your help will be greatly appreciated, especially by other travellers. In return we will send you details about our special guidebook offer.

email Footprint at:
thai3_online@footprintbooks.com

or write to:

Elizabeth Taylor
Footprint Handbooks
6 Riverside Court
Lower Bristol Road
Bath
BA2 3DZ
UK

Sales & distribution

Footprint Handbooks
6 Riverside Court
Lower Bristol Road
Bath BA2 3DZ England
T 01225 469141
F 01225 469461
discover
@footprintbooks.com

Australia
Peribo Pty
58 Beaumont Road
Mt Kuring-Gai
NSW 2080
T 02 9457 0011
F 02 9457 0022

Austria
Freytag-Berndt Artaria
Kohlmarkt 9
A-1010 Wien
T 01533 2094
F 01533 8685

Freytag-Berndt
Sporgasse 29
A-8010 Graz
T 0316 818230
F 3016 818230-30

Belgium
Craenen BVBA
Mechelsesteenweg 633
B-3020 Herent
T 016 23 90 90
F 016 23 97 11

Waterstones
The English Bookshop
Blvd Adolphe Max 71-75
B-1000 Brussels
T 02 219 5034

Canada
Ulysses Travel Publications
4176 rue Saint-Denis
Montréal
Québec H2W 2M5
T 514 843 9882
F 514 843 9448

Europe
Bill Bailey
16 Devon Square
Newton Abbott
Devon TQ12 2HR. UK
T 01626 331079
F 01626 331080

Denmark
Nordisk Korthandel
Studiestraede 26-30 B
DK-1455 Copenhagen K
T 3338 2638
F 3338 2648

Scanvik Books
Esplanaden 8B
DK-1263 Copenhagen K
T 3312 7766
F 3391 2882

Finland
Akateeminen Kirjakauppa
Keskuskatu 1
FIN-00100 Helsinki
T 09 121 4151
F 09 121 4441

Suomalainen Kirjakauppa
Koivuvaarankuja 2
01640 Vantaa 64
F 09 852751

France
FNAC – major branches

L'Astrolabe
46 rue de Provence
F-75009 Paris 9e
T 01 42 85 42 95
F 01 45 75 92 51

VILO Diffusion
25 rue Ginoux
F-75015 Paris
T 01 45 77 08 05
F 01 45 79 97 15

Germany
GeoCenter ILH
Schockenriedstrasse 44
D-70565 Stuttgart
T 0711 781 94610
F 0711 781 94654

Brettschneider
Feldkirchnerstrasse 2
D-85551 Heimstetten
T 089 990 20330
F 089 990 20331

Geobuch
Rosental 6
D-80331 München
T 089 265030
F 089 263713

Gleumes
Hohenstaufenring 47-51
D-50674 Köln
T 0221 215650

Globetrotter Ausrustungen
Wiesendamm 1
D-22305 Hamburg
T040 679 66190
F 040 679 66183

Dr Götze
Bleichenbrücke 9
D-2000 Hamburg 1
T 040 3031 1009-0

Hugendubel Buchhandlung
Nymphenburgerstrasse 25
D-80335 München
T 089 238 9412
F 089 550 1853

Kiepert Buchhandlung
Hardenbergstrasse 4-5
D-10623 Berlin 12
T 030 311 880
F 030 311 88120

Greece
GC Eleftheroudakis
17 Panepistemiou
Athens 105 64
T 01 331 4180-83
F 01 323 9821

India
India Book Distributors
1007/1008 Arcadia
195 Nariman Point
Mumbai 400 021
T 91 22 282 5220
F 91 22 287 2531

Israel
Eco Trips
8 Tverya Street
Tel Aviv 63144
T 03 528 4113
F 03 528 8269

For a fuller list, see www.footprintbooks.com

Italy
Librimport
Via Biondelli 9
I-20141 Milano
T 02 8950 1422
F 02 8950 2811

Libreria del Viaggiatore
Via dell Pelegrino 78
I-00186 Roma
T/F 06 688 01048

Netherlands
Nilsson & Lamm bv
Postbus 195
Pampuslaan 212
N-1380 AD Weesp
T 0294 494949
F 0294 494455

Waterstones
Kalverstraat 152
1012 XE Amsterdam
T 020 638 3821

New Zealand
Auckland Map Centre
Dymocks

Norway
Schibsteds Forlag A/S
Akersgata 32 - 5th Floor
Postboks 1178 Sentrum
N-0107 Oslo
T 22 86 30 00
F 22 42 54 92

Tanum
Karl Johansgate 37-41
PO Box 1177 Sentrum
N-0107 Oslo 1
T 22 41 11 00
F 22 33 32 75

Olaf Norlis
Universitetsgt 24
N-1062 Oslo
T 22 00 43 00

Pakistan
Pak-American Commercial
Hamid Chambers
Zaib-un Nisa Street
Saddar, PO Box 7359
Karachi
T 21 566 0418
F 21 568 3611

South Africa
Faradawn CC
PO Box 1903
Saxonwold 2132
T 011 885 1787
F 011 885 1829

South America
Humphrys Roberts
Associates
Caixa Postal 801-0
Ag. Jardim da Gloria
06700-970 Cotia SP
Brazil
T 011 492 4496
F 011 492 6896

Southeast Asia
APA Publications
38 Joo Koon Road
Singapore 628990
T 865 1600
F 861 6438

In Hong Kong, Malaysia,
Singapore and Thailand:
MPH, Kinokuniya, Times

Spain
Altaïr
C/Balmes 69
08007 Barcelona
T 933 233062
F 934 512559

Altaïr
Gaztambide 31
28015 Madrid
T 0915 435300
F 0915 443498

Libros de Viaje
C/Serrano no 41
28001 Madrid
T 01 91 577 9899
F 01 91 577 5756

Il Corte Inglés – major
branches

Sweden
Hedengrens Bokhandel
PO Box 5509
S-11485 Stockholm
T 08 611 5132

Kart Centrum
Vasagatan 16
S-11120 Stockholm
T 08 411 1697

Kartforlaget
Skolgangen 10
S-80183 Gavle
T 026 633000
F 026 124204

Lantmateriet Kartbutiken
Kungsgatan 74
S-11122 Stockholm
T 08 202 303
F 08 202 711

Switzerland
Office du Livre OLF
ZI3, Corminboeuf
CH-1701 Fribourg
T 026 467 5111
F 026 467 5666

Schweizer Buchzentrum
Postfach
CH-4601 Olten
T 062 209 2525
F 062 209 2627

Travel Bookshop
Rindermarkt 20
Postfach 216
CH-8001 Zürich
T 01 252 3883
F 01 252 3832

Tanzania
A Novel Idea
The Slipway
PO Box 76513
Dar es Salaam
T/F 051 601088

USA
Publishers Group West
1700 Fourth Street
Berkeley
CA 94710
T 510 528 1444
F 510 528 9555

Barnes & Noble, Borders,
specialist travel bookstores

Footnotes

Advertisers

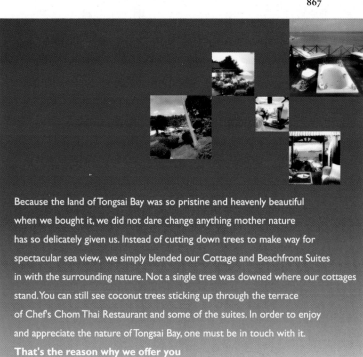

Because the land of Tongsai Bay was so pristine and heavenly beautiful when we bought it, we did not dare change anything mother nature has so delicately given us. Instead of cutting down trees to make way for spectacular sea view, we simply blended our Cottage and Beachfront Suites in with the surrounding nature. Not a single tree was downed where our cottages stand. You can still see coconut trees sticking up through the terrace of Chef's Chom Thai Restaurant and some of the suites. In order to enjoy and appreciate the nature of Tongsai Bay, one must be in touch with it. **That's the reason why we offer you**

Great Outdoor Living

The Tongsai Bay
Ko Samui Thailand

84 Moo5, Bo Phut, Ko Samui,
Suratthani, Thailand.
Tel: 077 425015-28,
Fax: 077 425462.
Bangkok office
Tel: 02 254 0056-63
Fax: 02 254 0054-55
www.tongsaibay.co.th
Email: info@tongsaibay.co.th

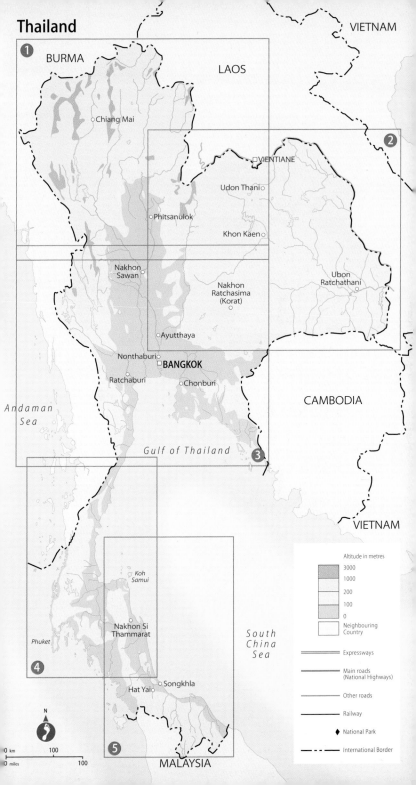

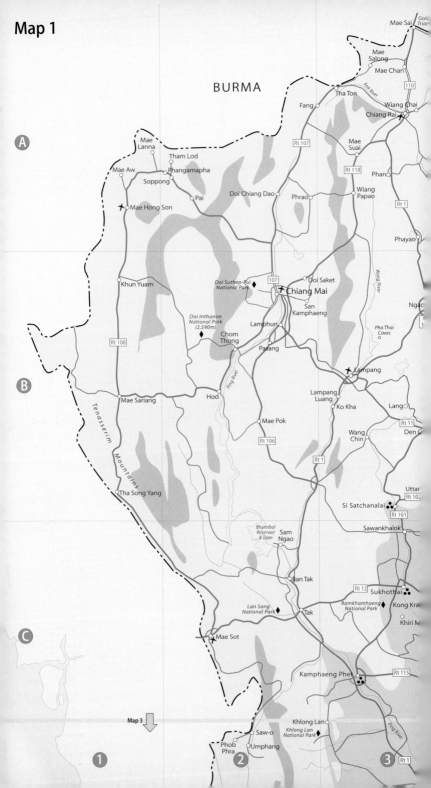

LAOS

Chiang
Khong

Mekong River

ng Kham

Tha Wang Pha

Ban Nong Bua Nan

Nan River

Rt 101

Men

Sirikit
Reservoir

Mekong River

Pak
Chom

Sang
Khom   **VIENTIANE**

Si Chiangmai   Friendship
Bridge

Chiang Khan   Tha Bo

Phu Phra Bat   Nong
Historical Park   Khai

Ban Phu

Rt 211   Rt 2

Loei   Ngoi

Rt 2020   Udon Thani

Rt 210

Nong Bua   Erawan Cave
Lamphu

Rt 11

Rt 203

Phu Kradung
National Park

Phu Hin
Rongkla National Park   Rt 201

Yaeng   Ubon Rat
Reservoir

Phitsanulok   Thung Salaeng
Luang NP   Rt 12   Lom Sak

Phu Kradung

Phra Cave

Phetchabun Hills

Rt 2

Khon Kaen

Phetchabun

hit

phan
Hin

Rt 113   Rt 21

Po Sak River

Rt 201   Rt 2057

Chonnabot

Bang Mun Nak   Samran   Ban Phai   Rt 23

4   **5**   **6**

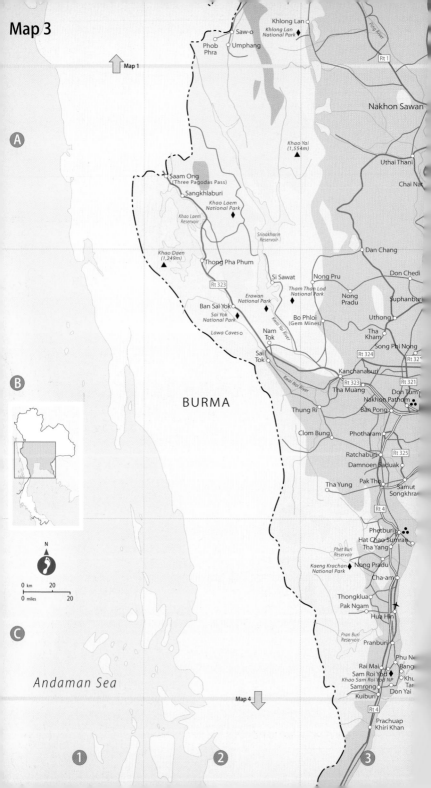

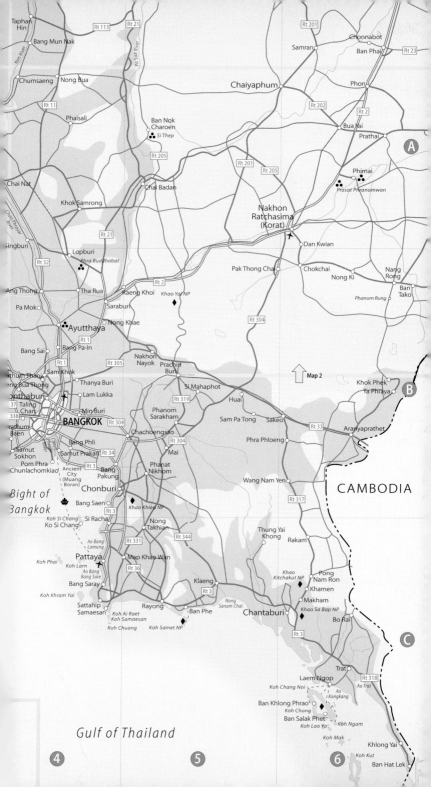

BTS Skytrain

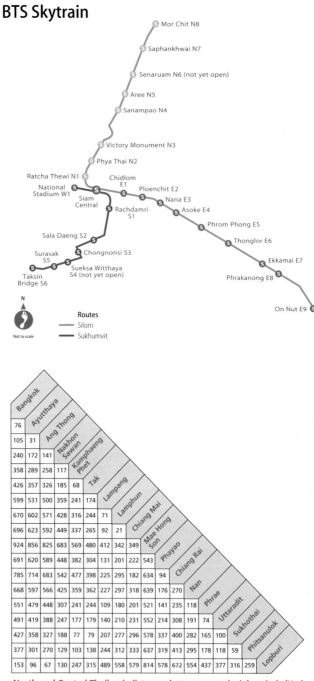

North and Central Thailand, distances between provincial capitals (Km)

Bangkok	Ayutthaya	Ang Thong	Nakhon Sawan	Kamphaeng Phet	Tak	Lampang	Lamphun	Chiang Mai	Mae Hong Son	Phayao	Chiang Rai	Nan	Phrae	Uttaradit	Sukhothai	Phitsanulok	Lopburi
76																	
105	31																
240	172	141															
358	289	258	117														
426	357	326	185	68													
599	531	500	359	241	174												
670	602	571	428	316	244	71											
696	623	592	449	337	265	92	21										
924	856	825	683	569	480	412	342	349									
691	620	589	448	382	304	131	201	222	543								
785	714	683	542	477	398	225	295	182	634	94							
668	597	566	425	359	362	227	297	318	639	176	270						
551	479	448	307	241	244	109	180	201	521	141	235	118					
491	419	388	247	177	179	140	210	231	552	214	308	191	74				
427	358	327	188	77	79	207	277	296	578	337	400	282	165	100			
377	301	270	129	103	138	244	312	333	637	319	413	295	178	118	59		
153	96	67	130	247	315	489	558	579	814	578	672	554	437	377	316	259	

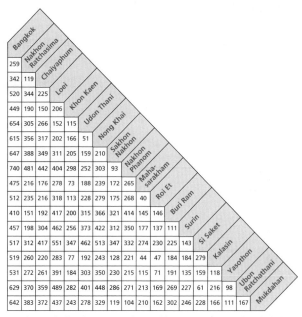

Northeast Thailand: Distances by road between provincial capitals (Km)

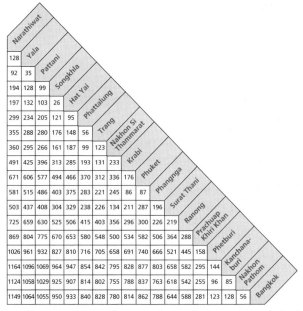

South and West Thailand, distances between provincial capitals (Km)

What the papers say

Mail order

Available worldwide in bookshops and on-line. Footprint travel guides can also be ordered directly from us in Bath, via our website **www.footprintbooks.com** or from the address at the beginning of this book.